ASPEN PUBLISHERS

SIMPLE, SEP, and SARSEP Answer Book

Eighteenth Edition

by Gary S. Lesser

This comprehensive, authoritative volume provides up-to-date coverage of recent legislative and regulatory developments in simplified employee pension (SEP) plans and savings incentive match plans for employees (SIMPLEs). It provides clear and concise guidance on the complex design, administration, and compliance issues that arise in connection with SIMPLEs, SEPs, and salary reduction SEPs (SARSEPs).

Highlights of the Eighteenth Edition

Highlights of *SIMPLE, SEP, and SARSEP Answer Book, Eighteenth Edition*, includes:

- Discussion of the final exemption procedure from the prohibited transaction rules that apply after December 26, 2011. (See Q 4:22.)
- How to compute the compensation a self-employed individual needs to be allocated the maximum amount ($50,000) for 2012. (See Q 6:30.)
- Why the Code Section 164(f) deduction for half of the self-employment taxes will be close to, but not equal to half, of the self-employment tax shown on Schedule C of Form 1040 or Form 1040NR for 2011 and 2012. (See Q 7:2.)
- The statutory changes under GOZA, TIPRA, HERO, PPA, HEART, and WRERA relating to qualification of IRAs that became effective after the mandatory amendments were announced in 2002. (See Q 3:6.)
- How the deduction for one-half of the self-employed health insurance (SEHI) was treated when calculating one-half of the self-employment tax under Code Section 164(f) for 2011 and 2010. (See Q 7:18.)
- When a person providing investment advice becomes a fiduciary under the proposed fiduciary advice regulations issued in 2010. (See Qs 4:24–4:39.)

- What an Employer Plans Compliance Unit (EPCU) examination program request involving a SIMPLE or SEP is looking for and how to respond. (See Q 3:7.)
- How a prototype traditional IRA, SEP-IRA, or SIMPLE IRA may be amended to incorporate statutory changes without affecting reliance on a favorable opinion letter. (See Q 3:19 and Appendix G for model language.)
- How the designated Roth account (DRA) rules apply to a 401(k) SIMPLE IRA plan. (See Q 15:21.)
- How the law about retirement plans' death benefits is sometimes similar to, but often quite different from, the law that applies to the disposition of other wealth. (See Chapter 16.)
- How the DOL's seven-day safe harbor rules for elective contribution are applied after a delinquent contribution is made. (See Q 4:45.)
- Why the *pro rata allocation rule* applies to direct rollovers and the *taxable first rule* applies to 60-day rollovers from an employer's plan to an IRA, and why Roth IRAs are treated differently. (See Q 15:51.)
- Whether inherited IRAs are protected from creditors or included in the debtor's bankruptcy estate under the Bankruptcy Abuse Prevention and Consumer Protection Act of 2005. (See Q 4:79.)
- When an ACA (automatic contribution arrangement) may be used in connection with a SEP or SARSEP arrangement. (See Q 12:1.)
- The extent to which IRAs are protected from creditors and the amount under state and federal law. (See Qs 4:68–4:73.)
- The Form 1099-R reporting codes and changes to Form 5498 and Form 8606. (See Chapter 13.)
- Restorative payments (of a good-faith claim of liability) and the annual IRA and SEP contribution limits. (See Q 5:6.)
- Limitations on deductions to combined plans and their effect on deductions for SEP contributions. (See Q 1:3.)
- Integration and participant exclusion rules that permit larger contributions to be made for employees earning above a specified amount, but that also require that the $50,000 (for 2012) allocation limit be reduced. (See Chapter 9.)
- Procedures for correcting excess contributions and the reporting of contributions, revocations, rollovers, and conversions. (See Chapters 10, 11, 12, and 13.)

- Review of the tax credits available to individuals for IRA contributions and elective deferrals, as well as the tax credits available to businesses establishing new SIMPLE or SEP arrangements. (See Qs 1:33, 14:168, and 15:61.)

11/12

For questions concerning this shipment, billing, or other customer service matters, call our Customer Service Department at 1-800-234-1660.

For toll-free ordering, please call 1-800-638-8437.

Aspen Publishers

SIMPLE, SEP, and SARSEP Answer Book

Eighteenth Edition

Gary S. Lesser

Published by Wolters Kluwer Law & Business in New York.

Wolters Kluwer Law & Business serves customers worldwide with CCH, Aspen Publishers and Kluwer Law International products.

Printed in the United States of America

ISBN 978-1-4548-0864-0

1 2 3 4 5 6 7 8 9 0

About Wolters Kluwer Law & Business

Wolters Kluwer Law & Business is a leading global provider of intelligent information and digital solutions for legal and business professionals in key specialty areas, and respected educational resources for professors and law students. Wolters Kluwer Law & Business connects legal and business professionals as well as those in the education market with timely, specialized authoritative content and information-enabled solutions to support success through productivity, accuracy and mobility.

Serving customers worldwide, Wolters Kluwer Law & Business products include those under the Aspen Publishers, CCH, Kluwer Law International, Loislaw, Best Case, ftwilliam.com and MediRegs family of products.

CCH products have been a trusted resource since 1913, and are highly regarded resources for legal, securities, antitrust and trade regulation, government contracting, banking, pension, payroll, employment and labor, and healthcare reimbursement and compliance professionals.

Aspen Publishers products provide essential information to attorneys, business professionals and law students. Written by preeminent authorities, the product line offers analytical and practical information in a range of specialty practice areas from securities law and intellectual property to mergers and acquisitions and pension/benefits. Aspen's trusted legal education resources provide professors and students with high-quality, up-to-date and effective resources for successful instruction and study in all areas of the law.

Kluwer Law International products provide the global business community with reliable international legal information in English. Legal practitioners, corporate counsel and business executives around the world rely on Kluwer Law journals, looseleafs, books, and electronic products for comprehensive information in many areas of international legal practice.

Loislaw is a comprehensive online legal research product providing legal content to law firm practitioners of various specializations. Loislaw provides attorneys with the ability to quickly and efficiently find the necessary legal information they need, when and where they need it, by facilitating access to primary law as well as state-specific law, records, forms and treatises.

Best Case Solutions is the leading bankruptcy software product to the bankruptcy industry. It provides software and workflow tools to flawlessly streamline petition preparation and the electronic filing process, while timely incorporating ever-changing court requirements.

ftwilliam.com offers employee benefits professionals the highest quality plan documents (retirement, welfare and non-qualified) and government forms (5500/PBGC, 1099 and IRS) software at highly competitive prices.

MediRegs products provide integrated health care compliance content and software solutions for professionals in healthcare, higher education and life sciences, including professionals in accounting, law and consulting.

Wolters Kluwer Law & Business, a division of Wolters Kluwer, is headquartered in New York. Wolters Kluwer is a market-leading global information services company focused on professionals.

Wolters Kluwer
Law & Business

Preface

SIMPLE, SEP, and SARSEP Answer Book, Eighteenth Edition, provides coverage of recent developments in simplified employee pension (SEP) plans and savings incentive match plans for employees (SIMPLEs) and discusses various technical changes and clarifications reflecting the changes made by the Tax Reform Act of 1986, the Uniformed Services Employment and Reemployment Rights Act of 1994, the Small Business Job Protection Act of 1996, the Taxpayer Relief Act of 1997, the Economic Growth and Tax Relief Reconciliation Act of 2001, the USA Patriot Act of 2001, the Job Creation and Worker Assistance Act of 2002, the Bankruptcy Abuse Prevention and Consumer Protection Act of 2005, Working Families Tax Relief Act of 2004, American Jobs Creation Act of 2004, the Pension Protection Act of 2006, the Heroes Earnings Assistance and Relief Tax Act of 2008, the Emergency Economic Stabilization Act of 2008, Worker, Retiree, and Employer Recovery Act of 2008, the Small Business Jobs Act of 2010, the Tax Relief, Unemployment Insurance Reauthorization, and Job Creation Act of 2010, and other legislation. Additional guidance, many new examples, and illustrations are provided to assist practitioners in complying with the new rules.

Included in this book are several appendices that will also be of assistance to the practitioner. Appendix L contains guidance on appropriate codes to enter on Form 1099-R when reporting revocations of contributions and CIP failure to SEPs, SIMPLEs, and salary reduction SEPs (SARSEPs). Appendix D contains extracts from the Employee Plans Compliance Resolution System applicable to SEP and SIMPLE IRA plans. Updated charts comparing various types of plans and plan features are provided in Appendices E, N, and O. COLA adjusted limits are provided in Appendix G, and an excess SEP/SARSEP contribution flow chart is provided in Appendix M. Appendix H reproduces illustrations of the many examples used in this book.

Designing plans that best meet a specific company's unique requirements is a difficult task. *SIMPLE, SEP, and SARSEP Answer Book* offers practitioners in-depth understanding of such issues as establishing, maintaining, and terminating the plan; employer and employee eligibility; catch-up contributions; SEP integration with Social Security contributions; and the operation and administration of SIMPLEs and SEPs. Among the many other key areas covered are the meaning of the terms *compensation* and *earned income* for various purposes, IRS reporting requirements, participant disclosures, ERISA fiduciary requirements, and earnings from self-employment.

SIMPLE, SEP, and SARSEP Answer Book is the most comprehensive, up-to-the-minute, and authoritative resource on the market, answering the complex questions surrounding SIMPLEs, SEPs, and SARSEPs. The question-and-answer format, with its breadth of coverage and its plain-language explanations, provides practitioners with clear, concise answers to hundreds of practical questions. Practice pointers and numerous examples offer additional insight into the complexities of designing, administering, and reporting SIMPLEs, SEPs, and SARSEPs. Citations to authorities are provided as research aids for those who need to pursue particular subjects in greater detail.

Numbering System. The questions are numbered consecutively within each chapter (e.g., Q 1:1, Q 1:2, and Q 1:3).

List of Questions. The detailed List of Questions that follows the Contents helps the reader locate areas of immediate interest. The list is similar to a detailed table of contents, providing both the question number and the page on which the question appears.

Tables. For easy access to a particular section of the Internal Revenue Code, Treasury regulations, Department of Labor regulations and advisory opinions, the United States Code, and IRS documents (revenue rulings, revenue procedures, letter rulings, notices, and announcements), tables of the sections, documents, and cases cited in the text, referenced by question number, have been included.

Index. A detailed topical index is provided at the back of the book as a further aid to locating specific information. All references are to question numbers and appendices.

Abbreviations and Acronyms. A number of the terms and statutory references that appear repeatedly in this book are referred to by their abbreviations and/or acronyms after the first mention. The most common of the abbreviations and acronyms are:

- Ann.—IRS Announcement
- BAPCPA—Bankruptcy Abuse Prevention and Consumer Protection Act of 2005
- C.B.—Cumulative Bulletin of the IRS
- CCA—Chief Counsel Advice
- COBRA—Comprehensive Omnibus Budget Reconciliation Act of 1985
- Code; I.R.C.—Internal Revenue Code
- DO—Delegation Order

- DOL—Department of Labor
- DOL Adv. Op.—Department of Labor Advisory Opinion
- EBSA—Employee Benefits Security Administration
- EGTRRA—Economic Growth and Tax Relief Reconciliation Act of 2001
- EPCRS—Employee Plans Compliance Resolution System
- ERISA—Employee Retirement Income Security Act of 1974
- E-SIGN—Electronic Signatures in Global and National Commerce Act
- FUTA—Federal Unemployment Tax Act
- FICA—Federal Insurance Contributions Act
- GOZA—Gulf Opportunity Zone Act of 2005
- HEART—Heroes Earnings Assistance and Relief Tax Act of 2008
- HIPAA—Health Insurance Portability and Accountability Act of 1996
- I.R.C.—Internal Revenue Code
- ILM—IRS Legal Memorandum
- IR—IRS Information Release
- IRA—individual retirement arrangement (account and annuity)
- I.R.B.—Internal Revenue Bulletin
- IRS or I.R.S.—Internal Revenue Service
- JCWAA—Job Creation and Worker Assistance Act of 2002
- JOBS—American Jobs Creation Act of 2004
- KETRA—Katrina Emergency Tax Relief Act of 2005
- Ltr. Rul.—Private Letter Ruling
- PPA—Pension Protection Act of 2006
- Prop. Treas. Reg.—Proposed Treasury Regulation
- P.T.E.—Prohibited Transaction Exemption
- Pub. L.—Public Law
- RA '78—Revenue Act of 1978
- RRA '98—IRS Restructuring and Reform Act of 1998
- Rev. Proc.—Revenue Procedure
- Rev. Rul.—Revenue Ruling
- SBJA—Small Business Jobs Act of 2010
- SBJPA—Small Business Job Protection Act of 1996

- SEC—Securities and Exchange Commission
- SEC Rel.—Securities and Exchange Commission Release
- TAMRA—Technical and Miscellaneous Revenue Act of 1998
- Temp. Treas. Reg.—Temporary Treasury Regulation
- TRA '86—Tax Reform Act of 1986
- TRA '97—Taxpayer Relief Act of 1997
- Treas. Reg.—Treasury Regulation
- USERRA—Uniformed Services Employment and Reemployment Rights Act of 1994
- WRERA—Worker, Retiree, and Employer Recovery Act of 2008.

Gary S. Lesser
October 2012

About the Authors

Gary S. Lesser, Esq., is the principal of GSL Galactic Consulting, located in Indianapolis, Indiana. Mr. Lesser maintains a telephone-based consulting practice providing services and plan illustrations to other professionals and business owners. Mr. Lesser is a nationally known author, educator, and speaker on retirement plans for individuals and smaller businesses. He has broad technical and practical knowledge of both qualified and nonqualified retirement plans.

Mr. Lesser is also the technical editor and coauthor of Wolters Kluwer Law & Business' *Health Savings Account Answer Book, Roth IRA Answer Book, 457 Answer Book,* and *Quick Reference to IRAs*. Mr. Lesser is also the principal author and technical editor of *The Adviser's Guide to Retirement Plans for Small Businesses* and other publications of the American Institute of Certified Public Accountants (AICPA). In 2010, Mr. Lesser published *Basic Accounting Simplified.* He has developed several software programs that are used by financial planners, accountants, and other pension practitioners to allocate contributions and market retirement plans for smaller businesses. His two software programs—*QP-SEP Illustrator*™ and *SIMPLE Illustrator*®—are marketed and distributed nationally. He has also been published in the *IRS EP/EO Digest, Journal of Taxation of Employee Benefits, Journal of Compensation and Benefits, Journal of Pension Benefits, Life Insurance Selling, Rough Notes,* and *NAPFA Advisor.*

In 1974, Mr. Lesser started his employee benefits career with the Internal Revenue Service, as a Tax Law Specialist/Attorney in the Employee Plans/Exempt Organizations (*EP/EO*) Division. He later managed and operated a pension administration and actuarial service organization, was an ERISA marketing attorney for a national brokerage firm, and was a senior vice president/director of retirement plans for several nationally known families of mutual funds and variable annuity products. Mr. Lesser graduated from New York Law School and received his B.A. in accounting from Fairleigh Dickinson University. He is admitted to the bars of the state of New York and the United States Tax Court. Comments and suggestions can be forwarded to Mr. Lesser at GSL Galactic Consulting, 944 Stockton St., Indianapolis, IN 46260-4925, (317) 254-0385, or to *QPSEP@aol.com.* Information is also available on his Web site at *http://www.GaryLesser.com.*

Contributing Authors

Denise Appleby, CISP, CRC, CRPS, CRSP, APA, is a retirement plans consultant, trainer, freelance writer, editor, and owner of Appleby Retirement Plans Consulting, located on the Internet at *http://www.applebyconsultinginc.com* and *http://www.RetirementDictionary.com*. Ms. Appleby's retirement-plans-related experiences include working as a retirement plans product manager, training manager, compliance consultant, technical help desk manager, and writer. She has written over 200 articles for many financial newsletters including *http://www.Investopedia.com*, Pershing LLC's "Sixty Something," "The Pershing Press," and "Ed Slott's IRA Advisor."

Ms. Appleby is a frequent speaker at seminars, where she explains the importance of saving for retirement, and how to prevent paying avoidable taxes and penalties on distributions from retirement plans.

Ms. Appleby has appeared on CNBC's "Business News," where she gave insights on saving and planning for retirement. She has earned the following professional designations: The Accredited Pension Administrator (APA) from the National Institute of Pension Administrators, the Certified IRA Services Professional (CISP) designation from the Institute of Certified Bankers; the Chartered Retirement Plans Specialist (CRPS) designation from the College for Financial Planning; Certified Retirement Services Professional (CRSP) designation from the Institute of Certified Bankers; and the Certified Retirement Counselor (CRC) designation from the International Foundation for Retirement Education (InFRE).

Peter Gulia, Esq., is the shareholder of Fiduciary Guidance Counsel, a law firm that advises retirement plans' fiduciaries.

After more than 21 years of experience with one of America's largest retirement services businesses, Mr. Gulia now counsels the people who manage employee-benefit plans. In addition, he offers advice about employers' and executives' smart use of plan designs permitted under Code Sections 125, 401(k), 403(b), 409A, and 457(b) or (f).

Although Mr. Gulia concentrates his practice on advising an employee-benefit plan's lead fiduciary, he also counsels investment advisers about their fiduciary duties and compliance procedures under the Investment Advisers Act, Employee Retirement Income Security Act of 1974 (ERISA), and other laws. Likewise, he advises lawyers and certified public accountants about their professional conduct.

Since 1984, Mr. Gulia has focused on the design, governance, fiduciary investment procedures, and administration of retirement plans. His groundbreaking solutions to resolve then-novel ERISA, tax, and securities issues for asset-allocation investment advice and other retirement plan services remain models that practitioners continue to use today. Beyond ERISA-governed plans, he has wide experience with church plans and governmental plans, and with how securities law and other laws beyond ERISA and the Internal Revenue Code affect retirement plans.

He is a widely published expert on plan investments (including qualified default investment alternatives), beneficiary designations, and domestic relations orders. Mr. Gulia has published primarily with Wolters Kluwer Law & Business. He is a contributing author of six books in its Answer Book series, and is a contributing editor of *401(k) Advisor*. He is an author of *The CPA's Guide to Retirement Plans for Small Businesses* (AICPA), and recently expanded the book's coverage of fiduciary issues. He is an *Insights* author and speaker with Bloomberg BNA.

Mr. Gulia is an adjunct professor in Temple University's law school, and teaches a broad range of professional-education programs, including for the National Association of Personal Financial Advisors (NAPFA), *Pensions & Investments* magazine, Financial Research Associates, and The American Law Institute Continuing Legal Education. He is a member of the ASPPA Benefits Council of the Delaware Valley, the American Bar Association, and the Philadelphia Bar Association, serving on its Employee Benefits Committee and Professional Guidance Committee.

Readers may call Peter Gulia at (215) 732-1552, or e-mail him at *Peter@PeterGulia.com.* Further information is available at *http://www.FiduciaryGuidanceCounsel.com.*

Christine P. Roberts, Esq., is a partner in the Santa Barbara law firm of Mullen & Henzell L.L.P. Ms. Roberts received her B.A. from Wellesley College and her juris doctorate degree from the University of California at Los Angeles.

Ms. Roberts practices exclusively in the employment benefits and employment law area, with particular emphasis on pension and health plans under the ERISA. She is an author of chapters on voluntary compliance programs in The Adviser's Guide to Retirement Plans for Small Businesses, published by the AICPA (3d Ed. 2012), and Quick Reference to IRAs (2012), published by Wolters Kluwer Law & Business. Ms. Roberts is a member of the Santa Barbara County Bar Association, the Santa Barbara Human Resources Association, and the Society for Human Resources Management. She currently serves on the board of trustees of the Santa Barbara Public Library. She writes frequently about benefit related topics at *http://www.eforerisa.com.*

Acknowledgments

Many individuals have contributed to the book you hold in your hand. I value their friendship and assistance greatly. You know who you are.

I wish to express my great appreciation and deep gratitude to Lisa Yi Hamond and the rest of the professional staff at Wolters Kluwer Law & Business for making the *SIMPLE, SEP, and SARSEP Answer Book* a reality. Although they hide behind firewalls and routers, I would also like to thank the individuals involved in the maintenance of the electronic version of this book.

I wish to express my deep appreciation and gratitude to Denise Appleby, Benjamin Botwick, Mac Brown, Alex DiMuro, Kevin Donovan, Richard Epstein, Seymour Goldberg, Joan Gucciardi, Peter Gulia, Mike Flintoff, David Powell, Christine Roberts, Michelle Ward, and Derrin Watson for their ongoing support and assistance whenever called upon. Special thanks to Christine Roberts for expanding her coverage of IRS and DOL plan correction programs. And to Peter Gulia for his keen insight and expertise in updating chapter 16 on Beneficiary Designations and Estate Planning—a treatise in its own right, a delightful read, and sprinkled with humor. And finally, to Denise Appleby, for her expertise and practical experience in revising and updating chapter 13 on IRS and DOL Disclosure, Filings, Penalties, and Withholding Issues.

I thank Lawrence C. Starr, President of Qualified Plan Consultants, Inc., in Springfield, Massachusetts, for helping me understand the intricacies of "ultra-net" earned income and how to get there from nowhere.

Over the years contributing authors have changed. I'd like to thank the former contributing author, Susan D. Diehl, for taking the time—when she could and for as long as she could—to share her expertise. Some of her contributions remain intact and we thank her for it.

And finally, my thanks to Hi-Ho Silver Zorro and Butch the Beast Slayer for their astute feline conversation, companionship, warmth, and occasional assistance in the typing of the manuscript. Special thanks to Kelso III for his canine security services and for protecting the manuscript during its preparation.

G.S.L.

Contents

Chapter 13

List of Questions

Chapter 1 Overview: SEPs and SARSEPs

Overview

Highly Compensated Employees

Chapter 2 SEP Establishment and Employer Qualification

Establishing SEPs

Establishing SARSEPs

SEP Establishment Dates

Employee Eligibility

Employees of Limited Liability Partnerships and Limited Liability Companies

Forcing Employees to Participate

Classification of Employees

Employees of Predecessor Employers

Repeal and Grandfathering of SARSEPs

Examination Guidelines

Chapter 3 SEP and SARSEP Documents

Model SEP and SARSEP Plan Documents

Mass Submitter Document Approval

Individually Designed SEPs

Approval for Combined Plans and Prior Plans

Chapter 4 ERISA Considerations and Related Laws

Overview

Alternative Reporting Methods

Disclosure Requirements When Using Form 5305-SEP

Disclosure Requirements When Not Using Form 5305-SEP

Payroll Deduction IRA

Use of Electronic Media

Forwarding Contributions

Federal Securities Laws

Option Securities and Margin Accounts

Impact of State and Local Laws

Creditor Protection

Bankruptcy

Automatic Rollover of Mandatory Distributions

Bonding

FDIC Coverage

Chapter 5 Making Contributions and Taking Distributions: SEPs and SARSEPs

Making Contributions to SEPs and SARSEPs

SEPs with Other Plans and Annual IRAs

Distributions and Deemed Distributions

Excess Contributions

Traditional IRA Excess Reporting Requirements

Compensation Limits

Multiemployer and Multiple-Employer Plans

Chapter 7 Special Rules for Self-Employed Individuals

Earned Income as Compensation

Calculating Earned Income

Self-Employment Tax

Disclosure Rules

Chapter 10 Deduction of SEP Contributions by Employer

Conditions for Deduction

Fees and Commissions

Elective Salary Reduction Contributions

Affiliated Service Group Member

Deduction in Future Years

Penalty

Reporting

Chapter 11 Taxation of SEP Contributions

Percentage Exclusion Limit

Dollar Exclusion Limit

Reporting

Overall Limit

FICA, FUTA, and Other Taxes

Chapter 12 Elective SARSEP Deferrals

Elective Salary Reduction Deferrals

Disallowed Deferrals—Failing the 50 Percent Participation Rate Requirement

Catch-up Contributions

Chapter 13 IRS Disclosure, Filings, Penalties, and Tax Withholding

Disclosure

Revocation Period

Reports to the IRS and the IRA Owner

Taxpayer Reporting

Withholding

Reporting Penalties

Early Distributions

Excess Contributions

Minimum Distributions

Reporting Form 5329 Penalties on Form 1040

Excess Distributions and Excess Accumulations

Calculating and Reporting Nondeductible Contributions on Form 8606

Filing Information and Requirements

IRS Form 990-T

IRS Form 1040

IRS Form 1099-R

Substitute Statements

Filing Corrected Forms 1099-R

Magnetic Media Filing Requirements

Paper Document Reporting

Noncompliance Penalties

Early Withdrawal Certificate of Deposit Penalty

Intended Rollover of IRA Distribution

Reporting Revoked IRAs

Renewed Investments

Fees Deducted from IRA Accounts

Miscellaneous Rules

IRS Form 5329

IRS Form 5330

IRS Form 5498

Annual Participant Statements

Required Minimum Distribution Statement

Magnetic Media Filing Requirements

Paper Document Reporting

Filing Corrected Returns

Noncompliance Penalties

Miscellaneous Reporting Requirements

Reporting Revoked IRAs

IRS Form 5500

IRS Form W-2

Other Filings and Registrations

Chapter 14 SIMPLE IRA Arrangements

Basic Concepts

Establishing a SIMPLE IRA Plan

Model IRS Forms

Prototype SIMPLE IRAs and SIMPLE IRA Plans

Employer Eligibility

Employee Eligibility

Compensation

Contributions

Employee Elections

Vesting Requirements

Employer Notification and Administrative Requirements

Trustee Administrative Requirements

Tax Treatment of SIMPLE IRAs

Contributions

Deduction of Contributions

Distributions

Designated Financial Institutions

Fiduciary Responsibility

Miscellaneous Rules

Remedial Correction Programs

Excess Contributions

Tax Credits

Chapter 15 401(k) SIMPLE Plans

Introduction

Vesting Require ments

Employer Eligibility

Exclusive Plan Requirement

Employee Eligibility

Compensation

Contributions

Discrimination Testing

Tax Treatment of Contributions

Distributions

Rollovers and Transfers

Notice and Reporting Requirements

Adopting a 401(k) SIMPLE Plan

Excess Contributions and Plan Deficiencies

Termination in Favor of a SIMPLE IRA

Tax Credits

Chapter 16 Beneficiary Designations and Estate Planning

About Beneficiary Designations

Substantial Compliance

Lost Beneficiary Designation

Default Beneficiary Designation

Laws and External Documents That Might Affect a Beneficiary Designation

Using Trusts

Pets

Charitable Gifts

Simultaneous Death; Absentees

Family Rights That Restrain a Beneficiary Designation

Failing to Provide for a Spouse

Failing to Provide for a Child

Marriage

Ceremonial Marriage

Common-Law Marriage

Same-Sex Marriage

Spouse's Rights

ERISA Survivor Benefits or Spouse's-Consent Rights

Tenancy by the Entirety

Disclaimers

Tax-Oriented Estate Planning

Marital Deduction

Qualified Domestic Trust for an Alien

Giving Advice

Common Mistakes

Chapter 17 Correction Programs

IRS Correction Program

DOL Correction Program

Chapter 1

Overview: SEPs and SARSEPs

A SEP arrangement allows an employer to make tax-deductible contributions to fund its eligible employees' retirement. A SARSEP also allows employees to reduce their taxable income, and the amount of federal income tax withheld, by electing to make pretax salary reduction contributions. This chapter explains the basic rules that apply to SEPs and SARSEPs.

Overview

Q 1:1 What is a *simplified employee pension plan*?

A *simplified employee pension plan* (SEP) is a written arrangement or program (a plan) that allows an employer to make tax-deductible contributions on a discretionary basis toward an employee's retirement. In form, a SEP is merely an individual retirement account or an individual retirement annuity (IRA) that meets several additional rules (see Q 1:6). If those rules are satisfied, an employer may make retirement contributions into the SEP of each eligible employee.

Under certain circumstances, employees may be permitted to make elective (salary reduction) contributions made with pretax dollars (see Qs 1:2, 2:18). A SEP arrangement that permits employees to make elective contributions is frequently called a SARSEP, or salary reduction SEP (see chapter 12). [Prop.

Treas. Reg. § 1.408-7(c)(2)] If elective contributions are allowed, the employer must promptly forward them to the IRA trustee or custodian (see Qs 4:44–4:50).

Although the employer must establish the SEP [Prop. Treas. Reg. § 1.408-7(b)], each IRA generally is in the name of the *employee*—as any other IRA would be—and is referred to variously as a SEP IRA, an IRA SEP, a SEP, or simply an IRA (see Q 1:8). Usually, an employee selects, establishes, and maintains the IRA into which employer SEP contributions are made.

An employer (or employee association) IRA under Section 408(c) of the Internal Revenue Code (Code) may also qualify as a SEP if additional rules are met (see Qs 5:30, 5:31).

Note. SEPs became effective for taxable years beginning after 1978. [RA '78 § 152]

Q 1:2 What is a *salary reduction SEP*, or *SARSEP*?

A *salary reduction SEP* (SARSEP), also called an *elective SEP*, is a SEP arrangement that allows eligible employees to reduce their taxable income by making pretax elective contributions (see Q 12:1) toward their own retirement. [I.R.C. § 408(k)(1); Prop. Treas. Reg. §§ 1.408-7, 1.408-8] That is, because contributions are made with pretax dollars, they reduce currently taxable income. Amounts deferred by an eligible employee are contributed by the employer into an IRA on behalf of the employee.

An employer that establishes a SEP may choose whether or not to allow eligible employees to make elective salary reduction contributions. Not all employers are eligible to offer a salary reduction feature (see Q 2:19).

Note. SARSEPs became effective for taxable years beginning after 1986. [TRA '86 § 1108(a)] The enabling legislation for SARSEPs was repealed for years beginning after 1996; existing SARSEPs were grandfathered (see Q 2:93).

Q 1:3 Are there any limits on the dollar amounts that may be contributed to a SEP?

Yes. No fewer than eight separate limits may apply to SEP contributions. Be that as it may, it is generally true that employer contributions that do not exceed 25 percent of includible taxable compensation not in excess of $250,000 for 2012 are deductible by the employer and (to the extent that the employer contributions do not exceed 25 percent of the employee's includible gross income) are excluded from the gross income of the employee (see Q 10:3). (See Appendix G.)

The eight limits that may apply to a SEP are as follows:

1. *The 25 percent exclusion limit.* Contributions allocated to a participant's SEP IRA that exceed 25 percent of that participant's includible taxable compensation are not excludable from the participant's gross income. In addition to the 25 percent exclusion limit, catch-up contributions, but not

other elective deferrals, are excludable from a participant's gross income (see Qs 11:1, 11:2).

Note. In years beginning before 2002, both the participant exclusion limit (item 1) and the employer's deduction limit (item 2) were limited to 15 percent (rather than 25 percent).

2. *The 25 percent deduction limit.* Within limits, all SEP contributions are deductible. The 25 percent limit for 2012 is based on the aggregate compensation, including (for this purpose) elective deferrals, of all plan participants (see Q 10:3). In addition to this 25 percent deduction limit, elective and catch-up contributions are deductible. Contributions, although deductible, may be includible in a participant's gross income to the extent that the amount allocated exceeds the participant's exclusion allowance (see item 1) or other limit.

Note. It should not be overlooked that profit-sharing plans, stock bonus plans, and SEPs share a combined 25 percent of aggregate compensation deduction limit. [I.R.C. §§ 404(h)(2), 404(h)(3)] An allowable SEP contribution would, therefore, reduce an employer's profit-sharing deduction limit under Code Section 404(a)(3)(A).

It should also be kept in mind that when a SEP is combined with a qualified defined contribution plan, the $50,000 (the 2012 limit) or 100 percent of aggregate compensation qualified plan limit also applies to the total contributions made by the employer—not only to the SEP but also to all the employer's qualified defined contribution plans (see items 3 and 4 below). [I.R.C. §§ 402(h), 415(c)(1)(A)] Nondeductible (excess) contributions to a SEP may subject the employer to a 10 percent excise tax (see Qs 10:12, 13:144). [I.R.C. § 4972(d)(1)(A)(iii)] A self-employed individual is treated as an employer for this purpose. [I.R.C. § 4972(d)(2)]

Note. Under the Pension Protection Act of 2006 (PPA), the limitation on deductions to combined plans was relaxed for taxable years starting after 2005. For taxable years starting in 2006, the limitation on deductions to combined plans only applies to single employer plans, not insured by the Pension Benefit Guaranty Corporation (PBGC), and only to contributions in excess of 6 percent of amounts otherwise paid to beneficiaries, where contributions to the defined contribution plans are in a form other than elective deferrals. Thus, when employer contributions to defined contribution plans (other than elective deferrals) *do not exceed* 6 percent of compensation of participants in those plans, the combined limit of Code Section 404(a)(7) does not apply to any employer contributions to defined contribution plans. In such a case, the combined limit under Code Section 404(a)(7) (i.e., the greater of 25 percent of compensation, or the contributions to the defined benefit plan or plans to the extent such contributions do not exceed the amount necessary to satisfy the minimum funding standard for the defined benefit plans, treating a contribution that does not exceed the unfunded current liability as an amount necessary to satisfy the minimum funding standard for each defined benefit plan) applies only to contributions to the defined benefit plans. Conversely, when employer contributions to defined contribution plans (other than elective deferrals) exceed 6 percent of compensation of participants in those plans, the amount of employer contributions to defined contribution plans to which the combined limit of Code Section 404(a)(7) applies is equal to the amount of employer contributions for the plan year less 6 percent of compensation of participants in those plans. Thus, the combined limit of Code Section 404(a)(7) (i.e., the greater of 25 percent of compensation, or the contributions to the defined benefit plan or plans to the extent such contributions do not exceed the amount necessary to satisfy the minimum funding standard for the defined benefit plans, treating a contribution that does not exceed 100 percent of the unfunded current liability as an amount necessary to satisfy the minimum funding standard for each defined benefit plan) applies to the total of employer contributions to defined benefit plans and employer contributions to defined contribution plans (other than elective deferrals), less 6 percent of compensation of participants in the defined contribution plans. Amounts carried over from preceding taxable years are treated as employer contributions to one or more defined contributions to the extent attributable to employer contributions to such plans in such preceding taxable years. If contributions to the defined contribution plan or plans are less than 6 percent of compensation, the defined benefit plan is not subject to the overall deduction limit. [PPA §§ 801–803, amending I.R.C. § 404(a)(7); I.R.S. Notice 2007-28, Q&As 8 and 9, 2007-14 I.R.B. 880]

Example 1. Emery Corporation maintains a SEP and contributed $100,000 to the SEP for the 2012 plan year. Emery also established a defined benefit plan and contributed $300,000, the amount required under the minimum funding standard, during the year to fund the plan. Both plans are maintained on a calendar-year basis. Aggregate compensation of all plan participants is $1 million. Amounts not in excess of 6 percent of compensation are deductible under the provisions of the PPA. Therefore, $40,000 is not deductible ($100,000 – (.06 × $1,000,000)), the amount that exceeds 6 percent of compensation. The maximum deduction is $360,000 ($300,000 + $60,000). [I.R.C. § 404(a)(7)(C), effective for years starting in 2006] The $40,000 nondeductible contribution will remain subject to a 10 percent penalty each year until the excess can be deducted. Emery should consider terminating its SEP or reducing its contribution to 6 percent of compensation.

Note. The Job Creation and Worker Assistance Act of 2002 (JCWAA) made a change to allow a contribution to a plan that accepts only elective deferrals not to be included in the maximum employer deduction described previously. In other words, the defined benefit plan's "contribution" for the year could exceed 25 percent of a participant's compensation, and the participant would still be permitted to make an elective deferral to a defined contribution plan (including a SARSEP that is not top heavy). For this special rule to apply, however, no employee may be a participant in more than one plan. For example, the employer maintains a defined benefit plan for collectively bargained employees and a SEP for all other employees that excludes collectively bargained employees.

3. *The $50,000 contribution limit.* Under Code Section 415(c), contributions other than catch-up contributions may not exceed $50,000 for 2012. The amount by which the contribution exceeds the Section 415 dollar limit is neither deductible by the employer nor excludable from the participant's gross income (see Q 10:8). Thus, structurally, a SEP participant cannot receive more than $50,000 for 2012. In the case of a SARSEP, the $50,000 limit may be increased by catch-up contributions (up to $5,500 for 2012) if the participant is age 50 or older at any time during the calendar year).

Caution. The $50,000 SEP contribution limit is reduced in the case of any highly compensated employee (HCE) if the SEP plan is integrated with contributions to Social Security (see Qs 10:8, 11:8).

Practice Pointer. In general, the only SEP limit that has an effective date of the year "in which the plan year ends" is the Code Section 415 dollar limit ($50,000 for 2012); all others are limited to the year in which the plan year began. This is not an issue for plans that are maintained on the basis of the calendar year. Elective contribution limits, however, are always determined on a calendar-year basis. (See Appendix G, Employee Benefit Limits.)

Example 2. Ambrosia maintains a SEP for its business. The plan year ends on September 30, 2012. Although $50,000 (the 2012 limit) applies to the plan year starting in 2011, other limits, such as the compensation cap, would utilize the limit in effect when the plan year began (in 2011). Thus, for the plan year beginning in 2011, compensation not in excess of $245,000 (the 2011 limit) may be considered under the plan, and no more than $50,000 (the 2012 limit, plus catch-up contributions) may be contributed/allocated to any single participant. Salary reduction SEPs have unique problems when the plan is not maintained on a calendar-year basis (see Q 12:54, Examples 3 and 4).

4. *The 100 percent of compensation limit.* Under Code Section 415(c)(1)(A), the total amount allocated to the SEP may not exceed the participant's gross compensation (see Q 10:9).

Example 3. Manny Bucks spends most of his days buying and selling securities for his own account. He has no other income. Manny does not have "compensation"; thus, the 100 percent of compensation limit prevents Manny from making a SEP contribution. Code Section 1402(a)(3)(A) specifically excludes from the term *net earnings from self-employment* (and thus by extension from the term *earned income*) any gain or loss that is considered a gain or loss from the sale of a capital asset. [*See, e.g.*, I.R.C. §§ 401(c)(2)(C)[B], 1402(a)(3)(C)] Similarly, Code Section 1402(a)(2) specifically excludes from that term *dividends* and *interest*. [*See* Miller v. Commissioner, 77 T.C. 97 (1981) (the court did not make a determination as to whether the enterprise (income generated from investments) constituted a "trade or business," for it did not matter); Kobel v. Commissioner, T.C. Memo 2011-66 (Mar. 17, 2011) ("investor/trader" had no compensation).

But see Levin v. United States, 220 Ct. Cl. 197, 597 F.2d 760 (1970).] But, in *Robinda v. Commissioner* [460 F.2d 1172 (9th Cir. 1972)], the taxpayer derived income from the manipulation of slot machines. The court held it to be "earned income." However, the expenditure of labor does not always produce earned income. [Vianello v. Commissioner, T.C. Memo 2010-17 (Feb. 1, 2010) (determination that taxpayer was engaged in farming was irrelevant); *see* Mayo v. Commissioner, 136 T.C. 81 (Feb. 2011) (regarding expenses of an individual engaged in the trade or business of gambling on horse races)]

5. *The excess deferral limit.* Under Code Section 402(g), the limit on normal elective deferrals is $17,000 for 2012 (see Qs 12:6, 12:19).
6. *The excess contribution limit.* Excess SEP contributions (failing the 125 percent nondiscrimination test of Code Section 408(k)(6)(A)(iii)), which affect only HCEs (see Q 12:24).
7. *The disallowed deferral limit.* Deferrals failing the 50 percent participation rate requirement of Code Section 408(k)(6)(A)(ii) (see Q 12:36).
8. *The catch-up contribution limit.* Under Code Sections 402(h)(2) and 414(v)(3)(A), the limit on catch-up contributions is $5,500 for participants who attain age 50 by the end of the 2012 calendar year (see Q 12:40). [Treas. Reg. § 1.414(v)-1(c)(1)]

Note 1. Except for nondeductible contributions (see item 2), all excess amounts are includible in gross income at different times and in different ways. Some excess amounts require notification (e.g., items 5, 6, and 7); others must satisfy Internal Revenue Service (IRS) reporting requirements (see chapter 13). Different types of excess amounts are treated in different ways. For example, items 6, 7, and 8 do not apply to the extent that item 1 (the 25 percent exclusion limit) is exceeded (see Qs 11:1, 11:9, 11:10).

Note 2. The 15 percent exclusion rule under Code Section 402(h) was not amended by the Economic Growth and Tax Relief Reconciliation Act of 2001 (EGTRRA), which was enacted on June 7, 2001. The JCWAA, enacted on March 9, 2002, contained a technical correction increasing the exclusion to 25 percent, but it did not make elective contributions separately excludable from a participant's gross income.

Employees may be permitted to contribute up to $17,000 for 2012 by entering into a salary reduction agreement to make elective SEP contributions that reduce the employee's taxable income and the amount of federal income tax withheld. Certain employees are eligible to make additional contributions, called catch-up contributions, to a SARSEP (see Q 1:30). In addition, nearly all SEP arrangements provide for an allocation limit of 25 percent of includible taxable compensation, up to $50,000 ($55,500 if age 50 or older at any time during the year) for 2012 (see Q 11:5). Elective contributions that are in excess of the $17,000 limit for 2012 (excess elective deferrals) are generally included in the participant's income for the year of deferral. In addition, elective contributions exceeding the 125 percent actual deferral percentage (ADP) limit (excess SEP contributions) and elective contributions made while the employer is ineligible to maintain a SARSEP (disallowed deferrals) are generally included in the participant's income for the year of deferral for plan years beginning after 2007 (see Qs 12:19, 12:22, 12:35, 12:41, 12:43). Elective deferrals do not, however, reduce the compensation on which the 25 percent employer deduction limit is computed.

Note. Participant reporting rules for contributions that exceed the 25 percent exclusion limit and the 100 percent of compensation allocation limit under Code Section 415 appear to require that amounts exceeding those limits be included in box 1 of Form W-2, Wage and Tax Statement, but do not appear to require that the participant be notified of the reason for the erroneous contribution—even though the amounts are to be included in the participant's taxable income (see Qs 11:15, 13:53). Perhaps it is contemplated that the employer will notify the employee of any amounts included in income when it discovers the erroneous contribution. [*See* Preamble, Prop. Treas. Reg. § 1.408-7 (published in the Federal Register on July 14, 1981)] If it does so, the participant can inform the SEP IRA trustee of the erroneous contribution. The trustee can then properly report the amount (when necessary) as a regular IRA contribution or distribute any excess to the participant upon the participant's request. Participant notification appears to be required only for some types of erroneous contributions (see Qs 12:29–12:44).

Q 1:4 Are the cost-of-living adjustments to dollar limits affecting SEPs rounded?

Yes. For taxable years beginning after 1994, the cost-of-living adjustments (COLAs) to several dollar limits affecting SEPs are simplified by a rounding-down process. For taxable years in which the total of the inflation adjustments is less than the incremental amount, the maximum amount will remain unchanged. Once the total of the inflation adjustments equals or exceeds the incremental amount, the limit will be increased by that increment. The rounding rule increments applicable to SEPs are listed in Table 1-1. (See Appendix G for limits applicable to other years.)

Table 1-1. Inflation Adjustment Increments

Employee Benefit Limit	*Base Amount*	*2012 Amount*	*Incremental Adjustment Amount*
Elective deferral limit	$ 7,000	$ 17,000	$ 500
Section 415 defined contribution limit	$ 30,000	$ 50,000	$ 1,000
Minimum compensation amount	$ 300	$ 550	$ 50
Maximum compensation limit	$150,000	$250,000	$10,000
Defined benefit limit	$ 90,000	$200,000	$ 5,000

[I.R.C. §§ 401(a)(17)(B), 402(g)(5), 404(l), 408(k)(8), 414(q)(1), 415(d); I.R.S. Notice 2011-90, 2011-47 I.R.B. 791 for 2012]

Q 1:5 May elective deferrals to a SEP be based on bonuses?

Yes. A SEP may contain a cash bonus option. The employer may permit eligible employees to make elective deferrals on bonuses that, at the employee's election, may be contributed into the SEP or received by the employee in cash. The elective contribution is deemed made on the day that the cash would have been paid had the election to defer amounts into the SEP not been made. The restrictions applicable to regular elective contributions apply fully to elective deferrals based on bonuses (see chapter 10).

Note. The updated Listing of Required Modifications (LRM) for SARSEPs released by the Internal Revenue Service (IRS) in 2002 deleted the separate option for making elective deferrals from bonuses. This makes it apparent that employers should design their salary reduction agreements to either include a separate election with respect to bonuses or make it clear that bonuses are part of the salary reduction agreement (see Appendix A). [LRMs are available at *www.irs.gov* (search for "LRM").]

Q 1:6 In addition to complying with the appropriate limits on dollar amounts, what rules must be met before an IRA may be treated as a SEP?

Five rules, in addition to those addressing limits on dollar amounts (see Q 1:3), must be met before an IRA may be treated as a SEP:

1. The SEP plan may not provide for minimum age and service requirements that are more stringent than those allowed by law (see Qs 2:42–2:57).
2. Contributions may not discriminate in favor of any HCE (see Qs 1:14, 5:26).
3. Employer contributions may not be conditioned on the retention of the employee's contribution in the SEP IRA, and withdrawals must be permitted (see Q 5:25). A special rule regarding elective deferrals may also apply (see Qs 5:17, 5:18).
4. There must be a definite written allocation formula for contributions, although the contribution itself may be discretionary (see Q 5:22).
5. If the SEP is part of a top-heavy plan (i.e., a plan or group of plans that primarily benefits key employees; see Q 3:16), the employer may have to make a minimum contribution to every non-key employee's IRA (see Q 8:8). (When an IRS model SEP (Form 5305-SEP) or a nonintegrated prototype SEP is the only plan maintained by an employer and no elective contributions are being made, a minimum top-heavy contribution is not required because all contributions will be allocated in proportion to compensation.)

Q 1:7 When must the election to make deferrals to a SEP be executed?

The election to make deferrals to a SEP must be executed before the amount would have been payable to the employee in cash (see Q 12:1). Employees whose wages are reported on Form W-2 frequently make elective contributions each payroll period to avoid contributions of larger amounts from end-of-year earnings. Elections for self-employed individuals must be in effect before such individuals' compensation (earned income) is determined on the last day of the business's taxable year. (A sample SEP deferral form appears in Appendix A.)

Example 1. Paul is paid $1,000 per month on the 15th day of each month. His employer, Jupiter Corporation, established an elective SEP arrangement in 1990. For the 2012 calendar year, Paul defers 4.166 percent of his annual wages by electing to defer $500 on December 7. After Social Security and other appropriate payroll taxes are withheld, Paul will receive a check for less than $500 on December 15. Paul's federal taxable income, $11,500, is reported in box 1 of his W-2 form for 2012, and $12,000 is reported in box 2 (Social Security wages). Jupiter Corporation deposits $500 into Paul's SEP IRA. Paul's election was made before he would have received the amount in cash on December 15.

Example 2. All partners of the Star Partnership receive a draw of $10,000 per month from the partnership. Star expects a large profit for 2012. On December 31, 2012, the partners meet and elect to defer a fixed percentage of their earned income (to be determined by their accountant in March). The partners' elective contributions are deposited by the partnership into a SEP IRA on March 5, 2013. Subject to any limits that may apply, the 2012 elective contribution was timely made (see Q 4:45) and is included in the earned income of each partner for 2012. Each partner will deduct a corresponding amount on his or her 2012 Form 1040, U.S. Individual Income Tax Return.

Q 1:8 Into what sort of accounts are SEP contributions made?

Generally, SEP contributions are made into the traditional IRA that is established by each eligible employee. An employer IRA under Code Section 408(c) may also be used to receive contributions in connection with a SEP program. An employer IRA trust (group trust) may be established by an employer or employee association (see Qs 5:30, 5:31).

An IRA is a written trust or custodial account. An IRA may be a nontransferable annuity contract or, if issued before November 7, 1978, an endowment contract. An employer IRA trust (or group trust) is treated as an individual retirement account under Code Section 408(a). [I.R.C. §§ 408(a), 408(b), 408(c), see, also, Rev. Rul. 81-100, 1981-1 C.B. 326 and I.R.S. Notice 2012-6, 2012-3 I.R.B. 293, modifying Rev. Rul. 2011-1, 2011-2 I.R.B. 251, and Rev. Rul. 2008-40, 2008-2 C.B. 166, regarding group trusts.]

Q 1:9 What are the differences between a trustee and custodian?

The differences between a *trustee* and a *custodian* are minor. A trust is a legal entity under which assets are actually owned and held on behalf of a beneficiary. As the legal owner, a trustee has some level of discretionary fiduciary authority over the assets of the fund. The trustee must exercise that authority in the best interests of the beneficial owner (i.e., the account owner).

A custodial arrangement is similar to a trust, but the custodian simply holds the assets on behalf of the owner of the assets. Other than holding the assets and doing as the owner orders, the custodian has no fiduciary obligations to the owner.

Q 1:10 May an employer require that an eligible employee participate in a SEP?

Yes. An employer may require that an eligible employee establish an IRA as a condition of employment (see Q 2:67). It may wish to do so because if one or more eligible employees elect not to participate in a SEP that the employer establishes, adverse tax consequences can result (see Qs 1:11, 5:4).

Q 1:11 What action may an employer take if an employee is unable or unwilling to execute SEP IRA documents or the employer is unable to locate a former employee?

An employer may execute any necessary documents on behalf of an employee who is eligible to make a contribution to a SEP if the employee is unable or unwilling to execute such documents. Similarly, an employer may execute any necessary documents on behalf of an eligible former employee if the employer is unable to locate the former employee. Failure to establish a valid SEP IRA on behalf of an eligible employee could result in the employer's SEP arrangement's being disqualified. [Prop. Treas. Reg. § 1.408-7(d)(2); I.R.S. Notice 81-1, 1981-1 C.B. 610; Ann. 80-112, 1980-36 I.R.B. 35]

> **Example.** Thelma, an employee eligible to receive a SEP contribution, dies before establishing an IRA. Her employer may establish an IRA in Thelma's name. Thelma's estate is designated as the beneficiary of the IRA. (An interest-bearing investment is generally selected for an IRA established in such a manner.)

> **Note.** The IRS has the authority to require reports with respect to employees who cannot be located, but so far it has not done so. [Prop. Treas. Reg. § 1.408-9(c)] (See also Q 5:21, regarding employment on a certain date.)

Q 1:12 Must an employer make SEP contributions?

Generally, no. A SEP arrangement is merely an agreement under which contributions, discretionary on a year-to-year basis, are made by the employer. The documents establishing a SEP arrangement may allow an employer to specify a contribution amount or fixed percentage, but such a provision may be changed by amendment at any time (see Q 5:23). If, however, elective contributions are made under a SARSEP and the arrangement is top heavy, or if any key employee makes an elective contribution and the employer uses model

Form 5305A-SEP to establish the SARSEP, then a minimum top-heavy contribution may have to be made (see Q 8:1).

Highly Compensated Employees

Q 1:13 May a SEP favor higher-paid employees?

Yes. A SEP arrangement may not discriminate in favor of any HCE (see Q 1:14). Nevertheless, contributions may be allocated to favor more highly paid employees without being considered discriminatory, provided certain rules are followed (see Q 5:26 and chapter 9). [I.R.C. § 408(k)(3)]

Q 1:14 Who is a *highly compensated employee*?

For years beginning after 1996, the definition of *highly compensated employee* under Code Section 414(q) has been simplified; the term now refers to the following:

1. An individual who was a 5 percent owner at any time during the current or preceding year, or
2. An individual who had compensation from the employer exceeding $80,000 (indexed for inflation; $115,000 for 2012) for the preceding year and was in the top-paid group.

[I.R.C. § 414(q)(1)]

Note 1. The statutory language of Code Section 414(q) uses the term *5 percent owner* but defines that term to mean a "more than" 5 percent owner. In addition, the Code Section 318 attribution rules are used to determine an individual's ownership interest (see discussion of "attribution rules" in Q 8:7). [I.R.C. § 414(q)(2)]

Note 2. The employer may elect to limit highly compensated treatment for a year to employees who were in the top-paid group of employees for that year (see Q 1:15).

Dollar Amount/Compensation. The applicable dollar amount (item 2) for a particular plan year (current year) or look-back year (i.e., preceding year) is the dollar amount for the calendar year in which the plan year or look-back year begins (see Appendix G). Compensation is the compensation received by the employee from the employer for the current year, including elective or salary reduction contributions to a cafeteria plan, cash or deferred arrangement, or tax-sheltered annuity. [Temp. Treas. Reg. § 1.414(q)-1T, Q&A-3(c)(1), Q&A-13]

The rule requiring the highest paid officer to be treated as an HCE was repealed for plan years beginning after 1996. [SBJPA § 1431]

Example 1. Garage maintains a calendar-year SEP plan. Ronald, the only employee, is a nonowner. Ronald earned $120,000 in 2011 but earned only

$60,000 in 2012. Ronald is an HCE in 2012 because he earned more than $115,000 (the 2012 limit) in the preceding year (2011).

Example 2. Dumpster maintains a calendar-year SEP plan. Hank, the only employee, is a nonowner. Hank earned $90,000 in 2011, but earned $150,000 in 2012. Hank does not have a 5 percent or greater ownership interest in Dumpster, nor did he earn more than the 2012 limit of $115,000 in 2011; therefore, he is not treated as an HCE in 2012. Hank will be treated as an HCE in 2013.

Example 3. Dumpster maintains an SEP plan with a plan year that begins on December 1, 2010. Sheila, the only employee, is a nonowner. For the plan year that ends in 2011, the 2010 limit ($110,000) is used to determine if Sheila is an HCE. Assume Sheila earned $90,000 in 2010, but earned $150,000 in 2011. Sheila does not have a 5 percent or greater ownership interest in Dumpster, nor did she earn more than the 2010 limit of $110,000 in 2010; therefore, she is not treated as an HCE in 2011. Sheila will be treated as an HCE in 2012.

Q 1:15 Who is included in the top-paid group, and how is a top-paid group election made?

In general, the top 20 percent of employees, ranked by compensation paid during a given year, are considered members of the top-paid group once the top-paid group election is made or once the SEP document makes the election automatic. [I.R.C. § 414(g)(3)]

Notice 97-45 [1997-2 C.B. 296] and Notice 98-1 [1998-1 C.B. 610] indicate that an employer may make a top-paid group election in its plan document. Once such an election is made, it will apply to all future years unless changed by the employer. Furthermore, if such an election is made, only 5 percent owners and employees in the top-paid group are considered HCEs.

Practice Pointer. An employer should keep track of whether the top-paid group election applies and, if so, to which years the election applies for purposes of making amendments in the future.

Q 1:16 Do the family aggregation rules apply to the post-1996 definition of highly compensated employee?

No. The family aggregation rules were repealed by the Small Business Job Protection Act of 1996 (SBJPA). The definition of *5 percent owner* as amended, however, requires family attribution under Code Section 318. This is because the definition of a 5 percent owner in Code Section 414(q)(2) refers to Code Section 416(i)(1), which in turn refers to the attribution rules of Code Section 318.

Q 1:17 Which employees are *non-highly compensated employees?*

Any employee who is not a highly compensated employee (see Q 1:14) is a *non-highly compensated employee (NHCE)*.

Establishment

Q 1:18 What kinds of documents may be used to establish a SEP or SARSEP arrangement?

Documents that an employer may use to establish a SEP or SARSEP arrangement come in several forms: IRS model documents, IRS-approved prototype plans, individually designed plans, and non-IRS-approved plans. In addition, if a qualifying entity can establish that at least 10 sponsoring organizations will sponsor the identical prototype IRA or SEP, a mass submitter plan may be approved for use by sponsors of prototypes (see Q 3:28).

Q 1:19 Where can an employer obtain an IRS-approved SEP or SARSEP document?

Many sponsors of IRAs (banks, mutual funds, insurance companies, and other financial institutions) have either prototype SEP or SARSEP plan documents (or both) or permit employers to use the IRS's model SEP document (Form 5305-SEP) or model SARSEP document (Form 5305A-SEP) (or both).

Termination

Q 1:20 How is a SEP or SARSEP terminated?

A SEP may be terminated by an amendment prepared by the employer. Employees must be given notice of the amendment (see chapter 13). Because contributions are generally discretionary, a formal termination is not usually necessary to terminate a SEP.

To discontinue elective contributions under a SARSEP, however, an employer must formally terminate the elective portion of the plan by notifying the financial institution handling the SEP-IRAs that SARSEP contributions will no longer be made and that the contract or agreement relating to the SARSEP is being terminated. [IRS Pub. 4336, available at: *http://www.irs.gov/pub/irs-pdf/p4336.pdf* (visited on Aug. 22, 2012)] No notice to the IRS that the SARSEP has been terminated is required.

Qualified Status

Q 1:21 Is a SEP a *qualified plan*?

No. A *qualified plan* is a plan that satisfies special requirements contained in Code Section 401(a). A SEP is a tax-sanctioned plan, the rules for which are contained in Code Section 408. Because a SEP is not qualified, distributions from a SEP do not qualify for the favorable tax treatment—such as 10-year income averaging and capital gains treatment (see Q 5:50) that is applicable to certain qualifying lump-sum distributions from qualified plans. [I.R.C. § 402(d)] When a SEP is "disqualified," it loses its tax-exempt status (i.e., it is no longer tax sanctioned) and ceases to be a SEP.

Q 1:22 Is a SEP IRA exempt from tax?

A SEP IRA is exempt from tax unless it ceases to be an IRA. An IRA loses its exemption from tax when the owner or beneficiary engages in a prohibited transaction (see Qs 4:20, 5:45 to 5:46) or borrows money from the IRA. In addition, IRAs are subject to tax on their unrelated business taxable income under Code Section 511. [*See* Ltr. Rul. 8830061 regarding payment and reimbursement to IRA of taxes on unrelated business taxable income and investment indebtedness, also treated as contributions; see Q 10:5.]

All assets are treated as distributed as of the first day of the taxable year that the IRA ceases to be treated as an IRA. To the extent that SEP IRA assets are pledged, they are treated as distributed. [I.R.C. §§ 408(e)(2)(B), 408(e)(3), 408(e)(4)] If someone other than the owner or beneficiary of an IRA (or SIMPLE IRA) engages in a prohibited transaction, that person may be subject to prohibited transaction penalty taxes (see Qs 4:20–4:22).

Q 1:23 May a participant roll over a distribution from an employer's retirement plan to a SEP-IRA?

Yes. Eligible rollover distributions are permitted between a qualified plan and 403(b) annuity and custodial account plans and governmental 457(b) plans, including the rollover of an eligible governmental 457(b) plan into a traditional IRA (which includes a SEP-IRA), subject to certain conditions (see Q 1:36 and Qs 15:50–15:52).

Compliance

Q 1:24 What voluntary compliance program has the IRS established for SEPs?

The IRS is aware of the difficulties employers have in establishing and maintaining SEP arrangements. In many cases, employers fail to cover their eligible employees. The IRS has therefore added a voluntary compliance program for employer plans and, in 2002, added SEPs to the types of plans that could be corrected (see chapter 17). The program became available for the first time in 1998 and generally is updated annually. The program includes a streamlined submission application procedure that applies to IRA-based plans, such as a SEP, a SARSEP, or a SIMPLE.

Furthermore, the Department of Labor (DOL) has established the Voluntary Fiduciary Correction Program (VFCP), which provides a means for plans to correct certain fiduciary breaches without fear of penalties (see chapter 17).

> **Note.** In 2009, the IRS began an Employee Plans Compliance Unit (EPCU) project that focuses on a sampling of taxpayers who either sponsored a SEP and/or received a Form 5498, IRA Contribution Information, which reflected an amount in Box 8 (SEP contribution) of Form 5498. The SEP project focuses on determining the accuracy of the information reported on Form 5498 and compliance with regard to the SEP plan.

Pros and Cons

Q 1:25 What are the advantages of a SEP arrangement?

Advantages of a SEP arrangement flow to both the employer and the employee. For the employer, they include the following:

- Less costly to establish and administer than a qualified plan
- Easily obtainable plan documents and (for most employers) automatic document reliance (see Q 3:2)
- Exclusion of employees who do not satisfy a minimum service requirement of up to three years (see Q 2:42)
- May be established on or before the due date of the business tax return (see Q 2:30)
- Less costly legal review than that required for a qualified plan
- Low trustee, custodian, issuer, or management fees (generally) for assets held in IRAs
- No qualified nonelective contributions; no qualified matching contributions
- Simple elective ADP test (compared with a traditional 401(k) plan), although the test may be harder to pass than in a 401(k); no average contribution percentage (ACP) test (see chapter 12 on SARSEPs)
- No summary plan descriptions; no summary annual reports (see Qs 4:11, 4:12)
- Annual Form 5500 filings generally not required (see Qs 4:11, 4:12)
- No joint and survivor annuity requirements
- Limited fiduciary liability (see chapter 4)

- Easy to terminate

For the employee, the advantages include the following:

- Accumulation of pretax dollars
- Exclusion of elective contributions from current income (see chapter 11)
- Not subject to rules governing qualified domestic relations orders
- May be transferred to former spouse without tax as a "transfer incident to divorce" (see Q 5:60)
- Possible creditor protection (see Q 4:72)

Q 1:26 What are the disadvantages of a SEP arrangement?

Following are some disadvantages of a SEP arrangement:

- Prototype and model documents may have limited features (see chapter 3)
- Large employers, tax-exempt organizations, and government employers may not provide for salary reduction feature (see Qs 2:22, 2:23)
- Must include most part-time and seasonal employees (see Qs 2:42, 2:46)
- Full vesting of all contributions (see Q 2:55)
- No matching contributions
- Limited employer deduction when elective deferrals are made by the employee
- No loan features
- Life insurance not permitted
- No last-day requirements for contributions
- No exclusion for employees who work less than 500 or 1,000 hours
- Limited creditor protection in most states, but may be exempt from federal bankruptcy estate (see Q 4:72)
- Loss of IRA deduction in many cases
- Possible need to determine HCEs for ADP testing in a SARSEP and key employees for top-heavy testing in an integrated SEP
- Integration (permitted disparity) may not be as advantageous as it is in a qualified plan
- 125 percent ADP test (see Q 1:3)
- 50 percent SARSEP participation rate requirement (see Q 2:20)

Q 1:27 What should an employer consider when attempting to select the best retirement plan?

Generally, the best retirement plan is the plan that most nearly satisfies the needs and expectations of the employer. Selecting the most appropriate retirement plan for a specific organization requires an analysis of many factors, including whether the employer is concerned about how much its employees will receive or how much must be contributed on their behalf.

SEP arrangements and SARSEPs are easily installed and simple to administer. They are not accompanied by the expenses and burdensome administration often associated with qualified plans. Nevertheless, only after considering many factors—including potential growth of the business, work patterns, employee turnover, employee age, and whether employees were employed on the last day of the plan year or worked at least 500 or 1,000 hours—and analyzing a group's eligibility to participate initially and then to receive contributions (and the extent to which those contributions will be vested upon an employee's termination) can the plan that offers the least employer cost at all points along an employment time line be determined (see Q 2:55).

Other factors that can play a role in determining the most appropriate plan choice are dates of hire and plan entry dates, the number of part-time employees, whether service is continuous, the date the business commenced, the plan year, the availability of other retirement programs, and whether the employer wishes to exclude certain employees for reasons other than failure to meet minimum age or service requirements.

Legislation

Q 1:28 How did the Economic Growth and Tax Relief Reconciliation Act of 2001 (EGTRRA) affect retirement plans?

Numerous changes to both qualified and nonqualified retirement plans were brought about by EGTRRA, including the following changes:

SIMPLEs Created. Under a SIMPLE, employees may choose to make salary reduction contributions (up to $11,500 for 2012) to the plan or to receive those amounts as part of their regular compensation. In addition, the employer makes a matching contribution or nonelective contribution on behalf of eligible employees. [I.R.C. § 408(p); SBJPA § 1421] (See chapter 14.)

Definition of Highly Compensated Employee. For years beginning after 1996, the definition of *highly compensated employee* under Code Section 414(q) has been simplified (see Qs 1:14, 1:15).

Family Aggregation. The family aggregation rules have been repealed for plan years beginning after 1996; however, the family attribution rules of Code Section 318 still apply in determining who is a 5 percent owner (see Qs 8:7, 12:10).

Five-Year Averaging. Five-year forward income averaging for qualified plans has been repealed effective for taxable years beginning after 1999. The 10-year grandfather provision contained in the Tax Reform Act of 1986 (TRA '86) has been preserved for individuals born before 1936, however.

$5,000 Death Benefit Exclusion. The $5,000 death benefit exclusion under Code Section 101(b) has been repealed effective for decedents dying after August 20, 1996. Amounts that had qualified for the death benefit exclusion were not permitted to be rolled over. [SBJPA § 1402]

Required Distributions. The "later of separation from service" rules that were in effect before TRA '86 have been reinstated. These rules, which prohibited most in-service distributions under qualified plans, do not (and never did) apply to distributions from IRAs, SEPs, SARSEPs, and SIMPLEs, which must commence by April 1 following attainment of age 70½.

Excess Distribution Tax. Before its repeal, Code Section 4980A imposed a 15 percent excise tax on any excess distribution, generally defined for 1997 as a distribution exceeding $155,000 in any year ($775,000 for certain lump-sum distributions). SBJPA Section 1452(b) suspended the excise tax for distributions received in 1997, 1998, and 1999. The Taxpayer Relief Act of 1997 (TRA '97) repealed the excess distribution tax entirely for distributions received after 1996 and repealed the excess accumulation tax for decedents dying after 1996. [I.R.C. § 4980A, repealed; TRA '97 § 1073(a)]

IRA Withdrawal Exceptions. Code Section 72(t) generally imposes a 10 percent premature distribution penalty on most distributions received from a qualified plan or an IRA (including a SEP, SARSEP, or SIMPLE) before the participant or owner attains age 59½. Legislation has added several more exceptions for penalty-free distributions from IRAs, SEPs, SARSEPs, and SIMPLEs (see Q 5:56).

Qualified Plan Minimum Participation Requirement. For years beginning after 1996, the minimum participation rules under Code Section 401(a)(26) apply only to defined benefit plans. Those rules never applied to SEPs, SARSEPs, or SIMPLEs, but may affect plan choice. [SBJPA § 1432]

Definition of Compensation. For years beginning after 1997, Section 415 compensation includes most elective deferrals—but not for all purposes (see Q 6:4).

Combined Plan Limit. Employers that maintain a defined benefit plan in addition to a defined contribution plan (including a SEP or SARSEP) are no longer subject to the combined plan limit of Code Section 415(e) for limitation years beginning after 1999. [SBJPA § 1452(a)]

Since the repeal of Code Section 415(e), the maximum employer deduction for contributions to a combination of defined benefit and defined contribution plans (including a SEP, a SARSEP, and a SIMPLE) is the greater of 25 percent of the participant's compensation or the amount necessary to fund the defined benefit plan. The JCWAA made a change effective for years beginning after 2001 to allow the combination of plans to exceed the 25 percent of compensation limit if the defined contribution plan accepts only elective deferrals. In other words, the defined benefit plan's "contribution" for the year may exceed 25 percent of the participant's compensation, and that participant will still be permitted to make an elective deferral contribution to a defined contribution plan (including a SARSEP). [I.R.C. § 404(a)(7)(C)(ii)]

Recovery of Basis. A simplified basis recovery method based on the employee's age on the annuity starting date, similar to the simplified method provided by the IRS in Notice 88-118 [1988-2 CB 450], is available if the annuity starting date is after November 18, 1996. *The change does not apply to IRAs, SEPs, or SIMPLEs,* under which distributions must commence by April 1 following attainment of age 70½. [I.R.C. § 72(d)(1)(G); SBJPA § 1403; I.R.S. Notice 98-2, 1998-2 I.R.B. 22]

Roth IRA. Available for taxable years beginning after 1997 [I.R.C. § 408A], the Roth IRA allows an individual to make a nondeductible contribution. For 2012, the Roth IRA annual contribution limit is $5,000, plus catch-up contributions of up to $1,000 if age 50 or over on the last day of the calendar year. The account must be designated as a Roth IRA at the time of establishment. The maximum contribution for 2012 is phased out for single taxpayers with adjusted gross income (AGI) between $110,000 and $125,000 ($173,000 to $183,000 for a joint return). Contributions to a Roth IRA may continue to be made after age 70½, and the mandatory distribution rules do not apply before the Roth IRA owner's death. Excess contributions are subject to the 6 percent excise tax under Code Section 4973.

A qualified distribution from a Roth IRA is not includible in income. A *qualified distribution* is a distribution

1. Made after the five-taxable-year period beginning with
   a. The first day of the first taxable year for which a contribution was made by the individual to a Roth IRA; or
   b. If earlier, the first day of the taxable year in which the first conversion contribution was made, if the distribution is allocable to a rollover from a non-Roth IRA; or
2. Made after the Roth IRA owner attains age 59½, or to the beneficiary on the owner's death, or attributable to the owner's being disabled, or up to a $10,000 lifetime limit for first-time homebuyer expenses.

If the distribution is not a qualified distribution, the Roth IRA owner may recover the full amount contributed before any (taxable) earnings are received.

A taxpayer whose modified AGI (MAGI) is less than $100,000 (before 2010) may roll over or convert an IRA into a Roth IRA. The taxable portion of the amount transferred is taxable, but it is not subject to the 10 percent premature distribution penalty under Code Section 72(t). If the conversion was made before 1999, ratable income inclusion over a four-year period was available. The taxable portion of a conversion made in 2010 is spread out over two years (2011 and 2012) unless the taxpayer elects to have the amount taxed in the conversion year (2010).

Education IRA (Coverdell ESA). Among numerous tax incentives for education, TRA '97 introduced the Education IRA, effective for taxable years beginning after 1997. In 2001, the Education IRA was renamed the Coverdell

Education Savings Account (Coverdell ESA). The annual contribution to an ESA, which is not deductible, is limited to $2,000 per designated beneficiary after 2001 ($500 per designated beneficiary for years prior to 2002), and is phased out ratably for contributors whose MAGI (AGI plus any amount excluded by Code Section 911, 931, or 936) is between $95,000 and $110,000 ($190,000 to $220,000 for a joint return). Excess contributions are subject to the 6 percent excise tax under Code Section 4973.

No contribution may be made to the ESA after the designated beneficiary attains age 18 (unless the designated beneficiary is a "special needs beneficiary"). Neither the contribution nor the account's investment income is included in the designated beneficiary's gross income, and distributions are excludable from the designated beneficiary's gross income to the extent that they do not exceed qualified education expenses incurred during the year of the distribution. Generally, any balance remaining when the beneficiary (other than a special needs beneficiary) reaches age 30 must be distributed.

The earnings portion of any distribution not used for qualified education expenses is subject to income tax and to a 10 percent penalty. Before the designated beneficiary reaches age 30, however, the balance may be transferred tax free to an ESA for another member of the original beneficiary's family; the new designated beneficiary (other than a special needs beneficiary) must be under age 30.

Q 1:29 When did EGTRRA become effective?

EGTRRA has various effective dates. Most of its provisions became effective in 2002 and were phased in over several years. Some of its provisions became effective immediately (i.e., on June 7, 2001), and some were set to expire sooner than others. On August 17, 2006, the Pension Protection Act of 2006 (PPA) (H.R. 4) was enacted into law. The PPA contains a number of significant tax incentives to enhance retirement savings. The PPA makes the EGTRRA changes (see Qs 1:30–1:36) permanent and also provides for the indexing of the income limits for traditional, spousal, and Roth IRA phaseout rules to prevent these benefits from being eroded by inflation (see Qs 1:33–1:34). If it were not for the PPA, the increased contribution limits, enhanced portability options, catch-up contributions provisions, and so on, would have expired after 2010 and reverted to their pre-EGTRRA limits.

The EGTRRA changes and their effective dates that apply to IRA, SIMPLE, SEP, and SARSEP arrangements are more fully discussed next (see Qs 1:30–1:36).

Q 1:30 How did EGTRRA affect IRAs?

EGTRRA made numerous changes that affected IRAs. As of 2002, it increased the overall annual contribution limit for traditional IRAs and Roth IRAs. Individuals age 50 or older (as of the end of the taxable year) may make catch-up contributions if otherwise eligible to contribute to an IRA or Roth IRA. As of

2003, an employer may permit employees to make voluntary traditional IRA (or Roth IRA) contributions into the employer's plan (referred to as deemed IRAs). The EGTRRA changes that affect traditional IRAs are as follows.

Increase in Annual IRA Contribution Limit. For taxable years beginning after 2001, EGTRRA increased the annual IRA contribution limit from $2,000 to $5,000, as follows:

Year	*Increased Limit*
2002–2004	$3,000
2005–2007	$4,000
2008–2012	$5,000

[I.R.C. §§ 219(b)(1)(A), 219(b)(5)(A)]

After 2008, the annual contribution limit of $5,000 is subject to COLAs, rounded to the next lower $500 increment. [I.R.C. § 219(b)(5)(C)] Within applicable limits (see Q 1:3), catch-up contributions are excludable from the participant's income (see Q 11:1) and are deductible by the employer (see Q 10:4). For 2012, the contribution limit remains at $5,000.

Spousal IRAs. Nothing in EGTRRA changes the requirements for spousal IRAs, except for the increased limits and liberalization of the rollover rules (see Q 1:35).

Catch-up Contributions for Individuals Age 50 or Older. For taxable years beginning after 2001, if an individual has attained the age of 50 before the close of the calendar year (e.g., for 2012, an individual born before 1962) and meets the other eligibility requirements, the annual IRA contribution limit for that individual is increased as follows:

Tax Year	*Normal Limit*	*Catch-up Amount*	*Total Contribution*
2002	$3,000	$ 500	$3,500
2003	$3,000	$ 500	$3,500
2004	$3,000	$ 500	$3,500
2005	$4,000	$ 500	$4,500
2006	$4,000	$1,000	$5,000
2007	$4,000	$1,000	$5,000
2008	$5,000	$1,000	$6,000
2009	$5,000	$1,000	$6,000
2010	$5,000	$1,000	$6,000
2011	$5,000	$1,000	$6,000
2012	$5,000	$1,000	$6,000

[I.R.C. § 219(b)(5)(B)]

Note. The catch-up amount for a traditional IRA (and a Roth IRA) is not subject to COLAs. Therefore, after 2010, when COLAs increase the $5,000 normal limit to $5,500, the catch-up amount will remain $1,000. [I.R.C. § 219(b)(5)(C)]

Example. Marvin, age 52, and Lydia, age 48, are married, and they file a joint return. For 2012, Marvin's IRA contribution limit is $6,000, and Lydia's IRA contribution limit is $5,000. Marvin and Lydia must have compensation, in the aggregate, equal to at least the amount they contribute.

Calculation of Deductible Contributions. Although EGTRRA does not modify the AGI phaseout ranges for calculating an individual's deductible contribution to a traditional IRA, if an individual or an individual's spouse is an active participant in an employer-sponsored plan, the calculation of the deductible portion of the contribution may be affected by the catch-up contribution permitted under EGTRRA.

[*See* IRS Publication 590, *Individual Retirement Arrangements (IRAs)*, Worksheets 1-1 and 1-2 (pages 14 and 19) for computing IRA contribution deduction calculations for different filing statuses and for an individual whose spouse is an active participant in an employer's plan.]

Deemed IRAs under Employer Plans. For plan years beginning after 2002, a qualified plan, a 403(b) plan, or a governmental 457(b) plan may accept traditional IRA or Roth IRA contributions, or both, if such contributions are permitted under the employer's plan and other requirements are satisfied. When established in an employer's plan, these accounts are called deemed IRAs, and contributions to them are treated as if they were made into an IRA or Roth IRA trust, annuity, or custodial account established at a financial institution (see Q 13:102). Thus, the employer's plan is subject to the same information reporting as other IRAs (i.e., Form 5498, IRA). In addition, the amount contributed as a deemed IRA contribution is part of the individual's IRA limit for the year. [I.R.C. §§ 408(q)(1), 408(q)(3)]

Update of Life Expectancy Tables. The IRS was required to modify the life expectancy tables to reflect current life expectancy. The 2001 proposed regulations for required minimum distributions (RMDs) changed the RMD rules, but did not change the old life expectancy rules. Instead, the regulations established a uniform table that can be used to determine lifetime RMDs. This table has the effect of lengthening the payout period and reducing minimum payouts. [EGTRRA § 634]

On April 17, 2002, the IRS finalized the 2001 proposed regulations under Code Section 401(a)(9) regarding RMDs. Changes and clarifications made include the following:

1. *New mortality table*. The final regulations contain a new mortality table. Single life divisors used by Roth IRA beneficiaries were changed slightly. [Treas. Reg. § 1.401(a)(9)-9, Q&A-1]

2. *Determination of designated beneficiary.* The designated beneficiary of the account will be determined as of September 30 (instead of December 31) of the year following the year of the IRA owner's death. This rule applies in 2003, regardless of when the account owner died. In most cases, there will be no change in the identity of the beneficiary under the new and old rules. [Treas. Reg. § 1.401(a)(9)-4, Q&A-1]
3. *Death of designated beneficiary.* If the designated beneficiary dies between the date of the account owner's death and the September 30 determination date, that beneficiary will still be the measuring life for postlife RMDs, regardless of who the successor beneficiary may be. [Treas. Reg. § 1.401(a)(9)-4, Q&A-4(c)]
4. *Shortest trust beneficiary life expectancy used.* All beneficiaries of the trust are generally considered in determining the beneficiary with the shortest life expectancy. An individual whose benefit is contingent on another beneficiary's dying before the payout of the entire plan balance is ignored. However, a beneficiary whose benefit is merely postponed until the death of another beneficiary (e.g., the remainder beneficiary of a trust where another individual is entitled only to the income from the trust) is not ignored. [Treas. Reg. § 1.401(a)(9)-4, Q&A-4(a); *see* Ltr. Rul. 200537044 (Mar. 29, 2005) where the beneficiary form specifically named each subtrust as a partial beneficiary allowing use of individual life expectancy of each separate-share beneficiary. This issue is more fully discussed in the *Roth IRA Answer Book*, 6th edition, chapter 8, CCH Incorporated, 2012.]
5. *Disclaimer rules revised.* An individual may disclaim an interest to make a contingent beneficiary a primary designated beneficiary and use the new designated beneficiary's life expectancy as the measuring life. The disclaimer must, however, be valid under Code Section 2518. The final regulations clarify that beneficiaries can be removed by disclaimer or payout, but they cannot be added. [Treas. Reg. § 1.401(a)(9)-4, Q&A-4(a)]

Q 1:31 How are required minimum distributions from a SEP IRA computed?

RMDs from a SEP IRA are computed in the same manner as RMDs are computed for a traditional IRA. The RMD for each year is determined by dividing the SEP IRA account balance as of the close of business on December 31 of the preceding year by the applicable distribution period or life expectancy. Contributions made after the end of the year for the preceding year are disregarded in determining the RMD for that preceding year; thus, contributions increase the account balance in the year in which they are made. Distributions made after December 31 of last year are disregarded in determining the RMD for this year; thus, distributions reduce the account balance in the year they are made. [I.R.C. §§ 408(a)(6), 408(b)(3), matching the distribution rules under § 401(a)(9)]

Q 1:32 When must RMDs from a SEP IRA commence?

RMDs from a SEP IRA must commence in the same manner as in a traditional IRA. These distributions must start by April 1 of the year following the year in which age 70½ is reached. That April 1 is referred to as the required beginning date. If the RMD was not received in the year that age 70½ was reached, then that distribution must be made by the required beginning date. Distributions for each year after the year age 70½ is reached must be made by December 31 of such later year.

If an IRA owner dies before April 1 of the year following attainment of age 70½, no RMD is required because death occurred before the required beginning date. [I.R.C. § 401(a)(9)(C)]

> **Note.** The WRERA waived the application of the RMD rules for 2009. [WRERA § 201 (Pub. L. No. 110-4580); *see also* I.R.S. Notice 2009-9, 2009-5 I.R.B. 419, *modifying* Notice 2002-27, 2002-18 I.R.B. 814]

Q 1:33 How did EGTRRA provide incentives for employers to establish new plans and for employees to make contributions?

EGTRRA provided a tax credit for the administrative expenses of small employers that adopt new plans and another credit to encourage certain low-income taxpayers to make elective contributions.

Tax Credits for Retirement Plan Expenses. A small business that adopts a new SIMPLE or SEP can generally claim an income tax credit for 50 percent of the first $1,000 of administrative and retirement-education expenses for each of the first three years of the plan. This credit is available only to employers that did not have more than 100 employees with compensation in excess of $5,000 during the previous tax year and that did have at least 1 NHCE during the previous tax year. The credit is taken as a general business credit on the employer's tax return. The other 50 percent of the expenses may be taken as a business deduction. The expenses must be paid or incurred in taxable years beginning after 2001 and with respect to plans established or made effective after 2001. [I.R.C. § 45E]

Low-Income Taxpayer Contribution Credit. Beginning after 2001, certain individuals may receive a nonrefundable tax credit for a percentage of their contributions. This credit is based on a sliding scale percentage of up to $2,000 contributed to a traditional IRA or Roth IRA; elective deferrals made to a SIMPLE, a SEP, a 401(k) plan, a 403(b) plan, or a governmental 457(b) plan; and voluntary after-tax contributions to a qualified plan. The credit also applies to designated Roth contributions made to a 403(b), 401(k), or governmental 457(b) plan. The credit is in addition to any other tax benefit (i.e., the possible tax deduction) that the contribution gives the taxpayer. [I.R.C. §§ 25B(a), 25B(b)]

> **Note.** The maximum saver's credit is $1,000 ($2,000 for married couples). However, the credit amount is often much less, and due to the impact of other deductions and credits, may be zero (0).

To be eligible for the contribution tax credit, the taxpayer must be 18 years of age or older and must not be a full-time student or be claimed as a dependent on another taxpayer's tax return. [I.R.C. § 25B(c)]

The amount of the credit for any year is reduced by any distribution taken during the testing period from a qualified plan, a 403(b) plan, a governmental 457(b) plan, or a traditional IRA, whether or not the distribution is taxable. The *testing period* consists of the two preceding taxable years, the taxable year, and the period after the taxable year and before the due date of the federal income tax return of the individual (and spouse of the individual if a joint return is filed) for the taxable year, including extensions. [I.R.C. § 25B(c)] Form 8880 and its instructions have details on making this computation.

Example 1. John requests an extension of time to file his 2012 tax return until October 15, 2013. John will be ineligible for a tax credit for 2012 if he took distributions totaling at least $2,000 at any time between January 1, 2010, and October 15, 2013.

Example 2. Sally takes an IRA distribution of $2,000 on March 1, 2012. She is ineligible to claim the contribution tax credit for 2011, 2012, and 2013.

Certain types of withdrawals, including the return of an excess contribution, a rollover, and a loan from an annuity contract, are not treated as distributions for this purpose. [I.R.C. § 25B(d)(2)(C)]

Caution. Amounts withdrawn for first-time home purchases and for either medical or educational expenses may reduce or eliminate the credit for contributions or deferrals to retirement savings plans for the current year or future years even though they may not be subject to the 10 percent early withdrawal penalty (see Q 14:170).

Credit rates are based on 2012 AGI levels as outlined next.

Joint Filers		*Heads of Household*		*All Other Filers**		*Credit Rate*
Over	Not Over	Over	Not Over	Over	Not Over	
$ 0	$34,500	$ 0	$25,875	$ 0	$17,250	50%
$34,500	$37,500	$25,875	$28,125	$17,250	$18,750	20%
$37,500	$57,500	$28,125	$43,125	$18,750	$28,750	10%
$57,500	N/A	$43,125	N/A	$28,750	N/A	0%

* This column includes single filers, married filers filing separately, and surviving spouses. When it comes to computing this credit, EGTRRA puts a surviving spouse in an adverse position compared to a head of household.

Note. The PPA provides for indexing of the income limits applicable to the saver's credit beginning in 2007, which was also permanently extended by the PPA (see Q 1:38). [I.R.C. § 25B(h), stricken by PPA § 812; *see* I.R.S. Notice 2011-90, 2011-47 I.R.B. 791 for 2012]

[I.R.C. § 25B(b)]

Example 1. Harry is married and files a joint tax return with his wife, Ann. Harry's AGI for 2012 is $36,000. He contributes $2,000 to an IRA or as an elective deferral to a SARSEP. His tax credit for 2012 is $400 ($2,000 × .20). If Harry's contribution for 2012 is only $1,500, his tax credit for 2012 will be $300 ($1,500 × .20). If Harry contributed $5,000 to his IRA for 2012, his credit amount remains at $400 because only up to $2,000 of contributions may be considered for purposes of the low-income contribution credit.

Example 2. Janice, who is not married, has an AGI of $28,000 for 2012. Janice contributes (or makes an elective deferral of) $1,000 to an IRA. Janice's tax credit for 2012 is $100 ($1,000 × .10).

Although the contribution tax credit could be an incentive to contribute to a Roth IRA rather than to a traditional IRA, particularly if the credit could eliminate any income tax entirely, situations exist in which the IRS is paying for the traditional IRA contribution because the IRA deduction is included in the calculation of the AGI.

Example 3. Gary and Candace file a joint tax return. Each contributes $2,950 to a Roth IRA for 2012. Their AGI is $34,600. Because Gary and Candace are under age 50, their contribution limit for 2012 is $5,000. They are entitled to a credit of $800 (($2,000 + $2,000) × .20). If Gary or Candace contributes an additional $100 to a traditional IRA, their AGI will become $34,500, and the credit percentage will jump from 20 percent to 50 percent. Their combined credit will increase from $800 to $2,000 (($2,000 + $2,000) × .50), giving them a $1,200 reduction in tax for the additional IRA contribution.

Taxpayers qualify for the contribution tax credit even if they are over age 70½. However, distributions, including RMDs, may make taxpayers ineligible for the credit. For older taxpayers, a Roth IRA or a transfer to an employer's plan (if the individual is not a 5 percent owner and is not retiring) might be a good idea.

Practice Pointer. The fact that the credit is available to spouses who file separate returns means that a lower income spouse can qualify for the credit even if the couple's joint income is too high. For example, if a husband has an AGI of $60,000, and the wife has an AGI of $15,000, the wife qualifies for a credit of 50 percent of any qualified contribution on a separate return, even though the couple cannot take a credit for the contribution on a joint return.

Q 1:34 Can the low-income saver's credit be claimed after age 70½?

Yes. There is no maximum age for claiming the low-income saver's credit. However, distributions including RMDs may make taxpayers ineligible for the credit. In that case, an acceptable solution may be the conversion of a traditional

IRA to a Roth IRA or, if the taxpayer is not a 5 percent owner (and not retiring), a transfer to an employer's plan.

> **Caution.** Amounts withdrawn for a first-time home purchase or for payment of medical or educational expenses also have the potential to reduce or eliminate the credit for contributions or deferrals to retirement savings plans for the current year or future years. These withdrawals are not subject to the 10 percent premature distribution penalty.

Certain types of withdrawals, including the return of an excess contribution, a rollover, and a loan from an annuity contract, are not treated as distributions for this purpose. [I.R.C. § 25B(d)(2)(C)]

Q 1:35 How did EGTRRA and the JCWAA affect SEP, SARSEP, and SIMPLE arrangements?

EGTRRA changed many of the rules and increased many of the limits applicable to SEP, SARSEP, and SIMPLE arrangements. Those changes included the following.

Increase in Maximum Compensation Limits for SEPs and SIMPLEs. The maximum compensation that can be considered on behalf of any participant in a SEP or SIMPLE was increased (see Qs 6:1, 7:1). For 2012, the maximum compensation limit is $250,000. (See Appendix G for annual limitations in earlier years.)

The definition of *compensation* is also amended for SEPs and SIMPLEs to include an individual's net earnings that would be subject to self-employment taxes but for the fact that the individual is covered by a religious exemption. [I.R.C. §§ 401(a)(17), 404(l), 408(k)]

Increase in SEP Deduction Limit. The employer's deduction for SEP contributions is increased from 15 percent to 25 percent of the *aggregate* compensation of all participants (see Q 10:3). For purposes of the deduction limit, compensation is no longer reduced by elective deferrals (see Q 10:7). [I.R.C. § 404(a)(12)] All elective salary reduction contributions (including catch-up contributions) that are within appropriate limits are also deductible by the employer, separately from the 25 percent deduction limit. [I.R.C. §§ 404(a)(3), 404(a)(7), 404(a)(9), 404(n)]

Increase in SEP Contribution Limits under Code Section 415.

1. *Dollar limit.* For 2002, annual additions to a defined contribution plan for any participant cannot exceed $35,000 (or, if less, 25 percent of that participant's compensation). Generally, for years beginning after 2001, the annual additions limit per participant increases to $40,000. [I.R.C. § 415(c)(1)(A)] Beginning in 2003, the $40,000 annual additions limit was increased for COLAs in increments of $1,000. For 2012, the annual addition limitation was increased to $50,000 due to cost-of-living adjustments. [I.R.C. § 415(d)] Catch-up contributions (up to $5,500 for 2012) are separately deductible and may be deducted in addition to the

$50,000 (for 2012) limit (see Q 10:7). For this annual additions limit, a SEP is generally treated as a defined contribution plan (see Q 5:7). (See Appendix G for annual limitations in earlier years.)

2. *Percentage limit.* EGTRRA replaces the 25 percent of compensation limit with a 100 percent of compensation limit (not to exceed $40,000, as indexed) for years beginning after 2001. [I.R.C. § 415(c)(1)(B)] This change will permit, for example, a participant in a SARSEP to defer 100 percent of compensation not to exceed the applicable deferral limit for the year and receive other employer contributions, as long as the total contributions do not exceed $40,000 (as indexed) or the exclusion limit. The indexed amount for 2012 is $50,000.

Note. The 100 percent and $50,000 (for 2012) limits on annual additions are account limits and apply separately to each participant. [I.R.C. § 404(h)]

Increase in SEP Exclusion Limit. Although EGTRRA generally increased the maximum contribution to a SEP to the lesser of $40,000 (with cost-of-living adjustments) or 100 percent of compensation, Code Section 402(h)(2)(A), regarding the exclusion of SEP contributions from a participant's gross income, is based on includible compensation (see Qs 5:13, 11:1–11:3). That section provides that any contributions to a SEP that exceed 25 percent of a participant's "includible" compensation are includible in the employee's gross income *and* treated as regular IRA contributions. This 25 percent exclusion from income limit also includes amounts deferred under a SARSEP. A technical correction made by the JCWAA increased the exclusion percentage limit to 25 percent, but Congress neglected to amend Code Section 402(h)(2)(A) to include elective deferrals (see Q 11:1). Therefore, the sum of deferrals and the employer's regular SEP contributions cannot exceed 25 percent of the participant's first $250,000 (2012 limit) of includible compensation (i.e., compensation reduced by elective deferrals). The $50,000 limit may be lower. [I.R.C. § 402(h)] (However, see *Caution* next.)

Caution. It is unclear whether compensation used for the 25 percent exclusion under Code Section 402(h) includes catch-up elective deferrals. For example, if an employee who has $100,000 of pre-plan W-2 wages makes an elective deferral of $17,000 and a catch-up contribution of $5,500 for 2012, it is unclear whether the maximum exclusion amount is based on $77,500 ($100,000 – $17,000 – $5,500) or $83,000 ($100,000 – $17,000) of compensation. Code Section 414(v)(3), regarding the treatment of catch-up contributions, states:

In the case of any contribution to a plan under paragraph (1):

A. Such contribution shall not, with respect to the year in which the contribution is made

   i. be subject to any otherwise applicable limitation contained in section 402(g), 402(h), 403(b), 404(a), 404(h), 408(k), 408(p), 415, or 457, or

   ii. be taken into account in applying such limitations to other contributions or benefits under such plan or any other such plan.

Arguably, the exclusion amount should be based on $83,000; otherwise, the maximum employer contribution for the employee in question would be reduced by $1,375 ($20,750 – $19,375), computed as follows:

Contributions	*Not Excluding Catch-up Contributions*	*Excluding Catch-up Contributions*
a. Pre-plan wages	$100,000	$100,000
b. Section 402(g) elective	$ 17,000	$ 17,000
c. Catch-up	$ 0	$ 5,500
d. Includible compensation	$ 83,000	$ 77,500
e. Exclusion rate	× .25	× .25
f. Initial exclusion amount (line d × line e)	$ 20,750	$ 19,375

The statutory construction of Code Section 402(h)(2)(A) also suggests that $83,000 is the amount of compensation used for the participant exclusion limit. Code Section 402(h)(2)(A) states:

Limitations on employer contributions:

> Contributions made by an employer to a simplified employee pension with respect to an employee for any year shall be treated as distributed or made available to such employee and as contributions made by the employee to the extent such contributions exceed the lesser of

A. 25 percent of the compensation (within the meaning of Section 414(s)) from such employer includible in the employee's gross income for the year (determined without regard to the employer contributions to the simplified employee pension) or

B. The limitation in effect under Section 415(c)(1)(A), reduced in the case of any highly compensated employee (within the meaning of Section 414(q)) by the amount taken into account with respect to such employee under Section 408(k)(3)(D).

In the authors' opinions, statutory construction would appear to favor the $83,000 amount. Thus, catch-up contributions may be made in addition to the amount computed under the 25 percent exclusion limit, which is computed without reducing compensation for catch-up contributions (see Q 11:1).

Increase in the Elective Deferral Limit for SARSEP Plans. The elective deferral limit for a SARSEP increases from $10,500 (see Q 5:12) to the following levels in years beginning after 2001:

Year	*Increased Deferral Limit*
2002	$11,000
2003	$12,000

Year	*Increased Deferral Limit*
2004	$13,000
2005	$14,000
2006	$15,000
2007	$15,500
2008	$15,500
2009	$16,500
2010	$16,500
2011	$16,500
2012	$17,000

[I.R.C. § 402(g)(1)]

Beginning after 2006, the elective deferral limit is increased for COLAs in increments of $500 after 2006. [I.R.C. § 402(g)(5); *see* I.R.S. Notice 2011-90, 2011-47 I.R.B. 791 for 2012 limits] For 2012, the elective deferral limit is $17,000.

Catch-up Elective Deferral Contributions under a SARSEP for Individuals Age 50 or Older. For taxable years beginning after 2001, if an individual participates in a SARSEP and will attain age 50 by the end of the taxable year, that participant may make additional elective deferrals up to an applicable dollar limit. This catch-up amount is in addition to the normal deferral limit for the calendar year. The catch-up amount may be contributed without regard to the $50,000 (for 2012) contribution limit.

Example. Jane is a participant in a non-top-heavy SARSEP. In 2012, she earns $85,000, of which $17,000 is deferred into the SARSEP. The 25 percent exclusion limit is not more than, and in this case equal to the amount Jane defers (($85,000 – $17,000) × .25), or $17,000. (If Jane is age 50 or over, she may make an additional contribution of up to $5,500.) Her W-2 form will report $68,000 as her taxable compensation for 2012 ($62,500 if she makes a $5,500 catch-up contribution).

The maximum amount of a catch-up contribution is the lesser of the participant's compensation for the year or the applicable dollar amount. Applicable dollar amounts are as follows:

Year	*Applicable Dollar Amount*
2002	$1,000
2003	$2,000
2004	$3,000
2005	$4,000
2006	$5,000
2007	$5,000

Year	*Applicable Dollar Amount*
2008	$5,000
2009	$5,500
2010	$5,500
2011	$5,500
2012	$5,500

[I.R.C. § 414(v)]

For taxable years beginning after 2006, the catch-up limit of $5,000 will be subject to COLAs in increments of $500. This COLA is separate from the COLA applicable to the normal elective deferral limit. [I.R.C. § 414(v)(2)(C); *see* I.R.S. Notice 2011-90, 2011-47 I.R.B. 791 for 2012 limits]

Note. Catch-up elective deferrals are not subject to the SARSEP deferral test or any other nondiscrimination requirements.

Increase in the Elective Deferral Limit for SIMPLE IRA Plans and SIMPLE 401(k) Plans. The elective deferral limit for SIMPLE IRAs (see Qs 14:69, 14:84) and SIMPLE 401(k) plans (see Qs 15:20, 15:23) increases from $6,000 (actually, $6,500 for 2001 because of COLAs) for years beginning after 2001, as follows:

Year	*Increased Deferral Limit*
2002	$ 7,000
2003	$ 8,000
2004	$ 9,000
2005	$10,000
2006	$10,000
2007	$10,500
2008	$10,500
2009	$11,500
2010	$11,500
2011	$11,500
2012	$11,500

[I.R.C. § 402(p)(2)(A)(ii)]

The elective SIMPLE deferral limit is increased for COLAs in increments of $500 after 2005. [I.R.C. § 408(p)(2)(E); *see* I.R.S. Notice 2011-90, 2011-47 I.R.B. 791 for 2012 limits] For 2012, the SIMPLE deferral limit is $11,500.

Catch-up Elective Deferral Contributions under a SIMPLE Plan for Individuals Age 50 or Older. If an individual participates in a SIMPLE and will attain age 50 by the end of the taxable year, that participant may make additional elective deferrals up to an applicable dollar limit. This catch-up amount is in addition to the normal deferral limit for the applicable year.

The maximum amount of a catch-up contribution is the lesser of the participant's compensation for the year or the applicable dollar amount. The applicable dollar amounts are as follows:

Year	*Applicable Dollar Amount*
2002	$ 500
2003	$1,000
2004	$1,500
2005	$2,000
2006	$2,500
2007	$2,500
2008	$2,500
2009	$2,500
2010	$2,500
2011	$2,500
2012	$2,500

[I.R.C. §§ 414(v), 414(v)(6)(A)(iv); *see* I.R.S. Notice 2011-90, 2011-47 I.R.B. 791 for 2012 limits]

Employer's matching contributions and nonelective contribution rates have not changed. This means that under a SIMPLE IRA plan, a participant may defer 100 percent of compensation or $11,500 (or $14,000 if age 50 or older), whichever is less, for 2012. The participant will receive a matching contribution of 3 percent of compensation (or less if permitted) based on his or her total compensation (with no $250,000 ceiling) or receive a 2 percent of compensation nonelective contribution based on his or her total compensation (capped at $250,000) for 2012.

Example. Gloria, age 55, participates in a SIMPLE IRA plan. For 2012, her compensation is $300,000, and she defers the maximum of $14,000. If her employer matches her deferrals at 3 percent of compensation, Gloria's matching contribution would be limited to $9,000 ($300,000 × .03 = $9,000). To receive a 3 percent matching contribution of $14,000, Gloria would have to earn $466,666.66 ($466,666.66 × .03 = $14,000).

Alternatively, if Gloria's employer uses the 2 percent nonelective contribution option, Gloria's nonelective contribution would be $5,000 ($250,000 compensation limit × .02).

Modification of Top-Heavy Rules for SARSEPs. For years beginning after 2001, an employee is considered a key employee if, at any time during the plan year, the employee is

1. An officer with compensation in excess of $130,000 (adjusted for COLAs in $5,000 increments—$165,000 for 2012);
2. A 5 percent or more owner; or
3. A 1 percent or more owner with compensation in excess of $150,000.

The four-year look-back and "top 10" owner rules are eliminated; however, the family ownership attribution rule continues to apply in determining whether an individual is a more than 5 percent owner of the employer for purposes of these rules. For purposes of determining a plan's top-heavy status, the five-year look-back period applicable to distributions is generally reduced to one year for former employees (see Q 8:7), except for in-service distributions. In addition, if an individual has not performed services for the employer during the one-year period ending on the date the top-heavy determination is made, the individual's account balance is not taken into account in determining top-heavy status. [I.R.C. § 416(i)]

Contributions for Household Workers. Currently, an employer may make a contribution on behalf of domestic and similar workers other than the employer or a member of the employer's family. The employer is not afforded a deduction, however, because such contributions are not made in connection with a trade or business. For taxable years beginning after 2001, EGTRRA permits such contributions to continue to be made on a nondeductible basis, and the 10 percent excise tax on nondeductible contributions does not apply to a 401(k) SIMPLE plan or a SIMPLE IRA plan solely because the contributions are not a trade or business expense. [I.R.C. § 4972(c)(6)]

Note. This provision is intended to apply only to employers that have paid and continue to pay all applicable employment taxes, but the statute does not include this limitation. [EGTRRA § 637; H.R. Conf. Rep. No. 107-51, pt. 1 (2001)]

Practice Pointer. Similar provisions were not enacted for a SEP or SARSEP covering only a domestic or household worker. Thus, the nondeductible contributions (see Q 2:1) may be subject to a 10 percent penalty.

Q 1:36 How have the rollover rules changed under EGTRRA?

EGTRRA contained numerous provisions that expanded portability between various types of retirement plans for the purpose of retaining tax-favored treatment of the amounts distributed. The incentives for individuals to retain benefits in tax-favored accounts include the following new rollover rules.

Eligible Rollover Distributions. After 2001, eligible rollover distributions are permitted between a qualified plan and 403(b) annuity and custodial account plans and governmental 457(b) plans without restriction, including the rollover of an eligible governmental 457(b) plan into a traditional IRA, subject to the following conditions:

1. The employer's plan must agree to accept rollovers from unlike plans and agree to keep separate accounts for such rollover amounts.

2. The rollover notice (for all plans) must include a description of the provisions under which distributions from the plan into which the distribution is rolled over may be subject to restrictions and tax consequences different from those applicable to distributions from the distributing plan.

After 2001, the rollover notice under Code Section 402(f) and the direct rollover requirements of Code Section 401(a)(31) apply to governmental 457(b) plans. A distribution from a governmental 457(b) plan that is rolled over will be reported on Form 1099-R, Distributions from Pensions, Annuities, Retirement or Profit-Sharing Plans, IRAs, Insurance Contracts, etc., in the same manner as distributions from other plans. Furthermore, the 20 percent mandatory withholding rules applicable to eligible rollover distributions that are not directly rolled over in a trustee-to-trustee transfer will apply to governmental 457(b) plans. [I.R.C. §§ 72(o)(4), 402(c)(8)(B)(vi), 403(b)(8)(A)(ii); *see* I.R.S. Notice 2009-68, 2009-39 I.R.B. 423, for the model 402(f) rollover notices.]

Note. If a distribution from a qualified plan or a 403(b) plan is rolled over into a governmental 457(b) plan, subsequent distributions from the 457(b) plan attributable to the qualified plan or 403(b) plan rollover will still be subject to the 10 percent additional tax on premature distributions under Code Section 72(t) (see Q 5:56).

The rollover notice required under Code Section 402(f) contain provisions under which distributions from the plan receiving the rollover may be subject to restrictions and tax consequences that are different from those applicable to distributions from the plan making the rollover distribution.

Surviving Spouse Rollover Rules Liberalized. A surviving spouse beneficiary is permitted to roll over a distribution received after 2001 from any of the plans mentioned above into any plan in which the surviving spouse is a participant, rather than just to a traditional IRA (as is the case for distributions received prior to 2002). [I.R.C. § 402(c)(9)] The PPA provides that benefits of a beneficiary other than a surviving spouse may be directly rolled over to an IRA or Roth IRA (see Q 1:39).

Rollovers of After-Tax Contributions. After-tax employee contributions to a defined contribution plan that are distributed after 2001 are permitted to be rolled over into another defined contribution plan or into a traditional IRA. The receiving plan must accept rollovers of after-tax employee contributions and agree to account separately for such amounts and the earnings on those amounts. If the rollover from a qualified plan is going into another qualified plan, the rollover must be a direct rollover. [I.R.C. §§ 402(c)(2), 408(d)(3)(H)] After-tax contributions may not be rolled over from an IRA into a qualified plan, a 403(b) annuity or custodial account plan, or a 457(b) plan. A distribution from a traditional IRA that is rolled over into an eligible qualified plan other than an IRA is considered to be distributed first from any amounts in an individual's combined traditional IRAs other than after-tax contributions. [I.R.C. § 408(d)(3)(H)] After-tax contributions are considered to be distributed last from an IRA to maximize the amount available for rollover into an employer's qualified plan.

Example. Samantha has contributed $1,000 to an IRA every year since 1981. She now has four separate IRAs worth $7,500, $15,000, $20,000, and $30,000, respectively. For 2003 through 2012, her contributions were designated as nondeductible contributions. Her basis in the combined IRAs is therefore $10,000 ($1,000 × 10). Samantha may roll over the entire balance in any of her four IRAs into her employer's plan (which provides for such contributions to be made), because the amount remaining in her combined IRAs will exceed her basis of $10,000. If she does this, any remaining basis will be allocated to future IRA distributions.

Note. Form 8606 is used for reporting such transactions. Unlike qualified plans, IRAs are not required to account separately for after-tax employee contributions. [I.R.C. § 402(c)(2)]

Rollovers of IRAs into Employer Plans. Distributions made after 2001 from a traditional IRA are permitted to be rolled over into a qualified plan, a 403(b) annuity or custodial account plan, or a governmental 457(b) plan. This rule applies to all amounts in a traditional IRA (except nondeductible contributions), including a conduit IRA, SEP IRA, and SIMPLE IRA (but only after the two-year period applicable to SIMPLE IRAs has expired). This rule does not apply to any amounts in a Roth IRA or Coverdell ESA. [I.R.C. §§ 408(d)(3)(A), 408(d)(3)(D)(i)]

Practice Pointer. It appears that certain individuals must keep qualified plan distributions that could qualify for capital gains treatment (with respect to pre-1974 participation) or 10-year averaging for lump-sum distributions (for taxpayers born before 1936) in a conduit IRA to qualify or requalify for favorable tax treatment by transferring that IRA back into a qualified plan (see Q 2:41). If applicable, capital gains treatment or the 10-year averaging method of lump-sum distribution taxation may be preferable to a taxable IRA distribution, which is subject to ordinary income taxation. (See Appendix F.)

Extension of 60-Day Rollover Period. EGTRRA grants the IRS the authority to extend a taxpayer's 60-day rollover period for any eligible rollover distribution made after 2001 in cases of casualty, disaster, or other events beyond the reasonable control of the individual subject to the rollover period. [I.R.C. § 402(c)(3)(B)]

Rollovers of Hardship Distributions Not Permitted. All hardship distributions made after 2001 from all qualified plans and 403(b) plans (not just those applicable to elective deferrals) are not eligible rollover distributions. [I.R.C. § 402(c)(4)(C)] In addition, distributions from an eligible governmental 457(b) plan for an unforeseen emergency may not be rolled over.

Rollovers Disregarded in Determining $5,000 Cash-Out Amount. After 2001, a plan subject to the involuntary cash-out rules under Code Section 411(a)(11) is permitted to exclude rollover contributions (including earnings allocable to rollover contributions) in determining whether a participant's benefit exceeds $5,000. [I.R.C. § 411(a)(11)(D)]

Mandatory Direct Rollovers. On September 28, 2004, the DOL issued final regulations for a default option for distributions that (1) exceed $1,000, (2) are subject to the $5,000 cash-out provisions, and (3) are eligible rollover distributions. Direct rollovers are mandatory for such distributions and are to be made to a designated traditional IRA unless the participant affirmatively elects otherwise.

The final regulation not only covers mandatory distributions of more than $1,000, as required by the Code, but also extends safe-harbor relief to distributions of $1,000 or less. [DOL Reg. § 2550.404a-2(d)] Mandatory distribution must also be directed to an IRA described in Code Sections 408(a) or 408(b). The preamble confirms that the safe harbor does not establish a minimum or maximum number of IRA providers for any plan of an employer. Thus, one plan may designate multiple IRA providers, or multiple plans of an employer may designate the same IRA provider. [Preamble, DOL Reg. § 2550.404a-2, 69 Fed. Reg. 187, 58018, 58020]

The plan fiduciary must also enter into a written agreement with the IRA provider that is enforceable by the participant and that specifically addresses, among other things, the investment of rolled-over funds and the IRA fees and expenses. To the extent that the agreement meets the safe-harbor conditions, the plan fiduciary can rely on the IRA provider's commitments in the agreement and is not required to monitor the IRA provider's performance after funds are properly rolled over. The fees and expenses charged must be comparable to what the IRA provider charges for IRAs (and eliminated the requirement in the proposed regulations that fees and expenses may be paid only from income earned on the rollover amount). (Note, however, that the limitation on fees and expenses in the related prohibited transaction exemption, discussed next, was not modified in the final exemption.) [DOL Reg. § 2550.404a-2 (69 Fed. Reg. 187, 58018–58029 (Sept. 28, 2004)); EGTRRA § 657(a)(2); H.R. Conf. Rep. No. 107-84 (2001)] Simultaneously with the release of the final regulation, the DOL released a proposed prohibited transaction class exemption that allows a financial institution to select itself or an affiliate to serve as the IRA provider for automatic rollovers from its own plan and to select proprietary investment products. [Application No. D-11203, 69 Fed. Reg. 9846 (Mar. 2, 2004), as corrected at 69 Fed. Reg. 11043 (Mar. 9, 2004), *http://www.dol.gov/ebsa/regs/fedreg/notices/2004004552.htm* (visited on Aug. 20, 2012); *see also* Field Assistance Bulletin (FAB) 2004-02 (Sept. 30, 2004), *http://www.dol.gov/ebsa/pdf/fab-2004-2.pdf* (visited on Aug. 20, 2012), regarding automatic rollovers for missing participants in terminated defined contribution plans]

Q 1:37 Did EGTRRA make other changes that affect retirement planning?

Yes. In addition to changing the income tax rates and possibly eliminating the estate tax, EGTRRA clarified rules regarding retirement advice provided to employees by employers and provided certain relief to employers with crew members engaged in transportation between the United States and a foreign country or possession of the United States.

Clarification of Employer-Provided Retirement Education. EGTRRA clarified that retirement planning advice provided to employees (and their spouses) after 2001 on an individual basis is a nontaxable fringe benefit to the extent that such services are made available on substantially equivalent terms to all employees. [I.R.C. §§ 132(a)(7), 132(m)(1)] (See Q 4:21.)

Permitted Exclusion of Nonresident Aliens for Coverage Purposes. After 2001, if a nonresident alien (NRA) is a regular member of a crew of a foreign vessel engaged in transportation between the United States and a foreign country or a possession of the United States, compensation received by such NRA is not considered U.S. source income for any qualified retirement plan, including a SEP, a SARSEP, and a SIMPLE. [I.R.C. § 861(a)(3)]

Q 1:38 Are SEPs subject to the nonqualified deferred compensation plan rules of Code Section 409A?

No. Code Section 409A provides special rules for certain types of nonqualified deferred compensation plans. The rules, however, do not apply to a SEP or SIMPLE arrangement of an employer. [I.R.S. Notice 2005-1, Pt. IV, Q-3(c), 2005-2 I.R.B. 274]

Q 1:39 How did the Pension Protection Act of 2006 (PPA) affect retirement planning?

On August 17, 2006, the Pension Protection Act of 2006 (PPA) (H.R. 4) was enacted into law. The PPA contained a number of significant tax incentives to enhance retirement savings. EGTRRA (2001) substantially increased pension and IRA contribution limits through 2010. The PPA made many of the EGTRRA changes (see Qs 1:28–1:37) permanent and also provided for the indexing of the income limits for traditional, spousal, and Roth IRA phaseout rules to prevent these benefits from being eroded by inflation (see Qs 1:33–1:35). If it were not for the PPA, the increased contribution limits and catch-up contributions provisions would have expired in 2010 and reverted to their pre-EGTRRA limits. Significant changes that affect IRAs and IRA-based plans under the PPA include the following.

1. Permanency of EGTRRA Pension and IRA Provisions

In order to comply with reconciliation procedures, EGTRRA included a "sunset" provision, pursuant to which many of the provisions of EGTRRA expire at the end of 2010. The PPA makes permanent the EGTRAA pension and IRA provisions. [EGTRRA, Title IX; PPA § 811(a)] The savers' credit for certain low-income individuals, set to expire after 2006, was also made permanent (see Q 1:33).

See Qs 1:24 through 1:36 for increased contributions (including catch-up contributions) and other provisions that will no longer be affected by the general EGTRRA 2010 "sunset" as a result of the PPA.

2. Improvements in Portability, Distribution, and Contribution Rules

- *Allow direct rollovers (conversions) from retirement plans to Roth IRAs.* Distributions from tax-qualified retirement plans, tax-sheltered annuities, and governmental 457 plans may be rolled over directly from such plan into a Roth IRA, subject to the present law rules that apply to rollovers from a traditional IRA into a Roth IRA. For example, a rollover from a tax-qualified retirement plan into a Roth IRA is includible in gross income (except to the extent it represents a return of after-tax contributions), and the 10 percent early distribution tax does not apply. Similarly, an individual with AGI of $100,000 or more could not roll over amounts from a tax-qualified retirement plan directly into a Roth IRA before 2010. (Roth IRAs are more fully discussed in the *Roth IRA Answer Book*, 6th edition, CCH Incorporated, 2012.)

Effective date: The provision is effective for distributions made after December 31, 2007. [PPA § 825(c); I.R.C. § 408A(e), as amended by PPA § 824]

Note. After-tax amounts may also be rolled over between different types of employer plans (e.g., qualified plans and 403(b) plans) in taxable years beginning after 2006. [PPA § 822]

- *Treatment of distributions to individuals called to active duty prior to December 31, 2007 and for at least 180 days (or an indefinite period).* Under the PPA, the 10 percent early withdrawal tax does not apply to a qualified reservist distribution (see Q 5:56).
- *Rollovers by nonspouse beneficiaries.* The PPA provides that benefits of a beneficiary other than a surviving spouse may be directly rolled over to an IRA. [Beech v. Commissioner, T.C. Summ. Op. 2012-74 (July 26, 2012)] The IRA is treated as an inherited IRA of the nonspouse beneficiary. Thus, for example, distributions from the inherited IRA are subject to the distribution rules applicable to beneficiaries. The provision applies to amounts payable to a beneficiary under a qualified retirement plan, an eligible governmental 457(b) plan, a 403 annuity contract or 403(b) tax-sheltered annuity or custodial account plan. To the extent provided by the Secretary of the Treasury, the provision applies to benefits payable to a trust maintained for a designated beneficiary to the same extent it applies to the beneficiary as long as the trust meets certain requirements (see Q 16:25).

Effective date: The provision is effective for distributions made on or after January 1, 2007. [PPA § 829(c), I.R.C. §§ 402(c)(11), 403(a)(4)(B), 457(e)(16)(B), as amended by PPA § 829(a)]

- *Direct deposit of tax refunds to IRA or Roth IRA.* The PPA directs the Treasury Department to develop forms under which all or a portion of a taxpayer's refund may be deposited in an IRA or Roth IRA of the taxpayer (or the spouse of the taxpayer in the case of a joint return). The provision does not modify the rules relating to IRAs, including the rules relating to timing and deductibility of contributions. In the case of 5 percent owners and distributions from a traditional IRA, distributions must begin by April 1 of the calendar year following the year in which the individual attains age 70½. The IRS has issued new Form 8888 to be used for the 2006 tax year and beyond. [IRS Fact Sheet 2008-5 (FS-2008-5, Jan. 2008)]

Practice Pointer. Individuals who want to deposit tax refunds directly should check with their IRA trustee/custodian to obtain the proper routing information. Not all institutions using correspondent banks have the ability to accept direct deposits.

- *Inflation indexing of gross income limitations on certain retirement savings incentives.*
  - *Saver's credit.* Eligibility for the saver's credit is dependent in part on an individual's MAGI. Beginning in 2007, the PPA provides for indexing of the income limits applicable to the saver's credit, which was also permanently extended by the PPA (see Qs 1:33, 14:170). Indexed amounts are rounded to the nearest multiple of $500. Under the indexed income limits, as under present law, the income limits for single taxpayers is one-half that for married taxpayers filing a joint return, and the limits for heads of household are three-fourths that for married taxpayers filing a joint return.
  - *IRA and Roth IRA contribution income limits.* Traditional IRA deductibility and Roth IRA eligibility are dependent in part on an individual's MAGI. To prevent erosion of these benefits, the PPA indexes the income limits for IRA contributions beginning in 2007 (see Q 1:30). The indexing applies to the income limits for deductible contributions for active participants in an employer-sponsored plan, the income limits for deductible contributions if the individual is not an active participant but the individual's spouse is, and the income limits for contributions to a Roth IRA. Indexed amounts are rounded to the nearest multiple of $1,000. The $150,000 threshold applicable to IRA deductibility for a nonactive participant who is married to an active participant is also indexed beginning after 2006. For 2012, the threshold applicable to IRA deductibility was increased to $183,000 for an individual who is not an active participant in an employer's plan but whose spouse is an active participant.

Effective date: The provisions relating to indexing and contribution income limits are effective for taxable years beginning after December 31, 2006. For 2012, the lower end of the income phaseout for active participants filing a joint return is $92,000 as adjusted to reflect inflation. For an active participant, IRA deductions are phased out completely once MAGI reaches $112,000. [PPA § 833(d), I.R.C. §§ 25B, 219(g)(8), 408A(c)(3); *see* I.R.S. Notice 2011-90, 2011-47 I.R.B. 791 for 2012 indexed limits]

- *Additional IRA contributions for participants in certain 401(k) plans.* An individual who has been a participant in a plan of a bankrupt company for more than 6 months may make additional IRA contributions of up to $3,000 to his or her IRA if (1) in the year preceding the year of contribution, the employer (or a controlling company of the employer) was a debtor in bankruptcy, or (2) the employer or any other person was subject to indictment or conviction resulting from a business transaction related to the employer or a controlling employer. To be eligible for the additional IRA contribution, the participant's plan must contain a matching contribution program that provides for a 50 percent or greater matching contribution in employer securities.

3. Prohibited Transaction Exemptions

Investment advice. The PPA adds a new category of prohibited transaction exemption under ERISA and the Code in connection with the provision of investment advice through an "eligible investment advice arrangement" to beneficiaries of IRAs and to participants and beneficiaries of a defined contribution plan who direct the investment of their accounts under the plan (e.g., a designated Roth contribution program) (see Q 4:21).

Transactions with service providers. The PPA offers relief in that a transaction between a plan and a party in interest (e.g., a service provider), who is not a fiduciary, is not a prohibited transaction (i.e., sale, exchange, lease, loan, or use of plan assets) under ERISA Section 406 so long as the plan receives no less than, or pays no more than, adequate consideration for the transaction (see Q 4:18). [I.R.C. § 4975(d)(20); ERISA §§ 406(a)(1)(A), (B), and (D); 408(b)(17); *see* PPA § 611(j)]

Block trades. Additional relief is provided for "block trades" (any trade of at least 10,000 shares or a fair market value of at least $200,000) that will be allocated among two or more client accounts of a fiduciary. [PPA § 611]

Electronic communication networks. An exemption is provided for certain transactions on electronic communication networks. [PPA § 611(c)]

Foreign exchange transactions. An exemption is provided for certain foreign exchange transactions. [PPA § 611(e)]

Cross-trading. An exemption for certain cross-trading transactions is provided. [PPA § 611(g); *see also* EBSA Adv. Op. 2011-08A (June 21, 2011), available at http://www.dol.gov/ebsa/regs/aos/ao2011-08a.html (visited on Sept. 20, 2012)]

Special correction period. A prohibited transaction involving securities or commodities generally would be exempt if the correction is completed within 14 days after the fiduciary discovers (or should have discovered) that the transaction was prohibited. However, the prohibited transaction exemption does not apply to transactions involving employer securities. It also does not apply if, at the time of the transaction, the fiduciary or other party-in-interest (or any person knowingly participating in the transaction) knew (or should have known) that the transaction was prohibited. [PPA § 612]

Effective date: The new exemptions are effective for transactions occurring after the PPA's enactment date, August 17, 2006. The correction period exemption applies to prohibited transactions that the fiduciary discovers (or should have discovered) after the date of enactment.

4. Coercive Interference with ERISA Rights

ERISA prohibits any person from using fraud, force, or violence (or threatening force or violence) to restrain, coerce, or intimidate (or attempt to intimidate) any plan participant or beneficiary in order to interfere with or prevent the exercise of his or her rights under the plan. Willful violation of this prohibition is a criminal offense subject to fine or imprisonment (see Q 4:1).

5. Administrative Provisions

- *Updating of Employee Plans Compliance Resolution System (EPCRS).* The PPA clarifies that the Secretary has the full authority to establish and implement EPCRS (or any successor program) and any other employee plans correction policies, including the authority to waive income, excise, or other taxes to ensure that any tax, penalty, or sanction is not excessive and bears a reasonable relationship to the nature, extent, and severity of the failure. See Chapter 17, Correction Programs.

Effective date: The provision became effective on August 17, 2006. [PPA § 1101]

- *No reduction in unemployment compensation as a result of a rollover.* Under the PPA, a state is prohibited from reducing unemployment compensation for any pension, retirement or retired pay, annuity, or other similar payment or distribution that is nontaxable because the payment or distribution is rolled over.

Effective date: The provision became effective on August 17, 2006. [I.R.C. § 3304(a), as amended by PPA § 1105]

6. Charitable Giving Incentives

- *Tax-free distributions from individual retirement plans for charitable purposes.* The PPA provides an exclusion from gross income for otherwise taxable IRA distributions from a traditional or a Roth IRA in the case of qualified charitable distributions. The provision does not generally apply to distributions from employer-sponsored retirement plans, including SIMPLE IRAs and SEPs (see Q 5:50). The provision for qualified charitable distributions was set to expire on December 31, 2009, but was extended to distributions made in 2010 and 2011. A special rule permits distribution made in January 2011 to be treated as having been made in 2010. [Tax Relief, Unemployment Insurance Reauthorization, and Job Creation Act of 2010 (Pub. L. No. 111-312) § 725]

7. Bonding Relief and Modifications

- The PPA provides an exception to the ERISA bonding requirement for an entity registered as a broker or a dealer under the Securities Exchange Act of 1934 if the broker or dealer is subject to the fidelity bond requirements of a self-regulatory organization (within the meaning of the Securities Exchange Act of 1934). (See Q 4:78.)

Effective date: The bonding exception provision is effective for plan years beginning on or after 2007. [PPA § 611(c); ERISA § 412(a)(2), as amended by PPA § 611(b)]

Q 1:40 How did the Heroes Earnings Assistance and Relief Tax (HEART) Act of 2007 provide tax relief to members of the armed service and others volunteering on behalf of the United States?

In general, the Heroes Earnings Assistance and Relief Tax (HEART) Act of 2007 (Pub. L. No 110-245) requires certain retirement plans to provide benefits to former employees who die or become disabled while performing qualified military service. The HEART Act was signed into law by President Bush on July 17, 2008. In addition the HEART Act:

- Requires employers to include differential wage payments made to an employee while on active military duty in the calculation of retirement plan benefits (see Qs 5:95, 6:4, 6:14);
- Military differential wage payments are treated as wages for withholding purposes and treated as compensation under a SEP and SARSEP. These payments are also treated as compensation for IRA contribution purposes.
- Makes permanent the expiring tax provision that permits active duty reservists to make penalty-free withdrawals from retirement plans (see Q 5:56); and
- Permits recipients of military death benefit gratuities and Servicemember's Group Term Life Insurance (SGLI) proceeds to roll over the amounts received to a Roth IRA or an education savings account (Coverdell ESA).
- All amounts held in IRAs, Coverdell ESAs, qualified tuition programs (I.R.C. § 529 plans), HSAs, and Archer MSAs will be treated as distributed for tax purposes as if they had been distributed on the day before a taxpayer's expatriation date, and therefore become fully taxable in that year. The 10 percent penalty that normally would apply to distributions before age 59½ will not apply. The assets may remain in the account (even though they are taxed). The amount that remains in the account will be treated as basis and "appropriate adjustments shall be made to subsequent distributions from the account to reflect such treatment." [HEART § 301; I.R.C. § 877A(e)]

Caution. No special rules (see below) are provided for amounts that are rolled over from an employer's plan into an IRA. Thus, such expatriated amounts would be treated as distributed from an IRA.

- In the case of an employer-sponsored plan such as a SEP or SIMPLE, any distribution received by an expatriate is subject to non-waivable withholding of 30 percent. [I.R.C. § 877A(d)(1)(A)] The withholding requirement applies to the distribution to the extent and at the time it would be included in gross income of the covered expatriate if such person were subject to tax as a citizen or resident of the United States. [HEART § 301; I.R.C. § 877A(d)] The SEP-IRA or SIMPLE-IRA account under an employer-sponsored plan is not treated as distributed and fully taxable.

Caution. No special rules are provided for an expatriated SEP-IRA that contains non-SEP assets. Thus, the extent to which non-SEP assets in an account registered (or previously registered) as a SEP-IRA would be treated as distributed and fully taxable is not known.

Chapter 2

SEP Establishment and Employer Qualification

This chapter examines the types of employers that are qualified to establish SEP and SARSEP arrangements and the types of related entities that are required to be treated as a single employer for plan establishment and contribution purposes. It also explains SEP establishment dates and employee participation requirements, and discusses establishment of SEPs by limited liability companies and limited liability partnerships.

Establishing SEPs

Q 2:1 What types of businesses may establish a SEP arrangement?

A SEP arrangement may be established by a business entity of any type and with any number of eligible employees. A SEP arrangement can be established by a corporation, an S corporation, a partnership, or a sole proprietorship, including a sole proprietorship in which the only employee is the sole proprietor. A SEP may also be established by an organization exempt from tax (see Q 2:3), a limited liability partnership, or a limited liability company (see Qs 2:58–2:65).

An employer of a domestic servant can maintain a SEP arrangement, but none of the employer's SEP contributions would be deductible. In addition, the employer would be subject to a 10 percent excise tax on the nondeductible employer contribution. Section 162 of the Internal Revenue Code (Code) prohibits deductions for personal or household expenses.

Q 2:2 Is there a maximum number of employees who may participate in a SEP?

No. SEPs may be established by employers of any size and with any number of participants. SEPs allowing for elective contributions (SARSEPs), however, are restricted to small employers (see Q 2:20).

Q 2:3 May a SEP arrangement be established by an organization exempt from tax?

Yes. However, a tax-exempt organization cannot establish a SEP that allows employees to make elective salary reduction (pretax) contributions (see Q 2:22). [I.R.C. § 408(k)(6)(E); Ltr. Rul. 8833047]

Q 2:4 Must all related businesses establish the SEP or SARSEP arrangement?

Yes. The SEP or SARSEP must be established by all businesses related to an employer that establishes a SEP or SARSEP. All employees of related entities must be treated as if employed by a single employer for the SEP requirements to be satisfied. For the purpose of any benefit requirement, service with a member of an affiliated service group must also be counted (see Q 2:14). [*See* I.R.C. § 414(b), (c), (m), (n), (o) (relationships requiring entities to be treated as a single employer); Ltr. Rul. 8041045; Prop. Treas. Reg. § 1.414(m)-3(a)(5)]

> **Note.** A business that is part of a controlled group, group under common control, or affiliated service group, or that hires leased employees, cannot use the model Form 5305-SEP or Form 5305A-SEP to establish a SEP or maintain a SARSEP (see Qs 2:42, 3:10). Leased employees, if otherwise eligible, must be treated as any other eligible employee. [I.R.C. § 414(n)(1)(A)]

The proposed regulations under Code Section 414(o) relating to shared employees were withdrawn by the Internal Revenue Service (IRS) on April 27, 1993. [Prop. Treas. Reg. § 1.414(o)-1(f)(2), withdrawn] Each employer of a shared employee is deemed to contribute its pro rata share of the employee's compensation. [Rev. Rul. 68-391, 1968-2 C.B. 180, still in effect; *see also* Rev. Rul. 67-101, 1967-1 C.B. 82, amplified by Rev. Rul. 68-391] Because the shared-employee rules were only proposed and have been formally disavowed by the IRS, very little confidence should be placed in them. To avoid problems, a shared employee is frequently treated as performing service for all businesses that use the employee's services. [*See also* obsolete (pre-ERISA) Rev. Ruls. 73-447, 1973-2 C.B. 135; 67-101, 1967-1 C.B. 82]

Example. The Cats Paw, a clinic, is operated by three physicians. Natalie, the receptionist, is age 24 and has compensation of $15,000. Donna, a nurse, is age 30 and has compensation of $30,000. Both have rendered services to the physicians for over three years. Day-to-day operation of the clinic is governed by an agreement between the physicians. For example, they must be in agreement as to the hiring and firing of employees, fixing of wages, assignment of duties, altering or renovating the clinic, and so forth. Liability insurance for injuries that might occur on the premises is carried jointly. Each physician has his or her own medical practice, and each carries his own malpractice and wage continuation insurance. The earnings derived from their individual practice of medicine are considered the individual income of each physician. Although the cost of operating the clinic is shared equally, the clinic is not operated as a partnership for federal income tax purposes. If any of the physicians established a SEP for his or her individual practice, the two employees would have to be considered for participation. The pro-rata share of compensation that each physician would consider for plan purposes is $15,000 ($15,000/3 + $30,000/3). Presumably, this applies for all plan purposes. However, problems could nonetheless arise. For example, if separate W-2s were issued by each of the physicians, state labor agencies might claim that each employer should be paying for full work at or above the prevailing minimum wage. The pivotal question is whether, in the absence of a recognized partnership for federal income tax purposes with regard to the physicians' operation of the clinic, the employees of the clinic are employed full time with each physician as a separate employer. The amount of services rendered to each physician will vary from day to day. The characteristics of an employee do not change when the efforts of such employee are shared by more than one employer. Therefore, the receptionist and nurse who work in the clinic are the full-time employees of each of the three physicians. [*See* S. Derrin Watson, "Who's the Employer?" 6th ed. (Goleta, CA 2012), Qs 7:1, 7:5 and other resources at *http://www.employerbook.com* (visited on Aug. 20, 2012) that discuss strategies to deal with shared employee situations.]

Q 2:5 When is an employer related to or affiliated with another employer?

An employer is related to or affiliated with another employer when it is a corporation that is a member of a controlled group of corporations that includes the other employer; a trade or business (whether or not incorporated) that is under common control with the other employer (see Q 2:13); an organization (whether or not incorporated) that is a member of an affiliated service group that includes the other employer (see Q 2:14); or any other entity required to be aggregated with the other employer pursuant to regulations under Code Section 414(o).

Under Code Section 414, entities having one of three types of relationships are treated as a controlled group of corporations. Entities may be related by being a parent-subsidiary controlled group (see Q 2:8), a brother-sister controlled group (see Q 2:9), or a combined group of corporations (see Q 2:12). [I.R.C. § 414(b), (c), (m), (n), (o)]

Q 2:6 Can controlled-group status be avoided?

Yes. The test for controlled-group status is strictly mechanical. Special rules for determining ownership and constructive ownership apply. Under the constructive ownership rules, there is generally attribution from partnerships, estates, trusts, children, and a spouse. [*See* I.R.C. § 1563(d), (e); Fujinon Optical Inc. v. Commissioner, 76 T.C. 499 (1981); Treas. Reg. § 1.414(b)-1] An entity that is not part of an affiliated service group (see Q 2:14) can avoid controlled-group treatment because the intent of the parties is immaterial as long as the statutory requirements to be a controlled group are not met.

Q 2:7 Do community property rules apply in determining stock ownership?

Yes. Community property rules, where present, apply in determining stock ownership for the purpose of determining which entity or entities are treated as the employer (see examples in Q 5:26). Under the constructive ownership rules of Code Section 1563, one of the conditions for an exception from attribution is that the spouse not own directly or indirectly any stock of the corporation; that is not likely in a community property state. [I.R.C. § 1563(e)(5); Aero Indus. Co. v. Commissioner, T.C. Memo 1980-116] In addition, certain states have community property laws that may require the spouse to be the beneficiary of an IRA unless the spouse consents in writing to the naming of another beneficiary (see Qs 16:92–16:97).

Note. When applying the dollar limit on elective deferrals and for other purposes under Code Section 408, community property laws are ignored. [I.R.C. §§ 402(g)(6), 408(g)] Federal tax law overrides state community property law in determining the taxation of distributions. The IRS was unsuccessful in taxing the spouse of the IRA holder on her community property share of taxable distributions made to her husband, the IRA holder. [I.R.C. §§ 408(d), 408(g); Angela C. Morris v. Commissioner, T.C. Memo 2002-17; Bunney v. Commissioner, 114 T.C. 259 (2000)]

Although IRA provisions are applied without regard to community property rules, Code Section 408(g) doesn't affect actual property rights. Thus, applicable state law determines property what is, or is not, community property. [Ltr. Rul. 200928043 (Apr. 14, 2009), ruling that "which of three subtrusts was/is to receive said IRA X lies outside of Code Section 402(g)."]

Q 2:8 What is a *parent-subsidiary controlled group* of corporations?

The term *parent-subsidiary controlled group* refers to one or more chains of corporations connected through stock ownership with a common parent corporation if the following two conditions are met:

1. Stock representing at least 80 percent of the total combined voting power of all classes of stock entitled to vote or at least 80 percent of the total value of shares of all classes of stock of each of the corporations, except the common parent corporation, is owned by one or more of the other corporations; and
2. The common parent corporation owns stock representing at least 80 percent of the total combined voting power of all classes of stock entitled to vote or at least 80 percent of the total value of shares of all classes of stock of at least one of the other corporations, excluding, in computing such voting power or value, stock owned directly by such other corporations. [I.R.C. § 1563(a)(1)]

For purposes of the 100 percent/$50,000 limit on overall contributions to SEPs and qualified plans under Code Section 415 for 2012, the phrase "more than 50 percent" is substituted for the phrase "at least 80 percent" (see Q 2:10).

Example 1. PeeWee Corporation owns stock possessing 80 percent of the total combined voting power of all classes of stock of SoSo Corporation entitled to vote. PeeWee is the common parent of a parent-subsidiary controlled group consisting of member corporations PeeWee and SoSo.

Example 2. The facts are the same as those in Example 1, except that SoSo owns stock possessing 80 percent of the total value of shares of all classes of stock of Toad Corporation. PeeWee is the common parent of a parent-subsidiary controlled group consisting of member corporations PeeWee, SoSo, and Toad. The result would be the same if PeeWee, rather than SoSo, owned the Toad stock.

Example 3. Light Corporation owns 80 percent of the only class of stock of Motor Corporation, and Motor, in turn, owns 40 percent of the only class of stock of Orbit Corporation. Light also owns 80 percent of the only class of stock of Nifty Corporation, and Nifty, in turn, owns 40 percent of the only class of stock of Orbit. Light is the common parent of a parent-subsidiary controlled group consisting of member corporations Light, Motor, Nifty, and Orbit.

Q 2:9 What is a *brother-sister controlled group* of corporations?

The term *brother-sister controlled group* refers to two or more corporations if the same five or fewer persons that are individuals, estates, or trusts own stock in each corporation representing

1. At least 80 percent of the total combined voting power of all classes of stock entitled to vote or at least 80 percent of the total value of shares of all classes of the stock of each corporation; and

2. More than 50 percent of the total combined voting power of all classes of stock entitled to vote or more than 50 percent of the total value of shares of all classes of stock of each corporation, taking into account the stock ownership of each such person only to the extent such stock ownership is identical with respect to each such corporation. [I.R.C. §§ 1563(a)(2), 1563(f)(5); Treas. Reg. § 1.1563(a)(3)(i)]

Note. Although the 80 percent requirement was excluded by the 2004 JOBS Act for applying Code Section 1561 to certain tax benefits (e.g., graduated tax brackets, the accumulated earnings credit, the general business credit against the first $25,000 of tax liability, and the ability to expense the cost of depreciable assets), the 80 percent requirement continues to apply for all other provisions that use the 1563(a) definition of a controlled group—*see, e.g.*, Code Section 414 addressing retirement plans of controlled employers and Code Section 415(h) regarding annual addition limitations. [I.R.C. § 1563(f)(5); American Jobs Creation Act of 2004 (JOBS) (Pub. L. No. 108-357) § 900]

Example 1. The outstanding stock of corporations *P*, *Q*, *R*, *S*, and *T*, which have only one class of stock outstanding, is owned by the following unrelated individuals:

	Corporations					
Individuals	*P*	*Q*	*R*	*S*	*T*	*Ownership*
A	55%	51%	55%	55%	55%	51%
B	45	49	0	0	0	(45% in *P* and *Q*)
C	0	0	45	0	0	
D	0	0	0	45	0	
E	0	0	0	0	45	
Total	100%	100%	100%	100%	100%	

Corporations *P* and *Q* are members of a brother-sister controlled group of corporations. Individuals *A* and *B* have a controlling interest in companies *P* and *Q*, because together they own 80 percent or more in company *P* (55% + 45% = 100%). They also have effective control for purposes of the more than 50 percent test because their identical ownership adds up to more than 50 percent (*A*'s identical ownership in *P* and *Q* is 51 percent, and *B*'s identical ownership in *P* and *Q* is 45 percent; together this is 96 percent, which exceeds 50 percent). The more than 50 percent identical ownership requirement is met for all five corporations; however, corporations *R*, *S*, and *T* are not members because at least 80 percent of the stock of each of those corporations is not owned by the same five or fewer persons whose stock ownership is considered for purposes of the more than 50 percent identical ownership requirement.

Example 2. The outstanding stock of corporations *U* and *V*, which have only one class of stock outstanding, is owned by the following unrelated individuals:

Individuals	*Corporations* U	V
A	12%	12%
B	12	12
C	12	12
D	12	12
E	13	13
F	13	13
G	13	13
H	13	13
Total	100%	100%

Any group of five of the shareholders will own more than 50 percent of the stock in each corporation, in identical holdings; however, *U* and *V* are not members of the brother-sister controlled group, because at least 80 percent of the stock of each corporation is not owned by the same five or fewer persons.

Historical Note. In *U.S. v. Vogel Fertilizer Co.* [455 U.S. 16 (1982)], the Supreme Court held that the same five or fewer individuals, estates, trusts must be used for both the "controlling interest" (80 percent or more) and "effective control" (greater than 50 percent) tests of Code Section 1563. Moreover, because those whose interest is zero under the effective control test are not counted in performing that test, they cannot be counted in performing the controlling interest test. Since the Supreme Court ruling, the relevant IRS regulations have been modified to incorporate this principle. The decision is available at *http://supreme.justia.com/us/455/16/* (visited on Aug. 22, 2012).

Q 2:10 Can the Section 415 limits apply to a group of businesses not otherwise treated as a controlled group?

Yes. For purposes of the percentage and dollar limits on overall contributions to SEPs and qualified plans under Code Section 415, the phrase "more than 50 percent" is substituted for the phrase "at least 80 percent" (see Q 2:9) when determining an individual's 415 limitation. [I.R.C. § 415(h)] Thus, the Section 415 limits on overall contributions and benefits could apply to an individual even if a group of businesses are not required to cover all employees of all members of the group for eligibility, discrimination, and testing purposes.

Example 1. Jack owns 100 percent of Master Corporation. Master owns 65 percent of Sub Corporation (the other 35 percent is owned by an unrelated individual). Master and Sub are not a controlled group, but because of Code Section 415(h), Jack has a combined 415 limit.

Example 2. Don is a CPA and operates as a sole proprietor. Don also owns a 51 percent interest in MaxGate, a partnership. Don and MaxGate are treated as one employer for purposes of Code Section 415(h); thus, Don has one 100 percent/$50,000 limit (for 2012) on contributions to a SEP (see Q 2:17).

If an individual participates in a 403(b) tax-sheltered annuity or custodial account and a qualified plan or SEP, the individual must combine contributions made to the 403(b) plan with contributions to a qualified plan and simplified employee pensions of all corporations, partnerships, and sole proprietorships in which the individual has more than 50 percent control. [I.R.C. §§ 403(b)(1)(E), 415(a)(2), 415(h); *see also* Treas. Reg. § 1.415(f)-1(f)]

Example 3. Larry has a 51 percent interest in a small business that established a SEP for 2012. Larry is also a participant in a 403(b) plan maintained by a tax-exempt entity. Larry must aggregate contributions to both plans for purposes of the 100 percent/$50,000 limits under Code Section 415. [Treas. Reg. § 1.415(f)-1(f)(1)-(32)]

Q 2:11 Did the final 415 regulations make any changes in combining a 403(b) plan with a SEP or other plan?

Yes and no. On April 5, 2007, the IRS issued the final 415 regulations with some unexpected modifications. The final rules adopt most of the provisions in the May 2005 proposed regulations, with a few notable exceptions, and add provisions reflecting amendments to Code Section 415 made by the Pension Protection Act of 2006 (PPA).

Generally, tax-sheltered annuity (or mutual fund custodial account) under Code Section 403(b) is not aggregated with other plans of the employer because the employee is deemed to control the 403(b) plan and not the employer. [Treas. Reg. §§ 1.415(f)-1(f)(1)] This rule has permitted employees to fully fund their 403(b) plan ($17,000 for regular deferrals, plus $3,000 for long-term service, plus $5,500 for age 50 catch-up deferrals) and still receive an employer contribution into another plan (where the employee does not control the employer) up to the maximum Code Section 415 limit ($50,000 for 2012).

There is one exception to this general rule. If an employee participates in a 403(b) plan and maintains a business that he or she controls, then the plans will be aggregated for Code Section 415 purposes. [Treas. Reg. § 1.415(f)-1(f)(2)]

Example. Manny, a university professor, contributes to the university's 403(b) plan and maintains a small consulting business on the side. Because Manny is deemed to control the 403(b) plan and owns 100 percent of the consulting business, he may only contribute $50,000 ($55,500 if age 50) between the two plans for 2012. This is also common where a doctor participates in the hospital's 403(b) program and maintains a plan for his or her private practice.

The final Code Section 415 regulations issued in April 2007 state that if an excess occurs in multiple plans, the excess will be treated as being in the 403(b) plan. Also, the excess must be separately accounted for from the date that the excess was created in the 403(b) plan; otherwise, the contract is not a qualified

403(b). [Treas. Reg. §§ 1.415(a)-1(b)(2) and 1.415(a)-1(b)(3) regarding I.R.C. § 403(b)(7) custodial accounts]

However, if a participant on whose behalf a Section 403(b) annuity contract (including a mutual fund custodial account) is purchased is in control of any employer for a limitation year, the annuity contract for the benefit of the participant is treated as a defined contribution plan maintained by both the controlled employer and the participant for that limitation year; accordingly, the Section 403(b) annuity contract is aggregated with all other defined contribution plans maintained by the employer. The preamble to the final Code Section 415 regulations places an additional burden on employers. It states:

> [T]he employer that contributes to the section 403(b) annuity contract must obtain information from participants regarding employers controlled by those participants and plans maintained by those controlled employers to monitor compliance with applicable limitations to comply with applicable reporting and withholding obligations. [Preamble, Treas. Reg. § 1.415 (T.D. 9319, 2007-18 I.R.B. 1041 (Apr. 30, 2007)]

Note. It is common practice for a doctor in private practice or a professor who maintains a consulting business to establish a SEP plan for his or her separate businesses. All excesses will be in the 403(b) plan and not the SEP plan.

Q 2:12 What is a *combined group of corporations*?

A *combined group of corporations* consists of three or more corporations, each of which is a member of a parent-subsidiary group or a brother-sister group, and one of which is both a parent of a parent-subsidiary group and a member of a brother-sister group. [I.R.C. § 1563(a)(3)]

Example 1. Rachel, an individual, owns stock possessing 80 percent of the total combined voting power of all classes of the stock of corporations *X* and *Y*. *Y*, in turn, owns stock possessing 80 percent of the total combined voting power of all classes of the stock of corporation *Z*. In as much as

1. *X*, *Y*, and *Z* are all members of either a parent-subsidiary or brother-sister controlled group of corporations, and
2. *Y* is the common parent of a parent-subsidiary controlled group of corporations consisting of *Y* and *Z*, and is a member of a brother-sister controlled group of corporations consisting of *X* and *Y*,

X, *Y*, and *Z* are members of the same combined group.

Example 2. The facts are the same as those in Example 1, except that corporation *X* owns 80 percent of the total value of shares of all classes of stock of corporation *T*. *X*, *Y*, *Z*, and *T* are members of the same combined group.

Q 2:13 How is common control determined for groups including unincorporated trades or businesses?

Regulations under Code Section 414(c) provide that unincorporated trades or businesses are under common control if they constitute a parent-subsidiary group of trades or businesses, a brother-sister group of trades or businesses, or a combined group of trades or businesses. Rules similar to those applicable to corporations are used for determining the existence of commonly controlled trades or businesses (see Q 2:5). Thus, two or more trades or businesses that, if incorporated, would have been a controlled group of corporations under Code Section 414(b) are a group of businesses under common control under Code Section 414(c). *Trades or businesses* include partnerships, sole proprietorships, trusts, estates, and corporations. [Treas. Reg. §§ 1.414(c)-1, 1.414(c)-2]

Example 1. Comet Partnership owns stock possessing 80 percent of the total combined voting power of all classes of stock of Dust Corporation entitled to vote. Comet is the common parent of a parent-subsidiary group of trades or businesses under common control consisting of Comet Partnership and Dust Corporation.

Example 2. The facts are the same as those in Example 1, except that Dust Corporation owns 80 percent of the profits interest in the Meteor Partnership. The Comet Partnership is the common parent of a parent-subsidiary group of trades or businesses under common control consisting of Comet, Dust, and Meteor. The result would be the same if Comet, instead of Dust, owned 80 percent of the profits interest in Meteor.

Example 3. MOM Partnership owns 75 percent of the only class of stock of BRO Corporation and SIS Corporation; BRO owns all the remaining stock of SIS, and SIS owns all the remaining stock of BRO. Because interorganization ownership is excluded (i.e., treated as not outstanding) for purposes of determining whether MOM owns a controlling interest in at least one of the other organizations, MOM is treated as the owner of stock possessing 100 percent of the voting power and value of all classes of stock of BRO and SIS. Therefore, MOM is the common parent of a parent-subsidiary group of trades or businesses under common control consisting of the MOM Partnership, BRO Corporation, and SIS Corporation.

Example 4. The outstanding stock of corporations Sun and Moon, which have only one class of stock outstanding, is owned by the following unrelated individuals:

	Corporations	
Individuals	*Sun*	*Moon*
Anne	12%	12%
Ben	12	12
Chuck	12	12
Dennis	12	12
Edward	13	13

	Corporations	
Individuals	*Sun*	*Moon*
Frank	13	13
Greg	13	13
Hillary	13	13
	100%	100%

Any group of five of the shareholders will own more than 50 percent of the stock in each corporation, in identical holdings; however, Sun and Moon are not members of a brother-sister group of trades or businesses under common control, because at least 80 percent of the stock of each corporation is not owned by the same five or fewer persons.

Example 5. Juanita, an individual, owns a controlling interest in Wood Partnership and Stone Partnership. Wood, in turn, owns a controlling interest in Coal Corporation. Because Wood, Stone, and Coal are all members of either a parent-subsidiary group or a brother-sister group of trades or businesses under common control, and Wood is the common parent of a parent-subsidiary group of trades or businesses under common control consisting of Wood and Coal and a member of a brother-sister group of trades or businesses under common control consisting of Wood and Stone, Wood Partnership, Stone Partnership, and Coal Corporation are members of the same combined group of trades or businesses under common control.

The terms *interest* and *stock* do not include an interest that is treated under Treasury regulations as not outstanding in the case of a parent-subsidiary group of trades or businesses under common control or in the case of a brother-sister group of trades or businesses under common control. In addition, the term *stock* does not include Treasury stock or nonvoting stock that is limited and preferred as to dividends. In some cases, the ownership of stock is disregarded. [Treas. Reg. §§ 1.414(c)-1 through 1.414(c)-4]

Q 2:14 What is an *affiliated service group*?

Proposed regulations under Code Section 414(m) contain rules and examples that explain what types of entities are treated as an affiliated service group. The rules are extremely complex. [*See* I.R.S. Notice 84-11, 1984-2 C.B. 469] Code Section 414(m)(2) defines an *affiliated service group* as a first service organization (FSO) and one or more of the following:

1. Any service organization (A-Org) that is a shareholder or partner in the FSO and regularly performs services for the FSO or is regularly associated with the FSO in performing services for third persons; and
2. Any other organization (B-Org) if
   a. A significant portion of the business of that organization is the performance of services for the FSO or A-Org (or both) of a type historically performed in the service field of the FSO or A-Org by employees, and

b. 10 percent or more of the interest of the B-Org is held by persons who are officers, highly compensated employees, or owners of the FSO or A-Org.

An *FSO* is an organization where the principal business is the performance of services. The proposed regulations under Code Section 414(m) provide that a *service organization* is any organization engaged in the fields of accounting, actuarial science, architecture, consulting, engineering, health, insurance, law, and performing arts.

Example. Three unrelated individuals, Iris, Cornelius, and Lenz (one optometrist and two ophthalmologists in separate practices), equally own Spectacle Shop, a partnership that makes eyeglasses. Each of the three partners refers patients to Spectacle, and a majority of Spectacle's clientele comes from the partners. The following is an estimate of the shop's revenues:

Patients of Iris	50%
Patients of Cornelius	30%
Patients of Lenz	15%
Other	5%

Spectacle is not a service organization because it is not in one of the industries enumerated by the IRS. [Rev. Rul. 87-41, 1987-1 C.B. 296] The proposed regulations say that a firm is not a service organization merely because it manufactures or sells health-related equipment or supplies. Under the proposed regulations, revenue is a determining factor. Spectacle Shop receives its revenue from providing eyeglasses to customers and not from performing services. Spectacle probably would not be treated as an affiliated service group under the proposed regulations. [Prop. Treas. Reg. §§ 1.414(m)-1–1.414(m)-4; *see* S. Derrin Watson, *Who's the Employer?* 6th ed. (Goleta, CA 2012), ch. 13; at *http://www.employerbook.com* (visited on Aug. 20, 2012). Examples used with permission. *See also* Rev. Rul. 81-105, 1981-1 C.B. 256]

Q 2:15 Do the special control rules under Code Section 401(d) apply to SEPs?

No. Code Section 401(d), regarding special rules for self-employed individuals, "the section that Congress forgot, does not reference SEPs, nor do any of the SEP rules reference it." [S. Derrin Watson, American Society of Pension Actuaries, Eastern Regional Seminar, "ASG/Controlled Groups" (audiotape) (June 1995)] Except for requiring that a qualified plan provide that contributions on behalf of an owner-employee be made only with respect to the earned income of the owner-employee that is derived from the trade or business with respect to which the plan is established (see Q 10:2), Code Section 401(d) has been largely repealed for years after 1996. [I.R.C. § 401(d); SBJPA § 1441(a)]

Q 2:16 When are the controlled group, common control, and affiliated service group rules applied?

The controlled group, common control, and affiliated service group rules are applied *before* determining which employees are highly compensated employees (HCEs) under Code Section 414(q)(1).

Q 2:17 How long do the controlled group, common control, and affiliated service group rules apply to sole proprietorships?

It has been informally reported that the IRS takes the position that a sole proprietorship continues until the death of the sole proprietor.

> **Note.** Form 1040, Schedule C, Profit or Loss from Business (Sole Proprietorship), of Form 1040, U.S. Individual Income Tax Return, is used only to report the gain or loss of a self-employed individual. The instructions for Schedule C require that box H be checked if a self-employed individual is reopening or restarting a business after temporarily closing and did not file Schedule C or Schedule C-EZ, Net Profit from Business (Sole Proprietorship), for the prior taxable year.

In a 1995 letter ruling, the IRS held that two entities that did not exist at the same time at some point in their existence could not, by definition, be part of a controlled group or an affiliated service group. [Ltr. Rul. 9541041] It is unclear whether that position would have any merit when there is a mere change in form or location (e.g., incorporating a sole proprietorship or relocating to another state).

> **Example.** A sole proprietor terminated a Keogh plan in 2011. In 2012, the sole proprietor incorporated and established a corporate plan. The sole proprietor and the corporation would be treated as a single employer. [*See* Treas. Reg. § 1.416-1, Q&A T-6, Ex. 2]

By assuming that the sole proprietorship exists until the death of the sole proprietor, Letter Ruling 9541041 and the Treasury regulations can be reconciled. That is, if the sole proprietorship in the previous example continues until the sole proprietor's death, the corporation and the sole proprietorship existed at the same time. Some commentators believe that the letter ruling is contradicted by the regulations. Others believe that the change of form can simply be ignored because there was no real change in the ownership of the business. In all likelihood, the IRS would find some way to categorize a situation like that in the example above as one involving a controlled group.

Establishing SARSEPs

Q 2:18 What is an *elective SEP*, or *SARSEP*?

An *elective SEP*, or *salary reduction SEP* (*SARSEP*), is a SEP arrangement that allows an eligible employee to make elective contributions (see Q 12:1) toward his or her own retirement. SARSEPs were added by the Tax Reform Act of 1986 (TRA '86). [TRA '86 § 1108(d)] They may be adopted or amended only by employers that had SARSEPs in effect on December 31, 1996 (see Q 2:93). For years beginning after 1986, contributions of up to $7,000 (as indexed) may be made with pretax dollars; thus, elective contributions reduce taxable income. For 2012, the indexed amount is $17,000 ($22,500 with catch-up contributions if age 50 or older). Amounts deferred by an eligible employee are contributed by the employer into an individual retirement account or an individual retirement annuity (IRA) on behalf of the eligible employee. Not all employers are eligible to offer a salary reduction feature in a SEP (see Q 2:19).

Q 2:19 What types of businesses may establish a SARSEP?

A SARSEP arrangement may be established by any type of *taxable* business entity (see Qs 2:22, 2:23, 2:25). A corporation, an S corporation, a partnership, or a sole proprietorship may establish a SARSEP. A limited liability partnership or a limited liability company may also establish a SARSEP (see Qs 2:58, 2:60). It should be noted, however, that elective contributions may be made only in plan years in which the employer is qualified to permit elective deferrals to be made under its SEP (see Q 2:20). It is unclear whether an entity that is merged with or becomes related to, affiliated with, or controlled by an entity that has a SARSEP may become a signatory to or may establish a SARSEP. Presumably, such an entity would at least be permitted to become a signatory to an existing grandfathered SARSEP (as amended for changes in the law) (see Q 2:93).

Q 2:20 When does an employer qualify to offer a SARSEP?

An employer qualifies to offer a SARSEP (i.e., an elective SEP) if all of the following conditions are met:

1. The SARSEP is grandfathered (see Q 2:93).
2. The employer had fewer than 26 eligible employees at all times during the prior plan year (determined as if the plan were in existence during that year). [I.R.C. § 408(k)(6)(B)]
3. At least 50 percent of the eligible employees elect to defer a portion of their wages during the current plan year. [I.R.C. § 408(k)(6)(A)(ii)]
4. If the employer uses model Form 5305A-SEP, Salary Reduction and Other Elective Simplified Employee Pension–Individual Retirement Accounts Contribution Agreement, and any eligible key employee participates by making elective contributions, the employer will make a minimum contribution of up to 3 percent for all non-key employees.
5. If the plan is top heavy, the employer will make the minimum required top-heavy contribution (up to 3 percent) for every non-key employee.
6. Unless the employer uses a prototype document, the employer does not have any leased employees (see Qs 2:85, 3:17). [I.R.C. § 414(n)(2)]
7. The employer does not have any eligible employees whose taxable year is not the calendar year. It may be difficult for an employer to verify the tax

year of each participant. [SARSEP—Listing of Required Modifications (LRM) (3-2002)]

Q 2:21 Is there a minimum elective contribution for purposes of the 50 percent rule?

No. The Code does not specify any minimum amount or percentage of compensation that must be deferred into a SARSEP. Thus, any employee who makes an elective contribution is counted for the requirement that at least 50 percent of the eligible employees make elective contributions.

Q 2:22 May a SARSEP arrangement be established by a tax-exempt organization?

No. SARSEP arrangements cannot be established by employers that are exempt from tax; however, such employers may establish SEPs providing for employer contributions only. [I.R.C. § 408(k)(6)(E)]

Q 2:23 May state and local governments or political subdivisions thereof establish a SARSEP?

No. State and local governments and their political subdivisions are prohibited from establishing a SARSEP; however, they may establish SEPs (or SIMPLEs; see Q 14:51) providing for employer contributions only. [I.R.C. § 408(k)(6)(E); *see* SEP Examination Guidelines § 4.72.17.7.1, issued as Internal Revenue Manual, Employee Plans Technical Guidance (Sept. 12, 2006)]

Q 2:24 What happens if elective contributions are made to a SEP in a year in which the employer does not qualify to permit such contributions?

When an employer does not initially qualify to offer elective contributions, any elective contributions made to its SEP are treated as regular wages at the time of the deferral and should be reported by the employer as wages on Form W-2, Wage and Tax Statement. Unless the individual can claim (offset) the amount of the elective contribution (up to $5,000; $6,000 if age 50 or over for 2012) as an annual IRA contribution (whether or not deductible), the amount must be withdrawn from the IRA (along with any gain) by the due date of the individual's federal income tax return to avoid the 6 percent excise tax on excess IRA contributions under Code Section 4973 (see Q 5:78). If the individual is under age 59½, any gain withdrawn may be subject to the 10 percent tax on premature distributions.

> **Example 1.** Calcium Corporation has employed at least 50 eligible employees for the last several years. Because it does not initially qualify to offer a SARSEP, any elective deferrals should be reported by Calcium as wages on Form W-2.

Example 2. Charity, Inc., a tax-exempt organization, establishes a SARSEP. Because it does not initially qualify to offer a SARSEP, any elective deferrals should be reported by Charity as wages on Form W-2.

Example 3. Calico Cat Company has 20 eligible employees on January 1 of the current plan year. Half of the 20 eligible employees elect to have a portion of their compensation paid into the plan. Calico's SARSEP provides for immediate eligibility upon hire. On December 20, a new employee is added to the workforce but does not elect to make an elective contribution to the SARSEP. At the end of the year, it is discovered that half of the eligible employees did not choose to make elective contributions to the SARSEP. Although Calico initially qualified to offer a SARSEP, all contributions are disallowed deferrals (see Q 12:41) and should be reported by Calico as wages on Form W-2.

Q 2:25 Do new employers that had no employees during the prior year qualify to establish a SARSEP?

Yes. New employers that had no employees during the prior year qualify under the "fewer than 26 employees" rule, which states that to establish a SARSEP, the employer must have had fewer than 26 eligible employees at all times during the prior plan year if the employer had 25 or fewer employees during the first 30 days that the business was in existence. [Rev. Proc. 91-44, 1991-2 C.B. 733] This rule has no applicability for tax years beginning after 1996 (see Q 2:20).

Q 2:26 Can it be determined whether the SARSEP employer eligibility requirements are satisfied on or before the first day of the plan year?

Yes. When a plan uses a one-year-or-more eligibility requirement, the employer should know on the first day of the plan year whether 50 percent or more of the eligible employees have elected to make elective contributions and whether the "fewer than 26 employees" rule has been satisfied. The 50 percent rule may not always be satisfied, however, when elective deferrals based on bonuses are permitted.

Example. Big Cat Corporation adopts a SARSEP that provides for a two-year service requirement. During the current year, five employees are eligible to participate. Big Cat offers employees the option of receiving cash bonuses on December 25 or of having the amount contributed into a SEP IRA. Only two employees elect to defer a portion of their annual bonus under the SARSEP. The 50 percent rule is not satisfied with a participation rate of only 40 percent.

Q 2:27 May a SARSEP have more than 25 participants for any single year?

Yes. Because the "fewer than 26 employees" rule is based on the prior year's service, a SARSEP can have an unlimited number of participants for any single year but not for two or more consecutive years.

Example. Intertech Corporation was established in 1976 and maintains a SARSEP arrangement for 2012. The SARSEP arrangement provides for immediate participation of all employees provided they have attained age 21. During 2011, Intertech had 10 employees at all times. On January 2, 2012, Intertech hired 200 employees over the age of 21 to work in its new factory. At least 50 percent of all employees elect to make salary reduction contributions. Because Intertech had fewer than 26 eligible employees during the prior year (2011), it is allowed to make contributions to a SARSEP for 2012.

Intertech may not maintain the SARSEP in 2013 because it had more than 25 eligible employees at all times during the prior year, 2012.

Q 2:28 May SEP and SARSEP arrangements be combined into one prototype document?

Yes. SEP and SARSEP arrangements may be combined into one prototype document; however, it should be noted that they are not required to be. It should also be noted that neither a SEP nor a SARSEP may be combined with an IRA into one prototype document (see Q 3:22).

Q 2:29 May elective contributions be based on bonuses?

Yes. Bonuses may be treated as compensation that may be deferred at the election of the employee (see Q 1:5).

The March 2002 LRM for SARSEPs deleted the separate option for making elective deferrals. This means that the employer should either amend the SARSEP to treat bonuses as other compensation or insert a separate election with respect to bonus payments. For example, an employee may elect not to defer from the bonus payment or elect to defer a lower or higher percentage of the bonus payment merely by completing a new salary reduction form for the employer. Alternatively, the employee may make the election on a revised form on which the employer has provided for bonus payment elections separate from other compensation. [*See http://www.irs.gov* (visited on Aug. 20, 2012), then search site for "LRM."]

SEP Establishment Dates

Q 2:30 What is the last day an employer may establish a SEP arrangement for a prior taxable year?

SEP arrangements may be established after an employer's fiscal year-end. That is, an employer has until the due date of the business's tax return, including extensions, to establish and make a contribution to a SEP arrangement for a prior taxable year. [I.R.C. §§ 404(h)(1)(B), 6072(a), 6072(b)] Contributions may not, however, be based on compensation paid after the end of the taxable year. [Rev. Rul. 90-105, 1990-2 C.B. 69] Documents establishing the employer's SEP must be in writing and signed by a responsible officer or owner at the time the contribution is made. [Ann. 97-42, 1997-17 I.R.B. 19; Ltr. Rul. 8450051; Prop. Treas. Reg. § 1.408-7(b)]

Note. Contributions are treated as made on the last day of the business's taxable year if the contributions are made by the due date of the business's tax return, plus any extensions to which the employer is entitled.

Q 2:31 How does a corporation apply for an automatic extension for filing its tax return?

To apply for an automatic extension for filing its tax return, a corporation must file Form 7004, Application for Automatic Extension of Time to File Corporation Income Tax Return, by the regular due date of its Form 1120, U.S. Corporation Income Tax Return, or Form 1120S, U.S. Income Tax Return for an S Corporation. The automatic extension is six months. The automatic extension does not extend the time for payment of any tax due on the return being extended. [Treas. Reg. §§ 1.6081-3(a), 1.6081-3(b)]

Q 2:32 What are the establishment dates for corporations?

A calendar-year corporation has until March 15, plus any filing extensions, to establish a SEP arrangement and claim a deduction for the prior taxable year. The due dates for a non-calendar-year corporation, and the extended due dates if an automatic extension is obtained, are listed in Table 2-1.

Table 2-1. SEP Establishment Dates for Corporations

2012 Year-End	*Business's Tax Return Due Date*	*Last Day If Six-Month Automatic Extension Obtained*
12/31	3/15/13	9/16/13
11/30	2/15/13	8/15/13
10/31	1/15/13	7/15/13
9/30	12/17/12	6/17/13
8/31	11/15/12	5/15/13

Table 2-1. SEP Establishment Dates for Corporations (cont'd)

2012 Year-End	*Business Tax Return Due Date*	*Last Day of Six-Month Automatic Extension Obtained*
7/31	10/15/12	4/15/13
6/30	9/17/12	3/15/13
5/31	8/15/12	2/15/13
4/30	7/16/12	1/15/13
3/31	6/15/12	12/17/12
2/28	5/15/12	11/15/12
1/31	4/18/12	10/15/12

If an entity is tax exempt, it has until the due date of its Form 990 (generally, the 15th day of the 5th month following the close of its accounting period) to establish a SEP (but not a SARSEP) arrangement.

Q 2:33 How does a partnership apply for an automatic extension for filing its tax return?

A partnership must file Form 7004, Application for Automatic Extension of Time to File Certain Business Income Tax, Information, and Other Returns, by the regular due date of its Form 1065, U.S. Partnership Return of Income. The automatic partnership extension is six months. All partners should have their personal income tax returns extended to the date that the partnership's tax return is due. The automatic extension does not operate to extend the time for payment of any tax due on the return being extended.

Q 2:34 How does an individual apply for an automatic extension to file Form 1040 or Form 1040A?

An individual may file Form 4868, Application for Automatic Extension of Time to File U.S. Individual Income Tax Return. In general, a six-month extension will be granted. The automatic extension does not operate to extend the time for payment of any tax due on the return being extended. [Treas. Reg. §§ 1.6081-5(a)(1),1.6081-5(a)(5)]

Q 2:35 What are the establishment dates for unincorporated entities?

A calendar-year partnership or sole proprietorship has until April 15, plus any filing extensions, to establish a SEP arrangement and claim a deduction for the prior taxable year. The due dates for a non-calendar-year partnership or sole proprietorship, and the extended due dates if an automatic extension is obtained, are listed in Table 2-2.

Table 2-2. SEP Establishment Dates for Unincorporated Entities

2012 Year-End	*Business's Tax Return Due Date*	*Due Date If Automatic Extension Obtained*
12/31	4/15/13	9/16/13
11/30	3/15/13	8/15/13
10/31	2/15/13	7/15/13
9/30	1/15/13	6/17/13
8/31	12/17/12	5/15/13
7/31	11/15/12	4/15/13
6/30	10/15/12	3/15/13
5/31	9/17/12	2/15/13
4/30	8/15/12	1/15/13
3/31	7/16/12	12/17/12
2/28	6/18/12	11/15/12
1/31	5/15/12	10/15/12

Example. For The Gold Partnership, a calendar-year partnership of three individuals, Form 1065 will need to be filed by September 16, 2013, if an automatic extension is obtained for the 2012 partnership return.

Note. Corporations and S corporations receive an automatic six-month extension period.

Practice Pointer. *Husband-wife business.* Generally, if married business owners are the sole owners and operate an unincorporated business and share in the profits and losses, they are partners in a partnership and must file Form 1065. However, as of 2007, if married sole owners materially participate as the only members of a jointly owned and operated business, and they file a joint federal income tax return for the tax year, they can make an election to be treated as a qualified joint venture instead of a partnership. By making the election, the individuals will not be required to file Form 1065 for any year the election is in effect and will instead report the income and deductions directly on their joint return. To make this election, the individuals must divide all items of income, gain, loss, deduction, and credit between the individuals in accordance with their respective interests in the venture. Each must file a separate Schedule C, C-EZ, or F. On each line of the separate Schedule C, C-EZ, or F, enter each individual's share of the applicable income, deduction, or loss. Both individuals must also file a separate Schedule SE to pay self-employment tax. The six-automatic extension period applies to a joint venture that elects to file Schedule C, C-EZ, or F instead of Form 1065.

Q 2:36 Must SEPs be maintained on a calendar-year basis?

For years beginning after 1986, an employer may elect to use either the calendar year or its taxable year for participation, contribution, and allocation purposes. The same year must be used for participation, contribution, and allocation purposes. [I.R.C. § 408(k)(7)(C)]

IRS-approved model documents must be established and maintained on a calendar-year basis. IRS-approved prototype documents, however, frequently allow an employer to choose a plan year that matches its business's taxable year.

Q 2:37 Can an employer change its plan year?

Yes. The plan year selected may be either the calendar year or the employer's taxable year. Plans that permit a change of plan year (generally from the calendar year to the fiscal year of the employer) must include specific provisions to ensure that the proper amount of service is credited to the employee. (*See* Listing of Required Modifications for Simplified Employee Pension Plans, Note to Reviewer (first) (March 2002).)

If the employer already maintains a SEP arrangement and changes its plan year, an employee who has any service during the resulting short year must be given credit for that service in determining whether he or she has performed service in three of the last five years. Such an employee must also receive a contribution for the short year if he or she would have been entitled to a contribution for the plan year in which the short year began had there been no change.

> **Example.** Fish Corporation adopts a SEP based on the calendar year ending December 31, 2012. The corporation's tax year ends on June 30. If the SEP is amended to operate on the basis of Fish's fiscal taxable year ending on June 30, 2012, an employee must receive a contribution for the short plan year beginning on January 1, 2012, and ending on June 30, 2012, if he or she would have been entitled to a contribution for the original plan year that began on January 1, 2012, and would have ended on December 31, 2012, had there been no change.

Q 2:38 Why would an employer change its plan year to match its fiscal taxable year?

When a fiscal-year business maintains a SEP or SARSEP on a calendar-year basis, its deduction for plan contributions may be postponed until the end of the business's taxable year in which the calendar-year plan year ends and the employer's deduction limit is based on compensation earned during the calendar year that ends within the business's fiscal taxable year (see Q 10:1). When the plan year matches the employer's fiscal year, contributions are currently deductible, and the employer's deduction limit is based on compensation earned during the plan year.

Example. Bakery, Inc., maintains a SEP and SARSEP for 2012 using the IRS-approved model documents, which provide that the calendar year be used as the SEP's plan year. Bakery's taxable year ends June 30. Contributions made to the SEP for the 2012 calendar-year plan year will be deductible on the business's federal income tax return for the taxable year ending June 30, 2013—in this case, six months after the last day of the plan year. If Bakery were to change the plan year to coincide with its taxable year (see Q 2:37), it could accelerate the timing of its deduction for SEP contributions.

Q 2:39 What is the last day for employees to establish their IRAs?

An employee has until the employer's contribution due date (determined under Code Section 404(h)) to establish the IRA into which the employer's SEP contribution will be made (see Qs 2:32, 2:35).

Practice Pointer. It is advisable for an employer to establish a SEP arrangement before its contribution due date because eligible employees must be given sufficient time to establish their IRAs.

Q 2:40 What happens if an employee refuses to establish an IRA or dies without having established an IRA?

If an employee eligible to receive a SEP contribution for a given year refuses to establish an IRA, or dies without having established one, the employer must establish an IRA on behalf of that employee. Otherwise, the employer is prohibited from establishing or maintaining a SEP for that year. In such cases, the employer may execute any necessary documents on behalf of an employee entitled to a contribution (see Qs 2:65–2:73). [Prop. Treas. Reg. § 1.408-7(d)(2) and I.R.S. Announcement 80-112, 1980-36 I.R.B. 35]

Q 2:41 May SEP contributions be combined with IRA or SIMPLE IRA contributions?

SEP contributions may be combined with annual IRA contributions without adverse tax consequences. SEP contributions should not, however, be combined with amounts in an IRA that came from a qualified plan or a tax-sheltered annuity under Code Section 403(b). When rollovers from a qualified plan or tax-sheltered annuity under Code Section 403(b) are kept in a separate account (not combined with annual IRA or SEP assets), they may be transferred back into a qualified plan or tax-sheltered annuity, respectively, and retain their original character. If applicable, capital gains treatment or the 10-year averaging method of lump-sum distribution taxation may be preferable to a taxable IRA distribution that is subject to ordinary income taxation.

Until an individual has been a participant in a SIMPLE IRA for two years (see Qs 14:133, 14:135), SIMPLE IRA contributions must not be combined with SEP, SARSEP, or regular annual IRA contributions.

Employee Eligibility

Q 2:42 Must all employees be eligible for a SEP or SARSEP arrangement?

No. SEP and SARSEP arrangements do not have to cover all employees. An employer can choose to exclude employees under the age of 21, employees who have not performed any service (see Q 2:43) during at least three of the immediately preceding five plan years, and employees who have not received a *de minimis* amount of compensation from the employer for the current plan year (see Q 2:46). The employee's participation begins "as of" the first day of the plan year in which the three eligibility requirements (age, service, and minimum compensation) are satisfied. [I.R.C. § 408(k)(2)] The plan year is generally the calendar year. Prototype plans generally allow for some other 12-month period to be used (see Q 2:54). [I.R.C. § 408(k)(2); *see* SEP Examination Guidelines § 4.72.17 (Sept. 12, 2006)] Other exclusions (see Qs 2:45–2:52) may also apply. An eligible employee may not opt out of a SEP; that is, such an employee may not refuse to participate in a SEP (see Qs 2:96, 5:4). [*See* IRS Publication 15-A, *Employer's Supplemental Tax Guide, Part 1, Who Are Employees?*]

> **Caution.** The failure to allocate contributions (if any are made) to an eligible employee may destroy the entire deduction for contributions for the plan year.

> **Example.** PugMugs established a SEP using the IRS model Form 5305-SEP in 2005. Cody, the owner, and his wife Mardou are its only eligible employees. The business contributed $10,000 to Cody's SEP-IRA for 2012. PugMugs did not make any contribution for Mardou (i.e., no amount was allocated to Mardou's SEP-IRA) for 2012. None of PugMug's contribution is deductible. It may also be subject to penalty as an excess contribution (see Qs 5:24, 10:12). [Brown v. Commissioner, T.C. Summ. Op. 2008-56 (T.C. 2008)]

Q 2:43 What is *service*?

Service means any work performed for an employer for any period of time, however short; it need not be continuous, and no specified number of hours is required. The term *service* is undefined in the Treasury regulations.

If a successor employer continues a plan for another employer (predecessor employer), all employees who worked for the predecessor employer must be given credit for the years of service for that predecessor employer (see Q 2:91). [I.R.C. § 414(a)(1)] If a successor employer maintains a plan that is not the plan maintained by the predecessor employer, service for the predecessor employer, to the extent provided under as yet unissued regulations, must be treated as service for the successor employer (see Q 2:92). [I.R.C. § 414(a)(2)]

> **Example.** Doris has been performing services for her friend Sol's sole proprietorship for three years on a part-time basis (she receives no compensation). Each year, Doris stuffs and addresses thousands of marketing brochures for Sol's business, signing Sol's name to each one. The

following year (year 4), she begins to receive compensation—more than $550—for her services and attains age 21 on the last day of the plan year (Dec. 31). Absent an exclusion (e.g., nonresident alien, collectively bargained), Doris is eligible to participate in Sol's SEP and receive a contribution if any are made for year 4, because she has met all three participation requirements (age, service, and minimum compensation).

Q 2:44 Must service with a related, controlled, or affiliated employer be considered?

Yes. Service includes service with any related entity (see Q 2:4); that is, service with an entity that is under common control or is a member of a controlled group must be counted. Service with a member of an affiliated service group must also be counted (see Q 2:14). [Treas. Reg. § 1.414(m)-3(a)(5); Ltr. Ruls. 9033061, 9026056, 8945070, 8928008]

Q 2:45 When must the SEP eligibility requirements be satisfied?

The age, compensation, and service requirements (if any are provided) for a SEP or SARSEP arrangement are satisfied if they are met at any time during the plan year. [Prop. Treas. Reg. § 1.408-7(d)(1)] The death of an eligible employee does not eliminate the requirement that an amount be allocated to the deceased employee's IRA if employer contributions are made for the plan year. Neither would a separation from service or a requirement that an employee be employed on a specified date (see Qs 2:51, 2:66). [Prop. Treas. Reg. § 1.408-7(d)(3)]

A SEP may not impose a length of service requirement. For example, if a plan requires an employee to work during at least one of the five years immediately preceding the current year, and the employee is otherwise eligible, the length of time he or she worked for the employer in that period is irrelevant. Even if the employee worked for one day he or she is eligible, assuming the employee otherwise meets the requirements for SEP participation.

Example 1. Total Green maintains a SEP arrangement for eligible employees. The plan year is the calendar year. The SEP provides for immediate participation regardless of age, service, or minimum compensation. Paul is age 18, and begins working part-time for Total Green in 2012. Paul is an eligible individual for 2012 and is entitled to share in SEP contributions if any are made by Total Green with respect to the 2012 plan year.

Example 2. Ace Corporation maintains a SEP arrangement for its employees. The plan year is the calendar year. The SEP arrangement requires an employee to have attained age 21 and to have performed service for the employer for at least three of the immediately preceding five calendar years. The plan does not have a minimum compensation requirement. Alice worked for Ace while in college in 2009, 2010, and 2011. She never worked more than 25 days in any particular year. In October 2012, Alice began to work for Ace on a fulltime basis. She earned $5,000 from Ace in 2012. Alice became 21 years old on December 31, 2012. She is entitled to share in any SEP contributions made by Ace with respect to 2012. As of December 31, 2012, Alice had met the minimum age and compensation requirements, as well as the service requirements, because she worked for Ace in three of the five years preceding 2012. [Prop. Treas. Reg. § 1.408-7(d)(5)] Had Alice commenced employment in 2010, she would not have met the plan's three-year eligibility requirement because she would have completed only two years of service for the plan year ending December 31, 2012.

Example 3. Wizard Software, Inc. adopts a SEP arrangement that requires an employee to have performed service for at least three of the immediately preceding five calendar years. Tommy had been continuously employed by Wizard since 1984 and shared in Wizard's contribution for 2008; however, he performed no service in 2009, 2010, or 2011 and thus received no contributions for those years. Tommy returned to work for Wizard in 2012, but he is not entitled to share in Wizard's contributions for 2012 because he worked during only two of the immediately preceding five years—2007 and 2008.

Q 2:46 May part-time employees be excluded from participation in a SEP?

A special *de minimis* rule allows part-time employees with compensation below $300 (as indexed; $550 for 2012) to be excluded from participation in a SEP for the current plan year. [I.R.C. § 408(k)(2)] For tax years beginning after 1994, the cost-of-living adjustments (COLAs) to the *de minimis* amount are simplified by a rounding-down process (see Q 1:4). The incremental amount is $50. For plan years beginning in 2012, employees with compensation of less that $550 may be excluded.

Note. For purposes of the *de minimis* rule only, the term *compensation* is defined in Code Section 414(q)(7) and has the same meaning as compensation for the 100 percent/$50,000 limit for 2012 (see Qs 6:3, 6:9). [I.R.C. § 408(k)(8)]

Example. Gemstones, Inc., adopted a SEP arrangement for 2011 that requires an employee to have performed service for one of the immediately preceding five calendar years and earn at least $550 during the current year. Donna's first day of work was December 31, 2011, and she earned $100 from Gemstones for 2011. Donna became a full-time employee of Gemstones during 2012 and earned $12,000 in that year. Donna is entitled to share in Gemstones's contribution for 2012 because she performed service during at least one of the immediately preceding five calendar years and earned more than $550 in 2012. Although Donna earned below the *de minimis* amount during the 2011 eligibility year, she is not precluded from participating during 2012. If Donna had earned less than $550 during 2012, she would not be eligible to participate for the 2012 plan year. [I.R.C. § 408(k)(2)(C)]

Q 2:47 Does an employer have to specify minimum compensation, age, or service requirements?

No. An employer does not have to specify service, age, or compensation requirements. When an employer does not establish any eligibility requirements, all employees performing service during the year would participate in the SEP for that year.

Q 2:48 May an employee on the effective date of the plan be treated as satisfying the age and/or service requirements specified in the SEP or SARSEP?

Yes. The IRS has allowed a prototype plan sponsor to provide a provision that allows an employer to waive the age and/or service requirement for an individual employed on the effective date of the plan (see Q 2:56). In such case, an employee employed on the effective date will be considered to have met the age and/or service requirement as of the effective date. An employee who was not employed on the plan's effective date must satisfy the age and service requirements specified in the plan (see Q 2:56).

Q 2:49 May union employees be excluded from participation in a SEP?

Yes, if certain conditions apply. A statutory exclusion similar to that applicable to qualified plans allows certain union employees to be excluded from participation in SEP or SARSEP arrangements. [I.R.C. § 408(k)(2)] For the exclusion to apply, there must be a unit of employees covered by an agreement that the Secretary of Labor finds to be a collective bargaining agreement between representatives of the employees and one or more employers. There must also be evidence that retirement benefits were the subject of good-faith bargaining between such employee representatives and such employer or employers. The exclusion does not necessarily require that retirement benefits be provided as a result of the good-faith bargaining. The SEP or SARSEP arrangement must specifically exclude certain employees for the union exclusion to apply.

Example. Matrix Company, a calendar-year taxpayer, establishes a SEP arrangement that covers all its employees who have attained age 21, except for employees whose retirement benefits are the subject of good-faith collective bargaining. Five employees belong to Local 999 and work for Matrix. The company has an agreement with representatives of those five union employees that the Secretary of Labor found to be a collective bargaining agreement. The official resolutions of the annual Local 999 collective bargaining meeting were approved by the membership (after a lengthy discussion) and provided that the union employees would accept four additional paid holidays instead of a retirement benefit program that would have provided the union employees with retirement contributions. This provision became effective on January 1, 2012. Those five employees may be excluded from the SEP arrangement adopted by Matrix for its 2012 taxable year.

Q 2:50 May nonresident alien employees be excluded from participation in a SEP?

Yes, if certain conditions apply. A statutory exclusion similar to that applicable to qualified plans allows nonresident alien employees to be excluded from participation in SEP or SARSEP arrangements. [I.R.C. § 408(k)(2)] For the exclusion to apply, the nonresident alien employee must receive no earned income (within the meaning of Code Section 911(d)(2)) from the employer that constitutes income from sources within the United States (within the meaning of Code Section 861(a)(3)).

Q 2:51 May SEP contributions be made contingent on employment on a certain date or on completion of a certain number of hours of service?

No. Unlike contributions to many qualified plans, SEP contributions cannot be made contingent on an employee's being employed on the last day of the plan year or on an employee's completion of a fixed number of hours of service. [I.R.C. § 408(k)(2); Prop. Treas. Reg. §§ 1.408-7(d), 1.408-7(d)(3)]

Q 2:52 Are exclusions for attaining a maximum age permitted?

No. SEP contributions otherwise due cannot be denied to an employee on account of his or her exceeding a specified age.

Q 2:53 Are contributions permitted after age 70½?

Yes. A SEP, SARSEP, or SIMPLE may not contain a maximum age restriction. Therefore, contributions cannot be denied to an employee after the employee has attained age 70½. Code Section 219(d), which prohibits annual IRA contributions (other than contributions to a Roth IRA) beyond age 70½, does not apply to SEP, SIMPLE, or SARSEP contributions. [I.R.C. § 219(b)(2)]

Q 2:54 May an employer amend its plan each year to lengthen the service requirement for eligibility?

Yes. It should be noted, however, that if new employees are added to the workforce, the successive amendments are likely to result in prohibited discrimination under Code Section 408(k)(3) (but see Q 2:48). That may be so because the present employees who are highly compensated employees could not meet the eligibility requirements for new employees at the time the plan was originally established (see Q 2:56). Another way to achieve the same effect is to terminate the plan each year and establish a new plan. In either case, it might be prudent to seek written assurances from an attorney who is familiar with the Employee Retirement Income Security Act of 1974 (ERISA) or submit a request to the IRS for a private letter ruling on such a scheme. [Rev. Rul. 73-382, 1973-2 C.B. 134; Rev. Rul. 70-75, 1970-1 C.B. 94]

Note. Code Section 414(o) provides that the Secretary of the Treasury shall prescribe such regulations as may be necessary to prevent the avoidance of any employee benefit requirement listed in Code Section 414(m)(4) or 414(n)(3). Both of those subsections refer to SEPs.

The employer must provide a copy of the amendment and a clear explanation of the amendment's effect to employees. A failure to clearly explain the effect of the amendment may subject the plan to the full reporting and disclosure requirements of ERISA (see Qs 4:7, 4:17).

Note. In an explanation of audit techniques, the IRS provided the example that follows. Unfortunately, the example does not address discrimination issues.

Example. Prior to 1997, an employer adopted the IRS model plan 5305A-SEP and completed the form to specify that employees are eligible to participate (1) upon attainment of age 21 and (2) after performing services in any year during the last five years. However, in operation, the employer uses the maximum permitted eligibility criteria: That is, the employer kept out employees until they were age 21 and had performed services for the employer in three of the last five years. Employers must follow the terms of their plans, and in this case the employer did not do so. The employer could amend the plan to require three years of performed service, but only for future eligibility. [*See* Chapter 13, *SEP, SARSEP Audit Techniques, Examination Case Examples*, at 13–22, available at *http://www.irs.gov/pub/irs-tege/epche1303.pdf* (visited on Aug. 20, 2012)]

Q 2:55 How do SEP and SARSEP eligibility rules compare to the eligibility rules under most qualified plans?

A SEP arrangement can be less costly to an employer than a qualified plan and can compare favorably to a qualified plan even though fully vested SEP contributions would generally be made for part-time employees with three or more years of service. A qualified plan's shorter eligibility requirement (generally one year and 1,000 hours of service) may result in contributions having to be made or allocated to more employees. Although the qualified plan would most likely apply a vesting schedule to employer-derived accrued benefits or account balances, a vesting schedule is generally applied to an additional two years of contributions made by the employer.

Only after considering many factors (e.g., potential growth of the business, employee turnover, age of employees, number of employees, and hours worked (500 or 1,000)) and analyzing a group's eligibility to participate initially and then to receive contributions (and the extent to which those contributions will be vested upon an employee's termination of service) can the plan that offers the least cost to an employer at all points along an employee's employment time line be determined.

Additional factors affecting appropriate plan choice will also need to be considered. Those factors may include the following:

- Administrative burdens and costs, including IRS and Department of Labor (DOL) reporting requirements;
- Plan documentation charges;
- Protection of plan assets from creditors;
- Loan availability;
- Existence of another plan, including a defined benefit plan that has been terminated; and
- Availability and usefulness of the special forward income averaging tax treatment available for qualifying lump-sum distributions from qualified plans (but see Q 5:50).

[I.R.C. § 402(d); see comparison chart at Appendix E]

Example 1. Big Boat, Inc., is comparing a SEP to a profit-sharing plan. Except for the owner, all of its 20 employees work part time. To maximize contributions for the owner, Big Boat adopts a profit-sharing plan and excludes employees who work fewer than 1,000 hours during the year. Although the profit-sharing plan may be more complex and more costly to administer and service, it is nonetheless more cost efficient because the owner is its sole participant.

Example 2. David's Muncheria employs college students on a part-time basis. All employees complete over 1,000 hours of service during the year. The students always seem to quit before working two or three years. David adopts a SEP and excludes employees who have completed fewer than three years of service. David is the plan's only participant.

Example 3. The Clock Shop, established in 1988, has one owner-employee and four full-time nonowner-employees who work from three to five years before terminating employment. If The Clock Shop adopts a SEP with a three-year service requirement, it will make fully vested contributions for recently hired nonowner-employees for one or two years. If it adopts a profit-sharing plan, The Clock Shop will make contributions for its employees for between two and five years. The profit-sharing plan would have a one-year (1,000 hours of service) eligibility requirement and would apply a vesting schedule to employer contributions. Thus, some of the benefits under the profit-sharing plan will be forfeited by terminating employees and reallocated to remaining participants in proportion to compensation. As presented in Table 2-3, the owner (who receives wages of $80,000) would receive 64.5 percent ($40,000) of a $62,000 SEP contribution, or 62.6 percent ($43,821) of a $70,000 profit-sharing contribution. In this simple example, the SEP compares favorably to the qualified plan.

Table 2-3 compares a 10 percent contribution under a SEP (with a three-year service requirement) to a profit-sharing plan (with a one-year service requirement and a vesting schedule). For purposes of these calculations, the following assumptions apply: two of the nonowner-employees were hired during the first year and will commence participation in the fourth year, all other employees are eligible and quit when indicated, the average profit-sharing forfeiture rate is 50 percent, and all gains on account balances are disregarded.

Table 2-3. Comparison of SEP and Profit-Sharing Contributions

Wages	*Year One*	*Year Two*	*Year Three*	*Year Four*	*Year Five*	*Total Contribution*	*Total to Be Received after Forfeiture*
$80,000 SEP	$ 8,000	$ 8,000	$ 8,000	$ 8,000	$ 8,000	$40,000	$40,000
P/S	$ 8,000	$ 8,000	$ 8,000	$ 9,713	$10,107	$40,000	$43,821
$20,000 SEP	$ 2,000	$ 2,000	$ 2,000	$ 2,000	Quit	$ 8,000	$ 8,000
P/S	$ 2,000	$ 2,000	$ 2,000	$ 2,429	Quit	$ 8,000	$ 4,213
$20,000 SEP	$ 2,000	$ 2,000	$ 2,000	Quit	—	$ 6,000	$ 6,000
P/S	$ 2,000	$ 2,000	$ 2,000	Quit	—	$ 6,000	$ 3,000
$20,000 SEP	$ 0	$ 0	$ 0	$ 2,000	$ 2,000	$ 4,000	$ 4,000
P/S	$ 0	$ 2,000	$ 2,000	$ 2,429	$ 3,053	$ 8,000	$ 9,428
$20,000 SEP	$ 0	$ 0	$ 0	$ 2,000	$ 2,000	$ 4,000	$ 4,000
P/S	$ 0	$ 2,000	$ 2,000	$ 2,429	$ 3,053	$ 8,000	$ 9,428
Cost* SEP	$12,000	$12,000	$12,000	$14,000	$12,000	$62,000	$62,000
P/S	$12,000	$16,000	$16,000	$14,000	$12,000	$70,000	$70,000

* Excludes forfeitures

Q 2:56 May future employees be required to satisfy an age or service condition not applicable to current employees?

No. Provisions allowing current employees to participate whether or not they have satisfied the eligibility requirements applicable to future employees are not expressly prohibited; however, the IRS model plan does not contain provisions for dual eligibility. Some prototype SEP plans contain provisions that allow individuals who are employed on the effective date of the plan to participate, notwithstanding the age and service requirements applicable to employees hired after the effective date of the SEP (see Qs 2:48; 2:54). A sponsor for such a plan informed the author that the IRS indicated that the provision allowing current employees to participate whether or not they have satisfied the eligibility requirements applicable to future employees would have to be removed when the plan is next amended. Arguably, adopting employers of such plans may rely on the provisions of their plan.

> **Example.** New Corp. was organized on April 1, 2012, and adopts a SEP for its 2012 taxable calendar year. The plan has a one-year service requirement. Because no service was performed before 2012, no employee is eligible to

participate for 2012. If SEPs were permitted to have dual eligibility provisions, all current employees could be permitted to participate, but future employees could be required to satisfy an age or service requirement to commence participation (see Q 2:48).

Q 2:57 May an employer adopt a SARSEP and a nonelective SEP with different eligibility requirements?

Yes. For example, an employer that adopts a model SEP using Form 5305-SEP may also establish a model elective SEP using Form 5305A-SEP or another SEP to which either elective or nonelective contributions are made. If the arrangement primarily benefits key employees, however, it is top heavy, and the required minimum top-heavy contribution would have to be made for all employees eligible under any plan that includes a key employee (see Q 8:1).

Employees of Limited Liability Partnerships and Limited Liability Companies

Q 2:58 What is a *limited liability partnership*?

A *limited liability partnership (LLP)* is a recognized business entity in most states, the specifics for which are governed by state law. Generally, an LLP is established as a partnership for federal income tax purposes and files Form 1065, U.S. Partnership Return of Income.

In general, a *partnership* is the relationship between two or more persons who join to carry on a trade or business, with each person contributing money, property, labor, or skill and each expecting to share in the profits and losses of the business, whether or not a formal agreement is made. The term *partnership* includes a limited partnership, syndicate, group, pool, joint venture, or other unincorporated organization through or by which any business, financial operation, or venture is carried on that is not, within the meaning of the regulations under Code Section 7701, a corporation, trust, estate, or sole proprietorship.

A *general partner* is a partner who is personally liable for partnership debts. A general partnership is composed only of general partners. A *limited partner* is a partner in a partnership formed under a state limited partnership law whose personal liability for partnership debts is limited to the amount of money or other property that the partner contributed or is required to contribute to the partnership. Some members of other entities, such as domestic or foreign business trusts or limited liability companies that are classified as partnerships, may be treated as limited partners for certain purposes. [*See, e.g.*, Temp. Treas. Reg. § 1.469-5T(e)(3) (treating all members with limited liability as limited partners for purposes of Code Section 469(h)(2), relating to limitations on passive activity losses and certain credits)]

A limited partnership is formed under a state limited partnership law and is composed of at least one general partner and one or more limited partners. An LLP is formed under a state LLP law. Generally, a partner in an LLP is not personally liable for the acts or omissions of any other partner solely by reason of being a partner.

An LLP is designed to protect a partner individually against lawsuits filed against the partnership or against one of the other partners. For example, to protect themselves against medical malpractice suits, a group of doctors may establish their business as an LLP. Although the business will be taxed and treated as a partnership for SEP purposes, the partners will have limited their liability for the acts of others. An LLP, however, may not protect against all liability, and state law should be closely reviewed. [Lurie, "Changing to an LLP or LLC Raises Special Pension Considerations for Professionals," 4 *J. of Taxation of Employee Benefits* 1 (May/June 1996) 38]

Q 2:59 What type of business may form an LLP?

Generally, an LLP is available only to professionals. State law defines which types of professionals qualify. For example, in New York, the term *professional* includes attorneys and other individuals "duly authorized to a profession." [N.Y. State Consolidated Laws, art. XII—Limited Liability Company, § 1207(c); *see also* Consolidated Laws of New York, ch. 16, "Education Law"]

Q 2:60 What is a *limited liability company*?

A *limited liability company (LLC)* is a recognized business entity in most states, the specifics for which are governed by state law. Like an LLP, an LLC is designed to protect an owner individually against lawsuits filed against the business entity. [Lurie, "Changing to an LLP or LLC Raises Special Pension Considerations for Professionals," 4 *J. of Taxation of Employee Benefits* 1 (May/June 1996) 38] Unlike partners in an LLP, members of an LLC are personally liable for the entity's debts. For federal tax purposes, an LLC may be classified as a partnership, a corporation, or an entity disregarded as an entity separate from its owner (by applying the rules in Treasury Regulations Section 301.7701-3). (*See* Form 8832, Entity Classification Election, for details.) Plan creation will rarely be a determining factor in deciding whether to conduct a business through an LLC, but there may be other benefits of doing so. [Pratt, "Focus On—Limited Liability Companies," 3 *J. of Pension Benefits* 3 (Spring 1996) 57; *see also* Frost, Steven G., "Square Peg, Meet Round Hole:" Classifying LLC Members as "General Partners" or "Limited Partners" for Federal Tax Purposes, *The Tax Magazine*, Vol. 73 (Dec. 12, 1995); *see also* Hennig, *The Adviser's Guide to Retirement Plans for Small Businesses*, chapter 2, Entity Choice (American Institute of Certified Public Accountants (AICPA), 2010)]

The entity classification regulations (generally referred to as the check-the-box regulations) under Code Section 7701 are generally effective January 1, 1997. The check-the-box regulations allow certain business entities to choose their classification for federal tax purposes under an elective regime. "Per Se" corporations are statutory corporations and are not allowed to choose their classification. [Treas. Reg. § 301.7701-2(b), and list in Treas. Reg. § 301.7701-2(b)(8)]

Classification rules. An eligible entity with at least two members can elect to be classified as a partnership or as a corporation for federal tax purposes. An eligible entity with a single owner can elect to be classified as a corporation or can be disregarded as an entity separate from its owner. [*See* Treas. Reg. § 301.7701-3(a)] If the entity is disregarded, it is treated as a sole proprietorship if it is owned by an individual; if it is owned by a corporation, it is treated as a branch or division of such corporation. Under default rules, unless the entity elects otherwise, a domestic eligible entity is classified as a partnership if it has at least two members; if it has a single owner, it is disregarded. Thus, under the default rules, a domestic general partnership, a limited partnership or an LLC is classified as a partnership for federal tax purposes if an election is not filed. A foreign entity is classified as a corporation if all members have limited liability. If it has a single owner, it is disregarded if the owner does not have limited liability. [*See* Treas. Reg. § 301.7701-3(b)]

An eligible entity that wants to elect out of its default classification or change its classification can do so by filing Form 8832, Entity Classification Election. If an eligible entity makes an election to change its classification, the entity cannot change its classification again for five years. [*See* Treas. Reg. § 301.7701-3(c)] This limit applies only to changes by election. Accordingly, a new eligible entity that elects out of its default classification may change its classification by election at any time. In addition, an entity generally may change its classification if the entity's business is transferred to another entity.

A domestic eligible entity in existence before January 1, 1997, retains the classification it claimed before that date. However, an eligible entity with a single owner that claimed to be a partnership is disregarded as a separate entity. A foreign eligible entity is treated as being in existence before the effective date only if the entity's classification was relevant at any time during the five years before January 1, 1997.

Tax consequences. A change in an entity's classification may have income tax consequences. For example, if an entity that was previously classified as a corporation elects to be classified as a partnership, the entity and its owners are subject to the tax rules applicable to both corporate liquidations and to the formation of a partnership.

Q 2:61 May a sole practitioner establish an LLC or LLP?

Depending on the state, a sole practitioner may be permitted to establish an LLC. That may be a solution for a sole practitioner seeking to limit its liability because, presumably, a one-person partnership cannot exist. In New York and Texas, for example, one-person LLCs are explicitly authorized. [Rev. Proc. 95-10, § 4.01, 1995-1 C.B. 501; N.Y. State Consolidated Laws, art. XII—Limited Liability Company, § 203]

Q 2:62 What is the compensation of a partner in an LLC or LLP?

The compensation of a partner in an organization established as an LLP or LLC is his or her earned income (see Qs 2:58, 2:60, 6:8). In general, a partner in an LLC owes self-employment taxes (Self-Employment Contributions Act of 1954 [SECA]) if the owner is personally liable for the LLC's debts; can sign a contract for the firm; or works for an LLC that provides services, such as law, accounting, health, engineering, architecture, or consulting. In addition, owners that perform services for 500 or more hours per year owe SECA tax. [*See* Prop. Treas. Reg. §§ 1.1402(a)-2(g), 1.1402(a)-2(h)]

In general, Treasury regulations allow entities such as a limited partnership, a general partnership, a sole proprietorship, an LLC, an LLP, a joint venture, or any other unincorporated business organization to elect how it is treated for federal tax purposes. Once an entity has made its choice, it may not elect out of that status. [Treas. Reg. § 301.7701-2(b)]

If a corporation does not or cannot elect S corporation status, it is taxed as a C corporation. [Treas. Reg. § 1.1361-1(c)] The election to be taxed as a C corporation is made by filing Form 8832, Entity Classification Election, within 75 days after the election's effective date, and a copy of the form must be attached to the organization's first federal income tax return.

> **Practice Pointer.** Corporations (entities) with reasonable cause for not timely filing Form 2553 can request to have the form treated as timely filed by filing Form 2553 as an attachment to Form 1120S, U.S. Income Tax Return for an S Corporation. An entry space for an explanation was added to page 1 of the form.

The election to be taxed as an S corporation is made on Form 2553, Election by Small Business Corporation. If any entity other than an LLC formed by a corporation does not choose to be taxed as a corporation, it is (1) taxed as a partnership if it has more than one owner or (2) disregarded as a separate entity if it has only one owner. [Treas. Reg. § 301.7701-3(a)] Thus, a sole proprietor that forms an LLC is still treated as a sole proprietorship. [Treas. Reg. §§ 301.7701-1–301.7701-3; S. Derrin Watson, *Who's the Employer?* 6th ed. (Goleta, CA 2012), Q&A 2:4; at *http://www.employerbook.com* (visited on Aug. 20, 2012)]

An LLC formed by a corporation is treated as a division of that corporation; its income is included on the corporation's tax return.

Foreign entities are subject to different rules. [Treas. Reg. § 301.7701-3(b)(2)]

> **Note.** QR and SEP—It should be noted that an IRA or Roth IRA does not qualify as an eligible shareholder of an S corporation. [Taproot Administrative Services v. Commissioner, Case No. 10-70892 (C.A. 9, Mar. 21, 2012); Rev. Rul. 66-266, 1966-2 C.B. 356; Rev. Rul. 92-73, 1992-2 C.B. 224; see too, Ltr. Rul. 201119022 (rel. May 13, 2011), 201114009 (rel. Apr. 8, 2011), 200940013 (June 25, 2009), 200931039 (Apr. 24, 2009), 200915020 (Dec. 19, 2008)]

Q 2:63 What is the compensation of an employee (including an owner) of an LLC established as a corporation or S corporation?

Generally, W-2 wages are used to determine the compensation of an employee of an LLC established as a corporation or as an S corporation (see Compensation disguised as dividends may be subject to payroll taxes. [NU-Look Design. TC Memo 2003-52, Docket No. 10368-01 (Feb. 26, 2003)]). S corporation dividends can never be treated as compensation (see Q 6:14).

Q 2:64 Where is the deduction for SEP contributions claimed?

Except for contributions made on behalf of a partner in a partnership, LLP, or LLC (see Q 2:65), the deduction for SEP contributions is claimed on the business's Form 1065, U.S. Partnership Return of Income (line 18), if the organization is taxed as a partnership. An unincorporated business other than a partnership claims the deduction for SEP and SARSEP contributions of nonowner-employees on Schedule C (line 19) or Schedule F (line 23), Profit or Loss from Farming, of Form 1040. If the organization is taxed as a corporation, the deduction for contributions made on behalf of owners and nonowners is claimed on the corporation's Form 1120 (line 23) or Form 1120S (line 17). These rules also apply to SIMPLE contributions. (Line numbers are from the 2012 version of forms.)

Q 2:65 Where is the deduction for SEP contributions on behalf of a partner in a partnership, LLP, or LLC claimed?

The deduction for SEP contributions made on behalf of a partner in a partnership, LLP, or LLC is claimed on the partner's individual federal income tax return Form 1040 (line 28) or Form 1040NR (line 28). SIMPLE contributions are treated in a similar fashion. (Line numbers are from the 2012 version of Form 1040 and Form 1040NR.)

Forcing Employees to Participate

Q 2:66 Are eligible employees required to participate in a SEP?

Yes. Participation in a SEP is automatic within the eligible group of employees. [I.R.C. § 408(k)(2)] A SEP is created by the employer's contribution, which must be allocated to the employees who are covered by year-end, even if the contribution was made earlier in the year before coverage was established.

Q 2:67 May an employer force each eligible employee to participate in a SEP?

Yes. Model Form 5305-SEP, Simplified Employee Pension-Individual Retirement Accounts Contribution Agreement, indicates that an employer may require an employee to join its SEP as a condition of continued employment (see Q 2:69).

Q 2:68 May an employer that requires an employee to join a SEP as a condition of continued employment require the employee to make elective contributions?

No. An employer cannot require or pressure an employee to make elective contributions to a SARSEP. An employee may, however, be required to sign an investment form and any other documents that are necessary to create an IRA required to be used under the SEP.

Example. Greg's employer, Illustrations, Inc., establishes a SARSEP using model Form 5305-SEP. Greg does not want to participate. Because owners participate in the SEP, the plan is deemed top heavy, and, consequently, a top-heavy contribution is required. Greg must receive the required minimum top-heavy contribution, and Illustrations may establish a traditional IRA on his behalf if he does not do so in a timely manner.

Q 2:69 Must an eligible employer provide a summary plan description to an employee before SEP coverage begins?

At least one state court has addressed the issue of providing a summary plan description (SPD) for a SEP. In *Schultz v. Production Stamping Corp.* [434 N.W. 2d 780 (Wis. 1989)], the court held that ERISA does not require that an SPD be given to an employee before SEP coverage begins. That ruling was less broad than it would appear because the employer distributed a copy of Form 5305-SEP to its employees. Form 5305-SEP was the plan document and contained summaries and disclosures (see Qs 4:1, 4:5). In addition, the employer held a meeting at which the plaintiff-employee asked no questions. The employee signed up, but her husband persuaded her to go back the next day and cross her name out. The employer warned the employee that she would be fired, and she was. The court, reversing a lower court damage award of $173,000, concluded that it was reasonable for the employer to discharge the employee because one employee should not have the power to destroy the pension arrangement for all the other employees. (The explanation portion of the standard SEP plan document confirms that the employer may terminate an uncooperative employee.) [*See* Form 5305-SEP, Information for the Employee, SEP Participation.]

The court in *Schultz* also had to rule on the issue of whether, in Wisconsin, such a discharge would be impermissible as a matter of public policy. Again, the court noted that the employer's disclosure exceeded the minimum requirements of ERISA; there could be no bar to a dismissal authorized by ERISA.

Q 2:70 What is the result if an employer does not require all employees to participate in its SEP?

If any eligible employee does not enroll in the employer's SEP, the IRS will refuse to allow tax deferral for the SEP contributions. The employer will lose tax deductions for the employees who are covered, and the employees who thought they were covered may be taxed on the amounts contributed. They may also be subject to a 6 percent penalty for excess contributions to their IRAs (see Q 5:24). [I.R.S. Notice 81-1, 1981-1 C.B. 610] Many types of plan failures may be corrected by the plan sponsor (generally the employer). (See chapter 17.)

Q 2:71 Should plans such as SEPs be announced early to avoid employee confusion?

Yes. Where possible, educating employees about a SEP before it is put into place is the better practice. In *Schultz v. Production Stamping Corp.* [434 N.W. 2d 780 (Wis. 1989)] (see Q 2:69), however, special circumstances existed. The decision to adopt the SEP was made on April 10, and the employer needed to complete the paperwork within a few days (i.e., by April 15). Apparently, the SEP law had just been changed to allow participation after age 70. The employer acted promptly after learning of the change. It did not, however, allow the employee to telephone her husband for advice. This contributed to the employee's rescinding her enrollment the next day.

Practice Pointer. Employers in situations similar to that in *Schultz* may prefer to delay the effective date of a SEP (instead of running the risk of litigation) or else announce the effective date early enough to avoid employee confusion.

Q 2:72 Why are the SEP participation rules so strict?

The SEP was conceived as a way for small employers to use their employees' own IRAs as vehicles for a pension arrangement that would involve little administrative work once contributions were made to those IRAs. To allow less than 100 percent participation would have necessitated compliance with complex provisions that usually require professional help—exactly what was intended to be avoided. By requiring 100 percent participation, lawmakers aimed to keep the SEP simple.

Q 2:73 Do state laws apply when determining whether disclosure regarding a SEP has been reasonable?

Maybe. In *Schultz v. Production Stamping Corp.* [434 N.W. 2d 780 (Wis. 1989)] (see Q 2:69), the court cited a general Wisconsin law that required full disclosure as a matter of state policy. It did not consider ERISA preemption, which consideration might have answered the question. Instead, the court stated that the Wisconsin law was a statement of general policy not applying to any specific statute and that, in any event, the employer had acted reasonably within the bounds of that policy.

Q 2:74 What harm could an employee suffer by being forced to participate in a SEP?

One consequence of SEP coverage is the possible reduction of the deduction that would otherwise be available for an employee's own IRA contributions.

Such a reduction could occur because participation in a SEP invokes the IRA deduction limits that apply above certain income levels when the IRA owner or his or her spouse actively participates in certain types of retirement plans, qualified plans, or SEPs (see Q 5:33). This negative might be counterbalanced by an employer's contributions to a SEP, depending on the size and regularity of those contributions. Of course, the nondeductibility of an IRA contribution is taken into account when distributions are made, and, at that time, the appropriate portion is treated as a tax-free return of contributions (see Q 13:47).

Classification of Employees

Q 2:75 What are the four types of business relationships?

The four types of business relationships are

1. Independent contractor (see Q 2:76),
2. Common-law employee (see Q 2:84),
3. Statutory employee (see Q 2:87), and
4. Statutory nonemployee (see Q 2:87).

[For additional information, *see* S. Derrin Watson, *Who's the Employer?* 6th ed. (Goleta, CA 2012), chs. 2 & 4; at *http://www.employerbook.com* (visited on Aug. 20, 2012)]

Q 2:76 What is an *independent contractor*?

The general rule is that an *independent contractor* is an individual whose employer has the right to control or direct only the result of the work and not the means and methods of accomplishing the result. Individuals such as lawyers, accountants, contractors, subcontractors, public stenographers, and auctioneers who follow an independent trade, business, or profession in which they offer their services to the public are generally not employees. Whether such people are employees or independent contractors in any particular case, however, depends on the facts of the case. [*See* McWhorter v. Commissioner, T.C. Memo 2008-263 (Nov. 24, 2008); not paying FICA does not necessarily trigger self-employment tax if an individual is an employee.]

Q 2:77 Is an independent contractor eligible to be included in another employer's SIMPLE plan?

Rarely. Independent contractors (see Qs 2:76, 2:78, 2:79) are not considered employees. Employers should take note, however, that in many cases part-time employees are misidentified as independent contractors. [*See* Treas. Reg. § 31.3401(c)-1(b); Rev. Rul. 87-41, 1987-1 C.B. 296]

Q 2:78 Can an individual work for one entity in a dual capacity?

It is possible. In Revenue Ruling 58-505 [1958-2 C.B. 728], the IRS recognized that an individual can work for one entity in a dual capacity, provided the two types of work are sufficiently different. Thus, it is possible, though not certain, that the employee will be treated as working in two capacities.

Q 2:79 Can an employee's status be changed?

If a worker meets the tests as a common-law employee, that worker continues to be an employee regardless of how he or she is classified. This is true even if the employee consents to being treated as an independent contractor, and even if working conditions change. It is possible that an employee could later become an independent contractor for the same payer, but only if the facts and circumstances indicate that the new work arrangement is truly not in the nature of employment.

Q 2:80 What penalties apply if an employee is misclassified as an independent contractor?

Unpaid taxes and penalties may apply if employees are misclassified as nonemployees. The exclusion of an otherwise eligible employee (see Qs 14:56, 14:57) could cause the plan to fail to be treated as a SEP or SIMPLE plan. See correction of eligible plan failures in Qs 14:162–14:166, 17:1. [Leb's Enters., Inc., 85 A.F.T.R.2d ¶ 2000-450, (Jan. 24, 2000) regarding misclassification of car shufflers as independent contractors] The status of certain workers is specifically determined by law; these workers are known as statutory employees and statutory nonemployees (see Q 2:87). [*See* IRS Publication 15-A, *Employer's Supplemental Tax Guide*]

Q 2:81 Will the IRS assist an employer or employee in determining whether an individual is an employee?

Yes. In doubtful cases, the facts will determine whether there is an actual employer-employee relationship. For IRS assistance, an employer or employee may file Form SS-8, Determination of Worker Status for Purposes of Federal Employment Taxes and Income Tax Withholding, with the district director of the appropriate IRS district. The IRS will issue a written determination. [*See* I.L.M. 200117003 (Jan. 26, 2001)]

Generally, a worker who receives a Form 1099 for services provided as an independent contractor must report the income on Schedule C and pay self-employment tax on the net profit, using Schedule SE. However, sometimes the worker is incorrectly treated as an independent contractor when he or she is actually an employee. When this happens, Form 8919, Uncollected Social Security and Medicare Tax on Wages, may be used beginning for tax year 2007 by workers who performed services for an employer but whose employer did not withhold the worker's share of Social Security and Medicare taxes. In addition, workers must meet one of several criteria indicating they were an employee while performing the services (see Q 2:82). By using Form 8919, the worker's Social Security and Medicare taxes will be credited to his or her Social Security record. To facilitate this process, the IRS will electronically share Form 8919 data with the Social Security Administration. In the past, misclassified workers often used Form 4137, Social Security and Medicare Tax on Unreported Tip Income, to report their share of Social Security and Medicare taxes. Misclassified workers should no longer use Form 4137. [I.R.S. Information Release, IR-2007-203 (Dec. 20, 2007)]

Q 2:82 May all employees that are incorrectly treated as an independent contractor use Form 8919?

No. To be eligible to use Form 8919, the worker must meet one of several criteria indicating he or she was an employee while performing the services. The criteria include:

- The worker has filed Form SS-8, Determination of Worker Status for Purposes of Federal Employment Taxes and Income Tax Withholding, and received a determination letter from the IRS stating he or she is an employee of the firm.
- The worker has been designated as a "Section 530" employee by the employer or by the IRS prior to January 1, 1997. Section 530 relief requirements are available at: *http://www.irs.gov/pub/irs-pdf/p1976.pdf* (visited on Aug. 20, 2012).
- The worker has received other correspondence from the IRS that states he or she is an employee.
- The worker was previously treated as an employee by the firm and is performing services in a similar capacity and under similar direction and control.
- The worker's co-workers are performing similar services under similar direction and control and are treated as employees.
- The worker's co-workers are performing similar services under similar direction and control and filed Form SS-8 for the firm and received a determination that they were employees.
- The worker has filed Form SS-8 with the IRS and has not yet received a reply.

[I.R.S. Information Release, IR-2007-203 (Dec. 20, 2007)]

Q 2:83 What facts have been considered by the courts in deciding whether a worker is an employee or an independent contractor?

The courts have considered many facts in deciding whether a worker is an independent contractor or an employee. These facts fall into three main categories:

1. Behavioral control—Facts that show whether the business has a right to direct and control. These include:
   a. Instructions—an employee is generally told:
      i. When, where, and how to work
      ii. What tools or equipment to use
      iii. What workers to hire or to assist with the work
      iv. Where to purchase supplies and services
      v. What work must be performed by a specified individual
      vi. What order or sequence to follow
   b. Training—An employee may be trained to perform services in a particular manner.
2. Financial control—Facts that show whether the business has a right to control the business aspects of the worker's job include:
   a. The extent to which the worker has unreimbursed expenses
   b. The extent of the worker's investment
   c. The extent to which the worker makes services available to the relevant market
   d. How the business pays the worker
   e. The extent to which the worker can realize a profit or loss
3. Type of relationship—Facts that show the type of relationship include:
   a. Written contracts describing the relationship the parties intended to create
   b. Whether the worker is provided with employee-type benefits
   c. The permanency of the relationship
   d. How integral the services are to the principal activity

[These and other issues are more fully discussed by S. Derrin Watson, in *Who's the Employer?* 6th ed. (Goleta, CA 2012), ch. 3; at *http://www.employerbook.com* (visited on Aug. 20, 2012); *see also* I.R.S. Notice 989 (rev. July 2009), commonly asked questions when IRS determines a taxpayer's status as an employee]

Q 2:84 What is a *common-law employee*?

A *common-law employee* is an individual who performs services subject to the will and control of another (the employer), as to both what must be done and how it must be done. It does not matter that the employer allows the employee discretion and freedom of action, as long as the employer has the legal right to control both the method and the result of the service. Two usual characteristics of a common-law employer-employee relationship are that the employer has the right to discharge the employee, and the employer supplies the employee with tools and a place to work.

If an employer-employee relationship exists, it makes no difference how it is described. It does not matter if the employee is called an employee, partner, co-adventurer, agent, or independent contractor. Employees may be leased (see Q 2:85). It does not matter how compensation is measured, how it is paid, or what it is called, nor does it matter whether the individual is employed full time or part time.

For plan purposes, no distinction is made between classes of employees. Superintendents, managers, and other supervisory personnel are all employees. An officer of a corporation is generally an employee, but a director is not. An officer who performs no services or only minor services, and neither receives nor is entitled to receive any pay, is not considered an employee.

Relying on factors enumerated in Treasury regulations, the IRS has issued a letter ruling illustrating the application of three of the categories—behavioral control, financial control, and the relationship of the parties—in determining whether a worker is an employee subject to FICA, FUTA, and income tax withholding. [Ltr. Rul. 200835025 (May 21, 2008, released Aug. 29, 2009); I.R.C. § 3121(d)(2); Treas. Reg. § 31.3121(d)-1 relating to the FICA, and Treas. Reg. § 31.3401(c)-1 relating to federal income tax withholding]

Q 2:85 What is a *leased employee*?

A *leased employee* is generally any person who is not an employee of the person for whom he or she performs services (called the *recipient*) but is instead the employee of the organization furnishing the worker to the recipient (called the *leasing organization*). [I.R.C. § 414(n)] For example, nurses, secretaries, or similarly trained workers who are leased by their employer (the leasing organization) to provide services to the leasing organization's subscribers (the recipients) may, under certain circumstances (see below), be considered leased employees.

Although the employee leasing rules of Code Section 414(n) apply to SEPs, a business that uses the services of a leased employee (i.e., the recipient) may not establish a SARSEP using an IRS model or prototype plan document. Only prototype SEPs (not SARSEPs) may be established by a business that uses the services of leased employees. Of course, the language of the prototype should be examined to make sure a restriction does not exist. In combination prototypes (SEP and SARSEP provisions contained in one prototype), there is a requirement under the IRS's Listing of Required Modifications to restrict the use of the SARSEP portion of the plan if the business uses the services of leased employees. [I.R.C. § 414(n)(3)(B); Rev. Proc. 91-44, § 3.014, 1991-2 C.B. 733]

A leased employee is not treated as the recipient's employee if all the following conditions are met:

1. Leased employees constitute not more than 20 percent of the recipient's non-highly compensated workforce.
2. The employee is covered by the leasing organization under its qualified pension plan.
3. The leasing organization's plan is a money purchase pension plan that has all the following provisions:

a. Immediate participation,
b. Full and immediate vesting, and
c. A nonintegrated employer contribution rate of at least 10 percent of compensation for each participant.

If the leased employee is the recipient's common-law employee (see Q 2:84), however, that employee will be treated as the recipient's employee for all purposes, regardless of any pension plan of the leasing organization. [I.R.C. § 414(n)(5)(A), (B)]

Changes Effected by SBJPA. Under prior law, a leased employee was treated as the employee of the recipient only if, among other requirements, the services provided by the leased employee were of a type historically performed by employees in the recipient's service field. The Small Business Job Protection Act of 1996 (SBJPA) replaced this requirement with a requirement that the services be performed under the primary direction or control of the recipient. In general, this requires that the recipient exercise the majority of direction and control over the individual. The SBJPA Conference Report identifies relevant factors, gives examples, and states that

> clerical and similar support staff (e.g., secretaries and nurses in a doctor's office) generally would be considered to be subject to primary direction or control of the service recipient and would be leased employees provided the other requirements of Section 414(n) are met.

[SBJPA § 1454; H.R. Conf. Rep. No. 104-737, IV(D)(17) (1996)]

The change is effective for tax years beginning after 1996, but it does not apply to any relationship previously determined by an IRS ruling not to involve leased employees. [I.R.C. § 414(n)(2)(C); SBJPA § 1454; H.R. Conf. Rep. No. 104-737, IV(D)(17) (1996)]

Q 2:86 How does a leasing arrangement work?

Generally, a service corporation enters into a contract with the recipient under which the recipient specifies the services to be provided and the fee to be paid to the service corporation for each individual furnished. The service corporation has the right to control and direct the workers' services for the recipient, including the right to discharge or reassign the workers. The service corporation hires the workers, controls the payment of their wages, provides them with unemployment insurance and other benefits, and is the employer for employment tax purposes. An employer that has leased employees generally may not establish a SEP using IRS model documents (see Qs 2:85, 3:10).

Q 2:87 What are *statutory employees* and *statutory nonemployees*?

A *statutory employee* is a worker who falls into one of the following four categories:

1. A driver who distributes beverages (other than milk) or meat, vegetable, fruit, or bakery products, or who picks up and delivers laundry or dry cleaning, if the driver is an agent or is paid on commission;
2. A full-time life insurance sales agent whose principal business activity is selling life insurance or annuity contracts, or both, primarily for one life insurance company;
3. An individual who works at home on materials or goods that are supplied to him or her and that must be returned, if specifications are furnished for the work to be done; or
4. A full-time traveling or city salesperson who works on behalf of another and turns in orders from wholesalers, retailers, contractors, or operators of hotels, restaurants, or similar establishments. The goods sold must be merchandise for resale or supplies for use in the buyer's business operation. The work performed must be the salesperson's principal business activity.

[I.R.C. § 3131(d); *see also* Rosemann v. Commissioner, T.C. Memo 2009-185 (T.C. 2009), salesman did not qualify as a statutory employee.]

Example. Joel sells life insurance. His Form W-2 states that he is a statutory employee of Alpha Corp. Can Joel establish a SEP for himself if he participates in Alpha's 401(k) plan, because his wages are reported on Schedule C of Form 1040 as profit from a sole proprietorship? Most likely he can if he is not a full-time life insurance salesperson and is a statutory employee and not a common-law employee. Joel's Form W-2 may be incorrect. For Joel to be a statutory employee, two principal tests must be satisfied. First, Joel must fall into one of the four groups listed in the statute. [I.R.C. § 3131(d)] Second, Joel must not be a common-law employee. If Joel is a statutory employee, then either he is a full-time insurance salesperson or he is not. If he is, he is treated as though he were an employee for qualified plan purposes. [I.R.C. § 7701(a)(20)] That means Joel can be covered under Alpha's 401(k) plan. It also means that for qualified plan purposes, Joel is not a self-employed individual and cannot set up a SEP, SIMPLE, or any type of qualified plan. If, however, Joel is not a full-time insurance salesperson and is truly a statutory employee, his inclusion in the 401(k) plan may violate the exclusive benefit rule applicable to qualified plans. [I.R.C. §§ 401(c)(4), 408(k)(7)(A), 408(p)(6)(B)]

Practice Pointer. A professional must always determine whether a client is a common-law employee and should never assume that the client or his or her employer has made a correct evaluation.

Two categories of statutory nonemployees have been established: direct sellers and licensed real estate agents. They are treated as self-employed for federal income tax and employment tax purposes if

1. Substantially all payments for their services as direct sellers or real estate agents are directly related to sales or other output, rather than to the number of hours worked; and

2. Their services are performed under a written contract providing that they will not be treated as employees for federal tax purposes.

A *direct seller* is a person engaged in selling (or soliciting the sale of) consumer products

1. In the home or at a place of business other than a permanent retail establishment; or
2. To any buyer on a buy-sell basis, a deposit-commission basis, or any similar basis, for resale in the home or at a place of business other than a permanent retail establishment.

Direct selling includes activities of individuals who attempt to increase direct sales activities of their direct sellers and who earn income based on the productivity of their direct sellers. Such activities include providing motivation and encouragement; imparting skills, knowledge, or experience; and recruiting.

Q 2:88 What is a *minister*?

A *minister* is an individual who is duly ordained, commissioned, or licensed by a religious body constituting a church or church denomination. A minister is given the authority to conduct religious worship, perform sacerdotal functions, and administer ordinances and sacraments according to the prescribed tenets and practices of a particular religious organization.

The common-law rules should be applied to determine whether a minister is an employee or a self-employed person (see Q 2:89). A self-employed minister covered under a church plan is treated as his or her own employer. [I.R.C. § 414(e)(5)(A)(ii)(I)] In such a situation, the minister's compensation is his or her earned income, and the minister can deduct any contribution to the church plan. The earnings of a minister are not subject to Social Security and Medicare tax withholding. They are, with some exceptions, subject to self-employment tax. [I.R.C. § 1402(a)(8)]

Q 2:89 Are salaried ministers treated as employees or as self-employed persons?

Salaried ministers or other members of the clergy employed by a congregation are common-law employees of the congregation for plan purposes, even though for Social Security purposes their compensation is treated as net earnings from self-employment. On the other hand, amounts received directly from members of the congregation, such as fees for performing marriages, baptisms, or other personal services, are treated as income from self-employment and therefore may be used to establish a Keogh or SEP arrangement.

Q 2:90 Are insurance salespersons treated as employees or as self-employed persons?

Full-time life insurance salespersons are treated as common-law employees for Social Security, qualified plan, and SEP purposes (see Q 2:87). Special statutory provisions prohibit full-time life insurance salespersons (as defined in the Social Security Act) from establishing a qualified plan and, presumably, a SEP arrangement. [I.R.C. § 7701(a)(20); Treas. Reg. § 1.401-10(b)(3)] Nevertheless, it appears that general agents and most general lines insurance agents and brokers are considered self-employed individuals and thus are eligible to establish a qualified plan and, presumably, a SEP arrangement for themselves and their employees.

Example. Jorge is a full-time life insurance agent with the Rock Insurance Company. In his spare time, Jorge is a general lines agent with Hub and Spoke Insurance Companies. Jorge may establish a SEP using self-employment income from Hub and Spoke.

Employees of Predecessor Employers

Q 2:91 What are *predecessor employers* and *successor employers*?

There are no rules, regulations, or guidance under Code Section 414(a) to define the terms *successor employer* and *predecessor employer*. The IRS has stated verbally that when there has been a more than 50 percent change in ownership of the employer, a new employer exists. Conversely, if there has been a 50 percent or less change in ownership, the relationship of successor employer and predecessor employer may exist. If a successor employer continues a plan for another employer (predecessor employer), all employees who worked for the predecessor employer must be given credit for the years of service for that predecessor employer (see Q 2:43). [I.R.C. § 414(a)(1); Ltr. Rul. 9336046]

A SEP does not constitute a predecessor plan for purposes of Code Section 411(a)(4)(C). That section, relating to qualified plans and qualified annuity plans, requires an employer to treat a plan (or plans) as a predecessor plan and to count service with an employer maintaining that plan in calculating an employee's nonforfeitable percentage under certain circumstances when an employer establishes a qualified retirement plan within the five-year period immediately preceding or following the date another such plan terminates. [I.R.C. §§ 411(a)(4), 7476(c); Treas. Reg. § 1.411(a)-5(b)(3)(v)(B)(1)]

However, final regulations issued under Code Section 415 in April 2007 provide that, for purposes of Code Section 415,

> former employer is a predecessor employer with respect to a participant in a plan maintained by an employer if the employer maintains a plan under which the participant had accrued a benefit while performing services for the former employer, but only if that benefit is provided under the plan maintained by the employer. In addition, with respect to

> an employer of a participant, a former entity that antedates the employer is a predecessor employer with respect to the participant if, under the facts and circumstances, the employer constitutes a continuation of all or a portion of the trade or business of the former entity. This will occur, for example, where formation of the employer constitutes a mere formal or technical change in the employment relationship and continuity otherwise exists in the substance and administration of the business operations of the former entity. . . .

[Treas. Reg. § 1.415(f)-1(c)]

Q 2:92 May past service with a former or predecessor employer be considered for eligibility purposes in a new SEP of the present employer?

If the employer maintains the plan of a predecessor employer, service with such predecessor must be counted for eligibility purposes. [I.R.C. § 414(a)(1)] In other situations, the model plan documents do not provide for service with a former or predecessor employer to be considered for SEP eligibility purposes. Arguably, however, an individually designed SEP arrangement could consider service with one or more former employers, or predecessor employers, even though the other entity did not maintain a SEP. In Letter Ruling 7742003 under Code Section 414(a), the IRS determined that a plan was not discriminatory when prior service as either a partner or a common-law employee with a predecessor partnership that did not maintain a plan was taken into account, but service of common-law employees with employers other than the partnership was not considered. [Farly Funeral Home Inc. v. Commissioner, 62 T.C. 150 (1974) (pre-ERISA)] When the plan is not the plan maintained by a predecessor employer (and in the absence of regulations under Code Section 414(a)(2)), the IRS would probably base its decision on whether the plan discriminated significantly in favor of HCEs or former HCEs based on all of the facts and circumstances. That being said, the IRS has permitted some sponsors to include a provision in their prototype SEP documents that counts service with a specifically named predecessor employer without mentioning any limitations.

In Letter Ruling 8240003, a husband and wife who were the sole proprietors of a business incorporated their business. The corporation adopted a defined benefit pension plan that had a one-year service requirement but recognized service with the predecessor proprietorship. Because the taxpayers were sole proprietors of the new corporation's predecessor, their years of service with the predecessor were counted for eligibility purposes under the plan. Thus, a sole proprietorship that incorporated its business could be treated as a predecessor employer if provision for recognizing such was included in the plan documents.

Repeal and Grandfathering of SARSEPs

Q 2:93 Have SARSEPs been repealed?

Yes. SARSEPs were repealed for years beginning after December 31, 1996, but SARSEPs established before January 1, 1997, have been grandfathered and must be amended from time to time. An employer is not permitted to establish a SARSEP for the first time after December 31, 1996, but SARSEPs established before January 1, 1997, can continue to receive contributions under present-law rules, and new employees of a SARSEP employer hired after December 31, 1996, can participate in their employer's SARSEP in accordance with those rules. Grandfathered SARSEPS are required to be amended from time to time (see Q 3:5). [I.R.C. § 408(k)(6)(H)]

Example 1. Blaze Inc. established a cash-bonus SARSEP on December 31, 1996. At least half of all eligible employees elect to defer a portion of their 1996 bonuses under the SARSEP instead of receiving those amounts in cash during 1996. The 1996 contribution is deposited into the employees' IRAs on January 10, 1997. Blaze may continue to maintain its SARSEP arrangement because it has been grandfathered.

Example 2. Green Company established a cash-bonus SARSEP on June 1, 1996. All of the eligible employees elected to defer 10 percent of their bonuses and established IRAs. To its dismay, Green had a poor year and was unable to pay any bonuses for 1996; consequently, no contributions were made for the year. It is unclear whether a SARSEP has been established for purposes of the grandfather rule.

If using the IRS model SARSEP, the plan is effective on *adoption* and establishment of IRAs for all eligible employees. [*See* Form 5305A-SEP, art. VII] The employer should fully implement the program by following the instructions for the employer on Form 5305A-SEP (or, alternatively, in the prototype being used).

Example 3. Light Company has never maintained a retirement program. On December 31, 1996, it established a SARSEP using the IRS model document (Form 5305A-SEP). No IRAs were established by the employees. The grandfather rule did not apply to Light (or any successor) because it did not establish a SARSEP program by December 31, 1996.

Example 4. Ambergris, Inc., has never maintained a retirement program. On December 31, 1996, it established a SARSEP using the IRS model document (Form 5305A-SEP). All employees established IRAs. Less than half of the eligible employees elected to participate. It is unclear whether a SARSEP was established for purposes of the grandfather rule.

Q 2:94 When is a model SARSEP considered "adopted"?

A SARSEP agreement using Form 5305A-SEP is considered adopted when IRAs have been established for all eligible employees, all blanks on the form have been completed, the form is executed by the employer, and all eligible employees have been given the following information:

1. A copy of Form 5305A-SEP (any individual who in the future becomes eligible to participate must also be given Form 5305A-SEP on becoming an eligible employee);
2. A statement that IRAs, other than the IRAs into which employer contributions will be made, may provide different rates of return and different terms concerning, among other things, transfers and withdrawals of funds from the IRAs;
3. A statement that, in addition to the information provided to an employee at the time the employee becomes eligible to participate, the administrator of the program must furnish each participant with a copy of any amendment to the SARSEP and a written explanation of its effects within 30 days of the amendment's effective date; and
4. A statement that the administrator will give written notification to each participant of any employer contributions made under the SARSEP to that participant's IRA by the later of January 31 of the year following the year for which a contribution is made or 30 days after the contribution is made.

Caution. An otherwise valid adoption without the creation of IRAs may not constitute an establishment for purposes of the grandfather rule. Article VII of the model SARSEP (Form 5305A-SEP) states: "This SEP will become effective upon adoption and establishment of IRAs for all eligible employees."

Q 2:95 Must contributions be made to a SARSEP established for 1996 for the SARSEP to be treated as established?

It does not appear that making a contribution into the SARSEP IRA by December 31, 1996, was a condition of establishment, provided the adoption of the program is otherwise valid for that year (see Q 2:94). Still, it is unclear whether a SARSEP program established in 1996 that did not satisfy the 50 percent participation rate requirement or a program into which no amount of compensation was deferred prior to December 31, 1996, will meet the requirements for grandfathering. The IRS may also have to consider the adoption of an illusionary program, that is, the establishment of the program after all compensation has been paid to the employee (whether on or before December 31, 1996).

Examination Guidelines

Q 2:96 Has the IRS issued examination guidelines for SEPs?

Yes. On July 31, 2001, the IRS issued Internal Revenue Manual Section 4.72.17, providing guidance for examining SEPs and SARSEPs. (See Appendix O for text of guidelines.) The provisions were revised on September 12, 2006. The guidelines provide technical background as well as guidance on issues that should be considered during an examination (audit) by the IRS. They are not all-inclusive, and they may be modified based on specific issues encountered by the examiner.

The guidelines offer little if any guidance on a number of difficult points, nine of which are examined next.

1. Whether amounts that exceed the individual 25 percent of compensation limit under Code Section 402(h)—which are treated as wages—are subject to Social Security and other employment taxes, except to the extent that elective contributions have already been subject to FICA and FUTA taxes.
2. Whether amounts that exceed the individual 25 percent of compensation limit are required to be reported on the employee's W-2 form and whether those amounts are subject to withholding taxes (see Q 11:10).

Note. To the extent that the individual 25 percent limit or $50,000 (for 2012) amount under Code Section 402(h) is exceeded, the employer should enter the excess in box 1 of Form W-2, without any offsetting deductions. If, however, at the time, it is not reasonable for the employer to believe that the employee on whose behalf the excess contribution is made will be entitled to an exclusion under Code Section 402(h) for the contribution, then the excess amount could arguably be subject to withholding taxes under Code Section 3401(a)(12). It is not clear whether withholding is required on amounts that exceed the 25 percent or the $50,000 (for 2012) exclusion limit under Code Section 402(h). Furthermore, the specific instructions for box 1 of Form W-2 make no mention of excess contributions.

3. Whether the designated distribution withholding rules apply when the participant makes a corrective distribution. When an excess employer nonelective contribution—alone or in combination with an excess SEP contribution, disallowed deferral, or excess deferral—is corrected during the tax year in which the excess arose, the designated distribution may be subject to the federal income tax withholding rules, unless the participant elects not to have withholding apply. In such situations it is not clear how Forms W-2 and Forms W-3, Transmittal of Wage and Tax Statements, are to be issued (or reissued) or whether Form 940, Employer's Annual Federal Unemployment Tax Act Tax Return (FUTA), and Form 941, Employer's Quarterly Federal Tax Return, have to be filed or refiled.
4. Whether the employer is required to notify the employee of an amount that exceeds the individual 25 percent of compensation limit. No rule or published guidance requires that the participant be notified of the reason for the erroneous contribution even though the amounts are to be included in the participant's taxable income (see Qs 11:15, 13:51). Perhaps it is contemplated that the employer will notify the employee of any amounts included in income when it discovers the erroneous contribution. If it does so, the participant can inform the SEP IRA trustee of the erroneous contribution. [Prop. Treas. Reg. § 1.408-7, Preamble] The trustee can then properly report the amount (when necessary) as a

regular IRA contribution on Form 5498, IRA Contribution Information, or distribute any excess to the participant on the participant's request. Participant notification appears to be required only for some types of erroneous contributions (see Qs 12:30–12:46). Distributions from SEP IRAs are reported directly to the IRS on Form 1099-R, Distributions from Pensions, Annuities, Retirement or Profit-Sharing Plans, IRAs, Insurance Contracts, etc., by the SEP IRA trustee (see Qs 13:95–13:102). Without modification, the reporting rules do not properly reflect contributions made to IRAs or SEPs.

5. Determining the taxable year in which an elective excess is includible in the participant's income. For example, is it taxable to the participant
   a. In the year the excess amount was contributed? It should be noted that, in some cases, the excess is created by a contribution made after the end of the year. Such a contribution is treated for deduction and establishment purposes as being contributed on the last day of the prior year (or the year designated if the contribution is made under an extension).
   b. In the year of notification?
   c. On April 15 following the year of contribution?
   d. On April 16 following the year of notification? (What if notification is never made?)

If the amount is treated as an excess on the day after the employee is required to remove it, it would seem to become an IRA contribution on that day—over two years later. Thus, it could be treated as an IRA contribution at that time and could not be claimed or used up any sooner. In addition, the 6 percent excise tax would not seem to apply until that time.

Example. Susan makes a $2,000 nondeductible IRA contribution into an interest-bearing IRA every year on January 2. She also makes a $1,000 elective contribution under her employer's SARSEP. In January 2013, Susan is notified by her employer that she made a disallowed deferral of $1,000 during 2012; the $1,000 deferral amount is reported on her 2012 Form W-2 (box 12). The IRA custodian calculates that $25 of interest was earned on the $1,000. If Susan removes $1,000 on the day after her 2013 tax return is due, she is subject to a 6 percent penalty tax on the $1,000 deferral, which becomes an IRA contribution on that date (April 15, 2014). The $1,000 is not included in income or subject to a premature distribution penalty even if Susan is under age 59½. If Susan also withdraws the gain, which is not required to be withdrawn after the due date of her 2013 return, the $25 will be subject to income tax. After the due date of the 2013 return, if Susan is under age 59½, the $25 would also be subject to the 10 percent premature distribution penalty unless an exception applies. The disallowed deferral is included in line 7 of Susan's 2012 Form 1040. The disallowed deferral is not taxed twice. [I.R.S. Notice 88-33, 1988-1 C.B. 513] Susan can eliminate the premature distribution penalty tax (if applicable) on the gain by making a correcting distribution of the disallowed deferral (plus gain) by April 15, 2014. The example in the guidelines would (incorrectly) require that that amount be withdrawn by April 15, 2013 (by April 15 of the year of a timely notification).

If Susan gives her IRA trustee or custodian a copy of the notice she receives from her employer, it would help the trustee or custodian to code the contribution on Form 5498 and (if requested) to report the corrective distribution on Form 1099-R.

6. Whether, for purposes of the 10 percent tax on nondeductible employer contributions, excess amounts that are *in fact* reported on the employee's W-2 form are deemed distributed (regardless of whether they are removed from the IRA by the employee).
7. Circumstances under which the *equivalency method* (reducing the rate called for in the plan) can be used to calculate employer contributions under plans benefiting self-employed individuals that are integrated with Social Security contributions or into which elective contributions are made. To reduce the likelihood of excess contributions, the guidelines should point out that only when the plan is the only plan of the employer, the plan is not integrated, and the owner's self-employment tax deduction and share of the common-law employee plan contribution expense are known can the equivalency method be used to determine the contributions for owners of unincorporated businesses. If elective *and* nonelective contributions are made, special adjustments are generally required to avoid exceeding the 15 percent (now 25 percent) limit.
8. Whether employer contributions made on behalf of nonowners of an unincorporated entity can create a loss for the self-employed individual or individuals.
9. When and how partners elect to make salary reduction contributions, and making contributions before determining the amount of earned income for the year.

Some of the audit steps announced in the guidelines appear to be incorrect. The reporting requirements under the guidelines are based on Notice 89-32 [1989-1 C.B. 671], which was designed primarily for 401(k) plans but was nonetheless made applicable to SARSEPs (probably in haste). Notice 89-32 modified Notice 87-77 [1987-2 C.B. 385], relating to excess contributions, and also modified Notice 88-33 [1988-1 C.B. 513].

Q 2:97 What is covered by the examination guidelines for SEPs?

The examination guidelines for SEPs provide guidance and confirmation in several areas, including the following:

1. A SEP must provide total coverage; that is, every employee who is a qualifying employee must be covered. Thus, an eligible employee cannot opt out.
2. The SEP must be part of a written arrangement. [I.R.C. § 408(k)(1), (5)]

3. Contributions to a SEP must be made under a definite written allocation formula. The formula must specify the requirements an employee must satisfy to receive an allocation and the manner in which the allocation is computed. [I.R.C. § 408(k)(5)(A)–(5)(B)]
4. The model forms generally may not be used by an employer who
   a. Maintains any other qualified retirement plan;
   b. Wants an integrated SEP;
   c. Has one or more eligible employees who have not established an IRA;
   d. Uses the services of leased employees, or is a member of an affiliated service group; or
   e. Wants a plan other than a calendar-year plan.
5. An employer can request an opinion letter for a prototype SEP from the IRS stating that the SEP arrangement is acceptable in form. [Rev. Proc. 87-50, 1987-2 C.B. 647]
6. An employer can set less restrictive participation requirements for its employees than is allowed but not more restrictive ones.
7. The person or firm for whom services are performed may have to include in a SEP plan any leased employee who is treated as an employee of the recipient (see Qs 2:85, 2:86).
8. Contributions to a SEP must be made for all employees who satisfy the definition of qualifying employee. There are no exclusions or percentages of employees that must be covered. All qualifying employees must be covered and receive the appropriate contribution. [I.R.C. § 408(k)(2)]
9. The SEP under which contributions are made can be set up after the close of the year for which contributions are made; however, the plan must exist at the time the contributions are made, and the contributions must be made within the time limit. [I.R.C. § 404(h)]
10. To deduct contributions for a year, the employer must make the contributions not later than the due date (including extensions) of the employer's return for the year. [I.R.C. § 404(h)(1)]
11. Contributions to a SEP are discretionary, but, if made, they must not discriminate in favor of any HCE. [I.R.C. § 404(k)(3)]
12. An employer may deduct up to 15 percent (now 25 percent) of each employee's compensation each year and contribute it to each participating employee's SEP IRA. [I.R.C. § 404(h)(1)(C)]
13. All employees must receive the same (uniform) rate of contribution; however, a rate of contribution that decreases as compensation increases is considered uniform. [I.R.C. §§ 401(l), 408(k)(3)(D)]
14. Except in the case of a SARSEP, the plan formula may take into account permitted disparity (integration). [I.R.C. § 408(k)(3)(D)]
15. Special rules apply for self-employed individuals when figuring the maximum deduction. For determining the 15 percent (now 25 percent) limit on contributions, *compensation* means "net earnings from self-employment."

16. The amount of the contribution to the IRA is subject to the same limit that applies to the amount allowed as a deduction. [I.R.C. § 404(a)(8)(C)]
17. Because a SEP is considered a defined contribution plan, employer contributions to a SEP must be considered with other contributions to defined contribution plans. [I.R.C. § 415(k)(1)(D)]
18. Elective deferrals, not exceeding the actual deferral percentage (ADP) test, made by the employer to the SEP IRA are subject to the overall 15 percent (now 25 percent) of compensation limit or $35,000 (now $50,000 for 2012), whichever is less. [I.R.C. § 408(k)(6)(A)]
19. For purposes of determining whether a plan is top heavy under Code Section 416, elective deferrals are considered employer contributions. Elective deferrals may not, however, be used to satisfy the top-heavy minimum contribution requirements (see Q 8:6).

Q 2:98 What are the examination steps in the examination guidelines for SEPs?

The examination guidelines for SEPs require that the examining agent follow a number of clearly specified procedures.

The prescribed general procedures direct the examiner to do the following:

1. Verify that the employer has a written plan document and determine if there is an approval letter issued by the IRS National Office or an IRS district office.
2. Determine whether the plan document contains provisions relating to
   a. Participation requirements (e.g., age and service),
   b. A contribution/allocation formula, and
   c. Top-heavy minimum contribution requirements.
3. Determine whether there are resolutions, minutes, or any other documentation relating to the original adoption of the SEP or to a subsequent amendment or termination amendment relating to the SEP document. (It is unclear why an employer would need to formally terminate a nonelective SEP arrangement, presumably by an amendment, inasmuch as SEP contributions are discretionary.)
4. Determine whether any other plans are maintained by the employer and verify the filing of any Form 5500 series return with applicable schedules (if any).
5. Determine whether any other plan was ever maintained by the employer. If so, develop information as to plan type, effective date, and date of termination, if applicable.
6. Check the payroll records and census information used to determine employees eligible to participate in the plan. Check, if available, dates of birth, hire, participation, and termination and any reason for nonparticipation, if applicable.

7. Ensure that all employees who were required to receive contributions did so.

The prescribed contribution procedures direct the examiner to do the following:

1. If the arrangement is a SARSEP, determine whether the plan satisfies the ADP test; that is, determine whether the deferral percentage for each HCE is less than or equal to the deferral percentage for the non-highly compensated employees (NHCEs) multiplied by 1.25 percent.
2. Verify whether the appropriate compensation limits were met.
3. Determine whether all applicable notices were provided, particularly in the case of
   a. Any excess contributions to HCEs, or
   b. Disallowed deferrals if the SEP failed to satisfy the 50 percent test.
4. Determine whether the SEP was top heavy, and if so, whether the appropriate contributions were made. Verify that elective contributions were not used to satisfy the top-heavy minimum contribution requirement (see Q 8:6).
5. Determine whether the compensation limits and any applicable limits on elective deferrals under Code Section 402(g) were met.

The prescribed distributions and deduction procedures direct the examiner to do the following:

1. Determine whether the appropriate Forms 940 and 941 (if applicable) were filed. Check whether Forms W-2 and W-3 were correctly prepared and timely filed.
2. Determine whether Forms 1099 were correctly prepared and filed. Verify with any canceled checks.

Note. The examination guidelines appear to be incorrect. Employers do not prepare, issue, or file Form 1099 with respect to a SEP. Trustees and other issuers file Form 1099-R with respect to SEP distributions.

3. Determine whether appropriate information regarding any distributions was provided to participants.
4. If the employer is self-employed and files Form 1040, verify the amount deducted. If there is any discrepancy, ask for an explanation.
5. Check documentation that would verify the establishment of IRAs or amounts of contributions, such as a copy of any bank or other institutional statement.

Note. In most cases, an employer will have very little to substantiate the existence of an employee's IRA except, perhaps, a canceled contribution check, an account number, or some other transmittal.

Chapter 3

SEP and SARSEP Documents

Documents prepared by the Internal Revenue Service, by a financial institution, or by an employer's tax or legal adviser may be used to establish a SEP or SARSEP arrangement. This chapter examines those documents—IRS model plans, prototype plans, individually designed plans, and mass submitter plans—and the rules that govern their approval and subsequent use.

Model SEP and SARSEP Plan Documents

Q 3:1 Is IRS approval of a SEP or SARSEP required?

No. Approval of a SEP or SARSEP arrangement by the Internal Revenue Service (IRS) is not required. Without such approval, however, there is no assurance that the form of the plan documents will guarantee the deferral of income taxes and the deductibility of employer contributions. In addition, an employer may not use the correction procedures of the Employee Plans Compliance Resolution System (EPCRS) (see chapter 17), including self-correction, unless the SEP or SARSEP plan has received IRS approval.

Q 3:2 Are there model SEP and SARSEP plan documents that are preapproved by the IRS?

Yes. The IRS has released model SEP and SARSEP documents that meet the requirements of Section 408(k) of the Internal Revenue Code (Code). Employers that want to adopt a SEP can use Form 5305-SEP, Simplified Employee Pension—Individual Retirement Accounts Contribution Agreement (revised December 2004). Employers that qualify to permit employees to make elective SEP contributions can use Form 5305A-SEP, Salary Reduction and Other Elective Simplified Employee Pension—Individual Retirement Accounts Contribution Agreement (revised June 2006), to amend older forms.

Note. Not all employers are eligible to use the IRS model documents (see Qs 3:10, 3:12).

Q 3:3 May the model SEP and SARSEP forms issued by the IRS be reproduced and used without making any reference to the IRS or its forms?

Yes. The provisions of the model SEP and SARSEP forms issued by the IRS may be reproduced on the letterhead of an employer or in pamphlets that omit all reference to the IRS and its forms.

Note. Such omission is not permitted for traditional individual retirement account or individual retirement annuity (IRA) documents or Roth IRA documents. A reference to the form number must appear somewhere in the document. [Rev. Proc. 98-59, § 3.05, 1998-2 C.B. 727, modified by Rev. Proc. 2010-48; 2010-50 I.R.B. 1]

Q 3:4 Should a SEP or SARSEP established using a model form issued by the IRS be submitted to the IRS for approval by the adopting employer?

No. An eligible employer that adopts a SEP or SARSEP arrangement using a model form issued by the IRS and follows its terms is assured that the arrangement meets the requirements of Code Section 401(k). Because automatic approval has been granted to model SEP and SARSEP arrangements, no ruling, opinion, or determination letter from the IRS is necessary, and none will be issued. [Rev. Proc. 87-50, § 2.07, 1987-2 C.B. 647]

Q 3:5 Do the model SEP and SARSEP forms issued by the IRS expire or have to be replaced?

Yes. Model Forms 5305-SEP and 5305A-SEP with a pre-1994 revision date expired on June 30, 1994. An employer that wanted to continue using a model form had to adopt one of the new forms by March 31, 1995, and distribute a copy of the new form to all eligible employees. [Ann. 94-52, 1994-15 I.R.B. 19]

The model SEP and SARSEP forms have been released in several versions. The version dated March 1994 should have been signed by an employer no later than March 31, 1995 [Ann. 94-52, 1994-15 I.R.B. 19]; however, another IRS ruling required that model SEPs and SARSEPs be amended to reflect the increase in the compensation limit to $150,000 by December 31, 1994. [Rev. Proc. 94-13, 1994-1 C.B. 566] If an employer used the March 1994 version of Form 5305A-SEP to establish or amend a SARSEP before May 1996, that employer was not required to use the new version of the form unless the employer wanted to change any elections on the previously adopted plan document.

In the December 1997 version of Form 5305A-SEP, the "Instructions for the Employer" section stated that if an employer wished to continue using a model elective SEP, the form would have to be adopted by December 31, 1998. In the January 2000 revised model SARSEP form, the instructions indicate that an employer whose arrangement is predicated on the December 1997 version of Form 5305A-SEP is not required to use the January 2000 version of the form.

Note. The Small Business Job Protection Act of 1996 (SBJPA) repealed the enabling legislation for the establishment of SARSEPs but grandfathered existing SARSEPs. Therefore, SARSEPs in effect as of December 31, 1996, may continue to be maintained, but no new ones may be established.

The most recent version of model SARSEP Form 5305A-SEP was issued in June 2006. The June 2006 version of the model SARSEP (Form 5305A-SEP) does not require that it be adopted if the 2002 version of Form 5305A-SEP was used.

The most recent version of model SEP Form 5305-SEP was issued in December 2004. The December 2004 version of the model SEP (Form 5305-SEP) does not require that it be executed by an employer that had previously adopted a SEP using the model form. However, an employer initially establishing a SEP should use the December 2004 version of the model SEP.

Revenue Procedure 2002-10 [2002-4 I.R.B. 401], released by the IRS on January 3, 2002, provides guidance on amending certain IRA agreements, including SEP and SARSEP documents, to incorporate the changes made by the Economic Growth and Tax Relief Reconciliation Act of 2001 (EGTRRA). SEP and SARSEP documents must also be amended to reflect the new required minimum distribution (RMD) rules. [Treas. Reg. §§ 1.401(a)(9)-1–1.401(a)(9)-9] Model SEPs that have been amended for EGTRRA and the RMD regulations must be used to establish a new SEP plan beginning after October 1, 2002. [Ann. 2002-49, 2002-19 I.R.B. 919]

On January 13, 2010, the IRS announced that existing model SEP, SARSEP, and SIMPLE IRA plan documents do not have to be amended for GOZA, TIPRA, HERO, PPA, HEART, and WRERA in order to operate in accordance with statutory requirements (see Q 3:6). The IRS expects to issue revised model documents "shortly," and although the use of the new models will not be required, the IRS recommends adoption of the latest form. [Rev. Proc. 2010-48, § 4.01, 2010-50 I.R.B. 828]

Q 3:6 What statutory changes relating to qualification of IRAs have been issued since 2002?

Statutory changes relating to qualification of IRAs became effective after the mandatory amendments were announced in 2002. The changes include:

- Allowing for the repayment of qualified hurricane distributions (see Q 13:158). [GOZA (Pub. L. No. 109-135) § 201]
- Eliminating the $100,000 modified adjusted gross income limit and the joint filing requirement for individuals wanting to make qualified rollover contributions (other than from a designated Roth account or from a Roth IRA) to Roth IRAs, effective for distributions after 2009 (see Qs 1:28, 1:39). [TIPRA (Pub. L. No. 109-222) § 512]
- Permitting compensation earned by members of the armed forces in 2004 and 2005 for service in a combat zone to be taken into account for purposes of making IRA and Roth IRA contributions, effective for taxable years beginning after 2003 and before May 28, 2009. [HERO (Pub. L. No. 109-227) § 2]
- Allowing qualified reservist distributions to be repaid to an IRA or Roth IRA, effective for individuals called to active duty after September 11, 2001 (see Q 5:56). [PPA (Pub. L. No. 109-280) § 827, as amended by WRERA (Pub. L. No. 110-458) § 108(e), extended by HEART (Pub. L. No. 110-245) § 107]
- Allowing a nonspouse beneficiary of a deceased participant's accrued benefit in an eligible retirement plan, other than an IRA, to roll over any portion of the benefit in a direct trustee-to-trustee transfer to an IRA or Roth IRA established to receive such rollover, effective for distributions made after 2006 (see Q 1:39). [PPA (Pub. L. No. 109-280) § 829, as amended by WRERA (Pub. L. No. 110-458) § 108(f)]
- Allowing certain individuals who were participants in a Code Section 401(k) plan maintained by certain indicted employers could make special catch-up contributions equal to three times the otherwise applicable IRA or Roth IRA contribution limit, effective for taxable years beginning after 2006 and before 2010. [PPA (Pub. L. No. 109-280) § 831]
- Permitting compensation for purposes of making IRA contributions to include differential wage payments, effective for years beginning after 2008 (see Qs 5:95, 6:4, 6:14). [HEART (Pub. L. No. 110-245) § 105]
- Allowing certain amounts received in connection with the Exxon Valdez litigation to be contributed to an eligible retirement plan (see Q 13:164). [Emergency Economic Stabilization Act of 2008 (Pub. L. No. 110-343) § 504 of Division C]
- Eliminating the requirement to take 2009 required minimum distributions from IRAs and Roth IRAs. [WRERA (Pub. L. No. 110-458) § 201] IRAs do not have to be amended for the temporary waiver of the 2009 required minimum distribution under Code Section 401(a)(9)(H), pending the issuance of further guidance (see chapter 5). [Rev. Proc. 2010-48, § 2.04, 2010-50 I.R.B. 828; Notice 2009-82, 2009-41 I.R.B. 491]

Q 3:7 What penalties will apply if an employer has not updated its SEP document prior to an IRS audit?

If the IRS becomes aware of a plan that has not been updated for EGTRRA, and the employer has operated the plan in accordance with EGTRRA, then the penalty will likely be calculated as if the plan was disqualified. The IRS will first determine the total contributions made for all employees into their SEP IRA accounts for the past three tax years, multiply that amount by 28 percent (the percentage used in practice by the IRS for disqualified plans), and add on interest and penalties for not paying the tax on these invalid contributions for the three-year period. The employer will then have to execute an updated document. The solution for SIMPLE IRAs had been an extension until the end of the 2006 calendar year for employers to reexecute updated SIMPLE IRA plans (see Q 14:23). According to the IRS, there will not be a similar grace period for SEP employers. Correction is also possible under the Compliance Resolution System (EPCRS). With the payment of an additional sanction, correction of qualification failures identified upon an IRS examination (audit) of a plan is also possible (see chapter 17). [Rev. Proc. 2008-50, § 13.01, 2008-35 I.R.B. 464]

EPCU examination program. The Employer Plans Compliance Unit (EPCU) examination program includes a SIMPLE project to check for potential non-amenders and a SEP project. Because an EPCU check is not an audit or investigation, it does not preclude a sponsor's use of the EPCRS to inexpensively correct plan errors. An EPCU check generally involves identifying certain information and filings; books and records are not inspected. Failure to respond to a letter from the EPCU or provide the information requested within the time frame allowed could result in further action. Nonresponders could be later audited. The EPCU SEP project focuses on taxpayers who either sponsored a SEP or received a Form 5498 that reflected a SEP contribution amount in box 8 of Form 5498, IRA Contribution Information. The initial phase of this project will focus on determining the accuracy of information reported on Forms 5498. [Employee Plan News, Issue 2011-4 (Mar. 23, 2011), available at *http://www.irs.gov/pub/irs-tege/epn_2011_4.pdf* (visited on Aug. 22, 2012)]

Q 3:8 What special reporting or disclosure rules apply to a SEP established using the IRS model form?

An employer that establishes a SEP arrangement using the IRS model form must provide eligible employees with a copy of the completed model form. The plan administrator (generally the employer) must also provide all eligible employees with the following:

1. A statement that the administrator will notify a participant of any contributions made under the SEP arrangement into the participant's IRA by the later of (a) January 31 of the year following the year for which the contribution is made or (b) 30 days after the contribution is made;
2. A statement that the administrator will notify a participant of any amendments to the SEP arrangement and will provide a copy of the

amendment and a written explanation of the amendment's effects to the participant within 30 days of the amendment's effective date; and

3. A statement that IRAs other than the IRAs into which employer SEP contributions will be made may provide different rates of return and different terms concerning, among other things, transfers and withdrawals of funds from the IRAs.

Form 5305-SEP contains the statements and information necessary to comply with the reporting and disclosure requirements set forth in Part 1 of Title I of the Employee Retirement Income Security Act of 1974 (ERISA) that are applicable to IRS-approved model plans. [DOL Reg. § 2520.104-48]

Q 3:9 How are contributions allocated under model Form 5305-SEP?

Model Form 5305-SEP provides that all contributions will be allocated to eligible employees in proportion to compensation. Contributions may not be made to different participants at different times.

Q 3:10 May all employers use model Form 5305-SEP to establish a SEP?

No. Model Form 5305-SEP may not be used to establish a SEP arrangement if any of the following conditions exists:

1. The employer currently maintains any other qualified retirement plan (see Qs 3:39, 3:40);
2. The employer has any eligible employees for whom IRAs have not been established;
3. The employer uses the services of leased employees as described in Code Section 414(n) (see Q 2:85);
4. The employer is a member of an affiliated service group (see Q 2:14), a member of a controlled group of corporations (see Q 2:5), or a trade or business under common control (see Q 2:13), unless all eligible employees of those related employers participate in the SEP arrangement; or
5. The employer will pay the cost of SEP contributions.

The restrictions listed previously do not prevent an employer that is maintaining a model SEP from also maintaining a model SARSEP or other SEP to which either elective or nonelective contributions are made.

Q 3:11 What special reporting or disclosure rules apply to a SARSEP established using the IRS model form?

Employees make contributions under a SARSEP arrangement (including one established using Form 5305A-SEP) by agreeing to defer a portion of their compensation. The contributions, which are treated as employer contributions for deduction purposes, are deposited by the employer into IRAs established by or for each employee. A form on which employees can make their elections must be provided, and employees must be informed about how they can make, change, or terminate elective deferrals.

The employer must also give eligible employees a copy of the completed Form 5305A-SEP. The plan administrator (generally the employer) must provide all eligible employees with the following:

1. A statement that the administrator will notify a participant of any top-heavy contributions made under the SEP arrangement into the participant's IRA by the later of (a) January 31 of the year following the year for which the contribution is made or (b) 30 days after the contribution is made; and
2. A statement that the administrator will notify a participant of any amendments to the SEP arrangement and will provide a copy of the amendment and a written explanation of the amendment's effects to the participant within 30 days of the amendment's effective date.

Form 5305A-SEP contains the statements and information necessary to comply with the reporting and disclosure requirements set forth in Part 1 of Title I of ERISA that are applicable to IRS-approved model plans. [DOL Reg. § 2520.104-48]

Note. When Form 5305A-SEP is used to establish a SARSEP arrangement, the IRAs established by employees must be IRS model, master, or prototype IRAs for which the IRS has issued a favorable opinion letter.

Q 3:12 May all employers use model Form 5305A-SEP to establish a SARSEP?

No. Model Form 5305A-SEP may not be used by an employer that

1. Currently maintains any other qualified retirement plan (this does not prevent an employer from also maintaining a model SEP (Form 5305-SEP) or other SEP to which either elective or nonelective contributions are made);
2. Has any eligible employees for whom IRAs have not been established;
3. Is a member of a group of related employers (see Q 2:5), unless all eligible employees within the entire group are eligible to participate in the SARSEP;
4. Is a state or local government or a tax-exempt organization;
5. Has any leased employees as described in Code Section 414(n) (see Q 2:85); or
6. Has more than 25 eligible employees at any time during the prior calendar year.

Q 3:13 What plan year must a SARSEP established by adopting Form 5305A-SEP use?

Form 5305A-SEP may be used only in connection with a calendar-year plan year, regardless of the employer's taxable year. (The Internal Revenue Code permits SEPs to operate on a calendar-year plan year or on the employer's taxable year. [I.R.C. § 408(k)(7)(C)] Prototype SARSEPs will usually permit any 12-month period to be the plan year.)

Q 3:14 May an employer make regular SEP contributions into an elective SEP established using Form 5305A-SEP?

No. The IRS model elective SEP (Form 5305A-SEP) is a stand-alone salary reduction plan into which no regular SEP contributions may be made. If an employer wishes to make both elective and nonelective contributions and adopts Form 5305A-SEP, it must also adopt Form 5305-SEP (or another approved plan, e.g., a prototype SEP) to be able to make nonelective contributions over and above the minimum required top-heavy contribution (see Q 3:16).

Q 3:15 How is compensation defined in model and prototype SEPs?

Although the term *compensation* is defined in the Code (see chapter 6), documents used to establish a SEP or SARSEP frequently specify their own definition of compensation.

Model SEP Plans

Under the model SEP (Form 5305-SEP), compensation for purposes of the contribution limits "does not include employer contributions to the SEP or the employee's compensation in excess of $205,000," increased for cost-of-living adjustments. [Form 5305-SEP, Instructions, p. 1 (2004)] The compensation limit is $250,000 for 2012.

The definition of compensation under the model SARSEP (Form 5305A-SEP), however, is quite different. It provides that:

- Compensation does not include any employer SEP contributions, including elective deferrals. Compensation, for purposes of the minimum compensation rule for participation during the current plan year ($550 for 2012), is the same, except it includes deferrals made to this SEP and any amount not includible in gross income under Code Section 125 or Code Section 132(f)(4).
- The maximum an employee may elect to defer under this SEP for a year is the smaller of 25 percent of the employee's compensation or the limitation under Code Section 402(g), as explained next.

Note. The deferral limit is 25 percent of compensation (minus any employer SEP contributions, including elective deferrals). Compute this amount using the following formula: Compensation (before subtracting employer SEP contributions) × 20%.

- If nonelective contributions are made to this SEP for a calendar year, or maintain any other SEP to which contributions are made for that calendar year, then contributions to all such SEPs may not exceed the smaller of $50,000 (the 2012 limit) or 25 percent of compensation for any employee.
- Catch-up elective deferral contributions are not subject to the 25 percent exclusion limit (see Q 11:2).

Caution. An employer that has adopted a SEP and SARSEP using the model forms will find administering two different definitions of compensation awkward, if not impossible. The definition found in the model SARSEP (Form 5305A-SEP) appears to violate the top-heavy contribution rules (which require that compensation not be reduced by elective deferrals to the plan). It is equally unclear whether allocations, under the model forms, can be based on compensation that includes elective deferrals (subject to various overall limits that do require that compensation be reduced by elective deferrals). The model SARSEP states that an employer "may need to use" IRS Publication 560, which appears to allow unreduced compensation to be used for allocation purposes. Publication 560 defines compensation as follows:

> *Compensation.* Compensation for plan allocations is the pay a participant received from you for personal services for a year. You can generally define compensation as including all the following payments.
>
> 1. Wages and salaries.
> 2. Fees for professional services.
> 3. Other amounts received (cash or noncash) for personal services actually rendered by an employee, including, but not limited to, the following items.
>   a. Commissions and tips.
>   b. Fringe benefits.
>   c. Bonuses.
>
> For a self-employed individual, compensation means the earned income, discussed later, of that individual.
>
> Compensation generally includes amounts deferred in the following employee benefit plans. These amounts are elective deferrals.
>
> - Qualified cash or deferred arrangement (Section 401(k) plan).
> - Salary reduction agreement to contribute to a tax-sheltered annuity (Section 403(b) plan), a SIMPLE IRA plan, or a SARSEP.
> - Section 457 nonqualified deferred compensation plan.
> - Section 125 cafeteria plan.
>
> However, an employer can choose to exclude elective deferrals under the preceding plans from the definition of compensation.

Other options. In figuring the compensation of a participant, you can treat any of the following amounts as the employee's compensation.

- The employee's wages as defined for income tax withholding purposes.
- The employee's wages you report in box 1 of Form W-2, Wage and Tax Statement.
- The employee's social security wages (including elective deferrals).

Compensation generally cannot include either of the following items.

- Nontaxable reimbursements or other expense allowance
- Deferred compensation (other than elective deferrals).

[IRS Publication 560, *Retirement Plans for Small Business*, p. 4]

Caution. The IRS does not provide any guidance on how an employer can choose to exclude elective deferrals from the definition of compensation for allocation purposes under a SARSEP.

Note. Contributions to a designated Roth account (DRA) under an employers' plan are contributions made under a "qualified cash or deferred arrangement." [I.R.C § 402A]

Prototype SEP Plans

Compensation under a prototype SEP is defined differently than under the model documents. Under a prototype SEP,

> except where specifically stated otherwise in this plan, a participant's compensation shall include any elective deferral described in Code § 402(g)(3) or any amount that is contributed by the employer at the election of the employee and that is not includible in the gross income of the employee under Code §§ 125, 132(f)(4) or 457.

[SEP LRM (Mar. 2002), item 7]

The SEP LRM also provides that

> [i]n no event can the amount allocated to each participant's IRA exceed the lesser of 25% of the participant's compensation or $42,000, as adjusted under Code § 415(d). For purposes of the 25% limitation described in the preceding sentence, a participant's compensation does not include any elective deferral described in Code § 402(g)(3) or any amount that is contributed by the employer at the election of the employee and that is not includible in the gross income of the employee under Code §§ 125, 132(f)(4) or 457.

[SEP LRM (Mar. 2002), p. 5]

Note. Although reduced compensation must be used to determine the overall limit on allocations under the participant exclusion rule, in the author's opinion, compensation should not be reduced by catch-up elective contributions in computing the 25 percent exclusion limit or 100 percent limit under Code Section 415. To do so would violate Code Section 414(v), which lists Code Section 402(h) as a section to which the catch-up contribution would have no effect on a limit or be taken into account. [I.R.C. § 414(v)(3)]

After 2001, the 25 percent exclusion limit (previously 15 percent) is equal to 20 percent of pre-plan compensation (see Q 11:1). Catch-up elective contributions are not subject to the 25 percent participation exclusion limit or to the $50,000 Code Section 415 limit for 2012 and may be separately excluded from a participant's gross income (see Q 11:2).

Example 1. For a model SARSEP participant with pre-plan wages of $10,000, the maximum regular elective contribution is $2,000:

$\$10{,}000 \times .20 = \$2{,}000$

$\$10{,}000 - \$2{,}000 = \$8{,}000$

$\$8{,}000 \times .25 = \$2{,}000$

Example 2. If the model SARSEP in Example 1 is top heavy (see Q 8:1), only $1,760 of the participant's pre-plan wages of $10,000 can be excluded and contributed so that the minimum required top-heavy contribution (assume 3 percent) can be made without the total contribution's exceeding the 25 percent of net compensation maximum allocation/exclusion limit. The maximum regular contribution taking into account the minimum 3 percent contribution can be computed as follows, where *x* is equal to the maximum elective deferral:

$(\$10{,}000 - x) \times .25 = x + (\$10{,}000 \times .03)$

$\$2{,}500 - .25x = x + \$300$

$\$2{,}200 = 1.25x$

$\$1{,}760 = x$

Proof: $\$1{,}760 + \$300 = .25\ (\$10{,}000 - \$1{,}760)$

Q 3:16 When is a model SARSEP established by adopting Form 5305A-SEP deemed top heavy?

The instructions to Form 5305A-SEP state that if *any* key employee makes an elective contribution in any amount, the plan is deemed top heavy. In other words, if a key employee participates in a SARSEP established using Form 5305A-SEP, then all non-key employees must receive the minimum top-heavy contribution whether or not the plan actually is top heavy (see Q 8:1). It should be noted that the model form provides that in such a case the employer *may* make both elective and nonelective contributions and the minimum top-heavy contribution (which is really a nonelective contribution) under the same plan only by not checking box B under Form 5305A-SEP Article VI (see chapter 8).

Example. Great Jay Corporation maintains a SARSEP for its employees using Form 5305A-SEP. Great Jay's three non-highly compensated employees (NHCE) elect to participate in the SARSEP. The only other eligible employee is the owner, Birdie, and she too elects to participate. Because Birdie (a key employee) participates, the SARSEP arrangement is deemed top heavy, and Great Jay Corporation must make a top-heavy contribution for each non-key employee (see Q 8:2).

Prototype Document Approval

Q 3:17 May a prototype SEP include features not available in the IRS model document?

Yes. Some financial institutions have developed prototype SEP arrangements that contain language allowing features not currently available in the IRS model document. For example, Form 5305A-SEP does not allow for SEP contributions to be integrated with Social Security contributions or for a SEP to be maintained when the employer maintains any qualified retirement plan (see Q 3:10), but a prototype SEP document may. In addition, an eligible leased employee is treated as any other employee under a prototype (see Q 2:20). Further, the model document requires that the calendar year be used for all purposes under the arrangement; prototype SEP documents need not include that restriction.

The IRS has allowed a prototype plan sponsor to provide a provision that allows an employer to waive the age and/or service requirement for an individual employed on the effective date of the plan (see Qs 2:48, 2:56).

Q 3:18 Is IRS approval required for a prototype SEP?

No. Receipt of a favorable opinion letter or letter ruling on a SEP arrangement is not required as a condition of receiving favorable tax treatment. It is important to note, however, that the form of a nonapproved plan may not be relied on by an adopting employer. In addition, an employer that does not have a favorable determination letter from the IRS may not use the self-correction procedures under the Employee Plans Compliance Resolution System (see chapter 17).

Q 3:19 Must a preapproved prototype SEP IRA or SIMPLE IRA document be amended for statutory changes made after 2002?

No. A prototype IRA may, but need not, be amended to reflect a statutory change listed in Q 3:6 in order for a trustee, custodian, or issuer to take advantage of the change. Thus, a trustee, custodian, or issuer may accept the additional IRA contributions listed in Q 3:6 without specific authorizing language in the prototype IRA. (See Q 14:22.) Similarly, a currently approved employer or association IRA or Roth IRA (a group trust, custodial account, or annuity) under Code Section 408(c) may, but need not, be amended. [Rev. Proc. 2010-48, § 3.01, 2010-50 I.R.B. 828]

Permissive amendment. A prototype traditional IRA, Simple IRA, or Roth IRA may be amended, solely to incorporate the statutory changes listed in Q 3:6, without affecting reliance on a favorable opinion letter. Similarly, a currently approved employer or association IRA or Roth IRA (a group trust, custodial account, or annuity) under Code Section 408(c) may be amended without affecting reliance on a favorable ruling. Sample language for these changes is available (see SEP LRM in Appendix G). [Rev. Proc. 2010-48, § 3.02, 2010-50 I.R.B. 828]

Application for new opinion letters. A prototype sponsor may apply to the Service any time for an IRA opinion letter, including an opinion letter for an amendment solely to incorporate the statutory changes listed in Q 3:6. [Rev. Proc. 2010-48, §§ 2.06 and 3.03, 2010-50 I.R.B. 828]

Q 3:20 May a prototype sponsor of individual retirement annuities that uses one IRA endorsement with one or more annuity contracts submit only the IRA endorsement for approval?

Yes. Beginning with applications submitted after December 13, 2010, prototype sponsors of individual retirement annuities that use one IRA (or Roth IRA) endorsement with one or more annuity contracts may submit only the IRA endorsement (and not the contracts) to the IRS for approval. Sponsors that take advantage of this new procedure will be issued an opinion letter referencing the IRA endorsement, thereby reducing the number of opinion letters issued and, correspondingly, the applicable user fees. In September 2010, the IRS issued a revised Form 5306 reflecting the new procedures. The IRA endorsement must include all IRA qualification rules and must provide that the terms of the IRA endorsement supersede any conflicting terms in the annuity contracts to which the IRA endorsement applies. Sponsors that use different IRA endorsements for each contract, that use no endorsements, or that simply want an opinion letter for each contract may submit applications to the IRS, including with such applications the document or documents that constitute the IRA.

Q 3:21 Will the IRS issue an opinion letter approving or rejecting the form of a document intended to be a prototype SEP?

Yes. The IRS will issue an opinion letter, if requested by a sponsoring organization, as to whether a prototype SEP arrangement meets the requirements of Code Section 408(k). The organization sponsoring a prototype SEP must submit Form 5306-A, Application for Approval of Prototype Simplified Employee Pension (SEP) or Savings Incentive Match Plan for Employees of Small Employers (SIMPLE IRA Plan) (revised September 2010), to the National Office of the IRS. A user fee is payable on submission of the approval request (see Q 3:24). The application forms may be computer generated. [Rev. Proc. 2011-61; 2011-52 I.R.B. 990]

[*See* Rev. Proc. 87-50, 1987-2 C.B. 647; Rev. Proc. 97-29, 1997-1 C.B. 698; and Rev. Proc. 98-59, 1998-2 C.B. 727, as referenced in Rev. Proc. 2005-16, 2005-1

C.B. 674, regarding the procedures for requesting an opinion letter on a SEP or SIMPLE prototype arrangement.]

Q 3:22 May a SEP and an IRA be combined into one prototype document?

No. The IRS will not issue an opinion letter on a prototype SEP arrangement that consolidates a SEP and an IRA into one document. [Rev. Proc. 87-50, § 5.03, 1987-2 C.B. 647]

Q 3:23 Should Form 5306-A be filed to request approval of a model SEP?

No. Instead of adopting an individually designed or a prototype SEP, a sponsor may use IRS model Form 5305-SEP or Form 5305A-SEP to establish a SEP arrangement that meets the requirements of Code Section 408(k) (see Q 3:2). If it does so, the sponsor should not file Form 5306-A, Application for Approval of Prototype Simplified Employee Pension (SEP) or Savings Incentive Match Plan for Employees of Small Employers (SIMPLE IRA Plan) (revised September 2010), to seek IRS approval of the SEP (see Q 3:4).

Q 3:24 What is the fee for requesting IRS approval of prototype plan documents?

The IRS imposes a user fee for the review of prototype plan documents and their amendments, and for related purposes. For 2012, typical user fees for requests are as follows:

- Opinion letter on a mass submitter prototype IRA or SEP, including a SARSEP (or a mass submitter prototype SIMPLE IRA, SIMPLE IRA plan, or Roth IRA)—$3,000
- Opinion letter on a non-mass submitter prototype IRA or SEP, including a SARSEP (or a non-mass submitter prototype SIMPLE IRA, SIMPLE IRA plan, or Roth IRA)—$3,000
- Sponsoring organization's word-for-word identical adoption or amendment of a mass submitter prototype IRA or SEP, including a SARSEP (or a mass submitter prototype SIMPLE IRA, SIMPLE IRA plan, or Roth IRA)—$200
- Non-mass submission (new or amended) by a sponsoring organization for approval of a prototype IRA or SEP (or a prototype SIMPLE IRA, SIMPLE IRA plan, or Roth IRA)—$3,000
- Computation of exclusion for annuitant under Code Section 72—$1,000
- Approval to become a nonbank trustee—$20,000
- Sponsoring organization's minor modification of a mass submitter prototype IRA or SEP, including a SARSEP (or a mass submitter prototype SIMPLE IRA, SIMPLE IRA plan, or Roth IRA)—$750

- Opinion letters on dual-purpose (combined traditional and Roth) IRAs
  - Mass submission of a prototype dual-purpose (combined traditional and Roth) IRA, per plan document, new or amended—$4,500
  - Sponsoring organization's word-for-word identical adoption or amendment of a mass submitter prototype dual-purpose IRA, per plan document—$200
  - Sponsoring organization's minor modification of a mass submitter prototype dual-purpose IRA—$750
  - Sponsoring organization's non-mass submission of a prototype dual-purpose IRA, new or amended, per plan document—$4,500
- Individually designed SEP—$10,000
- Letter ruling requests on Roth IRA recharacterizations—$4,000
- Certain waivers of 60-day rollover period:
  - Rollover less than $50,000—$500
  - Rollover equal to or greater than $50,000 and less than $100,000—$1,500
  - Rollover equal to or greater than $100,000—$3,000

[Rev. Proc. 2012-8, 2012-1 I.R.B. 235]

Q 3:25 What types of organizations qualify to sponsor a prototype SEP?

An organization seeking to qualify as a sponsor of a prototype SEP must be a trade or professional organization (other than an employee association; see Q 5:31) having characteristics similar to those described in Treasury Regulations Section 1.501(c)(6)-1, a bank (as defined in Code Section 581), an insured credit union (within the meaning of Section 101(6) of the Federal Credit Union Act), a regulated investment company (as defined in Code Section 851), an investment adviser under a contract with one or more regulated investment companies, a principal underwriter that has a principal underwriting contract with one or more regulated investment companies, or a person that, under the Treasury regulations, may act as a trustee or custodian of an IRA (nonbank trustee or custodian). [Rev. Proc. 87-50, § 3.01, 1987-2 C.B. 647] The IRS maintains a list of entities (other than most banks and insurance companies, which are automatically approved) that have been approved to act as nonbank trustees or custodians. [*See* I.R.S. Ann. 2007-47, 2007-20 I.R.B. 1260, 121] This list includes names, addresses, and the date each application was approved.]

When the sponsoring organization is an insurance company, the IRS will issue an opinion letter, if requested to do so, as to whether a specific prototype individual annuity contract, within the meaning of the regulations, meets the requirements of Code Section 408(b). [Rev. Proc. 87-50, § 3.01, 1987-2 C.B. 647; *see also* Rev. Proc. 97-29, 1997-1 C.B. 698 (regarding SIMPLE IRAs) and Rev. Proc. 98-59, 1998-2 C.B. 727 (regarding Roth IRAs)]

Practice Pointer. A copy of the IRS opinion letter approving the prototype SEP must be furnished to employers using that agreement. [Rev. Proc. 87-50, § 3.01, 1987-2 C.B. 647]

Q 3:26 May an employer that adopts a prototype SEP document rely on the opinion letter received from the IRS by the prototype sponsor?

Yes. If a particular employer adopts a prototype SEP arrangement in accordance with the form approved by the IRS and observes its provisions, that employer may rely on the opinion letter as long as

1. SEP contributions are made to a model IRA or an IRS-approved master or prototype IRA and
2. Contributions under the SEP arrangement do not (in combination with another SEP arrangement or any terminated qualified defined benefit plan of the employer) fail to satisfy the requirements of Code Section 415 (see Q 5:6).

[Rev. Proc. 87-50, § 5.03, 1987-2 C.B. 647]

Q 3:27 May a prototype SEP be used by an employer that currently maintains a master or prototype defined contribution plan?

Yes. If an employer maintains a master or prototype defined contribution plan (see Q 3:40), the plan document most likely contains language that will coordinate contributions under that plan with any other master or prototype defined contribution plan or SEP maintained by the same employer. [IRS Modifications for Defined Contribution Plans (Aug. 2005)] If a qualified plan does not contain language that coordinates contributions made under it with a SEP and is maintained with a SEP, it may not satisfy Code Section 415. [Rev. Proc. 87-50, § 5.05, 1987-2 C.B. 647]

Mass Submitter Document Approval

Q 3:28 May an entity that is not eligible to submit a prototype SEP as an approved sponsoring organization receive an opinion letter?

Yes. The IRS may issue an opinion letter to an entity whether or not the entity qualifies to submit a prototype SEP document as an approved sponsoring organization. First, however, the entity must establish that there are at least 10 sponsoring organizations that will sponsor the identical prototype SEP. The entity that initially submits the document to the IRS is called a *mass submitter.* A user fee is payable upon submission of the mass submitter documents for approval and upon submission of each subsequent prototype approval request (see Q 3:24).

Example. Galactic Pension Consulting has 19 clients that are interested in sponsoring an identical plan document. Galactic does not qualify to sponsor a prototype document (see Q 3:25); however, it may submit a document for approval as a mass submitter. After IRS approval has been granted, Galactic's clients may sponsor the document and have it approved as a prototype.

Q 3:29 Must the IRS be informed of the names of the sponsoring organizations behind the mass submitter of a prototype SEP?

Yes. A list of the sponsoring organizations committed to the entity that is the mass submitter of a prototype SEP document must be included with the application for the opinion letter; however, the opinion letter and any correspondence relating to it will only be issued to (and will apply only to) the mass submitter.

Q 3:30 Must each sponsoring organization behind the mass submitter of a prototype SEP seek approval to sponsor a prototype plan document?

Yes. Each sponsoring organization behind the mass submitter of a prototype SEP document must obtain an opinion letter so that the form of the SEP arrangement will be treated by the IRS as a prototype SEP. [Rev. Proc. 87-50, § 7.01, 1987-2 C.B. 647]

Q 3:31 Who submits the request for an opinion letter on behalf of the sponsoring organization's prototype SEP?

The application for an opinion letter must be submitted by the mass submitter of the prototype SEP document on behalf of the sponsoring organization. A user fee applies to such a request (see Q 3:24). Although the mass submitter must complete all items on Form 5306-A, the application for IRS approval of a prototype SEP document, it is the sponsoring organizations that must sign the completed form, unless a power-of-attorney form is completed and submitted with the application.

In addition, if the prototype SEP replaces any other SEP(s) of the sponsoring organizations, the mass submitter must attach (a list of) the plan number(s) and file folder number(s) of the prototype SEP(s) replaced. Upon receipt of the opinion letter application and related material (i.e., plan, adoption agreement, and power-of-attorney form), the IRS will issue an opinion letter to the mass submitter for distribution to the sponsoring organizations. Any interim correspondence will be addressed to the mass submitter. [Rev. Proc. 87-50, § 7.02, 1987-2 C.B. 647]

Q 3:32 When will the IRS accept requests for an opinion letter on behalf of a sponsoring organization's mass submitter prototype SEP?

Submissions by individual sponsors wishing to use a mass submitter prototype SEP may be made only after an opinion letter has been issued to the mass submitter.

Q 3:33 May a mass submitter of a prototype SEP make its opinion letter available to others?

If a mass submitter of a prototype SEP document also qualifies as a sponsoring organization (see Q 3:25), it may make its opinion letter available to individuals and businesses wishing to establish a prototype SEP.

Q 3:34 Must a sponsoring organization's prototype SEP adopt the mass submitter's original document word for word?

It depends. The first 10 submissions made to the IRS for approval of a prototype SEP document must contain a declaration by the mass submitter, under penalty of perjury, that the sponsoring organizations have adopted the identical prototype SEP of the mass submitter, which SEP must be identified by the serial number and date of the opinion letter issued to the mass submitter with respect to that SEP. The submission must also include a copy of the SEP.

After 10 sponsoring organizations have adopted the identical SEP, other sponsoring organizations may adopt the plan word for word or with minor modifications. Requests on behalf of sponsoring organizations that have adopted the SEP with minor modifications must contain a statement indicating the purpose and effect of each change. The mass submitter must submit the request on behalf of the sponsoring organization and must certify, under penalty of perjury, that the SEP of the sponsoring organization, except for the delineated changes, is identical to the plan document for which the mass submitter received a favorable opinion letter. The IRS will review the changes on a priority basis and issue an opinion letter to the sponsoring organization as soon as possible. Any interim correspondence will be addressed to the mass submitter. [Rev. Proc. 87-50, § 7.03, 1987-2 C.B. 647]

Q 3:35 Must a sponsor that uses a mass submitter prototype SEP use the post-1996 definition of highly compensated employee if the mass submitter prototype plan has not been amended?

Yes. Even if a mass submitter prototype plan has not been amended to reflect the changes effected by the SBJPA, an employer must use the definition of *highly compensated employee* (HCE) that became effective after 1996 (see Q 1:14).

Individually Designed SEPs

Q 3:36 What is an individually designed SEP?

An *individually designed SEP* is a SEP arrangement that is not preapproved by the IRS for use as either a model or a prototype plan. An individually designed plan is sponsored directly by the employer establishing the plan.

Q 3:37 Is there a procedure for obtaining IRS approval of an individually designed SEP or SARSEP?

Yes. An employer may submit a request for a letter ruling to the National Office of the IRS regarding the acceptability of an individually designed SEP or SARSEP arrangement. The IRS imposes a one-time user fee of $10,000 (see Q 3:24). [Rev. Proc. 87-50, 1987-2 C.B. 647, as modified by Rev. Proc. 91-44, 1991-2 C.B. 733 (relating to SEPs and SARSEPs); Rev. Proc. 2012-8, 2012-1 I.R.B. 235 for 2012]

Approval for Combined Plans and Prior Plans

Q 3:38 May an employer that adopts more than one SEP obtain IRS approval of its SEP documents?

Yes. If an adopting employer maintains more than one SEP covering any of the same employees, the employer may request a letter ruling as to whether the SEP, in combination with the other SEP (or SEPs), satisfies the requirements of Code Section 415 (see Q 3:41). The instructions set forth in Revenue Procedure 2005-4 should be followed, and the material submitted should include a single copy of each SEP. [Rev. Proc. 2012-4, § 6.02, 2012- 1 I. R. B. 125; Rev. Proc. 87-50, § 4.01, 1987-2 C.B. 647] A user fee of $10,000 must also be submitted. [Rev. Proc. 2012-8, § 6.01(14), 2012-1 I.R.B. 235]

Q 3:39 May a prototype or model SEP be combined with a prototype or model SARSEP?

Yes. The instructions contained in the IRS model documents (Forms 5305-SEP and 5305A-SEP) permit SEPs and SARSEPs to be used with one another. Multiple SEPs or SARSEPs are also permitted. Similar rules apply to SEPs and SARSEPs established with IRS-approved prototypes. It should be noted, however, that if an employer has ever maintained a defined benefit pension plan that is now terminated, the employer may request a letter ruling from the IRS confirming that the requirements of Code Section 415 are satisfied (see Q 3:41).

Q 3:40 May a prototype or individually designed SEP or SARSEP be used in conjunction with a qualified defined contribution plan without violating Code Section 415?

Yes. Language coordinating Code Section 415 with a SEP or SARSEP is contained in the qualified plan (non-SEP) documents and should be followed. The SEP limits are not deemed to have been exceeded merely because an employer has made a contribution to a qualified plan.

Q 3:41 May an employer that once maintained a defined benefit plan (now terminated) request IRS approval of a SEP document?

Yes. If an adopting employer ever maintained a qualified defined benefit plan that is now terminated and that plan covers any of the same employees covered by the employer's SEP, the employer *may* request a letter ruling stating whether the SEP (in combination with the terminated defined benefit plan) satisfies the requirements of Code Section 415. The instructions set forth in Revenue Procedure 87-50 [1987-2 C.B. 647] should be followed, and the material submitted should include a single copy of each SEP and qualified plan. [Rev. Proc. 87-50, § 4.01, 1987-2 C.B. 647]

For plan years beginning before 2000, an employer that once maintained a defined benefit plan (even if since terminated) was *required* to seek a determination of whether the plan, in combination with a SEP agreement, satisfied the requirements of Code Section 415. Seeking such a determination is no longer required because, effective for plan years beginning in 2000, the combination limit under Code Section 415(e) was repealed. In addition, the 2002 Model SEP and SARSEP (Forms 5305-SEP and 5305A-SEP) and the 2002 Prototype SEP plan language was amended to remove this restriction. Form 5305-SEP was amended in December 2004 for new adoptions (see above).

> **Note.** For plan years beginning before 2000, an employer that once maintained a qualified defined benefit plan that has since terminated could not rely on the form of a model or prototype plan. The SEP plan used in the submission for IRS approval had to have been an individually designed plan that contained specific language that was not contained in a model SEP or prototype plan. [Rev. Proc. 87-50, § 4.05, 1987-2 C.B. 647; Ltr. Ruls. 200003057, 9709008, 9706009, 9552055, 9445070, 9036038, 8942081, 8932078, 8928008, 8927036]

Chapter 4

ERISA Considerations and Related Laws

The Employee Retirement Income Security Act of 1974 (ERISA), the most sweeping overhaul of the pension and employee benefit rules in U.S. history, gave rise to the concept of savings for retirement with the creation of the individual retirement arrangement. SEPs were established five years later. This chapter examines the rules that affect SEP reporting and disclosure requirements under ERISA, the protection of employee benefits rights, and the security of plan assets. Aspects of federal securities law and state law considerations are also presented. Regulations encouraging payroll deduction individual retirement arrangements (IRAs) are also discussed. Additional information is provided on SIMPLE IRAs in chapter 14, on 401(k) SIMPLE plans in chapter 15, and on matters pertaining to the Voluntary Fiduciary Correction Program (VFCP) in chapter 17.

Overview

Q 4:1 What is an *employee pension benefit plan* under Title I of ERISA?

Under Section 4(a) of the Employee Retirement Income Security Act of 1974 (ERISA), the only employee benefit plans subject to Title I of ERISA (regarding the protection of employee benefit rights) are those within the meaning of ERISA Section 3(3), provided such a plan is established or maintained by an employer engaged in commerce or in any industry or activity affecting commerce, by an employee organization or organization representing employees engaged in commerce or in any activity affecting commerce, or by both.

The term *employee benefit plan* includes an "employee pension benefit plan." [ERISA § 3(3)] Most SEPs and SARSEPs are employee benefit plans under ERISA; however, many exclusions and exceptions apply. As a general matter, a SEP would be a "pension plan" within the meaning of ERISA Section 3(2). [29 U.S.C. § 1002(2); *see also* DOL Reg. § 2520.104-4 and -49 presuming the applicability of ERISA to a SEP] SIMPLE IRA plans are subject to special rules (see chapter 14).

Section 3(2)(A) of Title I of ERISA defines the term *employee pension benefit plan* as follows:

> [A]ny plan, fund, or program which was heretofore or is hereafter established or maintained by an employer or by an employee organization, or by both, to the extent that by its express terms or as a result of surrounding circumstances such plan, fund, or program
>
> i. provides retirement income to employees, or
> ii. results in a deferral of income by employees for periods extending to the termination of covered employment or beyond,
>
> regardless of the method of calculating the contributions made to the plan, the method of calculating the benefits under the plan or the method of distributing benefits from the plan.

[*See also LaChapell,* 901 F. Supp. at 24 n. 1; 45 Fed. Reg. 24866, 24867; *see also* Cline v. Industrial Maint. Eng'g & Contracting Co., 200 F.3d 1223 (9th Cir. 2000)]

Moreover, a Code Section 408(a) or (b) individual retirement account or annuity is governed by ERISA as "employee pension benefit plan[s]" if they receive employer contributions or if the employer is otherwise actively involved with the account or annuity. [29 C.F.R. § 2510.3-2(d)]

Plans without employees are not covered under Title I of ERISA. [DOL Reg. § 2510.3-3] Thus, for purposes of Title I, the term *employee benefit plan* does not include any plan, fund, or program under which only a sole proprietor or only partners are participants covered under the plan. An individual and his or her spouse will not be deemed to be employees with respect to a trade or business, whether incorporated or unincorporated, that is wholly owned by the individual or by the individual and his or her spouse, and a partner in a partnership and his or her spouse will not be deemed to be employees with respect to the partnership. It is unclear, however, whether a limited liability company that is treated as a partnership for tax purposes and that has no common-law employees is excluded from coverage under Title I.

Example 1. Puck establishes a SEP for his sole proprietorship. Puck and his wife, Mookie, are the SEP's only participants. A third employee is ineligible to participate for the current plan year. Puck causes his SEP IRA trustee to unwittingly purchase a piece of real estate as an investment for the IRA that Puck indirectly owns. Although the plan is exempt from Title I of ERISA, the transaction is, nonetheless, a prohibited transaction under the Code (see Q 4:20).

Example 2. Blueberry maintains a SEP. In 2008, several employees terminated employment, leaving only the owner and his spouse as participants. Although the plan was at one time governed by ERISA, it is no longer an ERISA plan. [See Meiszner v. Suburban Bank & Trust Co., 397 F. Supp. 2d 952 (N.D. Ill. 2005); International Resources, Inc. v. New York Life Insurance Co., 950 F.2d 294 (6th Cir. 1992)]

Note. ERISA prohibits any person from using fraud, force, or violence (or threatening force or violence) to restrain, coerce, or intimidate (or attempt to) any plan participant or beneficiary in order to interfere with or prevent the exercise of their rights under the plan. Willful violation of this prohibition is a criminal offense subject to a $10,000 fine or imprisonment of up to one year, or both. The Pension Protection Act of 2006 (PPA) increases the penalties for willful acts of coercive interference with participants' rights under an ERISA plan. The amount of the fine is increased to $100,000, and the maximum term of imprisonment is increased to 10 years. [ERISA § 511, as amended by PPA § 623(a). The provision is effective for violations occurring on and after August 17, 2006, the date the PPA was enacted. PPA § 623(b)]

Q 4:2 Can a participant or former participant bring a claim for a breach of fiduciary duty when the loss to an account does not necessarily affect the entire plan?

Possibly. In February 2008, the U.S. Supreme Court in *LaRue v. DeWolff, Boberg & Associates* expanded the remedies available for fiduciary breach claims brought under ERISA. [LaRue v. DeWolff, Boberg & Assoc., 128 S. Ct. 1020 (2008), reversing a decision by the U.S. Court of Appeals for the Fourth Circuit, and remanding the case for further proceedings, available at *http://www.supremecourt.gov/qp/06-00856qp.pdf* (visited on Aug. 15, 2012)]

Under a long-standing decision, *Massachusetts Mutual Life Ins. Co. v. Russell* [473 U.S. 134 (1985)], involving a disability plan, any relief granted for fiduciary breach was required to benefit the *entire plan*, rather than an individual participant. Under the *Russell* rationale, participants who claim to have suffered a loss due to a breach of fiduciary duty generally faced an uphill battle. If a participant sought money damages, but those money damages were not recoverable on behalf of the plan "as a whole," the participant often had no available remedy. Thus, in the context of investment-related breaches, the "entire plan" rule effectively limited fiduciary claims to defined benefit and similar insurance plans, under which all benefits are funded from a common asset pool. However, the plan in *LaRue* was a defined contribution plan. In respect to *Russell*, the *LaRue* decision stated: "Whether a fiduciary breach diminishes plan assets payable to all participants or only to particular individuals, it creates the kind of harms that concerned § 409's draftsmen. Thus, *Russell's* 'entire plan' references, which accurately reflect § 409's operation in the defined benefit context, are beside the point in the defined contribution context."

In *LaRue*, the plaintiff, Mr. LaRue, claimed that he directed his former employer, the plan's administrator under ERISA, to change the investments in his 401(k) account, that the administrator failed to carry out the directive, breaching its fiduciary duty, and that as a result, he suffered a loss of approximately $150,000. Having lost at the trial-level court [450 F.3d 570 (4th Cir. 2006)], he appealed to the Fourth Circuit Court of Appeals, which held that money damages are not available under ERISA when the claim is that only the account of an individual participant, or subset of participants, has been damaged, since the recovery in such a case would not be for the benefit of the plan "as a whole."

In three opinions, the majority opinion by Justice Roberts, and two opinions concurring in the judgment, the Supreme Court Justices concluded that the Fourth Circuit Court of Appeals was "flawed." Unfortunately, the opinions represent three distinct philosophical approaches to the same problem that will have to be considered (and interpreted) by the lower courts. (The Supreme Court remanded *LaRue* to the lower court for further consideration.)

Although ERISA Section 502(a) does not specifically provide a remedy for individual injuries distinct from plan injuries, it does authorize recovery for fiduciary breaches that impair the value of plan assets in a participant's individual account. ERISA Sections 502(a)(1) and 502(a)(2) read as follows:

> (a) Persons empowered to bring a civil action
>
> A civil action may be brought—(1) by a participant or beneficiary—
>
> (A) for the relief provided for in subsection (c) of this section [regarding relief for participants when an administrator fails or refuses to comply with a request for information], or
>
> (B) to recover benefits due to him under the terms of his plan, to enforce his rights under the terms of the plan, or to clarify his rights to future benefits under the terms of the plan;

(2) by the Secretary, or by a participant, beneficiary or fiduciary for appropriate relief under section 409; . . .

ERISA Section 502(a)(2) provides for suits to enforce the liability-creating provisions of ERISA Section 409, concerning breaches of fiduciary duties that harm plans. ERISA Section 409 provides:

> Any person who is a fiduciary with respect to a *plan* who breaches any of the responsibilities, obligations, or duties imposed upon fiduciaries by this title shall be personally liable to make good to such *plan* any losses to the plan resulting from each such breach, and to restore to such *plan* any profits of such fiduciary which have been made through use of assets of the plan by the fiduciary, and shall be subject to such other equitable or remedial relief as the court may deem appropriate, including removal of such fiduciary. [Emphasis added.] A fiduciary may also be removed for a violation of section 411 of this Act.

[88 Stat. 886, 29 U. S. C. § 1109(a)]

Note. Other sections of ERISA would appear to confirm that the "entire plan" language from *Russell,* which appears nowhere in ERISA Sections 409 or, does not apply to defined contribution plans. Most significant is ERISA Section 404(c), which exempts fiduciaries from liability for losses caused by participants' exercise of control over assets in their individual accounts. [*See also* 29 C.F.R. § 2550.404c-1 (2007)]

The Supreme Court assumed in *LaRue* that the plan administrator "breached fiduciary obligations defined in § 409(a), and that those breaches had an adverse impact on the value of the plan assets in petitioner's individual account." Whether Mr. LaRue could prove his allegations and whether the respondent had valid defenses to the claim were not matters before the Supreme Court. For example, the Court did not decide whether petitioner made the alleged investment directions in accordance with the requirements specified by the plan, or whether Mr. LaRue was required to exhaust his administrative (or other) remedies set forth in the plan before seeking relief in Federal court pursuant to ERISA § 502(a)(2) for breach of fiduciary duty, or even whether Mr. LaRue asserted his rights in a timely fashion. (The lower courts are currently divided on this issue; and whether this turns out to be a foothold or a valid defense will remain to be seen.) In actuality there were three decisions, the majority opinion and two opinions concurring in the judgment. The opinions represent three distinct philosophical approaches to the same problem.

Despite the language of ERISA Section 502(a)(2) and ERISA Section 409(a) specifically referring to recovering money for the "plan," not an individual, Justice John Paul Stevens (joined by Souter, Breyer, Ginsburg, and Alito) focused their decision on the fact that individual account defined contribution plans, rather than defined benefit plans, are now the dominant form of retirement plan in the workplace. In that context, they stated that "[f]iduciary misconduct need not threaten the solvency of the entire plan to reduce benefits below the amount that participants would otherwise receive." The ruling appears to open the door for an individual participant in an ERISA covered plan to commence litigation against a plan administrator for breach of fiduciary duty. If that is so, the ruling may also lead to innovative ways to protect plan fiduciaries from liability from individual plan participants. However, the decision only holds that, if the plaintiff can prove the facts that he or she has alleged, then the individual may have viable legal claim. There has been no decision, for instance, that Mr. LaRue's investment instructions were not properly carried out (see above).

In the first concurring *LaRue* opinion, Chief Justice Roberts (joined by Justice Kennedy) wrote that, while he agreed that the analysis of the Fourth Circuit Court of Appeals was "flawed," it was not clear that LaRue brought his claim under the correct provision of ERISA. Justice Roberts wrote that lower federal courts in the future should consider whether ERISA Section 502(a)(1)(B) applies in a case like this, and if so, whether there must be an exhaustion of internal remedies before the (a)(2) issue is reached, if at all. Arguably, if appropriate relief is available under ERISA Section 502(a)(1)(B) as a denial of benefits case, there is no need to consider an 502(a)(2) fiduciary breach remedy, which would not provide any meaningful remedy for a participant to make up their losses from their individual account. Thus, for example, if LaRue or Rogers did not exhaust their internal remedies under ERISA Section 502(a)(2), they may still lose. [*See* Varity Corp. v. Howe, 516 U.S. 489 (1996); *see also* Stephen D. Rosenberg, Boston ERISA and Insurance Blog, "Interpreting LaRue" (2008), available at *http://www.bostonerisalaw.com/archives/401k-plans-interpreting-larue.html* (visited on Aug. 15, 2012); Paul M. Secunda, Workplace Prof. Blog, "Reflections on the LaRue Decision" (2008) available at *http://lawprofessors.typepad.com/laborprof_blog/2008/02/reflections-on.html* (visited on Aug. 15, 2012)] Thus, to the extent that it is relied upon by future courts, the Roberts opinion suggests that claims of this nature should not even be decided under ERISA's fiduciary breach provisions, but rather, should be approached as a claim for benefits (which, arguably, would favor plan administrators, sponsors, and fiduciaries).

In the second concurring *LaRue* opinion, Justice Thomas, joined by Justice Scalia, wrote that whether a claim is available to LaRue does not depend on "trends in the pension plan market" (i.e., the trend away from defined benefit plans to defined contribution plans) nor to the ostensible "concerns" of ERISA's drafters that were mentioned in the majority decision. Rather, according to Justice Thomas, the losses to LaRue's individual account resulting from purported breaches of fiduciary duty were losses of "plan assets," which, once recovered, were simply attributable to Mr. LaRue's individual account." Thus, ostensibly under this view, LaRue's claim could have been brought under either ERISA Section 502(a)(1) or 502(a)(2).

[*See also* Joe Faucher and Mike Vanic, Reish Luftman Reicher & Cohen Bulletin, "The Supreme Court's Decision in *LaRue v. DeWolff, Boberg & Associates*: How It Affects You, What You Should Do, and Ruminations Regarding the Fractured Opinion" (Apr. 10, 2008), available at *http://www.reish.com/publications/pdf/larue.pdf* (visited on Aug. 15, 2012)]

Note. With the ink barely dry on the Supreme Court's opinion in *LaRue*, the Seventh Circuit has applied it in deciding *Rogers v. Baxter International Inc.* [521 F.3d 702 [521 F.3d 702 (7th Cir. Ill. 2008)] The Seventh Circuit held in *Rogers* that a participant in a defined contribution plan may use ERISA Section 502(a)(2), and thus ERISA Section 409(a), to obtain relief if losses to an account are attributable to a pension plan fiduciary's breach of a duty owed to the plan.

On April 21, 2008, a federal judge in Iowa ruled that former participants in a 401(k) plan lacked standing to pursue legal remedies under ERISA, despite the Supreme Court's recent ruling in *LaRue*. [Young v. Principal Fin. Group, Inc., 2008 U.S. Dist. LEXIS 32732 (S.D. Iowa Apr. 21, 2008)] However, in *Young*, the court held that standing was proper to pursue equitable relief under ERISA Section 502(a)(3), which provides that a civil action may be brought—

> by a participant, beneficiary, or fiduciary (A) to enjoin any act or practice which violates any provision of this title or the terms of the plan, or (B) to obtain other appropriate equitable relief (i) to redress such violations or (ii) to enforce any provisions of this title or the terms of the plan.

[29 U.S.C. § 1132(a)(2)]

In *Young*, the court also noted that it was not alleged that the breach or deception

> directly caused harm to either an employee benefit plan or to an individual ERISA benefit account while the assets were invested in an ERISA plan, nor do Plaintiffs claim that Defendants' breach reduced the amount of money Plaintiffs received when they cashed out of their employers['] retirement plan. Instead, Plaintiffs only allege that after they removed their money from their employers' ERISA plans, their investments have performed poorly and that the fees that Principal has charged caused their current investments to be substantially less valuable than they would have been had Plaintiffs remained in their ERISA plans.

The court noted that ERISA Section 502(a)(3) provides a "catchall" remedy for participants to sue for injury to their own account, and that "former participants" have standing if they were deceived into leaving an ERISA plan. In discussing the remedies available under ERISA Section 502(a)(3), the court noted that they are limited to "classic equitable remedies," and held that, depending on the factual development of the case, plaintiffs might be entitled to the traditional equitable remedy of a disgorgement of Principal's profits, or to having their assets transferred back out of their IRAs into their 401(k) plans.

Note. In a well-reasoned opinion, a recent district court decision held that *LaRue* did not revive the plaintiffs' breach of fiduciary duty claims. Although the plans involved were defined contribution ESOPs, the participants (unlike in *LaRue)*, did not direct the investment of their own contributions (whereas the ESOP did). The individual relief permitted in *LaRue* was a direct result of the plan's failure to follow LaRue's investment direction. Since the ESOP did not permit participant direction of accounts, the district court was able to distinguish the *LaRue* holding. [Cook v. Campbell, 2008 U.S. Dist. LEXIS 38336 (M.D. Ala. May 12, 2008)]

Although the plaintiffs in *Cook* claimed that the trustees' breach of fiduciary duty negatively impacted the value of the company stock, and thus negatively impacted all ESOP participants, the district court found that the plaintiffs were still only seeking individualized recoveries and not recovery to the plan as a whole. *LaRue* sought recovery *to the plan* of his individual losses, even though no other participants were affected. Because LaRue sought damages to flow through the plan to himself, the district court reasoned (in this matter) that *LaRue* did nothing to alter the law in *Russell*, which required that recoveries for breach of fiduciary duty be paid to the plan, and not to individual participants.

Finally, in viewing the plaintiffs' claims as claims for benefits, the district court adhered to Chief Justice Roberts's concurring opinion in *LaRue*, requiring exhaustion of administrative remedies under ERISA Section 501(a)(1)(B).

After the parties returned to the very early stages of litigation on remand, LaRue voluntarily dismissed his case. Although LaRue reported to the court "that it [was] not financially feasible to continue to pursue his claim," observers are left to speculate whether he was ultimately discouraged by the legal obstacles that remained in his case, including the ultimate burden of proving a breach of fiduciary duty.

Practice Pointer. The *Cook* decision essentially treats ESOPs more like defined benefit plans subject to the Supreme Court's prior holding in *Russell*, which requires that damages in ERISA cases flow through the plan for the benefit of all plan participants. Perhaps other courts will limit relief in other circumstances *à la LaRue*.

In *Metropolitan Life Insurance Co. v. Glenn* [128 S. Ct. 2008 (2008)], a divided Supreme Court attempted to resolve the question of how much deference a court must pay to a benefit determination by a welfare plan fiduciary that has an inherent conflict because it also pays the benefits. The Court held that (1) a conflict had resulted because of the dual roles; (2) the decision nevertheless is entitled to deference and may be reviewed only for an abuse of discretion; and (3) the conflict is to be taken into account (along with other factors) in determining whether abuses occurred.

In Bendaoud v. Hodgson [45 Employee Benefit Cas. 1026 (D. Mass. 2008)], the court attempted to limit the scope of *LaRue* by holding that a participant cannot sue on behalf of other participants because he or she cannot have an economic interest in the account of any other participant. If this holding is followed by other courts, it should at least reduce or eliminate the number of class action lawsuits that *LaRue* could have created. [Arthur Woodard, "Supreme Court Continues to Wrestle With Questions on Benefits" (Jan. 1, 2010), available at *http://eba.benefitnews.com/news/supreme-court-continues-to-wrestle-with-questions-on-benefits-2682726-1.html* (visited on Aug. 15, 2012)]

Q 4:3 Is it unlawful to discharge or to discriminate against a participant for exercising his or her ERISA rights?

Yes. ERISA Section 510 provides that "[i]t shall be unlawful for any person to discharge, fine, suspend, expel, discipline, or discriminate against a participant or beneficiary for exercising any right to which he is entitled under the provisions of an employee benefit plan . . . or for the purpose of interfering with the attainment of any right to which such participant may become entitled under the plan. . . . [29 U.S.C. § 1140] ERISA Section 510 protects against two types of conduct: (1) adverse action for exercising any right under a plan or ERISA, and (2) interference with the attainment of any right under a plan or ERISA. This protection is necessary to prevent the "circumvent[ion] of promised benefits." [Ingersoll-Rand Co. v. McClendon, 498 U.S. 133, 143 (1990)]

In *Garratt v. Walker* (rehearing en banc), the Tenth Circuit addressed when an employer maintaining a SEP can condition another employee's participation in the plan upon a reduction in salary without violating the antidiscrimination provision of ERISA Section 510. Many of the operative facts involve salary discussions after the employer requested that the employee switch to a salary arrangement in lieu of hourly wages. When she declined, the employer advised that she should look for another job. She gave notice, but stayed on two weeks at the employer's request. Ultimately, the employer contributed to the plan on his own behalf. Having done so, he also contributed on behalf of the employee, given the rules that require allocation of contributions among SEP participants uniformly based upon compensation, and prohibit discrimination in favor of certain highly compensated employees. [Garratt v. Walker, 164 F.3d 1249 (10th Cir. 1998), available at *http://vlex.com/vid/18481528* (visited on Aug. 15, 2012)]

The civil enforcement mechanism of ERISA Section 502, allows a plan participant to bring a civil action not only for recovery of plan benefits and enforcement of plan rights, but also "to clarify his rights to future benefits under the terms of the plan." ERISA Section 510 cross-references ERISA Section 502, and the courts have recognized the relationship between the two sections in safeguarding ERISA "rights and expectations." [*See* Ingersoll-Rand Co. v. McClendon, 498 U.S. 133, 137 (1990); *see also* Humphreys v. Bellaire Corp., 966 F.2d 1037, 1043 (6th Cir. 1992)]

A unilateral oral decision to require a salary reduction would not satisfy the requirement of a written allocation formula, nor is it consistent with other plan documentation, publication, or amendment requirements. [Garratt v. Walker, 164 F.3d 1249 (10th Cir. 1998), available at *http://vlex.com/vid/18481528* (visited on Aug. 15, 2012); *see* I.R.C. § 408(k)(5); *see* ERISA §§ 102 (regarding plan descriptions), 104 (regarding filings and furnishing information), 402 (regarding establishment of plan); *see also* 29 C.F.R. § 2520.104-49] The imposition of requirements not contained in the plan has been held to be arbitrary and capricious. [*See* Blau v. Del Monte, 748 F.2d 1348, 1354 (9th Cir. 1984)]

In *Garratt*, the court held that a trier of fact could find that a motivating factor behind the employer's terms was to discriminate in favor of himself and against the employee in order to save the cost of the employee's participation in the plan. Similarly, a trier of fact could find that a motivating factor behind the employer's terms was the employee's assertion of rights under the plan. The case was reversed and remanded.

[Garratt v. Walker, 164 F.3d 1249 (10th Cir. 1998), available at *http://vlex.com/vid/18481528* (visited on Aug. 15, 2012), *reversing and remanding* Garratt v. Walker, 121 F.3d 565, 570 (10th Cir. 1997)]

Q 4:4 May any contributions, plan assets, or funds ever revert to an employer that maintains a SEP?

No. Generally, a SEP arrangement is an employee pension benefit plan within the meaning of ERISA Section 3(2) (see Q 4:1). The assets of an employee pension benefit plan may never inure to the benefit of any employer (but see Q 17:29 regarding correction under the EPCRS). [ERISA § 403(c)]

Q 4:5 Who is the *plan administrator of a SEP*?

The *plan administrator of a SEP* may be any person specifically designated by the terms of the written arrangement under which the SEP is operated. If a plan administrator is not so designated, the plan sponsor (generally the employer or employee organization that establishes or maintains the plan) is the plan administrator. In the case of a plan for which an administrator is not designated and a plan sponsor cannot be identified, such person as the Secretary of Labor may by regulations prescribe is the plan administrator. [DOL Reg. § 2520.104-48(a)]

Q 4:6 What rules apply to the paperless administration and electronic storage of SEP records?

Under the authority of Section 7805 of the Internal Revenue Code (Code), the Secretary of the Treasury has issued rules relating to paperless administration and requirements for electronic storage of records relating to matters under its jurisdiction. For example, Notice 99-1 [1999-2 I.R.B. 8] relates to paperless administration of qualified plans and states: "As a result of developments in electronic technologies, a variety of electronic media (such as e-mail, the Internet, intranet systems, and automated telephone systems) are now available for many plan transactions." The Employee Benefits Security Administration (EBSA), formerly the Pension and Welfare Benefits Administration (PWBA) of the Department of Labor (DOL), has also issued regulations that set forth standards regarding the use of electronic media for any transactions involving plan participants and beneficiaries under Title I of ERISA. [DOL Reg. § 2520.104b-1]

Revenue Procedure 98-25 [1998-1 C.B. 689] specifies the requirements that the Internal Revenue Service (IRS) considers to be essential when a taxpayer's records are maintained within automated data processing systems. The requirements of that revenue procedure apply to employee plans and thus to SEPs.

Revenue Procedure 97-22 [1997-1 C.B. 652] provides guidance to taxpayers maintaining books and records by using an electronic storage system that either images their hard-copy (paper) books and records or transfers their computerized books and records to an electronic storage medium (e.g., an optical disk). The requirements of Revenue Procedure 97-22 also apply to employee plans and thus to SEPs.

The EBSA has issued final rules under Title I of ERISA concerning the disclosure of certain employee benefit plan information through electronic media and standards for the maintenance and retention of employee benefit plan records in electronic form. [DOL Reg. § 2520.104b-1(c); 29 C.F.R. pt. 2520, 67 Fed. Reg. 68, 17263–17276 (2002)] The rules establish a safe harbor pursuant to which all pension plans covered by Title I may satisfy their obligations to furnish summary plan descriptions (SPDs), summaries of material modifications, updated SPDs, and summary annual reports using electronic media. With respect to recordkeeping, the rules provide standards for the use of electronic media, including electronic storage and automatic data processing systems, and for the maintenance and retention of records. It is unclear to what extent the rules would affect SEPs, which are generally subject to special rules (see Qs 4:9–4:17, 4:42).

Alternative Reporting Methods

Q 4:7 Are alternative methods of compliance with ERISA reporting requirements available to SEPs?

Yes. SEPs are generally subject to the reporting requirements of Title I of ERISA that apply to employee pension benefit plans; however, two alternative methods of compliance are available to SEPs. One method applies only to SEPs established using IRS model Form 5305-SEP, Simplified Employee Pension–Individual Retirement Accounts Contribution Agreement (see Qs 4:9–4:11). The other method applies to SEPs established using other documents (see Qs 4:12–4:17). The information provided under both methods is nearly identical. SEP arrangements that do not qualify under either of the alternative methods generally must comply with the reporting requirements of ERISA that apply to employee pension benefit plans. Generally, a SEP IRA or SIMPLE IRA arrangement that satisfies (in operation) either of the alternate methods of compliance is not treated as a Title I plan under ERISA (see Q 4:11).

Accordingly, sponsors of "nonmodel" SEPs that satisfy the limited disclosure requirements of the regulation are relieved from otherwise applicable reporting and disclosure requirements under Title I of ERISA, including the requirements to file annual reports (Form 5500 Series) with the DOL, and to furnish summary plan descriptions and summary annual reports to participants and beneficiaries.

Information compliance request. On April 22, 2011, the EBSA announced that it is soliciting comments "on the proposed extension of the collection of information included" in the alternative method of compliance for certain SEP regulation (ERISA Regulation Section 2520.104-49). The announcement only applies to "nonmodel" SEPs. The information compliance request (ICR) includes four separate disclosure requirements. The ICR will seek to determine if—

1. At the time an employee became eligible to participate in the SEP, the administrator of the SEP furnished the employee in writing specific and general information concerning the SEP (see Qs 4:12–4:13); a statement on rates, transfers, and withdrawals; and a statement on tax treatment (see Qs 4:9, 4:14)
2. Whether the administrator of the SEP furnished participants with information concerning any amendments (see Q 4:16)
3. Whether the administrator notified participants of any employer contributions made to the IRA (see Q 4:10)
4. In the case of a SEP that provides integration with Social Security, whether the administrator provided participants with a statement on Social Security taxes and the integration formula used by the employer.

A nonmodel SEP does not include (1) those SEPs which are created through use of Form 5305-SEP (see Q 4:12), and (2) those SEPs in which the employer limits or influences the employees' choice to IRAs into which employers' contributions will be made and on which participant withdrawals are prohibited (see Q 4:17). No changes are being proposed or made to the regulation at this time. [Proposed Extension of Information Collection Request Submitted for Public Comment and Recommendations; Alternative Method of Compliance for Certain SEPs pursuant to 29 C.F.R. § 2520.104-49, 76 Fed. Reg. 22728 (Apr. 22, 2011)]

Q 4:8 Must an employer provide an IRA disclosure statement to its eligible employees?

No. The IRA disclosure statement is provided to eligible employees by the financial institution, trustee, custodian, or other person that sponsors the IRA(s) into which contributions will be made under the SEP arrangement, not the employer. Still, the employer must provide a description of the disclosure statement and the information that the IRS requires to be given to individuals for whose benefit an IRA is established (see Q 4:14). [DOL Reg. § 2520.104-49(a)(3)]

Note. In 2010, the EBSA issued a final rule addressing fiduciary disclosure requirements of plan and investment-related information, including fee and expense information, in participant-directed individual account plans subject to ERISA. [DOL Reg. § 2550.404a-5, 75 Fed. Reg., 64910–64941 (Oct. 20, 2010)] Although the requirements would apply to nearly all defined contribution plans subject to ERISA, the disclosure requirements do not apply to plans involving IRA accounts or IRA annuities that are part of a SIMPLE or SEP. [DOL Reg. § 2550.404a-5(b)(2), 75 Fed. Reg., 64910, 64937 (Oct. 20, 2010)]

Disclosure Requirements When Using Form 5305-SEP

Q 4:9 What information must be disclosed to each eligible employee under the alternative method of compliance for a SEP established using Form 5305-SEP?

Under the alternative method of compliance applicable to a SEP established using model Form 5305-SEP, the employer must furnish each eligible employee with a copy of that form and a statement to the effect that IRAs other than the IRA(s) into which employer contributions will be made may yield different rates of return and may have different terms concerning, among other things, transfers and withdrawals of funds from the IRA(s). [DOL Reg. § 2520.104-48]

Q 4:10 Must a participant be notified of any contribution made to his or her IRA under a SEP established using Form 5305-SEP?

Yes. A participant in a SEP established using model Form 5305-SEP must receive a written notification from the plan administrator of any contribution made to his or her IRA by either (1) January 31 of the year following the year in which the contribution is made or (2) 30 days after the contribution is made, whichever date is later. (See Appendix C.) [DOL Reg. § 2520.104-48(c)] An employer's failure to provide the contribution notification (annual statement) may subject the employer to a $50 penalty per failure, unless the failure is due to reasonable cause. This requirement is satisfied if the information is contained on the employee's Form W-2 for the calendar year for which the contribution is made [I.R.C. § 408(l); Prop. Treas. Reg. § 1.408-9(b)]

Q 4:11 Must an employer that selects, recommends, or influences the selection of IRAs by its employees file Form 5500 for a SEP established using Form 5305-SEP?

Possibly. An employer maintaining a SEP or SARSEP arrangement does not have to file Form 5500, Annual Return—Report for Employee Benefit Plans, if the employer conforms to an alternative method of compliance. Under Title I of ERISA, however, relief from the annual reporting requirements is not generally available to an employer that selects, recommends, or in any other way influences employees to choose an IRA or type of IRA "subject to restrictions on a participant's ability to withdraw funds (other than restrictions imposed by the Code that apply to all IRAs)." [DOL Reg. § 2520.104-48(c)]

An exception is made for a SEP created with Form 5305-SEP if the plan administrator gives each employee a clear explanation of any such restrictions and a statement to the effect that other IRAs, into which rollovers or *employee* contributions may be made, may not be subject to such restrictions. The statement must be in writing and must be given at the time the employee becomes eligible to participate in the SEP. [DOL Reg. § 2520.104-49(a)(3)(i)]

It should be noted that an employer is permitted to select the IRA that an employee must establish.

Disclosure Requirements When Not Using Form 5305-SEP

Q 4:12 What general information must be given to eligible employees under the alternative method of compliance for a SEP not established using model Form 5305-SEP?

ERISA Section 110 provides for an alternative method of complying with the reporting and disclosure requirements set forth in Part 1 of Title I of ERISA for IRS-approved SEP arrangements not established by use of model Form 5305-SEP. [Prop. Treas. Reg. § 1.408-6; DOL Reg. § 2520.104-49] When a SEP is established without using the model IRS form, eligible employees should be provided with general information concerning SEP arrangements and IRAs, including a clear written explanation of the following:

- What a SEP arrangement is and how it operates
- The statutory provisions prohibiting discrimination in favor of highly compensated employees
- A participant's right to receive contributions under a SEP and the allowable sources of contributions to a SEP
- The statutory limits on contributions to SEP IRAs
- The consequences of excess contributions to a SEP IRA and how to avoid such contributions
- A participant's rights with respect to contributions made to a SEP IRA
- How a participant must treat contributions to a SEP IRA for tax purposes
- The statutory provisions concerning withdrawal of funds from a SEP IRA and the consequences of a premature withdrawal
- A participant's ability to roll over or transfer funds from one SEP IRA to another and how such a rollover or transfer may be effected without causing adverse tax consequences

[DOL Reg. § 2520.104-49(a)(2)]

Q 4:13 What specific information must be furnished to eligible employees under the alternative method of compliance for a SEP not established using model Form 5305-SEP?

At the time an employee becomes eligible to participate in a SEP arrangement not established using model Form 5305-SEP (whether at the initial creation of the arrangement or thereafter), the plan administrator must furnish the employee, in writing, with the following:

- The requirements for employee participation in the SEP arrangement,
- The formula to be used to allocate employer contributions made under the SEP arrangement to each participant's IRA, and
- The name or title of the individual designated by the employer to provide additional information to participants concerning the SEP arrangement

These requirements may be met by giving the eligible employee a copy of the SEP agreement, provided it is written in a manner that may be understood by the average plan participant. [DOL Reg. § 2520.104-49(a)(1)] (See Appendix C.) Failure to timely furnish this disclosure requirement may subject the employer to a $50 penalty per failure, unless the failure is due to reasonable cause. [I.R.C. § 6693(a); Prop. Treas. Reg. § 1.408-9]

Q 4:14 What statements must be provided to each eligible employee under the alternative method of compliance for a SEP not established using model Form 5305-SEP?

An employer must provide each eligible employee under a SEP not established using model Form 5305-SEP with a written statement to the effect that

1. IRAs other than the IRA(s) into which employer contributions will be made under the SEP arrangement may provide different rates of return and may have different terms concerning, among other things, transfers and withdrawals of funds;
2. In the event a participant is entitled to make a contribution or rollover to an IRA, it may be made to an IRA other than the one into which employer contributions under the SEP arrangement are to be made; and
3. Depending on the terms of the IRA into which employer contributions are made, a participant may be able to make rollovers or transfers of funds from that IRA to another IRA.

[DOL Reg. § 2520.104-49(a)(3)]

Q 4:15 Must an employee be notified of any contribution made to his or her IRA under a SEP not established using Form 5305-SEP?

Yes. A participant in a SEP not established using model Form 5305-SEP must receive a written notification from the plan administrator of any contribution made to his or her IRA by the later of either (1) January 31 of the year following the year for which the contribution is made or (2) 30 days after the contribution is made. [DOL Reg. § 2520.104-49(a)(5)] An employer's failure to provide the contribution notification (annual statement) may subject the employer to a $50 penalty per failure, unless the failure is due to reasonable cause. This requirement is satisfied if the information is contained on the employee's Form W-2 for the calendar year for which the contribution is made [I.R.C. § 408(l); Prop. Treas. Reg. § 1.408-9(b)]

Q 4:16 Must a participant in a SEP not established using Form 5305-SEP be notified of any amendments to the SEP?

Yes. The plan administrator (usually the employer establishing or maintaining the SEP) must furnish each participant in a SEP not established using model Form 5305-SEP with a copy of any amendments and a clear written explanation of their effects within 30 days of their effective date. [DOL Reg. § 2520.104-49(a)(5)]

Q 4:17 May an employer that selects, recommends, or influences the selection of IRAs by its employees for a SEP not established using Form 5305-SEP still qualify for alternative compliance?

Yes. The alternative compliance method (see Q 4:9) is not available to an employer that selects, recommends, or in any other way influences employees to choose a particular IRA or type of IRA subject to restrictions that prohibit the withdrawal of funds for any period of time (other than restrictions imposed by the Code that apply to all IRAs). [DOL Reg. § 2520.104-48(c)] Nonetheless, if an employer that maintains a SEP that was not established using model Form 5305-SEP selects the IRAs into which employer contributions will be made and those IRAs make available to participants an option that imposes a restriction on withdrawals, the plan administrator for the SEP will not be precluded from using the alternative method of compliance under DOL Regulations Section 2520.104-49, provided that

1. Other meaningful investment options that do not restrict withdrawals are available to participants;
2. The employer does not select, recommend, or otherwise influence any participant's choice of an available investment option under the IRAs; and
3. All other conditions of the regulation are satisfied.

[DOL Reg. §§ 2520.104-48(c), 2520.104-49(a)(1)(iv); DOL Adv. Op. 82-3A; Form 5305A-SEP, Instructions for the Employer Completing the Agreement, at 2; Form 5305-SEP, Instructions to the Employer Completing the Agreement, at 1]

Example. The Five Cents Savings Bank (the Bank) establishes a SEP for its employees without using model Form 5305-SEP. The terms of the SEP require all eligible employees to establish their IRAs with the Bank. The plan contains no restriction on withdrawals, and the Bank has added no withdrawal restriction. Investments under the plan are at the direction of the participant and not under the control of any other person. Through its IRAs, the Bank offers various investment options to participants, including regular savings, term certificates, and "special notice accounts." Neither the regular savings nor the term certificates impose any restriction on withdrawals by the participant; however, the special notice accounts do not allow withdrawal of funds held on deposit for less than 90 days. The Bank is not precluded from using the alternative method of compliance for its SEP, because other meaningful investment options that do not restrict withdrawals are available to participants; the employer does not select, recommend, or otherwise influence any participant's choice of an available investment option under the IRAs; and all other conditions of the regulation are satisfied. (See Appendix J.)

It should be noted that an employer may select the IRA that an employee must establish. Unlike the alternative method of compliance for a SEP established using model Form 5305-SEP (see Qs 4:9–4:11), the alternative method of compliance for a SEP not created with a model form does not apply if the IRA required to be established by employees prohibits withdrawals for any length of time.

Prohibited Transactions and Related Definitions

Q 4:18 What is a *plan* for purposes of the prohibited transaction rules?

For purposes of the prohibited transaction rules, the term *plan* means (1) a trust described in Code Section 401(a) that forms a part of a plan, or a plan described in Code Section 403(a) exempt from tax under Code Section 501(a), and (2) an IRA. [I.R.C. § 4975(e)(1); ERISA § 3]

Q 4:19 Is a SEP or a SEP IRA subject to the prohibited transaction provisions of the Code?

Yes. Notwithstanding whether an IRA is a plan within the meaning of Title I of ERISA, the prohibited transaction provisions of Code Section 4975 are applicable to transactions by a SEP and related SEP IRAs (see Qs 4:20–4:31, 5:42–5:46).

Q 4:20 What is a *prohibited transaction*?

Under ERISA, the prohibited transaction rules apply to employer-sponsored retirement plans and to welfare benefit plans. Under the Code, the prohibited transaction rules apply to qualified retirement plans and qualified retirement annuities, as well as to individual retirement accounts and annuities (IRAs), SEPs, SARSEPs, and SIMPLE IRA. The prohibited transaction rules also apply to health savings accounts (HSAs), Archer medical savings accounts (MSAs), and Coverdell education savings accounts. [I.R.C. § 4975(e)(1)(A)–I.R.C. § 4975(e)(1)(G)]

ERISA and the Code prohibit certain transactions between an employer-sponsored retirement plan and a disqualified person (see Q 4:23), referred to as a "party in interest" under ERISA. [ERISA § 406; I.R.C. § 4975] Absent an exemption, a *prohibited transaction* includes any direct or indirect

- Sale, exchange, or lease of any property between a plan and a disqualified person (see Q 4:23);
- Loan of money or other extension of credit between a plan and a disqualified person;
- Provision of goods, services, or facilities between a plan and a disqualified person;

- Transfer to, or use by or for the benefit of, a disqualified person of the income or assets of a plan;
- Act by a disqualified person who is a fiduciary whereby he or she deals with the income or assets of a plan in his or her own interest or for his or her own account; or
- Receipt of any consideration for his or her own personal account by any disqualified person who is a fiduciary from any party dealing with the plan in connection with a transaction involving the income or assets of the plan.

[I.R.C. § 4975(c); ERISA § 406; *see* DOL Interpretive Bull. 94-3, 59 Fed. Reg. 66735 (1994) (in-kind contributions to satisfy statutory or contractual funding obligations); Marshall v. Snyder, 430 F. Supp. 1224 (E.D.N.Y. 1977), *aff'd in part and remanded in part,* 572 F.2d 894 (2d Cir. 1978) (furnishing of goods, services, or facilities); Leigh v. Engle, 727 F.2d 113 (7th Cir. 1984) (self-dealing); New York State Teamsters Council Health & Hosp. Fund v. Estate of De Perno, 816 F. Supp. 138 (N.D.N.Y. 1993), *aff'd in part and remanded,* 18 F.3d 179 (2d Cir. 1994) (self-dealing, financial loss to trust fund not necessary); *see also* DOL Adv. Ops. 86-01A, 88-03A, 89-089A, 93-06A (direct expenses of salary and related cost of employees that work on plans)]

Example 1. Damian Corporation established a SEP for its 750 employees and makes contributions into a group (employer) IRA trust under Code Section 408(c). Damian, a fiduciary, retains his daughter Miriam to provide much-needed administrative services to the plan's trust for a fee. Miriam's provision of services to the trust is a prohibited transaction. The prohibited transaction may, however, be exempt from the excise tax if it meets certain conditions (see Qs 4:21–4:22). As a fiduciary, Damian's action causing the plan to pay a fee to his daughter is a separate prohibited transaction, which would not be exempt. [I.R.C. § 4975(d)(2); I.R.M. 4.72.11.3.5, Fiduciary Self-Dealing; *see* David A. Pratt, "Focus on Prohibited Transactions—Part I," 10 *J. Pension Ben.* 2 (Winter 2003), which outlines transactions that are prohibited by ERISA and the transactions that are exempt from ERISA prohibitions]

Note. The penalty for initial violations is 15 percent of the amount involved for prohibited transactions occurring after August 5, 1997. If the transaction is not corrected, there is a second-tier excise tax of 100 percent of the amount involved. [I.R.C. § 4975(a); SBJPA § 1453(a); TRA '97 § 1074(a); Ralf Zacky v. Commissioner, T.C. Memo 2004-130 (May 27, 2004), sole shareholder liable for the first- and second-tier I.R.C. § 4975 excise tax on prohibited loan transactions]

Example 2. Biggs Bank is the trustee of an IRA. Biggs extends a line of credit to the IRA. The line of credit is a prohibited transaction. Biggs, but not the owner of the IRA, is subject to the prohibited transaction tax. Because the account ceases to be treated as an IRA, the owner is not subject to the prohibited transaction tax (see Q 1:22).

Example 3. Moola Bank is the trustee of an IRA. The account beneficiary accesses the funds in the IRA through a debit card. In addition, Moola extends a line of credit to the account beneficiary, which is not secured by the account beneficiary's IRA, and amounts in the IRA cannot be used to repay the line of credit. The line of credit is not a prohibited transaction.

Pledging IRA as security for a loan. A prohibited transaction occurs when an account beneficiary pledges his or her IRA as security for a loan. Any direct or indirect extension of credit between the account beneficiary and his or her IRA is a prohibited transaction (see Q 1:22).

Example 4. Paolo is an account beneficiary of an IRA. Marine Bank is the trustee of the IRA. Marine extends to Paolo a line of credit secured by the IRA. The pledge securing the line of credit is a prohibited transaction (see Q 1:22).

Rollovers as business startups (ROBS). On October 1, 2008, the IRS released initial guidelines on the acceptability of arrangements referred to in the guidelines as Rollovers as Business Startups, or ROBS. These arrangements provide a business owner with the apparent ability to convert retirement accounts into business capital by using the rollover process. Though not stating that these arrangements are noncompliant per se, the guidelines warn that the IRS will scrutinize these transactions very carefully.

By creating a new corporation that sponsors a new retirement plan, the individual can roll over proceeds from a prior employer's retirement account (such as an IRA) into the new plan. Then, through an exchange of corporate stock for the rollover money, the owner receives instant business capital. The plan owns all the stock, for the benefit of the individual, and the business receives needed cash. The distribution restrictions normally associated with taking money out of a retirement plan are circumvented, and the capital, which includes previously untaxed income, is not taxed at this time. Other than the risk of gambling one's retirement savings on business success, this transaction appears to be too good to be true.

The IRS guidance states that ROBS plans are questionable in "that they may solely benefit one individual's exchange of tax-deferred assets for currently available funds. This stock exchange occurs inside what should otherwise be a retirement plan for the benefit of employees. Yet, from our review, few, if any, employees other than the individual who initiates the transaction will actually benefit from the exchange. Furthermore, these arrangements are predicated on stock valuations that are frequently superficial and are administered more as a corporate funding vehicle than a bona fide employee benefit program." Regardless of whether this is true, the IRS intends "to scrutinize ROBS arrangements" because they "may endanger the qualified status of otherwise tax-qualified employee plans and may be prohibited transactions, requiring complete undoing of the transaction, and imposition of excise taxes."

If other employees are in the plan, the IRS will likely assert that the plan is discriminatory in operation. On the other hand, a plan without employees cannot be discriminatory. Although the IRS's position may be flawed, it will turn any such transaction inside out—and likely find something wrong with the plan document, how it is being administered, or worse yet, find discrimination in operation. [*See also*, Kaleda, David C., *Do You Really Want to Do That? IRAs and the Prohibited Transaction Provisions*, 19 The Investment Lawyer 5 (May 2012)]

Exemptions for Investment Advice

Q 4:21 Is the provision of investment advice by a fiduciary a prohibited transaction?

It depends. The prohibited transaction provisions of ERISA and the Code prohibit an investment advice fiduciary from using the authority, control, or responsibility that makes it a fiduciary to cause itself, or a party in which it has an interest that may affect its best judgment as a fiduciary, to receive additional fees. As a result, in the absence of a statutory or administrative exemption, fiduciaries are prohibited from rendering investment advice to plan participants regarding investments that result in the payment of additional advisory or other fees to the fiduciaries or their affiliates. The Pension Protection Act of 2006 (PPA) [Pub. L. No. 109-280, 120 Stat. 780] adds a new category of prohibited transaction exemption—under ERISA Section 408(b)(14) and Code Section 4975(d)—applicable to the provision of investment advice through an "eligible investment advice arrangement" to beneficiaries of HSA accounts who direct the investment of their accounts under the plan. A statutory exemption permits investment advice to be given either on a level-fee basis or via a computer model certified as unbiased by a fiduciary adviser. If the requirements of the exemption are met, the restrictions under ERISA Sections 406(a) and (b), relating to certain prohibited transactions, and the sanctions resulting from the application of the prohibited transaction rules under Code Sections 4975(c)(1)(A) through (F), do not apply to those transactions. [*See* DOL Reg. § 2550.408(g)-1, issued Oct. 25, 2011, and effective on Dec. 27, 2011.] Previously, to avoid conflicts of interest, advisors were prohibited from recommending investments if they were paid for other services. To provide investment advice, providers were required to hire an independent advisor. Under the final regulations and the exemption, for example, the distributor of a mutual fund family can now offer investments (without using an independent advisor) using an "eligible investment advice arrangement" to plan participants as long as they avoid conflicts of interest by meeting one of two conditions:

- Any fee the advisor receives cannot vary based on the investments it recommends. Thus, it cannot get more money by promoting ("pushing") one type of fund over another.
- The advice must be provided through a computer model that has been certified as unbiased by an independent expert.

[DOL Reg. § 2550.408(g)-1(b), 76 Fed. Reg. 66136 (Oct. 25, 2011)]

If the conditions for the exemption are satisfied, the person who develops the computer model, or markets the investment advice program or computer model, is treated as the fiduciary of the plan by reason of the provision of investment advice. The statutory exemption limiting fiduciary status does not permit an advisor to actually render investment advice to participants or beneficiaries. Furthermore, the regulations do not affect the proposed regulations on the definition of fiduciary investment advice, which the DOL recently announced that it will re-propose.

Investment advice is given under an eligible investment advice if it is provided under an arrangement that is either a fee-leveling arrangement or a computer model arrangement. Under a fee-leveling arrangement, any fees received by the investment advisor do not vary based on the investment option selected. Under a computer model arrangement, a computer model certified by an independent third party is used under an investment advice program. Specific regulatory requirements apply to fee-leveling arrangements and computer model arrangements.

In addition to satisfying the regulatory requirements applicable to a fee-leveling arrangement or a computer model arrangement, all eligible investment advice arrangements must meet certain other requirements. An arrangement must be authorized by a plan fiduciary and annually audited by an independent auditor. In addition, an arrangement must be disclosed to participants in a comprehensive written notification that is understandable by the average plan participant.

Historical Note. Prior to the PPA, the prohibited transaction rules generally prohibited any provision of investment advice where the adviser could benefit based on the advice given. The only exception to this rule was for class and individual exemptions granted by the DOL, where the DOL had specifically determined that an advice arrangement had enough safeguards in place to remove or substantially diminish any real or potential conflict, so that the use of such arrangement was in the best interests of the participants. Prior to the PPA, it was clear that certain advice arrangements did not involve any conflict of interest and thus did not violate the prohibited transaction rules. For example, many advice arrangements relied on a DOL Advisory Opinion generally referred to as "SunAmerica Opinion." [DOL Adv. Op. 2001-09A (Dec. 14, 2001)] Under the SunAmerica Opinion, generally a plan adviser, which may be a financial institution, arranges for advice to be given to participants based solely on a computer model designed and exclusively controlled by an independent third party. The advisory opinion articulates objective rule for determining whether the third party is truly independent. Because all advice is provided pursuant to an independently designed computer model, and because that advice cannot be modified by the plan adviser, the advice is not conflicted. Another example of non-conflicted advice is advice given by an adviser that receives the same compensation regardless of which investment option is chosen (the "pre-PPA level fee rule"). For example, if advice is given by an employee of a financial institution, the investment option chosen cannot affect the compensation received by the employee, the financial institution, or any affiliate of the financial institution. As discussed above, the DOL took an additional step in the 2009 class exemption (since withdrawn). Under the "class exemption level-fee rule," investment advice to a participant is permitted as long as the investment options chosen cannot affect the compensation of the adviser giving the advice. The compensation of the adviser's employer or such employer's affiliate may, however, vary based on the investment option chosen (and thus, possibly conflicted).

Exemption for investment advice fiduciaries. In 2011, EBSA issued guidance in the form of an Advisory Opinion concerning the application of Prohibited Transaction Class Exemption 86-128, which permits a plan fiduciary (or affiliate) to engage in securities transactions for a fee as an agent on behalf of a plan. [PTE 86-128, 51 Fed. Reg. 41686 (Nov. 18, 1986), amended at 67 Fed. Reg. 64137 (Oct. 17, 2002); EBSA Adv. Op. 2011-08A (June 21, 2011), available at *http://www.dol.gov/ebsa/regs/aos/ao2011-08a.html* (visited on Aug. 25, 2012)]

The class exemption [PTE 86-128] provides that the prohibited transaction provisions of ERISA Section 406(b) do not apply to:

1. A plan fiduciary using its authority to cause a plan to pay a fee for effecting or executing securities transactions to that person as agent for the plan, to the extent that such transactions are not excessive in either amount or frequency;
2. A plan fiduciary acting as the agent in an agency cross transaction for both the plan and one or more other parties to the transaction; and
3. The receipt by a plan fiduciary of reasonable compensation for effecting or executing an agency cross transaction to which a plan is a party from one or more other parties to the transaction.

In the view of EBSA, PTE 86-128 provides relief for covered transactions engaged in by any person who meets the definition of fiduciary as that term is defined in ERISA Section 3(21)(A), including a person who is a fiduciary solely by reason of rendering investment advice. Further, a fiduciary or an affiliate who receives a fee for executing securities transactions carried out in accordance with the fiduciary's investment advice would be using its authority as a fiduciary to cause the plan to pay a fee within the meaning of the prohibited transaction exemption.

Caution. On October 22, 2010, the EBSA issued a proposed regulation (the "2010 proposed regulation") that would have turned many consultants, advisors, and appraisers into ERISA fiduciaries. [Prop. DOL Reg. § 2510.3-21(c), since withdrawn, 75 Fed. Reg. 65263, 65264 (Oct. 22, 2010)] The withdrawn proposed regulation would have given a broader and clearer understanding of the circumstances that will cause persons providing investment advice to be subject to ERISA's fiduciary standards. The DOL proposed that the changes to the fiduciary standards set out in the proposed regulations would take effect on April 20, 2011. However, in the wake of considerable criticism of the proposed regulation, the DOL has indicated an intention to re-propose and expand upon its rule on the definition of fiduciary in 2012. [*See* EBSA News Rel. Number 11-1382-NAT (Sept. 19, 2011)]

Exemption for Transactions with Service Providers

The PPA offers relief in that a transaction between a plan and a party in interest (e.g., service provider), who is not a fiduciary, is not a prohibited transaction (i.e., sale, exchange, lease, loan, or use of plan assets) under ERISA Section 406 so long as the plan receives no less than adequate consideration, or pays no more than adequate consideration, for the transaction (see Qs 4:18, 4:19, 4:22–4:31). [I.R.C. § 4975(d)(20); ERISA §§ 406(a)(1)(A), (B) and (D); 408(b)(17); *see* PPA § 611]

Other Prohibited Transaction Exemptions

The PPA also added exemptions from the prohibited transaction rules for several types of transactions.

- *Block trades.* Additional relief is provided for "block trades" (any trade of at least 10,000 shares or a fair market value of at least $200,000) between a plan and a disqualified person, which will be allocated among two or more client accounts of a fiduciary. At the time of the transaction, the interest of the plan (together with the interests of any other plans maintained by the same plan sponsor) may not exceed 10 percent of the aggregate size of the block trade. [ERISA § 408(b)(15); I.R.C. § 4975(f)(9); PPA § 611(a)]
- *Electronic communication networks.* An exemption is provided for certain transactions on electronic communication networks. [ERISA § 408(b)(16); I.R.C. § 4975(d)(18); PPA § 611(c)]
- *Foreign exchange transactions.* An exemption is provided for certain foreign exchange transactions. [ERISA § 408(b)(18); I.R.C. § 4975(d)(21); PPA § 611(e)]
- *Cross-trading.* An exemption for certain cross-trading transactions that allows cross-trades between accounts managed by the same investment manager is provided. [PPA § 611(g); ERISA § 408(b)(19); I.R.C. § 4975(d)(22); DOL Reg. § 2550.408b-19, 73 Fed. Reg. 58, 450 (Oct. 7, 2008)]
- *Special correction period.* A prohibited transaction involving securities or commodities would be exempt if the correction is completed within 14 days after the fiduciary discovers (or should have discovered) that the transaction was prohibited. This prohibited transaction exemption does not apply to transactions involving employer securities. It also does not apply if, at the time of the transaction, the fiduciary or other party in interest (or any person knowingly participating in the transaction) knew (or should have known) that the transaction was prohibited. [PPA § 612]
- *Temporary Relief for Owners Entering Into Certain Agreements with Brokers and Financial Institutions.* In 2011, the IRS announced temporary relief to IRA owners who pledged other assets as security for their IRAs, or

who agreed to indemnify the IRA custodian for losses in excess of the assets in their IRAs. [*See* I.R.S. Ann. 2011-81 (2011-52 I.R.B. 1052) granting temporary relief from the holdings in EBSA Adv. Op. 2011-09A (Oct. 20, 2011), available at *http://www.dol.gov/ebsa/regs/aos/ao2011-09a.html* (visited on Aug. 1, 2012) and in EBSA Adv. Op. 2009-3A (Oct. 27, 2009), available at *http://www.dol.gov/ebsa/regs/aos/ao2009-03a.html* (visited on Aug. 25, 2012)] Although the DOL is considering further action and the possibility of issuing a class exemption, the temporary relief is in effect pending further action by the DOL and the IRS. Under the temporary relief, entering into certain indemnification agreements or granting certain security interests would not be treated as an "impermissible extension of credit," which would otherwise be a prohibited transaction and the IRA would no longer be treated as an IRA and cease to exist.

Q 4:22 May the prohibited transaction rules be waived?

Yes. The Secretary of the Treasury has established a procedure under which a conditional or unconditional exemption from all or part of the prohibited transaction rules may be granted to any disqualified person or transaction or to any class of disqualified persons or transactions. The procedures were updated in 2011 to clarify and consolidate the DOL's exemption procedures governing the filing and processing of applications for administrative exemptions from the prohibited transaction provisions of ERISA. The final rule applies to all exemption procedures filed after December 26, 2011. [*See* Prohibited Transaction Exemption Procedures, Employee Benefit Plans (RIN 1210-AB49), 76 Fed. Reg. 208, 66637 (Oct. 27, 2011), codified at DOL Reg. §§ 2570.30–2570.52.] The Secretary of Labor generally may not grant an exemption unless he or she finds that such an exemption is

1. Administratively feasible,
2. In the interests of the plan and its participants and beneficiaries, and
3. Protective of the rights of participants and beneficiaries of the plan.

[I.R.C. § 4975(c)(2)] The authority of the Secretary of the Treasury to issue rulings under Code Section 4975 has been transferred, with certain exceptions, to the Secretary of Labor. [Presidential Reorg. Plan No. 4 of 1978, § 102, 43 Fed. Reg. 47713 (Oct. 17, 1978)] This transfer of jurisdiction clarified the Reorganization Plan No. 4 of 1978 and was accomplished in meetings held between the two agencies on Aug. 4, 1987, which were memorialized by letter dated Oct. 6, 1987, from the Assistant Commissioner (Employee Plans and Exempt Organizations) to the DOL.

Although the IRS has the final authority to determine if an IRA is disqualified under Code Section 408(e)(2), the DOL has the authority to issue waivers that are binding under ERISA Section 408 and Code Section 4975. In the Field Service Advice publication, the IRS explained that authority to define prohibited transactions has been transferred to the DOL, although the IRS retains enforcement authority along with DOL. [F.S.A. 1999-524]

Q 4:23 Who is a *disqualified person* under the Code, and who is a *party in interest* under ERISA?

For purposes of the Code, the term *disqualified person* refers to any of the following:

1. A fiduciary (see Q 4:24);
2. A person providing services to a plan;
3. An employer with any employees who are covered by a plan;
4. An employee organization with any members who are covered by a plan;
5. An owner, direct or indirect, of 50 percent or more of the combined voting power of all classes of stock entitled to vote or the total value of shares of all classes of stock of a corporation, the capital interest or the profits interest of a partnership, or the beneficial interest of a trust or unincorporated enterprise that is an employer or an employee organization described in item 3 or 4;
6. A member of the family (spouse, ancestor, lineal descendant, or any spouse of a lineal descendant) of a person described in item 1, 2, 3, or 5;
7. A corporation, partnership, or trust or estate of which (or in which) 50 percent or more of the combined voting power of all classes of stock entitled to vote or the total value of shares of all classes of stock of such corporation, the capital interest or profits interest of such partnership, or the beneficial interest of such trust or estate is owned directly or indirectly or held by a person described in item 1, 2, 3, 4, or 5;
8. An officer or director (or an individual having powers or responsibilities similar to those of an officer or a director), a 10 percent or more shareholder, or a highly compensated employee (earning 10 percent or more of the yearly wages of an employer) of a person described in item 3, 4, 5, or 7; or
9. A 10 percent or more (in capital or profits) partner or joint venturer of a person described in item 3, 4, 5, or 7.

Note. ERISA prohibits certain transactions between a plan and a party in interest. Under the Code, the term *disqualified person* is used instead of *party in interest*, and it is defined slightly differently.

[I.R.C. § 4975(e)(2)]

For purposes of ERISA, the term *party in interest* refers to the following:

1. Any fiduciary (including, but not limited to, any administrator, officer, trustee, or custodian), counsel, or employee of an employee benefit plan;
2. A person providing services to a plan; [*see* Harris Trust & Sav. Bank v. Solomon Smith Barney, 530 U.S. 238 (2000) (broker-dealer providing nondiscretionary equity trades to plan automatically classified as party in interest)]
3. An employer with any employees who are covered by a plan;
4. An employee organization with any members who are covered by a plan;

5. An owner, direct or indirect, of 50 percent or more of the combined voting power of all classes of stock entitled to vote or the total value of shares of all classes of stock of a corporation, the capital interest or the profits interest of a partnership, or the beneficial interest of a trust or unincorporated enterprise that is an employer or an employee organization described in item 3 or 4;
6. A relative (spouse, ancestor, lineal descendant, or any spouse of a lineal descendant) of any person described in item 1, 2, 3, or 5;
7. A corporation, partnership, or trust or estate of which (or in which) 50 percent or more of the combined voting power of all classes of stock entitled to vote or the total value of shares of all classes of stock of such corporation, the capital interest or profits interest of such partnership, or the beneficial interest of such trust or estate is owned directly or indirectly or held by persons described in item 1, 2, 3, 4, or 5;
8. An employee, an officer or director (or an individual having powers or responsibilities similar to those of an officer or a director), a 10 percent or more shareholder, or a highly compensated employee (earning 10 percent or more of the yearly wages of an employer) of a person described in item 2, 3, 4, or 5; or
9. A 10 percent or more (in capital or profits) partner or joint venturer of a person described in item 2, 3, 4, 5, or 7.

[ERISA § 3(14); *see also* F.S.A. 200128011 (July 13, 2001); Ltr. Rul. 200917030 (May 24, 2009); Treas. Reg. § 1.6011-4-(d)]

Example 1. George is the general partner and owner of a 6.5 percent interest in an investment club partnership formed by various family members. The partnership is managed by an outside brokerage firm, and George receives no compensation. George instructs his IRA trustee to purchase an interest in the partnership. Is this a prohibited transaction? No. Because of George's status in the partnership and his control over the investment of his assets, George is a disqualified person, but because he owned less than a 10 percent interest in the partnership, the partnership itself is not a disqualified person. Therefore, transactions between it and the partnership would not be prohibited. [DOL Op. Ltr. 2000-10A (July 27, 2000)]

Caution. In the preceding example, George does not and will not receive any compensation from the partnership and will not receive any compensation by virtue of the IRA's investment in the partnership. However, if an IRA fiduciary causes the IRA to enter into a transaction where, by the terms or nature of that transaction, a conflict of interest between the IRA and the fiduciary (or persons in which the fiduciary has an interest) exists or will arise in the future, that transaction may violate either Code Sections 4975(c)(1)(D) or (E). The DOL stated:

> Moreover, the fiduciary must not rely upon and cannot be otherwise dependent upon the participation of the IRA in order for the fiduciary (or persons in which the fiduciary has an interest) to undertake or to continue his or her share of the investment. Furthermore, even if at its

inception the transaction did not involve a violation, if a divergence of interests develops between the IRA and the fiduciary (or persons in which the fiduciary has an interest), the fiduciary must take steps to eliminate the conflict of interest in order to avoid engaging in a prohibited transaction.

Nonetheless, a violation of Code Section 4975(c)(1)(D) or (E) will not occur merely because the fiduciary derives some incidental benefit from a transaction involving IRA assets. [DOL Op. Ltr. 2000-10A (July 27, 2000)]

Example 2. Greta established an IRA. She instructs her IRA custodian to execute a subscription agreement to purchase newly issued shares of a corporation that she recently formed. The IRA became the sole shareholder of the corporation of which Greta was and remains the director. The payment of dividends by the corporation to the IRA did not constitute a prohibited transaction. The corporation is not a disqualified person. A corporation without shares or shareholders does not fit the definition of a disqualified person under Code Section 4975(e)(2)(G). The newly issued shares were not owned by anyone at the time of sale; thus, their sale to the IRA was not a sale or exchange of property between the plan (IRA) and a disqualified person [I.R.C. § 4975(c)(1)(A)] The dividends did not become income of the IRA until unqualifiedly made subject to the demand of the IRA; thus, there was no use of the IRA assets for the benefit of a disqualified person. [I.R.C. § 4975(c)(1)(D); Treas. Reg. § 1.301-1(b); Swanson v. Commissioner, 106 T.C. 76 (1996); *see also* F.S.A. 1994-524, conceding *Swanson*]

Note. The *Swanson* court addressed the actions of arranging for IRA ownership of stock and for the subsequent payment of dividends by the corporation to the IRA by stating: "[C]onsidered together, [the actions] did not constitute an act whereby a fiduciary directly or indirectly 'deals with income or assets of a plan in his own interest or for his own account,'" within the meaning of Code Section 4975(c)(1)(E). The court noted that the Commissioner had not alleged that the taxpayer had ever dealt with the corpus of the IRA for his own benefit, but stated that the "receipt by a disqualified person of any benefit to which he may be entitled as a participant or beneficiary in the plan, so long as the benefit is computed and paid on a basis which is consistent with the terms of the plan as applied to all other participants and beneficiaries" does not violate Code Section 4975(c). [*See* exception at I.R.C. § 4975(d)(9)]

In Field Service Advice 200128011, a father owned the majority of the shares of a U.S. corporation. His three children owned the remaining shares in equal amounts. The father and each of the children owned separate IRAs. Each acquired a 25 percent interest in a new foreign sales corporation (FSC). The U.S. corporation then entered into service and commission agreements with the FSC: the FSC made cash distributions to the IRAs out of earnings and profits from foreign trade income from exports of the U.S. corporation. The IRS concluded that neither the original issuance of the stock of the FSC to the IRAs nor the payment of dividends is a prohibited transaction under Code Section 4975(c)(1)(D). In light of *Swanson v. Commissioner* [106 T.C. 76 (1996)], the

IRS determined that the IRAs' ownership of FSC stock was not considered to be a prohibited transaction under Code Section 4975(c)(1)(E). However, the father's arrangement to have 75 percent of the FSC owned by his children, and for the FSC to earn profits under agreements with the U.S. corporation, results in a taxable gift to the children because the father did not receive any consideration for the arrangement. The IRS stated that the value of the gift is the difference between the children's combined beneficial interest in the amount of earnings and profits realized by the FSC and distributed to the IRAs, and the children's combined interest in the profits the U.S. corporation would have earned on the sales had the corporation not used the FSC. [F.S.A. 200128011, July 13, 2001]

Example 3. Herb and Marilyn established several tiered corporations in a series of complex transactions that were ultimately owned by a domestic international sales corporation (DISC) owned, in part, by their Roth IRAs. Each of the Roth IRAs acquired its interest in the DISC by subscribing to 25 percent of previously unissued stock of a corporation that elected to be treated as a DISC. The corporations were active business entities and paid taxes on their profits. Annual dividend payments (up to $100,000) were made to the Roth IRA. The IRS alleged that the transactions were prohibited transactions and that the dividend payment to the Roth IRA was an excess contributions. The Tax Court held that there was no prohibited transaction in the creation of the business or in the payment of the dividend to the Roth IRA. [Hellweg v. Commissioner, T.C. Memo 2011-58 (Mar. 9, 2011); *see also* Ohsman v. Commissioner, T.C. Memo. 2011-98 (May 3, 2011); and Ice, "When Can An IRA or Qualified Plan Invest in a Closely Held Business?," available at *http://www.leimbergservices.com/all/lisiice_111010.html* (visited on Aug. 15, 2012)]

Q 4:24 Who is a *fiduciary* for purposes of ERISA?

The term *fiduciary* refers to any person who

1. Exercises any discretionary authority or discretionary control respecting management of a plan or exercises any authority or control respecting management or disposition of its assets;
2. Renders investment advice for a fee or other compensation, direct or indirect, with respect to any monies or other property of a plan (see Q 4:30), or has any authority or responsibility to do so; or
3. Has any discretionary authority or discretionary responsibility in the administration of a plan.

[ERISA § 3(21)]

Because the administration of a plan (including a SEP arrangement) is the responsibility of the plan administrator, under ERISA the plan administrator is a fiduciary and thus is subject to the fiduciary duties imposed by ERISA.

Note. A person that is designated by a named fiduciary to carry out fiduciary responsibilities (other than trustee responsibilities under the plan) is treated as a fiduciary (see Q 4:30).

Accountants, attorneys, actuaries, insurance agents, and consultants who provide services to a plan are generally not considered fiduciaries unless they exercise discretionary authority or control over the management or administration of the plan or the assets of the plan, even if such activities are unauthorized. [ERISA § 3(21); DOL Reg. § 2509.75-5, D-1]

Note. Accountants, attorneys, actuaries, insurance agents, and consultants (although not generally fiduciaries) may be liable to a plan according to traditional theories of malpractice.

The ERISA statute, however, is not the only source of law in this area. The DOL, acting pursuant to a statutory grant of authority, has adopted regulations defining when a person is deemed to be providing investment advice for purposes of ERISA Section 3(21)(A)(ii). The regulations significantly narrow the class of stockbrokers who might otherwise fall within the statutory definition. The regulation's definition of the term *fiduciary*, as applied to stockbrokers, therefore includes two classes. The regulation includes stockbrokers who actually have discretionary authority with regard to buying and selling securities. The second alternative, however, does not require that the stockbroker have discretion or control. It merely requires rendering of investment advice pursuant to a mutual agreement that the stockbroker's advice will serve as a primary basis for investment decisions and that the broker will render "individualized investment advice" as defined by the regulations.

The law, as implemented by the regulations, requires only that the stockbroker (1) render investment advice to the plan on a regular basis; (2) pursuant to a mutual agreement, arrangement, or understanding, written or otherwise between the broker and a plan fiduciary; (3) that such services will serve as a primary basis for investment decisions with respect to plan assets; and (4) that the broker will render "individualized investment advice" to the plan based on the particular needs of the plan. [Ellis v. Rycenga Homes, Inc., 40 Employee Benefits Cas. (BNA) 1889 (W.D. Mich. 2007); 29 C.F.R. § 2510.3-21(c)(1)(ii)(B)] Thus, to be "individualized" within the meaning of the regulation, advice must pertain to investment policies or strategy or portfolio composition or diversification. [29 C.F.R. § 2510.3-21(c)(1)(ii)(B)] In other words, the advice must address the individual needs of the plan.

Note. Since an IRA account owner likely exercises discretionary authority or discretionary control with respect to management or disposition of its assets, the account owner will likely be a fiduciary. In addition, although accountants, attorneys, actuaries, insurance agents, and consultants may not be considered fiduciaries, such individuals may be liable to a plan under traditional theories of malpractice.

Caution. The EBSA believes that there is a need to reexamine the types of advisory relationships that should give rise to fiduciary duties on the part of those providing advisory services. Specifically, the EBSA notes that an increasing number of plan fiduciaries rely on advice and recommendations from service providers such as pension consultants and financial asset appraisers in making investment-related decisions regarding plan assets. Because the current regulatory definition of fiduciary limits the ability of ERISA to protect plans from such individuals that act imprudently, or that subordinate their client's interests to the interest of others, the EBSA issued proposed regulations in 2010 subjecting these individuals to ERISA fiduciary responsibility rules that will foster quality, impartial advice, and recommendations (see Qs 4:26–4:29). [EBSA Fact Sheet, "Definition of Fiduciary Regulation (Investment Advice)" (Dec. 10, 2009), available at *http://www.dol.gov/ebsa/regs/unifiedagenda/ebsafall2009/1210-AB32fs.html* (visited on July 15, 2012); *see also* DOL Reg. § 2510.3-21(c), five-part test (see Q 4:27) used to determine whether the provision of investment advice is a fiduciary function]

Service provider disclosure. On February 3, 2012, the EBSA issued final regulations requiring that certain service providers to employee pension benefit plans disclose information to plan fiduciaries in accessing the reasonableness of contracts or arrangements, including the reasonableness of the service provider's compensation and potential conflicts of interest that may affect the service provider's performance. [Described in ERISA § 3(2)(A) and not described in § 4(b)] The final regulations on fee disclosure are effective on July 1, 2012. A covered service provider that fails to provide written disclosures about their services, fiduciary status and compensation to the responsible plan fiduciary of an existing plan client by July 1 made their service arrangements prohibited transactions under ERISA.

Although the final regulations cross reference provisions of Code Section 4975 regarding prohibited transactions, the final service provider fee disclosure rules do not apply to IRA accounts and annuities, SEP plans, or simple retirement accounts. [DOL Reg. § 2550.408b-2(c)(1)(ii), 77 Fed. Reg. 5632, 5655 (Feb. 3, 2012); *see also* Field Assistance Bulletin (FAB) 2012-02R (July 30, 2012)] In addition, the rules do not apply to a service provider of a covered plan that reasonably expects to earn, directly or indirectly, less than $1,000 from the plan. [Final DOL Reg. § 2550.408b-2(c)(1)(iii)]

Note. It is unclear whether commissions from pure sales of an investment product to a plan from a party without an existing relationship to a plan, either on its own or through an affiliate, is governed either by ERISA Section 408(b)(2) or by the prohibited transaction rules. A "sale," by itself, does not seem to be a service covered by Code Section 408(b)(2), and the payment of a commission to a someone who is not a party of interest may raise fiduciary concerns if too much is paid, but it is not, in itself, a prohibited transaction."But there are times where sales and the payment of commission may eventually be considered services, where there becomes an ongoing, supportive relationship." [Toth, "ERISA Metaphysics, Mysticism and Alchemy: Sales Compensation" (Mar. 7, 2011), available at *http://www.businessofbenefits.com/2011/03/articles/complex-prohibited-transaction/erisa-metaphysics-mysticism-and-alchemy-sales-compensation/* (visited on Aug. 15, 2012); *see also* Toth, "Annuity Investment Account and 408(b)(2)" (Apr. 7, 2011), available at *http://www.businessofbenefits.com/2011/02/articles/complex-prohibited-transaction/annuity-investment-accounts-and-408b2/* (vi sited on July 15, 2012) and Toth, "Guidelines for Keeping It Simple Under

408(b)(2)" (Mar. 18, 2011), available at *http://www.businessofbenefits.com/2011/03/articles/408b2-1/guidelines-for-keeping-it-simple-under-408b2/* (visited on Aug. 15, 2012)]

Q 4:25 When is the provision of investment advice a prohibited transaction?

Directing the investment of a plan constitutes the exercise of authority and control over the management or disposition of plan assets and the person directing the investments is a fiduciary, even if the person is chosen by the participant and has no other connection to the plan. Under existing DOL Regulation Section 2510-3.21(c):

> a person will be deemed to be rendering investment advice if such person renders advice to the plan as to the value of securities or other property, or makes a recommendation as to the advisability of investing in, purchasing, or selling securities or other property and such person either directly or indirectly has discretionary authority or control, whether or not pursuant to an agreement, arrangement or understanding, with respect to purchasing or selling securities or other property for the plan; or renders any such advice on a regular basis to the plan pursuant to a mutual agreement, arrangement or understanding, written or otherwise, between such person and the plan or a fiduciary with respect to the plan, that such services will serve as a primary basis for investment decisions with respect to plan assets, and that such person will render individualized investment advice to the plan based on the particular needs of the plan regarding such matters as, among other things, investment policies or strategy, overall portfolio composition, or diversification of plan investments. [DOL Adv. Op. 2005-23A (Dec. 7, 2005]

Immediately after the enactment of ERISA, DOL promulgated in 1975 investment advice regulations (the 1975 regulations), which it now seeks to replace (see Q 4:28), specifying the circumstances in which a person providing investment advice becomes a fiduciary. For an adviser who does not have discretionary management authority, the 1975 regulations provide that the adviser is a fiduciary only if he or she satisfies a five-part test (see Q 4:27).

Q 4:26 When does a person providing investment advice become a fiduciary under the 1975 investment advice regulations?

Under the 1975 regulations, an adviser who does not have discretionary management authority is a fiduciary only if he or she satisfies a five-part test (see Q 4:27). The DOL has taken the position (under the 1975 regulations) that this definition of fiduciary also applies to investment advice provided to a participant or beneficiary in an individual account plan that allows participants or beneficiaries to direct the investment of their accounts. [DOL Reg. § 2509.96-1(c)]

The other fiduciaries of the plan would not be liable as fiduciaries for either the selection of the investment manager or investment adviser or the results of the investment manager's decisions or investment adviser's recommendations.

Other fiduciaries of the plan may have co-fiduciary liability if, for example, they knowingly participate in a breach committed by the participant's fiduciary. [DOL Reg. § 2509.96-1(c)] Other plan fiduciaries would not have any obligation to advise the participant about the investment manager or investment adviser or their investment decisions or recommendations. [DOL Reg. § 2550.404c-1(f)—Example (9); *see also* DOL Adv. Op. 84-04A (Jan. 4, 1984), which states that if a person is deemed to be giving investment advice within the meaning of DOL Reg. § 2510.3-21(c)(1)(ii)(B), the presence of an unrelated second fiduciary acting on the investment advisor's recommendations on behalf of the plan is not sufficient to insulate the investment advisor from fiduciary liability under ERISA § 406(b)]

The regulations (DOL Regulation Section 2510.3-21(c)(1)(B)) presuppose the existence of a second fiduciary who by agreement or conduct manifests a mutual understanding to rely on the investment adviser's recommendations as a primary basis for the investment of plan assets. In the presence of such an agreement or understanding, the rendering of investment advice involving self-dealing will subject the investment adviser to liability under ERISA Section 406(b). The DOL believes that the same principles enunciated in Advisory Opinion 84-04A apply in the context of a financial planner or investment adviser rendering investment advice to a participant in a participant-directed plan.

Q 4:27 What is the five-part test under the 1975 investment advice regulations?

Over the years, the second fiduciary category—the investment advice fiduciary—has perhaps required the most elaboration. Immediately after the enactment of ERISA, DOL promulgated the 1975 regulations specifying the circumstances in which a person providing investment advice becomes a fiduciary. For an adviser who does not have discretionary management authority, the 1975 regulations provide that the adviser is a fiduciary only if he or she satisfies a five-part test, specifically, if he or she for a direct or indirect fee or other compensation:

1. Renders advice as to the value of securities or other property, or makes recommendations as to the advisability of investing in, purchasing, or selling securities or other property,
2. On a regular basis,
3. Pursuant to a mutual agreement, arrangement, or understanding, with the plan or a plan fiduciary, that
4. The advice will serve as a primary basis for investment decisions with respect to plan assets, and that
5. The advice will be individualized based on the particular needs of the plan.

Q 4:28 Why does the DOL seek to replace the five-part test?

The DOL has made a judgment that, after 35 years, the 1975 fiduciary investment advice regulations require reconsideration. The DOL argues that the five-part test should be replaced with a new definition more faithful to the statutory definition that makes more investment service providers accountable as ERISA fiduciaries. [Preamble, 2010 Prop. DOL Reg. § 2510.3-21(c), since withdrawn, 75 Fed. Reg. 65263, 65264 (Oct. 22, 2010)] The DOL has indicated an intention to re-propose and expand upon its rule on the definition of fiduciary in 2012. [*See* EBSA News Rel. No. 11-1382-NAT (Sept. 19, 2011)]

The arguments include the following:

- Since 1975, ERISA retirement plans have shifted from predominantly defined benefit to predominantly defined contribution. The financial markets have also changed and have become more complex. As a result, the investment practices of plans, along with their relationships with their advisers, have changed.
- In this more complex environment, plan fiduciaries seek out impartial assistance and expertise from consultants, advisers, and appraisers to advise them on investment-related matters.
- In structuring their relationships with plans, however, these advisers can too readily take advantage of the five-part test to avoid fiduciary status.
- In recent years, non-fiduciary service providers, such as consultants, appraisers, and other advisers, have abused their relationships with plans by recommending investments in exchange for undisclosed kickbacks from investment providers, engaging in bid-rigging, misleading plan fiduciaries about the nature and risks associated with plans investments, and giving biased, incompetent, and unreliable valuation opinions. "Yet, no matter how egregious the abuse, plan consultants and advisers have no fiduciary liability under ERISA, unless they meet every element of the five-part test." [Preamble, Prop. DOL Reg. § 2510.3-21(c), since withdrawn, 75 Fed. Reg. 65,263, 65,271 (Oct. 22, 2010)]
- The DOL feels hampered in its enforcement efforts, both by its need to allocate substantial resources for investigating and proving each and every element of the five-part test and by its inability to redress cases it deems abusive if it cannot do so.
- The five-part test is not compelled by the plain language of ERISA Section 3(21). The DOL contends that the plain terms of the statute are simpler and broader than the 1975 regulations.

Note. By claiming that the statutory definition is broad, the DOL assumes a result that also is not compelled by the plain text of ERISA Section 3(21). That section provides no content for the term *investment advice*. The Supreme Court has instructed that, absent guidance from Congress to the contrary, terms used in ERISA should be given their ordinary meaning in the law and should not be stretched to accomplish some perceived remedial objective. [Preamble, Prop. DOL Reg. § 2510.3-21(c), since withdrawn, 75 Fed. Reg. 65,263, 65,264 (Oct. 22, 2010]

Q 4:29 Is there an exemption for invest advice fiduciaries?

Yes. In 2011, the EBSA issued guidance in the form of an Advisory Opinion concerning the application of Prohibited Transaction Class Exemption 86-128 [51 Fed. Reg. 41686 (Nov. 18, 1986), amended at 67 Fed. Reg. 64137 (Oct. 17, 2002)], which permits a plan fiduciary (or affiliate) to engage in securities transactions for a fee as an agent on behalf of a plan. [EBSA Adv. Op. 2011-08A (June 21, 2011), available at *http://www.dol.gov/ebsa/regs/aos/ao2011-08a.html* (visited on Aug. 1, 2012)] The class exemption [PTE 86-128] provides that the prohibited transaction provisions of ERISA Section 406(b) do not apply to:

4. A plan fiduciary using its authority to cause a plan to pay a fee for effecting or executing securities transactions to that person as agent for the plan, to the extent that such transactions are not excessive in either amount or frequency;
5. A plan fiduciary's acting as the agent in an agency cross transaction for both the plan and one or more other parties to the transaction; and
6. the receipt by a plan fiduciary of reasonable compensation for effecting or executing an agency cross transaction to which a plan is a party from one or more other parties to the transaction.

In the view of the EBSA, PTE 86-128 provides relief for covered transactions engaged in by any person who meets the definition of fiduciary as that term is defined in ERISA Section 3(21)(A), including a person who is a fiduciary solely by reason of rendering investment advice. Further, a fiduciary or an affiliate who receives a fee for executing securities transactions carried out in accordance with the fiduciary's investment advice would be using its authority as a fiduciary to cause the plan to pay a fee within the meaning of the prohibited transaction exemption.

Caution. On October 22, 2010, the EBSA issued a proposed regulation (the "2010 proposed regulation") that would have turned many consultants, advisors, and appraisers into ERISA fiduciaries. [Prop. DOL Reg. § 2510.3-21(c), since withdrawn, 75 Fed. Reg. 65263, 65264 (Oct. 22, 2010)] The DOL proposed that the changes to the fiduciary standards set out in the proposed regulations would take effect on April 20, 2011. However, in the wake of considerable criticism of the proposed regulation, the DOL has indicated an intention to re-propose and expand upon its rule on the definition of fiduciary in 2012. [*See* EBSA News Rel. No. 11-1382-NAT (Sept. 19, 2011)]

Note. Securities and Exchange Commission Chairman Mary Schapiro has said in a letter to Representative Scott Garett (R-NJ) that the commission is conducting further analysis of the costs and benefits of a fiduciary rule for brokers, resulting in a delay in the SEC's proposal (authorized by the 2010 Dodd-Frank Act), which would impose a fiduciary standard on broker-dealers that is as rigorous as the one for investment advisers, requiring them to put retail clients' interests before their own. Currently, brokers are required by the SEC only to provide advice "suitable" to customers at the moment of the sale. [Letter dated January 10, 2012]

Q 4:30 May investment-related information be provided to employees without becoming a fiduciary?

Yes. An employer is permitted, but not required, to educate its employees about investment principles, financial planning, and retirement; however, the employer must be cautious when it does so. Providing investment-related information may be considered the rendering of investment advice and could raise questions about fiduciary conduct under ERISA in plans that permit participants to direct their own investments. [ERISA § 3(21)(A)(ii); PWBA Interpretive Bull. 96-1; DOL Reg. §§ 2509.96-1, 2510.3-21(c)]

An employer that selects, recommends, or in any other way influences employees to choose a particular IRA or type of IRA into which contributions under a SEP or SARSEP are to be made is likely to be treated as a fiduciary. If, however, employees are given the opportunity to exercise control over assets in their IRAs and there is a broad range of investment alternatives available, the employer will not be deemed a fiduciary. If the employer is treated as a fiduciary, it must (like all fiduciaries under ERISA) carry out its duties with the care, skill, prudence, and diligence that a prudent person acting in a like capacity would use under conditions prevailing at the time. A fiduciary must also conduct all transactions solely in the interests of plan participants and their beneficiaries. [ERISA § 404(c); DOL Reg. § 2550.404c-1]

The EBSA has finalized guidance designed to help plan sponsors and service providers educate participants about plan investments without providing investment advice; the guidance applies to plans that permit participants to direct their own investments. Several safe harbors or types of information and materials may be provided to participants without giving investment advice under ERISA, including the following:

1. *Plan information.* Information about plan participation, the benefits of increasing plan contributions, the impact of preretirement withdrawals on retirement income, the terms and operation of the plan, and investment alternatives, including a description of investment objectives and philosophies, risk and return characteristics, historical return information, and investment prospectuses.

2. *General financial and investment information.* Information about general financial and investment concepts, historic differences in rates of return between different asset classes, effects of inflation, estimating future retirement income needs, determining investment time horizons, and assessing risk tolerance.

3. *Asset allocation models.* Information and materials, such as pie charts, graphs, or case studies that provide models of asset allocation portfolios for hypothetical individuals with different time horizons and risk profiles.

Asset allocation models identifying a specific investment alternative under the plan must provide an accompanying statement indicating that other investment alternatives with similar risk and return characteristics may be available under the plan. The statement must also specify where information on those investment alternatives may be obtained. It is not necessary to specifically describe other investment alternatives with similar risk and return characteristics. Asset allocation models may take into account a participant's nonplan assets, income, investments, and other information, and service providers may assist individual participants in developing asset allocation models.

4. *Interactive investment materials.* Questionnaires, worksheets, software, and similar materials that provide a participant or a beneficiary with the means to estimate future retirement income needs and assess the impact of different asset allocations on retirement income.

Caution. Despite the safe harbors, an employer's designation of a service provider to provide investment educational services or investment advice is an exercise of discretionary authority and, thus, is a fiduciary act that could result in fiduciary liability for the employer.

Q 4:31 Does a recommendation that a participant roll over his or her retirement plan account balance to a traditional IRA or to then convert that IRA to a Roth IRA to take advantage of investment options not available under an employer's plan constitute investment advice with respect to plan assets?

Merely advising a plan participant to take an otherwise permissible plan distribution, even when that advice is combined with a recommendation as to how the distribution should be invested, does not constitute "investment advice" within the meaning of DOL Regulation Section 2510-3.21(c). (See Caution below.) The 1975 investment advice regulations define when a person is a fiduciary by virtue of providing investment advice with respect to the assets of an employee benefit plan. The DOL does not view a recommendation to take a distribution as advice or a recommendation concerning a particular investment (i.e., purchasing or selling securities or other property) as contemplated by the 1975 regulations. [DOL Reg. § 2510.3-21(c)(1)(ii)] However, a person recommending that a participant take a distribution may be subject to federal or state securities, banking, or insurance regulation. [DOL Adv. Op. 2005-23A (Dec. 7, 2005)] Any investment recommendation regarding the proceeds of a distribution would be advice with respect to funds that are no longer assets of the plan.

Note. Automatic rollovers are subject to special rules which include, among other requirements, that the rolled-over funds be invested in an investment product designed to preserve principal and provide a reasonable rate of return, whether or not such return is guaranteed, consistent with liquidity. [*See* DOL Reg. § 2550.404a-2 (69 Fed. Reg. 58,018 (Sept. 28, 2004))]

Caution. Concerns have been expressed that, as a result of this position, plan participants may not be adequately protected from advisers who provide distribution recommendations that subordinate participants' interests to the advisers' own interests. The DOL, therefore, is requesting comment on whether and to what extent the final regulation should define the provision of investment advice to encompass recommendations related to taking a plan distribution. The DOL is specifically interested in information on other laws that apply to the provision of these types of recommendations, whether and how those laws safeguard the interests of plan participants, and the costs and benefits associated with extending the regulation to these types of recommendations (see Qs 4:26–4:30). [Preamble, Prop. DOL Reg. § 2510.3-21, since withdrawn, 75 Fed. Reg. 65,263, 65,266 (Oct. 22, 2010)] However, in the wake of considerable criticism of the proposed regulation (since withdrawn), the DOL has indicated an intention to re-propose and expand upon its rule on the definition of fiduciary in 2012. [*See* EBSA News Rel. No. 11-1382-NAT (Sept. 19, 2011)]

On the other hand, where a plan officer or someone who is already a plan fiduciary responds to participant questions concerning the advisability of taking a distribution or the investment of amounts withdrawn from the plan, that fiduciary is exercising discretionary authority respecting management of the plan and must act prudently and solely in the interest of the participant. [*See* Varity Corp. v. Howe, 516 U.S. 489, 502–503 (1996] Moreover, if, for example, a fiduciary exercises control over plan assets to cause the participant to take a distribution and then to invest the proceeds in an IRA account managed by the fiduciary, the fiduciary may be using plan assets in his or her own interest, in violation of ERISA Section 406(b)(1). Thus, there are potential implications for how financial service institutions cross-sell their products to ERISA plan participants. Courts will view the sales process through the lens of hindsight and often look critically at practices that have any appearance of impropriety. Each case is likely to turn on its particular facts and circumstances. [Young v. Principal Fin. Group, 547 F. Supp. 2d 965 (S.D. Iowa 2008)]

A recommendation by someone who is not connected with the plan, that a participant take an otherwise permissible distribution, even when combined with a recommendation as to how to invest distributed funds, is not investment advice within the meaning of the 1975 DOL Regulation Section 2510-3.21(c), nor is such a recommendation, in and of itself, an exercise of authority or control over plan assets that would make a person a fiduciary within the meaning of ERISA Section 3(21)(A). Accordingly, a person making such recommendations would not be a fiduciary solely on the basis of making such recommendations, and would not engage in an act of self-dealing if he or she advises the participant to roll over his account balance from the plan to an IRA that will pay management or other investment fees to such person. (See Caution above.) On the other hand, this position applies only to advice provided by a person who is not a plan fiduciary on some other basis. Advice of this nature given by someone who is already a fiduciary of the plan would be subject to ERISA's fiduciary duties. Moreover, if the person exercised control over the participant's account in making the distribution and reinvestment outside the plan, the person would be a fiduciary and would be subject to the ERISA's fiduciary obligations. [DOL Adv. Op. 2005-23A (Dec. 7, 2005)]

Payroll Deduction IRA

Q 4:32 Is a *payroll deduction IRA* a SEP?

No. An IRA into which an employee is allowed to make contributions with after-tax dollars is called a *payroll deduction IRA*. An IRA used in connection with an employer's SEP arrangement may also be used in connection with a payroll deduction IRA. Contributions to the payroll deduction IRA are subject to the 100 percent/$5,000 limit, plus catch-up contributions (up to $1,000) if age 50 or older, under Code Sections 219 and 408 for 2012. An employer that establishes a payroll deduction IRA will be treated as maintaining an ERISA plan, unless certain conditions are satisfied.

DOL regulations provide a safe harbor under which IRAs will not be considered to be pension plans when the conditions of the regulation are satisfied. Thus, with few constraints, employees may be provided an additional opportunity for saving for retirement. The safe-harbor rules require that

1. No contributions are made by the employer or employee association;
2. Participation must be completely voluntary for employees or members;
3. The sole involvement of the employer or employee organization is without endorsement to permit the sponsor to publicize the program to employees or members, to collect contributions through payroll deductions or dues checkoffs and to remit them to the sponsor (see Qs 2:64–2:66); and
4. The employer or employee organization receives no consideration in the form of cash or otherwise, other than reasonable compensation for services actually rendered in connection with payroll deductions or dues checkoffs (see Q 2:67).

[DOL Reg. § 2510.3-2(d)]

An employer may forward contributions made under a payroll deduction IRA program into the same IRAs that are used to receive employer SEP contributions.

Note. Although a Roth IRA is not a traditional IRA, it has been the DOL's long-held view that an employer who provides employees with the opportunity for making contributions to an IRA through payroll deductions does not thereby establish a "pension plan" within the meaning of ERISA Section 3(2)(A). In the authors' opinion, the DOL's view would apply equally to a payroll deduction Roth IRA program. In addition, IRS Announcement 99-2, 1999-1 C.B. 305, states that employers may permit employees to contribute to traditional IRAs or Roth IRAs by direct deposit through payroll deductions.

Q 4:33 May employees make pretax salary reduction contributions to a payroll deduction IRA program?

No. All contributions are made with after-tax dollars and generally treated as wages or as earned income if the individual is self-employed.

Q 4:34 When is an employer considered to "endorse" a payroll deduction IRA program?

When the employer does not maintain "neutrality" with respect to the sponsor it selects. For purposes of the regulations, if an employer maintains neutrality with respect to the sponsor in its communications with its employees, the employer will not be considered to "endorse" an IRA payroll deduction program (see also Q 4:35). [DOL Reg. § 2509.99-1(c)(1)]

Q 4:35 May an employer encourage participation in the payroll deduction IRA program?

Yes. An employer may encourage participation by employees by providing general information on the payroll deduction program and other educational materials that explain the prudence of retirement savings, including the advantages of contributing to an IRA, without thereby converting the wage contribution withholding program to an ERISA-covered plan.

> **Caution.** The employer must make it clear that its involvement in the program is limited to collecting the deducted amounts and remitting them promptly to the sponsor and that it does not provide any additional benefit or promise any particular investment return on the employee's retirement savings.
>
> [DOL Reg. § 2509.99-1(c)(1)]

Q 4:36 How may an employer demonstrate its neutrality with respect to a sponsor?

An employer may demonstrate its neutrality with respect to a sponsor in a variety of ways, including (but not limited to) ensuring that materials distributed to employees in connection with a payroll deduction program clearly and prominently state, in language reasonably calculated to be understood by the average employee, that

1. The IRA payroll deduction program is completely voluntary;
2. The employer does not endorse or recommend either the sponsor or the funding media;
3. Other IRA funding media are available to employees outside of the payroll deduction program;
4. An IRA may not be appropriate for all individuals; and
5. The tax consequences of contributing to an IRA through the payroll deduction program are generally the same as the consequences of contributing to an IRA outside of the program.

The employer would not be considered neutral to the extent that the materials distributed to the employees identified the funding medium as having as one of its purposes investing in securities of the employer or its affiliates or the funding medium has significant investments in such securities.

If the program resulted from an agreement between the employer and an employee organization, then informational materials that identified the funding medium as having as one of its purposes investing in an investment vehicle that is designed to benefit an employee organization by providing more jobs for its members, or loans to its members, or similar direct benefits (or the funding medium's actual investments in any such investment vehicles) would indicate that the employee organization's involvement in the program is less than neutral.

[DOL Reg. § 2509.99-1(c)(1), n. 2]

Q 4:37 What is considered *reasonable compensation*?

Reasonable compensation does not include any profit to the employer. Payments that an employer receives from an IRA sponsor for the employer's cost of operating the IRA payroll deduction program do constitute reasonable compensation to the extent that they constitute compensation for the actual costs of the program to the employer.

Example. The IRA sponsor agrees to make or to permit particular investments of IRA contributions in consideration for the employer's agreement to make a payroll deduction program available to its employees. Such an arrangement would exceed "reasonable compensation" for the services actually rendered by the employer in connection with the program.

[DOL Reg. § 2509.99-1(f)]

Q 4:38 What else may an employer do without converting the payroll deduction program into an ERISA-covered plan?

Specifically, without converting the payroll deduction program into an ERISA-covered plan, an employer may

1. Answer employees' specific inquiries about the mechanics of the IRA payroll deduction program and may refer other inquiries to the appropriate IRA sponsor;
2. Provide to employees informational materials written by the IRA sponsor describing the sponsor's IRA programs or addressing topics of general interest regarding investments and retirement savings, provided that the material does not itself suggest that the employer is other than neutral with respect to the IRA sponsor and its products;
3. Request that the IRA sponsor prepare such informational materials, and it may review such materials for appropriateness and completeness.

Note. The fact that the employer's name or logo is displayed in the informational materials in connection with describing the payroll deduction program would not in and of itself suggest that the employer has endorsed the IRA sponsor or its products, provided that the specific context and surrounding facts and circumstances make clear to the employees that the employer's involvement is limited to facilitating employee contributions through payroll deductions (see Q 4:36).

[DOL Reg. § 2509.99-1(c)(2)]

Q 4:39 May an employer that established a payroll deduction IRA limit the number of IRA trustees/custodians that are available to its employees?

Yes, an employer may limit the number of IRA trustees/custodians to which its employees may make payroll deduction contributions, provided that any limitations on, or costs or assessments associated with, an employee's ability to transfer or roll over IRA contributions to another IRA trustee/custodian are fully disclosed in advance of the employee's decision to participate in the program. In addition, an employer may violate the limitations of such a program if the employer negotiates with an IRA trustee/custodian and thereby obtains special terms and conditions for its employees that are not generally available to similar purchasers of the IRA. The employer's involvement in the IRA program would also be in violation of the limitations if the employer exercises any influence over the investments made or permitted by the IRA sponsor (see Q 4:30).

[DOL Reg. § 2509.99-1(d)]

Q 4:40 May an employer that established a payroll deduction IRA pay the fees imposed by the sponsors?

Yes. The employer may pay any fee the IRA sponsor imposes on employers for services the sponsor provides in connection with the establishment and maintenance of the payroll deduction process itself. The employer may also assume the internal costs (e.g., for overhead and bookkeeping) of implementing and maintaining the payroll deduction program without reimbursement from either employees or the IRA sponsor.

Caution. If, in connection with operating an IRA payroll deduction program, an employer pays any administrative, investment management, or other fee that the IRA sponsor would require employees to pay for establishing or maintaining the IRA, the employer would fall outside the safe harbor and, as a result, may be considered to have established an ERISA-covered plan.

[DOL Reg. § 2509.99-1(e)]

Q 4:41 May an employer that offers IRAs to the general public in the normal course of its business, or an affiliate of an employer-sponsor, establish a payroll deduction IRA program for its employees?

Generally, an employer that offers IRAs in the normal course of its business to the general public or that is an affiliate of an IRA sponsor may provide its employees with the opportunity to make contributions to IRAs sponsored by the employer or the affiliate through a payroll deduction program as long as

1. The IRA products offered to the employees for investment of the payroll deduction contributions are identical to IRA products the sponsor offers the general public in the ordinary course of its business; and

2. Any management fees, sales commissions, and the like charged by the IRA sponsor to employees participating in the payroll deduction program are the same as those charged by the sponsor to employees of nonaffiliated employers that establish an IRA payroll deduction program.

Note. Although the funding medium offered by an employer that is an IRA sponsor or an affiliate of an IRA sponsor might be considered an employer security when offered to its own employees, the fact that informational materials provided to employees identify the funding medium as having as one of its purposes investing in securities of the employer would not involve the employer beyond the safe-harbor limits, nor would the fact that the funding medium may actually be so invested. However, if the informational materials that the employer provides to employees suggest that the employer, in providing the IRA payroll deduction program for purposes of investing in employer securities, is acting as an employer in relation to persons who participate in the program, instead as an IRA sponsor acting in the course of its ordinary business of making IRA products available to the public, then the employer would have gone beyond the safe-harbor limits (see Q 4:36).

Caution. If an employer that is an IRA sponsor waives enrollment and management fees for its employees' IRAs, and it normally charges those fees to members of the public who purchase IRAs, then the employer would be considered to be so involved in the program as to be outside the "safe harbor" and be deemed to have established a "pension plan" within the meaning of ERISA Section 3(2)(A) (see Q 4:30).

[DOL Reg. § 2509.99-1(g)]

Use of Electronic Media

Q 4:42 To what extent may an employer use electronic technologies for providing employee benefit notices and transmitting employee benefit elections and consents?

The Treasury Department and IRS issued final regulations regarding the use of electronic media to provide notices to employee benefit plan participants and beneficiaries and to transmit elections or consents from participants and beneficiaries to employee benefit plans. The standards set forth in these regulations would apply to any "notice, election, or similar communication" made to or by a participant or beneficiary under a SEP, SARSEP, or SIMPLE IRA.

The regulations state that they are meant to constitute the "exclusive rules relating to the use of electronic media" to satisfy a requirement under the Code that a communication be in written form, but would also act as "safe harbor" with respect to any communication that is *not* required to be in written form. However, the regulations would not apply to any notice, election, consent, or disclosure required under the provisions of Title I or IV of ERISA over which the DOL has interpretative and regulatory authority "or any other Code provision over which DOL has similar interpretative authority." Although it is not entirely clear, it would appear that participants must receive, for example, a *written* copy of Form 5305-SEP (and/or Form 5305A-SEP) completed by the adopting employer, as well as a written explanation of any amendments and explanation thereof (see Qs 1:19, 3:7, 3:10, 12:28, 14:18). Notices of excess contributions (see Q 12:42) and the employer's annual notice of the annual contribution (see Q 4:15) must be in writing. On the other hand, the salary reduction deferral form could be provided electronically to participants. (See Appendix A, page A-4.) It is unlikely that many SEP plans will utilize the electronic media rules to enroll participants.

Effective date: The final regulations were effective on October 20, 2006.

[Treas. Reg. § 1.401(a)-21, 71 Fed. Reg. 61877–61888, Oct. 20, 2006, reflecting the provisions of the Electronic Signatures in Global and National Commerce Act, Pub. L. No. 106-229, 114 Stat. 464 (2000) (E-SIGN)); Treas. Reg. § 35.3405-1; *see also* chapter 13] The DOL and the Pension Benefit Guaranty Corporation (PBGC) have also issued regulations relating to the use of electronic media to furnish notices, reports, statements, disclosures, and other documents to participants, beneficiaries, and other individuals under Titles I and IV of ERISA. [DOL Reg. § 2520.104b-1]

Forwarding Contributions

Q 4:43 Are both elective and nonelective contributions to a SEP treated as plan assets under ERISA?

Yes. All contributions to a SEP are plan assets [DOL Reg. § 2510.3-102(a)] and must be segregated from the employer's general assets on the earliest date possible (see Q 5:28).

Q 4:44 When must an employer forward salary reduction contributions under an ERISA plan?

ERISA regulations generally require employee contributions to be deposited as soon as they can reasonably be segregated from the employer's general assets, but in any event within 15 business days after the end of the month in which the payroll deduction is made. [DOL Reg. § 2510.3-102] Up to an additional 15 days is allowed in the case of a SIMPLE IRA (see Q 14:105). The DOL also provides a seven-day safe-harbor rule for smaller ERISA-covered plans (see Qs 4:45–4:47). The general rule—providing that amounts paid or withheld by an employer become plan assets on the earliest date they can reasonably be segregated from the employer's general assets—did not change. The DOL does not currently permit the self-correction of late deposits.

Depending on the facts and circumstances, even one day may be a reasonable time in which to segregate employee contributions from an employer's general assets. Thus, until the DOL announces a safe-harbor rule specifying the number of days in which to remit deferrals, the "as soon as possible" rule still applies. (See chapter 17 regarding IRS and DOL correction programs.)

Contributions by Partners. When the plan asset regulations were initially proposed, comments were received by the DOL relating to when contributions by partners become plan assets. Under the final regulations the monies that are to go to a qualified 401(k) plan by virtue of a partner's election become plan assets at the earliest date they can reasonably be segregated from the partnership's general assets after those monies would otherwise have been distributed to the partner, but no later than 15 business days after the month in which those monies would, but for the election, have been distributed to the partner. [DOL Reg. § 2510.3-102, Preamble; *see* Treas. Reg. § 1.401(k)-2(a)(4)(ii) (T.D. 9169, 69 Fed. Reg. 78144–78201 (Dec. 29, 2004)); *see also* Treas. Reg. § 1.401(k)-1(a)(6)(iii) and (iv)]

The following example is an interpretation of the plan asset regulations and illustrates how the rule might apply to a SARSEP maintained by a partnership.

> **Example.** The Able-7 Partnership maintains a SARSEP. On December 31, 2012, the last day of its taxable and plan year, all the partners individually elect to defer the maximum amount into their SARSEP IRAs (not to exceed $17,000 per partner). During the year, each partner had a monthly draw of $750 cash against eventual earnings. The firm's accountant, Bob, is ill and will not be able to compute Able-7's net earnings by the due date of Able-7's return; therefore, he files for an extension on behalf of the partnership and each of the partners (see Table 2-2, Q 2:34). On June 27, Bob notifies the partnership that it indeed had a profit and that each of the partners is due an additional $37,000. Able-7 must deposit $119,000 ($17,000 × 7) as contributions to the SARSEP IRAs of its seven partners as soon as the amounts can reasonably be segregated from the partnership's general assets, but no later than 15 business days after the end of June. For deduction purposes, elective contributions must (arguably) be made no later than the close of the 30-day period following the last day of December, the month with respect to which the contributions are to be made under Code Section 408(p)(5)(A)(i). (see Qs 2:33–2:35, 10:1).

Although very little guidance has been issued on this subject, the IRS has ruled that a partnership making periodic advances of earnings to each partner throughout the plan year (designed to be equivalent to periodic payments of compensation to each partner as if such partner were a common-law employee) could be contributed as "elective contributions" under a 401(k) plan, where the partnership intended to withhold an amount from each partner's periodic advances pursuant to a deferral election. [Ltr. Rul. 200247052]

With respect to the prohibited transaction provisions of ERISA, the employer of employees covered by the plan is a party in interest with respect to the plan under ERISA Section 3(14)(C). [ERISA §§ 3(14)(C), 406] The failure to segregate and forward participant contributions to a plan from the general assets of the employer in the prescribed time frames would result in a prohibited use of plan assets in violation of ERISA Section 406(a)(1)(D). Similarly, because an employer that retains plan assets commingled with its general assets would be a fiduciary with respect to those assets pursuant to ERISA Section 3(21)(A)(i), any actions taken by the employer with respect to the participant contributions that become plan assets, other than the actual contribution of such assets to the plan's trust or custodial account, would be a prohibited transaction under ERISA Sections 406(b)(1) and (2). The DOL has announced civil and criminal action to enforce timely deposits of employee contributions in retirement plans. [EBSA New Release 10-1416-NT (Nov. 16, 2010), available at *http://www.dol.gov/ebsa/newsroom/2010/10-1614-NAT.html* (visited on Aug. 15, 2012)]

Although the failure to forward participant contributions in a timely fashion would not, in itself, constitute an extension of credit between the plan and the employer in violation of ERISA Section 406(a)(1)(B), depending on the particular facts and circumstances, a separate arrangement, agreement, or understanding to extend credit to pay the delinquent amounts to the plan could occur that would give rise to a violation of that section. Such arrangement, agreement, or understanding could be express or implied. For example, a fiduciary's consistent failure to exercise diligence in its collection efforts regarding participant contributions may serve as the basis to assert that an implied understanding existed to extend credit between the fiduciary and the employer.

[DOL News Release, 06-80-CHI (Jan. 18, 2006), business owner to restore funds timely forwarded to SIMPLE IRA] [*see* Frequently Asked Questions about Reporting Delinquent Participant Contributions on the Form 5500 at *http://www.dol.gov/ebsa/faqs/faq_compliance_5500.html* (visited on Aug. 15, 2012)]

Excise tax on failure to remit timely. Guidance on determining the amount of the excise tax imposed when an employer fails to timely remit employee deferrals is contained in Revenue Ruling 2006-38. [2006-29 I.R.B. 80] According to the hypothetical example included in that Revenue Ruling, an employer's failure to remit until December 30, 2012, employee deferrals that could reasonably be segregated from the employer's general assets as of December 8, 2010, would constitute a prohibited transaction for taxable years 2011 and 2012. Revenue Ruling 2006-38 makes clear that if an employer does not timely pay participant deferrals or contributions to an employee benefit plan, the excise tax is based on the interest on those elective deferrals or contributions measured from the earliest date those contributions could have been reasonably segregated from the employer's general assets. In addition, the Revenue Ruling states what interest rate to use in computing the excise tax and how the interest should be calculated.

Q 4:45 What is the DOL's seven-day safe-harbor rule for forwarding participant contributions?

Under the DOL's safe harbor final regulations, participant contributions to a pension or welfare benefit plan (see Q 4:1) with fewer than 100 participants at the beginning of the plan year will be treated as having been made to the plan in accordance with the general rule (i.e., on the earliest date on which such contributions can reasonably be segregated from the employer's general assets, see Q 4:44) when contributions are deposited with the plan no later than the seventh business day following the day on which such amount is received by the employer (in the case of amounts that a participant or beneficiary pays to an employer) or the seventh business day following the day on which such amount would otherwise have been payable to the participant in cash (in the case of amounts withheld by an employer from a participant's wages). [DOL Reg. § 2510.3-102(a) and (f); *see* 75 Fed. Reg. 2068 (Jan. 14, 2010)]

Example 1. Interstate Trucking sponsors a SARSEP plan. There are 30 participants in plan. Interstate has one payroll period for its employees and uses an outside payroll processing service to pay employee wages and process deductions. Interstate has established a system under which the payroll processing service provides payroll deduction information to Interstate within 1 business day after the issuance of paychecks. Interstate checks this information for accuracy within three business days (assumed to be a reasonable period) and then forwards the withheld employee contributions to the plan. The amount of the total withheld employee contributions is deposited into IRAs established by participating employees under the plan on the fourth business day following the date on which the employees are paid. Under the safe-harbor rule, when the participant contributions are deposited with the plan on or before the seventh business day following a pay date, the participant contributions are deemed to be contributed to the plan on the earliest date on which such contributions can reasonably be segregated from Interstate's general assets. The result would be the same if Interstate maintained a SIMPLE-IRA plan and contributions were deposited into SIMPLE IRAs within the seven-day period.

Example 2. Assume the same facts as in Example 1, except that during a single pay period in 2012, Interstate Trucking inadvertently delays making the contribution until the eighth business day following the end of the pay period. It cannot rely on the seven-day safe harbor for that pay period. Therefore, its contributions had to be submitted on the earliest date on which such contributions could have been reasonably be segregated from Interstate's general assets. In all likelihood, Interstate could have segregated the contributions by the fourth day—the date interest will begin to accrue on the delinquent contributions. Interstate will also have to file Form 5330, *Return of Excise Taxes Related to Employee Benefit Plans for 2012.* The 15 percent prohibited transaction excise tax is reported in Part 1 (line 3a) of Form 5330. Form 5330 is due on the last day of the seventh month following the end of the 2012 plan year. In the unlikely event the plan was subject to 5500 Annual Return–Report for Employee Benefit Plans filings, the delinquent contributions would have to be indicated (see Qs 4:11, 4:12).

As under the current regulation, participant contributions will be considered deposited when placed in an account of the plan. An amount is considered deposited without regard to whether the contributed amounts have been allocated to specific participants or investments of such participants.

Q 4:46 What is the effect on employers of the seven-day safe-harbor rule for forwarding employee contributions?

This seven-day safe harbor rule is likely to encourage some eligible employers whose current remittance practices involve holding participant contributions for longer than seven business days to change their remittance practices to conform to the seven-business day time limit. In deciding whether to rely on the safe harbor, employers will weigh the benefits of compliance certainty against the cost of changes needed to make quicker and possibly more frequent deposits.

Because the rule is not mandatory and changes in remittance practices are likely to entail some cost to employers, only those employers that believe they will benefit from the protection of the safe harbor will elect to take advantage of the safe harbor.

> **Example.** Timely, Inc., which currently remits contributions on the day they are withheld and responds to the safe harbor by delaying remittances to the seven-business day safe-harbor limit, would gain use of the funds for seven business days. At an annual rate of 8 percent, the value of the float gain would be less than one-quarter of 1 percent of employee contributions.

> **Caution.** As under current regulations, the rule affects the application of ERISA and Code provisions, it has no implications for and may not be relied upon to bar criminal prosecutions under 18 U.S.C. Section 644. [*See* ERISA § 2510.3-102(a)] 18 U.S.C. Section 664 prohibits the embezzlement and theft of property by any person from an employee pension or welfare benefit plan subject to title I of ERISA. [29 U.S.C. § 1001 *et seq.*] The statute also prohibits embezzlement and theft from a "fund connected" with such an employee benefit plan. Employee benefit plans that are excluded from regulation by ERISA include church plans and benefit plans that are established or maintained by the United States or state or local governments on behalf of their employees. [*See* 29 U.S.C. § 1003]

Q 4:47 When was the seven-day safe-harbor rule effective?

The safe harbor was effective on January 14, 2010, the date the DOL published final regulations in the *Federal Register*. [DOL Reg. § 2510.3-102, 75 Fed. Reg. 2068 (Jan. 14, 2010] However, the regulations indicate that the DOL will not assert violation of the plan asset regulations if a small plan is in compliance with the safe harbor. [*See* 73 Fed. Reg. 11074 (Feb. 29, 2008)]

Q 4:48 How did the DOL enforce the "plan asset" regulations before the effective date of the final safe-harbor rule?

Before the effective date of the final seven-day safe-harbor regulation, the DOL did not assert a violation of ERISA based on the general rule that participant contributions (or loan repayments in a qualified plan) become plan assets on the earliest date on which they can reasonably be segregated from the employer's general assets, so long as such contributions or repayments to a plan with fewer than 100 participants have been transferred to the plan in accordance with the seven-business-day safe-harbor period. [*See* 73 Fed. Reg. 11074 (Feb. 29, 2008)]

Q 4:49 Does the seven-day safe-harbor rule apply on a payroll-by-payroll basis?

Yes. The safe harbor is available on a deposit-by-deposit basis, such that a failure to satisfy the safe harbor for any deposit of participant contribution amounts to a plan will not result in the unavailability of the safe harbor for any other deposit to the plan. [Preamble, DOL Reg. § 2510.3-102, 75 Fed. Reg. 2068, 2070 (Jan. 14. 2010)] Thus, the failure to meet the safe harbor during one payroll period does not result in the application of the general rule for determining when participant contributions are plan assets for an entire plan year. (See Example 2 in Q 4:45.)

Federal Securities Laws

Q 4:50 Is an IRA or a SEP a security?

An IRA established, managed, and maintained to receive contributions made under a SEP arrangement by the individual who owns it is not likely to be treated as a security. A SEP is similar, although not identical, to a 401(a) qualified defined contribution plan and is not likely to be viewed as a security. [International Bhd. of Teamsters v. Daniel, 439 U.S. 551 (1979); SEC v. W.J. Howey Co., 328 U.S. 293 (1946); SEC Rel. 33-6188 (Feb. 1, 1980); SEC Rel. 33-6281 (Jan. 15, 1981)]

> **Note.** The Private Litigation Securities Reform Act of 1995 [Pub. L. No. 104-67] requires the Securities and Exchange Commission (SEC) to determine if qualified plans (including SEPs) need increased protection against securities fraud.

Q 4:51 Do securities laws apply to the interests of participants when the assets of unrelated SEP IRAs are commingled and managed by a third party?

Yes. If the assets of several otherwise unrelated SEP IRAs are commingled in a common trust or other investment fund managed by a third party and invested in securities, the interests of the participants in such a fund will normally constitute securities. Unless an exemption applies, those interests will be subject to registration as a security under the Securities Act of 1933. [SEC Rel. 33-6188 (Feb. 1, 1980); SEC Rel. 33-6281 (Jan. 15, 1981)]

Q 4:52 Do securities laws apply to the fund that holds and invests the assets of unrelated SEP IRAs that are commingled and managed by a third party?

Yes. If the assets of several otherwise unrelated SEP IRAs are commingled in a common trust or other investment fund managed by a third party and invested in securities, the fund may be required to be registered as an investment company under the Investment Company Act of 1940.

Q 4:53 Under what circumstances might an employer or plan sponsor be concerned about securities laws?

Securities laws may come into play in situations involving an employer (group) SEP IRA's (see Q 5:29) using a single trust or investing in securities of the employer or a plan sponsor's pooling or commingling IRA funds in pooled and collective investment vehicles.

Q 4:54 How may a SEP avoid the potential difficulty of establishing an IRA for a minor?

Very simply. Establishing a minimum age requirement for participation in a SEP generally eliminates the potential difficulty of establishing an IRA for a minor. That difficulty may arise because some financial institutions are prohibited from establishing an account in the name of a minor. Others are concerned that a minor would rescind unprofitable transactions on becoming an adult. Furthermore, broker-dealers and mutual funds are prohibited under rules of the National Association of Securities Dealers (NASD) from registering a brokerage account in the name of a minor. Guardian registrations are sometimes used to get around that rule, but their status under Code Section 408(k) is not clear.

Option Securities and Margin Accounts

Q 4:55 What is an *option*?

An *option* is the right either to buy or to sell a specified amount or value of a particular underlying interest at a fixed exercise price by exercising the option before its specified expiration date. Calls and puts are distinct types of options, and the buying or selling of one type does not involve the option (i.e., the put or call may be bought and sold before exercising the option rights). All options are securities and are sold by prospectus.

Q 4:56 Does ERISA prohibit the purchase of options as an investment in a SEP IRA?

No. An option is a security and thus may be purchased as an investment in a SEP IRA. Nevertheless, unless the plan document allows option transactions, they may not be made. Some brokerage firms do not allow the buying and selling of options in an IRA or SEP IRA because certain types of option transactions are considered imprudent investments or may result in a prohibited loan to the account owner. Other firms will limit the types of option transactions allowed.

Q 4:57 Why might a brokerage firm limit the types of securities that can be purchased in an IRA or SEP IRA?

A brokerage firm may limit the types of investments it allows in an IRA or SEP IRA to limit its liability under federal and state laws. Some firms are concerned about investments that produce little or no income (wasting assets). A decision not to allow calls without an underlying position in a security (naked calls) and unhedged puts is generally made to avoid any allegation of investment unsuitability.

Some brokerage firms prohibit any type of option trading in an ERISA account. Others allow a broader range of options in a non-IRA ERISA account. In all cases, the plan document and the option's prospectus must allow for the purchase in the account.

Q 4:58 Why is a margin account used to trade options in a SEP IRA?

The NASD requires that an option be bought or sold in a margin account because some types of margin transactions may be financed with money belonging to the broker (see Q 4:60).

Q 4:59 Does a margin account established in connection with a brokerage account in a SEP IRA create a prohibited loan to an individual?

No. A margin account established in connection with a brokerage account in a SEP IRA does not create a prohibited loan. That is so because an IRA is not pledged as security for a loan to an individual under Code Section 408(e). Furthermore, even though a margin account is used, no loan is likely to result (see Qs 4:53, 4:55, 4:56). If a loan were nevertheless to result, the margined security would be considered debt-financed property within the meaning of Code Section 514, and realized profits would be taxable as unrelated business taxable income (see Q 13:74). [I.R.C. §§ 511, 514; Ltr. Rul. 8830061 (May 4, 1998); Elliot Knitwear Profit Sharing Plan v. Commissioner, 614 F.2d 347 (3d Cir. 1980), *aff'g* 71 T.C. 765 (1979); Ocean Cove Corp. Retirement Plan & Trust v. United States, 657 F. Supp. 776 (S.D. Fla. 1987); DOL Adv. Op. 82-49A]

Q 4:60 Would an extension of credit in a margin account between a party in interest or a disqualified person and an IRA be a prohibited transaction?

It is extremely unlikely that a brokerage firm would allow an option strategy that could result in a debit balance. Be that as it may, an extension of credit is allowable, provided the broker-dealer is not a fiduciary with respect to the account (see Q 4:24).

Many firms do not allow margin accounts in an IRA just in case the firm inadvertently becomes a fiduciary with respect to an account (see Qs 4:24, 4:52). A margin account allows for securities to be purchased with money borrowed from the broker. The establishment of a margin account is frequently required to purchase options even when no loan is likely to result. [P.T.E. 75-1, pt. V, 40 Fed. Reg. 50845 (1975)] It makes no difference whether the SEP IRA is covered by Title I of ERISA, so long as it is covered under the prohibited transaction provisions of Code Section 4975. [I.R.C. § 4975(c)(2); DOL Adv. Op. F-3055A; Reorg. Plan No. 4 of 1978, 43 Fed. Reg. 47713 (1978) (transferring the authority of the Secretary of the Treasury to issue rulings under Code Section 4975 to the Secretary of Labor)]

Prohibited Transaction Exemption 75-1 (P.T.E. 75-1) permits various classes of transactions involving employee benefit plans and certain broker-dealers, reporting dealers, and banks, provided the relevant conditions specified in the class exemption are met. Part V of P.T.E. 75-1 provides that the restrictions of ERISA Section 406 and the taxes imposed by Code Section 4975(a) and 4975(b) will not apply to any extension of credit to an employee benefit plan by a party in interest or disqualified person with respect to the plan if the following conditions are met:

1. The party in interest or disqualified person
   a. Is a broker or dealer registered under the Securities Exchange Act of 1934; and
   b. Is not a fiduciary with respect to any assets of such plan, unless no interest or other consideration is received by such fiduciary or any affiliate thereof in connection with such extension of credit
2. Such extension of credit
   a. Is in connection with the purchase or sale of securities,
   b. Is lawful under the Securities Exchange Act of 1934 and any rules and regulations promulgated thereunder, and
   c. Is not a prohibited transaction under Code Section 503(b), relating to exempt organizations.

The preamble to Part V of P.T.E. 75-1 states that a normal part of the execution of securities transactions by broker-dealers on behalf of their customers, including employee benefit plans, is the extension of credit to the customers in order to permit settlement within the usual three-day period. The preamble further states that extensions of credit by broker-dealers are also customary in connection with certain kinds of securities transactions, such as short sales and the writing of option contracts. It is important to note, however, that the phrase "in connection with the purchase or sale of securities" does not encompass an extension of credit as a result of a prior purchase of securities by a plan, regardless of the period of time that has elapsed since the purchase of securities by the plan. Thus, a loan from a broker-dealer to an IRA to permit a plan to make a distribution to a participant (or his or her beneficiaries) or to pay unexpected expenses, in both cases without necessitating the liquidation of existing securities positions, would not encompass an extension of credit that arises directly in connection with the purchase of specific securities and is prohibited. [DOL Adv. Op. 87-06A]

Q 4:61 What option strategies are generally allowed in a SEP IRA?

Subject to client suitability, selling (writing) covered calls and buying hedged or protective puts are generally allowed in an IRA or SEP IRA. The underlying security cannot be sold while a covered call is held in the account. (Selling the cover is called "lifting one leg up.") In most cases, the option will have to be closed (bought back) before the underlying security can be sold.

Q 4:62 Why might an IRA sell (write) a covered call?

A covered call gives the purchaser the right to purchase a set quantity of shares at a specified price from the seller of the option. Selling a covered call is generally considered an income strategy. The IRA receives income (the premium) from the purchaser of the option. If the stock increases in value, however, the purchaser might exercise the option and call the shares away at the lower price. Thus, the upside potential of the investment for the option period is limited. If the option was exercised by the purchaser, the IRA would be forced to sell the shares. The IRA would receive the stated price (in addition to the premium), but it would have to deliver the securities to the purchaser's brokerage account. If the stock declined in value, it would be unlikely that the purchaser would exercise the option because the security could be purchased on a national exchange at a lower price; the seller gets to keep the premium income. In no event can the option loss exceed the value of the account, because the underlying shares are "held long" in the brokerage account. Thus, the margin account will never have a debit balance (no loan will be created) as a result of selling a covered call. The "right" to buy shares at a price lower than the market price may be an attractive strategy in a declining market.

Q 4:63 Why might an IRA invest in a *hedged put*?

A *hedged put* gives the purchaser the right to sell a set quantity of shares at a specified price to the seller of the option. Buying a hedged put is generally considered an income strategy. The IRA pays a premium to the seller of the option. If the stock declines in value, however, the IRA might exercise the option and sell ("put") the shares at the higher price. Thus, the downside potential of the investment for the option period is limited. If the option were to be exercised by the IRA, the seller of the option would be forced to buy the shares. The seller would receive the stated price (in addition to the premium) and the IRA would receive the shares in return. If the stock increased in value, it would be unlikely that the IRA would exercise the option because the security could be sold on a national exchange at a higher price; the seller gets to keep the premium income.

In no event can the option loss exceed the value of the account, because the underlying shares are "held long" in the brokerage account. Thus, the margin account will never have a debit balance (no loan will be created) as a result of buying a hedged put.

Q 4:64 What option strategies are generally not allowed in an IRA or SEP IRA?

The following option strategies are generally not allowed in an IRA or SEP IRA:

- Covered writing on convertibles
- Naked call buying
- Naked spreads
- Combinations or straddles
- Index options (but index funds are allowed when suitable)
- Foreign currency options
- Short equity puts (selling a put that is not owned) versus short-term Treasury bill or certificate of deposit

Impact of State and Local Laws

Q 4:65 Are elective and nonelective SEP contributions subject to state income taxes?

It depends on the state. State and municipal tax laws do not always grant the same deductions and exemptions allowed by federal law for SEP IRA contributions. Some states do not permit tax deduction for contributions made to retirement accounts—such as 401(k) plans, IRAs, and SEP IRAs—but neither do they tax withdrawals (e.g., Pennsylvania and Florida). New Jersey, which does not permit a tax deduction, taxes the growth in the account on distribution. New York residents may take up to $20,000 a year in retirement income from pensions and other sources free of state tax.

Practice Pointer. In some cases, an individual could profit (with regard to taxes) by moving from one state to another.

Q 4:66 Are distributions from a SEP to a nonresident subject to state taxation?

It appears not (but see Note below). The Pension Source Act [Pub. L. No. 104-95] prohibits any state, including any political subdivision of a state, the District of Columbia, and the possessions of the United States, from imposing income tax on any retirement income of any individual who is not a resident or domiciliary of the state (as determined under the laws of that state). [Lesser, "State Taxation of Pension Income Curtailed," 4 *J. of Taxation of Employee*

Benefits 2 (July/Aug. 1996) 88; Mazawey, "New Federal Limitations on State Taxation of Retirement Income," 22 *J. of Pension Planning & Compliance* 2 (Summer 1996) 1]

For purposes of the Pension Source Act, retirement income includes any income from a qualified retirement or annuity plan, a SEP, a tax-sheltered annuity plan, or an IRA. There are no dollar limits on the amount of income that may be treated as retirement income.

Note. The Pension Source Act does not prevent a state from denying deductions for contributions made to a retirement or deferred compensation plan or from including the amount contributed currently in the participant's income. Thus, with only the front door closed, states are still able to walk in the back door by not allowing business deductions or by limiting exclusions from the employee's income (or both). In addition, it remains to be seen how aggressive states will be in determining when an individual is domiciled within a state and then subjecting the unprotected benefits to taxation.

Q 4:67 What aspects of state law other than income tax might apply to SEPs?

Once contributions are made into a SEP IRA, certain aspects of state law may apply—for example, estate, inheritance, and gift taxes, as well as the rules of escheat and applicability of power-of-attorney documents. Intangible property taxes on account balances (or values) may be imposed. Some states impose taxes on the annual income or the realized gains (or both) generated by a SEP IRA. As a general rule, the validity of a trust is determined under state law.

Escheat Law. The ERISA status of SEP IRAs under applicable escheat law cannot be definitely determined. Treasury Regulations Section 1.411(a)-4(b)(6) provides that a benefit "lost by reason of escheat under applicable state law will not be deemed an impermissible forfeiture." That regulation does not apply to SEPs, however, and it provides no guidance as to whether a particular application of state escheat law is preempted under ERISA Section 514. Most states provide for an unclaimed or abandoned IRA to escheat to the state after a number of years, and many documents provide for compliance by the trustee or custodian of such laws.

Creditor Protection

Q 4:68 Are SEP IRA assets subject to the claims of creditors or the IRS in a non-bankruptcy situation?

Nearly all states grant creditor protection for assets held in an IRA, including a SEP IRA. Most states, however, do not offer any protection from creditors for assets held in an IRA that is established and maintained by a participating employee for the holding of SEP contributions. Recently, the Sixth Circuit affirmed a district court order holding that an attorney's SEP was subject to garnishment to satisfy a judgment for violating ERISA. [Lampkins v. Golden, 28 Fed. App. LEXIS 409, 2002 WL 74449 (6th Cir. Jan. 17, 2002)] The status of assets held in an employer IRA under Code Section 408(c) has not been determined, but, in the authors' opinion, a participant's interest should be treated no differently from a regular, "self-settled" IRA.

Note. The IRS can enforce a federal lien against an IRA. [I.R.C. § 6334] Amounts distributed from an IRA, even if used to satisfy a federal lien, are generally (but not always) subject to the premature distribution penalty if the IRA owner is under age 59½. [Chief Counsel Notice N(36)000-2 (Jan. 21, 2000)]

Caution. It does not appear that an inherited IRA is exempt from creditors in a non-bankruptcy situation. [*See* Steve Leimberg's Employee Benefits and Retirement Planning Newsletter No. 422 (June 5, 2007) available at *http://www.leimbergservices.com* (visited on Aug. 15, 2012), regarding spendthrift trusts and decedent revocable trusts.] Even in states that have spendthrift trust provisions, almost 20 states permit any creditor to attach the required minimum distribution (RMD) amount from a standalone IRA trust. If a beneficiary is concerned regarding creditor attachment of the RMD amount, the IRA trust should reside in a state that statutorily codifies the asset protection benefits such as South Dakota or Delaware. [*See* UTC § 506 and Restatement 50, comment a; *see* South Dakota SB 98 (2007) or Delaware SB 117 (2007)]

Q 4:69 Are retirement benefits protected from creditors under ERISA?

Yes, but only if the plan is an employee benefit plan subject to Title I of ERISA (an "ERISA-covered plan"). An asset that is held in trust and subject to an enforceable non-bankruptcy restriction on transfer (a "spendthrift clause") is not part of the debtor's bankruptcy estate under federal or state law bankruptcy schemes (see Q 4:70). [11 U.S.C. § 541(c)(2); ERISA § 206(d)(1); 11 U.S.C. § 1056(d)(1)] In 1992 the Supreme Court ruled that an ERISA-required "anti-alienation" clause in a qualified pension plan is an enforceable non-bankruptcy law restriction on transfers within the meaning of 11 United States Code Section 541(c)(2). [Paterson v. Schumate, 504 U.S. 753 (1992)] SEP and SIMPLE IRA plans are not generally treated as ERISA plans for bankruptcy purposes (see Qs 4:1, 4:7, 4:11). The new bankruptcy rules provide protection for IRS qualified plans. Not all IRS qualified retirement plans are ERISA-covered plans. ERISA's anti-alienation clause applies only to "employee benefit plans." [*See* ERISA § 3(3); 29 U.S.C. § 1056(d)(1)] Under Department of Labor regulations, for purposes of determining whether a plan is an "employee benefit plan" covered by Title I of ERISA, an individual and his or her spouse are not deemed to be "employees" with respect to any business wholly owned by either or both of them, and a partner and his or her spouse are not "employees" with respect to the partnership. [DOL Reg. § 2510.3-1] Therefore, unless the plan covers one or more employees (other than the business owner, partners, and/or their spouses), the plan is not an employee benefit plan that is subject to ERISA's anti-alienation clause. [*See* Yates v. Hendon, 541 U.S. 1 (2004)] In such a case (for a plan without employees), the only exemptions for a non-ERISA "qualified plan" are found in Bankruptcy Code Section 522 (see Q 4:73). Although qualified plans are exempt in bankruptcy (see Q 4:73), the *Paterson* decision may still be useful when an ERISA-covered plan is not (or not treated as) a qualified plan, and state exemptions do not apply or are unavailable. To be an ERISA plan, the plan must cover at least one or more employees. If a plan also covers one or more employees (in addition to the business owner, partners, and/or their spouses), then it is an employee benefit plan under Title I of ERISA, and the sole business owner, partners, and/or their spouses are treated as "employees" and "plan participants" for ERISA Title I purposes. [*See* Yates v. Hendon, 541 U.S. 1 (2004)] A plan treated as an ERISA Title I plan is also exempt from creditors in the event of bankruptcy.

> **Caution.** On April 4, 2005, the Supreme Court unanimously ruled in *Rousey v. Jackoway,* [2003 WL 22382955 (8th Cir. 2003)] that IRA assets are protected from bankruptcy under Bankruptcy Code Section 522(e)(10)(E) to the extent that it "is reasonably necessary to support the account holder or his dependents." However, *Rousey* was an interpretation of pre-BAPCPA (Bankruptcy Abuse Prevention and Consumer Protection Act of 2005) rules. In light of the express provisions regarding IRAs (and other "retirement funds") in the BAPCPA, the court's holding in *Rousey* may no longer be applicable.

Bankruptcy

Q 4:70 What is a federal bankruptcy "exemption"?

In general, the debtor's bankruptcy estate includes, among other things, "all legal or equitable interests of the debtor in property." [11 U.S.C. §§ 541(a), 541(a)(1)] Once an item is included in the bankruptcy estate, an exemption may apply to exclude the item. Obviously, if an item is not considered part of the debtor's estate in the first place (e.g., spendthrift trust), it certainly will not be treated as part of the bankruptcy estate. [11 U.S.C. § 541(c)(2)] State and local law, when applicable, may also provide for additional exemptions. (See Q 4:69 regarding ERISA Title 1 covered plans.)

Q 4:71 What property is exempt in bankruptcy?

Exactly what property is protected in bankruptcy depends on the exemption scheme chosen.

Two exemption schemes are used. Bankruptcy Code Section 522(b)(1) provides that a debtor may exempt from property of the bankruptcy estate the property specified in Bankruptcy Code Section 522(b)(2), which is called the "federal law only" scheme, or Section 522(b)(3), which is called the "federal plus state law" scheme. Residency requirements determine which state's exemptions may be used, when applicable. [11 U.S.C. § 522(b)(3)(A)] If the petitioner is not properly domiciled (for federal bankruptcy purposes) in a state to be entitled to use that state's exemptions, the individual must use the "federal law only" scheme (i.e., 11 U.S.C. § 522(b)(3)). On the other hand, if the petitioner is properly domiciled (for federal bankruptcy purposes) in a state that requires the petitioner to use the "federal plus state law" scheme, the individual must do so. Otherwise, the debtor may choose one of the two schemes.

The exemptions for Bankruptcy Code Section 522(b)(2) (the federal law only scheme) are listed in Section 522(d). The Sections 522(d) and 522(b)(3) exemption lists are different; however, both lists include the following:

> [R]etirement funds to the extent that those funds are in a fund or account that is exempt from taxation under sections 401, 403, 408, 408A, 414, 457, or 501(a) of the Internal Revenue Code of 1986.

[*See* 11 U.S.C. §§ 522(b)(3)(C) (if federal plus state law scheme) and 522(d)(12) (if federal law only scheme)]

Regardless of which scheme is chosen, many types of retirement funds are protected in bankruptcy. For assets in an IRA or Roth IRA, other than those assets attributable to a SEP or a SIMPLE IRA, the aggregate value of such assets exempted shall not exceed $1 million (increased for inflation) in a case filed by a debtor who is an individual, except that such amount may be increased if the interests of justice so require. The $1 million cap (as increased for inflation) does not apply to amounts attributable to rollover contributions under Code Sections 402(c), 402(e)(6), 403(a)(4), 403(a)(5), and 403(b)(8). [11 U.S.C. §§ 522(b)(1), 522(b)(2), 522(b)(3), 522(d), 522(n); *see also* 11 U.S.C. § 522(d)(E)(10)]

An unlimited exemption applies to amounts attributable to contributions made by an employer (including elective contributions) to a SEP IRA or SIMPLE IRA. [11 U.S.C. §§ 522(b)(1), 522(b)(3)(C), 522(d) (referenced by § 522(b)(2))]

Caution. In a case of first impression, a bankruptcy court has concluded that, unlike a debtor's own traditional individual retirement account, a debtor's inherited IRA is not an exempt asset of her bankruptcy estate under Bankruptcy Code Section 522(d)(12). [*In re* Chilton (2010-1 U.S.T.C 50-275; Bankr. Tex. Mar. 5, 2010)] However, on March 16, 2011, the *Chilton* decision was reversed by the U.S. District Court for the Eastern District of Texas. [Chilton v. Moser, 444 B.R. 548 (E.D. Tex. 2011)]

However, *In re Nessa* [105 AFTR 2d 2010-609 (Jan. 11, 2010)], held that inherited IRAs transferred to another trustee remain retirement funds prior to distribution, and can be claimed exempt under Section 522(d)(12) of the Bankruptcy Code by debtor beneficiaries who are their equitable owners. Further, the Bankruptcy Court in *Nessa* stated that the funds did not lose their character as retirement funds and the account was exempt from tax under Bankruptcy Code Section 522(d)(12) [BAPCPA (Pub. L. No. 109-8) § 224; *see also In re* Tabor, 2010-1 U.S.T.C. 50,479 (Bankr. M.D. Pa.) (inherited IRAs). *See also In re* Mathusa, 446 B.R. 601 (Bankr. M.D. Fla. 2011) (following *Nessa*); Robertson v. Deeb, 16 So. 3d 936 (Fla. Dist. Ct. App. 2d Dist. 2009); *In re* Theim, 443 B.R. 832 (Bankr. D. Ariz. 2011) (exemption allowed under Bankruptcy Code § 522(d)(12) or § 522(b)(3)(C)); *In re* McClelland, 2008 WL 89901 (Bankr. D. Idaho 2008) (exemption allowed under Arizona statute); *In re* Tabor, 433 B.R. 469, 474 (Bankr M.D. Pa. 2010), and *In re* Kuchta, 434 B.R. 837 (Bankr. N.D. Ohio 2010) (exemption allowed under

Bankruptcy Code § 522(b)(3)(C))] There appears to be some consistency now that in herited IRAs are exempt assets under Bankruptcy Code Section 522(d)(12). [*See, e.g.*, *In re Stephenson*, 2011 U.S. Dist. LEXIS 142360 (E.D. Mich. 2011); *In re Weilhammer*, 2010 Bankr. LEXIS 2935 (Bankr. S.D. Cal. 2010); *In re Clark, 2012 U.S. Dist. LEXIS 8219 (W.D. Wis. Jan. 5, 2012), rev'g, 450 B.R. 858 (Bankr. W.D. 2011)] The courts' rulings in these cases do not appear to be limited by the kind of plan that was the source of the inherited IRA.*

Q 4:72 When are the new bankruptcy rules effective?

The Bankruptcy Abuse Prevention and Consumer Protection Act of 2005 (BAPCPA) changes to the Bankruptcy Code are generally effective with respect to cases filed after its effective date, October 17, 2005 (180 days after the date of enactment of BAPCPA, Apr. 20, 2005). [BAPCPA (Pub. L. No. 109-8) § 1501 (S. 246)] Special residency tests may apply in determining applicable state law. [11 U.S.C. § 522(b)(3)(A)]

Q 4:73 Are retirement plan assets protected in bankruptcy?

It depends, unless the plan is an ERISA plan (see Qs 4:1, 4:7, 4:11). Sweeping bankruptcy reforms were passed by the Senate as BAPCPA. [Pub. L. No. 109-8] The BAPCPA makes significant changes to the protection afforded to a debtor's interest in pension plans, benefits plans, and retirement accounts. In general, BAPCPA excludes from the bankruptcy estate retirement funds to the extent that those funds are in a fund or account that is exempt from tax, as follows:

- A traditional IRA and/or Roth IRA (other than SEP IRA or SIMPLE IRA), up to $1 million (as adjusted for inflation) in the aggregate, except that such amount may be increased if the interests of justice so require
- A SEP IRA or SIMPLE IRA, unlimited exemption. However, a $1 million cap (as adjusted for inflation) applies, in the aggregate, to annual amounts attributable to traditional IRA contributions (i.e., including earnings) that may be in a SEP IRA or SIMPLE IRA

Note. The $1 million exemption amount is adjusted every three years to reflect the change in the Consumer Price Index for All Urban Consumers published by the DOL for the three-year period ending December 31, 2009, and rounded to the nearest $25. For cases filed on or after April 1, 2010, the exemption amount increased from $1,095,000 to $1,171,650. The next three-year automatic adjustments of these dollar amounts will be published before March 1, 2013, and take effect April 1, 2013. [11 U.S.C. § 104(a); *see* 75 Fed. Reg. 8747 (Feb. 25, 2010) for revised amounts]

- A plan under Code Section 414 (governmental plans, church plans, multiemployer plans)
- A plan under Code Section 457 (eligible § 403(b) plans, ineligible 457(f) plans)

- A plan under Code Section 403 (qualified annuity plan, § 403(b) annuities, § 403(b)(7) mutual fund custodial accounts, § 403(b)(9) retirement income church accounts)
- A debtor's interest in retirement funds that are exempt from tax under Code Section 501(a)
- A direct rollover or distribution that is rolled over within the requisite 60-day period from a plan listed above to another such eligible plan
- Distributions from the plans listed previously that are rolled over within the requisite 60-day period from one plan listed previously to another such eligible plan. Thus, the rollover may be completed after the bankruptcy petition is filed (but within 60 days). [11 U.S.C. §§ 522(b)(4)(D)(i), 522(b)(4)(D)(ii)]

In addition, an employee benefit plan subject to Title I of ERISA is protected in bankruptcy. [Patterson v. Schumate, 504 U.S. 753 (1992)] Most, but not all qualified plans, are subject to Title I of ERISA (see Q 4:1).

> **Note.** The House legislative history accompanying S. 256 (BAPCPA) states that the "intent of section 224 is to expand the protections for tax-favored retirement plans or arrangements that may not be already protected under Bankruptcy Code Section 541(c)(2) . . ." [regarding property of the estate] ". . . pursuant to Patterson v. Schumate, 504 U.S. 753 (1992)." [House Rep. No. 109-31] Senator Orrin Hatch (R-UT) provided similar explanatory language when the Senate passed the bill on March 10, 2005. No conference committee was necessary because the House and Senate-passed bills were identical.

[11 U.S.C. §§ 522(b)(1), 522(b)(2), 522(b)(3), 522(n); *see also* 11 U.S.C. § 522(d)(E)(10)]

> **Note.** The $1 million cap (as adjusted for inflation) applicable to traditional IRAs (other than funds attributable to SEP IRA or a SIMPLE IRA contributions) may be raised, presumably on a case-by-case basis, "if the interests of justice so require." [11 U.S.C. § 522(n)] Although the economic value of a Roth IRA (which generally allows for tax-free distributions) is worth more than a traditional IRA (where distributions are generally taxable, except to the extent that nondeductible contributions are distributed), the new bankruptcy rules make no distinction. Thus, all traditional IRAs (other than funds attributable to SEP IRA or SIMPLE IRA contributions) and Roth IRAs are aggregated and generally subject to the $1 million cap.

Once a debtor goes into bankruptcy, they become subject to the bankruptcy law exemption limitations. Thus, under BAPCPA, the following are likely results for traditional IRA funds under both bankruptcy schemes:

1. If the federal law only scheme is used under Bankruptcy Code Section and the state-law traditional IRA exemption is
   a. $100,000. The exemption amount is increased to $1 million ($1,171,650 for federal bankruptcy cases filed on or after April 1, 2010

(was $1,095,000)). [11 U.S.C. § 522(d)(12)] The state exemption is trumped.

b. $1 million. Remains at $1 million ($1,171,650 for federal bankruptcy cases filed on or after April 1, 2010 (was $1,095,000)).

c. $2 million. The state exemption amount is capped at $1 million ($1,171,650 for federal bankruptcy cases filed on or after April 1, 2010 (was $1,095,000)). [11 U.S.C. § 522(n)]

2. If the federal plus state law exemption scheme is used (e.g., in an opt-out state) under Bankruptcy Code Section 522(b)(3) and the state-law traditional IRA exemption is

    a. $100,000. The exemption amount is increased to $1 million ($1,171,650 for federal bankruptcy cases filed on or after April 1, 2010). [11 U.S.C. § 522(b)(3)(C)]

    b. $1 million. Remains at $1 million ($1,171,650 for federal bankruptcy cases filed on or after April 1, 2010).

    c. $2 million. The state exemption amount is capped at $1 million ($1,171,650 for federal bankruptcy cases filed on or after April 1, 2010). [11 U.S.C. § 522(n)]

Thus, under BAPCPA, the new retirement plan rules apply both to the federal exemption scheme and override all opt-out state exemption schemes. [*In re* Baker, 590 F.3d 1261 (11th Cir. 2009); Foster, "Protection of Tax Qualified Retirement Benefits from Creditors under the Bankruptcy Abuse Prevention and Consumer Protection Act of 2005," available at *http://www.lawmh.com/uploads/publications/TrustandEstatesArticle.pdf* (visited on Aug. 15, 2012)]

An IRA that ceases to be an IRA because of a prohibited transaction (see Q 1:22) would not be exempt from the bankruptcy estate. [*In re* Ernest W. Willis (Bankr. FL Aug. 6, 2009), 104 AFTR 2d 2009-5195]

Note. In the authors' opinion, Bankruptcy Code Section 522(n) solely, only, and exclusively provides protections to IRAs in a federal bankruptcy proceeding.

Note. A taxpayer should consider segregating their voluntary contribution IRAs from rollover arrangements so that accounting and calculation to determine what is protected in future years will not be an expensive or uncertain process.

Caution. It would appear that amounts attributable to an inherited IRA that originated from a qualifying rollover distribution from a "qualified plan" are not subject to the $1 million (as adjusted for inflation) cap. [11 U.S.C. § 522(n)]

The following examples assume the new bankruptcy provisions of BAPCPA are in effect.

Example 1. John has a SEP IRA. His employer SEP contributions (including elective contributions if a SARSEP) aggregated $3 million (with earnings). He rolled over $1.5 million from a qualified plan that is now worth $2 million.

John also made annual contributions into his IRA that are now worth $500,000. John's entire IRA is protected from creditors. Amounts in the IRA attributable to the SEP contributions and the rollover contributions from the qualified plan have an unlimited exemption. The portions representing annual contributions to the traditional IRA are also exempt because they do not exceed the $1 million exemption limit amount ($1,171,650 as adjusted for inflation).

Example 2. Same facts as in Example 1, except that the portion of John's SEP IRA attributable to annual traditional contributions is worth $4 million. John's bankruptcy estate will include $2,828,350 of the $4 million because only the first $1,171,650 is covered by the exemption (unless the interests of justice require a larger amount to be exempt). [11 U.S.C. § 522(n)]

Example 3. Same facts as in Example 2, except John is responsible for supporting a wife and seven children; he is also disabled and has limited resources outside of his bankruptcy estate. If the "interests of justice so require," the bankruptcy trustee could exempt more than the $1,171,650 attributable to annual traditional IRA contributions. [11 U.S.C. § 522(n)]

Note. Under the new bankruptcy law (as changed by BAPCPA), a state's homestead exemption will only protect the debtor's interest in excess of $125,000 ($146,450, effective April 1, 2010 through March 21 2013), if allowed by local state law, if the interest was acquired at least 1,215 days (3 years and 4 months) before the filing of the bankruptcy petition. [11 U.S.C. § 104(a)] Interests in excess of $146,450 (the current limit) that are acquired within the 1,215-day period are not protected. Thus, a debtor no longer can pay down a home mortgage immediately before bankruptcy and expect the new home equity to be exempted from the bankruptcy estate if the equity in the homestead exceeds $146,450.

Note. The $125,000 homestead exemption amount is increased every three years for the Consumer Price Index for All Urban Consumers. Effective April 1, 2007, the $125,000 amount was increased to $136,875. The amount was increased to $146,450 effective on April 1, 2010. [11 U.S.C. § 104(a); *see* 75 Fed. Reg. 8747 (Feb. 25, 2010) for revised amounts]

Note. It may be possible for a state homestead exemption law to be given extraterritorial effect to exempt property located in another state. [E.g., Debtor moves from a state that has a $300,000 exemption amount (e.g., Rhode Island) to another state, Florida (which has an unlimited exemption amount), but does not qualify for Florida's homestead exemption with respect to a home recently purchased (within 730 days) in Florida. The court applied the Rhode Island exemption to the Florida property, and explained when extraterritorial effect can be given to a state's homestead exemption for property located in another state. *See In re Jevne* (Bankr. S.D. Fla. 2008)]

Example 4. Joe lives in a state with an unlimited homestead exemption but no exemption for retirement assets. His home is worth $7 million. He has a traditional IRA and a Roth IRA worth $800,000. None of the funds in the traditional IRA consist of assets that were rolled over from a protected plan or are attributable to SEP IRA or SIMPLE IRA contributions. If Joe does not file for bankruptcy, his IRA and Roth IRA funds may not be protected, but if he does file for bankruptcy, then his homestead may be limited to $146,450.

Example 5. Same facts as in Example 4, except Joe's Roth IRA and traditional IRA are worth $2 million. Only $1,171,650 of the IRA assets will be protected in bankruptcy (unless the interests of justice require a greater amount to be exempt). [11 U.S.C. § 522(n)]

Example 6. Same facts as in Example 4, except Joe is domiciled (for federal bankruptcy purposes) in an opt-out state that requires him to use the "federal plus state-law exemptions." Joe's IRA is not treated as an ERISA plan; therefore, the IRA will only be exempt to the extent provided by Bankruptcy Code Section 522(b)(3) and other federal, state, and local law. Although the state does not provide for an exemption, Section 522(b)(3) excludes the IRA. [11 U.S.C. § 522(b)(3)(D)] Thus, $1,171,650 is exempt property and cannot be reached in bankruptcy. The result would be the same if state or local law exempted less than $1 million (say, $250,000) or more (say, $2 million). Because Joe is precluded from using the "federal law only" scheme, he may not use the exemptions found in Bankruptcy Code Section 522(d); the exemptions found in Section 522(b)(A) through (D) are applicable (which include federal nonbankruptcy law and applicable state and local laws. [11 U.S.C. § 522(b)(3)(A)]

Note. Asset protection plans were also attacked by BAPCPA by giving bankruptcy trustees broad powers to avoid transfers made to such trusts. [11 U.S.C. §§ 548, 548(a), 548(b)] Before BAPCPA, a debtor could threaten to file a bankruptcy petition to wipe out creditors' claims. Now, creditors may threaten to force a debtor into bankruptcy so that the debtor's assets can be reached.

Automatic Rollover of Mandatory Distributions

Q 4:74 May an employer adopt an IRA for a missing participant to comply with the mandatory direct rollover rules under ERISA?

Yes. Beginning March 28, 2005, an employer must generally directly roll (transfer) to an IRA any mandatory distribution (cash out) of more than $1,000, but less than $5,000, if the distribution is eligible for rollover treatment and such participant does not elect another payment method. [DOL Reg. § 2550.404a-2(e), 69 Fed. Reg. 187 (Sept. 28, 2004); I.R.C. § 401(a)(31)(B); *see also* EGTRRA § 657; HR Conf. Rep. No. 107-84 (2001)] The final regulations generally apply, with some exceptions, to any rollover of a mandatory distribution made on or after March 28, 2005. [*See* I.R.S. Notice 2005-5, Part III, Qs 5–9, 16 (2005-3 I.R.B. 337) for effective dates for various plan types and transitional rules.]

The 402(f) notice ("Special Tax Notice" or "Rollover Notice"), which is provided to terminated participants who are entitled to a distribution, is required to indicate the IRA into which the rollover will be made if the participant does not affirmatively elect a distribution from the plan. In addition, the summary plan description will be required to also contain information about the IRA that is selected for the mandatory direct rollover. [DOL Reg. § 2550.404a-2(c)(4), 69 Fed. Reg. 187 (Sept. 28, 2004); *see* I.R.S. Notice 2009-69, 2009-39 I.R.B. 423]

On December 28, 2004, the IRS issued Notice 2005-5 containing guidance and clarifications and addressed some of the practical applications of these rules to IRA providers. [I.R.S. Notice 2005-5, Part III, 2005-3 I.R.B. 337] The notice also contains a sample plan amendment for employer plans. Some of the guidance in the notice included the following:

1. Clarification that the plan administrator may sign the IRA plan agreement and any other documents necessary to establish an IRA on the participant's behalf;
2. Indicated that the plan administrator must use the participant's most recent mailing address on record when establishing the IRA;
3. The trustee or custodian may satisfy the written disclosure and revocation requirements by mailing the disclosure statement to the address provided by the plan administrator, even if it is returned as undeliverable;
4. Indicated that the automatic rollover requirement will be satisfied if the employer rolls over such distribution to deemed IRAs within the employer's plan; and
5. The type of IRA receiving the automatic direct rollover must be a traditional IRA and includes an Employer IRA under Code Section 408(c) or a Deemed IRA under 408(q).

Q 4:75 What must the trustee/custodian do to permit future distributions from the account?

Because the employer is required to update and amend certain plan documentation, before the employer indicates which IRA trustee/custodian will be used, the employer should confirm that the selected IRA trustee/custodian will be offering these rollover accounts. Once the IRA trustee/custodian is selected by the employer, the IRA trustee/custodian should set up internal procedures to handle these accounts. It should be specified, for example, what forms must be signed by the employer to establish the IRA and where the statements should be mailed.

The Treasury Department, along with other agencies, has determined that the customer identification program (CIP) requirements under the USA Patriot Act will become applicable only when the former participant or beneficiary contacts the IRA institution to claim ownership or exercise control over the assets in the IRA Account. Therefore, the CIP requirements will not apply at the time the assets are automatically rolled over into the IRA, but rather upon distribution. The trustee/custodian would, therefore, apply its own internal policy to comply with the USA Patriot Act at the point of distribution. [USA Patriot Act (Pub. L. No. 107-56) § 326, amending Bank Secrecy Act (Pub. L. No.

91-508, 31 U.S.C. § 5311; Preamble, DOL Reg. § 2550.404a-2, 69 Fed. Reg. 58018 (Sept. 28, 2004); I.R.S. Notice 2005-5, 2005-3 I.R.B. 337, n. 1]

Q 4:76 Does the establishment of a traditional IRA by an employer violate the USA Patriot Act?

No. There was a concern by many financial institutions that there might be legal problems under the USA Patriot Act concerning setting up an IRA without a participant's signature and other information that may not be available. [USA Patriot Act § 326, amending 31 U.S.C. § 5318]

In January 2004, the Treasury Department, along with other agencies, determined that the customer identification and verification requirements under the USA Patriot Act will become applicable only when the former participant or beneficiary first contacts the IRA institution to claim ownership or exercise control over the assets in the IRA. Therefore, these CIP requirements will not apply at the time the assets are automatically rolled over into the IRA. [*See* Preamble, DOL Reg. § 2550.404a-2, 69 Fed. Reg. 187, 58018-58028, 58023 (Sept. 28, 2004). *See also Interagency Interpretive Guidance on Customer Identification Program Requirements under Section 326 of the USA PATRIOT Act* (Apr. 28, 2008) available at: *http://www.fincen.gov/statutes_regs/guidance/pdf/faqsfinalciprule.pdf* (visited on Aug. 15, 2012)]

Bonding

Q 4:77 Are SEP IRA and SIMPLE IRA plans subject to the ERISA bonding requirements?

Maybe. In most cases, an employer that handles funds or other property belonging to an ERISA plan (see Qs 4:1, 4:32) is required to be bonded to protect the plan against "fraud and dishonesty" by plan officials. The basic standard is determined by the possibility of risk of loss in each situation; thus, it is based on the facts and circumstances in each situation. The amount of a bond is determined at the beginning of each year. It may not be less than 10 percent of the amount of funds handled, and the minimum bond is $1,000. Contributions made by withholding from an employee's salary are not considered funds or other property of a SEP IRA or SIMPLE IRA plan for purposes of the bonding provisions as long as they are retained in, and not segregated in any way from, the general assets of the withholding employer. Because employer contributions are made into traditional or SIMPLE IRAs established by each employee (which are outside the control of an employer once made), bonding would not generally apply. [ERISA §§ 404(c), 412; DOL Reg. §§ 2510.3-3, 2550.412-5; Field Assistance Bulletin 2008-4 (Nov. 25, 2008)] A payroll deduction IRA is not subject to the bonding rules, provided the arrangement is not treated as a pension plan (see Q 4:32).

Bonding Exception. An exception to the bonding requirement generally applies for a fiduciary (or a director, officer, or employee of the fiduciary) that is a corporation authorized to exercise trust powers or conduct an insurance business if the corporation is subject to supervision or examination by federal or state regulators and meets certain financial requirements. The PPA provides an exception to the ERISA bonding requirement for an entity registered as a broker or a dealer under the Securities Exchange Act of 1934 if the broker or dealer is subject to the fidelity bond requirements of a self-regulatory organization (within the meaning of the Securities Exchange Act of 1934).

The plan must be the named insured or otherwise be identified on the bond to enable plan representatives to make a claim in the event of a covered loss. Deductibles are not allowed, at least up to the amount of the mandated coverage. A one-year discovery period upon termination of the bond is required so that a plan may assert for claims for events occurring during the term of the bond.

Effective date: The bonding exception provision is effective for plan years beginning on or after 2007. [PPA § 611(c); ERISA § 412(a)(2), as amended by PPA § 611(b)]

In addition, the PPA raises the maximum bond amount from $500,000 to $1 million in the case of a plan that holds employer securities. A plan would not be considered to hold employer securities within the meaning of this section where the only securities held by the plan are part of a broadly diversified fund of assets, such as mutual or index funds.

Effective date: The bonding provisions relating to employer securities is effective for plan years beginning on or after January 1, 2008. [PPA § 622(b), ERISA § 412(i), as amended by PPA § 412(a)]

The taxpayer's obligation under the bond must be secured by a surety, and the company acting as surety on the bond must hold a Certificate of Authority from the Department of the Treasury, Financial Management Service. These companies are listed in Treasury Department Circular 570, Companies Holding Certificates of Authority as Acceptable Sureties on Federal Bonds and as Acceptable Reinsuring Companies. [Circular 570 is available at *http://www.fms.treas.gov/c570/c570.html* (visited on Aug. 15, 2012); *see also* DOL Field Assistance Bulletin 2008-04 (Nov. 24, 2008), providing guidance to regional offices regarding bonding requirements under ERISA;DOL Adv. Op. 2004-07A (July 1, 2004), addressing technical bonding issues and exceptions for certain corporations]

FDIC Coverage

Q 4:78 Has the Federal Deposit Insurance Corporation raised the coverage limit for a SEP-IRA or SIMPLE-IRA?

Yes. The Federal Deposit Insurance Corporation (FDIC) raised the coverage threshold from $100,000 to $250,000 for most types of retirement plans. There also are strategies for insuring greater amounts in other accounts. On February 8, 2006, Congress passed legislation and President Bush signed it into law. Any changes in the insurance rules and their effective dates will be noted on the FDIC Web site at *http://www.fdic.gov* (visited on Aug. 15, 2012). Strategies to increase coverage above $250,000 for most retirement accounts are available. In March 2006, the FDIC's Board of Directors approved final rules that raised the deposit insurance coverage on certain retirement accounts at a bank or savings institution from $100,000 to $250,000. The increase became effective on April 1, 2006. [*See* Federal Deposit Insurance Act (12 U.S.C. § 1811 *et seq.*) and the FDIC's regulations relating to insurance coverage (12 C.F.R. Part 330); *see also http://www.fdic.gov/deposit/deposits/index.html* (visited on Aug. 15, 2012)]

Deposits owned by one person and titled in the name of that person's retirement account qualify for coverage up to $250,000. The following types of retirement accounts which are owned by the same person in the same FDIC-insured bank are added together and the total is insured to $250,000:

- All types of traditional IRAs (including Roth IRAs and SIMPLE IRAs);
- 457(b) deferred compensation plan accounts (regardless of whether they are self-directed); and
- Self-directed qualified defined contribution plan accounts, including self-directed Keogh plan accounts (or H.R. 10 plan accounts) designed for self-employed individuals.

Chapter 5

Making Contributions and Taking Distributions: SEPs and SARSEPs

This chapter examines the basic rules that govern the making of contributions, the effect of participation in other retirement plans, the general rules pertaining to distributions, and the mechanics of removing excess IRA, SEP, and SARSEP contributions. This chapter also discusses the impact of USERRA (Uniformed Services Employment and Reemployment Rights Act of 1994), which requires that employers treat certain rehired military employees as employed during their military service.

Making Contributions to SEPs and SARSEPs

Q 5:1 Must SEP contributions be based on business profits?

No. SEP contributions made by employers on behalf of their employees do not need to be based on profits or accumulated retained earnings. Special rules apply, however, to contributions made on behalf of owners of unincorporated entities. The deduction for contributions made on behalf of such an owner cannot exceed the owner's earned income (see chapter 7).

Q 5:2 May SEP contributions be made after the end of an employer's taxable year?

Yes. An employer may make nonelective SEP contributions until the due date of the employer's Federal Business Tax Return, including extensions (see Qs 2:32, 2:35).

Q 5:3 May employer SEP contributions be claimed on a tax return filed before the date that they are actually made?

Yes. An employer may deduct contributions to a SEP on its business tax return, even when the contributions are made after the business tax return is filed, if the contributions are made on or before the due date of the return. [Rev. Rul. 84-18, 1984-1 C.B. 88]

Q 5:4 May an employee or owner opt out of a SEP arrangement?

No. There is no provision in the Internal Revenue Code (Code) that allows an employee, including an owner-employee, to opt out of a SEP. If an employer contribution is made, the contribution must be allocated among all eligible employees in accordance with the plan's written allocation formula. Presumably, a plan that did not make a contribution for an eligible employee would fail to be a plan, as described in Code Section 408(k), for that year. [I.R.C. § 408(k)(2)]

> **Example.** Oscar and Oswald, both age 61 (i.e., older than age 59½), are the owners of Double-O, Inc. They want to establish a SEP for their nonowner-employees but do not want to receive company contributions. Their second goal is not possible. All eligible employees must participate; thus, Oscar and Oswald must receive contributions from Double-O. Oscar and Oswald may, however, withdraw the contributions after they are made, and may even be able to defer tax on the contributions for a year or more because the contributions may be made and withdrawn after the end of the year. Double-O will not have to pay Social Security (FICA) or federal unemployment (FUTA) tax on the contributions because nonelective contributions to, and distributions from, SEPs are not subject to FICA or FUTA tax (see Qs 11:9–11:11, 11:15).

> **Note.** Before the EGTRRA restatement of SEP plans, the IRS had approved some prototype SEPs that did permit highly compensated employees to receive less as a contribution (including zero) than the non-highly compensated employees. This is no longer permitted. A sponsor that has such a provision should contact the IRS.

Q 5:5 Are all SEP and SARSEP contributions excludable from an employee's gross income and deductible by the employer?

No. There are limits on how much of an employer's SEP contribution may be excluded from an employee's gross income (see Q 11:1). Separate rules determine how much of the contribution may be deducted by the employer (see chapter 10).

Q 5:6 Is there an overall limit on how much may be contributed to a SEP or SARSEP?

Yes. Code Section 415 establishes an overall limit on how much may be contributed to a SEP or SARSEP arrangement on behalf of any individual employee. Two 25 percent limits also apply for years after 2001 (see Qs 5:11, 11:1). If the Section 415 limit is exceeded, the SEP or SARSEP may be disqualified (see Qs 5:8, 5:10). Any other defined contribution plans maintained by the employer must be aggregated with the SEP or SARSEP for the purpose of determining whether the Section 415 limit has been exceeded. The Section 415 limit applies whether or not the contributions are excludable from the gross income of the employee or are deductible by the employer.

The total amount, including elective deferrals, that may be contributed to a SEP and any other defined contribution plans of an employer on behalf of an employee for 2012 is the lesser of $50,000 or 100 percent of compensation includible in gross income. [*See* I.R.S. Notice 2011-90, 2011-47 I.R.B. 791 for 2012 limits] (See Appendix G for other limits.) The Section 415 dollar limit for earlier years is as follows:

$49,000 for 2009 through 2011

$46,000 for 2008

$45,000 for 2007

$44,000 for 2006

$42,000 for 2005

$41,000 for 2004

$40,000 for 2002 and 2003

$35,000 or 25 percent for 2001

(See Q 6:1.) [I.R.C. §§ 415(c)(1)(A), 415(c)(1)(B), 415(c)(3); Treas. Reg. §§ 1.415(c)-1(a)(1),1.514(c)-1(a)(2)(i)(C)]

Note. The $50,000 limit does not prohibit the catch-up contribution (see Q 1:34) from being made. Thus, up to $55,500 may be contributed for 2012 if the employee is age 50 or older (see chapter 12). For 2012, the catch-up contribution limit is $5,500.

Practice Pointer. *After* 1997, elective deferrals under Code Sections 402(g), 125, and 457 do not reduce compensation for purposes of the Section 415 limit. [I.R.C. § 415(c)(3)(D)] However, for purposes of the 25 percent allocation limit, compensation does not include elective deferrals (I.R.C. § 402(g)) or any amount that is contributed by the employer at the election of the employee and that is not includible in the income of the employee under a cafeteria plan (I.R.C. § 125), a Code Section 457 deferred compensation plan, or that is an excluded qualified transportation fringe benefit. [I.R.C. § 132(f)(4)]

In some cases, business entities are treated as a single employer for purposes of the Section 415 limit. Two or more entities must be aggregated (treated as a single employer) under the following Code sections:

- Code Section 414(b) (relating to controlled groups of corporations)
- Code Section 414(c) (relating to commonly controlled businesses)
- Code Section 414(m) (relating to affiliated service groups)
- Code Section 414(o) (containing special rules to prevent the avoidance of certain employee benefit requirements through the use of separate organizations or employee-leasing arrangements)

(See Qs 2:4–2:17.)

Note. Special rules apply to contribution limits if an employer has any leased employees (see Q 2:85). Special rules also apply to employees covered under both a SEP and a 403(b) plan (see Q 2:10).

Restorative payments. In Letter Ruling 200738025 (June 26, 2007), the IRS ruled that amounts received by married taxpayers from a company broker-dealer pursuant to an arm's length settlement of a good faith claim of liability were "restorative" payments, rather than additional contributions subject to the annual IRA contribution limits. Here, the taxpayers withdrew from a pending class action lawsuit and converted to an arbitration action. The IRS allowed the arbitration settlement agreement amount that was designated as the amount associated with the IRA losses to be contributed to the IRA, notwithstanding the annual IRA contribution limits of $5,000/$6,000 for 2012. [*See also* Rev. Rul. 2002-45, 2002-2 C.B. 116; Ltr. Rul. 200921039 (Feb. 25, 2009), interest accrued on settlement not part of the restorative IRA payment]

Q 5:7 Are specific plan provisions required to be incorporated in a SEP to address the limits under Code Section 415?

No. A plan simply may not allow the limits imposed by Code Section 415 to be exceeded. [I.R.C. § 415(k)(1)(F); Treas. Reg. § 1.415(a)-1(d)(1)] Although plan provisions regarding Code Section 415(e) are not specifically required in a SEP arrangement, all SEPs contain provisions that limit the allocation of contributions to a participant to the lesser of 100 percent of compensation or $50,000/$55,500 for 2012 (see Q 3:2). The 100 percent limit under Code Section 415 is rarely exceeded, because the 25 percent of taxable compensation participant exclusion allowance is always lower (see Q 11:1).

Q 5:8 What happens if the overall Section 415 limit is exceeded?

A SEP arrangement that violates the limits of Code Section 415 is disqualified after all other nonterminated plans have been disqualified. That is, if two or more plans are available, and if one of the plans is a SEP (as defined in Code Section 408(k)), the SEP will not be disqualified until all other plans have been disqualified. If, however, an employer has terminated a plan, the SEP will be disqualified before the terminated plan is disqualified. [Treas. Reg. § 1.415(g)-1(b)(3)(iv) (special rules for SEPs)]

Q 5:9 Can Section 415 violations be corrected?

Yes. Under Revenue Procedure 2008-50 [2008-35 I.R.B. 464], the Internal Revenue Service (IRS) allows employers to correct a Section 415 violation either by self-correction or by submission of an appropriate correction method to the IRS (see chapter 17).

Q 5:10 What happens if a SEP is disqualified?

If a SEP arrangement is disqualified, none of the contributions are deductible by the employer as SEP contributions, and the employer must include all contributions (including salary reduction amounts) in the employee's gross income when they are made. [I.R.C. § 402(h)(1)] The disqualification of a SEP means that it no longer meets the requirements of Code Section 408(k). [Treas. Reg. § 1.415(g)-1(b)(3)(iv)] The failure may generally be corrected under the EPCRS (see Q 17:1).

Q 5:11 How much may be contributed to a SEP arrangement and deducted by an employer for 2012?

Generally, 25 percent of each participant's includible taxable compensation, up to $250,000 (as indexed), may be contributed to a SEP, excluded by the employee from gross income, and deducted by an employer for 2012 (see Qs 1:3, 6:14, 6:15, 6:16 and chapters 10 and 11). [I.R.C. § 404(h)(2)(A)]

Because 25 percent of $250,000 exceeds the overall Section 415 contribution limit of the lesser of 100 percent of gross compensation or $50,000 (see Q 5:6), the maximum amount that generally may be contributed on behalf of any participant in a SEP or a SARSEP for 2012 is $50,000 ($55,500 with a catch-up contribution) (but see Q 11:5). If the employer maintains or maintained a defined benefit plan, other limits may apply (see Q 5:6).

For purposes of calculating the 25 percent employer deduction limit, the compensation of each participant (up to $250,000 for 2012) is aggregated. For taxable years beginning after 2001, compensation for *deduction* purposes includes elective deferrals; that is, compensation is gross compensation (see Q 10:3). Because the participant exclusion limit is only based on includible compensation, it is possible that an employer would have to include a portion of a fully deductible contribution under a SARSEP in a participant's gross income (see Q 11:2). [I.R.C. §§ 404(l), 414(s)(2)] The participant exclusion limit is also always based on calendar year compensation, regardless of when the plan year ends (see Q 11:1).

Q 5:12 To what extent may eligible employees make contributions with pretax dollars under a SARSEP?

An employer may allow its eligible employees to reduce their taxable income by as much as $17,000 for 2012 by means of a salary reduction agreement (see Qs 1:2, 2:18). In addition, catch-up contributions may be permitted (see Q 12:6). Amounts in excess of the dollar limit are included in the individual's gross income (see Qs 12:6, 12:19). [I.R.C. § 402(g)(1)]

Elective contributions (other than catch-up contributions) are also subject to the general 25 percent (15 percent before 2002) exclusion limit (see Qs 5:13, 10:3, 11:1).

Q 5:13 To what extent are contributions excludable from an employee's taxable compensation?

SEP contributions are generally excluded from an employee's taxable compensation to the extent that the employer's contribution does not exceed 25 percent of the employee's taxable compensation actually included in gross income or $50,000, whichever is less for 2012 (see Qs 11:1, 11:7). [I.R.C. § 402(h)(2)(A) (referencing I.R.C. § 414(s))] The $50,000 amount is reduced slightly if the plan is integrated with Social Security (see Qs 9:1, 9:3, 11:8). [I.R.C. § 402(h)(2)(B); Treas. Reg. § 1.219-3(e), ex. (2)] The compensation limit may be adjusted upward for cost-of-living increases. [I.R.C. § 415(d)(2)(C)] Catch-up elective contributions are not subject to the 25 percent participation exclusion limit or to the $50,000 Code Section 415 limit and may be separately excluded from a participant's gross income (see Q 11:2).

If the elective and nonelective SEP contributions exceed $50,000 (as indexed and adjusted) or 25 percent of includible compensation, the elective contributions must be reduced (or the excess included in income). [Rev. Proc. 91-44, § VI(C), 1991-2 C.B. 733] That, in turn, could require a recalculation of the percentage of salary allowed to be deferred by each eligible highly compensated employee (HCE) (see Qs 1:13–1:17). Conversely, if the overall contribution for 2012 is less than $50,000 or 25 percent of includible compensation, recalculation of each employee's actual deferral percentage (ADP) is not required.

For purposes of the individual 25 percent exclusion limit, compensation is not limited to $250,000 (as indexed for 2012). Neither Code Section 401(a)(17) nor Code Section 404(l) applies to Code Section 402(h)(2)(A) or limits the amount of compensation that can be taken into account in calculating the 25 percent of compensation exclusion limit. Nonetheless, a plan must provide language that would prohibit more than $50,000 ($55,500 with a catch-up contribution) from being allocated to any one participant (see Q 11:5).

Q 5:14 Are SEP and SARSEP contributions that exceed the $5,000/$6,000 annual IRA deduction limit treated as excess IRA contributions?

No. Elective and nonelective contributions to a SEP or SARSEP that are not includible in an employee's income under Code Section 402(h) (see Q 5:13) are treated as amounts allowed as regular individual retirement account or individual retirement annuity (IRA) contributions for the year (see Q 2:55). Thus, the normal traditional IRA contributions limits are increased for allowable SEP contributions.

Q 5:15 May SEP contributions be forfeited?

No. Contributions made to IRAs, SEP IRAs, or SARSEP IRAs of employees are nonforfeitable; that is, they are fully vested at all times in the name of the employee. [I.R.C. § 408(a)(4), (b)(4), (k)(1)]

Q 5:16 May SEP contributions or any assets in a SEP IRA be returned to the employer?

No. Generally, any reversion of SEP contributions or assets in a SEP IRA to the employer is prohibited by the Employee Retirement Income Security Act of 1974 (ERISA) (see Q 4:4). Under the IRS's EPCRS program (see chapter 17), there are correction methods available that require certain "nondeductible employer contributions" to be returned to the employer, but reported in the employee's name indicating the taxable amount as zero by placing "0" in box 2a on Form 1099-R (see Q 17:28).

> **Note.** The EPCRS program recognizes the SEP as an employer plan. The employer, however, is not a party to the agreements establishing the SEP IRAs and has neither dominion nor control over the assets in such an arrangement, nor does the employer have any control as to their investment or disposition. The employer is not authorized to order, direct, or effectuate any distribution from the SEP IRA accounts; all such rights in the account reside solely with the employee who established the account. Arguably, the participant could approve of the distribution but is not required to do so. In practice, however, institutions have developed distribution forms that require both the employer's and the employee's signatures.

Q 5:17 May SEP contributions be withdrawn by an employee at any time?

Generally, yes. It must be noted, however, that elective contributions made to a SARSEP may not be withdrawn or transferred to another IRA or SEP IRA until a determination is made by the employer that the special 125 percent nondiscrimination test has been satisfied (see Q 12:9) or until the March 15 following the plan year-end, whichever is earlier. This is referred to as the *determination date*. The trustee or custodian of the IRA may enforce that restriction; failure to do so could result in penalties to the employee and loss of

SEP status for the arrangement (see Qs 5:18, 5:19). Special rules may apply to the removal of elective contributions made under an automatic contribution arrangement (see Q 12:1).

Q 5:18 What happens to amounts withdrawn from a SEP before the determination date?

Until the determination date (see Q 5:17), any transfer or distribution of restricted funds (salary reduction contributions and income attributable to such contributions) from a SEP is subject to tax and may be subject to the 10 percent premature distribution penalty tax, regardless of whether an exception to the penalty tax would otherwise apply. Excess elective deferrals (see Q 5:20) may be withdrawn before the determination date but may not be rolled over or transferred to another IRA. Special rules may apply to the removal of elective contributions made under an automatic contribution arrangement (see Q 12:1).

Any distribution, transfer, or rollover of restricted funds before the determination date is treated as other than an excess contribution permitted to be withdrawn without penalty. The penalty tax, if any, is reported in Part I of Form 5329, Additional Taxes on Qualified Plans (Including IRAs) and Other Tax Favored Accounts.

Although only HCEs can fail the 125 percent nondiscrimination test (see Q 12:9), the withdrawal restriction appears to apply to all participating employees. That is probably so because HCEs might not be identified until, or after, the end of the year (see Q 1:14). The model elective SEP deferral form, Form 5305A-SEP, provides notice to *all* participating employees that they should not withdraw or transfer any amount from the IRA until either March 15 or earlier notification by the employer that the 125 percent nondiscrimination test has been satisfied and that the withdrawal restriction no longer applies. The instructions for the employer on Form 5305A-SEP, however, state only that "highly compensated employees may not withdraw or transfer" restricted funds.

> **Note.** Under Code Section 408(k)(6)(F), the Secretary of the Treasury has broad discretion to issue reporting and other requirements to "insure" that contributions (and any income allocable thereto) may not be withdrawn until the 125 percent nondiscrimination test has been satisfied. The rules and legislative history of Code Section 408(k)(6)(F) are very vague, but, in the authors' opinion, it could easily be inferred that the penalty tax applies to *any* employee who withdraws restricted funds. [I.R.C. § 408(d)(7)(A); TAMRA § 1011(f)(1)–1011(f)(5); *see* Listing of Required Modifications and Information Package (LRM), Simplified Employee Pensions, Item V (March 2002)]

Q 5:19 What happens if an IRA containing restricted funds is revoked by the participant within the seven-day revocation period?

If an IRA is revoked during the first seven days following its establishment, the distribution from the IRA is reported on Form 1099-R, Distributions from

Pensions, Annuities, Retirement or Profit-Sharing Plans, IRAs, Insurance Contracts, etc., as a taxable distribution (see Q 13:119). Form 5498, IRA Contribution Information, must also be filed with the IRS by the trustee or issuer to report the fair market value of the SEP IRA, if any. [Treas. Reg. § 1.408-6(d)(4)(ii); TD 7714, 45 Fed. Reg. 52795 (Aug. 8, 1980)]

It is not entirely clear whether the distribution may be delayed until employer notification requirements concerning restricted funds are satisfied. The instructions to Form 1099-R state that if an IRA is timely revoked, the distribution from the IRA must be reported. Thus, it appears that a distribution may be required upon revocation, notwithstanding the general prohibition against removing restricted funds.

Q 5:20 May amounts in excess of $17,000 be withdrawn before the 125 percent nondiscrimination test has been satisfied?

Yes. Excess elective deferrals (amounts generally in excess of $17,000 for 2012 are not subject to the withdrawal restriction discussed previously (see Qs 5:17, 5:18).

Q 5:21 May an employer deny a contribution to an employee because he or she was not employed on a certain date?

No. An employer may not require that an otherwise eligible employee be employed as of a particular date to receive a contribution for a plan year. [I.R.C. § 408(k)(2); Prop. Treas. Reg. § 1.408-7(d)(3)]

Q 5:22 How are contributions allocated to employees under a SEP?

Employer contributions to a SEP arrangement must be made under a definite written allocation formula that specifies the following:

1. The requirements that an employee must satisfy to share in an allocation and
2. The manner in which the amount allocated to each employee's account is computed.

[I.R.C. § 408(k)(5); Prop. Treas. Reg. § 1.408-7(e)]

Allocations are generally based on compensation (see chapter 6).

A unilateral oral decision to require a salary reduction in a SEP would not satisfy the requirement of a written allocation formula. [Garratt v. Walker, 164 F.3d 1249 (10th Cir. 1998), available at *http://vlex.com/vid/18481528* (visited on Aug. 22, 2012)]

Employer's contribution for each calendar year are generally allocated to the IRA of each participant in the same ratio that the participant's compensation bears to all participants. Nonetheless, allocating a contribution to some, but not all, employees eligible to receive a contribution would not be in accordance with a plan's written allocation formula (an operational failure). Arguably, problems could arise if employer nonelective contributions are allocated (whether or not plan contributions are integrated with Social Security contributions and benefits, see chapter 9) to owners in the beginning of a plan year and to nonowners later in the year. [See Listing of Required Modifications and Information Package (LRM), Simplified Employee Pensions, Item 3(b)-(d) (Mar. 2002)]

Practice Pointer. If more than one employee is eligible to receive a contribution, an employer's contribution must be allocated to the accounts of all eligible employees in accordance with the terms of the plan.

Example. Joe, a sole-proprietor, has a SEP plan. Joe and two of his employees are eligible to participate under the terms of the plan. A contribution is made to the SEP for the current year in January. Five percent of Joe's compensation is contributed and allocated to Joe's SEP-IRA. In March of the following year, a 5 percent of compensation contribution (for the prior year) is made and allocated to the remaining employees. An operational failure has resulted. The plan's definite written allocation formula was violated.

Example. Firefly makes contributions to a SEP and also has a money purchase pension plan that requires a 10 percent of compensation contribution for each eligible employee. For deduction purposes, assume all employees participate in both plans. The 10 percent of compensation contributions made under the money purchase plan must be made and take precedence over any SEP contributions. Thus, most excesses will be treated as having been made under the SEP plan. (See Q 7:23, examples 1 through 3.) Assume that Firefly make a 20 percent of compensation contribution to the SEP. In addition to exceeding the overall 25 percent deduction limit, the 25 percent participant allocation exclusion limit under the SEP has also been exceeded by 5 percent (25%–10%–20%). (See Qs 10:1, 11:1.)

Q 5:23 May the written contribution allocation formula be changed?

Yes. An employer may vary the definite written allocation formula from year to year provided the SEP arrangement is amended by the due date for making contributions under Code Section 404(h) to indicate the new formula. [Prop. Treas. Reg. §§ 1.408-7(c), 1.408-7(e)(2)] Problems may arise if contributions for any one year are made under different allocation formulas (see Q 5:26).

Q 5:24 How are SEP contributions that exceed the written allocation formula treated?

To the extent that employer contributions to a SEP do not satisfy the written allocation formula, the contributions are generally deemed to be contributions that are not made under the SEP arrangement. [Prop. Treas. Reg. § 1.408-7(f)(1)] Instead, such contributions are deemed to be made to employee IRAs not maintained as part of the SEP. [Prop. Treas. Reg. § 1.408-7(f)(2)] Elective contributions are not treated as employer contributions for allocation purposes.

It is contemplated that the employer will notify the employee of the amount of the non-SEP contribution made in excess of the allocation formula when it discovers the erroneous contribution. [Prop. Treas. Reg. § 1.408-7, Preamble] Because such a contribution may result in an excess contribution when made, the employee may wish to take appropriate action in order to avoid IRS penalties.

The normal IRA rules under Code Section 219 apply in such a situation and prevent the entire SEP arrangement from being disqualified because of an inadvertent error on the part of the employer, such as an incorrect calculation of employee compensation. Under Code Section 408(k), the entire SEP arrangement could be disqualified on account of the excess contribution. The rule treating the amounts as IRA contributions provides relief in such cases. Similarly, other contributions, such as voluntary contributions made by the employee, or on behalf of the employee by the employer as the agent for the employee (e.g., by payroll withholding to a "payroll deduction IRA"), are treated as employee contributions and not employer contributions for allocation purposes.

Example. In 2012, Weed Corporation adopts an IRS model SEP (Form 5305-SEP) arrangement that calls for Weed to contribute the same percentage of each participant's compensation exclusive of SEP contributions (allocation compensation). Weed has three employees, Al, Bill, and Carl, who satisfy the participation requirements of the SEP arrangement. Carl also makes the maximum annual IRA contribution on January 2, each year. The compensation, the contributions to the SEP, and the contributions as a percentage of compensation are set forth in the following table.

Employee	*Gross Income*	*SEP IRA Contribution*	*Contribution as % of Compensation*
Al	$ 10,000	$ 1,000	10
Bill	10,000	1,500	15
Carl	160,000	24,000	15
	$180,000	$26,500	

Because only 10 percent of compensation was allocated to Al, and the allocation formula provides that the same percentage must be allocated to each participant, portions of the contribution under the SEP are deemed to be made to Bill's and Carl's IRAs that are not part of the SEP arrangement.

To determine Bill's and Carl's allocation compensation, the total compensation included in gross income must be divided by 1.10 (1 plus the percentage of allocation compensation contributed to Al's IRA under the SEP arrangement) for each of them. The excess of compensation included in gross income over the allocation compensation is considered to be a contribution under the SEP arrangement.

Employee	*Total Compensation*	*Allocation Compensation*	*SEP IRA Contribution*	*Deemed Traditional IRA Contribution**
Al	$ 11,000	$ 10,000	$ 1,000	$ 0
Bill	11,500	$ 10,455	1,045	455
Carl	184,000	$167,273	16,727	7,273
	$206,500	$187,728	$28,772	$7,728

* Also included in allocation compensation.

Under Code Section 404(h), for purposes of computing Weed Corporation's deduction, only $28,772 is considered to be a contribution to a SEP arrangement described in Code Section 408(k). The allowable Section 404(h) deduction of $28,772 (25 percent of the excess of total compensation of $206,500 over the SEP contribution of $28,772, or 25 percent of $206,500) is not exceeded. The $7,728 amount is treated as a payment of compensation and is subject to the deduction rules of Code Section 162 or 212 (see Q 10:2). Code Section 404(h)(1) treats employer SEP contributions as if they were made to a plan subject to the requirements of Code Section 404. Code Section 404(a) provides special rules for deducting contributions and places limits on amounts that "would otherwise be deductible." Similarly, the deemed traditional IRA contribution of $7,728 would not be considered an employer SEP contribution for purposes of exemption from FICA and FUTA taxes under Code Sections 3121 and 3306.

The effect of treating the $7,728 as a contribution to a SEP arrangement for purposes of Code Sections 408(a)(1), 408(b)(2)(B), and 408(d)(5) is to prevent disqualification of Carl's IRA for accepting non-SEP contributions in excess of the annual $5,000 (for 2012) individual IRA limit [I.R.C. § 219(b)(1)] and to allow Carl to withdraw the excess contribution of $2,728 ($7,728 – $5,000 limit for 2012) without including that amount in income under Code Section 408(d)(1). [Prop. Treas. Reg. § 1.408-7(f)(2)] The deemed IRA contribution should be included on Carl's Form W-2 as wages for 2012.

> **Caution.** If the employer had instead adopted a prototype SEP plan and had elected a flat rate of 15 percent of compensation, then the correction would have been to contribute an additional 5 percent of compensation (.05 × $10,000 = $500) plus "reasonable" lost earnings on the undercontributions through the date of the corrective contribution. (See chapter 17.)

Q 5:25 May an employer require that its contributions remain in a SEP IRA or prohibit withdrawals?

No. Employer contributions to a SEP arrangement may "not be conditioned on the retention in the SEP of any portion of the amount contributed," and there must be "no prohibition imposed by the employer on withdrawals from the SEP arrangement." [I.R.C. § 408(k)(4); Prop. Treas. Reg. § 1.408-7(g)] Notwithstanding this rule, it is generally understood that elective SEP contributions may not be withdrawn either until a determination is made by the employer that certain tests have been satisfied or until the March 15 following the plan year-end, whichever is earlier (see Q 5:17).

Q 5:26 May contributions discriminate in favor of highly compensated employees?

No. SEP contributions made by the employer may not discriminate in favor of HCEs. Contributions are considered discriminatory unless they bear a uniform relationship to each participating employee's total compensation not in excess of $250,000 for 2012 (but see Qs 9:14, 9:15, 9:22). The uniform contribution requirement applies on a plan-year basis. [Prop. Treas. Reg. § 1.408-8(c); *see also* Ltr. Rul. 8224019 (March 17, 1988), regarding an individually designed rate per hour SEP plan that was not discriminatory] An allocation formula under which contributions decrease as compensation increases meets the uniform contribution requirement. [Prop. Treas. Reg. §§ 1.408-8(c)(1) and 1.408-8(e)] There are other exceptions to the "uniformity" rule that are deemed not to be discriminatory.

Example 1. Trio Corporation maintains a calendar-year SEP arrangement. Employer contributions made by June 30 of each year are allocated in proportion to compensation paid from January 1 to June 30. Contributions made between July 1 and December 31 are allocated in proportion to compensation paid during that period. Salaries paid and contributions allocated in 2012 are shown in the following table.

Participant	*Compensation 1/1/12–6/30/12*	*6/30/12 Allocation*	*Compensation 7/1/12–12/31/12*	*12/31/11 Allocation*
Alice	$10,000	$500	$10,000	$1,000
Beth	$10,000	$500	$ 1,000	$ 100
Cathy	$10,000	$500	$15,000	$1,500

For 2012, Alice, Beth, and Cathy received allocations equal to 7.5 percent, 5.45 percent, and 8 percent of compensation, respectively. Those contributions are discriminatory because they do not bear a uniform relationship to total compensation. [Prop. Treas. Reg. § 1.408-8(c)(3)]

Example 2. Widget Corporation adopts a SEP arrangement, under which it contributes 7.5 percent of an employee's first $10,000 in compensation and 5 percent of all compensation above $10,000. The SEP arrangement Widget has adopted will not be considered discriminatory because the rate of contribution decreases as compensation increases. A rate of contribution which decreases as compensation increases shall be considered uniform. [Prop. Treas. Reg. § 1.408-8(c)(1)]

Example 3. Brown Corporation adopts a SEP arrangement that covers all of its employees. Brown plans to contribute 5 percent of the total compensation of each employee who has completed up to five years of service and 7 percent of the total compensation of each employee who has completed more than five years of service. This SEP arrangement will be considered discriminatory because the employer contributions do not bear a uniform relationship to each employee's total compensation. [Prop. Treas. Reg. § 1.408-8(e), Ex. (2)]

Q 5:27 Into what vehicles are SEP contributions placed?

All SEP contributions are placed into IRAs in the names of individual employees. An employer may establish an employer IRA to receive contributions (see Q 5:30).

Q 5:28 How soon must an employer segregate elective contributions and forward them to the IRA trustee or custodian?

Most SEP plans and SARSEPs are subject to Title I of ERISA (see Q 4:1); that is, unless specifically excluded from coverage under ERISA (e.g., church plans and state or local governmental plans), SEP IRA plans are covered by ERISA. Regulations under ERISA require that employee contributions be deposited as soon as they can reasonably be segregated from an employer's general assets, but not later than 15 business days after the end of the month in which the payroll deduction is made (see Q 4:44). [DOL Reg. § 2510.3-102] Special rules apply if the individual is self-employed. That is so because the compensation (earned income) of such an individual may not be available for several months (see Q 4:44). The DOL has finalized a seven-day safe-harbor rule for forwarding elective contributions (see Qs 4:45–4:49).

Note. A different rule applies for SIMPLE IRAs (see Q 14:105); although the seven-day safe-harbor rule is also available (see Qs 4:45–4:49).

Q 5:29 What is an *employer IRA trust* under Code Section 408(c)?

An employer IRA may be established by an employer for the exclusive benefit of its employees or their beneficiaries or by an association of employees (see Q 5:31) for the exclusive benefit of its members. An *employer IRA trust* is an employer-sponsored IRA. [I.R.C. § 408(c)] It is treated as an IRA under Code Section 408(a) and may be part of a SEP or SARSEP arrangement. The trust or custodial agreement must provide for separate accounting of the interest of each employee or member (or the interest of a spouse or beneficiary of an employee or member) and must be created or organized in the United States. An employer IRA trust should be considered for qualified plan distributions of property that cannot be easily divided or sold.

Note. Unless it is part of a SEP arrangement, an employer-sponsored IRA is subject to the regular IRA contribution limits.

Q 5:30 May contributions be made to an employer IRA?

Yes, contributions may be made to an employer IRA. Such a choice is rare, however, because of the expense involved in establishing such a trust and the federal and state securities law issues that may arise regarding both the trust fund and the interests of participants (see Qs 4:50–4:53). In some cases, the trust fund itself may have to be registered as an investment company (see Q 4:51). The assets of an IRA may be commingled in a common trust fund or common investment fund for the IRAs of all individuals who have an interest in the common trust (see Q 4:51). [I.R.C. § 408(a)(5)]

If an employer IRA is not used in connection with a SEP program, the employer IRA program may be discriminatory and cover a select group of employees. In such a case, the non-SEP traditional IRA contributions are included in the income of the employee in the year the contributions are made; however, unless the sponsor is a church or governmental body, other ERISA rules are likely to apply (see Qs 4:32–4:38).

Practice Pointer. An employer or employee association that wants a ruling under Code Section 408(c) that the trust may be used for IRAs may file Form 5306, Application for Approval of Prototype or Employer Sponsored Individual Retirement Account.

Q 5:31 What is an *employee association*?

An *employee association* is any organization composed of two or more employees and includes, but is not limited to, any civic league or organization not organized for profit but operated exclusively for the promotion of social welfare or any local association of employees, the membership of which is limited to employees of a designated person or persons in a particular municipality and the net earnings of which are devoted exclusively to charitable, educational, or recreational purposes. [Treas. Reg. § 1.408-2(c)(4)(ii)] An employee association may establish an IRA trust to receive SEP contributions.

An employee association may include self-employed individuals; however, there must be some connection between the employees—for example, employment by the same employer or employment in the same trade or industry—for an organization to qualify as an employee association. [Treas. Reg. § 1.408-2(c)]

Q 5:32 How are SEP contributions reported to the IRS?

Form W-2 and Form 5498, IRA Contribution Information, are used to report SEP contributions to the IRS (see chapter 13).

SEPs with Other Plans and Annual IRAs

Q 5:33 Are employees who receive contributions or accrue benefits under a SEP, SARSEP, or other type of retirement program treated as active participants for IRA deduction limitation purposes?

Yes. Employees who receive any SEP contributions or make elective contributions to a SARSEP are treated as active participants for purposes of the limit on the deductibility of IRA contributions. [I.R.C. § 219(g)(5)(A)(v)] Annual contributions of up to $5,000 for 2012 may be made to an IRA by an employee participating in a SEP arrangement, although the IRA contribution may not be deductible (see Q 5:35). An individual who is age 50 or older may also make a catch-up contribution of $1,000 for 2012.

Participation in a SIMPLE, a tax-sheltered annuity program under Code Section 403(b), or a qualified plan, such as a profit-sharing, stock bonus, defined benefit, or money purchase pension plan, must also be considered in determining an individual's active participant status. Although participation in most governmental retirement plans and in certain trusts described in Code Section 501(c)(18) is treated as active, participation under a deferred compensation plan described in Code Section 457(b) or (f) does not cause an individual to be treated as an active participant for IRA deduction limitation purposes. [I.R.C. § 219(g)(5)]

In the case of a defined benefit plan, an individual who is not excluded under the eligibility provisions of the plan for the plan year ending with or within the individual's taxable year is an active participant in the plan, regardless of whether he or she has elected not to participate in the plan, has failed to make a mandatory contribution specified under the plan, or has failed to perform the minimum service required to accrue a benefit under the plan. [I.R.S. Notice 87-16, § I(A), 1987-1 C.B. 446] The existence of a vesting schedule is ignored in determining active participant status.

Example. Wayne waives participation in his company's new defined benefit pension plan because he plans to retire in two years (before the plan's normal retirement date), and his retirement will occur before any of his benefits would have vested. Even though Wayne is certain that he will not receive any benefit under the defined benefit pension plan, he is treated as an active participant.

Q 5:34 How do employer contributions made after the end of the year affect active participant status?

If, with respect to a particular plan year, no employer or employee elective contributions have been allocated to the SEP IRA by the last day of the plan year, and contributions are purely discretionary for the plan year, an employee is not treated as an active participant for the taxable year in which the plan year ends. It must be noted, however, that when discretionary contributions to a SEP for two plan years are made in one calendar year, the contribution for the later plan year is deemed to be made in the next taxable year solely for the purpose of determining active participant status.

If an allocation must be made to the SEP IRA of an employee with respect to a particular plan year, the employee will be an active participant in the taxable year in which the plan year ends. For example, top-heavy minimum contributions are not discretionary—and thus an allocation must be made. On the other hand, elective contributions cause active participation for the plan year as of which the deferral contribution is allocated.

Example 1. In 2012, but before the due date of its 2011 federal tax return, Acme Corporation establishes a SEP for 2011. Discretionary contributions are made to the SEP in January 2012 for the 2011 taxable year. Participating employees will be treated as active participants for their 2012 taxable year. If Acme also makes a 2012 SEP contribution in 2012, participating employees will be treated as active participants for the 2012 taxable year. [I.R.S. Notice 87-16, § I(A), Qs A-21–A-26, 1987-1 C.B. 446; Ltr. Rul. 9008056]

Example 2. In 1995, Bonus Corporation established a cash-bonus SEP. The plan is not top heavy. On December 31, 2012, employees are informed that they may elect in writing to have all or a portion of their annual bonuses treated as an elective contribution under the SEP or receive them in cash on December 31. The employees who make elective contributions based on their bonuses are treated as active participants for 2012 even though the amounts may be contributed or deposited into the SEP IRA several days after December 31, 2012.

Q 5:35 How is the annual IRA deduction limit applied to active participants?

If either an employee or his or her spouse is an active participant in a SEP, SIMPLE, or SARSEP arrangement, the allowable annual IRA deduction (100 percent of compensation, up to $5,000 per individual, $6,000 with a catch-up contribution) for 2012 will generally be reduced by $25/$30 for every $50 ($100 if married, active participants, filing jointly) of adjusted gross income above certain amounts (threshold levels) until it is completely phased out, as presented in Table 5-1.

Table 5-1. 2012 Threshold Levels for Employees and Their Spouses

2012 Filing Status	*Threshold Level*	*Complete Phaseout*
Unmarried	$ 58,000	$ 68,000
Married, filing jointly, active participant	$ 92,000	$112,000
Married, filing separately, active participant	$ 0	$ 10,000
Married, filing jointly, only spouse active participant	$173,000	$183,000

A minimum deductible contribution of $200 is allowed for active participants with adjusted gross income below the phaseout level, and all deductible amounts are rounded up to the next $10. An individual will not be treated as married if his or her spouse files a separate return and lives apart from the individual at all times during the taxable year. [I.R.C. § 219(g)(4), (5); I.R.S. Notice 2011-90, 2011-47 I.R.B. 791 for 2012]

Q 5:36 How is active participation reported to the IRS?

The employer marks the "Pension plan" box in box 12 of Form W-2 to indicate active participation (see Q 5:34).

Q 5:37 May an employer maintain a SEP and a qualified plan at the same time?

Yes, an employer may maintain a SEP and a qualified plan simultaneously; however, special rules and limitations may apply. (See chapter 3 regarding document approval.) [I.R.C. §§ 402(h)(1)(C), (2)(A), 404(a), 415(c)(1)(A)] For 2012, the Code Section 415 dollar limit is $50,000, plus catch-up contributions (up to $5,500) if the employee is age 50 or older.

After 2001, there is no need to establish a SEP plan in combination with a pension plan such as a 10 percent money purchase pension plan to reach the 25 percent overall employer deduction limit. [I.R.C. § 415(k)(1)(D), (E), (F)]

Q 5:38 May a SEP be combined with a profit-sharing or stock bonus plan?

Yes, a SEP may be combined with a profit-sharing or stock bonus plan. It should be noted, however, that each such plan and a SEP share a 25 percent aggregate deduction limit for 2012 to the extent employees participate in both plans. The otherwise allowable profit-sharing contribution is reduced by the amount of allowable SEP contributions (see Q 10:3) [*See* I.R.C. § 404(a)(7)] [I.R.C. § 404(h)(2), (3)] Thus, an allowable SEP contribution would reduce an employer's profit-sharing deduction limit under Code Section 404(a)(3)(A).

Q 5:39 May an employer establish a SEP and a tax-sheltered annuity under Code Section 403(b)?

Yes. If an individual participates in a 403(b) tax-sheltered annuity or custodial account and a qualified plan or SEP, the individual must combine contributions made to the 403(b) plan with contributions to a qualified plan and simplified employee pensions of all corporations, partnerships, and sole proprietorships in which the individual has more than 50 percent control. [I.R.C. §§ 415(a)(2), 415(h); *see also* Treas. Reg. § 1.415(f)-1(f)(2)]

Example. Larry has a 51 percent interest in a small business that established a SEP for 2012. He is also a participant in a 403(b) plan maintained by a tax-exempt entity. Larry must aggregate contributions to both plans for purposes of the 100 percent/$50,000 limit under Code Section 415.

A participant's 403(b) employer is not considered to maintain the tax-sheltered annuity contract (or custodial account) under Code Section 403(b) unless the participant has more than 50 percent control in another employer. Thus, absent the element of control, contributions under a SEP and a non-ERISA 403(b) arrangement (elective deferral plan only) need not be aggregated for purposes of the 100 percent/$50,000 limit under Code Section 415, nor for purposes of the prior limits under Code Section 415(e) regarding defined benefit plans and SEPs. [*See* I.R.C. § 415(k)(4); Treas. Reg. §§ 1.415(f)-1(f)(1), 1.415(g)-1(b)(iv)(C)]

Q 5:40 May amounts be contributed to a SARSEP under a tandem or "wrap" SARSEP and nonqualified deferred compensation plan arrangement?

Probably. The IRS has allowed a tandem qualified plan under Code Section 401(k) and a nonqualified deferred compensation plan arrangement in many situations. Unfortunately, no private letter rulings have ever been requested on creating a "wrap SARSEP" plan, where the employer combines a SARSEP and a nonqualified deferred compensation plan. [I.R.C. § 402(e)(3), (g)(1); Ltr. Ruls. 200116046, 9807027, 9701057, 9530038] In Letter Ruling 9530038, amounts in the nonqualified plan remained the assets of the employer and were available to the employer's general creditors. An irrevocable election was made no later than December 31 of the calendar year preceding the year in which the compensation (otherwise payable during the year) was earned to have elective amounts contributed to the qualified plan. At the same time, the employee elected to enter into the salary reduction agreement under the nonqualified plan. Amounts not transferred to the qualified plan after the end of the plan year and by January 31 were paid to the employee within two and one-half months after the end of the plan year. Earnings in the nonqualified plan could not be transferred to the qualified plan. Amounts paid to the employee—because the employee did not elect to have them contributed to the qualified plan as an elective contribution—would be includible in the employee's gross income in the year in which the compensation to which the salary deferral under the nonqualified plan related was earned, and the employer would include that amount as compensation on the employee's Form W-2 for that year.

To qualify for the alternate reporting and disclosure requirements under ERISA, the nonqualified plan would have to be established as a top-hat plan covering a select group of management or highly compensated employees. Although an employee may be classified as highly compensated under the Code for ADP testing purposes, he or she would not necessarily be so classified under the Department of Labor (DOL) regulations for purposes of the top-hat exemption.

Under a tandem or "wrap" SEP arrangement, shortly after the end of the year the employer determines the maximum amount that may be deferred by an HCE under the ADP test. The least of that amount, the Section 402(g) dollar limit ($17,000 for 2012), or the amount in the nonqualified deferred compensation plan would be transferred by the employer to the SEP arrangement so that the maximum amount allowable could be deferred by the employee. To avoid any question about the application of the constructive receipt doctrine, the election to have amounts contributed to the SARSEP must be made before the performance of services to which the deferral amounts would relate. [Ltr. Ruls. 200116046, 9807027, 9701057, 9530038; Ltr. Rul. 9414051, revoking Ltr. Rul. 9317037]

In the letter rulings just cited, the HCEs involved in the nonqualified plan all deferred the maximum permitted under the plan for the year. The IRS cautioned that if one HCE had not deferred the maximum permitted under the plan, other participants would be able to increase their deferrals, thereby possibly permitting employer discretion as to who may increase their deferrals. In such situations, both plans (the nonqualified plan and the SEP plan) would be required to contain language to preclude employer discretion in determining how much any particular participant could contribute.

In Letter Ruling 200116046, a nonqualified plan provided for participants to execute a salary reduction agreement by January 31 indicating whether they wanted to receive the salary deferrals in cash after the close of the plan year or, instead, to have them transferred to the 401(k) plan. To the extent an employee's salary deferrals fell short of the permitted maximum, employee deferrals and employer matching contributions to the nonqualified plan would be transferred to the 401(k) plan. The IRS ruled that elective salary deferrals made to the 401(k) plan from the nonqualified plan would be excluded from participants' income (1) to the extent that the Section 402(g) and Section 401(k) limits were not exceeded, (2) if the transfer election was timely made, and (3) as long as the transfer occurred by March 15. The IRS also ruled that the transfers would be treated as made in the year in which the deferred income was earned rather than in the year of transfer, as would deferrals returned to participants.

It should be noted that under a SARSEP, the percentage that may be deferred by each eligible HCE is *not* contingent on what other HCEs elect to defer (see Q 12:13).

Distributions and Deemed Distributions

Q 5:41 Does the employer process distributions and issue checks?

No. No distribution checks are cut when an employee retires or separates from service because all contributions and earnings are in separate IRAs belonging to each employee. Distributions are effected by the participant's requesting funds from the trustee or custodian of the IRA. (Under Code Section 408(c), the interests of the participants in an employer IRA, although separately accounted for, might be invested in a common fund or in an omnibus account under a single-employer IRA plan document.)

Q 5:42 When is an employee taxed on amounts contributed to a SEP or a SARSEP?

Generally, an employee includes contributions in his or her federal gross income when the amounts are withdrawn (distributed) from the IRA. Pledging an IRA as security (see Q 5:43), engaging in a prohibited transaction (see Q 5:44), or failing to make a required minimum distribution after age 70½ (see Q 5:47) could also subject the assets of the IRA to taxation. Premature distributions before age 59½, death, or disability may also be subject to an additional tax of 10 percent (see Q 5:56). Contribution amounts that exceed applicable limits are also taxable.

Q 5:43 May IRA assets be used or pledged as security?

Yes and no. If an individual uses his or her individual retirement *account* as security for a loan, the portion so used is treated as distributed to that individual. The pledge of security is not treated as a prohibited transaction (see Q 5:44) in the case of an individual retirement account (or SIMPLE IRA). If any portion of an individual retirement *annuity* is pledged as security for a loan, however, the full market value of the entire annuity must be included in income. [I.R.C. § 408(e)(3)–408(e)(4); *see* Griswold v. Commissioner, 85 TC 869 (1985)] The account may no longer be protected (exempt) in bankruptcy.

On the other hand, the granting of a security interest in a personal account to cover indebtedness in an IRA (or vice versa) is a prohibited extension of credit and thus a prohibited transaction. [I.R.C. § 4975(c)(1)(B); DOL Adv. Op. 2009-03A (Oct. 27, 2009) and DOL Adv. Op. 2011-09A (Oct. 20, 2011)] However, the IRS granted relief on December 12, 2011, by announcing a temporary waiver that results from the execution of an account agreement that is an indemnification agreement or a cross-collateralization agreement similar to the agreements described in DOL Advisory Opinions 2009-03A and 2011-09A, provided there has been no execution or other enforcement pursuant to the agreement. Thus, even though a prohibited transaction results when the pledge is (or was) executed, the IRS will treat the security interest or cross-collateralization agreement as a prohibited transaction if, and only if, any non-IRA monies were actually used to satisfy outstanding debts of an IRA (or vice versa). The DOL is considering issuing an exemption that would allow these types of agreements without being a prohibited transaction. [*See* I.R.S. Ann. 2011-81, 2011-52 I.R.B. 1052, granting temporary relief from the holdings in EBSA Adv. Op. 2011-09A (Oct. 20, 2011), available at *http://www.dol.gov/ebsa/regs/aos/ao2011-09a.html* (visited on Aug. 24, 2012) and in EBSA Adv. Op. 2009-3A (Oct. 27, 2009), available at *http://www.dol.gov/ebsa/regs/aos/ao2009-03a.html* (visited on Aug. 24, 2012)]

Q 5:44 What is a *prohibited transaction*?

Under Code Section 4975, a *prohibited transaction* (see Qs 4:18–4:31) is generally any direct or indirect

- Sale, exchange, or lease of any property between a plan and a disqualified person;
- Loan of money or other extension of credit between a plan and a disqualified person;
- Provision of goods, services, or facilities between a plan and a disqualified person; or
- Transfer to, or use by or for the benefit of, a disqualified person of the income or assets of a plan.

Q 5:45 What are the consequences of a prohibited transaction?

If an individual engages in a prohibited transaction with his or her IRA, the IRA is disqualified. In such a case, the assets are deemed distributed, and the appropriate taxes apply, including the additional 10 percent penalty on premature distributions (see Q 1:22). The individual is not subject, however, to the prohibited transaction excise tax of 15 percent under Code Section 4975(a). [I.R.C. § 4975(c)(3)]

Q 5:46 How are prohibited transactions handled in a union or employer-sponsored IRA?

Where there is a union or employer-sponsored IRA (see Q 5:29) and the IRA covers more than one employee, only the employee who engages in the prohibited transaction is subject to disqualification of his or her portion of the IRA. If, however, the employer (or union) sponsoring the IRA is the party engaging in the prohibited transaction, the employer (or other party) will be liable for the excise tax, but the individual participants will not.

Q 5:47 Are required minimum distributions subject to tax if not withdrawn?

Yes. Required minimum distributions (RMDs) payable after age 70½ are treated as distributed even if they are not actually removed from the IRA. To enforce the requirement that minimum distributions be taken after age 70½, there is an excise tax of 50 percent of the amount, if any, by which the amount of the distribution from the IRA fails to equal the RMD for the year. [I.R.C. §§ 408(a)(6), 408(b)(3), 4973] The removal of an excess SEP contribution, excess deferral, or disallowed deferral cannot be used to satisfy the RMD rules. The requirement to take an RMD for 2009 was waived (see Q 1:32).

Q 5:48 Do all the traditional IRA distribution rules apply to SEP IRAs?

Yes. All the traditional IRA distribution rules apply to IRAs used in connection with a SEP or SARSEP arrangement, except that the contribution limit is higher for SEP IRAs and contributions may be made to SEP IRAs after the participant attains age 70½ and after the participant's death (posthumous contributions). [I.R.C.

§ 408(k)(1)] Subject to the one rollover per year rule, an IRA established to receive SEP or SARSEP contributions can generally be rolled over or transferred to another IRA. [I.R.C. § 408(d)(3)(B)] The suspension of the required minimum distributions rule for 2009 also applied to an IRA that holds SEP assets.

Note. The joint and survivor annuity rules do *not* apply to a SEP or SEP IRA. [I.R.C. §§ 401(a)(12), 408(d), 408(k)(1)] Those rules require that a qualified plan provide for a "qualified joint and survivor annuity" if the plan provides for any method of payment in the form of an annuity. Even if a SEP plan is an ERISA-governed plan, an IRA is exempt from Part 2 of Subtitle B of Title I of ERISA. The survivor-annuity or spouse's-consent rules of ERISA Section 205 do not apply to an IRA. [ERISA §§ 201(6), 205; *see, e.g.*, Cline v. Industrial Maint. Eng'g & Contracting Co., 200 F.3d 1223 (9th Cir. 2000)]

Q 5:49 Does the requirement to take minimum distributions affect an employee's right to receive SEP contributions?

No. Even though some of the IRA assets may have to be distributed to an employee after the employee attains age 70½ because of the RMD rules, an employer must allocate SEP contributions (if any are made) for an employee otherwise eligible to receive contributions regardless of the employee's age (see Q 2:53).

Example. Jill, age 75, has been an employee of the Bucket Company for over 20 years. Since 1985, Bucket has been making annual contributions under its SEP on Jill's behalf. Jill properly commenced distributions from her SEP IRA following the year she attained age 70½, except in 2009 when the RMD rules were waived. Because SEP (and SIMPLE IRA) plans are not subject to a maximum age restriction, Bucket must continue to make annual SEP contributions on her behalf. Jill, however, may not make an annual traditional IRA contribution because she is over age 70½.

Q 5:50 How are distributions from an IRA taxed?

Generally, for federal income tax purposes, an individual has a zero basis in his or her IRA, and the proceeds are fully taxable as ordinary earned income when distributed or deemed distributed. [Pub. L. No. 93-406, Joint Conference Committee Explanation § 2002(b); I.R.C. § 408(d)(1)] Exceptions are made for tax-free rollovers, nondeductible contributions, and the return of excess contributions that are included in the participant's gross income. [Treas. Reg. § 1.408-4(a)]

Qualified charitable distribution. The Pension Protection Act of 2006 (PPA) provided an exclusion (up to $100,000) from gross income for otherwise taxable IRA distributions from a traditional or a Roth IRA in the case of a qualified charitable distribution (QCD). The provision for qualified charitable distributions was set to expire on December 31, 2009, but was extended to distributions made in 2010 and 2011. A special rule permits distribution made in January 2011 to be treated as having been made in 2010. [I.R.C. § 408(d)(8); Tax Relief, Unemployment Insurance Reauthorization, and Job Creation Act of 2010 (Pub. L. No. 111-312) § 725]

A QCD could not be made from an "ongoing" SEP IRA or SIMPLE IRA. A SEP IRA or SIMPLE IRA is treated as *ongoing* if it is maintained under an employer arrangement under which an employer contribution is made for the plan year ending with or within the IRA owner's taxable year in which the QCD would be made.

[I.R.C. § 408(d)(8)(A); I.R.S. Notice 2007-7, Q&A 36, 2007-5 I.R.B. 395]

Q 5:51 Are there special basis recovery rules?

In the case of a traditional IRA that contains "basis" (such as nondeductible contributions or rollovers of after-tax employee contributions from an employer's plan), the normal pro rata basis recovery rules do not apply to the QCD. The first amounts transferred to the qualifying charity are deemed coming from the taxable portion of the traditional IRA. In the case of a Roth IRA, the normal ordering rules that apply where the earnings are deemed distributed last do not apply. The first amounts transferred to the charity are deemed coming from the earnings portion of the Roth IRA.

Practice Pointer. After making a QCD, a greater portion of subsequent distributions that are subject to the pro rata recovery rule may be treated as taxable.

Q 5:52 Are IRA distributions eligible for capital gains treatment or special income averaging?

No. Distributions from an IRA are not eligible for capital gains treatment or the special 10-year forward income averaging rules applicable to lump-sum distributions from qualified plans.

Q 5:53 Do federal estate and gift taxes apply to IRA assets?

Yes. Amounts in IRAs are not excluded for purposes of federal estate and gift taxes. Exemptions and exclusions may, however, reduce the amount of tax otherwise due.

Q 5:54 Are nontaxable distributions before age 59½ subject to the 10 percent premature distribution penalty tax under Code Section 72(t)?

No. The penalty tax under Code Section 72(t) applies to a traditional IRA or SEP only if the distribution is otherwise taxable (see Q 5:56).

Q 5:55 On what day does an individual attain age 59½?

In practice, the half-year mark is reached on the date that is six months after the individual's date of birth. Thus, for example, a person born on February 22, 1953, attains age 59½ on August 22, 2012. [Treas. Reg. § 1.401(a)(9)-1(b), Q&A B-3]

Q 5:56 Are taxable distributions before age 59½ subject to the 10 percent premature distribution penalty?

Yes. In addition to federal income tax and, in most cases, state income tax, distributions removed from IRAs before age 59½ may be subject to a premature distribution penalty in the form of a nondeductible excise tax. [I.R.C. § 72(t)] The tax equals 10 percent of the amount includible in income. Form 5329, Additional Taxes on Qualified Plans (Including IRAs) and Other Tax Favored Accounts, is sometimes used to report the tax (see Q 13:129).

Exceptions to the premature distribution penalty are as follows:

- Distributions of gain (if removed by April 15 following the year of notification) accompanying a withdrawal of an excess SEP contribution, excess deferral, or disallowed deferral
- Distributions after age 59½
- Distributions for medical expenses (see below)
- Distributions made to a beneficiary (or to the estate of a beneficiary) on or after the individual's death
- Distributions to unemployed individuals for medical insurance (see below)
- Distributions attributable to the individual's disability as defined under Code Section 72(m)(7). [Treas. Reg. § 1.72-17(f); Rideaux v. Commissioner, TC Summ. Op. 2006-74 (T.C. 2006) (indefinite disability avoids penalty tax); Johnson v. Commissioner, TC Summ. Op. 2006-62 (2006) (temporary disability for depression does not qualify for penalty tax exception)] An individual must establish that he or she was not able to work in the year of the distribution at an activity comparable to the one in which he or she would customarily engage. The regulations under Code Section 72(m) require that with reasonable effort and safety, the impairment cannot be diminished to the extent that the individual will not be prevented by the impairment from engaging in his or her customary or any other comparable substantial gainful activity. [Treas. Reg. § 1.72-17(f)(3)-(4); Chief Counsel Advice (CCA) 200922041 (Apr. 16, 2009); Ltr. Rul. 201011036 (Mar. 22, 2010)]
- Distributions, commencing at any age, that are part of a series of substantially equal periodic payments made not less frequently than annually for the life of the employee or the joint lives of the employee and his or her designated beneficiary for a period which is the longer of five years or the attainment of age 59½ (see Qs 5:57–5:61). The Tax Court determined that an IRA distribution that escaped the 10 percent tax on pre-59½ distributions because it is used to pay for qualified higher education expenses does not constitute a "modification" to a series of substantially equal periodic payments. [Benz et ux. v. Commissioner, 132 T.C. No. 15, Docket No. 15867-07 (May 11, 2009)] In the authors' opinion, the Benz decision is technically flawed and the IRS is not likely to follow the decision in Benz.
- Distributions used to pay qualified higher education expenses (see below)

- Distribution for first-time homebuyer expenses (see below)
- Distributions made to an individual on account of an IRS levy (see below)
- Distributions of tax-free amounts from an IRA for charitable purposes (see below)
- Distributions to qualified reservists (see below)
- Distributions of stimulus payments (see below)

Withdrawal of Stimulus Payment That Was Deposited Directly into an IRA. An amount not to exceed the economic stimulus payment that was deposited into an IRA may be removed from that IRA. Such amounts, when timely withdrawn, are treated as neither contributed nor distributed from the IRA account. In general, the deadline for these withdrawals is the due date or extended due date for filing a 2009 return. This means April 15, 2010, for most taxpayers, or October 15, 2010, for those who obtain tax-filing extensions. [Ann. 208-44 (IR-2008-44) (Apr. 30, 2008)]

Distributions for Medical Expenses. There is an exception to the 10 percent premature distribution penalty for qualified plan, IRA, SEP, SARSEP, or SIMPLE distributions used to pay medical expenses that are not deductible on the individual's federal income tax return because they do not exceed 7.5 percent of adjusted gross income (AGI). Before passage of the Health Insurance Portability and Accountability Act of 1996 (HIPAA), this exception applied only to qualified plan distributions. [I.R.C. § 72(t)(2)(B)]

Distributions to Unemployed Individuals. The 10 percent premature distribution penalty does not apply to a withdrawal from an IRA (including a SEP, SARSEP, or SIMPLE) that is made after separation from employment and is used to pay for medical insurance for the individual and his or her spouse and dependents (without regard to the 7.5 percent of AGI floor) if the individual (including a self-employed individual) has received unemployment compensation under federal or state law for at least 12 consecutive weeks by reason of such separation and the withdrawal is made in a year in which such unemployment compensation is received (or in the following year). This provision, which was added by HIPAA, is effective for distributions made after 1996.

The unemployment exception does not apply if the individual has been reemployed for at least 60 days. The exception is also limited to payments made during the year of distribution. [Davis v. Commissioner, TC Summ. Op. 2009-61 (Apr. 30, 2009); *see also* Vetere v. Commissioner, TC Summ. Op. 2011-138 (Dec. 19, 2011)]

To the extent provided in as yet unissued regulations, a self-employed individual who is not eligible for unemployment compensation is treated as having received unemployment compensation if that individual would have received unemployment compensation but for the fact that he or she was self-employed. [I.R.C. § 72(t)(2)(D); Chief Counsel Advice (CCA) 200920052 (Apr. 8, 2009)]

Distribution Used to Pay Qualified Higher Education Expenses. The 10 percent premature distribution penalty does not apply to an IRA distribution used to pay qualified higher education expenses (including graduate education expenses) for the individual, the individual's spouse, or any child or grandchild of either. This provision, which was added by the Taxpayer Relief Act of 1997 (TRA '97), is effective for distributions made after December 31, 1997, with respect to expenses paid after that date for education furnished in academic periods beginning after that date. [TRA '97 § 303; I.R.C. §§ 72(t)(2)(E), 72(t)(7)]

Distribution for First-Time Homebuyer Expenses. Effective for taxable years beginning after 1997, TRA '97 added an exception to the 10 percent premature distribution penalty for an IRA distribution for first-time homebuyer expenses. The homebuyer may be the individual, his or her spouse, or any child, grandchild, or ancestor of either. A person qualifies as a first-time homebuyer if he or she (and his or her spouse) had no present ownership interest in a principal residence during the preceding two years. There is a lifetime maximum of $10,000 per individual. [TRA '97 § 303; I.R.C. §§ 72(t)(2)(F), 72(t)(8)]

Distribution by IRS Levy. The government was entitled to garnish the IRA of an individual convicted of conspiracy to defraud the United States, tax evasion, and filing a false federal income tax return in order to satisfy the criminal fine imposed on him. The taxpayer contended that IRAs were not garnishable under the Federal Debt Collection Procedures Act (FDCPA) and that the anti-alienation provision of ERISA also exempted his IRA from garnishment. Because none of the limitations to the government's authority to enforce judgments under the FDCPA applied, the taxpayer's IRA was property the government could garnish. In addition, Treasury Regulations Section 1.401(a)-13 stipulates that the anti-alienation provision of ERISA does not preclude the government's collection of an unpaid tax assessment. Finally, ERISA contains a "saving clause," which provides that it does not change, invalidate, or supersede any other laws, including the FDCPA. [*See* United States v. Anthony J. Grico, Beneficial Sav. Bank, No. 99-202-01, 2003 WL 21244024 (E.D. Pa. May 22, 2003)] Amounts seized by federal government under a plea agreement would not be subject to the early distribution penalty. [Larotonda v. Commissioner, 89 T.C. 287 (1987); Murillo v. Commissioner, T.C. Memo 1998-13, *aff'd,* 166 F.3d 1201 (2d Cir 1998)] If distributions to the owner are used to pay such amounts, the exception would not apply. [*See* Baas v. Commissioner, T.C. Memo 2002-130 (2002)] The payment of federal income taxes by way of a levy constitutes an involuntary assignment of income and may be included in gross income in the year of levy pursuant to the doctrine of constructive receipt. [Judith A. Swanston v. Commissioner, T.C. Memo 2010-140 (No. 7181-08L)] Exempt property under Bankruptcy Code Section 541(c)(2)—an ERISA pension plan—can be subject to an IRS lien following discharge in bankruptcy and the trustee in bankruptcy has no power over it. It may be possible to convert pension assets to an IRA before bankruptcy to have the lien on the IRA (an exempt asset) discharged in bankruptcy (IRS failed to file a Notice of Federal Tax Lien (NFTL) under Code Section 6321). [Wadleigh v. Commissioner, 134 T.C. No. 14 (Jun. 15, 2010); *see also* Paterson v. Shumate, 504 U.S. 743 (1992)]

Treatment of Distributions to Individuals Called to Active Duty for at Least 180 Days (or an Indefinite Period). Under the PPA, the 10 percent early withdrawal tax does not apply to a qualified reservist distribution. A qualified reservist distribution is a distribution (1) from an IRA or attributable to elective deferrals under a 401(k) plan, 403(b) annuity, or certain similar arrangements; (2) made to an individual who (by reason of being a member of a reserve component as defined in section 101 of title 37 of the U.S. Code) was ordered or called to active duty for a period in excess of 179 days or for an indefinite period; and (3) that is made during the period beginning on the date of such order or call to duty and ending at the close of the active duty period. A 401(k) plan or 403(b) annuity does not violate the distribution restrictions applicable to such plans by reason of making a qualified reservist distribution.

An individual who receives a qualified reservist distribution may, at any time during the two-year period beginning on the day after the end of the active duty period, make one or more repayments (or "recontributions") to an IRA of such individual in an aggregate amount not to exceed the amount of such distribution. The dollar limitations otherwise applicable to contributions to IRAs do not apply to any contribution made pursuant to the provision. No deduction is allowed for any contribution made under the provision.

Because of this exception to the 10 percent additional tax and the retroactive application of this rule, eligible reservists who already paid the 10 percent premature distribution tax can claim a refund by filing Form 1040X to amend their return for the year in which the early distribution was taken. Eligible reservists should write the words *active duty reservist* at the top of the form. In Part II, Explanation of Changes, the reservist should write the date he or she was called to active duty, the amount of the early distribution, and the amount of the premature distribution tax that was paid.

Two-Year Repayment Period

The qualified reservist has a two-year period after the end of active duty to repay (recontribute) the distribution to an IRA. However, if the reservist's active duty ended before August 17, 2006 (the date of enactment of the PPA), he or she had until August 17, 2008, to make a repayment of the distribution into an IRA.

Two-Year Period Is Not a Rollover Period. The two-year period is called a "repayment" period, rather than being called a "rollover" period. This means that if the reservist repaid the distribution into an IRA, he or she would not be entitled to also claim a refund for the normal taxes that were already paid on the distribution. Further, the IRS announcement refers to these repayments as "special contributions." The statutory language in the PPA is,

> Any individual who receives a qualified reservist distribution may, at any time during the two-year period beginning on the day after the end of the active duty period, make one or more contributions to an IRA in an aggregate amount not to exceed the amount of such distribution. The dollar limitations otherwise applicable to contributions to IRAs shall not apply to any contribution made pursuant to the preceding sentence. No deduction shall be allowed for any contribution pursuant to this clause.

The repayment of a qualified reservist distribution is *not* a rollover, but merely repayments of a qualified reservist distribution where normal income taxes apply even if the taxpayer repays the distribution to an IRA. Thus, the only tax that can be claimed as a refund is the 10 percent premature distribution tax on qualified reservist distributions that have already been included in gross income. The conclusion, therefore, is that if the reservist repays the distribution, such recontribution should then be treated as additional "basis" in the IRA because income taxes are still paid.

No special reporting is required for qualified charitable distributions. The repayment of a qualified reservist distribution is, however, reported on Form 5498. The repayment amount is reported in box 14a. In box 14b enter Code "QR." If the distribution was treated as subject to penalty (distribution code 1 is incorrectly shown in box 7 of Form 1099-R) Form 5329 must be filed.

Effective date: This provision applies to individuals ordered or called to active duty after September 11, 2001. The two-year period for making recontributions of qualified reservist distributions does not end before August 17, 2008, the date that is two years after the date the PPA was enacted. If refund or credit of any overpayment of tax resulting from the provision would be prevented at any time before the close of the one-year period beginning on the date of the enactment by the operation of any law or rule of law (including *res judicata*), such refund or credit may nevertheless be made or allowed if claim therefore is filed before the close of such period. [PPA § 827(c), I.R.C. § 72(t)(2)(G), as amended by HEART § 107]

> **Note.** Prior to June 17, 2008, the ability to make qualified reservist distributions was limited to individuals ordered or called to active duty after September 11, 2001, and before December 31, 2007. [I.R.C. § 72(t)(G)(iv), prior to amendment] The rules governing qualified reservist distributions were amended by the HEART Act (Pub. L. No. 110-245). [HEART, § 107, amending I.R.C. § 72(t)(2)(G)(iv), by striking ", and before December 31, 2007." The amendment was effective for individuals ordered or called to active duty on or after December 31, 2007.

> **Example.** Bill, a qualified reservist, was called to active duty on January 1, 2012. Bill takes an IRA distribution on December 1, 2013. The 10-percent penalty tax for early withdrawal will not apply. Assuming that Bill is relieved of active duty on January 1, 2014, he will have until January 1, 2016 (the later of two years after the date of enactment or two years after the end of his active duty) to roll over the 2013 distribution amount and avoid having to pay federal income tax.

> **Note.** The PPA provides an exclusion from gross income for otherwise taxable IRA distributions from a traditional or a Roth IRA in the case of qualified charitable distributions (see Q 5:50). The provision does not apply to distributions from employer-sponsored retirement plans, including SIMPLE IRAs and SEPs. If the distribution is excluded from gross income, the 10 percent penalty tax does not apply.

Q 5:57 What happens if the IRA distribution method is modified before age 59½?

When distributions to an individual from an IRA are not subject to the premature distribution penalty because of the application of the substantially equal payment exception, the penalty will nevertheless be imposed, except upon death or disability, if the individual modifies the distribution method before age 59½.

Q 5:58 What happens if the IRA distribution method is modified after age 59½?

If an individual does not receive substantially equal payments from an IRA under a method that qualifies for the substantially equal payment exception, the 10 percent premature distribution penalty will apply for five years or upon the individual's attainment of age 59½, whichever is later.

Example. Myra began receiving substantially equal and penalty-free payments when she reached age 58 in 2011. To avoid penalties, she must wait until at least 2016 before changing the distribution method, even though she will reach age 59½ in an earlier year.

Q 5:59 When will the premature distribution penalty be imposed on modifications that are subject to tax?

The premature distribution penalty will be imposed in the first taxable year in which the modification that is subject to tax is made and will be equal to the tax that would have been imposed had the exception not applied, plus interest for the deferral period.

Q 5:60 Are distributions to a former spouse pursuant to a divorce decree subject to taxation or to the 10 percent premature distribution penalty if he or she is under age 59½?

No. An individual may transfer an IRA without tax, and therefore without penalty, to an IRA of his or her spouse or former spouse pursuant to a divorce or separate maintenance decree or a written instrument incident to divorce. Thereafter, such an IRA is treated as maintained for the benefit of the spouse. [I.R.C. §§ 408(d)(6), 414(p)(9)]

Q 5:61 If a traditional IRA is converted to a Roth IRA, are substantially equal payments subject to penalty?

No. A taxpayer who is receiving substantially equal payments before age 59½ may convert his or her traditional IRA to a Roth IRA and not be subject to the recapture of the 10 percent premature distribution penalty retroactively, so long as the series of payments continues from the Roth IRA after the conversion.

For this rule to apply, the entire IRA subject to substantially equal payments must be converted to the Roth IRA.

Q 5:62 Has the IRS provided any further guidance on substantially equal payments?

Yes. On October 3, 2002, the IRS issued Revenue Ruling 2002-62 [2002-2 C.B. 710], which was intended to help certain taxpayers calculate substantially equal periodic payments to avoid the additional 10 percent income tax on premature distributions. Although this revenue ruling still does not answer all the questions taxpayers may have, it replaces the only substantive guidance that had previously been released, in Q&A 12 of Notice 89-25 [1989-1 C.B. 662]. Before a taxpayer acts on the provisions in this ruling, he or she should seek professional advice and, in some cases, should apply for a private letter ruling.

Q 5:63 What three calculation methods are provided under Revenue Ruling 2002-62?

Revenue Ruling 2002-62 [2002-2 C.B. 710] continues, with modification, the three calculation methods provided in Q&A 12 of Notice 89-25 [1989-1 C.B. 662].

Method 1: Required Minimum Distribution Method (RMD Method)

Method 2: Fixed Amortization Method

Method 3: Fixed Annuitization Method

Each method is described in Q 5:66, and each includes other clarifications contained in the revenue ruling.

Q 5:64 What is the intent of Revenue Ruling 2002-62?

The primary intent of Revenue Ruling 2002-62 [2002-2 C.B. 710] is to address taxpayer concerns in preserving retirement savings when there is a decrease in the value of the individual's IRA or employer plan. Depending on the original method chosen by the taxpayer, many taxpayers will literally "run out of money" sooner than expected as a result of substantial declines in the financial markets. The ruling at least provides *some* relief in this regard.

Q 5:65 What is the effective date and transitional rule under this revenue ruling?

The guidance in Revenue Ruling 2002-62 applies in calculating substantially equal periodic payments from IRAs and employer plans for payments commencing on or after January 1, 2003. If payments commenced before 2003, the method being used that satisfied the prior guidance may be changed *at any time* to the RMD method explained in Q 5:66, including the use of a different life expectancy table.

[*See, e.g.*, Ltr. Ruls. 200720023 (Feb. 21, 2007), 200716032 (Jan. 23, 2007), 200631025 (May 12, 2006), 200634033 (Apr. 25, 2006), 200544023 (Aug. 09, 2005), 200532062 (May 20, 2005)]

Q 5:66 What are the three methods of calculating the substantially equal payments?

The three methods used in calculating substantially equal payments are the following:

Method 1: RMD Method

Under this method, the annual payment is calculated by dividing the account balance for that year by the chosen life expectancy table for that year. The account balance, life expectancy factor, and resulting annual payment are redetermined each year and will fluctuate from year to year. If a taxpayer uses the RMD method, he or she cannot change to another method in any subsequent year.

Although the annual payment will not remain constant from year to year, the IRS provides that using this method will not be deemed to be a modification of the series of payments.

Method 2: Fixed Amortization Method

Under this method, level annual payments are calculated by amortizing the account balance over the chosen life expectancy table using a chosen interest rate.

The account balance, life expectancy factor, interest rate, and resulting annual payment are determined *once* in the first distribution year. Therefore, the annual payment is fixed in the first year and is the same amount for each subsequent year.

Method 3: Fixed Annuitization Method

Under this method, level annual payments are calculated by dividing the account balance by an annuity factor (the present value of an annuity of $1 per year) beginning at the taxpayer's age and continuing for life (or joint lives) using a chosen interest rate.

The annuity factor used for this method can be obtained from the mortality table in Appendix B of Revenue Ruling 2002-62. The account balance, annuity factor, chosen interest rate, and resulting annual payment are determined *once* in the first distribution year. Therefore, the annual payment is fixed in the first year and is the same amount for each subsequent year.

Q 5:67 Which life expectancy tables may be used?

A taxpayer may use any of the following life expectancy tables in calculating the appropriate substantially equal periodic payments:

1. Uniform Lifetime Table in Appendix A of Revenue Ruling 2002-62. This Uniform Lifetime Table is the same as the table under final Treasury Regulations Section 1.401(a)(9)-9, Q&A 2, except that it has been expanded to begin at age 10 instead of at age 70. This table assumes a beneficiary who is exactly 10 years younger than the taxpayer.
2. Single Life Table in final Treasury Regulations Section 1.401(a)(9)-9, Q&A 1
3. Joint and Last Survivor Table in final Treasury Regulations Section 1.401(a)(9)-9, Q&A 3

For all methods, to find the appropriate life expectancy, use the taxpayer's attained age as of his or her birthday in the first distribution year.

If the Joint and Last Survivor Table is used, find the beneficiary's attained age as of the beneficiary's birthday in the first distribution year.

For the RMD method, use the taxpayer's attained age (and the beneficiary's attained age, if applicable) as of his or her birthday in each subsequent year, and the same table must be used for all years. For example, if the Single Life Table is used in the first distribution year, that same table must be used in all subsequent years.

If the Joint and Last Survivor Table is used, the beneficiary must be the actual beneficiary of the retirement account. If the participant has multiple primary beneficiaries, the "designated" beneficiary with the shortest life expectancy (the oldest in the group) is the beneficiary whose life expectancy will be used along with the participant.

The determination of the designated beneficiary is made as of January 1 of the year without regard to any changes in the list of beneficiaries in that year. Under the RMD method only, if the beneficiary used in one year is subsequently removed, that beneficiary is not taken into account in future years. In addition, if in any year there is no beneficiary, the Single Life Table must be used that year.

Example. Marvin begins payments in 2012. Marvin's attained age on his birthday in 2012 is age 50. Marvin has two primary beneficiaries, Marvella and Martina. During 2012 Marvella attains age 55, and Martina attains age 25. If Marvin were to choose the Uniform Lifetime Table, the factor would be 46.5. If Marvin were to choose the Single Life Table, the factor would be 34.2. If Marvin were to choose the Joint and Last Survivor Table, the factor would be 38.3 by using ages 50 and 55.

For subsequent years under the RMD method, the factors would be (1) 45.5 if using the Uniform Lifetime Table for age 51, (2) 33.3 if using the Single Life Table for age 51, or (3) 37.4 if using the Joint and Last Survivor Table for ages 51 and 56.

Q 5:68 What interest rate may be used?

The interest rate that may be used for the fixed amortization method or the fixed annuitization method is any interest rate that is not greater than 120 percent of the federal midterm rate for either of the two months immediately preceding the month in which the payments commence. The revenue rulings that contain the federal midterm rates may be found at *http://www.irs.gov* (search for "federal rates").

As of August 2012, the 120 percent annual federal midterm rate was 1.06 percent. [View "Applicable Federal Rates" at *http://www.brentmark.com/#rates* (visited on Aug. 22, 2012)]

Q 5:69 What account balance may be used?

The revenue ruling provides a rather ambiguous definition of the term *account balance* that needs further clarification by the IRS (see Q 5:65). The ruling states that "the account balance that is used to determine payments must be determined in a reasonable manner based on the facts and circumstances." What exactly does that statement mean?

In the authors' opinion, the IRS wanted this definition to be as flexible as possible, but we are certain that the industry, especially the affected taxpayers, would like to have seen a more precise definition. The ruling provides the following example.

> **Example.** For an IRA with daily valuations that made its first distribution on July 15, 2012, it would be reasonable to determine the yearly account balance under the RMD method based on the value of the IRA from December 31, 2011, to July 15, 2012. For subsequent years, under the RMD method, it would be reasonable to use the value either on the December 31 of the prior year or on a date within a reasonable period before that year's distribution.

Although the example was for the RMD method only, it can be assumed that for any of the three methods, it is possible to use the value of the account (including the most recent statement value) on a date that coincides with or precedes the date of the first payment, including the account value on the prior December 31.

Q 5:70 What constitutes a change to the account balance?

Under all three methods, payments are calculated with respect to an account balance as of the first valuation date selected under the heading above. The ruling provides a very important distinction here. The ruling states that a modification to the series of payments will occur if, after such date, any of the following occurs:

1. Any addition to the account balance, other than gains or losses (no additional contributions or transfers);

2. Any nontaxable transfer of a portion of the account balance to another retirement plan (no partial transfers from the account); or
3. A rollover of the amount received (no tax-free rollovers of any payment received in the series of payments).

This provision in the revenue ruling makes clear that once payments commence under an acceptable method of determining substantially equal periodic payments, no further contributions (including transfers) to the account, partial transfers from the account, or rollovers of any payments from the account are permitted (see Q 5:65). The Tax Court recently determined that an IRA distribution that escaped the 10 percent tax on pre-59-1/2 distributions because it is used to pay for qualified higher education expenses does not constitute a "modification" to a series of substantially equal periodic payments. [Benz et ux. v. Commissioner 132 T.C. No. 15, Docket No. 15867-07 (May 11, 2009)] In the authors' opinion, the *Benz* decision is technically flawed and the IRS is not likely to follow the decision in *Benz*. It remains to be seen whether the IRS will acquiesce or appeal. [Ltr. Ruls. 200943044 (July 28, 2009), proposed method results in substantially equal periodic payments; 200925044 (Mar. 23, 2009), partial transfer to another IRA deemed a modification; 200634033 (Apr. 25, 2006), early distribution treated as a modification]

However, what happens if, pursuant to a divorce decree, a portion of the participant's account is required to be transferred into an IRA for the benefit of the divorced spouse, or required to be distributed under a qualified domestic relations order (QDRO) that can be rolled over by the divorced spouse? In these cases, the taxpayer should seriously consider filing for a private letter ruling. Failure to do so could result in the series of payments to be considered modified, and thus retroactive 10 percent additional taxes may apply. [*See* Ltr. Ruls. 200202076 (Oct. 15, 2001), 200202075 (Oct. 15, 2001), 200116056 (Jan. 26, 2001)]

As a general rule, a "material modification" is considered to be any change to the account, other than gains/losses or the substantially equal periodic distributions themselves. Thus, if a taxpayer took an additional distribution from an IRA or rolled a portion of the IRA balance to another IRA during the five-year period, the distribution/rollover would cause a "material modification," regardless of whether the distribution was taxable or the distribution qualified for another exception under Code Section 72(t). [Rev. Rul. 2002-62, 2002-2 C.B. 710, flush language; *see however*, Ltr. Ruls. 2010051025 (Sept. 30, 2010), make-up distribution allowed following custodian error; 201030038 (May 5, 2010), nontaxable transfer to former spouse with proportionate reduction not deemed a modification; 200930053 (Apr. 27, 2009), trustee error and offsetting adjustment not deemed a modification; 200929021 (Apr. 21, 2009), inadvertent error by financial institution]

Q 5:71 What is the result when there is a complete depletion of the assets in the IRA?

As previously mentioned, the IRS has addressed the concerns of many taxpayers who began substantially equal payments several years ago under the amortization method or the annuitization method.

By using these two methods, the required fixed payment amounts (until the modification period expires) has resulted in, or will soon result in, the entire account balance being distributed sooner than expected. This is because the account balance used under these two methods and the interest rate used in the calculation reflected such values when the payments first commenced without future market declines. Taxpayers were obviously reluctant to change the fixed annual payments under those two methods unless they filed for a private letter ruling. Consequently, the IRS provides the following relief in Revenue Ruling 2002-62 [2002-2 C.B. 710]:

> If a taxpayer is using an acceptable method of calculating substantially equal periodic payments, but the account balance is exhausted, the taxpayer will not be subject to the 10 percent additional income tax and the resulting cessation of payments will not be treated as a modification of the series of payments.

Q 5:72 Is a one-time change permitted?

Yes. Revenue Ruling 2002-62 [2002-2 C.B. 710] permits a taxpayer who is calculating substantially equal periodic payments using either the fixed amortization method or the fixed annuitization method to "switch" to the RMD method in any subsequent year. In the year that the taxpayer switches to the RMD method, the RMD method must be used to calculate that year's payment amount. Such RMD method must then be used to determine each subsequent year's payment amount. In other words, if a taxpayer switches to the RMD method, he or she cannot switch back to either of the other two methods.

The ruling also provides that this one-time switch to the RMD method will not be considered as a modification of the payment series. However, any subsequent change will be treated as a modification for purposes of the retroactive application of the 10 percent additional tax.

Example. Jack began substantially equal payments in 2011 using the fixed amortization method, which resulted in an annual payment of $40,000. The annual payment for 2012 has not yet occurred. Thus, Jack can switch to the RMD method for determining the payment for 2012, but must continue using the RMD method for all future years. However, assume that Jack has already received $30,000 of the fixed $40,000 for the 2012 payment calculated under the fixed amortization method. Further assume that the use of the RMD method for 2012 results in a payment of $20,000. Because Jack has already received more than the $20,000, he would need to satisfy the 2012 payment amount of $40,000 under the same method he previously used and would not be able to switch to the RMD method until 2013. If he had received only

$15,000 so far this year (2012), he could switch to the RMD method and receive an additional amount of $5,000 to satisfy the $20,000 payment amount determined under the RMD method for 2012.

However, in Private Letter Ruling 200419031 (Feb. 11, 2004), the IRS permitted a one-time change and allowed the taxpayer to return the excess withdrawal (as a rollover) even though more than 60 days had expired. [Ltr. Ruls. 200437038 (June 17, 2004), proposed computation method not approved; 200419031 (Feb. 11, 2004), method approved and excess permitted to be rolled over]

Note. Another method may be used in a private letter ruling request, but, of course, it would be subject to individual analysis.

[*See also* Ltr. Ruls. 200720023 (Feb. 21, 2007) modification caused by transfer; 200616046 (Jan. 21, 2006) inadvertent rollover by broker; 200503036 (Oct. 25, 2004) mistake not treated as a modification; 200419031 (Feb. 11. 2004) combined with I.R.C. § 408(d)(3)(I) to change method retroactively]

Q 5:73 Are SEPs and IRAs subject to the qualified domestic relations order rules?

No. Trustees and custodians of SEPs and IRAs are not subject to the qualified domestic relations order rules of Code Section 414(p)(1) (allowing for transfers of plan assets to satisfy certain domestic issues between spouses or former spouses) (see Q 5:60).

Q 5:74 How are distributions from SEP IRAs reported to the IRS?

Form 1099-R is used to report distributions from SEP IRAs (see chapter 13).

Excess Contributions

Q 5:75 What types of excesses may occur in a SARSEP?

Three types of excesses may occur in a SARSEP; certain notification procedures and correction deadlines apply to each. Failure to correct any such excess appropriately and in a timely manner will result in adverse tax consequences and, in some cases, will disqualify the entire plan. In addition, depending on the type of excess and when the excess is corrected, special reporting requirements apply. [I.R.S. Notice 97-77, 1997-2 C.B. 342; I.R.S. Notice 88-33, 1988-1 C.B. 513; Rev. Proc. 91-44, 1991-2 CB 733; Instructions to Form 1099-R] (See Appendix M.) (See also Qs 12:18–12:44.)

Excess SEP Contribution: SEP Contributions That Fail the 125 Percent Nondiscrimination Test. A SEP contribution that fails the 125 percent nondiscrimination test is an elective contribution made for a plan year on behalf of eligible HCEs that exceeds the maximum permissible amount of such contributions (i.e., the amount determined under the ADP test; see Q 12:9). [I.R.C. § 408(k)(6)(C); Treas. Reg. § 1.401(k)-1(g)(7)] Such an excess can be incurred only by HCEs.

Excess Deferrals: Elective Deferrals That Exceed the Limit of $7,000 Per Taxpayer, as Indexed. The annual dollar limit per taxpayer on elective deferrals is $7,000, indexed annually, based on cost-of-living adjustments (see Table 5-2). For 2012, the indexed amount is $17,000. A SARSEP will not qualify unless it provides that elective deferrals may not exceed that dollar limit. [I.R.C. §§ 408(k)(6)(A)(iv), 401(a)(30)] The limit applies to the aggregate amount that an individual elects to defer under a SARSEP other than catch-up elective deferrals. [Treas. Reg. § 1.402(g)-1(b)]

Table 5-2. Annual Elective Deferral Limit

Year	*Elective Deferral Limit*	*Catch-up Amount*
1987	$ 7,000	n/a
1988	$ 7,313	n/a
1989	$ 7,627	n/a
1990	$ 7,979	n/a
1991	$ 8,475	n/a
1992	$ 8,728	n/a
1993	$ 8,994	n/a
1994	$ 9,240	n/a
1995	$ 9,240	n/a
1996	$ 9,500	n/a
1997	$ 9,500	n/a
1998	$10,000	n/a
1999	$10,000	n/a
2000	$10,500	n/a
2001	$10,500	n/a
2002	$11,000	$1,000
2003	$12,000	$2,000
2004	$13,000	$3,000
2005	$14,000	$4,000
2006	$15,000	$5,000
2007	$15,500	$5,000
2008	$15,500	$5,000
2009	$16,500	$5,500
2010	$16,500	$5,500
2011	$16,500	$5,500
2012	$17,000	$5,500

[*See* Notice 2011-90, 2011-47 I.R.B. 791 for 2012]

Disallowed Deferrals (Less Than 50 Percent Participation of Eligible Employees). If less than 50 percent of eligible employees choose to make elective deferrals for the plan year, any deferrals made for that year will be disallowed. Unless the disallowed deferrals are timely corrected, they will be treated as regular contributions to an IRA instead of as contributions to a SARSEP, and the regular IRA contributions may be subject to the 6 percent excise tax on excess regular IRA contributions. Disallowed deferrals can affect both HCEs and non-highly compensated employees (NHCEs).

Note. When an employer contributes more than it can deduct, it is referred to as a "nondeductible employer contribution," not an "excess contribution." For example, if an employer contributes 25 percent of compensation to each participant's SEP IRA, and the SEP document provides for 15 percent of compensation under a definite contribution formula, the 10 percent difference is a "nondeductible employer contribution." Such amounts may be corrected under EPCRS, not under the "excess contribution rules" (see chapter 17).

Traditional IRA Excess Reporting Requirements

As discussed in this chapter, the rules for distributing the three types of excess contributions that are unique to SARSEPs are not the same as the rules for distributing excess (or unwanted) contributions that are made by an individual into a traditional IRA. The correction of an excess or an unwanted traditional IRA contribution made "during a year" are corrected as discussed below (see Q 5:75).

Correction Before Due Date of Federal Income Tax Return. For a distribution of an excess traditional IRA contribution (or an unwanted traditional IRA contribution) plus earnings from a traditional IRA before the due date of the return under Code Section 408(d)(4), report the gross distribution in box 1 of Form 1099-R, only the earnings in box 2a, and enter code 8 (taxable in 2012) or P (taxable in 2010), whichever is applicable, in box 7. Also enter code 1 (not attained age 59½, no known exception) or code 4 (death), if applicable. If the earnings amount is negative (a loss), enter 0 (zero) in box 2a.

Note. The earnings on an excess (or unwanted) traditional IRA contribution are taxable for the year "during which" the contribution is made, even though they may have been contributed in respect to the prior (the "for which") taxable year. [I.R.C. § 408(d)(4)]

Example 1. Sue, age 40, established a traditional IRA in 2012 and contributed $3,000 in February 2012. In January, Sue contributed an additional $2,000 and designated that contribution as having been made for the prior year (2012). Sue changes her mind and decides to withdraw the entire $5,000 contribution as an "unwanted" contribution—by treating it as an excess contribution. At the time of removal, the $3,000 "excess" contribution had earned $30, and the $2,000 "excess" contribution had earned $20. If removed on a timely basis (on or before the return due date), none of the excess (unwanted) contributions are subject to the 6 percent tax on excess contributions.

Example 2. The facts are the same as in Example 1, except Sue removes the $5,000 unwanted contribution in March 2013. Because the earnings are taxable in different years, two separate Forms 1099-R (for 2013) will have to be issued. The trustee or custodian will have to issue the 2013 versions of Form 1099-R, reflecting the return of $3,000 in box 1 and the earnings of $30 in box 2a. In box 7, code P (taxable in prior year—2012) and code 1 (under age 59½, no known exceptions) is entered. In addition, another 2013 version of Form 1099-R is completed, showing $2,000 in box 1, $20 in box 2a, and with code 1 because Sue is under age 59½. The earnings on the $2,000 excess amount are taxable in the year during which the contributions were made (2013). Neither code 8 (taxable in prior year—2012) or code P (taxable in second prior year—2011) is entered because the earnings ($20) on the $2,000 excess amount are taxable in 2013, the year the excess contribution of 2,000 was made and distributed.

Example 3. The facts are the same as in Example 1, except that Sue had made the entire 2012 traditional IRA contribution in 2012 and removed the unwanted contribution in March of 2013. The trustee or custodian will have to issue the 2013 versions of Form 1099-R, reflecting the return of $5,000 in box 1 and the earnings of $50 in box 2a. In box 7, code P (taxable in prior year—2012) and code 1 (under age 59½, no known exceptions) are entered.

Example 4. The facts are the same as in Example 1, except that Sue had made the entire 2012 traditional IRA contribution in February 2013 and removed the excess in March of 2014 (before the due date of the return for the year during which the $5,000 unwanted contribution was made—2013). The trustee or custodian will have to issue the 2014 version of Form 1099-R, reflecting the return of $5,000 in box 1 and the earnings of $50 in box 2a. In box 7, code P (taxable in prior year—2013) and code 1 (under age 59½, no known exceptions) are entered.

Example 5. The facts are the same as in Example 4, except that Sue decides only to treat $2,000 of her 2012 traditional IRA contribution as an unwanted excess contribution. She would have until the due date of her 2013 Federal Income Tax Return to remove the $2,000 under Code Section 408(d)(4), regarding corrections before the due date of the return for the year 2013, during which the $2,000 contribution was made.

Correction after Due Date of Federal Income Tax Return. For a distribution of excess contributions from a traditional IRA without earnings after the due date of the individual's return under Code Section 408(d)(5), leave box 2a blank, and check the "Taxable amount not determined" checkbox in box 2b. Use code 1 (has not attained age 59½, no known exception) or code 7 (has attained age 59½) in box 7, depending on the age of the participant. [I.R.C. § 408(d)(5)]

The payer must determine which part of the corrective distribution is taxable in which year and report such amount in boxes 1 and 2a, using the following code or codes in box 7:

1. Code 1. The taxpayer has not attained age 59½, and it is not known whether any of the early distribution penalty exceptions apply to the payment (e.g., death or disability).
2. Code 4. The payment is being made after the owner's death to a beneficiary, estate, or trust.
3. Code 7. The taxpayer has attained age 59½.
4. Code 8. The amount reported is taxable in the year of distribution (e.g., 2012).
5. Code P. The amount reported is taxable in the year before distribution (e.g., 2011).

Note. The rules discussed previously regarding excess traditional IRA contributions do not apply to the three types of excess contributions that can be made in a SARSEP. However, after appropriate notifications have been made, uncorrected excess contributions; in a SARSEP are treated as traditional IRA contributions; in which time, the traditional IRA rules discussed previously are used to correct any excess (see Q 5:80).

Q 5:76 How should excess SEP contributions that fail the 125 percent nondiscrimination test be corrected and reported?

The following steps should be taken to correct and report excess SEP contributions that fail the 125 percent nondiscrimination test. (See examples in Q 12:37.)

Notification. The employer must notify each affected HCE by March 15 of the amount of any excess SEP contribution made to that employee's SEP IRA for the preceding calendar year. If the employer fails to notify the employee by March 15, it is subject to an excise tax of 10 percent on the excess SEP contribution. [I.R.C. § 4979] That tax is reported on line 13 of Form 5330, Return of Excise Taxes Related to Employee Benefit Plans.

The employer's notification to each affected HCE must specifically state the following in a manner calculated to be understood by the average employee:

1. The amount of the excess SEP contribution attributable to that HCE's elective deferrals;
2. The calendar year in which the excess SEP contribution is includible in gross income; and
3. That the employee must withdraw the excess SEP contribution (and earnings attributable to it) from the SEP IRA by April 15 (plus extensions) following the calendar year of notification by the employer, in accordance with the details described in "Distribution," below.

Note. If the employer fails to notify the employee by December 31 following the calendar year in which the excess SEP contribution arose, the SEP is no longer considered to meet the requirements of Code Section 408(k)(6). In such a case, all elective contributions made for that year to an employee's SEP IRA will be subject to the regular IRA contribution limit (generally $5,000 for 2012) and thus may be considered an excess contribution to the employee's IRA subject to a 6 percent excise tax to be paid by the employee.

Inclusion in Income. The excess SEP contribution amount is included in the employee's gross income in the year that it is distributed from the IRA.

Income Attributable to Excess Contribution. The employer determines the income attributable to the excess SEP contribution using the formula for computing earnings attributable to excess IRA contributions (see Q 5:86). The income attributable to the excess SEP contribution is included in income in the year the income is distributed from the IRA.

Distribution. If the excess SEP contribution amount plus income attributable to the excess is distributed to the employee by April 15 following the calendar year of notification by the employer, no additional excise tax is assessed.

An excess SEP contribution not withdrawn by April 15 following the calendar year of notification will be subject to the regular IRA contribution limit (generally $5,000 for 2012) for the preceding year and may be considered an excess contribution to an IRA. Thus, the employee may be subject to the 6 percent excise tax on excess IRA contributions. If the income attributable to the excess SEP contribution is not withdrawn by April 15 following the calendar year of notification by the employer, the employee may also be subject to the 10 percent premature distribution penalty.

Reporting Requirements. Excess SEP contributions are reported in the following manner.

Form 1099-R. The principal amount of an excess SEP contribution is included in income in the year the excess amount is distributed from the IRA (along with any distributed income). Thus, both the excess SEP contribution and the income attributable to the excess SEP contribution is included in income in the year of the corrective distribution. Therefore, in most corrective distribution cases, two different Forms 1099-R must be produced: one reporting the amount of the excess SEP contribution being distributed as fully taxable in boxes 1 and 2a and the other reporting the amount of the income attributable to the excess as fully taxable in boxes 1 and 2a. The separate Forms 1099-R will usually have different codes in box 7 because each part of the distribution is generally taxable in a different year. If, however, the corrective distribution occurs in the same year as the deferral, just one Form 1099-R is needed to report the total amount in boxes 1 and 2a, with code 8 in box 7.

If the excess SEP contribution (not including the income attributable to it) is less than $100, the excess SEP contribution is included in income in the year of notification by the employer (see "Inclusion in Income," above). Even in such a case, however, two Forms 1099-R may be required if the actual corrective distribution is made in the year following the year of notification by the employer.

For a distribution of contributions plus earnings from an IRA before the due date of the return under Code Section 408(d)(4), report the gross distribution in box 1, only the earnings in box 2a, and enter code 8 (taxable in 2012) or P (taxable in 2011), whichever is applicable, in box 7. Also enter code 1 (not attained age 59½, no known exception) or code 4 (has attained age 59½) also, if applicable.

For a distribution of excess contributions without earnings after the due date of the individual's return under Code Section 408(d)(5), leave box 2a blank, and check the "Taxable amount not determined" checkbox in box 2b. Use code 1 (has not attained age 59½, no known exception) or code 7 (has attained age 59½) in box 7 depending on the age of the participant.

Practice Pointer. Payers making corrective distributions must advise the plan participant at the time of the distribution that the receipt of amounts includible in income in a prior year will require the participant to file Form 1040X, Amended U.S. Individual Income Tax Return, if he or she has already filed an income tax return for that year.

Form 1040. Instead of being reported as an IRA distribution, an excess SEP contribution that is timely withdrawn in accordance with prescribed procedures is included as wages on line 7 of the Form 1040 for the year it is taxable (the deferral year). Income attributable to the excess SEP contribution is also reported as wages on line 7 of the Form 1040 for the year it is taxable (the distribution year). If a loss is being reported, the loss should be shown as a bracketed amount on the "Other Income" line of the Form 1040 for the appropriate taxable year (usually the distribution year).

Form W-2. All elective deferrals should be reported, even if some or all of the amount is an excess SEP contribution, in box 12 of Form W-2 for the year of deferral. No elective deferrals should be included in box 1, but they should be included in boxes 3 and 5 for FICA purposes.

Form 5498. When excess SEP contributions are not withdrawn by April 15 following the calendar year of notification by the employer, such amounts are considered regular IRA contributions, which are generally limited to $5,000 for 2012. Thus, excess SEP contributions that are not timely corrected in accordance with prescribed procedures may be subject to the 6 percent excise tax applicable to excess IRA contributions. Such a tax would apply first to the year the excess SEP contribution arose and then to each year thereafter until corrected.

Note. All SEP contributions (whether regular employer contributions or elective deferrals) are separately identified on the original Form 5498 for the year of the deposit.

Caution. The IRS has not issued any formal guidance regarding corrective Form 5498 reporting procedures, and the regulations have not been updated for SARSEPs.

Note. Line numbers are from the 2012 version of the various forms.

Q 5:77 How should elective deferrals that exceed the $17,000 per taxpayer (as indexed for 2012) limit be corrected and reported?

The following steps should be taken to correct and report elective deferrals that exceed the limit of $17,000 per taxpayer (as indexed). (See examples in Q 12:25.)

Determination. The employee is responsible for determining whether the $17,000 limit for 2012 has been exceeded.

Inclusion in Income. The excess elective deferral is included in the employee's gross income in the calendar year of the deferral.

Income Attributable to Excess Elective Deferral. The method used to determine the income attributable to the excess elective deferral is the same as that used to determine earnings attributable to excess IRA contributions (see Q 5:86). The income attributable to the deferral is included in income in the year of withdrawal from the IRA.

Distribution. The employee must withdraw the excess elective deferral and any income attributable to it by April 15 following the year to which the deferral relates.

If the employee fails to withdraw the excess elective deferral and any income attributable to it by the April 15 deadline, the deferral will be subject to the regular IRA contribution limit (generally $5,000 for 2012) and thus may be subject to the 6 percent excise tax on excess IRA contributions for each year it remains in the IRA. If the income attributable to the excess elective deferral is not withdrawn by the April 15 deadline, it may be subject to the 10 percent premature distribution penalty when withdrawn.

Note. If an employee has both an excess elective deferral and an excess SEP contribution, the amount of the excess elective deferral that is withdrawn by the April 15 deadline will reduce the amount of the excess SEP contribution.

Reporting Requirements. Excess elective deferrals are reported in the following manner.

Form 1099-R. The excess deferral amount is included in income in the year the deferral is made. The income attributable to the excess deferral is included in income in the year of the corrective distribution. Therefore, in most corrective distribution cases, two different Forms 1099-R must be produced: one reporting the amount of the excess deferral being distributed as fully taxable in boxes 1 and 2a and the other reporting the amount of the income attributable to the excess deferral as fully taxable in boxes 1 and 2a. The separate Forms 1099-R will usually have different codes in box 7 because each part of the distribution is generally taxable in a different year. If the corrective distribution occurs in the same year as the deferral, however, only one Form 1099-R is needed to report the total amount distributed in boxes 1 and 2a, with code 8 in box 7.

The payer must determine which part of the corrective distribution is taxable in which year and report such amount in boxes 1 and 2a using the following codes in box 7:

Code 8. The amount being reported is taxable in the year of distribution.

Code P. The amount being reported is taxable in the year before the distribution year.

Note. Code D should probably never apply to the corrective distribution of an excess deferral because such an amount must be distributed no later than April 15 following the calendar year to which the deferral relates.

Practice Pointer. Payers making corrective distributions must advise the plan participant at the time of the distribution that the receipt of amounts includible in income in a prior year will require the participant to file Form 1040X, Amended U.S. Individual Income Tax Return, if he or she has already filed an income tax return for that year.

Form 1040. Instead of being reported as an IRA distribution, an excess deferral that is timely withdrawn in accordance with prescribed procedures is included as wages on line 7 of Form 1040 for the year it is taxable (the deferral year) and must be unadjusted for any gains or losses. Income attributable to the excess deferral is also reported as wages on line 7 of Form 1040 for the year it is taxable (the distribution year). If a loss is being reported, the loss should be shown as a bracketed amount on the "Other Income" line of Form 1040 for the appropriate taxable year (the distribution year).

Form W-2. All elective deferrals should be reported, even if some or all of the amount is an excess deferral, in box 12 of Form W-2 for the year of deferral. Elective deferrals should not be included in box 1, but they should be included in boxes 3 and 5 for FICA purposes.

Form 5498. When excess deferrals are not withdrawn by April 15 following the calendar year of deferral, such amounts are considered regular IRA contributions, which are generally limited to $5,000 for 2012. Thus, excess deferrals that are not timely corrected in accordance with prescribed procedures may be subject to the 6 percent excise tax applicable to excess IRA contributions. Such a tax would apply first to the year the excess deferral arose and then to each year thereafter until the excess was corrected.

See *Caution* in Q 5:76.

Note. Line numbers are from the 2012 version of the various forms.

Q 5:78 How should disallowed deferrals be corrected and reported?

If an employer determines at the end of any year that more than half of its eligible employees did *not* make elective deferrals to the SEP for that year, *all* elective deferrals made by any employee for that year will be considered disallowed deferrals. If not withdrawn within the prescribed time limit (see below), the deferred amounts will be treated as regular IRA contributions rather than SEP contributions. (See examples in Q 12:44.)

Notification. The employer must notify each affected employee by March 15 that the employee's deferrals for the previous year are no longer considered SEP contributions. That notification must clearly state the following in a manner calculated to be understood by the average employee:

1. The amount of the disallowed deferrals;
2. The year in which the disallowed deferrals and income attributable to them are includible in gross income; and
3. That the employee must withdraw the disallowed deferrals (and income attributable to them) from the IRA by April 15 following the calendar year of notification by the employer, in accordance with the details described in "Distribution" below.

Inclusion in Income. Disallowed deferrals are includible in the employee's income in the year that the deferrals were made.

Income Attributable to Disallowed Deferrals. The method used to determine the income attributable to disallowed deferrals is the same as that used to determine earnings attributable to excess IRA contributions (see Q 5:86). Income attributable to the disallowed deferrals is includible in the employee's gross income in the year of distribution from the IRA.

Distribution. The employee must withdraw the disallowed deferrals and income attributable to them by April 15 following the calendar year of notification by the employer.

Disallowed deferrals not withdrawn by April 15 following the calendar year of notification by the employer will be subject to the regular IRA contribution limit (generally $5,000 for 2012) and thus may be subject to the 6 percent excise tax on excess IRA contributions. If the income attributable to disallowed deferrals is not withdrawn by April 15 following the calendar year of notification by the employer, the employee may also be subject to the 10 percent premature distribution penalty when the disallowed deferrals are withdrawn.

Reporting Requirements. Distributions of disallowed deferrals are reported in the same way that excess SEP contributions are reported (see Q 5:76).

Q 5:79 In addition to correction and reporting requirements, what other rules apply to the distribution of excess SEP contributions, excess elective deferrals, and disallowed deferrals?

Various rules apply to the distribution of excess SEP contributions, excess elective deferrals, and disallowed deferrals, in addition to those regarding correction and reporting.

One such rule is that excess SEP contributions, excess elective deferrals, and disallowed deferrals may not be rolled over or transferred to another IRA. Such amounts must be corrected by distribution.

In addition, a 10 percent excise tax is imposed on the employer for excess SEP contributions. [I.R.C. § 4979(a), (b)] The tax is due by the employer's income tax filing deadline for the employer's taxable year with or within which the plan year containing the excess ends; it is reported on Form 5330. [Treas. Reg. § 54.4979-1(a)(3)] If a corrective distribution is made on a timely basis, however, the penalty does not apply. [Treas. Reg. § 54.4979-1(c)]

Further, a timely distribution of excess SEP contributions, excess elective deferrals, or disallowed deferrals (plus earnings) is not subject to the 10 percent premature distribution penalty. [Treas. Reg. § 1.401(k)-1(f)(4)(v)]

As well, a corrective distribution of an excess SEP contribution, an excess deferral, or a disallowed deferral is treated as a distribution for purposes of the minimum distribution rules under Code Section 401(a)(9). Therefore, if an employee is required to receive a minimum distribution for the year the excess is distributed, the excess is disregarded for purposes of satisfying the minimum distribution requirements. [Treas. Reg. § 1.401(k)-1(f)(4)(vi)]

It should also be noted that, unlike excess contributions to a 401(k) plan, excess contributions to a SARSEP cannot be recharacterized (see Q 5:83).

Q 5:80 How are excess SEP contributions, excess elective deferrals, and disallowed deferrals treated?

After the relevant April 15 date, when an excess SEP contribution, excess elective deferral, or disallowed deferral occurs, such excess is deemed an IRA contribution. Thus, on April 16, an excess SEP contribution, excess elective deferral, or disallowed deferral is no longer treated as an excess SEP contribution, excess elective deferral, or disallowed deferral, respectively—it is an IRA contribution and presumably deemed made on that day, April 16, unless April 15 is a Saturday, Sunday, or legal holiday, in which case the taxpayer has until the next business day after April 15 to make the corrective distribution (see Qs 5:76–5:78). As shown in some of the following examples, excess IRA contributions are treated differently from excess elective contributions under a SARSEP. (See additional examples in Qs 12:23–12:24, 12:37, and 12:44.)

Q 5:81 What happens if an employer's SEP contributions exceed the amount that is excludable?

If a SEP contribution exceeds the 25 percent exclusion limit under Code Section 402(h), the excess amount is treated as wages and reported in box 1 of Form W-2 (see Qs 10:15, 11:1). Unlike elective deferrals under a SARSEP, regular employer SEP contributions in excess of applicable limits have not generally been reported for FICA purposes. It is unclear, however, whether such amounts are subject to FICA or other withholding taxes (see Qs 11:9–11:11, 11:15). The amount treated as wages is also considered an amount immediately contributed to an IRA and is not treated as an elective SARSEP excess. Thus, the gain distributed in a correcting distribution is subject to the 10 percent premature distribution tax if the employee is under age 59½ (unless another exception applies).

The exception to the premature distribution penalty found in Code Section 401(k)(6)(D) does not apply to excess employer nonelective contributions. [I.R.C. §§ 72(t), 408(k)(6)(C)(i)] An individual who owns 80 percent or more of an unincorporated business is treated as the employer for purposes of payment of any tax on a nondeductible contribution. [I.R.C. §§ 401(c)(5), 401(c)(6), 4972(d)(2)]

Q 5:82 What is a returned contribution?

IRA contributions that can be returned pursuant to Code Section 408(d)(4) include either excess contributions or "unwanted" contributions. That section provides that the principal amount of the returned contribution is not taxable so long as the net income attributable to such contribution is also distributed. The net income attributable can be a negative amount. Therefore, losses attributable to the returned contribution will reduce the amount of the distribution. However, any attributable earnings are taxable in the year in which the contribution was made and will also be subject to the 10 percent additional income tax of Section 72(t) if the individual is under the age of 59½.

Q 5:83 What is a recharacterized contribution?

IRA contributions that can be recharacterized pursuant to Code Section 408A(d)(6) include regular contributions made to a traditional IRA or a Roth IRA and conversion contributions made to a Roth IRA. Any recharacterized contribution must be increased by any attributable earnings or decreased by any attributable losses. A recharacterization must be accomplished as a direct transfer of assets and is not considered a taxable event. Any gains or losses are deemed to have occurred in the second IRA and not the first IRA.

Q 5:84 What guidance has been issued by the IRS?

Treasury Regulations Section 1.408-4(c)(2)(ii) was first published on August 7, 1980, and contained the original formula for calculating the attributable earnings on a returned IRA contribution. This regulation is referred to as the "old method." Under this "old method," the attributable net income could not be a negative amount. Thus, even where there were no earnings, the contribution being returned could not be reduced by any losses. In addition, this method required that the computation period begin on January 1 of the year in which the contribution was made. The calculation included a period of time when the contribution being returned was not even in the IRA.

On July 10, 2000, the IRS issued Notice 2000-39 [2000-2 C.B. 132] that provided a "new method" for calculating the net income on a returned contribution or a recharacterized contribution. This "new method" based the calculation on the actual earnings and losses during the time that the IRA held the contribution and also permitted net income to be a negative amount. Then on July 23, 2002, proposed regulations were issued that generally adopted the "new method" of Notice 2000-39 with certain modifications. IRS permitted a comment period on the proposed regulations.

On May 5, 2003, the IRS published these final regulations. The preamble to the final regulations states that "few comments were received on the proposed regulations . . . consequently, these final regulations adopt the rules in the proposed regulations *without modification* [emphasis added]." [T.D. 9056, 68 Fed. Reg. 23586–23590 (May 5, 2003)]

Q 5:85 Who is responsible for the calculation?

This answer is still unclear. Neither the prior guidance nor the final regulations identify who is responsible for determining the net income amount. Clearly, either the taxpayer is responsible, or the IRA vendor is responsible. The final regulations state, "These regulations will affect IRA owners and IRA trustees, custodians and issuers." The current version of Publication 590 also states that "[i]n most cases, the net income you must withdraw is determined by your IRA trustee or custodian." [IRS Publication 590, *Individual Retirement Arrangements (IRA)*]

When SARSEP language was first issued by the IRS, in the employee disclosure information there was a sentence that very clearly required that the IRA trustee or custodian determine the earnings attributable to an excess contribution. As a matter of fact, the language told the employee to go to the IRA custodian who *will* calculate the earnings on the excess. Each organization should make a decision after carefully considering the provisions of the final regulations.

Q 5:86 How is net income attributable to an excess contribution determined for years after 2004?

Under the new method, the formula for calculating the net income (positive or negative) on a returned contribution or a recharacterized contribution after 2004 is:

Net income[1] = Contribution[2] × (ACB[3] – AOB[4]) / AOB

[1] Net income can be positive or negative.

[2] The amount of the contribution that is being returned or recharacterized.

[3] ACB is the adjusted closing balance (see Q 5:87).

[4] AOB is the adjusted opening balance (see Q 5:88).

Q 5:87 How is the *adjusted closing balance* determined?

The *adjusted closing balance (ACB)* is the fair market value of the IRA at the end of the computation period plus the amount of any distributions or transfers (including recharacterizations) made from the IRA during the computation period. Thus, the ACB is the value just before the distribution or recharacterization.

Q 5:88 How is the *adjusted opening balance* determined?

The *adjusted opening balance (AOB)* is the fair market value of the IRA at the beginning of the computation period plus the amount of any contributions (including the contribution that is being returned) or transfers (including recharacterizations) made to the IRA during the computation period.

Q 5:89 What is the new *computation period*?

The *computation period* is the period beginning immediately before "the time" that the contribution being returned or recharacterized was made to the IRA and ending immediately prior to the removal of the contribution (or transfer in the case of a recharacterization).

The preamble to the final regulations implies that if an IRA is valued on a daily basis, for purposes of determining the AOB, the computation period begins the exact day before the contribution was made that is being returned or recharacterized. If the IRA is not valued on a daily basis, for purposes of determining the AOB, the fair market value at the beginning of the computation period is deemed to be the most recent, regularly determined, fair market value of the asset as of a date that coincides with or precedes the first day of the computation period (i.e., the most recent statement value).

Q 5:90 How are the final regulations structured?

There are actually two different regulations:

1. Final Treasury Regulations Section 1.408-11 governs the net income calculation for returned contributions under Code Section 408(d)(4). Returned contributions can be either excess contributions or "unwanted" contributions made to a traditional IRA or to a Roth IRA.
2. Final Treasury Regulations Section 1.408A-5, A-2(c) governs the net income calculation for recharacterized contributions. Recharacterized contributions include regular contributions made to a traditional IRA or a Roth IRA or conversions made to a Roth IRA.

In general, both regulations are identical except in the following areas:

1. For returned contributions under Code Section 408(d)(4) where a series of regular contributions were made, the contribution being returned is deemed to be the last contribution made, up to the amount of the contribution identified as the amount to be distributed.

2. For recharacterized contributions under Code Section 408A(d)(6) where a series of contributions were made that are eligible for recharacterization, the IRA owner can choose by date and by dollar amount which contribution, or portion thereof, is to be recharacterized. However, the IRA owner may not identify by a specific asset acquired with those dollars.

The final regulations clarify that the net income calculation is performed only on "the IRA" containing the particular contribution being returned or recharacterized, and that IRA is the IRA from which the distribution or recharacterizing transfer must be made.

The final regulations also clarify that if regular and conversion contributions are commingled in a single Roth IRA, the calculation of net income is still performed on the entire IRA, and any net income, including losses, must be allocated pro rata.

Practice Pointer. It may be advisable to establish a separate Roth IRA when making a conversion from a traditional IRA, so that a subsequent recharacterization will not affect the assets in an existing Roth IRA because of the pro-rata recovery rule. After the expiration of the recharacterization period (tax filing date plus extensions for the conversion year), the assets then could be combined into a single Roth IRA.

USERRA

Q 5:91 Does USERRA affect SEP and SIMPLE IRA plans?

Yes. USERRA generally applies to all plans subject to ERISA. These plans satisfy the definition of an "Employee Pension Benefit Plan" under ERISA Section 3. This definition applies to qualified plans, SEP IRAs, and SIMPLE IRAs that cover common-law employees and also includes ERISA 403(b) plans.

Additionally, USERRA also applies to certain plans that are non-ERISA plans, such as those plans sponsored by a state, governmental entity, or church for its employees. This would include 457(b) plans as well as non-ERISA 403(b) plans that are adopted by a state or local government (i.e., public schools or state colleges or universities).

USERRA does not apply to pension benefits under the Federal Thrift Savings Plan because there is another law that takes care of that plan.

Q 5:92 What does USERRA stand for?

The Uniformed Services Employment and Reemployment Rights Act of 1994 (USERRA) added Section 414(u) to the Code. Since that time, various pieces of guidance related to USERRA have been issued. It was not until September 20, 2004, that the DOL issued proposed regulations under USERRA with the anticipation of quickly making them final. More than a year later, on December

19, 2005, the USERRA regulations, along with some additional changes, were made final.

Q 5:93 What is the effective date of the USERRA regulations?

The effective date of the final regulations was January 18, 2006. It is unclear whether plan documents will need to be amended further to take into consideration these final regulations. Most qualified plans were amended during the GUST restatement to (at least) reference Code Section 414(u). According to the IRS, model SEPs, model SARSEPs, and model SIMPLE IRAs will not be updated. Compliance with Code Section 414(u) is still required, but the SEP or SIMPLE "plan" document will not need to be updated.

Note. GUST is an abbreviation for a decade's worth of laws affecting pension plans. Those laws are:

- Uruguay Round Agreements Act, Pub. L. No. 103-464 ("GATT");
- Uniformed Services Employment and Reemployment Rights Act of 1994, Pub. L. No. 103-353 ("USERRA");
- Small Business Job Protection Act of 1996, Pub. L. No. 104-188 ("SBJPA");
- Taxpayer Relief Act of 1997, Pub. L. No. 105-34 ("TRA '97").

Q 5:94 Will compliance with USERRA be a problem?

During the comment process for the proposed USERRA regulations, the DOL was made aware of the fact that in order for certain employers to comply with USERRA, they may actually violate the Code. In the preamble to the final regulations, the DOL states that "the Internal Revenue Service and the Department of the Treasury have indicated that a health or pension plan will be deemed not to be in conflict with the applicable IRC requirements merely because of compliance with USERRA or its related regulations."

Q 5:95 What general requirements does USERRA mandate?

Generally, contributions and distributions are affected. Below is an overview of the final USERRA regulations:

1. *Break-in-service rules.* Generally, upon reemployment, the employee is treated for all plan purposes as never incurring a break in service. This is true for purposes of participation, vesting, and accrual of benefits.
2. *Reporting back to work.* Depending on the employee's length of military service, he or she is required to report back to work with the employer within specific time frames:
3. *Employer make-up contributions.* Once the employee is reemployed, the employer must, within 90 days after the employee returns to service, make up any contributions to which the employee would have been entitled had he or she not gone into military service. For example, if the employer maintained a profit-sharing plan or a SEP plan and provided for

an employer contribution of 15 percent of compensation for the years that the employee was in the military, then the employer must, within the later of the 90 days after the reemployment date or the normal deadline for funding the plan for the year, determine the amount of the missed employer contribution and contribute that amount for the employee's benefit under the plan. If it is impossible or unreasonable for the employer to make this contribution within 90 days after the employee is reemployed, then the employer will have a reasonable amount of time to contribute the make-up contribution.

4. *Make-up elective deferrals into SARSEP plans.* Once employees are reemployed, they may begin to make up deferrals from salary for years in which they were not able to defer into the plan. Caution must be exercised because the limitations on elective *deferrals* have changed, and employees must limit the amount that they are deferring into the plan to the 402(g) limit for the make-up year.
   a. An *employee* will have up to three times the length of military service, not to exceed five years, to make up elective deferrals for past years.
   b. The *employee* is not required to make up the full amount of the elective deferrals for any given year.
   c. If the employee was making elective deferrals while in the military, the maximum 402(g) amount for such year will be reduced to take into consideration the amounts already contributed for that year.
   d. The employee is neither required nor permitted to include interest with any make-up elective deferral.
5. *Employer matching formula requirements.* If the plan contains an employer matching formula, and such match is contingent on the employee contributing an elective deferral or an after-tax contribution, then the match is not required until the time that the employee elects to defer into the plan. This does not apply to SARSEP plans.
6. *Differential pay.* The final regulations also address situations where certain employers have provided differential pay to employees who leave employment and entered the military. *Differential pay* is pay provided by the employer that is partial pay or *civilian pay* while the employee is in active military service. The *amount* and duration of differential pay varies from employer to employer and is not required by USERRA. Instead, it is merely an employer-provided benefit. Military differential wage payments are treated as wages for withholding purposes and treated as compensation under a SEP and SARSEP for purposes of the limitations on annual additions (see Q 6:4). These payments are also treated as compensation for traditional IRA and Roth-IRA contribution purposes. [HEART § 105, amending I.R.C. §§ 219(f)(1), 414(u)(12)] The Treasury and the IRS have issued regulations on the treatment of differential pay and the ability of employees in the military to defer from this compensation even though they are technically not employed by the employer paying these amounts. [Treas. Reg. § 1.415(c)-2(e)(4)]

IRS Notice 2010-15 provides that differential wage payments and the ability to make contributions based on such payments must be made available to all employees on reasonably equivalent terms. However, contributions and benefits provided as a result of differential wage payments need not be included in a plan's nondiscrimination testing. But, if such benefits and contributions are taken into account for any employee, they must be taken into account for all employees. Although differential wage payments are not required to be treated as compensation for calculating benefits and contributions under a SEP or SIMPLE plan, such amounts are treated as compensation for purposes of the annual limitation on benefits and contributions under Code Section 415 (see Q 6:4). [I.R.S. Notice 2010-15, 2010-10 I.R.B. 390]

7. *Repayment of distributions.* The proposed regulations provided that an employee could have repaid a distribution received from any plan subject to USERRA. This provision caused much confusion in the defined contribution plan community, especially for SEP plans and SIMPLE IRAs, for which contributions are reported. The final regulations modify this rule and only permit the repayment of distributions where the plan is a defined benefit plan. In this case, interest is included in the determination of the repayment. The employee must be permitted to repay this amount starting with the day of reemployment and ending three times the length of military service, not to exceed five years. The final regulations also do not address the ramifications to employer plans where the employer has already permitted the employee to repay a distribution before the final regulations are issued.
8. *Benefit amounts may vary.* In a defined contribution plan, including SEPs and SIMPLE IRAs, the benefit may actually not be the same as if the employee had remained in the service of the employer due to the following rules:
    a. During the actual years of allocations, the reemployed employee is not entitled to forfeitures;
    b. The employee and the employer are not restoring earnings to the plan along with the make-up contributions; and
    c. The employee's make-up contributions are also not subject to losses incurred in the plan for the period of military service.
9. *Determination of rate of pay.* For purposes of make-up employer contributions, the employer must be able to determine the rate of pay once the employee is reemployed. If the rate of pay is not reasonably ascertainable (e.g., due to commissions earned), the average rate of compensation during the 12-month period prior to military service is used.

    If the *employee* had not been employed for 12 months prior to military service, then the average rate of pay is determined using the shorter period.
10. *Special rules for multiemployer plans.* The last employer that employed the employee is responsible for making any make-up contributions,

unless such employer provides otherwise. If the prior employer no longer exists, the plan must still provide coverage for the employee. An employer that contributes to the multiemployer plan is required to notify the plan administrator of the plan within 30 days after the date the employee is reemployed.

Chapter 6

Compensation for SEPs and SARSEPs

Numerous limits and restrictions are placed on the amount of compensation that may be considered in the design and operation of a SEP or SARSEP. This chapter examines the definition of compensation for employees whose earnings are reported on Form W-2. A SEP or SARSEP plan document may define compensation as modified W-2 earnings or wages used for income tax withholding at the source, or it may use some other definition allowed by the Internal Revenue Service. Clarifications made by the final regulations are also discussed in this chapter. The rules for determining earned income and the effect of the 2 percent reduction in SECA taxes for 2011 and 2012 are discussed in chapter 7.

Defining Compensation

Q 6:1 Is there a general definition of compensation for purposes of a SEP or SARSEP?

Yes. Section 415 of the Internal Revenue Code (Code) contains a general definition of compensation (see Qs 6:4, 6:14). The Code sections that apply to SEPs and SARSEPs include 408(k)(7)(B) and 402(h)(2), which reference Code Section 414(s). Code Section 414(s)(1), in turn, refers to the definition of compensation found in Code Section 415(c)(3), as does Code Section 414(q)(7). Thus, Code Section 415(c)(3) is the starting point for determining compensation for a SEP or SARSEP. In revenue rulings, notices, and other guidance of general applicability, the Internal Revenue Service (IRS) may provide additional definitions of compensation that are treated as satisfying Code Section 415(c)(3).

[I.R.C. §§ 414(s)(1), 414(s)(2), 415(c)(3); Treas. Reg. §§ 1.414(s)-1(b)(1), 1.415(c)-2(d)(1)]

The definition under Code Section 415(c)(3) is also used for purposes of applying the limits on overall contributions under Code Section 415. Special rules apply to self-employed individuals (see Qs 6:2, 6:18).

Although the term *compensation* is defined in the Code, documents used to establish a SEP or SARSEP frequently specify their own definition of compensation (see Q 3:15).

> **Note 1.** Documents used to establish a SEP or SARSEP frequently specify their own definition of compensation (see Q 3:15).

> **Note 2.** Prior to the issuance of the proposed regulations in 2005, comprehensive Section 415 regulations were last issued in 1981. For more than 25 years, updates to the 1981 regulations to reflect statutory and other changes were incorporated in a series of revenue rulings and notices. The proposed regulations both consolidated all of the Section 415 rules in updated regulations and reflected certain statutory changes not previously addressed in IRS guidance. The final 2007 rules adopt the 2005 proposed regulations with certain changes, including changes made by the Pension Protection Act (PPA). [*See* Preamble, Treas. Reg. § 1.415 (T.D. 9319, 2007-18 I.R.B. 1041 (Apr. 30, 2007))] Most calendar year plans began applying the new rules as of January 1, 2008 (see Q 6:6).

Q 6:2 Are contributions that are not excludable from gross income treated as compensation?

Yes. Contributions that are not excluded from gross income are treated as compensation for purposes of Code Section 415. For example, an elective SARSEP contribution that is in excess of the 25 percent exclusion limit (see Q 11:1) is treated as compensation. Similarly, an employer contribution that is not excludable from gross income (e.g., an excess contribution) is also treated as compensation under Code Section 415. [Treas. Reg. § 1.415(c)-2(b)(1)] Nonetheless, amounts that are not excluded from a participant's gross income may be deductible. This is because compensation used for deduction purposes does not exclude elective deferrals (see Q 6:3).

Q 6:3 Is Section 415 compensation used for all purposes?

No. Compensation determined under Code Section 415 includes elective contributions made by participants. Such contributions may be included or excluded from compensation for the purpose of allocating the employer's SEP contribution (see Q 6:21). Elective contributions are included in compensation for the purpose of determining the limit on the employer's deduction for contributions for plan years beginning after 2001 (see Qs 6:20, 6:23). For the purpose of determining the minimum amount of compensation required for an employee to participate in a SEP arrangement, compensation includes all of a participant's elective contributions, but does not generally include nonelective contributions made by the employer (see Qs 6:2, 6:19). For the purpose of determining the exclusion of contributions from an employee's gross income, elective contributions (other than elective contributions that are treated as catch-up contributions) are not treated as compensation (see Q 11:1).

Q 6:4 What does Section 415 compensation include?

Under Code Section 415, the term *compensation* includes the following:

1. An employee's wages, salaries, fees for professional services, and other amounts received (without regard to whether an amount is paid in cash) for personal services actually rendered in the course of employment with the employer maintaining the plan, to the extent that the amounts are includible in gross income (see Q 6:14). Such amounts include, but are not limited to, commissions paid to salespersons, compensation for services on the basis of a percentage of profits, commissions on insurance premiums, tips, bonuses, fringe benefits, and reimbursements or other expense allowances under a nonaccountable plan, as described in Treasury Regulations Section 1.62-2(c)(3).
2. Elective deferrals made to a SARSEP, a 403(b) plan, a 401(k) plan, a SIMPLE, a 457 plan, or a cafeteria plan under Code Section 125 (see Qs 6:20, 6:21, 6:24, 6:26). [Treas. Reg. § 1.415(c)-2(b)(1)]

   Differential military pay. Effective for taxable years beginning after 2008, and to remuneration paid after 2008, differential military pay is treated as compensation for purposes of the limitations on contributions and benefits under a plan (Code Section 415) and treated as wages for withholding purposes. A differential wage payment is defined as any payment which: (i) is made by an employer to an individual with respect to any period during which the individual is performing service in the uniformed services while on active duty for a period of more than 30 days; and (ii) represents all or a portion of the wages that the individual would have received from the employer if the individual were performing services for the employer. The final Code Section 415 regulations issued in 2007 generally permitted a plan to treat differential pay as compensation for purposes of that section. [Treas. Reg. § 1.415(c)-2(e)(4), 72 Fed. Reg. 16,878 (Apr. 5, 2007)] More recent legislation mandates this result. [Heroes Earnings Assistance and Relief Tax Act of 2008 (HEART) § 105; I.R.C. §§ 219(f)(12), 414(u)(12), 3401(h)(12)]

   IRS Notice 2010-15 provides that differential wage payments and the ability to make contributions based on such payments must be made available to all employees on reasonably equivalent terms. However, if such benefits and contributions are taken into account for any employee, they must be taken into account for all employees. Although differential wage payments are not required to be treated as compensation for calculating benefits and contributions under a SEP or SIMPLE plan (see Q 5:95), such amounts are treated as compensation for purposes of the annual limitation on benefits and contributions under Code Section 415. [I.R.S. Notice 2010-15, 2010-10 I.R.B. 390]

3. Elective reductions made for qualified transportation fringe benefits under Code Section 132(f)(4).
4. Foreign earned income (as defined in Code Section 911(b)), whether or not excludable from gross income under Code Section 911.
5. Amounts described either in Code Section 104(a)(3), relating to compensation for certain injuries or sickness, or in Code Section 105(a), relating to accident or health insurance for personal injuries or sickness, or amounts described in Code Section 105(h) paid to certain highly compensated common-law employees under a discriminatory self-insured medical expense reimbursement plan, but only to the extent that the amounts are includible in the gross income of the employee under those sections.
6. Amounts paid or reimbursed by the employer for an employee's moving expenses, but only to the extent that at the time of the payment it is reasonable to believe that the amounts are not deductible by the employee under Code Section 217.
7. The value of a nonqualified stock option granted to an employee by the employer, but only to the extent that the value of the option is includible in the employee's gross income for the taxable year in which the option is granted.
8. The amount includible in gross income of an employee who makes an election (described in Code Section 83(b)) relating to the current inclusion in gross income of property transferred in connection with the performance of services.
9. Amounts included in the gross income of an employee under an ineligible 457(f) plan, or under the rules of Code Section 409A regarding the inclusion in gross income of deferred compensation under nonqualified deferred compensation plans, or because the amounts are constructively received by the employee. [Treas. Reg. § 1.415(c)-2(b)(1)-(7)]

[I.R.C. §§ 414(s)(1), 414(s)(2), 415(c)(3); Treas. Reg. § 1.414(s)-1(b)(1); Treas. Reg. § 1.415(c)-2]

Note. Compensation under Code Section 415 is determined without regard to the exclusions from gross income in Code Section 931, relating to income from sources within Guam, American Samoa, or the Northern Mariana Islands, and Code Section 933, relating to income from sources within Puerto Rico.

Q 6:5 How does Code Section 415 limit annual additions to a SEP plan?

Code Section 415 limits the annual additions that may be allocated to an individual's account in any limitation year (generally $50,000 for limitation years beginning in 2012). [I.R.C. § 415(c)(1)]

Q 6:6 What is the limitation year in a SEP?

The limitation year is the calendar year unless another 12-month period is designated in the plan document. (Nearly every plan will designate the plan year as its limitation year.) For limitation years that begin after December 31, 2001, the maximum annual addition is the lesser of 100 percent of compensation or $40,000 (indexed for inflation). For 2012, the Code Section 415 dollar limitation is $50,000. [I.R.C. § 415(c)(1)] Proration is required in the event the plan year is changed. [*See* Treas. Reg. § 1.415(j)-1(d)] (See Appendix G for limits in earlier years.)

Caution. The adjusted dollar limitation applicable to a SEP is effective as of January 1 of each calendar year and applies with respect to limitation years ending with or within that calendar year. For example, if a SEP has a plan year beginning July 1, 2012, and ending June 30, 2013, the annual contribution limit in effect on January 1, 2012 ($250,000), applies to the plan for the entire plan year (rather than the 2013 limit which is generally announced in October of each year). Thus, anticipation of the increased dollar limit is not permitted until the new limit (if increased) becomes effective after it is announced by the IRS. [Treas. Reg. § 1.415(d)-1(b)(2)(iii); I.R.S. Notice 2011-90, 2011-47 I.R.B. 791 for 2012 limits]

Q 6:7 When are amounts contributed to a SEP deemed allocated to a participant's account?

Amounts contributed to a SEP are treated as allocated to the individual's account as of the last day of the limitation year ending with or within the taxable year for which the contribution is made. [Treas. Reg. § 1.415I-1(b)(6)(ii)(C)]

Q 6:8 Has the $40,000 limit been indexed for inflation?

Yes, the $40,000 limit has been indexed for inflation in increments of $1,000 beginning after 2001. The original Employee Retirement Income Security Act of 1974 (ERISA) limit on annual additions was $25,000. The limit was increased by the Tax Equity and Fiscal Responsibility Act of 1982 (TEFRA) to $30,000. The limit was later increased to $40,000 by the Economic Growth and Tax Relief Reconciliation Act of 2001 (EGTRRA). [I.R.C. § 415(d)(4)(B); Treas. Reg. § 1.415(d)-1(b)] Table 6-1 shows the limits in effect for 1997 and later years.

Table 6-1. Code Section 415 Dollar Limitations

Plan Year Ending in	*Code Section 415 Dollar Limit*
2012	$50,000
2011	$49,000
2010	$49,000
2008	$46,000

Table 6-1. Code Section 415 Dollar Limitations (*cont'd*)

Plan Year Ending in	*Code Section 415 Dollar Limit*
2009	$49,000
2007	$45,000
2006	$44,000
2005	$42,000
2004	$41,000
2002-2003	$40,000
2001	$35,000
1997–2000	$30,000

[*See* I.R.S. Notice 2011-90, 2011-47 I.R.B. 791 for 2012 limits]

Q 6:9 May compensation that is paid after a limitation year be used for the prior limitation year?

Maybe. A *de minimis* timing rule states that compensation paid after the end of a limitation year may be used provided

1. The amounts are earned during the year but paid in the first few weeks of the next limitation year.
2. The amounts are included on a uniform and consistent basis with respect to all similarly situated employees.
3. The same amount is not included in more than one limitation year.

[Treas. Reg. § 1.415(c)-2(e)(2); Treas. Reg. § 1.415(c)-2(e)(2)]

Example. Jean defers from her salary into her employer SARSEP plan during 2012. On January 15, 2013, she receives a check for the pay period that ends on December 31, 2012. Jean may defer from the check received on January 15, 2013, for the 2012 plan limitation year.

Note. This rule was clarified under the proposed 415 regulations issued May 31, 2005. These regulations were finalized in April 2007 and are effective for years beginning after December 31, 2007. Arguably, the rule would apply to a SEP plan, although there is no reference to SEP plans under these new final regulations with respect to this rule.

Q 6:10 May severance payments be treated as compensation for purposes of making elective deferrals under a SARSEP?

Generally not. Severance payments are not generally considered compensation and may not have elective deferrals taken from these payments. However, a special rule applies to payments made shortly after the end of the year (see Q 6:11). [Treas. Reg. § 1.415(c)-2(e)(1)(ii)]

Q 6:11 May an employee defer from compensation received after termination from employment?

Maybe. An employee may defer from post-severance payments they would have been entitled to had the employee continued service with the employer. Such payments must also be paid by the later of the end of the limitation year in which the employee terminated service or within two and a half months after severance from employment.

Generally, this would include compensation paid for services before severance from employment (e.g., regular compensation, overtime, bonuses, and accrued sick or vacation pay), as long as the employee would have been entitled to these payments had he or she continued to work, and to payments with respect to leave that would have been available for use if employment had not terminated. Based on the final 415 regulations, it is unclear whether this rule will apply to a SEP or SARSEP plan. [*See* Preamble, Treas. Reg. § 1.415 (T.D. 9319, 2007-18 I.R.B. 1041, 1044 (Apr. 30, 2007)), referring only to I.R.C. § 401(k) and § 457(b) plans; Treas. Reg. § 1.415(c)-2(e)] Such amounts are also treated as compensation under Code Section 415. [Treas. Reg. § 1.415(c)-2(e)(3)]

> **Note 1.** Severance pay, unfunded nonqualified deferred compensation, and parachute payments (under Code Section 280G(b)(2)) are not treated as compensation under Code Section 415, because the amounts would not have been paid absent the severance from employment (see Q 6:10).

> **Note 2.** With respect to bona fide leave payments, the final regulations under Code Section 415 require that the plan explicitly provide that such post-severance payments are included in compensation. The final regulations also permit payments made postemployment from a nonqualified unfunded deferred compensation plan to be treated as compensation, if the payments would have been made at the same time if the employee had continued employment and the payments are includible in gross income. Such amounts are also treated as compensation under Code Section 415. [Treas. Reg. § 1.415(c)-2(e)(3)(i)]

> **Note 3.** Under the final regulation, severance "regular pay" must be included as compensation, but other payments are optional. Code Section 415(c)(3) compensation must include certain post-severance "regular pay" that is paid within the specified time frame described above and that would have been paid had the participant remained employed (e.g., regular, overtime, and shift differential pay, commissions, bonuses, and other similar compensation). In addition, the final regulations permit, but do not require, plan provisions to specify that any of the following types of post-severance payments be included in Code Section 415(c)(3) compensation: (1) certain payments within the specified time frame for accrued bona fide sick, vacation, or other leave (if the participant would have been able to use the leave if employment had continued); (2) certain payments within the specified time frame under a nonqualified deferred compensation plan (if the payments are taxable and would have been made at that time if the

employee had continued in employment); (3) certain payments to a permanently and totally disabled participant (not limited to specified time frame); or (4) certain differential payments to individuals in qualified military service (see Q 6:4). [Treas. Reg. § 1.415(c)-2(e)(3)(i)]

Q 6:12 May payments made after severance from employment by reason of qualified military service be treated as compensation?

Yes. The rule generally excluding payments after severance from employment (see Q 6:11) from compensation does not apply to payments to an individual who does not currently perform services for the employer by reason of qualified military service to the extent those payments do not exceed the amounts the individual would have received if the individual had continued to perform services for the employer rather than entering qualified military service. [Treas. Reg. § 1.415(c)-2(e)(4)] Thus, compensation paid after the two-and-a-half-month period described in Q 6:11 may be taken into account (treated as compensation) for contribution purposes.

Q 6:13 What is *qualified military service*?

Qualified military service means any service in the uniformed services (as defined in chapter 43 of Title 38, United States Code) by any individual if such individual is entitled to reemployment rights under such chapter with respect to such service. [I.R.C. § 414(u)(1); Treas. Reg. § 1.415(c)-1(b)(6)(ii)(D)]

Q 6:14 What does Section 415 compensation exclude?

Under Code Section 415, the term *compensation* does *not* include the following:

1. Employer nonelective contributions made on behalf of an employee to a SEP, a qualified plan, or a 403(b) plan, or contributions made to governmental plans as "pick up" contributions
2. Contributions made by the employer to a deferred compensation plan, to the extent that, before the application of the Section 415 limits to that plan, the contributions are not includible in the gross income of the employee for the taxable year in which contributed
3. Distributions from a deferred compensation plan, regardless of whether such amounts are includible in the gross income of the employee when distributed. It should be noted, however, that any amounts received by an employee from an unfunded nonqualified plan are permitted to be considered compensation for Section 415 purposes in the year the amounts are includible in the gross income of the employee.
4. Amounts realized from the exercise of nonqualified stock options or when restricted stock (or property) held by an employee either becomes freely transferable or is no longer subject to a substantial risk of forfeiture [I.R.C. § 83]

5. Amounts realized from the sale, exchange, or other disposition of stock acquired under a qualified stock option
6. Amounts qualifying for special tax benefits, such as premiums for group term life insurance (but only to the extent that the premiums are not includible in the gross income of the employee)

[I.R.C. § 415(c)(3); Treas. Reg. § 1.415(c)-2(b)]

Note 1. Dividend income (S corporation or otherwise) is a return on invested capital, not a return on labor (wages). It does not count for plan establishment or plan contribution purposes. If a taxpayer improperly, in the view of the IRS, either inflates his or her S corporation dividend and correspondingly reduces his or her earned income to, for example, reduce Social Security or Medicare taxes, or deflates his or her S corporation dividend and correspondingly increases his or her earned income to get a higher pension contribution (not likely to be challenged by the IRS, but it is possible), the IRS maintains that it has the right to recharacterize the split between the two to reflect what it says is the "economic reality." If the filed return reflects economic reality, dividends do not count toward compensation for plan purposes. [Durando v. United States, 70 F.3d 548 (9th Cir. 1995)] In *Joseph M. Grey Public Accountant, P.C. v. Commissioner* [119 T.C. No. 5], the owner of a Sub S treated himself as an independent contractor and reported payments for services on Form 1099. The Tax Court held that the owner was an employee and that the wages were subject to employment taxes FICA and FUTA (i.e., not Self-Employment Contributions Act of 1954, SECA). Can an individual be an independent contractor for and the sole shareholder of an S corporation? Maybe, depending on the facts. In *Veterinary Surgical Consultants, P.C.* [117 T.C. No. 141, Oct. 15, 2001], the facts worked against the taxpayer. The corporation did veterinary consulting and had only one employee who was a veterinarian, the president and sole shareholder, and his services were essential to the business. He claimed to be an independent contractor. The Tax Court held that he was an employee. The Court also held, as in *Grey,* that the corporation could not avail itself of the benefits of Section 530 of the Revenue Act of 1978 (which provides for reduced penalties) because the corporation did not have a reasonable basis for treating the worker as an independent contractor. The taxpayer was the only employee, and his services were essential to the operation of the business. Arguably, an individual might be considered an independent contractor if his or her services are not essential to the business and the he or she has another business. For example, Joe is a 25 percent owner in a building contractor, but he also does business as a lawyer. Joe does legal work for the contractor and bills them through his law firm. See the following Note. [*See also Yeagle Drywall,* T.C. Memo 2001-284 (the taxpayers' services were essential and 99 percent stockholder treated as an employee and not an independent contractor)]

Note 2. It may be questionable "whether it is ever reasonable for a taxpayer to treat a statutory employee as a nonemployee for employment tax purposes." [See discussion in Joseph M. Grey Public Accountant, P.C. v. Commissioner, ¶ 26 (119 T.C. No. 5).]

Relying on Revenue Ruling 1959-221 [1959-1 C.B. 225], the IRS advised an S corporation shareholder that his distributive share of earnings could not be treated as self-employment income for retirement plan purposes because his services were not a material income producing factor. [Field Service Advice 1999-526 (undated)] In Revenue Ruling 1959-221, the IRS issued guidance on whether the amounts required to be included in the gross income of a shareholder of an electing small business corporation (S corporation) constitute "net earnings from self-employment" for purposes of SECA. After noting the various Code provisions affecting self-employed individuals, such as Code Sections 1402(a) and (c), the ruling stated:

> [I]t is apparent that income not resulting from the conduct of a trade or business by an individual or by a partnership of which he is a member is not includible in computing the individual's net earnings from self-employment. Amounts which must be taken into account in computing a shareholder's income tax by reason of the provisions of Section 1373 of the Code are not derived from a trade or business carried on by such shareholder. Neither the election by a corporation as to the manner in which it will be taxed for Federal income tax purpose nor the consent thereto by the persons who are shareholders results in the consenting shareholder's being engaged in carrying on the corporation's trade or business. Accordingly, amounts which a shareholder is required to include in his gross income by reason of the provisions of Section 1373 of the Code should not be included in computing his net earnings from self-employment for Self-Employment Contributions Act purposes. [Rev. Rul. 1959-221, 1959-1 C.B. 225–227]

However, an appeals court decision held that only a portion (less than half) of an S corporation's net profits was reportable as salaries and subject to FICA taxes where employees who were not partners performed significant services. [David E. Watson, P.C. v. United States, 668 F.3d 1008 (8th Cir. Iowa 2012), providing a road map to "reasonable compensation"; *see also* Storey v. Comm., T.C. Memo 2012-115 (Apr. 19, 2012), night-time filmmaker was self-employed despite large losses] This easing would not be available if all of the services were performed by S firm owners.

Q 6:15 Does a plan that uses the general Section 415(c)(3) definition of compensation satisfy Code Section 408(k)?

Yes. A plan that defines compensation for purposes of applying the limits of Code Section 415 to include only the items specified previously (see Q 6:4) and to exclude all the items specified previously (see Q 6:14), if applicable, is automatically considered to be using a definition that satisfies Code Section 415 and, thus, to satisfy the provisions of Code Section 408(k). [I.R.C. §§ 408(k)(7)(B), 414(s)(1)]

Q 6:16 Are there alternative safe harbor definitions of compensation?

Yes. As an alternative to the Section 415 definition of compensation, a plan (including a SEP or a SARSEP) may define *compensation* using one of the following three definitions used for wage-reporting purposes and automatically be deemed to satisfy Code Section 415(c)(3). The three alternatives do *not* apply to self-employed individuals treated as employees within the meaning of Code Section 401(c)(1) (see Q 6:18). [Treas. Reg. § 1.415(c)-2(d)(2)]

W-2, Box 1, Earnings (excludes elective deferrals that reduce compensation). This alternative includes amounts required to be reported under Code Sections 6041, 6051, and 6052 (wages, tips, and other compensation box on Form W-2, Wage and Tax Statement). That is, *compensation* is defined as wages within the meaning of Code Section 3401(a) and all other payments of compensation to an employee by his or her employer (in the course of the employer's trade or business) for which the employer is required to furnish the employee a written statement under Code Sections 6041(d), 6051(a)(3), and 6052. [Treas. Reg. §§ 1.6041-1(a), 1.6041-2(a)(1), 1.6052-1, 1.6052-2; *see also* Treas. Reg. § 31.6051-1(a)(1)(i)(C)] This definition of compensation may be modified to exclude amounts paid or reimbursed by the employer for an employee's moving expenses, but only to the extent that at the time of the payment it is reasonable to believe that the employee may deduct such amounts under Code Section 219. Compensation is to be determined without regard to any rules under Code Section 3401(a) that limit the remuneration included in wages based on the nature or location of the employment or the services performed, for example, the exception for agricultural labor in Code Section 3401(a)(2). Although treated as elective deferrals, designated Roth contributions made to an employer's 401(k) plan, 403(b) plan, and governmental 457(b) plan under Code Section 402A, *are* included in box 1 of Form W-2.

Section 3401(a) Wages (Social Security wages; includes elective deferrals). Under this alternative, *compensation* is defined as wages within the meaning of Code Section 3401(a) (which generally includes, for purposes of income tax withholding at the source, all remuneration for services performed as an employee other than fees paid to a public official) but determined without regard to any rules that limit the remuneration included in wages based on the nature or location of the employment or the services performed, for example, the exception for agricultural labor in Code Section 3401(a)(2).

Safe Harbor—Section 415 Compensation (includes elective deferrals). The Section 415 safe harbor definition of compensation is generally a streamlined version of the full Section 415 definition. It is intended to simplify the full definition by including an employee's basic wages without the required adjustments of the full Section 415 definition. Under this alternative, *compensation* is defined as wages, salaries, fees for professional services, and other amounts received (without regard to whether an amount is paid in cash) for personal services actually rendered in the course of employment with the employer maintaining the plan, to the extent that the amounts are includible in gross income. Such amounts include, but are not limited to, commissions paid to salespersons, compensation for services on the basis of a percentage of profits, commissions on insurance premiums, tips, bonuses, fringe benefits, and reimbursements or other expense allowances under a nonaccountable plan (as described in Treasury Regulations Section 1.62-2(c)(3)) and exclude the items enumerated in Q 6:14.

> **Note.** The Commissioner of Internal Revenue may—in revenue rulings, notices, and other guidance of general applicability—provide additional definitions of compensation that are treated as satisfying Code Section 415(c)(3).

> **Example.** Marvin, an insurance agent, retired in 2011. In 2012, he received commissions on policies that he sold in prior years. Although Marvin retired from day-to-day operations in 2011, he spent about two hours every day in the office. His commissions are compensation, reportable on Schedule C, and subject to self-employment tax. [Edwards v. Commissioner, T.C. Memo 2008-24 (Feb. 7, 2008)]

Q 6:17 Are SEP contributions treated as compensation under Code Section 415?

Maybe. For the purpose of Code Section 415, compensation includes elective (but not nonelective) contributions to a SEP. [I.R.C. § 415(c)(3)(D)] Before 1998, most types of elective deferrals were not treated as compensation.

> **Note.** In April 2002, the IRS released an updated model SEP form (Form 5305-SEP), an updated model SARSEP form (Form 5305A-SEP), and an updated Listing of Required Modifications (LRM) for both SEPs and SARSEPs. In the 2002 LRM, the definition of compensation was amended to reflect the changes made by the Small Business Job Protection Act of 1996 (SBJPA), the EGTRRA, and the technical corrections made by the Job Creation and Worker Assistance Act of 2002 (JCWAA). The model SEP form now has a revision date of December 2004. The model SARSEP now has a revision date of June 2006. Both model forms have also been updated to reflect the changes made by the SBJPA and EGTRRA.

Q 6:18 What is the compensation of a self-employed individual?

For purposes of applying the limits under Code Section 415, the earned income of a self-employed individual who is an employee within the meaning of Code Section 401(c)(1) is treated as his or her compensation, plus amounts deferred at the election to the extent they are excludable from gross income. [Treas. Reg. § 1.415(c)-2(b)(2)] Finding a suitable starting point for calculating earned income is discussed in chapter 7.

The earned income of a partner in an organization established as a limited liability partnership (LLP) or limited liability company (LLC) is also treated as his or her compensation. [Treas. Reg. § 1.1402(a)-2] Amounts earned by partners and shareholder-partners of an LLC are not wages subject to FICA, FUTA, or federal income tax withholding. [IRS Legal Mem. 200117003 (Apr. 27, 2001)] See also Note 1 in Q 6:14 regarding how the courts view the treatment of an employee whose remuneration for services are reported on Form 1099 or treated as dividends.

> **Note.** Compensation includes the net income from operating oil, gas, or mineral interests or the net earnings of a self-employed writer, inventor, or artist; however, a royalty paid for the right to use a copyright or patent or an oil, gas, or mineral property is taxable, although it is not generally treated as earned income.

The definition of *compensation* for a self-employed person as determined in the plan document is extremely important in applying the limits applicable to SEPs and SARSEPs. A SEP may provide for employer contributions to be allocated to employees, including self-employed individuals, based on their compensation, including or excluding their elective contributions. After all adjustments are made, a maximum of $250,000 of compensation for plan years beginning in 2012 may be taken into account (see Q 6:21). If a plan's definition of compensation includes the elective contributions of nonowner-employees, a self-employed individual's earned income for purposes of SEP allocations must be increased by the amount of the elective deferrals made by the employer on behalf of the self-employed individual, up to the maximum limit of $250,000 (the 2012 limit). A special rule allows a plan to consider only a portion, instead of all, of the earned income of a self-employed individual who is also a highly compensated employee (HCE). Few plans, however, contain such a provision. [Treas. Reg. § 1.414(s)-1(g)(1)(i)]

Additional complications arise when contributions are integrated with Social Security or when participants, including self-employed individuals, are employed by more than one employer (see Qs 7:5, 7:24, 9:3, 9:9).

Q 6:19 What is compensation for purposes of the *de minimis* compensation requirement for eligibility?

Employees who receive less than $550 in compensation (for 2012) during the plan year may be excluded from participation in a SEP or SARSEP (see Q 2:46). The 2012 minimum compensation limit of $550 is effective for plan years beginning in 2012. (See Q 6:27 and Appendix G for limits in earlier years.) For such purpose, compensation means Section 415 compensation (see Qs 6:4, 6:14), which does not include employer nonelective contributions made to a SEP arrangement. Compensation earned in prior years is irrelevant; the *de minimis* compensation requirement is applicable only for current-year exclusion purposes. [I.R.C. §§ 408(k)(2)(C), 414(q)(4)] The rounding rule for the *de minimis* amount is set in increments of $50 after 1994 (see Q 1:4).

Q 6:20 What is compensation for employer deduction purposes?

For taxable years beginning after 2001, compensation for employer deduction purposes includes elective deferrals, even though they are not includible in gross income. [I.R.C. § 404(a)(12)] The maximum amount of compensation per participant that may be considered for employer deduction purposes of plan years beginning in 2012 is $250,000.

> **Historical Note.** Before 2002, compensation for deduction purposes was limited to the compensation paid by the employer to participating employees that was includible in gross income.

> **Example 1.** Eunice, an employee of Sew-Right, is the only participant in Sew-Right's SEP arrangement. She earns $10,000 in 2001 and elects to defer $500 of her wages. Sew-Right makes a $950 SEP contribution for 2001. Eunice's Form W-2 (for 2002) will show taxable wages of $9,500. Sew-Right will be able to take the maximum permitted SEP deduction of $1,425 ($9,500 × .15).

> **Example 2.** The facts are the same as those in Example 1, except that it is 2012 and the maximum permitted SEP deduction has increased to 25 percent of gross compensation plus elective deferrals (beginning in 2002). The amount allowed to be contributed on an elective basis is also fully deductible. Eunice again elects to defer $500 of her wages. For 2012, Sew-Right will be able to deduct $3,000 ($10,000 × .25 + $500). (See Qs 6:24, 11:3 for discussion of how to determine how much is excludable from Eunice's income.)

Q 6:21 What is compensation for the purpose of allocating employer contributions?

For plan years beginning after 1997, compensation for allocation purposes may include elective contributions as defined in Code Section 402(g), as well as amounts excludable from income at the election of an employee under Code Section 125 or 457 (see Q 6:4, item 2).

> **Example.** Harry and Gloria have pre-plan compensation of $10,000 each for 2012. Their employer, Gumdrops, Inc., adopts a SEP arrangement with provisions for employees to reduce their taxable income. Harry elects to defer $500 by salary reduction, and Gloria elects to defer $1,000. In addition, Gumdrops elects to contribute 3 percent of compensation for each employee. For the purpose of allocating contributions, the plan specifically includes elective contributions as compensation. Harry and Gloria will therefore receive $300 ($10,000 × .03) each. The 25 percent employer deduction limit is based on $20,000 ($10,000 + $10,000). [I.R.C. § 404(h)] Harry's Form W-2 will show $9,500 as includible taxable income, and Gloria's W-2 will show $9,000. Because the total of the contributions made on their behalf does not exceed 25 percent of their includible taxable compensation, determined separately, none of the contributions are includible in either Harry's or Gloria's gross income for the year. Harry's total contribution of $800 does not exceed $2,375 ($9,500 × .25), and Gloria's total contribution of $1,300 does not exceed $2,250 ($9,000 × .25).

IRS Publication 560, *Retirement Plans for Small Business* (for 2011) (page 4), specifically defines compensation for allocation purposes as follows:

Compensation. Compensation for plan allocations is the pay a participant received from you for personal services for a year. You can generally define compensation as including all the following payments:

1. Wages and salaries
2. Fees for professional services
3. Other amounts received (cash or noncash) for personal services actually rendered by an employee, including, but not limited to, the following items:
   a. Commissions and tips
   b. Fringe benefits
   c. Bonuses

For a self-employed individual, compensation means the earned income, discussed later, of that individual.

Compensation generally includes amounts deferred in the following employee benefit plans. These amounts are elective deferrals.

4. Qualified cash or deferred arrangement (Section 401(k) plan)
5. Salary reduction agreement to contribute to a tax-sheltered annuity (Section 403(b) plan), a SIMPLE IRA plan, or a SARSEP
6. Section 457 nonqualified deferred compensation plan
7. Section 125 cafeteria plan

However, an employer can choose to exclude elective deferrals under the above plans from the definition of compensation.

Other options. In figuring the compensation of a participant, you can treat any of the following amounts as the employee's compensation.

8. The employee's wages as defined for income tax withholding purposes
9. The employee's wages you report in box 1 of Form W-2, *Wage and Tax Statement*
10. The employee's social security wages (including elective deferrals)

Compensation generally cannot include either of the following items:

1. Nontaxable reimbursements or other expense allowances
2. Deferred compensation (other than elective deferrals)

Note. Contributions to a designated Roth account (DRA) under an employers' 401(k) plan, 403(b) plan, and governmental 457(b) plan are contributions made under a "qualified cash or deferred arrangement." [I.R.C § 402A]

The IRS does not provide any guidance in Publication 560, or elsewhere, regarding how an employer can choose to exclude elective deferrals from the definition of compensation for allocation purposes under a SARSEP (see Q 3:15).

Publication 560 also allows any of three alternate definitions to be used as compensation for allocation purposes (see Q 6:16).

Compensation Limits

Q 6:22 How much compensation may be considered when allocating employer contributions among employees?

For purposes of allocating employer contributions among employees participating in a SEP for plan years beginning in 2012, Code Section 408(k)(3)(C) imposes a $250,000 annual limit on compensation that may be considered for each participating employee (see Q 6:27). The limit is adjusted annually in the same manner as the compensation limit under Code Section 401(a)(17)(B), applicable to qualified plans. [I.R.C. §§ 401(l), 408(k)(8)] That is, a SEP arrangement will not satisfy Code Section 408(k)(1) unless it provides that an employee's compensation in excess of the annual limit is not used in determining plan benefits or contributions for a plan year in which the annual limit applies.

Rounding Rule. The rounding rule for the annual compensation limit is set in increments of $5,000 for plan years beginning after 2002.

Caution. Although the family aggregation rules have been repealed for plan years beginning after 1996, the ownership attribution rules of Code Section 318 still apply in determining who is a 5 percent owner under the HCE rules (see Q 8:7, examples). Thus, for instance, the true owner's spouse or child whose compensation is less than $115,000 for 2012 may still be an HCE by virtue of the family relationship. The family, however, would no longer be treated as a single HCE. [SBJPA § 1431]

Q 6:23 How much compensation may be considered in determining the employer's deduction?

For plan years beginning in 2012, Code Section 404(l) imposes a $250,000 limit on compensation that may be considered for purposes of determining the employer's 25 percent aggregate deduction limit for contributions to a SEP arrangement. The limit is based on the aggregate compensation that is includible in the gross income of the employees participating in the plan plus elective deferrals under Code Section 402(g).

Example. Catrina owns the Darn Knit Corporation. Her W-2 income is $375,000 for 2012. The compensation of the three employees that participate in the employer's SEP plan is $100,000. Darn's 25 percent deduction limit under Code Section 404 is based on aggregate compensation of $550,000 because only the first $250,000 that Catrina earns may be considered for deduction purposes. Elective contributions are separately deductible (see also examples in Q 6:24).

Note. Contributions that exceed 415 limits are not deductible. For example, an employer nonelective contribution of $52,000 for a plan year starting in 2012, would exceed the 415 dollar limit by $2,000 (assuming the catch-up contribution rules do not apply). The employer may only deduct $50,000. The 100 percent limit under Code Section 415 is rarely exceeded because the participant exclusion limit is lower (see Q 11:1). [I.R.C. § 404(j)]

Q 6:24 How much compensation may be considered in determining the amount of the contribution excludable from an employee's gross income?

There has never been a dollar limit on the amount of compensation that may be considered for the purpose of determining the amount of the contribution that may be excluded from an employee's gross income under Code Section 402(h) (see Q 11:1). For exclusion purposes, compensation includes only the compensation from the employer making the contribution to the SEP. Thus, for example, neither the compensation of a husband and wife nor that of a family member need be aggregated. In addition, elective deferrals that are not treated as catch-up contributions are *not* considered compensation in determining the exclusion limit, which is 25 percent of includible compensation (15 percent before 2002).

Example 1. In 2012, Barbara earns $50,000 from one employer, Atlantis Tours, Inc., and $20,000 from another employer, Eurobike, Inc. Eurobike contributes $4,000 to a SEP on Barbara's behalf. The maximum amount that Barbara will be able to exclude under Code Section 402(h) is 25 percent of $20,000, or $5,000. [I.R.C. § 402(h)]

Example 2. Joe, age 40, an employee of Bainbridge, Inc., earned $12,000 in 2012 and elected to defer $500 of it into Bainbridge's SARSEP. Thus, $11,500 of taxable income was reported on Joe's W-2. For purposes of the 25 percent aggregate limit on the employer's deduction for 2012, Joe's compensation is $12,000. Elective contributions are separately deductible (not subject to the 25 percent deduction limit). If Joe were the only employee, Banbridge's deductible SEP contribution would be limited to $3,500 (.25 × $12,000 plus the $500 elective contribution that is separately deductible by Bainbridge). Assume Bainbridge makes a nonelective contribution of $3,000. Bainbridge may claim a deduction for the full $3,500 ($3,000 + $500) contributed. Unfortunately, however, Joe will have to include $625 ($3,500 – (.25 ($12,000 – $500))) in his gross income because the 25 percent participant exclusion allowance is less (see Q 11:1).

Example 3. Same facts as those in Example 2, except Joe is age 50 or older and the plan permits catch-up contributions to be made by participants. Thus, Joe is catch-up eligible. Bainbridge's contribution of $3,000 would be equal to Joe's exclusion allowance based on his pre-plan compensation of $12,000 (assuming no normal elective amounts are considered). Thus, none of Joe's elective contributions can be treated as normal elective contributions because of the statutory limit (the 25 percent exclusion limit) and can be treated as catch-up contributions (up to $5,500 for 2012). Because catch-up contributions are not subject to the exclusion limit, Joe does not have to include any of the $3,500 elective contribution in gross income. Thus, $3,500 may be deducted by Bainbridge. In fact, if Joe's elective contributions were $5,500, $8,500 ($5,500 elective contribution plus the nonelective contribution of $3,000) would be deductible by Bainbridge and the full amount excluded from Joe's gross income as a catch-up contribution.

Example 4. Same facts as in Example 2, except Bainbridge contributes $2,500. Joe may make an elective contribution of $400 for 2012 on a fully excludable basis.

Proof: .25 × ($12,000 – $400) = $2,900 ($2,500 + $400)

Example 5. Same facts as in Example 4, except Joe is catch-up eligible and makes elective contributions of $6,100. As indicated in Example 4, Joe's maximum excludable elective contribution is $400. Because only amounts up to $5,500 may be considered a catch-up contribution for 2012, the balance is $200 ($6,100–$5,500–$400). The balance of his elective contribution is an excess contribution because it exceeds Joe's exclusionary limit and should be reported on Form W-2 for Bainbridge to avoid any penalties for nondeductible contributions (see chapter 10). Joe will be deemed to have made a $200 annual IRA contribution for 2012, whether or not deductible (see Q 10:11).

Although the $200 amount that exceeded the exclusion limit under Code Section 402(h) is treated as wages for reporting purposes, it is unclear whether the amount is subject to FICA and FUTA tax (see Q 11:15). The amount may be exempt from withholding tax, notwithstanding that it may not be reasonable to believe that Joe will be entitled to an exclusion for the amount under Code Section 402(h) (see Q 11:17).

Q 6:25 What rule applies if an individual participates in more than one SEP?

The maximum exclusion under Code Section 402(h) for an individual who receives SEP contributions from two or more unrelated employers' SEP arrangements may not exceed the sum of the maximum deduction limits computed separately for that individual under each employer's arrangement. [I.R.C. § 402(h); Prop. Treas. Reg. § 1.219-3(a)(3)(iii)]

Example. James is employed by Heavy Metal Corporation and Light Crude Corporation. The two companies are not members of a controlled or related group of employers. Both companies maintain a SEP arrangement, and each contributes 25 percent of compensation, but not more than $50,000, on behalf of each employee for 2012. James earns $240,000 from Heavy Metal and $250,000 from Light Crude, and each company contributes $50,000 under its SEP arrangement to an IRA maintained on James's behalf. James will be allowed to exclude $100,000 for employer contributions to SEPs because each employer has a SEP arrangement and the SEP contributions by the unrelated corporations, determined separately, do not exceed the applicable $50,000/25 percent deduction limit for 2012.

In contrast, contributions by (and compensation received from) employers that are related—that is, under common control or members of a controlled group—must be aggregated for purposes of the Section 402(h) exclusion limit. [I.R.C. §§ 414(b), 414(c), 414(o)] The IRS may also require aggregation when the employers are members of an affiliated service group (see Q 2:14).

Furthermore, it appears that in the case of an employee who is self-employed within the meaning of Code Section 401(c)(1) with respect to more than one trade or business, the maximum exclusion limit under Code Section 402(h) may not exceed the lesser of the limit applied separately to each employer or such limit determined by treating all such employers as a single employer. [Prop. Treas. Reg. § 1.219-3(c)(2)(iii)]

Q 6:26 How much compensation may be considered for integration and nondiscrimination test purposes?

The maximum annual compensation that may be taken into account to comply with certain nondiscrimination rules is $250,000 for 2012. [I.R.C. §§ 408(k)(3)(C), 408(k)(6)(D)(ii), 408(k)(8)] Thus, in determining the allocation rates and applying the integration rules to SEPs, an employee's compensation in excess of the annual limit is disregarded.

Note. The annual compensation limit applies separately to each group of plans that is treated as a single plan for purposes of the applicable nondiscrimination requirement.

Q 6:27 What have been the limits on compensation since 1989?

The maximum amount that a participant's contribution may be based on is limited to the annual compensation limit under Code Section 401(a)(17). This limit applies to SEPs, qualified plans, and 403(b) plans. The maximum annual compensation limits for a plan year beginning in the indicated year that have been (and are) used for nearly all purposes since 1989 are as follows:

1989	$200,000
1990	$209,200
1991	$222,220
1992	$228,860
1993	$235,840
1994	$150,000
1995	$150,000
1996	$150,000
1997	$160,000

1998	$160,000
1999	$160,000
2000	$170,000
2001	$170,000
2002	$200,000
2003	$200,000
2004	$205,000
2005	$210,000
2006	$220,000
2007	$225,000
2008	$230,000
2009	$245,000
2010	$245,000
2011	$245,000
2012	$250,000

After 2002, the $200,000 limit increases for cost-of-living adjustments in increments of $5,000. [I.R.C. § 408(k)(8)]

Q 6:28 How is the compensation limit determined for a fiscal year plan?

Any increase in the annual compensation limit is effective as of January 1 of a calendar year and applies to any plan year beginning in that calendar year. For example, if a plan has a plan year beginning July 1, 2012, and ending June 30, 2013, the annual compensation limit in effect on January 1, 2012 ($250,000), applies to the plan for the entire plan year (see Q 6:6). [Treas. Reg. § 1.401(a)(17)-1(a)(3)(i)]

Q 6:29 Will the relationship between Code Section 401(a)(17) and Code 415 affect contributions made under a SARSEP?

The proposed regulations under Code Section 415 issued in 2005 (since finalized) state that a plan's definition of compensation used for applying Code Section 415 cannot exceed to Code Section 401(a)(17) limit—$250,000 for 2012. Many practitioners viewed this position as a departure from the generally accepted rule that Section 415 compensation was not subject to the Section 401(a)(17) compensation limit. [Treas. Reg. § 1.415(c)-2(f)] Arguably, once a participant has received $250,000 (for 2012), he or she must cease making elective contributions for the remainder of that plan year even though the individual's contributions were not in excess of the amounts permitted under the calendar year limits of Code Section 401(g)—generally $17,000, $22,500 with catch-up contributions if age 50 or older. The IRS chose to retain the rule from the proposed regulations. [*See* Preamble, Treas. Reg. §§ 1.415 (T.D. 9319, 2007-18 I.R.B. 1041 (Apr. 30, 2007), 1.415(c)-2(f)]

Q 6:30 How much must a self-employed individual earn to contribute the maximum for 2012?

A self-employed individual who has no employees must have $260,310.19 in net profit and a plan with a 25 percent of compensation contribution formula to make the maximum contribution to a SEP for 2012. The maximum contribution can also be made at a lower rate with higher net profits.

Note. For the purpose of calculating the deduction under Code Section 164(f), which is used in calculating earned income for contribution purposes, the Tax Relief, Unemployment Insurance Reauthorization, and Job Creation Act of 2010 reduced the old-age, survivors, and disability insurance (OASDI) SECA tax rate for 2011 by 2 percent (from 12.4 percent to 10.4 percent). The "payroll tax holiday" was extended through 2012. (See Q 7:2.) The maximum compensation is $250,000 for 2012. Compensation for a self-employed person is earned income, not net profit. A self-employed person would need earned income of $200,000 in 2012 to contribute the maximum of $50,000 ($200,000 × .25). If a self-employed individual's net profit shown on Schedule C, Profit or Loss from Business (Sole Proprietorship), for 2012 equals or exceeds $260,310.19, the earned income will equal or exceed $200,000, which is the amount of earned income needed to make the $50,000 maximum contribution to a SEP. That figure may be confirmed by applying the basic earned income formula (modified for the payroll tax holiday), as follows:

Net Profit (*NP*) = Earned Income + Contribution + Code Section 164(f) Deduction

$260,310.19 = $200,000 + $50,000 + $10,310.19

To determine the preceding net profit amount, apply the following formula:

NP = $200,000 + $50,000 + ($110,100 × .076484*) + .0145 (NP.9235 – 110,100**)

NP = $200,000 + $50,000 + $8,420.89 + .0145 (NP.9235 – $110,100)

NP = $258,420.89 + (.01339075 × NP) – $1,596.45

NP = $256,824.44 + .01339075NP

(Subtract .01339075NP from both sides)

.98660925NP = $256,824.44

NP = $260,310.19.

* The decimal .076484 is equal to the 10.4% reduced OASDI rate multiplied by "59.6," plus 1.45%. For years other than 2011 and 2012, use "7.65." For 2011 and 2012, the Code Section 164(f) deduction will be close to, but not equal to, one-half of the self-employment tax shown on Schedule SE of Form 1040 or Form 1040 NR. If this adjustment was not made, the resulting value for NP would be $260,311.97, a difference of less than $2.

** $110,100 is the 2012 taxable wage base amount (limit) for the OASDI portion of SECA taxes (12.4%, reduced to 10.4% for 2011 and 2012).

Proof 1: $260,310.19 × .9235 = $240,396.46

($110,100 × .061984) + ($240,396.46 × .0145)

$6,824.44 + $3,485.75 = $10,310.19 (*I.R.C. § 164(f) deduction*)

$260,310.19 – $50,000 – $10,310.19 = $200,000 (*earned income*)

$200,000 × .25 = $50,000 (*contribution*).

Proof 2: (using equivalency method, see Q 7:9)

$260,310.19 – $10,310.19 = $250,000 × .20 = $50,000.

The $50,000 limit for 2012 can also be achieved at a lower contribution rate if the owner has sufficient net profits. For 2012, net profits of $310,988.81 would be required to contribute $50,000 at a 20 percent contribution rate. With a contribution rate of less than 20 percent, the $50,000 limit cannot be reached because the maximum compensation limit of $250,000 for 2012 would have to be exceeded. The $250,000 compensation limit is generally determined (the normal method) after all reductions are applied to arrive at the individual's earned income. The equivalency method does not consider the reduction for the owner's contribution and cannot be used in all circumstances (see Q 7:8) without exceeding the $250,000 maximum contribution limit for 2012. (See chapter 7 regarding special rules for self-employed individuals.)

Proof:

$310,988.81 × .9235 = $287,198.16 (application of the "in-lieu" deduction to compute self-employment tax)

$287,198.16 × .0145 = $4,164.37

$110,100 × .061984 = $6,824.44

$4,164.37 + $6,824.44 = $10,988.81 (*I.R.C. § 164(f) deduction*)

$310,988.81 – $10,988.81 – $50,000 = $250,000

$250,000 × .20 (contribution rate) = $50,000 (maximum contribution using regular method)

$310,988.81 – $10,988.81 = $300,000

.20/1.20 = .166666667 (the equivalency rate, see Q 7:9)

$300,000 × .166666667 = $50,000 (maximum contribution using equivalency method, see Q 7:8 for restrictions on using equivalency method)

(See Appendix H; see also Q 7:23, example 4.)

Multiemployer and Multiple-Employer Plans

Q 6:31 How is compensation determined in multiemployer and multiple-employer plans?

A multiemployer plan is a collectively bargained plan where more than one employer contributes, but there is some sort of relationship between the participants. For example, the Steelworkers Union may establish a multiemployer plan where steelworkers who belong to local unions (different employers) may participate in the plan. Unlike a multiemployer plan, a multiple-employer plan is not maintained pursuant to a collective bargaining agreement, and the employers participating in the plan are not related. Under a multiple-employer plan, each employer is tested separately for all limitations under the law. Under both types, the annual compensation limit applies separately to each employee from each unrelated employer maintaining the plan instead of to the total compensation from all employers maintaining the plan. Thus, for example, if during a year in which the compensation limit was $250,000 (the 2012 limit) an employee participating in a multiemployer plan was employed by three of the employers maintaining the plan and received compensation of $90,000 a year from one employer, $85,000 from the second, and $75,000 from the third, the plan would be permitted to take into account up to $250,000 of the employee's compensation from the three employers for the plan year (see Q 6:28) without violating Code Section 401(a)(17) (and, presumably, Code Section 408(k)(3)(C)). [Treas. Reg. § 1.401(a)(17)-1, Preamble (T.D. 9319, 2007-18 I.R.B. 1041 (Apr. 30, 2007))]

Note. SEPs are not usually adopted as part of a multiemployer or multiple-employer arrangement, which is defined in ERISA Section 3(37). [*See* Form 5500, Kinds of Filers] In addition, a multiple-employer plan must be an individually designed plan.

Chapter 7

Special Rules for Self-Employed Individuals

The meaning of the term *compensation* changes according to the purpose for which it is used. For a self-employed individual (including a partner in a partnership), compensation for purposes of a SEP or SARSEP means that individual's earned income. Determining the amount of usable earned income is extremely complex and requires both interdependent and circular (indirectly calculated) calculations. Less complicated rules apply to SIMPLE plans (see chapter 14). The rules for determining earned income and the effect of the 2 percent reduction in SECA taxes for 2011 and 2012 are also discussed in this chapter.

Earned Income as Compensation

Q 7:1 For SEP purposes, who is a *self-employed individual*, and what is such a person's *compensation*?

An owner of an unincorporated business is called a *self-employed individual*. A self-employed individual's *compensation* for qualified plan and SEP purposes is defined as his or her earned income (see Q 7:2). [I.R.C. §§ 408(k)(7)(B), 414(s)(1), 415(c)(3)] (Net earnings from self-employment are used for a SIMPLE plan (see chapter 14).)

Q 7:2 What is *earned income*?

Under Section 401(c)(2) of the Internal Revenue Code (Code), *earned income* for a self-employed person (including a partner in a partnership) refers to net earnings from self-employment (NESE) in a trade or business in which the personal services of that individual are a material income-producing factor. [I.R.C. § 1402(a)] Generally, for 2012, after several adjustments, up to $250,000 of earned income may be considered for plan allocation and employer deduction purposes (see Qs 7:6, 7:12). [I.R.C. §§ 401(a)(17), 404(l)]

The adjustments discussed in this chapter not only affect one another but also may be affected by other factors. Under Code Section 401(c)(2), net earnings from self-employment must be reduced by all contributions made by or on behalf of the owner and by the deduction for half of the self-employment tax under Code Section 164(f).

> **Caution.** For the purpose of calculating the deduction under Code Section 164(f), which is used in calculating earned income for contribution purposes, the Tax Relief, Unemployment Insurance Reauthorization, and Job Creation Act of 2010 reduced the OASDI (old-age, survivors, and disability insurance) portion of the SECA tax rate for 2011 by 2 percent (from 12.4% to 10.4%). The "payroll tax holiday" was extended through 2012.

For 2011 and 2012 only, the Code Section 164(f) deduction for one half of the self-employment tax is equal to "59.6" percent of the 10.4 percent of the OASDI portion of SECA tax (6.1984%) up to the taxable wage base of $110,100, plus 1/2 of the 2.9 percent Medicare portion of the SECA tax with no ceiling (i.e., 6.1984% + 1.45%, respectively). The 59.6 percent statutory rate for use in 2011 and 2012 only can be computed as follows:

$$\frac{\text{7.65\% SECA tax rate less 1.45\% Medicare tax rate (6.2\%)}}{\text{10.4 (6.2\% + 4.2 (reduced rate))}} = 59.6$$

Thus, for 2011 and 2012, the Code Section 164(f) deduction for half of the self-employment taxes will be close to, but not equal to, half of the self-employment tax shown on Schedule C of Form 1040 or Form 1040NR.

[*See* I.R.C. § 1401(a) regarding SECA tax rates and § 3101(a) regarding FICA tax rates; Tax Relief, Unemployment Insurance Reauthorization, and Job Creation Act of 2010 (Pub. L. No. 111-312), Section 601 for 2011, and the Temporary Payroll Tax Cut Continuation Act of 2011 (H.R. 3765) (Pub. L. No. 112-78), Section 101, and the Middle Class Tax Relief and Job Creation Act of 2012 (H.R. 3630) (Pub. L. No. 112-95), Section 1001, for 2012]

It should be noted that the owner's share of the allowable contribution expense for nonowner-employees must also be subtracted from business income to arrive at the amount of net earnings from self-employment.

In general, an individual's earned income is the amount subject to federal income tax. After 2001, elective contributions are added back for some purposes (see Q 7:6), up to the $250,000 (for 2012) limit.

Caution. For taxable years beginning after 2001, elective contributions are added back for the purpose of calculating the employer's maximum deduction, but not generally for the purpose of computing the 25 percent participant exclusion limit. Catch-up elective contributions do not, however, reduce the base upon which the 25 percent participation exclusion allowance is computed (see chapter 11). Elective contributions may be added back when allocating an employer's nonelective contributions among employees (see Q 7:6).

In the case of a partnership or a limited liability company (see Qs 2:58–2:62), earned income may include guaranteed payments to members. [Ltr. Ruls. 9525058, 9452024, 9432018l; *see* Form 1065, Schedule K-1, line 4] Code Section 1402 defines the term *self-employment income* as net earnings from self-employment derived by an individual during any taxable year. Code Section 1402(a) provides that the term *net earnings from self-employment* includes an individual's distributive share (whether or not distributed) of income or loss described in Code Section 702(a)(8) from any trade or business carried on by a partnership of which the individual is a member. Code Section 1402(a)(13) provides that the distributive share of any item of income or loss of a limited partner is not included under the definition of *net earnings from self-employment* unless the distributive share is a guaranteed payment to that partner for services actually rendered to or on behalf of the partnership to the extent that such payment is established to be in the nature of remuneration for those services. In the view of the IRS, it is generally not essential that an individual currently be engaged in the day-to-day conduct of a trade or business in order to be carrying on a trade or business. A taxpayer can still be engaged in a trade or business even if there is a temporary hiatus in the conduct of the activities of that trade or business. [Newberry v. Commissioner, 76 T.C. 441, 444 (1981); *see also Reisinger v. Commissioner*, 71 T.C. 568, 572 (1979); *Haft v. Commissioner*, 40 T.C. 2, 6 (1963); *see also* Rev. Rul. 75-120, 1975-1 C.B. 55 (job search costs may be deductible trade or business expenses even if taxpayer is temporarily unemployed); Storey v. Comm., T.C. Memo 2012-115 (Apr. 19, 2012), night time filmmaker was "self-employed" despite large losses]

Some tax court cases have adopted more narrow interpretations of what constitutes *self-employment income* for self-employment tax purposes. [I.R.C. § 1402(a)-(b)] Whether a payment is derived from a trade or business carried on by an individual for purposes of Code Section 1402 depends on whether, under all the facts and circumstances, a nexus exists between the payment and the carrying on of the trade or business. The Tax Court articulated this "nexus" requirement in *Newberry v. Commissioner* [76 T.C. 441, 444 (1981)], where it observed that, under Code Section 1402,

> there must be a nexus between the income received and a trade or business that is, or was, actually carried on. Put another way, the construction of the statute can be gleaned by reading the relevant language all in one breath: the income must be derived from a trade or business carried on.

Thus, the trade or business must be "carried on" by the individual, either personally or through agents or employees, in order for the income to be included in the individual's "net earnings from self-employment." [S. Rep. 1669, 81st Cong., 2d Sess. (1950), 1950-2 C.B. 302, 354] Generally, the required nexus exists if it is clear that a payment would not have been made but for an individual's conduct of a trade or business. [Newberry v. Commissioner, 76 T.C. 441, 444 (1981)]

Although the IRS agreed with the Tax Court in *Newberry* that a nexus must exist, it did not agree with the court's conclusion in that case that such a nexus cannot exist if an individual is not currently engaged in the day-to-day conduct of a trade or business. Therefore, the IRS declared that it will not follow the decision in *Newberry*. [Rev. Rul. 91-19, 1991-1 C.B. 186; *see also* Ltr. Ruls. 9235040 (June 2, 1992), 200111044 (Jan. 25, 2001)]

> **Example 1.** Sirus, a farmer, suffered an $80,000 crop loss resulting from a drought. Sirus received an $80,000 loan from the Farmers Home Administration, of which $50,000 of the principal was immediately canceled. The amount of the canceled portion of the loan represents a replacement of a portion of the farmer's lost profits, and must be taken into account in computing Sirus's net earnings from self-employment. [Rev. Rul. 76-500, 1976-2 C.B. 254; *see also* Rev. Rul. 60-32, 1960-1 C.B. 23; I.R.S. Notice 87-26, 1987-1 C.B. 470; Ltr. Rul. 200111044 (Jan. 25, 2001)]

> **Example 2.** Herman was performing services as an independent contractor for a government agency. His contract was terminated after four years due to an act of war. He promptly accepted a position as an employee for a corporation after his contract was terminated. Eighteen months later, Herman was given an unexpected severance payment of $10,000 minus $2,500 for each year of prior service. Although the IRS would likely view this as earned income because there was a previous nexus, the courts may be more lenient because Herman's severance payment was not derived from a trade or business *carried on*.

Income received from rental real estate generally is not NESE unless services are provided with the property. [I.R.C. § 1402(a)(1); Treas. Reg. § 1.1402(a)-4(c)] Except for a securities dealer, investment interest and dividends are not NESE. [I.R.C. § 1402(a)(3); *see also* Rev. Rul. 58-195, 1958-1 C.B. 329] Dealers in real property, who are in the business of buying property for resale (as opposed to mere speculators), derive NESE from their rentals. [Treas. Reg. § 1.1402(a)-4(a)] Limited partners generally do not have NESE, except to the extent of guaranteed payments for services they perform for the partnership. An unincorporated business generates NESE only if it is a trade or business under Code Section 162 relating to trade or business expenses. [I.R.C. § 1402(c)]

Service as an Employee. The performance of service as an employee does not generally constitute a trade or business, but several exceptions exist. A trade or business does not include the performance of service by an individual as an employee, except in the following situations:

- *Duly ordained, commissioned, or licensed minister.* The performance of service by a duly ordained, commissioned, or licensed minister of a church in the exercise of his ministry or by a member of a religious order in the exercise of duties required by such order. [I.R.C. §§ 1402(c)(2)(D), 1402(c)(4)]

- *Christian science practitioners.* The performance of service by an individual in the exercise of his profession as a Christian Science practitioner, provided the individual has not received an exemption from the tax on self-employment income (e.g., has taken a vow of poverty) for such year. [I.R.C. § 1402(c)(5); Treas. Reg. § 1.1402(e)-2A]
- *Members of certain religious faiths.* The performance of service by members of certain religious faiths during which time they are exempt from the tax on self-employment income. [I.R.C. §§ 1402(c)(6), 1402(g); Treas. Reg. § 1.1402(c)-7]
- *Functions of public office.* The performance of the functions of a public office, other than the functions of a public office of a State or a political subdivision thereof with respect to fees received in any period in which the functions are performed in a position compensated solely on a fee basis and in which such functions are not covered under an agreement entered into by such State and the Commissioner of Social Security. [I.R.C. § 1402(c)(1)(d); *see also* Soc. Sec. Act § 218 (42 USC 418)]
- *Newspaper and magazine vendors and carriers.* An individual is engaged in the trade or business of selling newspapers or magazines, and thus is subject to the self-employment tax if: (1) he has attained the age of 18, and (2) the newspapers or magazines are sold to the ultimate consumers under an arrangement whereby the individual purchases the items at a fixed price and his compensation is based upon the retention of the excess of his sales price over the amount at which the items were charged to him. [I.R.C. §§ 1402(c)(2)(A), 3121(b)(16); Treas. Reg. § 1.1402(c)-3(b)]
- *Arrangement with owner or tenant of land.* Service described in Code Section 3121(b)(16), regarding service performed under an arrangement with the owner or tenant of land pursuant to which (i) such individual undertakes to produce agricultural or horticultural commodities (including livestock, bees, poultry, and fur-bearing animals and wildlife) on such land, (ii) the agricultural or horticultural commodities produced by such individual, or the proceeds therefrom are to be divided between such individual and such owner or tenant, and (iii) the amount of such individual's share depends on the amount of the agricultural or horticultural commodities produced. [I.R.C. §§ 1402(c)(2)(B), 3121(b)(11)]
- *Government or international organization service.* Service performed in the United States by a citizen is when the service is:
  - –Performed in the employ of a foreign government (including service as a consular or other officer or employee or a non-diplomatic representative). [I.R.C. §§ 1402(c)(2)(C), 3121(b)(11)]
  - –Performed in the employ of an instrumentality wholly owned by a foreign government if the service is of a character similar to that performed in foreign countries by employees of the U.S. Government or of an instrumentality thereof; and if the Secretary of State shall certify to the Secretary of the Treasury that the foreign government, with respect

to whose instrumentality and employees thereof exemption is claimed, grants an equivalent exemption with respect to similar service performed in the foreign country by employees of the U.S. Government and of instrumentalities thereof. [I.R.C. §§ 1402(c)(2)(C), 3121(b)(12)]

–Service performed in the employ of an international organization, except service that constitutes "employment" under Code Section 3121(y) relating to certain transferred federal employees. [I.R.C. §§ 1402(c)(2)(C), 3121(b)(15)]

- *Representative of railway labor organization.* Service performed by an individual as an employee or employee representative as defined in Code Section 3231 relating to any officer or official representative of a railway labor organization (with certain exceptions, who before or after June 29, 1937, was in the service of an employer and who is duly authorized and designated to represent employees in accordance with the Railway Labor Act [45 U.S.C., chapter 8], and any individual who is regularly assigned to or regularly employed by such officer or official representative in connection with the duties of his office). [I.R.C. §§ 1402(c)(3), 3231]

Note 1. The "tax on self-employment income" imposed by Code Section 1401, unlike the employment taxes imposed on wages in subtitle C, is technically an income tax because Code Section 1401 is part of subtitle A of the Code.

Note 2. A partner's compensation is deemed currently available on the last day of the partnership's taxable year. Accordingly, an individual partner may not make a cash or deferred election with respect to compensation for a partnership taxable year after the last day of that year. [*See* Treas. Reg. § 1.401(k)-1(a)(6)(ii)(B)] Periodic advances made by partners throughout the year, pursuant to an election of the partner, are "elective contributions," assuming the plan otherwise satisfies the applicable requirements of Code Section 408(p). [Ltr. Rul. 200247052; *see also* Treas. Reg. §§ 1.401(k)-1(a)(3)(i), 1.401(k)-1(g)(3)] A sole proprietor can make elective contributions of "advances" pursuant to an election to defer compensation made before the end of the year (see Q 4:45).

Net earnings from self-employment do not include income passed through to shareholders of an S corporation (see Q 6:14).

Example 3. During the years 1970 through 2012, Yolanda wrote and had published 38 books, from which she has received royalties in excess of $400 for each year. During the years 1970 through 2002, Yolanda performed teaching services in a private school as an employee, and the employee Federal Insurance Contribution Act (FICA) tax was deducted from her "wages" for each such year. She retired from all activities as an employee on December 31, 2012. Whether or not Yolanda is engaged in a trade or business depends upon the facts in the particular case. As a general rule, a person who is regularly engaged in an occupation or profession for profit which constitutes his or her livelihood, in whole or in part, and who is not regarded as an employee for FICA purposes, is engaged in a trade or business for self-employment tax purposes. If an individual writes only one book as a sideline and never revises it, he or she would not be considered "regularly engaged" in an occupation or profession and his or her royalties therefrom would not be considered net earnings from self-employment. However, where an individual prepares new editions of the book from time to time, and writes other books and materials, such activities reflect the conduct of a trade or business, and, if it is not one of the excluded service/professions listed in Code Section 1402(c), the income from it is includible in computing net earnings from self-employment. Since authorship is not a listed excluded service/profession, Yolanda's income is subject to SECA tax and is treated as compensation for plan purposes. If Yolanda was not treated as having a trade or business, then her income would be reported as a royalty on Schedule E of Form 1040 and it would be exempt from self-employment tax. [*See* Rev. Ruls. 68-498, 1968-2 C.B. 377; 68-499, 1968-2 C.B. 421; 55-385, 1955-1 C.B. 100]

Practice Pointer. Code Section 401(c)(2) provides that the sale, exchange, or licensing of property (other than a capital asset created by an individual) is earned income, whether or not these are net earnings from self-employment. In such a case, and for plan establishment purposes, the activity generating the earned income must constitute a trade or business. Establishing a corporation and receiving wages may alleviate the problem.

Q 7:3 What might happen if earned income is miscalculated?

An erroneous calculation of earned income (see Q 7:2) could result in the violation of various nondiscrimination rules or could cause the Section 415 dollar or percentage limits on allowable contributions and benefits to be exceeded (see Q 11:13). A miscalculation could also result in operational discrimination in favor of highly compensated employees and could jeopardize the tax-sanctioned status of a SEP arrangement. Nondeductible employer contribution amounts and deemed distributions could be subject to income tax, as well as to nondeductible excise taxes (see Q 10:11). [I.R.C. §§ 72(t), 4972(a); I.R.M. 4.72.17, rev. Sept. 12, 2006]

Q 7:4 Is determining the amount of earned income difficult?

Yes. Except when no common-law employees exist or when the contribution amount for the nonowner-employees is known, calculating earned income for both plan and self-employment tax purposes can be extremely complicated (see Qs 7:12-7:15). Even practitioners with a thorough understanding of how plan limits are applied and how earned income is figured will find the process of designing plans, calculating contributions, and applying limits a complex, nearly impossible, task. It is difficult to design a plan around an owner because the owner's compensation fluctuates as the contribution amount is changed. Circular and interdependent calculations are required to solve for a particular result. Absent a legislative change, the practitioner must use caution.

Spreadsheet software and programs offer a welcome solution for practitioners who need to design plans for owners of unincorporated businesses with common-law employees. [*See http://www.benefitslink.com/GSL* (visited on Aug. 22, 2012)]

Q 7:5 Does a self-employment loss from a separate unincorporated business reduce the employer's earned income from another business that has a SEP and is owned by the same individual?

Maybe. A self-employment loss from a separate unincorporated business that is unrelated to the employer adopting the SEP but is owned in part by the same individual does not directly offset the earned income of the employer adopting the SEP. There is no such thing as negative compensation. Nevertheless, the loss will affect the calculation of the individual's self-employment tax, and the amount of that tax will have an effect on the calculation of earned income that can be considered for the plan (see Qs 7:2, 7:18, 7:24).

Q 7:6 Must elective and nonelective contributions of owners be taken into account to arrive at the amount of earned income?

It depends. For purposes of determining the 25 percent (15 percent before 2002) limit on the amount that may be excluded from a participant's gross income, contributions on behalf of a self-employed owner, including elective contributions, must be deducted from the owner's net earnings from self-employment to arrive at the owner's earned income (see Q 11:12). [I.R.C. § 404(h)(1)(C)] On the other hand, elective contributions made on behalf of a self-employed individual are added back in determining plan compensation for company deductions (see Q 6:19) and in applying the $550 for 2012 *de minimis* participation rule (see Q 6:19) [I.R.C. § 404(n)] For the purpose of allocating other employer contributions, a plan *may* provide for elective salary reduction contributions to be included in the participant's compensation (or earned income) up to the $250,000 limit for 2012 (see Q 6:21). [I.R.C. § 414(s)(2); Treas. Reg. § 1.414(s)-1(c)(4)] (See Appendix G for limits in earlier years.)

Example. Nancy operates a sole proprietorship that has $10,000 of pre-plan net profits. She establishes a SEP arrangement for 2012. After subtracting her own contribution ($1,858.73) and the deduction for half of the self-employment tax, $706.33 (see below), Nancy has only $7,434.94 of earned income for plan contribution and limit purposes. Nancy's maximum contribution of 25 percent equals $1,858.73. The 25 percent SEP exclusion limit is an individual limit and is applied separately to each participant, rather than to the aggregate taxable compensation of all participants as is done in computing the employer's 25 percent deduction limit. Because Nancy has no other employees participating in her business's plan, her income from self-employment is known, and her deduction for self-employment tax under Code Section 164(f) can be calculated. From this, the plan contribution is calculated as follows:

Pre-plan earned income	$10,000.00
Less half of self-employment tax deduction ($10,000 × 92.35% × .104% × 59.6% × 1.45%) (See Q 7:2)	–706.33
Adjusted pre-plan earned income	$9,293.67

Nancy's plan contributions must also be subtracted from her earned income before applying the 25 percent contribution rate. A mathematical equivalent can be calculated to take that reduction into account automatically by dividing the contribution rate (expressed as a decimal) by the sum of 1 plus the contribution rate:

.25/1.25 = .20 (the equivalency percentage)

Adjusted pre-plan earned income	$ 9,293.67
Multiply by equivalency percentage	× .20
Nancy's maximum SEP contribution	$1,858.73

The maximum contribution can be verified as follows:

Pre-plan earned income	$10,000.00
Less half of self-employment tax deduction	– 706.33
Less plan contribution	–1,858.73
Earned income for plan purposes	$7,434.94
Multiply by contribution rate	× .25
SEP contribution	$1,858.73

See Appendix H for an illustration of this example.

Q 7:7 How are contributions calculated for self-employed individuals?

When a self-employed person's contribution amount is not known, his or her earned income cannot be determined. In such case, the equivalency method may generally be used to calculate the contribution amount (and, in turn, earned income). The equivalency method does not work when contributions are allocated to participants under an integrated plan. In other cases, it works only some of the time (see Q 7:8). Under the equivalency approach, a lower percentage of a higher (pre-plan) amount is used.

When a self-employed person's earned income amount is known, the percentage method is used to calculate contributions.

Regardless of whether the percentage method or the equivalency method is used, one must know the owner's share of the deduction expense for the nonowner's contributions and the deduction for half of the self-employment tax under Code Section 164(f) to allocate contributions (see Q 7:2).

Example. Decor, a sole proprietorship that maintains a SEP, is owned by Seymour and has no common-law employees. To calculate Seymour's earned income for purposes of applying the 25 percent of compensation limit (for 2012), Seymour's SEP contribution must be subtracted from his earned income. If Seymour has $100,000 of pre-plan earned income after subtracting his self-employment tax from his earned income, Decor may contribute 20 percent of $100,000 (a known amount) or 25 percent of $80,000 ($100,000/1.25) on his behalf. Under either method, $20,000 may be contributed.

Q 7:8 When can the equivalency approach for calculating contributions be used?

If a plan is the only plan of the employer, if the plan is not integrated, and if the owner's self-employment tax deduction and share of the common-law employee plan contribution expense are known, the equivalency approach to calculating SEP contributions can be used. If the above conditions apply, and a self-employed individual has two plans, the contribution rates must be added together to determine the equivalency percentage. The total contribution would be calculated and then prorated between the plans. Once any required contributions are made (e.g., to a money purchase pension plan), the remainder may generally be contributed to the discretionary contribution plan such as a SEP. If contributions under either plan were integrated with Social Security benefits (see chapter 9), the equivalency approach for calculating contributions cannot be used. (See examples in Q 7:23.)

Q 7:9 How is the equivalency method used to determine the contribution amount for an unincorporated business owner (self-employed individual)?

When an unincorporated business owner's earned income is not known, the contribution can be calculated in an indirect manner using the equivalency method. The pre-plan profits from self-employment are first reduced by the allocable share of all nonowners' contributions and one-half of the self-employment tax deduction. The resulting "net earnings from self-employment" is then multiplied by an equivalency percentage to determine the contribution.

The equivalency rates shown in Table 7-1 may be used to determine contributions for owners of unincorporated businesses. It should be noted that if elective and nonelective contributions are made, special adjustments are generally required so as to avoid exceeding the 25 percent of compensation limit (see Qs 7:6, 12:14).

Table 7-1. Equivalency Rates for Owners of Unincorporated Businesses

If the plan contribution rate is	*The self-employed individual's equivalency rate is*
1%	.009901
2	.019608
3	.029126

Table 7-1. Equivalency Rates for Owners of Unincorporated Businesses (*cont'd*)

If the plan contribution rate is	*The self-employed individual's equivalency rate is*
4	.038462
5	.047619
6	.056604
7	.065421
8	.074074
9	.082569
10	.090909
11	.099099
12	.107143
13	.115044
14	.122807
15	.130435
16	After 2001 .137931
17	.145299
18	.152542
19	.159664
20	.166667
21	.173554
22	.180328
23	.186992
24	.193548
25	.200000

Example 1. Tasha, age 45, an owner of an unincorporated business, contributed 25 percent of her employee's compensation to a SEP for 2012. After deducting her share of the common-law employee's plan contribution expense, Tasha's net profit from self-employment is $10,760.01. The self-employment tax deduction on $10,760.01 is $760.01. Using the equivalency method, Tasha's maximum excludable contribution (25 percent) can be computed as follows:

($10,760.01 – $760.01) = $10,000 (equivalency compensation)

$10,000 × .20 (equivalency factor from Table 7-1) = $2,000

Proof: ($10,000 – $2,000) × .25 = $2,000

Example 2. The facts are the same as those in Example 1, except that Tasha makes a $500 elective contribution. Her maximum excludable employer contribution ($1,500) can be determined as follows:

($10,760.01 – $760.01) = $10,000 (equivalency compensation)

$10,000 × .20 (equivalency factor from Table 7-1) = $2,000

$2,000 – $500 = $1,500

Proof: ($10,000 – $500 – $1,500) × .25 = $2,000

Note 1. Although the deductible limit in Example 2 is higher, the amount over $2,000 may not be allocated to Tasha on an excludable basis (see Qs 7:6, 11:2). The deductible limit of $2,125 (($10,000 – $1,500) × .25) is computed without taking into account elective deferrals. The deductible limit is then increased by the amount of the elective contributions. Thus, the deductible limit is $2,625 ($2,125 + $500). If the maximum deductible amount were to be contributed to the SEP, the $125 ($2,125 – $2,000) would not be deductible as a SEP contribution and would result in an excess IRA contribution that should be corrected timely (unless the amount can be contributed (absorbed) as an annual traditional IRA contribution).

Note 2. Code Section 404(n) provides that elective deferrals are not subject to the deduction limits, and that elective deferrals are not taken into account when computing the deduction limit to any other contributions.

Q 7:10 How is the equivalency percentage determined?

The equivalency percentage (expressed as a decimal) can be calculated as follows:

$$\frac{\text{Contribution Percentage (expressed as a decimal)}}{1 + \text{Contribution Percentage}} = \text{Equivalency Percentage}$$

Thus, for example, the equivalency percentage for a 25 percent contribution (.20) can be calculated as follows:

$$\frac{.25}{1.25} = .20$$

Q 7:11 Which method of calculating the compensation limit is better, the percentage method or the equivalency method?

When the equivalency method can be used (see Q 7:8), it will produce the same contribution as the percentage method. However, before 2002, when the SEP contribution limit was based on, for example, compensation not in excess of $170,000, the percentage method would provide a higher contribution than the equivalency method when compensation, after adjustment for one-half of the self-employment tax deduction, exceeded the annual compensation limit.

Practice Pointer. With a compensation limit of $250,000 (applied after the reduction for one-half of the self-employment tax and the owner's share of the nonowner contributions expense), both methods produce the same contribution, up to the maximum contribution of $50,000 ($250,000 × .20 = $50,000 ($250,000 – $50,000) × .25). (See Qs 6:22, 10:3.)

Most employers *calculate* SEP contributions for self-employed individuals using the equivalency method when the plan is not integrated. (See Q 7:7 and chapter 9.) [Treas. Reg. § 1.401(a)(17)-1(b)(6)]

Calculating Earned Income

Q 7:12 How do nonowner contributions affect the calculation of earned income?

Business expenses, including the owner's share of contributions on behalf of nonowner-employees, must be deducted when calculating earned income. [I.R.C. § 1402(a)] If a plan's contribution formula does not result in a fixed contribution (as with profit-sharing plans, stock bonus plans, and SEP arrangements), earned income fluctuates as the plan contribution rate is changed (e.g., when the annual plan contribution is being determined).

As contributions for nonowner-employees increase, the calculation changes as follows:

1. Earned income is directly reduced to the extent of the owner's share of nonowner-employee contribution expense.

   Example. Gabrielle has a 25 percent interest in a partnership. The partnership decides to increase its contribution to nonowner-employees by $1,000. Gabrielle's earned income for allocating contributions decreases by $250 (i.e., her share of the $1,000 partnership-level expense).

   Note. The reduction in earned income will actually be slightly less than $250, because Gabrielle's self-employment tax is lower as a result of the additional $250 partnership expense (see item 2).

2. The base for calculating self-employment taxes changes. Earned income is determined "with regard to" self-employment taxes (see Q 7:16). Here, increased expenses result in a decrease in the self-employment tax deduction and therefore a slight increase in the owner's earned income for plan purposes (up to the $250,000 maximum for 2012).

   Example. Gabrielle will show $250 less of self-employment earnings on Schedule SE of Form 1040, U.S. Individual Income Tax Return. Earned income for plan purposes must be reduced by the deduction for half of Gabrielle's self-employment tax. Thus, Gabrielle's earned income for plan purposes will decrease slightly less than $250 as a result of the lower self-employment tax deduction.

   Plan allocations are now based on less earned income, the net effect of the preceding changes.

The $250 downward adjustment is slightly offset by Gabrielle's self-employment tax savings; both of these are caused by the $1,000 increase in nonowner contributions.

3. There is less excess compensation to consider if plan contributions are integrated with Social Security benefits.

   Example. The partnership's plan is designed to favor employees earning above a certain amount; therefore, the amount of excess compensation will decrease by almost $250 (for the same reason stated in items 1 and 2).

4. The limits on maximum contributions and deductibility of contributions are now based on less earned income.

Q 7:13 Is it difficult for all plans in which a self-employed individual participates to calculate earned income?

No. Money purchase and defined benefit pension plans, as well as plans with no common-law employee participants, do not have as much difficulty with fluctuating earned income as other plans do. That is so because nonowner contributions are known and remain fixed. When nonowner contributions are not known, the self-employment tax cannot be calculated. In that case, the owner's compensation and resulting contribution (another subtraction to arrive at earned income) are also unknown. Circular and interdependent calculations are required to determine earned income and the resulting contribution.

Q 7:14 How do guaranteed payment partners and ineligible owners affect the calculation of an owner's plan compensation?

The presence of ineligible owners and guaranteed payment partners means that additional factors must be considered when designing a plan. Although ineligible owners do not receive a contribution, their pro rata share of the nonowner contribution expense must be set aside and not allocated to remaining participating owners. A guaranteed payment partner is promised a stated amount, and that amount is not reduced by nonowner contributions. The nonowner contribution expense is allocated to regular partners only. Generally, the nonowner contribution expense is allocated among all regular partners in proportion to their pre-plan earned income. In some cases, there is a written agreement that specifies how the nonowner contribution expense is to be allocated among regular partners.

Q 7:15 Is calculating a self-employed individual's contribution ever easy?

Generally, no. If owner contributions were the only reduction to be considered, there would always be a pre-plan equivalency percentage. For example, 25 percent of net earned income would always equal 20 percent of pre-plan compensation; 15 percent would equal 13.04348 percent of pre-plan compensation; and so on. Such a time-honored equivalency approach does not work, however, when other adjustments must be made to earned income or when the plan is integrated (see Q 7:4).

When a plan is designed to favor highly compensated employees, such as a plan that is integrated with Social Security benefits, different rates of contribution are applied to compensation earned above and below the integration level. In such cases, contributions cannot be calculated easily or quickly because the results keep changing the starting point (see Q 7:4).

Self-Employment Tax

Q 7:16 How does the deduction for 50 percent of the self-employment tax affect earned income?

In addition to other factors that affect the calculation of earned income, that amount must be determined under Code Section 1402(a) "with regard to" the deduction for half of the self-employment tax allowed the taxpayer by Code Section 164(f). [I.R.C. § 401(c)(2)(A)(v)] Code Section 1402(a) defines net earnings for self-employment tax purposes, and Code Section 1402(a)(12) provides for a deduction "in lieu of" the deduction under Code Section 164(f).

That is not to say that there are two different deductions. The Section 164(f) deduction, taken on the self-employed individual's Form 1040, is used by Code Section 401(c)(2) in computing earned income. The purpose of the "in lieu of" deduction in Code Section 1402(a)(12) is to calculate the self-employment tax.

Q 7:17 Why is an "in lieu of" deduction required to calculate self-employment tax?

Code Section 1402(a)(12) provides that self-employment taxes are not payable on the self-employment tax deduction claimed. That results in a small break—but also another riddle—for the taxpayer. Because the tax is an unknown, Schedule SE of Form 1040 takes into account .9235 (1 – (15.3% ÷ 2)), 15.3 percent being the total self-employment tax rate) of total self-employment earnings in computing the tax, thereby excluding the Form 1040 deduction for half of the self-employment tax. The "with regard to" deduction under Code Section 401(c)(2), on the other hand (see Q 7:16), is used in calculating earned income for plan purposes. This interpretation by the authors has also been suggested by other practitioners. [L.C. Starr, American Society of Pension Professionals and Actuaries (ASPPA), "Sole Proprietorship and Partnership Compensation and Deduction Issues" (Webcast) (June 2010]

Q 7:18 How was the deduction for one-half of the self-employed health insurance treated when calculating one-half of the self-employment tax under Code Section 164(f) for 2010?

The IRS has indicated that for retirement plan purposes in 2010 "[w]hen calculating the deduction for one-half of the self-employment tax, the deduction for self-employed health insurance is disregarded." [IRS Publication 560, *Retirement Plans for Small Business*, p. 5 (see 2010 version)]

Thus, based on IRS Publication 560 for retirement plan purposes, the self-employed health insurance (SEHI) amount is not taken into account when calculating the Code Section 164(f) deduction for 1/2 of the self-employment tax. Thus, SEHI can be completely disregarded in computing earned income for retirement plan purposes. This means that the Code Section 164(f) deduction for 50 percent of self-employment tax may be greater than the deduction actually shown on the return. In effect, the Code Section 164(f) deduction must be recomputed without regard to SEHI for retirement plan purposes (see example below).

A temporary provision under the Small Business Jobs Act of 2010 (SBJA) allows self-employed individuals who claim a deduction for health insurance premiums to reduce their earnings for self-employment tax purposes for one year (i.e., for 2010 only). [SBJA (Pub. L. No. 111-240) § 2042; I.R.C. § 162(l)(4). The one-year temporary provision is effective for the tax year (generally the calendar year) beginning after 2009. SBJA (enrolled version), available at *http://www.gpo.gov/fdsys/pkg/BILLS-111hr5297enr/pdf/BILLS-111hr5297enr.pdf* (visited on Aug. 22, 2012)] The Technical Explanation of the Tax Provisions in the Senate Amendment 4594 to H.R. 5297 prepared by the Joint Committee on Taxation states that "It is intended that earned income within the meaning of section 401(c)(2) be computed *without regard* to this deduction for the cost of health insurance." (Emphasis added.) (See example below.) The SBJA Technical Explanation indicates that "A technical correction may be needed to achieve this result." [SBJA, Official Explanation (JCX-47-10), available at *http://www.jct.gov/publications.html?func = startdown&id = 3707* (visited on Aug. 22, 2012)]

Q 7:19 What external factors may affect the calculation of the self-employment tax deduction?

The self-employment tax deduction may be affected by such external factors as income on Form W-2, Wage and Tax Statement, or gains and losses from other self-employment activities.

Both of these factors affect an owner's earned income. When an individual has W-2 wages, he or she gets a credit for the contribution to Social Security, and the self-employment tax is reduced. The reduction in self-employment tax has the effect of increasing earned income, and the partner will receive a larger contribution. Similarly, an unrelated loss from self-employment also has the effect of reducing the self-employment tax and increasing earned income for plan purposes, and the partner will receive a larger contribution. Conversely, an unrelated gain from self-employment has the effect of increasing self-employment tax and reducing earned income, and the partner will receive a smaller contribution. When there is an unrelated gain from self-employment, the self-employment tax must be apportioned between the entities. (See Q 7:14 for more information regarding guaranteed payment partners and ineligible owner situations.)

Example. Unusual Facts, a partnership, maintains a SEP plan for its employees. Unusual Facts makes a contribution of $45,908.79. Three nonowner-employees earn wages of $10,000 each. The following chart reflects the status of the owner, pre-plan earned income, allocation of nonowner contributions, one-half of the self-employment tax deduction, allocation of the 2012 contribution, and the compensation upon which the allocation was made. (See Appendix H.)

Employee Name/Status	*A Pre-Plan Compensation*	*B Share of $3,000 Nonowner Contributions*	*Self-Employment Income for SE Tax*	*C 1/2 of the Self-Employment Tax Deduction***	*D 10% Contribution $45,908.79*	*Allocation Compensation (for owners: A-B-C-D)*
Owners						
Joe Normal	$100,000	$600.00	$ 99,400.00	$7,020.92	$ 8,398.10	$83,979.65
Lou has $20,000 of W-2 income from an unrelated entity	100,000	600.00	99,400.00	6,915.80	8,407.65	84,531.78
Tom has a $10,000 loss from self-employment from an unrelated entity	100,000	600.00	89,400.00	6,314.59	8,462.31	84,621.90
Tim has a $10,000 gain from self-employment from an unrelated entity	100,000	600.00	109,400.00	7,024.77*	8,397.75	83,976.15
Abe is ineligible to participate	100,000	600.00	n/a	n/a	Ineligible	n/a
Ros is a guaranteed payment partner (GPM) with $109,400 of guaranteed payment	109,400	GPM none allocated	109,400.00	7,727.25	9,242.98	92,428.31
Nonowners						
Employees (combined)	$ 30,000	n/a	n/a	n/a	$ 3,000	$ 30,000

* The self-employment tax on $109,400 ($100,000 + $10,000 – $600) is $7,727.25 for 2012. The result is a pro rata allocation of the self-employment tax attributable to this entity of $7,024.77 (see Q 7:24). That

amount ($7,727.25) is multiplied by .90909090 (pre-plan earned income of $100,000, divided by $110,000 (the sum of the pre-plan earned income ($100,000) and the outside earned income ($10,000).

** The special calculation of the Code Section 164(f) deduction for 2012 is reflected. For 2011 and 2012 only, the Code Section 164(f) deduction for one-half of the self-employment tax is equals "59.6" percent of the 10.4 percent old-age portion of FICA tax up to the taxable wage base of $110,100 for (2012), plus 1/2 of the 2.9 percent Medicare portion of the FICA tax on $99,400 (with no ceiling). See Q 7:2. That amount would have to be allocated to each entity in accordance with the proceeding paragraph. The results of both the special calculation of the Code Section 164(f) deduction and the special "entity" allocation of the self-employment tax is shown in an illustration in Appendix H.

Practice Pointer. Frequently, partners have different tax preparers. Information from the uncompleted federal income tax returns of some partners may be needed to compute the contributions to be made under the plan and to complete the federal income tax returns of the partnership, and, in turn, the individual federal income tax returns of the individual partners can be completed. Return preparation is much easier when all partners and the partnership have the same tax preparer; privacy issues are also minimized.

Earned Income: Where to Start

Partners

Note. Line and box numbers from the 2012 tax forms are used.

Q 7:20 What is the correct starting point for calculating the earned income and self-employment tax of a partner?

No specific line number or amount on any tax return, worksheet, or schedule can be used as the correct starting point for calculating a partner's pre-plan earned income or self-employment tax. It does seem prudent, however, to start with Schedule K-1, line 14a, on Form 1065 (box 9 of Form 1065-B, codes F (guaranteed payments) and J1 (net earnings from self-employment)), U.S. Return of Partnership Income. (Up to four adjustments are possible when using the amount from that box.) The amount in that box is initially determined using a worksheet provided in the instructions to Form 1065 and then is allocated to the individual partners. Thus, line 14a, on Schedule K-1 of Form 1065 cannot always be determined simply by adding box 1 (ordinary income) and box 4 (guaranteed payments to partner) of Schedule K-1 (see Q 7:21). (See Form 1065 instructions and worksheet for Schedules K and K-1, line 14a.)

Practice Pointer. If an individual's tax return is properly completed, line 14a on Schedule K-1 of Form 1065 is a suitable starting point for calculating earned income (see Q 7:22).

Table 7-2 lists the factors that must be considered to calculate the earned income of a partner (see Q 7:22).

Table 7-2. Adjustments to Arrive at Earned Income of a Partner

Pre-Plan Form 1065, Schedule K-1 (line 14a)

Subtract gains and add back any losses on sale of business property (only if "off-sheet" adjustment not properly considered; see worksheet, Form 1065 instructions and worksheet for Schedule K-1, line 14*)

Less:

- Section 179 depreciation expenses deduction claimed
- Unreimbursed partnership expense claimed
- Depletion claimed on oil and gas properties
- Share of common-law employee contributions
- Contributions on behalf of owner
- Contributions by owners (salary reduction and catch-up)
- Half of the Social Security tax deduction**

---

* Gains or losses from the sale of business property are "unearned."

** When calculating the deduction for one-half of the self-employment tax, the deduction for self-employed health insurance is disregarded (see Q 7:18).

Practice Pointer. Similar rules apply to calculate self-employment income to electing large partnerships using Form 1065-B, Return of Income for Electing Large Partnership, except that line 13a is the relevant starting point for Schedule K and box 9 (codes F and JI) for Schedule K-1 (of Form 1065-B). The Form 1065-B worksheet is similar, but not identical, to the Form 1065 worksheet (see Form 1065-B, Instructions).

Note. *Husband-wife business.* Generally, if married business owners are the sole owners and operate an unincorporated business and share in the profits and losses, they are partners in a partnership and must file Form 1065. However, beginning in 2007 if married sole owners materially participate as the only members of a jointly owned and operated business, and they file a joint return for the tax year, they can make an election to be treated as a qualified joint venture instead of a partnership. By making the election, the individuals will not be required to file Form 1065 for any year the election is in effect and will instead report the income and deductions directly on your joint return. To make this election, the individuals must divide all items of income, gain, loss, deduction, and credit between the individuals in accordance with their respective interests in the venture. Each must file a separate Schedule C, C-EZ, or F. On each line of the separate Schedule C, C-EZ, or F, each individual's share of the applicable income, deduction, or loss must be entered. Both individuals must also file a separate Schedule SE to pay self-employment tax. (See Q 7:23.)

Q 7:21 Why is it not possible to determine line 14a of Schedule K-1 to Form 1065 by adding line 1 and line 4 of Schedule K-1?

When there is an ordinary gain or loss on the sale of business property (from Form 4797 Part II, Sales of Business Property), the worksheet contained in the instructions to Form 1065 provides for included losses to be added back and included gains to be subtracted out before allocation to each partner. That adjustment (sometimes referred to as an "off-sheet" adjustment) appears in the instructions to Form 1065 but not on Schedule K or K-1. Its absence from Form 1065 (and its relevance to determining the correct amount on line 14a explains why line 14a of Schedule K-1 to Form 1065 cannot always be determined simply by adding line 1 (ordinary income) and line 4 (guaranteed payments to partner) of Schedule K-1. [L.C. Starr, ASPPA, "Sole Proprietorship and Partnership Compensation and Deduction Issues" (Webcast) (June 2010)]

Q 7:22 In addition to an adjustment for ordinary gains or losses on the sale of business property reflected on Schedule K-1, what other adjustments are required if line 14a of Schedule K-1 is used as the starting point for calculating a partner's earned income?

The instructions for Form 1065, Schedule K-1, line 14a (other than farming) provide for the amount on that line to be entered on Schedule SE to Form 1040 after three more "off-sheet" reductions are made (in addition to that for ordinary gains or losses on the sale of business property):

1. *Section 179 expense deduction claimed.* Schedule K-1 shows only the Section 179 deduction being passed through to the partner (line 12). The deduction actually claimed, however, is on Form 4562, Depreciation and Amortization, line 12. For example, if an individual is a partner in several partnerships, not all of the Section 179 expenses may be deductible.
2. *Claimed unreimbursed partnership expenses.* Not all legitimate partnership expenses are run through the business. Such expenses, although not technically nonpassive losses, are reported on Form 1040, Schedule E, Supplemental Income and Loss, Part II, line 28(i). Unreimbursed partnership expenses that partners are required to pay under the terms of the partnership agreement are deductible. (*See* Form 1040, Schedule E, Instructions to Parts II and III, Partnerships.)
3. *Depletion on oil and gas properties claimed.* (*See* Form 1065, Instructions, Adjustments, and Tax Preference Items.)

Practice Pointer. If the net earnings from self-employment from line 14a of a partner's Schedule K-1 are reduced, the instructions for Schedule SE require an explanation to be attached.

Note. Line and box numbers from the 2012 tax forms are used.

Sole Proprietors

Q 7:23 What is the starting point for calculating a sole proprietor's earned income?

The calculation of a sole proprietor's earned income generally starts with line 31 of Schedule C, Profit or Loss from Business (Sole Proprietorship), to Form 1040, although the amount that appears there will need to be adjusted slightly (see Table 7-3). That line is also reported on Form 1040, Schedule SE.

Table 7-3. Adjustments to Arrive at Earned Income of a Sole Proprietor in a SEP

Sole Proprietor's Schedule C (line 31) or Schedule F (line 36)

Less:

- Share of common-law employee contributions
- Contributions on behalf of owner
- Contributions by owner (salary reduction)
- Half of the self-employment tax deduction [I.R.C. § 164(f)]

Practice Pointer. Similar rules apply to farmers using Form 1040, Schedule F, Profit or Loss from Farming, except that line 36 is the relevant starting point.

Example 1. Matty is a sole proprietor, and her 2012 net earnings from self-employment (not taking into account any plan contributions and not reduced by her self-employment tax deduction) is $100,000. Matty decides to make a 15 percent SEP contribution for an eligible employee earning $25,000. The net earnings amount ($100,000) is reduced to $96,250 (by subtracting the employee contribution of $3,750) and is further reduced to $89,451.58 (by subtracting half of the self-employment tax deduction of $6,798.42). The owner equivalency percentage of 13.043478 percent is then multiplied by $89,451.58 (the adjusted net earned income) to calculate Matty's deductible contribution of $11,667.60 (see Q 7:8). (Numbers need to be carried out to only six decimal places.) (See Appendix H.)

Example 2. Matty also maintains a money purchase pension plan requiring that 10 percent of compensation be contributed each year. The employee will receive a 25 percent contribution, or $6,250. After subtraction of the employee contribution of $6,250 and half of the self-employment tax deduction of $6,621.84, Matty's adjusted net earned income is $87,128.16. With a 20 percent equivalency percentage, Matty will contribute and deduct $17,425.63. Her "ultra net" (after all adjustments) earned income (see Q 7:24) is $69,702.53 ($87,128.16 – $17,425.63). After the required 10 percent contribution of $6,970.25 ($69,702.53 × .10) is made to the money purchase plan, there is $10,455.38 ($17,425.63 – $6,970.25) left over for the SEP. (See Appendix H.)

Example 3. Matty elects not to contribute to the SEP arrangement for 2012; however, the required pension plan contribution of 10 percent must be made for her. Matty's resulting net earned income is multiplied by the 10 percent equivalency percentage of 9.090909 percent. Her pension plan contribution is $8,237.57 ($100,000 is reduced by the required employee contribution of $2,500 and half of the self-employment tax deduction of $6,886.71; the result, $90,613.29, is multiplied by Matty's 10 percent equivalency percentage of 9.090909 percent). (See Appendix H.)

Note. An employer no longer needs to maintain a 10 percent money purchase pension plan to achieve a 25 percent/$50,000 contribution (see Q 1:35).

Example 4. Myron's net profit from self-employment for 2012 is $260,310.19 (see Q 6:30). His earned income after making a $50,000 deductible contribution is $200,000 ($260,310.19 – $50,000 – $10,310.19 (deduction for half of the self-employment tax deduction)). In addition to a SEP, Myron maintains a money purchase pension plan requiring that 11 percent of compensation be contributed each year. Myron has no employees. In this case, $27,500 ($250,000 × .11) is contributed to the money purchase pension plan to meet minimum funding standards. [I.R.C. § 412] The remainder of the contribution, $22,500 ($50,000 – $27,500), may be contributed to the SEP. Here, the SEP contribution is limited by Code Section 415 to $50,000 reduced by the 11 percent money purchase plan contribution of $27,500 ($250,000 × .25 would exceed the $50,000 limit for 2012). Thus, only $22,500 ($50,000 – $27,500) may be contributed to the SEP for 2012. (See Appendix H.)

Practice Pointer. Similar rules apply to calculate self-employment income to farmers using Form 1040, Schedule F, Profit or Loss from Farming, except that line 36 is the relevant starting point.

Note. If a self-employed individual has two plans, the contribution rates must be added together to determine the equivalency percentage. The total contribution would be calculated and then prorated between the plans; other factors may apply (see Q 7:25 and example 4 above).

"Ultra Net" Earned Income

Q 7:24 How is "ultra net" earned income calculated for deduction, exclusion, and allocation purposes?

Following is a worksheet for calculating "ultra net" earned income under Code Section 401(c)(2) for purposes of allocating contributions and calculating the employer's deduction and the amount of contributions that may be excluded from the employee's gross income.

1. Total earned income before any plan contributions (for 2012, Schedule K-1, line 14a, plus partner's share of nonowner-employee contributions shown on Form 1065, line 18) $_____

2. Less any unreimbursed partnership expense claimed (data from the accountant or Form 1040, Schedule E, Part II, line 28, column (i)) –$_____
3. Less Section 179 expense deduction claimed (see Schedule K-1, line 12, and confirm on Form 4562, line 12) –$_____
4. Less depletion claimed on oil and gas properties (see Schedule SE, Instructions, Partnership Income or Loss) –$_____
5. **Pre-plan compensation (items 1–4): Sole Proprietorships, start here.** =$_____
6. Less owner's share of common-law employee allocations (Form 1065, line 18, multiplied by partner's share percentage, or line 19 from Schedule C if self-employed) –$_____
7. **Net amount** for determining ½ of the self-employment tax deduction Code Section 164(f) (Items 5 and 6) =$_____
8. Less half of self-employment tax deduction (if individual also has W-2 income, complete long Schedule SE to reflect the proper SE tax and *in lieu* of deduction) See Q 7:2. –$_____
9. Less elective and nonelective contributions for owner –$_____
10. **Earned income** for SEP exclusion purposes (Items 7–9; up to $250,000 for plan years beginning in 2012) =$_____
11. Plus elective contributions of owner* +$_____
12. **Earned income** for deduction purposes (not to exceed $250,000) =$_____
13. **Earned income** for the allocation of plan contributions (Items 10 and 11 up to $250,000 for 2012)* =$_____

---

* Not all plans provide for elective contributions to be included in the definition of earned income for the purpose of allocating employer contributions. For contribution allocation purposes after 1997, compensation generally may include elective contributions (see Qs 6:4, 6:14). Under a prototype SEP document, but not a model SEP, elective contributions may be treated as compensation (see Qs 3:14, 6:21) for contribution allocation purposes. (*See* Form 5305A-SEP, Salary Reduction Simplified Employee Pension-Individual Retirement Accounts Contribution Agreement.)

Note. Line and box numbers from the 2012 tax forms are used.

Interests in Multiple Entities

Q 7:25 If a self-employed individual has an interest in more than one entity, must each entity be considered differently?

Yes. More than one entity may have to be considered in designing a SEP, testing for various limits, and avoiding discrimination initially or in operation.

The employers may be related or unrelated, or they may be considered related for some purposes but not all.

Many complexities may arise. For instance, if a sole proprietor has an interest in multiple related or controlled employers, in most cases those employers will all adopt the plan. What if one of the entities was unrelated and did not adopt the plan? Would the deduction for half of the owner's self-employment tax have to be prorated? Possibly, says one commentator. [L.C. Starr, ASPPA, "Sole Proprietorship and Partnership Compensation and Deduction Issues" (Webcast) (June 2010)]

Further, knowing the total amount of all the outside earned income subject to self-employment tax presupposes that the formulas and contributions for each separate employer's nonowner participants are known. That is unlikely (see Q 7:2).

When the "ultra net" (after all adjustments) earned income (see Q 7:24) is less than the $250,000 maximum for 2012, the proration of the self-employment tax deduction among multiple entities (to increase the amount of earned income that is considered for plan purposes) would seem preferable to allocating all of the earned income to the entity that adopted the plan. [*See* Ann. 94-101, § 684, Ex. I, 1994-35 I.R.B. 53] At the same time, it should be noted that allocating all of the self-employment tax to a nonadopting entity (to maximize the amount of earned income that is considered for plan purposes) might be considered aggressive.

Chapter 8

Top-Heavy Plans Benefiting Key Employees: SEPs and SARSEPs

A plan or group of plans that primarily benefits key employees is called a top-heavy plan. If a SEP or SARSEP is top heavy, the employer must make a minimum contribution to each non-key employee. This chapter focuses on determining which SEPs or SARSEPs are top heavy, who are key and non-key employees, and when and how much of a minimum contribution is required. The treatment of frozen plans and plan-to-plan transfers, as well as the family attribution rule under Code Section 318, used in determining whether an individual is a more than 5 percent owner, are also discussed in this chapter. (The rules discussed in this chapter do not apply to SIMPLEs, which are fully discussed in chapter 14.)

Introduction

Q 8:1 When is a SEP or SARSEP top heavy?

A SEP arrangement that primarily benefits key employees (see Q 8:7) as of the determination date (see below) is top heavy and becomes subject to the top-heavy rules of the Internal Revenue Code (Code). [I.R.C. § 408(k)(1)(B); Treas. Reg. § 1.416-1, Q&A G-1] A SEP primarily benefits key employees when 60 percent or more of the aggregate account balances under the plan as of the determination date belong to key employees (see Qs 8:10, 8:16). [I.R.C. § 416(g)(1)(A)(ii)]

Special rules allow an employer to determine whether a SEP or SARSEP arrangement is top heavy for any plan year by taking into account aggregate contributions rather than by taking into account aggregate account balances of all employees. [I.R.C. § 416(i)(6)(B); *see also* Treas. Reg. § 1.416-1, Q&A T-21] Internal Revenue Service (IRS) prototype documents use this approach. Special rules also apply to elective SEPs when any key employee makes an elective contribution (see Q 3:16). In the authors' opinion, excess contributions (elective and nonelective) are *not* taken into account when performing the top-heavy test, provided the excess amount was included in the employee's income and the employee was notified in accordance with plan provisions of statutory requirements (see Qs 12:18–12:44).

Note. It would be very difficult for an employer maintaining a SEP to ascertain the balances of all employees' individual retirement arrangements (IRAs), including their growth. It would be impossible unless employees furnished the balance information to the employer. That is why there are special rules for SEPs allowing the employer to use only the *contributions* made to the plan—and not account balances—to determine top-heavy status.

Generally, the determination date for deciding whether a plan is top heavy is the last day of the *preceding* plan year. In the case of the first plan year of any plan, the determination date is the last day of that plan year; however, contributions made after the determination date that are allocated as of a date in that first plan year are not considered. [I.R.C. § 416(g)(4)(C); Treas. Reg. § 1.416-1, Q&A T-22] When calculating a participant's account balance for the purpose of determining whether a plan is top heavy, the account balance is increased for distributions made to the participant within the five-year period (which, after 2001, is generally reduced to a one-year look-back period) ending on the determination date. [I.R.C. §§ 408(k)(1)(B), 416(g)(3)] The five-year period is retained unless the distribution is made because of severance from employment, death, or disability.

Catch-up contributions for prior years are taken into account in determining whether a SEP or SARSEP is top heavy. [Treas. Reg. § 1.414(v)-1(d)(3)(i)]

Note 1. *Prototype SARSEPs*. Regardless of which method is used to determine the top-heavy status of a prototype SEP, elective contributions (including catch-up elective contributions) for the current year are not taken into account in determining whether a plan is top heavy for the current year.

Note 2. *Model SARSEPs (Form 5305A-SEP)*. Under a model SARSEP, catch-up contributions are not taken into account in determining whether a key employee has made a contribution for the current year under the special rule discussed previously (see also Q 3:16). [Form 5305A-SEP, Art. VI(A)]

Example. Giant Gumball Corporation has maintained a SEP for its tax years ending on December 31, 2005, through 2012. All contributions are made on December 31. The following table lists contributions, cumulative contributions, and gain to date; data in the Gain to Date column are used only in the aggregate account balance method of determining top-heavy status and would be moot in determining the top-heavy status of a SEP using the aggregate contribution method.

	Key Employees			Non-Key Employees		
Year	*Contributions*	*Cumulative Contributions*	*Gain to Date*	*Contributions*	*Cumulative Contributions*	*Gain to Date*
2012	$12,000	$75,640	$20,940	$6,800	$50,750	$13,126
2011	10,000	63,640	15,177	8,100	43,950	9,392
2010	7,600	53,640	10,643	5,350	35,850	6,433
2009	13,000	46,040	6,573	9,100	30,500	4,016
2008	10,000	33,040	3,804	5,350	21,400	2,354
2007	7,000	23,040	1,885	5,350	16,050	1,150
2006	8,000	16,040	653	5,350	10,700	375
2005	8,040	8,040	0	5,350	5,350	0

The calculations in the table that follows show how top-heavy status is determined under the two methods for determining whether a plan is top heavy for a particular year. The years for which the Giant Gumball SEP would be top heavy under each method are indicated by T-H.

Determination Year		*Aggregate Contribution Method*		*Balance Method Aggregate Account*
2012		$75,640 ÷ ($75,640 + $50,750) is < 60%	T-H	($75,640 + $20,940) ÷ ($75,640 + $20,940 + $50,750 + $13,126) is > 60%
2011		$63,640 ÷ ($63,640 + $43,950) is < 60%		($63,640 + $15,177) ÷ ($63,640 + $15,177 + $43,950 + $9,392) is < 60%
2010		$53,640 ÷ ($53,640 + $35,850) is < 60%	T-H	$53,640 + $10,463) ÷ ($53,640 + $10,463 + $35,850 + $6,433) is > 60%
2009	T-H	$46,040 ÷ ($46,040 + $30,500) is > 60%	T-H	($46,040 + $6,573) ÷ ($46,040 + $6,573 + $30,500 + $4,016) is > 60%
2008	T-H	$33,040 ÷ ($33,040 + $21,400) is > 60%	T-H	($33,040 + $3,804) ÷ ($33,040 + $3,804 + $21,400 + $2,354) is > 60%
2007		$23,040 ÷ ($23,040 + $16,050) is < 60%	T-H	($23,040 + $1,885) ÷ ($23,040 + $1,885 + $16,050 + $1,150) is > 60%
2006		$16,040 ÷ ($16,040 + $10,700) is < 60%	T-H	($16,040 + $563) ÷ ($16,040 + $563 + $10,700 + $375) is > 60%
2005*	T-H	$8,040 ÷ ($8,040 + $5,350) is > 60%	T-H	$8,040 ÷ ($8,040 + $5,350) is > 60%

* Current (initial) year (2005) used for determining whether plan is top heavy.

Minimum Required Contribution

Q 8:2 How much is the employer required to contribute if a SEP or SARSEP arrangement is top heavy?

When a SEP or SARSEP arrangement is top heavy, the employer must make a minimum contribution for each eligible non-key employee that is equal to the lesser of

1. Three percent of each eligible non-key employee's compensation or
2. A percentage of each eligible non-key employee's compensation equal to the percentage of compensation at which elective (not counting catch-up elective deferral contributions) and nonelective contributions are made under the SEP or SARSEP (and under any other SEP or SARSEP maintained by the employer) for the year for the key employee for whom the percentage is the highest for the year.

[I.R.C. §§ 408(k)(1)(B), 416(b)(2)]

Q 8:3 Must all employees receive the minimum required top-heavy contribution?

No. If a top-heavy contribution is required, it must be given to all *non-key* employees (see Q 8:8) who are eligible to participate, not to all employees.

Q 8:4 May the minimum required top-heavy contribution be made to all employees?

Yes. Provided no other limits are exceeded, the minimum required top-heavy contribution may be made to all employees.

Note 1. The required minimum top-heavy contribution percentage may change as additional contributions are made for key employees.

Note 2. If a 3 percent nonelective contribution is made to all participants for the plan year, a plan would not be top heavy (or treated as top heavy) for that year.

Q 8:5 Must the minimum required top-heavy contribution be made into the SEP or SARSEP?

No. Plan documents of a SEP or SARSEP may provide for the top-heavy requirements of Code Section 416 to be satisfied by contributions to a non-key employee's elective SEP, to a nonelective SEP, or to a qualified plan maintained by the employer. (IRS model Form 5305A-SEP, Article VI, Part B, provides an option for the employer to satisfy the elective SEP's top-heavy requirements by contributing to a nonelective SEP.)

Q 8:6 May elective deferrals be treated as employer contributions to satisfy an employer's top-heavy contribution requirement?

No. Elective deferrals under a SARSEP may not be used to satisfy an employer's top-heavy contribution requirement. [I.R.C. §§ 408(k)(6)(D), 401(k)(4)(A), 416(c)(2)(A); Form 5305A-SEP, Top-Heavy Requirements, at 4; Treas. Reg. § 1.401(k)-1(e)(6)(i)]

Example 1. Jerry, a participant in a top-heavy SARSEP requiring a 3 percent contribution to satisfy the top-heavy rules, made a 2 percent elective SARSEP contribution. To satisfy the top-heavy rules, Jerry's employer must make a 3 percent contribution on Jerry's behalf.

Example 2. Vikki, a participant in a top-heavy SARSEP requiring a 3 percent contribution of $1,200 to satisfy the top-heavy rules, made a 20 percent elective SARSEP contribution ($8,000 based on her pre-plan compensation of $40,000). To satisfy the top-heavy rules, Vikki's employer must make a 3 percent contribution on Vikki's behalf. Unless Vikki is eligible to make catch-up contributions (generally has attained age 50 by the end of the calendar year), the 25 percent participant exclusion limit under Code Section 402(h) has also been exceeded (see Q 11:1).

Had the plan not been required to make a top-heavy contribution (and no other nonelective contributions were made by the employer), the 25 percent exclusion limit would not have been exceeded. In that case, Vikki's elective contribution of $8,000 is equal to her exclusion limit ($40,000–$8,000) × .25). Here, however, the 3 percent contribution made by Vikki's employer lowered the amount of her allowable elective contribution (see formula in Q 12:14) under the exclusion limit rules to $7,040 (($40,000–$7,040) × .25 = $8,240), which is further reduced by the employer's contribution of $1,200). If Vikki is age 50 by December 31, the elective contribution $960 ($8,000–$7,040) that exceeded the exclusion limit of $7,040 would be treated as a catch-up contribution under the plan. If not, the $960 is treated as wages (see Q 12:14).

Key Employees

Q 8:7 Which employees are key employees?

For years beginning after 2002, the term *key employee* is generally any employee who was one of the following during the *prior* year:

1. An officer with compensation in excess of $130,000 (adjusted for cost-of-living increases in $5,000 increments ($165,000 for 2012)),
2. A 5 percent or more owner, or
3. A 1 percent or more owner with compensation in excess of $150,000.

[I.R.C. § 416(i)(1)(A), 416(i)(1)(B); *see* I.R.S. Notice 2011-90, 2011-47 I.R.B. 791 for 2012 limits]

The constructive ownership rules of Code Section 318 are used to determine ownership. [I.R.C. § 416(i)(1)(B)(iii)]

> **Note.** The statutory language of Code Section 416(i)(1)(A) uses the terms *5 percent owner* and *1 percent owner*, but defines those terms to mean a "more than" 5 percent or 1 percent owner, respectively. [I.R.C. § 416(i)(1)(B)(i), 416(i)(1)(B)(ii)]

The number and identity of the officers treated as key employees are limited to the greater of 3 (individuals) or 10 percent of all employees, but in no event may more than 50 individuals, ranked by compensation, be treated as key employees. The term *officer* does not include any officer or employee of an entity referred to in Code Section 414(d) (relating to governmental plans). Certain other officers may also be excluded. [*See* I.R.C. § 416(i)(1)(A), referring to § 414(q)(5) regarding the exclusion of certain employees from the definition of *highly compensated employee*; such exclusions also apply in determining the number and identity of officers under the key employee rules.]

The four-year look-back rule and the "top 10" owner rule have been eliminated. The family attribution rule, however, continues to apply in determining whether an individual is a more than 5 percent owner of the employer for purposes of determining which employees are key employees.

An individual is deemed to own stock (or other ownership interests) held by his or her spouse unless they are divorced or legally separated under a decree of separate maintenance. Unlike the controlled group rules, there apparently is attribution between spouses even if there is an interlocutory decree of divorce, and even if the nonowning spouse is not involved in the business. [I.R.C. § 318(a)(1)(A)(i)]

An individual is also deemed to own stock (or other ownership interests) held by his or her parents, children, and grandchildren. [I.R.C. § 318(a)(1)(A)(ii)] Notice that there is attribution from grandchild to grandparent, but not from grandparent to grandchild. No "age 21" rule limits the attribution of stock between parent and child. Adopted children are treated as blood relatives. [I.R.C. § 318(a)(1)(B)]

No double attribution occurs under the family rules, although stock deemed to be owned under one of the other rules, such as attribution from trusts or options, can then be deemed to be owned by a family member.

Example 1. *Family attribution.* The Robinson family members consist of Dad and Mom, a married couple, and their children (Brother and Sister), and Sister's daughter, Grandkid. Brother was adopted. Their ownership of Xavier Corporation is as follows:

Dad	500 shares
Mom	400 shares
Sister	300 shares
Brother	200 shares
Grandkid	100 shares

Example 2. Mom and Dad are each deemed to own all 1,500 shares. Sister is deemed to own 1,300 shares, all but Brother's. Brother is deemed to own 1,100 shares, missing Sister's and Grandkid's. Grandkid is deemed to own 400 shares, just her own and her mother's.

Example 3. *Key employee family attribution.* Each of the following owns 1 percent of Trout Corporation: Sam, Sam's wife, Sam's mother, Sam's grandmother, Sam's son, and Sam's granddaughter (the daughter of Sam's son). Sam is deemed to own the stock of all those individuals other than Sam's grandmother. That gives Sam exactly 5 percent. Because a "5 percent owner" is one who owns more than 5 percent of a company, Sam is not a 5 percent owner. Sam and each of his five family members is a 1 percent owner, however, because each is deemed to own more than 1 percent.

Example 4. *No double family attribution.* Son, Daughter, and Mother each own 2.5 percent of The Chrysanthemum Corporation. Son and Daughter are each deemed to own 5 percent, while Mother is deemed to own 7.5 percent. Son's stock cannot be attributed to Daughter through Mother. Son and Daughter are not 5 percent owners (again, that requires more than 5 percent), while Mother is a 5 percent owner.

Example 5. *Option precedence.* The facts are the same as in the preceding example, except that Mother has an option to buy Son's stock. Mother is deemed to own Son's stock because of option attribution, not because of the family rules, which means it can be attributed from her to Daughter. Accordingly, both Mother and Daughter are deemed to own 7.5 percent of Chrysanthemum. Son is still deemed to own 5 percent.

Example 6. *Stepchildren.* Mabel owns 4 percent of Second Chance, Inc., and her stepson, Roy, owns 2 percent. On these facts, neither is a 5 percent owner. There is no attribution between stepchild and stepparent. That would require double family attribution through Roy's father (Mabel's husband).

Example 7. *Stock attribution, not compensation attribution.* Dad owns 3 percent of Nepotism, Inc. His salary from the company is $175,000 per year, and hence he is an HCE and a key employee. Daughter does not own any stock in the company, but does receive an annual salary of $40,000. Daughter is not an HCE or a key employee. She is deemed to own Dad's stock, but 3 percent ownership will not make her an HCE. His compensation is not attributed to her, and her compensation is insufficient to make her an HCE or a key employee.

[*See* S. Derrin Watson, *Who's the Employer?* Q 14:7 (6th ed. (Goleta, CA 2012)) at *http://www.employerbook.com* (visited on Aug. 22, 2012). Examples used with permission.]

Q 8:8 Which employees are *non-key employees*?

All employees who are not key employees (see Q 8:7) are *non-key employees*. [I.R.C. § 416(i)(2)]

Determining Top-Heavy Status

Q 8:9 Must each plan of an employer take into account all other plans of the employer for purposes of determining whether the plan is top heavy?

Yes. All of an employer's plans, including distributions from plans that have terminated during the last five years (see Q 8:16), have to be considered when determining whether a particular plan is top heavy. [I.R.C. § 416(g)] Thus, all stock bonus, pension, or profit-sharing plans intended to qualify under Code Section 401(a), annuity contracts described in Code Section 403(a), and SEPs described in Code Section 408(k) are subject to the top-heavy rules and must be considered for top-heavy testing purposes.

Q 8:10 What factors must be considered in determining whether a SEP is top heavy?

To determine whether a plan is top heavy for a plan year, it is necessary to determine which employers will be treated as a single employer for purposes of Code Section 416; what the determination date is for the plan year; which employees are, or were, key employees; which former employees have not performed any service for the employer maintaining the plan at any time during the five-year period ending on the determination date; which plans of such employers are required or permitted to be aggregated to determine top-heavy status; and the present value of the accrued benefits (including distributions made during the plan year containing the determination date and the four preceding plan years) of key employees, former key employees, and non-key employees.

Q 8:11 What is a *required aggregation group*?

All employers that are aggregated under Code Sections 414(b), 414(c), and 414(m) must be taken into account as a single employer for the plan year in question. All plans maintained by the employers in which a key employee participates, and certain other plans, must then be aggregated (the required aggregation group).

For purposes of determining whether an employer's plans are top heavy for a particular plan year, the *required aggregation group* includes each plan of the employer in which a key employee participates in the plan year containing the determination date or any of the four preceding plan years.

> **Example.** By Design, a sole proprietor, terminated a Keogh plan in 2009. In 2012, By Design incorporated and established a SEP with a calendar-year plan year. For purposes of determining whether the corporate SEP is top heavy for its 2012 plan year, the terminated Keogh plan and the corporate SEP would be part of a required aggregation group. By Design and By Design Inc. would be treated as a single employer under Code Section 414(c). The terminated plan would be aggregated with the corporate SEP because it was maintained within the five-year period ending on the determination date for the 2012 plan year and because, but for the fact that it terminated, it would be aggregated with the corporate plan because it covered a key employee (see Q 8:16).

Q 8:12 Must a collectively bargained plan be aggregated with other plans of an employer to determine whether some or all of the employer's plans are top heavy?

Yes. A collectively bargained plan that includes a key employee of an employer must be included in the required aggregation group for that employer. [Treas. Reg. § 1.416-1, Q&A T-6]

Q 8:13 What plans will be treated as top heavy if they are part of a required aggregation group that is top heavy?

For plans that must be aggregated, each plan in the required aggregation group (see Q 8:11) will be top heavy if the group is top heavy. Obviously, no plan in the required aggregation group will be top heavy if the group is not top heavy.

Q 8:14 What types of SEPs are likely to be top heavy?

Integrated SEPs and SARSEPs may be top heavy. Situations in which the employer has more than one plan or had a defined benefit plan that has been terminated may also cause a SEP to be top heavy. Plans of smaller businesses and plans with many owners tend to be or are designed to be top heavy.

Treatment of Various Plans

Q 8:15 Are multiemployer plans and multiple-employer plans subject to the top-heavy requirements of Code Section 416?

Yes. Multiemployer plans described in Code Section 414(f) and multiple-employer plans described in Code Section 413(c), to which an employer makes contributions on behalf of its employees, are treated as plans of that employer to the extent that benefits under the plan are provided to employees of the employer because of service with that employer. [Treas. Reg. § 1.416-1, Q&A T-2]

Q 8:16 How is a *terminated plan* treated for purposes of the top-heavy rules?

A terminated plan is treated the same as any other plan for purposes of the top-heavy rules. A *terminated plan* is a plan that has been formally terminated, has ceased crediting service for benefit accruals and vesting, and has been or is distributing all plan assets to participants or their beneficiaries as soon as administratively feasible. Such a plan must be aggregated with other plans of the employer if it was maintained within the last five years ending on the determination date for the plan year in question and would, but for the fact that it terminated, be part of a required aggregation group for that plan year. Distributions that have taken place within the five years ending on the determination date must be considered. [Treas. Reg. § 1.416-1, Q&A T-4]

Q 8:17 How is a *frozen plan* treated for purposes of the top-heavy rules?

For purposes of the top-heavy rules, a frozen plan is treated the same as a nonfrozen plan. A *frozen plan* is a plan in which benefit accruals have ceased, but all assets have not been distributed to participants or their beneficiaries. Because no key employees are receiving contributions under the frozen plan, a top-heavy contribution to non-key employees is not required. [Treas. Reg. § 1.416-1, Q&A T-5]

Q 8:18 How are rollovers and plan-to-plan transfers treated when testing whether a plan is top heavy?

The rules for handling rollovers and transfers depend on whether they are unrelated (both initiated by the employee and made from a plan maintained by one employer to a plan maintained by another employer) or related (either not initiated by the employee or made from one plan to another plan maintained by the same employer). Generally, a rollover or transfer made incident to a merger or consolidation of two or more plans or the division of a single plan into two or more plans will not be treated as being initiated by the employee. The fact that the employer initiated the distribution does not mean that the rollover was not initiated by the employee. For purposes of determining whether two employers are to be treated as the same employer, all employers aggregated under Code Section 414(b), 414(c), or 414(m) are treated as the same employer.

In the case of *unrelated* rollovers and transfers, (1) the plan making the distribution or transfer is to count the distribution as part of the accrued benefit for a five-year period, and (2) the plan accepting the rollover or transfer is not to consider the rollover or transfer as part of the accrued benefit (if the rollover or transfer was accepted after Dec. 31, 1983).

In the case of *related* rollovers and transfers, (1) the plan making the distribution or transfer is not to count the distribution or transfer, and (2) the plan accepting the rollover or transfer is to count the rollover or transfer in the present value of the accrued benefits. [I.R.C. §§ 416(g)(1)–416(g)(3); Treas. Reg. § 1.416-1, Q&A T-32]

Chapter 9

Integration of Contributions with Social Security

If a SEP arrangement is integrated with Social Security, employer contributions will not be shared in proportion to compensation by employees eligible to participate for a given year. That is, in an integrated plan, contributions will favor higher paid employees: Employees who earn above a certain amount will receive a percentage of the contributions that is higher than their pro rata share of the compensation paid to all participants.

Two general methods for allocating integrated contributions are available; plan documents determine the method that must be used. The allocation formula may be changed if the employer amends the plan in a timely manner and the amendment indicates the new formula.

Integration rules for SEPs were provided when SEPs were first permitted—that is, for taxable years beginning after 1978. [I.R.C. § 408(k)(3)(D) and (E)] It should be noted that top-heavy contributions and salary reduction contributions under a SARSEP may not be integrated.

Overview

Q 9:1 How does an integrated plan work?

In theory, the integration rules avoid a duplication of benefits by not requiring that contributions be made twice on the same compensation. The retirement portion of Social Security, or self-employment tax if self-employed, covers compensation up to, but not above, a certain amount for 2012—the taxable wage base (TWB; $110,100). (See Appendix G for limits in earlier years.)

Q 9:2 How does a nonintegrated plan work?

In a nonintegrated plan, contributions do not take into account payments made into the Social Security retirement system by employers and self-employed individuals. Generally, contributions are allocated in proportion to compensation determined under applicable plan provisions. Thus, for example, if a participant's plan compensation represents 8 percent of the total plan compensation of all eligible employees, that participant will receive 8 percent of any employer contributions made for that year.

Q 9:3 Have the SEP integration rules changed since 1979?

Yes. For taxable years beginning after 1986, Code Section 408(k)(3)(D), which provided SEP integration rules, was amended and a new participant exclusion allowance created. The new rules eliminated the coordination of nonelective contributions with employer-paid Old-Age, Survivors, and Disability Insurance (OASDI) contributions under Code Section 3111. [I.R.C. §§ 401(l), 402(h), 408(k)(3)]

Note. The OASDI limit (5.7 percent) under Code Section 3111 was not changed by the Patient Protection and Affordable Care Act (PPACA) [Pub. L. No. 111-148] as amended by the Health Care and Education Reconciliation Act. [Pub. L. No. 111-152]

Note. Before 1987, the contribution allocated to each eligible employee was permitted to be reduced (offset) by the employer's share of the OASDI tax. [I.R.C. § 408(k)(3)(D), as it then existed; I.R.C. § 3111(a)] The employer's SEP contribution (expressed as a uniform percentage of compensation) for each employee was reduced (offset) by the employer-paid OASDI tax. Assume it is 1987, the taxable base is $43,800, and the OASDI rate is 5.7 percent. The employer establishes an integrated SEP for its only two employees: Jill, earning $80,000, and Dee, earning $14,000. The employer contributes the maximum percentage (15 percent in 1987). The integration level is set at $15,000. The employees' integrated contribution under the pre-1987 offset integration rules can be computed as follows.

Jill: $12,000 (.15 × $80,000) reduced by $855 (.057 × $15,000) = $11,145.

Dee: $2,100 (.15 × $14,000) reduced by $798 (.057 × $14,000) = $1,302.

In place of those "offset" rules, SEPs became subject to the new rules applicable to defined contribution plans, which allowed "permitted disparity" between the contribution percentages applicable to compensation below and compensation above the TWB (see Q 9:10). Although the new qualified plan integration rules—now made applicable to SEPs—do not require any reduction, as the prior rules did, the new participant exclusion limit in part created a new reduction (offset) that is applied to the maximum annual SEP contribution limit ($50,000 for plan years beginning in 2012 instead of to the actual contribution amount allocated to the employee as under the prior rules. [I.R.C. § 402(h)(2)(B)] Thus, the maximum contribution dollar limit is reduced to the extent of the integrated contribution (see Q 9:5).

In addition, the maximum reduction rate under the prior rules was fixed at the OASDI rate under Code Section 3111(a). Under the new rules, the statutory rate is the rate attributable to the old age insurance only portion of OASDI (5.7 percent after 1990), but it must be adjusted downward when the integration level is set at an amount lower than the TWB and above 20 percent of the taxable wage base (see Q 9:12). [Treas. Reg. § 1.401(a)(4)-7 (T.D. 8360, 56 Fed. Reg. 47,568 (Sept. 19, 1991), corrected by 57 Fed. Reg. 4,719 (Feb. 7, 1992); T.D. 8485, 58 Fed. Regs. 46,773–46,828 (Sept. 3, 1993)); Treas. Reg. § 1.401(l)-2 (T.D. 8359, 56 Fed. Reg. 47,614 (Sept. 19, 1991), corrected by 57 Fed. Reg. 10,818 (Mar. 31, 1992), 57 Fed. Reg. 10,951 (Mar. 31, 1992); *amended by* T.D. 8486, 58 Fed. Reg. 46,828–46,835 (Sept. 3, 1993))]

When the intent is to place a $50,000 limit on total retirement contributions, the foregoing interpretation seems to make sense as a policy matter—it puts the amount deemed to be contributed by the employer under Social Security into the same category as the SEP contributions. Notwithstanding that the IRS has approved SEP arrangements that provide for a nondiscriminatory contribution of a flat dollar amount per hour for each participant [Ltr. Ruls. 8824019, 8441067], the interpretation presented above is also in keeping with the structure of Code Section 408(k)(3), which, while calling for a uniform percentage to be contributed under the SEP arrangement, in effect allows the employer to consider FICA contributions to be SEP contributions.

Note. The $50,000 or $50,000 (as reduced) limit on allocations for 2012 may be increased by as much as $5,500 with catch-up contributions if age 50 or older in an elective SEP (SARSEP) (see Qs 11:5, 12:55).

Q 9:4 Was the reduction that applied to all participants in the original integration rules retained under the new rules?

Yes and no. When originally enacted in 1978, the reduction to the annual contribution amount applied to all eligible employees, including owners. [Prop. Treas. Reg. § 1.408-8(d)] The new reduction under the participant exclusion limit (see Q 11:1) applies only to a highly compensated employee (HCE) (see Q 1:14). Thus, after 1986, a reduction is applied to limit the maximum permitted SEP contribution (see Q 9:3) that can be made on behalf of an HCE (see Q 1:14 for definition).

Practice Pointer. The reduction (offset) does not apply to qualified plans. A qualified defined contribution plan may generally provide an HCE with an integrated contribution allocation of $50,000 (the 2012 limit), plus catch-up contributions if age 50 or older in an elective SEP.

Q 9:5 How is the reduced annual exclusion limit computed in the case of a highly compensated employee?

The reduction to the $50,000 annual exclusion limit in an integrated SEP is equal to the plan's spread percentage (see Qs 6:5, 9:9) multiplied by the HCE's compensation not in excess of the plan's integration level or the TWB, whichever is less (see Q 9:7). Compensation in excess of $250,000 (the limit for plan years beginning in 2012 limit) is not considered.

For 2012, using an integration level of $110,100 (with the maximum 5.7 percent offset) produces a limit of $43,724.30 ($50,000 *reduced by* the maximum integration level of $110,100 *multiplied by* .057) ($49,224.30 with catch-up contributions if age 50 or older). The following chart contains examples of typical maximum limits for 2012.

Plan Integration Level	*Percent of TWB*	*Max Spread*[1]	*Adjusted $50,000 Limit*[2]
$110,100	100%	5.7%	$43,724.30
$ 88,081	80%+$1	5.4	$45,243.63
$ 55,050	50%	4.3	$47,632.85
$ 22,020	20%	5.7	$48,744.86
$ 10,000	9.082652%	5.7	$ 49,430
$ 1	0.000908265%	5.7	$49,999.94

[1] The maximum spread is 5.7% when the integration level is equal to the TWB or is set at 20% of TWB or less. The maximum 5.7% spread is reduced to 5.4% when the integration level is less than the TWB and more than 80% of the TWB. If the integration level is set at more than 20% of the TWB but does not exceed 80% of the TWB, the maximum spread is 4.3%. Thus, if a SEP is integrated at 50 percent of the 20120 TWB ($55,050), the resulting maximum HCE allocation would be $47,632.85 ($50,000 reduced by ($110,100 × .50 × .043)). [I.R.C. §§ 401(l)(2), 408(k)(3)(D)]

[2] Catch-up contributions for individual age 50 or older may be contributed in addition to the $50,000 or $50,000 (as reduced if integrated) limit. [I.R.C. § 414(v)(3)(A)]

Practice Pointer. With few employees or when employees do not earn significant amounts, it may be necessary to determine the additional nonowner cost to provide an owner with a $50,000 contribution instead of the reduced limit. The additional cost of the nonowner contributions may be insignificant, especially if there is more than one owner.

Example 1. The Darn Knit Store established a SEP for its employees. Under the plan, contributions are integrated with Social Security. The plan's integration level is set at $10,000 (9.082652% of the TWB) for 2012 and uses the maximum permitted spread of 5.7 percent. Donna Darn, the owner, has W-2 compensation of $250,000. Mona, the only employee, earns $10,000. Darn Knit contributes the smallest amount ($50,860) that will result in an allocation to Donna of $49,430 (her maximum for 2012, see above). When the contribution is expressed as a formula, it results in a contribution of 14.3 percent of compensation plus 5.7 percent of compensation (the spread) in excess of $10,000 (the integration level).

a. Donna receives a contribution of $49,430 ($250,000 × .143) + (($250,000 – $10,000) × .057). Mona will receive $1,430 ($10,000 × .143).

b. Hypothetically, if the plan were not integrated, Donna could receive a contribution of $50,000 ($250,000 × .20). Mona could receive $2,000 ($10,000 × .20).

Analysis. The difference in plan costs is $1,140 ($52,000 – $50,860). For Donna to receive an additional $570 ($50,000 – $49,430) under a nonintegrated plan, an additional nonowner contribution of an equal amount would be required. From Donna's point of view, the additional cost is only 50 percent effective ($570/$1,140); an integrated plan may be a better alternative for the Darn Knit Store.

Example 2. Beaver Hat Shop established a SEP for its employees. Under the plan, contributions are integrated with Social Security. The plan's integration level is set at the TWB ($110,100) for 2012 and uses the maximum permitted spread of 5.7 percent. Clarence, the owner, has compensation of $250,000. Joe, the sole employee, earns $15,000. Beaver Hat contributes the smallest amount ($45,869.30), which will result in an allocation to Clarence of $43,724.30 (his maximum for 2012). When the contribution is expressed as a formula, it results in a contribution of 14.3 percent of compensation plus 5.7 percent of compensation (the spread) in excess of $110,100 (the integration level)

a. Clarence receives a contribution of $43,724.30 ($250,000 × .143) + (($250,000 – $110,100) × .057). Joe would receive $2,145 ($15,000 × .143).

b. Hypothetically, if the plan were not integrated, Clarence could receive a contribution of $50,000 ($250,000 × .20). Joe could receive $3,000 ($15,000 × .20). Hypothetical plan cost is $53,000.

Analysis. The difference in plan costs is $7,130.70 ($53,000 – $45,869.30). For Clarence to receive an additional $6,275.70 ($50,000 – $43,724.30) under a nonintegrated plan would require an additional nonowner contribution of $855 ($3,000 – $2,145). From Clarence's point of view, the additional cost is 88 percent effective ($6,275/$7,130); an integrated plan may be a better alternative for the Beaver Hat Shop.

Example 3. The facts are the same as those in Example 2, except that there are five employees with compensation of $30,000.

a. Clarence receives the same contribution of $43,724.30. Each of the employees would receive $4,290 ($30,000 × .143). Total plan cost is $65,174.30.

b. Hypothetically, if the plan were not integrated, Clarence could receive a contribution of $50,000. Each of the employees would receive $6,000 ($30,000 × .2). Hypethetical plan cost is $80,000.

Analysis. The difference in plan costs is $14,825.70 ($80,000 – $65,174.30). For Clarence to receive an additional $6,275.70 ($50,000 – $43,724.30) under a nonintegrated plan would require an additional nonowner contribution of $8,550 (($6,000 – $4,290) × 5). Because there are more employees and/or higher levels of compensation, Clarence would receive only 42.3 percent ($6,275/ $14,825) of the additional $14,825.70. Clarence is likely to find the integrated plan the more efficient method of allocating employer contributions.

(See Appendix H for illustrations of the preceding examples.)

In the previous examples, the maximum contribution limit of $50,000 in the case of the HCE is being reduced. Non-highly compensated employee (NHCE) contributions are not being reduced. NHCEs are merely receiving the allocation percentage provided under the integrated plan. If the amounts contributed by the employers in the above examples were increased, only the allocations of the NHCEs would be increased.

Practice Pointer. Only an NHCE can receive an allocation of $50,000 in an integrated SEP. For example, at an integration level of $110,100 (the TWB for 2012) and with compensation of $174,897.18 or more, an HCE is limited to a SEP allocation of $43,724.30 (see previous examples). However, an NHCE earning $200,000 or more (for the current year—2012, but not previous year—2011) could receive an allocation of $50,000 ($55,500 with catch-up contributions if age 50 or older) in an integrated SEP plan for 2012.

Q 9:6 Can a nonintegrated, nonelective SEP be top heavy?

It depends. If a nonintegrated, nonelective SEP is the only plan that has ever been maintained by the employer, it cannot be top heavy. Inasmuch as no disparity (see Q 9:9) exists in contributions based on earnings above and below a certain point, the minimum required top-heavy contribution rules will always be satisfied. [I.R.C. §§ 416(g)(1)(A)(ii), 416(g)(2)(B), 416(i)(6)(B)] If, however, the employer maintains other plans (whether or not terminated) or allows employees to make elective salary reduction contributions, the arrangement may be top heavy (see Qs 8:1, 8:9) or may be treated as top heavy (see Q 3:16).

Q 9:7 What effect do the top-heavy rules have on an integrated SEP?

If a SEP arrangement is integrated with Social Security but is not top heavy (does not primarily benefit key employees; see Q 8:10), no minimum contribution is required beyond the amount required to satisfy the integration rules themselves. If, on the other hand, the integrated SEP arrangement is top heavy, the employer is required to make a minimum contribution to every non-key employee. [IRS News Release IR-96-43]

For 2012, the term *key employee* (see Qs 1:35, 8:7) generally includes employees who, at any time during the plan year, were

1. Officers earning over $165,000,
2. More than 5 percent owners, or
3. More than 1 percent owners earning more than $150,000.

[I.R.C. § 416(i)(1)(A)]

Caution. The Code Section 318 attribution rules apply (see Q 8:7).

Q 9:8 Are integrated SEPs discriminatory?

No. It is true that SEP contributions may not discriminate in favor of HCEs, as defined in Code Section 414(q); however, integration is intended to prevent a duplication of benefits and is specifically authorized. [I.R.C. § 408(k)(3)(D)] Under Code Section 402(h)(2)(B), the maximum amount that may be excluded from an HCE's gross income, $50,000 ($55,500 with catch-up contributions if age 50 or older) for 2012, is reduced if the plan is integrated with Social Security (see Q 9:5).

Allocating Integrated Contributions

Q 9:9 What are the fundamental terms used in the discussion of allocation of contributions in an integrated SEP?

When a SEP arrangement is integrated with Social Security, the percentage contributed (rate) on compensation above a certain amount (the *integration level*) is higher than the percentage contributed on compensation at or below that amount. The difference between the two rates is called the *spread* or the *disparity rate*. The compensation in excess of the integration level is referred to as *excess compensation*, and the compensation at or below the integration level is referred to as *base compensation*.

Q 9:10 What is the maximum integration level permitted?

The integration level cannot exceed the TWB (see Q 9:1) in effect at the *beginning* of the plan year ($110,100 for 2012). (See Appendix G for limits in earlier years.) The integration level may be changed by plan amendment; it may also be designed to change automatically whenever the TWB is increased (see Q 9:21).

Example. A SEP is established on a fiscal year basis that begins on December 1. For the plan year ending November 30, 2012, the maximum integration level that may be used is $106,800 (the 2011 limit). $110,100 is the maximum integration level that may be used for plan years beginning in 2012.

Caution. The integration level should not be changed if any contributions have been made for the year. Because contributions must be made under a definite written plan formula, a midyear change after a contribution has been made may cause the plan to be discriminatory in operation and may create excess contributions under the plan (see Q 5:26). In other cases, the plan may be amended before the contribution is made and up until the due date of the business's tax return, including extensions.

Q 9:11 What is the maximum *spread*, or *disparity rate*, permitted in an integrated SEP?

The *spread,* or *disparity rate,* is the difference between the excess and base contribution percentages. The excess contribution percentage (the rate of contributions made to the plan by the employer with respect to compensation above the integration level, expressed as a percentage of such compensation) may not exceed the base contribution percentage (the rate of contributions made to the plan by the employer with respect to compensation at or below the integration level, expressed as a percentage of such compensation) by more than the lesser of (1) the base contribution percentage or (2) 5.7 percent. [I.R.C. § 401(l)(2)(A)] The 5.7 percent factor must be reduced under certain circumstances (see Q 9:12).

In light of the foregoing, the following, for example, would be true:

1. A contribution formula of 10 percent below and 20 percent above a specified dollar level would violate the "lesser of" rules.
2. A contribution formula of 2 percent below and 4 percent above a specified dollar level would be permitted, but the plan might be top heavy.
3. A contribution formula of 3 percent below and 6 percent above a specified dollar level would be permitted.
4. A contribution formula of 6 percent below and 12 percent above a specified dollar level would violate the 5.7 percent rule.

Q 9:12 When must the 5.7 percent maximum spread, or disparity rate, be reduced?

The maximum spread, or disparity rate, of 5.7 percent depends on the integration level selected for the plan year. A rate of 5.7 percent may be used when the plan is integrated at the TWB or the integration level is set at 20 percent or less of the TWB. If, however, the integration level is set above $10,000 (or, if greater, 20 percent of the TWB) and below the TWB, the maximum spread factor of 5.7 percent must be reduced. Table 9-1 summarizes the applicable rules.

Table 9-1. Adjusting the Maximum Disparity Rate

If the integration level is more than	*But not more than*	*The 5.7% maximum disparity rate is reduced to*
The greater of $10,000 or 20% of the TWB	80% of the TWB	4.3%
80% of the TWB	An amount less than 100% of the TWB	5.4%

Based on the 2012 TWB of $110,100, the maximum 5.7 percent spread would be reduced, as summarized in Table 9-2.

Table 9-2. Adjustments Based on 2012 TWB of $ 110,100

If the integration level is more than	*But not more than*	*The 5.7% maximum disparity rate*
$ 0	$ 22,020	Remains at 5.7%
$22,020	$ 88,080	Is reduced to 4.3%
$88,080	$110,099	Is reduced to 5.4%
n/a	$110,100	Remains at 5.7%

Q 9:13 Must the contribution rates above and at or below the selected integration level be uniform for all participants?

Yes. Treasury Regulations Section 1.401(l)-2(c) requires that the excess contribution percentage exceed the base contribution percentage by an amount that is uniform for all participants. There is, however, an exception for special employees (other than self-employed individuals) who are not subject to FICA taxes—that is, employees for whom the employer makes no Social Security contributions (see Q 9:15).

> **Example.** An integrated plan formula provides for a contribution of 2 percent of compensation up to $10,000 and 4 percent of compensation in excess of $10,000. The plan is not top heavy. For all employees, the contribution rate for compensation above the integration level is 4 percent, and the contribution rate for compensation at or below the integration level is 2 percent. The excess contribution percentage therefore exceeds the base contribution percentage by an amount that is uniform for all participants.

Q 9:14 Is the uniformity rule violated if a key employee with compensation at or below the plan's integration level does not receive a top-heavy contribution that is made to other employees who earn the same amount?

No. A contribution that is made under the top-heavy rules is required to be made to non-key employees. Because the contribution is required under the top-heavy rules, the introduction of a third percentage does not violate the uniformity rule for an integrated plan. Introduction of a third percentage, relative to the integration level, can occur if the base contribution percentage is less than 3 percent and the plan is top heavy. In such a case, the minimum required top-heavy contribution may be made to some but not necessarily all employees with compensation at or below the plan's integration level.

Example. Lorenzo and Ben are key employees in Tiny Corporation's integrated SEP. Lorenzo earns $50,000, and Ben earns $10,000. Asia, the only other eligible employee, earns $10,000 and is not a key employee. The integrated plan formula calls for contribution rates of 2 percent of compensation up to $10,000 and 4 percent of compensation in excess of $10,000. Further, Tiny Corporation must make a 3 percent contribution to satisfy the top-heavy rules.

The compensation, contribution, and contribution rate for each of the two employees (Ben and Asia) who earn an amount equal to the integration level ($10,000) are shown in Table 9-3. The rate of contribution for Ben is 2 percent, and the rate of contribution for Asia is 5 percent. Lorenzo will receive a 4 percent contribution on his excess compensation. Lorenzo's 4 percent excess contribution percentage does not exceed the base contribution percentage by an amount that is uniform for all participants. Thus, if a top-heavy contribution is required to be made for Asia, and if key employees Lorenzo and Ben earn below the TWB, the key employees get a lower contribution percentage than the non-key employee with compensation at or below the integration level. In such a circumstance, the introduction of a third percentage does not cause the uniformity rule to be violated.

Table 9-3. Uniformity Rule Satisfied with Third Rate

Employee	*A Compensation*	*B 3% Top-Heavy Contribution on Base Compensation*	*C 2% Contribution on Base Compensation*	*Percentage Rate on Base Compensation (B + C) ÷ A*
Ben	$10,000	n/a (key employee)	$200 ($10,000 × .02)	2%
Asia	$10,000	$300 ($10,000 × .03)	$200 ($10,000 × .02)	5%

Q 9:15 May a non-FICA employee receive a percentage of compensation that falls below the plan's excess contribution percentage?

No. For each employee under an integrated SEP for whom no tax under Code Section 3111(a), 3221, or 1401 is required to be paid, employer contributions must be allocated to the account of the employee with respect to the employee's total plan-year compensation at the excess contribution percentage rate. That is, if the employer does not pay employment, railroad retirement, or self-employment taxes on behalf of an eligible employee, contributions must be allocated to the account of the employee at the excess contribution percentage rate. [Treas. Reg. § 1.401(l)-2(c)(2)(iii)]

Example. Fern owns and operates a successful business, Fernway, and employs her 17-year-old son Tommy on a full-time basis. Tommy earns $30,000. Because Tommy is under the age of 18 and is in the employ of his parent, his income is not subject to employment taxes. [I.R.C. § 3121(b)(3)(A)] Fernway maintains an integrated SEP, and this year it will contribute 5 percent of compensation up to $17,000 and 10 percent of compensation that is in excess of $17,000. The contribution for Tommy will not be integrated. He will receive $3,000 ($30,000 × .10) because Fernway is not subject to employment taxes on Tommy's wages.

Note. Presumably, contributions must also be allocated to the account of a non-FICA employee at the excess contribution percentage in the unlikely event that the employee's cumulative permitted disparity years exceed 35 (see Q 9:22). [*See* I.R.C. §§ 1402(c), 1402(e), 3121(b)]

Q 9:16 What are some rules of thumb for selecting an appropriate integration level?

Selecting an appropriate integration level to meet the employer's goal and spread requires careful analysis. Nevertheless, for 2012 contributions, the following rules of thumb may be considered:

1. The integration level should be set at the amount of compensation below which the employer does not want to contribute the maximum employer contribution, but not more than the current TWB (see Q 9:1).
2. The guidelines presented in Table 9-4 should be taken into consideration.
3. These figures should always be tried: $110,100 (the 2012 TWB), $88,081 (80 percent of the TWB + $1), $22,020 (20 percent of the TWB) or less.
4. If a spread greater than 4.3 percent is used, it should be determined whether the integration level selected falls within the compensation bands for that year (see Table 9-4). If 5.7 percent is used, it should be determined whether the integration level should be set at $110,100, or at $22,020 or less.
5. Owners with slightly higher compensation than employees should consider using a 5.7 percent spread at the $22,020 level (or less).
6. Several approaches should be tried.

Obviously, nonowners will not always fall into convenient compensation bands. At any given contribution amount, aggregate contributions and the effective contribution rate for the group of employees being favored will fluctuate as the various combinations of integration level and spread are applied. Setting the integration level at an amount equal to the highest paid employee that the employer does not want to favor does not always result in the most efficient plan (see Q 9:19, examples). It does not result in the lowest overall cost at the specified contribution level. Software is available that can determine the most efficient integration level. [*See http://www.BenefitsLink.com/GSL* (visited on Aug. 22, 2012)] If the integration level is changed, the employer must amend the plan before the contribution is made.

Table 9-4. Guidelines for Determining the 2012 Integration Amount

If all nonowners earn	*Maximum spread factor is*
$110,100	5.7%
$88,081–$110,099	5.4%
$22,020–$88,080	4.3%
$22,020 or less	5.7%

Q 9:17 How may a participant receive a contribution percentage greater than the base contribution percentage?

Generally, the only way that a participant may receive a contribution percentage greater than the base contribution percentage (aside from increasing the base contribution percentage or making elective contributions) is to earn more than the plan's integration level (see Qs 9:14, 9:15).

Q 9:18 How are contributions allocated in an integrated plan?

An integrated SEP may provide for contributions to be allocated by formula or, in the case of contributions of a fixed dollar amount, by use of the "four-step" method (see Q 9:20).

Both allocation methods produce the same results when the amount contributed equals or exceeds 3 percent of aggregate compensation. When the amount contributed falls below 3 percent, however, the four-step method does not provide for integration; that is, everyone first receives an identical contribution of up to 3 percent of compensation before integration takes effect. In contrast, the formula method would, for example, allow participants to receive a contribution of 2 percent of compensation, plus an additional 2 percent contribution on excess compensation, unless the plan was top heavy. If the plan was top heavy, the employer would have to provide a minimum contribution (generally 3 percent) to each non-key employee in any event. Thus, the four-step method always satisfies the top-heavy rules (see chapter 8).

Allocation by Formula Method

Q 9:19 How are contributions to an integrated SEP allocated by formula?

Using the basic rules set forth previously (see Qs 9:9–9:12), contributions are made to employees in accordance with the formula contained in the plan.

Example 1. The owners of Bonefish, Inc., will have earned 66.67 percent of the total compensation paid to all eligible employees during 2012. Bonefish will make a $30,000 SEP contribution that is equal to 10 percent of the corporate payroll. Because the plan is not integrated, the owners receive 66.67 percent of the $30,000 contribution being made, as listed in Table 9-5.

Table 9-5. Nonintegrated SEP: Contributions Shared Equally

Employee	*Wages*	*10% of All Wages*	*Total Plan Contribution*	*Percentage of Wages*	*Percentage of Contribution*
Owners:					
Joe	$100,000.00	$10,000.00	$10,000.00	10	33.33
Sally	100,000.00	10,000.00	10,000.00	10	33.33
Subtotals			20,000.00		66.67
Nonowners:					
Ruth	30,000.00	3,000.00	3,000.00	10	10.00
Tom	25,000.00	2,500.00	2,500.00	10	8.33
Ned	20,000.00	2,000.00	2,000.00	10	6.67
Lee	15,000.00	1,500.00	1,500.00	10	5.00
Sarah	10,000.00	1,000.00	1,000.00	10	3.33
Subtotals			$10,000.00		33.33
Grand Totals			$30,000.00		100.00

Example 2. Bonefish, Inc., will make a $30,000 SEP contribution integrated at an amount equal to the highest paid employee's compensation that Bonefish does not wish to favor (in this case, $30,000). The contribution can be expressed as 7.9933330 percent of compensation up to $30,000, plus 12.2933330 percent of compensation in excess of $30,000. (This formula could also be expressed as follows: 7.9933330 percent of all compensation, plus 4.3 percent of compensation in excess of $30,000.)

Here, the integrated formula provides each owner with a larger contribution amount and a higher percentage (73) of the overall contribution, as presented in Table 9-6. (See Appendix H.) However, the integration level precludes the use of the maximum 5.7 percent spread (see Q 9:16). A more effective plan could be designed (see Example 3), the contribution ($30,000) could be optimized (see Example 4), or the owners could receive the maximum permitted contribution (25 percent) in an integrated plan (see Example 5).

Table 9-6. Integrated SEP with a $30,000 Contribution, $30,000 Integration Level, 4.3% Spread

Employee	*Wages*	*7.9933317% on First $30,000 of Wages*	*12.2933317 7% on Excess Above $30,000*	*Total Plan Contribution*	*Percentage of Wages*	*Percentage of Contribution*
Owners:						
Joe	$100,000.00	$2,398.00	$8,605.33	$11,003.33	11.00	36.678
Sally	100,000.00	2,398.00	8,605.33	11,003.33	11.00	36.678
Subtotals				$22,006.66		73.356
Nonowners:						
Ruth	30,000.00	2,398.00	0.00	2,398.00	7.99	7.993
Tom	25,000.00	1,998.33	0.00	1,998.33	7.99	6.661
Ned	20,000.00	1,598.67	0.00	1,598.67	7.99	5.329
Lee	15,000.00	1,199.00	0.00	1,199.00	7.99	3.997
Sarah	10,000.00	799.33	0.00	733.34	7.99	2.664
Subtotals				$ 7,993.34		26.644
Grand Totals				$30,000.00		100.00

Example 3. Bonefish's contribution has been lowered to 3 percent (satisfying all top-heavy rules), and the maximum spread of 3 percent is used (lesser of 5.7 percent or the 3 percent base contribution percentage; see Q 9:11). The plan is integrated at $32,040. The formula becomes 3 percent of compensation up to $32,040, plus 6 percent of compensation in excess of $32,040. (This formula could also be expressed as follows: 3 percent of all compensation, plus 3 percent of compensation in excess of $32,040.) Although the overall contribution has been more than halved, the percentage going to the owners has increased to over 77 percent, creating a more favorable outcome ("effective contribution") for the two owners. (See Appendix H.)

Table 9-7. Integrated SEP with 3 Percent/6 Percent to Satisfy Top-Heavy Rules

Employee	*Wages*	*3% on First $ 32,040 of Wages*	*6% on Excess Above $32,040*	*Total Plan Contribution*	*Percentage of Wages*	*Percentage of Contribution*
Owners:						
Joe	$100,000.00	$961.20	$4,077.60	$ 5,038.80	5.04	38.53
Sally	100,000.00	961.20	4,077.60	5,038.80	5.04	38.53
Subtotals				$10,077.60		77.06

Table 9-7. Integrated SEP with 3 Percent/6 Percent to Satisfy Top-Heavy Rules (*cont'd*)

Employee	*Wages*	*3% on First $ 32,040 of Wages*	*6% on Excess Above $32,040*	*Total Plan Contribution*	*Percentage of Wages*	*Percentage of Contribution*
Nonowners:						
Ruth	30,000.00	900.00	0.00	900.00	3.00	6.88
Tom	25,000.00	750.00	0.00	750.00	3.00	5.73
Ned	20,000.00	$600.00	0.00	600.00	3.00	4.59
Lee	15,000.00	450.00	0.00	450.00	3.00	3.44
Sarah	10,000.00	300.00	0.00	300.00	3.00	2.29
Subtotals				$ 3,000		22.94
Grand Totals				$13,077.60		100.00

Example 4. To optimize the contribution in favor of higher-paid individuals, Bonefish uses an integration level of $22,020 (20 percent of the TWB) and contributes $30,000, the same amount as in the previous examples). Each of the owners receives a higher contribution ($11,273) at this integration level. No other integration level would allocate more than $11,273 to each owner with an overall contribution of $30,000. The maximum spread of 5.7 percent is used. The resulting formula can be expressed as 6.828519 percent of compensation plus 5.7 percent of compensation in excess of $22,020. (See Appendix H.)

Table 9-8. Integrated SEP with Optimized $30,000 Contribution

Employee	*Wages*	*6.828519 % on Total Wages*	*5.7% on Excess Wages Above $22,020*	*Total Plan Contribution*	*Percentage of Wages*	*Percentage of Contribution*
Owners:						
Joe	$100,000.00	$6,828.52	$4,444.86	$11,273.38	11.3	37.6
Sally	100,000.00	6,828,52	4,444.86	11,273.38	11.3	37.6
Subtotals				$22,546.76		75.2
Nonowners:						
Ruth	30,000.00	2,048.56	454.86	2,503.42	8.3	8.3
Tom	25,000.00	1,707.12	169.86	1,876.99	7.5	6.3
Ned	20,000.00	1,365.70	0.00	1,365.70	6.8	4.5
Lee	15,000.00	1,024.28	0.00	1,024.28	6.8	3.4
Sarah	10,000.00	682.85	0.00	682.85	6.8	2.3
Subtotals				$ 7,453.24		24.8
Grand Totals				$30,000.00		100.00

The owners, Joe and Sally, receive the greatest percentage (75%) of the $30,000 contribution when the contributions are allocated at the $22,020 level. Table 9-9 reflects the percentage of the $30,000 contribution that would be allocated to the owners at different integration levels.

Table 9-9. $30,000 Allocation to Owners at Different Integration Levels

Integration Level	*Amount to Each Owner*	*Contribution Percentage to Owners*[1]
$0[2]	$10,000.00	66.67%
1	10,000.07	66.67
11,010	10,818	72.12
22,020	11,273	75.16 (highest)
33,030	10,960	73.07
44,040	10,802	72.01
55,050	10,664	70.96
66,060	10,486	69.91
77,070	10,329	68.86
88,080	10,170	67.81
99,090	10,016	66.78
110,100	10,000.00	66.67

[1] Maximum permitted spread used in each instance.

[2] Nonintegrated plan.

Example 5. For Bonefish, Inc., to maximize contributions to owners at 25 percent of compensation, it selected an integration level of $22,020 (20 percent of the TWB) and contributed $71,179.85, as listed in Table 9-10. (Selecting an integration level above $22,020 and below $110,100 would require the maximum spread to be reduced to 5.4 percent or 4.3 percent, whichever was applicable, and (in this case) would decrease the percentage of contribution allocated to the owners.)

Table 9-10. Integrated SEP with 5.7 Percent Maximum Spread, $71,179.85 Contribution

Employee	*Wages*	*20.555136% on Total Wages*	*5.7% Wages Above $22,020*	*Total Plan Contribution*	*Percentage of Wages*	*Percentage of Contribution*
Owners:						
Joe	$100,000.00	$20,555.14	$4,444.86	$25,000.00	25.00	35.12
Sally	100,000.00	20,555.14	4,444.86	25,000.00	25.00	35.12
Subtotals				$50,000.00		70.24

Table 9-10. Integrated SEP with 5.7 Percent Maximum Spread, $71,179.85 Contribution (*cont'd*)

Employee	*Wages*	*20.555136% on Total Wages*	*5.7% Wages Above $22,020*	*Total Plan Contribution*	*Percentage of Wages*	*Percentage of Contribution*
Nonowners:						
Ruth	30,000.00	6,166.54	454.86	6,621.40	22.07	9.30
Tom	25,000.00	5,138.78	$169.86	5,308.64	21.24	7.46
Ned	20,000.00	4,111.03	0.00	4,111.03	20.56	5.78
Lee	15,000.00	3,083.27	0.00	3,083.27	20.56	4.33
Sarah	10,000.00	2,055.51	0.00	2,055.51	20.56	2.89
Subtotals				$21,179.85		29.76
Grand Totals				$71,179.85		100.00

The owners, Joe and Sally, receive the maximum permitted contribution percentage (25%) of the $71,179.85 contribution when the contributions are allocated at the $22,020 level. Other integration levels would not be as effective. Table 9-11 reflects the amount and percentage of a $71,179.85 contribution that would be allocated to the owners at different integration levels.

Table 9-11. $71,179.85 Allocation to Owners at Different Integration Levels

Integration Level	*Amount to Owners*	*Contribution Percentage to Owners*[1]
$0[2]	$23,726.62	66.67%
1	23,726.69	66.7
11,010	24,544.19	68.9
22,020	25,000.00	70.2 (highest)
33,030	24,686.52	69.4
44,040	24,528.71	68.9
55,050	24,370.90	68.5
66,060	24,213.09	68.0
77,070	24,055.28	67.6
88,080	23,897.47	67.2
99,090	23,743.00	66.7
110,100	23,726.62	66.7

[1] Maximum permitted spread used in each instance.

[2] Nonintegrated plan.

Four-Step Allocation Method

Q 9:20 How are integrated contributions allocated when the contribution amount is known?

If the amount to be contributed is known, the contribution can be allocated in four steps. (See Q 9:19, Example 3.)

Step 1. Contributions are allocated to each participant's account in the ratio of each participant's total compensation to all participant's total compensation, but not in excess of 3 percent of each participant's compensation.

Step 2. Any contributions remaining after the allocation in step 1 are allocated to each participant's account in the ratio of each participant's compensation in excess of the integration level to the excess compensation of all participants, but not in excess of 3 percent of each participant's compensation in excess of the integration level.

Step 3. Any contributions remaining after the allocation in step 2 are allocated to each participant's account in the ratio of the sum of each participant's total compensation plus compensation in excess of the integration level to the sum of all participants' total compensation plus compensation in excess of the integration level, but not in excess of the maximum disparity rate multiplied by the sum of each participant's total compensation plus compensation in excess of the integration level. For 2012, the maximum disparity rate is equal to the lesser of

a. 2.7 percent (the 5.7 percent maximum is reduced by the 3 percent allocated in step 2) or

b. The applicable percentage determined in accordance with Tables 9-12 and 9-13.

Using the 2012 TWB of $110,100, the maximum 2.7 percent spread would be reduced for other integration levels, as presented in Table 9-13.

Table 9-12. Maximum Percentage for Allocations under Step 3

If the integration level is more than	*But not more than*	*The 2.7% maximum rate disparity is reduced to*
The greater of $10,000 or 20% of the TWB	80% of the TWB	1.3%
80% of the TWB	An amount less than 100%of the TWB	2.4%

Table 9-13. Maximum Percentage for 2012 Allocations under Step 3

If the integration level is more than	*But not more than*	*The 2.7% maximum disparity rate*
$ 0.00	$ 22,020	Remains at 2.7%
$ 22,020	$ 88,080	Is reduced to 1.3%
$ 88,080	$110,099	Is reduced to 2.4%
$110,099.99	$110,100	Remains at 2.7%

Step 4. Any remaining employer contributions are allocated to each participant's account in the ratio of each participant's total compensation for the plan year to all participants' total compensation for that year, but not in excess of plan limits.

Example. A plan is integrated at $10,000; the contribution amount is $6,910. The four steps needed to allocate the contribution are listed in the following table.

Employee Compensation	*Step 1*	*Step 2*	*Step 3*	*Step 4*	*Totals (1–4)*
$10,000	$300	$0	$270 (2.7% maximum × $10,000)	10,000 ÷ 70,000 × 70 = $10	$580
$60,000	$1,800	$1,500 ($50,000 × 3%)	$2,970 (2.7% maximum × $110,000 ($60,000 + $50,000))	$60,000 ÷ 70,000 × 70 = $60	$6,330
Contribution to be allocated: $6,910	Remaining contribution: $4,810	Remaining contribution: $3,310	Remaining contribution: $70	Remaining contribution: $0	Total allocated: $6,910

Related Integration Rules

Q 9:21 May the integration level be changed?

Yes. The integration level is generally expressed as the TWB or as a percentage of the TWB. When expressed as a percentage, the integration level (and possibly the allowable spread percentage) will change automatically whenever the TWB is increased. The allocation formula and integration level may be changed provided the employer amends the plan in a timely manner (see Q 9:10) and the amendment indicates the new formula or integration level.

When the TWB or 20 percent of the TWB is not used as the integration level, the maximum spread (5.7 percent) must be reduced to either 4.3 percent or 5.4 percent (see Q 9:12).

Q 9:22 May SEP contributions be integrated with Social Security contributions indefinitely?

No. In general, the maximum period for which contributions may be integrated with Social Security contributions is 35 integration years (cumulative permitted disparity years) per employee (see Qs 9:15, 9:23). [Treas. Reg. § 1.401(l)-2(c)(2)(i) and (ii)]

Q 9:23 What are *integration years* for purposes of the maximum permitted disparity limit rules?

Integration years, or cumulative permitted disparity years, generally are the number of years credited to a participant for allocation or accrual purposes under an integrated SEP or any integrated qualified plan described in Code Section 401(a) (whether or not terminated) ever maintained by the employer. For purposes of determining a participant's cumulative permitted disparity limit, all years ending in the same calendar year are treated as the same year.

If the participant has not benefited under a defined benefit or target benefit plan for any year beginning on or after January 1, 1994, the participant has no cumulative disparity limit, and the rules are deemed satisfied. [I.R.C. § 408(k)(3)(D); Treas. Reg. §§ 1.401(l)-5(a)(3) through 1.401(l)-5(a)(5), 1.401(l)-5(c)(1)(i), 1.401(l)-5(c)(1)(ii)]

Q 9:24 May an employer have more than one integrated plan?

Yes, an employer may have more than one integrated plan, although the rules can be somewhat unwieldy. It should be noted, however, that the extent of integration may not exceed 100 percent for any year. For example, an employer contributing 6 percent of total compensation may not also provide for a 5.7 percent contribution on compensation in excess of the TWB in two separate plans; however, a contribution of 2.85 percent on compensation in excess of the TWB in two separate plans would be permitted.

If an adopting employer maintains more than one SEP or another plan in conjunction with a SEP covering any of the same employees, the employer must request a letter ruling on whether one SEP, in combination with the other SEP or other plan, satisfies the requirements of Code Section 401(l) if both plans are integrated with Social Security contributions (see also Q 3:38).

Disclosure Rules

Q 9:25 What disclosure requirements apply to a SEP that allows for integration with Social Security contributions?

A SEP arrangement that provides for integration with Social Security contributions must provide the following to each participant:

1. A statement that the employer's portion of Social Security taxes paid on behalf of a participant will be considered employer contributions under the plan's allocation formula to the participant's SEP IRA for purposes of determining the amount contributed by the employer to the participant's SEP IRA;
2. A description of the effect that integration with Social Security contributions has an employer's contributions under the SEP arrangement; and
3. The integration formula, which may also constitute part of the allocation formula mentioned in item 1.

The three requirements may be met by giving each participant a copy of the SEP agreement provided the agreement is written in a manner reasonably calculated to be understood by the average participant. [DOL Reg. §§ 2520.104-49(a)(6), 2520.104-49(b)(1)] Providing an employee with a copy of the SEP agreement does not relieve an employer from providing written notification to participants receiving contributions (see Qs 4:10, 4:15). (See Appendix C.)

Chapter 10

Deduction of SEP Contributions by Employer

Special rules determine whether contributions made under a SEP arrangement are deductible by the employer. This chapter focuses on the amount of the employer's deduction and when contributions may be claimed as a business expense. It should be noted that contributions that are deductible by the employer are not necessarily excludable from the employee's gross income (see chapter 11). In addition, the treatment of administrative fees, commissions, and wrap fees is reviewed.

Conditions for Deduction

Q 10:1 When are employer contributions deductible?

Within prescribed limits, all SEP and SARSEP contributions are deductible by the employer in accordance with the following rules:

1. In the case of a plan maintained by a calendar-year employer on a calendar-year basis, contributions are deductible for the calendar year for which the contribution is made.
2. Contributions made to a plan maintained on the basis of the employer's taxable year are deductible for the taxable year for which the contribution is made.

3. When a fiscal-year business maintains a plan on a calendar-year basis, contributions are deductible for the fiscal taxable year that includes the last day of the calendar plan year.

Note. SEP contributions are reported to the IRS by trustees and custodians for the year in which they are received, even if made with respect to the prior year.

[I.R.C. § 404(h)]

Example 1. Inner Space Corporation is a calendar-year taxpayer and adopts a calendar-year SEP for 2012. Contributions made with respect to the 2012 SEP plan year are deductible by Inner Space on its 2012 federal corporate income tax return.

Example 2. On Time Corporation adopts a SEP with a plan year that corresponds to its taxable year ending on June 30. Contributions made with respect to the plan year ending on June 30, 2012, are deductible by On Time when it timely files its federal corporate income tax return on September 15, 2012.

Example 3. La Tisane Corporation's taxable year ends on February 28. La Tisane adopts a SEP arrangement with a calendar-year plan year. On March 5, 2012, La Tisane makes a 2012 SEP contribution. La Tisane will claim its deduction on its federal corporate income tax return for the taxable year ending February 28, 2012.

Example 4. Sunset Corporation's taxable year ends on November 30. Sunset adopts a SEP arrangement with a calendar-year plan year. On April 10, 2012, Sunset makes a 2012 SEP contribution. Sunset will claim its deduction on its federal corporate income tax return for the taxable year ending November 30, 2013.

Other rules determine how much is deductible and the measuring period used to compute compensation (see Q 10:3). Elective salary reduction contributions, if permitted to be made by employees, are treated as employer contributions for deduction purposes (see Q 10:7).

Note. Provisions relating to the deductibility of employer contributions and the exclusion of those contributions from a participant's income are not required to be included in the plan document. Maxgate maintains a calendar-year SEP. The 2012 federal income tax return is due on March 15 for the 2012 tax year.

Example 5. Maxgate made its 2012 contribution on February 1, 2013, and notified the trustee that the contribution was being made for the prior year. On April 5, 2013, Maxgate is informed by its bookkeeper that it had already made a prior year contribution on January 25, 2013, and that the SEP was now overfunded by $10,000. Although the trustee/custodian will report both contributions as being made in 2013, there is no requirement that the report indicate for which year the contribution is intended to be made. Arguably, a SEP contribution made between January 1 and Monday April 15, 2013, can be for either 2012 or 2013, and Maxgate does not have a problem at all, unless participant compensation for 2013 cannot support the additional $10,000 contribution. Although issued a few years before the existence of SEPs, Revenue Ruling 76-28 [1976-1 C.B. 106] (modified slightly by Rev. Rul. 76-77 [1976-1 C.B. 107]) would appear to support such a conclusion because the language of Code Section 404(h) is similar to the "special rules for SEPs" under Code Section 404 regarding the time contributions are deemed made. [I.R.C. §§ 404(h), 404(a)(6)] On the other hand, the IRS might consider whether employees were notified that the contribution was made for the current or prior taxable year. The employer's contribution notice would have been required, in this case, by January 31, or within 30 days after the contribution is made (see Qs 4:10, 4:15). In the authors' opinion, the notice requirement should not affect the timing of the deductibility of employer contributions. Thus, employer nonelective contributions can be made after the end of the taxable year and on or before the due date of the business's federal income tax return in respect to the prior or current plan year. The IRS might argue that it would be difficult, if not impossible, to determine if and when an excess contribution was made unless the notice requirements were given some effect. No legislative history is available to support such a position. SEP contributions are reported to the IRS by trustees and custodians for the year in which they are received, even if made in respect to the prior year.

Q 10:2 Must SEP contributions meet the "ordinary" and "necessary" tests and be limited to a self-employed individual's earned income to be deducted by an employer?

Yes and no. Contributions to a SEP arrangement are made to a plan subject to Section 404 of the Internal Revenue Code (Code). Therefore, the contributions must be an ordinary and necessary business expense that relates to the production of income to be deductible. [I.R.C. §§ 404(a), 404(h)(1) (Section 162 or Section 212 test applies)]

To be deductible, as an ordinary and necessary business expense under Code Section 162(a), the activity of a trade or business must be conducted with continuity and regularity and the taxpayer's primary purpose for engaging in the activity must be for income or profit. [Vianello v. Commissioner, T.C. Memo 2010-17 (Feb. 1, 2010)]

A contribution on behalf of a self-employed individual automatically meets the ordinary and necessary business expense rules to the extent that the amount does not exceed the individual's earned income (determined without regard to the deduction for the contribution).

Example. Stone, Inc., an S corporation that reports its earnings on a calendar-year basis, maintains a SEP arrangement. Solely as a result of Stone's contribution to a SEP IRA (individual retirement arrangement) for Barney, its only employee and owner, Stone has a loss for the year. Barney's wages are reported on Form W-2, Wage and Tax Statement. To reduce any net positive income Barney may have for the current year, Stone's loss is deductible on Barney's federal individual income tax return in accordance with the applicable timing rules (see Q 10:1).

Note. For 2012, a contribution allocation of more than $50,000 ($55,500 with catch-up) is not permitted and is not allowed to be deducted. [*See* I.R.S. Notice 2011-90, 2011-47 I.R.B. 791 for 2012 limits] Contributions, including elective contributions, above the $50,000/$55,500 limits are neither "ordinary" nor "necessary."

Q 10:3 Are there percentage limits on contributions that may be deducted by an employer?

Yes. The amount that may be deducted by an employer for any plan year may not exceed 25 percent of the compensation (not in excess of $250,000 for 2012, see Q 6:22) paid to eligible employees during the plan year (15 percent before 2002), provided the plan is maintained on the basis of the employer's taxable year. If the plan year is not the same as the employer's taxable year, compensation is compensation paid to eligible employees during the calendar year ending within the employer's taxable year. [I.R.C. § 404(h)(1)(A); Rev. Rul. 90-105, 1990-52 I.R.B. 6] Employer contributions to a SEP arrangement are not taken into account in determining an individual's compensation for deduction purposes. After 2001, elective salary reduction contributions made by employees do not reduce the compensation base to which the 25 percent employer deduction limit is applied (see Q 6:20). Thus, for purposes of the 25 percent deduction limit, compensation includes all elective deferrals made to the SARSEP.

Example 1. During the 2012 calendar year, Jerry earned $80,000. Jerry is the only employee of Solo, Inc. Solo's fiscal year ends on June 30, 2013. Jerry earned $100,000 during the fiscal year. Solo maintains a SEP on a calendar-year basis. The deduction for the 2012 plan year—deductible on Solo's return for the tax year ending June 3, 2013—is limited to 25 percent of $80,000, rather than 25 percent of compensation earned during the 2012–2013 fiscal year.

After 2001, elective contributions (within appropriate limits), as well as 25 percent of aggregate compensation, are fully deductible up to a maximum of $50,000/$55,500 (the limits for plan years ending in 2012). [I.R.C. § 404(n)] The SEP employer deduction limit is similar to the 25 percent of aggregate compensation limit (15 percent before 2002) applicable to a qualified profit-sharing plan. [I.R.C. § 404(a)(3); Prop. Treas. Reg. § 1.404(h)-1(a)] Generally, nondeductible contributions may be carried forward by the employer to succeeding taxable years (see Q 10:10).

Note. The maximum allowable profit-sharing deduction is reduced by the employer's allowable SEP deduction, but only with respect to participants covered in both plans (see Examples 3 and 4). [I.R.C. § 404(h)(2)] If the employer maintains a defined benefit plan, the SEP arrangement is treated as a profit-sharing or stock bonus plan for deduction limit purposes. [I.R.C.

§ 404(h)(3)] If the combined plan deduction limit rules under Code Section 404(a)(7) apply, then only defined contribution plan contributions in excess of 6 percent of a participant's compensation will count against the combined plan limit. [I.R.C. § 404(a)(7), as amended by the Pension Protection Act of 2006 (PPA), § 801, effective for tax years beginning on or after Jan. 1, 2006]

Example 2. Kahuna Corporation is a fiscal-year taxpayer with a taxable year ending on June 30, 2012. It adopts a nonelective SEP arrangement maintained on a calendar-year basis. Kahuna makes a timely contribution in August 2012 for its prior taxable year ending June 30, 2011. The 25 percent deduction limit will be based on compensation earned by the employees during the 12-month period ending December 31, 2011.

Example 3. Jupiter Corporation is a calendar-year taxpayer. On January 2, 2012, it adopts a nonelective SEP arrangement. At the end of 2012, it determines that it has paid $400,000 to all its employees. Eight of its employees met Jupiter's eligibility requirements for contributions to the SEP, and their compensation totaled $300,000 before any contributions were made to their SEPs. None of the employees earns in excess of $250,000. Jupiter will be allowed to deduct its contributions to its employees' SEPs, not to exceed 25 percent of $300,000, or $75,000.

Note. Unless a participant earns in excess of $200,000 ($50,000 ÷ .25), all amounts contributed would be excludable from a participant's gross income (see Q 11:1).

Example 4. Tetra Corporation is a calendar-year taxpayer that maintains a SEP and a noncontributory profit-sharing plan. Tetra has 100 employees. None of the employees earn in excess of $250,000. For the 2012 taxable year, Tetra makes contributions to the SEP for 75 of its employees who are also participants in the corporation's profit-sharing plan. The 75 employees received total compensation of $1,125,000 in 2012, and Tetra made SEP contributions of 10 percent of their compensation. Tetra can deduct $112,500 under Code Section 404(h) as its contribution to the SEP arrangement and must reduce the otherwise applicable allowable deduction for contributions to the profit-sharing plan on behalf of the 75 employees by $112,500.

Example 5. Sunlight Corporation, a calendar-year taxpayer with 100 employees, maintains a SEP arrangement and a profit-sharing plan. Each employee has compensation of $15,000. For the 2012 taxable year, Sunlight makes contributions to the SEP for 75 of its employees. The contributions are 25 percent of compensation received in 2012. Twenty-five of the 75 employees are also participants in the corporation's profit-sharing plan. The corporation deducts $281,250 (75 × $15,000 × .25) under Code Section 404(h) as its contribution to the SEP arrangement. Sunlight must reduce the otherwise applicable allowable deduction for contributions to the profit-sharing plan on behalf of the 25 employees by $93,750 (25 × $15,000 × .25), the amount contributed to the SEP IRAs on behalf of the employees covered by the profit-sharing plan.

Note. The employer deduction limit is based on the aggregate compensation and earned income paid or accrued during the taxable year to all beneficiaries under a plan. Generally, those are the employees and former employees who are benefiting under the plan, that is, employees who would receive an allocation if a nonelective contribution were made by an employer. If the plan year is not the same as the employer's taxable year, calendar-year compensation is used for computing the 25 percent deduction limit (see Q 10:3). [Treas. Reg. § 1.404(a)-9(c)]

Caution. The 25 percent participant exclusion limit may be lower than the 25 percent deduction limit. Unlike the 25 percent deduction limit, the 25 percent participant exclusion limit is generally based separately on each participant's taxable plan-year compensation (see Q 11:1). Thus, the portion of a fully deductible contribution that exceeds a participant's individually computed exclusion limit, although deductible, is nonetheless included in the affected participant's gross income for the taxable year. Practitioners may find it easier to compute SEP contribution amounts by solving for a favored employee's maximum excludable contribution when (1) employee elective contributions are permitted (see Q 12:14), (2) employer nonelective contributions are integrated with Social Security contributions (see Qs 9:1, 9:5), or (3) when a participant earns in excess of $200,000 for 2012 (see Q 6:30).

Example 6. Ashley, the only employee of the Wooly Coat Company, has compensation of $280,000. For the purpose of computing the SEP deduction limit, only the first $250,000 may be considered. The deduction limit amount of $62,500 ($250,000 × .25) exceeds the $50,000 annual contribution limit. If allocated, Ashley will have received an excess contribution ($12,500) that may be subject to the 6 percent excess contribution penalty tax. Wooly will be subject to the 10 percent nondeductible contribution penalty tax (see Q 10:11). Amounts that exceed the $50,000 ($55,500 with catch-up) contribution limit are not deductible.

Example 7. Bunny, age 40, the only employee of Bubbles, Inc., has compensation of $10,000 and elects to defer $500 of that amount into her employer's SARSEP. Bubbles makes a SEP contribution of $2,500. The deduction limit appears to be $3,000 (.25 × $10,000 + $500), but it is not. Because the contribution made by Bubbles cannot be allocated to Bunny on an excludable basis (see Q 12:15), it is not treated as an allowable elective contribution and must be reduced (in this case, to zero). Thus, Bunny's participant exclusion limit and Bubble's deduction limit remain at $2,500 (.25 × $10,000). Bunny must include $500 ($3,000 - $2,500) in gross income, and Wooly may be subject to the 10 percent nondeductible contribution penalty tax on $500 if that amount is not included in box 1 of Form W-2 (see Q 11:10).

Example 8. The facts are the same as those in Example 6, except that Bubbles contributes only $2,000. Because the contribution made by Bubbles and by Bunny ($500) cannot be fully allocated to Bunny on an excludable basis (see Q 12:15), it is not all treated as an allowable elective contribution and must be reduced (in this case, to $400). The maximum allowable basic elective contribution can be computed as follows (see Q 12:14):

$$\$10{,}000 \times \frac{(.25 - (\$2000/\$10{,}000))}{1.25} = \$400$$

Proof: .25 × ($10,000 - 400) = $2,400

Bunny must include $100 ($2,500 – (($10,000 – $400) × .25)) in gross income, but Wooly's $2,500 ($2,000 + $500) contribution does not exceed the deductible limit of $2,900 (($10,000 × .25) + $400).

Fees and Commissions

Q 10:4 Are administrative fees charged to participants by the employer or by the IRA trustee treated as SEP contributions?

No. Administrative fees charged to participants by the employer or by the IRA trustee are not plan contributions under Code Section 408(k), but instead are deductible by the payer under Code Section 162 or 212. Administrative fees may include the following:

- An annual flat fee per participant paid by the plan administrator or by the sponsoring employer
- A one-time fee to cover the administrative start-up costs associated with opening an individual's account
- An annual fee for providing recordkeeping services to the SEP
- A mutual fund subaccounting fee designed to cover recordkeeping costs for mutual fund subaccounts
- An early close-out fee on time deposit accounts (a special fee assessed for closing out time deposit accounts before maturity)
- A fee for closing out a plan participant's account
- A service charge for additional plan investment selections by a plan participant
- A fee for additional statements of account balances and activities

To the extent that a deduction for administrative costs is permitted under Code Section 162, it will be considered an expense of the trade or business. If the deduction is claimed under Code Section 212, it will be considered an expense for the production (or management) of income. To claim a deduction under Code Section 212, the taxpayer must not use the standard deduction, and the amount that may be claimed is only the amount by which total miscellaneous deductions exceed 2 percent of adjusted gross income. [Treas. Reg. § 1.212-1(g); Rev. Rul. 84-146, 1984-2 C.B. 61; Ltr. Rul. 8711095]

Q 10:5 Are sales charges and commissions deductible?

Maybe. Sales charges and commissions that are billed separately and paid by the SEP IRA holder are treated as additional non-SEP IRA contributions and are to be reported by the trustee or issuer as IRA contributions on Form 5498, IRA Contribution Information. Commissions are intrinsic to the value of the assets held in the IRA. Buying commissions are part of the cost of the securities purchased, and selling commissions are an offset against the sales price. Thus, commissions are not like recurring administrative or overhead expenses, such as trustee or actuary fees, incurred in connection with the maintenance of the IRA trust and are not deductible. Administrative fees paid directly from the IRA and sales charges and commissions are not deductible by the IRA holder under Code Section 212. [Rev. Rul. 86-142, 1986-2 C.B. 60; Ltr. Ruls. 8835062, 8833047, 8830061, 8747072, 8711095] Taxes on unrelated business income and other costs, such as interest, attributable to an extension of credit for investments in an IRA are not administrative fees or trustee's fees. To treat them as such would be to create a device to circumvent the contribution limits. Rather, they are costs linked directly to specific investment transactions or investment opportunities and are treated as annual contributions to the IRA. [Ltr. Rul. 8830061]

Wrap fees. In some cases, sales charges, commissions, and administrative fees may be combined in what is referred to as a *wrap fee*. [Ltr. Rul. 200507021; Ltr. Rul. 9124037, revoking Ltr. Rul. 8840014; Ltr. Rul. 9124036, revoking Ltr. Rul. 8940013; *see also* I.L.M. 200721015 (Jan. 16, 2007]

In Letter Ruling 200507021 (Nov. 23, 2004), a securities broker-dealer and an investment adviser provided a variety of financial services—investment banking, securities brokerage, trading (representing no more than 15 percent of the wrap fee cost), investment management, retirement planning, estate planning, and trust services—to their clients. The company instituted several programs that provide a combination of investment advisory services and securities trade execution services for various clients for their IRAs, for which the clients pay a single fee (a "wrap fee"). In each of the programs, either the company or one of its affiliates was the custodian and delegated investment and reporting responsibilities to the company. The company focuses its resources on its investment advisory service, a policy that is reflected in a wrap fee structure. Under the wrap fee structure, fees are based on a percentage of assets under management and bear no relation to the number of trades an individual causes the company to execute, and were distinct from the cost or volume of any assets purchased or sold by the IRA (or Roth IRA). The IRS ruled that the payment of wrap fees by clients that participated in the wrap fee programs (several factual scenarios were presented) were recurring expenses and would not be deemed contributions to the clients' IRAs (or Roth IRAs) if the clients paid the wrap fees with funds that were not part of their respective IRAs (or Roth IRAs).

In Letter Ruling 201104061 (Nov. 4, 2010), which is similar to the 2005 ruling (issued in 2004), no mention of the percentage of the wrap fee that could be used for securities trading service is mentioned and, unlike Letter Ruling 200507021, none of the accounts were non-advisory programs (but, in the authors' opinion, non-advisory accounts would likely be treated the same). The ruling listed numerous other expenses that were not part of the wrap fee; therefore, the ruling does not address the proper tax treatment of the payment of those other expenses that include commissions charged by other brokers, interest on debit account balances, interest charges on margin loans, the entire public offering price on securities purchased from an underwriter or dealer involved in a distribution of securities, bid-ask spreads, off-lot differentials, exchange fees, transfer taxes and other fees required by law, transaction charges on the liquidation of assets not eligible for the account, and short-term trading charges for purchases and redemptions of certain mutual fund shares within short periods of time. Also, under one arrangement, a $55 "active trader" fee is imposed (presumably for exceeding frequency limitations specified in the account terms and conditions) that also would not be covered by the wrap fee. [*See also* Dold, Elizabeth T., and Levine, David N., *Tax Treatment on the Payment of IRA Fees Gets a New (but Familiar) Private Letter Ruling*, Taxes-The Tax Magazine, page 17, CCH, Inc. (May 2011); *Knight v. Commissioner*, 128 S. Ct. 782 (2008); *see also* Prop. Reg. § 1.67-4T (REG-128224-06), 76 Fed. Reg. 55322–55325, issued in light of the *Knight* decision.]

Q 10:6 Are administrative fees and charges of the trustee deductible?

It depends. If administrative fees are paid directly by the employer, they are deductible by the employer. [Treas. Reg. § 1.404(a)-3(d)] If administrative fees are paid directly by the IRA holder, they are deductible subject to the 2 percent floor on miscellaneous itemized deductions.

Miscellaneous deductions are not available if the standard deduction is taken. [Rev. Rul. 86-146, 1986-2 C.B. 61; Rev. Rul. 86-142, 1986-2 C.B. 60; Ltr. Ruls. 8941010, 8835062, 8711095, 8432109, 8329058, 8329055, 8329049]

Administrative fees paid directly from the IRA merely decrease the overall balance in the SEP IRA and are not reported to the Internal Revenue Service (IRS). Reimbursement to an IRA once administrative fees have been paid directly from the IRA would be treated as a reportable contribution. [Ltr. Rul. 8830061]

Practice Pointer. Plan documents determine which methods of paying administrative fees are permissible under the terms of the plan.

Elective Salary Reduction Contributions

Q 10:7 How are elective salary reduction contributions treated for deduction purposes?

Elective salary reduction contributions made by employees are treated as employer SEP contributions for deduction purposes. [I.R.C. § 404(h); Treas. Reg. § 1.402(g)-1(e)(1)(ii)] Excess elective contributions are not reflected on an employee's Form W-2 as gross wages unless other limits are exceeded (see Q 10:10). Elective deferrals, including excess elective deferrals, are reported in box 12 of Form W-2 (see Q 12:23).

Elective salary reduction contributions are separately deductible. In addition, catch-up contributions may be contributed and deducted without regard to the 25 percent deduction limit, or when combined with nonelective contributions, the 100 percent limit under Code Section 415 (see Qs 10:8, 10:9). [I.R.C. §§ 404(n), 414(v)]

> **Note.** Although unincorporated business owners are employees, they deduct elective (and nonelective) SEP contributions that are made on their behalf to the extent allowable on line 28 of Form 1040, U.S. Individual Income Tax Return or line 28 of Form 1040NR, U.S. Nonresident Alien Income Tax Return.
>
> Although not deductible, excess elective deferrals (amounts in excess of $17,000 and in excess of $22,500 with catch-up contribution for 2012) are treated as employer contributions for purposes of the employer deduction limit and the limits under Code Section 415 (see Q 5:6). [Treas. Reg. § 1.402(g)-1(e)(1)(ii)]

Q 10:8 Are SEP contributions that exceed the $50,000 ($55,500 with catch-up contribution) limit under Code Section 415 deductible by the employer?

No. SEP contributions that exceed the $50,000 limit under Code Section 415 ($55,500 with catch-up contribution for 2012) are not deductible by the employer. If the limit is exceeded, other problems may arise (see Qs 5:8–5:10). [I.R.C. § 415(j)(1)]

Q 10:9 Are SEP contributions that exceed the 100 percent limit under Code Section 415 deductible by the employer?

Possibly. The 100 percent limit can be exceeded by the $5,500 catch-up amount for employer deduction purposes. The IRS issued a worksheet in IRS Publication 560, *Retirement Plans for Small Business*. The worksheet on page 23 of the publication, titled "Deduction Worksheet for Self-Employed," indicates that the sum of the employer's contributions and elective deferral plus the catch-up contribution may exceed the self-employed individual's earned income (compensation).

> **Note 1.** Elective deferrals are not treated as catch-up (elective) contributions unless the individual is age 50 or older and the elective contributions exceed 25 percent of taxable compensation ($17,000 for 2012), or other limits applicable to normal elective contributions (see Qs 12:46, 12:52).
>
> **Caution.** The IRS worksheet clearly states on page 22 that it is applicable to computing the maximum deductible contribution in the case of a SEP (but not SARSEP). And indeed it is. The publication only cryptically mentions on

page 6 that SEP contributions may not generally exceed 25 percent of reduced (taxable) compensation. [I.R.C. § 402(h)] The IRS has never addressed the interplay of the SEP deduction rules under Code Sections 404(h) and 404 and the participant exclusion rules under Code Section 402(h). Publication 560 also states: "Compensation generally does not include your contributions to the SEP." [Pub. 560, Retirement Plans for Small Business (2011), How Much Can I Contribute—Contribution Limits, p. 6]

Example. Based on the worksheet, a self-employed individual whose earned income is $10,000 (after reduction for one-half of the self-employment tax deduction) may make an employer contribution of $2,000 (.25 × ($10,000–$2,000)) and an $8,000 elective deferral, plus defer an additional $1,000 (if the individual is age 50 or over) and still be within the qualified plan 25 percent deduction limit under Code Section 404(a)(3)(A). Thus, the individual may make $9,000 in overall contributions with only $8,000 of remaining compensation ($10,000–$2,000). (It should be noted that the 25 percent deduction limit is based on the eligible compensation of all plan participants.) In the authors' opinion, the contribution amount that exceeds $2,000 (25 percent of $8,000 ($10,000–$2,000)) must be included in gross income in the case of a SARSEP; or $7,000 (the $2,000 nonelective contribution + $5,000), if age 50 or older, for 2012 (see chapter 11). The IRS worksheet does not take into account the effect of the 2 percent reduction in SECA taxes in effect for 2012. The 2 percent SECA tax reduction, however, has a negligible effect on the allowable contribution (see Q 7:2). The payroll tax holiday was extended through 2012.

Note 2. When an employer has a deduction for a profit-sharing plan contribution, a contribution on behalf of a self-employed individual may not create a net operating loss; that is, it may not exceed the individual's earned income (determined without regard to the deduction for the contribution). Contributions made for a 10 percent or less owner, however, may exceed the owner's earned income and create a net loss from self-employment. Contributions made to nonowner-employees may exceed the owner's earned income and create a net loss from self-employment. [I.R.C. §§ 404(1)(8)(C), 404(h)(2); Treas. Reg. § 1.404(a)-8]

Caution. Absent nonelective employer contributions, it is difficult to imagine the source of contributions that exceed an individual's earned income. As a rule, individuals may only make elective contributions from amounts that, had the election not been made, they would have received in cash.

Affiliated Service Group Member

Q 10:10 May a member of an affiliated service group deduct contributions on behalf of individuals who are not employees of that member?

It depends. If a SEP maintained by a member of an affiliated service group covers an individual who is not an employee of that member but who is an employee of another member, the plan will be considered to be maintained by the member that does employ that individual. Thus, the plan will be considered to be maintained by more than one employer. Therefore, a member of an affiliated service group may deduct contributions on behalf of individuals who are not employees of that member if the individuals are employed by another member of that affiliated service group. This multiple-employer plan rule does not apply, however, in the case of a controlled group of corporations or a group of trades or businesses under common control. [Prop. Treas. Reg. § 1.414(m)-3(a)(5)]

Example. Train Corporation is a partner in Track Partnership, a service organization. Train employs only its sole shareholder and maintains a SEP. Walter and Zeb, other partners in Track, are not incorporated. Each partner has a one-third interest in Track, which has eight common-law employees. Train and Track are members of an affiliated service group. The SEP maintained by Train covers some of the common-law employees of Track; thus, it benefits individuals who are not employees of the member of the affiliated service group maintaining the plan (Train). The plan will be considered to be maintained by more than one employer. Contributions by Train on behalf of those individuals will not fail to be deductible under Code Section 404 merely because the individuals are not employees of Train.

Deduction in Future Years

Q 10:11 May nondeductible employer contributions be deducted in future years?

Yes. The excess of the amount contributed over the amount deductible by an employer for a taxable year is generally deductible in succeeding taxable years (in order of time); however, the amount deducted is subject to the 25 percent limit (see Q 10:3). [I.R.C. § 404(h)(1)(C); Prop. Treas. Reg. § 1.404(h)-1(a)(3), (4)]

Example. Crane Corporation, a calendar-year business, establishes a SEP for its 2011 taxable year. It contributed 25 percent of compensation for all participants on December 31, 2011. In addition, on March 1, 2012, Crane accidentally makes a 2 percent contribution for the prior taxable year (2011) and the maximum contribution (25 percent) for the current year (2012). If less than the maximum is contributed for 2013, the amount of the 2011 excess may be deductible on Crane's 2013 tax return.

A contribution on behalf of a self-employed individual may not create a net operating loss; that is, it may not exceed the individual's earned income (determined without regard to the deduction for the contribution) (but see Q 10:8). Contributions made to nonowner-employees, however, may exceed the owner's earned income and create a net loss from self-employment. [I.R.C. §§ 404(a)(8)(C), 404(h)(2); Treas. Reg. § 1.404(a)-8]

> **Example 1.** Theo's sole proprietorship has no employees and makes a 26 percent SEP contribution for 2012. There is no carryforward. The nondeductible employer SEP contribution is not deductible on Theo's tax return for 2012. Theo should include the excess amount on line 7 of his Form 1040 for 2012.

> **Example 2.** Max, a sole proprietor, makes a 25 percent SEP contribution for himself and all eligible employees. Max later discovers that he overestimated his earned income; in fact, he did not have any earned income for the year. The contributions made on behalf of the nonowner-employees create a net operating loss that Max may use to offset personal income. Any balance attributable to the nonowner-employees may be carried forward.

A special rule requires a proper reduction of the carryforward where an excess deduction was allowed for closed year. Proper reduction must be made in the amount allowed as a deduction for a prior taxable year for which the period for assessing a deficiency has expired if the amount so allowed exceeds the amount that should have been allowed for such prior taxable year. [Prop. Treas. Reg. § 1.408-9]

> **Caution.** The specific instruction for line 7 (wages, salaries, tips, etc.) of Form 1040 states that excess elective contributions (generally amounts that exceed $17,000, excluding catch-up contributions, for 2012) are reported on line 7. However, the instructions were updated beginning in 2007 to include a statement that this does not apply to a self-employed person who does not receive a deduction for an "excess" contribution.

Penalty

Q 10:12 Is there a penalty for making nondeductible employer contributions?

Yes. An employer is subject to a 10 percent penalty tax on any nondeductible contributions. [I.R.C. § 4972(a)] Under Code Section 4972(d), a SEP is treated as a qualified employer plan for this purpose and is therefore subject to the penalty tax on nondeductible contributions. The term *nondeductible contributions* is defined as the sum of (1) contributions in excess of the allowable deduction for the taxable year plus (2) the amount of contributions in all preceding years that were not allowed as a deduction, minus the amounts that became deductible for the current year. [I.R.C. § 4972(c)] However, employer contributions to one or more defined contribution plans, or to one or more defined benefit plans that are not deductible because they exceed the combined plan limits under Code

Section 404(a)(7), are generally not subject to the 10 percent tax unless they exceed 6 percent of compensation in the tax year for which they are made (see Q 1:3). [*See* I.R.C. § 4972(c)(6) for exceptions.]

It would appear that a participant's inclusion in income of an elective contribution in excess of $17,000/$22,500 (the 2012 limits, in box 12 of Form W-2; see Q 11:15) or of a contribution exceeding the 25 percent of compensation exclusion limit (see Q 11:1) or the 100 percent of compensation limit under Code Section 415 (reported in box 1 of Form W-2; see Q 10:8) reduces the nondeductible amount subject to the 10 percent penalty in the case of a SEP. [I.R.C. § 4972(c)(3); Treas. Reg. §§ 1.402(g)-1(e)(1)(i), 1.402(g)-1(e)(1)(ii)] Clearly, an excess amount actually withdrawn by the employee from his or her IRA reduces the nondeductible amount subject to the penalty. Arguably, in the case of a SEP, a proper and timely notification (when required) of a nondeductible employer SEP contribution or a disallowed deferral would reduce the nondeductible amount subject to the penalty.

Reporting

Q 10:13 On which IRS forms are employer contributions claimed?

Contributions by corporations and on behalf of common-law employees of unincorporated businesses are claimed as an expense on the federal business income tax return. If the organization is taxed as a corporation, the deduction for contributions made on behalf of owners and nonowners is claimed on line 23 of Form 1120, U.S. Corporation Income Tax Return, or line 17 of Form 1120S, U.S. Income Tax Return for an S Corporation. An unincorporated business, other than a partnership, claims the deduction for SEP and SARSEP contributions of nonowner-employees on line 19 of Schedule C, Profit or Loss from Business (Sole Proprietorship), or line 23 of Schedule F, Profit or Loss from Farming, of Form 1040. [I.R.C. § 404(h)] Self-employed individuals combine their SEP and Keogh contributions and deduct them on Form 1040 (line 28) or Form 1040NR (line 28).

A partnership reports owner contributions on line 13(d) of Schedule K (Partner's Distributive Share Items) of Form 1065 (U.S. Return of Partnership Income) and as a memo entry. It also reports owner contributions on line 13 of Schedule K-1 (Partner's Share of Income, Credits, Deductions, etc.) of Form 1065, U.S. Return of Partnership Income. Code R is used to reflect partnership payments to a SEP on Schedule K (Form 1065) and on Form K-1. [Instructions for Form 1065, Specific Instructions (Schedules K, line 13(d); K-1, line 13)] In the authors' opinion, however, elective deferrals on behalf of guaranteed payment partners should be reported on line 4 (guaranteed payments for nonpersonal service income) instead of on Schedules K (line 13(d)) and K-1 (line 13); otherwise, Form 1065 will not flow properly. When elective deferrals on behalf of guaranteed payment partners are reported on line 4, the income (loss) per books will reconcile with income (loss) per return on Schedule M-1

(Reconciliation of Income (Loss) per Books with Income (Loss) per Return) of Form 1065.

Note. Line numbers are based on the 2012 version of these forms.

Q 10:14 Must an employer notify an employee of employer contributions made into an employee's SEP IRA?

Yes. ERISA requires an annual notification of employer contributions to an employee's IRA under a SEP (see Qs 4:10, 4:15). (See Appendix C.)

Q 10:15 How is an excess deferral corrected if the participant is also participating in a 403(b) program?

Generally, tax-sheltered annuity (or mutual fund custodial account) under Code Section 403(b) is not aggregated with other plans of the employer because the employee is deemed to control the 403(b) plan and not the employer. [Treas. Reg. § 1.415(f)-1(f)(1)] This rule has permitted employees to fully fund their 403(b) plan ($17,000 for regular deferrals, plus $3,000 for long-term service, plus $5,500 for age 50 catch-up deferrals) and still receive an employer contribution into another plan (where the employee does not control the employer) up to the maximum Code Section 415 limit ($50,000 for 2012).

There is one exception to this general rule. If an employee participates in a 403(b) plan and maintains a business that he or she controls, then the plans will be aggregated for Code Section 415 purposes. [Treas. Reg. § 1.415(f)-1(f)(2)]

Example. In 2012, Manny, a university professor, contributes to the university's 403(b) plan and maintains a small consulting business on the side. Because Manny is deemed to control the 403(b) plan and owns 100 percent of the consulting business, he may only contribute $50,000 ($55,500 if age 50) between the two plans. This is also common where a doctor participates in the hospital's 403(b) program and maintains a plan for his or her private practice.

Although there were rumors to the contrary, the final Code Section 415 regulations issued in April 2007 state that if an excess occurs in multiple plans, the excess will be treated as being in the 403(b) plan. Also, the excess must be separate accounted for from the date that the excess was created in the 403(b) plan; otherwise, the contract is not a qualified 403(b). [Treas. Reg. §§ 1.415(a)-1(b)(2), 1.415(a)-1(b)(3) regarding I.R.C. § 403(b)(7) custodial accounts]

However, if a participant on whose behalf a Section 403(b) annuity contract (including a mutual fund custodial account) is purchased is in control of any employer for a limitation year, the annuity contract for the benefit of the participant is treated as a defined contribution plan maintained by both the controlled employer and the participant for that limitation year; accordingly, the Section 403(b) annuity contract is aggregated with all other defined contribution plans maintained by the employer.

The preamble to the final Code Section 415 regulations places an additional burden on employers. It states: "[T]he employer that contributes to the Section 403(b) annuity contract must obtain information from participants regarding employers controlled by those participants and plans maintained by those controlled employers to monitor compliance with applicable limitations to comply with applicable reporting and withholding obligations." [Preamble, Treas. Reg. § 1.415 (T.D. 9319, 2007-18 I.R.B. 1041 (Apr. 30, 2007))]

Note. It is common practice for a doctor in private practice or a professor who maintains a consulting business to establish a SEP plan for their separate businesses. All excesses will be in the 403(b) plan and not the SEP plan.

Chapter 11

Taxation of SEP Contributions

Contributions to a SEP that are deductible by the employer are not necessarily excludable from employees' gross income. This chapter focuses on the amount of contributions that may be excluded from an employee's gross income, as well as the reporting and treatment of excess SARSEP contributions. Issues related to individual retirement accounts and individual retirement annuities (IRAs) and the 100 percent/$50,000/$55,500 limit under Section 415 of the Internal Revenue Code are also discussed. In addition, this chapter discusses FICA, FUTA, and other taxes.

Percentage Exclusion Limit

Q 11:1 What is the percentage exclusion limit for SEP contributions?

Unlike a qualified plan under Section 401(a) of the Internal Revenue Code (Code), deductible contributions made by an employer under a SEP are not necessarily excluded from a participant's gross federal taxable income. Code Section 402(h) provides special rules for a SEP that are applied on a participant level. That is, the amount of aggregate contributions that may be excluded from each participant's gross income is applied on a per-participant basis. Under the participant exclusion limit rules there are actually two limits: a dollar limit (see Q 11:5) and a percentage limit.

Under the percentage exclusion limit for SEP contributions, contributions to a SEP that do not exceed 25 percent of taxable plan-year compensation are generally excluded from an employee's taxable compensation. For purposes of the percentage exclusion limit, only compensation that is included in the employee's gross income is considered. Catch-up contributions for employees age 50 or older are not, however, taken into account in computing the 25 percent exclusion limit (see Q 11:2). For plan years before 2002, the percentage exclusion limit was 15 percent.

The year to be used in determining an employee's compensation seems to be the SEP's "limitation year," generally the calendar year (or plan year). The $50,000 annual addition limit imposed by Section 415 of the Code, which limit is also part of Code Section 402(h), is clearly applied on a plan-year basis (see Qs 6:6, 11:13). Contributions to a SEP are treated as allocated to the SEP IRA as of the last day of the limitation year (generally the plan year (see Q 6:6)) ending with or within the employer's taxable year for which the contribution is made. [Treas. Reg. § 1.415(c)-1(b)(6)(ii)(C)]

Elective contributions in excess of $17,000 plus a catch-up contribution of up to $5,500 for 2012 must be included in gross income for the calendar year, notwithstanding the percentage exclusion limit under Code Section 402(h). [Treas. Reg. § 1.402(g)-1(a)]

The Economic Growth and Tax Relief Reconciliation Act of 2001 (EGTRRA) did not make any changes to the rules regarding a participant's exclusion of contributions to a SEP or a SARSEP under Code Section 402(h). Technical corrections made by the Job Creation and Worker Assistance Act of 2002 (JCWAA), however, corrected a portion of Code Section 402(h), as follows:

1. The percentage limit on the exclusion of contributions from a participant's compensation was increased to 25 percent from 15 percent for taxable years beginning after 2001. [I.R.C. § 402(h)(2)(A)]
2. Elective contributions were made deductible by the employer *in addition* to the amount deductible under the 25 percent of aggregate compensation deduction limit (but not in excess of the $50,000 per participant limit under Code Section 415; $55,500 with a catch-up contribution of $5,500 for 2012) (see chapter 10). [I.R.C. § 404(n)]

Note. Disharmony and confusion resulted from having a participant exclusion limit, which, in some cases, was lower than the employer's deduction limit. EGTRRA increased the SEP deduction limit from 15 percent to 25 percent. EGTRRA, as amended by the JCWAA, increased the participant exclusion limit from 15 percent to 25 percent (of taxable compensation, which does not include basic elective contributions) and provided that elective contributions would be deductible in addition to the amount determined under the 25 percent deduction limit (which is determined without reducing compensation by any elective contributions). Although the JCWAA made some improvements, it also broadened the disparity between excludable allocations of contributions and deductible amounts, primarily by treating elective contributions differently. These anomalies were well known. It is also well known that the Treasury Department and the IRS urged Congress on numerous occasions to correct the exclusion from income limit in the statute. It never happened.

The technical corrections did not clarify the following issues:

1. Whether elective contributions, including catch-up contributions, are excluded for the purpose of applying the percentage exclusion limit, that is, whether only "includible" (taxable) compensation is considered (see Q 11:2). In the authors' opinion, catch-up contributions do not reduce the amount upon which the 25 percent participant exclusion limit is applied. [I.R.C. §§ 414(v)(3), 402(h)(2)(A)]
2. Whether the compensation cap of $250,000 (as indexed for 2012) under Code Section 401(a)(17) applies for the purpose of the percentage exclusion limit. In the authors' opinion, the percentage exclusion limit has never been subject to the compensation cap (see Qs 11:5, 11:6), although the compensation cap does apply to Code Section 415. Nonetheless, IRS model language precludes more than $250,000, as adjusted for additional increases in the cost of living, from being used for allocation purposes. [*See* Listing of Required Modifications and Information Package (LRMs), Simplified Employee Pensions, items 3 & 7 (March 2002)]
3. Whether catch-up contributions can exceed the 100 percent of compensation limit under Code Section 415(c) when combined with nonelective contributions and whether total contributions that exceed that limit are deductible by the employer (see Qs 11:13, 12:5). [I.R.C. §§ 404(j), 414(v)(3)(A)]

The IRS issued a worksheet for Publication 560, *Retirement Plans for Small Business* (2011). The worksheet, titled "Deduction Worksheet for Self-Employed," indicates that the sum of the employer's contributions and elective deferral plus the catch-up contribution may exceed the self-employed individual's earned income (compensation) (see Q 10:9). [The worksheet is available at *http://www.irs.gov/pub/irs-pdf/p560.pdf* (visited on Aug. 22, 2012)] Even if so, this would not apply to a common-law employee or nonowner who is paid on Form W-2.

Example. Based on the 2011 worksheet, a self-employed individual whose earned income is $10,000 (after reduction for one-half of the self-employment tax deduction) may receive an employer contribution of $2,000 (.25 × ($10,000 – $2,000)) and make an $8,000 elective deferral, plus defer an additional $5,500 (the 2012 limit, if the individual is age 50 or over) and still be within the 25 percent deduction limit under Code Section 404(a)(3)(A). Thus, the individual may receive $15,500 in overall contributions with only $8,000 of compensation. (It should be noted that the 25 percent deduction limit is based on the eligible compensation of all plan participants.) The 25 percent participant exclusion limit, however, has been exceeded. In the authors' opinion, the contribution amount that exceeds $2,000 ((.25 × ($10,000 – $2,000)); $7,500 if age 50 or older for 2012) is an excess contribution. The IRS worksheet clearly states on page 22 that it is applicable to computing the maximum deductible contribution in the case of a SEP (but not SARSEP). And indeed it is. The publication, however, mentions only briefly, on page 6, that contributions may not generally exceed 25 percent of reduced (taxable) compensation. Based on the IRS worksheet, an individual with only $8,000 of compensation could receive an overall contribution of $15,500 ($2,000 + $8,000 + $5,500) for 2012. The IRS has never issued any guidance on the interplay of the SEP deduction rules under Code Sections 404(h) and 404(n) and the participant exclusion rules under Code Section 402(h). [I.R.C. §§ 404(1)(8)(C), 404(h)(2); Treas. Reg. § 1.404(a)-1]

Caution. It is difficult to imagine the source of contributions that exceed an individual's earned income. As a rule, individuals may only make elective contributions from amounts that, had the election not been made, they would have received in cash.

Historical Note. Before the Tax Reform Act of 1986 (TRA '86) was enacted, amounts contributed to a SEP and elective deferrals under a SARSEP were deductible by the employee (under Code Section 219(b)(2)), instead of excludable from gross income as they are under current law.

Q 11:2 Why must the 25 percent participant exclusion limit be applied after subtracting elective salary reduction contributions from compensation?

Code Section 402(h)(2)(A), referring to Section 414(s) compensation, includes such compensation only to the extent that it is includible in the employee's gross income. Elective salary reduction SEP contributions, within limits (see Q 11:1), are excludable from gross income.

Note. Catch-up contributions are not subject to the percentage exclusion limit or to the $50,000 Section 415 limit and may be separately excluded from a participant's income. [I.R.C. § 414(v)]

Example 1. Quest Corporation maintains a SEP arrangement for its employees. The plan year is the calendar year. Elise, age 40, a nonowner-employee, earns $10,000 and makes an elective contribution of $2,500 for 2012. If no other contributions are made, the 25 percent exclusion limit of $2,000 is computed as follows:

$$\$10,000 \times .25/1.25 = \$2,000$$

Quest should report $500 in box 1 on Elise's 2012 Form W-2, Wage and Tax Statement. It is unclear what other amounts have to be withheld (see Qs 11:15, 11:17).

Example 2. Pattern Corporation maintains a SEP arrangement for its employees. The plan year is the calendar year. Frank, age 40, a nonowner-employee, earns $10,000 and elects to defer $1,000 under a SARSEP for 2012. The 25 percent exclusion limit of $2,250 is computed as follows:

$$(\$10,000 - \$1,000) \times .25 = \$2,250$$

The maximum employer SEP contribution amount not includible in Frank's income (if an elective contribution of $1,000 is made) can be calculated as follows:

$2,250 – $1,000 = $1,250

The maximum elective contribution (if no nonelective contributions are made by the employer) can be computed as follows:

$10,000 × .25/1.25 = $2,000

Proof: ($10,000 – $2,000) × .25 = $2,000

Example 3. Thyme Corporation maintains a SEP arrangement for its only employee in 2012. The plan year is the calendar year. Grace, the employee, age 40, earns $100,000 and elects to defer $18,000 under a SARSEP. Thyme makes a nonelective SEP contribution of $7,750 for Grace.

The 25 percent exclusion limit can be computed as follows:

($100,000 – $17,000 (the 2012 limit)) × .25 = $20,750

Amounts in excess of the Section 402(g) elective deferral dollar limit (currently $17,000) are not excludable from income; therefore, it appears that $83,000 ($100,000 – $17,000) is used as Grace's compensation. The 25 percent exclusion limit of $20,750 has been exceeded by $5,000 ($18,000 + $7,750 – $20,750). For tax reporting purposes, the excess should be treated as exceeding the 25 percent exclusion limit under Code Section 402(h). Thus, $5,000 should be included in box 1 of Grace's Form W-2 for 2012 (the calendar year that includes the last day of the plan year). The $1,000 amount, which is an excess deferral (the amount exceeding the $17,000 deferral limit for 2012), would be included in box 12 of Form W-2, along with the maximum allowable elective deferral amount (see Q 13:204).

Thyme Corporation's 25 percent deduction limit (which does not consider catch-up contributions, which are separately deductible) is $25,000 (.25 × $100,000). As a result, Thyme may deduct $20,750 ($17,000 + $3,750; $26,250 if Grace were age 50 or older and made a $5,500 catch-up contribution) for 2012. [I.R.C. §§ 402(h)(2), 402(h)(3), 4972, 4979; Treas. Reg. §§ 1.402(g)-1(e)(1)(i), 1.402(g)-1(e)(1)(ii)]

Example 4. Assume the same facts as in Example 3, except Thyme Corporation makes a contribution of $12,000 for Grace. Grace may make a salary reduction contribution of $10,000 and exclude the entire contribution of $22,000 ($10,000 + $12,000) from her gross income. If Grace were age 50 or older and made a salary reduction contribution of $13,000, $3,000 ($13,000 + $12,000 – $22,000), but not more than $5,500 for 2012) would be treated as a catch-up contribution instead of treated as exceeding the participant exclusion limit, in which case the entire contribution of $27,500 may be excluded from Grace's gross income and deducted by Thyme for 2012.

Proof: .25 ($100,000 – $12,000) = $22,000 ($10,000 + $12,000)

If Grace were age 50 or older:

Proof: .25 ($100,000 – $12,000) + $3,000 = $25,000 ($12,000 + $13,000)

Example 5. In 2012, Jim, age 40, chose to have his salary reduced by $7,500 and to have that amount contributed by his employer, Moore Inc., to a SEP IRA (individual retirement account) under a salary reduction arrangement. Jim's salary for the year is $30,000. On Jim's Form W-2, Moore will show total wages of $22,500 ($30,000 – $7,500), Social Security wages of $30,000, and Medicare wages of $30,000. Jim will report $22,500 as wages on Form 1040, U.S. Individual Income Tax Return.

Jim's 25 percent exclusion limit under Code Section 402(h)(2)(A) has been exceeded. Form 5305A-SEP explains that the maximum limit on elective deferrals is computed by using the following formula: compensation (before subtracting employer SEP contributions) multiplied by 20 percent. Thus, Jim's excess of $1,500 is computed as follows: $7,500 – ($30,000 × .20). The excess is treated as compensation in calculating the maximum elective amount. Jim would have to include the excess amount of $1,500 on line 7 of Form 1040 for 2012. The $7,500 would be reported in box 12 and $1,500 reported in box 1 of Form W-2.

Example 6. Joe, age 50, is a participant in SEP. His pre-plan compensation is $100,000. For 2012, Joe contributes $22,500 as an elective contribution. The 25-percent-of-compensation exclusion allowance and maximum excludable SEP contribution can be computed as follows:

Pre-plan compensation	$100,000
Less normal elective contributions	– 17,000 (max)
Exclusion compensation [I.R.C. § 402(h)]	$ 83,000
Exclusion percentage	× .25
Maximum excludable contribution	$ 20,750
Less total normal elective contribution	– 17,000
Excludable SEP contribution	$ 3,750
Catch-up elective contribution	+ 5,500
Normal elective contribution	+ 17,000
Maximum excludable contribution	$ 26,250

In Example 6, Joe's participant exclusion allowance is based on $83,000 ($100,000 – $17,000) instead of $77,500 ($100,000 – $17,000 – $5,500). This is due to Code Section 414(v) regarding the treatment of catch-up contributions. Although catch-up contributions are excluded from gross income (in addition to amount computed under the 25 percent participant exclusion limit), the catch-up amount is not taken into account in computing the limits applicable to SEPs. Code Section 414(v)(3), regarding the treatment of catch-up contributions, reads:

In the case of any contribution to a plan under paragraph (1)—

(A) such contribution shall not, with respect to the year in which the contribution is made—

i. be subject to any otherwise applicable limitation contained in Sections 402(h), 403(b), 408, 415(c), and 457(b)(2) (determined without regard to Section 457(b)(3)), or

ii. taken into account in applying such limitations to other contributions or benefits under such plan or any other such plan, and

(B) . . . .

In the authors' opinion, reducing compensation for the catch-up contribution would conflict with clause (i) because the catch-up contribution would be taken into account in applying an "otherwise applicable limitation" (i.e., Code Section 402(h)), and with clause (ii) because the catch-up contribution would reduce the maximum excludable employer contribution by $1,375 ($5,500 × .25 for 2012).

Q 11:3 How are SEP contributions in excess of the 25 percent exclusion limit treated?

Contributions made by an employer to a SEP that exceed the 25 percent exclusion limit (see Qs 11:1, 11:2) are subject to the IRA contribution limits of Code Sections 219 and 408 and may be considered excess IRA contributions for the calendar year that includes the last day of the plan year.

For purposes of the 25 percent exclusion limit, compensation for a plan year is not limited to $250,000 (as indexed for 2012). Neither Code Section 401(a)(17) nor Code Section 404(l) appears to limit the amount of compensation that can be taken into account under Code Section 402(h)(2)(A) or in calculating the 25 percent of compensation exclusion limit. Nonetheless, nearly all IRS-approved SEP documents contain provisions that limit the allocation (and hence the deduction) to 25 percent of the first $250,000 of compensation earned by an individual (see Qs 11:1, 11:5), but capped at $50,000 (or at $55,500 with a $5,500 catch-up contribution) for 2012.

Note. Special correction procedures and rules apply to the three types of excess contributions that can only be made into a SARSEP (see Qs 5:75, 12:18). However, after appropriate notifications have been made, uncorrected excess contributions in a SARSEP are treated as (deemed) traditional IRA contributions; in which time, the traditional IRA rules discussed in Q 5:75 are used to correct any deemed excess traditional IRA contributions.

Q 11:4 How can the maximum elective or employer SEP contribution percentage be calculated?

When the salary deferral percentage contributed by the employee is known, the maximum elective or employer SEP contribution percentage that is not includible in the employee's income (see Q 11:2) can generally be calculated as follows:

$$(20\% - x) \times 1.25$$

where x equals the salary deferral percentage contributed by the employee and x does not represent an amount that exceeds the dollar limit ($17,000 for 2012)

Example 1. Mary, age 40, an employee of Klein Co., makes an elective contribution of 10 percent. The maximum SEP contribution percentage for Klein Co. that is not includible in Mary's income is 12.5 percent and is calculated as follows:

$$(20\% - 10\%) \times 1.25 = 12.5\%$$

Example 2. Joe, age 58, has pre-plan wages of $100,000 and defers $22,500 to a SARSEP for 2012. Of the SARSEP amount, $5,500 is treated as a catch-up contribution.

If the 25 percent SEP exclusion limit is based on $83,000, not more than $26,250 ($20,750 + $5,500 catch-up contribution) may be contributed to the SARSEP and excluded from Joe's income, computed as follows:

$100,000 – $17,000 = $83,000

$83,000 × .25 = $20,750

$20,750 + $5,500 catch-up contribution = $26,250

Thus, a 3.75 percent SEP contribution of $3,750 ($100,000 × .0375), when combined with $17,000 of elective contributions, would produce the maximum excludable contribution of $20,750 ($26,250 with the $5,500 catch-up contribution). The employer's deduction limit of $47,500 (($100,000 × .25) + ($17,000 + $5,500)) has not been exceeded.

The maximum nonelective employer SEP contribution that may be excluded from Grace's gross income can be computed as follows:

(.20 – 17% ($17,000 divided by $100,000)) × 1.25 = 3.75%

.0375 × $100,000 = $3,750 (maximum excludable nonelective contribution).

Example 3. The facts are the same as those in Example 2, except that Joe has wages or earned income (net earnings from self-employment as reduced under Code Section 401(c)(2)) of $250,000 or more. The 25 percent deduction limit of $85,000 ($250,000 × .25) + $22,500 (elective and catch-up contributions)) is reduced to $55,500 (the $50,000 Section 415 limit plus the $5,500 catch-up contribution limit for 2012).

Q 11:5 May an employee be allocated more than $50,000?

Possibly. For 2012, up to $50,000 may generally be allocated to an employee; however, because catch-up contributions are not subject to the $50,000 Section 415 limit, an additional $5,500 for 2012 may be allocated to employees who are age 50 or older. Thus, $55,500 may be allocated to an eligible employee who makes a catch-up contribution of $5,500, for 2012. (See Appendix G for compensation limits in other years.)

Q 11:6 Was the failure to coordinate the $250,000 limit (as indexed) of Code Sections 401(a)(17), 404(l), and 408(k)(3)(C) with Code Section 402(h) intentional?

Possibly. The failure to coordinate the $250,000 (as indexed for 2012) limit referred to in Code Sections 401(a)(17), 404(l), and 408(k)(3)(C) for purposes of the 25 percent exclusion limit under Code Section 402(h)(2)(A) may be intentional instead of the result of legislative oversight. Qualified profit-sharing plans that are integrated may provide for an allocation of more than 25 percent of compensation even if an individual earns below $250,000 for 2012 (see Q 11:5). Arguably, the omission of the compensation cap places SEP arrangements and SARSEPs on a more equal footing with the limit on annual additions under Code Section 415 for qualified plans.

Dollar Exclusion Limit

Q 11:7 What is the maximum dollar amount that may be excluded from an employee's gross income?

Under Code Section 402(h)(2)(B), the maximum dollar amount that may be excluded from an employee's gross income is $50,000 ($55,500 with a $5,500 catch-up contribution) for 2012. This is an annual limit applied on a participant-by-participant basis by aggregating contributions made for the limitation year (presumably the plan year 6:6)) to all SEP arrangements and qualified defined contribution plans maintained by the employer, including contributions made by any related, 50 percent controlled, or affiliated employers (see Qs 2:4–2:17). [I.R.C. §§ 402(g)(6), 414(b), 414(c), 414(m), 414(o), 415(h); Treas. Reg. § 1.415(a)-1(f)(1); I.R.S. Notice 2011-90, 2011-47 I.R.B. 791 for 2012]

For a SEP plan integrated with Social Security, the $50,000 exclusion limit is reduced slightly when the individual is a highly compensated employee (HCE) (see Q 11:8). [I.R.C. §§ 402(h)(2)(A), 402(h)(2)(B)] There is also a $50,000 annual limit on total contributions to all defined contribution plans, including SEPs (see Qs 11:13, 11:14). [I.R.C. § 408(k)(7)(C); Ann. 94-101, §§ 541.2(4), 541.3(2)(b), 1994-35 I.R.B. 53] Elective contributions are subject to a separate dollar limit (see Q 12:6), and, with the exception of catch-up elective contributions, may not exceed $50,000—or $50,000 as reduced—if the plan contributions are integrated with Social Security contributions.

Q 11:8 How is the $50,000 exclusion limit adjusted if the plan is integrated?

It is possible that the $50,000 (as indexed for 2012) limit under Code Section 415 will be reached because of the application of the annual compensation limit and the 25 percent limit on allocations (See Q 11:5). Code Section 402(h)(2)(B) states that the maximum dollar amount that can be allocated each year to an HCE's SEP IRA ($50,000) is "reduced . . . by the amount taken into account with respect to such employee under Section 408(k)(3)(D)." Code Section

408(k)(3)(D) does not provide a concrete amount, but instead refers to "the rules of 401(l)(2), which are the integration rules (see Q 9:5).

For the reasons more fully discussed in Q 9:5, the reduction to the $50,000 annual contribution limit in an integrated SEP is equal to the plan's spread percentage (see Q 9:9) multiplied by the HCE's compensation not in excess of the plan's integration level or the TWB, whichever is less (see Q 9:7). Compensation in excess of $250,000 (the 2012 limit) is not considered.

For 2012, the maximum offset produces a limit of $43,724.30 ($50,000 reduced by the maximum integration level of $110,100 multiplied by .057; $49,224.30 with catch-up contributions if age 50 or older). The following chart presents examples of typical maximum limits at various integration levels for 2012.

Plan Integration Level	*Percent of TWB*	*Max Spread Limit**	*Adjusted $50,000*
$110,100	100%	5.7%	$43,724.30
$ 88,081	80% + $1	5.4	$45,243.63
$ 55,050	50%	4.3	$47,632.85
$ 22,020	20%	5.7	$48,744.86
$ 10,000	.000908265%	5.7	$49,430

* Catch-up contributions for individual age 50 or older by December 31 may be contributed in addition to the $49,000 or $49,000 (as reduced) limit. [I.R.C. § 414(v)(3)(A)]

Q 11:9 How are SEP contributions in excess of the $50,000/$55,500 exclusion limit treated?

To the extent that the $50,000/$55,500 exclusion limit (see Q 11:7) is exceeded, the excess is included in the income of the employee. Presumably, the year of inclusion would be the taxable year of the employee in which the plan year ends. Any such excess contributions are subject to the IRA contribution limits of Code Sections 219 and 408 and may be considered excess contributions to the participant's IRA (see Q 5:75). Such excesses are also treated as compensation for purposes of the 100 percent limit under Code Section 415. However, the 25 percent exclusion limit is always lower than the 100 percent Section 415 limit. [I.R.C. §§ 402(h), 415(c); Treas. Reg. § 1.415(a)-1(f)]

Except for salary reduction amounts described in Code Section 408(k)(6), any payment made to or on behalf of an employee is generally not treated as wages for purposes of FICA (Social Security) and FUTA (federal unemployment) taxes (see Q 11:15). The exemption is not limited in amount and generally applies whether or not the payments are includible in the gross income of the employee (see Q 11:15). [I.R.C. § 3121(a)(5)(C)]

Note. It is unclear whether federal income tax withholding at the source applies when it is not reasonable for the employer to believe that the employee on whose behalf a contribution was made would be entitled to an exclusion for the contribution under Code Section 402(h) (see Qs 11:10, 11:17).

Reporting

Q 11:10 How are excess employer SEP contributions reported to the IRS?

To the extent that the 25 percent or $50,000/$55,500 exclusion limit under Code Section 402(h) is exceeded, the employer should include the excess in box 1 of Form W-2, without any offsetting deductions. If, however, at the time the excess contribution is made, it is not reasonable for the employer to believe that the employee on whose behalf the contribution is made will be entitled to an exclusion under Code Section 402(h) for the contribution, the excess amount could arguably be subject to withholding taxes under Code Section 3401(a)(12). The 2002 version of IRS Publication 590, *Individual Retirement Arrangements (IRAs)*, chapter 3, "Are My Employer's Contributions Taxable?" stated that excess employer contributions must be included in "your gross income, without any offsetting deduction." The 2003 version discontinued coverage of SEP plans, which are now covered in IRS Publication 560, *Retirement Plans for Small Business*. Publication 560 for 2012 more simply states:

> Excess contributions are included in the employee's income for the year and are treated as contributions by the employee to his or her SEP IRA. For more information on employee tax treatment of excess contributions, see chapter 1 in Publication 560. (See Qs 5:75, 11:1.)

Chapter 1 of Publication 560 does not contain any information on the employer's tax treatment of excess contributions. Thus, it is not clear whether withholding is required on amounts that exceed the 25 percent or $50,000/ $55,500 exclusion limit under Code Section 402(h) (see Q 11:15). Furthermore, Instructions for Form W-2 (2012), Specific Instructions—wages, tips, other compensation, box 1, makes no mention of excess contributions.

It is also unclear how the designated distribution withholding rules apply when a participant makes a corrective distribution. When an excess employer nonelective contribution—alone or in combination with an excess SEP contribution, disallowed deferral, or excess deferral—is corrected *during the tax year in which the excess arose*, the designated distribution may be subject to the federal income tax withholding rules, unless the participant elects not to have withholding apply (see Qs 13:24, 13:25).

Notwithstanding the preceding, an amount allocated to a participant under a SEP in excess of the plan's written allocation formula is treated as compensation and is subject to FICA and FUTA tax and to the deduction limits under Code

Section 162 or 212 (see Q 5:24). [Prop. Treas. Reg. § 1.408-8(e)(2), ex. (v)] In some cases, excess amounts may not be determined until after the end of the year. Similarly, excess amounts may be contributed by the employer after the end of the year.

Q 11:11 How does an employer report excess elective deferrals, disallowed deferrals, and excess SEP contributions to the IRS?

Excess elective deferrals (generally deferrals exceeding the taxpayer's $17,000 deferral limit for 2012, disallowed deferrals (deferrals failing the 50 percent participation rate requirement), and excess SEP contributions (contributions failing the 125 percent nondiscrimination test) are reported (in total) in box 12 of Form W-2 (see Qs 11:12, 12:6, 12:18). They are not included in box 1 of Form W-2. The preparer should also not include excess amounts in box 3 or box 5 because the amounts are already included as FICA (Social Security) wages and are not subject to FICA or FUTA (federal unemployment) taxes twice. Such excess amounts are also not subject to income tax withholding. [Rev. Proc. 91-44, 1991-2 C.B. 733; I.R.S. Notice 87-77, 1987-2 C.B. 385; I.R.S. Notice 89-32, 1989-1 C.B. 671 (requiring inclusion of excess elective contributions, an "administrative pronouncement" that may be relied on to the same extent as a revenue procedure or a revenue ruling)]

Note. In the event of a disallowed deferral or an excess SEP contribution, the employer must provide a notice to the employee (see Qs 12:31, 12:43).

When an excess elective deferral, disallowed deferral, or excess SEP contribution is corrected by the participant *during the tax year in which the excess arose*, the designated distribution may be subject to the federal income tax withholding rules, unless the participant elects not to have withholding apply (see Qs 13:24, 13:25)

Q 11:12 How are elective SEP contributions reported to the IRS?

The full amount of elective SEP contributions is reported by the employer on Form W-2, box 12. Code F is included for elective SEP contributions. Thus, for example, if an elective contribution of $22,500 is made to a SEP for 2012, the entry in box 12 would be F 22500.00. Report the code to the left of the vertical line in boxes 12a-d and the money amount to the right of the vertical line. Use decimal points, but not a dollar sign and leave at least one blank space after the code. The 2012 instructions to Form W-2 provide an example in which an excess elective contribution was made. The instructions state: "The excess is not reported in box 1." Presumably, the same rules apply for excess SEP contributions and disallowed deferrals.

If the excess also causes the 25 percent or the $50,000/$55,500 (for 2012) exclusion limit under Code Section 402(h) to be exceeded, elective contributions are required to be reduced by the excess. The IRS does not specify how such a situation is to be handled. [Rev. Proc. 91-44, § VI, Item C, 1991-2 C.B. 733] The actual deferral percentage (ADP) rate may also have to be redetermined, taking into account only the allowable elective contribution.

Overall Limit

Q 11:13 Is a SEP treated as a defined contribution plan for purposes of the 100 percent/$50,000 limit under the overall limit?

Yes. Under Code Section 415(k), a SEP arrangement is treated as a defined contribution plan and is subject to the annual addition limit of $50,000 or 100 percent of plan-year compensation (see Q 11:1), whichever is less, for 2012 (see Q 5:6). That is an overall limit on the amount that can be placed into an account, whether or not the amount is includible in the employee's gross income. The overall limit is especially applicable when more than one plan must be considered. It should be noted that catch-up contributions are not subject to the 100 percent limit nor subject to the $50,000 limit. [I.R.C. § 414(v)(3); Treas. Reg. § 1.415(a)-1(f)]

Q 11:14 Must annual IRA contributions be taken into account when computing the overall limit?

No. As part of the changes effected by the Small Business Job Protection Act of 1996 (SBJPA), IRAs were removed from the list of plans that must be taken into account when computing the overall limit. [I.R.C. § 415(k)] Before that removal, authorities questioned whether annual contributions made to an IRA were to be aggregated in a controlled situation. [Brown, "Are IRAs Included in Section 415 Calculations?" 21 *J. of Pension Planning & Compliance* 4 (Winter 1996)30]

FICA, FUTA, and Other Taxes

Q 11:15 Are employer contributions to SEPs subject to FICA or FUTA taxes?

No. Employer contributions (except elective salary reduction contributions) for owners and employees whose wages are reported on Form W-2 are not treated as wages and are exempt from FICA and FUTA taxes under Code Section 3306(b)(5)(C). [*See* IRS Publication 15-A, *Employer's Supplemental Tax Guide*, supplement to IRS Publication 15, *Circular E, Employer's Tax Guide*, 2012.] The amount of exemption from FICA and FUTA taxes is not limited and seems to apply whether or not the contributions are includible in the gross income of the employee. If the contributions were subject to FICA and FUTA taxes, they would be reported in boxes 3 and 5 on Form W-2. Publication 15-A states:

> An employer's SEP contributions to an employee's individual retirement arrangement (IRA) are excluded from the employee's gross income. These excluded amounts are not subject to social security, Medicare, FUTA taxes, or federal income tax withholding. However, any SEP contributions paid under a salary reduction agreement (SARSEP) are included in wages for purposes of social security and Medicare taxes and for FUTA.

[IRS Publication 15-A, *see* "Contributions to a Simplified Employee Pension (SEP)," p. 14 (2011)]

Contributions (both elective and nonelective) that exceed the 25 percent of compensation exclusion limit or the 100 percent of compensation limit under Code Section 415 are treated as wages. When the excess is attributable to nonelective employer contributions (for which no FICA or FUTA tax has been paid), it is unclear whether the excess amount—treated as wages—is subject to FICA or FUTA tax. The only guidance on the issue was last found in the 2002 version of IRS Publication 590, *Individual Retirement Arrangements (IRAs)*, chapter 3, "Are My Employer's Contributions Taxable?" which stated that excess employer contributions must be included in "your gross income, without any offsetting deduction." (See Q 11:10.) Thus, it is not clear whether FICA or FUTA tax is required on nonelective contributions that exceed the following limits:

- The 25 percent of compensation exclusion limit under Code Section 402(h)(2)(A),
- The dollar limit on annual contributions (currently $50,000) under Code Section 415(c)(1)(A),
- The 100 percent of compensation limit on annual contributions under Code Section 415(c)(1)(B), or
- The special dollar limit (see Q 11:8) applicable to an integrated SEP plan under Code Section 402(h)(2)(B).

Notwithstanding the preceding, an amount allocated to a participant under a SEP in excess of the plan's written allocation formula is treated as compensation and is subject to FICA and FUTA tax and to the deduction limits under Code Section 162 or 212 (see Q 5:24). [Treas. Reg. §§ 1.408-8(e)(2), ex. (v), 1.415(c)-1(b)(1)(ii)]

In some cases, excess amounts may not be determined until after the end of the year. Similarly, excess amounts may be contributed by the employer after the end of the year.

> **Note.** In response to general information letters requested in 1995 and 1996, the IRS told the authors that it is examining the issue of FICA and FUTA taxation of excess nonelective contributions. As of publication of the 18th edition of this book, the IRS has not issued any guidance. Until guidance is issued, it will remain difficult to determine whether an excess amount that is "treated" as wages is also treated as a SEP contribution for FICA and FUTA exemption under Code Section 3306(b)(5)(C).

Q 11:16 Are contributions to SEPs on behalf of self-employed individuals subject to self-employment tax?

Yes. Elective and nonelective contributions made by or on behalf of unincorporated business owners, including partners in a partnership, do not reduce their self-employment tax obligations. [I.R.C. § 1402(d)]

Q 11:17 Are contributions to SEPs subject to federal income tax withholding at the source?

Generally, no. SEP contributions are not generally treated as wages; therefore, they are not subject to federal income tax withholding. The statutory exemptions from such tax apply if it is reasonable to believe that the employee is entitled to exclude the contribution from income under Code Section 402(h).

The term *wages*, under Code Section 3401(a)(12)(C), does not include SEP contributions described in Code Section 402(h)(1) and 402(h)(2) if, at the time of the contribution, it is reasonable to believe that the employee will be entitled to an exclusion, under Code Section 402(h)(1) and 402(h)(2), for the contribution. (See Qs 11:10, 11:15, 11:18.)

Example. Jerry, an employee of Big Box Co., excludes a beginning-of-the-year bonus from income as an elective deferral under a SEP. Soon thereafter Jerry resigns. The deferral exceeds 25 percent of Jerry's compensation for the year. Even though the contribution was more than 25 percent of Jerry's compensation, it arguably could be considered reasonable when made. On the other hand, under Code Section 415, amounts contributed in excess of $50,000 or 100 percent of compensation for 2012 may cause the entire arrangement to be disqualified (see Q 5:8).

Q 11:18 Are excess SEP contributions, excess deferrals, and disallowed deferrals subject to federal income tax withholding at the source?

No. Although excess SEP contributions and excess deferrals (even if less than 25 percent of compensation for 2012) are included in an employee's gross income, they are not subject to federal income tax withholding at the source. [I.R.S. Ann. 97-42, 1997 I.R.B. 17, 19, employer required to report excess SEP contributions in the manner described in I.R.S. Notice 89-32, 1989-1 C.B. 671. This Notice modified I.R.S. Notice 87-77, 1987-2 C.B. 385 and I.R.S. Notice 88-33, 1988-1 C.B. 513. *See also* Rev. Proc. 91-44, 1991-2 C.B. 735] Portions of Notice 87-77 are antiquated, however, and cannot be relied on in light of recent changes made under EGTRRA and the JCWAA (see Qs 2:94–2:96).

Excess contributions (reported in box 1) are deducted by the employer as "wages."

In the case of a self-employed individual, excess contributions (of any type) are not to be deducted on Form 1040.

Presumably, the same rules would apply to disallowed deferrals when less than 50 percent of eligible employees fail to make elective contributions.

Chapter 12

Elective SARSEP Deferrals

This chapter defines elective salary reduction deferrals, including catch-up deferrals, and discusses how they may be made to a grandfathered salary reduction SEP (SARSEP). It also examines how excess contributions may occur under a SARSEP and how such contributions are treated. Relevant employee notifications are explained as well. The special problems that arise when the plan year (which is used for most plan limitation purposes) is not the same as the calendar year (which is used for elective contribution limitation purposes) are also discussed in this chapter. The forwarding of elective contributions and the Department of Labor's (DOL's) seven-day safe harbor under the Employee Retirement Income Security Act (ERISA) are discussed in chapter 4 (see Q 4:45).

Elective Salary Reduction Deferrals

Q 12:1 How does a SEP contribution qualify as an elective SEP contribution?

A SEP contribution qualifies as an elective SEP contribution only if there is a voluntary election by the employee to reduce current compensation or to forgo a compensation increase. Although subject to various limits, an elective deferral generally reduces an employee's taxable income.

A contribution that precludes an individual election by the employee is treated as a nonelective employer contribution. [Prop. Treas. Reg. § 1.408-7(c)(2)] Thus, a unilateral decision by the employer to reduce an employee's compensation and to make a contribution of all or a portion of the reduction amount is considered a nonelective employer SEP contribution.

Note 1. In 2009, the IRS released final regulations providing guidance on automatic contribution arrangements (ACAs or negative elections) in 401(k) cash-or-deferred arrangements (CODAs), 403(b) tax-sheltered annuities, or 457(b) governmental plans. Section 401(k) plans that adopt qualified automatic contribution arrangements (QACAs) are deemed to have satisfied the tax code's special nondiscrimination tests that would otherwise apply to employee elective deferrals and employer matching contributions. In addition, such plans generally will be exempt from the top-heavy rules. [74 Fed. Reg. 8200–8214 (Feb. 24, 2009); *see* Rev. Rul. 2009-30, 2009-39 I.R.B. 391 (Sept. 28, 2009)]

Caution. An eligible automatic contribution arrangement (EACA) is an automatic contribution arrangement (ACA) that may allow employees to withdraw automatic enrollment contributions, up to 90 days from the date these contributions first start, without incurring the 10 percent early withdrawal tax. The default percentage must be applied uniformly to all eligible employees, and they must be given notice before each plan year or when eligible to join the plan if that occurs after the beginning of the plan year.

In September 2009, the Internal Revenue Service (IRS) issued guidance that facilitates automatic enrollment in SIMPLE IRA (Savings Incentive Match Plan for Employees) plans, including questions and answers relating to the inclusion in a SIMPLE IRA plan of an ACA. [I.R.S. Notice 2009-66, 2009-39 I.R.B. 418] Under an ACA, in the absence of an affirmative election by an employee, a default election applies whereby the employee is treated as having elected to have a portion of his or her compensation contributed to a tax-favored retirement plan as default elective contributions rather than paid to the employee in cash (see Q 14:80). In addition, the IRS has provided a sample plan amendment that a prototype sponsor of a SIMPLE IRA plan (providing for a designated financial institution) can use in drafting an amendment to add an ACA to the SIMPLE IRA plan. The guidance explains the additional notification requirements that would apply to a SIMPLE IRA plan containing an ACA and provides that the percentage of compensation at which default salary reduction contributions are made for an employee may increase based on the number of years or portions of years for which default salary reduction contributions have been made for the employee. The IRS is also requesting comments on whether it should issue guidance regarding SIMPLE IRA plans that include an eligible ACA and for SIMPLE IRA plans that contain an ACA that is not an eligible ACA, and if so, what issues should be discussed in such guidance.

The IRS has not issued any guidance regarding ACAs under a SARSEP or a SIMPLE IRA plan. Thus, it is not known under what circumstance an ACA can be treated as an elective contribution under a SARSEP or SIMPLE IRA plan. It is also not known whether the IRS will permit an ACA feature in a model and/or prototype document, or whether a private letter ruling request will be required to include such a feature.

Note 2. The IRS expects to issue a revised Form 5305-SIMPLE, Savings Incentive Match Plan for Employees of Small Employers (SIMPLE) for Use with a Designated Financial Institution. [I.R.S. Notice 2009-67, 2009-39 I.R.B. 420] The IRS did not indicate when additional guidance or a sample plan amendment would be available for other model forms, or for a SIMPLE IRA plan that does not provide for a designated financial institution (see Q 14:143), or for a SARSEP plan. The IRS will likely issue revised LRMs (Listings of Required Modifications) and new model forms in 2012 (see Qs 3:19, 3:20). The current versions of Form 5305-SIMPLE (rev. Sept. 2008) and SIMPLE LRM (rev June 2010) do not contain provisions for ACAs.

Note 3. Final regulations under Code Section 414(w) provide special withdrawal rules for an ACA that also satisfies special requirements, called an eligible ACA (or EACA), and the rules include an EACA in a SEP or SIMPLE IRA. However, the regulations do not reflect: (1) the additional time to correct excess contributions under a SARSEP that includes an EACA; (2) the tax treatment of excess contributions and earnings thereon under a SARSEP; and (3) guidance on SIMPLE IRA plans that include an EACA. [Treas. Reg. § 1.414(w)-1(e)(1)(iv) and (v); Preamble, Treas. Reg. § 1.414(w)-1 (T.D. 9447, 74 Fed. Reg. 8200, 8206 (Feb. 24, 2009))]

Q 12:2 May elective SEP contributions be based on bonuses?

Yes. A SEP may contain a cash-bonus option. That is, an employer may allow eligible employees the option to base elective deferrals on bonuses that, at the employee's election, may be contributed to the SEP or received in cash during the plan year (see Qs 1:5, 6:9). In other cases, compensation subject to deferral would include bonus payments.

Q 12:3 May an employee choose not to make elective contributions to a salary reduction SEP?

Yes. Participation in a SARSEP must be voluntary. That is, an employee must elect to participate and cannot be required to make elective salary reduction contributions.

Q 12:4 Are elective deferrals deductible by the employer?

Yes. Amounts deferred by employees (including owner employees) are treated as employer contributions and are deducted by the employer in the case of an entity not treated as a corporation, or by the self-employed individual (see Q 10:12). In general, elective deferrals are also treated as plan assets and must be forwarded timely to the trustee or custodian (see Q 4:45).

Q 12:5 May the employer make matching contributions based on the elective deferrals of employees?

No. If an employer makes a contribution, it must be allocated to all employees in accordance with the plan's written allocation formula.

Q 12:6 Is there a dollar limit on elective deferrals?

Yes. An employee may normally defer up to $17,000 for 2012 by means of a salary reduction agreement. The limit is computed on a calendar-year basis. [I.R.C. § 402(g)(1)] Amounts that exceed the dollar limit are called excess deferrals or excess elective deferrals (see Q 12:18). The maximum amount of catch-up contributions is based on the participant's taxable year, which will almost always be the calendar year (see Q 12:53). Special considerations apply if the plan year is not the calendar year (see Q 12:54). This is because statutory limits, as well as employer-provided limits (if any), may be based on the plan year (or other 12-month period) and can affect the amount of elective deferrals that can be treated as catch-up contributions (see Q 12:52).

For 2012, an elective contribution that exceeds the $17,000 limit or other statutory limit is automatically treated as a catch-up elective contribution (up to $5,500 for 2012; see Q 12:45). Thus, there is no need for an employee to separately contribute catch-up contributions. In a sense, catch-up contributions are what remains of elective contributions for the calendar year that cannot be treated as normal elective contributions that are subject to the $17,000 limit, actual deferral percentage (ADP) testing, and other limitations for 2012. A plan must contain written catch-up provisions if they are to apply (see Q 12:50).

If the dollar limit is exceeded (after considering amounts that may be treated as catch-up contributions), the excess SEP contribution is includible in the participant's income in the year for which the deferral was made, but any earnings (upon correction) are taxable when distributed.

For years beginning after 2001, the normal elective deferral limit for a SARSEP will increase as follows:

Year	*Increased Deferral Limit*
2002	$11,000
2003	$12,000
2004	$13,000
2005	$14,000
2006	$15,000
2007	$15,500
2008	$15,500
2009	$16,500

Year	*Increased Deferral Limit*
2010	$16,500
2011	$16,500
2012	$17,000

[I.R.C. § 402(g)(1) *see* I.R.S. Notice 2011-90, 2011-47 I.R.B. 791 for 2012 limits]

The normal elective deferral limit is increased for cost-of-living adjustments (COLAs) in increments of $500 after 2006. [I.R.C. § 402(g)(5)]

In addition, for taxable years beginning after 2001, if an individual participates in a SARSEP and is at least age 50 or will attain age 50 by the end of the plan year, that participant may make additional elective deferrals up to an applicable dollar limit. This catch-up amount is in addition to the normal deferral limit for the applicable year (see Q 12:46).

The maximum amount of the catch-up contribution is the lesser of the participant's compensation for the year or the applicable dollar amount. The applicable dollar amounts are as follows:

Year	*Normal Limit*	*Applicable Dollar Amount*	*Total Deferral*
2002	$11,000	$1,000	$12,000
2003	$12,000	$2,000	$14,000
2004	$13,000	$3,000	$16,000
2005	$14,000	$4,000	$18,000
2006	$15,000	$5,000	$20,000
2007	$15,500	$5,000	$20,500
2008	$15,500	$5,000	$20,500
2009	$16,500	$5,500	$22,000
2010	$16,500	$5,500	$22,000
2011	$16,500	$5,500	$22,000
2012	$17,000	$5,500	$22,500

Note. Catch-up deferrals are not subject to the ADP test or to any other nondiscrimination requirements (see Qs 12:55–12:61). [I.R.C. § 414(v)]

For taxable years beginning after 2006, the catch-up limit of $5,000 is subject to COLAs in increments of $500. This adjustment is separate from the adjustment applicable to the normal elective deferral limit. [I.R.C. § 414(v)(2)(C)]

All deferrals (including excess deferrals) are generally treated as employer contributions for purposes of the employer's deduction limit and the limits under Section 415 of the Internal Revenue Code (Code) (see Qs 5:6, 10:7).

[Treas. Reg. § 1.402(g)-1(e)(1)(ii)] Catch-up deferrals, however, are not subject to the $50,000 Section 415 limit for 2012; see Qs 11:5, 11:7) or to the 25 percent exclusion limit (see Q 11:1) or the 100 percent limit under Code Section 415 (see Qs 11:1, 11:13, 12:15). Failure to properly report elective contributions in box 12 of Form W-2, Wage and Tax Statement, could result in disqualification of the SEP if the dollar limit on elective deferrals is exceeded. [I.R.C. § 401(k)(6)(A)(iv) (imposing the requirements of I.R.C. § 401(a)(30) on a SARSEP)]

Elective contributions (other than catch-up contributions) must be reduced to the extent the 25 percent participant exclusion limit would be exceeded (see Q 12:15). Elective contributions may not exceed a participant's compensation (determined without taking elective contributions into account). [Treas. Reg. § 1.414(v)-1(c)(1)]

It is possible to have a catch-up contribution without a normal contribution.

Example. Elective contributions are made to a SARSEP for 2012. The employer makes a 25 percent of pre-plan compensation contribution for 2012. Those employees that are eligible to make elective contributions may do so. In this case, elective contributions will be treated as catch-up contributions up to the catch-up contribution limit ($5,500 for 2012).

Practice Pointer. In computing the dollar limit on elective deferrals, community property laws are ignored. [I.R.C. § 402(g)(6)]

Practice Pointer. If the plan year is not the calendar year, it will be difficult to determine the elective deferral and catch-up limits (and amounts) in overlapping "plan year" periods. This problem could be avoided if all of a participant's yearly elective deferrals (for all years) were contributed (made) during only one of the periods during any calendar year (see Q 12:54 and examples).

Q 12:7 What is the maximum percentage that an employee may elect to defer?

Generally, an employee who is not a highly compensated employee (HCE; see Q 1:14) may elect to defer 25 percent of his or her includible taxable compensation up to $17,000 for 2012 (see Q 11:1) plus catch-up contributions of up to $5,500 if age 50 or older.

Example. Marcy, age 40, has pre-plan compensation of $10,000. Marcy's employer, Quincy Market Corp., adopts a SEP arrangement with provisions for Quincy Market employees to reduce their taxable income. Marcy contributes $2,000, which is the maximum amount excludable from her income if no employer contributions are made.

Proof: .25 ($10,000 – $2,000) = $2,000

If Marcy were age 50 or older, she could contribute an additional $5,500 as a catch-up contribution for 2012.

Q 12:8 How much may each eligible HCE elect to defer as a normal contribution?

The percentage of total compensation elected to be deferred by each eligible HCE (see Q 1:14) cannot exceed the lesser of

1. 25 percent of the HCE's taxable plan year compensation that will be includible in gross income [I.R.C. § 402(h)]; or
2. The average of the individual percentages, determined separately and without taking catch-up contributions into account (see Q 12:56), elected to be contributed by each eligible non-highly compensated employee for the plan year (NHCE) multiplied by 1.25 (the 125 percent rule). [I.R.C. §§ 408(k)(6)(A)(iii), 414(v)(3)]

Q 12:9 What is the 125 percent rule?

Under the *125 percent rule* (also known as the ADP test), the percentage of total compensation (expressed to 2 decimal places) elected to be deferred by each eligible HCE for the current plan year, *excluding* catch-up contributions, must not exceed the average of the individual deferral percentages, computed separately and without regard to catch-up contributions (see Q 12:56), for all eligible NHCEs multiplied by 1.25. [I.R.C. §§ 408(k)(6)(A)(iii), 414(v)(3)]

Example 1. Pisces Corporation's NHCEs earn the following amounts and defer the following percentages for 2012:

NHCE 1	$10,000/8%
NHCE 2	$10,000/4%
NHCE 3	$10,000/4%
NHCE 4	$10,000/0%

The average of the NHCEs' deferral percentages is computed as follows:

(.08 + .04 + .04 + 0)/4 = .04

The amount that may be deferred by each eligible HCE is computed as follows:

.04 × 1.25 = .05, up to $17,000 for 2012

Caution. Except as otherwise indicated, the examples in this chapter assume a prototype SARSEP is used that defines compensation for ADP testing purposes as gross compensation (before reduction for elective deferrals) (see chapter 6). In a model SARSEP (Form 5305A-SEP), the term *compensation* generally excludes elective contributions that are made by the participant to the plan. Under the model document, the ADP percentage for an employee that deferred $500 from gross wages of $10,000 would be 5.26 percent ($500/$9,500). If a model document were used in Example 1, the average of the NHCEs' deferral would be 4.26 percent ((8.7 + 4.17 + 4.17 + 0)/4) rather than 4. An HCE employee could defer 5.32 percent (4.26% × 1.25) under the model plan. However, if any nonelective employer SEP contributions are made, plan provisions would generally require that they be allocated based on reduced compensation (i.e., excluding the elective deferrals). It should be noted that the 25 percent exclusion limit (see Q 11:1) is always based on reduced compensation. [*See also* IRS Publication 4336, *Salary Reduction Plans for Small Businesses* (Mar. 2010), which uses unreduced compensation for the ADP denominator without distinguishing between plan types (i.e., model or prototype plan document). Publication 4336 is available at *http://www.irs.gov/pub/irs-pdf/p4336.pdf* (visited on Aug. 22, 2012)]

Example 2. The facts are the same as those in Example 1, except that one HCE is over age 50 on December 31, 2012. That HCE may defer 5 percent of total compensation, up to $17,000, plus a catch-up contribution of up to $5,500 (see Q 12:6).

Note. The percentage that may be deferred by any one eligible HCE is *not* dependent (as generally is the case in a traditional 401(k) plan) on percentages or amounts that other HCEs elect to defer (see Q 12:13).

Example 3. Marlin Corporation maintains a SARSEP for its employees using Form 5305A-SEP. Its three NHCEs elect to defer 2 percent, 3 percent, and 4 percent, respectively, of their compensation. The only other eligible employee is the owner, Vicki, and she contributes her allowed maximum of 3.75 percent, computed by taking the average of the deferral rates of each eligible NHCE (separately determined for each employee) and multiplying it by 1.25. Because Vicki is a key employee and a plan participant, the SARSEP arrangement is deemed top heavy and Marlin must contribute 3 percent (i.e., the lesser of 3 percent or 3.75 percent) to each non-key employee (see Q 3:16).

Note. Elective contributions must be reduced if the 25 percent of includible compensation limit is exceeded (see Q 12:15). Elective contributions in excess of the 25 percent limit may possibly be treated as a catch-up contribution (see Q 12:54).

Q 12:10 How are family members treated for purposes of the 125 percent rule?

For purposes of the 125 percent rule, certain family members of 5 percent or more owners must be treated as HCEs under the family attribution rules (see Qs 1:14, 12:13).

Q 12:11 Must related employers be considered for purposes of the 125 percent rule?

Yes. For purposes of the 125 percent rule (see Q 12:9), the determination of the identity of the HCEs, and the calculation of the number of HCEs and their deferral percentages, must take into account all employees of members of an affiliated service group, all employees of a controlled group of corporations, and all employees of trades or businesses under common control (see Q 2:5). [I.R.C. §§ 414(b), 414(c), 414(m), 414(n), 414(o)]

Q 12:12 May elective contributions be made to a plan in which there are only HCEs?

Yes. Although there is no express authority on point, a plan without any eligible NHCEs for a year should not fail the 125 percent rule. [Treas. Reg. § 1.401(k)-1(b)(2)(B)] One of the listed restrictions in the original version of Form 5305A-SEP was that it could not be used if only HCEs were participants. That restriction was deleted from the subsequent version of the form to permit the model form to be used when only HCEs participate in the plan.

Q 12:13 Does nonparticipation by one highly compensated employee in a SEP affect another HCE's maximum deferral percentage?

No. In a SEP, the result of the 125 percent calculation is applied separately to each HCE (see Qs 12:8, 12:10).

Q 12:14 How can the maximum elective contribution rate be determined if the employer's contribution is known?

If the employer contribution is known, the maximum normal elective SEP contribution rate for 2012 generally can be calculated as follows:

$$\frac{25 - x}{1.25}$$

where x equals the employer contribution percentage of pre-plan compensation.

Example. Ariana, age 25, has pre-plan compensation of $10,000 for 2012. Her employer, Kitchen Goods, Inc., adopts a SEP arrangement with provisions for employees of Kitchen Goods to reduce their taxable income. Ariana contributes $2,000, which is 25 percent of her taxable income of $8,000 ($10,000 – $2,000) and the maximum amount excludable from her income (see Q 11:1) if no employer contributions are made. After the end of the year, Kitchen Goods is informed that it must make a 3 percent top-heavy contribution for the year. Given the employer contribution rate of 3 percent, the maximum SEP contribution, including Ariana's salary reduction contribution, may be calculated as follows:

$$\frac{25 - 3}{1.25} = 17.60\%$$

$10,000 × .1760 = $1,760

Proof: .25 ($10,000 – $1,760) – (.03 × $10,000) = $1,760

Kitchen Goods makes the 3 percent contribution; $300 must be included in Ariana's income under Code Section 402(h)(2). The $300 amount, which exceeds the 25 percent exclusion limit under Code Section 402(h), is treated as wages. It is unclear whether the amount is subject to FICA (Social Security) and FUTA (federal unemployment) tax (see Q 11:15) or to federal income tax withholding (see Q 11:17). If Ariana were age 50 or older, the $300 could possibly be treated as a catch-up contribution (see Q 12:52).

Q 12:15 Are elective contributions reduced if a participant's Section 415 limits are exceeded?

Yes. If elective and nonelective SEP contributions exceed the Section 415 limit of $50,000 or 100 percent of includible compensation for plan years ending in 2012, the elective contributions must be reduced; however, catch-up contributions are not subject to the $50,000 Section 415 limit (see Q 11:5), and the 25 percent exclusion limit is always lower than the 100 percent Section 415 limit (see Qs 11:1, 11:2). Reduction of the elective contributions could require a recalculation of the percentage of compensation allowed to be deferred by each eligible HCE. Of course, if the overall contribution is less than $50,000 or 25 percent of includible compensation for 2012, recalculation of each HCE's deferral percentage is not required. [Rev. Proc. 91-44, § 7, 1991-2 C.B. 733]

If the $50,000/100 percent limit is exceeded, the plan may be disqualified (i.e., lose its tax-sanctioned status).

Q 12:16 May a SARSEP provide for salary reduction contributions only and no employer contributions?

It depends. A SARSEP known as a zero-contribution SARSEP can be designed to avoid the top-heavy rules and thus to be limited to salary deferrals only. In such a case, no employer contributions are required. When an employer has too many key employees (or they earn too much), however, such a plan cannot be designed because a zero-contribution SARSEP must not be top heavy or become top heavy in operation. Furthermore, Form 5305A-SEP may not be used to establish a zero-contribution SARSEP arrangement if any key employee makes an elective deferral (see Q 3:16).

Example. Grouper Corporation established a prototype SARSEP that is now grandfathered. It has never maintained a SEP or qualified plan in the past. Grouper's NHCEs each elect to defer 4 percent of compensation for 2012 (see Table 12-1). Although Grouper's owner and key employee could defer 5 percent, he defers only 4.1538462 percent, so that the total amount allocated to him ($5,400/$9,000) is not more than 60 percent. Because key employees have never received more than 60 percent of all contributions, the plan is not top heavy (see Q 8:1), and employer contributions are not required. Without nonelective employer contributions, the plan is 100 percent effective (see Q 12:17). (Prototype documents that use the formula allocation method are being used.)

Table 12-1.
Zero-Contribution SARSEP: 60 Percent to Owner

Employee	*W-2 Compensation*	*Salary Reduction Contributions*	*Taxable Federal Compensation*
Owner	$130,000	$5,400	$124,600
Employee B	40,000	1,600	38,400
Employee C	30,000	1,200	28,800
Employee D	20,000	800	19,200
Total	$220,000	$9,000	$211,000

Q 12:17 Why might an employer combine a SEP and a SARSEP?

Combining SEP and SARSEP arrangements can increase an employer's effectiveness ratio that is, the percentage of employer dollars going into the tax-deferred individual retirement accounts (IRAs) of higher paid owners. Salary reduction amounts contributed by employees cost the employer nothing but allow owners to defer their own income, which would otherwise be taxable.

Example. Combo Co., owned by Mark, makes an integrated contribution of 3 percent of compensation up to $40,000, plus 6 percent of compensation in excess of $40,000, to a combined SEP and SARSEP. Combo's NHCEs, Linda, Donna, and Christine, each elect to defer 4 percent, whereas Mark elects to defer the maximum of 5 percent. The plan's effectiveness ratio is 82.9 percent, computed as follows:

Table 12.2. Combined SEP and SARSEP

Employee	*W-2 Compensation*	*Salary Reduction Contributions*	*Deductible Employer Contribution*	*Total IRA Contribution*
Mark	$130,000	$ 6,500	$6,600	$13,100
Linda	40,000	1,600	1,200	2,800
Donna	30,000	1,200	900	2,100
Christine	20,000	800	600	1,400
Total	$220,000	$10,100	$9,300	$19,400
Effectiveness Ratio	59%	100%	71%	82.9%*

* $13,100 divided by $15,800 ($19,400 – $3,600 of nonowner salary reduction) equals an effectiveness ratio of 82.9 percent.

Excess Amounts Unique to SARSEPs

Special rules govern the correction of contributions that exceed the special limits applicable to a SARSEP. If correction is not timely made, the employer can still correct most failures under the EPCRS. A streamlined application procedure that enables a plan sponsor to fix certain types of plan failures became available in 2008. The procedure follows a mostly "fill-in-the-blank" approach. (See chapter 17.) The correction procedures available under the EPCRS are generally not as favorable as those described in Qs 12:18–12:44 for corrective distributions timely made. Although rules "similar to" the rules of Code Section 401(k)(8) apply to excesses under a SARSEP, the IRS has not updated the regulations. [I.R.C. § 408(k)(6)(C)] Although all three types of excess become traditional IRA contributions if not timely corrected by the participant (as discussed in Q 3:21), this does not relieve an employer from correcting any failures that might have occurred. (See chapter 17.)

Q 12:18 How many types of excess contributions might be made to a SARSEP for 2012?

In addition to contributions in excess of the 100 percent (up to $50,000/ $55,500) overall limit on total contributions to any one participant's account (see Q 5:6), the participant's exclusion limit of 25 percent of compensation, up to $50,000/$5,500 (as indexed and adjusted; see Q 11:1), and the employer's 25 percent of aggregate compensation deduction limit (see Q 10:3), three other kinds of excess contributions might occur in a SEP arrangement that allows for elective deferrals (see Q 5:75 and Appendix M):

1. Excess deferrals (deferrals exceeding the taxpayer's deferral limit under Code Section 402(g), $17,000 for 2012) (see Q 12:19);
2. Excess SEP contributions (contributions failing the 125 percent nondiscrimination test of Code Section 408(k)(6)(A)(iii)), which would affect only HCEs (see Q 12:26); and
3. Disallowed deferrals (deferrals failing the 50 percent participation rate requirement of Code Section 408(k)(6)(A)(ii)) (see Q 12:41).

(See also Qs 5:75–5:81.) [I.R.S. Notice 89-32, 1989-1 C.B. 671; I.R.S. Notice 88-33, 1988-1 C.B. 513; I.R.S. Notice 87-77, 1987-2 C.B. 385; and the regulations under I.R.C. §§ 401(k), 401(m), and 402(g)] Plan failures may also be corrected under the EPCRS (see chapter 17). (See Qs 12:19–12:44.)

Note. To the extent that the 25 percent exclusion limit or $50,000 is exceeded, different rules apply (see Qs 11:3, 11:9, 11:10, 12:15).

Excess Deferrals—Exceeding Deferral Dollar Limit

Q 12:19 What are *excess deferrals*, and who is responsible for monitoring the deferral limit?

Excess deferrals, sometimes called excess elective deferrals, are the salary reduction contributions that exceed the dollar limit under Code Section 402(g) ($17,000 plus catch-up contribution for 2012). The employer and each employee are separately responsible for monitoring the limit for the calendar year.

> **Note.** The excess deferral of an NHCE is not taken into account in calculating the NHCE's deferral percentage for purposes of testing a SARSEP's compliance with the 125 percent rule (see Q 12:9). [Treas. Reg. § 1.402(g)-1(e)(1)(ii)]

Q 12:20 Are plans other than the SARSEP taken into account in determining the Section 402(g) dollar limit?

Yes. The Section 402(g) dollar limit ($17,000 for 2012; $22,500 with catch-up contributions) is an annual limit imposed on an individual employee and includes any elective contributions made to a 401(k) plan or to a tax-sheltered annuity or custodial account under Code Section 403(b), but not an eligible governmental plan under Code Section 457(b).

Q 12:21 May the dollar limit imposed by Code Section 402(g) be increased?

Under certain circumstances, yes. The dollar limit imposed by Code Section 402(g), which is $17,000 for 2012, may be increased by as much as $3,000 if an employee makes elective deferrals to a tax-sheltered annuity or custodial account under Code Section 403(b). The additional amount, however, applies only to employees with 15 or more years of service with a qualifying organization. [I.R.C. § 402(g)(7)] In addition, for years beginning after 2001, the Section 402(g) dollar limit may also be increased for catch-up contributions (see Qs 12:6, 12:45).

Q 12:22 Is an employer required to provide an employee with formal notification of an excess deferral?

No. An employer is not required to provide an employee with any type of formal notification that an elective contribution in excess of the Section 402(g) dollar limit (an excess deferral) has been made.

Q 12:23 How are excess elective deferrals treated by an employee?

The total amount of the elective deferral is reported in box 12 of Form W-2. The Form W-2 Notice to Employee (Form W-2, box 12) instructs the employee to include in income elective SEP deferral amounts that exceed the overall elective limit (generally $17,000 plus catch-up contributions, if applicable, for 2012). Unless the participant includes the excess deferral in his or her income on Form 1040, U.S. Individual Income Tax Return (line 7), in the year to which the deferral relates, the employee may have to file an amended income tax return.

The employee should generally withdraw the excess deferral and any allocable income by April 15 following the calendar year to which the deferral relates because after that date, the excess deferral is deemed an IRA contribution subject to the IRA contribution limits of Code Sections 219 and 408 and may be considered an excess contribution to his or her IRA (see Q 5:77). [I.R.C. §§ 402(g)(2)(A)(ii), 408(d)(4), 408(d)(5)] That is, on April 16 of the calendar year following the deferral, it is no longer treated as an excess deferral, but as an IRA contribution.

If, on the other hand, the employee withdraws the excess deferral in a proper correcting distribution before April 16 (no extensions) of the year following the calendar year to which the deferral relates, the gain is not subject to the 10 percent premature distribution penalty tax (see Q 5:77). [I.R.C. §§ 401(k)(8)(D), 408(k)(6)(C)(i)]

Example. Harvey, age 40, makes an elective contribution of $18,000 during 2012 to his employer's elective SEP (SARSEP); however, the dollar limit on his normal elective contribution is $17,000. After April 15, 2013 (no extensions), to the extent that the excess deferral ($1,000) is not allowable as an annual IRA contribution (deemed made on April 16, 2013), the amount is treated as an excess IRA contribution for 2013. Before April 16, 2013 (the year following the year to which the deferral relates), the amount is a SARSEP excess deferral that Harvey can remove (adjusted for gains, negative or positive) without having to pay a premature distribution penalty (see Q 5:77). If Harvey were age 50 or older, an additional $5,500 could be treated as a catch-up contribution (but not in excess of Henry's compensation, including elective deferrals).

Q 12:24 Is a corrective distribution of an excess deferral subject to income tax withholding, social security, or Medicare taxes?

No. A corrective distribution of an excess deferral is not subject to income tax withholding, social security, or Medicare taxes (see Q 11:1).

Q 12:25 How are corrective distributions of 2012 excess deferrals reported on Form 1099-R?

If distributed by April 15 of the year following the year of deferral, the excess is taxable in the year of deferral, but the earnings are taxable in the year of distribution. If a correction of an excess deferral is made after the end of the year, but before April 15 of the following year, a separate Form 1099-R will be necessary to reflect the taxable year. Corrective distributions of a 2012 excess deferral plus earnings are reported on Form 1099-R by the trustee or custodian of the SEP IRA, depending upon when the correcting distribution is made. An investment incident to a correcting distribution is treated differently (see Q 12:39).

If a corrective distribution of an excess deferral is made during the year of deferral, the excess amount and the earnings will be taxable in the same year. If corrected in the year of deferral, enter the gross distribution in box 1 (gross distribution) of the 2012 version of Form 1099-R. Enter the amount of the excess contribution plus earnings in box 2a (taxable amount). Box 2b (taxable amount not determined) is left blank. Enter code 8 (taxable in 2012) in box 7 (distribution codes) on the 2012 version of Form 1099-R.

On the other hand, if the correcting distribution was made after the end of the year, but on or before April 16, 2013, two separate Form 1099-Rs will be required, as follows:

1. *To report the distribution of the excess deferral taxable in the prior year.*

   Enter the gross distribution in box 1 (gross distribution) of Form 1099-R. Enter the amount of the excess deferral in box 2a (taxable amount). Box 2b (taxable amount not determined) is left blank. Enter code P (taxable in 2012) in box 7 on the 2013 version of Form 1099-R.

2. *To report the distribution of earnings on the excess deferral taxable in the year of distribution.*

   Enter the gross distribution in box 1 (gross distribution) of Form 1099-R. Enter the amount of the earnings in box 2a (taxable amount). Enter code 8 (taxable in 2013) in box 7 on the 2013 version of Form 1099-R.

If not corrected before April 16 of the year following the year the excess elective deferral was made, the excess deferral is treated as a traditional IRA contribution for the year. Thus, if not timely corrected as an excess elective deferral, on April 16, 2013, the excess amount is treated as a traditional IRA contribution. If this happens, the individual's traditional IRA contribution limit may be exceeded and result in an excess traditional IRA contribution for that year (see Q 5:75). An unwanted traditional IRA contribution can also be removed (see Q 5:75).

> **Note.** In all cases, code 1 (early distribution, no known exception), code 2 (early distribution, exception applies), or code 4 (death) should also be entered in box 7, if applicable.

> **Caution.** An individual should know that the Code Section 402(g) dollar limit is exceeded. Therefore, the relevant April 15th for correcting an excess elective contribution does not depend upon any employer notification being provided to the participant. In fact, no employer notification of an excess deferral is required.

> **Example 1.** Lucy, age 45, an employee of Faux Furs, makes the maximum permitted nondeductible IRA contribution into an interest-bearing IRA every year on January 2. She also makes an elective contribution of $18,000 under her Faux Furs SARSEP in 2012; the $18,000 deferral amount is also reported on Lucy's 2012 Form W-2 (box 12). The Code Section 402(g) limit ($17,000

for 2012) has been exceeded, and Lucy does not qualify to make catch-up contributions. Lucy reports $1,000 on line 7 of her 2012 tax return.

The IRA custodian calculates that $25 of interest was earned on the $1,000. If Lucy does not make a correcting distribution (with gain) in 2013 on or before by April 15, 2013 (no extensions), the excess elective contribution is then treated as a 2013 traditional IRA contribution "deemed" made on April 16, 2013.

Assume Lucy makes a correcting distribution of $1,025 on December 22, 2012. Here, the excess elective contribution and correcting distribution are made in the same calendar year. Lucy can eliminate the premature distribution penalty (if applicable) on the gain by making a corrective distribution of the excess (plus gain) before April 15, 2013. However, because the correcting distribution was made in 2012, only one Form 1099-R is needed. Form 1099-R for 2012 would show $1,025 in box 1 (gross distribution) and box 2a (taxable amount). Code 8 (taxable in 2012) would be entered in box 7 to show that both the excess elective contribution and gain distributed are taxable—in this case, in the same year.

Example 2. The facts are the same as those in Example 1, except Lucy makes a correcting distribution of the excess deferral and gain ($1,025) on April 15, 2013—the day before the $1,000 would be deemed a 2013 traditional IRA contribution if not timely corrected as an excess elective contribution.

Because the correcting distribution is made in 2013, two Form 1099-Rs are needed: one to show the excess elective contribution ($1,000) is taxable in 2012 (the deferral year) and another to show the gain is taxable in the year of distribution (2013).

Form 1099-R for 2013 would show $1,000 in box 1 (gross distribution) and box 2a (taxable amount). Code P (taxable in 2012) would be entered in box 7 to show that the excess elective contribution is taxable in the deferral year. The other Form 1099-R for 2013 would show $25 in box 1 (gross distribution) and box 2a (taxable amount). Code 8 (taxable in 2013) would be entered in box 7 to show that the gain on the excess elective contribution is taxable in the distribution year.

Note 1. The $1,000 is not subject to a premature distribution penalty, even if Lucy is under age 59½. The excess elective contribution is reported on line 7 of Lucy's 2012 Form 1040. The excess elective contribution is not taxed twice. [I.R.S. Notice 88-33, 1988-1 C.B. 513] Lucy can eliminate the premature distribution penalty (if applicable) on the gain by making a corrective distribution of the excess elective contribution (plus gain) by April 15, 2013.

Note 2. In all cases, code 1 (early distribution, no known exception), code 2 (early distribution, exception applies), or code 4 (death) should also be entered in box 7, if applicable.

Note 3. Line numbers are from the 2012 version of the various forms.

Example 3. The facts are the same as those in Example 1, except Lucy does correct the excess elective contribution. On April 16, 2013, the $1,000 amount is treated as a 2013 traditional IRA contribution. Because she has already contributed the maximum annual contribution to her IRA, the traditional IRA excess can be corrected in accordance with the traditional IRA correction rules (see Q 5:75). The $1,000 can no longer be corrected as an excess elective contribution.

Excess SEP Contributions—Failing the 125 Percent Nondiscrimination Test

Q 12:26 Is it possible for anyone to make an excess SEP contribution?

It depends. Generally, only an HCE is in a position to make an excess SEP contribution; that is, to make an elective deferral in excess of the 125 percent deferral limit (see Q 12:9). If, however, an employer fails to notify an HCE of excess SEP contributions in a timely manner (if applicable), then all employees who made elective deferrals may be treated as having made excess SEP contributions (see Q 12:28 and Appendix M).

Excess SEP contributions of a catch-up eligible employee are reduced to the extent he or she has not reached the catch-up deferral limit for the plan year to which the deferral relates (see Q 12:6). [Treas. Reg. § 1.414(v)-1(d)(2)(A)(iii)]

Q 12:27 Who must determine whether an excess SEP contribution has been made?

The employer must determine whether any HCEs have made excess SEP contributions. Whether or not the employer notifies affected employees of any excess SEP contributions (see Q 12:28), the amounts are includible in gross income. The amounts may also be subject to the IRA contribution limits of Code Sections 219 and 408 and thus may be considered excess IRA contributions (see Q 5:76 and Appendix M).

Q 12:28 Must an employer notify employees of any excess SEP contributions?

Yes. An employer must notify employees of any elective contributions that do not satisfy the 125 percent rule (see Q 12:9) within two and one-half months following the end of the plan year (generally March 15).

Q 12:29 What must the excess SEP contribution notification say?

The employer's notification to each affected employee of the excess SEP contributions must specifically state, in a manner calculated to be understood by the average plan participant,

1. The amount of the excess contributions attributable to that employee's elective deferrals;
2. The calendar year for which the excess contributions were made;
3. That the excess contributions are includible in the affected employee's gross income for the specified calendar year; and
4. That failure to withdraw the excess SEP contributions and income attributable to them by the due date (plus extensions, for plan years beginning after 2007) of the tax return for the tax year following the year of notification may result in significant penalties.

Note. For plan years beginning after 2007, the relevant April 15 for making a correcting distribution is extended by an extension of the taxpayer's income tax return. Thus, for a taxpayer under an automatic six-month extension, the relevant April 15 would change to October 15.

[Treas. Reg. § 54.4979-1(a)(4)]

Q 12:30 What should an employee do upon receiving notification of an excess SEP contribution?

The employee should withdraw the excess SEP contribution (and allocable income) from his or her IRA by the April 15 (plus extensions) following the calendar year in which he or she is notified by the employer of the excess SEP contribution. Excess SEP contributions not withdrawn by April 15 (plus extensions) will be subject to the IRA contribution limits of Code Sections 219 and 408 and may be considered excess IRA contributions (see Q 5:76). In most cases, the employee will be notified shortly after the end of the plan year. The gain (negative or positive) on the excess SEP contribution withdrawn in a proper correcting distribution made on or before April 15 (plus extensions) of the year following the year of notification by the employer is *not* subject to the 10 percent premature distribution penalty. [I.R.C. §§ 401(k)(8)(D), 408(k)(6)(C)]

Unless the excess SEP contribution is included by the participant in his or her income (line 7 of Form 1040) in the year to which the deferral relates, the employee may have to file an amended income tax return.

Q 12:31 What happens if an employee is not timely notified of an excess SEP contribution?

If an affected employee is not timely notified of an excess SEP contribution (see Q 12:28), the employer is subject to a 10 percent tax on the contribution. [I.R.C. § 408(k)(6)(C)(i); Treas. Reg. § 54.4979-1(a)(1)] The tax is reported on line 13 of Form 5330, Return of Excise Taxes Related to Employee Benefit Plans (rev. Apr. 2009) after completing Schedule H on page 6 of the form. [I.R.C. § 408(k)(6)(C); see Treas. Reg. § 54.4979-1(a)(4)(i) exempting "excess contributions" (usually referred to by the IRS as excess SEP contributions) when an employee is properly and timely notified of the excess from the 10 percent tax under I.R.C. § 4979] The 10 percent penalty for not providing a proper or timely notification is not a "cumulative" excise tax for the reasons specified below. An excess contribution of this type (excess SEP contribution) means, with respect to an HCE, "the excess of elective employer contributions . . . over the maximum amount of such contributions allowable" under the 125 percent deferral percentage test (see Q 12:26). [I.R.C. §§ 408(k)(6)(C)(ii), 4979(c)]

Furthermore, if the employer fails to notify the affected employee by the end of the plan year following the plan year in which the excess arose, the elective SEP will no longer be considered to meet the requirements of Code Section 408(k)(6). [Treas. Reg. § 54.4979-1(a)(4)(iii)] As a result, all elective contributions that are made to the SEP IRAs of any of the employees will be subject to the IRA contribution limits of Code Sections 219 and 408, and thus may be considered excess IRA contributions (see Q 5:76).

Q 12:32 Is any method provided to cure the failure to make a timely notification of excess SEP contributions?

Possibly. Although no specific method is available to cure an employer's failure to timely notify participants of excess SEP contributions, the plan could possibly regain its qualified status by submitting an application for the significant operational failure under the IRS Employee Plans Compliance Resolution System (EPCRS) (see chapter 17). Nonetheless, a request could be submitted to the appropriate IRS district director, attached to Form 5330, Return of Excise Taxes Related to Employee Benefit Plans, to abate any penalties for reasonable cause.

Practice Pointer. By curing a defect in a prior year, which caused automatic disqualification, deduction for later years could be preserved and resulting excess contributions avoided. The excess amounts will also have to be reported on Form W-2. Under the EPCRS, the IRS may allow all prior years excess to be reported in the current year; thus avoiding amending W-2s for previous years. In addition, the filing of Form 5330 by the employer and the filing of amended income tax returns by employees could possibly be avoided. Affected employees, possibly all employees if automatic disqualification occurred, may have to remove the excess contribution from their IRA to avoid the 6 percent penalty tax on excess contributions.

If the notification is made after the end of the plan year following the year in which the excess arose, or if the notification is never made, it is not clear in what year the elective contributions are subject to the IRA contribution limits of Code Sections 219 and 408. [Rev. Proc. 91-44, pt. IX, 1991-2 C.B. 733] (See Appendix M.) It is also unclear whether the employer's failure to give notification within the 12-month period has any effect on the contributions made in the current or prior year, and, if so, to what extent. Equally unclear is whether the excess amount may be subject to the cumulative nondeductible contribution excise tax under Code Section 4973 with respect to those prior contributions, and, if so, to what extent.

Practice Pointer. The IRS requires that certain information be provided to the employee that clearly indicates that the excess SEP contribution should be withdrawn by "April 15 following the calendar year of notification by your employer." [Form 5305A-SEP, Instructions for the Employee, Excess SEP Contribution, at 6; Rev. Proc. 91-44, pts. IX, XIII, 1991-2 C.B. 733] The form has not been updated for recent changes (see Q 3:6).

Q 12:33 Which excess SEP contributions become subject to the IRA limits: all or only those of *highly compensated employees*?

Generally, only the elective contributions of the HCEs that fail the 125 percent rule or ADP test (see Q 12:9) and that cannot be treated as catch-up contributions may become subject to the IRA limits.

For years beginning after 1996, the definition of *highly compensated employee* under Code Section 414(q) generally refers to the following:

1. An individual who was a 5 percent owner at any time during the current or preceding year, or
2. An individual who had compensation from the employer exceeding $95,000 (indexed for inflation for 2012 at $115,000) for the preceding year (see Q 1:14).

The attribution rules of Code Section 318 are used in determining which individuals are 5 percent owners (see Q 1:14 and examples in Q 8:7 regarding Section 318 attribution). [I.R.C. 414(q)(2)]

Example. Jerry is a participant in a SEP maintained on a calendar year basis. He does not have any ownership interest, directly or indirectly, in his employer. During 2012, Jerry's compensation was $60,000. During the previous year (2011), Jerry's compensation was $116,000. Jerry is treated as a highly compensated employee for 2012 because his prior year's compensation exceeded the 2012 limit ($110,000) for the prior year (2011). Assuming his ownership interest does not change, Jerry will not be treated as a highly compensated employee in 2013, because his compensation for the prior year (2012) is less that the statutory limit (as indexed).

Q 12:34 May the employer establish a new elective SEP if there was no timely notification of an excess SEP contribution?

No explicit prohibition exists against establishing a new elective SEP for a year subsequent to the year in which excess grandfathered SEP contributions were made nor any absolute support for such a position (see Q 12:31).

Q 12:35 What happens if there are both excess deferrals and excess SEP contributions?

If both excess deferrals (i.e., amounts generally in excess of the Section 402(g) dollar limits; see Q 12:6) and excess SEP contributions (i.e., amounts in excess of the 125 percent rule; see Q 12:9) exist, the amount of excess elective deferrals withdrawn will reduce any excess SEP contributions that must be withdrawn for the corresponding calendar year.

Q 12:36 When are excess SEP contributions includible in the gross income of the employee?

Beginning in taxable years after 2007, excess SEP contributions are included in income for the calendar year in which they are distributed. Income earned on excess SEP contributions is included in gross income when withdrawn from the IRA.

Q 12:37 How are excess SEP contributions reported on Form 1099-R?

The trustee or custodian will report the gross distribution in box 1 and the excess SEP contribution plus earnings in box 2a of Form 1099-R. The distribution code used depends upon when the notification to the participant is provided and whether the correction is made in the year of the deferral, or in either of the next two years. The excess SEP contribution (plus gain) is reported in box 1 (gross distribution) and box 2a (taxable distribution).

For correction on the 2012 version of Form 1099-R, use codes 8 (taxable in 2012), P (taxable in 2011), or, in some cases, D (taxable in 2009) in box 7 (distribution codes). For correction of a 2012 excess with a notification in 2013, a timely correction could be made in 2013 or 2014.

If the notification was provided in 2013 and the correction occurred in 2013, use code P (taxable in 2012) on the 2013 version of Form 1099-R. However, if the correction occurred in 2014 and before April 15, 2014, code D (taxable in 2012) would be entered in box 7 of the 2014 version of Form 1099-R.

Example 1. Joe, age 40 and an employee of Speedy Shipping Co., makes the maximum permitted nondeductible contribution into an interest-bearing IRA every year on January 2 ($5,000 for 2012). He also makes elective contributions of $3,000 to Speedy's grandfathered SARSEP during 2012. Joe is a highly compensated employee. The actual deferral percentage test for the plan is computed. In January 2013, Joe is notified by Speedy that he made excess SEP contributions of $500 during 2012. The $500 excess is not specifically reported on Joe's 2012 W-2 form; however, $3,000 is reported in box 12 of his W-2 form. The SEP IRA custodian calculates that $25 of interest was earned on the $500. Joe removes the excess plus the gain in February 2013.

The custodian will report the distribution on the 2013 version of Form 1099-R: the timely distribution of an excess SEP contribution is reported as fully taxable (box 1 and box 2a) in 2013, the year of distribution (for plan years beginning after 2009). In addition, the income attributable to it is also reported as fully taxable (box 1 and box 2a) for the year of distribution (2013). Code 8 will be used to show that the distribution of the excess SEP contribution and gain attributable to the excess SEP contribution is taxable in 2013 (the distribution year). Only one Form 1099-R is required.

Example 2. The facts are the same as those in Example 1, except that Joe is notified of his excess SEP contribution on December 20, 2012, and Joe removes the excess SEP contribution plus gain in December 2012. (This is before April 16 of the year following the calendar year of the notification; therefore, the amount is still an excess SEP contribution.) Joe included the $500 as income on line 7 of his 2012 Federal Income Tax Return. The 2012 version of Form 1099-R is used. One Form 1099-R will be issued by the IRA custodian; $525 is entered in box 1 (gross distribution) and in box 2a (taxable amount). Code 8 will be used in box 7 of Form 1099-R to show that the distribution of the excess SEP contribution and gain is taxable in 2012 (the distribution year). Joe will include an additional $25 on line 7 of his tax return for 2012.

Example 3. The facts are the same as those in Example 1, except that Joe does not remove the "excess SEP contribution."

If Joe was notified within 2½ months after the end of the year that the excess SEP contribution (Example 1) was made, he will be deemed to have made a 2014 IRA contribution of $500 on April 16, 2014. Joe will have to pay a 6 percent penalty for 2014, depending upon whether he can use up any portion of his excess as a 2014 annual IRA contribution.

On the other hand, if the employer notification was made instead on December 20, 2012, Joe will be deemed to have made a traditional IRA contribution of $500 on April 16, 2013 (the day after the April 15th of the year following the notification).

The amount treated as an IRA contribution is deemed contributed on the day after the last day that the excess elective SARSEP contribution could have been withdrawn—that is, in the examples above, is deemed made on the relevant April 16—and becomes subject to the annual limits on IRA contributions under Code Sections 219 and 408.

Note. Joe should give his IRA custodian a copy of the notice he receives from Speedy to help the custodian code the distribution properly on Form 1099-R. In the following examples, the relevant April 16 changes depending upon when the employer's notification is made. In some cases, more than one Form 1099-R is required to show that the excess and gain are taxable in different years.

Example 4. Tony, age 35, makes an elective contribution of $17,500 during 2012. His allowable "ADP" limit is $17,000. If Tony removes the excess elective deferral of $500 ($17,500 – $17,000 for 2012), plus the gain attributable to it, on or before April 15, 2013, he will also eliminate his excess SEP contribution of $500 ($17,500 – $17,000) that exceeded his ADP limit. A code is entered in box 7 (distribution codes). The excess elective deferral is taxable in 2012, and the gain is taxable in the year of distribution.

Note 1. In all cases, code 1 (early distribution, no known exception), code 2 (early distribution, exception applies), or code 4 (death) should also be entered in box 7, if applicable.

Note 2. Line numbers are from the 2012 version of the various forms.

Q 12:38 Is a corrective distribution of an excess SEP contribution subject to income tax withholding, social security, or Medicare taxes?

No. A corrective distribution of an excess SEP contribution is not subject to income tax withholding, social security, or Medicare taxes (see Q 11:1).

Q 12:39 How is an investment loss on an excess deferral reported on Form 1099-R?

If a corrective distribution of an excess deferral is made in a year after the year of deferral and an investment loss has been allocated to the excess deferral, the trustee or custodian of the SEP IRA will report the corrective distribution amount in box 1 (gross distribution) and box 2a (taxable amount) on Form 1099-R for the year of distribution.

Q 12:40 How is an investment loss on an excess deferral treated?

The total amount of the excess deferral (unadjusted for loss) must be included in income in the year of deferral. That amount is reported on line 16a and line 16b of Form 1040. However, a taxpayer may report a loss on the tax return for the year the corrective distribution is made. The loss is shown as a negative number on line 21 of Form 1040 and "Loss on Excess Deferral Distribution" is written on the dashed line to the left.

Disallowed Deferrals—Failing the 50 Percent Participation Rate Requirement

Q 12:41 What causes *disallowed deferrals*?

Disallowed deferrals occur when more than half of an employer's eligible employees choose not to make elective deferrals for a year. When that happens, all elective deferrals made by employees for that year are considered disallowed deferrals. Thus, if less than 50 percent of an employer's eligible employees choose to make elective deferrals in a plan year, no employee may participate for that plan year. In such a case, catch-up contributions are not allowed. The employer determines if there are disallowed deferrals. (See Appendix M.)

Q 12:42 How are employees notified of disallowed deferrals?

If the 50 percent participation rule is not met, the employer must notify affected employees within two and one half months after the end of the plan year (usually March 15) of the amount of the disallowed deferrals (and allocable income, if known) and that the elective contributions will not be considered SEP contributions. The notification must also state that the amount must be withdrawn by April 15 following the calendar year of notification and that deferrals not withdrawn by April 15 will be subject to the IRA contribution limits of Code Sections 219 and 408 and may be considered excess IRA contributions (see Q 5:78).

Note. Disallowed deferrals are includible in the employee's gross income in the year made, but the income allocable to the excess is includible in the employee's gross income in the year in which the income is withdrawn from the IRA.

Disallowed deferrals and any income (negative or positive) the deferrals have earned may be withdrawn without penalty until April 15 following the calendar year in which the affected employee is notified of the disallowed deferrals, which may or may not be the year of the deferral. After April 15, the disallowed deferrals will be subject to the IRA contribution limits of Code Sections 219 and 408 and may be considered excess IRA contributions (see Q 5:78).

Q 12:43 What happens if an employer fails to notify employees of disallowed deferrals?

The consequences of an employer's failure to notify employees of disallowed deferrals are not known. If the notification is not made on time, it is not clear in what year the disallowed deferrals (and other amounts) are subject to the IRA contribution limits of Code Sections 219 and 408.

Practice Pointer. The IRS requires that certain information be provided to the employee that clearly indicates that the disallowed deferrals should be withdrawn by "April 15 following the calendar year in which you were notified of the disallowed deferral." [Form 5305A-SEP, Instructions for the Employee, Disallowed Deferrals, at 6; Rev. Proc. 91-44, pts X, XIII, 1991-2 C.B. 733] If a penalty is assessed against an employee, the employee should request that the appropriate district director of the IRS abate the penalty.

Q 12:44 How should disallowed deferrals be corrected, and how are they treated?

Disallowed deferrals and any income (negative or positive) should be withdrawn by the employee from the IRA by April 15 (no extensions) following the calendar year in which he or she was notified by the employer of the disallowed deferral. Disallowed deferrals not withdrawn by April 15 are subject to the IRA contribution limits of Code Sections 219 and 408 and may be considered excess IRA contributions (see Q 5:78).

The gain on the disallowed deferrals withdrawn in a proper correcting distribution made on or before April 15 (no extensions) of the year following the year of notification by the employer is *not* subject to the 10 percent premature distribution penalty. [I.R.C. §§ 401(k)(8)(D), 408(k)(6)(C)]

Unless the participant includes the disallowed deferral in his or her income (line 7, Form 1040) in the year to which the deferral relates, he or she may have to file an amended income tax return. A disallowed deferral is included in income in the year deferred, but any gain is taxable in the year distributed.

Example 1. Susan, an employee of the Latke Company, makes the maximum nondeductible IRA contribution into an interest-bearing IRA every year on January 2. She also makes a $1,000 elective contribution under Latke's SARSEP in 2012. The $1,000 deferral amount is reported on her 2012 Form W-2 (box 12). Susan includes the $1,000 on line 7 of her 2012 tax return. Assume that $25 of interest is earned on the $1,000 at the end of each year.

Latke notifies Susan on November 14, 2012, that she made a disallowed deferral of $1,000 during 2012. In this case, the notification and the disallowed deferral fall in the same calendar year. Susan can avoid the premature distribution penalty on the gain (if the penalty is applicable) by taking a correcting distribution of the disallowed deferral (plus gain) by April 15, 2013. The early notification accelerates the date by which a disallowed deferral may be removed without any penalty. Assume Susan makes a correcting distribution of $525 on December 20, 2012.

The trustee or custodian will show the $1,025 in box 1 (the gross distribution) and $1,025 in box 2a (taxable amount) on the 2012 version of Form 1099-R. Code 8 (taxable in 2012) will be entered in box 7 (distribution codes).

The $1,000 is not included in income or subject to a premature distribution penalty, even if Susan is under age 59½. The disallowed deferral and the excess distributed are not taxed twice. [I.R.S. Notice 88-33, 1988-1 C.B. 513] Susan can eliminate the premature distribution penalty tax (if applicable) on the gain by taking a correcting distribution of the disallowed deferral (plus gain) by April 15 of the year following the year of notification of the disallowed deferral—by April 15, 2013.

Note. If Susan gives her IRA custodian a copy of the notice she receives from Latke, it will help the custodian to code the distribution properly when completing Form 1099-R, titled Distributions from Pensions, Annuities, Retirement or Profit-Sharing Plans, IRAs, Insurance Contracts, etc.

Example 2. The facts are the same as those in Example 1, except that Latke notifies Susan on March 5, 2013, that she made a disallowed deferral of $1,000 during 2012. In this case, the notification and the disallowed deferral occur in different years. Susan can avoid the premature distribution penalty on the gain (if the penalty is applicable) by taking a correcting distribution of the disallowed deferral (plus gain) by April 15, 2014. Assume Susan makes a correcting distribution of $1,050 on June 1, 2013. The trustee or custodian will complete two Form 1099-Rs, as follows:

a. $1,000 will be entered in box 1 (the gross distribution) and $1,000 in box 2a (taxable amount) on the 2013 version of Form 1099-R. Code P (taxable in 2012) will be entered in box 7 (distribution codes).

b. The trustee or custodian will show the $50 in box 1 (the gross distribution) and $50 in box 2a (taxable amount) on the 2013 version of Form 1099-R. Code 8 (taxable in 2013) will be entered in box 7 (distribution codes).

If Susan did not include the $1,000 on her 2012 tax return, she would have to file an amended return.

The $1,000 is not included in income or subject to a premature distribution penalty. The disallowed deferral and the excess distributed are not taxed twice. Susan can eliminate the premature distribution penalty tax (if applicable) on the gain by taking a correcting distribution of the disallowed deferral (plus gain) by April 15 of the year following the year deferral.

Example 3. The facts are the same as those in Example 2, except that Susan makes a correcting distribution of $1,050 on April 15, 2014, the day before the $1,000 would become an IRA contribution if not removed.

a. The trustee or custodian will show the $1,000 in box 1 (the gross distribution) and $1,000 in box 2a (taxable amount) on the 2014 version of Form 1099-R. Code D (taxable in 2012) will be entered in box 7 (distribution codes).
b. The trustee or custodian will show the $50 in box 1 (the gross distribution) and $50 in box 2a (taxable amount) on the 2014 version of Form 1099-R. Code 8 (taxable in 2014) will be entered in box 7 (distribution codes).

The $1,000 is not included in income or subject to a premature distribution penalty. The disallowed deferral and the excess distributed are not taxed twice. Susan eliminated the premature distribution penalty tax (if applicable) on the gain by taking a correcting distribution of the disallowed deferral (plus gain) by April 15 of the year following the year of notification of the disallowed deferral—by April 15, 2014.

If Susan did not include the $1,000 on her 2012 tax return, she would have to file an amended return. If Susan does not make a correcting distribution, the $1,000 would become ("deemed") a 2014 traditional IRA contribution made on April 16, 2014, and subject to the annual IRA contribution limits for 2014 as well as the traditional IRA excess contribution correction rules (see Q 5:75) and distribution rules. If excess traditional IRA contributions do result, they may be subject to a cumulative 6 percent penalty tax until corrected. Distributions may also be subject to a 10 percent penalty tax if Susan is under age 59½ at the time of distribution, unless an exception applies.

Catch-up Contributions

Q 12:45 When are the final catch-up contribution regulations effective?

The final regulations are applicable to contributions for tax years beginning on and after January 1, 2004, and plans are permitted to rely on the final regulations or proposed regulations for taxable years beginning before January 1, 2004. [Preamble, Treas. Reg. § 1.414(v)-1 (68 Fed. Reg. 40510–40520 (July 8, 2003)); Treas. Reg. § 1.414(v)-1(i)(2)] The final regulations generally mirror the proposed regulations with certain modifications.

The legislative history of Section 631 of the Economic Growth and Tax Relief Reconciliation Act of 2001 (EGTRRA) indicates that the intent of Congress in enacting the catch-up provisions was to allow a participant who is eligible for catch-up contributions to make elective deferrals over and above any otherwise applicable limit, up to the catch-up contribution limit for the taxable year.

Q 12:46 What are *catch-up contributions*?

Catch-up contributions generally are elective deferrals, made by a catch-up eligible participant (see Q 12:48), that exceed an otherwise applicable limit (see Qs 1:3, 12:6, 12:52) and that are treated as catch-up contributions under the plan, but only to the extent they do not exceed the maximum amount of catch-up contributions permitted for the taxable year (generally the calendar year). [Treas. Reg. §§ 1.402(g)-2, 1.414(v)-1(a)(1), 1(b)]

Q 12:47 Do the Section 414(v) catch-up regulations apply to a SARSEP?

Yes. The Section 414(v) catch-up regulations apply generally to all retirement plans that permit elective deferrals, including SARSEPs. [I.R.C. § 414(v)(6)(A)(iv); Treas. Reg. §§ 1.414(v)-1(a)(1), 1.414(v)-1(g)]

Q 12:48 What is a *catch-up eligible participant*?

A *catch-up eligible participant* is a participant who is age 50 or older and otherwise eligible to make elective deferrals under a SARSEP. [I.R.C. § 414(v)(5); Treas. Reg. § 1.414(v)-1(g)(3)(i)]

Q 12:49 How is a participant who is expected to attain age 50 by the end of the taxable year treated?

A participant who will attain age 50 before the end of the participant's taxable year is treated as having attained age 50 as of the first day of that year. [Treas. Reg. § 1.414(v)-1(g)(3)(ii)]

In describing the catch-up rules, the EGTRRA Conference Report states:

> [T]he otherwise applicable dollar limit on elective deferrals under a section 401(k) plan, section 403(b) annuity, SEP, or SIMPLE, or defer-

rals under a section 457 plan is increased for individuals who have attained age 50 by the end of the year.

[HR Conf. Rep. No. 107-84, at 236 (2001)]

Q 12:50 Is an employer required to permit catch-up contributions under its SARSEP?

Yes and no. Although, technically, an employer is not required to provide for catch-up contributions in any of its plans, plan documents determine whether catch-up contributions are permitted. The model SARSEP form, Form 5305A-SEP (revised in June 2006), provides no choice as to whether catch-up contributions are permitted. Prototype plan language does not appear to preclude an option to exclude a catch-up provision. [Listing of Required Modifications and Information Package (LRMs) for Salary Reduction Simplified Employee Pension Plans, see Part III—Note to Reviewer (March 2002)]

Note. By way of comparison, catch-up contributions must generally be matched under a SIMPLE IRA plan. A SARSEP is not permitted to have a matching contribution formula.

If an employer provides for catch-up contributions, all plans of that employer that provide for elective deferrals generally must comply with the regulations' universal availability requirement and contain a catch-up provision. [Treas. Reg. §§ 1.414(v)-1(a)(1), 1.414(v)-1(e)]

Q 12:51 What is the *universal availability requirement*?

In general, the *universal availability rule* would require that if a plan permits catch-up eligible participants to make catch-up contributions, then all plans in the employer's controlled group that permit participants to make elective deferrals also must permit participants to make the same dollar amount of catch-up contributions. The final regulations make three substantive changes to the universal availability rule.

1. Collectively bargained employees and nonresident aliens are excluded from the universal availability rule.
2. It has been clarified that a plan does not violate the universal availability rule by restricting elective deferrals, including the elective deferrals of any catch-up eligible participant, to amounts available after taxes and other withholdings are deducted from an employee's pay.
3. The final regulations eliminate the "as soon as practicable" requirement. The proposed regulations provided that a plan did not violate the universal availability rule if an employer in the controlled group acquired a plan that did not offer catch-up contributions, provided that the acquired plan was amended as soon as practicable following the acquisition, but no later than the end of the plan year following the plan year in which the plan was acquired. The final regulations permit the amendment to be made no

later than the end of the plan year following the plan year in which the plan was acquired.

[*See also* I.R.S. Notice 2002-4, 2002-2 I.R.B. 298, regarding situations involving a plan qualified under Puerto Rico law.]

The final regulations also provide for the following:

1. Coordination between catch-up contributions and the special eligible 457 plan limit of $17,000. [I.R.C. § 414(v)(6)(c)] and
2. Transition rules for collectively bargained employees and newly acquired plans.

The final regulations retain the proposed regulations' rule that the amount of an elective deferral in excess of an applicable limit is determined as of the end of the plan year by comparing the total elective deferrals for the plan year with the applicable limit for the plan year. For annual limits measured on the basis of a year other than a plan year—such as the calendar year limit on annual deferrals under Code Section 402(g)—the determination of whether the limit is exceeded is based on the other year.

The final regulations also explain how catch-up contributions in excess of employer-provided limits should be coordinated on a controlled group basis (or same employer basis in the case of a 457 plan). A plan is generally permitted to treat elective deferrals in excess of the plan's employer-provided limit as a catch-up contribution to the extent of the amount remaining under the employee's catch-up contribution limit for the year in any other plan of the employer.

[I.R.C. § 403(b)(3); Treas. Reg. §§ 1.414(v)-1(e)(2), 1.414(v)-1(e)(3), 1.414(v)-1(f)]

Caution. If an employer provides for catch-up contributions under a qualified plan, all other employer plans in the controlled group that provide for elective deferrals, including plans not subject to Code Section 401(a)(4), such as a SARSEP or a SIMPLE, must provide catch-up eligible participants with the same effective opportunity to make catch-up contributions. To provide catch-up eligible participants with an effective opportunity to make catch-up contributions, the plan would have to permit each such participant to make sufficient elective deferrals during the year to give him or her the opportunity to make elective deferrals up to the otherwise applicable limit plus the catch-up contribution limit. For example, a plan that limits elective deferrals on a payroll-by-payroll basis might also provide participants with an effective opportunity to make catch-up contributions that are administered on a payroll-by-payroll basis (by allowing catch-up eligible participants to increase their deferrals above the otherwise applicable limit by a prorated portion of the catch-up limit for the year). Whether such elective deferrals are treated as catch-up contributions would not be determined until the end of the year (see Q 12:54). [Treas. Reg. § 1.414(v)-1(b)(2)]

Q 12:52 How are catch-up contributions determined?

Catch-up contributions are determined by reference to the following limits:

- *Statutory limits.* Statutory limits are imposed on elective deferrals or annual additions permitted to be made under a SARSEP without regard to Code Section 414(v). They include the requirement under Code Section 401(a)(30) that the plan limit all elective deferrals within a calendar year under the plan and other plans (or contracts) maintained by members of a controlled group to the amount permitted under Code Section 402(g). [I.R.C. § 408(k)(6)(A)(iv)] The 25 percent of includible compensation exclusion limit is also a statutory limit (see Q 11:1). [Treas. Reg. § 1.414(v)-1(b)(1)(i)]
- *Employer-provided limits.* An employer-provided limit is a limit contained in the terms of the plan on the elective deferrals an employee can make under the plan. SARSEPs do not generally contain plan limitations on elective deferrals. Some employers, however, cap elective deferrals when they intend to make a top-heavy or other nonelective employer contribution.
- *ADP limit.* For purposes of ADP testing (see Q 12:9), the regulations provide that any elective deferral for the plan year that is treated as a catch-up contribution because it is in excess of a statutory limit or an employer-provided limit be disregarded for purposes of calculating the participant's actual deferral ratio. That is, catch-up contributions are subtracted from the participant's elective deferrals for the plan year before determining the participant's ADP ratio. The subtraction is made without regard to whether the catch-up eligible participant is an HCE or an NHCE. [Treas. Reg.§ 1.414(v)-1(b)(1)(ii)]

Q 12:53 Which elective contributions are treated as catch-up contributions?

Elective deferrals in excess of an applicable limit are treated as catch-up contributions only to the extent that the elective deferrals do not exceed the catch-up contribution limit for the taxable year reduced by elective deferrals previously treated as catch-up contributions for the taxable year. For 2012, the catch-up contribution limit for a SARSEP is $5,500 (see Q 11:1).

Q 12:54 When are elective deferrals in excess of an applicable limit treated as catch-up contributions?

The amount of elective deferrals in excess of an applicable limit is generally determined as of the end of a plan year, by comparing the total elective deferrals for the plan year with the applicable limit for the plan year. For a limit that is determined on the basis of a year other than a plan year (such as the calendar-year limit on elective deferrals under Code Section 401(a)(30)), the determination of whether elective deferrals are in excess of the applicable limit is made on the basis of such other year. [Treas. Reg. § 1.414(v)-1(b)(2)]

The regulations include a timing rule for purposes of determining when elective deferrals in excess of an applicable limit are treated as catch-up contributions. A timing rule is necessary because the maximum amount of catch-up contributions is based on the participant's taxable year, but the determination of whether an elective deferral is in excess of an applicable limit is determined on the basis of the taxable year, the plan year, or the limitation year, depending on the underlying limit. Under the regulations, whether these elective deferrals in excess of an applicable limit can be treated as catch-up contributions would be determined as of the last day of the relevant year, except that if the limit is determined on the basis of a taxable year or calendar year, then whether elective deferrals in excess of the limit can be treated as catch-up contributions would be determined at the time they are deferred. [Treas. Reg. § 1.414(v)-1(d)]

Caution. The timing rule is most significant for a plan with a plan year that is not the calendar year. For example, in a SEP with a plan year ending on June 30, 2012, elective deferrals in excess of the ADP limit for the plan year ending June 30, 2012 would be treated as catch-up contributions as of the last day of the plan year, up to the catch-up contribution limit for 2012. Any amounts deferred after June 30, 2012 that are in excess of the catch-up elective limit for the 2012 calendar year ($5,500) would also be treated as catch-up contributions at the time they are deferred, up to the catch-up contribution limit for 2012, reduced by elective deferrals treated as catch-up contributions as of June 30, 2012. [Preamble, Treas. Reg. § 1.414(v)-1 (68 Fed. Reg. 40510–40520 (July 8, 2004))] Thus, the elective contribution limits (which are calendar year limits) have to be reviewed, initially, as of the end of the plan year, and then taken into account together with elective contributions made during remainder of the calendar year (in which the plan year ends).

The following examples illustrate the application of catch-up contributions under a SARSEP. Except as specifically provided, the plan year is the calendar year. In addition, it is assumed that the participant's elective deferrals under all plans of the employer do not exceed the 100 percent of compensation limit under Code Section 415 and that the taxable year of the participant is the calendar year. The full amount of a participant's elective deferrals (including excess) is reported by the employer in box 12 of Form W-2, with Code F (see chapter 13). Difficulties are likely to arise in a SARSEP when the plan year is maintained on a 12-month period that is not the calendar year (see Examples 4 and 5 next).

Example 1. David, age 55, is eligible to make elective deferrals under a SARSEP. The plan does not limit elective deferrals, except as necessary to comply with the $17,000 (for 2012) limit under Code Section 408(k)(6)(a) and the 100 percent/$50,000 limits under Code Section 415. The SARSEP also provides that a catch-up-eligible participant is permitted to defer amounts in excess of the normal $17,000/$50,000 limits up to the applicable dollar catch-up limit for the year ($5,500 for 2012). David defers $22,500 during 2012.

David's elective deferrals in excess of the Section 408(k)(6)(a) limit ($5,500 ($22,500 – $17,000)) do not exceed the applicable dollar catch-up limit for 2012 ($5,500). Thus, $5,500 is treated as a catch-up contribution and is not taken into account in determining David's allowable ADP rate (see Qs 12:9, 12:56) under the SARSEP for the year. [I.R.C. § 408(k)(6)(A)(iv); Treas. Reg. §§ 1.414(v)-1(a), 1.414(v)-1(d)(2)(i)]

Example 2. Ben and Carl, both age 55, are HCEs who each earn $165,000, and are eligible to make elective deferrals under a model SARSEP (Form 5305A-SEP). The plan limits elective deferrals as necessary to comply with the normal $17,000 elective deferral limit as well as the 100 percent/$50,000 limits on overall contributions for 2012. [I.R.C. §§ 401(a)(30), 408(k)(6)(A)(iv), 415(c)] The plan provides that no HCE may make an elective deferral at a rate that exceeds 10 percent of compensation. However, the plan also provides that a catch-up-eligible participant is permitted to defer amounts in excess of 10 percent during the plan year up to the applicable dollar catch-up limit for the year. In 2012, Ben and Carl both elect, pursuant to plan provisions, to defer 10 percent of compensation ($1,375 monthly) plus $425 monthly ($4,800 for the 2012 calendar year). Ben continues this election in effect for the entire year, for a total elective contribution for the year of $21,600. However, in September 2012, after deferring $16,200 (9 × ($1,375 + $425)), Carl discontinues making elective deferrals.

Once Ben's elective deferrals for the year exceed the normal elective limit ($17,000 for 2012), subsequent elective deferrals are treated as catch-up contributions as they are deferred, provided that such elective deferrals do not exceed the catch-up contribution limit for the taxable year. The October deferral ($1,800) causes the elective deferral limit $17,000 to be exceeded by $1,000 ($17,000 – ($1,800 × 10)). Because the $1,000 elective deferrals made after Ben reaches the Code Section 402(g) limit for the calendar year does not exceed the applicable dollar catch-up limit for 2012, the $1,000 is treated as a catch-up contribution.

As of the last day of the plan year, Ben has exceeded the employer-provided limit of 10 percent (10 percent of $165,000 ($170,000)) by $3,600 (($1,800 × 12) – $17,000 – $1,000). Because the additional $3,600 in elective deferrals does not exceed the $5,500 applicable dollar catch-up limit for 2012, reduced by the $1,000 in elective deferrals previously treated as catch-up contributions, the entire $3,600 of elective deferrals is treated as a catch-up contribution. Ben is treated as having made a $4,600 ($3,600 + $1,000) catch-up contribution for 2012. In determining Ben's ADP rate, the $4,600 of catch-up contributions are subtracted from Ben's elective deferrals for the plan year. [Treas. Reg. § 1.414(v)-1(d)(2)(i)] Accordingly, Ben's participation rate for ADP purposes is 11.486487 percent ($17,000 ($21,600 – $4,600)/ $148,000 ($165,000 – $17,000)). Ben is treated as having regular elective deferrals of $17,000 and catch-up deferrals of $4,600.

Carl's elective deferrals for the year do not exceed an applicable limit for the plan year. Accordingly, Carl's $16,200 of elective deferrals must be taken into account in determining his participation rate for ADP purposes.

Note. In Examples 3 and 4, which follow, the difficulties in determining elective deferral and catch-up limits (and amounts) in overlapping periods could be avoided if the plan year were the calendar year (instead of coinciding with the business's fiscal taxable year). A deduction timing issue may also result when the plan year and the business's taxable year are not the same (see Q 10:1).

Practice Pointer. If the plan year is not the calendar year, some of the difficulties in determining elective deferral and catch-up limits (and amounts) in overlapping periods (as illustrated) could be avoided if all of a participant's yearly elective deferrals (for all years) were contributed (made) during only one of the periods (e.g., Jan. 1 through Oct. 31 in Examples 3 and 4).

Note. Increases to the normal elective limit and the catch up limit do not always occur each year. In Examples 3 and 4, which follow, the normal elective limit amount and the catch-up limit amount that applies for any plan year may be different (e.g., a 2011 limit for normal elective deferrals—$16,500—combined with the 2012 limit for catch-up elective deferrals of $5,500). The catch-up and regular deferral limits are always applied on a calendar-year basis.

Example 3. Edward is an HCE who is a catch-up-eligible participant under a SARSEP with a plan year ending October 31, 2012. The plan does not limit elective deferrals, except as necessary to comply with applicable Code provisions. The plan permits all catch-up-eligible participants to defer an additional amount equal to the applicable dollar catch-up limit for the calendar year ($5,500) in excess of the $17,000 (for 2012) limit. Edward made $11,500 of elective contributions during the first 10 months of 2011. Edward made $5,000 of deferrals in the period November 1, 2011, through December 31, 2011, and an additional $17,500 of deferrals in the first 10 months of 2012, for a total of $22,500 in elective deferrals for the plan year ending in 2012. Edward did not exceed the $16,500 limit in 2011 and did not exceed the ADP limit for the plan year ending October 31, 2011.

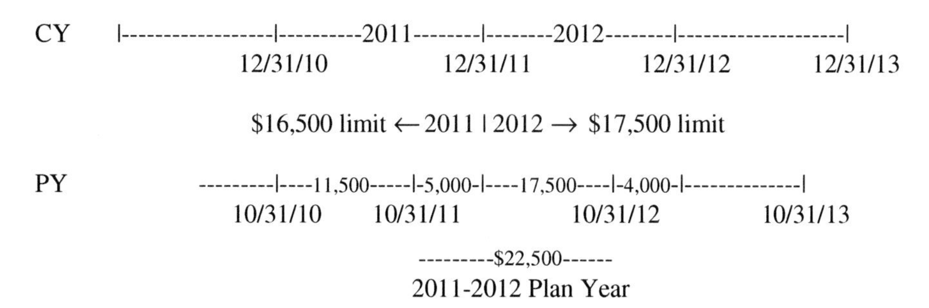

Once Edward's elective deferrals for calendar year 2012 ($17,500) exceed $17,500 (the 2012 limit), subsequent elective deferrals are treated as catch-up contributions at the time they are deferred, provided that such elective deferrals do not exceed the applicable dollar catch-up limit for the calendar year. Because the $500 ($17,500–$17,000) in elective deferrals made after Edward reaches the

$17,000 (Code Section 402(g)) limit for the calendar year does not exceed the applicable dollar catch-up limit for 2012, the entire $500 is a catch-up contribution. The $500 is subtracted from Edward's $17,500 in elective deferrals for the plan year ending October 31, 2012, in determining Edward's ADP rate for that plan year, to wit, $17,000. [Treas. Reg. § 1.414(v)-1(d)(2)(i)]

The 125 percent SARSEP ADP test is run for the plan after excluding the $500 in elective deferrals in excess of the $17,000 (for 2012) elective deferral limit for the calendar year. The maximum deferrals that may be retained by Edward (an HCE), under the SARSEP for the plan year ending October 31, 2012, (the ADP limit) is $17,000 (assumed).

Edward is treated as having contributed $21,000 ($4,000 + $17,500 – $500) of elective deferrals to the plan ($4,000 + $17,000) for the plan year ending in 2012. The amount of elective deferrals in excess of $17,000 for calendar year 2012 can be treated as a catch-up contribution. In this case, $4,000 ($21,000 – $17,000) is less than the excess of the applicable dollar catch-up limit ($5,500) over the elective deferrals previously treated as catch-up contributions under the plan for the taxable year ($500).

Although Edward's elective deferrals for the calendar year 2012 have exceeded the $17,000 (for 2012) limit, he can continue to make elective deferrals during the last two months of the calendar year because his catch-up contributions for the taxable year ($4,500) are not taken into account in applying the $17,000 deferral limit amount for 2012.

Thus, Edward can make an additional contribution of $4,000 ($17,000 – ($17,500 – $4,000 – $500)) without exceeding the $17,000 (for 2012) limit for the calendar year, and without regard to any additional catch-up contributions. In addition, Edward may make additional catch-up contributions of $1,000 (the $5,500 applicable dollar catch-up limit for 2012, reduced by the $4,500 ($500 + $4,000) of elective deferrals previously treated as catch-up contributions during the taxable year). The $1,000 of catch-up contributions will not be taken into account in the ADP test for the plan year ending October 31, 2013. [*See* Treas. Reg. § 1.414(v)-1(h), ex. 6 for additional information.]

Note. In Example 3, it is necessary to determine the elective contributions that were made during the following periods for the plan year ending in 2012 to determine the 2011–2012 plan year and 2012 calendar year elective limits.

- January 1, 2011, through October 31, 2011 ($11,500)
- November 1, 2011, through December 31, 2011 ($5,000)
- January 1, 2012, through October 31, 2012 ($17,000)
- November 1, 2012, through December 31, 2012 ($4,000 allowed)

Example 4. The facts are the same as in Example 3, except that Edward made $16,500 of elective contributions during the first 10 months of 2011. He made $4,500 of deferrals in the period November 1, 2011, through December 31, 2011, and an additional $13,000 of deferrals in the first 10 months of 2012, for a total of $17,500 in elective deferrals for the plan year ending in 2012. Edward did not exceed the $16,500 limit in 2011 by more than his catch-up limit and did not exceed the ADP limit for the plan year ending October 31, 2011.

```
CY   |-----------------|-----------2011--------|--------2012---------|--------------------|
                   12/31/10          12/31/11           12/31/12           12/31/13

               $16,500 limit ←— 2011 | 2012 → $17,000 limit

PY          ---------|----16,500-----|-4,500-|----13,000----|-8,500-|--------------|
                  10/31/10      10/31/11          10/31/12          10/31/13

                               ---------$17,500------
                                2011-2012 Plan Year
```

Once Edward's elective deferrals for calendar year 2011 ($21,000) exceed $16,500 (the 2011 limit), subsequent elective deferrals are treated as catch-up contributions at the time they are deferred, provided that such elective deferrals do not exceed the applicable dollar catch-up limit for the calendar year. Because the $4,500 in elective deferrals made after Edward reaches the $16,500 (Code Section 402(g)) limit for the calendar year (2011) does not exceed the applicable dollar catch-up limit for 2011, the entire $4,500 is a catch-up contribution. The $4,500 is subtracted from Edward's $13,000 in elective deferrals for the plan year ending October 31, 2012, in determining Edward's ADP rate for that plan year. [Treas. Reg. § 1.414(v)-1(d)(2)(i)]

The 125 percent SARSEP ADP test is run for the plan after excluding the $4,500 in elective deferrals treated as catch-up contributions in excess of the $17,000 (for 2012) elective deferral limit for the calendar year. The maximum deferrals that may be retained by Edward (an HCE) under the SARSEP for the plan year ending October 31, 2012 (the ADP limit) is $17,000 (assumed).

Edward is treated as having contributed $17,500 of elective deferrals to the plan ($4,500 + $13,000) for the plan year ending in 2012.

Edward's elective deferrals for the calendar year 2012 have not exceeded the $17,000 (for 2012) limit; he can continue to make elective deferrals during the last two months of the calendar year because his catch-up contributions for the taxable year ($4,500) are not taken into account in applying the $17,000 deferral limit amount for 2012.

Thus, Edward can make an additional contribution of $8,500 ($17,000 – ($13,000 – $4,500)) without exceeding the $17,000 (for 2012) limit for the calendar year, and without regard to any additional catch-up contributions. In addition, Edward may make additional catch-up contributions of $1,000 (the $5,500 applicable dollar catch-up limit for 2012, reduced by the $4,500 of elective deferrals previously treated as catch-up contributions during the taxable year). The $4,500 of catch-up contributions will not be taken into account in the ADP test for the plan year ending October 31, 2013. [*See* Treas. Reg. § 1.414(v)-1(h), ex. 6 for additional information.]

Note. In Example 4, it is necessary to determine the elective contributions that were made during the following periods for the plan year ending in 2012 to determine the 2011–2012 plan-year and 2012 calendar-year elective limits.

- January 1, 2011, through October 31, 2011 ($16,500)
- November 1, 2011, through December 31, 2011 ($4,500)
- January 1, 2012, through October 31, 2012 ($13,000)
- November 1, 2012, through December 31, 2012 ($8,500 allowed)

Q 12:55 Are catch-up contributions subject to otherwise applicable limits under the SEP?

No. If an elective deferral is treated as a catch-up contribution, it is not subject to otherwise applicable limits under the SEP and the plan would not be treated as failing otherwise applicable nondiscrimination requirements because of the catch-up contributions. Under the regulations, catch-up contributions would not be taken into account in applying the limits of certain sections of the Code, including Sections 401(a)(30), 402(h), 404(h), 408, 415, and 457(b)(2), to other contributions or benefits under the plan offering catch-up contributions or under any other plan of the employer (see Q 11:2). [Treas. Reg. § 1.414(v)-1(d)]

Q 12:56 How are catch-up contributions treated for purposes of ADP testing?

For purposes of ADP testing for a SARSEP, any elective deferral for the plan year that is treated as a catch-up contribution because it exceeds a statutory or employer-provided limit (see Q 12:52) is disregarded for calculating a participant's ADP ratio. [Treas. Reg. § 1.414(v)-1(d)(2)]

Caution. Because an amount treated as a catch-up contribution is not taken into account in calculating the ADP, the ADP may have to be recalculated if unanticipated catch-up amounts are determined to exist for any participating NHCE.

Q 12:57 How are catch-up contributions treated for top-heavy testing purposes?

Catch-up contributions for the *current* plan year are not taken into account for purposes of Code Section 416, regarding contribution requirements to top-heavy plans (see Q 8:1). Thus, if the only contributions made for key employees for a plan year are catch-up contributions, the applicable percentage is zero, and no top-heavy minimum contribution is required for the year. [Treas. Reg. § 1.414(v)-1(d)(2)]

Catch-up contributions for prior years are taken into account for purposes of Code Section 416. Thus, catch-up contributions for prior years are included in the account balances that may be used in determining whether the plan is top heavy under Code Section 416(g). [Treas. Reg. § 1.414(v)-1(d)(3)(i)]

Q 12:58 How are catch-up contributions treated for purposes of the 25 percent of includible compensation exclusion limit under Code Section 402(h)?

Catch-up contributions are treated as includible compensation for purposes of the 25 percent of includible compensation exclusion limit (see Q 11:2) and are separately excludable from gross income. [I.R.C. § 414(v)(3)(A)]

Q 12:59 How are catch-up contributions treated for purposes of the 100 percent limit under Code Section 415?

Catch-up contributions are not taken into account in determining whether the 100 percent limit under Code Section 415 has been exceeded (see Q 11:13). Other limits on contributions (e.g., the participant's 25 percent of includible compensation exclusion limit) are always lower than the 100 percent limit under Code Section 415 (see chapter 11). [I.R.C. § 414(v)(3)(A)(1)]

Q 12:60 How are catch-up contributions treated for purposes of the $50,000 limit under Code Section 415?

The $50,000 limit under Code Section 415 may be exceeded (increased) for allowable catch-up contributions (see Q 11:5).

Q 12:61 How are catch-up contributions treated for purposes of the 25 percent of aggregate compensation deduction limit?

Catch-up contributions are separately deductible. Catch-up contributions do not reduce compensation for purposes of computing a participant's 25 percent of aggregate compensation deduction limit (see Q 11:2).

Q 12:62 May a catch-up contribution in excess of $5,500 for 2012 be excluded from income?

Possibly. Unless an individual also participates in an eligible governmental 457 plan, he or she is entitled to exclude from income only catch-up amounts that do not exceed $5,500 in the aggregate for 2012 (see Qs 12:20, 12:21). [Treas. Reg. § 1.414(v)-1(f)]

> **Note.** Catch-up contributions in an eligible governmental 457 plan are not treated as elective deferrals subject to Code Section 402(g). [I.R.C. § 402(g)(3)]

Q 12:63 May catch-up contributions be made to more than one plan?

Yes. Catch-up contributions are generally not treated as exceeding the dollar amount of Section 402(g)(1) ($17,000 for 2012). The regulations provide that a catch-up-eligible participant who participates in more than one plan may treat an elective deferral as a catch-up contribution (up to the maximum amount of catch-up contributions permitted for the taxable year) because it exceeds the catch-up-eligible participant's Section 402(g) dollar limit for the taxable year. This rule allows a catch-up-eligible participant who participates in plans of two or more employers an exclusion from gross income for elective deferrals that exceed the Code Section 402(g) limit, even though the elective deferrals do not exceed an applicable limit for either employer's plan. The treatment by an individual of such elective deferrals as catch-up contributions will not have any impact on either employer's plan. [Treas. Reg. § 1.414(v)-1(f)]

This treatment is parallel to the treatment of excess deferrals for an individual under age 50 who exceeds the Section 402(g) dollar limit in the plans of two unrelated employers. Accordingly, the regulations did not provide for the ADP test to be rerun to disregard elective deferrals that an individual treats as catch-up contributions because they exceed the Section 402(g) limit; however, the total amount of elective deferrals in excess of the Section 402(g) dollar limit that are not includible in income because they are treated as catch-up contributions cannot exceed that limit ($17,000 for 2012) by more than the catch-up contribution limit for the taxable year ($5,500 for 2012). [Treas. Reg. § 1.414(v)-1(f)]

Chapter 13

IRS Disclosure, Filings, Penalties, and Tax Withholding

Denise Appleby, CISP, CRC, CRPS, CRSP, APA;
Appleby Retirement Consulting Inc., Grayson, GA

Financial institutions that serve as custodians and trustees (custodians) for individual retirement arrangements (IRAs) are subject to disclosure, tax reporting, and notifications requirements, and may be subject to penalties if any of these requirements are not met.

IRA owners must also comply with tax reporting requirements for certain transactions that occur within their IRAs. Failure to meet these requirements can result in the IRA owner paying taxes on amounts that should be tax-free and paying penalties when the penalties should be waived. IRA owners may also need to file certain reports with the IRS in order to pay excise tax owed.

This chapter covers the disclosure, reporting, and tax withholding requirements, including the steps that custodians, plan sponsors, and IRA owners should follow to ensure that they satisfy these requirements. All reference to tax forms applies to the 2012 versions of these forms, unless they have not yet been released at the time this chapter was written.

For the purpose of this chapter, *IRA* includes traditional IRAs, Roth IRAs, SEP IRAs, and SIMPLE IRAs unless otherwise noted.

Note. Line and box numbers are based on 2012 versions of the forms unless otherwise indicated.

Disclosure

Q 13:1 What documentation must be provided to the IRA owner when an IRA is established?

The IRA Custodian must provide the IRA owner with an IRA plan agreement and disclosure statement (see Qs 13:2, 13:3) when the IRA is established. [Treas. Reg. § 1.408-6(d)(4)(ii)(A)(1)] The IRA is not considered established until the IRA owner signs the IRA plan agreement. The disclosure statement must be given to the IRA owner before (or at the time) the IRA is established. The IRA owner must be given the right to revoke the IRA within seven calendar days of receiving the disclosure statement (see Qs 13:4–13:7), or seven days after the date on which the IRA is opened, whichever is later. [Treas. Reg. § 1.408-6(d)(4)(ii)(A)(2)]

Q 13:2 What is the purpose of the IRA plan agreement?

The IRA plan agreement serves as the contract between the IRA owner and the Custodian, and provides an explanation of the rights of the IRA owner and the Custodian, as well as their duties. The plan agreement must contain the following requirements:

- Except in the case of a rollover contribution described in Code Sections 402(c), 403(a)(4), 403(b)(8), 408(d)(3), or 457(e)(16), an employer contribution to a simplified employee pension plan as described in Code Section 408(k), or a recharacterized contribution described in Code Section 408A(d)(6), the custodian will accept only cash contributions up to the limit in effect for the year under Code Section 219(b)(1)(A).
- The custodian must be a bank (as defined in Code Section 408(n)), or a nonbank entity that has received approval from the IRS to serve as a nonbank trustee or nonbank custodian.
- No part of the IRA funds will be invested in life insurance contracts.
- The IRA is nonforfeitable.
- The IRA assets will not be commingled with other property except in a common fund.
- The required minimum distribution (RMD) rules under Code Section 401(a)(9) and the incidental death benefit requirements of Code Section 401(a) applies to the IRA.

[I.R.C. § 408(a)]

For individual retirement annuities, the following requirements apply:

- The contract is not transferable by the owner.
- Under the contract—

the premiums are not fixed;

the annual premium on behalf of any individual will not exceed the contribution limit in effect for the year under Code Section 219(b)(1)(A); and

- any refund of premiums will be applied before the close of the calendar year following the year of the refund toward the payment of future premiums or the purchase of additional benefits.
- The RMD rules under Code Section 401(a)(9) and the incidental death benefit requirements of Code Section 401(a) apply to the IRA.
- The entire interest of the owner is nonforfeitable.

[I.R.C. § 408(b)]

Custodians generally use the IRS model Forms 5305, Traditional Individual Retirement Trust Account, if they have trust powers over the IRA; Form 5305-A, Traditional Individual Retirement Custodial Account, if they have custodial powers; or their own prototype IRA agreement.

The IRA is not considered established until the plan agreement is fully executed by both the IRA owner and the Custodian. [Treas. Reg. § 1.408-6(d)(4)(ii)(A)(1)]

Q 13:3 What information must be included in the IRA disclosure statement?

The disclosure statement must include a nontechnical explanation of the rules that apply to the IRA and the financial projections. The information that must be disclosed include:

- Requirements for establishing an individual retirement account or individual retirement annuity
- Financial projections indicating whether the return on the IRA is guaranteed, projectable, or not projectable
- Deductibility rules for regular IRA contributions
- Revocation rights, including the name, address, and telephone number of the representative of the trustee or custodian who is designated to receive revocations
- Distribution rules, including the RMD rules that apply to IRA owners and beneficiaries
- Prohibited transactions and their consequences, including the effect of using the IRA as security for a loan
- When additional tax (early distribution penalties) under Code Section 72(t) may apply
- Estate and gift tax consequences
- Whether approval of the IRS has been obtained for the IRA and, if it has, that the approval does not address the financial merits or the advisability of the taxpayer's establishing the IRA
- Rollover availability
- Non-availability of forward averaging or capital gain treatment
- Advice about commissions payable, expressed as a percentage of an assumed contribution
- Any additional information required by Treasury regulations (which must not be false or misleading)

The IRA plan agreement establishes the terms under which the IRA will be governed and serves as a contract between the IRA owner and the financial institution. The following are some of the terms that should be included in the plan agreement:

For individual retirement accounts:

- Except for rollover contributions, where securities were distributed and are being rolled over to the IRA, contributions must be made in cash.
- The financial institution must satisfy the requirements for serving as a trustee or nonbank custodian.
- No part of the IRA can be invested in life insurance.
- The IRA balance is nonforfeitable.
- The IRA assets will not be commingled with other property, except in a common trust fund or common investment fund.
- The RMD rules under Code Section 401(a)(9) will apply to the IRA.

For individual retirement annuities:

- The contract is nontransferable by the owner.
- Premiums are not fixed.
- The annual premium on behalf of any individual will not exceed the dollar amount in effect under Code Section 219(b)(1)(A).
- Any refund of premiums will be applied before the close of the calendar year following the year of the refund toward the payment of future premiums or the purchase of additional benefits.
- The IRA is nonforfeitable.

[I.R.C. §§ 408(a), 408(b); Treas. Reg. §§ 1.408-6(d)(4)(iii)–1.408-6(d)(4)(vii)]

Revocation Period

Q 13:4 What can an individual do during the seven-day revocation period?

The IRA owner may revoke (cancel) the IRA within a seven-day period. The IRA can be revoked orally or in writing, as specified in the IRA disclosure statement.

If the IRA owner is provided with the disclosure statement and a copy of the IRA plan agreement on the same day the IRA is established (see Qs 13:1–13:2), he or she has seven days after the establishment date to revoke the IRA. If the IRA owner is provided with the disclosure statement and a copy of the IRA plan agreement at least seven days before the IRA is established, no additional period for revocation is required. The IRA plan agreement need not be filled in with information pertaining to the IRA owner; however, it must be complete in all other respects. [Treas. Reg. § 1.408-6(d)(4)(ii)(A)(2)]

If a timely revocation is received by the IRA custodian, the IRA owner is entitled to receive the entire amount contributed without any adjustments for sales commissions, administrative fees (including certificate of deposit penalties), or fluctuation in market value. [Treas. Reg. § 1.408-6(d)(4)(ii)(A)(2)]

To protect themselves from having to restore investment losses upon revocation, some IRA custodians do not allow initial contributions to be invested in anything other than a government-guaranteed investment or government-guaranteed security until the seven-day revocation period has expired. Unless the IRA document provides otherwise, investment gains do not have to be distributed from an IRA that is timely revoked.

Example. The Friendly family of mutual funds custodian provides that contributions made during the first seven days after the IRA is established will be invested in the Friendly U.S. Government Cash Fund. After the seven-day period, assets in the IRA may be transferred to any of the Friendly stock or bond funds. Friendly has limited its loss in the event that an IRA is revoked.

Q 13:5 When does the seven-day revocation period commence?

The seven-day revocation period commences on the date that the prospective IRA owner is provided with the disclosure statement. If the disclosure statement is provided less than seven days before the IRA is established, the seven-day period begins when the IRA is established. [Treas. Reg. § 1.408-6(d)(4)(ii)(A)(2)]

Q 13:6 Is a revocation of an IRA reportable?

Yes. Financial institutions must report contributions made to the IRA on Form 5498, *IRA Contribution Information,* even if the contribution is revoked. This includes regular IRA contributions, rollover contributions, SIMPLE IRA contributions and SEP IRA contributions. Form 1099-R, *Distributions from Pensions, Annuities, Retirement or Profit-Sharing Plans, IRAs, Insurance Contracts, etc.*, must also be issued to report the distribution of the amount from the IRA as a revocation. Form 5498 will show the year-end fair market value (FMV) as zero (0) unless the transaction was initiated just before the end of the year and revoked early in the following year (see Qs 13:12, 13:13, 13:119, 13:120). Revocation of transfers are not reported on Form 5498, but are reported on Form 1099-R.

Note. In many cases, the revocation of an IRA may have tax consequences, depending on the type of contribution being revoked.

Q 13:7 What mailing rules affect the right of revocation?

Treasury regulations provide that if an IRA disclosure statement or an IRA governing instrument (or an amendment to either) is mailed to the taxpayer, it will be deemed to have been received seven days after the date of mailing, unless there is evidence to the contrary. If the mailing is received less than seven days before the earlier of the date of establishment (date the IRA agreement is signed) or the date of purchase (date of the initial contribution), the right of revocation must be granted. If an individual's written revocation is required or permitted, the postmark or certification date determines when the revocation was mailed. [Treas. Reg. § 1.408-6(d)(4)]

Generally, a disclosure statement is considered to be mailed on the date of the postmark stamped on the cover in which it was properly mailed. Therefore, if the cover containing the disclosure statement bears a postmark, the statement is considered mailed on the postmark date even if it is received after the date it is normally required to be received. [Prop. Treas. Reg. §§ 301.7502-1, 301.7502-2] The sender has the burden of proving when the postmark was made. (See Qs 13:63–13:72 for additional mailing rules.)

Reports to the IRS and the IRA Owner

Q 13:8 What form must the financial institution file to inform the IRS and the IRA owner about IRA contributions?

The financial institution must file Form 5498 with the IRS to report regular IRA contributions, rollover contributions, recharacterized contributions, Roth IRA conversion contributions, SEP IRA contributions, and SIMPLE IRA contributions made to the IRA. Form 5498 must also be issued to the IRA owner, unless no contributions were made to the IRA for the year (see Qs 13:158–13:199).

Each IRA owner must receive either the official IRS Form 5498 or a substitute Form 5498 that meets the requirements of IRS Publication 1179, *Rules and Specifications for Private Printing of Substitute Forms 1096, 1098, 1099, 5498, and W-2G*. IRS Publication 1179 is a revenue procedure that is revised annually and contains the requirements for the format and content of substitute statements to recipients.

> **Note.** If the financial institution furnished the December 31 FMV statement by January 31 as required (see Q 13:10) and no reportable contributions were made to the IRA, the IRA custodian need not issue Form 5498 (see Q 13:9) to the IRA owner. In such cases, the FMV statement, which is required to be issued by January 31, must contain the following legend, indicating which information is being provided to the IRS: "This information is being furnished to the Internal Revenue Service."

Q 13:9 When must Form 5498 be filed with the IRS?

Form 5498 must be filed with the IRS annually. It is due by May 31 of the year that follows the year for which the contribution is being reported. For 2012 forms, the due date is May 31, 2013.

Q 13:10 What other information is reported on Form 5498?

The FMV of the IRA as of December 31 is also reported on Form 5498. The December 31 FMV is also reported on the Fair Market Value Statement, which can be in any written format and must be issued to the IRA owner by January 31 of the year following the year for which the FMV is being reported. If Form 5498 is not issued to the IRA owner for the year because no contributions were made to the IRA, the Fair Market Value Statement must include a legend designating which information is being provided to the IRS.

Q 13:11 Must Form 5498 be filed if an IRA has no value at the end of the year because of investment loss?

It depends. Form 5498 must be filed to report any contributions made during the year. However, if no contributions were made for the year, the financial institution is not required to issue Form 5498 to the IRA owner (see Q 13:9).

Q 13:12 Must Form 5498 be filed if an IRA is revoked by December 31?

Yes. Form 5498 must be filed if any contributions were made during the year, even if the IRA was revoked by December 31 of that year.

Q 13:13 Must Form 5498 be filed if an IRA is revoked in the year that follows the year in which it was established?

Yes. The December 31 FMV of the IRA, if any, must be included on Form 5498. Even if the IRA has a zero FMV on December 31, and the contribution is timely revoked, Form 5498 must be filed to report the contribution.

Q 13:14 Should Form 5498 be issued to an IRA owner?

Yes. Each IRA owner must receive either the official Form 5498 developed by the IRS or a substitute Form 5498 that meets the requirements of IRS Publication 1179, *Rules and Specifications for Private Printing of Substitute Forms 1096, 1098, 1099, 5498, and W-2G*. IRS Publication 1179 is a revenue procedure that is revised annually and contains the requirements for the format and content of substitute statements to recipients.

> **Note.** If the IRA trustee or custodian furnished the December 31 FMV statement by January 31 as required (see Q 13:10) and no reportable contributions were made to the IRA, the IRA custodian need not issue Form 5498 to the IRA owner (see Q 13:9). In such a case, the FMV statement must contain the following legend, indicating which information is being provided to the IRS: "This information is being furnished to the Internal Revenue Service."

Q 13:15 How must distributions from an IRA be reported?

Distributions from an IRA must be reported to the IRS on Form 1099-R (see Qs 13:95–13:127), which must be filed with the IRS by the custodian by February 28 (March 31 if filed electronically) following the calendar year for which the distribution is being reported. A copy must be sent to the IRA owner by January 31 of the year that follows the year for which the distribution is being reported.

Q 13:16 What are the distribution reporting requirements when an IRA has been revoked?

All distributions from a revoked IRA must be reported on Form 1099-R (see Qs 13:6, 13:119, 13:120). The reporting requirements vary depending on the type of transaction being revoked.

Q 13:17 Must a report be filed when a trustee transfers an IRA to another trustee?

Generally no. Transfers are nonreportable transactions and, as such, require no tax reporting. However, certain transactions where the assets are delivered via a trustee-to-trustee transfer are reported on IRS Forms 1099-R and 5498. These include direct Roth IRA conversions, recharacterizations, qualified charitable donations under Code Section 408(d)(8), direct rollovers, and qualified HSA funding distributions as defined under Code Section 408(d)(9) (see Qs 13:21, 13:102, 13:164).

Practice Pointer. The IRS often uses the term *trustee-to-trustee transfer* to refer to the *delivery method* for some reportable transactions. Examples include direct Roth IRA conversions and direct rollovers, where the assets are paid by the issuing custodian or plan trustee to the receiving custodian or trustee for credit to the participant's retirement account.

Q 13:18 Are the reporting requirements for a transfer of an IRA different when the transfer is made or received by a custodian?

No. The IRA rules specifically allow for choosing a trustee or a custodian without any change in IRA attributes.

Q 13:19 How is the fair market value of a transferred IRA reported at the end of the calendar year?

Although the value of the actual transfer activity is not reported, the custodian that held the IRA on December 31 must issue the December 31 FMV statement by the following January 31 (see Q 13:10). In addition, the custodian must issue Form 5498 to the IRS by May 31 of the year that follows the year for which the reporting is issued (see Q 13:9).

Taxpayer Reporting

Q 13:20 How must a taxpayer report the receipt of a distribution from an IRA?

A taxpayer must report an IRA distribution received during the year on his or her tax return for the year (Form 1040, 1040A, or Form 1040NR, U.S. Individual Income Tax Return). (See Qs 13:90–13:94 for additional information regarding Form 1040.) The tax return must generally be filed on April 15 following the year of distribution, or by an extended due date when permitted.

Q 13:21 How does a taxpayer indicate on Form 1040 whether any portion of a distribution from an IRA is nontaxable because it was rolled over to an eligible retirement plan?

An IRA-to-IRA rollover should be documented by copies of Form 1099-R, which shows the distribution, and Form 5498, which shows the rollover contribution. If the distribution was processed as a direct rollover, the amount is reported on line 11a ,15a or 16a, and zero (0) is entered on line 11b, 15b or 16b. If the distribution was paid to the IRA owner and rolled over within 60 days, the amount is reported on line 11a, 15a or 16a, and the taxable amount is reported on line 11b, 15b or 16b. The taxable amount is usually any amount not properly rolled over within 60 days, less any nontaxable amount of the distribution.

Direct Rollovers. A direct rollover from an IRA occurs when a direct payment of the distribution from a traditional IRA, SEP IRA, or SIMPLE IRA is made to a qualified plan, a 403(a) or 403(b) annuity plan, or an eligible governmental 457(b) plan.

Q 13:22 If any portion of a distribution from a traditional IRA, SEP IRA, or SIMPLE IRA is not rolled over, is that portion automatically reported as a fully taxable distribution?

Not necessarily. The IRA trustee will report the distribution as "taxable amount not determined." However, if the IRA owner made nondeductible IRA contributions or rolled over after-tax amounts (from a qualified plan or 403(b) account), a calculation must be done to determine the portion of the distribution that represents a return of basis (i.e., nondeductible IRA contributions and rollover of after-tax amounts). The IRA participant must file Form 8606 to determine the nontaxable portion of the distribution. Form 8606 includes a formula for determining the taxable amount of the distribution.

Q 13:23 Are other IRAs taken into account when calculating the portion of a distribution that represents a return of basis?

Yes. A taxpayer's entire non-Roth IRA portfolio (including SEP IRAs and SIMPLE IRAs) must be taken into account when calculating the portion of an IRA distribution (from an IRA other than a Roth IRA) that represents a return of basis (any nondeductible IRA contributions or rollover of after-tax contributions). That is so even if the other IRAs do not include basis. (See Qs 13:47–13:58.)

Withholding

Q 13:24 How much income tax must a payor withhold from an IRA distribution in the absence of a waiver of withholding?

Under federal law, 10 percent of an IRA's nonperiodic distributions (see Q 13:25) must be withheld unless the taxpayer elects to waive withholding, or elects to withhold more than 10 percent. The financial institution should provide the taxpayer with Form W-4P, Withholding Certificate for Pension or Annuity Payments (or a substitute Form W-4P or a form that is designed by the organization and meets the language requirements for the waiver), so that such a waiver can be executed before the distribution is made. [Treas. Reg. § 35. 3405-1, Q&A D-26; I.R.S. News Releases IR-83-3, IR-83-32]

Periodic distributions should generally be treated in the same manner as wages under the usual withholding tables, under rules more fully described on Form W-4P or a substitute form.

No waiver is required when the distribution is processed as a direct rollover to a qualified plan, 403(b), or governmental 457(b) plan, as direct rollovers are not subject to withholding tax.

Q 13:25 What is a nonperiodic distribution?

Generally, periodic distributions are annuity payments made for more than one year that are not eligible rollover distributions. For wage withholding purposes, these payments are treated as if they are wages. Withholding on a periodic distribution may be waived by filing Form W-4P or a substitute form (as is the case for nonperiodic distributions; see Q 13:24).

Q 13:26 Is there any mandatory withholding from a distribution from an IRA?

No. IRA owners have the option of electing to have taxes withheld from a distribution or electing to have no taxes withheld. If no election is made, the financial institution is required to withhold 10 percent of the gross distribution amount for federal taxes from nonperiodic distributions.

Q 13:27 Can the IRA owner elect to have an amount other than 10 percent withheld for federal income tax?

Yes. The taxpayer may elect to have from 10 percent to 100 percent withheld for federal income tax. The withholding amount cannot be less than 10 percent (except in cases where the taxpayer elects to have zero percent withheld), for nonperiodic distributions.

Q 13:28 Is there withholding required on distributions made to U.S. citizens and resident aliens who have the distributions delivered outside the United States?

Yes. The payor is required to withhold 10 percent for federal income tax on distribution amounts paid to U.S. citizens and resident aliens, if the distribution is delivered to the taxpayer at a home address that is outside the United States. The taxpayer can choose to waive the withholding, if a home address in the United States or in a U.S. possession is provided to the payor. The payor must withhold tax if the U.S. address provided is that of a nominee, trustee, or agent to whom the benefits are to be delivered, and the taxpayers own home address in the United States or in a U.S. possession is not provided. [IRS Publication 505, *Tax Withholding and Estimated Tax*]

An individual who meets either the green card test of the substantial presence test for a year is considered a resident alien of the United States for tax purposes. An individual who does not meet either of these tests may be able to choose to be treated as a U.S. resident for part of the year. [IRS Publication 519, *U.S. Tax Guide for Aliens*]

Green card test. Under the green card test, an individual is generally considered to be a resident for tax purposes, by being a lawful permanent resident of the United States at any time during calendar year. This is known as the "green card" test. Under the green card test, an individual is considered to be a lawful permanent resident of the United States at any time if approval has been given under the immigration laws (by the U.S. Citizenship and Immigration Services (USCIS), or its predecessor organization) for the individual to reside permanently in the United States as an immigrant.

Substantial presence test. An individual is generally considered a U.S. resident for tax purposes if the substantial presence test is met for the calendar year. To meet this test, the individual must be physically present in the United States on at least:

1. 31 days during the calendar year for which the test applies, and
2. 183 days during the three-year period that includes the year for which the test is being performed and the two preceding calendar years, counting:
   (a) All the days the individual was present in the United States for the year for which the test is being done, and
   (b) 1/3 of the days in the immediately preceding year, and
   (c) 1/6 of the days in the year that precedes the immediately preceding year

For this purpose, the term *United States* includes the following areas.

- All 50 states and the District of Columbia,

- The territorial waters of the United States, and
- The seabed and subsoil of those submarine areas that are adjacent to U.S. territorial waters and over which the United States has exclusive rights under international law to explore and exploit natural resources.

The term does not include U.S. possessions and territories or U.S. airspace.

Q 13:29 Is there withholding required on distributions made to nonresident aliens (NRAs)?

It depends. Distributions paid to nonresident aliens are usually subject to a withholding requirement of 30 percent. [I.R.C. § 1441; T.D. 8881] Nonresident aliens can apply for a rate under a U.S. tax treaty for their country by providing the payor with a properly completed Form W-8BEN, Certificate of Foreign Status of Beneficial Owner for United States Tax Withholding.

Note. The payor generally must request that the nonresident alien provide a U.S. taxpayer identification number (TIN), and include the TIN on forms and other tax documents. The TIN may be a Social Security number (SSN), an IRS individual taxpayer identification number (ITIN), or, for any person other than an individual, an employer identification number (EIN).

Q 13:30 How is withholding determined on a distribution made to an NRA?

IRA distributions being delivered outside the United States to a non-U.S. person (referred to as a nonresident alien) may be subject to higher income tax withholding at the rate of 30 percent under Code Section 1441, in lieu of the normal 10 percent withholding rate under Code Section 3405. [*See* Treas. Reg. § 1.401(a)-21, T.D. 9294, 71 Fed. Reg. 61877–61888 (Oct. 20, 2006)]

A nonresident alien is an individual who is not a U.S. citizen or resident alien. A nonresident alien is not a "resident alien." A resident alien is an alien who meets either the green card test or the substantial presence test for the calendar year. [*See* IRS Publication 519, *Withholding of Tax on Nonresident Aliens and Foreign Entities*, which provides information on resident and nonresident alien status, the tests for residence, and the exceptions to those tests]

Electing out of the Normal 10 Percent Withholding under Code Section 3405. If an IRA distribution is being made to an NRA, the individual may elect out of (waive) the normal 10 percent withholding requirement by

1. Filing Form W-8BEN—Certificate of Foreign Status of Beneficial Owner for United States Tax Withholding, with the payer (see new W-8 "family" of forms below); and
2. Signing a written certification, under penalties of perjury, with the payer that the individual is not a U.S. citizen or resident alien, and is not an expatriate of the United States (one who expatriates for the principal purpose of avoiding U.S. taxes).

An NRA who elects out of Code Section 3405 withholding is now subject to withholding under Code Section 1441, usually at the rate of 30 percent. In such case, report the distribution on IRS Form 1042-S—Foreign Person's U.S. Source Income Subject to Withholding, and file Form 1042—Annual Withholding Tax Return for U.S. Source Income of Foreign Persons.

Publication 515 contains more information on the various types of income, including retirement plan income, that are subject to tax withholding and includes when exemptions or reduced withholding rates apply to certain types of income.

Can Lower Treaty Rates Apply to IRA Distributions? If an NRA elects no withholding under Code Section 3405 (the normal retirement plan withholding rules) by filing Form W-8BEN and providing the statement under penalties of perjury described above, the recipient may be able to claim the benefits under the country's income tax treaty with the United States. If any lower treaty rate applies (including 0 percent), such payments are still reportable on IRS Form 1042-S—Foreign Person's U.S. Source Income Subject to Withholding.

Caution. Using the lower treaty rate is not automatic. Each country's tax treaty with the United States defines *pension and annuity income* for purposes of using the treaty rate for retirement plan distributions. In some specific treaties, IRAs are included in the definition of *pension income,* and thus the treaty rate can be used. However, other specific treaties define IRAs as "other income," or the treaty may be silent, which means that the 30 percent withholding rate applies with no reduction.

If the NRA individual elects for no withholding under Code Section 3405, most payers will automatically withhold at the rate of 30 percent and report the payment on Form 1042-S. The only other option is for the payer to research each country's tax treaty with the United States in order to determine how IRAs are defined under the treaty.

W-8 "Family" of Forms. Without proper documentation, the full 30 percent withholding rate applies. The IRS has issued the following forms referred to as the "W-8" "Family of Forms":

W-8BEN	Certificate of Foreign Status of Beneficial Owner for U.S. Tax Withholding. When this form is filed with the payer, the individual is claiming to be a foreign person and is also claiming whether or not treaty benefits apply.
W-8ECI	Certificate of Foreign Person's Claim for Exemption from Withholding on Income Effectively Connected with the Conduct of a Trade or Business in the United States.

In general, foreign persons are subject to U.S. tax at a 30 percent rate on income they receive from U.S. sources. However, no withholding is required on income that is, or is deemed to be, effectively connected with the conduct of a trade or business within the United States and is includible in the beneficial owner's gross income for the tax year.

W-8EXP	Certificate of Foreign Government or Other Foreign Organization for United States Tax Withholding
W-8IMY	Certificate of Foreign Intermediary, Foreign Partnership, or Certain U.S. Branches for United States Tax Withholding

Validity of Forms. A Form W-8BEN provided without a taxpayer identification number (TIN) will remain in effect for a period starting on the date the form is signed and ending on the last day of the third succeeding calendar year, unless a change in circumstances makes any information on the form incorrect. For example, a Form W-8BEN signed on September 30, 2010, remains valid through December 31, 2013.

A Form W-8BEN furnished with a TIN will remain in effect until the status of the person whose name is on the form changes, or a change in circumstances makes any information on the form incorrect, provided that the withholding agent reports on Form 1042-S at least one payment annually. Thus, a Form W-8BEN containing a TIN remains valid for as long as the filer's status and the information relevant to the filer's certification on the form remain unchanged.

A TIN is either a U.S. Social Security number or an ITIN (Individual Tax Identification Number). An ITIN can be obtained by an NRA who either does not have or is not entitled to a U.S. Social Security number.

Claim by NRA for a Refund of Tax Withheld. Whether the payer withholds under Code Section 3405 and files Form 1099-R reporting the IRA distribution or withholds under Code Section 1441 and files Form 1042-S reporting the IRA distribution, the NRA can file Form 1040-NR—U.S. Nonresident Alien Income Tax Return, in order to claim a refund of taxes.

IRS Amends Final NRA Regulation to Include IRAs. On May 16, 2000, the IRS published amendments [T.D. 8881, 65 Fed. Reg. 32151–32212 (May 22, 2000)] to the final regulations [T.D. 8734, 62 Fed. Reg. 53387–53498 (Oct. 14, 1997)] on the income tax withholding requirements on payments made to nonresident aliens.

These amendments extended the "presumption rules" applicable to qualified plans and Code Section 403(b) plans to IRAs described under Code Section 408. Code Section 408 includes traditional IRAs, SEP IRAs, and SIMPLE IRAs, but it does not include Roth IRAs that are governed under Code Section 408A.

Although IRAs are now mentioned in the NRA regulations, it does not necessarily change the final results when making payments to a nonresident alien individual.

Presumption Rules. Payments from a qualified plan, a Code Section 403(b) account, or a Code Section 408 IRA that a withholding agent cannot reliably associate with documentation is presumed to be made to a U.S. person *only if* the payee has a Social Security number (not just an ITIN) *and* a mailing address in the United States, or in a foreign country with which the United States has an income tax treaty in effect and the treaty provides that the payee, if an individual resident in that country, would be entitled to an exemption from U.S. tax on retirement plan payments. In such cases, withhold income tax at the appropriate rate under Code Section 3405 depending on the type of plan and frequency of payments, and report the payments on Form 1099-R.

Note. A U.S. person residing in a foreign country cannot elect out of withholding under Code Section 3405.

Any payment that does not meet the above requirements can be presumed to be made to a foreign person. In these cases, withhold income tax under Code Section 1441 at the rate of 30 percent, and report the payments on Form 1042-S.

Claiming Foreign Status by Filing Form W-8BEN. If the payer receives from the payee a completed Form W-8BEN, the withholding agent can usually presume the payee is foreign, unless the withholding agent has reason to believe that the payee is a U.S. person. When a Form W-8BEN is received, the withholding agent applies the 30 percent withholding rate. However, if the payment is from a qualified plan or a Code Section 403(b) account *and* the payee either has a Social Security number or an ITIN, the withholding agent can apply the lower treaty rate (if any) found in the tables in IRS Publication 515.

Lower Treaty Rates Are Not Automatic for IRAs. In order to apply any lower treaty rates for payments from an IRA, the treaty itself must specifically state that IRAs are treated as "pension income." If such treaty does not specifically so state, or if the treaty is silent, the 30 percent withholding rate cannot be reduced, even if the payee has an SSN or ITIN.

Reporting Penalties

Q 13:31 What role does Form 1099-R play in assessing penalties?

As noted above (see Q 13:15), Form 1099-R is a statement provided to both the IRS and the recipient of IRA distributions made during the year. Box 7 of the form contains a number or letter (see Q 13:102) that indicates whether the distribution is subject to the 10 percent early distribution penalty. If box 7 incorrectly indicates whether the 10 percent early distribution penalty applies, the taxpayer may file IRS Form 5329 to correct the reporting.

Q 13:32 What is the purpose of Form 5329?

Form 5329 is used by a taxpayer to calculate excise tax penalties on qualified plans (including IRAs) and other tax-favored accounts. There are eight parts to Form 5329.

Part I. Penalty (10 percent) for distributions made before age 59½ (without meeting one of the exceptions allowed for IRAs; see Qs 13:33, 13:34).

Part II. Penalty (10 percent) for distributions from a Coverdell education savings account (ESA) not used for educational expenses.

Part III. Reconciliation of over contribution corrections from traditional IRAs and calculation of the 6 percent excise tax on portions not yet corrected (see Qs 13:37–13:39).

Part IV. Determination of tax (6 percent) on excess contributions to Roth IRAs.

Part V. Determination of tax (6 percent) on excess contributions to Coverdell ESAs.

Part VI. Determination of tax (6 percent) on excess contributions to Archer medical savings accounts (Archer MSAs).

Part VII. Determination of 6 percent excise tax on excess contributions to health savings accounts (HSAs).

Part VIII. Penalty (50 percent of the undistributed portion) for distributions after age 70½ not meeting the minimum distribution requirements (see Q 13:40).

Penalties reported on Form 5329 are not reimbursable by the IRS unless the excise tax is waived. If a taxpayer does not have to file an income tax return for 2012, Form 5329 should be filed by itself at the time and place the taxpayer would be required to file Form 1040 or Form 1040-NR.

Early Distributions

Q 13:33 How does Part I of Form 5329 address the 10 percent penalty for early distributions?

Part I of Form 5329 (with accompanying instructions) begins by enumerating the types of distributions that are to be considered in determining the 10 percent penalty for early distributions. In each case, the distribution must have been made before the taxpayer reached age 59½.

Distributions should be shown net of current-year contributions already withdrawn and earlier contributions withdrawn as excess contributions, as explained in the form. Also to be excluded are nondeductible contributions as determined under Form 8606, Nondeductible IRAs and Coverdell ESAs.

The following distributions should also be included:

1. Annuity contract distributions,
2. Modified endowment contract distributions, and
3. Prohibited transaction-caused distributions.

With regard to item 3, for example, if the taxpayer borrowed from either an individual retirement account or an individual retirement annuity, such account or annuity is disqualified as of the first day of the tax year in which the borrowing occurred. If the taxpayer was then younger than age 59½ (even if he or she was age 59½ or older when the borrowing occurred), the early distribution penalty applies. The result is the same if an individual retirement *annuity* was pledged as security for a loan. If an individual retirement *account* is pledged as security for a loan, the date of the pledge determines the age at which the distribution was received. If the taxpayer was then under age 59½ a pre-age-59½ distribution of the individual retirement account would be deemed to have occurred on the date of the pledge and the amount of the pledge would be reported on line 1 of Form 5329. (For detailed information about reporting prohibited transactions on Form 5330, Return of Excise Taxes Related to Employee Benefit Plans, see Qs 13:147–13:157.)

Investment of an IRA in a collectible is deemed a distribution of the IRA on the date of the investment. The age at which the distribution was received is determined at that time. Collectibles include the following:

- Works of art
- Rugs or antiques
- Metals or gems
- Stamps and coins, other than certain gold and silver U.S. coins (see Qs 13:137, 13:138)
- Alcoholic beverages
- Any other tangible personal property specified by the IRS

If the taxpayer was under age 59½ on the investment date, the distribution is a pre-age-59½ distribution.

Q 13:34 What exceptions to the tax on early distributions are recognized in Part I of Form 5329 for IRAs?

Certain distributions that are excluded from the tax on early distributions are reported on line 2 in Part I of Form 5329 (see Q 5:56). In addition, an exception Code number from the instructions is entered on the blank line to the left of line 2. The following is a list of these exceptions that apply to IRAs:

- Distributions made as part of a series of substantially equal periodic payments (made at least annually) for the life (or life expectancy) or the joint lives (or joint life expectancies) of the IRA owner and designated beneficiary
- Distributions due to total and permanent disability
- Distributions due to death
- Distributions up to (1) the amount paid for unreimbursed medical expenses during the year minus (2) 7.5 percent of the IRA owner's adjusted gross income for the year.
- Distributions made to unemployed individuals for health insurance premiums.
- Distributions made for higher education expenses.
- Distributions made for purchase of a first home, up to $10,000.
- Distributions due to an IRS levy on the IRA.
- Qualified distributions to reservists while serving on active duty for at least 180 days.

- Distributions incorrectly indicated as early distributions by code 1, J, or S in box 7 of Form 1099-R. Include on line 2 the amount received when the IRA owner was age 59½ or older.

Q 13:35 What can be done if Form 1099-R incorrectly indicates that a distribution is subject to the 10 percent early distribution penalty?

If Form 1099-R incorrectly indicates that the distribution is subject to the 10 percent early distribution penalty, a correction can be made on Form 5329. In such a case, line 2 of Form 5329 should be completed according to the instructions.

Note. In 2011, the IRS added a new Employee Plans Compliance Unit (EPCU) project, the Form 1099R-72(t) Project, focusing on taxpayers who were issued a Form 1099-R documenting receipt in 2009 of an early taxable distribution from an IRA or qualified plan, but who did not report the taxable distribution on their personal income tax returns (Form 1040). Information request letters sent to selected taxpayers in this group require the taxpayer to verify, among other things, if the 1099-R information is correct. Information on the EPCU is found at *http://www.irs.gov/retirement/article/0,,id=250532,00.html* (visited on Aug. 27, 2012), which contains a link to the information request letter.

Q 13:36 How does a financial institution report a deemed distribution?

A financial institution must report a deemed distribution in exactly the same manner as it reports an actual distribution. Like the value of an actual distribution, the value of a deemed distribution will be the basis of the 10 percent premature distribution penalty. Amounts attributable to distribution of basis will not be subject to the 10 percent premature distribution penalty.

Excess Contributions

Q 13:37 How does Part III of Form 5329 address excess contributions?

Part III of Form 5329 helps the IRS and the taxpayer trace the recovery of excess contributions and determine what portion was not corrected during the year and thus is to be taxed again at 6 percent. It is also used to compute the tax for new over-contributions. (Returns of excess contributions before age 59½ may include earnings that will be taxed at 10 percent under Part I of Form 5329, unless an exception applies.)

Q 13:38 How does Form 5329 determine the amount of excess contributions subject to tax, and what are the reporting guidelines for excess contributions?

To determine the amount of excess contributions subject to tax, Form 5329 considers the following: (1) prior-year excess contributions that were not previously eliminated, (2) under-contributions for the current year that may be applied, (3) certain withdrawals of prior-year excess contributions, and (4) any other distributions made in the current year that are taxable. [I.R.C. § 4973(b)]

The four methods for correcting excess contributions follow; the examples under each method include reporting guidelines.

Method 1. Withdrawing current-year contributions before that year's tax return due date.

Before 1986, Code Section 408(d)(4) permitted only the withdrawal of IRA contributions that were not allowed as a deduction; however, an individual may now withdraw any contribution, whether it is deductible or nondeductible. For this method to apply, all of the following requirements must be met:

1. The excess or unwanted contribution must be distributed to the individual no later than the deadline (including extensions) for filing the federal income tax return for the year in which the contribution was made.
2. The earnings attributable to the excess or unwanted contribution must accompany the distribution. Treasury Regulations Section 1.408-4(c)(2) prescribes a rather complicated formula for determining the earnings attributable to an unwanted contribution being returned before the due date of the return for the year in which the contribution was made. The earnings attributable to the contribution are taxable to the individual in the year in which the contribution was made, regardless of when the distribution occurs and regardless of the year for which the contribution was made. Gains attributable to excess SEP contributions, disallowed deferrals, and excess deferrals under an elective SEP (SARSEP) are treated differently (see chapter 12).
3. The individual may not deduct the excess or unwanted contribution.

Example 1. Harriet makes an IRA contribution for 2012 on January 10, 2013. She has until the deadline for filing her 2012 federal income tax return, including extensions, to remove any current-year excess or unwanted contribution (whether or not deductible) because the contribution was made for 2012.

If the three rules set forth above are satisfied, the distribution of the excess or unwanted contribution is not taxable; however, the accompanying earnings on the excess or unwanted contribution are considered a taxable IRA distribution. In addition, if the individual is under age 59½, the 10 percent additional income tax applies to the premature distribution of the earnings attributable to the unwanted contribution. If the contribution is a true excess contribution (rather than an unwanted current-year contribution), the otherwise applicable 6 percent excise tax under Code Section 4973 does not apply.

Note. On May 5, 2003, the IRS published final regulations (T.D. 9056, 68 Fed. Reg. 23586–23590 (May 5, 2003)) that provide a new method for calculating the net income attributable to IRA contributions that are recharacterized under Code Section 408A(d)(6) or distributed as a returned contribution under Code Section 408(d)(4).

Effective on May 5, 2003, the final regulations incorporate, without change, the methods provided in the proposed regulations (REG-124256-02). The final regulations apply to income calculations of IRA contributions made on or after January 1, 2004.

The new formula for calculating the net income on a returned contribution or a recharacterized contribution is:

$$\text{Net income}^{1} = \text{Contribution}^{2} \times \frac{(\text{Adjusted closing balance}^{3} - \text{Adjusted opening balance}^{4})}{\text{Adjusted opening balance}}$$

---

[1] Net income can be positive or negative.

[2] The amount of the contribution that is being returned or recharacterized.

[3] Adjusted closing balance (ACB) is the Fair Market Value (FMV) of the IRA at the end of the computation period plus the amount of any distributions or transfers (including recharacterizations) made from the IRA during the computation period. Thus, the ACB is the value just prior to the distribution or recharacterization.

[4] Adjusted opening balance (AOB) is the FMV of the IRA at the beginning of the computation period, plus the amount of any contributions (including the contribution that is being returned) or transfers (including recharacterizations) made to the IRA during the computation period.

The computation period is the period beginning immediately before "the time" that the contribution being returned or recharacterized was made to the IRA and ending immediately before the removal of the contribution (or transfer in the case of a recharacterization).

The preamble to the final regulations implies that if an IRA is valued on a daily basis, for purposes of determining the adjusted opening balance (AOB), the computation period begins the exact day before the contribution was made that is being returned or recharacterized. If the IRA is not valued on a daily basis, for purposes of determining the AOB the FMV at the beginning of the computation period is deemed to be the most recent, regularly determined, FMV of the asset as of a date that coincides with or precedes the first day of the computation period (i.e., the most recent statement value). The IRS believes that if an IRA asset is normally valued on a daily basis, these values must be used so that the calculation of the amount of net income is based on the actual earnings and losses during the time the IRA actually held the contribution. The IRS also believes that using the most recent statement value would produce anomalous results.

Example 2. On January 1, 2012, Ronald, age 40 and a calendar-year taxpayer, contributes $5,100 to an IRA established for his benefit. For 2012, he is entitled to a deduction of $5,000 under Code Section 219, he does not claim as deductions any other items listed in Code Section 62, and his gross income is $11,334. On April 3, 2012, $103.29 is distributed to Ronald from his

IRA. As of that date, the closing balance of the IRA before any distribution is $5,268. There were no other distributions from the IRA as of that date. The net amount of income earned by the IRA is $100 × (($5,268 – ($0 initial-year balance + $5,100))/$5,100). The net income attributable to the excess contribution is $3.29 ($100 × ($168/$5,100)). Ronald's adjusted gross income for 2012 is his gross income for 2012 ($11,334), reduced by the amount allowable as a deduction under Code Section 219 ($5,000), or $6,334. Ronald will include $3.29 of the $103.29 distributed on April 3, 2012, in his gross income for 2012. [I.R.C. § 408(d)(4)] Furthermore, he will pay a premature distribution penalty of $.33 on the income attributable to the excess contribution ($3.29) for 2012 under Code Section 72(t).

The contribution and distribution would be reported as follows:

1. Ronald would report the contribution and distribution on his Form 1040 for 2012 (the year the excess contribution was made) as follows:
   a. $5,000 as a regular contribution;
   b. $103.29 as a total distribution, but only $3.29 as a taxable distribution; and
   c. $.33 as a 10 percent premature distribution penalty.
2. Ronald would complete Form 5329 (and attach it to Form 1040). He would complete Part I and report the 10 percent premature distribution penalty of $.33.
3. The trustee or custodian would
   a. Report the full amount contributed ($5,100) on Form 5498 for 2012 (the year the excess contribution was made); and
   b. Report the gross distribution as $103.29 and the taxable distribution as $3.29 on Form 1099-R (2012 version). Distribution code 8 would be used to indicate that the taxable distribution (which represented earnings attributable to the excess) was taxable to Ronald in 2012. Had Ronald taken the corrective distribution during the following year (2013) the excess contribution was made, the trustee or custodian would have issued Form 1099-R for that year. All of the boxes would reflect the same information, except that code P would be used rather than code 8.

Example 3. Tania makes a contribution of $2,000 to her existing IRA on July 12, 2012. Her compensation for the year is only $1,500. Thus, Tania has a $500 excess contribution. On April 1, 2013, Tania withdraws the $500, plus the earnings attributable thereto, calculated as follows, with the following givens: the FMV immediately prior to the contribution being made on July 12, 2012 was $15,300; Tania did not receive any distributions during the computation period; no penalties or fees are imposed; and the FMV on April 1, 2013, immediately prior to the distribution, is $19,553, which includes accrued but not yet credited interest.

The items in the excess equation are determined as follows: the amount of the unwanted contribution or excess contribution is $500; the AOB is $15,300 plus all contributions made during the computation period ($2,000), or $17,300; and the adjusted closing balance (ACB) is $19,553. The total income earned on the IRA excess during the computation period, determined as follows:

1. FMV on the date of corrective distribution is $19,553. This amount would be reduced by early withdrawal or transaction fees if any applied.
2. Add back any distributions to the result of step 1. In this case, no distributions were made, so the result is $19,553. This is the ACB.
3. FMV of the IRA immediately prior to the excess contribution being made was $15,300.
4. Add any contributions or transfers made during the computation period ($2,000). Therefore, the AOB is $17,300.

The earnings calculation can now be expressed as follows:

Net Earnings = $500 × (($19,553 – $17,300)/$17,300)

Net Earnings = $500 × ($2,253/$17,300) = $500 × .130231214 = $65.12

The result ($65.12) represents the earnings attributable to the $500 excess contribution. Tania will withdraw a total of $565.12 on April 2, 2012.

The $500 is not subject to either income taxes or the 6 percent excess contribution penalty. The $65.12, however, is taxable to Tania for the year in which the contribution was made (2012), even though the corrective distribution occurs in the following year (2013).

The remaining balance in Tania's IRA is $18,987.88 ($19,553 – $565.12).

The contribution and distribution would be reported as follows:

1. Tania would report the contribution and distribution on her Form 1040 for 2012 (the year the excess contribution was made) as follows:
   a. $1,500 as a regular contribution;
   b. $565.12 as a total distribution, but only $65.12 as a taxable distribution; and
   c. $6.51 as a 10 percent premature distribution penalty if Tania is under age 59½.
2. If Tania is under age 59½ she would complete Form 5329 (and attach it to Form 1040). She would complete Part I and report the 10 percent premature distribution penalty of $6.51. If Tania is age 59½ or older, she does not complete Form 5329 because she would not be subject to the 10 percent premature distribution penalty.
3. The trustee or custodian would
   a. Report the full amount contributed ($2,000) on Form 5498 for 2012 (the year the excess contribution was made); and
   b. Report the gross distribution as $565.12 and the taxable distribution as $65.12 on Form 1099-R (2013 version). Distribution code P would be

used to indicate that the taxable distribution (which represents earnings attributable to the excess) was taxable to Tania in the prior year. Had Tania taken the corrective distribution during the year the excess contribution was made, the trustee or custodian would have issued Form 1099-R for that year. All the boxes would reflect the same information, except that code 8 would be used rather than code P.

The reporting requirements for returning an unwanted contribution that is not a true excess contribution would be the same as those listed previously.

Method 2. Withdrawing true excess contributions after the tax return due date. (This method does not apply to withdrawing nondeductible contributions that are not true excess contributions.)

After the time to file a federal individual income tax return has expired, the excess may still be withdrawn under the following rules:

1. Because the tax return due date has passed, the taxpayer is immediately subject to the 6 percent excise tax penalty applied first to the excess in the year the excess contribution was made and then to any remaining uncorrected excess in each subsequent year until the excess is corrected.
2. Only the excess amount is withdrawn; earnings attributable to the excess are not required to be distributed as they were in the case of Method 1.
3. The taxpayer does not deduct the excess contribution amount.

Note. Whereas the principal amount of an excess contribution being withdrawn under Method 1 is always treated as a nontaxable IRA distribution, that may not always be the case under Method 2. (See the discussion of the $5,000 rule that follows.)

Caution. Method 2 does not apply to a nondeductible contribution. Thus, a taxpayer who made such a contribution and did not withdraw the contribution plus the earnings attributable to it as described in Method 1 must attach Form 8606 to the tax return and report the amount as a nondeductible contribution.

The $5,000 Rule. When the principal amount of an excess contribution is withdrawn after the tax filing deadline for the year the excess contribution was made, it is not taxable—provided the taxpayer's total aggregate contributions during the year the excess contribution was made do not exceed the applicable maximum for the year ($5,000 for 2012). If the taxpayer's total aggregate contributions during the year the excess contribution was made do exceed $5,000, the principal amount of the excess contribution withdrawn under Method 2 will be taxable for the year of the withdrawal. In addition, it may be subject to the 10 percent premature distribution penalty for the year of the withdrawal if the taxpayer is not yet age 59½. Because an individual may not deduct an excess contribution, such a circumstance would result in double taxation. After 1997, the statutory amount changed from $2,250 to the amount of the IRA contribution limit, currently $5,000, as a result of the change allowing spousal IRA contributions of up to $5,000 per spouse versus a total IRA contribution of $2,250 for both spouses. [I.R.C. § 408(d)(5)]

Example 4. In 2012, Mavis, age 40, inadvertently contributes a total of $5,500 to her IRA for 2012, although $5,000 is her contribution limit for the year. Thus, Mavis has a $500 excess contribution. If she allows the deadline for using Method 1 for correcting this excess to expire (the tax filing deadline, plus extensions, for her tax return filed for the year in which the excess contribution was made), Mavis is immediately subject to the 6 percent excess contribution penalty on the $500 excess.

When Mavis withdraws the $500 under Method 2, the $500 will be taxable to her for the year the distribution occurs, and will also be subject to the 10 percent premature distribution penalty for that year because Mavis is not yet age 59½. Because the total contribution was in excess of $5,000 and Mavis does not get a deduction for the excess contribution, she will pay taxes twice on the same money. If eligible, Mavis may be better off using Method 3 (see below), even though she would have to pay a 6 percent penalty.

Under Method 2, Mavis would

1. Report the contribution on her Form 1040 for 2012 (the year the excess contribution was made) as follows:
   a. $5,000 as a regular contribution, and
   b. $30 ($500 × 6%) as an excess contribution penalty.
2. Complete Form 5329 (and attach it to Form 1040). She would complete Part I and report a 10 percent premature distribution penalty of $50 ($500 × 10%) and complete Part II of Form 5329 to report $30 as an excess contribution penalty.

Under Method 2, the trustee or custodian would

1. Report the full amount contributed ($5,500) on Form 5498 for 2012 (the year the excess contribution was made), and
2. Report the gross distribution as $500 and the taxable distribution as $0 on Form 1099-R (2012 version).

Because no earnings attributable to the $500 excess are required to be distributed, the trustee or custodian is not required to determine the taxable distribution, as it was in the case of Method 1 when earnings were distributed. The 2012 instructions to Form 1099-R, however, say to report the gross amount in box 1 and leave box 2a blank. (This is a change from prior years.) Codes P and 8 do not apply to a distribution of an excess contribution after the tax filing deadline (because no earnings are distributed). The trustee or custodian would use the premature distribution code (code 1) because Mavis is under age 59½.

Exceptions to the $5,000 Rule. There are two exceptions to the $5,000 rule ($5,000 for 2012) applicable to corrections of true excess contributions after the due date of an individual's federal income tax return for the year in which the excess contribution was made:

1. If an employer makes an excess contribution into an employee's IRA under a SEP or SARSEP arrangement, the $5,000 amount is increased by the excess SEP contribution.
2. If an employee makes an excess rollover contribution based on erroneous information received from his or her employer with respect to the amount eligible to be rolled over, the $5,000 amount is increased by the portion of the rollover contribution attributable to the erroneous information.

Method 3. Treating a prior-year excess as a regular contribution made in a subsequent year for which the taxpayer has an unused contribution limit.

Under Method 3, there is no distribution from the IRA. The taxpayer merely under contributes in subsequent years until the excess amount is used up. Still, as in the case of Method 2, the taxpayer is immediately subject to the 6 percent excess contribution penalty because a corrective distribution did not occur on a timely basis (see Method 1). The 6 percent penalty is applied first to the year in which the excess contribution was made, then to any remaining uncorrected excess amount in each subsequent year until the excess is used up. [I.R.C. § 219(f)(6)]

Thus, an IRA owner who makes an excess contribution in any year is permitted to carry over that excess as a contribution made for a subsequent year for which he or she has an unused contribution limit. The carryover is reported on the individual's income tax return, but it is not reported to the IRS on Form 5498.

Under Method 3, it should be noted, the taxpayer must be eligible to make a regular IRA contribution for the subsequent year. That may pose a problem if the taxpayer is nearing or has attained age 70½ or has no compensation during the subsequent year.

Practice Pointer. The 6 percent penalty may not be as costly as the result under Method 1, where the taxpayer receives a taxable distribution of the earnings attributable to the excess amount and may be subject to a 10 percent premature distribution penalty assessed on earnings and an early withdrawal penalty or other fee assessed by the trustee or custodian. The taxpayer should consult his or her tax or legal adviser.

Example 5. In 2011 Linda, age 23, made a contribution of $5,000 to her IRA for 2011. Her compensation for the year was only $2,200. Therefore, she has a 2011 excess IRA contribution of $2,800. If Linda decides not to withdraw the $2,800 excess under Method 1, she is immediately subject to the 6 percent excess contribution penalty for the year the excess was made (2011).

Linda's compensation for 2012 is $9,000, making her eligible to contribute the maximum of $5,000. Linda contributes $2,200 of new money for 2012 and applies the prior-year excess amount of $2,800 toward her overall limit of $5,000 for 2012. Because she uses up her entire prior-year excess in the following year, no 6 percent penalty is reapplied.

Under Method 3, Linda would

1. Report the contribution on her Form 1040 for 2011 (the year the excess contribution was made) as follows:
   a. $2,200 as a regular contribution, and
   b. $168 ($2,800 × 6%) as the excess contribution penalty.
2. Complete Form 5329 (and attach it to Form 1040). She would complete Part III and report the excess contribution penalty of $168.

Under Method 3, the trustee or custodian would

1. Report the full amount contributed ($5,000) on Form 5498 for 2011 (the year the excess contribution was made), and
2. Report the full amount contributed ($2,200) on Form 5498 for 2012.

Linda would report $5,000 ($2,200 + $2,800) as a regular contribution on her Form 1040 for 2012 (the year the excess was corrected). No further reporting would be required from the trustee or custodian because no distributions are being made.

Q 13:39 How is the 6 percent penalty tax on excess contributions applied?

The 6 percent penalty on excess contributions is applied to the total excess contribution remaining after the deadline by which the excess is required to be removed and the amount that remains at the end of each year for subsequent years (see Q 13:38). It should be noted, however, that the amount of the tax for any year cannot exceed 6 percent of the value of the IRA determined at the end of the year. [I.R.C. § 4973(a)]

Minimum Distributions

Q 13:40 How does Part VIII of Form 5329 address the 50 percent penalty tax on excess accumulations?

The instructions to Part VIII of Form 5329 confirm that the IRS may excuse the 50 percent penalty tax on excess accumulations when it is shown that a reasonable error has occurred and the taxpayer is taking appropriate steps to correct the error. The IRS suggests that if a taxpayer believes that he or she qualifies for relief, Form 5329 should nevertheless be filed, a letter of explanation attached. Prior to 2007, the 50 percent penalty tax was required to be paid with the submission of Form 5329.

As of the publication of the Form 5329 instructions for 2007, the taxpayer may file a letter of explanation if he or she believes the under distribution was due to reasonable error and is being corrected. The taxpayer may file Form 5329 without making the payment of the 50 percent tax and wait to see if the IRS accepts the explanation. The amount of the tax requested to be waived should be indicated on the dotted line next to line 52 with "RC" next to the amount. If the IRS does not accept the explanation, the taxpayer will receive a letter and a bill for the penalty and any interest owed. The taxpayer will, of course, want to consult a tax adviser as to whether such an approach is the best one to take.

Reporting Form 5329 Penalties on Form 1040

Q 13:41 Where are Form 5329 penalties reported?

Any penalties determined using Form 5329 are reported on line 59 of Form 1040 or line 54 of Form 1040NR. In such instances, Form 5329 must be attached to the taxpayer's Form 1040 or Form 1040NR.

Q 13:42 Does the filing of Form 5329 affect what is to be reported on Form 1040 or Form 1040NR?

Yes. With respect to Part I of Form 5329, because a distribution may be fully taxable even if it is not subject to the 10 percent tax, the distribution (but not the penalty) should be reported in full on lines 15a and 15b of Form 1040 (lines 11a and 11b of Form 1040A; lines 16a and 16b of Form 1040-NR). The penalty, if applicable, is reported on line 59 of or line 54 of Form 1040NR.

Part III of Form 5329 reflects the fact that any excess contribution may be left in the IRA as long as the 6 percent penalty is regularly (annually) paid.

With respect to Part VIII of Form 5329, a distribution is fully reported on lines 15a and 15b of Form 1040, even though the 50 percent penalty applies.

Excess Distributions and Excess Accumulations

Q 13:43 Was Form 5329 used to calculate the excise tax on excess distributions from IRAs?

Yes. The excess distribution tax was repealed for tax years beginning after December 31, 1996. Before that, IRAs were classified as one of the distribution sources that could trigger the 15 percent excise tax on excess distributions.

Q 13:44 Was Form 5329 used to calculate the 15 percent excise tax imposed on an excess accumulation?

No. Note that the 15 percent excess accumulation tax has been repealed for decedents who die after December 31, 1996. [I.R.C. § 4980A, repealed]

Q 13:45 Must the 15 percent excess accumulation tax be reported and paid for years after 2001?

No. Many accounts remain in a decedent's name for up to five years after death, because of the beneficiary distribution options that are available. Therefore, unlike the excess distribution tax, the 15 percent excess accumulation tax disappeared at the end of 2001.

Q 13:46 Was the 15 percent excess accumulation tax reported on Schedule S of Form 706 for years after 2001?

No. For years before 1997, the 15 percent excess accumulation tax was determined by filing Schedule S of Form 706.

Calculating and Reporting Nondeductible Contributions on Form 8606

Q 13:47 What form is used to determine the portion of a distribution that is a tax-free return of nondeductible contributions?

For the taxable year in which a distribution is made, Form 8606, Nondeductible IRAs and Coverdell ESAs, is used to determine the portion of the distribution that is nontaxable as a result of being attributable to nondeductible contributions now being returned (also referred to as a return of basis).

Form 8606 must therefore be filed with an individual's tax return (Form 1040, Form 1040A, or Form 1040NR) unless there is no history of nondeductible contributions to the individual's IRA (or IRAs). If a portion of a current contribution is nondeductible, Form 8606 starts or continues the data history that will be needed to determine the nontaxable portion of a distribution when it occurs.

Practice Pointer. It is likely that Form 8606 will be needed long after the individual's tax return is discarded. Therefore, it or the information it contains should be kept as part of a permanent tax record (see Q 13:49).

Q 13:48 Must a taxpayer file Form 8606 if neither a nondeductible contribution nor a distribution occurs in a particular year?

No. In addition, if there has never been a nondeductible contribution, there is no need to file Form 8606. If there is a history to preserve, however, there seems to be no harm in filing Form 8606 again to keep the file current, even if no nondeductible contribution was made in the tax year at issue. The decision is one the individual's tax preparer should make.

Note. If a taxpayer is not filing a tax return for the year, but nondeductible contributions or distributions (or both) have occurred, Form 8606 must still be filed. It should be filed when and where the Form 1040, Form 1040A, or Form 1040NR would have been filed.

Q 13:49 What recordkeeping is suggested for Form 8606 filers?

In the instructions to Form 8606, the IRS provides a list of records that are to be kept until all distributions from an individual's IRAs have been made:

1. Page 1 of each year's Form 8606 for years in which nondeductible contributions were made;

2. Forms 5498 to confirm each year's traditional IRA contributions and Coverdell ESA contributions;
3. Forms 5498 or similar statements to confirm year-end values for each year in which a distribution occurred from a traditional IRA or Coverdell ESA; and
4. Forms 1099-R and W-2P for each year in which a distribution was received. (Form W-2P, formerly used for partial distributions from IRAs, has been discontinued and replaced by Form 1099-R.)

Practice Pointer. It is advisable to keep a separate IRA file that contains photocopies of the items needed for filing Form 8606, rather than removing them from the taxpayer's general tax return files.

Q 13:50 Must information similar to that needed to file Form 8606 be maintained for all IRAs, including those for which Form 8606 never needs to be filed?

Information similar to that needed to file Form 8606 should be maintained for all IRAs, even those for which Form 8606 never needs to be filed, until all distributions from an individual's IRAs have been made. The rules for allocating nondeductible and deductible portions of an IRA take into account all of an individual's IRAs. That is, when a distribution is being made, all IRAs are combined so that the taxpayer cannot make distributions from an IRA with the highest amount of nondeductible contributions to delay taxability.

It should be noted, however, that Forms 8606 are separately prepared for each spouse, even if the parties file jointly.

Q 13:51 What information does Form 8606 call for, and how should it be prepared?

Part I of Form 8606 takes the taxpayer through the various steps required to calculate the previously nondeductible portion of an IRA distribution. It applies whenever there have been some nondeductible contributions to any traditional IRA the taxpayer owns. By not filing Form 8606, the taxpayer may forfeit the chance to treat some of the distribution as nontaxable, even though not all contributions were deductible.

Line 1. Current-year contributions that are being reported as nondeductible are shown on line 1 of Form 8606. They include contributions that could have been deducted but that the taxpayer elected not to deduct (presumably, so they would be nontaxable in a later year).

Example. Amy contributed $500 to each of two IRAs, and $500 of the $1,000 contributed is to be nondeductible. Amy contributed an additional $1,000 the following year but attributed the amount to the current tax year, since it was paid before the tax filing date. Amy should enter $500 (the nondeductible amount).

Line 2. Total basis for all IRAs to date is shown on line 2. Total basis is total nondeductible IRA contributions reduced by distributions of those nondeductible contributions in prior years. If Form 8606 has not been required before, because there were never any nondeductible contributions, the correct entry is 0 (zero).

Example. Amy previously made nondeductible contributions of $2,500 to each of two IRAs and previously received distributions of basis of $500 from each IRA. Amy should enter $4,000, the result of reducing $2,500 by $500 for a net of $2,000 for each IRA.

Line 3. This line represents the total of lines 1 and 2. It brings the basis up to date. If no distributions were received in the current year, the rest of the form may be disregarded, and the line 3 amount is simply entered at line 12. That is the case when Form 8606 is being filed only because nondeductible contributions were made for the tax year being reported.

Example. The correct entry for Amy is $4,500. That amount is not to be repeated at line 12, because Amy has received distributions.

Line 4. This line is used to determine the portion of the nondeductible contribution for the tax year that was actually made in the following year, before the filing date, and that was reported for the tax year being reported.

Example. Amy has decided to treat the $500 nondeductible contribution as part of the $1,000 actually contributed during the tax year. Because no nondeductible amount was paid in the following three and one-half months, line 4 should be 0 (zero).

Line 5. This line shows the portion of the basis that relates to the allocation as of the end of the tax year. Making part of the nondeductible contribution in the following year reduces the basis as of the end of the tax year. Nondeductible contributions made after the tax year are not relevant to the apportionment calculation, even though they are reported as made for the tax year.

Example. For Amy, line 5 is $4,500 because there is no adjustment to line 3.

Line 6. This line addresses overall asset valuation. The taxpayer is to add outstanding rollovers, including distributions that the taxpayer has not rolled over as of the end of the tax year but that he or she intends to roll over early the next year (before the 60-day period expires).

Example. The IRA from which the distribution was made is valued at $50,000 at year-end, and Amy's other IRA holding is valued at $25,000 at year-end. One of the IRA balances was reduced by a $5,000 distribution that was received on November 30 and rolled over on the following January 15 and then added back. Line 6 would show $80,000 ($50,000 + $25,000 + $5,000).

Line 7. This line reports the total amount distributed from all IRAs during the tax-year. Distributions that were rolled over before the end of the tax year are to be excluded, and outstanding rollovers already included on line 6 are not to be reported again. Contributions that were returned on or before the due date of the return (under Code Section 408(d)(4)) and excess contributions that were returned after the due date (under Code Section 408(d)(5)) are also to be excluded.

> **Example.** Assume that another $5,000 was distributed from each of Amy's two IRAs, and there were no rollovers or contribution returns other than outstanding rollovers already referred to. The correct entry for line 7 would be $10,000 ($5,000 from each of the two IRAs).

Line 8. This line reports all amounts converted from traditional IRAs to Roth IRAs.

> **Example.** Amy enters 0 (zero) on line 8 because she did not convert any traditional IRAs to Roth IRAs during the calendar year.

Line 9. The purpose of this line is to adjust the year-end value to bring back into play all amounts that relate to the year-end balance.

> **Example.** For Amy, line 6 brought back the outstanding rollover of $5,000 because, effectively, it is in transit back to an IRA and would not otherwise be reflected in the year-end balance. Similarly, the $10,000 distributed (at any time during the tax year) needs to be shown as part of the pre-distribution balance that is being measured as of the end of the tax year. Form 8606 would show $90,000 here ($80,000 from line 6 plus $10,000 from line 7).

Line 10. A percentage that shows the portion of the total IRA funds represented by nondeductible contributions is calculated. It is important to note that earnings resulting from nondeductible contributions are not segregated from earnings resulting from deductible contributions. No such record is necessary because the earnings are taxable on distribution regardless of their source. Only the nondeductible contributions as originally contributed and not yet recouped through the distribution process need to be measured.

> **Example.** The correct decimal for Amy's Form 8606 is .05, arrived at by dividing $4,500 (see line 3) by $90,000.

Line 11. This line is used to determine the nontaxable amount of the conversion from a traditional IRA to a Roth IRA.

> **Example.** Because Amy did not convert her traditional IRA to a Roth IRA, 0 (zero) is entered on this line.

Line 12. This line is used to determine the amount of distributions during the year that will be free of tax. The calculation is based on the factor determined in line 9, which measured the portion of the fund represented by nondeductible contributions.

> **Example.** The decimal .05 is deemed to be the portion of the distribution that, on a pro rata basis, represents the nondeductible contributions. Because total distributions were $10,000, $500 is tax free, and $9,500 is fully taxable. It is not necessary to do so, but the $500 tax-free return could be allocated between the two IRAs for Amy's own records. For Form 8606 purposes, such

an allocation does not appear to be crucial, because the aggregate IRA history must be maintained, including the history of any discontinued IRAs.

Line 13. On this line, nontaxable distributions for the year are subtracted from line 5.

Example. Amy should subtract $500 from $4,500 to reduce the basis to $4,000.

Line 14. On this line, the amount on line 4 is added back to arrive at the total IRA basis.

Example. In Amy's case, the amount on line 14 is 0 (zero).

Line 15. This line adjusts distributions for the nontaxable portion for the current year's Form 1040.

Example. For Amy, distributions of $10,000 are reduced to a $9,500 net taxable amount.

Q 13:52 Why is it practical for an IRA owner to maintain separate Form 8606 records for each IRA owned when the IRAs have different beneficiaries?

If an IRA owner dies owning more than one IRA, the beneficiary of one of those IRAs might wish to continue that IRA and not accelerate distributions. If the deceased made nondeductible contributions, the basis would not have been fully recovered, and at least some of it would remain because the IRA itself remains. In such cases, Form 8606 must continue to be filed for distributions from the inherited IRA that is effectively owned by the beneficiary. If there are two IRAs and separate beneficiaries, the beneficiary of the other IRA must file a separate Form 8606. Therefore, the decedent's basis would need to be split between the two IRAs. If either beneficiary also maintains one or more IRAs that were not inherited, distributions from that individual's IRAs would be combined on the individual's Form 8606, but not with distributions from the inherited IRA, which would continue to have its own separate basis and its own Form 8606.

Q 13:53 What penalties may arise from a failure to follow the requirements of Form 8606?

Unless reasonable cause can be established, a $50 fine results from failing to file Form 8606 in a year when nondeductible contributions are made. Further, unless reasonable cause is shown, there is a $100 fine for each overstatement of nondeductible contributions on the form.

Q 13:54 In addition to the penalties, what other consequences may result from failing to file a required Form 8606 correctly?

The taxpayer may lose out on recovery of basis if Form 8606 is not filed correctly. In the absence of evidence to the contrary, the IRS will assume that all distributions are of amounts previously deducted and that the entire distribution is fully taxable.

Furthermore, if Form 8606 is not prepared regularly, the taxpayer loses an important means of ensuring that recovery of basis is not inadvertently omitted.

Q 13:55 What is the procedure to follow when redesignating a nondeductible contribution as a deductible contribution?

Changing a nondeductible contribution to a deductible contribution requires that a new Form 8606 be filed, along with Form 1040X, Amended U.S. Individual Income Tax Return.

Q 13:56 When is basis fully recovered?

Basis should be fully recovered automatically when the final distribution from all of an individual's IRAs has occurred. In any event, it would seem reasonable to correct any mathematical errors so that 100 percent of the unapplied nondeductible contributions is applied at that time. If there has been a loss, the unamortized basis may become a deductible loss.

Q 13:57 How are the various distributions reported on Form 1040?

Total taxable distributions are entered on line 15b of Form 1040. If the distribution has been rolled over, line 15a will show the total distributed, and line 15b will show only the portion not rolled over along with the reduction for the Form 8606 calculation. Lines 11a and 11b of Form 1040A and lines 16a and 16b are completed in the same manner, when applicable.

Q 13:58 May distributions be reduced for death payments other than those attributable to nondeductible contributions?

No. The $5,000 exclusion for death benefits is not available for distributions from an IRA. Indeed, there is no reduction for death benefits paid from an IRA other than the usual recovery of any basis from nondeductible contributions not previously applied.

Filing Information and Requirements

Q 13:59 How can information about form reporting be obtained?

Forms and Publications. To order IRS forms and publications, taxpayers can call (800) TAX-FORM (800-829-3676).

Telephone Queries. The IRS operates a centralized telephone site to answer questions about reporting on Forms W-2 (Wage and Tax Statements), W-3 (Transmittal of Wage and Tax Statements), the Form 1099 series, and other information returns. For questions related to reporting on information returns, taxpayers can call (304) 263-8700. For questions about magnetic media filing taxpayers can also call (866) 455-7438.

Forms, instructions, publications, and other information are also available through online computer services. Subscribers to online services should ask if IRS information is available and, if so, how to access it.

Q 13:60 What happens if the IRS makes an error when answering a question?

If the IRS makes an error when answering a taxpayer's question, the taxpayer will not be charged any penalty. It should be kept in mind, however, that the taxpayer is nonetheless responsible for payment of the correct tax. As a matter of good recordkeeping, a taxpayer should always get a written answer from the IRS.

Q 13:61 How is a compliance deadline met if it falls on a weekend or legal holiday?

Generally, if the due date for a specific act of compliance or for filing a return falls on a Saturday, Sunday, or legal holiday, the act or filing is considered timely if it is performed by the next succeeding day that is not a Saturday, Sunday, or legal holiday. [I.R.C. § 7503; Treas. Reg. § 301.7503-1(a)]

Q 13:62 What is a *legal holiday*?

The term *legal holiday* means the legal holidays in the District of Columbia, as follows:

- New Year's Day, January 1, 2013
- Dr. Martin Luther King Jr.'s Birthday, the third Monday in January
- Inauguration Day, Monday, January 21, 2013. Inauguration Day, January 20, 2013, falls on a Sunday. Therefore, the next succeeding day selected for the public observance of the inauguration of the President is a legal public holiday in some areas
- Presidents' Day, the third Monday in February
- Emancipation Day in Washington, D.C., April 16, 2013
- Memorial Day, the last Monday in May
- Independence Day, July 4
- Labor Day, the first Monday in September
- Columbus Day, the second Monday in October
- Veterans Day, November 11, 2013
- Thanksgiving Day, the fourth Thursday in November
- Christmas Day, December 25

[I.R.C. § 7503; Treas. Reg. § 301.7503-1(b); D.C. Code Ann. § 28-2701]

Furthermore, for any act required to be performed at an office of the IRS, return, statement, or other document required to be filed at an office of the IRS, the term *legal holiday* includes, in addition to the legal holidays in the District of Columbia, any statewide legal holiday of the state where the act is required to be performed or the document filed or any legal holiday that is recognized throughout the territory or possession in which the IRS office is located. [Treas. Reg. § 301.7503-1(b)] For example, if the tax filing date falls on the third Monday in April, those taxpayers filing in the Massachusetts office of the IRS will have an extra day to file as Patriots' Day is an official holiday in Massachusetts.

Q 13:63 When is a document or payment that is mailed deemed filed or paid?

Generally, a document or payment is considered to be filed or paid on the date of the postmark stamped on the cover in which it was properly mailed. Thus, if the cover containing the document or payment bears a timely postmark, the document or payment is considered timely filed or paid even if it is received after the date it is normally required to be filed or paid (see Qs 13:64–13:72). [Treas. Reg. §§ 301.7502-1, 301.7502-2]

Q 13:64 What date controls if a document or a payment is considered not timely filed?

If a document or a payment is considered not timely filed or paid, the date of the postmark stamped on the cover in which it was mailed will *not* be considered the filing or payment date. For purposes of computing any penalties and additions to tax, the date that the document or payment is received will be considered the date the document or payment was filed or paid.

Q 13:65 Must a document actually be received to be considered timely filed?

No. For a document (but not a payment; see Q 13:68) sent by registered or certified mail, proof that the document was properly registered or that a postmarked certified mail sender's receipt was properly issued for it, and that the envelope or wrapper was properly addressed to an agency, officer, or office, constitutes prima facie evidence that the document was delivered to that agency, officer, or office. However, Final Treasury Regulations "clarify" that a registered or certified mail receipt or proof of the proper use of a private delivery service (as designated by IRS) are the only ways, other than direct proof of delivery, to raise the presumption that a tax document was delivered to the IRS. [Treas. Reg. §§ 301.7502-1(e)(1), 301.7502-1(g)(4)]

Q 13:66 Must a payment actually be received to be considered timely paid?

Yes. Whether made in the form of currency or another medium, a payment is not treated as paid unless it is actually received and accounted for. For example, if a check is used as the form of payment, the check does not constitute payment unless it is honored upon presentation.

Q 13:67 What are the requirements for a valid mailing?

Forms must be mailed in accordance with the following requirements:

1. They must be in an envelope or other appropriate wrapper and be properly addressed to the agency, officer, or office with which the document is required to be filed or to which the payment is required to be made.
2. They must be mailed flat (not folded).
3. They must be mailed first class, and sufficient postage must be affixed.
4. They must be deposited within the prescribed time in the domestic mail service of the U.S. Postal Service (including mail transmitted within, among, and between the United States, its possessions, and Army-Air Force (APO) and Navy (FPO) post offices) or must be sent via IRS-approved private delivery companies (see below). The mail services of other countries are not considered. [Treas. Reg. § 301.7502-1]
5. If there are many forms, they must be sent in conveniently sized packages, numbered consecutively, with the payer's name and TIN written on each package, and Form 1096 (Annual Summary and Transmittal of U.S. Information Returns) placed in the first package.

Before the Taxpayer Bill of Rights [Pub. L. No. 104-168 § 1210] was enacted in 1996, only taxpayers who sent returns via the U.S. Postal Service had the assurance that their returns would be considered to be timely filed if they were timely mailed. The change in the law permitted the IRS to extend the timely mailing as timely filing or paying rule to certain private delivery companies, also called designated delivery services. The IRS has designated three private delivery companies that last-minute filers can use with the same assurance as those who use the U.S. Postal Service that a return mailed on time will be considered filed on time:

1. DHL Express (DHL): DHL Same Day Service; DHL Next Day 10:30 a.m.; DHL Next Day 12:00 p.m.; DHL Next Day 3:00 p.m.; and DHL 2nd Day Service;
2. Federal Express (FedEx): FedEx Priority Overnight, FedEx Standard Overnight, FedEx 2 Day, FedEx International Priority, and FedEx International First; and
3. United Parcel Service (UPS): UPS Next Day Air, UPS Next Day Air Saver, UPS 2nd Day Air, UPS 2nd Day Air A.M., UPS Worldwide Express Plus, and UPS Worldwide Express.

[I.R.S. Notice 2004-83, 2004-2 C.B. 1030]

Note. Airborne Express, Inc. was removed from the list due to its acquisition by DHL Worldwide. [I.R.S. Notice 2004-83, 2004-52 I.R.B. 1030, superseding I.R.S. Notice 2002-62, 2002-39 I.R.B. 574]

Only the types of delivery services specified qualify, not other services offered by the four companies.

The date on which an item given to any one of the IRS-approved private delivery companies is recorded electronically in the company's database is treated as the postmark date. It should be noted that the private delivery companies are required to maintain their electronic databases for only six months. [I.R.S. Notice 2004-83; 2004-2 C.B. 1030] Confirmation of the date recorded can be obtained by contacting the company in question, using the following toll-free telephone numbers:

- DHL "Same Day" Service: (800) 345-2727; DHL USA Overnight: (800) 225-5345
- FedEx: (800) 463-3339
- UPS: (800) 742-5877

Q 13:68 What is the result if the postmark date is wrong or not legible?

The person required to file the document or make the payment has the burden of proving when the postmark was made. Furthermore, if the cover containing a document or payment bearing a timely postmark made by the U.S. Postal Service is received later than the date a document or payment postmarked and mailed at that time would ordinarily be received, the sender may be required to prove that it was timely mailed.

Q 13:69 What rules apply to postmarks of foreign postal services?

Special rules apply if the postmark on an envelope or wrapper is made by a foreign postal service. When the document or payment is received later than it would have been received if it had been duly mailed and postmarked by the U.S. Postal Service, it is treated as having been received when a document or payment so mailed and so postmarked would ordinarily be received. Still, the person required to file must establish that it was actually and timely deposited in the mail before the last collection of the mail from the place of deposit. The person must also show that the delay in receipt was due to a delay in the transmission of the mail and must explain the cause of that delay.

Q 13:70 How can the risk that a document or payment will not be postmarked on the day that it is posted be overcome?

The risk that a mailing will not be postmarked on the day it is posted may be overcome by use of registered or certified or proof of the proper use of a private delivery service (as designated by IRS) (see Qs 13:64–13:66, 13:71, 13:72).

Q 13:71 What is the postmark date for U.S. registered mail?

If a document or a payment is sent by U.S. registered mail, the date of registration of the document or payment is treated as the postmark date.

Q 13:72 What is the postmark date for U.S. certified mail?

If a document or a payment is sent by U.S. certified mail and the sender's receipt is postmarked by the postal employee to whom that document or payment is presented, the date of the U.S. postmark on the receipt is treated as the postmark date of the document or payment.

IRS Form 990-T

Q 13:73 What is the purpose of Form 990-T?

In general, Form 990-T, Exempt Organization Business Income Tax Return, is used by tax-exempt organizations and by certain IRAs to report their unrelated business taxable income under Code Section 511 and to obtain a refund of income tax paid on undistributed long-term capital gains. [I.R.C. §§ 408(e)(1), 852; Treas. Reg. § 1.408-1(b)] Failure of the IRA trustee to recover undistributed long-term capital gains tax may result in liability to the IRA owner.

> **Example.** Cathy establishes a large rollover IRA in an actively managed mutual fund. Gains from trading are reported to her on Form 2439, Notice to Shareholder of Undistributed Long-Term Capital Gains. To obtain a refund of income tax paid on undistributed long-term capital gains, the IRA trustee should make a regulated investment company filing on Form 990-T (see Qs 13:83–13:84).

Q 13:74 What is unrelated trade or business income?

Unrelated trade or business income is the gross income derived from any trade or business that is regularly carried on and not substantially related to an IRA's exempt purpose or function. [I.R.C. §§ 512, 513]

> **Example.** Myra establishes a large rollover IRA in a real estate limited partnership, which invests all of its assets in real estate. The partnership borrows $9 out of every $10 it invests in real estate. As a result of the leveraging, the IRA is subject to a tax on its unrelated business taxable income.

Q 13:75 How much unrelated trade or business income must an IRA have before it is required to file Form 990-T?

Form 990-T is not required to be filed unless the IRA has gross income of $1,000 or more from an unrelated trade or business. However, a Form 990-T may be filed if there is unrelated trade or business income (UBI) loss that may be deducted in a future year.

Q 13:76 When must Form 990-T be filed?

Form 990-T must be filed by the 15th day of the 4th month after the end of the tax year (April 15 for calendar-year tax years).

Q 13:77 Who must sign Form 990-T?

Form 990-T should be signed and dated by the trustee or custodian of the IRA.

Q 13:78 Can the trustee or custodian of an IRA request an extension of time to file Form 990-T?

Yes. A trust may request an initial automatic three-month extension of time to file Form 990-T by using Form 8868, Application for Extension of Time to File an Exempt Organization Return.

Q 13:79 When must any tax from Form 990-T be paid?

The financial institution must pay the tax due in full when Form 990-T is filed, but no later than the 15th day of the 5th month after the end of the tax year. The trustee may be required to use the electronic funds transfer system.

Q 13:80 Is interest charged on any underpayment of taxes due under Form 990-T?

Yes. Interest is charged on taxes not paid by the due date for Form 990-T even if an extension of time to file is granted. Interest is also charged on penalties imposed for failure to file, negligence, fraud, gross valuation overstatements, and substantial understatements of tax from the due date (including extensions) to the date of payment. The interest charge is figured at the underpayment rate determined under Code Section 6621(a)(2).

Q 13:81 What is the penalty for late filing of Form 990-T?

A financial institution that fails to file Form 990-T when due (including any extension of time for filing) is subject to a penalty of 5 percent of the unpaid tax for each month or part of a month the return is late, up to a maximum of 25 percent of the unpaid tax, unless it can show reasonable cause for the delay. A trustee or custodian filing after the due date (including extensions) must attach an explanation to the return. The minimum penalty for a Form 990-T that is more than 60 days late is the lesser of the tax due or $100.

Q 13:82 What is the penalty for late payment of tax due under Form 990-T?

The penalty for late payment of taxes is usually 0.5 percent of the unpaid tax for each month or part of a month the tax is unpaid. The penalty cannot exceed 25 percent of the amount due.

Q 13:83 How must Form 990-T be completed?

All filers must complete the applicable items in the heading area at the top of page 1 and the signature area on page 2. Except in the case of a regulated investment company (RIC) filing (see Q 13:84), Part I, column (A), lines 1 through 13, on page 1 should be completed. If the amount on line 13, column (A), is $10,000 or less, only line 13 of columns (B) and (C), lines 29 through 34 of Part II, and Parts III through V should be completed. Filers who enter $10,000 or less on line 13, column (A), do not have to complete Schedules A through K; however, they should refer to applicable schedules when completing column (A) and in determining the deductible expenses to include on line 13 of column (B). If the amount on line 13, column (A), Part I, is more than $10,000, all lines and schedules that apply must be completed.

Q 13:84 Which parts of Form 990-T should be completed in a regulated investment company filing?

To obtain a refund of income tax paid on undistributed long-term capital gains (only), the financial institution should make a RIC filing on Form 990-T as follows:

1. Write “Claim for refund shown on Form 2439” at the top of the form;
2. Complete the heading (using the name and Employer Identification Number (EIN) of the exempt trustee or custodian);
3. Enter the credit on line 44e;
4. Sign the return; and
5. Attach copy B of Form 2439, Notice to Shareholder of Undistributed Long-Term Capital Gains.

Q 13:85 May a trustee or custodian of multiple IRAs that have invested in regulated investment companies file a composite return?

Yes. Instead of filing a separate Form 990-T for each IRA that has been invested in a RIC that elected to retain a long-term capital gain, a financial institution may file a composite return for all such IRAs to claim a refund under Code Section 852(b).

Q 13:86 How is a composite filing accomplished?

A composite filing for IRAs that have invested in RICs is accomplished as follows:

1. The trustee or custodian must apply to its Internal Revenue Service Center for a special EIN on Form SS-4, Application for Employer Identification Number. The special EIN will be effective only for making a composite claim for refund of tax under Code Section 852(b) on behalf of the IRAs administered by the trustee. (The trustee or custodian should *not* apply for a special EIN for each year it makes a claim for refund.)
2. The trustee or custodian must indicate that the application is for a special EIN by writing "Notice 90-18" on the top of the Form SS-4.
3. The trustee or custodian must file one composite return on Form 990-T for each year it makes a claim.
4. The trustee or custodian must attach a list of the IRAs for which the claim is being made showing the names and Social Security numbers of the persons who established the IRAs and the allocated shares of tax paid by the RICs.
5. The IRAs must be grouped according to the RIC in which each IRA has made an investment.
6. Form 2439 must be attached for each RIC according to such grouping.
7. The trustee or custodian must write "Composite return per Notice 90-18" on the top of the Form 990-T.
8. The trustee or custodian must enter the special EIN assigned for the composite return (and only that EIN) in the block provided for EINs.

Q 13:87 Under what circumstances is a composite return not available to an IRA trustee or custodian?

A composite return may be filed only by a common trustee or custodian of more than one IRA. It cannot be filed by a person acting merely as a nominee (owner of record) of RIC shares owned by an IRA. An IRA that has unrelated business taxable income may not be included in the claim for refund on the composite return. The trustee or custodian of such an IRA must file a separate Form 990-T for the IRA reporting the income on that return and claiming a credit for any RIC that elected to retain a long-term capital gain.

Q 13:88 To whom will a refund check flowing from Form 990-T be issued?

The IRS will issue a check for any amounts refundable under Form 990-T to the IRA trustee or custodian.

Q 13:89 What is the responsibility of the financial institution with respect to the refund from Form 990-T?

The financial institution must allocate the refund from Form 990-T to the IRA trusts in accordance with the amounts due as shown on the composite return. [I.R.S. Notice 90-18, 1990-1 C.B. 327]

IRS Form 1040

Q 13:90 How does an individual report a distribution from an IRA?

The gross distribution amount is reported on line 11a of Form 1040A, line 16a of Form 1040NR, or line 15a of Form 1040. The amount should be the same as that reported in box 1 of Form 1099-R.

The taxable portion of the distribution is reported on line 11b of Form 1040A, line 16b of Form 1040NR, or line 15b of Form 1040.

Q 13:91 Is there an exception to using line 15 of Form 1040 or line 11 of Form 1040A to report IRA distribution?

Yes. There is one exception to using line 15 of Form 1040 or line 11 of Form 1040A to report IRA distributions. Corrective distributions of excess deferrals, excess contributions, or disallowed deferrals, plus income allocable thereto, under a SARSEP must be reported on the wage line of the tax return for the appropriate year (line 7 of Form 1040 or Form 1040A; line 8 of Form 1040NR). The principal amount is taxable in the year it was deferred; the income allocable to that amount is taxable in the year it was distributed. Because parts of the distribution may be taxed in two or three different years, in most corrective distribution cases the payer must issue separate Forms 1099-R.

Q 13:92 Where on Form 1040 are corrective distributions under SEP or SARSEP IRAs reported?

Corrective distributions under SEP IRAs are reported on line 7 of Form 1040 or Form 1040A; line 8 of Form 1040NR.

Corrective distributions to SARSEP participants are reported on different forms:

- Excess salary deferrals (deferrals exceeding the dollar limit on elective contributions, generally $17,000 for 2012) and the total deferred are reported on Form W-2.
- Excess contributions (contributions failing the 125 percent actual deferral percentage test) are reported on Form 1099-R.
- Disallowed deferrals (deferrals failing the 50 percent participation rate requirement) are reported on Form 1099-R.

- Deferrals of an ineligible employer (deferrals failing the "fewer than 26 employees in prior year" requirement) are reported on Form 1099-R.
- Nonexcluded contributions (contributions exceeding the applicable dollar amount under Code Section 402(h)(2)(B) if the plan is integrated or 25 percent of compensation or earned income) are reported on Form W-2.
- Amounts that exceed the $50,000/100 percent of compensation limit other than catch-up contributions under Code Section 415 are reported on Form W-2.

Q 13:93 How is a rollover of SEP IRA assets reported on Form 1040?

A rollover of SEP IRA assets is treated in the same manner as a rollover from a traditional IRA, because a SEP IRA is a traditional IRA to which SEP contributions have been made. The distribution and rollover is reported on lines 15a and 15b of Form 1040. The total distribution is entered on line 15a. If the total on line 15a was rolled over, 0 (zero) is entered on line 15b. If the total distribution was not rolled over, the taxable portion of the amount not rolled over is entered on line 15b. Form 8606 is used to figure the taxable portion that is inputted on line 15b. Use lines 11a and 11b if filing Form 1040A and lines 16a and 16b if filing Form 1040NR.

Q 13:94 Is there a special Form 1040 help line for people with impaired hearing?

Yes. In the continental United States and in Alaska, Hawaii, Puerto Rico, and the U.S. Virgin Islands, hearing-impaired persons may call (800) 829-4059 for assistance regarding Form W-2 or Form 1040 (TDD only). TDD requires special telephone equipment.

IRS Form 1099-R

Q 13:95 What does a financial institution report on Form 1099-R?

A financial institution reports all distributions, except for certain *de minimis* distributions, on Form 1099-R, Distributions From Pensions, Annuities, Retirement or Profit-Sharing Plans, IRAs, Insurance Contracts, etc., even if the IRA owner exercises his or her right to revoke the IRA. A trustee or custodian must report certain information to both the recipient of the distribution and the IRS each year. [I.R.C. § 408(i); Treas. Reg. § 1.408-7]

Note. If the recipient of an IRA distribution is not an individual (e.g., an estate or trust), the distribution is taxable to that entity. Items of income taxable to such an entity for purposes of federal income tax are reported on Form 1041, U.S. Income Tax Return for Estates and Trusts.

Q 13:96 What other information may be provided on Form 1099-R?

If a distribution includes a distribution from an annuity contract, its value will be shown on Form 1099-R even though it is not taxable until (and only as) distributions are received from the contract under Code Section 72. [Treas. Reg. § 1.408-4(e)] For purposes of applying Code Section 72 to a distribution from such a contract, the investment in such a contract is zero.

The percentage of the total distribution belonging to the recipient, if distribution is also made to another person or persons, may also be included on Form 1099-R.

Q 13:97 Is withholding shown on Form 1099-R?

Yes. Form 1099-R shows federal income tax withholding, as well as state and local tax information. As might be expected, there is a wide array of possibilities for state and local tax information.

> **Practice Pointer.** Form 1099-R is not required to be attached to the taxpayer's federal tax return, unless it shows amounts withheld for federal income tax.

Q 13:98 What is the deadline for filing Form 1099-R?

Form 1099-R must be provided to the recipient of the distribution no later than January 31 following the calendar year in which the distribution was made; it must be transmitted to the IRS no later than February 28, following the calendar year in which the distribution was made. If the payer files electronically, the deadline to file with the IRS is March 31 following the calendar year in which the distribution was made. Leap years are ignored for these deadlines. [Ann. 91-179, 1991-49 I.R.B. 78] If either deadline falls on a Saturday, a Sunday, or a legal holiday, the deadline becomes the next business day as shown above.

Q 13:99 How may an extension of time for filing Forms 1099-R be granted?

For paper or magnetic media filing, a request for an extension to file Form 1099-R with the IRS is made by completing Form 8809, Request for Extension of Time to File Information Returns, which is sent to the following address:

Enterprise Computing Center—Martinsburg
Information Reporting Program
Attn: Extension of Time Coordinator
240 Murall Drive
Kearneysville, WV 25430

The IRS suggests that Form 8809 be filed as soon as the need for an extension becomes apparent. Be that as it may, Form 8809 *must* be filed no later than the due date of Form 1099-R (February 28) for the IRS to consider granting the extension. If the IRS approves the extension request, the taxpayer will be granted an additional 30 days to file. The extension will apply only to the due date for filing the returns with the IRS; it will not extend the due date for providing statements to recipients (see Q 13:100). If more time to file is needed, an additional 30 days may be requested by submitting another Form 8809 before the end of the initial extension period.

On June 10, 2003, the IRS issued proposed and temporary regulations that provide an automatic extension of time to file certain information returns. These regulations were effective on June 11, 2003. Under Regulations Section 1.6081-8, filers and transmitters of certain information returns may obtain an automatic 30-day extension of time to file.

The forms covered by this regulation include the 1099 series, 1098 series, 5498 series, W-2 series, 1042-S, and 8027. In the past, filers could obtain a 30-day extension by filing a signed Form 8809 and providing an explanation of the reasons needed for the extension. In current practice, the explanation is not a determining factor for the initial extension and such initial extension is routinely granted.

These new regulations permit filers to request an automatic 30-day extension by filing Form 8809 without having to sign the form and provide an explanation. The new rules allow the IRS to develop an online version of the extension request that will provide immediate approval to the filer requesting the automatic extension.

However, an extension beyond the initial 30-day period will not be granted unless the filer provides a signed Form 8809 and a detailed explanation and the filer has first obtained an automatic extension.

> **Note.** An extension of time to file an information return with the IRS does not extend the due date for providing a statement to the person with respect to whom the information is required to be reported.

Q 13:100 How may an extension of time for providing Forms 1099-R to recipients be requested?

To request an extension of time for providing Forms 1099-R to recipients, a letter should be sent to the Enterprise Computing Center—Martinsburg (see Q 13:99 for the address). The letter must include the following:

- Payer's name
- Payer's TIN
- Payer's address
- Type of return
- Statement that the request is for an extension for providing statements to recipients
- Reason for the delay
- Payer's signature

The request must be postmarked by the date Form 1099-R is due to plan participants (January 31). If the request for extension is approved, an additional 30 days will be granted to furnish the recipient statements.

Q 13:101 What changes/clarifications were made to Form 1099-R and Form 5498 for 2012?

The following changes were made to Form 1099-R and Form 5498 for 2012:

Truncating recipient/participant identification number on paper payee statements. Notice 2011-38 allows filers of Forms 1099-R and 5498 to truncate a recipient's (Form 1099-R) or participant's (Form 5498) identification number (social security number (SSN), individual taxpayer identification number (ITIN), or adoption taxpayer identification number (ATIN)) on paper payee statements for tax years 2011 and 2012. See part M in the 2012 General Instructions for Certain Information Returns.

The following changes were made to Form 5498 for 2011:

- *Successor beneficiary reporting.* A new paragraph has been added to the instructions under Inherited IRAs for reporting successor beneficiary(ies).
- *Fair market valuation.* A Caution has been added to the instructions for box 5, Fair market value of account.

The following changes were made to Form 1099-R for 2010:

- *Renumbering of boxes.* Boxes 10 through 15 have been renumbered as boxes 12 through 17, respectively. The blank box formerly to the left of former box 10 has been numbered and labeled "10 Amount allocable to IRR within 5 years" and a dollar sign ($) has been added. The box "1st year of desig. Roth contrib." has been numbered 11.
- *Prohibited transactions.* Information regarding identifying and reporting prohibited transactions relating to an IRA has been added to *Specific Instructions for Form 1099-R*.
- *Reporting excess employer contributions returned to an employer.* Instructions for reporting excess employer contributions (plus earnings on them) returned to an employer have been added to *Distributions under Employee Plans Compliance Resolution System (EPCRS)*.
- *Rollovers to designated Roth accounts within the same plan (in-plan Roth rollovers).* Instructions for reporting in-plan Roth rollovers that are direct rollovers have been added to *Designated Roth accounts* starting on page 4 and the instructions for boxes 1 and 2a. Also, for more information on in-plan Roth rollovers, see Notice 2010-84. [2010-51 I.R.B. 872 (Dec. 20, 2010)]
- *Distributions from designated Roth accounts allocable to in-plan Roth rollovers.* Instructions for reporting distributions from a designated Roth account allocable to an in-plan Roth rollover have been added to *Designated Roth Account Distributions* on pages 2 and 8 and the instructions for

new box 10. Also, for more information on in-plan Roth rollovers, see Notice 2010-84. [2010-51 I.R.B. 872 (Dec. 20, 2010)]

Guide to Distribution Chart

- *Code B.* Distribution Code B has been reworded for reporting all distributions from designated Roth accounts.
- *Code D.* Distribution Code D has been eliminated. (See Distribution Codes 8 and P.)

The following changes were made to Form 1099-R and Form 5498 for 2010:

- *Truncating recipient's/participant's identification number on paper payee statements.* Notice 2009-93 allows filers of Forms 1099-R and 5498 to truncate a recipient's (Form 1099-R) or participant's (Form 5498) identification number (Social Security number (SSN), individual taxpayer identification number (ITIN), or adoption taxpayer identification number (ATIN)) on the paper payee statement for tax years 2009 and 2010. [*See* Part M in the 2010 General Instructions for Certain Information Returns (Forms 1098, 1099, 3921, 3922, 5498, and W-2G)]
- *Form 1099-R. Reporting IRA distributions:* For 2009 and preceding years, distribution amounts were required to be reported in box 2a. This was changed for 2009, requiring the amount to be reported in box 1 and box 2a to be left blank. The instructions for 2010 reinstated the previous rule, requiring the reporting of distributions from traditional, SEP, and SIMPLE IRAs in boxes 1 and 2a, unless an exception applies. Box 2b "taxable amount not determined" should be checked.
- *Form 5498. Additional contribution rules for 2004 and 2005.* References to additional contribution rules for 2004 and 2005 under special reporting for U.S. Armed Forces in designated combat zones have been removed due to expiration of the provision on May 28, 2009.
- *Special reporting for 2009.* References to catch-up contributions in special reporting for 2009 and the reporting instructions for boxes 15a and 15b have been removed due to expiration of this provision.

Q 13:102 How is the 2012 Form 1099-R completed, and what are the reporting codes applicable to IRA distributions?

Following is a box-by-box explanation of the 2012 Form 1099-R, including the reporting codes applicable to IRA distributions.

Box 1: Gross Distribution

- *All plans.* Enter the total amount of the distribution before income tax or other deductions were withheld. Include direct rollovers, IRA rollovers to accepting employer plans, and the gross amount of any IRA distribution, including a recharacterization and a Roth IRA conversion. Also include in this box distributions to plan participants from governmental 457(b) plans.

- Report the total amount of the distribution, including income taxes that were withheld (if any). Do not include any fees that were charged (e.g., certificate of deposit (CD) penalties for early withdrawal). For a distribution of property other than cash, report the FMV of the property on the date of distribution.
- *Recharacterizations*. Recharacterizations of eligible IRA contributions are reportable on Form 1099-R. Enter the amount of the recharacterized contribution, plus earnings, in this box. In the case of a loss on the recharacterized contribution, enter the actual amount recharacterized. Recharacterizations must be accomplished via a trustee-to-trustee transfer, rather than via a distribution and rollover.

  The IRA from which the recharacterized amount is being transferred is referred to as the "first IRA." Therefore, the trustee must issue Form 1099-R. (The trustee of the first IRA must also report the original contribution and its character on Form 5498 issued with respect to the first IRA.)

  If the first IRA is a traditional IRA, the only type of contribution that is eligible to be recharacterized to a Roth IRA is a regular contribution. If the first IRA is a Roth IRA, the eligible recharacterized contribution to a traditional IRA can be either a regular contribution or a conversion. Earnings (or losses) attributable to the recharacterized contribution must be included in the transfer. "Prior year" recharacterizations must be reported on a separate Form 1099-R from "same year" recharacterizations (as different reporting codes apply for box 7). Code R is used for a prior year recharacterization; code N is used for a same year recharacterization.

  A prior year recharacterization is a recharacterization of a contribution made for 2011 and recharacterized in 2012, even if the 2011 contribution was made in 2012. In the case of a recharacterization of a conversion where the amount was distributed from a traditional IRA in 2011 but was not deposited as a conversion contribution until 2012 (but within the requisite 60-day period), treat such a recharacterization as a prior year recharacterization for these reporting purposes. A same year recharacterization is a recharacterization of a contribution made for 2012 and recharacterized in 2012.
- *Roth IRA Conversions/reconversions*. Report the total amount converted or reconverted from a traditional IRA, SEP IRA, or SIMPLE IRA to a Roth IRA in boxes 1 and 2a. A conversion or reconversion is considered a distribution and must be reported even if it is with the same trustee and even if the conversion is done by a trustee-to-trustee transfer. When an IRA annuity is converted to a Roth IRA, the amount that is treated as distributed is the FMV of the annuity contract on the date the annuity contract is converted. This rule also applies when a traditional IRA holds an annuity contract as an account asset and the traditional IRA is converted to a Roth IRA. For a Roth IRA conversion, use code 2 in box 7 if the participant is under age 59½ or code 7 if the participant is at least age 59½. Also check the IRA/SEP/SIMPLE box in box 7.

Note. An annuity's valuation must include the present value of any additional benefits included in the contract.

- *Losses.* If a distribution is a loss, do not enter a negative amount in this box. For example, if stock is distributed from a profit-sharing plan but the value is less than the employee's after-tax contributions or designated Roth account contributions, enter the value of the stock in box 1, leave box 2a blank, and enter the employee's contributions or designated Roth account contributions in box 5. For a plan with no after-tax contributions or designated Roth account contributions, even though the value of the account may have decreased, there is no loss for reporting purposes. Therefore, if there are no employer securities distributed, show the actual cash and/or FMV of property distributed in boxes 1 and 2a, and make no entry in box 5. If only employer securities are distributed, show the FMV of the securities in boxes 1 and 2a and make no entry in box 5 or 6. If both employer securities and cash or other property are distributed, show the actual cash and/or FMV of the property (including employer securities) distributed in box 1, the gross less any net unrealized appreciation (NUA) on employer securities in box 2a, no entry in box 5, and any NUA in box 6.
- *Revocations and CIP Failures.* (See Appendix L, Chart of Revocations and CIP Failures.) A newly established IRA can be revoked within its first seven days; if the individual also made an initial deposit during such period, the individual is entitled to receive the amount deposited without reduction for changes in the market value. If an IRA is involuntarily closed by the trustee due to not receiving the information to satisfy the CIP requirements under the USA Patriot Act, report the distribution in the same manner as if the individual actually revoked the account. The manner of reporting depends on the type of contribution that was made.
  - If a traditional or Roth IRA is revoked during its first seven days or is closed at any time by the financial institution due to a failure of the taxpayer to satisfy the Customer Identification Program (CIP) requirements, the distribution from the IRA must be reported. [Treas. Reg. § 1.408-6(d)(4)(ii)); USA Patriot Act (Pub. L. No. 106-102) § 326] In addition, Form 5498, IRA Contribution Information, must be filed to report a regular, rollover, Roth IRA conversion, SEP IRA, or SIMPLE IRA contribution to an IRA that is subsequently revoked or closed by the trustee or custodian.
  - If a regular contribution is made to a traditional or Roth IRA that later is revoked or closed, and distribution is made to the taxpayer, enter the gross distribution in box 1. If no earnings are distributed, enter 0 (zero) in box 2a and code 8 in box 7 for a traditional IRA and code J for a Roth IRA. If earnings are distributed, enter the amount of earnings in box 2a. For a traditional IRA, enter codes 1 and 8, if applicable, in box 7; for a Roth IRA, enter codes J and 8, if applicable. These earnings could be subject to the 10 percent early distribution tax. If a rollover contribution is made to a traditional or Roth IRA that later is revoked or closed, and distribution is made to the taxpayer, enter in boxes 1 and 2a of Form

1099-R the gross distribution and the appropriate code in box 7 (code J for a Roth IRA). Follow this same procedure for a transfer from a traditional or Roth IRA to another IRA of the same type that later is revoked or closed. The distribution could be subject to the 10 percent early distribution tax.

- If an IRA conversion contribution is made to a Roth IRA that later is revoked or closed, and a distribution is made to the taxpayer, enter the gross distribution in box 1 of Form 1099-R. If no earnings are distributed, enter 0 (zero) in box 2a and code J in box 7. If earnings are distributed, enter the amount of the earnings in box 2a and code J in box 7. These earnings could be subject to the 10 percent early distribution tax.
- If an employer SEP (simplified employee pension) IRA or SIMPLE (savings incentive match plan for employees) IRA plan contribution is made and the SEP IRA or SIMPLE IRA is revoked by the employee or is closed by the trustee or custodian, report the distribution as fully taxable. [*See also* Rev. Proc. 91-70, 1991-2 C.B. 899]

(See Qs 13:5–13:7, 13:12–13:13, 13:120 and 13:199 for a discussion of revocation of contributions.)

- *Designated Roth Contribution (DRC) Account.* If a Section 401(k) plan or Section 403(b) is accepting Designated Roth Contributions (DRC), such contributions must be either held in a separate account or be separately accounted for under the plan. Any distributions from the DRC must be reported on a separate Form 1099-R from distributions made from the other portions of the plan.
- *Deemed IRAs.* A qualified employer plan may allow employees to make voluntary employee contributions to a separate account or annuity established under the plan. Under the terms of the qualified employer plan, the account or annuity must meet the applicable requirements of Code Section 408 or 408A for a traditional IRA or Roth IRA. Under Code Section 408(q), the "deemed IRA" portion of the qualified employer plan is subject to the rules applicable to traditional and Roth IRAs, and not to those of the applicable plan under Code Section 401(a), 403(a), 403(b), or 457. Accordingly, the reporting and withholding rules on plan and IRA distributions apply separately depending on whether the distributions are made from the deemed IRA or the qualified employer plan. For example, the reporting rules for RMDs apply separately for the two portions of the plan. A total distribution of amounts held in the qualified employer plan portion and the deemed IRA portion is reported on two separate Forms 1099-R—one for the distribution from the deemed IRA portion and one for the rest of the distribution. Also, the 20 percent withholding rules of Code Section 3405(c) do not apply to a distribution from the deemed IRA portion but would apply to a distribution from the qualified employer plan portion, and Code Section 72(t) applies separately to the two portions.
- *IRAs other than Roth IRAs.* Distributions from any IRA, except a Roth IRA, must be reported in boxes 1 and 2a regardless of the amount. The "Taxable

amount not determined" box in box 2b should be checked, unless an exception applies.

- *Roth IRAs.* For distributions from a Roth IRA, report the gross distribution in box 1 but generally leave box 2a blank. Check the "Taxable amount not determined" box in box 2b. Enter code J, Q, or T as appropriate in box 7. Do not use any other codes with code Q or code T. Code 8 or P with code J may be entered. For the withdrawal of excess contributions, it is not necessary to mark the IRA/SEP/SIMPLE checkbox.
- *Roth IRA conversions.* You must report an IRA that is converted or reconverted this year to a Roth IRA in boxes 1 and 2a, even if the conversion is a trustee-to-trustee transfer or is with the same trustee. Enter code 2 or 7 in box 7 depending on the participant's age.
- *Conduit IRAs.* If you know the distribution is from a conduit IRA, follow these rules. If a distribution from a conduit IRA is paid to the participant, report the full amount in boxes 1 and 2a, and use code 1 or 7 in box 7 depending on the participant's age. If a distribution from a conduit IRA is paid to the trustee of, or is transferred to, an employer plan, report the distribution in box 1, enter 0 (zero) in box 2a, and use code G in box 7.

Box 2a: Taxable Amount

Generally, report the same amount as reported in box 1. However, in certain cases, the amount in box 2a may differ from the amount in box 1. In the case of a traditional IRA the amount in box 2a may be 0 (zero). However, if you are unable to reasonably obtain the data needed to compute the taxable amount, leave this box blank. Do not enter excludable or tax-deferred amounts reportable in boxes 5, 6, and 8.

For a direct rollover from a qualified plan (including a governmental 457(b) plan) or 403(b) plan, for a distribution from a conduit IRA that is payable to the trustee of or is transferred to an employer plan, for an IRA recharacterization, or for a nontaxable Code Section 1035 exchange of life insurance, annuity, or endowment contracts, enter 0 (zero) in box 2a.

- *Designated Roth account.* Generally, a distribution from a designated Roth account that is not a qualified distribution is taxable to the recipient under Code Section 402 in the case of a plan qualified under Code Section 401(a), and under Code Section 403(b)(1) in the case of a 403(b) plan. For purposes of Code Section 72, designated Roth contributions are treated as employer contributions (that is, as includible in the participant's gross income).

Example. Participant A received a nonqualified distribution of $5,000 from the participant's designated Roth account. Prior to the distribution, the participant's account balance was $10,000, consisting of $9,400 of designated Roth contributions and $600 of earnings. The taxable amount of the $5,000 distribution is $300 ($600/$10,000 × $5,000). The nontaxable portion of the distribution is $4,700 ($9,400/$10,000 × $5,000). The issuer would report on Form 1099-R:

- Box 1, $5,000 as the gross distribution;
- Box 2a, $300 as the taxable amount;
- Box 5, $4,700 as the designated Roth contribution basis (nontaxable amount); and
- The first year of the five-taxable-year period in the box to the left of box 10.
- *Traditional IRAs or SEP IRAs*. Generally, you are not required to compute the taxable amount of a traditional IRA or SEP IRA nor designate whether any part of a distribution is a return of basis attributable to nondeductible contributions. Therefore, unless the instructions require otherwise, such as reporting the earnings on a return-of-excess contribution, leave box 2a blank. Check the "Taxable amount not determined" box in box 2b. However, for a distribution by a trust representing CDs redeemed early, report the net amount distributed. Do not include any amount paid for IRA insurance protection in this box.
- For a distribution of contributions plus earnings from an IRA before the due date of the return under Code Section 408(d)(4), report the gross distribution in box 1, only the earnings in box 2a, and enter code 8 or P, whichever is applicable, in box 7. Enter code 1 or 4, if applicable.
- For a distribution of excess contributions without earnings after the due date of the individual's return under Code Section 408(d)(5), leave box 2a blank, and check the "Taxable amount not determined" checkbox in box 2b. Use code 1 or 7 in box 7 depending on the age of the participant.
- For a traditional IRA and a SEP IRA rolled over to an accepting employer plan, enter the gross amount in box 1, 0 (zero) in box 2a, and code G in box 7.
- *SIMPLE IRA*. Enter the total amount distributed from a SIMPLE IRA in box 2a. For a SIMPLE IRA rolled over to an accepting employer plan after the two-year period, enter the gross amount in box 1, 0 (zero) in box 2a, and code G in box 7.
- *Roth IRAs*. For a distribution from a Roth IRA, report the total distribution in box 1 and leave box 2a blank except in the case of an IRA revocation or account closure (see page R-2) and a recharacterization (see page R-4). Use code J, Q, or T as appropriate in box 7. Use code 8 or P, if applicable, in box 7 with code J. Do not combine code Q or T with any other codes. However, for the distribution of excess Roth IRA contributions, report the gross distribution in box 1 and only the earnings in box 2a. Enter code J, and code 8 or P in box 7.
- *Roth IRA conversion*. Report the total amount converted or reconverted from a traditional IRA, SEP IRA, or SIMPLE IRA to a Roth IRA in boxes 1 and 2a. A conversion or reconversion is considered a distribution and must be reported even if it is with the same trustee and even if the conversion is done by a trustee-to-trustee transfer. When an IRA annuity is converted to a Roth IRA, the amount that is treated as distributed is the FMV of the annuity contract on the date the annuity contract is converted. This rule also applies when a traditional IRA annuity contract as an account asset

and the traditional IRA is converted to a Roth IRA. Determining the FMV of an individual retirement annuity issued by a company regularly engaged in the selling of contracts depends on the timing of the conversion. [Treas. Reg. § 1.408A-4T, Q&A 14; *see also* Rev. Proc. 2006-13 [2006-1 C.B. 315] for a safe harbor determination of the FMV when an IRA is converted to a Roth IRA. Rev. Proc. 2006-13 is available at *www.irs.gov/pub/irs-irbs/irb06-03.pdf* (visited on Aug. 1, 2012)]

- For a Roth IRA conversion, use code 2 in box 7 if the participant is under age 59½ or code 7 if the participant is at least age 59½. Also check the IRA/SEP/SIMPLE box in box 7.
- *Losses.* If a distribution is a loss, do not enter a negative amount in this box. For a plan with no after-tax contributions or designated Roth account contributions, even though the value of the account may have decreased, there is no loss for reporting purposes. Therefore, if there are no employer securities distributed, show the actual cash and/or FMV of property distributed in boxes 1 and 2a, and make no entry in box 5. If only employer securities are distributed, show the FMV of the securities in boxes 1 and 2a and make no entry in box 5 or 6. If both employer securities and cash or other property are distributed, show the actual cash and/or FMV of the property (including employer securities) distributed in box 1, the gross less any NUA on employer securities in box 2a, no entry in box 5, and any NUA in box 6.
- *Corrective distributions.* Enter in box 2a the amount of excess deferrals, excess contributions, or excess aggregate contributions (other than employee contributions or designated Roth account contributions). *Deemed IRAs under an employer's plan.* An employer's plan (qualified plan, Section 403(b) plan, or governmental 457 plan) can permit participants to make "deemed" traditional and/or Roth IRA contributions to the plan. In general, the deemed IRA portion of the plan follows the rules applicable to traditional or Roth IRAs and the other portion of the plan follows the rules applicable to the employer's plan for purposes of taxation, RMDs, premature distribution exceptions, and withholding. Thus, distributions of the deemed IRA portion of the plan must be reported on a separate Form 1099-R from distributions of the other portion of the plan. The Form 1099-R reporting the distribution from the deemed IRA portion of the plan uses the distribution codes applicable to traditional or Roth IRAs, as applicable. In addition, if the participant has both a deemed traditional IRA and a deemed Roth IRA, distributions from the two types of IRAs must be reported on separate Forms 1099-R.

Box 2b: Taxable Amount Not Determined

Enter an *X* in this box only if it is not possible to reasonably obtain the data needed to compute the taxable amount.

If this box is marked, leave box 2a blank unless the distribution being reported is from a SIMPLE IRA distribution or represents a Roth IRA conversion. If the distribution is from a traditional IRA or a SEP IRA, leave box 2a blank. If the distribution is from a Roth IRA, generally mark this box, and leave box 2a blank (unless the distribution is a return of excess plus earnings, a recharacterization, or a revocation as explained in box 2a).

Do not mark this box if the distribution is a return of an excess contribution plus earnings from a Roth IRA. In that case, the earnings are taxable (and reported in box 2a), and thus the taxable amount is determined. Do not mark this box if the Form 1099-R is reporting a recharacterization transfer from a Roth IRA to a traditional IRA. In that case, 0 (zero) is entered in box 2a, and thus the taxable amount is determined to be zero. Do not mark this box if the distribution is a revocation of a Roth IRA. In this case, either the earnings or 0 (zero) will be entered in box 2a, and thus the taxable amount is determined.

Except in the case of IRAs, the IRS strongly encourages payers to make every effort to compute the taxable amount.

(Second) Box 2b: Total Distribution

Enter an *X* in this box only if the payment shown in box 1 is a total distribution. A total distribution is one or more distributions within one tax year in which the entire balance of the account is distributed. If periodic or installment payments are made, mark this box in the year the final payment is made.

Box 3: Capital Gain (Included in Box 2a)

For lump-sum distributions from qualified plans only, enter the amount reported in box 2a that is eligible for the capital gain election for participants born before 1936. Leave this box blank for a direct rollover or any IRA distribution.

Box 4: Federal Income Tax Withheld

Enter any federal income tax withheld. This withholding is subject to the deposit rules and the withholding tax return Form 945, Annual Return of Withheld Federal Income Tax. No withholding is required until the annual aggregate distribution exceeds $200.

- *Traditional IRAs (including SEP IRAs) and SIMPLE IRAs.* All IRA distributions that are "payable upon demand" are generally subject to a flat 10 percent withholding rate, unless the recipient elects to have more than 10 percent withheld. If the recipient is eligible for and elects no withholding, leave this box blank. For IRA annuities, the issuer of the annuity contract generally withholds under the periodic payment rules.

  For withholding purposes, assume that the entire amount of any IRA distribution is taxable, except for the distribution of contributions under Code Section 408(d)(4), in which case only the earnings are taxable, and for Section 408(d)(5) distributions of excess contributions.

  A traditional IRA that is converted (or reconverted) to a Roth IRA is subject to withholding, unless the recipient is eligible for and elects no withholding. This is true regardless of the method used for the conversion (transfer or rollover), and even if the conversion is accomplished within the same financial institution.

- *Roth IRAs.* Most Roth IRA distributions are exempt from any federal income tax withholding as a result of the Consolidated Appropriations Act of 2000. Therefore, do not withhold on any Roth IRA distribution, except in the case of a returned contribution plus earnings under Code Section 408(d)(4), or revoked contributions plus earnings. These earnings are always treated as a taxable distribution, even where the Roth IRA owner otherwise meets the definition of a *qualified distribution* (see Code Section 408A(d)(2)(C) and final Regulations Section 1.408A-6, Q&A 1(d)). Thus, withholding applies only on the earnings being distributed. The recipient can elect no withholding on the earnings.

  Recharacterizations. Do not withhold on any IRA recharacterization. Recharacterizations are not treated as distributions.
- *All plans subject to withholding.* If a payee fails to furnish his or her TIN, or if the IRS notifies the trustee before any distribution that the TIN furnished is incorrect, the payee cannot claim exemption from these withholding requirements. Backup withholding under Code Section 3406 does not apply to any retirement plan distribution.

Box 5: Employee Contributions/Designated Roth Contributions or Insurance Premiums

Enter the employee's contributions to a profit-sharing or retirement plan, designated Roth account contributions, or insurance premiums that the employee may recover tax free this year. Also report after-tax contributions directly rolled over to an IRA. Do not include contributions to any DEC, 401(k) plan, or any other contribution to a retirement plan that was not an after-tax contribution.

- *Designated Roth contributions.* Distributions from a designated Roth contribution account are reported on a separate Form 1099-R. Enter in box 5 the amount distributed that is attributable to the employee's basis in the DRC. Earnings are reported in box 2a.

Box 6: Net Unrealized Appreciation in Employer's Securities

Use this box if a distribution from a qualified plan (except a qualified distribution from a designated Roth account) includes securities of the employer corporation (or a subsidiary or parent corporation) and you can compute the NUA in the employer's securities. Enter all the NUA in employer securities if this is a lump-sum distribution. If this is not a lump-sum distribution, enter only the NUA in employer securities attributable to employee contributions. Include the NUA in box 1 but not in box 2a. You do not have to complete this box for a direct rollover.

Box 7: Distribution Code

Enter an *X* in the IRA/SEP/SIMPLE checkbox if the distribution is from a traditional IRA, SEP IRA, or SIMPLE IRA. It is not necessary to check the box for a distribution from a Roth IRA or for an IRA recharacterization.

Enter the appropriate code(s) from the Guide to Distribution Codes that shows the type of distribution. In certain cases, double codes must be entered. For example, for a corrective distribution plus earnings from a traditional IRA where the earnings are taxable in the prior year and the participant is under the age of 59½ enter 1P in box 7. In addition, for a direct rollover from an employer's qualified plan, Section 403(b) plan, or governmental 457(b) plan to a traditional IRA or employer's plan of the surviving spouse of a deceased participant, enter double code 4G.

Only three numeric combinations are permitted: (1) codes 8 and 1, (2) 8 and 2, or (3) 8 and 4. If two other numeric codes are applicable, more than one Form 1099-R must be filed. For example, if a distribution during the first part of 2012 is a premature distribution, and later on the participant takes another distribution during 2012 on or after age 59½, two Forms 1099-R must be issued. The premature distribution would use code 1, and the normal distribution would use code 7. If a second code applies, it is listed under the code descriptions below. If an alpha and numeric code is used, there is no required ordering of the codes. (See Qs 13:119, 13:120 for a discussion of revocations.)

The Guide to Distribution Codes shows the distribution codes that are used in box 7 of Form 1099-R for 2012.

Box 7 (Form 1099-R) Distribution Codes

Distribution Codes	*Explanations*	*Used with Code (if applicable)*
1—Early distribution, no known exception.	Use code 1 only if the employee/taxpayer has not reached age 59, and you do not know if any of the exceptions under distribution code 2, 3, or 4 apply. Use code 1 even if the distribution is made for medical expenses, health insurance premiums, qualified higher education expenses, or a first-time home purchase under Code Section 72(t)(2)(B), (D), (E), (F). Code 1 must also be used even if a taxpayer is 59 or older and he or she modifies a series of substantially equal periodic payments under Code Section 72(q), (t), or (v) prior to the end of the five-year period. Use code 1 for a qualified reservist distribution.	8, B, D, L, or P

Box 7 (Form 1099-R) Distribution Codes (*cont'd*)

Distribution Codes	*Explanations*	*Used with Code (if applicable)*
2—Early distribution, exception applies.	Use code 2 only if the employee/ taxpayer has not reached age 59 and the distribution is: • A Roth IRA conversion (an IRA converted to a Roth IRA). • A distribution made from a qualified retirement plan or IRA because of an IRS levy under Code Section 6331. • A 457(b) plan distribution that is not subject to the additional 10 percent tax. • A distribution from a qualified retirement plan after separation from service where the taxpayer has reached age 55 or older in the year of separation. • A distribution from a governmental defined benefit plan to a public safety employee after separation from service where the taxpayer has reached age 50 or older. • A distribution that is part of a series of substantially equal periodic payments as described in Code Section 72(q), (t), or (v). • Any other distribution subject to an exception under Code Section 72(q), (t), or (v) that is not required to be reported using code 1, 3, or 4. • Permissible withdrawals under an eligible automatic contribution arrangement.	8, B, D, or P
3—Disability.	Disability is defined in Treasury Regulations Section 1.72-17(f).	None
4—Death.	Use code 4 regardless of the age of the employee/taxpayer to indicate payment to a decedent's beneficiary, including an estate or trust. Also use it for death benefit payments made by an employer but not made as part of a pension, profit-sharing, or retirement plan.	8, A, B, D, G, H, L, or P
5—Prohibited transaction.	Use code 5 if there was a prohibited (improper) use of the account. Code 5 means the account is no longer an IRA (or Roth IRA).	None

Box 7 (Form 1099-R) Distribution Codes (*cont'd*)

Distribution Codes	*Explanations*	*Used with Code (if applicable)*
6—Code Section 1035 exchange.	Use code 6 to indicate the tax-free exchange of life insurance, annuity, or endowment contracts under Code Section 1035.	None
7—Normal distribution.	Use code 7: (a) for a normal distribution from a plan, including a traditional IRA, Code Section 401(k), or Code Section 403(b) plan, if the employee/taxpayer is at least age 59½, or (b) for a Roth IRA conversion or reconversion if the participant is at least age 59½, and to report a distribution from a life insurance, annuity, or endowment contract and for reporting income from a failed life insurance contract under Code Sections 7702(g) and (h). Use code 7 with code A, if applicable. Generally, use code 7 if no other code applies. Do not use code 7 for a Roth IRA. **Note.** Code 1 must be used even if a taxpayer is 59½ or older and he or she modifies a series of substantially equal periodic payments under Code Section 72(q), (t), or (v) prior to the end of the five-year period.	A
8—Excess contributions plus earnings/excess deferrals (and/or earnings) taxable 2012.	Use code 8 for an IRA distribution under Code Section 408(d)(4), unless code P applies. Also use this code for corrective distributions of excess deferrals, excess contributions, and excess aggregate contributions, unless code D or P applies. (Special rules apply to corrective distributions and IRA revocation or account closures (discussed above).) (See Appendix L.)	1, 2, 4, B, or J
9—Cost of current life insurance protection.	Use code 9 to report premiums paid by a trustee or custodian for current life or other insurance protection.	None
A—May be eligible for 10-year tax option.	Use code A to indicate the distribution may be eligible for the 10-year tax option method of computing the tax on lump-sum distributions (on Form 4972, Tax on Lump-Sum Distributions). This code does not apply to any IRA or Roth IRA.	4 or 7

Box 7 (Form 1099-R) Distribution Codes (*cont'd*)

Distribution Codes	*Explanations*	*Used with Code (if applicable)*
B—Designated Roth account distribution.	Use code B for a distribution from a designated Roth account that is not a qualified distribution. But use code E for a Code Section 415 excess under a DRC.	1, 2, 4, 8, D, G, L, P or U
E—Distributions under the Employee Plans Compliance Resolution System (EPCRS).	Use this code for distributions under EPCRS, including excess annual additions under Code Section 415. Use code E for a Code Section 415 excess under a DRC.	None
F—Charitable gift annuity.	This code does not apply to an IRA or Roth IRA.	None
G—Direct rollover and rollover contribution.	Use code G for a direct rollover from a qualified plan (including a governmental 457(b) plan) or Section 403(b) plan to an eligible retirement plan (another qualified plan, a Section 403(b) plan, or an IRA). Also use code G for certain distributions from conduit IRAs to an employer plan and IRA rollover contributions to an accepting employer plan. **Note.** Do not use code G for a direct rollover from a designated Roth account to a Roth IRA. Use code H.	4 or B
H—Direct rollover of a designated Roth account distribution to a Roth IRA.	Use code H for a direct rollover of a distribution from a designated Roth account (DRA) to a Roth IRA. Use with code 4 if a spouse or nonspouse beneficiary makes distribution from a DRA to a Roth IRA.	4
J—Early distribution from a Roth IRA.	Use code J for a distribution from a Roth IRA when code Q or code T does not apply. But use code 2 for an IRS levy and code 5 for a prohibited transaction.	8 or P
L—Loans treated as deemed distributions under Code Section 72(p).	Do not use code L to report a loan offset. This code does not apply to an IRA or Roth IRA.	1, 4, or B

Box 7 (Form 1099-R) Distribution Codes (*cont'd*)

Distribution Codes	*Explanations*	*Used with Code (if applicable)*
N—Recharacterized IRA contribution made for 2012.	Use code N for a recharacterization of an IRA contribution made for 2012 and recharacterized in 2012 to another type of IRA by a trustee-to-trustee transfer or with the same trustee. **Caution.** The Form 1099-R instructions differ from the description of codes N and R in the *Instructions for Recipient* on Form W-2.	None
P—Excess contributions plus earnings/excess deferrals taxable in 2011.	The IRS suggests that anyone using code P for the refund of an IRA contribution under Code Section 408(d)(4), including excess Roth IRA contributions, advise payees, at the time the distribution is made, that the earnings are taxable in the year in which the contributions were made.	1, 2, 4, B, or J
Q—Qualified distribution from a Roth IRA.	Use code Q for a distribution from a Roth IRA if you know that the participant meets the five-year holding period and: • The participant has reached age 59½, or • The participant died, or • The participant is disabled. **Note.** *If any other code, such as 8 or P, applies, use code J.*	None
R—Recharacterized IRA contribution made for 2011.	Use code R for a recharacterization of an IRA contribution made for 2011 and recharacterized in 2012 to another type of IRA by a trustee-to-trustee transfer or with the same trustee. See Caution above.	None
S—Early distribution from a SIMPLE IRA in the first two years, no known exception.	Use code S only if the distribution is from a SIMPLE IRA in the first two years, the employee/taxpayer has not reached age 59½ and none of the exceptions under Code Section 72(t) are known to apply when the distribution is made. The two-year period begins on the day contributions are first deposited in the individual's SIMPLE IRA. Do not use code S if code 3 or 4 applies.	None

Box 7 (Form 1099-R) Distribution Codes (*cont'd*)

Distribution Codes	*Explanations*	*Used with Code (if applicable)*
T—Roth IRA distribution, exception applies.	Use code T for a distribution from a Roth IRA if you do not know if the five-year holding period has been met but: • The participant has reached age 59½, or • The participant died, or • The participant is disabled. **Note.** *If any other code, such as 8 or P, applies, use code J.*	None
U.—Dividends distributions from an employee stock ownership plan (ESOP) under Code Section 404(k).	Use code U for a distribution of dividends from an ESOP under Code Section 404(k). These are not eligible rollover distributions. **Note.** *Do not report dividends paid by the corporation directly to plan participants or their beneficiaries. Continue to report those dividends on Form 1099-DIV.*	B

Q 13:103 How are IRA distributions reported on the federal income tax return?

Individual Recipients. If the recipient of an IRA distribution is an individual, that individual must report the distribution on his or her federal income tax return. Form 1040 filers use lines 15a and 15b; Form 1040A filers use lines 11a and 11b; Form 1040NR filers use lines 16a and 16b.

Line 15a (or 11a or 16a) shows the gross amount of the distribution. This amount should be the same as reported in box 1 of Form 1099-R. If your IRA distribution is fully taxable, enter it on line 15b; do not make an entry on line 15a. If only part is taxable, enter the total distribution on line 15a and the taxable part on line 15b.

Line 15b (or 11b or 16b) shows the taxable amount of the distribution. This amount should be the same as reported in box 2a of Form 1099-R.

If the payer is unsure of the taxable amount reported in box 2a, the payer can check "tax amount not determined" in box 2b. This should alert the recipient to check with his or her accountant for assistance in determining the taxable amount.

Exception. There is one exception to using line 15 (or line 11 or 16) of a tax return to report IRA distributions. For corrective distributions of excess deferrals, excess contributions, and/or disallowed deferrals, plus income allocable, under a SARSEP plan, the recipient must report these amounts on the wage line of the tax return for the appropriate year (line 7 of Form 1040 or Form 1040A, line 8 of Form 1040NR). The principal amount is taxable the year it was deferred; the income allocable is taxable the year it was distributed. Therefore, in most corrective distribution cases, the payer must issue separate 1099-Rs because parts of the distribution may be taxed in two or three different years.

Nonindividual Recipients—If the recipient of an IRA distribution is a nonindividual (e.g., the estate or a trust), the distribution is taxable to such entity. Items of income taxable to such entity for purposes of federal income taxes are reported on Form 1041.

Substitute Statements

Q 13:104 What requirements must substitute statements for Form 1099-R satisfy?

Substitute statements for Form 1099-R, which can be sent to recipients of distributions in lieu of Forms 1099-R, must meet the following requirements:

1. They must prominently display in one area the tax year, the form number, and the form name that appears on the official form. For example, that information could be shown in the upper right part of the statements.
2. The filer and form recipient identifying information required on the official IRS form must be included.
3. All applicable money amounts and information, including box numbers, required to be reported to the form recipient must be titled on the recipient statement in substantially the same manner as they are on the official IRS form.
4. Appropriate instructions to the form recipient, similar to those on the official IRS form, must be provided to aid in the proper reporting of the items on the recipient's income tax return.
5. The following language must be included: "This information is being furnished to the Internal Revenue Service."
6. The Office of Management and Budget (OMB) number must be shown as it appears on the official IRS form.
7. The quality of carbon used to produce substitute statements to recipients must meet the following standards:
   a. All copies must be clearly legible;
   b. All copies must be legible enough to be photocopied; and
   c. Fading must not preclude legibility and the ability to photocopy. In general, black chemical transfer inks are preferred; other colors are permitted only if the required standards are met. Hot wax and cold carbon spots are not permitted.

Filing Corrected Forms 1099-R

Q 13:105 How are corrected Forms 1099-R filed?

It is sometimes necessary to correct Forms 1099-R after the originals have been submitted to the IRS. Although Form 1099-R is not subject to the three-tiered penalty structure applicable to other reporting forms, all corrections for a year must be submitted to the IRS in accordance with special rules contained in IRS Publication 1220, *Specifications for Filing Forms 1096, 1098, 1099, 5498, and W-2G Magnetically or Electronically*. Publication 1220 is published annually by the IRS and can be ordered by calling (800) 829-3676. The instructions emphasize the requirement to file a corrected Form 1099-R if the form has already been filed with the IRS and an error is later discovered. [*See also* Rev. Proc. 2012-30, 2012-33 I.R.B. 165]

> **Example.** A direct rollover to an eligible recipient plan was made and Form 1099-R was filed with the IRS reporting that none of the direct rollover was taxable by entering 0 (zero) in box 2a. It is later discovered that part of the direct rollover was not eligible to be rolled over; in this instance, part of the distribution consisted of the taxpayer's RMD. The original Form 1099-R must be corrected by issuing a new Form 1099-R with the account number box completed, so the IRS can determine which 1099-R is being corrected, if there were multiple forms filed for the same taxpayer on the same IRA plan.

Corrections should be filed as soon as possible. Corrections filed after August 1 may be subject to the maximum penalty of $50 per return; corrections filed on or before August 1 may be subject to a lesser penalty (see Q 13:113). All fields must be completed with the correct information, not just the data fields needing correction. Some types of corrections—such as correcting an erroneous Social Security number—require two separate steps. Only returns filed in error should be corrected and submitted, not the entire file. The participant's copy, clearly marked "corrected," should be furnished as soon as possible. [IRS Publication 1220, *Specifications for Filing Forms 1096, 1098, 1099, 5498, and W-2G Magnetically or Electronically*, § 13.02]

If a trustee discovers errors for prior years that affect a large number of payees, in addition to sending the IRS the corrected return and notifying the payees, the trustee should send a letter containing the following information to the IRS magnetic media coordinator:

- Name and address of payer
- Type of error (explained clearly)
- Tax year
- Payer TIN
- Transmitter control code
- Type of return
- Number of payees

That information will be forwarded to the appropriate office in an attempt to prevent erroneous notices from being sent to the payees. [IRS Publication 1220, *Specifications for Filing Forms 1096, 1098, 1099, 5498, and W-2G Magnetically or Electronically*, § 13.02]

The correction must be submitted on an actual information return document or filed magnetically or electronically. The correct tax year should be shown in box 2 of Form 4804, Transmittal of Information Returns Reported Magnetically/ Electronically (see Q 13:109), and on the external media label. [IRS Publication 1220, *Specifications for Filing Forms 1096, 1098, 1099, 5498, and W-2G Magnetically or Electronically*, § 13.05]

Prior-year data, original or corrected, must be filed according to the requirements of Revenue Procedure 2011-60 [2011-52 I.R.B. 934]. If submitting prior-year corrections, the trustee should use the record format for the current year and submit on separate media; however, it should use the actual-year designation of the correction in field positions 2–3 or positions 3–4 for eight-inch diskette filing. For electronic filing, a separate transmission must be made for each tax year. [IRS Publication 1220, *Specifications for Filing Forms 1096, 1098, 1099, 5498, and W-2G Magnetically or Electronically*, § 13.06]

In general, filers should submit corrections for returns to be filed within the last three calendar years (four years if the payment is a reportable payment subject to backup withholding under Code Section 3406). [IRS Publication 1220, *Specifications for Filing Forms 1096, 1098, 1099, and W-2G Magnetically or Electronically*, § 13.07]

If the corrected Forms 1099-R are being submitted on paper documents, an *X* should be placed in the corrected box at the top of a new Form 1099-R. For paper transmissions of corrected Forms 1099-R, the accompanying paper transmittal (Form 1096) must also be marked "corrected" at the top. For magnetic media submissions, the procedures contained in the appropriate revenue procedure for that year should be followed.

Magnetic Media Filing Requirements

Q 13:106 What are the magnetic media filing requirements for original and corrected Forms 1099-R?

If a trustee is required to file 250 or more Forms 1099-R, the original submission must be filed electronically or via an approved magnetic media submission. The 250-forms requirement applies separately to original and corrected returns. For example, if the count for the original submission was 1,000 and the count for the corrections is 225, the original submission must be via magnetic media, whereas the corrections may be submitted either on paper forms or via magnetic media.

Q 13:107 Must IRS approval to file magnetically be sought?

Yes. Form 4419, Application for Filing Information Returns Magnetically or Electronically, must be filed at least 30 days (45 days for some electronic filings) before the due date of the return. Only one Form 4419 need be filed for all types of returns that will be filed on magnetic media. Once the trustee has received approval, no additional approvals are required for subsequent years.

The IRS will reply to the applicant in writing and provide instructions at the time of the approval, usually within 30 days. A magnetic-media reporting package will be sent to all approved filers each year; it includes the necessary transmittals (Forms 4804), labels, and instructions.

Q 13:108 What is the due date for filing Form 1099-R magnetically?

The due date for magnetic media reporting of Form 1099-R is the same as that for paper reporting—that is, February 28, 2013, for the 2012 version of the form. Leap years are ignored for electronic filing purposes.

Q 13:109 Where are magnetic media filings made?

All information returns filed magnetically should be sent to the following address:

IRS—Martinsburg Computing Center
Information Reporting Program
230 Murall Drive
Kearneysville, WV 25430

Electronic submissions are filed using the Filing Information Returns Electronically (FIRE) system. The FIRE system operates 24 hours a day, 7 days a week, and is accessed through a personal computer and modem by calling (304) 262-2400.

Form 4804, Transmittal of Information Returns Reported Magnetically/Electronically, must accompany the submissions.

Q 13:110 Should a magnetic media filer also file paper copies with the IRS?

No. A magnetic media filer should not file on both paper and magnetic media.

Q 13:111 May a trustee organization request a waiver from filing on magnetic media?

Yes. Form 8508, Request for Waiver from Filing Information Returns on Magnetic Media (Forms W-2, W-2G, 1099 Series, 5498, and 8027), may be submitted to request an undue hardship waiver from magnetic media filing for a period not to exceed one tax year. Requests for waivers from filing information returns on magnetic media must be filed on Form 8508 at least 45 days before the return is due and should be sent to the following address:

Enterprise Computing Center—Martinsburg
Information Reporting Program
240 Murall Drive
Kearneysville, WV 25430

Paper Document Reporting

Q 13:112 What rules must be followed by a trustee organization filing Form 1099-R on paper documents?

Paper forms are read by machines (optical scanner recognition equipment). A payer permitted to file its original or corrected Forms 1099-R (or both) on paper documents must follow these rules or risk a penalty of $50 per incorrectly filed form:

1. Do not cut or separate copies A of the forms that are printed two or three to a sheet. Forms 1099-R are printed two to an 8½ by-11-inch sheet. Form 1096 (the transmittal form) is printed on an 8½ by-11-inch sheet and must be submitted to the IRS on such a sheet. If at least one form on the page is correctly completed, the entire page must be submitted. Send the forms to the IRS in a flat mailing, not folded.
2. No photocopies of the form are acceptable.
3. Do not staple, tear, or tape any of the forms. That will interfere with the IRS's ability to scan the documents.
4. Pinfeed holes on the form are not acceptable. Pinfeed holes outside the 8½-by-11-inch area must be removed before submission, without tearing or ripping the form. Substitute forms prepared in continuous or strip form must be burst and stripped to conform to the size specified for a single sheet (8½ by-11-inches) before filing with the IRS.
5. Do not change the title of any box on the form. Do not use a form to report information that is not properly reportable on that form. (For assistance regarding where to report the data, call (304) 263-8700.)
6. Report information only in the appropriate boxes provided on the forms. Make only one entry in each box unless otherwise indicated in the instructions.
7. Do not submit any copy other than copy A to the IRS.
8. Use the current-year form to report current-year information. Do not use prior-year forms unless reporting prior-year information; do not use subsequent-year forms for the current year.
9. Use the official forms or substitute forms that meet the specifications in the current IRS Publication 1179. If substitute forms that are not machine scannable and do not meet the current specifications are submitted, a penalty of $50 for each return may apply.

10. Type or machine print, using a carbon-based black ink ribbon. Use 10-pitch (pica) or 12-pitch (elite) block print, not script characters. Take measures to guarantee a dark black, clear, sharp image. Insert data in the middle of the boxes, well separated from other printing and lines.
11. Use decimal points to indicate dollars and cents. Do not use dollar signs, ampersands, asterisks, commas, or other special characters in money-amount boxes.
12. Do not enter number signs (#) and do not enter zeros or "none" in money-amount boxes unless specifically so instructed; leave them blank when no entry is required.

Noncompliance Penalties

Q 13:113 What are the consequences if a filer fails to transmit Forms 1099-R via magnetic media when required or fails to follow the paper document format?

Failure to transmit Forms 1099-R via magnetic media when required and failure to follow the paper document format are treated as failure to file the form (see penalty structure below) unless the filer has an approved waiver on file and can establish reasonable cause or, in some cases, due diligence.

Form 1099-R is subject to different penalties depending on when the correct report is submitted to the IRS. In general, for corrections submitted within 30 days after the required filing date (February 28), the penalty is $15 per failure, with a maximum annual penalty of $75,000. For corrections submitted on or before August 1 of the calendar year in which the required filing date occurs, the penalty is $30 per failure, with a maximum annual penalty of $150,000. Corrections submitted after such August 1 are subject to a penalty of $50 per failure, with a maximum annual penalty of $250,000. If filing requirements are intentionally disregarded, the IRS may impose penalties of $100 per failure with no ceiling. Special penalty rules apply to certain *de minimis* failures and certain payers with gross receipts of not more than $5 million.

Q 13:114 What are the consequences if errors in taxpayer identification numbers appear on Forms 1099-R?

Form 1099-R was included in the Information Returns Name/TIN Matching Program beginning in tax year 1996. In Announcement 98-73 [1998-31 I.R.B. 14], the IRS granted penalty relief for missing or incorrect TINs for Forms 1099-R. The announcement also stated that the Notice 972CG (Notice of

Proposed Civil Penalty) provided to the payer with respect to TIN errors would constitute a "notice" under Code Section 3405(e)(12) for purposes of income tax withholding on future retirement distributions for that payee.

IRS Publication 1586, *Reasonable Cause Regulations and Requirements for Missing and Incorrect Name/TINs* (Sept. 2007), sheds some light on the issue. The publication implies that the penalty for missing and incorrect names or TINs will be assessed to the filer beginning with Forms 1099-R filed for tax year 1999 and beyond. TIN errors for 1999 Forms 1099-R appeared on the Notice 972CG that filers received in August 2001. It is anticipated that future Notice 972CG mailings will be received in August for the applicable year (i.e., payers will receive penalty notices for forms filed for tax year 2007 in August 2008).

Because the Forms 1099-R will become subject to TIN penalties beginning with the Notice 972CG received by the payer, the payer must generally begin withholding federal income tax on the next scheduled distribution.

Q 13:115 What steps must a payer take if taxpayer identification numbers are missing?

According to IRS Publication 1586, *Reasonable Cause Regulations and Requirements for Missing and Incorrect Name/TINs* (Sept. 2007), absent any regulations or other guidance, a payer should take the following actions if TINs for Forms 1099-R are missing or incorrect:

1. Complete an initial solicitation at the time the account is opened.
2. If no response to the initial solicitation is received, withhold federal income tax from any retirement plan distribution as the payer normally would, depending on the type of plan and frequency of payment.

   Note. An eligible rollover distribution from an employer's plan that is not paid as a direct rollover to another eligible plan is subject to withholding at the rate of 20 percent; the payee cannot elect out of this withholding requirement.
3. If no TIN is received as a result of the initial solicitation, the payer should complete a *first annual* solicitation by December 31 of the calendar year in which the payer receives a Notice 972CG notifying it of a missing TIN.
4. If no TIN is received as a result of the first annual solicitation, the payer should complete a *second annual* solicitation by December 31 of the year immediately following the calendar year in which the payer receives a Notice 972CG notifying it of a missing TIN.

   Note. A solicitation is a request from the trustee of the IRA for the payee to furnish a correct TIN. Solicitations may be accomplished by U.S. mail, telephone, or other electronic means (e.g., e-mail) as long as the time frames indicated in the paragraphs above are met.

Q 13:116 What steps must be taken by a payer when a taxpayer identification number is incorrect?

A payer should make every effort to ensure that its records reflect correct TINs. It should begin with a complete initial solicitation when the payee opens the account. It should also complete a first annual solicitation by the later of (1) 30 business days from the date on a Notice 972CG in which the IRS notifies the payer of an incorrect name/TIN combination or (2) 30 business days from the date on which the payer receives a Notice 972CG.

If the payee responds to the first annual solicitation within 45 days and confirms that the name/TIN combination in the payer's records is correct, the payer may continue to treat as valid any withholding election the payee previously made by completing Form W-4P (or a substitute form).

If the payee responds to the first annual solicitation within 45 days and furnishes a different name/TIN combination, any existing withholding election based on the prior name/TIN combination must be disregarded. To notify the payer regarding the amount to be withheld from future distributions, the payee must submit a new withholding election by completing Form W-4P (or a substitute form). The new withholding election will be effective on the date provided in Treasury Regulations Section 35.3405-1, Q&A D-21 (no later than Jan. 1, May 1, July 1, or Oct. 1 after it is received, as long as it is received at least 30 days before that date). The payer must withhold at the appropriate rate, depending on the type of plan and the frequency of the payments, until a new withholding election is received.

If the payee does not respond to the first annual solicitation within 45 days, the payer must withhold from any distribution at the appropriate rate.

Alternatively, upon receipt of a Notice 972CG in which the IRS notifies the payer of an incorrect name/TIN combination, the payer may choose to disregard any prior withholding elections made by the payees whose name/TIN combinations are identified as incorrect in the Notice 972CG. In that event, the payer should consider such payees to have no withholding election in effect until receipt of new withholding elections.

The payer must complete a second annual solicitation within the same time frame as required for the first annual solicitation if it is notified of an incorrect name/TIN combination in any calendar year following the first notification.

Early Withdrawal Certificate of Deposit Penalty

Q 13:117 How is an early withdrawal certificate of deposit penalty treated?

In no event will the assessment of an early withdrawal CD penalty or other permissible transaction fees be included as part of the gross distribution amount. The reportable distribution amount is *net* the penalty or fee.

Example 1. Beth requests a distribution from her IRA in the amount of $1,000. This is *not* a withdrawal of an unwanted contribution, plus earnings.

The trustee imposes an early withdrawal CD penalty of $50. The institution gives Beth a check for $1,000 and takes the $50 CD penalty from the remaining IRA balance. The reportable distribution is $1,000, even though $1,050 came out of Beth's IRA. Any withholding of 10 percent would be assessed on the reportable distribution amount of $1,000.

Example 2. The facts are the same as those in Example 1, except that the institution reduces the $1,000 by the $50 CD penalty. This results in a net check to Beth of $950. The reportable distribution is $950, even though $1,000 came out of Beth's IRA. Any withholding of 10 percent would be assessed on the reportable distribution amount of $950.

Intended Rollover of IRA Distribution

Q 13:118 How is a distribution reported when an IRA owner indicates that he or she will roll the distribution over into another IRA?

When making a distribution to an individual who indicates that he or she is going to roll the amount over into another IRA, the trustee or custodian should use code 1 if the IRA owner is under age 59½ or code 7 if the IRA owner is age 59½ or older. Because the *receiving* financial institution will produce a Form 5498 indicating the amount rolled over, the IRA owner must reflect the rollover transaction on the appropriate line of his or her personal income tax return. [Ann. 90-56, 1990-16 I.R.B. 22]

If the IRA owner is converting a traditional IRA to a Roth IRA, Form 1099-R should be prepared for the traditional IRA. Code 2 should be used if the participant is under age 59½; code 7 should be used if the participant is age 59½ or older.

Reporting Revoked IRAs

Q 13:119 How is a revoked IRA reported?

Revenue Procedure 91-70 [1991-2 C.B. 899] outlines the reporting requirements that apply when an IRA is timely revoked. Before Revenue Procedure 91-70 was issued, an IRA that was timely revoked was treated as though it had never existed, and no reporting was required. The IRS changed its position with respect to both the contribution and the distribution. Revenue Procedure 91-70 provides that even when a participant exercises the option to revoke the IRA, the IRS reporting requirements still apply. See Chart of Contribution Revocations and CIP Failures in Appendix L.

To the consternation of practitioners, the IRS has not revised Revenue Procedure 91-70 or the Form 1099-R instructions to deal with the revocation of a SIMPLE IRA within its first seven days. Until Revenue Procedure 91-70 is updated to include revocations of SIMPLE IRAs, the Form 1099-R instructions cannot be changed. It would appear, however, that if a SIMPLE IRA is revoked, the distribution should be reported on Form 1099-R in boxes 1 and 2a, and code S or code 7 should be entered in box 7 (depending on the age of the participant).

Q 13:120 Do the distribution reporting requirements vary according to the type of IRA contribution being revoked?

Yes. Proper distribution reporting depends on the type of IRA contribution being revoked, as follows. See Chart of Contribution Revocations and CIP Failures in Appendix L.

Revoked Regular Contributions. If a regular contribution is made to an IRA (whether it is a current-year or a prior-year contribution) that is timely revoked, and distribution is made to the taxpayer, the gross distribution should be entered in box 1 of Form 1099-R. If no earnings are distributed, 0 (zero) should be entered in box 2a and code 8 in box 7. If earnings are distributed, the amount of earnings should be entered in box 2a.

Such earnings could be subject to the early distribution tax under Code Section 72(t). If they are subject to that tax (i.e., the taxpayer is under age 59½), code 1 should be entered in box 7 regardless of the age of the taxpayer. If it is unknown whether the taxpayer deducted the contribution, the total amount distributed should be entered in box 2a.

Revoked Rollover Contributions and Revoked Transfers. If a rollover contribution or a transfer is made to an IRA that is timely revoked, the gross distribution amount should be entered in boxes 1 and 2a of Form 1099-R. For purposes of box 7, code 1 should be used if the taxpayer is under age 59½, and code 7 should be used if the taxpayer is age 59½ or older.

Revoked SEP or SIMPLE Contributions. If employer SEP or SIMPLE contributions are made to the IRA, and the IRA is timely revoked by the employee, the distribution should be reported as fully taxable in boxes 1 and 2a. Code 1 should be used if the taxpayer is under age 59½, code 7 if the taxpayer is age 59½ or older, and code S if the SIMPLE IRA was in existence for less than two years.

Revoked Roth IRA Contributions. If a regular contribution is made to a Roth IRA (whether it is a current-year or a prior-year contribution) that is timely revoked, and distribution is made to the taxpayer, the gross distribution should be entered in box 1 of Form 1099-R. If no earnings are distributed, 0 (zero) should be entered in box 2a and code J8 in box 7, regardless of age. If earnings are distributed, the amount of earnings should be entered in box 2a. Such earnings could be subject to the early distribution tax under Code Section 72(t). If they are subject to that tax (i.e., the taxpayer is under age 59½), code J should be entered in box 7 regardless of the age of the taxpayer.

Renewed Investments

Q 13:121 Are renewed investments treated as distributions?

No. When existing investments (e.g., CDs) within an IRA are renewed or reinvested in some other form of investment, no distribution occurs. Therefore, no Form 1099-R is issued in such instances and Form 5498 does not report the renewed investments as contributions.

Fees Deducted from IRA Accounts

Q 13:122 Are fees deducted from an IRA treated as distributions?

No. When such fees such as annual maintenance or transaction fees are deducted from an IRA, those amounts are not treated as distributions and are not reportable on Form 1099-R. In addition, once fees are deducted from the IRA, the participant may not reimburse the IRA. That is, if the IRA is reimbursed for the fees, the reimbursements are treated as regular IRA contributions, and they must be reported in box 1 of Form 5498. Such amounts would thus count toward the IRA owner's contribution limit for the year. [Ltr. Ruls. 9124037, 9124036, 8830061]

Miscellaneous Rules

Q 13:123 How is Form 1099-R filed if two corporations merge?

Revenue Procedure 99-50 [1999-52 I.R.B. 757] outlines procedures that permit a successor business to combine all information reporting following a merger or an acquisition. The revenue procedure covers information reporting with respect to Form 1042-S, all forms in the series 1099, Form 1098, Form 5498, and Form W-2G, hereinafter referred to as "appropriate forms."

The provisions of Revenue Procedure 99-50 apply only when all of the following conditions are met:

1. One business entity (the successor) acquires from another business entity (the predecessor) substantially all of the property (a) used in the trade or business of the predecessor or (b) used in a separate unit of the trade or business of the predecessor.
2. During the preacquisition portion of the calendar year in which the acquisition occurs, the predecessor files any of the information returns covered in Revenue Procedure 99-50.
3. During the postacquisition portion of the acquisition year, the predecessor or the separate unit of the predecessor does not make or receive any reportable payments and does not withhold or collect any tax.
4. The requirements described in Section 5 of Revenue Procedure 99-50 (relating to the alternative procedure) are met.
5. The IRS instructions to the appropriate forms do not prohibit use of the alternative procedure.

Under the standard procedure set forth in Section 4 of Revenue Procedure 99-50, each person who makes or receives payments or withholds or collects taxes that are reportable on any of the appropriate forms is responsible for separate information reporting of those transactions. Thus, both the predecessor and the successor must file the appropriate forms for reportable transactions occurring in the acquisition year.

For the successor to report the combined information for the year under the alternative procedure set forth in Section 5 of Revenue Procedure 99-50, the following requirements must be satisfied:

1. Both the predecessor and the successor must agree that the successor assumes the predecessor's entire information reporting obligations for the appropriate forms to which their agreement applies. In such a case, the predecessor is relieved of its information reporting obligations for reportable transactions occurring in the acquisition year only if and to the extent that their agreement meets and the successor satisfies the requirements of Revenue Procedure 99-50.
2. The predecessor and the successor must agree on the specific forms to which the alternative procedure applies. They may agree, for example, to use the alternative procedure for all appropriate forms or to limit the use of the alternative procedure to (a) certain specific forms or (b) specific reporting entities. In other words, the standard procedure may be used for some forms or by some reporting entities, and the alternative procedure may be used for other forms or by other reporting entities.
3. On each appropriate form, the successor must combine (a) any payments made or received on account of a person by the predecessor in the preacquisition portion of the acquisition year with (b) any payments made or received on account of that person by the successor in that year, if any, and must report the aggregate amount (or amounts) on account of that person for that year.
4. On each appropriate form, the successor must combine the amount of any withheld income tax withheld for a person by the predecessor in the preacquisition portion of the acquisition year with the amount (or amounts) withheld for that person by the successor in that year and, on the appropriate form(s), must report the aggregate amount withheld for the year.
5. The successor must file a statement with the IRS indicating that the appropriate forms are being filed on a combined basis in accordance with Revenue Procedure 99-50. If any income tax has been withheld by the predecessor during the acquisition year and reported by the predecessor on Form 945, the total of the withholding amounts shown on the successor's Forms 1099 for that year will exceed the total of the withholding amounts shown on the successor's Form 945. Therefore, the statement that must be filed with the IRS must reflect the amount of any income tax that has been withheld by the predecessor and by the successor for each type of form. Identical procedures apply to the filing of Forms 1042 and 1042-S.
6. The statement required to be filed with the IRS must include the name, address, telephone number, and EIN of both the successor and the predecessor and the name and telephone number of the person responsible for preparing the statement.

7. The statement for Form 1042-S must be attached to Form 1042 and mailed to the address appearing in its instructions on or before the due date of the Form 1042.
8. The statement for the forms in the series 1098 and 1099 and Forms 5498 and W-2G must be filed separately from such forms and Form 945. Unless otherwise directed by the form's instructions, the statement for Forms 1098, 1099, and 5498 and Forms W-2G must be mailed on or before the due date for such forms to: Internal Revenue Service, Martinsburg Computing Center, 230 Murall Drive, Attn: Chief, Information Returns Branch, Mail Stop 360, Kearneysville, WV 25430.

Revenue Procedure 99-50 is generally effective for appropriate forms filed after December 31, 1999. If, however, a successor filed forms before that date and the requirements of Revenue Procedure 99-50 were satisfied, the predecessor's filing obligations are deemed to have been satisfied, as long as the predecessor and successor have substantially complied with all of the requirements, except for the statement requirements described previously.

Q 13:124 How long should copies of Form 1099-R be kept?

Copies of information returns filed with the IRS, including Form 1099-R, or the information needed to reconstruct the data should be kept for at least three years from the due date of the return to which they relate.

Q 13:125 May more than one Form 1099-R be enclosed in a single envelope?

Generally, yes. If a trustee or custodian organization combines Form 1099-R with returns for interest, dividend, and royalty payments, very strict mailing requirements must be followed. In such a case, no additional enclosures are permitted. Additional enclosures include advertising or promotional material and quarterly or annual reports. The mere addition of a sentence or two on the year-end statement is also not permitted. Logos are permitted on the envelope and on any nontax enclosures.

If Form 1099-R is being mailed without any other forms, the rules regarding enclosures, described above, do not apply.

Q 13:126 Must Form 1099-R be sent by first-class mail to the IRS?

Yes. If sending many forms to the IRS, the filer should send them in conveniently sized packages. The filer should write the payer's name and TIN on each package. The packages should be numbered consecutively, and Form 1096 should be placed in the first package. Postal regulations require forms and packages to be sent by first-class mail.

Q 13:127 Must the account-number box on Form 1099-R be completed?

Beginning in 2004, yes. The account-number box is required to be used for an account-number designation. The number must not appear anywhere else on the form and must not be the taxpayer's SSN. It may be to the payer's benefit to include the account number in the event a customer has more than one IRA plan at that organization.

Practice Pointer. If window envelopes are used to mail statements to customers via a reduced-rate mail, the account number must not appear in the window. If it does, the U.S. Postal Service may not accept the envelopes for reduced-rate mail.

IRS Form 5329

Q 13:128 Who must file Form 5329?

An individual must file Form 5329, Additional Taxes on Qualified Plans (Including IRAs) and Other Tax-Favored Accounts, if any of the following applies:

1. A premature distribution was made from an IRA or a SEP IRA, but distribution code 1 (premature distribution) is not shown in box 7 of Form 1099-R. Part I of Form 5329 should be completed.
2. An exception to the tax on early IRA distributions applies, but distribution code 2, 3, or 4 is not shown in box 7 of Form 1099-R, or the distribution code shown is incorrect.
3. An excess contribution was made to an IRA (Part III of Form 5329 should be completed), a medical savings account (Part VI should be completed), a Roth IRA (Part IV should be completed), or a Coverdell ESA (Part V should be completed).
4. RMDs from an IRA were not made by April 1 of the first year following attainment of age 70½, or missed for any other year thereafter. (Part IV of Form 5329 should be completed.)

Q 13:129 Are there any exceptions to the requirements for filing Form 5329?

Yes. Form 5329 should not be filed if any of the following applies:

1. Only the 10 percent tax is owed on early distributions (distribution Code 1 must be shown in box 7 of Form 1099-R). (If Form 1040 is filed, Form 5329 should not be completed. Instead, 10 percent of the taxable part of the distribution is entered on Form 1040, line 59, or on Form 1040-NR, line 54. "No" is written under the heading "Other Taxes" to the left of line 59 or line 54 to indicate that Form 5329 does not have to be filed.)

2. An early distribution was received from an IRA, but the taxpayer meets an exception to the tax (distribution code 2, 3, or 4 must be correctly shown on Form 1099-R).
3. The taxable part of all qualifying distributions was rolled over.

Q 13:130 How is Form 5329 filed?

Form 5329 should be attached to Form 1040 and both should be filed by the due date of Form 1040 (including extensions). The due date is three and one-half months after the end of the individual's tax year. It is normally April 15 for calendar-year taxpayers.

Q 13:131 Must Form 5329 be filed even if Form 1040 does not have to be filed?

Yes. If tax is owed on Form 5329 or if the form is required to be filed even though no tax is due, Form 5329 must still be completed and filed with the IRS at the time and place Form 1040 would have been required to be filed. If Form 5329 is being filed by itself, the filer must be sure to include the taxpayer's address on page 1 and the taxpayer's signature and the date on page 2. A check or money order payable to the United States Treasury for the total amount of any tax due should be enclosed (but not attached). The taxpayer's Social Security number and "[year for which the form is being filed] Form 5329" should be written on the check or money order.

Q 13:132 Which version of Form 5329 is used to pay a tax for a previous year?

To pay a tax for a previous year, that year's version of Form 5329 must be used. For example, to pay tax for 2012, the 2012 version of the form must be used.

Q 13:133 How should Form 5329 be filed if tax is owed for a previous year?

If tax is owed for a previous year because of an early distribution, Part I of Form 5329 for that year should be completed and attached to Form 1040X, Amended U.S. Individual Income Tax Return. The filer must be sure to include the distribution that has not previously been reported as additional income on Form 1040X that has not previously been reported. If a tax other than the tax penalty on early distributions for a previous year is owed, Form 5329 should be filed by itself for that year. The other tax (i.e., excess contribution penalty tax) would be paid on a Form 5329 for the current year. The taxpayer's signature and the date should be included on page 2. A check or money order payable to the United States Treasury for the amount of tax due should be enclosed (but not attached). The taxpayer's Social Security number and "[year for which the form is being filed] Form 5329" should appear on the check or money order.

Q 13:134 How should Form 5329 be prepared if both spouses owe penalty taxes and are filing a joint return?

Each spouse must complete a separate Form 5329 for taxes attributable to his or her own IRA or SEP IRA. If both spouses owe penalty taxes and are filing a joint return, they should enter the combined total tax from Forms 5329 on Form 1040, line 59 or Form 1040-NR, line 54.

Q 13:135 How is line 1 of Form 5329 completed if the taxpayer engaged in a prohibited transaction?

If the taxpayer was under age 59½ on the first day of the year, the entire value of the account or annuity should be reported on line 1 of Form 5329. The value amount entered on line 1 of Form 5329 depends on the type of prohibited transaction engaged in and whether it was engaged in with respect to an individual retirement account or an individual retirement annuity.

If the prohibited transaction was, for example, borrowing from an individual retirement account, the account is no longer qualified as an individual retirement account or annuity on the first day of the tax year in which the borrowing or pledging occurred. The owner of the account is considered to have received a distribution of the entire value of his or her individual retirement account at that time. Therefore, if the owner was under age 59½ at that time, he or she must report the entire value of his or her individual retirement account on line 1 of Form 5329.

On the other hand, if any part of an individual retirement *account* was pledged as security for a loan, that part is considered distributed at the time pledged. Therefore, if the taxpayer was under age 59½ at the time of the pledge, the amount pledged must be entered on line 1 of Form 5329. Using an individual retirement account as a basis for obtaining a benefit is also a prohibited transaction.

Q 13:136 Must Form 5329 be filed if an IRA invests in collectibles?

Yes. If an IRA trustee invested IRA funds in collectibles, the IRA owner is considered to have received a distribution equal to the cost of the collectibles. Collectibles generally include works of art, rugs, antiques, metals, gems, stamps, coins (but see Qs 13:137, 13:138), alcoholic beverages, and certain other tangible personal property purchased after 1981. It should be noted that if the taxpayer was under age 59½ when the funds were invested, the cost of the collectibles should be included on line 1 of Form 5329.

> **Note.** A taxpayer must include the total cost of the collectibles in income on his or her Form 1040, line 15b. [I.R.C. § 408(m)] Because an IRA is the investment vehicle for SEPs, SARSEPs, and SIMPLE IRAs, the same investment restrictions apply.

Q 13:137 Are all coins considered collectibles?

No. An IRA trustee may invest IRA funds in U.S. gold coins of one ounce, one-half ounce, and one-tenth of an ounce and U.S. silver coins of one ounce minted after September 30, 1986. Under Code Section 408(m), any portion of an IRA that is invested in collectibles is currently taxable, subject to an exception for certain gold or silver coins and coins issued by a state. The Taxpayer Relief Act of 1997 (TRA '97) extended the exception to certain platinum coins and to certain gold, silver, platinum, or palladium bullion, effective for taxable years beginning after 1997. [I.R.C. § 408(m)]

Q 13:138 Are mutual funds that hold coins, precious metals, and the like treated as collectibles?

No. A registered security such as a mutual fund is not treated as a collectible, even if it holds coins or precious metals.

Q 13:139 Can the 50 percent excess accumulation tax for failure to withdraw the RMD be waived?

Yes. The IRS may waive the 50 percent nondeductible excise tax on excess accumulations if certain conditions are satisfied. The assets in the IRA must include an affected investment (see Q 13:140), or the shortfall must have been the result of reasonable error and reasonable steps must have been taken to remedy the shortfall. To request such relief, Form 5329 must be filed, any excise tax must be paid, and a letter of explanation must be attached. If the IRS grants the request, it will send out a refund. Special rules apply if the IRA is unable to make a minimum distribution because of the insolvency of an insurance company. [I.R.C. § 4974(d); Rev. Proc. 92-10, 1992-1 C.B. 661]

Q 13:140 What is an *affected investment*?

An *affected investment* is an annuity contract or a guaranteed investment contract (with an insurance company) for which payments under the terms of the contract have been reduced or suspended because of state insurer delinquency proceedings against the contracting insurance company. [Rev. Proc. 92-10, 1992-1 C.B. 661]

Q 13:141 Which assets must be used to satisfy the minimum IRA distribution requirement if the IRA contains an affected investment?

If an IRA includes assets in addition to the affected investment, all IRA assets, including the available portion of the affected investment, must be used to satisfy as much as possible the minimum IRA distribution requirement to the extent possible. If the affected investment is the only asset in the IRA, as much as possible of the required distribution must come from the available portion, if any, of the affected investment.

Q 13:142 What is the *available portion* of an affected investment?

The *available portion* of an affected investment is the amount of payments remaining after the payments have been reduced or suspended because of state insurer delinquency proceedings.

Q 13:143 What action must be taken if the reduction or suspension of payments is canceled?

If the payments under an annuity contract or a guaranteed investment contract increase because all or part of the reduction or suspension is canceled, the amount of any shortfall in a prior distribution pursuant to the proceedings must be made up.

Q 13:144 When must any shortfall be made up if the reduction or suspension of payments is canceled?

The shortfall in a minimum distribution must be made up by December 31 of the calendar year following the year that increased payments were received. Thus, the taxpayer may make up (reduce or eliminate) the shortfall with the increased payments that are received.

Q 13:145 Is the estate tax increased if there are excess accumulations in an IRA?

It depends on the date of death. For taxpayers who died after December 31, 1986, and before January 1, 1997, the estate tax will be increased by 15 percent of the excess accumulation. TRA '97, however, repealed the excess accumulation tax for taxpayers dying after 1996. [SBJPA § 1452; I.R.C. § 4980A, before repeal by TRA '97 § 1073(a)]

Q 13:146 May the excess accumulation tax be offset by any credits against the estate tax?

No. The excess accumulation tax may not be offset by any credits against the estate tax, such as the unified credit. [I.R.C. § 4980A(d)(2)]

IRS Form 5330

Q 13:147 What is the purpose of Form 5330?

With regard to IRAs, SEPs, and SARSEPs, Form 5330, Return of Excise Taxes Related to Employee Benefit Plans, is used to report the 10 percent excise tax on the following:

- Nondeductible employer contributions to SEPs and SARSEPs [I.R.C. § 4972(d)(1)(A)(ii)]

- Prohibited transactions [I.R.C. §§ 4975(a), 4975(e)(1)]
- Excess contributions to plans with cash or deferred arrangements [I.R.C. §§ 4979(a), 4979(e)(4)]

The nondeductible contributions are computed as of the end of the employer's tax year. The current-year nondeductible contributions are equal to the excess of the amount contributed during the employer's tax year over the amount of contributions allowable as a deduction under Code Section 404. In addition, prior-year nondeductible SEP contributions (for tax years beginning after December 31, 1986) continue to be subject to the 10 percent excise tax annually until eliminated by a carryforward deduction in years after the nondeductible contributions are made.

Q 13:148 May more than one type of excise tax be reported on the same form?

Yes. Generally, a single return can be filed for excise taxes with the same due date. The due date for the payment of tax on excess contributions to plans with cash or deferred arrangements (CODAs), however, falls after the due date for the payment of taxes on prohibited transactions and nondeductible employer contributions. Furthermore, the IRS requires a separate filing for reporting the tax on excess contributions to plans with CODAs.

Q 13:149 May an employer use one Form 5330 to report the prohibited transaction tax and the tax on nondeductible employer contributions?

Yes. It should be noted, however, that even though an employer may report two types of taxes on one Form 5330 (e.g., prohibited transaction tax and tax on nondeductible employer contributions), more than one "person" may be required to file Form 5330 in the event of a prohibited transaction.

Q 13:150 Who must file Form 5330?

Form 5330 must be filed by the following:

1. Any employer that is liable for the tax under Code Section 4972 for nondeductible employer contributions to SEPs and SARSEPs;
2. Any disqualified person (see Q 13:152) who is liable for the tax under Code Section 4975 for participating in a prohibited transaction (other than a fiduciary acting only as such or an individual (or his or her beneficiary) who engages in a prohibited transaction with respect to his or her IRA); and
3. Any employer that is liable for the tax under Code Section 4979 on excess contributions to plans with a CODA.

Q 13:151 Why is an individual (or his or her beneficiary) who engages in a prohibited transaction with respect to an IRA not required to file Form 5330?

There is no requirement that Form 5330 be filed by an individual (or his or her beneficiary) who engages in a prohibited transaction with respect to an IRA because the IRA is disqualified by such an action. As a result, the IRA itself becomes taxable (see Q 13:34).

Q 13:152 Who is a *disqualified person*?

A *disqualified person* is any one of the following:

1. A fiduciary;
2. A person providing services to the plan;
3. An employer, with any employees who are covered by the plan;
4. An employee organization, with any members who are covered by the plan;
5. Any direct or indirect owner of 50 percent or more of
   a. The combined voting power of all classes of stock entitled to vote,
   b. The total value of shares of all classes of stock of a corporation,
   c. The capital interest or the profits interest of a partnership,
   d. The beneficial interest of a trust or unincorporated enterprise that is an employer or an employee organization described in item 3 or 4, or
   e. Any direct or indirect owner of 50 percent or more of (i) the combined voting power of all classes of stock entitled to vote or the total value of shares of all classes of stock of a corporation, (ii) the capital interest or the profits interest of a partnership, or (iii) the beneficial interest of a trust or unincorporated enterprise that is an employer or an employee organization described in item 3 or 4;
6. A family member of any individual described in item 5a, b, c, or e (a family member is a spouse, ancestor, lineal descendant, or spouse of a lineal descendant);
7. A corporation, partnership, or trust or estate of which (or in which) any direct or indirect owner holds 50 percent or more of the interest described in item 5e(i), (ii), or (iii) (for purposes of (iii), the beneficial interest of the trust or estate is owned, directly or indirectly, or held by persons described in items 5a through e);
8. An officer, director (or an individual having powers or responsibilities similar to those of officers or directors), 10 percent or more shareholder, or highly compensated employee (earning 10 percent or more of the yearly wages of an employer) of a person described in item 5c, d, or e, or in item 7; or
9. A 10 percent or more (in capital or profits) partner or joint venturer of a person described in item 5c, d, or e, or in item 7.

Q 13:153 What is the due date for Form 5330?

Form 5330 must be filed by the last day of the seventh month after the end of the tax year of the employer or other person who must file the return for the tax on nondeductible contributions to SEPs and SARSEPs and for the tax on engaging in a prohibited transaction. An employer that is liable for the tax on excess elective contributions to SARSEPs must file Form 5330 by the last day of the 15th month after the close of the plan year to which the excess SEP contributions, disallowed deferrals, or excess deferrals relate.

Q 13:154 How may an extension of time to file Form 5330 be obtained?

Form 5558, Application of Extension of Time to File Certain Employee Plan Returns, can be filed to request an extension of time to file Form 5330. If the request is approved, an extension of up to six months may be granted. Beginning April 1, 2004, only the employer, an attorney, an accountant, an actuary, an enrolled agent, or an enrolled retirement plan agent may sign the extension form—Form 2848—on file with the IRS. [*See* Circular 230, Regulations Governing the Practice of Attorneys, Certified Public Accountants, Enrolled Agents, Enrolled Actuaries, Enrolled Retirement Plan Agents, and Appraisers before the Internal Revenue Service (4-2008)]

Q 13:155 May interest and other penalties be charged if the tax is not paid or Form 5330 is not timely filed?

Yes. In fact, even if an extension is granted (see Q 13:154), interest (determined under Code Section 6621) is charged on taxes not paid by the due date. Interest is also charged on penalties imposed for failure to file, negligence, fraud, gross valuation overstatements, and substantial understatements of tax from the due date (including extensions) to the date of payment. Interest and penalties will be billed separately after the return is filed.

Q 13:156 What is the penalty for not filing Form 5330 by the due date?

If Form 5330 is not filed by the due date, including extensions, there may be a penalty of 5 percent of the unpaid tax for each month or part of a month the return is late, up to a maximum of 25 percent of the unpaid tax. The minimum penalty for a return that is more than 60 days late is the lesser of the tax due or $100.

The penalty will not be imposed if failure to file on time can be shown to be attributable to reasonable cause. A request for abatement of any late filing penalties requires a statement explaining the reasonable cause to be attached to Form 5330.

Q 13:157 What is the penalty for the late payment of tax due on Form 5330?

If the tax due under Form 5330 is not paid when due, there may be a penalty of 0.5 percent of the unpaid tax for each month or part of a month the tax is not paid, up to a maximum of 25 percent of the unpaid tax. Such a penalty may also apply to any additional tax not paid within 10 days of the date of the notice and demand for payment. The penalty will not be imposed if it can be shown that the failure to pay on time was attributable to reasonable cause.

IRS Form 5498

Q 13:158 What is Form 5498 used to report?

Each year, an IRA trustee must submit contribution information to the IRS using Form 5498, IRA Contribution Information. [I.R.C. § 408(i); Prop. Treas. Reg. § 1.408-5]

Following is a summary of information required for the 2012 tax year. (See Q 13:164 for a detailed explanation of each box.)

- *Box 1:* Include regular traditional IRA contributions made in 2012 and through April 15, 2013, for 2012.
- *Box 2:* Enter rollover contributions to any IRA received during 2012 including direct and indirect (rollover) conversions from qualified plans, 403(b) plans, and governmental 457(b) plans to Roth IRAs.
- *Box 3:* Enter the amount converted from a traditional IRA, SEP, or SIMPLE IRA to a Roth IRA during 2012. Do not include a rollover from one Roth IRA to another Roth IRA.
- *Box 4:* Enter any amount recharacterized (plus earnings) to this IRA.
- *Box 5:* Include the FMV of the account as of December 31, 2012.
- *Box 6:* For endowment contracts enter any life insurance cost included in box 1.
- *Box 7:* A checkbox to indicate IRA, SEP, SIMPLE, or Roth IRA. The appropriate checkbox must be marked on each Form 5498 issued.
- *Box 8:* Enter employer contributions made into a SEP (including salary deferrals under a SARSEP) during 2012.
- *Box 9:* Enter any contributions made to a SIMPLE (including salary deferrals) during 2012.
- *Box 10:* Enter any regular contributions made to a Roth IRA in 2012 and through April 15, 2013, designated for 2012.
- *Box 11:* Check if RMD for 2013.
- *Box 12a:* Enter the RMD date if Form 5498 is being used to report additional information required for RMDs.

- *Box 12b:* Enter the amount if you are using Form 5498 to report the additional information under Alternative 1 (see Q 13:173) for providing the RMD information to the IRA owner.
- *Box 13a:* Report the amount of any postponed contribution made in 2012 for a prior year. If contributions were made for more than a prior year, each prior year's postponed contribution must be reported on a separate form.
- *Box 13b:* Enter the year for which the postponed contribution is made.
- *Box 13c:* Enter the applicable code to indicate the reason the participant made the postponed contribution.
- *Box 14a:* Enter the amount of a qualified reservist distribution or a designated disaster distribution payment, such as a hurricane disaster distribution.
- *Box 14b:* Enter the code for the payment of a qualified reservist distribution, or for repayment of a federally designated disaster distribution.
- *Box 15a:* Enter the amount of catch-up contributions made in the case of certain employer bankruptcies, up to $3,000. This does not include regular catch-up contributions.
- *Box 15b:* Enter the code for these special catch-up contributions.

Q 13:159 Who is responsible for determining the FMV for an IRA?

The IRA trustee, custodian, or issuer of the IRA is responsible for determining the FMV of the account or annuity.

Q 13:160 Must Form 5498 be filed if the account was closed before the end of the year?

Yes. Form 5498 is required to be submitted if any activity that should be reported on Form 5498 occurred, even if the account was closed before year-end (see Q 13:164).

Q 13:161 What is the deadline for submitting Form 5498 to the IRS?

The deadline for submitting Form 5498 to the IRS is May 31 of each year. If that date falls on a Saturday, Sunday, or legal holiday, the due date is the next business day. For 2012 filings, the applicable deadline date is May 31, 2013.

Note. Most trustees are required to transmit Form 5498 data to the IRS via magnetic media (see Qs 13:184, 13:190).

Q 13:162 How may an extension of time to file Form 5498 with the IRS be obtained?

For paper or magnetic media filing, an extension of time to file Form 5498 with the IRS may be requested by completing Form 8809, Request for Extension of Time to File Information Returns, and sending it to the following address:

Enterprise Computing Center—Martinsburg
Information Reporting Program
Attn: Extension of Time Coordinator
240 Murall Drive
Kearneysville, WV 25430

The IRS suggests that Form 8809 be filed as soon as the need becomes apparent; in any case, Form 8809 must be filed no later than the due date of the return (generally May 31) for the IRS to consider granting the extension. If the IRS approves the extension request, an additional 30 days to file will be granted. The extension will apply only to the due date for filing the returns with the IRS, however; it will not extend the due date for providing statements to recipients (see Q 13:163). If more time to file is needed, an additional 30 days may be requested by submitting another Form 8809 before the end of the initial extension period.

Q 13:163 How may an extension of time for providing Forms 5498 to recipients be requested?

If it is necessary to request an extension of time for providing Forms 5498 to IRA owners, a letter should be sent to the IRS–Martinsburg Computing Center (see Q 13:162 for the address). The letter must include the following:

- Payer's name
- Payer's TIN
- Payer's address
- Type of return
- Statement that an extension for providing statements to recipients (Form 5498) is being requested
- Reason for the delay
- Payer's signature

The request must be postmarked by the due date of the return (generally May 31).

If the request for extension is approved, an additional 30 days will be granted to furnish the recipient statements.

Q 13:164 How is the 2012 Form 5498 completed?

Following is a box-by-box explanation of the 2012 Form 5498.

Note. If an individual has only one IRA agreement, only one Form 5498 should be issued. If, on the other hand, an individual has established more than one IRA agreement—for example, one agreement for regular contributions, a second for SEP contributions, and a third for a rollover from an employer's plan—three Forms 5498 should be issued.

Box 1. IRA Contributions (Other Than Amounts in Boxes 2–4, 8–10, 13a, 14a, and 15a)

Enter contributions to a traditional IRA made in 2012 and through April 15, 2013, designated for 2012.

Report gross contributions, including the amount allocable to the cost of life insurance (see box 6) and including any excess contributions, even if the excess contributions were withdrawn. If an excess contribution is treated as a contribution in a subsequent year, do not report it on Form 5498 for the subsequent year. It has already been reported as a contribution on Form 5498 for the year it was actually contributed.

Also include employee contributions to an IRA under a SEP plan. These are contributions made by the employee, not by the employer, that are treated as regular IRA contributions subject to the 100% of compensation and $5,000 ($6,000 for participants 50 or older) limits of Section 219. Do not include employer SEP IRA contributions or SARSEP contributions under Section 408(k)(6). Instead, include them in box 8.

Also, do not include in box 1 contributions to a SIMPLE IRA (report them in box 9) and a Roth IRA (report them in box 10).

In addition, do not include in box 1 rollovers and recharacterizations (report rollovers in box 2 and recharacterizations in box 4), or a Roth IRA conversion amount (report in box 3).

Box 2. Rollover Contributions

Enter any rollover contributions (or contributions treated as rollovers) to any IRA received by you during 2012. These contributions may be any of the following:

- A direct or indirect rollover from a qualified plan (including a governmental Section 457(b) plan) or Section 403(b) plan
- Any qualified rollover contribution as defined in Section 408A(e) from an eligible retirement plan (other than an IRA) to a Roth IRA
- A military death gratuity
- An SGLI payment
- Qualified settlement income received in connection with the Exxon Valdez litigation
- Airline payment amounts

Note. For a limited time, the FAA Modernization and Reform Act of 2012 [Pub. L. No. 112-95] allows for the rollover of up to 90 percent of an airline payment to a traditional IRA, as well as, the recharacterization of up to 90 percent of an airline payment from a Roth IRA to a traditional IRA.

For the rollover of property, enter the FMV of the property on the date you received it. This value may be different from the value of the property on the date it was distributed to the participant.

For more details, see IRS Publication 590.

Box 3. Roth IRA Conversion Amount

Enter the amount converted or reconverted from a traditional IRA, SEP IRA, or SIMPLE IRA to a Roth IRA during 2012. Do not include a rollover from one Roth IRA to another Roth IRA. Include this type of rollover in box 2.

Box 4. Recharacterized Contributions

Enter any amounts recharacterized, plus earnings from one type of IRA to another.

Box 5. Fair Market Value of Account

Enter the FMV of the account on December 31.

Box 6. Life Insurance Cost Included in Box 1

For endowment contracts only, enter the amount included in box 1 allocable to the cost of life insurance.

Box 7. Checkboxes

Check the appropriate box.

- **IRA.** Check "IRA" if you are filing Form 5498 to report information about a traditional IRA account.
- **SEP.** Check "SEP" if you are filing Form 5498 to report information about a SEP IRA. If you do not know whether the account is a SEP IRA, check the "IRA" box.
- **SIMPLE.** Check "SIMPLE" if you are filing Form 5498 to report information about a SIMPLE IRA account. Do not check this box for a SIMPLE 401(k) plan. See Section 408(p).
- **Roth IRA.** Check "Roth IRA" if you are filing Form 5498 to report information about a Roth IRA account.

Box 8. SEP Contributions

Enter employer contributions made to a SEP IRA (including salary deferrals under a SARSEP) during 2012, including contributions made in 2012 for 2011, but not including contributions made in 2013 for 2012. Do not enter employee contributions to an IRA under a SEP plan. Report any employee contributions to an IRA under a SEP plan in box 1. Also include in box 8 SEP contributions made by a self-employed person to his or her own account.

Box 9. SIMPLE Contributions

Enter contributions made to a SIMPLE IRA during 2012. Do not include contributions to a SIMPLE 401(k) plan. A distribution from one SIMPLE IRA rolled over to another SIMPLE IRA is reported in box 2.

Box 10. Roth IRA Contributions

Enter any contributions made to a Roth IRA in 2012 and through April 15, 2013, designated for 2012. However, report Roth IRA conversion amounts in box 3.

Box 11. Check if RMD for 2013

Check the box if the participant must take an RMD for 2013.

You are required to check the box for the year in which the IRA participant reaches age 70½, even though the RMD for that year need not be made until April 1 of the following year. Then check the box for each subsequent year an RMD is required to be made.

> **Caution.** Boxes 12a and 12b are provided for your use to report RMD dates and amounts to participants. You may choose to complete these boxes or continue to provide a separate Form 5498, or a separate statement, to report the information required by Alternative 1 or Alternative 2.

Box 12a. RMD Date

Enter the RMD date if you are using Form 5498 to report the additional information.

Box 12b. RMD Amount

Enter the RMD amount if you are using Form 5498 to report the additional information under Alternative 1.

Box 13a. Postponed Contribution

Report the amount of any postponed contribution made in 2012 for a prior year. If contributions were made for more than one prior year, each prior year's postponed contribution must be reported on a separate form.

Box 13b. Year

Enter the year for which the postponed contribution in box 13a was made.

Box 13c. Code

From the following list of codes, enter the reason the participant made the postponed contribution.

- For participants' service in the combat zone or hazardous duty area, enter:
  - AF - Allied Force
  - JE - Joint Endeavor
  - EF - Enduring Freedom
  - IF - Iraqi Freedom
- For participants who are "affected taxpayers," as described in an IRS News Release relating to a federally designated disaster area, enter FD.

Box 14a. Repayments

Enter the amount of any repayment of a qualified reservist distribution or a designated disaster distribution repayment (e.g., a qualified hurricane distribution).

Box 14b. Code

Enter QR for the repayment of a qualified reservist distribution or DD for repayment of a federally designated disaster distribution.

Box 15a. Other Contributions

Enter the amount of any catch-up contributions made in the case of certain employer bankruptcies (maximum amount $3,000). The regular catch-up contributions for individuals 50 or older does not apply if this special catch-up contribution is made. [*See* I.R.C. § 219(b)(5)(C) for further information]

Box 15b. Code

Enter BK for these special catch-up contributions.

Q 13:165 Must Form 5498 be filed if no contributions were made and there was a total distribution made during the year?

No. If no reportable contributions were made and a total distribution was made during the year, Form 5498 does not have to be filed and an annual FMV statement does not have to be furnished. It should be noted, however, that special rules apply in the year of an IRA owner's death and in the case of a revoked IRA (see Q 13:16).

Q 13:166 Are separate Forms 5498 required for each investment under a single IRA arrangement?

No. It is not necessary to file a Form 5498 for each investment under one IRA plan. For example, if a participant has three CDs under one IRA plan, only one Form 5498 is required for all contributions to the IRA plan and for the FMVs of the CDs under the plan. In contrast, if an individual has established several IRA plans with the same financial organization, a separate Form 5498 must be filed for each plan.

Because the definition of an individual retirement account includes all assets within the same trust (or custodial) agreement, one Form 5498 should include all information associated with that agreement. On the other hand, in an individual retirement annuity, each contract is a separate plan.

Q 13:167 How should the "Account Number" box on Form 5498 be completed?

A box is provided on Form 5498 to identify the specific IRA plan being reported. This identifying number (which must be unique so that it will distinguish the specific IRA plan) is especially important when an individual maintains more than one IRA plan at the same trustee organization, for example, one plan for regular contributions and a separate plan for rollover contributions. The taxpayer's Social Security number may *not* be used in this box (see Q 13:101).

The Account Number box is required on all information returns if there are multiple accounts for the same taxpayer for whom more than one form of the same type is being filed, or if multiple forms of the same type for the same taxpayer are filed even if the taxpayer has only one account.

> **Example.** An IRA owner has one IRA. A premature distribution was made in March 2012 and a return of excess distribution was made in July 2012. Although both distributions came from the same account, two Forms 1099-R must be filed: one to report the premature distribution and a separate form to report the return of excess distribution. It would also be required that more than one Form 1099-Q be filed if a distribution and a trustee-to-trustee transfer was made in the same year from a Coverdell ESA because transfers must be reported on a separate Form 1099-Q from other distributions. The purpose of this box is to identify the proper information return if a correction is filed.

The account number must be unique to identify the specific "plan" being reported. The recipient's TIN cannot be used for this purpose. In addition, in cases where multiple reportable distributions are made from the same plan for different reasons that require separate forms, the account number must be able to identify the specific form being filed. Using a sequence of numbers or alpha characters (1, 2, 3, or A, B, C) is permitted for this purpose. In addition, using a dash between the primary account number and the sequence number or alpha character is acceptable. For example, the following distributions were made during 2012 from the same traditional IRA plan, Account Number 123456789:

- March distribution that is premature (code 1 applies)
- June distribution that is converted to a Roth IRA (code 2 applies)
- IRA owner attains age 59½ on July 14
- September distribution that is a return of excess (code 8 or P applies)
- November distribution that is a normal distribution (code 7 applies)

Although four distributions were made from the same "plan," separate Forms 1099-R are required because different codes apply. In this example, it would be acceptable to enter Account Number 123456789, along with -1, -2, -3, and -4 (or -A, -B, -C, and -D), or some other sequence, with or without dashes. If it becomes necessary to correct the Form 1099-R on which the September distribution was reported, the corrected Form 1099-R would indicate "Account Number 123456789-3," which would alert the IRS as to the specific form being corrected.

Annual Participant Statements

Q 13:168 What rules apply to annual participant statements vis-à-vis Form 5498?

Information may be required to be reported to IRA participants (or beneficiaries in certain cases) on annual participant statements. There are two general rules and one special rule regarding such statements.

Rule 1. In general, a copy of the Form 5498 that is submitted to the IRS must be provided to the participant. The deadline for providing such a copy to the participant is May 31, the same deadline as for IRS submission.

Rule 2. All IRA participants must receive another report before the May 31 deadline. By January 31 of each year, the trustees of IRAs, SEP IRAs, and SIMPLE IRAs must provide participants with a statement in written format of their IRAs' FMV as of the previous December 31. That is the same FMV that will eventually be reflected in box 4 on the Form 5498 submitted to the IRS in May of each year.

In addition, trustees of SIMPLE IRAs must provide a "statement of the account activity" by January 31 of each year. The instructions do not provide a definition of the term *account activity* because the IRS Chief Counsel has not yet issued one. The Forms and Publications Division has indicated informally that until such guidance is issued, a good-faith interpretation of account activity may be used.

Special Rule—Substitute Statement. An exact copy of the official Form 5498 is not required to be furnished to the IRA participant. A trustee organization may use a substitute Form 5498 that meets the requirements of IRS Publication 1179, *Rules and Specifications for Private Printing of Substitute Forms 1096, 1098, 1099, 5498, and W-2G.* Publication 1179 is updated each year and contains the current year's revenue procedure addressing substitute statements to inform recipients. Publication 1179 may be ordered from the IRS by calling (800) 829-3676.

Q 13:169 Must Form 5498 be filed if the trustee or issuer already furnished a timely statement of the fair market value of the IRA to the participant, and no contributions were made to the IRA by the participant?

If the trustee or issuer furnished a statement of the FMV of the IRA to the participant by January 31, and no contributions were made to the IRA by the participant for the prior year, the trustee or issuer need not furnish another statement (or Form 5498) to the participant. That is, if the IRA participant does not make any traditional contributions for the year, rollover contributions during the year, Roth IRA contributions for the year, Roth conversions during the year, Coverdell ESA contribution during the year, or an employer SEP or SIMPLE contribution during the year, there is no requirement to provide Form 5498 (or a substitute) by May 31.

Form 5498 must still be filed with the IRS by May 31 to report the FMV of the IRA as of the prior December 31. That is also true for beneficiary accounts under the inherited IRA rules.

If the trustee or issuer does not furnish another statement to the participant because no contributions were made for the year, the December 31 FMV statement provided by January 31 must contain a legend designating which information is being furnished to the IRS, although the FMV statement itself has no required format. [*See* IRS Publication 1179, *Rules and Specifications for Private Printing of Substitute Forms 1096, 1098, 1099, 5498, and W-2G*; Instructions to Form 5498]

Many organizations comply with the FMV statement and the Form 5498 requirements in the following manner:

1. In January, they produce and mail the official Form 5498 (or a substitute that meets the specifications of Publication 1179) for the prior year. The prior year-end value will be available from the system for any participant who has already made the prior year's traditional or Roth contribution, completed a conversion from a traditional IRA to a Roth IRA, made a rollover/direct rollover contribution during the prior year, or received an employer's SEP or SIMPLE contribution during the prior year. The Coverdell ESA (formerly Education IRA) contribution statement must be sent to the participant by February 1.
2. After April 15, they produce the official Form 5498 (or a substitute that meets the specifications of Publication 1179) only for those participants who made a prior-year regular contribution to a traditional IRA or Roth IRA between January 1 and April 15 of the following year. Only those participants need to receive a mailing before the May 31 deadline.
3. They transmit the entire tape (both the January information and the later information) to the IRS via the approved magnetic media after April 15 but before the May 31 deadline.

Practice Pointer. Because reporting requirements change yearly, it is always a good idea to discuss those reporting requirements with the filer's data processor at least once each year.

Q 13:170 What requirements must substitute statements for Form 5498 meet?

Substitute statements for Form 5498 must meet requirements nearly identical to those applicable to substitute statements for Form 1099-R (see Q 13:104), *except* that the following language must be included: "The information in boxes 1, 2, 3, 4, 5, 6, 7, 8, 9, 10, and 11 is being furnished to the Internal Revenue Service."

Required Minimum Distribution Statement

Q 13:171 What are the requirements for sending participants a required minimum distribution statement?

Code Section 408(i) delegates authority to the Secretary of the Treasury to require that the trustee, custodian, or issuer of an IRA (hereinafter referred to as "trustee") make reports regarding such accounts. Additionally, Section 1.408-8, Q&A-10, of the final regulations provides that the trustee of an IRA is required to report RMD information in accordance with guidance published by the IRS.

At this time, no reporting of any kind is required for "beneficiary IRAs," including Roth IRAs, or for 403(b) accounts. However, if the IRS determines at any time in the future that RMD reporting applies to these types of accounts, it will issue additional guidance that will be effective prospectively.

Q 13:172 What are the reporting requirements to the IRA owner?

If the IRA owner is alive at the beginning of the year, and an RMD is required for that year, the trustee that holds the IRA as of the prior December 31 must provide a statement to the IRA owner by January 31 regarding the RMD for that year under one of two alternative methods explained in Qs 13:173 and 13:174. This requirement coincides with the requirement that a December 31 FMV statement must be provided to the IRA owner by the following January 31. This "RMD statement" can be provided along with the FMV statement of the prior December 31 that is required by the following January 31. Under both alternatives, the statement must inform the IRA owner that the trustee will be reporting to the IRS (on the previous year's Form 5498) that the IRA owner is required to receive a minimum distribution for the calendar year.

Q 13:173 What is alternative one?

The trustee furnishes the IRA owner with a statement of the amount of the RMD with respect to the IRA for the calendar year and the date by which such amount must be distributed. This requirement clarifies that the trustee must calculate the RMD with respect to each separate IRA maintained by that individual. The trustee calculates the RMD amount for purposes of this statement for each IRA based on the same criteria for all IRA owners as follows:

1. Use the prior December 31 balance of the IRA without any adjustments for contributions received by that IRA after December 31. This balance will be the same as the amount already required to be reported on the year-end FMV statement.
2. Use the Uniform Lifetime Table based on the IRA owner's attained age during the calendar year for which the RMD is being determined, even though the IRA owner's spouse may be the sole beneficiary and is more than 10 years younger than the IRA owner.

Note. It is ultimately the IRA owner's responsibility to request the RMD. It is only the trustee's responsibility to notify the IRA account owner of the RMD requirement and to assist with the calculation.

Q 13:174 What is alternative two?

The trustee provides the IRA owner with a statement that (1) informs the IRA owner that an RMD with respect to the IRA is required for the calendar year and the date by which such amount must be distributed and (2) includes an offer to furnish to the IRA owner, upon request, with a calculation of the amount of the RMD with respect to the IRA for that calendar year. If the IRA owner requests a calculation, the trustee must calculate the RMD for the IRA owner and report that amount to the IRA owner.

Note. Under alternative 2, the notice does not prescribe a date by which the calculated amount of the RMD that has been requested by the IRA owner be provided to the IRA owner. We therefore conclude that there is no required date to provide the calculation to the IRA owner; however, it should be within a reasonable time after the IRA owner requests the calculation.

Alternative 2 also does not specifically permit the calculation of the RMD to be determined under the same criteria for each IRA owner as it does under alternative 1. Thus, we conclude that if the trustee uses alternative 2, it should calculate the actual RMD based on the exact facts of the particular IRA owner.

Q 13:175 What are the reporting requirements to the IRS?

The 2012 Form 5498 requires that a trustee indicate that an RMD is required with respect to an IRA *for* calendar year 2013. The actual amount of the RMD will appear in Box 12b of Form 5498 if Alternative 1 (see Q 13:173) is being used. If Alternative 1 is not being used, the RMD amount need not be included on Form 5498 and checking box 11 is sufficient. An RMD that is required *for* 2013 must be indicated on the prior year's Form 5498 (the 2012 Form 5498) because the 2012 Form 5498 will be provided to the IRA owner and to the IRS *during* 2013.

With respect to IRA owners who are already age 70½ in 2012 or before, you will already have the information from your system that the person is subject to RMDs; therefore, you can make the RMD indication on the 2012 Form 5498.

Example. Robert has an IRA with Lone Tree Bank as trustee. The trustee has opted to use alternative 1 in meeting its RMD reporting obligation. The FMV of Robert's IRA on December 31, 2012, was $85,000. Robert's attained age during 2013 was 73, and the factor from the Uniform Lifetime Table is 24.7. On the 12/31/09 FMV statement that the trustee furnished to Robert by January 31, 2013, the bank indicated that his RMD for 2013 was $3,441 ($85,000 ÷ 24.7).

The statement also indicated that this amount must be distributed no later than December 31, 2013, from this IRA or any other traditional IRA that Robert holds as the IRA owner. The statement informed Robert that the trustee will be required to report on Robert's 2012 Form 5498 (provided to Robert and IRS during 2013) that he is required to receive an RMD *for* calendar year 2013.

Q 13:176 Can both alternatives be used in the same year?

Yes. On December 20, 2002, the IRS published Notice 2003-3 [2003-2 I.R.B. 258] that clarifies that both alternatives can be used simultaneously by using alternative 1 for some IRA owners and alternative 2 for other IRA owners.

Q 13:177 Are there any special rules if annuity payments have not commenced on an irrevocable basis?

Yes. On December 20, 2002, the IRS published Notice 2003-2 [2003-2 I.R.B. 257] that provides that, until further guidance is issued, in the case of an IRA annuity where annuity payments have not commenced on an irrevocable basis (except for acceleration), the IRA issuer may determine the entire interest under the annuity contract as the dollar amount credited to the IRA owner under the contract without regard to the actuarial value of any other benefits (e.g., minimum survivor benefits) that will be provided under the contract. Otherwise, the RMD reporting requirements continue to apply to the IRA annuities.

Q 13:178 May RMD statements be provided electronically?

Yes. Notice 2003-3 also provides that an IRA trustee, custodian, or issuer may satisfy the RMD statement requirement by transmitting such statement electronically. Beginning in 2003, the electronic transmission must comply with a reasonable, good-faith interpretation of applicable law. For calendar years after 2003, the electronic transmissions of the IRA owner's RMD statement must comply with the procedures for transmitting Forms W-2 electronically. This procedure includes the consent requirements described in the regulations under Code Section 6051. Use of these regulations is a reasonable, good-faith interpretation of applicable law for 2003.

Regulations Section 31.6051-1 contains the procedures for filing Forms W-2 electronically, and these same procedures apply for furnishing the RMD statements electronically. For purposes of these procedures, the term *furnisher* means the IRA trustee, custodian, or issuer, and the term *recipient* means the IRA owner. In general, this article provides the details concerning the following six requirements:

1. Consent
2. Disclosure
3. Format
4. Posting
5. Notice
6. Retention

Q 13:179 What are the consent requirements?

The recipient must affirmatively consent to receive the RMD statement electronically and must not have withdrawn that consent before the RMD statement is furnished. The consent must be made electronically in a manner that demonstrates that the recipient can access the information in the format in which it will be furnished to the recipient.

If a change in hardware or software required to access the RMD statement creates a risk that the recipient will not be able to access the information, the furnisher must provide the recipient with a notice before changing the hardware or software.

The notice must describe the revised hardware or software and inform the recipient that a new consent to the revised electronic format must be provided to the furnisher. After implementing the revised hardware or software, the furnisher must obtain a new consent from the recipient to receive the RMD statement electronically.

Q 13:180 What disclosure requirements apply?

Before, or at the time of, a recipient's consent, the furnisher must provide a disclosure statement to the recipient that contains the following information:

1. The recipient must be informed that the RMD statement will be furnished on paper if the recipient does not consent to receiving it electronically.
2. The recipient must be informed of the scope and duration of the consent. For example, the recipient must be informed whether the consent applies to the RMD statement every year until the consent is withdrawn, or only to the RMD statement required to be furnished by January 31 immediately following the date on which the consent is given.
3. The recipient must be informed of any procedure for obtaining a paper copy of the RMD statement after giving consent for an electronic version.
4. The recipient must be informed that the recipient may withdraw a consent at any time by furnishing the withdrawal in writing, either electronically or on paper, to the person whose name, mailing address, telephone number, and e-mail address is provided in the disclosure statement.
5. The furnisher must confirm the withdrawal in writing, either electronically or on paper. A withdrawal of consent does not apply to an RMD statement that was furnished electronically before the withdrawal of consent is furnished.
6. The recipient must be informed of the conditions under which a furnisher will cease furnishing statements electronically to the recipients (e.g., termination of the account subject to RMD reporting).
7. The recipient must be informed of the procedures for updating the information needed by the furnisher to contact the recipient.
8. The recipient must be provided with a description of the hardware and software needed to access, print, and retain the RMD statement, and the date when the information will no longer be available on the Web site.

Q 13:181 What requirements apply for posting the RMD statement on the trustee's Web site?

The furnisher must post the RMD statement on a Web site accessible to the recipient on or before the deadline for providing the annual RMD statement (January 31 of the year to which the RMD applies).

The furnisher must notify the recipient that the RMD statement is posted on a Web site. The notice must be provided no later than the due date for that year's RMD statement. The notice may be delivered by mail, e-mail, or in person. The notice must provide instructions on how to access and print the statement. The notice must include the following statement in capital letters: "IMPORTANT TAX RETURN DOCUMENT AVAILABLE." If the notice is provided by e-mail, the foregoing statement should be on the subject line of the e-mail and sent with high importance.

If an electronic notice is returned as undeliverable, and the correct electronic address cannot be obtained from the furnisher's records or from the recipient, the furnisher must then furnish the notice by mail or in person within 30 days after the electronic notice is returned. A furnisher must also notify a recipient that it has posted any corrected RMD statement information on a Web site within 30 days of such posting. This notice must be furnished by mail or in person if (1) an electronic notice of the original posting of the RMD statement was returned as undeliverable or (2) the recipient has not provided a new e-mail address.

Q 13:182 Are there requirements to retain access to the Web site?

Yes. The furnisher must maintain access to the RMD statements on the Web site through October 15 of the year following the calendar year to which the statement relates. The furnisher must also maintain access to corrected RMD statements on the Web site based on the time frame in the preceding sentence or, if later, the date that is 90 days after the corrected statements are posted.

Q 13:183 May other forms be delivered electronically?

Yes. On January 20, 2004, the IRS issued Notice 2004-10 [2004-6 I.R.B. 433], which was subsequently revised and reissued on January 23, 2004. This notice provides guidance regarding the electronic delivery of certain payee statements to form recipients. Specifically, this notice applies to Forms 1099-R, 5498, 1099-Q, 5498-ESA, 1099-MSA, and 5498-MSA (the 1099-MSA and 5498-MSA were replaced later in 2004 by 1099-SA and 5498-SA, because of the health savings accounts (HSAs)) that must be furnished to the form recipient for 2003 and subsequent years. [Rev. Proc. 2012-30, 2012-33 I.R.B. 165]

Part F of the general instructions permits electronic delivery of the forms listed above if the furnisher satisfies the consent, format, posting, and notification requirements described in Part F of the general instructions and furnishes such payee statements by their respective due dates.

Briefly, the form recipient must consent in the affirmative and not have withdrawn the consent before the statement is furnished. The consent must be made electronically in a way that shows that he or she can access the statement in the electronic format in which it will be furnished.

Before furnishing the electronic statement, you must give the recipient a statement with certain information prominently displayed, such as

- The scope and duration of the consent
- How to obtain a paper copy after giving consent
- How to withdraw consent
- Procedures to update the recipient's information
- A description of the hardware and software required to access, print, and retain a statement
- A date that the statement will no longer be available on the Web site

Moreover, you must ensure that the electronic format contains all of the required information and complies with the substitute statement requirements of Publication 1179. You must post the statement on a Web site that is accessible to the form recipient through October 15 of that year. You must also inform the recipient, electronically or by mail, of the posting and how to access and print the statement.

Magnetic Media Filing Requirements

Q 13:184 When must a trustee or custodian organization file Form 5498 via an approved magnetic media submission?

If a trustee or custodian organization is required to file 250 or more Forms 5498, the transmission to the IRS must be filed electronically or via an approved magnetic media submission. The 250-forms requirement applies separately to original and corrected Forms 5498. For example, if the count for a trustee's original submission was 1,000, and the count for the trustee's corrections is 225, the original submission must be via magnetic media, whereas the corrections may be submitted either on paper forms or via magnetic media; however, if the corrections equal or exceed 250, the trustee must submit such corrections via magnetic media.

Q 13:185 Is it necessary to obtain IRS approval to file magnetically?

Yes. The requirements for requesting approval for magnetic media filing are discussed above (see Q 13:107).

The trustee or custodian organization should consult its data processing provider (which generally has signing authority for the trustee or custodian organization). In most cases, the steps necessary to become an approved magnetic media filer will have already been taken by the data processor. It should be noted, however, that the signing authority held by the data processor does not relieve the trustee or custodian organization of its liability for penalties for not timely filing correct and complete returns.

Q 13:186 What is the due date for filing Form 5498 magnetically?

The due date for magnetic media (or electronic) filing of Form 5498 is the same as for paper reporting—May 31.

Q 13:187 Where are magnetic media filings made?

All information returns filed magnetically should be sent to the following address:

Enterprise Computing Center—Martinsburg
Information Reporting Program
230 Murall Drive
Kearneysville, WV 25430

Form 4804, Transmittal of Information Returns Reported Magnetically/Electronically, must accompany the submissions.

> **Note.** Form 8508 may be submitted requesting an undue hardship waiver from magnetic media filing for a period not to exceed one tax year. Waiver requests on Form 8508 must be filed at least 45 days before the return is due.

IRS Publication 1220, *Specifications for Filing Forms 1096, 1098, 1099, 5498, and W-2G Magnetically or Electronically*, which is published each year by the IRS, contains the current year's magnetic media reporting requirements. It can be ordered from the IRS by calling (800) 829-3676.

Paper Document Reporting

Q 13:188 What steps should be taken if a trustee or custodian organization can file Form 5498 on paper documents?

Paper forms are read by optical scanner recognition equipment. If a trustee or custodian organization can file its original or corrected Forms 5498 on paper documents, the rules discussed above (see Q 13:112) apply.

Filing Corrected Returns

Q 13:189 How are corrected Forms 5498 filed?

Sometimes it is necessary to correct a Form 5498 after the original has been submitted to the IRS. Although Form 5498 is not subject to the three-tiered penalty structure applicable to other reporting forms, all corrections for a year should be submitted to the IRS in accordance with the rules discussed earlier (see Q 13:105).

Noncompliance Penalties

Q 13:190 What penalties may apply to a trustee or custodian organization required to file Form 5498?

The IRS strongly encourages the quality review of information returns before filing to avoid erroneous statements to participants. The following penalties apply to a trustee or custodian organization required to file Form 5498 with the IRS:

1. A $50-per-failure penalty applies to each failure to timely file a Form 5498.
2. A $50-per-failure penalty applies to each failure to file a Form 5498 when required.
3. A $50-per-failure penalty applies to each failure to timely furnish a statement to a participant as required.
4. If filing on paper returns, a $50-per-failure penalty applies to each failure to furnish paper forms that are machine scannable.
5. All the penalties listed may be waived by the IRS if the failure can be shown to be attributable to reasonable cause and not willful neglect.

Failure to transmit the Forms 5498 via magnetic media when required to do so and failure to follow the paper submission format are treated as failure to file the form unless the trustee or custodian organization has an approved waiver on file or can establish reasonable cause or, in some cases, due diligence.

In the case of intentional disregard of the filing and correct information requirements, penalties of $100 per failure may be imposed. [I.R.C. § 6693; Prop. Treas. Reg. § 1.408-5]

Miscellaneous Reporting Requirements

Q 13:191 Does Form 5498 indicate what amounts are deductible?

No. Form 5498 does not address the issue of whether a contribution is deductible or nondeductible or whether the amount is excludable from income under Code Section 402(h).

Q 13:192 Must a participant inform the IRA trustee or custodian, issuer, or employer if an IRA contribution is deductible?

No. A participant is not required to inform the IRA trustee or custodian, the issuer, or his or her employer as to whether a contribution is deductible or nondeductible.

Q 13:193 How is Form 5498 filed if two corporations merge?

The reporting requirements applicable to mergers for years after 1999 are discussed in Q 13:123.

Q 13:194 How long should copies of Form 5498 be kept?

Copies of information returns filed with the IRS, including Form 5498, or the information needed to reconstruct the data should be kept for at least three years from the due date of the return.

Q 13:195 May more than one Form 5498 be enclosed in a single envelope?

Generally, yes. If a trustee or custodian organization combines Form 5498 with returns for interest, dividend, and royalty payments, very strict mailing requirements must be followed. If the Form 5498 is being mailed without any other forms, however, the rules regarding enclosures are more lenient. Specific instructions can be found in the form's addenda.

Q 13:196 Must Forms 5498 be sent by first-class mail?

Yes. When sending many forms to the IRS, the filer should send them in conveniently sized packages, with the payer's name and TIN written on each package. The packages should be numbered consecutively, and Transmittal Form 1096 should be placed in the first package. Postal regulations require forms and packages to be sent by first-class mail.

> **Practice Pointer.** If window envelopes are used to mail Forms 5498 to customers via reduced-rate mail, the account number (see Q 13:167) must not appear in the window. If it does, the U.S. Postal Service may not accept the envelopes for reduced-rate mail.

Q 13:197 What are the special Form 5498 reporting requirements for a deceased IRA owner?

In the year of an IRA owner's death, Form 5498 (and the year-end FMV information due by January 31) must be issued in both the decedent's name and each beneficiary's name. An IRA owner must be able to identify the source of each IRA he or she holds for purposes of determining the taxation of a distribution from the IRA.

A spouse beneficiary (unless the spouse makes the IRA his or her own IRA) is treated as any other beneficiary for the special reporting purposes. If the spouse makes the IRA his or her own in the year of the IRA owner's death, the spouse's name should be reported on Form 5498 and on the annual statement without the beneficiary designation (see below).

On the decedent's Form 5498 and annual statement, either the FMV of the IRA on the date of death is entered, or the "alternate reporting method" is used, and the FMV as of the end of the year in which the decedent died is reported.

Under the alternate reporting method contained in Revenue Procedure 89-52 [1989-2 C.B. 632], any FMV reported on the beneficiary's Form 5498 should not also be reported on the decedent's Form 5498 for that year. Consequently, the value of the decedent's account as of the end of the year will frequently be zero—even though the money is still in the account.

Under the alternate reporting method, the financial institution will prepare a Form 5498 for the year during which the IRA owner died in the name (and Social Security number) of the original IRA owner reflecting any current-year contributions (box 1 information), any rollover contributions (box 2 information), and the FMV as zero (box 5 information). The SEP checkbox will be marked if an employer SEP contribution was made during the year of death (box 5 information). No further Forms 5498 will be issued in the name of the deceased IRA owner.

Note. Usually, no entry is required in box 5 of Form 5498 if the FMV is zero, absent specific instructions to the contrary.

In addition, the trustee or custodian will prepare a Form 5498 for the year during which an IRA owner died in the name of *each* primary beneficiary. The beneficiary's Form 5498 must be styled, for example, as "David Vetter as beneficiary of Kitty Ferguson." The only information to be reported on that Form 5498 will be the FMV of that *beneficiary's* portion of the decedent's IRA as of year-end. The trustee or custodian will continue issuing a Form 5498 on behalf of the beneficiary until the IRA is reduced to zero. If a beneficiary takes a total distribution of his or her share of the IRA in the year of death, it is not necessary to file Form 5498 or to furnish an annual statement for that beneficiary. A Form 1099-R in the name of the beneficiary reporting the amount of the death distribution must be issued. A Form 5498 must still be issued for the decedent, however.

If the trustee or custodian has no knowledge of the death of the IRA owner until after the reporting deadline (May 31), no corrective filing of the Form 5498 is required for that year. Be that as it may, the trustee or custodian should probably prepare Forms 5498 as described previously for the year it became knowledgeable of the IRA owner's death, provided the IRA has not yet been withdrawn by the beneficiary.

The Revenue Procedure also states that if the trustee/custodian uses this alternative method, it *must* inform the executor of the decedent's estate of his or her right to receive the IRA's FMV as of the date of the IRA owner's death. Prior to 1998, Form 5498 had language on the reverse side of copy B, the participant's copy, which referred to the executor's right to request the IRA's FMV on the date of death of the IRA participant. The IRS deleted these two sentences from the "Participant Instructions" on the reverse side of copy B beginning with the 1998 form. These two sentences refer to the executor's right to request the IRA's FMV on the date of death of the IRA participant. Beginning with the 2003 Form 5498, the IRS has added this language to the reverse side of the participant's copy. If you are using the official IRS form, you will automatically meet this notification requirement.

If you are using a substitute statement to participants in lieu of the official Form 5498, you will also meet this notification requirement if you use the same language located on the reverse side of the participant's copy (which is a requirement for preparing substitute statements anyway). The following two sentences have been added to the description of box 5, Fair Market Value, in order to be in compliance with Revenue Procedure 89-52:

> However, if a decedent's name is shown, the amount reported may be the FMV on the date of death. If the FMV shown is zero (0) for a decedent, the executor or administrator of the estate may request a date-of-death value from the financial institution.

If the trustee or custodian is sending the official Form 5498, the trustee's or custodian's legal counsel must decide whether to add the preceding two sentences as a separate statement on all the Forms 5498 or to add them only on the Forms 5498 being reported in the decedent's name and showing 0 (zero) in box 5.

Example. Diane Smith had an IRA with ABC Bank. The beneficiaries of her IRA were her three nephews: Tom Young, Bill Young, and Ron Young. During 2012, before Diane's death in that year, a direct rollover in the amount of $75,000 was added to Diane's IRA from her 401(k) plan. Upon Diane's death, Bill and Ron took a total distribution of their beneficial interest in the IRA, while Tom decided to have his portion paid out over a five-year period.

For 2012, the year of Diane's death, two Forms 5498 will be issued. One Form 5498 will be issued in Diane Smith's name and Social Security number and will report $75,000 in box 2 (representing the rollover from Diane's 401(k) plan) and 0 (zero) in box 5 (using the alternate method for reporting FMV). Tom will receive a Form 5498 styled "Tom Young as beneficiary of Diane Smith," using his Social Security number, and reporting a $25,000 FMV in box 5. That dollar amount represents Tom's one-third beneficial interest in his aunt's IRA. No Form 5498 will be issued for Bill or Ron because each took a total distribution of his beneficial interest in the IRA before year-end.

Bill will receive a Form 1099-R styled "Bill Young as beneficiary of Diane Smith," using his Social Security number, and reporting the $25,000 death distribution he received from his aunt's IRA during the year. Ron will receive a Form 1099-R styled "Ron Young as beneficiary of Diane Smith," using his Social Security number, and reporting the $25,000 death distribution he received from his aunt's IRA during 2012.

Reporting Revoked IRAs

Q 13:198 What are the Form 5498 reporting requirements for revoked IRAs?

Revenue Procedure 91-70 [1991-2 C.B. 899] outlines reporting requirements that apply whenever an IRA is timely revoked.

The requirements have been broken down into six categories, as follows:

1. *Regular contributions.* When an individual establishes an IRA with a regular contribution, including spousal contributions, but then timely

revokes the plan, the trustee or custodian is required to report the regular contribution in box 1 on Form 5498 and the revoked distribution on Form 1099-R.

2. *Rollover contributions.* When an individual establishes an IRA with a rollover contribution (regardless of whether the eligible rollover distribution came from another IRA, a qualified plan, or a 403(b) plan), but then timely revokes the plan, the accepting financial institution reports the rollover contribution in box 2 on Form 5498 and the revoked distribution on Form 1099-R.
3. *Transfer contributions.* When an individual requests a direct transfer between IRA trustees or custodians, the distributing (transferor) institution would already have issued a Form 5498 when the IRA was established and the original contribution was made. However, no Form 5498 is issued for the transfer. The accepting (transferee) institution need provide only a Form 1099-R when the transferred IRA is revoked.
4. *SEP contributions.* SEP contributions are made by the IRA owner's employer. Until the IRS issues guidance with respect to revoking an IRA that received a SEP contribution, the instructions for Form 5498 cannot be revised. Nonetheless, because calendar-year SEP contributions are reported in box 8, it could be assumed that those amounts, if any, should be reported even if the IRA was revoked within the first seven days. At any rate, the revoked distribution must be reported on Form 1099-R.
5. *SIMPLE IRA contributions.* SIMPLE IRA contributions are made by the SIMPLE IRA owner's employer. The revoked distribution must be reported on Form 1099-R (see Q 13:119) and is fully taxable.
6. *Roth contributions, Roth conversions.* The revoked distribution should be reported on Form 1099-R (see Q 13:119).

Q 13:199 How must a revocation of an IRA be reported if it crosses two calendar years?

If an IRA contribution is made in one calendar year and revoked in the next calendar year (but within seven days), an FMV statement must be prepared and an entry made in box 5 of Form 5498 accordingly. Most often, a revocation occurs in the same calendar year as the contribution, and therefore a year-end FMV statement and an entry in box 5 of Form 5498 are not usually required.

IRS Form 5500

Q 13:200 Who must file Form 5500?

Generally, any administrator or sponsor of an employee benefit plan subject to the Employee Retirement Income Security Act of 1974 (ERISA) must file with the Department of Labor (DOL) information about each such plan every year. [I.R.C. § 6058; ERISA §§ 104, 4065] In the case of a SIMPLE, a SEP, or a SARSEP, the employer is generally the plan administrator; however, such plans do not generally have to file Form 5500, Annual Return/Report of Employee Benefit Plan (see Qs 4:6–4:8, 14:107).

Generally, the Form 5500 series does not have to be filed to report any information required under Code Section 6058. However, a group IRA established by an employer under Code Section 408(c) is required to file an annual return/report. [Treas. Reg. § 301.6058-1(a)(2)]

Q 13:201 When must Form 5500 be filed for an IRA?

An employer-sponsored IRA established under Code Section 408(c) must file the Form 5500 series by the last day of the seventh month following the close of the plan year.

Q 13:202 Who signs Form 5500 returns or reports?

Generally, the plan administrator (employer) will sign and date all Form 5500 returns or reports. The name of the individual who signs as plan administrator must be typed or printed clearly on the line under the signature line. In addition, the employer must sign a return/report filed for a single-employer plan.

IRS Form W-2

Q 13:203 Is Form W-2 used in reporting elective deferrals?

Yes. All elective deferral contributions are reported in box 12 of Form W-2, Wage and Tax Statement, for the year of deferral, even if some or all of the amount is an excess contribution. Any elective deferrals should be excluded from box 1, but should be included in boxes 3 and 5 for purposes of FICA.

Q 13:204 How is the elective deferral reported on Form W-2?

If an employee makes an elective contribution to a SARSEP or SIMPLE IRA, the amount of the elective deferral must be shown in box 12 of Form W-2, and the employer must precede the contribution amount with a code F, which indicates that an elective deferral contribution was made to a SARSEP, or code S, which indicates that an elective deferral was made to a SIMPLE IRA. The code is entered using capital letters. One space is left blank after the code, and the dollar amount is entered on the same line. Decimal points—but not dollar signs or commas—are used. For example, $17,000 in elective deferrals would be expressed as F 17000. All elective deferrals are reported in box 12 in such manner, even if some or all of the amount is an excess contribution, excess elective deferral, or disallowed deferral.

The amount of any elective deferral contribution is not included in the amount of wages in box 1, even if some or all of the amount may be an excess;

however, elective deferrals are included in box 3, Social Security Wages, and box 5, Medicare Wages and Tips, because all elective deferral contributions are subject to FICA when contributed and not when distributed.

Q 13:205 When is box 13 checked for a SEP?

When an employee is participating in a SARSEP, the pension plan block in box 13 of the W-2 form must be checked if either

1. The employer made a nonelective (regular) SEP contribution on the employee's behalf *during* the year, or
2. The employee made an elective deferral contribution during the year.

If the employer makes a prior-year nonelective contribution, and no elective contributions were made, the employee is not considered an active participant for the year for which the contribution is made. For example, if an employer made a regular SEP contribution on behalf of an employee for the 2012 plan year on April 15, 2013, and that employee did not make an elective contribution during 2012, the employee is not considered an active participant for the 2012 plan year. In such a case, the employee would be an active participant for the 2013 year.

Please note however that if two contributions are made in 2012, one for 2011 and another for 2012, the employee will be considered an active participant in 2013 even if no contribution is made in 2013 (see Q 5:34).

Q 13:206 Do the box 13 reporting rules for a SEP also apply to a SIMPLE?

Yes. An employer reporting for a SIMPLE would place an *X* in box 13, and box 12 would show the deferral amounts preceded by the letter *S*.

Q 13:207 What should be done if Form W-2 is incorrect, lost, or not received?

If Form W-2 is incorrect, lost, or not received, the employee-taxpayer should request an amended form from the employer.

Q 13:208 What should be done if the employer fails to issue Form W-2?

If an employee does not receive a Form W-2 by January 31, the employee should ask his or her employer for that form. Even if Form W-2 is not received from the employer, a SEP or SIMPLE IRA participant may be responsible for including the proper amount in income. For 2012 reporting, the applicable due date is January 31, 2013.

Q 13:209 What should be done if Form W-2 is not received by February 15?

Any employee who has not received Form W-2 by February 15 should call the IRS Teletax number, (800) 829-4477; enter the Teletax topic number, 154; and follow the recorded instructions. Teletax topics are also available at *http:www. irs.gov.*

Q 13:210 What information does the IRS need to provide a taxpayer with assistance in getting Form W-2?

When asked for assistance in obtaining Form W-2, the IRS may request the following information:

- Employer's name
- Employer's address
- Employer's telephone number
- Employer's identification number (if known)
- Employee's address
- Employee's Social Security number
- Employee's daytime telephone number
- Dates of employment
- Estimate of missing income amount or amount of federal income tax withheld

The information just listed may also be used for requesting taxpayer assistance on general tax matters that affect Form 1040.

Other Filings and Registrations

Q 13:211 Are SIMPLEs, SEPs, SARSEPs, or IRAs required to file annual registrations and annual returns with the IRS under Code Sections 6057 and 6058?

No. Only plans to which the vesting standards of Section 203 of ERISA apply are required to file annual registrations. The vesting standards of Code Sections 6057 and 6058 do not apply to SIMPLEs, SEPs, SARSEPs, or IRAs. [ERISA § 201(6); I.R.C. §§ 408(a)(4), 408(b)(4)]

Chapter 14

SIMPLE IRA Arrangements

Section 1421 of the Small Business Job Protection Act of 1996 (SBJPA) established a simplified tax-favored retirement plan for small employers—a savings incentive match plan for employees (SIMPLE)—under Section 408(p) of the Internal Revenue Code (Code). SIMPLE IRAs are established by employees in conjunction with the SIMPLE plans adopted by their employers. Employees may choose to make salary reduction contributions to a SIMPLE IRA instead of receiving those amounts as part of their regular compensation. Employers may opt to make matching contributions or nonelective contributions to SIMPLE IRAs on behalf of eligible employees.

All contributions are deposited with a financial institution authorized to accept IRA deposits. The employer may stipulate the institution where employees establish their SIMPLE IRAs. Special rules apply to such an entity, known as a designated financial institution.

This chapter examines SIMPLE arrangements established in the form of an IRA, employer and employee eligibility, employee notifications, salary reduction agreements, summary plan descriptions, the time and manner of making contributions and elections, effective dates, and administrative requirements and deposit rules for financial institutions and employers. It also discusses how to use model documents (Form 5305-SIMPLE and Form 5304-SIMPLE), whether an employer should use a model document or a prototype document, and the steps in the establishment of SIMPLE IRAs by eligible employees. SIMPLE IRA arrangements are compared with 401(k) plans that employ some of the SIMPLE IRA rules to satisfy nondiscrimination requirements. (See Appendix N for a chart comparing a SIMPLE arrangement in IRA form to one in the form of a 401(k) plan.)

Note. Line and box numbers are from the 2012 version of the forms unless indicated otherwise (see chapter 13).

Basic Concepts

Q 14:1 What is a *SIMPLE IRA plan*, and what is a *SIMPLE IRA*?

A *SIMPLE IRA plan* (sometimes referred to as a SIMPLE) is a written arrangement established by an employer under Code Section 408(p) that provides a simplified tax-favored retirement plan for small employers. A *SIMPLE IRA* is an individual retirement account or an individual retirement annuity that satisfies the following rules in addition to the rules for traditional IRAs:

1. The vesting requirements of Code Section 408(p)(3);
2. The participation requirements of Code Section 408(p)(4);
3. The administrative requirements of Code Section 408(p)(5); and
4. The requirement that a qualified salary reduction arrangement exist under which, and only under which, contributions may be made.

[I.R.C. § 408(p)(1)]

When an employer establishes a SIMPLE, each eligible employee may choose to have the employer make payments as elective (salary reduction) contributions under the plan into a SIMPLE IRA or to receive those payments directly in cash (see Q 14:80). The employer must then make either matching contributions or nonelective contributions (see Q 14:69).

Q 14:2 Why did Congress create the SIMPLE IRA?

Although the law provides a number of ways for individuals to save for retirement on a tax-favored basis (including employer-sponsored retirement plans such as qualified plans and simplified employee pension (SEP) plans), such plans must comply with many rules in order to receive tax-favored treatment, including in some cases complex nondiscrimination and administrative rules. In addition, top-heavy rules may require an employer to make a minimum contribution (generally 3 percent of every non-highly compensated participant's compensation). Congress created the SIMPLE IRA to provide a simpler tax-favored retirement plan for small employers. A SIMPLE entails none of the top-heavy or complex nondiscrimination rules or administrative burdens associated with a qualified plan or SEP. Thus, a SIMPLE IRA may be a less burdensome alternative for some employers than other types of deferred compensation agreements.

Q 14:3 Do SIMPLEs replace SARSEPs?

No. Although a SIMPLE may contain a matching formula and may be less complex for some employers to administer, SIMPLEs do not entirely replace salary reduction simplified employee pension plans (SARSEPs). One reason an employer may wish to retain its SARSEP, rather than establish a SIMPLE plan, is that for 2012 the maximum contribution that may be made under a SIMPLE for any employee is generally $14,000 ($11,500, plus catch-up contributions of $2,500), but not more than $28,000 (with a 3% matching contribution), compared to $50,000/$55,500 for a SEP or SARSEP established using a model form or a prototype plan document. Furthermore, mandatory matching or required nonelective contributions under a SIMPLE may not suit the needs of all employers.

Q 14:4 What are the design parameters of a SIMPLE IRA plan?

A SIMPLE IRA plan may be established using a model form, a prototype plan document, or an individually designed plan. All of the plan types are approved by the Internal Revenue Service (IRS) as to form.

An eligible employee may use model Form 5305-S (SIMPLE Individual Retirement Trust Account) or model Form 5305-SA (SIMPLE Individual Retirement Custodial Account) to establish a SIMPLE IRA (see Q 14:22). The forms are quite similar to the model forms—Forms 5305 and 5305-A—used to establish regular IRAs. A model SIMPLE IRA, however, may be used only in connection with a contribution made under a SIMPLE IRA plan or to receive a transfer or rollover from another SIMPLE IRA. Thus, a traditional IRA contribution, transfer, or rollover from a qualified plan or 403(b) arrangement will not be accepted by a model SIMPLE IRA.

Model SIMPLE IRAs remain SIMPLE IRAs even after two years of participation (see Q 14:128) (i.e., they do not become IRAs or allow regular IRA contributions after that time); neither do prototype SIMPLE IRAs. [*See* Listing of

Required Modifications (LRM) and Information Package for SIMPLE IRAs, § 2 (June 2010), available at *http://www.irs.gov* (search for "LRM") (visited on Aug. 22, 2012)]

Q 14:5 When did SIMPLEs become effective?

The provision of the Small Business Job Protection Act of 1996 (SBJPA) relating to SIMPLEs became effective for taxable years beginning after December 31, 1996.

Q 14:6 Must a SIMPLE be maintained on a calendar-year basis?

Yes. A SIMPLE must be maintained on a calendar-year basis. [I.R.C. § 408(p)(6)(C)] Thus, employer eligibility to establish a SIMPLE (see Qs 14:42–14:55) and SIMPLE IRA contributions (see Qs 14:69–14:89) are also determined on a calendar-year basis. [I.R.C. § 408(p)(6)(C)] Nevertheless, a SIMPLE may be started during the year (see Q 14:15).

Q 14:7 Must a SIMPLE IRA arrangement be in writing?

Yes. SIMPLE IRA and qualified salary reduction arrangements must be written arrangements of an eligible employer. [I.R.C. §§ 408(a), 408(b), 408(c), 408(p)(1), 408(p)(2)(A)]

Q 14:8 Who may be covered under a SIMPLE IRA plan?

Only an employee may be covered under a SIMPLE IRA plan maintained by an employer. For purposes of a SIMPLE IRA plan, an *employee* is a common-law employee of the employer (see Q 2:76); the term also includes self-employed individuals and leased employees described in Code Section 414(n). [I.R.C. § 408(p)(6)(B)]

Independent contractors performing work for an unrelated employer (if properly classified) are not treated as employees. The business employing an independent contractor (often a self-employed individual) may, however, be entitled to establish its own SIMPLE IRA plan.

> **Note.** The IRS model form for a SIMPLE IRA plan does not treat as an employee any individual who is a nonresident alien who received no earned income from the employer that constitutes earned income from sources within the United States. To include such an individual, an employer would have to use a prototype or individually designed SIMPLE that contains no restrictions on employee eligibility.

A household employee may also be covered under a SIMPLE IRA plan (see Qs 1:35, 14:63).

Q 14:9 May contributions made under a SIMPLE IRA plan be made to any type of IRA?

No. Contributions made under a SIMPLE IRA plan may be made only to a SIMPLE IRA, not to any other type of IRA. Conversely, the only contributions that can be made to a SIMPLE IRA are contributions under a SIMPLE IRA plan and rollovers or transfers from another SIMPLE IRA.

Q 14:10 May SIMPLE IRA contributions be made into an employer IRA under Code Section 408(c)?

No. Accounts established by employers and certain associations of employees under Code Section 408(c)—commonly referred to as group IRAs or employer-sponsored IRAs—are generally treated as individual retirement accounts as described in Code Section 408(a). Very little guidance has been issued as to whether SIMPLE IRA contributions may be made to a group IRA. [*See* Rev. Proc. 97-29, §§ 7.01, 7.013, 1997-1 C.B. 698] Generally, group IRAs are submitted to the IRS for approval.

Q 14:11 Is a SIMPLE IRA subject to tax?

No. A SIMPLE IRA is generally not subject to tax. A SIMPLE IRA is, however, subject to tax on unrelated business taxable income that exceeds $1,000 (e.g., an amount in excess of $1,000 that results from operating a grocery store within the IRA). [I.R.C. §§ 408(e), 511]

Further, if an owner engages in a prohibited transaction, such as borrowing on any account's assets or pledging the account as security for a loan, the account ceases to be treated as a SIMPLE IRA. The 15 percent prohibited transaction tax does not apply if the account ceases to be a SIMPLE IRA; instead, all amounts in the account become subject to tax. [I.R.C. §§ 408(e)(1), 408(e)(2), 408(e)(3), 4975(c)(3)]

Q 14:12 What is a *qualified salary reduction arrangement*?

A *qualified salary reduction arrangement,* one of the basic requirements of a SIMPLE IRA plan, is the provision that contains the rules that govern the types of contributions permitted to be made to a SIMPLE IRA: elective, and matching or nonelective. Such an arrangement will provide for either an employer matching contribution or a 2 percent nonelective contribution. In effect, the nonelective contribution replaces the requirement that there be a true matching contribution.

Q 14:13 What are the statutory requirements for a qualified salary reduction arrangement?

Under a qualified salary reduction arrangement, an eligible employee may elect to have his or her employer make payments to the employee directly in cash or as elective employer contributions to a SIMPLE IRA on behalf of the employee (see Qs 14:69, 14:80). The amount the employee elects to be deferred must be expressed as a percentage of compensation (see Q 14:76) and generally may not exceed a total of $11,500 for 2012 (see Q 14:83). [I.R.C. § 408(p)(2)(A)] The contribution limits have continued to increase since 2006 (see Q 14:84).

An employer is required to make a matching contribution (or, alternatively, a nonelective contribution) to the SIMPLE IRA for any year in an amount equal to as much of the amount that the employee elects to defer as does not exceed the applicable percentage (i.e., 3 percent) of compensation for the year. No other contributions may be made. However, a transfer or rollover from another SIMPLE IRA is permitted to be made into a SIMPLE IRA. [I.R.C. § 408(p)(2)(A), 408(p)(2)(B)]

Note. An employer may elect to apply a percentage lower than 3 percent (but not less than 1 percent) for any year for all employees eligible to participate in the plan for that year under certain circumstances (see Q 14:86).

Q 14:14 How long does a salary reduction agreement remain in effect?

In general, a salary reduction agreement may remain in effect as long as the individual remains an eligible employee under the SIMPLE or until the employee requests that salary reduction contributions be discontinued, the plan is terminated (see Q 14:108), or the employee provides the employer with a new salary reduction agreement as permitted under the SIMPLE.

Establishing a SIMPLE IRA Plan

Q 14:15 Must an employer establish a SIMPLE IRA plan on January 1?

No. An existing employer may establish a SIMPLE IRA plan effective on any date between January 1 and October 1 of a year beginning after December 31, 1996, provided the employer (or any predecessor employer; see Q 14:16) did not previously maintain a SIMPLE. If, however, an employer (or predecessor employer) previously maintained a SIMPLE, it may establish a SIMPLE effective only on January 1. [I.R.S. Notice 98-4, Q&A K-1, 1998-2 I.R.B. 26]

Q 14:16 What is a *predecessor employer*?

The term *predecessor employer* has not been defined for SIMPLE purposes; however, Letter Ruling 8240003 may shed some light on the matter. In that ruling, a husband and wife who were the sole proprietors of a business incorporated that business. The corporation adopted a defined benefit pension plan that had a one-year service requirement but recognized service with the predecessor proprietorship. Because the taxpayers were sole proprietors of the new corporation's predecessor, their years of service with the predecessor were counted for eligibility purposes under the plan. In the ruling, the husband and wife were treated as active participants for IRA contribution deduction purposes. Thus, a sole proprietorship that incorporated its business could be treated as a predecessor employer. [*See, e.g.*, Ltr. Rul. 199916010 (Jan. 11, 1999), general partnership that transfers its assets to a limited liability company but continues to employ its employees until the end of the year is the same employer for FICA and FUTA purposes.]

As under the proposed regulations issued under Code Section 415 in 2005, the final regulations issued in 2007, provide that, for purposes of Code Section 415, where a plan is maintained by successor

> [f]or purposes of section 415 and regulations promulgated under section 415, a former employer is a predecessor employer with respect to a participant in a plan maintained by an employer if the employer maintains a plan under which the participant had accrued a benefit while performing services for the former employer (for example, the employer assumed sponsorship of the former employer's plan, or the employer's plan received a transfer of benefits from the former employer's plan), but only if that benefit is provided under the plan maintained by the employer.

Where a plan is not maintained by successor, the final regulations provide the following:

> With respect to an employer of a participant, a former entity that antedates the employer is a predecessor employer with respect to the participant if, under the facts and circumstances, the employer constitutes a continuation of all or a portion of the trade or business of the former entity. This will occur, for example, where formation of the employer constitutes a mere formal or technical change in the employment relationship and continuity otherwise exists in the substance and administration of the business operations of the former entity and the employer.

[Treas. Reg. § 1.415(f)-1(c)]

Q 14:17 Why may a SIMPLE not be adopted after October 1?

There are at least two reasons why an employer generally may not adopt a SIMPLE after October 1, as follows:

1. To lessen the likelihood of overlapping election periods (see Q 14:91). Overlapping election periods could occur, for example, if the election period for the second year starts later than November 2 (60 days before the beginning of any year).
2. To prevent possible abuses when the plan is adopted late in the year. The SBJPA Committee on Finance Report states:

   The Committee believes that the goal of the nondiscrimination rules, broad pension coverage, is an important one. Unfortunately, the complicated nature of these rules may prevent small employers from establishing any plan. The Committee believes that the purpose of the

> nondiscrimination rules will be served in the case of small employers if all full-time employees are given the *opportunity to participate in the plan.*
> . . . [Emphasis added]

[Sen. Rep. No. 104-281, at 66 (1996); *see* SBJPA § 1421 (a)]

Example. Swift Manufacturing established a SIMPLE IRA on December 25 providing for a 3 percent matching contribution. Although all Swift employees are eligible to participate (and have received summary descriptions, forms, notices, and elections), only one, the company's president, elects to participate. Arguably, the adoption is not a valid one because the legislatively mandated "opportunity to participate" did not occur.

Special rules apply to employers that come into existence after October 1 (see Qs 14:53, 14:54).

Q 14:18 When is a SIMPLE IRA plan considered adopted?

If model Form 5305-SIMPLE is used, the plan is considered adopted when all appropriate boxes and blanks have been completed and the form has been executed by an employer and a designated financial institution (see Q 14:143).

If model Form 5304-SIMPLE is used, the plan is considered adopted when all appropriate boxes and blanks have been completed and the form has been executed by an employer.

In the case of a prototype, the plan will be considered adopted when all instructions for the adoption of the prototype have been followed.

Q 14:19 What is the effective date of a SIMPLE?

In general, the effective date of a SIMPLE is the date that the provisions of the plan become effective (see Qs 14:15, 14:18).

For IRS model Forms 5305-SIMPLE and 5304-SIMPLE and for prototype SIMPLEs, January 1 is the effective date. In the first year that an employer adopts a SIMPLE, however, the effective date may be any date from January 1 through October 1 of the applicable year. Because SIMPLEs are effective for taxable years beginning after 1996, January 1, 1997, is the earliest effective date permitted by law.

Note. Unless a SIMPLE provides for multiple election periods, an employee's election to participate can be set to expire on the day before the plan's effective date (see Q 14:91).

Q 14:20 When must a SIMPLE IRA be established for an employee?

A SIMPLE IRA is required to be established for an employee on or before the first date by which a contribution is required to be deposited into the employee's SIMPLE IRA. [I.R.S. Notice 98-4, Q&A G-5, G-6, 1998-2 I.R.B. 26]

Q 14:21 Is IRS approval of a SIMPLE IRA plan required?

No. Receipt of a favorable opinion letter or letter ruling on a SIMPLE IRA plan is not required as a condition of receiving favorable tax treatment; however, the form of a nonapproved plan may not be relied on by either an adopting employer or an employee. Without approval, clearly, there is no assurance that the form of the document will guarantee the deferral of income taxes and the deductibility of employer contributions.

Model IRS Forms

Q 14:22 Are model SIMPLE IRA plans and model SIMPLE IRAs approved by the IRS available?

Yes. The IRS has issued the following four model documents pertaining to SIMPLE IRA arrangements:

1. *Form 5305-SIMPLE, Savings Incentive Match Plan for Employees of Small Employers (SIMPLE) (subject to the DFI rules) (revised* February 2012). This form provides small employers with a way to adopt a SIMPLE IRA plan by using a model plan document, notification to employees, and salary reduction agreement. It is a model SIMPLE for use by employers that require all contributions to be made to SIMPLE IRAs established for participants at a designated financial institution (see Qs 14:143, 14:144). [IRS News Release IR-96-46 (Oct. 31, 1996)]
2. *Form 5304-SIMPLE, Savings Incentive Match Plan for Employees of Small Employers (SIMPLE) (not subject to the DFI rules) (revised* January 2012). This form provides small employers with a way to adopt a SIMPLE IRA plan by using a model plan document, notification to employees, and salary reduction agreement. It is a model SIMPLE for use by employers that permit plan participants to select the financial institutions at which their SIMPLE IRAs are established. [IRS News Release IR-96-55 (Dec. 30, 1996)]
3. *Form 5305-S, SIMPLE Individual Retirement Trust Account (revised March 2002)*. This form provides eligible employees and financial institutions with a model trust account that meets the requirements of Code Sections 408(a) and 408(p). A SIMPLE individual retirement account is established after the form is fully executed by both the participant and the trustee.
4. *Form 5305-SA, SIMPLE Individual Retirement Custodial Account (revised March 2002)*. This form provides eligible employees and financial institutions with a model custodial account that meets the requirements of Code Sections 408(a) and 408(p). A SIMPLE individual retirement account is established after the form is fully executed by both the participant and the custodian.

On January 13, 2010, the IRS announced that existing model SEP, SARSEP, and SIMPLE IRA plan documents do not have to be amended for GOZA, TIPRA, HERO, PPA, HEART, and WRERA in order to operate in accordance with statutory requirements (see Q 3:6).

In 2012, the IRS revised model Forms 5304-SIMPLE and 5305-SIMPLE. An employer that used the March 2002, August 2005, or September 2008 version of Form 5304-SIMPLE or Form 5305-SIMPLE to establish a model SIMPLE are not required to use the 2012 versions of the form. However, the IRS recommends adoption of the latest form. [Rev. Proc. 2010-48, § 4.01, 2010-50 I.R.B. 828]

Q 14:23 What was the 2006 EGTRRA relief initiative for amending plans?

The EGTRRA relief initiative provided sponsors of SIMPLE IRA plans an extended time to update their plans to take into account the law changes enacted by the EGTRRA and retain the many tax benefits afforded by these plans. The EGTRRA relief initiative for SIMPLE IRA plans is simple. All a taxpayer needs to do is adopt an IRS model SIMPLE IRA Form 5304-SIMPLE or Form 5305-SIMPLE as needed, with an August 2005 revision date shown in the top left-hand corner by December 31, 2006, to have relief. However, if a taxpayer had an IRS SIMPLE IRA plan with a revision date of March 2002 or later, the taxpayer did not need to take any action as the plan is up to date. The relief initiative was not extended beyond 2006.

If a taxpayer's SIMPLE IRA plan is not an IRS model plan, one indicator that it may have been updated is if it contains language providing for "catch-up contributions." If so, it likely has already been updated for EGTRRA. In addition, if the SIMPLE IRA plan was adopted or amended after 2001 (the issue or revision date on the document should be 2002 or later), it is likely that the plan includes EGTRRA provisions. Adopting employers should check with the document provider or the financial institution holding the SIMPLE IRA to be sure. The Simple IRA Relief initiative has not been extended (see chapter 17).

[Employee Plans News, Simple IRA Relief Initiative, IRS National Office (Mar. 10, 2006)]

EPCU examination program. The Employer Plans Compliance Unit (EPCU) examination program that was announced in March 2011 includes a SIMPLE project to check for potential non-amenders and a SEP project. Because an EPCU check is not an audit or investigation it does not preclude a sponsor's use of the EPCRS to inexpensively correct plan errors. An EPCU check generally involves identifying certain information and filings; books and records are not inspected. Failure to respond to a letter from the EPCU or provide the information requested within the time frame allowed could result in further action. Nonresponders could be audited later. The EPCU SEP project focuses on taxpayers who either sponsored a SEP or received a Form 5498 that reflected a SEP contribution amount in box 8 of Form 5498, IRA Contribution Information. The initial phase of this project will focus on determining the accuracy of information reported on Forms 5498. (See Q 3:7.) [Employee Plan News, Issue 2011-4 (Mar. 23, 2011), available at *http://www.irs.gov/pub/irs-tege/epn_2011_4.pdf* (visited on Aug. 22, 2012)]

Q 14:24 May a model SIMPLE be submitted by an adopting employer for approval by the IRS?

No. Eligible employers that adopt a model SIMPLE and follow its terms are assured that the arrangement meets the requirements of Code Section 408(p). Because automatic approval has been granted to model SIMPLE arrangements, no ruling, opinion, or determination letter from the IRS is necessary, and none will be issued.

Q 14:25 Must Form 5305-SIMPLE or Form 5304-SIMPLE be used to establish a SIMPLE IRA plan?

No. A SIMPLE IRA plan may be established by using Form 5305-SIMPLE, Form 5304-SIMPLE, or any other document that satisfies the statutory requirements. [I.R.C. § 408(p)(2)(A)]

Q 14:26 May an employer amend its SIMPLE IRA plan?

Yes. An employer may amend model Form 5305-SIMPLE or Form 5304 SIMPLE. It should be noted, however, that an employer may amend only the entries inserted in the blanks or boxes on either form. A SIMPLE IRA plan established using an IRS approved prototype document (fill-ins and optional provisions) may also be amended. It would appear that any amendment to a SIMPLE IRA plan can become effective only at the beginning of the calendar year and must conform to the content of the plan notice (see Qs 14:100, 14:108) for the calendar year. [*See* LRM Savings Incentive Match Plan for Employees of Small Employers, item 18 (June 2010)]

Q 14:27 May the model SIMPLE IRA forms be reproduced and reduced in size?

Yes. The model SIMPLE IRA forms, Form 5305-S and Form 5305-SA, may be reproduced and their size reduced to, for example, passbook size.

Q 14:28 May model SIMPLE forms be reproduced and used without making any reference to the IRS or its forms?

Very possibly. Rules exist for the word-for-word adoption of the language contained in the model forms for SEPs and SARSEPs (see Q 3:3). Similar rules will apply to SIMPLEs that use model Form 5305-SIMPLE or Form 5304-SIMPLE. If so, the provisions of the model forms may be reproduced on the letterhead of the employer or in pamphlets that omit all reference to the IRS and its forms.

Q 14:29 When should an employer not use Form 5305-SIMPLE to establish a SIMPLE IRA?

An employer should not use Form 5305-SIMPLE in any of the following circumstances:

1. It does not meet the employer's needs and objectives. Prototype SIMPLEs may contain more flexible provisions that better suit the employer's objectives. A prototype plan may also offer greater protection to the financial institution that sponsors the plan document or invests the contributions.
2. Employees are to be given the right to choose a financial institution that will initially receive contributions (i.e., the employer will not be designating or selecting the financial institution). (Form 5304-SIMPLE may be used for this purpose.)
3. Nonresident alien employees receiving no earned income from the employer that constitutes income from sources within the United States are to be eligible under the plan (see Q 14:57).
4. The employer wants to establish a SIMPLE arrangement in the form of a qualified 401(k) plan (see chapter 15).

Prototype SIMPLE IRAs and SIMPLE IRA Plans

Q 14:30 Has the IRS issued procedures regarding the form of a document intended to be a prototype SIMPLE IRA or prototype SIMPLE IRA plan?

Yes. Procedures for the creation of SIMPLE IRA prototypes were initially announced in Revenue Procedure 97-29 [1997-1 C.B. 698]. On January 2, 2002, the IRS issued Revenue Procedure 2002-10 [2002-4 I.R.B. 401]. This revenue procedure provided guidance on how to amend SIMPLE IRAs and SIMPLE IRA plans and disclosures to incorporate the changes brought about by EGTRRA and the new required minimum distribution rules. In 2010, the IRS updated its SIMPLE IRA plan LRM for changes brought about by the WFTRA (see Q 14:22).

Q 14:31 How does a sponsor request IRS approval on the form of a document intended to be a prototype SIMPLE IRA?

The procedures contained in Revenue Procedure 97-29 [1997-1 C.B. 698] may be used by a sponsor to submit an opinion letter request for the IRS's approval of a prototype SIMPLE IRA plan.

Revenue Procedure 97-29 provides that the same procedures and user fees (see Q 14:22) that apply to a submission for an opinion letter for a traditional IRA also apply to a SIMPLE IRA plan. Thus, a sponsor may apply to the IRS for an opinion letter for a prototype SIMPLE IRA plan in accordance with Revenue Procedure 87-50 [1987-2 C.B. 647]. Sample language that the service finds acceptable can be found in the SIMPLE IRA plan LRM (June 2010). [Rev. Proc. 97-29, §§ 4.01–4.03, 1997-1 C.B. 698]

Q 14:32 How does a sponsor request IRS approval on the form of a document intended to be a SIMPLE IRA plan?

Revenue Procedure 87-50 [1987-2 C.B. 647], as modified by Revenue Procedure 97-29 [1997-1 C.B. 698] provides the procedures that may be used by a sponsor or mass submitter (a "prototype sponsor") to submit an application for an opinion letter on the form of a document intended to be a prototype SIMPLE IRA plan. The sponsor's request must be submitted to the IRS using Form 5306-A (revised Jan. 2010), Application of Prototype Simplified Employee Pension (SEP) or Savings Incentive Match Plan for Employees of Small Employers (SIMPLE IRA Plan). The user fees are the same as those for a SEP (see Q 3:24). Sample language that the service finds acceptable can be found in the SIMPLE IRA Plan Listing of Required Modifications and Information Package (LRM) (June 2010). [Rev. Proc. 97-29, §§ 6.01–6.04, 1997-1 C.B. 698] Form 5306-A is also used for amending the form of a previously approved SIMPLE IRA plan. Revenue Procedure 87-50 also contains procedures for employers and employee associations to apply for a ruling on a Code Section 408(c) IRA.

Q 14:33 Who may use the procedures for creating a prototype SIMPLE IRA plan?

The procedures for creating a prototype SIMPLE IRA plan may be used by a sponsoring organization. As defined in the instructions to Form 5306-A (revised Jan. 2010), Application of Prototype Simplified Employee Pension (SEP) or Savings Incentive Match Plan for Employees of Small Employers (SIMPLE IRA Plan), a *sponsoring organization* may be any of the following entities:

- An insurance company,
- A trade or professional organization (other than an employee association),
- A savings and loan association that qualifies as a bank,
- A bank,
- A regulated investment company,
- A federally insured credit union, or
- An approved nonbank trustee.

Q 14:34 Which organizations must receive approval from the IRS to serve as a nonbank trustee or nonbank custodian?

An entity that is not a bank (as defined in Code Section 408(n)) or an insurance company within the meaning of Code Section 816 must receive approval from the IRS to serve as a nonbank trustee or nonbank custodian. A prospective nonbank trustee or custodian must file a written application with the Commissioner of Internal Revenue demonstrating that the requirements of Treasury Regulations Sections 1.408-2(e)(2) through 1.408-2(e)(7) will be met. If the application is approved, a written notice of approval will be issued to the applicant. The notice of approval will state the day on which it becomes effective, and (except as otherwise provided therein) will remain effective until revoked by the IRS or withdrawn by the applicant. Entities that have received such approval from the IRS may also sponsor certain retirement plans, custodial accounts under Code Section 403(b)(7), IRAs, and Roth IRAs. [Rev. Proc. 2012-8, 2012-1 I.R.B. 235, and Rev. Proc. 87-50, 1987-2 C.B. 647, as modified] The IRS user fee for approval to become a nonbank trustee is $20,000.

Q 14:35 May a nonbank trustee or custodian accept an IRA-based account before such notice of nonbank approval becomes effective?

No. A prospective nonbank trustee or custodian may not accept any IRA-based fiduciary account before such notice of approval becomes effective. In addition, a nonbank trustee or custodian may not accept a fiduciary account until after the plan administrator or the person for whose benefit the account is to be established is furnished with a copy of the written notice of approval issued to the applicant. Contributions made to such account are not deductible from gross income and will be disallowed if claimed on an income tax return. This notice should be contained in the IRA plan document package provided to the individual establishing the IRA, SIMPLE IRA, or SEP IRA.

> **Note.** The IRS maintains a list of entities, other than most banks and insurance companies, which are automatically approved, that have been approved to act as a nonbank trustee or custodian. [*See* I.R.S. Ann. 2007-47, 2007 I.R.B. 20, 1260 (May 14, 2007); update (as of May 1, 2011) available at *http://www.irs.gov/pub/irs-tege/nonbank_trustee_list.pdf* (visited on Aug. 22, 2012)] This list includes names, addresses, and the date each application was approved.

Q 14:36 Must an employer using a prototype SIMPLE IRA plan amend the plan if the form of the plan is amended by the sponsor?

Yes. An employer using a currently approved prototype SIMPLE IRA plan must adopt an amended SIMPLE IRA plan no later than 180 days after the sponsoring organization receives a new approval letter for the plan.

Q 14:37 Must the disclosure statement of a SIMPLE IRA plan be modified?

Yes. Even though an employer generally has 180 days to adopt a revised SIMPLE plan after it has been approved by the IRS, all employees participating under the employer's current SIMPLE IRA plan must be notified of the changes made. In effect, notification will be accomplished by updating the plan's disclosure statement and providing the new statement to all participating employees.

Q 14:38 Is there a fee for requesting IRS approval of a prototype SIMPLE IRA or SIMPLE IRA plan?

Yes. The IRS imposes a user fee for the review of plan documents and their amendments (see Q 3:24), including the review of each prototype SIMPLE IRA or SIMPLE IRA plan established pursuant to Revenue Procedure 97-29. [Rev. Proc. 97-29, §§ 4.01, 6.02, 1997-1 C.B. 698]

Q 14:39 Should a prototype sponsor submit a copy of the underlying SIMPLE IRA when applying for prototype plan approval?

No. When using model amendments under Revenue Procedure 97-29 [1997-1 C.B. 698], the prototype sponsor should not submit the underlying SIMPLE IRA to the IRS.

Q 14:40 May a prototype document be designed to be used as a SIMPLE IRA or as a non-SIMPLE IRA?

No. The IRS will not issue an opinion with respect to any prototype sponsor concerning a SIMPLE IRA that, by its terms, can be used as either a SIMPLE IRA or a non-SIMPLE IRA (i.e., as a traditional IRA). [Rev. Proc. 97-29, § 4.02, 1997-1 C.B. 698]

Q 14:41 May a SIMPLE IRA and a SIMPLE IRA plan be combined in one document?

No. The IRS will not issue an opinion letter to a prototype sponsor for a SIMPLE IRA plan that combines a SIMPLE IRA plan and a SIMPLE IRA in the same document. [Rev. Proc. 97-29, § 6.05, 1997-1 C.B. 698]

Employer Eligibility

Q 14:42 May any employer establish a SIMPLE IRA plan?

No. A SIMPLE IRA plan may be established only by an employer that had no more than 100 employees who earned $5,000 or more in compensation (see Qs 14:56–14:59, 14:61–14:64) during the preceding calendar year (the 100-employee limit). [I.R.C. § 408(p)(2)(C)(i)]

Q 14:43 May any employees be excluded for purposes of the 100-employee limit?

No. For purposes of the 100-employee limit (see Q 14:42), all employees employed at any time during the prior calendar year are taken into account, regardless of whether they are eligible to participate in the SIMPLE IRA plan. Thus, certain unionized employees who are excludable under the rules of Code

Section 410(b)(3), nonresident alien employees, and employees who have not met the plan's minimum eligibility requirements (see Qs 14:56–14:62) must be taken into account. Employees also include self-employed individuals who received earned income from the employer during the year. [I.R.C. §§ 401(c)(1), 408(p)(4)(A), 408(p)(4)(B)]

Q 14:44 How are leased employees treated for purposes of the 100-employee limit?

If an employer has leased employees who are required to be treated as its own employees under Code Section 414(n), those leased employees must be treated as employees of the employer for purposes of the employer's eligibility to establish a SIMPLE IRA plan (see Q 14:42). [I.R.C. §§ 414(b), 414(c), 414(m), 414(n), 414(o)]

Q 14:45 How are related employers treated for purposes of a SIMPLE IRA plan?

Certain related employers (trades or businesses under common control) must be treated as a single employer (see Qs 2:5–2:9, 2:12–2:14, 2:17). As a result, individuals working for related employers are treated as if they were employed by a single employer for purposes of satisfying the SIMPLE requirements.

Related employers include the following:

- A controlled group of corporations under Code Section 414(b)
- A partnership or sole proprietorship under common control under Code Section 414(c)
- An affiliated service group under Code Section 414(m)

Example. Paul owns Peach, a computer rental agency that has 80 employees who received more than $5,000 in compensation in 2011. Paul also owns Pear, a company that repairs computers and has 60 employees who received more than $5,000 in compensation in 2011. Paul is the sole proprietor of both businesses. Code Section 414(c) provides that the employees of partnerships and sole proprietorships that are under common control are treated as employees of a single employer. Thus, for purposes of the SIMPLE rules, all 140 employees are treated as being employed by the same employer. Because together they employed over 100 employees who received more than $5,000 in compensation in 2011, neither Peach nor Pear is eligible to establish a SIMPLE IRA plan for 2012.

Q 14:46 Is there a grace period for an employer that no longer satisfies the 100-employee limit?

Yes. An employer that previously maintained a SIMPLE IRA plan is treated as satisfying the 100-employee limit (see Q 14:42) for the two calendar years immediately following the calendar year for which it last satisfied that requirement. [I.R.C. § 408(p)(2)(C)(i)(II)]A special transition rule applies if the failure to satisfy the 100-employee limit is the result of an acquisition, disposition, or similar transaction involving the employer (see Q 14:47). [I.R.C. § 408(p)(10)]

Example 1. Train Company employed 90 individuals during 2009 and 2010. It establishes a SIMPLE IRA plan for 2011 for employees who earned at least $5,000 from Train during any two previous years. During 2011, Train hires 50 additional employees. All employees earn at least $5,000. If it were not for the grace period, Train would not be eligible to maintain a SIMPLE for 2012 because it employed over 100 employees earning at least $5,000 in 2011 (the preceding year).

Example 2. Big Boat Company employed 90 individuals during 2009 and 2010. All employees earned at least $5,000. Big Boat established a SIMPLE IRA plan in 2010 for employees who earned at least $5,000 from the company during any two previous years. During 2011, Big Boat hires 50 new employees. Although Big Boat would be ineligible to maintain a SIMPLE for 2012 because it had over 100 employees earning at least $5,000 during 2011, it may continue to maintain its existing SIMPLE during the two-year grace period (i.e., for 2012 and 2013).

Example 3. Arch Company employed 85 individuals during 2009 and 2010. All employees earned at least $5,000. Arch establishes a SIMPLE IRA plan for 2011 for employees who earned at least $5,000 from the company during any two previous years. Sixty of the original 85 employees quit during the first half of 2011. During the second half of 2011, Arch hires 50 new employees. Arch would not be an eligible employer for 2012 if it were not for the grace period (because during 2011 it had more than 100 employees with compensation of $5,000 or more).

Note. Although it is not entirely clear, it appears that the two-year grace period applies to the year following the year that the employer was no longer an eligible employer at *any time* during the year. For instance, an employer that exceeds the 100-employee limit in mid-year would, for purposes of the grace period only, be treated as an ineligible employer for that year (even though it was an eligible employer on January 1 of that year). If the grace period is measured as of the first day of the preceding year (when the employer was an eligible employer), then the employer may continue the plan for three years, and the grace period in the examples above would have to be extended by one additional year.

Q 14:47 What transition rule applies to the 100-employee limit?

If the failure to satisfy the 100-employee limit (see Q 14:42) is the result of an acquisition, disposition, or similar transaction involving the employer, the qualified plan transition rule for coverage when there is an acquisition or disposition replaces the two-year grace period (i.e., the grace period runs through the end of the year following the acquisition or disposition). [I.R.C. §§ 408(p)(2)(C)(i)(II),408(p)(10), 410(b)(6)(C)]

Thus, an employer maintaining a SIMPLE IRA plan that fails to meet any applicable requirement because of an acquisition, disposition, or similar transaction will not be treated as failing to meet that requirement during a transition period. The transition period ends on the last day of the second calendar year in which the transaction occurs.

The term *applicable requirement* includes only the following:

1. That an employer be an eligible employer (see Qs 14:42, 15:6);
2. That, generally, the arrangement be the only plan of an employer (see Qs 14:48, 15:14); and
3. That all eligible employees who satisfy the compensation and service requirements, if any are specified, be given the opportunity to participate.

For the transition rules to apply, the qualified salary reduction arrangement maintained by the employer must satisfy the requirements of Code Section 408(p) after the transaction as if the employer that maintained the arrangement before the transaction had remained a separate employer. As well, coverage under the plan may not be significantly changed during the transition period (except by reason of the change in members of a group) and the plan must meet such other requirements as the Secretary of the Treasury may prescribe by regulation. [I.R.C. § 408(p)(10)]

Q 14:48 May an employer make contributions under a SIMPLE for a calendar year if it maintains another plan?

No. An employer may not make contributions under a SIMPLE IRA plan for a calendar year if the employer, or a predecessor employer, maintains a qualified plan (see Qs 14:49, 14:61) under which any of its employees receives an allocation of contributions (in the case of a defined contribution plan) or has an increase in a benefit accrued or treated as an accrued benefit under Code Section 411(d)(6) (in the case of a defined benefit plan) for any plan year beginning or ending in that calendar year. [I.R.C. § 408(p)(2)(D)(i)] Thus, for example, if the employer establishes a SEP, which is considered a qualified plan for this purpose (see Q 14:49), and makes a contribution to it for a plan year that includes any part of the SIMPLE year (which is always a calendar year), *all* SIMPLE contributions become excess contributions and should be treated as wages by the employer on Form W-2, Wage and Tax Statement (see Qs 14:163–14:166). However, an employer may adopt a SIMPLE IRA plan for non-collectively bargained employees without violating the exclusive plan requirement even though the employer also maintains a qualified plan for collectively bargained employees. [I.R.C. § 408(p)(2)(D)(i)]

Certain types of contributions to qualified plans are disregarded for this purpose; that is, they are not treated as contributions (see Q 14:50).

A special transition rule allows an employer to maintain a qualified plan and a SIMPLE IRA plan at the same time because of an acquisition, disposition, or other similar transaction (see Q 14:46). The special transition rule provides that the SIMPLE IRA will be treated as a qualified salary reduction arrangement for the year of the transaction and the following year (see Q 14:47).

Q 14:49 What types of plans are considered to be *qualified plans* for the purpose of denying a SIMPLE contribution?

For the purpose of denying a SIMPLE contribution, *qualified plan* means a plan, contract, pension, or trust described in Code Section 219(g)(5), as follows:

1. A qualified pension, profit-sharing, or stock bonus plan under Code Section 401(a) that includes a tax-exempt trust;
2. An annuity plan under Code Section 403(b);
3. A governmental plan (a plan established by the United States, a state, a political subdivision, or an agency of a state or a political subdivision) other than an eligible deferred compensation plan under Code Section 457(b);
4. Certain trusts funded solely with employee contributions under Code Section 501(c)(18);
5. A SEP or SARSEP; and
6. A SIMPLE.

It follows, then, from item 6 that an employer may not maintain more than one SIMPLE plan without losing its deduction (see also Q 14:52). [I.R.C. §§ 219(g)(5)(A), 408(p)(2)(D); *see* SIMPLE IRA LRM § 3 (June 2010)]

Q 14:50 Are forfeitures, transfers, and rollovers disregarded in determining whether a contribution has been made to a qualified plan?

Except to the extent forfeitures replace otherwise required contributions, transfers, rollovers, and forfeitures are disregarded in determining whether a contribution has been made to a qualified plan (see Q 14:49). [I.R.S. Notice 98-4, Q&A B-3, 1998-2 I.R.B. 26]

Q 14:51 Are tax-exempt organizations and governmental entities permitted to maintain a SIMPLE IRA plan?

Yes. In contrast to the IRS's explicit refusal to permit them to establish SARSEPs, tax-exempt organizations and governmental entities are permitted to establish SEP and SIMPLE IRA plans. [I.R.S. Notice 98-4, Q&A B-4, 1998-2 I.R.B. 26; I.R.C. § 408(k)(6)(E); Ltr. Ruls. 8833047, 8824019]

Excludable contributions may be made to the SIMPLE IRAs of employees of tax-exempt organizations and governmental entities on the same basis as contributions may be made to employees of other eligible employers. [I.R.S. Notice 98-4, Q&A B-4, 1998-2 I.R.B. 26]

It should be noted that a governmental entity may not maintain a SIMPLE arrangement in the form of a 401(k) plan. [I.R.C. §§ 401(k)(4)(B)(ii), 401(k)(4)(B)(iii)]

Q 14:52 May an individual participate in a SIMPLE IRA plan and an eligible plan under Code Section 457(b) without violating the only-plan-of-the-employer rule?

Yes. Contributions made under a 457 plan do not violate the only-plan-of-the-employer rule because such a plan is not a qualified plan, nor treated as a qualified plan for the purpose of denying SIMPLE contributions (see Q 14:49). [I.R.C. §§ 219(g)(5)(A), 219(g)(5)(B), 408(p)(2)(D)(ii)]

> **Note.** For 2001 and earlier years, the dollar limits under an eligible 457 plan (generally the lesser of $8,500 or 25 percent of gross compensation for 2001) were, however, reduced by the amount of elective employer contributions deferred by the employee under the SIMPLE (or 401(k) SIMPLE) (see Q 14:61). [I.R.C. § 457(c)(2)(B)(i) 457(c)(2)(B)(i)] The EGTRRA removed the coordination of limits and increased the general Section 457 deferral limit to the lesser of $11,000 (as indexed; $17,000 for 2012) or 100 percent of compensation for taxable years beginning after 2001.

Q 14:53 May a new employer establish a SIMPLE?

Yes. A new employer may qualify as an employer eligible to establish a SIMPLE; however, the employer would have to adopt extremely liberal eligibility requirements. Otherwise, the plan would have no participants.

In the case of a new employer, it is unclear whether the IRS may require that the 100-employee limit (see Q 14:42) be satisfied during the first 30 days that the business was in existence (as it does for the 25-employee limit for SARSEPs; see Q 2:25). [Rev. Proc. 91-44, pt. VI, § D, 1991-2 C.B. 733] Arguably, a new employer qualifies because it had no employees in the previous year.

Q 14:54 How are employers that come into existence after October 1 treated?

The requirement that a SIMPLE become effective on any date between January 1 and October 1 (see Q 14:19) does not apply to an employer that comes into existence after October 1 of the year the SIMPLE is established if the employer establishes the SIMPLE as soon as administratively feasible after it comes into existence.

Q 14:55 May an employer that terminates a SIMPLE start another SIMPLE in the same tax year?

No. If an employer (or predecessor employer) previously maintained a SIMPLE, it may establish a SIMPLE only effective on the following January 1 (see Q 14:108). [I.R.S. Notice 98-4, Q&A K-1, 1998-2 I.R.B. 26]

Employee Eligibility

Q 14:56 Which employees are eligible to participate in a SIMPLE IRA plan?

All employees (see Q 14:8) of an employer (see Q 14:45) who received at least $5,000 in compensation from the employer during any two preceding calendar years (whether or not consecutive) and who are reasonably expected to receive at least $5,000 in compensation during the calendar year are eligible to participate in the employer's plan for the calendar year. [I.R.C. § 408(p)(4)(A)] The term *reasonably expected* is not defined.

> **Example 1.** Harry's employer maintains a SIMPLE IRA plan in 2012. The plan uses the maximum service provision (two years) and the maximum compensation amount ($5,000) for determining eligibility. Harry earned $10,000 in 2004 and 2005 but did not perform any service during 2006, 2007, and 2008. During 2009, 2010 and 2011, Harry earned $4,000 each year. Harry is reasonably expected to earn $7,000 in 2012. He is eligible to participate in 2012 because he can reasonably be expected to earn at least $5,000 in compensation during the current year and he earned at least $5,000 in two previous years (2004 and 2005).

> **Example 2.** For 18 years, Donna has been a full-time employee of the Giant Motor Company, which maintains a SIMPLE. Donna's annual salary is $36,000. Shortly before the plan's election period (Nov. 2–Dec. 31), Donna requests and is granted an 11-month personal leave of absence to start on January 1, 2012. For 2012, Donna is reasonably expected to earn only $3,000 and will not be eligible to participate in the plan for 2012 because Giant imposed a $4,000 compensation requirement for the current year.

> **Example 3.** The facts are the same as those in Example 2, except that (1) on January 2, 2012, Donna decides not to take the leave of absence; (2) Giant had duly elected to make the 2 percent nonelective contribution; and (3) the plan requires that an employee have $5,000 of current compensation to participate but only $2,000 of previous compensation to be eligible. Donna is not entitled to receive a nonelective contribution because she was not an eligible employee; that is, she was not reasonably expected to earn $5,000 (even though she did earn more than $2,000).

Certain employees may be excluded from participation (see Q 14:57), although the plan may not impose an age requirement.

Caution. Independent contractors (see Qs 2:75–2:83) are rarely considered employees. Employers should take note, however, that in many cases part-time employees are misidentified as independent contractors (see Q 2:80). [*See* Treas. Reg. § 31.3401(c)-1(b); Rev. Rul. 87-41, 1987-1 C.B. 296]

Q 14:57 May an employee be excluded from participation in a SIMPLE IRA plan?

Yes. An employer, at its option, may exclude from eligibility for participation in a SIMPLE IRA plan any employee described in Code Section 410(b)(3). [I.R.C. § 408(p)(4)(B)] The document must affirmatively exclude such employees by classification.

The following employees may be excluded:

1. An employee who is included in a unit of employees covered by an agreement that the Secretary of Labor finds to be a collective bargaining agreement between employee representatives and one or more employers, if there is evidence that retirement benefits were the subject of good-faith bargaining between such employee representatives and such employer or employers.
2. In the case of a trust established or maintained pursuant to an agreement that the Secretary of Labor finds to be a collective bargaining agreement between air pilots represented in accordance with Title II of the Railway Labor Act and one or more employees, all employees are *not* covered by that agreement.
3. An employee who is a nonresident alien and who received no earned income (within the meaning of Code Section 911(d)(2)) from the employer that constitutes income from sources within the United States (within the meaning of Code Section 861(a)(3)).

The employer aggregation rules (see Q 14:45) and leased employee rules (see Q 14:44) apply for purposes of Code Section 408(p). Thus, for example, if two related employers must be aggregated under the rules of Code Section 414(b), then all employees of either employer who satisfy the eligibility criteria must be allowed to participate in the SIMPLE IRA plan.

The model SIMPLE forms (see Q 14:4) automatically exclude from participation nonresident alien employees receiving no earned income from an employer that constitutes income from sources within the United States, but they allow an employer to choose whether to exclude employees covered under a collective bargaining agreement for which retirement benefits were the subject of good-faith bargaining.

If the nonresident alien is a regular member of a crew of a foreign vessel engaged in transportation between the United States and a foreign country or a U.S. possession, compensation received by the nonresident alien is not considered U.S. source income for any qualified retirement plan, including a SEP, a SARSEP, or a SIMPLE. [I.R.C. § 861(a)(3)]

Q 14:58 May an employer impose less restrictive eligibility requirements for its SIMPLE IRA plan?

Yes. An employer may impose less restrictive eligibility requirements for its SIMPLE IRA plan by eliminating or reducing the compensation requirement for the previous years or for the current year, or both, under its plan. An employer could, for instance, allow participation for employees who received $2,500 in compensation during any preceding calendar year.

Example. Marden Company, an eligible employer, establishes a SIMPLE for 2012. All employees who received any compensation from Marden during any one preceding year are eligible. Nick worked for Marden in 2011; therefore, he will be eligible to participate in his second year of employment.

Q 14:59 May an employer impose eligibility requirements for its SIMPLE IRA plan that are more restrictive than those set out by SBJPA and the IRS?

No. An employer may not impose requirements for participating in its SIMPLE IRA plan that are more restrictive than those set forth by the SBJPA and the IRS.

Q 14:60 May an employer use a rolling eligibility period to exclude employees who become eligible for its SIMPLE IRA plan?

It is unclear whether a SIMPLE IRA plan may be amended each year to increase the number of years of service needed to participate.

Example. Marvin, the owner and only employee of a newly established small business, creates a SIMPLE IRA plan using a model SIMPLE for 2012. The plan does not have a service requirement. A new employee, Carlos, is hired in June, and Marvin amends the plan to provide for a one-year service requirement so that Carlos will not be eligible to participate until the following year. In 2012, Marvin amends the plan, this time to provide for a two-year service requirement. Again, Carlos is ineligible. It is not known whether such a rolling eligibility period will pass IRS scrutiny.

Q 14:61 What limitations apply when an employee participates in a SIMPLE IRA plan if that employee also participates in a plan of an unrelated employer for the same year?

An employee may participate in a SIMPLE IRA plan even if he or she also participates in a plan of an unrelated employer in the same year. The employee's salary reduction contributions are subject, however, to the limit of Code Section 402(g), which provides an aggregate limit on the exclusion for elective deferrals for any individual. For years beginning after 2001, an employee who participates in a SIMPLE IRA plan and an eligible deferred compensation plan described in Code Section 457(b) is not subject to any coordination rules. For 2012, the

Section 457(b) elective deferral limit is $17,000 ($22,500 with catch-up contributions if age 50 or older) or 100 percent of compensation. [I.R.C. § 402(g)(3), 402(k)]

> **Note.** An employer that establishes a SIMPLE plan is not responsible for monitoring compliance with the limit imposed by Code Section 402(g), provided the SIMPLE is the only plan maintained by the employer. [I.R.S. Notice 98-4, Q&A C-3, 1998-2 I.R.B. 26]

Q 14:62 How are rehired employees and employees who are eligible to participate immediately upon initial hire treated?

For rehired employees and employers who are eligible to participate immediately on initial hire, the requirement that specific information, notices, and elections regarding a SIMPLE be given before the 60-day period for making or modifying a salary reduction election may be waived (see Qs 14:91, 14:100, 14:101).

Compensation

Q 14:63 For purposes of the SIMPLE rules, how is *compensation* defined for an individual who is not self-employed?

For purposes of the SIMPLE rules, *compensation* for a person who is not self-employed generally means the amount described in Code Section 6051(a)(3) (wages, tips, and other compensation from the employer subject to income tax withholding under Code Section 3401(a)) and amounts described in Code Section 6051(a)(8), including elective contributions made under a SIMPLE IRA plan and compensation deferred under a 457 plan. [I.R.C. §§ 408(p)(6)(A)(i), 3401(a), 6051(a)(3), 6051(a)(8)]

The WFTRA (H.R. 1308, § 404(d)) amends the definition of *compensation,* for purposes of determining contributions to a SIMPLE plan, to be determined "without reference to Code Section 3401(a)(3)." The change is effective for tax years after 2001. As changed, wages paid to certain domestic workers may be treated as compensation, even though such amounts are not subject to income tax withholding. Thus, it is not necessary that the worker and the worker's employer elect to subject the worker's wages to income tax withholding for allowing SIMPLE IRA contributions to be made. [I.R.C. § 408(p)(6), *cross-referencing* I.R.C. §§ 6051(a)(3), 3401(a)(3); *see also* I.R.C. §§ 3101, 3111, 3121(a)(7) regarding FICA for domestic services in private home] IRS model documents (Forms 5304-SIMPLE and 5305-SIMPLE) were revised in September 2005 to include amounts paid for domestic service in a private home, local college club, or local chapter of a college fraternity or sorority (see Qs 1:34, 14:22) to the definition of compensation. The IRS model documents (Forms 5304-SIMPLE and 5305-SIMPLE) were last revised in 2012 (see Q 14:22).

For purposes of applying the 100-employee limit and determining whether an employee is eligible to participate in a SIMPLE IRA plan by virtue of previous amounts of compensation (see Qs 14:42–14:47), an employee's compensation also includes his or her elective deferrals under a 401(k) plan, a SARSEP, and a 403(b) annuity contract. [I.R.C. §§ 408(p)(6)(A), 6051(a)(3), 6051(a)(8)]

Compensation does not include amounts deferred under a Section 125 plan. [*See* SIMPLE IRA plan LRM §§ 6–7 (June 2010), available at *www.irs.gov* (search for "lrm")]

> **Example.** Ian, an eligible employee of Cork Products, Inc., earned $10,000 in 2012 and elected to defer 5 percent of that amount into an IRA established under Cork Products' SIMPLE. Although only $9,500 was reported on his Form W-2, Ian's compensation for plan purposes was $10,000 ($9,500 + $500). Cork Products elected to make a 2 percent nonelective contribution for 2012; Ian received $200 ($10,000 × .02).

At one time, it was unclear whether compensation earned before a new SIMPLE IRA plan's effective date (see Q 14:19) might be ignored or had to be prorated (see Q 14:87). Which course of action applies is important in determining the amount of compensation that is considered by the employer in making its contribution. IRS guidance now provides that nonelective and matching contributions are based on compensation "for the entire calendar year." [I.R.S. Notice 98-4, 1998-2 I.R.B. 26; I.R.C. §§ 401(a)(17), 408(p)(6)(A); Treas. Reg. § 1.401(a)(17)-1(b)(3)(iii)(A)]

Q 14:64 For purposes of the SIMPLE rules, how is *compensation* defined for a self-employed individual?

For purposes of the SIMPLE rules, *compensation* for a self-employed individual means net earnings from self-employment (NESE) determined under Code Section 1402(a), before subtracting any contributions made under the SIMPLE IRA plan on behalf of the individual. [I.R.C. § 408(p)(6)(A)(ii)] Code Section 1402(a)(12) provides for a deduction "in lieu of the deduction provided by section 164(f)." The IRS takes the position that the "in lieu of" deduction provided by Code Section 1402(a)(12) is taken into account (i.e., is subtracted to arrive at NESE).

> **Example.** Harriet, a sole proprietor, has $10,000 of personal service income from self-employment and is the only participant in a SIMPLE IRA plan. Harriet's contribution would be based on $9,235, according to the IRS. The IRS determines the amount by multiplying net profits ($10,000) by the Section 1402(a) percentage reduction (.9235).

After 2001, NESE are determined without regard to Code Section 1402(c)(6). Thus, NESE include earnings from services performed while claiming exemption from self-employment tax as a member of a group conscientiously opposed to Social Security benefits. [I.R.C. § 408(p)(6)(A)(ii)]

In the authors' opinion, unlike the definition used for SEPs, the definition of *compensation* used for SIMPLEs does not specifically require that compensation be determined with regard to the deduction allowed the taxpayer by Code Section 164(f) (i.e., net earnings do not have to be reduced by the deduction for half of an individual's self-employment tax). [I.R.C. §§ 401(c)(2), 408(p)(6)(A)(ii)] Because the deduction authorized by Code Section 1402(a)(12) is in lieu of a deduction that does not apply, no adjustment appears to be required under Code Section 1402(a)(12) in determining the compensation of a self-employed individual under Code Section 408(p). In the previous example, therefore, compensation is $10,000.

> **Note 1.** The definition of compensation for a self-employed individual that applies to a SEP or qualified plan is found in Code Section 401(c)(1), regarding the definition of *earned income*. That section also uses the Code Section 1402(a) definition (see below), but makes several adjustments. One of the adjustments is to specifically require that earned income be determined "with regard to the deduction allowed the taxpayer by section 164(f)" relating to the deduction for one-half of the individual's self-employment tax (reported on Form 1040, line 27). No such adjustment is mentioned in Code Section 408(p)(6)(A)(ii) referring to Code Section 1402(a). Why, then, is this adjustment made?

IRS guidance suggests that $9,235 is the correct amount of compensation. The Employee Plans Division of the IRS has offered a slightly different interpretation of the calculation. To the consternation of many practitioners, however, except for unofficial information appearing in an IRS publication that resulted in the $9,235 figure, it has not been clarified authoritatively. Thus, the issue is not settled.

Page 67 of IRS Publication 590, *Individual Retirement Arrangements (IRAs)*, for use in preparing 2011 returns, states the following:

> **Compensation**. For purposes of the SIMPLE plan rules, your compensation for a year generally includes the following amounts:
>
> 1. Wages, tips, and other pay from the employer that is subject to income tax withholding,
> 2. Deferred amounts elected under any 401(k) plans, 403(b) plans, government (section 457(b)) plans, SEP plans, and SIMPLE plans.
>
> **Self-employed individual compensation.** For purposes of the SIMPLE plan rules, if you are self-employed, your compensation for a year is your net earnings from self-employment (line 4, Section A, or line 6, Section B, of Schedule SE (Form 1040)) before subtracting any contributions made to a SIMPLE IRA on your behalf.
>
> For these purposes, net earnings from self-employment include services performed while claiming exemption from self-employment tax as a member of a group conscientiously opposed to social security benefits.

> **Note 2.** Line 4 and line 6 of Form 1040, Schedule SE are computed after taking into account the 92.35 percent "in lieu of" deduction required under Code Section 1402(a)(12), which states:

In lieu of the deduction provided by section 164(f) (relating to deduction for one-half of self-employment taxes), there shall be allowed a deduction equal to the product of—

(A) the taxpayer's net earnings from self-employment for the taxable year (determined without regard to this paragraph), and

(B) one-half of the sum of the rates imposed by subsections (a) and (b) of section 1401 for such year.

The result of (A) above is the actual net profit from the Schedule C and the result of (B) above is one-half of 15.3 percent, or 7.65 percent. (100% less 7.65% = 92.35%.) Thus, the formula for determining compensation for a self-employed individual is:

Net Profit (from Schedule C) × .9235 = Compensation

Caution. Code Section 1402(a)(12)(B), above, as amended by the Patient Protection and Affordable Care Act, § 9015 (Pub. L. No. 111-148), inserts "(determined without regard to the rate imposed under paragraph (2) of section 1401(b))" after "for such year" with respect to remuneration received, and tax years beginning, after December 31, 2012. In tax years beginning after 2012, Code Section 1402(a)(12) reads as follows:

(B) one-half of the sum of the rates imposed by subsections (a) and (b) of section 1401 for such year (determined without regard to the rate imposed under paragraph (2) of section 1401(b)).

Note 3. As amended, Code Section 1402(a)(12)(B) provides additional hospital insurance tax (0.9%) on self-employment income in excess of certain threshold amounts. The one-half of self-employment taxes that are deductible under Code Section 164(f), does not include the additional Medicare tax. Thus, no deduction is allowed under Code Section 1402(a)(12) for the additional SECA tax, and the deduction under Code Section 164(f) is determined without regard to the additional SECA tax.

Example 1. Shannon, a calendar year taxpayer, owns Travel Dreams, an unincorporated travel agency that maintains a SIMPLE IRA plan for 2012. She has two employees, Frank and Delilah, who earn $30,000 and $25,000, respectively. Shannon's net profit before any contribution is made and before the wage deduction is $130,000. Frank defers $4,000, and Delilah defers $1,000. Shannon has elected to make a 3 percent matching contribution.

	Gross Compensation	*Total Deferral*	*Match*	*Contribution*
Frank	$30,000	$4,000	$ 900	$4,900
Delilah	$25,000	$1,000	$ 750	$1,750
Totals	$55,000	$5,000	$1,650	$6,650

Shannon deducts the $6,650 total contributions for her employees on Schedule C, Profit or Loss from Business (Sole Proprietorship), to Form 1040 as a plan contribution. The wage deduction on her Schedule C is $50,000

($55,000 – $5,000). Shannon's pre-plan NESE is $75,000 ($130,000 – $55,000)

Shannon's profit of $130,000 minus the wage deduction and the total contributions for her employees is as follows:

$130,000 – $50,000 – $6,650 = $73,350

Shannon's "compensation" would be computed as follows:

$73,350 × .9235 = $67,738.73

Shannon decides to defer the maximum of $14,000. Her matching contribution would be calculated as follows:

$67,738.73 × .03 = $2,032.16

Shannon's total contribution for herself is $16,032.16 ($14,000 + $2,032.16). She would deduct the $16,032.16 on Form 1040 in the "Adjusted Gross Income" section on page 1.

It is the authors' opinion that, as a matter of legislative tax policy and interpretation, the 7.65 percent reduction that occurs when a methodology based on line 4 of Section A or line 6 of Section B of Schedule SE, Self-Employment Tax, is used should not apply to a SIMPLE IRA plan. Furthermore, the instructions offer no guidance and no suggestions as to what would happen if the individual had additional earned income (positive or negative) from a nonrelated or noncontrolled employer that would require the use of Section B of Schedule SE. Be that as it may, as a practical matter, until further guidance is issued by the IRS, it would appear prudent to use the IRS's "92.35 percent" approach, which is the interpretation presented by the IRS in Publication 590, Individual Retirement Arrangements (IRAs). That being said, using the Schedule SE amounts may be unwise when outside factors are present (e.g., self-employment gains/losses from unrelated employers). (See Appendix H.)

Note 4. The definition of *compensation* also includes an individual's net earnings that would be subject to SECA (Self-Employment Contributions Act) taxes but for the fact that the individual is covered by a religious exemption. [I.R.C. §§ 404(l), 408(p)(6)(A)(ii)]

Example 2. Assume the same facts as in Example 1, except that it is 2013. Assuming no changes to the annual limits on contributions, the results would be the same. Thus, the change made to Code Section 1402(a)(12)(B) that is discussed above, does not affect the calculation of a self-employed individual's SIMPLE IRA contribution.

Q 14:65 Must net earnings from self-employment be reduced by matching or nonelective contributions made by the employer on behalf of nonowner-employees?

Yes. Matching or nonelective contributions made on behalf of nonowner-employees (common-law employees) are deducted as an expense of the business. [I.R.C. §§ 404(a), 404(h), 404(k), 404(m), 1402(a)]

Q 14:66 Can SIMPLE contributions to nonowner-employees create a loss for a self-employed individual?

Yes. Contributions made on behalf of nonowners in an unincorporated business reduce the owners' income. A deductible loss could result. [I.R.C. § 1402(a)]

Q 14:67 Do matching or nonelective contributions to a SIMPLE made on behalf of a self-employed individual create a deductible loss or excess contribution?

The IRS has not issued any guidance on the matter. It is unclear whether a self-employed individual may claim a loss for the required matching contribution (or, alternatively, the nonelective contribution) made on his or her behalf. Most likely, recharacterization (see Q 14:68) will be required if compensation is insufficient to support a self-employed person's contributions to his or her own SIMPLE IRA. As a point of comparison, under a 401(a) qualified plan, contributions on behalf of self-employed individuals may not exceed their compensation. [I.R.C. § 404(a)(8)(C)]

Q 14:68 When may compensation be required to be recharacterized?

Recharacterization is the process of recasting a contribution to equal the amount actually available for contribution. It may be required when a self-employed individual does not earn a sufficient amount to support his or her contribution to his or her SIMPLE IRA (see Q 14:67). In general, that would be the case when net earnings from self-employment (NESE) (after reduction for the owner's share of the employer matching or nonelective contributions made to nonowners) are less than the total amount contributed on the self-employed individual's behalf under the SIMPLE.

Example 1. Mark, a self-employed individual with no other employees, has compensation of exactly $4,000. Mark's SIMPLE IRA plan provides for a matching contribution of up to 3 percent of compensation. Mark's recharacterized compensation is $3,880 ($4,000 – ($4,000 × .03)). If Mark contributes $4,000 and receives a $120 matching contribution, the excess amount may be subject to a penalty tax.

Note. To the extent contributions under a SIMPLE are not deductible by the employer, the employer, including a self-employed individual who is treated as the employer, is subject to a 10 percent nondeductible contribution penalty tax under Code Section 4972. [I.R.C. §§ 4972(d)(1)(A)(iv), 4972(d)(2)] Form 5330, Return of Excise Taxes Related to Employee Benefit Plans, is used for this purpose.

Example 2. Lauren, a sole proprietor, has $3,000 of NESE determined under Code Section 1402(a). She is the only participant in a SIMPLE IRA plan. The IRS has not issued any guidance on whether Lauren can elect to contribute the full $3,000 and, in addition, receive a matching or nonelective contribution.

As a point of comparison, in the case of a qualified defined contribution plan, Code Section 404(a)(8)(C) provides that the maximum allowable deduction cannot exceed the earned income of a self-employed individual. Because the rules of Code Section 404(a)(8)(C) do not apply to SIMPLE IRA plans, it appears that the amount that exceeded Lauren's $3,000 of NESE would be deductible; however, a technical correction to limit the contribution and to deny the deduction is a possibility.

Contributions

Q 14:69 What contributions must an employer make under a SIMPLE IRA plan?

When an employer establishes a SIMPLE IRA plan, it must make salary reduction contributions (see Qs 14:81, 14:82) out of compensation to the extent elected by employees. In addition, the employer must make matching contributions (see Q 14:85) or, alternatively, nonelective contributions (see Q 14:87).

Q 14:70 What is a *nonelective contribution*?

A *nonelective contribution* is an employer contribution that is not subject to a voluntary cash or deferred option. For example, a unilateral decision by the employer to reduce an employee's compensation and to make a contribution of all or part of the reduction amount is considered a nonelective contribution.

Q 14:71 May an employee choose not to make contributions to a SIMPLE IRA plan?

Yes. Participation in a SIMPLE IRA plan must be voluntary. An employee must elect to participate and cannot be required to do so (see Q 14:80). Furthermore, a participant may discontinue contributions at any time during the calendar year. [I.R.C. § 408(p)(5)(B)]

Q 14:72 May an employee elect not to receive nonelective contributions if the employer opts to make such contributions?

No. Although an employee may want to opt out of a small employer contribution under a SIMPLE IRA plan to preserve a deduction for a traditional IRA contribution (see Qs 5:33–5:35), he or she is not permitted to do so. An employer must make the matching contribution (or, alternatively, the nonelective contribution), as indicated in the notification to all eligible employees meeting the compensation requirements (if any are specified; see Q 14:87). [I.R.C. § 408(p)(4)(A)]

Q 14:73 May contributions be made from compensation earned before the date the salary reduction agreement is executed?

No. A salary reduction election may not apply to compensation that an employee received, or had a right to immediately receive, before execution of the salary reduction agreement or election.

Q 14:74 May an employer that maintains a SIMPLE make contributions under a SEP or SARSEP?

No. A SIMPLE must be the only plan of an employer (see Q 14:48); thus, the employer may not make contributions under a SEP or SARSEP.

Q 14:75 May contributions be made to a SIMPLE IRA for an employee who is age 70½ or older?

Yes. Contributions to an employee's SIMPLE IRA are not subject to a maximum age requirement. [I.R.C. §§ 219(d)(1), 408(b)(4)]

Q 14:76 How must elective deferrals under a SIMPLE IRA plan be expressed?

The amount deferred under a SIMPLE IRA plan must be expressed as a percentage of compensation. [I.R.S. Notice 98-4, D-2, 1998-2 I.R.B. 26] An eligible employee's percentage election includes bonuses that, at the employee's election, may be contributed to the SIMPLE IRA or received in cash during the calendar year. [I.R.C. § 408(p)(2)(A)(i)]

The following language may be appropriate for elective deferrals under a SIMPLE IRA plan and, at the same time, satisfy the requirement that deferrals be expressed as a percentage.

> Subject to the requirements of the employer's SIMPLE plan, I authorize (a) _____ percent or (b) $ _____ (which equals _____ percent of my current rate of pay) to be withheld from my pay for each pay period and contributed to my SIMPLE IRA as a salary reduction contribution.

[*See* Form 5305-SIMPLE]

Presumably, if (b) is completed, the dollar amount controls (the percentage in (b) is adjusted to equal the dollar amount in the event of a salary change or payment of a bonus). By adjusting the percentage, the employer will know how much to deposit into the SIMPLE IRA and will be able to comply with the administrative requirements of the IRS and the Department of Labor (DOL) regarding prompt forwarding of contributions to a SIMPLE IRA (see Q 14:105).

The language set out above is also suitable for a self-employed individual whose compensation is determined at the end of the business's taxable year. [*See* Treas. Reg. § 1.401(k)-1(a)(6)(ii)(B), 1.401(k)-1(b)(4)(iii)]

Q 14:77 Are contributions to a SIMPLE IRA excluded from the employee's gross income?

Yes. Within prescribed limits, contributions to a SIMPLE IRA are not included in a participant's federal gross income. [I.R.C. § 402(k)] To the extent contributions under a SIMPLE are not deductible by the employer, the employer (including a self-employed individual who is treated as the employer) is subject to the 10 percent nondeductible contribution penalty tax under Code Section 4972. [I.R.C. §§ 4972(d)(1)(A)(iv), 4972(d)(2)(A)]

If a SIMPLE IRA plan fails to meet the statutory requirements (participation, vesting, administrative, and qualified salary reduction arrangement), it is unclear whether and in what year contributions would have to be included in the participant's gross income. Furthermore, whether and when such amounts would be subject to the IRA contribution limits of Code Sections 219 and 408 are also unknown (see Q 14:79).

Practice Pointer. Individual states may or may not exclude SIMPLE IRA contributions from an employee's gross income. Employers and employees should verify state tax rules with regard to deductibility by the employer and exclusion by the employee of SIMPLE IRA plan contributions.

Q 14:78 Are matching contributions subject to the annual dollar limit in the case of a self-employed individual?

Effective with the establishment of SIMPLE IRAs in 1997 and for years beginning after 1997 for 401(k) SIMPLEs, matching contributions for a self-employed individual are treated in the same way as matching contributions are for an employee and thus are not subject to the annual dollar limit on elective deferrals ($11,500 plus catch-up contributions of up to $2,500 for 2012). [I.R.C. §§ 402(g)(9), 408(p)(8)-(9); TRA '97 § 1501]

Q 14:79 What happens if an employer fails to make the matching or nonelective contribution that it agreed to make under a SIMPLE IRA plan?

The IRS has not issued guidance on the issue of an employer's failure to make the contributions it agreed to make to employees' SIMPLE IRAs. It is possible that the plan would not qualify as a SIMPLE IRA plan for the year and all contributions would be reported as regular wages on the employees' Forms W-2; in the case of self-employed individuals, no deduction would be allowed.

It is unclear what happens if an employee does not remove the "excess" contribution (i.e., the contribution that should be treated as wages) or, for that matter, by what date excess contributions have to be removed, because IRA contributions are not permitted to be made to a SIMPLE IRA. Code Section 408(j) allows SEP and IRA contributions to be combined notwithstanding the $5,000/$6,000 limit (for 2012) under Code Section 408(a)(1) and 408(b)(2). Code Section 408(j) was not amended by the SBJPA to allow SIMPLE and IRA contributions to be combined. Thus, the prohibition against combining SIMPLE

IRAs with other plans (see Q 14:48) also applies to traditional, transferred, and rollover IRAs. Arguably, excess contributions may be corrected under Code Section 408(d)(4) and 408(d)(5) (see Qs 5:75, 14:164 and chapter 13).

Also unclear is what happens if an inadvertent error occurs.

Caution. An employer cannot stop making nonelective or matching contributions to a SIMPLE IRA plan in mid-year, or simply shut down the plan before the end of the year. An employer can, however, defer making the nonelective or matching contribution until the extended due date of their income tax return (see Q 14:122). [IRS Employee Plan News (Summer 2009), available at *http://www.irs.gov/pub/irs-tege/sum09.pdf* (visited on Aug. 22, 2012)]

In 2003, the IRS provided new correction procedures for SIMPLE IRA plan failures (see Q 14:162).

Q 14:80 What is a *salary reduction contribution*?

A *salary reduction contribution* (also known as an elective contribution) is a contribution made pursuant to an employee's election to have an amount contributed to his or her SIMPLE IRA rather than to receive the amount directly in cash. That is, the employee makes a voluntary election to reduce current compensation or to forgo a compensation increase.

If a contribution precludes an individual election by the employee, it will be treated as an employer nonelective contribution (see Q 14:70). Eligible automatic contribution agreements (ACAs) or negative elections are discussed in Q 12:1.

An employee must be permitted to elect to have salary reduction contributions made at the level he or she specifies, expressed as a percentage of compensation for the year. Additionally, an employer may permit an employee to express the level of salary reduction contributions as a specific dollar amount (see Q 14:76). [I.R.S. Notice 98-4, 1998-2 I.R.B. 26]

Q 14:81 May an employer place restrictions on the amount of an employee's salary reduction contributions?

No. An employer may not place any restrictions on the amount of an employee's salary reduction contributions—for example, by limiting the contribution percentage—except to the extent needed to comply with the annual limit on the amount of salary reduction contributions (see Qs 14:83, 14:84). [I.R.S. Notice 98-4, Q&A D-2, 1998-2 I.R.B. 26]

Q 14:82 May elective deferral amounts be limited to allow for FICA and FUTA taxes?

The IRS has not issued any guidance regarding limits on elective deferral amounts vis-à-vis FICA (Social Security) and FUTA (federal unemployment) taxes. It is unclear whether an employer may limit the amount that must be deposited in an employee's SIMPLE IRA to the portion that remains after applicable taxes and other amounts have been deducted from wages (see Q 14:81). (The question may arise when a low-paid employee elects to defer more than the amount of his or her net payroll check. Because only the net amount would have been received in cash (see Q 14:80), arguably only the net amount is available for deferral by the employee.)

Q 14:83 What is the maximum annual amount of salary reduction contributions under a SIMPLE?

For 2012, the maximum annual amount of salary reduction contributions that may be made on behalf of any participant under a SIMPLE IRA plan generally is $11,500. [I.R.C. § 408(p)(2)(A)(ii)] However, if the participant is expected to reach age 50 or higher by the end of the participant's taxable year (generally December 31), they may elect to contribute up to $14,000 for 2012.

Q 14:84 Will the maximum dollar limit for salary reduction contributions to a SIMPLE IRA be increased in the future?

Yes. The elective deferral limit for a SIMPLE IRA will increase for years beginning after 2003, as follows:

Year	*Increased Deferral Limit*
2004	$ 9,000
2005	$10,000
2006	$10,000
2007	$10,500
2008	$10,500
2009	$11,500
2010	$11,500
2011	$11,500
2012	$11,500

[I.R.C. § 402(p)(2)(A)(ii); I.R.S. Notice 2011-90, 2011-47 I.R.B. 791 for 2012 indexed limits]

After 2005, the elective SIMPLE IRA deferral limit will be increased for COLAs in increments of $500. [I.R.C. § 408(p)(2)(E)] In addition, a participant in a SIMPLE IRA plan who is age 50 (or older) before the end of the taxable year may make an additional elective deferral (catch-up contribution) up to an "applicable dollar limit." This catch-up amount is in addition to the normal deferral limit ($11,500 for 2012) for the applicable year.

The maximum amount of the catch-up contribution is the lesser of the participant's compensation for the year (see Qs 14:63, 14:64) or the applicable dollar amount.

The applicable dollar amounts are as follows:

Year	*Normal Limit*	*Applicable Dollar Amount*	*Total Deferral*
1997–2000	$ 6,000	n/a	$ 6,000
2001	$ 6,500	n/a	$ 6,500
2002	$ 7,000	$ 500	$ 7,500
2003	$ 8,000	$1,000	$ 9,000
2004	$ 9,000	$1,500	$10,500
2005	$10,000	$2,000	$12,000
2006	$10,000	$2,500	$12,500
2007	$10,500	$2,500	$13,000
2008	$10,500	$2,500	$13,000
2009	$11,500	$2,500	$14,000
2010	$11,500	$2,500	$14,000
2011	$11,500	$2,500	$14,000
2012	$11,500	$2,500	$14,000

[I.R.C. § 414(v)(2)(B)(i), 414(v)(2)(C); I.R.S. Notice 2011-90, 2011-47 I.R.B. 791 for 2012 indexed limits]

Q 14:85 What matching contribution is an employer generally required to make under a SIMPLE IRA plan?

Under a SIMPLE IRA plan, an employer is generally required to make a contribution on behalf of each eligible employee in an amount equal to the employee's salary reduction contributions, up to a limit of 3 percent of the employee's compensation for the entire calendar year (see Q 14:86). Instead of a matching contribution, however, the employer may elect to make a nonelective contribution (see Q 14:87).

Matching and nonelective contribution rates have not changed. Thus, under a SIMPLE IRA plan, a participant may defer $11,500 ($14,000 if the participant is age 50 or older) or 100 percent of compensation, whichever is less, for 2012. A participant may receive a matching contribution of up to 3 percent (or a lower percentage if permitted) of his or her total compensation (with no $250,000 ceiling). Alternatively, the participant may receive a nonelective contribution of 2 percent of his or her total compensation (capped at $250,000) for 2012.

Example 1. Gloria, age 55, participates in a SIMPLE IRA plan. For 2012, her compensation is $300,000, and she defers the maximum of $14,000. If

Gloria's employer matches her deferrals at 3 percent of compensation, Gloria's matching contribution would be $9,000 ($300,000 × .03 = $9,000). Alternatively, if Gloria's employer chooses to make a 2 percent nonelective contribution, Gloria's nonelective contribution would be $5,000 (compensation limit of $250,000 × .02). If Gloria had earned $466,666.67 or more, her matching contribution would be $14,000 ($466,666.67 × .03), the maximum permitted match.

Example 2. The facts are the same as those in Example 1, except that Gloria is currently age 49. She will turn 50 on December 25, 2012. Gloria is permitted to make a catch-up contribution (up to $2,500) to her SIMPLE IRA for the plan year ending in 2012 because she will have attained age 50 before the end of the calendar year. She will also be eligible to make catch-up contributions in subsequent years (see Q 14:84).

No other contribution may be made under a SIMPLE IRA plan; any other contributions are prohibited excess contributions. Thus, an amount from a qualified plan, a 403(b) plan, or a traditional IRA (including SEPs and SARSEPs) may not be transferred or rolled over to a SIMPLE IRA. Nonetheless, a transfer or rollover from a SIMPLE IRA may be made into another SIMPLE IRA (see Q 14:135). [I.R.C. § 408(p)(2)(A)(iv)] Furthermore, excess contributions made under a SIMPLE IRA cannot be treated as traditional IRA contributions (see Q 14:164).

Q 14:86 May the 3 percent limit on matching contributions to a SIMPLE IRA plan be reduced?

Yes. The 3 percent limit on matching contributions to a SIMPLE IRA plan may be reduced for a calendar year at the election of the employer, but only under the following conditions:

1. The limit is not reduced below 1 percent;
2. The limit is not reduced for more than two years out of the five-year period that ends with (and includes) the year for which the election is effective (see Q 14:88); and
3. Employees are notified of the reduced limit within a reasonable period (see Q 14:101) before the 60-day election period during which employees can enter into salary reduction agreements (see Q 14:91).

For purposes of determining whether the limit on matching contributions was reduced below 3 percent for a year, any year before the first year in which an employer (or a predecessor employer) maintains a SIMPLE IRA plan will be treated as a year for which the limit was 3 percent (see Q 14:88). If an employer chooses to make a 2 percent nonelective contribution for a year, that year will also be treated as a year for which the limit was 3 percent.

Q 14:87 How may an employer make nonelective contributions (rather than matching contributions)?

As an alternative to making matching contributions under a SIMPLE IRA plan (see Q 14:85), an employer may make nonelective contributions (see Q 14:70) equal to 2 percent of each eligible employee's compensation (presumably for the entire calendar year; see Q 14:63). The nonelective contributions must be made for each eligible employee regardless of whether such an employee elects to make salary reduction contributions for the calendar year. The employer may, but is not required to, limit nonelective contributions to eligible employees who have at least $5,000 (or some lower amount selected by the employer) of compensation for the year.

For purposes of the 2 percent nonelective contribution, the compensation taken into account must be limited to the amount of compensation that may be taken into account under Code Section 401(a)(17) for the year. The Section 401(a)(17) limit is $250,000 for 2012. The limit will be adjusted by the IRS for subsequent years to reflect changes in the cost of living. Any increase not a multiple of $5,000 will be rounded to the next lowest multiple of $5,000. [I.R.C. § 401(a)(17)(B)]

An employer may substitute the 2 percent nonelective contribution for the matching contribution for a year only if

1. Eligible employees are notified that a 2 percent nonelective contribution will be made instead of a matching contribution, and
2. The notice is provided within a reasonable period (see Q 14:101) before the 60-day election period during which employees may enter into salary reduction agreements (see Q 14:91).

Q 14:88 May a level of contributions be assumed for years before the first year a qualified salary reduction arrangement is in effect?

Yes. If any year in a five-year period that ends with (and includes) the year for which an election is effective is a year before the first year for which any qualified salary reduction arrangement is in effect with respect to the employer (or any predecessor), the employer is treated as if the matching contribution was 3 percent for that previous year. [I.R.C. § 408(p)(2)(C)(i)(III)]

Example 1. After graduating from high school in 1985, Alex formed the Tempura Company. Tempura established a SIMPLE in 2007. It may make a contribution of less than 3 percent (but not less than 1 percent) during any two years from 2008 through 2012 because it is deemed to have made a 3 percent matching contribution for all earlier years.

Example 2. The facts are the same as those in Example 1. During its first five years, Tempura elects to make the following contributions to employees' SIMPLE IRAs:

2008—1 percent *matching* contribution

2009—3 percent *matching* contribution

2010—2 percent *nonelective* contribution

2011—3 percent *matching* contribution

2012—3 percent *matching* contribution

Tempura may make a matching contribution of less than 3 percent (but not less than 1 percent) for the 2013 plan year because the 2008 year will have rolled away (i.e., it will no longer be a part of the five-year contribution history ending with the current year, 2013). If Tempura makes a matching contribution of less than 3 percent for 2012, it will not be able to elect that alternative again until 2017.

Example 3. The facts are the same as those in Example 2. Tempura elects to make a 2 percent nonelective contribution for 2012. It may elect to make a matching contribution of less than 3 percent (but not less than 1 percent) once from 2013 through 2017.

Q 14:89 Are SIMPLE IRA plans subject to minimum funding standards or state law?

No. The minimum funding standards under the Employee Retirement Income Security Act of 1974 (ERISA) and Code Section 412 do not apply to SIMPLEs. [ERISA § 302] It should nevertheless be noted that, under ERISA, employee deferrals must be timely deposited (see Q 14:105).

State law may create additional employer liability if agreed-to contributions are not made.

Q 14:90 Are nondeductible SIMPLE IRA plan contributions subject to penalty?

Yes. To the extent contributions under a SIMPLE are not deductible by the employer, the employer, including a self-employed individual who is treated as the employer, is subject to a 10 percent nondeductible contribution penalty tax under Code Section 4972. [I.R.C. §§ 408(d)(7)(B), 4972(d)(1)(A)(iv), 4972(d)(2)] Form 5330, Return of Excise Taxes Related to Employee Benefit Plans, is used for this purpose.

Employee Elections

Q 14:91 When must an employee be given the right to enter into a salary reduction agreement under a SIMPLE IRA plan?

For an existing or a new SIMPLE IRA plan (see Q 14:54), an eligible employee must be given the right to enter into a salary reduction agreement for a calendar year during the 60-day period immediately preceding January 1 of the calendar year (i.e., Nov. 2–Dec. 31 of the preceding calendar year).

In addition to the election period commencing before the beginning of any year, there is a 60-day period before an employee first becomes eligible to participate. Thus, for the year in which the employee becomes eligible to make salary reduction contributions, the period during which the employee may make or modify the election is a 60-day period that includes either the date he or she becomes eligible or the day before (see Q 14:62). In addition, for the year in which an employee becomes eligible to make salary reduction contributions, the employee must be able to commence those contributions as soon as he or she becomes eligible, regardless of whether the 60-day period has ended, but no earlier than the plan's effective date.

In all cases, the plan may provide for additional periods during which an employee may make a salary reduction election or modify a prior election. [I.R.C. § 408(p)(5)(C); I.R.S. Notice 98-4, 1998-2 I.R.B. 26]

Example 1. On November 1, 2012, Precision Company decides to establish its first retirement plan. It adopts a SIMPLE IRA plan with no service or compensation requirements for its 40 employees. The plan is duly adopted and effective on January 1, 2013. Employees are given a summary description, a model notification to eligible employees, and a model salary reduction agreement on November 1, 2012. The 60-day period starts on November 2 and ends on December 31, 2012. Here, the 60-day election period includes the day before (Dec. 31) the date the employees become eligible. Although contributions may be discontinued at any time (see Q 14:95), no modifications are permitted after the 60-day election period unless the plan provides for additional opportunities to modify (or make) an election to defer compensation.

Example 2. In May 2012, Big Bucks Inc. decides to establish its first retirement plan. It adopts a SIMPLE IRA plan with no compensation or service requirements to cover its 60 employees. The plan is duly adopted on May 25 but states an effective date of June 1, 2012. Employees are given a summary description, a model notification to eligible employees, and a model salary reduction agreement on June 2. The 60-day period starts on June 3. The summary description, salary reduction agreement, and model notification to eligible employees must generally be given before the 60-day election period. Salary reduction contributions may start as soon as administratively feasible, but not earlier than June 3 (the day after notification and delivery of the summary description). The plan may provide for salary deferrals to start at some later date during the year. Here, the 60-day period includes the date the employees become eligible (June 3). Employees may make or modify an election during the 60-day period that ends on August 2, 2012.

Example 3. Crawdad Company establishes a SIMPLE IRA plan effective as of July 1, 2012; each eligible employee becomes eligible to make salary reduction contributions on that date. The 60-day period must begin no later than July 1, 2012, and cannot end before August 31, 2012.

In certain situations, the requirement that specific information, notices, and elections regarding a SIMPLE be given before the beginning of the 60-day period for making or modifying a salary reduction election may be waived (see Qs 14:100, 14:101). Such situations include instances when an employee becomes an eligible employee other than at the beginning of a calendar year because

1. The plan does not impose a compensation requirement for prior years;
2. The employee satisfied the plan's compensation requirement for prior years during a prior period of employment with the employer; or
3. The plan is first effective after the beginning of a calendar year.

[I.R.C. §§ 408(l)(2)(C), 6693(c); ERISA § 101(g)]

If any of the foregoing circumstances apply, the eligible employee must be permitted to make or modify a salary reduction election during the 60-day period that *begins on the day plan notice is provided to the employee* and that includes the day the employee becomes an eligible employee or the day before. By allowing the 60-day period to start on the day plan notice is provided to the employee (instead of on the next day), a rehired employee, for example, will not have to wait until the following year to become eligible. It would be impractical to require notice before the date of eligibility in such situations because that day or the identity of the employee, or both, is not always known. [*See* SIMPLE IRA plan LRM §§ 6–7 (June 2010)]

It is the authors' opinion that the rules just discussed also apply to adopters of model plans.

> **Example 4.** Stacy was a participant in her employer's SIMPLE IRA plan until she severed her employment in January 2012. On May 1, 2012, Stacy was rehired and provided notice of the opportunity to make a salary reduction election. The 60-day period that started on May 1 includes the day Stacy became an eligible employee (May 1, 2012). If it were not for the special rule, the 60-day period could not start until May 2 and thus could not include the day Stacy became eligible (May 1) or the day before (Apr. 30). Therefore, Stacy would have to wait until the following year to participate (i.e., the first year for which the 60-day period could include the day she became an eligible employee for that year or the day before).

In all cases, the salary reduction agreement should become effective as soon as practical after receipt by the employer (or, if later, the date specified by the employee in the salary reduction agreement), but any election made by the eligible employee may be modified prospectively at any time during the 60-day period.

Q 14:92 May an employee modify his or her salary reduction elections under a SIMPLE IRA plan during the 60-day election period?

Yes. During the 60-day election period (see Q 14:91), an eligible employee must be given the right to modify his or her salary reduction agreement under a SIMPLE IRA plan without restrictions (including reducing the amount subject to any agreement to $0). Even an employee who commences participation during an election period may cancel or modify a previous election. Any such change is prospective and should be implemented by the employer as soon as administratively feasible or in accordance with the documentation submitted to the employee.

Q 14:93 May a SIMPLE IRA plan provide election periods longer than 60 days?

Yes. Nothing precludes a SIMPLE IRA plan from providing election periods longer than 60 days.

Q 14:94 May a SIMPLE IRA plan provide additional election periods?

Yes. Nothing precludes a SIMPLE IRA plan from providing additional election periods—for example, quarterly election periods during the 30 days before each calendar quarter.

Q 14:95 Does an employee have the right to terminate a salary reduction agreement outside a SIMPLE IRA plan's election period?

Yes. An employee must be given the right to terminate a salary reduction agreement for a calendar year under a SIMPLE IRA plan at any time during the year. The plan may provide that an employee who terminates participation outside of the normal cycle provided under the plan may not elect to resume participation until the beginning of the next year. [I.R.C. § 408(p)(5)(B)] If, however, an employee terminates a salary reduction election in accordance with the provisions (if any) adopted by the employer, the employee could resume participation in accordance with the normal cycle (if available) without having to wait until the following year.

> **Example 1.** The Lunar Company's SIMPLE IRA plan permits participants to elect to make a salary reduction contribution or modify an earlier election on the first day of any month. Cecil terminates his participation in the plan on August 1. On September 1, he again elects to make salary reduction contributions to start as soon as possible.

> **Example 2.** Solar Inc.'s SIMPLE IRA plan permits participants to elect to make a salary reduction contribution or modify an earlier election during the first week of any month. The plan provides that a participant who terminates participation outside of the normal cycle (which termination must be permitted) may not participate until the following year. Larry terminates his participation in the SIMPLE IRA plan during the third week of August 2012. Larry may not participate in Solar Inc.'s SIMPLE until 2013.

Q 14:96 May an employee be allowed to change his or her salary reduction election under a SIMPLE IRA plan outside of the 60-day election period?

Yes. A SIMPLE IRA plan may permit (but is not required to permit) an employee to make changes to his or her salary reduction contribution election during the year (i.e., increase or reduce the contribution percentage) at times other than during the 60-day election period.

Q 14:97 Must an employer allow an employee to select the financial institution to which the employer will make SIMPLE IRA contributions on behalf of the employee?

Generally, under Code Section 408(p) an employer must permit an employee to select the financial institution that will maintain the SIMPLE IRA to which the employer will make contributions on behalf of the employee. There is an exception, however, that allows an employer to designate the financial institution to which contributions will be made (see Qs 14:143–14:154).

Vesting Requirements

Q 14:98 Must contributions under a SIMPLE IRA plan be nonforfeitable?

Yes. All contributions under a SIMPLE IRA plan must be fully vested and nonforfeitable when made. [I.R.C. § 408(a)(4), 408(b)(4), 408(p)]

Q 14:99 May an employer impose any restrictions or penalties on an employee's withdrawals from his or her SIMPLE IRA?

No. An employer may not require an employee to retain any portion of the contributions in the employee's SIMPLE IRA or otherwise impose any withdrawal restrictions. [I.R.C. § 408(p)(3); Treas. Reg. § 1.408-6(d)(4)(ii)]

Employer Notification and Administrative Requirements

Q 14:100 What notifications must an employer provide each eligible employee before the 60-day election period can begin?

The two formal notifications that generally must be given to eligible employees before the 60-day election period (see Q 14:91) can begin are as follows:

1. *Summary description.* A summary description must be provided to an eligible employee before the 60-day election period. If using IRS model forms, an employer may satisfy that requirement by giving the employee a copy of Form 5305-SIMPLE or Form 5304-SIMPLE (whichever is applicable). The form must be completed and must include a copy of the

procedures for withdrawals and transfers from the SIMPLE IRA received from the financial institution at which the SIMPLE IRA is established (see Q 14:143). The employer receives the summary description from the trustee (see Q 14:109).

2. *Notification to eligible employees.* All employees must be notified before the 60-day election period that they may make or change salary reduction elections during that period. If applicable, such notification must disclose the employee's right to select the financial institution that will serve as the trustee of his or her SIMPLE IRA (see Q 14:97). In this notice, the employer must also indicate whether it will provide a matching contribution up to 3 percent of compensation, a matching contribution percentage that is between 1 and 3 percent of compensation, or a nonelective contribution equal to 2 percent of compensation.

An employer that uses either of the IRS model forms does not have to use the model salary reduction agreement portion of the form to enable employees to make or modify salary reduction elections. Likewise, the model notification to eligible employees does not have to be used. Nevertheless, the agreement and notice used must satisfy all statutory requirements.

There are exceptions to the requirement that certain information, notices, and elections be given before the 60-day election period begins (see Q 14:62). [I.R.C. §§ 408(l)(2)(C), 6693(c); ERISA § 101(g)]

Q 14:101 What is a reasonable period for providing the notification regarding a reduced matching contribution or a nonelective contribution in lieu of a matching contribution?

An employer is deemed to have provided the notification regarding a reduced matching contribution (see Q 14:86) or a nonelective contribution in lieu of a matching contribution (see Q 14:87) within a reasonable period before the 60-day election period if, immediately before the 60-day election period, the notification is included with the notification of an employee's opportunity to enter into a salary reduction agreement. [I.R.S. Notice 98-4, Q&A G-1, G-2, 1998-2 I.R.B. 26; I.R.C. § 408(p)(2)(C)(ii)(II)] Thus, a reasonable period is one day.

Q 14:102 May an employer change the matching contribution percentage once the 60-day election period has begun?

No. An employer may not change the matching contribution percentage after the 60-day election period (see Q 14:91) has begun.

Example. For 2012, Eric adopts a SIMPLE IRA plan for his business that provides for a dollar-for-dollar matching contribution not to exceed 1 percent of compensation. None of his employees participates. Realizing that he can take advantage of the situation, Eric increases the matching contribution to 3 percent of compensation and makes that contribution for 2012. The election to make a nonelective contribution or the new matching contribution rate must be communicated to employees before the 60-day election period. Eric has turned his SIMPLE IRA plan into a "complex" and will have to await further guidance from the IRS on how to correct the excess contributions that were made to the SIMPLE IRA (see Q 14:79).

Q 14:103 What reporting penalties apply under the Code if an employer fails to provide one or more of the required notices?

If an employer fails to provide one or more of the required notices (see Q 14:100), it will be liable under the Code for a penalty of $50 per day until the notices are provided. If an employer can show that the failure was attributable to reasonable cause, the penalty will not be imposed.

If an employee is permitted to select the trustee for his or her SIMPLE IRA (see Q 14:97) and is so notified (see Q 14:100), and the name and address of the trustee and its withdrawal procedures are not available at the time the employer is required to provide the summary description, the employer is deemed to have shown reasonable cause for failure to provide that information to eligible employees. [I.R.C. §§ 408(l)(2)(C), 6693(c)(1)]

Q 14:104 What action may an employer take if an eligible employee is unwilling or unable to establish a SIMPLE IRA?

If an eligible employee who is entitled to a contribution under a SIMPLE IRA plan is unwilling or unable to establish a SIMPLE IRA with any financial institution before the date on which the contribution is required to be made to his or her SIMPLE IRA, the employer may execute the necessary documents to establish a SIMPLE IRA on the employee's behalf with a financial institution selected by the employer. [I.R.S. Notice 98-4, Q&A C-4, 1998-2 I.R.B. 26] Most documents provide default options if a beneficiary is not selected. The default beneficiary is generally the employee's spouse or estate.

Q 14:105 When must an employer make salary reduction contributions under a SIMPLE IRA plan?

An employer must make salary reduction contributions to the financial institution maintaining an employee's SIMPLE IRA no later than the close of the 30-day period following the last day of the month in which amounts would otherwise have been payable to the employee in cash. [I.R.C. § 408(p)(5)(A)(i); DOL Reg. § 2510.3-102] Special considerations, however, apply under ERISA regarding the forwarding of contributions (see Qs 4:44–4:49). Most SIMPLE IREA plans are subject to ERISA (see Q 4:1). Under ERISA, salary reduction contributions under a SIMPLE IRA plan must be made to the SIMPLE IRA as of the earliest date on which the contributions can reasonably be segregated from the employer's general assets, but in no event later than the 30-day deadline described above. These rules also apply in the case of self-employed individuals. Thus, the latest day for the deposit of salary reduction contributions made on behalf of a self-employed individual for a calendar year is 30 days after the end of such year, which is January 30th. The 7-day safe harbor rules would also apply to a SIMPLE plan under ERISA (see Qs 4:45–4:47).

> **Example.** Juniper maintains a SIMPLE IRA plan for 2013. Its owner deducts $10,000, representing all contributions made on or before the due date of its federal income tax return for the year. The contribution includes $6,000 that was contributed by employees as elective deferrals, but that were deposited after the 30-day period following the last day of the month the employees would have received the amounts in cash (i.e., after Jan. 31, 2012). Only the $4,000 employer funded contribution is deductible. [Runyan v. Commissioner, T.C. Summary Opinion 2007-58 (Apr. 19, 2006)]

It is unclear whether amounts contributed after the 30-day period may be deducted in succeeding years. [I.R.C. §§ 404(m), 408(p)(5)] Unlike Code Section 404(h), which provided generally for a carryover of nondeductible SEP contributions, there is no express provision regarding nondeductible SIMPLE IRA contributions. Such amounts may also be subject to the 10 percent nondeductible contribution penalty tax (see Q 14:90). Although contributions are reported (on Form 5498) in the year received, many trustees and custodians are hesitant to accept salary reduction contributions for a prior year that are deposited after the 30-day period. In the author's opinion, it is not the trustee's or custodian's responsibility to determine whether contributions are timely made or deductible.

Q 14:106 Is an employer required to file a Form 5500 for a SIMPLE IRA plan?

No. For a SIMPLE IRA plan, an employer is not required to file any annual information returns, such as Form 5500 or 5500-EZ, Annual Return/Report of Employee Benefit Plan. [I.R.C. §§ 408(i), 408(l)(2)(A); ERISA § 101(g)]

Q 14:107 Is an employer that maintains a SIMPLE IRA plan required to report anything to the IRS?

Yes. An employer that maintains a SIMPLE IRA plan must report which eligible employees are active participants in the plan and the amount of the employees' salary reduction contributions to the SIMPLE plan on Form W-2 (see Q 13:206). Salary reduction contributions are subject to Social Security, Medicare, railroad retirement, and federal unemployment taxes.

Form W-2 (2012), Box 12. A salary reduction contribution (elective deferral) is reported in box 12 of Form W-2. Instructions on the back of copy C for code S state: "Employee salary reduction contributions to a section 408(p) SIMPLE (not included in box 1)." That language differs from the language used in the instructions for code F relating to SARSEPs, which omits the parenthetical language. Although it is unclear, it appears that excess contributions to a SIMPLE IRA are treated as wages and are included in boxes 1, 3, and 5.

> **Example.** Hortense earned $20,000 and elected to defer $3,000 to a SIMPLE IRA. Her employer, Dynamex Corporation, made a 2 percent nonelective

contribution ($400) for the year. Thus, $3,000 is reported in box 12, preceded by code S (S 3000.00) if the plan is a SIMPLE IRA or code D (D 3000.00) if the SIMPLE is part of a 401(k) arrangement. (Commas are not entered in the box.)

Note. The employer's nonelective (or matching) contribution is not reported on Form W-2.

No more than four codes should be entered in box 12. If more than four items need to be reported, a taxpayer should use a separate Form W-2 or a substitute Form W-2 to report the additional items. Reporting instructions for magnetic media filing may differ from the paper reporting instructions. For example, more than four entries in box 12 of an individual's wage report are permitted on one magnetic tape but not on one paper Form W-2.

Form W-2 (2012), Box 13. An individual who is a participant in a SIMPLE IRA plan is treated as an active participant for the purpose of claiming a deduction for the contribution made to an IRA. Thus, special limits may apply to the amount of IRA contributions that an individual may deduct (see Q 14:158). The employer indicates active participation by checking the "Retirement Plan" box. The "Retirement Plan" box is also checked if the individual is a participant in a SIMPLE IRA plan for any part of the year.

Form W-2 (2012), Box 14. The employer may enter in this box any other information it wants to give the employee (e.g., nonelective employer contributions, voluntary after-tax contributions deducted from the employee's pay, employer matching contributions to the employee's SIMPLE IRA). Each item entered should be clearly labeled.

Practice Pointer. An employer must retain books and records relating to a SIMPLE IRA plan as long as their contents may become material in the administration of any federal law. An individual should keep a copy of copy C of Form W-2 for at least three years after the due date for filing his or her federal income tax return.

Q 14:108 How can an employer amend or terminate a SIMPLE IRA plan?

Yes. Although SIMPLE IRA plans are established with the intention of being on-going, the time may come when a SIMPLE IRA plan no longer suits the business's purposes. In a joint IRS/DOL publication, the IRS and the DOL state that to

> terminate a SIMPLE IRA plan, notify the financial institution that you will not make a contribution for the next calendar year and that you want to terminate the contract or agreement. You must also notify your employees that the SIMPLE IRA plan will be discontinued. You do not need to give any notice to the IRS that the SIMPLE IRA plan has been terminated.

No further guidance is provided. [IRS Publication 4334, *Simple IRA Plans for Small Businesses,* p. 5 (Dec. 2011)] To be effective, the notice would have to be provided on or before November 1st of the year prior to the year of plan termination. Thus, to terminate a plan with a plan year ending on December 31, 2013, the notification to eligible employees (see Q 14:100) specifying the discontinuance of contributions must have been provided on or before November 1, 2012.

Example 1. If in 2012 an employer decides to terminate its SIMPLE IRA plan as soon as possible, the employer must inform employees within a reasonable period of time before the 60-day election period ending on December 31, 2012, that there will be no SIMPLE IRA plan for 2013. For 2013 the employer may establish and maintain another kind of qualified plan for its employees and, if this other qualified plan is not operative in 2014, re-establish a SIMPLE IRA plan for 2012.

Practice Pointer. Once notices are given to the employee, the employer cannot amend the plan to change the type of contribution it chose to make. Any such amendment is not effective until the beginning of the following year. If the plan is terminated, the employer must make the contributions it specified or lose the deduction for its contributions. State law may also require that the employer make its agreed-to contribution. On the other hand, an amendment that conforms to the content of the annual notification to eligible employees generally may be made effective sooner. The Listing of Required Modifications and Information Package for SIMPLE IRA plans state that "Any amendment to this SIMPLE IRA Plan can become effective only at the beginning of a calendar year and must conform to the content of the plan notice for the calendar year." [*See* LRM Savings Incentive Match Plan for Employees of Small Employers, item 18 (June 2010)]

Example 2. A SIMPLE IRA plan provides for an employer matching contribution of 3 percent. On November 1, 2012, the employees are notified that the employer will (instead) make a 2 percent nonelective contribution for the 2013 plan year. On December 15, 2013, the plan is amended to specify that a 2 percent nonelective contribution will be made for 2013. The amendment may be made effective on January 1, 2013, because the amendment conforms to the content of the notification to eligible employees.

Practice Pointer. If an employer maintains a SIMPLE IRA plan and adopts another retirement plan, the adoption of the second plan will likely violate the exclusive plan requirement (see Q 14:26) causing all contributions under the SIMPLE IRA plan for the plan year to be treated as excess contributions (see Q 14:163).

Trustee Administrative Requirements

Q 14:109 What information must a SIMPLE IRA trustee provide to an employer?

Each year, a SIMPLE IRA trustee must provide the employer sponsoring the SIMPLE IRA plan with a summary description containing the following information:

1. Name and address of the employer and the trustee;
2. Requirements for eligibility for participation;
3. Benefits provided with respect to the arrangement;
4. Time and method of making elections with respect to the arrangement; and
5. Procedures for, and effects of, withdrawals (including rollovers) from the arrangement.

The trustee must provide the summary description to the employer early enough to allow the employer to meet its notification obligation to its employees (see Q 14:100). A trustee is not, however, required to provide the summary description for the SIMPLE IRA plan before agreeing to be the trustee of a SIMPLE IRA.

Form 5305-SIMPLE. A trustee may satisfy its obligation for a SIMPLE IRA plan established using Form 5305-SIMPLE by providing the employer with a current copy of the model form, with instructions; the information required for completion of Article VI (regarding the procedures for withdrawal); and the name and address of the financial institution. The trustee should provide guidance to the employer concerning the need to complete the first two pages of Form 5305 SIMPLE in accordance with its plan's terms and to distribute completed copies to eligible employees.

Form 5304-SIMPLE. A trustee may satisfy its obligation for a SIMPLE IRA plan established using Form 5304-SIMPLE by providing the employer with a current copy of the model form, with instructions; the information required for completion of Article VI (regarding the procedures for withdrawal); and the name and address of the financial institution, unless the name and address are unavailable. The trustee should provide guidance to the employer concerning the need to complete the first two pages of Form 5304-SIMPLE in accordance with its plan's terms and to distribute completed copies to eligible employees. An employer is relieved from providing the procedures for withdrawal if the information is provided directly to the employee by the financial institution.

A procedure similar to that used for the model forms applies to prototype SIMPLE plans.

Q 14:110 What is the penalty if a trustee fails to timely provide an employer with a summary description for a SIMPLE IRA?

Under the Code, a trustee that fails to provide an employer with a summary description for a SIMPLE IRA incurs a $50 penalty for each day the failure continues, unless the trustee shows that the failure is the result of reasonable cause. To the extent that the employer or the trustee provides the information contained in a summary description (see Q 14:109) within the time period prescribed by law (see Q 14:100) to the employee for whom the SIMPLE IRA is established, the trustee of that SIMPLE IRA is deemed to have shown reasonable cause for failure to provide that information to the employer. Thus, for example, if an employer provides its name and address and other necessary information and the effects of withdrawal to all eligible employees in a SIMPLE IRA plan, and the trustee provides its name and address and its procedures for withdrawal to each eligible employee for whom a SIMPLE IRA is established with the trustee under the SIMPLE IRA plan, the trustee will be deemed to have shown reasonable cause for failing to provide the employer with that information. [I.R.S. Notice 98-4, Q&A H-1, 1998-2 I.R.B. 26]

Q 14:111 What is a transfer SIMPLE IRA?

According to Notice 98-4, Q&A H-1 [1998-2 I.R.B. 26], "A SIMPLE IRA is a transfer SIMPLE IRA if it is not a SIMPLE IRA to which the employer has made contributions under the SIMPLE plan."

Q 14:112 Is the trustee of a transfer SIMPLE IRA required to provide a summary description to an employer?

No. The trustee of a transfer SIMPLE IRA (see Q 14:111) is not required to provide a summary description to an employer. Presumably, the summary description was provided by a prior trustee. [I.R.S. Notice 98-4, Q&A H-1, 1998-2 I.R.B. 26]

Q 14:113 What information must a SIMPLE IRA trustee provide to participants in the SIMPLE IRA plan?

Within 31 days after the close of each calendar year, a SIMPLE IRA trustee (and presumably insurers that offer annuities for SIMPLE IRAs) must provide each individual on whose behalf a SIMPLE IRA is maintained with a statement of the individual's account balance as of the close of that calendar year and the account activity during that calendar year. A trustee that fails to provide individuals with such statement within the prescribed time incurs a $50 penalty under the Code for each day the failure continues, unless the trustee shows that the failure is attributable to reasonable cause.

Practice Pointer. Individuals should keep a copy of this information. They are not required to file it with the IRS, however, because the trustee or other issuer will do so.

A trustee must also provide any other information required to be furnished to IRA holders, such as disclosure statements for individual retirement plans referred to in Treasury Regulations Section 1.408-6. [I.R.C. § 408(i)]

Q 14:114 What information must a SIMPLE IRA trustee provide to the IRS?

Code Section 408(i) requires the trustee of an IRA or SIMPLE IRA to make reports regarding the IRA to the IRS (see Q 13:158). Form 5498, IRA Contribution Information, is used to report the amount of contributions and rollovers (including direct rollovers) to an IRA, SEP, or SIMPLE IRA and the fair market value of the IRA, SEP, or SIMPLE IRA. [Ann. 97-10, 1997-10 I.R.B. 64] A trustee that fails to file the reports incurs a $50 penalty under the Code for each failure, unless it is shown that the failure is attributable to reasonable cause. Do not file Form 5498 for a SIMPLE 401(k) plan.

Form 5498 must also be filed by an IRA trustee or custodian when an IRA is revoked within the first seven days of its establishment (see chapter 13). For 2012, complete Form 5498 as follows:

> **Caution.** Box numbers are based upon the 2012 version of the Form 5498 (see chapter 13).

Form 5498, Box 2. This box is used to report any rollover contributions (or contributions treated as rollovers) received during 2012. The repayment of a qualified reservist distribution is reported in box 14.

Form 5498, Box 5. The fair market value (FMV) of the SIMPLE IRA account as of December 31, 2012, should be entered in this box.

Form 5498, Box 7. This box contains a series of checkboxes to indicate the type of account: an IRA, a SEP, a SIMPLE, or a Roth IRA.

Form 5498, Box 9. This box is used to report SIMPLE contributions made during 2012.

For regular IRA contributions made between January 1, 2013, and April 15, 2013, trustees and issuers should obtain the participant's designation of the year for which the contributions are made. For purposes of Form 5498, contributions and rollovers do not include direct trustee-to-trustee transfers from one IRA to another, but do include direct rollovers from a plan other than an IRA or SIMPLE IRA.

Form 5498, Box 11. Check the box if the participant must take a required minimum distribution (RMD) in 2013. The box is checked for the year in which the individual attains age 70½ even though the RMD for that year need not be made until April 1 of the following year. The box is to be checked each year thereafter. A beneficiary SIMPLE IRA is not subject to RMD reporting.

Marking this box is in addition to the "RMD Statement" that is required to be provided to the IRA owner by each January 31 under either Alternative One or Alternative Two.

Under Alternative 1, Form 5498 informs the participant that a RMD is due, and the amount and date that the distribution is required to be made to the participant.

Under Alternative 2, a statement informs the participant that a RMD is required and the date such amount must be distributed.

Form 5498, Box 12a. The Form 5498 instructions provide that the IRA trustee or custodian can use this box to report the additional information if the trustee or custodian is using Alternative One.

Form 5498, Box 12b. Report the RMD amount if the trustee or custodian is using Alternative One.

Form 5498 does not address the issue of whether a contribution is deductible or nondeductible or whether the amount is excludable from income under the Code.

Q 14:115 Must distributions from a SIMPLE IRA be reported on Form 1099-R?

Yes. Pursuant to Code Section 6047 and Treasury Regulations Section 35.3405-1, the payer of a designated distribution from an IRA must report the distribution on Form 1099-R, Distributions from Pensions, Annuities, Retirement or Profit-Sharing Plans, IRAs, Insurance Contracts, etc. Inasmuch as a distribution from a SIMPLE IRA is a designated distribution from an IRA, it must be reported on Form 1099-R (see Q 13:102). The 2012 Form 1099-R reflects the requirements that apply to SIMPLE IRAs. The penalty for failure to report a designated distribution from an IRA (including a SIMPLE IRA) is $50 for each failure (but not more than $50,000) unless the failure is attributable to reasonable cause rather than willful neglect. [I.R.C. §§ 6047(f), 6704]

Form 1099-R, Box 1, Gross Distribution. This box is used to report the total amount of the distribution before income taxes were withheld but after any fees were charged, such as penalties for early withdrawal of a certificate of deposit. For a noncash distribution of property, the FMV of the property on the date of distribution should be reported.

Form 1099-R, Box 2a, Taxable Amount. Generally, the amount reported in box 1 is reported in this box. For an IRA, an amount *must* be entered in this box.

For IRA distributions (including those from a SIMPLE IRA), the filer is required to compute the taxable amount or to designate whether any part of a distribution is a return of basis attributable to nondeductible IRA contributions. Therefore, in most cases, the amount reported in box 2a will be the same as the amount reported in box 1. The filer may mark the "Taxable amount not determined" box in box 2b (if the trustee cannot reasonably obtain the data needed to compute the taxable amount), but an amount must be entered in box 2a.

Form 1099-R, Box 2b, Taxable Amount Not Determined. Only the taxpayer can compute the taxable amount by using Form 8606, Nondeductible IRA. An *X* should be entered in this box for a SIMPLE IRA.

Form 1099-R, Box 4, Federal Income Tax Withheld. Any federal income tax withheld is entered in this box. This withholding is subject to the deposit rules and is reported on Form 945, Annual Return of Withheld Federal Income Tax.

All IRA distributions (including those from a SIMPLE IRA) are subject to a 10 percent withholding rate. A filer should assume that the entire amount of an IRA distribution is taxable, except for the distribution of contributions under Code Section 408(d)(4), in which case only the earnings are taxable, and for Section 408(d)(5) distributions of excess contributions.

Form 1099-R, Box 7, Distribution Codes. The code that shows the type of distribution should be entered in this box (see Q 13:102). In addition, an *X* should be entered in the IRA/SEP/SIMPLE checkbox if the distribution is from a SIMPLE IRA.

The IRS has *requested* that filers of Form 1099-R include the telephone number of a person whom the recipient can contact to answer questions about the statement. The telephone number may be entered anywhere the payer chooses on the recipient's statement. [I.R.C. § 6722; Ann. 96-98, 1996-39 I.R.B. 42]

Q 14:116 Is a SIMPLE IRA trustee responsible for reporting a distribution to a participant during the initial two-year period of that participant's participation in a SIMPLE IRA plan?

Yes. A SIMPLE IRA trustee is required to report on Form 1099-R a distribution to a participant made during the two-year period that follows that participant's initial participation in a SIMPLE IRA plan (see Q 14:132).

A trustee is permitted to prepare that report on the basis of its own records with respect to the SIMPLE IRA. A trustee may, but is not required to, take into account other adequately substantiated information regarding the date on which an individual first participated in any SIMPLE IRA plan maintained by the individual's employer. [I.R.S. Notice 98-4, Q&A H-5, 1998-2 I.R.B. 26]

Tax Treatment of SIMPLE IRAs

Contributions

Q 14:117 Are contributions to a SIMPLE IRA excludable from a participant's federal income tax and thus not subject to federal income tax withholding?

Yes. Within prescribed limits, contributions to a SIMPLE IRA are excludable from a participant's federal income tax and thus not subject to federal income tax withholding. [I.R.C. §§ 402(k), 3401(a)(12)(D); I.R.S. Notice 98-4, Q&A I-1, 1998-2 I.R.B. 26]

Q 14:118 Are salary reduction contributions to a SIMPLE IRA subject to FICA, FUTA, or RRTA taxes?

Yes. Salary reduction contributions to a SIMPLE IRA are subject to FICA (Social Security) and FUTA (federal unemployment) taxes, as well as taxes arising under the Railroad Retirement Tax Act (RRTA). [I.R.C. §§ 3121(a)(5)(H), 3306(b)(5)(H); I.R.S. Notice 98-4, Q&A I-1, 1998-2 I.R.B. 26]

Q 14:119 How are salary reduction contributions to a SIMPLE IRA reported?

Salary reduction contributions to a SIMPLE IRA must be reported on Form W-2, Wage and Tax Statement. [I.R.S. Notice 98-4, Q&A I-1, 1998-2 I.R.B. 26] On the 2012 Form W-2, a code must be used to designate amounts reported in box 12. Code S—Savings Incentive Match Plan for Employees of Small Employers (SIMPLE) Retirement Account—is used to report salary reduction contributions made under a SIMPLE IRA plan (code D is used for a SIMPLE 401(k)). [Ann. 96-134, 1996-53 I.R.B. 60]

Q 14:120 Are matching and nonelective contributions to a SIMPLE IRA subject to FICA, FUTA, or RRTA taxes or to federal income tax withholding?

No. Matching and nonelective contributions to a SIMPLE IRA are not subject to FICA, FUTA, or RRTA taxes. On the other hand, elective (salary reduction) contributions are (see Q 14:117). [I.R.C. §§ 3121(a)(5)(H), 3131(v)(2)(C), 3231(e)(8)(B), 3306(b)(5)(H); I.R.S. Notice 98-4, Q&A I-1, 1998-2 I.R.B. 26]

Furthermore, because SIMPLE contributions are not includible in gross income, matching and nonelective contributions are exempt from federal income tax withholding. [I.R.C. § 3401(a)(12)(D); I.R.S. Notice 98-4, Q&A I-1, 1998-2 I.R.B. 26]

Q 14:121 Must matching and nonelective contributions be reported on Form W-2?

No. Matching and nonelective contributions are not treated as wages and are not required to be reported on Form W-2. [I.R.S. Notice 98-4, Q&A I-1, 1998-2 I.R.B. 26]

Deduction of Contributions

Q 14:122 When must an employer make matching or nonelective contributions under a SIMPLE IRA plan to be able to claim a deduction for such contributions for its current tax year?

For deduction purposes, an employer's matching or nonelective contributions under a SIMPLE IRA plan must be made to the financial institution maintaining an employee's SIMPLE IRA no later than the employer's due date (including extensions) for filing its income tax return for the taxable year that includes the last day of the calendar year for which the contributions are made (see Q 14:124). [I.R.C. § 408(p)(5)(A)]

> **Example 1.** Webster Corporation, whose tax year ends on November 30, adopts a SIMPLE IRA plan for 2012. On January 10, 2013 (and before its tax return due date), Webster makes a nonelective contribution to all employees for the 2012 plan year. Webster may claim a deduction for its contribution on its federal income tax return for the taxable year ending on November 30, 2013.

> **Example 2.** Comet Corporation, whose tax year ends on November 30, adopts a SIMPLE IRA plan for 2012. On August 10, 2012, Comet makes a matching contribution to all employees for the 2012 plan year. Comet received an automatic six-month extension to file its federal income tax return. Thus, its federal income tax return, normally due on February 15, 2013, is due on August 16, 2013. Comet may claim a deduction for its 2012 contribution made on August 10, 2013, on its federal income tax return for the taxable year ending on November 30, 2013.

If an entity is tax exempt, it has until the due date of its Form 990, Return of Organization Exempt from Income Tax (generally, the 15th day of the 5th month following the close of its accounting period) to make any contributions required of it under a SIMPLE IRA plan for any given year.

Q 14:123 How are deductions for contributions made under a SIMPLE IRA plan claimed?

Rules similar to the SEP and Keogh rules apply; that is, elective and non-elective contributions made on behalf of a self-employed individual (including a partner in a partnership) to a SIMPLE IRA plan are claimed on Form 1040, line 28. The deduction for SIMPLE contributions made on behalf of nonowners is claimed on line 18 of the business's Form 1065, U.S. Partnership Return of Income, if the organization is taxed as a partnership. An unincorporated business other than a partnership claims the deduction for SIMPLE contributions made on behalf of a nonowner-employee on line 19 of Schedule C or line 23 of Schedule F to Form 1040. If the organization is taxed as a corporation, the deduction for owners and nonowners is claimed on line 23 of Form 1120, U.S. Corporation Income Tax Return, or line 17 of Form 1120S, U.S. Income Tax Return for an S Corporation.

Q 14:124 When are employer contributions to a SIMPLE IRA plan deducted by an employer?

Within prescribed limits, all contributions made under a SIMPLE IRA plan are deductible by an employer. (Elective salary reduction contributions made by employees are treated as employer contributions for deduction purposes.) Contributions made under a SIMPLE IRA plan are deductible in the taxable year of the employer with or within which the calendar year for which the contributions were made ends. Contributions are therefore deductible by the employer in accordance with the following rules:

1. In the case of a SIMPLE IRA plan maintained by a calendar-year business, contributions are deductible for that calendar year.
2. When a fiscal-year business maintains a SIMPLE IRA plan, contributions are deductible for the fiscal taxable year that includes the last day of the calendar-year plan.

[I.R.C. §§ 404(m)(1), 404(m)(2)(A)]

Example 1. Ladybug Co. has a June 30 taxable year-end. Contributions made under its SIMPLE IRA plan for the calendar year 2012 (including contributions made for 2012 before June 30, 2013) are deductible in the taxable year ending June 30, 2013, as follows:

```
Contributions:
                                                $ $ $
          Calendar Plan Year:                   ↓ ↓ ↓
          |-----10-----|-----11-----|-----12-----|
                   12/31/10      12/31/11       12/31/12
Ladybug's Taxable Year:
|-----10-----|-----11-----|-----12-----|
         6/30/10      6/30/11       6/30/12
```

Example 2. Bee Corporation, with a tax year that ends on February 28, adopts a SIMPLE IRA plan. On December 31, 2012, Bee makes a nonelective contribution to all employees' SIMPLE IRAs for the 2012 plan year. Bee may claim a deduction on its federal income tax return for the taxable year ending on February 28, 2013.

Q 14:125 How are SIMPLE IRA plan contributions made after the end of the taxable year treated?

For the purpose of determining the timing of an employer's deduction for contributions made under a SIMPLE IRA plan, contributions made after the end of the tax year are treated as made for a taxable year if (1) they are made on account of that taxable year, and (2) they are made no later than the due date (including extensions) of the employer's federal income tax return for that taxable year. [I.R.C. § 404(m)] For deduction purposes, however, elective deferrals must be deposited sooner (see Q 14:105).

Example 1. Tibor is a sole proprietorship where the tax year is the calendar year. Nonelective contributions under a SIMPLE IRA plan for the calendar year 2012 (including contributions made in 2013 by April 15, 2013, including extensions) are deductible in the 2012 tax year.

Example 2. Garden Corporation, with a tax year that ends on June 30, adopts a SIMPLE IRA plan. Garden makes a nonelective contribution to all employees for the 2012 plan year on the day its tax return for the fiscal year ending in 2013 is due. Garden may claim its deduction on its federal income tax return for the taxable year ending on June 30, 2012.

[I.R.S. Notice 98-4, Q&A I-7, 1998-2 I.R.B. 26]

Q 14:126 Do the qualified plan contribution limits under Code Section 404(a) apply to a SIMPLE IRA plan?

No. The qualified plan contribution limits under Code Section 404(a) do not apply to a SIMPLE IRA plan; that is, the employer's 25 percent (15 percent before 2003) deduction limit (based on participants' aggregate compensation) does not apply. Instead, special limits apply to contributions under a SIMPLE IRA plan. Thus, in the case of a SIMPLE IRA, an employer is permitted a deduction for all contributions.

Q 14:127 Is a SIMPLE IRA subject to the $5,000/$6,000 or 100 percent of compensation limit that applies to regular IRAs?

No. The regular IRA contribution limit does not apply to a SIMPLE IRA. A technical correction was enacted to clarify that a SIMPLE IRA *can* accept more than $5,000 plus catch-up contributions of up to $1,000 for 2012. [I.R.C. §§ 219(b)(4), 408(p)(8)] (See Q 1:30 for traditional IRA contribution limits after 2001.)

Distributions

Q 14:128 What are the tax consequences when amounts are distributed from a SIMPLE IRA?

Generally, the tax consequences of distributions from a SIMPLE IRA are the same as the tax consequences of distributions from a traditional IRA (i.e., they are generally taxable except to the extent of any pro rata basis recovery). [I.R.C. § 408(d)] A special rule does apply, however, to a payment or distribution received from a SIMPLE IRA during the two-year period beginning on the date on which an individual first participated in any SIMPLE IRA plan maintained by that individual's employer ("the two-year period"; see Qs 14:129–14:135).

Q 14:129 When does participation in a SIMPLE IRA plan commence for the purpose of the two-year period?

Participation in a SIMPLE IRA plan commences for the purpose of the two-year period on the first day on which contributions made by an individual's employer are deposited in that individual's SIMPLE IRA.

Q 14:130 What is the penalty tax applicable to distributions made from a SIMPLE IRA during the two-year period?

If the additional income tax on early distributions under Code Section 72(t) applies to a distribution from a SIMPLE IRA within the two-year period, Code Section 72(t)(6) provides that the rate of additional tax is increased from 10 percent to 25 percent (unless an exception applies).

Q 14:131 Do the usual exceptions to the Section 72(t) tax that apply to IRA distributions apply to SIMPLE IRA distributions during the two-year period?

Yes. If one of the exceptions to application of the tax under Code Section 72(t) applies (e.g., for amounts paid after age 59½, after death, or as part of a series of substantially equal payments; see Q 5:55) to distributions from an IRA, the exception also applies to distributions from a SIMPLE IRA within the two-year period, and neither the 25 percent nor the 10 percent additional tax on premature distributions will apply.

Q 14:132 What special rollover rule applies to a distribution from a SIMPLE IRA during the two-year period?

Code Section 408(d)(3)(G) provides that the rollover provisions of Code Section 408(d)(3) apply to a distribution from a SIMPLE IRA during the two-year period beginning on the date on which the individual first participated in any SIMPLE IRA plan maintained by the individual's employer only if the distribution is paid into another SIMPLE IRA. Thus, a distribution from a SIMPLE IRA during that two-year period qualifies as a rollover contribution (and is therefore not includible in gross income) only if the distribution is paid into another SIMPLE IRA and satisfies the other requirements of Code Section 408(d)(3) for treatment as a rollover contribution.

Q 14:133 May an amount be transferred from a SIMPLE IRA to a traditional IRA in a tax-free trustee-to-trustee transfer?

Yes, an amount may be transferred from a SIMPLE IRA to a traditional IRA in a tax-free trustee-to-trustee transfer. As mentioned previously (see Q 14:132), however, during the two-year period beginning on the date on which the individual first participated in any SIMPLE IRA plan maintained by the individual's employer, an amount in a SIMPLE IRA may be transferred in a tax-free trustee-to-trustee transfer *only* to another SIMPLE IRA. [I.R.S. Notice 98-4, Q&A I-4, 1998-2 I.R.B. 26]

Q 14:134 May an amount be transferred from a SIMPLE IRA to a Roth IRA?

Yes, an amount may be transferred from a SIMPLE IRA to a Roth IRA as a direct conversion or as a rollover conversion. As mentioned previously (see Q 14:132), however, during the two-year period beginning on the date on which the individual first participated in any SIMPLE IRA plan maintained by the individual's employer, an amount in a SIMPLE IRA may be transferred in a tax-free trustee-to-trustee transfer *only* to another SIMPLE IRA. [I.R.S. Notice 98-4, Q&A I-4, 1998-2 I.R.B. 26]

Caution. Prior to 2010, the conversion is only permitted if the taxpayer's adjusted gross income (AGI) for the year does not exceed $100,000 (not including the taxable amount converted or any required minimum distributions) and, if married, the taxpayer must file a joint return.

Q 14:135 What is the result if, during the two-year period, an amount is paid from a SIMPLE IRA directly to the trustee of an IRA that is not a SIMPLE IRA?

If, during the two-year period, an amount is paid from a SIMPLE IRA directly to the trustee of an IRA or other plan that is not a SIMPLE IRA, the payment is neither a tax-free trustee-to-trustee transfer nor a rollover contribution. Instead, the payment is a distribution from the SIMPLE IRA and a contribution to the other IRA that does not qualify as a rollover contribution. The amount is treated as a regular annual IRA contribution and is subject to the IRA contribution limit of $5,000 plus catch-up contributions of up to $1,000 for 2012 under Code Sections 219 and 408.

The instructions to Form 1099-R indicate that the payer must report as a distribution on Form 1099-R any trustee-to-trustee transfer from a SIMPLE IRA to a non-SIMPLE IRA during the two-year period beginning on the day contributions are first deposited in the individual's SIMPLE IRA by the employer. That information is needed because tax-free transfers (and rollovers) are not permitted from a SIMPLE IRA to an IRA during the first two years regardless of the participant's age. Because the original SIMPLE IRA trustee will know that the transfer of assets is going into a non-SIMPLE IRA, Form 1099-R can be prepared and filed.

When a SIMPLE IRA distribution is made to a participant who is over age 59½ but is made before the expiration of the two-year period (which is reportable on Form 1099-R as a normal distribution, code 7) and the participant completes a 60-day rollover contribution into a non-SIMPLE IRA, the IRS will not know that the two-year rule has been violated.

Note. A transfer pursuant to a divorce or legal separation under an IRA is not considered a distribution and is not reportable on Form 1099-R.

Q 14:136 Do the required minimum distribution rules for persons age 70½ and over apply to a SIMPLE IRA?

Yes. The required minimum distribution rules for persons age 70½ or over that generally apply to IRAs apply to SIMPLE IRAs. [I.R.C. §§ 408(a)(6), 408(b)(4), 408(p)(1)] Those rules generally require that an IRA commence distributions beginning when an individual attains age 70½ over a period certain (e.g., 1/17th, 1/16th, 1/15th, . . . of the account balance) or based on joint or single life expectancy factors. The required minimum distributions requirements were waived for 2009 RMDs.

Q 14:137 May required distributions be postponed until the calendar year in which an employee retires?

No. The delayed payout rules applicable to a qualified plan under Code Section 401(a)(9)(C) do not apply to any type of IRA, including a SIMPLE IRA. The normal age 70½ IRA distribution rules apply. [I.R.C. § 401(a)(9)(C); I.R.S. Notice 96-97, 1996-2 C.B. 235]

Q 14:138 Do the qualification rules of Code Section 401(a) apply to contributions under a SIMPLE IRA plan?

No. None of the qualification rules under Code Section 401(a), which are applicable to pension, profit-sharing, and stock bonus plans, applies to a SIMPLE IRA plan. [I.R.C. § 408(p)(1)] For example, the joint and survivor annuity rules do *not* apply to SIMPLE IRAs. [I.R.C. §§ 401(a)(12), 408(p)(1), 408(d), 408(k)(1)] Those rules require that a qualified plan provide for a "qualified joint and survivor annuity" if the plan provides for any method of payment in the form of an annuity. Even if a SIMPLE plan is an ERISA-governed plan, a SIMPLE IRA is exempt from Part 2 of Subtitle B of Title I of ERISA. The survivor-annuity or spouse's-consent rules of ERISA Section 205 do not apply to an IRA or SIMPLE IRA. [ERISA §§ 201(6), 205; *see, e.g.*, Cline v. Industrial Maint. Eng'g and Contracting Co., 200 F.3d 1223 (9th Cir. 2000)]

Q 14:139 Do the qualified plan limits on contributions and benefits under Code Section 415 apply to contributions under a SIMPLE IRA plan?

No. The limits on annual additions and benefits that may be provided under a qualified plan or plans do not apply to contributions under a SIMPLE IRA plan. Thus, neither the contribution limit of 100 percent (25 percent before 2002) of compensation nor the dollar limit of $50,000 (for 2012) applies to a SIMPLE IRA. Such rules do apply, however, when a SIMPLE IRA is established as part of a qualified 401(k) plan (see Q 15:3). [I.R.C. § 415(k)(1)]

Q 14:140 Is the amount of compensation that may be taken into account for contributions limited to $250,000 under a SIMPLE IRA plan?

Although the Section 401(a)(17) limit of $250,000 for 2012 does not apply to salary reduction contributions and matching contributions made under a SIMPLE IRA plan, the amount of compensation that may be taken into account for purposes of the 2 percent nonelective contribution is limited by Code Section 401(a)(17) to $250,000 for 2012. [I.R.C. § 408(p)(2)(B)]

Example 1. Jo Ann has W-2 compensation of $250,000 from Latte Corporation and elects to make an $11,500 contribution into a SIMPLE IRA under Latte's SIMPLE IRA plan for 2012. Latte elects to make a 3 percent matching contribution. Jo Ann will receive $7,500 ($250,000 × .03) from Latte. The matching contribution is based on total compensation.

Example 2. For 2012, Martha, age 60, has W-2 compensation of $250,000 and elects to make a $14,000 contribution to a SIMPLE IRA under a SIMPLE IRA plan maintained by her employer, Space Carpenter, Inc. Space Carpenter elects to make a nonelective contribution (2 percent). Martha's nonelective contribution will be $5,000 ($250,000 × .02) because only $250,000 of compensation may be considered for the purpose of making a nonelective contribution for 2012.

Q 14:141 What are some possible results of different SIMPLE IRA contribution alternatives?

The possible results of three SIMPLE IRA contribution alternatives under the two contribution methods (matching and nonelective) are explained in the following example.

Example. The results that follow have been determined on the basis of data for 2012 available from the accompanying table, which employs various givens.

1. Employer elective contributions deferred by employees ($67,500) plus employer matching contributions ($30,750) at the applicable percentage (3 percent) specified in Code Section 408(p)(2)(C)(ii)(I) equals $98,250 (columns A + B).
2. Employer elective contributions deferred by employees ($67,500) plus employer matching contributions ($21,200) at the minimum alternative matching rate (1 percent) specified in Code Section 408(p)(2)(C)(ii)(II) equals $88,700 (columns A + C).
3. Employer elective contributions deferred by employees ($67,500) plus nonelective employer contributions ($21,400) at the rate (2 percent) provided in Code Section 408(p)(2)(B)(i) equals $88,900 (columns A + D). All eligible employees receive nonelective contributions.

				Employer Contributions		
			A *Elective*	*B* *Matching*	*C* *Matching*	*D* *Nonelective*
Name	*2012 Compensation*	*Percentage Elected by Employee Deferral Percentage*	*Deferral Amount*	*(May be elected any year employer matching contribution 3 percent maximum)*	*(May be elected instead of column B for any 2 years during any 5-year period at 1 percent)*	*(May be elected instead of columns B and C for any year 2 percent statutory rate)*
Alex	$1,400,000	1.0000	$14,000[1]	$14,000[2]	$14,000	$5,000[3]
Beth	250,000	2.4	6,000	6,000	2,500	5,000
Chris	150,000	7.6667	11,500	4,500	1,500	3,000
Dana	125,000	0	0	0	0	2,500
Ellen	100,000	8	8,000	3,000	1,000	2,000
Fred	100,000	1	1,000	1,000	1,000	2,000
Gary	50,000	286	14,000	1,500	500	1,000
Hugh	10,000	80	8,000	300	100	200
Isaac	10,000	10	1,000	300	100	200
Juan	5,000	80	4,000	150	50	100
Kim	5,000	0	0	0	0	100
Totals:	$2,200,000		$67,500	$30,750	$21,200	$21,400

Note. Alex, Chris, and Gary are age 50 or older. (See Appendix H.)

[1] Elective employer contribution dollar limit is $11,500 ($14,000 with catch-up) for 2012.

[2] Dollar-for-dollar employer matching contribution, up to the $11,500/$14,000 limit.

[3] Compensation used for nonelective contributions is limited to $250,000 for 2012.

Q 14:142 Do the top-heavy rules apply to a SIMPLE IRA plan?

No. The top-heavy rules do not apply to a SIMPLE IRA plan that uses the SIMPLE rules to meet nondiscrimination tests for a given year. [I.R.C. §§ 401(k)(11)(D)(ii), 416(a), 416(g)(4)(G)]

> **Example.** Anthony, a sole proprietor, established a SIMPLE IRA plan for his successful business. Although other employees are eligible to participate, only Anthony elects to make a salary reduction contribution. Although the plan primarily benefits a key employee, it is not subject to the top-heavy rules.

Designated Financial Institutions

Q 14:143 What is a *designated financial institution*?

A *designated financial institution* (DFI) is a trustee or custodian for a SIMPLE IRA plan that agrees to maintain IRAs on behalf of all individuals receiving contributions under the plan and to deposit those contributions in the SIMPLE IRAs of each eligible employee as soon as practical. The DFI must also agree to transfer the participant's account balance in a SIMPLE IRA to another SIMPLE IRA without cost or penalty to the participant (see Q 14:151). [I.R.C. § 408(p)(7)]

Only certain financial institutions, such as banks, savings and loan associations, insured credit unions, insurance companies that issue insurance contracts, or IRS-approved nonbank trustees, may serve as DFIs under a SIMPLE IRA plan (see Q 14:33). [I.R.C. § 408(n)]

Note. An employer that does not wish to use a DFI should not use Form 5305-SIMPLE to establish a SIMPLE.

Q 14:144 May an employer designate a particular financial institution to which all contributions under a SIMPLE IRA plan will be made?

Yes. Instead of making SIMPLE IRA plan contributions to the financial institution selected by each eligible employee (see Q 14:97), an employer may require that all contributions on behalf of all eligible employees under its SIMPLE IRA plan be made to SIMPLE IRAs at a DFI if the following requirements are met:

1. The employer and the financial institution agree that the financial institution will be a DFI under Code Section 408(p)(7) for the SIMPLE IRA plan;
2. The financial institution agrees that if a participant so requests, his or her balance will be transferred without cost or penalty to another SIMPLE IRA or, after the two-year period (see Qs 14:132, 14:133), to any IRA at a financial institution selected by the participant; and
3. Each participant is given written notification describing the procedures under which, if a participant so requests, his or her balance will be transferred without cost or penalty to another SIMPLE IRA or, after the two-year period, to any IRA at a financial institution selected by the participant.

[I.R.C. § 408(p)(7)]

Example 1. A representative of Lucky Investment Financial Institution contacts Top Brass Manufacturing Co. about the establishment of a SIMPLE IRA plan. Top Brass agrees to establish such a plan for its eligible employees. Because Top Brass would prefer to avoid writing checks to more than one financial institution on behalf of its employees, it is interested in making all contributions under the SIMPLE IRA plan to a single financial institution. Top

Brass and Lucky Investment agree that Lucky Investment will be a DFI, and Lucky Investment agrees that if a participant so requests, it will transfer the participant's balance, without cost or penalty, to another SIMPLE IRA or, after the two-year period, to any IRA at a financial institution selected by the participant.

A SIMPLE IRA is established for each participating employee of Top Brass at Lucky Investment. Each participant is provided with a written description of how and when he or she may direct that his or her balance attributable to contributions made to Lucky Investment be transferred without cost or penalty to a SIMPLE IRA or, after the two-year period, to any IRA at another financial institution he or she selects. Lucky Investment is a DFI, and Top Brass may require that all contributions on behalf of all eligible employees be made to SIMPLE IRAs at Lucky Investment.

Example 2. A representative of Metro Financial Institution (Metro) contacts Mirror Co. about the establishment of a SIMPLE IRA plan. Mirror invites Metro to make a presentation on its investment options for SIMPLE IRAs to Mirror's employees. Each eligible employee receives notification that he or she may select which financial institution will serve as the trustee of his or her SIMPLE IRA (see Q 14:100). All eligible employees of Mirror voluntarily select Metro to serve as the trustee of the SIMPLE IRAs to which Mirror will make all contributions on behalf of the employees. Metro is not a DFI merely because all eligible employees of Mirror selected Metro to serve as the trustee of their SIMPLE IRAs and Mirror consequently makes all contributions to Metro. Therefore, Metro is not required to transfer SIMPLE IRA balances without cost or penalty.

Example 3. The facts are the same as those in Example 2, except that two employees of Mirror Co. who made salary reduction elections, Harry and Henry, failed to establish SIMPLE IRAs to receive SIMPLE plan contributions on their behalf before the first date on which Mirror is required to make a contribution to their SIMPLE IRAs (see Q 14:122). Mirror establishes SIMPLE IRAs at Metro for Harry and Henry and contributes the amount required to their accounts. Metro is not a DFI merely because Mirror establishes SIMPLE IRAs on behalf of Harry and Henry.

Q 14:145 What IRS model forms may an employer use to establish a SIMPLE IRA plan with and without a designated financial institution?

Form 5305-SIMPLE may be used by an employer establishing a SIMPLE IRA plan with a financial institution that is a DFI (see Q 14:143). [I.R.S. News Release IR-96-46 (Oct. 31, 1996)]

Form 5304-SIMPLE may be used by an employer establishing a SIMPLE IRA plan that does not wish to use a DFI. [I.R.S. News Release IR-96-55 (Dec. 30, 1996); see Ann. 96-112, 1996-45 I.R.B. 7 (regarding the establishment of a non-DFI SIMPLE IRA plan before the availability of Form 5304-SIMPLE)]

Form 5305-SIMPLE and Form 5304-SIMPLE were revised in 2012 (see Q 14:22).

Q 14:146 May the time in which a participant may transfer his or her balance in a SIMPLE IRA without cost or penalty be limited without violating the requirements of Code Section 408(p)(7)?

Yes. Code Section 408(p)(7) will not be violated merely because a participant is given only a reasonable period of time (see Q 14:147) each year in which to transfer his or her balance in a SIMPLE IRA without cost or penalty.

Q 14:147 What is a reasonable period of time in which to choose whether to transfer contributions to a SIMPLE IRA without cost or penalty?

A participant will be deemed to have been given a reasonable period of time in which to transfer his or her SIMPLE IRA balance without cost or penalty if, for each calendar year, the participant has until the end of a 60-day period (see Q 14:91) to request a transfer, without cost or penalty, of his or her balance attributable to SIMPLE IRA plan contributions for the calendar year following that 60-day period (or, for the year in which an employee first becomes eligible to make salary reduction contributions, for the balance of that year) and subsequent calendar years.

Example 1. Orange Computer first establishes a SIMPLE IRA plan effective January 1, 2012, and intends to make all contributions to Starship Financial Institution, which has agreed to serve as a DFI. For the 2012 calendar year, Orange Computer provides the 60-day election period beginning November 2, 2011, and notifies each participant that he or she may request that his or her balance attributable to future contributions be transferred from Starship to a SIMPLE IRA at a financial institution that the participant selects. The notification states that the transfer will be made without cost or penalty if the participant contacts Starship before January 1, 2012. For the 2012 calendar year, the requirements of Code Section 408(p)(7) will not be violated merely because participants are given only a 60-day period in which to request the transfer of their balances without cost or penalty.

Example 2. The facts are the same as those in Example 1. Linda, a participant, does not request a transfer of her balance by December 31, 2011, but requests a transfer of her current balance to another SIMPLE IRA on July 1, 2012. Linda's current balance would not be required to be transferred without cost or penalty because she did not request such a transfer before January 1, 2012. During the 60-day period preceding the 2013 calendar year, however, Linda may request a transfer, without cost or penalty, of her balance attributable to contributions made for the 2013 calendar year and, if she so elects, for all future calendar years (but not her balance attributable to contributions for the 2012 calendar year).

Example 3. The facts are the same as those in Example 1. Under the terms of the SIMPLE IRA plan, Eli becomes an eligible employee on June 1, 2012, and, for him, the 60-day period (see Q 14:91) begins on that date. For the 2012 calendar year, Eli will be deemed to have been given a reasonable amount of time in which to request a transfer, without cost or penalty, of his balance attributable to contributions for the balance of the 2012 calendar year if Starship Financial Institution allows such a request to be made before July 31, 2012.

Q 14:148 How is any limitation on the time or manner in which a participant may transfer his or her SIMPLE IRA balance without cost or penalty disclosed?

If the time or manner in which a participant may transfer his or her balance without cost or penalty (see Q 14:151) is limited, any such limitation must be disclosed as part of a written notification regarding a DFI (see Q 14:144). In the case of a SIMPLE established using Form 5305-SIMPLE, if the summary description requirement is being satisfied by providing a completed copy of pages 1 and 2 of Form 5305-SIMPLE, Article VI (Procedures for Withdrawal) must contain a clear explanation of any such limitation.

Q 14:149 Is there a limit on the frequency with which a participant's SIMPLE IRA balance must be transferred without cost or penalty?

Yes. To satisfy Code Section 408(p)(7), if a participant acts within applicable reasonable time limits (see Q 14:147), if any, to request a transfer of his or her balance, the participant's balance must be transferred on a reasonably frequent basis. A participant's balance will be deemed to be so transferred if it is transferred on a monthly basis. [I.R.S. Notice 98-4, Q&A J-3, 1998-2 I.R.B. 26]

Q 14:150 To where must a participant's SIMPLE IRA balance be transferred?

A participant's SIMPLE IRA balance must be transferred in a trustee-to-trustee transfer directly to a SIMPLE IRA or, after the two-year period (see Q 14:128), to any IRA at the financial institution specified by the participant. [I.R.C. § 408(p)(7)]

Q 14:151 When is a transfer of a participant's SIMPLE IRA balance deemed to be made without cost or penalty?

A transfer of a participant's SIMPLE IRA balance is deemed to be made without cost or penalty if no liquidation, transaction, redemption, or termination fee or any commission, load (front-end or back-end), or surrender charge or similar fee or charge is imposed with respect to the balance being transferred. A transfer will not fail to be made without cost or penalty merely because contributions that a participant has elected to have transferred without cost or penalty are required to be invested in one specified investment option until transferred, even though a variety of investment options are available with respect to contributions that participants have not elected to transfer.

Example 1. Capture Financial Institution agrees to be a DFI for the SIMPLE IRA plan maintained by Cement Co. Cement provides a 60-day election period (see Q 14:91) beginning on November 2 of each year, and each participant is notified that he or she may request, before the end of the 60-day period, a transfer of his or her future contributions from Capture without cost or penalty to a SIMPLE IRA or, after the two-year period (see Q 14:128), to any IRA at a financial institution selected by the participant. The notification states that a participant's contributions that are to be transferred without cost or penalty will be invested in a specified investment option and will be transferred to the financial institution selected by the participant on a monthly basis.

Capture Financial Institution offers various investment options to account holders of SIMPLE IRAs, including investment options with a sales charge. Any participant who does not elect to have his or her balance transferred to another financial institution may invest the contributions made on his or her behalf in any investment option available to account holders of SIMPLE IRAs at Capture. Contributions that a participant has elected to have transferred, however, are automatically invested, before transfer, in a specified investment option that has no sales charge. The requirement that a participant's balance be transferred without cost or penalty is not violated.

Example 2. The facts are the same as those in Example 1. Capture Financial Institution generally charges its IRA accounts a reasonable annual administration fee. It also charges that fee with respect to SIMPLE IRAs, including SIMPLE IRAs from which balances must be transferred in accordance with participants' transfer elections. The requirement that participants' balances be transferred without cost or penalty will not be violated merely because a reasonable annual administration fee is charged to SIMPLE IRAs from which balances must be transferred in accordance with participants' transfer elections. [I.R.S. Notice 98-4, Q&A J-4, 1998-2 I.R.B. 26]

Q 14:152 Is the without-cost-or-penalty requirement violated if a designated financial institution charges an employer for the transfer of a participant's SIMPLE IRA balance?

No. The without-cost-or-penalty requirement (see Q 14:144) is not violated merely because a DFI charges an employer an amount that takes into account the financial institution's responsibility to transfer balances upon participants' requests or otherwise charges an employer for transfers requested by participants. [I.R.S. Notice 98-4, 1998-2 I.R.B. 26]

Q 14:153 May an employer pass on any cost or penalty associated with the transfer of a SIMPLE IRA balance to the participant?

No. If a DFI charge for transferring a participant's SIMPLE IRA balance is passed through to a participant, the without-cost-or-penalty requirement is violated.

Q 14:154 Should it be expected that all employers will use a designated financial institution?

Although it would seem convenient to issue just one check to one financial institution each month, it is expected that many employers will permit employees to choose where their SIMPLE IRA contributions are invested. Many institutions will accept SIMPLE IRAs under both the DFI and the non-DFI methods.

Fiduciary Responsibility

Q 14:155 Is an employer or other fiduciary responsible when an employee or beneficiary exercises control over the assets of a SIMPLE IRA?

No. An employer—or any other plan fiduciary (see Q 4:24) will not be subject to liability under ERISA when an employee or beneficiary exercises control over the assets in a SIMPLE IRA. [ERISA § 404(c)(2)]

Q 14:156 When is an employee treated as exercising control over his or her SIMPLE IRA?

An employee or beneficiary will be treated as exercising control over the assets in his or her SIMPLE IRA upon the earliest of

1. An affirmative election among investment options with respect to the initial investment of any contribution,
2. A rollover to any other SIMPLE IRA, or
3. One year after the SIMPLE IRA is established.

[ERISA § 404(c)(2)]

Q 14:157 Are SIMPLE IRA plans subject to the ERISA bonding requirements?

Maybe. In most cases, an employer that handles funds or other property belonging to an ERISA plan (see Q 4:1) is required to be bonded. The basic standard is determined by the possibility of risk of loss in each situation; thus, it is based on the facts and circumstances in each situation. The amount of a bond is determined at the beginning of each year. It may not be less than 10 percent of the amount of funds handled, and the minimum bond is $1,000.

Contributions made by withholding from an employee's salary are not considered funds or other property of a SIMPLE IRA plan for purposes of the bonding provisions as long as they are retained in, and not segregated in any way from, the general assets of the withholding employer. Because employer contributions are made into SIMPLE IRAs established by each employee (which are outside the control of an employer once made), bonding would not generally apply. (See also Q 4:77.) [ERISA §§ 404(c), 412; DOL Reg. §§ 2510.3-3, 2550.412-5]

Miscellaneous Rules

Q 14:158 Are the IRA contribution deduction limits affected if an employee participates in a SIMPLE IRA plan?

Yes. Participation in a SIMPLE IRA plan is treated as active participation for purposes of the IRA contribution deduction limit (generally, $5,000 plus catch-up contributions of up to $1,000 for 2012). Participation includes the receipt of an employer's nonelective contribution or matching contribution or an employee elective contribution. It appears that nonelective contributions made after the end of the year are treated as though made on the last day of that year because they are not discretionary. [I.R.S. Notice 87-16, 1987-1 C.B. 446; I.R.C. § 219(g)(5)(A)]

Example 1. Frame Corporation establishes a SIMPLE IRA plan for 2012 and elects to make a 2 percent nonelective contribution instead of a matching contribution for 2012. The nonelective contribution is made in January 2013. Employees will be treated as active participants for 2012.

Example 2. Beehive Corporation is formed in December 2012. It establishes a cash bonus SIMPLE IRA plan. Under the agreement, employees may elect in writing to have all or a portion of their annual bonus treated as an elective contribution under the plan or receive it in cash on December 31. The employees who make elective contributions based on their bonuses are treated as active participants for 2013 even though the amounts may be deposited into those employees' SIMPLE IRAs after the end of 2012.

Q 14:159 How is the annual IRA deduction limit applied to active participants in a SIMPLE IRA plan?

If either an employee or a spouse is an active participant in a SIMPLE IRA plan, the allowable annual IRA deduction—for 2012, 100 percent of compensation, up to $5,000 ($6,000 with a catch-up contribution), or $10,000 for spousal IRAs ($12,000 if both spouses are age 50 or older) will generally be reduced by $25/30 for every $50 ($100 if married filing jointly beginning in 2009) of adjusted gross income (AGI) above certain amounts (threshold levels) until it is completely phased out as listed in Table 14-1. The calculation of the deductible portion of a contribution on behalf of an active participant may be affected by the catch-up contribution permitted in 2002 and later years (see Q 1:30).

Table 14-1. Phaseout Levels for Employees and Their Spouses for Tax Years 1998–2012

Year	*Threshold Levels for Married Participants Filing Jointly*[*]	*Threshold Levels for Single Participants*
1998	$50,000–$60,000	$30,000–$40,000
1999	$51,000–$61,000	$31,000–$41,000
2000	$52,000–$62,000	$32,000–$42,000
2001	$53,000–$63,000	$33,000–$43,000
2002	$54,000–$64,000	$34,000–$44,000
2003	$60,000–$70,000	$40,000–$50,000
2004	$65,000–$75,000	$45,000–$55,000
2005	$70,000–$80,000	$50,000–$60,000
2006	$75,000–$85,000	$50,000–$60,000
2007	$83,000–$103,000	$52,000–$62,000
2008	$85,000–$105,000	$53,000–$63,000
2009	$89,000–$109,000	$55,000–$65,000
2010	$89,000–$109,000	$56,000–$66,000
2011	$90,000–$110,000	$56,000–$66,000
2012	$92,000–$112,000	$58,000–$68,000

[*] $0 to $10,000 for married individuals filing separate returns.

A minimum deductible contribution of $200 is allowed for active participants with AGI below the phaseout level, and all deductible amounts are rounded up to the next highest $10. An individual whose spouse files a separate return and lives apart from the individual at all times during the taxable year will not be treated as married. [I.R.C. §§ 219(g)(4), 219(g)(5)]

An individual is not treated as an active participant in a SIMPLE IRA plan merely because his or her spouse is an active participant. [I.R.C. § 219(g)(7)] The maximum deduction for such an individual, however, is phased out between $173,000 and $183,000 of AGI for 2012.

Q 14:160 Is a SIMPLE IRA subject to the nonqualified deferred compensation plan rules of Code Section 409A?

No. Code Section 409A provides special rules for certain types of nonqualified deferred compensation plans. The rules, however, do not apply to SEP or

SIMPLE arrangements of an employer. [Treas. Reg. § 1.409A-1(a)(2)(iv) and (v); I.R.S. Notice 2005-1, pt. IV, Q-3(c), 2005-2 I.R.B. 274]

Remedial Correction Programs

Q 14:161 How are plan revocations reported to the IRS?

If an IRA is timely revoked (usually within the first seven days after the date of establishment), the distribution must be reported on Form 1099-R. In general, Revenue Procedure 91-70 [1991-2 C.B. 899] provides the details on how to report revoked distributions and the proper codes to use in box 7 of Form 1099-R. The method of reporting depends on the type of contribution being revoked.

The IRS has not yet revised the revenue procedure to address the revocation of a SIMPLE IRA within its first seven days. The IRS has stated that until Revenue Procedure 91-70 is updated to include revocations of SIMPLE IRAs, the Form 1099-R instructions cannot be changed. If an employer SEP IRA or SIMPLE IRA plan contribution is made and the SEP IRA or SIMPLE IRA is revoked by the employee or is closed by the trustee or custodian, the distribution is reported as fully taxable.

If a SIMPLE IRA is revoked, it seems reasonable to report the distribution on Form 1099-R in box 1 and box 2a and enter code 1 if under age 59½ (S if SIMPLE IRA less than 2 years) or 7 (over age 59½) in box 7, depending on the age of the participant.

Q 14:162 How does EPCRS apply to SIMPLE IRA plans?

EPCRS is a comprehensive system of correction programs that permits sponsors of SEPs and SIMPLE IRA plans to correct eligible failures and to continue providing their employees with retirement benefits on a tax-favored basis. In general, a compliance qualification failure is any failure that adversely affects the tax-sanctioned status of a SEP under Code Section 408(k) or a SIMPLE IRA plan of an employer under Code Section 408(p).

On August 18, 2008, the IRS released updated guidance on EPCRS. Announced in Revenue Procedure 2008-50 [2008-35 I.R.B. 464], the IRS makes supervised voluntary compliance by plan sponsors easier and more fordable; however, it will still require a careful assessment of the defects to determine the most appropriate and effective form of correction.

Revenue Procedure 2008-50, updating and expanding the voluntary correction program is generally effective January 1, 2009; however, plan sponsors are permitted to apply its provisions to any failure on or after September 2, 2008. [Rev. Proc. 2006-27 (2006-22 I.R.B. 945) was superseded by Rev. Proc. 2008-50 (2008-35 I.R.B. 464] The EPCRS program continues to have a self-correction program (SCP) available to fix minor (non-egregious) errors; a voluntary submission program (VCP) involving submission to the IRS and a fixed fee for errors that cannot be corrected through SCP; and a correction program for errors discovered by the IRS on audit (Audit CAP).

SEP and SIMPLE IRA plan failures can be classified into the following categories:

1. Plan document failure—A provision (or the absence of a provision) within the plan's written document that violates Code Section 408(k) if a SEP or Code Section 408(p) in the case of a SIMPLE IRA plan of an employer. [Rev. Proc. 2008-50, § 5.01(2)(a), 2008-35 I.R.B. 464]
2. Operational failure—A problem that arises when a plan is not administered in accordance with its written terms. [Rev. Proc. 2008-50, § 5.01(2)(b), 2008-35 I.R.B. 464]
3. Demographic failure—A violation of the nondiscrimination and/or the participation and coverage requirements. [Rev. Proc. 2008-50, § 5.01(2)(c), 2008-35 I.R.B. 464]
4. Employer eligibility failure—The adoption of a plan by any ineligible employer (e.g., SARSEP adopted by a tax-exempt organization or a SIMPLE IRA plan adopted by an employer that is making contributions to a profit-sharing plan for its non-union employees). [Rev. Proc. 2008-50, § 5.01(2)(d), 2008-35 I.R.B. 464]

[Rev. Proc. 2008-50, 2008-35 I.R.B. 464]

Note 1. Although brought to the attention of the IRS, many of the correction methods provided under the EPCRS remain impractical when applied to SEP and SIMPLE IRA plans. (See chapter 17 for a full discussion of the EPCRS and VCP procedures.)

Note 2. Revenue Procedure 2008-50 expands the EPCRS program by including a streamlined submission procedure for the IRS correction of SEP, SARSEP, and SIMPLE plans, which follow a mostly "check the box" approach, and include a discussion of the new procedure that expands income and excise taxes that the IRS will exercise discretion not to pursue. [Rev. Proc. 2008-50, App. F, 2008-35 I.R.B. 464]

Excess Contributions

Q 14:163 How are excess SIMPLE IRA contributions created?

Excess SIMPLE IRA contributions are created when contributions are made in excess of the amounts permitted or when an employer does not qualify to establish or maintain a SIMPLE IRA plan (see Qs 14:69, 14:83). An amount contributed on behalf of an employee that is in excess of an employee's benefit under the plan or an elective deferral in excess of the dollar amount ($11,500/ $14,000 for 2012) under Code Section 402(g) is treated as an "excess amount" under the IRS's plan correction program (see Qs 14:166, 17:27).

Q 14:164 Has the IRS issued formal guidance on excess SIMPLE IRA contributions?

No. The IRS has not issued formal guidance on excess contributions to a SIMPLE IRA. Form 5329 does not provide for such excesses to be reported on that form (nor does Form 5330 apply) because a SIMPLE IRA is not a traditional IRA, although it is an IRA (just like a SEP or a SARSEP). Therefore, many financial organizations will not make a corrective distribution from a SIMPLE IRA. Instead, they consider any withdrawal an age-based distribution taxable when withdrawn and subject to the 25 percent penalty tax (unless an exception applies).

Example. An employer established a SIMPLE for 2012. On June 8, 2012, the employer adopted a qualified profit-sharing plan and made contributions to such plan for 2012. According to informal guidance, corrective distributions would not be subject to the 25 percent penalty. [ASPA National Conference, 2000, IRS Q No. 376] On September 25, 2000, in Arlington, Virginia, representatives of the American Society of Pension Actuaries (ASPA) met with three senior IRS employees: James E. Holland Jr., Chief, Actuarial Branch I; Paul Shultz, Director of Employee Plans, Rulings and Agreements; and Richard J. Wickersham, Chief, Projects, Branch 2. The IRS representatives stated that the 25 percent penalty would not apply when an employer adopted a 401(k) plan invalidating the qualified salary reduction plan a SIMPLE. The meeting served as the basis for discussions at the ASPA National Conference. Although accurate, the statements neither represent official positions of the IRS nor were they reviewed or approved by the IRS or the Treasury Department. Nonetheless, the trustee or custodian will code this distribution as occurring within the two-year period (see Q 14:166). The participant may have to explain why the 10/25 percent penalty does not apply.

Q 14:165 How else might excess SIMPLE IRA contributions be treated in the absence of formal IRS guidance?

With one exception (excess deferrals), none of the guidance issued with respect to SIMPLE IRAs or to other types of excess contributions suggests how excess SIMPLE IRA contributions should be treated or specifies any correction method. Because excess contributions are not deductible, the employer may be subject to a 10 percent penalty tax unless the excess is corrected (see Q 14:90). [I.R.C. § 4972] The EPCRS offers additional correction methods (see Q 14:167).

The correction methods applicable to qualified plans do not appear to apply to or are inadequate for SIMPLEs because the employer has no control over a SIMPLE IRA, which belongs to the employee (see Q 14:167). An excess amount cannot be used by the employee as a traditional IRA contribution because such contributions must be made to a *traditional IRA*, which does not include a SIMPLE IRA. [I.R.C. § 408(p)(1)(B)]

The traditional IRA excess contribution correction rules *do not* appear to apply to the employees because a SIMPLE retirement account is "an individual retirement plan (as defined in section 7701(a)(37)" that must meet additional rules specified in Code Section 408(p). [I.R.C. § 408(p)(1)] An *individual retirement plan* under Code Section 7701(a)(37) is defined as an individual retirement account or individual retirement annuity under Code Section 408(a) or 408(b), respectively. Thus, SIMPLE IRAs are not correctible under Code Sections 408(d)(4) and 408(d)(5).

The specific instructions for Form W-2 (2012), box 12, relating to 401(k) plan excesses, provide that the entire elective contribution is reported in box 12 (with code S). The instructions specifically state, "The excess is *not* reported in box 1" (emphasis added).

On the other hand, the instructions on the back of Form W-2 (2012) for completing box 12 state the following with respect to code S: "Employee salary reduction contributions under a section 408(p) SIMPLE (not included in box 1)." Arguably, excess contributions under a SIMPLE are to be reported in box 1 but should not be reflected in box 12. This approach appears to eliminate any *employer* penalty relating to nondeductible contributions by turning those amounts into personal SIMPLE IRA contributions made by the employee. Because traditional IRA contributions cannot be made to a SIMPLE IRA, in the authors' opinion the employee should remove the excess contribution as soon as possible. This approach also seems to eliminate the distinction between excess employer contributions and excess employee contributions, but leaves open the issue of income tax withholding and FICA and FUTA taxes.

Q 14:166 How are excess SIMPLE IRA contributions corrected?

It is a mystery. It is unclear whether including excess amounts on Form W-2 is an acceptable method of correcting excess contributions made to a SIMPLE IRA (see Q 14:165). Nonetheless, elective contributions that exceed the annual limit ($11,500/$14,000 for 2012) must be included on a taxpayer's federal income tax return. The instructions to the employee on copy C of Form W-2 state (for line 12): "Amounts in excess of the overall elective deferral limit must be included in income. See the 'Wages, Salaries, Tips, etc.' line instructions for Form 1040." It is equally unclear whether an employer can avoid the nondeductible contribution penalty tax by including excess contributions amounts in box 1 of Form W-2 (see Q 10:12). Until such time as additional guidance is issued, correction of excess contributions under the EPCRS is the only clearly sanctioned method of correction because the Code does not provide a remedy.

Excess traditional IRA contributions are subject to a 6 percent excise tax for each year that the excess remains in the IRA, but the tax cannot be more than 6 percent of the value of the IRA determined as of the end of the year. [I.R.C. § 4973(a)] Excess IRA contributions should be removed. The individual reports the excise tax in Part II of Form 5329, and reports the 10 percent premature distribution penalty tax in Part I of Form 5329 unless an exception applies. The 6 percent penalty tax does not appear, however, to apply to a SIMPLE IRA (see Note 3).

It could be argued that an excess contribution to a SIMPLE IRA should be treated in the same manner as an excess contribution to a SEP IRA. Under a SEP, contributions in excess of 25 percent of an individual's taxable compensation are includible in income and reported by the employer on Form W-2 as wages. [I.R.C. § 402(h)] No comparable provision applies in the case of a SIMPLE, nor does the 25 percent of compensation limit apply. Excess salary reduction contributions under a SARSEP are subject to special notification and timing rules, which in some cases treat the amount as an excess only after the notification is provided to the employee. In some cases, the entire arrangement is invalidated if no notification is provided. No notification requirements are applicable to excesses under a SIMPLE (other than including the amount in box 1) (see Q 14:165).

Note 1. An employer cannot force a corrective distribution from any type of IRA-based plan, such as a SEP, SARSEP, or SIMPLE. It appears evident that the IRS is hesitant to address this issue and other issues relating to the proper administration of the tax laws relating to distributions and the correction of excess contributions. Perhaps this is so because the Code did not provide a clear remedy.

Note 2. Code Section 402(k) provides for excess contributions to be included in the participant's income, and Code Section 404(m) does not provide for a carryforward of nondeductible employer amounts contributed to a SIMPLE IRA, whereas excesses under a SEP can be carried forward. [*See* I.R.C. § 404(h)(1)(C)]

Note 3. Although the 6 percent penalty tax does not appear to apply to an excess SIMPLE IRA contribution according to the IRS, the IRS will eventually have to address this issue as it relates to Form 5329 (discussed above) and Form 1099-R distribution reporting codes. The instructions for Form 1099-R require that SIMPLE IRA distributions be reported in box 2a (taxable amount). Code S is generally entered in box 7 of Form 1099-R if the amount is distributed within two years. The Form 1099-R instructions offer no clue as to the reporting codes that apply to the return of excess SIMPLE IRA contributions that are returned before (adjusted for earnings) or after the participant's tax filing deadline (including extensions). The requirement to report corrective distributions from nearly all types of plans are listed and extensively covered on page R-4 of the instructions to Form 1099-R; but the instructions contain no mention of excess contributions that are made to a SIMPLE IRA.

Q 14:167 How are excess amounts corrected under the EPCRS program?

An amount contributed under a SIMPLE IRA on behalf of an employee that is in excess of an employee's benefit under the plan or an elective deferral under Code Section 402(g) in excess of the dollar amount ($11,500/$14,000 for 2012) is treated as an "excess amount" under the IRS's EPCRS program (see chapter

17). The EPCRS program provides for two possible correction procedures to correct excess amounts, and another for *de minimis* excess amounts.

1. *Distribution of excess amounts.* If an excess amount is attributable to elective deferrals, the plan sponsor may effect distribution of the excess amount, adjusted for earnings through the date of correction, to the affected participant. The amount distributed to the affected participant is includible in gross income in the year of distribution. The distribution is reported on Form 1099-R for the year of distribution with respect to each participant receiving the distribution. In addition, the plan sponsor must inform affected participants that the distribution of an excess amount is not eligible for favorable tax treatment accorded to distributions from a SIMPLE IRA plan (and, specifically, is not eligible for tax-free rollover). If the excess amount is attributable to employer contributions, the plan sponsor may effect distribution of the employer excess amount, adjusted for earnings through the date of correction, to the plan sponsor. The amount distributed to the plan sponsor is not includible in the gross income of the affected participant. The plan sponsor is not entitled to a deduction for such employer excess amount. The distribution is reported on Form 1099-R issued to the participant indicating the taxable amount as zero. Self-correction under this method is generally available. [Rev. Proc. 2008-50, §§ 6:10(5), 9, 2008-35 I.R.B. 464]

   Note. It may be difficult for a plan sponsor to utilize this method unless the trustee/custodian and the employee participant or participants all agree. A recalcitrant employee's SIMPLE IRA could face possible disqualification and lose its tax-exempt status.

2. *Retention of excess amounts.* If an excess amount is retained in the plan, a special compliance fee of 10 percent of the retained amount (excluding earnings) will generally apply. This is in addition to the $250 submission compliance fee. If the error was egregious, special fees apply. [Rev. Proc. 2008-50, §§ 12.05, 12.06, 2008-35 I.R.B. 464] The plan sponsor is not entitled to a deduction for an excess amount retained in the SEP or SIMPLE IRA plan. In the case of an excess amount retained in a SEP that is attributable to a Section 415 failure, the excess amount, adjusted for earnings through the date of correction, must reduce affected participants' applicable Section 415 limit for the year following the year of correction (or for the year of correction if the plan sponsor so chooses), and subsequent years, until the excess is eliminated.

Note. De minimis *excess amounts.* If the total excess amount in a SIMPLE IRA plan, whether attributable to elective deferrals or employer contributions, is $100 or less, the plan sponsor is not required to distribute the excess amount and the special 10 percent compliance fee described in item 2 does not apply. [Rev. Proc. 2008-50, § 6.10(c), 2008-35 I.R.B. 464]

Tax Credits

Q 14:168 May a business that establishes a new SIMPLE IRA plan claim a tax credit?

Beginning in 2002, a small business that adopts a new SIMPLE IRA plan may generally claim an income tax credit for 50 percent of the first $1,000 in administrative and retirement-education expenses for each of the first three years of the plan. The credit is available only to employers that did not have more than 100 employees with compensation in excess of $5,000 during the previous tax year. At least one non-highly compensated employee (NHCE) must participate in the plan. The credit is taken as a general business credit on the employer's business tax return. The other 50 percent of the expenses may be taken as a business deduction. The expenses must be paid or incurred in taxable years beginning after 2001 and with respect to plans established for years after such date. [I.R.C. § 45E]

Q 14:169 What is the maximum credit amount for an employer that adopted a new SIMPLE IRA plan?

The maximum credit amount is $500 for the first year and each of the two taxable years immediately following the first year, thereby limiting the credit to $1,500 over a three-year period. [I.R.C. § 45E(b)]

Q 14:170 May an individual claim a tax credit for a contribution to a SIMPLE IRA?

It depends. Beginning after 2001, a low-income taxpayer savers' credit is available (see Q 1:33). This credit will allow certain individuals to receive a nonrefundable tax credit for a percentage of their contribution to a SIMPLE IRA. The credit is based on a sliding scale percentage of up to $2,000 contributed to a traditional IRA or a Roth IRA or elective deferrals made to a SIMPLE IRA, a SEP IRA, a 401(k) plan, a 403(b) plan, or a 457(b) plan, and voluntary after-tax contributions to a qualified plan. The credit is in addition to any other tax benefit (i.e., potential tax deduction) that the contribution gives the taxpayer. The maximum saver's credit is $1,000 ($2,000 if married). [I.R.C. §§ 25B(a), 25B(b)]

The eligibility requirements for the contribution tax credit are as follows [I.R.C. § 25B(c)]:

1. The taxpayer must be 18 years of age or older.
2. The taxpayer may not be a full-time student or be claimed as a dependent on another taxpayer's tax return.
3. The amount of the credit for any year is reduced by any distribution taken during the "testing period" (i.e., the two preceding tax years), the tax year, or the period after such tax year and before the due date of the federal income tax return of the taxpayer (and spouse of the taxpayer if a joint return is filed) for such year, including extensions.

Example 1. John obtains an extension for filing his 2012 tax return until October 15, 2012. He will be ineligible for the credit for 2013 if he took distributions totaling at least $2,000 at any time between January 1, 2009, and October 15, 2013.

Example 2. Sally takes a distribution of $2,000 from a traditional IRA on March 1, 2011. She is ineligible to claim this credit for 2009, 2011, 2012, and 2013.

4. The taxpayer's credit rates are based on AGI levels for 2012 (see Q 1:33).

Chapter 15

401(k) SIMPLE Plans

This chapter examines the basics of 401(k) SIMPLE plans, including employer and employee eligibility, employee notifications, salary reduction agreements, summary plan descriptions, the time and manner of making contributions and elections, effective dates, and the administrative requirements and deposit rules for employers. SIMPLE plans established in the form of individual retirement accounts or individual retirement annuities (IRAs) are more fully discussed in chapter 14. Appendix N contains a chart comparing a SIMPLE in IRA form to a SIMPLE in the form of a 401(k) plan.

The Economic Growth and Tax Relief Reconciliation Act of 2001 (EGTRRA) changed many of the rules and increased many of the limits applicable to 401(k) SIMPLE plans. Increased employer and employee contribution limits, compensation caps, and deduction limits, as well as administrative changes, will make these plans more popular than they were before.

A complete explanation of all the qualification requirements that apply to qualified plans is beyond the scope of this book. Those issues are more fully discussed in S. Krass, *The 2012 Pension Answer Book* (New York, CCH Incorporated, 2012).

Introduction

Q 15:1 What is a *401(k) SIMPLE plan*?

A *401(k) SIMPLE plan* is a qualified 401(k) plan that adopts some of the SIMPLE rules to satisfy annual nondiscrimination tests. SIMPLE is the acronym for savings incentive match plan for employees.

A 401(k) SIMPLE plan maintained by an eligible employer (see Q 15:16) is treated as satisfying the participation and discrimination standards of the Internal Revenue Code (Code) provided the arrangement satisfies special rules relating to contributions (see Q 15:20) and vesting (see Q 15:5) and is the only plan of the employer (see Q 15:13). [I.R.C. § 401(k)(11)(A)]

Although the 401(k) SIMPLE rules are in Code Section 401(k)(11), subparagraph (D) of that section states that "any term used in this paragraph which is also used in section 408(p) shall have the meaning given such term by such section." Thus, some of the 401(k) SIMPLE rules are borrowed from, and are the same as, the rules for SIMPLE IRAs (individual retirement accounts or individual retirement annuities).

The 401(k) SIMPLE rules apply to plan years beginning after December 31, 1996. [I.R.C. § 401(k)(11), 401(m)]

Q 15:2 Must a 401(k) SIMPLE plan be maintained on a calendar-year basis?

Yes. The plan year of a plan containing 401(k) SIMPLE provisions must be the calendar year. Thus, an employer maintaining a 401(k) plan on a fiscal-year basis must convert the plan to a calendar year to adopt 401(k) SIMPLE provisions. [I.R.C. § 401(k)(11)(D)(i); Rev. Proc. 97-9, § 2.04, 1997-1 C.B. 624; Rev. Proc. 87-27, 1987-1 C.B. 769 (regarding automatic approval of certain changes in accounting periods for qualified plans and trusts)]

Q 15:3 Do the qualification and other plan requirements of the Code apply to 401(k) SIMPLE plans?

For the most part, yes. Except as discussed in this chapter, all qualification requirements of the Code continue to apply to a plan that adopts 401(k) SIMPLE provisions, including the following:

1. The contribution limits of Code Section 415 must be met (see Q 15:25).

2. The compensation limits of Code Section 401(a)(17) must be met (see Q 15:19)
3. The plan as amended must operate in accordance with its terms.
4. In addition, all other requirements applicable to 401(k) plans continue to apply, including the following:
   a. The distribution restrictions of Code Section 401(k)(2)(B), which generally prohibit elective contributions from being distributed before a participant's severance from employment, attainment of age 59½, death, disability, or hardship; and
   b. The general prohibition set forth in Code Section 401(k)(4)(B) against state and local governments' maintaining a 401(k) plan.

Because of the limits, restrictions, and complexities of a 401(k) SIMPLE plan, some commentators believe it unlikely that many employers will establish SIMPLEs in 401(k) form. [*See* England, "SARSEP or SIMPLE? Smaller Plans Face a Choice between New and Old Savings Plans," 5 *Plan Sponsor* 1 (Feb. 1997)] Although statistics on 401(k) SIMPLE plans are not readily available, in the authors' opinion, other types of 401(k) plans (e.g., safe-harbor 401(k) plans) are more suitable for most employers.

Q 15:4 Is a 401(k) SIMPLE subject to the nonqualified deferred compensation plan rules of Code Section 409A?

No. Code Section 409A provides special rules for certain types of nonqualified deferred compensation plans. The rules, however, do not apply to a SIMPLE or SEP arrangement of an employer. [Treas. Reg. § 1.409A-1(a)(2)(iv) and (v); I.R.S. Notice 2005-1, Pt. IV, Q-3(c), 2005-2 I.R.B. 274]

Vesting Requirements

Q 15:5 Must contributions to a 401(k) SIMPLE plan be fully vested?

Yes. Like contributions made under a SIMPLE IRA plan, all contributions (adjusted for gains and losses) made under a 401(k) SIMPLE plan must be fully vested (nonforfeitable) at all times. [I.R.C. § 401(k)(11)(A)(iii)] (Contributions not made under the SIMPLE rules may continue under existing or other qualified plan vesting rules.)

Employer Eligibility

Q 15:6 Which employers may establish a 401(k) SIMPLE plan?

Generally, a 401(k) SIMPLE plan may be established only by an employer that had no more than 100 employees (the 100-employee limit) who earned

$5,000 or more in compensation during the preceding calendar year. [I.R.C. §§ 401(k)(11)(A), 401(k)(11)(D), 408(p)(2)(C)(i)(I)]

There is a two-year grace period if an eligible employer ceases to be eligible in a subsequent year (see Q 15:12).

Note. The 100-employee limit for a 401(k) SIMPLE plan is the same as the 100-employee limit for a SIMPLE IRA plan (see Qs 14:46, 14:47).

Q 15:7 Are tax-exempt employers and governmental entities permitted to maintain a 401(k) SIMPLE plan?

A tax-exempt employer may maintain a 401(k) SIMPLE plan after 1996. A governmental entity (other than an Indian tribal government), on the other hand, may not maintain a SIMPLE in the form of a 401(k) plan. It should be noted, however, that the Code does not expressly prohibit tax-exempt organizations or government employers from establishing a simplified employee pension (SEP) plan or SIMPLE IRA plan. [*See* I.R.C. § 401(k)(4)(B)(ii)] (This issue is more fully discussed in G. S. Lesser, *457 Answer Book*, 5th ed. (New York: CCH Incorporated, 2012).)

Q 15:8 May any employees be excluded for purposes of the 100-employee limit?

No. For purposes of the 100-employee limit, all employees employed at any time during the calendar year are taken into account, regardless of whether they are eligible to participate in the SIMPLE. Thus, certain unionized employees who are excludable under the rules of Code Section 410(b)(3), nonresident alien employees, and employees who have not met the plan's minimum eligibility requirements (see Qs 14:56–14:62) must be taken into account. Any such employee, however, can be excluded from participation in the SIMPLE (see Q 15:15). [I.R.C. §§ 401(c)(1), 408(p)(2)(C)(i)(I), 408(p)(4)(B)]

Q 15:9 Are self-employed individuals treated as employees for purposes of the 100-employee limit?

Yes. Employees counted for purposes of the 100-employee limit include self-employed individuals who received earned income from the employer during the year (see Q 15:18). [I.R.C. §§ 401(c)(1), 408(p)(2)(C)(i)(I), 408(p)(4)(B)]

Q 15:10 Must employees of related employers be considered for purposes of the 100-employee limit?

Yes. Certain related employers (trades or businesses under common control) must be treated as a single employer; thus, individuals working for related employers are treated as if they are employed by a single employer for purposes of satisfying the SIMPLE requirements (see Q 2:5).

Related employers include the following:

- A controlled group of corporations under Code Section 414(b)
- A partnership or sole proprietorship under common control under Code Section 414(c)
- An affiliated service group under Code Section 414(n)

Q 15:11 How are leased employees treated for purposes of the 100-employee limit?

For purposes of the 100-employee limit, leased employees are treated as employed by the employer for which they provide services if the services are performed on substantially a full-time basis for at least one year and pursuant to an agreement. [I.R.C. § 414(n)(3)(B); Rev. Proc. 97-9, Appendix § 1.2(a), 1997-1 C.B. 624]

Q 15:12 What rules apply to an employer that fails to be an eligible employer in a subsequent year?

An employer maintaining a 401(k) SIMPLE plan that fails to be an eligible employer may continue to maintain the plan for two years following the last year in which it was eligible. [Rev. Proc. 97-9, Appendix § 1.2(a), 1997-1 C.B. 624]

Further, if the failure to satisfy the 100-employee limit is the result of an acquisition, disposition, or similar transaction involving the employer, the qualified plan transition rule for coverage when there is an acquisition or disposition replaces the two-year grace period (i.e., the grace period runs through the end of the year following the acquisition or disposition). [I.R.C. § 410(b)(6)(C)]

Exclusive Plan Requirement

Q 15:13 Must a 401(k) SIMPLE plan be the exclusive plan of an employer?

Yes. Like a SIMPLE IRA plan, a 401(k) SIMPLE plan generally must be the only "qualified plan" of the employer (see Qs 14:48–14:50, 15:14, 15:17). However, if employees who are eligible to participate in the SIMPLE 401(k) plan do not receive contributions or accrue benefits under another qualified plan (as defined in Code Section 72(p)(4)(A)(ii) and includes an eligible 457(b) plan), the existence of the qualified plan will not violate the exclusive plan requirement. Thus, for example, an employer may adopt a SIMPLE 401(k) plan for non-collectively bargained employees without violating the exclusive plan requirement even though the employer also maintains a qualified plan for collectively bargained employees. In other cases, if the employer maintains another qualified plan, that plan generally must be frozen or terminated. [I.R.C.

§§ 401(k)(11)(A)(ii), 401(k)(11)(C), 408(k)(12)(D)(i), 410(b)(3)] It should also be noted that an employer may not maintain more than one SIMPLE plan.

Q 15:14 What rule applies to an employer that simultaneously maintains a qualified plan and a 401(k) SIMPLE plan as a result of an acquisition, disposition, or other similar transaction?

The Technical Corrections Act of 1998 provides for a uniform grace period during which a 401(k) SIMPLE plan may be maintained following an acquisition, disposition, or other similar transaction that affects the employer's ability to meet the following requirements:

1. The 100-employee limit,
2. The exclusive plan requirement, and
3. The plan coverage and eligibility rules.

If an employer with a 401(k) SIMPLE plan fails to meet any of the preceding requirements because of an acquisition, disposition, or other similar transaction, the plan may be maintained for a transition period that begins on the date of the transaction and ends on the last day of the second calendar year following the calendar year in which the transaction occurs. For the grace period to apply, coverage under the plan may not be significantly changed during the transition period.

For a 401(k) SIMPLE plan to be maintained during the transition period, it must meet the above requirements following the transaction as if the employer maintaining the plan had remained a separate employer.

> **Example.** Jackie, who owns a hair salon, Touch of Class, adopted a 401(k) SIMPLE plan for the company's 18 employees. On June 1, 2012, Jackie acquired a second salon called Nail Boutique, which had a money purchase pension plan for its 25 employees. Touch of Class can continue its 401(k) SIMPLE plan during the period June 1, 2012, to December 31, 2014. Coverage under the plan cannot be significantly changed during that period, and eligibility to participate is limited to individuals who would have been employees of Touch of Class if the acquisition had not occurred.

Employee Eligibility

Q 15:15 When may an employee of an eligible employer participate in a 401(k) SIMPLE plan?

Employee eligibility for a 401(k) SIMPLE plan is based on qualified plan rules, under which, for example, an employee may be eligible after the completion of one year of service (generally, 1,000 hours) and attainment of age 21. Any employee who is eligible to make elective deferrals under the regular 401(k) plan rules is eligible to participate in the 401(k) SIMPLE plan. As is the case with a SIMPLE IRA plan, collectively bargained employees, nonresident alien employees, and so on may be excluded from participating in a 401(k) SIMPLE plan (see Q 14:57). [Rev. Proc. 97-9, Appendix § 2.2, 1997-1 C.B. 624]

Contributions for Household Workers. An employer may make a contribution on behalf of each domestic (and similar) worker other than the employer or a member of the employer's family. The employer's contributions, however, do not qualify for a deduction, because the contributions are not made in connection with a "trade or business." For taxable years beginning after 2001, the 10 percent excise tax on nondeductible contributions does not apply to 401(k) SIMPLE or SIMPLE IRA plan contributions, simply because the contributions are not a trade or business expense. [I.R.C. § 4972(c)(6)]

> **Note.** Code Section 4972(c)(6) is intended to apply only to employers that have paid and continue to pay all applicable employment taxes. [EGTRRA § 637; see H.R. Rpt. No. 107-51, pt 1 (2001)] The Working Families Tax Relief Act of 2004 (Pub. L. No. 109-135) provides that wages paid to domestic workers may be treated as compensation even though such amounts are not subject to income tax withholding. [I.R.C. § 408(p)(6)(A), as amended]

> **Practice Pointer.** Similar provisions were not enacted for a SEP or salary reduction SEP (SARSEP) covering only a domestic or household worker. Thus, an employer's nondeductible contributions may be subject to a 10 percent penalty (see Qs 2:1, 10:11).

Q 15:16 May an individual who works for unrelated employers participate in more than one SIMPLE plan or in a SIMPLE plan of one employer and a qualified plan of another employer?

Yes. An employee may participate in a SIMPLE plan of one employer and in a SIMPLE plan or qualified plan of another employer without violating the exclusive plan requirement (see Q 15:13), provided the employers are unrelated. In such a case, the total elective deferrals that can be made under more than one plan generally may not exceed $17,000 for 2012. [I.R.C. §§ 402(g)(1), 402(g)(3)(D)] (See Q 15:23 for elective deferral limits for years after 2004.)

Q 15:17 May an individual participate in a 401(k) SIMPLE plan and an eligible plan under Code Section 457(b) without violating the only-plan-of-the-employer rule?

Yes. Contributions made under a 457(b) plan do not violate the only-plan-of-the-employer rule because such a plan is not a qualified plan, and is not treated as a qualified plan for the purpose of denying SIMPLE contributions (see Qs 14:48, 14:52). The dollar limit under an eligible 457(b) plan (generally $17,000 for 2012) is not reduced by the amount of elective employer contributions deferred by the employee under the 401(k) SIMPLE plan for years after 2001. [I.R.C. § 457(c)(2)(B)(i)]

Compensation

Q 15:18 What definition of *compensation* applies to a 401(k) SIMPLE plan?

The SIMPLE IRA plan definition of compensation is used for a 401(k) SIMPLE plan (see Qs 14:63–14:68). Therefore, in the case of a self-employed individual, *compensation* means net earnings from self-employment before subtracting any contributions made under the 401(k) SIMPLE plan on behalf of the individual (see Q 14:64). [I.R.C. § 401(k)(11)(D)(i); Rev. Proc. 97-9, Appendix § 2.1, 1997-1 C.B. 624]

Q 15:19 How much compensation may be considered in a 401(k) SIMPLE plan?

For 2012, the maximum compensation that may be considered on behalf of any participant in a 401(k) SIMPLE plan is $250,000. Therefore, for 2012, a nonelective contribution may not exceed $5,000 ($250,000 × .02), and the maximum matching contribution is $7,500 ($250,000 × .03). (See Qs 6:1, 7:1.) [I.R.C. § 401(a)(17)]

Contributions

Q 15:20 What types of contributions may be made under a 401(k) SIMPLE plan?

Under a qualified plan containing 401(k) SIMPLE provisions, each employee may elect to make salary reduction contributions of up to $11,500 ($14,000 with a catch-up contribution if age 50 or over) for 2012 (see Q 15:23). For 2012, the employer must make either a matching contribution or a nonelective contribution, as follows:

1. *Matching contribution*. Each year, the employer makes a matching contribution to the plan on behalf of each employee who makes a salary reduction election. The amount of the matching contribution is equal to the employee's salary reduction contribution, up to a limit of 3 percent of the employee's compensation (up to $7,350) for the full calendar year.
2. *Nonelective contribution*. For any year, instead of a matching contribution, the employer may choose to make a nonelective contribution of 2 percent of compensation (up to $5,000 for 2012) for the full calendar year for each eligible employee who received at least $5,000 (or less if elected) of compensation from the employer for the year.

[I.R.C. § 401(k)(11)(B); *see* I.R.S. Notice 2011-90, 2011-47 I.R.B. 791 for 2012 limits]

No other types of contributions are permitted. [I.R.C. § 401(k)(11)(B)(i)(III)]

Example. Sasha changed jobs and became a participant in her new employer's 401(k) SIMPLE plan. Shortly thereafter, Sasha received distributions from a SIMPLE IRA and from her previous employer's 401(k) SIMPLE plan. Neither distribution may be rolled over or transferred into the 401(k) SIMPLE of Sasha's new employer because a 401(k) SIMPLE plan may only receive elective and matching contributions.

Q 15:21 Do the designated Roth account rules apply to a 401(k) SIMPLE IRA plan?

Yes. Designated Roth account (DRA) contributions may be accepted by a new or existing 401(k) or 403(b) plans, and beginning in 2011 by a governmental 457(b) plan. If a plan adopts this feature, employees can designate some or all of their elective contributions as DRA contributions (which are included in gross income) rather than as traditional, pretax elective contributions. Starting in 2006 for Roth 401(k) and Roth 403(b) and in 2011 for governmental 457(b) plans, elective contributions come in two types: traditional, pretax elective contributions (elective contributions are also referred to as elective deferrals) and DRA contributions. [I.R.C. § 402A(e)(1) 402A(e)(1)] DRA contributions are more fully discussed in chapter 10 of the *Roth IRA Answer Book* (New York, CCH Incorporated, 2012).

Roth SIMPLE 401(k). It would appear that a 401(k) plan that is satisfying discrimination rules by adopting a 401(k) SIMPLE may provide for elective contributions to be made into a designated Roth contribution account. [Treas. Reg. § 1.402(g)-1(b)(6)]

Q 15:22 May an employer elect a matching contribution of less than 3 percent?

No. An employer does not have the option under a 401(k) SIMPLE plan of reducing the matching contribution to less than 3 percent of an employee's compensation. [I.R.C. § 401(k)(11)(B)] Such an option does exist for a SIMPLE IRA plan (see Q 14:86).

Q 15:23 Is the annual dollar limit on salary reduction contributions ever increased?

Yes. The elective deferral limit for a 401(k) SIMPLE plan increases each year, as follows:

Year	*Increased Deferral Limit*
2003	$ 8,000
2004	$ 9,000
2005	$10,000
2006	$10,000

Year	*Increased Deferral Limit*
2007	$10,500
2008	$10,500
2009	$11,500
2010	$11,500
2011	$11,500
2012	$11,500

After 2005, the elective 401(k) SIMPLE plan deferral limit is increased for COLAs in increments of $500. [I.R.C. §§ 408(p)(2)(A)(ii), 408(p)(2)(E)] For 2012, the normal limit on elective deferrals is $11,500 for individuals who are under age 50. [I.R.S. Notice 2011-90, 2011-47 I.R.B. 791 for 2012 limits]

In addition, if a participant in a 401(k) SIMPLE plan reaches age 50 by the end of the calendar year, he or she may make an additional elective deferral. The amount of this catch-up contribution is in addition to the normal deferral limit for the applicable year.

The maximum amount of a catch-up contribution is the lesser of the participant's compensation for the year or the applicable dollar amount. The applicable dollar amounts are as follows:

Year	*Normal Limit*	*Applicable Catch-up Dollar Amount*	*Total Deferral*
1997–2000	$ 6,000	n/a	$ 6,000
2001	$ 6,500	n/a	$ 6,500
2002	$ 7,000	$ 500	$ 7,500
2003	$ 8,000	$1,000	$ 9,000
2004	$ 9,000	$1,500	$10,500
2005	$10,000	$2,000	$12,000
2006	$10,000	$2,500	$12,500
2007	$10,500	$2,500	$13,000
2008	$10,500	$2,500	$13,000
2009	$11,500	$2,500	$14,000
2010	$11,500	$2,500	$14,000
2011	$11,500	$2,500	$14,000
2012	$11,500	$2,500	$14,000

[I.R.C. § 414(v); I.R.S. Notice 2011-90, 2011-47 I.R.B. 791 for 2012 limits]

This means that a 401(k) SIMPLE plan participant who is age 50 or over by the last day of participant's taxable year (generally Dec. 31) may defer 100 percent of compensation or $14,000, whichever is less, for 2012. The employer may choose to make a 3 percent of compensation matching contribution based on the participant's total compensation or a 2 percent of compensation nonelective contribution based on the participant's total compensation. In both cases, compensation is capped at $250,000.

Example. Karen, age 55, participates in a 401(k) SIMPLE plan. Her compensation is $300,000, and she defers the maximum of $14,000 for 2012. If Karen's employer is matching her deferrals at 3 percent of compensation, Karen's matching contribution will be $7,500 ($250,000 compensation limit × .03). Alternatively, if Karen's employer chooses the 2 percent nonelective contribution option, Karen's nonelective contribution will be $5,000 ($250,000 compensation limit × .02).

Q 15:24 May contributions under a 401(k) SIMPLE plan be integrated with Social Security contributions?

No. Contributions to a 401(k) SIMPLE plan may not be reduced or increased by taking into account Social Security or other similar contributions. [I.R.C. § 401(k)(3)(B)]

Q 15:25 Does the 100 percent of compensation limit apply to a 401(k) SIMPLE plan?

Yes. The 100 percent of taxable compensation limit under Code Section 415 (25 percent before 2002) applies to a 401(k) SIMPLE plan, although it does not apply to a SIMPLE IRA plan. This limit is referred to as the "Section 415 annual limit." For 2012, the Section 415 annual limit is the lesser of 100 percent of the employee's compensation or $50,000 ($55,500 with catch-up contribution). [I.R.C. § 415; I.R.S. Notice 2011-90, 2011-47 I.R.B. 791 for 2012 limits; Rev. Proc. 97-9, Appendix § 2.06, 1997-1 C.B. 624]

Q 15:26 Does the deduction limit of 25 percent of aggregate compensation apply to an employer maintaining a 401(k) SIMPLE plan?

No. The employer's deduction for contributions made to a 401(k) SIMPLE, including salary reduction contributions, is not limited to 25 percent of the participant's aggregate compensation under Code Section 404. [I.R.C. §§ 404(a)(3)(A)(i), 404(a)(3)(A)(ii), 404(m)]

Q 15:27 Are matching contributions made to a 401(k) SIMPLE plan for self-employed individuals treated as elective contributions?

No. Matching contributions made to a 401(k) SIMPLE plan for self-employed individuals are treated in the same way as matching contributions made for employees are treated, and thus are not subject to the annual dollar limit on elective deferrals after 1997 (see Qs 14:78, 15:23). [I.R.C. § 402(g)(9)] (See

Q 15:58 for a discussion of excess contributions that may have resulted from contributions made for 1996 or a later year.)

Q 15:28 May an employee choose not to make contributions to a 401(k) SIMPLE plan?

Yes. Participation in a SIMPLE plan must be voluntary. An employee must elect to participate and cannot be required to do so (see Q 15:30).

Q 15:29 May a participant discontinue making contributions to a 401(k) SIMPLE plan?

Yes. A participant in a 401(k) SIMPLE plan may discontinue contributions at any time during the calendar year. [I.R.C. § 408(p)(5)(B)]

Q 15:30 May an employee elect not to receive an employer's matching or nonelective contributions to a 401(k) SIMPLE plan?

No. An employee may not opt out of employer contributions to a 401(k) SIMPLE plan. The employer must make the matching contribution (or, alternatively, the nonelective employer contribution), as indicated in the notification to employees, to all eligible employees earning the compensation requirements (if any are specified). [I.R.C. § 408(p)(4)(A)]

Q 15:31 May contributions be made to a 401(k) SIMPLE plan from compensation earned before the date the salary reduction agreement or election is executed?

No. A salary reduction election may not apply to compensation that an employee received, or had a right to immediately receive, before execution of the salary reduction agreement or election.

Discrimination Testing

Q 15:32 Must a plan containing 401(k) SIMPLE provisions satisfy the actual deferral percentage or actual contribution percentage test?

No. For a year in which the SIMPLE rules are used to satisfy nondiscrimination standards, the nondiscrimination tests applicable to elective deferrals and matching contributions will be satisfied provided all SIMPLE contributions are fully vested and the employer makes the required contribution. [I.R.C. §§ 401(k)(11)(A), 401(k)(11)(B)] Thus, the plan does not have to satisfy the special nondiscrimination tests applicable to 401(k) plans, the actual deferral percentage (ADP) test, and the actual contribution percentage (ACP) test applicable to matching contributions, unless the employer fails to make SIMPLE contributions.

Q 15:33 Is it possible for a 401(k) SIMPLE plan to be top heavy?

A 401(k) plan that includes 401(k) SIMPLE provisions is not treated as top heavy (see Q 8:1) under Code Section 416. If the employer fails to make contributions as required, it appears unlikely that a minimum top-heavy contribution (up to 3 percent) will be required even if the plan primarily benefits key employees (but see Qs 15:57, 15:58). [I.R.C. §§ 408(k)(11)(D)(ii), 416(g)(4)(G)]

Tax Treatment of Contributions

Q 15:34 Are elective, nonelective, or matching contributions to a 401(k) SIMPLE plan includible in a participant's income?

Within allowable limits (see Qs 15:20, 15:23), 401(k) SIMPLE plan contributions are not includible in a participant's gross income for federal income tax purposes. [I.R.C. §§ 402(a), 404(m)] state income tax rules may differ.

Q 15:35 May an employee deduct salary reduction contributions to a 401(k) SIMPLE plan on his or her federal income tax return?

Except for a self-employed individual, whose contributions are deducted on Form 1040 (see Q 14:123), an employee may not deduct elective 401(k) SIMPLE plan contributions on his or her federal income tax return. State income tax rules may differ.

Q 15:36 Are salary reduction contributions to a 401(k) SIMPLE plan subject to FICA, FUTA, or RRTA taxes?

Yes. Salary reduction contributions to a 401(k) SIMPLE plan are subject to tax under the Federal Insurance Contributions Act (FICA), the Federal Unemployment Tax Act (FUTA), and the Railroad Retirement Tax Act (RRTA). [I.R.C. §§ 3121(a)(5)(H), 3306(b)(5)(H); I.R.S. Notice 98-4, Q&A I-1, 1998-2 I.R.B. 26]

Q 15:37 Are employer contributions to a 401(k) SIMPLE plan subject to FICA, FUTA, or RRTA taxes?

No. Matching and nonelective (i.e., employer) contributions to a 401(k) SIMPLE plan are not subject to FICA, FUTA, or RRTA taxes. [I.R.C. §§ 3121(a)(5)(H), 3121(v)(2)(C), 3231(e)(8)(B), 3306(b)(5)(H); I.R.S. Notice 98-4, Q&A I-1, 1998-2 I.R.B. 26]

Q 15:38 Are employer contributions to a 401(k) SIMPLE plan subject to federal income tax withholding?

No. SIMPLE contributions are not includible in gross income; therefore, employer contributions to a 401(k) SIMPLE plan are exempt from federal income tax withholding. [I.R.C. § 3401(a)(12)(D); I.R.S. Notice 98-4, Q&A I-1, 1998-2 I.R.B. 26]

Q 15:39 How are salary reduction contributions to a 401(k) SIMPLE plan reported?

Salary reduction contributions to a 401(k) SIMPLE plan must be reported on Form W-2, Wage and Tax Statement. [I.R.S. Notice 98-4, Q&A I-1, 1998-2 I.R.B. 26] On the 2012 Form W-2, a code must be used to designate amounts reported in box 12. Code D is used to report salary reduction contributions made under a 401(k) SIMPLE plan. [Ann. 96-134, 1996-53 I.R.B. 60]

Q 15:40 Must matching and nonelective contributions be reported on Form W-2?

No. Like other types of contributions made to qualified plans, matching and nonelective (i.e., employer) contributions are not required to be reported on Form W-2. [I.R.S. Notice 98-4, Q&A I-1, 1998-2 I.R.B. 26]

Q 15:41 When are 401(k) SIMPLE plan contributions deductible by the employer?

Within limits, contributions (including elective contributions made by employees) are deductible by the employer for its business taxable year that includes or coincides with the last day of the plan year, which is always December 31 in the case of a SIMPLE (see Q 15:2). Thus, if a taxpayer with a fiscal tax year ending June 30 adopts a 401(k) SIMPLE plan for 2012, the taxpayer may claim a deduction for 2012 contributions on its business tax return for the period ending June 30, 2011. [I.R.C. § 404(a)(3)]

Q 15:42 By what date must matching or nonelective contributions be made by an employer to a 401(k) SIMPLE plan for deduction purposes?

For deduction purposes only (see Qs 14:124, 14:125), employer matching or nonelective contributions to a 401(k) SIMPLE plan must be made on or before the date the employer's federal income tax return is due (including extensions; see Qs 2:32, 2:35). [I.R.C. § 404(a)(6)]

Q 15:43 How long does an employer have to place elective deferrals into a 401(k) SIMPLE plan's trust?

Elective contributions are assets of a 401(k) SIMPLE plan. The employer must promptly transmit any employee salary reduction contributions to the plan's trust on the earliest date such contributions can reasonably be segregated from the employer's general assets, but not later than the 15th business day of the month following the month in which the contributions were withheld or received by the employer. [DOL Reg. § 2510.3-102] (See Q 4:44 regarding special DOL rules for partnerships and sole proprietorships.)

The 15-day rule is not a safe harbor. In some cases, one or two days may be a reasonable period (e.g., for an employer that uses automatic payroll processing and makes electronic transfers of funds). Each situation depends on the specific facts and circumstances at the time the contribution amounts are withheld. The DOL has a seven-day safe harbor rule (see Q 4:45).

Distributions

Q 15:44 When may distributions be made from a 401(k) SIMPLE plan?

All 401(k) plans, including those that are SIMPLEs, must limit in-service distributions of elective contributions. [I.R.C. §§ 401(k)(2)(B), 408(k)(10); Rev. Proc. 97-9, Appendix § 2.06, 1997-1 C.B. 624] Except for loans, distributions to participants and beneficiaries of amounts attributable to elective deferrals may not be made to participants and beneficiaries earlier than upon any of the following:

1. Death;
2. Disability;
3. Severance from employment (before 2002, separation from service);
4. For distributions made before 2002, the disposition of 85 percent or more of the employer's assets to an unrelated corporation, provided the employee continues employment with the purchaser;
5. The disposition of the employer's subsidiary to an unrelated entity (or individual), provided the employee continues employment with the subsidiary;
6. The employee's hardship; or
7. The termination of the plan, provided a lump-sum distribution is received.

Separation from service occurred only upon a participant's discharge, retirement, resignation, or death. It did not occur if the employee continued on the same job for a different employer as a result of a consolidation, merger, liquidation, or some other corporate transaction.

Severance from employment occurs when a participant ceases to be employed by the employer that maintains the plan. Under the "same desk rule," a participant's severance from employment does not necessarily result in a separation from service. [Rev. Rul. 79-336, 1979-2 C.B. 187]

Note. The amount attributable to elective deferrals includes any gain thereon.

Q 15:45 How are distributions from a 401(k) SIMPLE plan taxed?

Generally, distributions from a 401(k) SIMPLE plan are taxable as ordinary earned income and thus are subject to federal income tax withholding. The withholding rate is 20 percent. [I.R.C. §§ 3405(b), 3405(e)(1); Treas. Reg. § 35.3405-1]

Individuals born before 1936 may be able to use the special 10-year income averaging method of computing the tax on a qualifying lump-sum (nonperiodic) distribution (see Appendix F). Five-year income averaging has been repealed for years after 1999. [I.R.C. §§ 402(d), 402(e)(4)(D)]

Q 15:46 When are hardship withdrawals from a 401(k) SIMPLE plan permitted?

Hardship withdrawals from a 401(k) SIMPLE plan are permitted upon the request of a participant if (1) the participant has an "immediate and heavy financial need" and (2) other resources are not reasonably available to meet the need. [Treas. Reg. § 1.401(k)-1(d)(3)(i)]

Withdrawals for medical expenses, tuition and related educational expenses, costs related to the purchase of a principal residence, and payments necessary to prevent eviction or foreclosure have all been deemed by the Internal Revenue Service (IRS) to satisfy the immediate and heavy financial need requirement. For years beginning after December 31, 2005, immediate and heavy financial needs will also include funeral expenses for the participant, the participant's spouse, or the participant's dependents, and, a financial disaster that caused damage to the participant's primary residence. These are referred to as "deemed" reasons for hardship, which means that if the employer wishes to add another definition to the list of six, they must get approval from the IRS. [Treas. Reg. § 1.401(k)-1(d)(3)(iii)(B)]

Hardship withdrawals are taxable and may be subject to a 10 percent premature distribution penalty unless the participant is age 59½ or older.

Note. The period during which an employee is suspended from making elective contributions (and after-tax contributions) following a hardship distribution was reduced from 12 months to 6 months. [Treas. Reg. § 1.401(k)-1(d)(3)(iv)(E)(2)]

Q 15:47 What are the restrictions on loans from a 401(k) SIMPLE plan?

Loans from a 401(k) SIMPLE plan must be made in accordance with plan provisions and the employer's written loan policy. There are restrictions on how much may be borrowed and when and how the loan must be repaid. Loans must be adequately secured, bear a reasonable rate of interest, and be made available to all participants (or beneficiaries) on a reasonably equivalent basis and must not be made to highly compensated employees (HCEs), officers, or shareholders in greater percentages than to other employees. [I.R.C. §§ 72(p)(1), 72(p)(2)]

Q 15:48 Are distributions from a 401(k) SIMPLE plan to a participant who has not reached age 59½ ever subject to a 25 percent premature distribution penalty?

No. The 25 percent penalty for distributions made within the first two years of the employee's participation in a SIMPLE IRA does not apply to a SIMPLE in the form of a 401(k) plan. [I.R.C. § 72(t)(6)]

Q 15:49 May distributions from a 401(k) SIMPLE plan commence after a participant reaches age 70½ if the participant is still employed?

Yes. Distributions may commence after age 70½ even if the participant is still employed. Because IRA distribution rules do not apply to 401(k) SIMPLE plans, if the participant is still employed at age 70½ and is not a 5 percent owner, distributions may be delayed until the employee retires, if the plan allows. [I.R.C. §§ 401(a)(9)(C)(i), 401(a)(9)(C)(ii)(II)]

Rollovers and Transfers

Q 15:50 Do the rollover rules apply to distributions from 401(k) SIMPLE plans?

Yes. All the regular rollover rules apply to 401(k) SIMPLE plans. Thus, a participant who receives a distribution from a 401(k) SIMPLE plan may generally defer tax on the taxable amount received by rolling it over within 60 days of receipt to another qualified employer-sponsored plan (except another 401(k) SIMPLE plan; see Q 15:20) or to an IRA or SEP IRA and after 2007, directly to a Roth IRA. A SIMPLE IRA may not, however, be used to receive a rollover from a qualified plan, including a 401(k) SIMPLE plan. [*See* SIMPLE IRA Listing of Required Modifications (LRM) and Information Package (June 2010)]

> **Caution.** The 60-day rollover period is measured in calendar days. If the 60th day falls on a Saturday, Sunday, or holiday, the rollover period is not extended to the next business day. [Ltr. Ruls. 200951044 (Sept. 24, 2009); 200930052 (Apr. 24, 2009)]

The 60-day rollover period does not apply to a direct rollover if the plan makes out the check to the trustee because the participant can make no use of the check (it is not a distribution but a direct transfer). The IRS ruled that, where a distributee gave the check to the trustee more than 60 days after receipt, the delay did not convert the rollover into a taxable distribution. [Ltr. Rul. 201005057 (Nov. 10, 2009)]

EGTRRA contains numerous provisions that expand portability between various types of retirement plans for the purpose of retaining tax-favored treatment of the amounts distributed. The incentives for individuals to retain benefits in tax-favored accounts include the following rollover rules.

- After 2001, rollovers are permitted between qualified plans, 403(b) annuity and custodial account plans, and governmental 457(b) plans without restriction, including rolling over an eligible governmental 457(b) plan to a traditional IRA.
- The employer's plan must agree to accept rollovers from unlike plans and agree to keep separate accounts for rollover amounts attributable to "after-tax" contributions.
- The rollover notice (for all plans) must include a description of the provisions under which distributions from the plan to which the distribution is rolled over may be subject to restrictions and tax consequences different from those applicable to distributions from the distributing plan.

[I.R.C. §§ 72(o)(4), 402(c)(8)(B)(vi), 403(b)(8)(A)(ii)]

Note. If a distribution from a qualified plan or 403(b) plan is rolled over to a governmental 457(b) plan, subsequent distributions from the 457(b) plan attributable to the qualified plan or 403(b) plan rollover will still be subject to the 10 percent premature distribution penalty under Code Section 72(t) (see Q 5:55). A rollover to a governmental 457(b) plan from a nongovernmental 457 plan must be separately accounted for (see Q 1:37). [I.R.C. § 402(c)(10)]

- The rollover notice required under Code Section 402(f) has been revised to contain provisions under which distributions from the plan receiving the rollover may be subject to restrictions and tax consequences that are different from those applicable to distributions from the plan making the distributions. There are two different 402(f) notices that the IRS provides as models. One covers rollovers from and to qualified plans and 403(b) plans; the other covers rollovers to and from governmental 457(b) plans.

Caution. The IRS has indicated that if the distributee elects to rollover only a portion of the distribution in a direct rollover (not a 60-day rollover) to an IRA or Roth IRA, an allocable portion of any after-tax contributions are considered rolled over (a "pro rata allocation" rule applies). In the case of a 60-day rollover, the taxable amount is considered rolled over first (the "taxable first rule"). (See Q 15:51.) [I.R.C. § 402(c)(2); I.R.S. Notice 2009-68, 2009-39 I.R.B. 423] There is an exception (grandfather rule) to the pro rata allocation rule for pre-1987 contributions maintained in a separate account from a plan that allows in-service withdrawals that are used to determine if after-tax contributions are included in the payment. [I.R.C. § 72(e)(8)(D); Ltr. Rul. 8747061 (Aug. 27, 1987); *but see* I.R.S. Notice 87-13, 1987-1 C.B. 432, A-13, regarding amounts transferred to another plan that did not permit in-service withdrawals] Under the "pre-1987" exception, if the amount of rolled over (converted) to a Roth IRA consists of just the amount pre-1987 after-tax contributions, none of the conversion amount would be included in income. Prior to 1987, there was a three-year recovery of basis rule (replaced by the grandfather rules).

- A surviving spouse beneficiary is permitted to roll over a distribution received after 2001 from any of the plans mentioned previously to any plan in which the surviving spouse is a participant, instead of just to a traditional IRA (as was the case for distributions received before 2002). [I.R.C. § 402(c)(9)]
- Employees' after-tax contributions to a defined contribution plan distributed after 2001 may be rolled over to another defined contribution plan or to a traditional IRA. The receiving plan must accept rollovers of after tax employee contributions and agree to account separately for such amounts and the earnings thereon. If a rollover from a qualified plan is going to another qualified plan, the rollover must be a direct rollover if the distribution is received before 2007. [PPA § 822; I.R.C. §§ 402(c)(2), 408(d)(3)(H)]
- After-tax contributions may not be rolled over from an IRA to a qualified plan, 403(b) annuity or custodial account plan, or 457(b) plan. A distribution from a traditional IRA that is rolled over to an eligible qualified plan (instead of an IRA) will be considered to have been distributed first from any amounts in an individual's combined traditional IRAs other than after-tax contributions. [I.R.C. § 408(d)(3)(H)]
- After-tax contributions will be considered to be distributed last from an IRA to maximize the amount available for rollover to an employer's qualified plan.

Note. The IRS has prescribed some rules and guidance for these transactions, including the reporting requirements. Form 8606, Nondeductible IRAs and Coverdell ESAs, has been amended to incorporate the after-tax rollovers, and the Form 1099-R instructions cover some of these transactions as well. Unlike qualified plans, IRAs are not required to account separately for after-tax employee contributions. The separate accounting is done by the taxpayer on Form 8606. [I.R.C. § 402(c)(2)]

Practice Pointer. It appears that certain individuals must keep qualified plan distributions that could qualify for capital gain treatment (with respect to pre-1974 participation) or 10-year averaging for lump-sum distributions (if a participant was born before 1936) in a separate conduit IRA to qualify or requalify for favorable tax treatment by possibly transferring that IRA back into a qualified plan.

Caution. Rollovers into 401(k) SIMPLE plans are not permitted (see Q 15:20).

In addition, EGTRRA grants the IRS the authority to extend the 60-day rollover period for any eligible rollover distribution made after 2001 in cases of casualty, disaster, or other events beyond the reasonable control of the IRA owner making the rollover. [I.R.C. § 402(c)(3)(B)]

Code Section 408(d)(3)(I) permits the IRS to allow a rollover after the expiration of the 60 days, if the failure to permit a late rollover would be against equity or good conscience. The new rule is effective only for distributions made after December 31, 2001. Revenue Procedure 2003-16 [2003-14 I.R.B. 359] requires that the IRS consider all appropriate facts and circumstances in determining whether a waiver is warranted. Facts and circumstances to be considered include the following:

1. Errors committed by an IRA custodian;
2. Inability to complete a rollover due to death, disability, incarceration, hospitalization, postal error, or restrictions placed by a foreign country;
3. How the amount distributed was used; and
4. The time elapsed since the distribution.

The IRS user fees for requesting waivers of the 60-day rollover period are as follows:

- Rollover less than $50,000: $500
- Rollover equal to or greater than $50,000 and less than $100,000: $1,500
- Rollover equal to or greater than $100,000: $3,000

[Rev. Proc. 2012-8, § 6.01(4), 2012-1 I.R.B. 235]

> **Caution.** The IRS views Revenue Procedure 2003-16 as all-inclusive, rather than as examples of situations. The true test should be whether the failure to waive the requirement would be "against equity or good conscience, including casualty, disaster, or other events beyond the reasonable control of individual subject to such requirement." [I.R.C. § 408(d)(3)(I); *see also* House Report 107-51—H.R. 10]

> **Note.** The IRS does not have the authority to waive the one-rollover-per-12-month period rule. [*See* Ltr. Rul. 200749016 (Sept. 12. 2007)]

[Rev. Proc. 2003-16, 2003-4 I.R.B. 359; *see e.g.*, approved requests, Ltr. Ruls. 201210046 (Dec. 15, 2011), granted for medical impairment; 201209026 (Dec. 6, 2011), incorrect advice from financial organization representative; 201209023 (Dec. 6, 2011), incorrect advice from financial organization representative; 201209022 (Dec. 8, 2011), granted for medical impairment; 201209015 (Dec. 8, 2011), incorrect advice from employer; 201208041 (Dec. 1, 2011), financial institution error; 201208040 (Nov. 30, 2011), financial institution error; *see also* denied requests, Ltr. Ruls. 201206023 (Nov. 18, 2011), *denied*, undocumented financial institution error; 201146024 (Aug. 24, 2011); *denied*, factors from Rev. Proc. 2003-16 not present; 201126041 (Apr. 5, 2011), *denied*, how factors outlined in Rev. Proc. 2003-16 affected ability to timely roll over not shown; 201015039 (Jan. 21, 2010), *denied*, mistaken distribution without any error by advisors; *denied*, Rev. Proc. 2003-16 factors not present; 200921039 (Feb. 25, 2009); *denied*, erroneous belief rollover period was 90 days; 200919070 (Feb. 10, 2009), *denied*, deposited into joint-ownership CD; 200919061 (Feb. 12, 2009), *denied*, Rev. Proc. 2003-16 factors not present; 200912042 (Feb. 24, 2008), waiver granted for dishonest advice; 200907049

(Nov. 19, 2008), denied for inadvertence in thinking; 200904031 (Oct. 30, 2008), denied for lack of rollover attempt; 200847023 (Aug. 29, 2008), enumerated factors of Rev. Proc. 2003-16 not present; 200809043 (Feb. 4, 2007), relief denied although taxpayer never informed of right to rollover; 200749016 (Sept. 12. 2007), relief granted, but not for second distribution within the one-year period; 200717021 (Jan 2, 2007), taxpayer deceased, rollover by spouse/executrix permitted; 200704042 (Nov. 30, 2006) request denied; 200738027 (June 26, 2006) declined to waive 60-day requirement where taxpayer's failure to accomplish the timely rollover was due to mistakenly entering the wrong account number; 200736036 (June 8, 2007) denied relief when taxpayer completed the wrong form over the Internet; 200608035 (Dec. 1, 2005), request not necessary because rollover period was extended to 120 days because amounts were used for purchasing a home that was not consummated, *see* I.R.C. § 72(t)(8)(E) regarding the first-time home buyer exception; 200602051 (Oct. 18, 2005), request denied because taxpayer had reasonable control but failed to note deadlines; 200602050 (Oct. 20, 2005), medical impairment and miscommunication between spouse beneficiary and son following death of IRA owner; 200602049 (Oct. 18, 2005), spouse beneficiary received no indication that death distribution made from an IRA; 200601042 (Oct. 13, 2005), request denied because taxpayer had reasonable control but failed to pay attention to correspondence received; 200601041 (Oct. 12, 2005), misunderstanding with financial institution that rollover occurred; 200551027 (Sept. 27, 2005), miscommunication caused too much to be distributed; 200551026 (Sept. 26, 2005), broker erred in making distribution from personal account; 200550040 (Sept. 20, 2005), bank erroneously deposited into personal account; 200550038 (Sept. 19, 2005), bank officer unavailable and holiday prevented communications; 200531036 (Mar. 1, 2005), 200530032 (Apr. 18, 2005), request denied, amounts placed in trust after owner's death with spouse having a life estate were not eligible to be rolled over; 200526024 (Apr. 6, 2005), request denied, no intent to roll over, owner died one day after 60-day period expired]

Note. The IRS cannot waive the one-rollover-per-year rule applicable to rollovers between IRAs. Thus, the extension of the 60-day rule is of no use to a taxpayer that has already taken a distribution within the one-year period from an IRA that was not includible in gross income.

> [D]eadlines, like statutes of limitations, necessarily operate harshly and arbitrarily with respect to individuals who fall just on the other side of them, but if the concept of a . . . deadline is to have any context, the deadline must be enforced.

[United States v. Lock, 471 U.S. 84 (1985); *see also* Dirks v. Commissioner, T.C. Memo 2004-138 June 10, 2004; Wood v. Commissioner, 93 T.C. 114 (1989), taxpayer did everything right and won; rollover transaction credited to wrong account]

Under EGTRRA, all hardship distributions made after 2001 from qualified plans and 403(b) plans (not just those applicable to elective deferrals) and distributions under Code Section 457(b) made pursuant to an unforeseen emergency will be ineligible for rollover distributions. [I.R.C. § 402(c)(4)(C)]

Rollovers are disregarded in determining the $5,000 cash-out amount. After 2001, a plan subject to the involuntary cash-out rules under Code Section 411(a)(11) is permitted to exclude rollover contributions (including earnings allocable thereto) in determining whether a participant's benefit exceeds $5,000. [I.R.C. § 411(a)(11)(A), 411(a)(11)(D); Treas. Reg. § 1.411(a)-11(c)(4)]

Q 15:51 How are after-tax contributions from an employer's qualified plan treated when rolled over to a traditional IRA or Roth IRA?

After-tax contributions included in a payment from an employer's plan are not taxed. If the payment is an eligible rollover distribution, the payment may be rolled over (converted) to a traditional IRA or to a Roth IRA either through a 60-day rollover or a direct rollover. [I.R.C. §§ 402(c), 402(e)] Rollovers from designated Roth accounts (DRAs) and deemed IRAs (not discussed) are treated differently.

In general, if only a portion of a participant's benefit is distributed from an employer's plan, an allocable portion (share) of after-tax contributions is generally included in the payment. This is called the *pro rata allocation rule.*

Caution. Once distributed from the plan, the tax treatment of the after-tax funds may depend on whether the amount is rolled over to an IRA or Roth IRA and how that rollover accomplished—through a direct rollover (e.g., trustee-to-trustee) or a 60-day rollover (where participant receives a distribution of the funds to be rolled over).

Taxable first rule. If a 60-day rollover is made of a portion of an amount distributed to the participant (a partial 60-day rollover, see Example 2), after-tax contributions are treated as being rolled over last (the taxable first rule) rather than allocated pro rata to each payment under the general rule (see examples below). [*See* I.R.C. § 402(c)(2), last sentence; I.R.S. Notice 2009-68, 2009-39 I.R.B. 423, see paragraphs following "If your payment includes after-tax contributions."]

Caution. The pro rata allocation rule (rather than the taxable first rule) appear to apply to a direct rollover (but not to a 60-day rollover) containing after-tax contributions. (See discussion below.)

The rollover provisions were expanded under EGTRRA to permit the rollover of after-tax amounts (directly and indirectly), and expressly provided in the flush language of Code Section 402(c)(2) that "the amount transferred shall be treated as consisting *first* of the portion of such distribution that is includible in gross income." [Emphasis added.] [I.R.C. § 402(c)(2); EGTRRA § 643]

Employer plans have historically permitted a participant to directly or indirectly roll over the entire pretax amount first. For example, if the participant took a full distribution of $80,000 of his account, which had $20,000 of after-tax contributions and the remainder as pretax amounts, the participant could elect to rollover the entire $80,000 pretax amount to a traditional IRA and receive the remaining $20,000 in cash tax free. Beginning in 2008, the $80,000 amount may be rolled over to a Roth IRA and $20,000 retained tax free.

However, an updated model 402(f) (rollover notice) issued in 2009 challenged the taxable first rule. [I.R.S. Notice 2009-68, 2009-39 I.R.B. 423, see paragraph following "If your payment includes after-tax contributions."] The Notice states that if the distributee elects to rollover only a portion of the distribution in a direct rollover, an allocable portion of any after-tax contributions are considered rolled over. A similar approach was taken for a partial direct rollover of Roth accounts; an allocable portion of the earnings are considered rolled over. More recently, the IRS issued another newsletter that appears to take the same pro rata allocation approach; unfortunately, it does not contain any examples to confirm the approach and by its terms is limited to conversions to Roth IRAs from an employer's plan. [EP Newsletter (Spring 2010), available at *http://www.irs.gov/pub/irs-tege/spr10.pdf* (visited on Aug. 22, 2012)]

Under the IRS's interpretation, it appears that each rollover/payment is being treated as a separate distribution (which is prior, under the IRS's analysis, to the annuity starting date) and therefore subject to Code Section 72(e)(8), which requires this pro rata allocation approach. Presumably, thereafter, Code Section 402(c)(2) flush language, providing for the rollover of taxable amounts first, can be applied. However, this language does not appear to apply to a payment that is directly rolled over (not a 60-day rollover). Thus, the ability to split distributions and preserve the segregation of pretax and after-tax funds if any portion is being transferred directly to an IRA or Roth IRA may be lost.

Mirroring the approach taken for designated Roth contributions under Treasury Regulations Section 1.402A-1, Q&A-5, where (1) the regulations expressly limit the special ordering rule to indirect rollovers—the part that is rolled over is deemed to consist first of the portion of the distribution that is attributable to income under Code Section 72(e)(8), and (2) following the Preamble to T.D. 9324, treat the portion of the distribution that is rolled over as a separate distribution for purposes of applying Code Section 402(c)(2). However, Roth accounts are different from after-tax amounts because Roth accounts are generally treated as a "separate account" for Code Section 72 purposes, which would prohibit commingling earnings on Roth contributions with other taxable amounts.

In the author's opinion, the clear language of Code Section 402(c)(2), which expressly applies to direct rollovers, would appear to trump the pro rata allocation rules under Code Section 72(e)(8). The legislative history, as noted above, does not make this pro rata allocation point clear. In addition, there is no policy reason for providing for a different result depending solely on whether the amount is directly rolled over or transferred in a 60-day rollover. Additional guidance is necessary to resolve the treatment of after-tax contributions that are directly rolled over to an IRA or directly converted Roth IRA.

The following examples show how after-tax contributions are treated in a rollover to a traditional IRA and Roth IRA in accordance with I.R.S. Notice

2009-68. In the following examples, none of the after-tax contributions were made prior to 1987 (see this question, first *Caution*) and for federal income tax withholding purposes the recipient is a U.S. citizen. In each example, the Form 1099-R issued to the participant will reflect the amount of the after-tax contributions.

Note. Guidance addressing eligible rollover distributions under Code Section 402(c) and Roth distributions under Code Section 402A that are "disbursed to multiple destinations" are expected to be forthcoming. [*See* Department of the Treasury 2011-2012 Priority Guidance Plan, 3rd Quarter Update (Apr. 27, 2012), available at *http://www.irs.gov/pub/irs-utl/2011-2012_pgp_3rd_update.pdf*. It is not known whether this guidance will address the sample 402(f) Notice that indicates a prorata basis allocation must be made for partial/split rollovers.]

Example 1. Sheila terminates employment at age 65 and received a total distribution of $12,000 in 2013, of which $2,000 is after-tax contributions. Sheila does not have an IRA or a Roth IRA. Assume the distribution is an eligible rollover distribution. Sheila rolls over the $12,000 to a traditional IRA within 60 days. None of the $12,000 is currently taxable. Sheila will have to keep track of the after-tax contributions in order to determine the taxable portion of later payments made from an IRA. Sheila must file Form 8606, Nondeductible IRAs, to keep track of her after-tax contributions.

Note. Since the amount was paid to Sheila, 20 percent would have been withheld for federal income tax. Sheila would need to make up the amount out of pocket, in order to rollover the entire taxable amount.

If instead, Sheila had directly converted (60-day rollover or direct rollover) the full amount ($12,000) to a Roth IRA within 60 days, she would have taxable conversion income of $10,000 ($12,000 - $10,000) and avoid federal withholding taxes.

On the other hand, had Sheila not rolled over any portion of the $12,000, $2,000 would be treated as a return of Sheila's after-tax contributions and $10,000 would be taxable under the general (pro rata) allocation rule.

Example 2. Assume the same facts as in Example 1, except Sheila transfers $10,000 to a Roth IRA within 60 days and keeps $2,000. Under the taxable first rule, after-tax contributions are treated as rolled over last in a partial 60-day rollover transfer. Thus, the taxable conversion amount is $10,000. The amount retained ($2,000) is a tax-free recovery of basis (the after-tax contributions).

Caution. The special rule treating after-tax contributions as being received last applies to a partial 60-day rollover, but not to a direct rollover (i.e., when no portion of the payment is distributed to the participant).

Partial Direct Rollover. If only a portion of an amount paid from the plan is directly rolled over (not a 60-day rollover), each payment will include an allocable portion of the after-tax contributions (see Examples 3 and 4).

Example 3. *Total direct rollover to Roth IRA.* Assume the same facts as in Example 1, except Sheila directly rolls (not a 60-day rollover) over $10,000 of her $12,000 benefit to a Roth IRA. $2,000 remains in the plan. As previously discussed, the IRS will treat the amount rolled over ($10,000) under the pro rata allocation rule as consisting of after-tax contributions of $1,667 ($10,000 × $2,000/$12,000). Therefore, the taxable conversion amount is $8,333 ($10,000 – $1,667). The remaining plan balance $2,000, will be treated as consisting of $333 of after-tax funds (basis) and $1,667 of pretax employer contributions (and gains).

Example 4. *Partial direct rollover to traditional IRA.* Assume the same facts as in Example 3 except that the $10,000 is directly rolled over to a traditional IRA and $2,000 is distributed to Sheila. This is a partial direct rollover. The special rule treating after-tax contributions as being received last does not apply when there is a direct rollover. Sheila must allocate a portion of the after-tax contributions to each payment. Thus, the $2,000 retained (and not rolled over) is taxable, except to the extent of any after-tax contributions. Thus, Sheila will include $1,667 ($2,000 × $10,000/$12,000)) of the $2,000 retained in gross income. The remaining portion $333 ($2,000 – $1,667) represents after-tax contributions and are not taxable. Of the $10,000 amount directly rolled over $1,667 ($10,000 – ($10,000 × $10,000/$12,000)) represents after-tax contributions in the traditional IRA. Sheila must file Form 8606, Nondeductible IRAs, to keep track of her after-tax contributions. None of the $10,000 is taxable at this time.

Partial direct rollover to Roth IRA. Assume instead that $10,000 is directly rolled over to a Roth IRA and $2,000 is distributed to Sheila. The special rule treating after-tax contributions as being received last does not apply when there is a direct rollover of a portion of the amount paid from the plan is directly rolled over and a portion is paid to the participant. Sheila must allocate a portion of the after-tax contributions to each payment. Thus, the $2,000 retained (and not rolled over) is taxable, except to the extent of any after-tax contributions. Thus, Sheila will include $1,667 ($2,000 × ($10,000 /$12,000)) of the $2,000 retained in gross income. The remaining portion $333 ($2,000 – $1,667) represents after-tax contributions and are not taxable.

Of the amount directly rolled over ($10,000) to the Roth IRA, $1,667 ($10,000 × $2,000 × $12,000), rounded) is treated as the allocable portion of the after-tax contributions and is not taxable. Sheila will have to include $8,333 ($10,000 × $1,667, rounded), in her gross income as the result of the partial direct rollover (a conversion). Sheila will have taxable income of $10,000 ($8,333 + $1,667 for 2013, see Example 5).

Example 5. Assume the same facts as in Example 4, except Sheila wants to roll over as much of the $2,000 distribution as she can to a traditional IRA or, alternatively, to a Roth IRA.

To traditional IRA. Sheila may roll over $2,000 within 60 days to a traditional IRA. No portion of the 60-day rollover will be currently taxable. Sheila's will have $333 of basis in the traditional IRA (see Example 4). Sheila will have taxable income for the year of $8,333 as a result of the partial direct transfer (see Example 4). Sheila must file Form 8606, Nondeductible IRAs, to keep track of her after-tax contributions.

To Roth IRA. If instead, Sheila rolls over the $2,000 (which included after-tax contribution of $333) to a Roth IRA, she would have to include $1,667 in gross income (see Example 4). Sheila will have taxable income for the year of $10,000 ($1,667 + $8,333).

In Letter Ruling 201005057 [Nov. 11, 2009], the taxpayer received an eligible rollover distribution in the form of a check that was made payable to a successor employer, as follows: "Company B, FBO Taxpayer A. Representatives of Plan Y." In addition, the check was endorsed for "deposit only." Form 1099-R reporting the distribution was coded "G" (direct rollover). No withholding taxes were withheld from the distribution. The taxpayer neglected to deposit the check within 60 days and sought a ruling from the IRS to waive the 60-day rollover requirement. The IRS ruled that the 60-day requirement did not apply because the rollover was a "direct transfer." The IRS noted the taxpayer's lack of control over the check's proceeds and could not deposit the check.

Practice Pointer. A direct conversion to a Roth IRA may be beneficial when an individual's retirement accounts hold substantial amounts of after-tax contributions (which could be recovered tax-free in a direct conversion).

Example 6. Lavonda is a single individual, age 60, and has an adjusted gross income of $80,000 from wages. Lavonda has an IRA worth $500,000. Deductions were claimed for all contributions made to this account. Lavonda is about to retire. She has $200,000 in her 401(k), of which $40,000 consists of after-tax contributions. Lavonda receives a distribution of her 401(k) account ($200,000) and rolls it over into a new IRA within 60 days. No amount is included in income as a consequence of the 60-day rollover to the new IRA. Lavonda converts $200,000 from either the new or existing IRA to a Roth IRA.

The $200,000 Roth conversion is treated as a partial conversion of the aggregate $700,000 ($200,000 + $500,000) balance in all of Lavonda's traditional IRAs. Because the after-tax contributions ($40,000) are recovered on a pro rata basis, Lavonda will not have to include $11,428.57 ($200,000 × $40,000/$700,000, or 5.714%) of the $200,000 distribution in her gross income. She will include $188,571.43 ($200,000–$11,428.57) as ordinary income on her tax return as a result of the indirect (60-day rollover) conversion. Alternatively, Lavonda could keep the $40,000 (as a non-taxable return of after-tax contributions) and rollover (within 60 days) the remaining taxable portion ($160,000) she received from the plan directly to a Roth IRA instead of to a traditional IRA (see Example 7). Special taxation rules apply to conversions made in 2010. [Roth rollover and conversion taxation is more fully discussed in the *Roth IRA Answer Book*, 6th ed., Ch. 3 (New York: CCH Incorporated, 2012]

Practice Pointer. Unless Lavonda needed temporary use of the $200,000, she could have directly rolled over that amount and avoided the 20 percent federal income withholding tax.

Example 7. Same facts as in Example 6, except Lavonda transfers her 401(k) account balance ($200,000) to a Roth IRA in a direct conversion (not a 60-day rollover). Because the IRA aggregation rules do not apply, $40,000 is treated as a return of principal (basis) and only $160,000 is taxable. As a result of the direct conversion, only $160,000 is taxable, compared to $188,571.43 if Lavonda were to receive the funds and roll over those funds within 60 days into a traditional IRA (which included after-tax contributions) and then converted $200,000 in her traditional IRA to a Roth IRA (see Example 6). Thus, Lavonda's taxable income is $28,571.43 ($188,571.43 - $160,000) less if she directly converts her 401(k) to a Roth IRA. It should be noted that the taxable portion of subsequent distributions from Lavonda's $500,000 IRA will be higher than had she indirectly (not through a traditional IRA) rolled her $200,000 401(k) to a Roth IRA. This is because the traditional IRA will be treated as containing after-tax contributions of only $11,428.57 ($200,000 – $188,571.43). Special taxation rules apply to conversions made in 2010.

Q 15:52 Must a distributee be given the option of having eligible rollover distributions from a 401(k) SIMPLE plan rolled over directly to an eligible retirement plan?

Yes. A distributee must be given the option of having eligible rollover distributions from a 401(k) SIMPLE plan rolled over directly to an eligible retirement plan. [I.R.C. §§ 401(a)(31), 402(c)]

Notice and Reporting Requirements

Q 15:53 Must eligible employees be given notice of their eligibility to participate in a 401(k) SIMPLE plan?

Yes. An employer must notify each eligible employee before the 60-day election period (see Q 14:91) that he or she can make a salary reduction election under a 401(k) SIMPLE plan or modify a prior election during that period. [Rev. Proc. 97-9, Appendix § 4.2(a), 1997-1 C.B. 624]

Note. As a result of an oversight, the Code did not expressly require an employer maintaining a 401(k) SIMPLE plan to notify each employee of the employee's opportunity to make or modify salary reduction contributions. That oversight was corrected by the Taxpayer Relief Act of 1997 (TRA '97). [I.R.C. § 401(k)(11)(B)(iii)]

Q 15:54 Must employees be notified of an employer's election to make a nonelective contribution to a 401(k) SIMPLE plan instead of a matching contribution?

Yes. As is the case with a SIMPLE IRA, an employer must notify its employees of its election to make the 2 percent nonelective contribution to a 401(k) SIMPLE plan within a reasonable period of time (see Q 14:101) before the 60-day period (see Q 14:91). [I.R.C. § 401(k)(11)(B); Rev. Proc. 97-9, Appendix § 4.2(b), 1997-1 C.B. 624]

Q 15:55 Do IRS and ERISA disclosure and reporting rules apply to 401(k) SIMPLE plans?

Yes. The adoption of SIMPLE provisions for a 401(k) plan does not change the employer's responsibility for providing summary annual reports or summary plan descriptions, filing annual returns/reports on Form 5500, Annual Return-Report of Employee Benefit Plan, or fulfilling other obligations required under the Code or the Employee Retirement Income Security Act of 1974 (ERISA).

Adopting a 401(k) SIMPLE Plan

Q 15:56 How may an employer go about adopting a plan that contains 401(k) SIMPLE provisions?

A new or existing plan may be submitted to the IRS for an opinion or notification letter in accordance with existing procedures for the submission of plans to the IRS. [*See* Rev. Proc. 2012-6, 2012-11 I.R.B. 197 and Rev. Proc. 2012-8, 2012-11 I.R.B. 235]

Excess Contributions and Plan Deficiencies

Q 15:57 How do the IRS remedial correction programs apply to a 401(k) SIMPLE plan?

All the remedial correction programs offered by the IRS under the Employee Plans Compliance Resolution System (EPCRS) can be used for a 401(k) SIMPLE plan because it is a qualified plan under Code Section 401(a). (See chapter 17.) [Rev. Proc. 2008-50, 2008-35 I.R.B. 464]

Q 15:58 How should excess contributions to a SIMPLE 401(k) plan be treated?

In the absence of well-established guidance, the position of the IRS regarding excess contributions to a SIMPLE 401(k) plan is, at best, unclear. Several possibilities exist, some of which offer solutions:

1. The plan becomes a traditional 401(k) plan and is taken out of the realm of a 401(k) SIMPLE plan. In the authors' opinion, this is an unlikely choice because of the information provided to the participant by the plan regarding the manner in which the plan would operate for that plan year.
2. The plan becomes a "bad" SIMPLE plan or a plan with a "bad" contribution allocation. Correction should be made under the EPCRS (see Q 15:57).
3. It may be possible to correct the excess contribution if plan contributions are the result of a mistake of fact. [ERISA § 403(c)(2)(A)] In the authors' opinion, this option is least likely; furthermore, the IRS has not included excess SIMPLE contributions among clear mistakes of fact.
4. It may be possible to correct the excess contribution (in accordance with plan provisions) if plan contributions are conditioned on their deductibility and the deduction for the contributions is subsequently denied. [ERISA § 403(c)(2)(C), I.R.C. § 4972(c)(2)]
5. In May 1999, the IRS informally agreed with propositions 2 and 4 in this list (see also Q 2:91). [General Information Letter issued to Gary S. Lesser, May 18, 1999; *see also* Rev. Rul. 91-4, 1991-1 C.B. 57]

Practice Pointer. Practitioners should proceed with caution when dealing with excess contributions to a 401(k) SIMPLE plan until further guidance is provided by the IRS.

Termination in Favor of a SIMPLE IRA

Q 15:59 If an employer that maintains a 401(k) plan or a 401(k) SIMPLE plan wishes to terminate the plan in favor of a SIMPLE IRA, is the SIMPLE IRA a defined contribution plan under Code Section 401(k)(10)(A)(i) to which the 401(k) plan assets must be rolled over?

Probably not, although no definitive guidance is currently in place. Under Code Section 401(k)(10)(A)(i), when a 401(k) plan terminates, participants may not receive a distribution of their account balances if the employer maintains a "successor" defined contribution plan (other than an employee stock ownership plan). Treasury Regulations Section 1.401(k)-1(d)(4)(i) indicates that a plan is a successor plan only if it exists at any time during the period beginning on the date of plan termination and ending 12 months after the distribution of all assets from the terminated plan. The regulation also indicates that a successor plan is any defined contribution plan, as defined in Code Section 414(i), excluding employer stock ownership plans and SEPs.

The Treasury regulations make sense from a policy perspective; that is, the purpose of Code Section 401(k)(10)(A)(i) is to prevent participants from gaining premature access to their funds. Once assets are in a SEP (i.e., an IRA), they are available to the participant. Requiring transfer of the account balances in a terminating 401(k) plan into a SEP maintained by the employer that is terminating the 401(k) plan would not prohibit the participants from receiving access to their 401(k) account balances. In fact, under the 1998 updates to the 401(k) LRM, the IRS added SIMPLE IRAs to the list of plans that should not be considered a "replacement plan." [*LRM for CODA Master or Prototype Plans*, § XVI, Distribution Limitations (Jan. 2006)]

Tax Credits

Q 15:60 May a business that establishes a new 401(k) SIMPLE plan claim a tax credit?

Starting in 2002, a small business that adopts a new 401(k) SIMPLE plan may generally claim an income tax credit for 50 percent of the first $1,000 in administrative and retirement-education expenses for each of the first three years of the plan. The credit is available only to employers that did not have more than 100 employees with compensation in excess of $5,000 during the previous tax year. The employer must also have had at least one non-highly compensated employee (NHCE). The credit is taken as a general business credit on the employer's business tax return. The other 50 percent of the expenses may be taken as a business deduction. The expenses must be paid or incurred in taxable years beginning after 2001 and with respect to plans established after 2001. [I.R.C. § 45E]

Q 15:61 May an individual claim a tax credit for a contribution to a 401(k) SIMPLE plan?

It depends. Beginning after 2001, there is a low-income saver's credit that allows certain individuals to receive a nonrefundable tax credit for a percentage of their contributions to a 401(k) SIMPLE plan (see also Q 1:33 and examples). The credit is based on a sliding scale percentage of up to $2,000 contributed to a traditional IRA or a Roth IRA, elective deferrals made to a SIMPLE, a SEP, a 401(k) plan, a 403(b) plan, or a 457(b) plan, and voluntary after-tax contributions to a qualified plan. The credit is in addition to any other tax benefit (i.e., the potential tax deduction) that the contribution affords the taxpayer. [I.R.C. § 25B(a)-25B(b)]

> **Note.** The maximum saver's credit is $1,000 ($2,000 for married couples). However, the credit amount is often much less, and due to the impact of other deductions and credits, may be zero (see Q 1:33).

Chapter 16

Beneficiary Designations and Estate Planning

Peter Gulia, Esq.
Fiduciary Guidance Counsel

Making a beneficiary designation is an important part of retirement and estate planning. While a simplified employee pension (SEP) or other retirement plan's benefit will not pass by a will, a participant's beneficiary designation affects his or her overall estate plan.*

---

* This chapter refers to the following kinds of plans:

- A SIMPLE plan under Internal Revenue Code Section 401(k)(11), or "401(k) SIMPLE";
- A SEP plan under Internal Revenue Code Section 408(k);
- A SEP plan that consists of, or includes, a salary-reduction arrangement under Code Section 408(k)(6) (SARSEP); and
- A SIMPLE retirement plan under Code Section 408(p).**Note**: The following words are used in this chapter in a specially defined manner:

- IRA. An individual retirement account under Code Section 408(a), an individual retirement annuity under Code Section 408(b), or a trust that is treated as an individual retirement account under Code Section 408(c).
- Non-ERISA. A governmental plan, a church plan that has not elected to be governed by the Employee Retirement Income Security Act of 1974 (ERISA), or an IRA that is not held under a plan.
- Non-probate. Property that is transferred or contract rights that are provided without a probate administration.
- Participant. A participant (instead of a beneficiary or alternate payee) under a retirement plan, or the original participant of an IRA. Participant also refers to the person who is the original holder or "owner" of an IRA.
- Payer. Any custodian, insurer, plan administrator, or other person responsible for deciding or paying a claim under a plan or IRA.
- Probate. Property that is transferred through a court-supervised administration or succession.
- Retirement plan. Any of the aforementioned plans (e.g., a SIMPLE or SEP plan). A retirement plan also includes an IRA that is used as the investment of a plan other than a 401(k) SIMPLE plan.
- State. The District of Columbia or any state, commonwealth, territory, possession, or similar jurisdiction of the United States. Because this chapter includes many references to state law, it makes parallel references to a state (instead of the lawyers' word, jurisdiction) for reading ease. For example, although the District of Columbia is not a state, law that applies to a person because he or she resides in the District of Columbia is state law, as distinguished from U.S. law or federal law, which applies throughout the United States.

This chapter focuses on a retirement plan participant's use of his or her valuable right to name a beneficiary. The chapter explains some opportunities and restrictions in making a beneficiary designation, including marriage and family rights that restrain a beneficiary designation. This chapter also explains how the law on retirement plans' death benefits is sometimes similar to, but often quite different than, the law that applies to a person's disposition of his or her other wealth.

The subject of tax-oriented estate planning warrants a book of its own. This chapter introduces the concept, because many retirement plan participants mistakenly assume that they lack enough wealth for federal or state estate and inheritance tax issues to be of concern. Although a participant might believe that he or she and his or her beneficiaries likely will not be subject to a federal estate tax, many states have a state estate or inheritance tax (or both), and most of these have a low exemption amount or none at all. Because a taxable estate can include non-probate assets, such as retirement benefits, this chapter describes some tax-treatment rules and planning opportunities.

Last but not least, this chapter ends with a list of common mistakes that people make with beneficiary designations, and how a practitioner might help his or her client avoid those mistakes.

Citations. This chapter includes many general explanations of state laws. To support each such statement with citations to more than 50 states' laws would be unwieldy in this chapter's summary. Moreover, an employee benefits practitioner usually is interested first in a general sense of the state laws. To these ends, the chapter frequently cites the Uniform Probate Code, Uniform Trust Code, and other uniform acts recommended by the Uniform Law Commission (http://www.nccusl.org). A reader who wants to find whether a particular state enacted a statute based on a uniform law might begin with this chapter's citations to Uniform Laws Annotated (ULA), which includes citations for states' adoptions of, and variations from, the recommended uniform laws. Because most employee-benefits practitioners do not use printed volumes to read federal or state statutes or regulations, this chapter's citations to statutes and regulations omit publisher and year references. The contributing author relies on several sources to check that these citations are current when he submits the chapter or its supplement.For citations to a section of the ERISA, as amended, the book omits parallel citations to the United States Code. Specialty citations are in the forms and with the abbreviations customary to employee benefits or tax practitioners, including the abbreviations shown in the book's front matter. Other citations are according to recognized legal writing styles, except as modified by the abbreviation and punctuation style of this book.

About Beneficiary Designations

Q 16:1 What law governs a beneficiary designation under a retirement plan?

For an ERISA plan, a participant must make a beneficiary designation according to the plan's provisions, a plan administrator must administer a plan according to its provisions, and ERISA preempts state laws. [ERISA §§ 404(a)(1)(D), 514(a); Kennedy v. Plan Adm'r for DuPont Sav. & Inv. Plan, 555 U.S. 285 (2009); Egelhoff v. Egelhoff, 532 U.S. 141 (2001)]

Caution. Some practitioners mistakenly assume that ERISA does not govern a SEP plan. A SEP or SARSEP plan is exempt from Parts 2 and 3 of Subtitle B of Title I of ERISA. [ERISA §§ 201(6), 301(a)(7); *see also* Cline v. Industrial Maint. Eng'g & Contracting Co., 200 F.3d 1223 (9th Cir. 2000)] A SEP or SARSEP plan might be excused from some of ERISA's reporting and disclosure requirements. [Labor Reg. §§ 2520.104-48, 2520.104-49] Parts 4 and 5 apply to a SEP or SARSEP plan if the plan provides (or previously provided) nonelective or matching contributions or an employer "endorsed" the plan or became involved in the plan's administration. [Labor Reg. § 2510.3-2(d)(1); *see also* DOL-EBSA, Interpretive Bull. [99-1] Relating to Payroll Deduction IRAs, 64 Fed. Reg. 33001 (June 18, 1999), *reprinted in* 29 C.F.R. § 2509.99-1] This means that ERISA's fiduciary responsibility, claims procedure, and civil enforcement provisions govern such an employer-maintained plan.

For a non-ERISA plan, state law may supplement the plan's or IRA's provisions concerning the manner of making a beneficiary designation. For example, New York law requires that a beneficiary designation be signed. [N.Y. Est. Powers & Trusts § 13-3.2]

Q 16:2 Is a retirement plan benefit distributed according to a participant's will?

No. A retirement plan usually includes a provision by which a participant may name his or her beneficiary or beneficiaries. The beneficiary designation applies even if the participant's will purports to state a contrary disposition or to revoke a beneficiary designation. [*See generally* Restatement (Third) of Property: Wills and Other Donative Transfers § 7.1 comment d (2003)] Indeed, if a beneficiary change could be effected by the participant's will, a responsible insurer or custodian would be unwilling to make any payment until a court had determined the correct distribution of a participant's estate or at least had appointed an executor. [*See, e.g.*, Stone v. Stephens, 155 Ohio 595, 600–601, 99 N.E.2d 766 (1951)]

Understanding that a will does not change a contract's beneficiary results simply from applying the terms of the contract. Yet some states, for convenience, provide a statute to recognize these non-testamentary transfers. [Unif. Probate Code §§ 1-201(4), 8 pt. I U.L.A. 33–46 (1998) & Supp. 13–23 (2011), 6-101, 8 pt. II U.L.A. 430–432 (1998) & Supp. 227–228 (2011), 6-104, 8 pt. II U.L.A. 467–475 (1998), 6-201, 8 pt. II U.L.A. 480–482 (1998)] Even without a statute, courts have held that a will cannot "override" a beneficiary designation. [Restatement (Third) of Property: Wills and Other Donative Transfers § 7.1 comment d (2003)]

Note. A beneficiary's right under a non-ERISA retirement plan arguably might be subject to the State of Washington's Testamentary Disposition of Nonprobate Assets Act. [*See* Wash. Rev. Code §§ 11.11.003–11.11.903] But even concerning a participant who is a resident or domiciliary of Washington, that statute might not always apply because many IRA "products" include a governing law clause, and few of these choose Washington law.

Concerning a non-ERISA plan, state law may supplement an IRA's provisions concerning the manner of making a beneficiary designation. For instance, New York law requires that a beneficiary designation be signed. [N.Y. Est. Powers & Trusts Law § 13-3.2]

For an ERISA plan, only the plan's provisions govern a beneficiary designation. [ERISA §§ 404(a)(1)(D),; Kennedy v. Plan Adm'r for DuPont Sav. & Inv. Plan, 555 U.S. 285 (2009); Egelhoff v. Egelhoff, 532 U.S. 141 (2001)]

Caution. In some circumstances, a will might be a beneficiary designation that supersedes an earlier designation if the plan's documents do not require that a beneficiary designation be made only on the form prescribed by the plan's administrator and the will/designation is submitted to the administrator according to the plan's conditions. [*See, e.g.*, Liberty Life Assurance Co. of Boston v. Kennedy, 358 F.3d 1295 (11th Cir. 2004)]

Q 16:3 Are there other reasons, beyond providing a death benefit, why a participant would want to name a beneficiary?

Yes. There are at least two kinds of benefits—other than the death benefit itself—that might be obtained by naming a beneficiary.

1. *A beneficiary, even if he or she is not a surviving spouse, may direct a rollover.* If an eligible retirement plan so provides, a designated beneficiary, even if he or she is not the participant's surviving spouse, may instruct a direct rollover into his or her inherited IRA. [I.R.C. § 402(c)(11)]

   Caution. A state might have an income tax law that does not follow the Internal Revenue Code. Before a beneficiary directs a rollover (or even decides to take a distribution), he or she should get expert advice about whether each state of which he or she is a resident or a domiciliary [*see* 4 U.S.C. § 114] would recognize the rollover, or would tax the distribution, even if rolled over for federal income tax purposes.

2. *A hardship distribution can be based on the need of a beneficiary who is not a spouse or dependent.* Without waiting for a participant to meet a plan's severance or other conditions that may permit a distribution, a retirement plan may permit a payment to meet a participant's hardship. A hardship must be based on the participant's need, which can include some needs concerning a participant's spouse or dependent. Further, a plan may provide that an event (including a medical expense) that would meet the plan's hardship conditions if it happened concerning the participant's spouse or dependent meets the conditions if it happens concerning "a person who is a beneficiary under the plan with respect to the participant." [Pub. L. No. 109-280, § 826 (Aug. 17, 2006)] In the IRS's view, such a rule applies only concerning a primary beneficiary—that is, one who "has an unconditional right to all or a portion of the participant's account balance under the plan upon the death of the participant." [I.R.S. Notice 2007-7, 2007-5 I.R.B. 395 (Jan. 29, 2007) at Q&A-5(a)]

Q 16:4 Who may make a beneficiary designation?

Before a participant's death, only the participant may make a beneficiary designation.

Although a typical retirement plan usually does not state a provision that permits a beneficiary to name his or her further beneficiary, some retirement plans do not preclude such a designation. Along with this, some IRA "products" permit a beneficiary to name a further contingent or successor beneficiary if the participant had not (before his or her death) designated all of the retirement plan benefit and the retirement plan lacked a "default" provision (or a beneficiary did not receive the full amount of his or her benefit). [Ltr. Rul. 199936052 (June 16, 1999)]

Caution. Depending on the plan's and account's provisions and other facts and circumstances, a power to name further beneficiaries might cause a retirement plan benefit that remains undistributed at each beneficiary's death to be subject to federal estate tax and state inheritance tax, notwithstanding that the same benefit was previously so taxed on the participant's death. [I.R.C. § 2041(a)(2); Treas. Reg. § 20.2041-1(b)] A federal estate tax might be postponed if the beneficiary names his or her spouse as the succeeding beneficiary and that spouse has power to take the entire remaining benefit. [I.R.C. § 2056; Ltr. Rul. 199936052 (June 16, 1999)]

Note. If any benefit remains after all participant-named beneficiaries are dead, a retirement plan might provide that the personal representative of the participant's estate is the "default" beneficiary (see Q 16:18). Although a participant's estate might have been closed, an estate may be "reopened" for subsequent administration on the discovery of property that was not disposed by the previous administration. [Unif. Probate Code § 3-1008, 8 pt. I U.L.A. 300–302 (1998) & Supp. 113–114 (2010)]

Practice Pointer. A careful participant should make a complete beneficiary designation that contemplates each possibility that is not remote. A participant who does not want to specify alternate beneficiaries may create a trust, which could include a power of appointment for a beneficiary to name a further beneficiary.

Practice Pointer. Whether a retirement plan or an IRA "product" permits a beneficiary to name his or her further beneficiary, or precludes such a designation, is not "hard-wired" by federal tax law, but rather is a provision of the particular plan and account documents together with applicable law. A person who cares about whether a particular plan or "product" allows a beneficiary to name his or her further beneficiary should read carefully all relevant documents.

Q 16:5 Who can be a beneficiary?

Unless a plan or contract otherwise provides, any person can be a beneficiary.

Q 16:6 May a participant designate his or her beneficiaries by describing a class?

Maybe. Some retirement plans expressly preclude a class beneficiary designation, and instead require a participant to specify each beneficiary by name. A few retirement plans expressly permit a class beneficiary. In the contributing author's experience, many retirement plans do not expressly preclude or permit a class beneficiary designation, and the text of many such plans could be argued to support or attack a wide range of interpretations concerning whether a class beneficiary designation is permitted.

Not recognizing a class beneficiary designation could result in an allocation of benefits that some people feel might not be what a participant intended.

Example. When Francine became a participant under her employer's SEP, she then had no spouse and had three children—Alan, Bart, and Charles.

Initially, Francine wrote on the plan's beneficiary-designation form: "to my children—in equal shares." Because the IRA expressly precluded a class beneficiary designation, the custodian rejected this attempted beneficiary designation. Francine completed and signed a form that stated: "Alan 33%, Bart 33%, Charles 33%." Two years later, Francine had a fourth child—Dorothy. Although Francine could do so any day, Francine never changed her beneficiary designation. Many years later, Francine died. It was unclear whether Francine intended to provide a share for Dorothy; her initial attempted beneficiary designation suggests she did, but her failure to change her beneficiary designation in the many years after Dorothy's birth might suggest that Francine did not intend to provide a benefit to Dorothy. Because the plan was unambiguous, Dorothy received nothing.

Those who favor allowing a class beneficiary designation often suggest that a retirement plan should be designed to accommodate a participant who is neglectful concerning his or her benefit.

However, allowing a class beneficiary designation sometimes results in difficult administration, which might lead to liability.

Example. Harry's beneficiary designation states: "to my children in equal shares." Anna and Ben file claims with the plan administrator, and each furnishes a birth certificate that shows him or her as Harry's child. The plan's administrator asks Anna and Ben to furnish proof that they are Harry's only children. Because Harry died with only nonprobate assets, there is no probate proceeding. Reluctantly, the plan's administrator accepts Anna's and Ben's affidavits stating that there is no other child of Harry. The plan pays Anna and Ben. A few months later, Irving files a claim and furnishes sound proof that Harry was his father. After the plan administrator denies the claim, Irving threatens a lawsuit that would include demands for the benefit, lost value, and his attorney's fees. The plan administrator's lawyer points out that the attorneys' fees for a defense would be more than the benefit at stake, and that a lack of prudence in the administrator's conduct calls into question whether defending that conduct would be a proper plan administration expense. The lawyer suggests a prompt approval of Irving's claim. Because the earlier payments to Anna and Ben exhausted Harry's plan account, the administrator pays Irving from its own money.

Observation. Most laws about determining the existence or nonexistence of a parent–child relationship assume only the needs of a minor child to whom a parent might owe support. A person who could not be either a parent or a child in the relationship that would be established might lack standing to begin a parentage court proceeding. Instead, a plan administrator might need to pursue an action to declare benefits, which might be heard in a court that lacks experience with the fact-finding methods of domestic-relations courts.

Practice Pointer. If a retirement plan does not preclude a class beneficiary designation, the plan sponsor should specify provisions that would resolve ambiguities and relieve the administrator from unworkable duties. For example, a plan sponsor could consider whether the plan's administrator would construe the words "child," "descendant," "heir," and "issue" according to customary legal meanings of those words, or according to a "typical" participant's misunderstanding of those words. Also, a plan sponsor should specify a rule of convenience that closes the class on the first distribution to any beneficiary of the class. [Restatement (Third) of Property: Wills and Other Donative Transfers § 15.1 (Tentative Draft No. 4 2004); Restatement (Third) of Trusts §§ 44–45 (2003)]

Q 16:7 May a plan administrator decide whether a document presented as a beneficiary designation is invalid because it is a forgery or was made under undue influence?

Yes. Although generally a plan's administrator administers the plan according to its documents and using the plan's internal records, this does not preclude a plan administrator from considering whether a document is what it purports to be. [*See* Tinsley v. General Motors Corp., 227 F.3d 700, 704 & n.1 (6th Cir. 2000)]

Q 16:8 Why should a participant read a beneficiary-designation form?

Plan administrators, custodians, and insurers design beneficiary-designation forms anticipating the possibility that a participant might give incomplete or ambiguous instructions. For example, many forms provide that if a participant has not specified how to divide his or her retirement plan, the account will be divided among all beneficiaries in equal shares.

A beneficiary designation form might include other "gap fillers" or "default" provisions, some of which might be surprising to a participant. For example, a beneficiary designation form might provide that a beneficiary change for one IRA will change the beneficiary for every IRA with the provider. Some retirement plans provide that the beneficiary designated under a pension or life insurance plan is the default beneficiary (see Q 16:18).

Practice Pointer. Because default provisions might frustrate a participant's intent, a participant should read, complete, sign, and deliver each beneficiary designation form.

Q 16:9 Must a beneficiary designation be witnessed?

Usually, no. For a non-ERISA plan, most states' laws do not require that a beneficiary designation be signed in the presence of a notary or otherwise witnessed. Even if a plan's administrator adopts a form that calls for witnesses, a plan administrator might have discretion to excuse an absence of witnesses. [*See, e.g.*, Lowing v. Public Sch. Employees' Ret. Bd., 776 A.2d 306 (Pa. Commw. Ct. 2001)] For an ERISA plan, a beneficiary designation must be made according to the plan and the plan's procedures. [ERISA §§ 404(a)(1)(D), 514(a)]

Q 16:10 Will a beneficiary designation made under a power of attorney be accepted?

Maybe. A trustee, custodian, insurer, or plan administrator may (but need not) accept a beneficiary designation made by an agent under a power of attorney. Typically, a trustee, custodian, insurer, or plan administrator will decline to act unless the power-of-attorney document expressly states a power to change beneficiary designations. [*See, e.g.*, Pension Comm. Heileman-Baltimore Local 1010 IBT Pension Plan v. Bullinger, 1992 U.S. Dist. LEXIS 17325 (D. Md. Oct. 29, 1992); Clouse v. Philadelphia, Bethlehem & New England R.R. Co., 787 F. Supp. 93 (E.D. Pa. 1992); *see also* Restatement (Second) of Agency § 37 (1957)]

Practice Pointer. If ERISA does not preempt state law, a practitioner should consider which state's law might apply, and should draft a power-of-attorney document to meet the state laws of all states that might be involved.

Example. Bill resides in Pennsylvania and works in New Jersey. His SEP plan, which Bill's employer adopted using forms furnished by an IRA custodian, provides that it is governed by Massachusetts laws and neglects to state any provision concerning conflict of laws. Instead of assuming that a power of attorney that meets the requirements of Pennsylvania's statute would be sufficient, Bill's lawyer drafts a document that conforms to the laws of Pennsylvania, New Jersey, and Massachusetts. Doing so is less expensive than researching which law would apply. Also, following all states' laws increases the likelihood that Bill's document will be relied on.

Q 16:11 May a participant's agent name the participant's beneficiaries?

Maybe not. Under some states' laws, an agent, even if he or she otherwise has powers to act concerning the principal's retirement plans, lacks authority to name or change the principal's beneficiaries, unless that power is expressly specified. [Unif. Power of Attorney Act (2006) §§ 201(4), 215]

Q 16:12 May a participant's agent appoint himself or herself as the participant's beneficiary?

Maybe not. Even if an agent generally has some power to name beneficiaries (see Q 16:11), state law might preclude the agent's power to name himself or herself as a beneficiary unless that power too is expressly specified.

Another approach looks to whether the agent is closely related to the principal: under Pennsylvania law's standard "power to engage in retirement plan transactions," an "agent cannot designate himself beneficiary of a retirement plan unless the agent is the spouse, child, grandchild, parent, brother or sister of the principal." [20 Pa. Cons. Stat. Ann. § 5603(q), *accord* § 5603(p) (insurance transactions)]

Even when ERISA preempts state laws relating to the retirement plan, or a different state's laws govern a retirement plan and its administration, the state law that governs a power of attorney remains relevant to discern the effect and meaning of the power of attorney.

Substantial Compliance

Q 16:13 Will a retirement plan participant's attempt to make a beneficiary designation be honored?

Maybe. For "standard-form" contracts, some states recognize the contract interpretation fiction of substantial compliance (see Q 16:14).

Q 16:14 What is the doctrine of *substantial compliance*?

When recognized, the doctrine of *substantial compliance* might excuse a contract holder's failure to effect a change of beneficiary according to the contract's terms if he or she intended to change his or her beneficiary and did everything reasonable in his or her power to effect the change. [*See, e.g.*, Teachers Ins. & Annuity Assoc. of Am. v. Bernardo, 683 F. Supp. 2d 344 (E.D. Pa. 2010)] Some courts find that this equitable doctrine of substantial compliance circumvents "a formalistic, overly technical adherence to the exact words of the change of beneficiary provision in a given [contract]." [Phoenix Mut. Life Ins. Co. v. Adams, 30 F.3d 554, 563 (4th Cir. 1994)]

A payer's interpleader or other circumstances that make a payer a mere stakeholder do not lessen the need for a claimant to show the participant's substantial compliance with a plan's or contract's procedure for making a beneficiary designation. [*See, e.g.*, MetLife Life & Annuity Co. of Conn. v. Sobie, 326 F. App'x 3, 5 (2d Cir. 2009); McCarthy v. Aetna Life Ins. Co., 681 N.Y.S.2d 790 (1998)]

Q 16:15 Does the doctrine of substantial compliance apply to a non-ERISA plan?

Yes, under most states' laws. If ERISA does not preempt state law, a state court likely would apply a relevant state's doctrine of substantial compliance if doing so is not contrary to the employer's plan. [*See* Restatement (Third) of Trusts § 63 comment i (2007), Unif. Trust Code § 602(c)(1), 7C U.L.A. 546–553 (2006) & Supp. 181–183 (2011)]

> **Caution.** Even if the decedent resided and all claimants reside in the same state, that state's law is not necessarily the governing law. A plan or a contract might include provisions concerning which state's law governs.

Q 16:16 Does the doctrine of substantial compliance apply to an ERISA plan?

Concerning an ERISA plan, the doctrine of substantial compliance should apply only if the plan administrator in its discretion decides to use the concept to aid its own interpretation or administration of the plan.

To decide who is the beneficiary under an ERISA plan, a court should hold that any state's doctrine of substantial compliance is preempted. [ERISA § 514(a); *see* Kennedy v. Plan Adm'r for DuPont Sav. & Inv. Plan, 555 U.S. 285 (2009); Egelhoff v. Egelhoff, 532 U.S. 141 (2001); *see, e.g.*, Schmidt v. Sheet Metal Workers' Nat'l Pension Fund, 128 F.3d 541 (7th Cir. 1997); Phoenix Mut. Life Ins. Co. v. Adams, 30 F.3d 554 (4th Cir. 1994); Prudential Ins. Co. of Am. v. Schmid, 337 F. Supp. 2d 325 (D. Mass. 2004); Continental Assurance Co. v. Davis, 24 Employee Benefits Cas. (BNA) 2273, 2000 U.S. Dist. LEXIS 810 (N.D. Ill. Aug. 11, 2000); Metropolitan Life Ins. Co. v. Hall, 9 F. Supp. 2d 560 (D. Md. 1998); Fortis Benefits Ins Co. v. Johnson, 966 F. Supp. 987 (D. Nev. 1997); First Capital Life Ins. Co. v. AAA Communications, 906 F. Supp. 1546 (N.D. Ga. 1995)] However, the Ninth and Tenth Circuits have held that a state's common-law doctrine of substantial compliance supplements an ERISA plan's provisions. [BankAmerica Pension Plan v. McMath, 206 F.3d 821 (9th Cir. 2000); Peckham v. Gem State Mut. of Utah, 964 F.2d 1043 (10th Cir. 1992); *see also* Metropolitan Life Ins. Co. v. Kubichek, 83 F. App'x 425, 529 (3d Cir. 2003)] In the absence of findings by the plan administrator, some federal circuits found that a state's doctrine of substantial compliance may be replaced by a federal common-law doctrine of substantial compliance. [Metropolitan Life Ins. Co. v. Johnson, 297 F.3d 558, 567–569 (7th Cir. 2002); Phoenix Mut. Life Ins. Co. v. Adams, 30 F.3d 554 (4th Cir. 1994)] Although some federal courts considering the question have held that ERISA does not necessarily preempt a state's doctrine of substantial compliance, the contributing author's view is that ERISA preempts any such law relating to an ERISA plan. [ERISA § 514(a)]

> **Practice Pointer.** Unless a plan provision is contrary to ERISA, an ERISA plan administrator must administer a plan according to the plan's documents. [ERISA § 404(a)(1)(D)] Therefore, if a plan states that any doctrine of substantial compliance will not apply, the plan administrator must interpret and administer the plan without using such a doctrine. [*See* Kennedy v. Plan Adm'r for DuPont Sav. & Inv. Plan, 555 U.S. 285 (2009)]

Further, if a plan grants the plan's administrator discretion in interpreting or administering the plan, a court will not interfere with the plan administrator's decision unless it was an abuse of discretion. [*See* Firestone Tire & Rubber Co. v. Bruch, 489 U.S. 101 (1989)]

> **Practice Pointer.** If a plan's administrator is worried that a court might decide that ERISA does not preempt the doctrine of substantial compliance or that ERISA permits a court to consider the doctrine as supplementary federal common law of ERISA, the administrator might, in appropriate circumstances, make an alternative discretionary finding on whether the participant's efforts to change his or her beneficiary designation were sufficient to

meet such a doctrine. It is difficult for a plaintiff to prove that a decision was so obviously wrong that it must have been an abuse of discretion.

Lost Beneficiary Designation

Q 16:17 What should a payer do if it cannot locate a beneficiary designation because records were destroyed?

Even with prudent efforts to safeguard records, circumstances beyond a plan administrator's control might result in the destruction of retirement plan records. If so, a payer should try to "reconstruct" a beneficiary designation using the best evidence available to it.

That records are lost or destroyed does not discharge a payer from its obligation to administer a retirement plan. When deciding whether to pay any benefit to a potential beneficiary, a payer must act in good faith and must use reasonable procedures, especially when deciding who is a participant's beneficiary. When a record is lost or destroyed, a payer may use the most reliable evidence available to it but also must use caution to consider whether the evidence is credible. For example, a claimant might furnish a copy of a beneficiary designation. A payer might use its discretion to rely on a document that appears to be a copy of a participant's beneficiary designation. A payer should do so, however, only if it has adopted and uses reasonable procedures designed to detect a forgery. Further, when a claimant submits evidence that he or she is the participant's beneficiary, a payer must take reasonable steps to consider whether the evidence is credible.

[*See generally* DOL PWBA (now EBSA), FAQs for Plan Sponsors, Fiduciaries and Service Providers Related to the Events of September 11th (2001)]

Default Beneficiary Designation

Q 16:18 What happens when a participant did not make a beneficiary designation?

A retirement plan or IRA may state a "default" beneficiary designation that applies when the participant did not make a valid beneficiary designation. For example, a plan governed by ERISA's Part 2 (see Q 16:40) might provide the plan's death benefit to a participant's surviving spouse, and then to a participant's personal representative only if there is no surviving spouse.

Note. If, under community-property law (see Qs 16:92–16:97), a portion of the participant's retirement plan benefit belongs or belonged to the participant's spouse but was paid to someone else, the spouse (or the spouse's beneficiaries or heirs) might have a claim against the participant's personal representative for payment of the spouse's community property. In Alaska, Arkansas, Colorado, Connecticut, Florida, Hawaii, Kentucky, Michigan,

Montana, New York, North Carolina, Oregon, Virginia, and Wyoming, a statute based on the Uniform Disposition of Community Property Rights at Death Act might apply. [Unif. Disp. Comm. Prop. Rights at Death Act (1971), 8A U.L.A. 213–227 (2003) & Supp. 204 (2011)]

Laws and External Documents That Might Affect a Beneficiary Designation

Q 16:19 Does a divorce revoke a beneficiary designation?

Whether a divorce revokes a beneficiary designation turns on

1. Whether ERISA or state law governs the retirement plan,
2. Which state law (if any) applies, and
3. What the chosen state law (if applicable) provides.

If a retirement plan is not part of an ERISA plan, state law may apply. In many states, a divorce will not revoke a beneficiary designation that names the ex-spouse. [*In re Declaration of Death of Santos, Jr.*, 282 N.J. Super. 509, 660 A.2d 1206 (1995); Hughes v. Scholl, 900 S.W.2d 606 (Ky. 1995); Stiles v. Stiles, 21 Mass. App. Ct. 514, 487 N.E.2d 874 (1986); O'Toole v. Central Laborers' Pension & Welfare Funds, 12 Ill. App. 3d 995, 299 N.E.2d 392 (3d Dist. 1973); Gerhard v. Travelers Ins. Co., 107 N.J. Super. 414, 258 A.2d 724 (Chancery Div. 1969)] Some states have a statute that provides that a divorce or annulment removes the former (or putative) spouse as a beneficiary, except as otherwise specified by a court order. [*See generally* Unif. Probate Code § 2-804(b), 8 pt. I U.L.A. Supp. 177–181 (2011)] Even when a relevant state has such a statute, however, it might not apply if the contract has contrary provisions. In any case, state law will protect a payer that pays the beneficiary of record unless the payer has received a court order restraining payment or at least a written notice that states a dispute about who is the lawful beneficiary. [Unif. Probate Code § 2-804(g)-(h), 8 pt. I U.L.A. Supp. 177–181 (2011)]

If the retirement plan is part of an ERISA plan, ERISA preempts state laws. [ERISA § 514(a)] Therefore, only the plan's terms will govern whether a divorce or other circumstance has any effect on the plan beneficiary designation. [ERISA §§ 404(a)(1)(D), 514(a); Kennedy v. Plan Adm'r for DuPont Sav. & Inv. Plan, 555 U.S. 285 (2009); Egelhoff v. Egelhoff, 532 U.S. 141 (2001); *see also* Boggs v. Boggs, 520 U.S. 833 (1997)]

Practice Pointer. A plan sponsor should consider whether it might be helpful for a plan to state expressly that any annulment, divorce, marital separation, or other event or circumstance has no effect under the plan.

Practice Pointer. After a divorce, a participant should remember to change or confirm his or her beneficiary designation.

Q 16:20 What happens when a beneficiary designation is contrary to an external agreement?

A retirement plan payer pays according to the contract's provisions and applicable law and need not consider external documents. However, once a payer has paid the retirement plan beneficiary, a person who has rights under an external agreement may pursue remedies under state law (if ERISA does not preempt state law). [*See, e.g.*, Kinkel v. Kinkel, 699 N.E.2d 41 (Ohio 1998) (a custodian correctly paid a participant's named beneficiary, but the participant's children later recovered from the participant's surviving spouse); *see also In re* Estate of Sauers, 971 A.2d 1265 (Pa. Super. 2009) (after an ERISA-governed welfare plan has paid its benefit, ERISA does not preempt a state law that permits a claim against the distributee), *appeal granted* 981 A.2d 1279 (Pa. 2009)]

Q 16:21 May an executor participate in a court proceeding concerning a disputed benefit?

Often, no. A personal representative of a participant's estate may participate in a court proceeding concerning a disputed benefit only if the personal representative is a bona fide claimant. If a personal representative does not make any claim of right to the benefit, however, such a personal representative has no claim or standing to participate in a court proceeding. [*See, e.g.*, Deaton v. Cross, 184 F. Supp. 2d 441 (D. Md. 2002)]

Q 16:22 Why would a divorced participant not want to name his or her young child as a beneficiary?

A divorced participant might not want to name his or her young child as a beneficiary if doing so might have the effect of putting money in the hands of the child's other parent—the participant's former spouse.

A retirement plan is a contract. A payer wants to be sure that a payment is a complete satisfaction of that contract. Ordinarily, a beneficiary's deposit or negotiation of a check that pays a retirement plan distribution is the beneficiary's acceptance of the payer's satisfaction of the beneficiary's claim under the retirement plan. A minor is a person still young enough that he or she cannot make a binding contract. At common law, the age of majority was 21. Now, all but three states' laws generally end a person's minor status at age 18.

Before a child reaches age 18 (or the other age of competence to make binding contracts), his or her guardian or conservator may disaffirm an agreement or promise the child made. After a child reaches age 18 (or the other "full age"), he or she may disaffirm an agreement or promise he or she made before he or she reached the age of competence to make contracts. A payer will not take the risk that paying a retirement plan distribution is not a complete satisfaction of retirement plan obligations. Thus, payers usually are unwilling to pay a retirement plan benefit to a minor.

To facilitate payment in these circumstances, most plans permit payment to a minor's conservator, guardian, or Uniform Transfers to Minors Act custodian. [*See generally* Susan N. Gary & Nancy E. Shurtz, *Nontax Considerations in Testamentary Transfers to Minors*, Tax, Estate, and Lifetime Planning for Minors 295–336 (Carmine Y. D'Aversa ed. 2006)] If a participant named his or her child as a beneficiary (rather than naming as beneficiary a custodian), a payer is likely to honor a claim made by the child's guardian. If a child's other parent is living, most courts would maintain or appoint the parent as the child's conservator. In some states, the law presumes that a court should consider a child's parent or natural guardian to serve also as the child's conservator. [*Compare* Manley v. Detroit Auto Inter-Insurance Exch., 127 Mich. App. 444, 339 N.W.2d 205 (1983), *motion denied*, 357 N.W.2d 644 (Mich. App. 1983), *remanded on other grounds*, 425 Mich. 140, 388 N.W.2d 216 (1986), *with In re Estate of Fisher, 503 So. 2d* 962 (Fla. Ct. App. 1987) (child's "natural guardian" was not the guardian of his property); *see generally* Unif. Probate Code § 5-413(6)-(7), 8 pt. II U.L.A. 390-395 (1998) & Supp. 234–235 (2011).]

Using Trusts

Q 16:23 What is a *living trust*?

A trust refers to a person's right to the beneficial enjoyment of property to which another person holds the legal title. A *living trust* is a trust that is created and takes effect during the settlor's lifetime. [*See generally Black's Law Dictionary*, 1018, 1651 (9th ed. 2009)] A typical living trust is revocable. If a living trust is irrevocable, it necessarily involves at least one beneficiary other than the trust's creator. [*See generally* Restatement (Third) of Trusts, § 2 (2003)]

Q 16:24 Can a participant hold his or her retirement plan in a living trust?

No, because the provisions of a typical "living trust" (see Q 16:23) are inconsistent with a plan's or IRA's exclusive-benefit and anti-alienation provisions.

A 401(k) SIMPLE plan (other than a church plan or governmental plan) must preclude assignment or alienation of a plan benefit (other than as required by a qualified domestic relations order or an offset to meet an obligation to the plan under a court order or settlement agreement). [ERISA § 206(d); I.R.C. § 401(a)(13)]

A SEP (including a SARSEP) or SIMPLE plan (other than a 401(k) SIMPLE plan) is "funded" by an IRA. [I.R.C. §§ 408(k)(1), 408(p)(1)] An individual retirement account must be for the exclusive benefit of the participant and his or her beneficiaries, and a participant's right to his or her account balance must be nonforfeitable. [I.R.C. §§ 408(a) (flush language), 408(a)(4)] An individual retirement annuity must provide that a participant cannot transfer the IRA, and that the participant's rights are nonforfeitable. [I.R.C. §§ 408(b)(1), 408(b)(4)]

Because a living trust can be revoked or amended, the trust declaration or agreement could not ensure that during the participant's lifetime the retirement plan benefit would be used only for the participant's benefit.

Practice Pointer. There is no particularly good reason to try to put a retirement plan benefit into a living trust. A retirement plan benefit already is non-probate rights that will pass according to the contract's beneficiary designation (see Q 16:2).

Q 16:25 Can a trust be a beneficiary?

Yes. A participant may name a trust as beneficiary under a retirement plan. To make a correct beneficiary designation, the participant should name the trustee, as trustee of the trust, as beneficiary. Most retirement plan administrators, however, will treat a designation of a trust as if it were a designation of the duly appointed and then currently serving trustee of the trust. The trust must be legally in existence (or completed such that it would be legally in existence on the trustee's receipt of money or property) before the participant makes the beneficiary designation.

Note. A beneficiary of a trust is not a designated beneficiary for minimum-distribution purposes unless the trust meets specified requirements, which include that the beneficiaries are identifiable under the trust instrument and that certain information is certified to the plan administrator (if any). [Treas. Reg. § 1.401(a)(9)-4, Q&As5 & 6]

Pets

Q 16:26 Can a participant name his or her dog or cat as a beneficiary?

No. A beneficiary must be a person, whether a natural person or a nonnatural person (e.g., a corporation), that can endorse a negotiable instrument—such as the check that pays the plan distribution.

For many people, living with a pet is an important and comforting part of life, and providing for the care of the pet is a real concern. Although it is usually more effective for a pet participant to plan for the care of the pet in the pet participant's will, some people might have insufficient probate property to provide for the pet's care and instead may use a beneficiary designation.

A person cannot give any part of his or her estate directly to an animal. However, a pet participant may leave a sum of money to a trustee (see Q 16:27) or to a person designated to care for the pet, along with a request (but not a direction) that the money be used for the pet's care.

Practice Pointer. A person should select as his or her pet's caretaker someone he or she trusts, because the caretaker often has no legal obligation to use the money for the purpose specified. If there is no suitable relative or friend who would take the pet, a person might consider a charity that cares for or places companion animals.

Q 16:27 May a trust provide for a pet's care?

State laws differ widely concerning whether and how a trust may provide for the care of animals; these differences may be grouped in the following broad categories:

1. In some states, a trust for the support of an animal is invalid because there is no beneficiary. However, a trust for a human beneficiary *may* include a provision that the trustee may use trust property to pay for the care of an animal since the animal's care might benefit the human beneficiary.
2. In some states, a person may create a valid trust for an animal (if the trust satisfies other trust law concerning the duration of a trust), but such a trust is an honorary trust. [*See generally* Restatement (Second) of Trusts, § 124 (1959)] A court will not order any remedy if the trustee fails to perform the honorary trust.
3. In some states, a trust for an animal's care may be enforced in the courts. [*See generally* Unif. Probate Code § 2-907, 8 pt. I U.L.A. 239–242 (1998) & Supp. 184–185 (2011); Unif. Trust Code §§ 408, 409, 7C U.L.A. 490–495 (2006) & Supp. 158–160 (2011)]

In some states, a trust recognized under categories 2 or 3 in the preceding list cannot exceed 21 years, even if the life span of a particular animal is longer. For a trust governed by a state law based on the Uniform Trust Code, a trust for the care of an animal ends on the animal's death, or a trust for the care of more than one animal (alive during the creator's life) ends on the death of the last surviving animal. [*See, e.g.*, 20 Pa. Consol. Stat. § 7738(a)] Colorado, however, permits a valid pet trust for the lifetime of the animals and "the animals' offspring in gestation." [Colo. Rev. Stat. Ann. § 15-11-901]

A trust does not necessarily mean that the trustee must be the animal's caretaker. If the trustee cannot or prefers not to take physical possession of the animal, a separate person may be named as the caretaker; but it is usually more efficient for one person to serve as both caretaker and trustee.

Q 16:28 How might a participant make a beneficiary designation to provide for his or her pet's care?

For an illustration of how to provide for the care of a pet without using a trust, consider the following example:

Example. Gary desires that his cat be properly cared for after Gary's death. Gary is a man of modest income and little wealth. He anticipates that almost none of his property will pass by his will. Gary has a small balance (to which he no longer contributes) under a retirement plan. To provide for his cat, he makes the following provisions:

Beneficiary designation: Mary Johnson 100%

Will

I give my cat, Lady Lucy of Canterbury Tails, and any other animals that I may own at the time of my death, to Mary Johnson (who currently resides at 234 Sunset Road, Indianapolis, Indiana) with the request that she treat them as companion animals. To provide for the care of these animals, I have made a separate financial provision for Mary Johnson, and I request (but do not direct) that she use that money for the care of these animals.

A bequest, gift, trust, or beneficiary designation in favor of a pet animal that is unreasonably large might be capricious and therefore legally ineffective. [*See generally* Restatement (Second) of Trusts § 124 (1959)] Sometimes, a court will reduce the amount set aside for the care of the pet animal. [*See generally* Unif. Probate Code § 2-907(c)(6), 8 pt. I U.L.A. 239–242 (1998) & Supp. 184–185 (2011)]

Practice Pointer. If a participant has relatives who might challenge the beneficiary designation, the participant should consider providing only a reasonable amount of money for the care of any pet. A large sum of money for the pet may prompt relatives to challenge the beneficiary designation.

Q 16:29 Who is taxed on a retirement plan distribution set aside for the care of a pet?

If a retirement plan distribution is paid to a pet's caretaker who does not serve as a trustee, the distribution is that person's income. If a retirement plan distribution is paid to a trustee who serves under a valid trust, the distribution is the trust's income. A valid pet trust that is legally unenforceable will nevertheless be treated as a trust for federal income tax purposes.

A pet trust is subject to federal income tax at the rates that apply to a married person who files a separate return. Although a trust normally has a deduction in the amount of trust distributions, "since the amounts of income required to be distributed . . . and amounts properly paid, credited, or required to be distributed under [the relevant Internal Revenue Code sections] are limited to distributions intended for beneficiaries, a deduction under those sections is not available for distributions for the benefit of a pet animal. Similarly, such distributions are not taxed to anyone[.]" [Rev. Rul. 76-476, 1976-2 C.B. 192] These rules are consistent with the idea that trust income generally should be taxed only once, but should be taxed.

Charitable Gifts

Q 16:30 May a participant name a charity as a beneficiary?

Yes, a participant may name a charitable organization as a beneficiary. Although some states previously had statutes that would have voided some charitable gifts made soon before a donor's death or for more than a specified portion of his or her estate, those statutes were unconstitutional. [*See, e.g.*, Estate of Cavill, 329 A.2d 503 (Pa. 1974)] States repealed all these statutes.

For a participant who already has fairly provided for his or her spouse and children, a charitable gift may be worthwhile. Many people who have worked for charity or in education are inclined to continue that work by making a gift to a charitable organization.

> **Caution.** A charitable organization employer should avoid inappropriately inducing its employees to name the charity as a beneficiary. In addition to consequences under other laws, doing so could interfere with rights under an ERISA plan. [*See* ERISA § 510]

> **Practice Pointer.** For someone who already has decided to make charitable gifts on death and expects his or her estate to be subject to a significant federal estate tax, some financial planners suggest that using a retirement plan benefit might be an efficient way to provide the gift. They suggest this because deferred compensation is subject to both federal income tax and federal estate tax, while a capital asset might enjoy a "stepped up" basis and might not be subject to income tax until the beneficiary sells the asset. Other planners point out that the federal income tax deduction for federal estate tax attributable to property that is income in respect of a decedent partially mitigates the "double tax." [*See* I.R.C. § 691(c)] Along with this, they argue that a retirement plan might permit longer income tax deferral, whereas post-death income on capital assets will subject the beneficiary to income tax. Considering which course might be "right" turns on the donor's (and the planner's) assumptions. Further, nontax factors might favor a particular approach.

Q 16:31 If a charity is the beneficiary, what is the tax treatment of the retirement plan benefit?

Although a retirement plan benefit will be included in the participant's taxable estate for federal estate tax purposes, the estate will have a deduction for the amount that properly passes to charity. [I.R.C. § 2055] Further, although some portion of a distribution from a retirement plan might be included in income for federal income tax purposes, a charitable organization does not pay federal income tax on its receipts from charitable gifts. [I.R.C. § 501(a)]

Simultaneous Death; Absentees

Q 16:32 What should a payer do if there is doubt as to the order of deaths?

For many retirement plans, the order of deaths between a participant and a beneficiary is irrelevant.

> **Practice Pointer.** A carefully drafted plan should state that a person cannot be a beneficiary if he or she is not living (or it is not in existence) when the plan's administrator receives the person's claim or, if later, a benefit is to be paid or becomes payable.

If an ERISA plan administrator must decide the order of deaths between a participant and a beneficiary (or among potential beneficiaries), and the plan does not provide a presumption concerning the order of deaths, the plan administrator need not follow any state's simultaneous-death statute. [ERISA § 514(a); *cf.* Apostal v. Laborer's Welfare & Pension Fund, 195 F. Supp. 2d 1052 (N.D. Ill. 2002)] If the plan does not provide a specific rule, a plan administrator might choose to follow the general pattern of state laws (see Q 16:33), treating such an invented rule as the plan administrator's interpretation.

Q 16:33 What is the typical simultaneous-death rule?

The "old" Uniform Simultaneous Death Act, adopted by many states, provides that if "there is no sufficient evidence that the persons have died otherwise than simultaneously, the property of each person shall be disposed of as if he [or she] had survived [the other person]." [Unif. Simultaneous Death Act § 1 (1940), 8A U.L.A. 141–158 & Supp. 97–99 (2009)] The 1991 version of the Uniform Simultaneous Death Act and the Uniform Probate Code each generally provide that a person cannot qualify as an heir unless he or she survives the first decedent for 120 hours. Further, the person who would claim through the heir has the burden of proving the duration that the heir survived the first decedent. [Unif. Probate Code §§ 2-104, 2-702, 8 pt. I U.L.A. 84, 182–186 (1998) & Supp. 42–44, 112 (2009)]

> **Practice Pointer.** For tax planning purposes, a wealthy participant may prefer to vary these "default" rules by express language in his or her beneficiary designation. [*See, e.g.*, Treas. Reg. § 20.2056(e)-2(e)] Even if state law applies to the plan, state law will permit a different provision if it is stated by the plan or the participant's beneficiary designation. [*See, e.g.*, N.Y. Est. Powers & Trusts Law § 2-1.6(b)]

Alternatively, a common-disaster clause or a delay clause of up to six months does not disqualify property for the federal estate tax marital deduction. [I.R.C. § 2056(b)(3); Treas. Reg. § 20.2056(b)-3(b)]

If it becomes necessary for an ERISA plan administrator to determine the order of deaths between or among potential beneficiaries and the retirement plan does not provide a presumption concerning the order of deaths, it may be prudent for the plan administrator to indulge a presumption that all persons who died within a few days of one another died at the same time and survived to the relevant time.

If a plan administrator decides claims under a non-ERISA plan, the plan administrator may be required to follow state law.

Q 16:34 Is there a federal common law of ERISA concerning simultaneous deaths?

No. At common law, when two or more persons died in a common disaster, there was no presumption for or against any person surviving another. [*See, e.g.*, People v. Eulo, 482 N.Y.S.2d 436, 472 N.E.2d 286 (1984)] Moreover, there is no clear consensus in states' statutes. [*See generally* Restatement (Third) of Property: Wills and Other Donative Transfers § 1.2, statutory note (2003)]

Q 16:35 What should a payer do when someone says a participant or beneficiary is absent and presumed dead?

Under ordinary circumstances, a plan administrator or payer should not presume a participant's or beneficiary's death. Instead, a plan administrator or payer should require the claimant (usually the next beneficiary) to prove the absentee's death by an appropriate court order.

Under the common law, a person was presumed dead if he or she had been absent for a continuous period of seven years. [*See, e.g.*, 20 Pa. Cons. Stat. Ann. § 5701(b) & comment] Likewise, an absentee's exposure to a specific peril was a sufficient ground for presuming death. [*See, e.g.*, 20 Pa. Cons. Stat. Ann. § 5701(c) and comment] Further, death may be inferred if survival of the absentee would be beyond human expectation or experience. [*See, e.g.*, *In re* Katz's Estate, 135 Misc. 861, 239 N.Y.S. 722 (Sup. Ct. 1930)] Courts sometimes required considerable evidence of an unexplained absence. For example, a person's absence from the places where his relatives resided together with his failure to communicate with his relatives was not enough to show that he was absent from his residence without explanation. [Estate of Morrison v. Roswell, 92 Ill. 2d 207, 441 N.E.2d 68, 65 Ill. Dec. 276 (1982)]

In 1939, the Uniform Absence as Evidence of Death and Absentees Property Act reversed the common-law rules: the fact that a person had been absent for seven years (or any duration) or had been exposed to a specific peril did not set up a presumption of death; instead, these facts were merely evidence for a court or jury to consider in making its own finding of whether the absentee's death had occurred. [*See, e.g.*, Armstrong v. Pilot Life Ins. Co., 656 S.W.2d 18 (Tenn. Ct. App. 1983)]

The Uniform Probate Code, portions of which have been adopted in many states, returns to a presumption. A person is presumed dead after he or she has been absent for a continuous period, such as three, four, five, or seven years. [*Cf.* Minn. Stat. § 576.141; N.J. Stat. Ann. § 3B:27-1; N.Y. Est. Powers & Trusts Law § 2-1.7; 20 Pa. Cons. Stat. Ann. § 5701(c)] However, a person who seeks a declaration of the absentee's death must demonstrate to a court's satisfaction that the absentee has not been heard from after diligent search or inquiry and that his or her absence is not satisfactorily explained. [*See, e.g.*, 20 Pa. Cons. Stat. Ann. §§ 5702–5705]

Unless sufficient evidence proves that death occurred sooner, the end of the waiting period is deemed the date of death. [*See, e.g.*, Hubbard v. Equitable Life Assurance Soc'y of the United States, 248 Wis. 340, 21 N.W.2d 665 (1946); Hogaboam v. Metropolitan Life Ins. Co., 248 Wis. 146, 21 N.W.2d 268 (1946)]

The presumption of an absentee's death does not necessarily apply to all property in the same way. For example, some states do not use the presumption to provide a life insurance death benefit. [*See, e.g.*, Armstrong v. Pilot Life Ins. Co., 656 S.W.2d 18 (Tenn. Ct. App. 1983)]

Usually, the person who would benefit from the absentee's death bears the burden of proof.

> **Note.** The terrorist attacks of September 11, 2001, focused attention on laws that permit a finding of death based on exposure to a specific peril. [*See* N.J. Stat. Ann. §§ 3B:27-1, -6; N.Y. Est. Powers & Trusts Law § 2.17(b); 20 Pa. Cons. Stat. Ann. § 5701(c); *see also* Chiaramonte v. Chiaramonte, 435 N.Y.S.2d 523 (Sup. Ct. 1981); Zucker's Will, 219 N.Y.S.2d 72 (Sup. Ct. 1961); Bobrow's Estate, 179 N.Y.S.2d 742 (Sup. Ct. 1958); Brevoort's Will, 73 N.Y.S.2d 216 (Sup. Ct. 1947)]

An ERISA plan's administrator need not follow state law and instead may make its own rules and use discretion in deciding whether or when a person's death occurred. [*See* Estate of Slack *ex rel.* Apostal v. Laborer's Welfare & Pension Fund, 195 F. Supp. 2d 1052 (N.D. Ill. 2002)]

Family Rights That Restrain a Beneficiary Designation

Failing to Provide for a Spouse

Q 16:36 May a participant make a beneficiary designation that does not provide for his or her spouse?

Yes, usually. Even if it is part of an ERISA plan, an IRA is exempt from Part 2 of Subtitle B of Title I of ERISA. Thus, the survivor-annuity rules of ERISA Section 205 do not apply to an IRA. [ERISA § 201(6)]

> **Caution.** A 401(k) SIMPLE plan usually is governed by ERISA Section 205, and almost always must meet Code Section 401(a)(11) and thereby Code Section 417. Therefore, such a plan must provide a qualified joint and survivor annuity for a distribution that begins before a participant's death and a qualified pre-retirement survivor annuity for a distribution that begins after a participant's death, or must provide an alternate survivor benefit (see Q 16:44).

A payer will, in the absence of a court order or written notice of a dispute, give effect to the participant's beneficiary designation. Even when a participant's beneficiary change has an obvious potential to frustrate a divorcing spouse's equitable distribution rights, a participant remains free to make his or her beneficiary designation unless a court's restraining order binds him or her. [*See, e.g.*, Titler v. State Employees' Ret. Bd., 768 A.2d 899 (Pa. Commw. Ct. 2001)] Further, an order that binds a participant might not bind a plan or its administrator.

If a participant's spouse did not receive his or her share provided by state law, any distributee might be liable to the participant's executor to the extent that state law provides for a spouse's elective share to be payable from non-probate property. [*See generally* Unif. Probate Code § 2-204, 8 pt. I U.L.A. 104-105 (1998) & Supp. 77–78 (2009)]

Note. If a distributee received a plan distribution in one year but paid over an amount to the participant's surviving spouse in a later year, the distributee recognizes income for the year he or she received the distribution and claims a deduction for the year he or she paid restoration to the surviving spouse. [I.R.C. § 1341; United States v. Lewis, 340 U.S. 590 (1951)]

Practice Pointer. A surviving spouse who is not the participant's named beneficiary and instead receives deferred compensation because of an elective-share law or community-property law is not a designated beneficiary when applying the plan's minimum distribution provisions. [Treas. Reg. § 1.401(a)(9)-4, Q&A-1] Thus, it might become necessary to compute a minimum distribution by reference to a different person's life.

In Louisiana, a payer may follow the participant's beneficiary designation. [La. Rev. Stat. Ann. §§ 23:638, 23:652] To the extent necessary to satisfy the spouse's community-property rights and usufruct, a distributee who receives benefits under a nongovernmental (and non-ERISA) retirement plan must account for and pay over benefits to the participant's surviving spouse. [T.L. James & Co. v. Montgomery, 332 So. 2d 834 (La. 1976)] A distributee who receives benefits under a retirement plan of "any public or governmental employer" is not subject to the claims of forced heirs. [La. Civ. Code Ann. art. 1505]

Caution. That ERISA's Part 2 of Subtitle B of Title I (which includes ERISA's surviving-spouse protection) does not apply to a plan does not mean that state law applies. If ERISA governs a plan (even without applying some Parts), ERISA preempts state laws. [ERISA § 514(a)]

Different law may apply to members of a Native American tribe. [Jones v. Meehan, 175 U.S. 1 (1899); *see also* 25 U.S.C. § 1301(1); Davis v. Shanks, 15 Minn. 369 (1870); Hasting v. Farmer, 4 N.Y. 293 (1850); Dole v. Irish, 2 Barb. 639 (N.Y. Sup. Gen. Term. 1848); *see generally* United States v. Wheeler, 435 U.S. 313 (1978)] A Native American tribe's law usually applies, however, between or among members of the tribe and often cannot be enforced against persons outside the tribe.

Even when a participant's beneficiary change has an obvious potential to frustrate a divorcing spouse's equitable distribution rights, a participant remains free to make his or her beneficiary designation unless a court's restraining order binds him or her. [*See, e.g.*, Titler v. State Employees' Ret. Bd., 768 A.2d 899 (Pa. Commw. Ct. 2001)] Further, an order that binds a participant might not bind a plan administrator or payer.

Note 1. If a distributee received a plan distribution in one year but paid over an amount to the participant's surviving spouse in a later year, the distributee recognizes income for the year he or she received the distribution and claims a deduction for the year he or she paid restoration to the surviving spouse. [I.R.C. § 1341; United States v. Lewis, 340 U.S. 590 (1951)]

Note 2. A surviving spouse who is not the participant's named beneficiary and instead receives a benefit because of an elective-share law or community-property law is not a designated beneficiary when applying the plan's minimum distribution provisions. [Treas. Reg. § 1.401(a)(9)-4, A-1] Thus, it might become necessary to compute a minimum distribution by reference to a different person's life.

Q 16:37 Must a payer tell an ex-spouse when a participant changes his or her beneficiary designation contrary to a court order?

No, in the absence of a court order that commands the payer to furnish specified information, a payer has no duty to furnish information about a particular beneficiary designation change:

> Absent a promise or misrepresentation, the courts have almost uniformly rejected claims by plan participants or beneficiaries that an ERISA administrator has to volunteer individualized information taking account of their peculiar circumstances. This view reflects ERISA's focus on limited and general reporting and disclosure requirements [citations omitted], and also reflects the enormous burdens an obligation to proffer individualized advice would inflict on plan administrators.

[Barrs v. Lockheed Martin Corp., 287 F.2d 202, 27 Empl. Benefits Cas. (BNA) 2409, Pens. Plan Guide (CCH) ¶ 23,979F (1st Cir. 2002)] Even when a plan administrator is governed by ERISA Section 404's greatest fiduciary duties, courts have not required a plan administrator to furnish an alternate payee information beyond that required by an express statutory or plan provision. For a non-ERISA plan, it seems unlikely that a court would impose a duty greater than federal courts have applied concerning ERISA plans.

Failing to Provide for a Child

Q 16:38 Can a participant make a beneficiary designation that does not provide for his or her child?

In the United States, only Louisiana and Puerto Rico have a forced-share provision for a decedent's children. [*See* La. Civ. Code Ann. arts. 1493–1495; P.R. Laws tit. 31, §§ 2362, 2411–2463] Therefore, a participant can usually "disinherit" his or her children. In some states, a modest family allowance is sometimes required for a decedent's children if there is no surviving spouse. [*See generally* Unif. Probate Code §§ 2-403–2-404, 8 pt. I U.L.A. 141, 142 (1998) & Supp 37–38 (2008)]

In Louisiana, a payer may follow the participant's beneficiary designation. [La. Rev. Stat. Ann. §§ 23:638, 23:652] A distributee who receives benefits under a church plan or another non-ERISA plan other than a governmental plan must account for and pay over benefits to the participant's surviving spouse as needed to satisfy his or her community-property rights and usufruct and to the participant's children or forced heirs as needed to satisfy their *légitime* (legitimate portions). [T.L. James & Co. v. Montgomery, 332 So. 2d 834 (La. 1976)] A distributee who receives benefits under a retirement plan of "any public or governmental employer" is not subject to the claims of forced heirs. [La. Civ. Code Ann. art. 1505]

Different law may apply to members of a Native American tribe. [Jones v. Meehan, 175 U.S. 1 (1899); *see also* 25 U.S.C. § 1301(1); Davis v. Shanks, 15 Minn. 369 (1870); Hasting v. Farmer, 4 N.Y. 293 (1850); Dole v. Irish, 2 Barb. 639 (N.Y. Sup. Gen. Term. 1848); *see generally* United States v. Wheeler, 435 U.S. 313 (1978)]

Whether it is called *légitime*, legitimate portions, or compulsory portions in civil law nations, family provision or family maintenance in nations following English law, or *ahl al-fara'id* under the Koran, in most nations a person is limited in his or her right or privilege to disinherit his or her children.

Practice Pointer. A participant who resides in a nation other than the United States should consult an expert lawyer before he or she makes a beneficiary designation that does not provide for his or her spouse and children.

Marriage

These questions explain some basics of marriage, as well as the differences between ceremonial marriage and informal or common-law marriage. Also, questions under this heading refer to same-sex marriages, including civil unions and domestic partnerships.

Q 16:39 Why is understanding the law of marriage important to beneficiary designations?

An important restraint on a beneficiary designation is a spouse's rights. Of course, these rights turn on a person's showing that he or she was a participant's spouse. Although many people are accustomed to thinking of a marriage certificate as evidence that a valid marriage occurred, sometimes it is unclear whether a marriage existed.

Q 16:40 What is *marriage*?

Marriage is a civil contract and a relation or status by which each of two persons agrees to live with the other as spouses, to the exclusion of others. States regulate marriage as part of their police power. Most states recognize a marriage contracted in another state, unless the marriage is contrary to a strong public policy of the forum state.

Q 16:41 What is a *void marriage*?

A *void marriage* is one that is invalid from its inception, and cannot be made valid. [Black's Law Dictionary 1062 (9th ed. 2009] A marriage is void if:

- The parties are too closely related, or
- Either party is married to someone else.

In some states, a later "marriage" becomes valid on the end of an earlier marriage, if both parties to the later "marriage" were unaware that the earlier marriage was undissolved when they entered into the later "marriage." In some states, a marriage is void if the parties are of the same sex and a restriction against such a marriage is not contrary to the U.S. Constitution or the state's constitution (see Qs 16:61–16:62).

Either party may "walk away" from a void marriage without waiting for a divorce or annulment.

> **Note.** A fraudulently obtained marriage license or a failure to obtain a license might not by itself invalidate a marriage. [*See, e.g.*, Carabetta v. Carabetta, 182 Conn. 344, 438 A.2d 109 (1980)]

Q 16:42 What is a *voidable marriage*?

A *voidable marriage* is one that is initially invalid but remains in effect unless ended by a court order. [Black's Law Dictionary 1062 (9th ed. 2009] For example, a marriage might be voidable if either party was underage, drunk, or otherwise legally incompetent. Likewise, a marriage is voidable if someone used fraud, duress, or force to induce a party to "agree" to the marriage. The parties may ratify an otherwise voidable marriage by words or conduct after the removal of the impediment that made the marriage voidable.

Ceremonial Marriage

Q 16:43 What is a *ceremonial marriage*?

A *ceremonial marriage* is a marriage performed according to a state statute (other than a statute that recognizes common-law marriage). Many people prefer a ceremonial marriage to an informal or common-law marriage because a ceremonial marriage is easier to prove.

A license to marry is required and is furnished by a state court or official upon approval of an application designed to check the parties' eligibility to marry. In most states, an application must state identifying information (i.e., information about each prior marriage of either applicant) that neither of the applicants is afflicted with a communicable disease and other facts necessary to find whether there is a legal impediment to the proposed marriage. A refusal to issue a marriage license is reviewable by a court. An application for a marriage license is a public record.

If either party is a minor or mentally incapacitated, most states require at least a guardian's approval, and sometimes a court's approval.

Most states provide that a judge or government official, or a church's, temple's, synagogue's, mosque's, congregation's, or tribe's minister, priest, rabbi, imam, or other leader may perform a ceremony. Some people use the term *civil marriage* to describe a ceremony led by a judge or government official, as distinguished from one solemnized by a religion's officiant, leader, or member. Some states permit the parties to perform their marriage ceremony. Some states permit (and others prohibit) a proxy marriage, a ceremony in which someone stands in for an absent party.

A failure to comply with statutory rules does not necessarily result in a void marriage. Sometimes a defect makes a marriage voidable rather than void. In a state that permits common-law marriage, a defective ceremonial marriage often results in a valid common-law marriage.

A fraudulently obtained marriage license or a failure to obtain a license might not by itself invalidate a marriage. [*See, e.g.*, Carabetta v. Carabetta, 182 Conn. 344 (1980); *but see, e.g.*, Edwards v. Franke, 364 P.2d 60, 63 (Alaska 1961); Abbott v. Abbott, 282 N.W.2d 561, 566 (Minn. 1979)] Likewise, a defect in recording a marriage will not by itself invalidate a marriage. [*See, e.g.*, Accounts Mgmt., Inc. v. Litchfield, 1998 S.D. 24 (1998)]

Q 16:44 What is the effect of a marriage certificate?

A person who wants to prove that a marriage exists (or existed until the other person's death) may refer to the marriage certificate as evidence of the marriage's validity. Unless someone else shows persuasive evidence of a defect, a marriage certificate usually is strong evidence that the marriage occurred.

Common-Law Marriage

Q 16:45 What is a *common-law marriage*?

A *common-law marriage* (perhaps more appropriately called an informal marriage) is a marriage that was not solemnized by a ceremony but was created by the simple agreement of the parties. Each person must be legally capable of making a marriage contract and must state, orally or in writing, his or her present agreement to the relation of spouses, agreeing to live with his or her spouse to the exclusion of all others. In general, the exchange of words that makes the marriage must be in the present tense, and must state the marriage itself instead of an intent to marry.

Some people mistakenly assume that a period of cohabitation results in a common-law marriage, but that is not true under any state's law. Conversely, cohabitation is not necessary; the present agreement to the marriage is all that is needed. [*See generally* James Kent, Commentaries on American Law, vol. II, pt. IV, lect. XXVI, pp. 86–93 (1794)] However, Alabama law seems to require cohabitation as further evidence of the agreement to a marriage. [Herd v. Herd, 194 Ala. 613, 69 So. 885 (Ala. 1915)] Likewise, Texas law suggests that an informal marriage "may be proved by evidence that . . . a man and woman . . . lived together in [Texas] as husband and wife[.]" [*See* Texas Family Code Ann. § 2.401(a)] Further, a "holding out" as spouses, though sometimes presented as evidence of a common-law marriage, is not always required. Even those who expressly denied to a third person that they were married may be married if they agreed (between themselves) to be married. [Polly v. Coffey, 2003 WL 231293 (Ohio Ct. App. Feb. 3, 2003)] Nonetheless, because a court's consideration of whether a common-law marriage existed usually involves disputed or ambiguous facts, courts often consider cohabitation and "reputation" (whether third persons believed the couple were spouses) as evidence that might suggest how likely it is that the couple agreed to a marriage.

> **Note.** Although England and Wales did not recognize informal marriages (other than of Jews or Quakers) made after 1753, early America (even before the 1776 Declaration of Independence) was permitted to recognize informal marriage because Britain's statute did not apply to Scotland, the Channel Islands, or Britain's colonies. [Lord Hardwicke's Act (Marriage Act), 1753, 26 Geo. II. c. 33 (Eng.)]

If the law of a state that recognizes common-law marriage (see Q 16:46) applies, a couple might be married, notwithstanding the absence of any ceremony or writing. Even an implication of consent to a marriage might be sufficient. [*In re* Garges' Estate, 474 Pa. 237, 378 A.2d 307 Garges' Estate, 474 Pa. 237, 378 A.2d 307 (Pa. 1977)] In addition, a marriage ceremony that had a defect is likely to result in a common-law marriage. [*See, e.g., In re* Larry's Estate, 29 Fiduc. Rep. (Bisel) 298 (Pa. Common Pleas Orphans Ct. Div. 1979)]

> **Practice Pointer.** Usually, the absence of a ceremony (and of witnesses, other than the parties) makes it difficult to prove that a common-law marriage exists or existed. Often, there is an evidence law rule or presumption against the claimant testifying to the creation of the relationship. [*See,*

e.g., 20 Pa. Cons. Stat. Ann. § 2209; 42 Pa. Cons. Stat. Ann. § 5930; *see also* Estate of Stauffer v. Stauffer, 476 A.2d 354 (Pa. 1984); Wagner's Estate, 398 Pa. 531 (1960); Estate of Corace v. Graeser, 527 A.2d 1058 (Pa. Super. Ct. 1987)] Courts consider evidence of how each person described the relationship to third persons and how third persons understood the relationship. The use of names might be significant. [*See, e.g.*, *In re* Erlanger's Estate, 145 Misc. 1, 259 N.Y.S. 610 (N.Y. Sur. 1932)] However, either spouse's denial of the marriage in records such as a driver's license, Social Security claims, tax returns, insurance applications, bank accounts, and wage records does not necessarily deny a common-law marriage. [*See, e.g.*, Dalworth Trucking Co. v. Bulen, 924 S.W.2d 728 (Tex. App. 1996); Estate of Giessel, 734 S.W.2d 27 (Tex. App. 1987)] The burden of proving a common-law marriage is on the person who asserts that it existed. [*See, e.g.*, Driscoll v. Driscoll, 220 Kan. 225, 227, 552 P.2d 629 (1976); *In re* Estate of Gavula, 490 Pa. 535, 417 A.2d 168 (Pa. 1980); *In re* Estate of Stauffer, 315 Pa. Super. 591, 462 A.2d 750 (1983), *rev'd on other grounds*, 504 Pa. 626, 476 A.2d 354 (1983); *but see* Fiedler v. National Tube Co., 161 Pa. Super. 155, 53 A.2d 821 (1947)]

Usually, the burden of proof is on the person who claims that a common-law marriage was made. [*See, e.g.*, White v. State Farm Mut. Auto Ins. Co., 907 F. Supp. 1012 (E.D. Tex. 1995)]

If a couple ever lived or even traveled in a state that recognizes or previously recognized common-law marriage (see Q 16:46), the couple may be married, notwithstanding the absence of any ceremony or writing.

Q 16:46 Which states recognize common-law marriage?

As of early 2012, Alabama, Colorado, Iowa, Kansas, Montana, New Hampshire, Oklahoma, Rhode Island, South Carolina, Texas, Utah, and the District of Columbia recognize a common-law marriage. [Creel v. Creel, 763 So. 2d 943 (Ala. 2000); Colo. Rev. Stat. §§ 14-2-104 to 14-2-109.5 (on and after September 1, 2006, only those who are at least 18 may contract a common-law marriage; earlier common-law marriages made when a party was under 18 continue to be recognized.); Nugent v. Nugent, 955 P.2d 584 (Colo. Ct. App. 1998); Iowa Code § 595.11; Iowa Dep't of Human Servs. *ex rel.* Greenhaw v. Stewart, 579 N.W.2d 321 (Iowa 1998); Shaddox v. Schoenberger, 19 Kan. App. 2d 361, 869 P.2d 249 (1994); Mont. Code Ann. § 40-1-403; N.H. Rev. Stat. Ann. § 457:39; *compare* Okla. Stat. Ann. 43 §§ 1, 7 *with* Mueggenborg v. Walling, 1992 Okla. 121, 836 P.2d 112 (Okla. 1992); Death of Boyd v. Monsey Constr. Co., 959 P.2d 612 (Okla. Civ. App. 1998); Lovegrove v. McCutcheon, 712 A.2d 874 (R.I. 1998); Barker v. Barker, 330 S.C. 361, 499 S.E.2d 503 (Ct. App. 1998); Tex. Fam. Code § 1.91-101, §§ 2.401 to 2.402; Utah Code Ann. § 30-1-4.5; Berryman v. Thorne, 700 A.2d 181 (D.C. Ct. App. 1997)] New Hampshire recognizes common-law marriage for survivorship, but not for divorce. [N.H. Rev. Stat. Ann. § 457:39] States that abolished common-law marriage in the 1990s and later include

Georgia, Idaho, Ohio, and Pennsylvania. [Ga. Code Ann. § 19-3-1.1; Idaho Code § 32-201; Ohio Rev. Code Ann. § 3105.12; 23 Pa. Cons. Stat. Ann. § 1103]

Note. Pennsylvania abolished common-law marriage for marriages made *after* January 1, 2005, and expressly preserved those "contracted *on or before* January 1, 2005[.]" [23 Pa. Cons. Stat. Ann. § 1103] Thus, words spoken on that New Year's morning might have resulted in a marriage.

All states recognize a marriage that, even if it does not meet all requirements of local law, was valid under the laws of the state in which the spouses lived at the time they entered into the marriage. [*See, e.g.*, *In re* Estate of Lamb, 99 N.M. 157, 655 P.2d 1001 (1982); People v. Badgett, 10 Cal. 4th 330, 41 Cal. Rptr. 635, 895 P.2d 877 (1995); *see generally* Restatement (Second) of Conflict of Laws § 283(2) (1971)] Likewise, states recognize a marriage made according to any Native American law or custom. [*See, e.g.*, Buck v. Branson, 34 Okla. 807, 127 P. 436 (1912); People *ex rel.* LaForte v. Rubin, 98 N.Y.S. 787 (1905); Kobogum v. Jackson Iron Co., 76 Mich. 498, 43 N.W. 602 (1899); Earl v. Godley, 42 Minn. 361, 44 N.W. 254 (1890); Wall v. Williamson, 8 Ala. 48 (1844); Morgan v. McGhee, 24 Tenn. 13 (1844)] Further, some states that recognize common-law marriage internally recognize a marriage that the spouses entered into while they lived in another state, notwithstanding that the marriage was invalid in the other state. [*See, e.g.*, Dibble v. Dibble, 88 Ohio App. 490, 100 N.E.2d 451 (1950)] In many states that do not recognize a common-law marriage made in the state, children born during the invalid marriage may nevertheless be presumed to be the children of both the child's mother and the man who would be her common-law husband.

Because of the recognition that states give to other states' and nations' laws, it is possible for a common-law marriage to exist anywhere in the United States. Although the states that recognize informal marriage are the minority, the mobility of the American people enables many informal marriages. Indeed, even a weekend or one-day trip across state lines can result in a marriage. [*See, e.g.*, Tornese v. Tornese, 233 A.D.2d 316, 649 N.Y.S. 2d 177 (1996); Carpenter v. Carpenter, 208 A.D.2d 882, 617 N.Y.S.2d 903 (1994); Kellard v. Kellard, 13 Fam. L. Rep. (BNA) 1490 (N.Y. Sup. Ct. 1987); *In re* Seymour, 113 Misc. 421, 185 N.Y.S. 373 (Sur. Ct. 1920)] Further, among states that currently do not recognize common-law marriage, almost half allowed it when persons still alive might have married.

Q 16:47 How does common-law marriage affect a non-ERISA benefit?

State law (or a Native American tribe's law) may provide that if a participant has a spouse, some or all of a retirement plan's death benefit belongs to the spouse (see Q 16:36). If the law of a state that recognizes common-law marriage (see Q 16:46) applies, the couple may be married notwithstanding the absence of any ceremony or writing.

A payer is protected in making a payment according to the beneficiary designation. For a benefit paid under a non-ERISA plan, the distributee receives any payment subject to the spouse's rights.

Example. George and Carmen lived in Pennsylvania throughout their working lives. In early 1999, before George met Carmen, George named his brother, Bill, as the beneficiary on George's retirement plan. Even after his marriage to Carmen in late 1999, and the birth of their children, Diana in 2000 and Samuel in 2001, it never occurred to George that he should change any beneficiary designation. After George's retirement, George and Carmen moved to a retirement community in Cazenovia, New York. George died without having made any will. After George died, Bill sent in a claim to the IRA custodian, which paid Bill all of George's retirement plan balance. On his death, George's retirement plan balance was $200,000, and his probate assets were $60,000. There was nothing else. (For ease of illustration, both parts of this example omit family exemption, homestead allowance, funeral and administration expenses, debts, taxes of all kinds, and attorneys' fees.) If Carmen does not elect to take an elective share of George's augmented estate (which includes non-probate retirement plan benefits), George's estate would be divided as follows:

	Retirement Plan Benefit	*Probate Estate*	*Augmented Estate*	*Share*
Carmen	$ 0	$55,000	$ 55,000	21%
Diana	$ 0	$ 2,500	$ 2,500	1%
Samuel	$ 0	$ 2,500	$ 2,500	1%
Bill	$200,000	$ 0	$200,000	77%
Total	$200,000	$60,000	$260,000	

[N.Y. Est. Powers & Trusts § 4-1.1(a)(1)]

If Carmen elects to take an elective share of George's augmented estate, George's estate would be divided as follows:

	Augmented Estate	*Share*
Carmen	$ 86,666.67	33.33%
Diana	$ 0	0%
Samuel	$ 0	0%
Bill	$173,333.33	66.66%
Total	$260,000.00	100.00%

[N.Y. Est. Powers & Trusts § 5-1.1-A(a)(2), (c); *see generally* Unif. Probate Code §§ 2-201, 2-202, 8 pt. I U.L.A. 101–103 (1998) & Supp. 73–77 (2011)]

Because George's probate estate is insufficient to pay Carmen the amount to which she is entitled, Bill must pay Carmen $26,666.67. [N.Y. Est. Powers & Trusts § 5-1.1-A(c); *see generally* Unif. Probate Code § 2-203, 8 pt. I U.L.A. 103–104 (1998) & Supp. 77–79 (2011)]

In some states, dower and curtesy might provide additional or related rights to a spouse. [Ark. Code Ann. §§ 28-11-301, 28-11-305, 28-12-103; Ohio Rev.

Code Ann. § 2103.02] In some states, a spouse's election of (or right to elect) a forced share is "in lieu of" dower and curtesy rights. [*See, e.g.*, N.Y. Est. Powers & Trusts § 5-1.1-A(c)(8)] Many states simply abolished dower and curtesy. [*See generally* Unif. Probate Code § 2-112, 8 pt. I U.L.A. 90–91 (1998); Restatement (Third) of Property: Wills and Other Donative Transfers § 9.1 comment c (2003)]

Q 16:48 How does common-law marriage affect a beneficiary designation?

A plan might provide that some or all of a death benefit belongs to a spouse. State law may provide that if a participant has a spouse, some or all of a retirement plan benefit belongs to the spouse (see Q 16:36). If a couple ever lived (or even traveled) in a state that recognizes or then recognized common-law marriage (see Q 16:46), the couple may be married, notwithstanding the absence of any ceremony or writing. A recognized common-law marriage is no less a marriage than a ceremonial marriage. [*Cf.* 5 C.F.R. § 630.1202] Many states recognize common-law marriage (see Q 16:46).

Example. Harold and Wendy lived together in Alabama. Harold never made any beneficiary designation under his employer's ERISA-governed 401(k) SIMPLE plan. The plan provides that in the absence of a beneficiary designation, a surviving spouse is entitled to the participant's account. When Wendy calls to ask about this plan benefit, the employer tells Wendy that it has no record that Wendy is Harold's spouse. Wendy files the plan's claim form and attaches to it an affidavit that states facts that, if correct, would prove that her relationship with Harold was a common-law marriage under Alabama law. Because the employer, acting as plan administrator, does not receive any contrary information, it decides that Wendy is Harold's surviving spouse. The plan administrator decides to pay the full benefit as Wendy requested.

Practice Pointer. A plan administrator must act as an expert when deciding plan claims. [ERISA § 404(a)(1)] Therefore, a plan administrator should obtain expert legal advice to evaluate person's claim that he or she is the common-law spouse of a participant. Although a plan administrator should consult a lawyer who has sufficient expert knowledge and skill, the lawyer need not be admitted to law practice in the state in which the claimant asserts that he or she married the participant; it is enough that the lawyer is admitted to law practice in *any* state. [*Cf.* DOL ERISA Adv. Op. 2005-16A (June 10, 2005)]

Some people assume that common-law marriage does not apply to a couple in which both persons are of the same sex. At least one court decision found that common-law marriage does not apply to a couple in which both persons are of the same sex. However, that decision has limited value as precedent because the intermediate appeals court did not consider arguments that had not been presented to the trial court. [DeSanto v. Barnsley, 328 Pa. Super. 181, 476 A.2d 952 (1984)] A discrimination against a same-sex couple or their marriage might be contrary to the U.S. Constitution or a state constitution, and therefore of no effect. (See Qs 16:61–16:62.)

Same-Sex Marriage

Q 16:49 In what ways might a same-sex couple be recognized as spouses?

A same-sex couple might be recognized as spouses in at least four ways.

1. The couple married in another nation.
2. The couple married in a state that provides (or then provided) same-sex marriage.
3. The couple are parties to a civil union or domestic partnership governed by the laws of a state that provides that the rights and burdens of such a relationship are identical to the state-law rights and burdens of another marriage.
4. The couple are domestic partners under a state's law and, for the particular plan purpose involved, a relevant state's law provides a right or burden that makes a domestic partner a spouse for the purpose involved.

Note. New Jersey law has two different statuses for opposite-sex couples and two different statuses for same-sex couples. Concerning same-sex couples, New Jersey law recognizes a civil union that has the same legal rights and burdens as an opposite-sex marriage or, if it was made before February 19, 2007, or by persons who are 62 or older, a domestic partnership, which under New Jersey law provides fewer rights and burdens.

Caution. New Jersey recognizes a same-sex relationship established under the law of another state or of a foreign nation, but the other state's or nation's name for a relationship does not control its treatment under New Jersey law. "Rather, it is the nature of the rights conferred by another jurisdiction that will determine how a relationship will be treated under New Jersey law." [N.J. Atty. Gen. Formal Opinion No. 3-2007 (Feb. 16, 2007) (available at *http://www.state.nj.us/health/vital/documents/legal_advice_ssm.pdf*) (last visited on April 29, 2012)] Therefore, a domestic partnership made under California law is a civil union under New Jersey law.

States recognize a marriage that, even if it does not meet all requirements of local law, was valid under the laws of the state in which the spouses lived at the time they entered into the marriage. [Restatement (Second) of Conflict of Laws § 283(2) (1971)] This rule is so strong that states have recognized an incestuous marriage. [*See, e.g.*, *In re* Estate Estate of May, 305 N. 486, 114 N.E.2d 4 (N.Y. 1953); *see also* Campione v. Campione, 201 Misc. 590 (N.Y. Sup. Ct. 1951)]

Q 16:50 Does a state of the United States recognize a foreign nation's marriage?

Yes, a state of the United States will recognize a marriage made according to the law of a foreign nation in which the marriage was made. [*See, e.g.*, Hallett v. Collins, 51 U.S. (10 How.) 174 (1850); Montano v. Montano, 520 So. 2d 52 (Fla. Dist. Ct. App. 1988); People v. Imes, 68 N.W. 157 (Mich. 1896); Miller v. Miller, 128 N.Y.S. 787 (Sup. Ct. 1911); Ferrie v. Public Adm'r, 3 Bradf. Sur. 151 (N.Y. Sur. 1855)] Even common-law or defective marriages in a foreign nation have been recognized as legitimate marriages in the United States. [*See, e.g.*, Overseers of Poor of Town of Newbury v. Overseers of Poor of Town of Brunswick, 2 Vt. 151 (1829). *Cf.* Metropolitan Life Ins. Co. v. Holding, 293 F. Supp. 854 (E.D. Va. 1968); *In re* Lamb's Estate, 655 P.2d 1001 (N.M. 1982)] *But see* Randall v. Randall, 345 N.W.2d 319 (Neb. 1984)] A court will even recognize a marriage that might be contrary to the norms of the forum state. [*See, e.g.*, United States v. Lee Sa Kee, 3 U.S. Dist. Ct. Haw. 265 (1908); Estate of Dalip Singh Bir, 83 Cal. App. 2d 256, 188 P.2d 499 (1948) (more than 50 years before the decedent's death in California, two women had married him in the Punjab Province of British India "according to the law and manner of the Jat community."); *see also* Sousa v. Freitas, 10 Cal. App. 3d 660, 89 Cal. Rptr. 485 (1970)] However, a court will not recognize as a marriage a relationship that under foreign law does not provide the usual rights of marriage. [*See, e.g.*, American Airlines v. Mejia, 766 So. 2d 305 (Fla. Dist. Ct. App. 2000)]

A state's refusal to recognize a foreign nation's marriage could lead to an international conflict. [*See generally* Universal Declaration of Human Rights; Covenant on Civil and Political Rights; Covenant on Economic, Social and Cultural Rights; Restatement (Third) Foreign Relations Law of the United States § 701 (1987)]

Q 16:51 Do other nations recognize same-sex marriages?

Many nations recognize various forms of same-sex marriages. However, not all of these relationships have the same rights and burdens as those of a U.S. state's opposite-sex marriage, and so some might not be recognized for some purposes under some states' laws.

Q 16:52 Which states provide marriage for same-sex couples?

As of early 2012, Connecticut, Iowa, Massachusetts, New Hampshire, New York, Vermont, and the District of Columbia expressly provide same-sex marriage. Further, at least California, Delaware, Illinois, Nevada, and New Jersey provide a status for a same-sex couple that does not use the word *marriage* but provides all the legal rights and duties that state law provides for an opposite-sex marriage. States that provide a same-sex relationship with fewer rights and burdens than an opposite-sex marriage include Colorado, Hawaii, Maine, Maryland, Oregon, Washington, and Wisconsin.

Q 16:53 How does a civil union of a same-sex couple affect a beneficiary designation?

As discussed elsewhere in this chapter, applicable law might provide that after the death of a participant who was a party to a civil union, some or all of a retirement plan benefit must be provided to the other party to the civil union to the extent necessary to provide such a spouse his or her property rights.

As mentioned under Q 16:82, some states provide a status for a same-sex couple that does not use the word *marriage* but provides all the legal rights and duties that state law provides for an opposite-sex marriage.

Q 16:54 What is a *domestic partnership*?

A *domestic partnership* is a quasi-marriage recognized for some (but not all) purposes under some states' laws.

Q 16:55 Which states provide for a domestic-partnership relationship?

As of early 2012, states that provide a same-sex relationship with fewer rights and burdens than an opposite-sex marriage include Colorado, Hawaii, Maine, Maryland, Nevada, Oregon, Washington, and Wisconsin.

Other states, including California, use the "domestic partner" label to refer to a relationship that has rights and burdens identical to those of an opposite-sex couple's marriage. [*See, e.g.*, Cal. Fam. Code § 297.5; *see also In re* Domestic Domestic P'ship of Ellis, 76 Cal. Rptr. 3d 401 (2008)]

Q 16:56 Who may form a domestic partnership?

In some (but not all) states that register domestic partnerships (see Q 16:55), a same-sex couple may form a domestic partnership.

In New Jersey, an opposite-sex couple may form a domestic partnership if *both* persons are 62 or older. [N.J. Domestic Partnership Act § 4.b.(5)] In California, an opposite-sex couple may form a domestic partnership if *one* person is older than 62 and is eligible for Social Security old-age benefits. [Cal. Fam. Code § 297(b)(6)(B)]

For either a same-sex or an opposite-sex domestic partnership, both partners must:

1. Be 18 or older,
2. Be unrelated,
3. Live together,
4. Be financially responsible for one another's living expenses,
5. Have some joint financial arrangements, and
6. Be in a committed relationship of mutual caring.

In addition, neither partner can be a spouse or domestic partner with anyone else. [*See, e.g.*, Haw. Rev. Stat. Ann. § 572C-4 (referring to a "reciprocal beneficiary" instead of a "domestic partner")]

Q 16:57 What are some of the rights of a domestic partner?

In the states that provide a domestic-partner relationship, a domestic partner's rights typically include civil rights concerning personal dignity, autonomy, and nondiscrimination; rights concerning health insurance (other than an employer-funded or noninsured health plan). Some states make a domestic partner similar to a spouse for state income tax purposes. [Cal. Rev. & Tax Code § 17021.7; N.J.S.A. §§ 54A:1-2.e, 54A:3-1(b)2, 54A:3-1(b)1] Likewise, some states treat a domestic partner as a spouse for inheritance tax purposes. [N.J. Rev. Stat. §§ 54:34-1.f, 54:34-2.a.(1), 54:34-4.j]

Q 16:58 Does a surviving domestic partner inherit from the other's estate?

Under the law of a state that provides a domestic-partnership relationship, a domestic partner has the same community-property rights or elective-share rights as a spouse.

Q 16:59 Is an opposite-sex domestic partner a spouse under federal laws?

It is unclear whether an opposite-sex domestic partner is a spouse. A domestic partner might be a spouse under some federal laws but not be a spouse under other federal laws.

The state legislatures that enacted domestic-partner laws appear to have intended that an opposite-sex domestic partner enjoy some or all incidents of marriage while avoiding the burdens of marriage under federal laws. [*See, e.g.*, N.J. Senate, Judiciary Committee Statement on a substitute for S. 2820 (Dec. 15, 2003) ("In authorizing domestic partnerships only for opposite sex couples who are age 62 and older, the committee recognizes that older persons often refrain from entering into marriage because remarriage could jeopardize their status as surviving spouse with regard to retirement income and benefits."); *see also* Cal. Stats. 2003, c. 421 (A.B. 205) § 15 ("This act shall be construed liberally in order to secure to eligible couples who register as domestic partners the full range of legal rights, protections and benefits, as well as all of the responsibilities, obligations, and duties to each other, to their children, to third parties[,] and to the state, as the laws of California extend to and impose upon spouses.")]

It is not clear that an opposite-sex couple can have it both ways; an opposite-sex domestic partner might be a spouse under some federal laws. [*See* 1 U.S.C. § 7] A domestic partnership includes the usual attributes of marriage: cohabitation, exclusivity, mutual dependence, financial responsibility, and (except in New Jersey) compulsory inheritance. Even in New Jersey, a domestic partner can obtain marital property rights by contract. And in every state, a spouse (including a "married" spouse other than a domestic partner) may release rights by contract. Therefore, a government agency or court might find that opposite-sex domestic partners live together as husband and wife and that the rights not provided by state law (if any) are irrelevant or insignificant in deciding whether the partners are spouses under a particular federal law.

Q 16:60 Is a same-sex domestic partner a spouse under federal laws?

If Section 7 of Title 1 of the United States Code is not unconstitutional, a same-sex domestic partner is not a spouse under any federal statute. [1 U.S.C. § 7] If Section 7 of Title 1 of the United States Code is unconstitutional, a same-sex domestic partner might be a spouse under some or all federal laws if the rights not provided by state law (if any) are irrelevant or insignificant in deciding whether the partners are spouses under a particular federal law. [*See* 1 U.S.C. § 7]

Q 16:61 Does the U.S. Constitution require recognition of a same-sex marriage?

Maybe. A discrimination against a same-sex couple or their marriage might be contrary to the U.S. Constitution, and therefore of no effect. [*See* U.S. Const. art. IV sec. 1 & Fifth Amendment]

Q 16:62 Could a state constitution require recognition of a same-sex marriage?

Maybe. A discrimination against a same-sex couple or their marriage might be contrary to a state constitution, and therefore of no effect. [*Compare* Goodridge v. Department of Public Health, 440 Mass. 309, 798 N.E.2d 941 (2003) (Massachusetts's constitution requires that the Commonwealth provide full marriage to a same-sex couple to the same extent that it provides marriage to an opposite-sex couple); Lewis v. Harris, 188 N.J. 415 (2006) (New Jersey constitution requires same-sex marriage); Baker v. Vermont, 744 A.2d 864 (1999) (Vermont's constitution requires that a same-sex couple must have the opportunity to obtain the same benefits and protections afforded by Vermont law to a married opposite-sex couple) *with* Hernandez v. Robles, 7 N.Y.3d 338 (2006) (New York constitution does not require same-sex marriage); Andersen v. King County, 138 P.3d 963 (Wash. 2006) (Washington constitution does not require same-sex marriage)]

Q 16:63 Must a state recognize a same-sex marriage made in another state?

Maybe. A federal statute states that a state need not recognize a same-sex marriage established in another state:

> No State . . . shall be required to give effect to any public act, record, or judicial proceeding of any other State . . . respecting a relationship between persons of the same sex that is treated as a marriage under the laws of such other State . . . or a right or claim arising from such relationship.

[28 U.S.C. § 1738C] It is unclear whether this statute is law because it might be unconstitutional. [*See* U.S. Const. art. IV sec. 1 & Fifth Amendment]

Spouse's Rights

Q 16:64 What are the ways a participant's surviving spouse might have rights to a participant's retirement plan benefit?

A participant's surviving spouse might have rights to a participant's retirement plan benefit as:

- Survivor-annuity or spouse's-consent rights provided by the plan (see Qs 16:65–16:88)
- Elective-share rights under state law (see Qs 16:89–16:91)
- Community-property rights under state law (see Qs 16:92–16:97)

ERISA Survivor Benefits or Spouse's-Consent Rights

Q 16:65 What rights does ERISA provide for a participant's surviving spouse?

A plan that is governed by Part 2 of Subtitle B of Title I of ERISA must provide some kind of benefit to a participant's spouse. [ERISA §§ 201, 205] The form of the required benefit turns on whether a distribution begins because of the participant's retirement or death.

For a distribution that begins before a participant's death, a plan must, unless an exception applies, provide a qualified joint and survivor annuity, which is often referred to by its abbreviation—a QJSA. [ERISA § 205(a)(1), 205(b)] Ordinarily, a defined-contribution plan that is not governed by ERISA funding standards need not provide a QJSA (see Q 16:66) as long as a participant does not elect that his or her retirement plan benefit be paid as a life annuity. [ERISA § 205(b)(1)(C)(ii)]

Practice Pointer. Previously, the IRS had an informal view that merely providing an annuity as a plan's default distribution option was in effect a participant's election of that annuity for the purposes of the survivor-annuity rule. The IRS no longer takes that position. Nonetheless, if a plan provides a life annuity as a normal form of benefit, a plan sponsor may amend the plan to provide that every annuity is an optional form of benefit, or to eliminate every annuity option. Such an amendment is not a cutback of accrued benefits. [ERISA § 204(g)(2)(B); Treas. Reg. § 1.411(d)-4/Q&A-2(e)] Once the amendment is effective, the plan need not provide a QJSA unless (if the plan permits) a participant affirmatively chooses it or chooses a different life annuity and fails to deliver a qualified election.

Practice Pointer. A practitioner should thoroughly consider all significant tax treatments before he or she suggests that a participant choose a single-sum or other short-term payout. In some states, only a life annuity or periodic payments similar to a life annuity will qualify for favorable treatment as a "pension" under state income tax law. [*See, e.g.*, N.Y. Tax Law §§ 612(c)(3-a); 72 Pa. Cons. Stat. §§ 7301(d)(3), 7303; 61 Pa. Code § 101.6(c); Bickford v. Commonwealth, 533 A.2d 822 (Pa. 1987)]

For a distribution that begins after a participant's death, a plan must provide a qualified pre-retirement survivor annuity or an alternate survivor benefit. [ERISA § 205(a)(2), 205(b)]

Q 16:66 What is a qualified joint and survivor annuity?

A *qualified joint and survivor annuity* (QJSA) is an annuity for the participant's life with a survivor annuity for his or her surviving spouse's life. The periodic payment of the survivor annuity must be no less than 50 percent (and no more than 100 percent) of the payment during the joint lives of the participant and his or her spouse. A QJSA is the actuarial equivalent of an annuity only on the participant's life. [ERISA § 205(d)]

Note. If a plan governed by Part 2 of Subtitle B of Title I of ERISA provides a qualified joint and survivor annuity, the plan must permit a participant to elect that his or her benefit be paid as a *qualified optional survivor annuity*. A qualified optional survivor annuity (QOSA) (see Q 16:67) means a QJSA that includes a recurring payment in its survivor phase that is equal to the *applicable percentage* of the payment during the participant's life. If a plan's normal QJSA provides a survivor-phase payment that is less than 75 percent of the payment during the participant's life, the applicable percentage is 75. If a plan's normal QJSA provides a survivor-phase payment that is at least 75 percent of the payment during the participant's life, the applicable percentage is 50. As with other survivor-annuity forms, a qualified optional survivor annuity must be at least the actuarial equivalent of a single-life annuity for the participant's life. A plan that is required to provide a survivor annuity must provide at least two different QJSAs, in addition to a qualified pre-retirement survivor annuity (QPSA). A plan administrator's written explanations of a plan's survivor-annuity options must explain *all* of the options, including the new qualified optional survivor annuity. The minimum election period for survivor-annuity choices is 180 days. A plan amendment made solely to meet the QOSA requirement generally does not violate the anti-cutback rule. However, this anti-cutback relief does not protect taking away a subsidized QJSA unless an equivalent or greater subsidy remains in at least one of the amended plan's other payout forms of that kind. [ERISA § 205(c)-(d)]

A surviving-spouse benefit under a QJSA vests irrevocably as of the annuity starting date. Only the person who was the participant's spouse on the annuity starting date—not any subsequent spouse—is entitled to the survivor benefit (if that spouse survives the participant). [Hopkins v. AT&T Global Info. Solutions Co., 105 F.3d 153 (4th Cir. 1997); Carmona v. Carmona, 544 F.3d 988 (9th Cir. 2008); Robinson v. New Orleans Employers ILA AFL-CIO Pension, Welfare, Vacation & Holiday Funds, 2007 U.S. Dist. LEXIS 25893 (E.D. La. Apr. 2, 2007); *see also* McGowan v. NJR Serv. Corp., 423 F.3d 241 (3d Cir. 2005), *cert. denied* 127 S. Ct. 1118 (2007)]

Practice Pointer. An exception to the rule that a participant's surviving spouse is the person that was his or her spouse on the relevant date—the participant's death for a QPSA or alternate survivor benefit, or the annuity starting date for a QJSA—is that a qualified domestic-relations order may specify that a person, even if he or she no longer is the participant's spouse, is deemed to be the participant's surviving spouse.

Q 16:67 What is a qualified optional survivor annuity?

Sometimes, a joint and survivor annuity provides the same recurring payment to the survivor as was payable to the first annuitant—this is a 100 percent survivor annuity. But sometimes the recurring payment of the survivor phase is less than that of the first phase. Under current law, the payment in the survivor phase of a QJSA may be anywhere from 50 to 100 percent.

If a plan must provide a survivor annuity, the plan must permit a participant to elect that his or her retirement benefit be paid as a QOSA.

A *qualified optional survivor annuity* means a QJSA that includes a recurring payment in its survivor phase that is equal to the applicable percentage of the payment during the participant's life. If a plan's normal QJSA provides a survivor-phase payment that is less than 75 percent of the payment during the participant's life, the applicable percentage is 75. If a plan's normal QJSA provides a survivor-phase payment that is at least 75 percent of the payment during the participant's life, the applicable percentage is 50.

Example. A plan that provides a participant a choice between a QJSA with a 100 percent survivor annuity and a QJSA with a 50 percent survivor annuity would meet the QOSA rule.

As with other survivor-annuity forms, a QOSA must be at least the actuarial equivalent of a single-life annuity for the participant's life.

Thus, a plan that is required to provide a survivor annuity (and does not subsidize the QJSA, which would be unlikely for a defined-contribution plan) must provide at least two different QJSAs, in addition to a QPSA.

A plan administrator's written explanation of a plan's survivor-annuity options must explain all the options, including the QOSA. The minimum election period for survivor-annuity choices is 180 days.

Q 16:68 What is a qualified pre-retirement survivor annuity?

For a defined contribution plan, a *qualified pre-retirement survivor annuity* is the annuity that results from using no less than half the participant's vested account balance to buy an annuity for the surviving spouse's life. [ERISA § 205(e)(2)]

Q 16:69 What is an alternate survivor benefit?

For a defined contribution plan that is not governed by ERISA's or the Internal Revenue Code's funding standards, a plan may omit both a qualified joint and survivor annuity and a qualified pre-retirement survivor annuity if the plan (in addition to meeting other conditions) provides that, absent a qualified election, the benefit that remains after a participant's death belongs to the participant's surviving spouse. [ERISA § 205(b)(1)(C)]

Q 16:70 What is a qualified election?

An ERISA plan may include a provision that assures a participant's surviving spouse some retirement income after the participant's death, and must include a provision that assures a survivor benefit if the participant dies before he or she receives or begins a distribution. [ERISA § 205] A plan must permit a participant to "waive" one or more of these benefits. [ERISA § 205(c)(1)(A)] To do so, a participant must deliver to the plan administrator a qualified election. [ERISA § 205(c)(2)] Ordinarily, such an election has no effect unless the participant's spouse consents to the election. [ERISA § 205(c)(2)(A)] In addition, a participant's qualified election must meet several form, content, and procedure requirements.

> **Note.** If a participant has a spouse when he or she makes a beneficiary designation but does not have a spouse on his or her death, an absence of the spouse's consent to the beneficiary designation "invalidates" it only until their marriage ends. If a participant does not have a spouse on his or her death, a plan may follow the participant's most recent beneficiary designation. [*See, e.g.*, Lehman v. University of Hartford Defined Contribution Ret. Plan, 28 Employee Benefits Cas. (BNA) 2796 (D. Conn. July 18, 2002)]

Q 16:71 Who is a spouse?

In some circumstances, it can be unclear, for the purposes of ERISA Section 205, whether a person is or is not a spouse, and which of two or more persons is a participant's spouse or surviving spouse.

ERISA states no definition for its use of the word *spouse*.

> **Note.** ERISA preempt state laws, and state law does not control whether a person is or is not a participant's spouse for an ERISA-governed plan's purposes. Nonetheless, a federal court might find facts based on acts of legal

significance under one or more state laws. [Tkachik v. Comerica, No. 05-72703, 40 Employee Benefits Cas. (BNA) 1952, 2006 U.S. Dist. LEXIS 92946 (E.D. Mich. Dec. 26, 2006)]

Further, ERISA states no provision concerning whether a putative spouse is or is not a spouse for any purpose of ERISA Section 205.

Practice Pointer. If a plan administrator makes a discretionary decision on whether a person does or does not have a spouse, the administrator should follow ERISA's claims-procedure rules, obtain information necessary to evaluate the claims and other questions presented, compile a sound administrative record, explain its decisions, and further act with care so that a court may defer to the administrator's decisions. [*See, e.g.*, Blessing v. Deere & Co., 985 F. Supp. 899–907 (S.D. Iowa 1997)]

Practice Pointer. If deciding whether a claimant was a participant's spouse turns not on unclear facts but rather on novel questions of law, a plan administrator might consider an interpleader. [*See, e.g.*, Cozen & Connor, P.C. v. Tobits & Farley, 2-11-cv-00045-CDJ (E.D. Pa. filed Jan. 4, 2011) (questions concerning whether an ERISA plan may, must, or must not recognize a same-sex marriage performed in Canada)] (By March 14, 2012, the court's record in this case includes at least 120 docket entries and hundreds of documents.)

Practice Pointer. An interpleader does not undo a court's deference to a plan administrator's decisions, at least for those decisions made before the interpleader. [Alliant Techsystems, Inc. v. Marks, 465 F.3d 864 (8th Cir. 2006)]

Q 16:72 Is a separated spouse considered a spouse for survivor-annuity or spouse's-consent purposes?

Yes. No matter how long a separation continues, a marriage does not end until a court orders the divorce.

Example. In 1984, Barbara and Alfred separated. In 1986, Alfred sued for divorce. In 1991, Alfred died. A divorce had not been ordered. Despite seven years' separation, Barbara was Alfred's wife until his death. Although the plan had previously paid distributions, she was entitled to the survivor portion of the QJSA that would have been paid in the absence of her consent. [Davis v. College Suppliers Co., 813 F. Supp. 1234 (S.D. Miss. 1993)]

Even a finding of fact that the spouse abandoned the participant does not end their marriage or the status of the spouses. [*In re Lefkowitz, 767 F. Supp.* 501, 508 (S.D.N.Y. 1991), *affirmed sub nom.* Lefkowitz v. Arcadia Trading Co. Ltd. Defined Benefit Pension Plan, 996 F.2d 600, 16 Employee Benefits Cas. (BNA) 2516, Pens. Plan Guide (CCH) ¶ 23880Z (2d Cir. 1993)]

Note. A separation or abandonment, although it does not end a marriage or the status of the spouses, might be relevant in considering whether a plan might excuse a spouse's consent. (See Q 16:76.)

Q 16:73 When a participant is survived by a spouse and a putative spouse, which one is treated as the participant's surviving spouse?

There is no rule; whether a putative spouse, a real spouse, both, or neither is treated as a participant's spouse depends on a plan administrator's, arbitrator's, or judge's thoughts about what might be desirable in the particular circumstances.

The following two cases had opposite results. In the contributing author's view, neither court explained the real reason for its decision. A third example illustrates a straightforward application of the law that a person whose marriage has not ended cannot marry another.

Example 1. In 1965, John and Susie married in Louisiana. In 1970, a Louisiana court ordered a judgment of separation, but not any divorce or dissolution of John and Susie's marriage. In 1973, Susie, while still married to John, "married" Milton. In 2000, John, while still married to Susie, "married" Gwendolyn in Texas. In 2001, John died (while still married to Susie and "married" to Gwendolyn). He was domiciled in Texas when he died. After John's death, Susie and Gwendolyn each submitted a claim to his pension plan for a survivor annuity; each claimed that she was John's surviving spouse. The pension plan included the following provision: "All questions pertaining to the validity of construction of this Pension Plan shall be determined in accordance with the laws of the State of Illinois and, to the extent of preemption[,] with the laws and regulations of the United States." (As cited below, these are the relevant facts of a real case.)

In resolving the plan administrator's interpleader, the court considered whether to apply Louisiana law, Texas law, Illinois law, or some combination of them in deciding which claimant (if either) was John's surviving spouse. Notwithstanding that neither of the claimants had argued for it, the court chose Texas law. Further, the court used Texas *property* law to resolve the *status* question needed to apply an ERISA plan's provision that preempts state law. Following this, the court found that Susie's acceptance of the benefits of her fraudulent "marriage" to Milton precluded her from asserting that she was John's surviving spouse, and recognized Gwendolyn as an innocent putative spouse to be treated as if she had been a spouse. [Central States, S.E. & S.W. Areas Pension Fund v. Gray, 31 Employee Benefits Cas. (BNA) 1748, 2003 U.S. LEXIS 18282 (N.D. Ill. Oct. 8, 2003)]

Example 2. In 1966, Douglas married Ann in Ohio. They lived together in Ohio from 1966 to 1982. In 1972, Douglas began a relationship with Rita. In 1982, Ann left Douglas and moved to Tennessee. In 1985, Douglas and Rita "married" in Nevada. Each of Ann and Rita submitted claims for several benefits to be provided to Douglas' surviving spouse. The pension plan provided that it "shall be construed, governed[,] and administered in accordance with the laws of the State of Michigan[,] except where [*sic*] otherwise required by Federal law."

In resolving the plan administrator's interpleader, the court considered whether to apply Federal law, Michigan law, or Ohio law, or some combination of them in deciding which claimant (if either) was John's surviving spouse. [*See, e.g.*, Croskey v. Ford Motor Co.-UAW, 2002 U.S. Dist. LEXIS 8824 (S.D.N.Y. May 2, 2002)]

Note 1. In both of these cases, the court did not apply the contractual choice of law and, even further, ignored the plan's provision that the plan be construed using the plan-specified state law.

Note 2. Courts' procedures for an interpleader, which focus on the arguments of the competing claimants and often do not require a stakeholder to assert a position, increase the likelihood that a court will render a decision that is unhelpful for future plan administration.

Practice Pointer. Before deciding to interplead competing claims, a fiduciary should consider which person or persons will pay the attorneys' fees and other expenses of the interpleader. If the plan might bear the expenses, a fiduciary should consider whether paying the expenses is a prudent or necessary use of plan assets. Instead, a plan administrator might use claims procedures and the deference afforded to a discretionary decision-maker to protect the plan against "double" liability, while setting up some opportunity for lower expenses (or at least delaying an expense), or even no incremental expense.

Example 3. Philadelphia Eagles running back Thomas Sullivan was a participant under the NFL Player Retirement Plan. Thomas married Lavona in 1979. Thomas and Lavona stopped living together around 1983, and last had contact with one another around 1985. In 1986, Thomas "married" Barbara. Thomas died in 2002. On the plan's interpleader, the federal court found that neither Barbara's unawareness of Thomas's marriage nor an assertion that Lavona "walked out on the marriage," even if both alleged facts were fully proven, could have changed the fact that Thomas and Lavona remained married until his death. Likewise, Barbara's belief that she was married to Thomas could not dissolve Thomas's marriage to Lavona or permit Thomas's marriage to anyone while he still was married to another. Lavona is entitled to the pension benefits that were the subject of the court proceeding. [Hill v. Bell, 50 Employee Benefits Cas. (BNA) 1220 (E.D. Pa. Nov. 4, 2010); *see also* Grabois v. Jones, 89 F.3d 97 (2d Cir. 1996) (Junior was married to Annie Marie from 1948 until his death in 1991, and was "married" to Kay from 1962 until his death. After two years of litigation, the appeals court decided that it lacked sufficient information to review the trial court's findings, including any finding concerning which claimant was the participant's widow, and so remanded the case to the trial court for it to pursue further development of relevant facts)]

Q 16:74 What is a spouse's consent?

An election is a qualified election only if the participant's spouse consents to it. In addition to meeting other form, content, and procedure requirements, a spouse's consent to a participant's election must

1. Be in writing;
2. Name a beneficiary that cannot be changed without the spouse's consent, or expressly consent to the participant's beneficiary designations (without further consent);
3. "Acknowledge" the effect of the participant's election; and
4. Be "witnessed by a plan representative or a notary public."

[ERISA § 205(c)(2)(A)(i)–(iii)]

The courts have held that a plan administrator must comply strictly with these requirements, even if there is no doubt that a spouse's consent was informed, voluntary, and genuine. [*See, e.g.*, McMillan v. Parrott, 913 F.2d 310 (6th Cir. 1990); Lasche v. George W. Lasche Basic Ret. Plan, 870 F. Supp. 336, 338, Pens. Plan Guide (CCH) ¶ 23905L (S.D. Fla. 1994); *see also* Alfieri v. Guild Times Pension Plan, 446 F. Supp. 2d 99, 112–113 (E.D.N.Y. 2006)] A spouse's sworn statement in his or her spouse's consent that the spouse consents to the participant's beneficiary designation is ineffective if in fact the beneficiary-designation part of the documents had not been completed when the spouse signed. [ERISA § 205(c)(2)(A); Davis v. Adelphia Commc'ns Corp., 475 F. Supp. 2d 600, 40 Empl. Benefits Cas. (BNA) 1731 (W.D. Va. 2007); *but see* Vilas v. Lyons, 702 F. Supp. 555 (D. Md. 1988) (a plan administrator may rely on a spouse's sworn statement that he or she received and read the required explanation of the spouse's rights)]

A premarital agreement cannot be a spouse's consent (see Q 16:100).

Q 16:75 May a spouse's guardian sign the spouse's consent?

A spouse's guardian may sign the spouse's consent, even if the electing participant is the spouse's guardian. [Treas. Reg. § 1.401(a)-20/Q&A-27] However, a guardian must act in the best interests of his or her ward. A guardian serves under a court's supervision and must account for his or her actions in court. Further, some guardianship decisions require a court's approval before the guardian implements the decision. [*See, e.g.*, Unif. Probate Code § 2-206 (1998), 8 pt. I U.L.A. 115–118 (1998) & Supp. 78 (2009)] It might be difficult to persuade a court that turning away money was in a surviving spouse's best interest. Although a participant might suggest making an irrevocable designation naming a trust for his or her spouse's benefit as the plan beneficiary, most retirement plans do not permit an irrevocable beneficiary designation.

Q 16:76 May a spouse's consent be excused if the spouse has abandoned the participant?

Maybe. According to the Treasury department's interpretation of not only Code Sections 401(a)(11) and 417 but also ERISA Section 205, a plan's terms may permit a participant's qualified election without his or her spouse's consent "if the participant is legally separated or the participant has been abandoned (within the meaning of local law) *and* the participant has a court order to such effect[.]" [26 C.F.R. § 1.401(a)-20, Q&A 27]

Q 16:77 May a spouse's consent be excused if the spouse cannot be located?

Maybe. According to the Treasury department's interpretation of not only Code Sections 401(a)(11) and 417 but also ERISA Section 205, a plan's terms may permit a participant's qualified election without his or her spouse's consent if the plan's administrator finds "that the spouse cannot be located[.]" [26 C.F.R. § 1.401(a)-20, Q&A 27]

Q 16:78 May proof of a spouse's consent be given in an electronic notarization?

Yes, but not really.

A Treasury regulation allows a notary's or plan representative's certificate to be furnished by electronic means, but requires that the spouse's consent have been signed in the physical presence of the notary or plan representative. [Treas. Reg. § 1.401(a)-21(d)(6)(i) & (ii)]

> **Note.** An electronic notarization is useful if each relying person has arranged in advance to receive and inspect an electronic apostille concerning a particular notary's electronic credentials. A capacity to accept electronic notarizations can be useful to those businesses and government agencies that process a large volume of transactions that depend on authenticated signatures. But a typical retirement plan, even if it has many claims and distributions, does not have enough claims that require a spouse's consent to motivate the plan's administrator to put effort and resources into arrangements for receiving electronic notarizations.

Q 16:79 Who is a *plan representative*?

ERISA does not define its use of the words *plan representative.* [ERISA §§ 3, 205] The Retirement Equity Act of 1984's legislative history does not explain what Congress meant. [S. Rep. No. 98-575 to accompany H.R. 4280, 98th Cong., 2d Sess. (1984), reprinted in 1984 USCCAN 2547, 2560]

A person might be a plan representative for the limited purpose of administering a plan's provisions required or permitted by ERISA's spouse's-consent rule or a plan's spouse's-consent provision if the plan administrator has authorized the person to witness such a spouse's consent.

In a case that involved facts and forms typical of a retirement plan's service arrangements, a federal court found that the litigants who asserted that a spouse's consent had been witnessed did not offer enough evidence even to allege that a securities broker-dealer's employee was a plan representative. [Lasche v. George W. Lasche Basic Ret. Plan, 870 F. Supp. 336, 339, Pens. Plan Guide (CCH) ¶ 23905L (S.D. Fla. 1994)]

Q 16:80 Must a plan representative be independent of the participant?

Yes. Although nothing in ERISA Section 205 requires that a witness to a spouse's consent be independent of the electing participant, at least one federal court has interpreted the statute to include such a requirement. A plan administrator who was the same person as the electing participant could not, even though he was a plan representative (or even if he was the only plan representative), witness his spouse's consent. [Lasche v. George W. Lasche Basic Ret. Plan, 870 F. Supp. 336, 339, Pens. Plan Guide (CCH) ¶ 23905L (S.D. Fla. 1994)]

> **Practice Pointer.** If a lawyer or financial planner who advises a participant about making a beneficiary designation that would provide for anyone other than the participant's spouse knows that the participant also is a plan administrator, trustee, or other fiduciary, the lawyer or planner should advise the participant to ask his or her spouse to sign the consent in the presence of an independent notary. Failing to give that advice might be malpractice.

Because ERISA permits a plan administrator to rely on a spouse's consent witnessed by a notary, it seems unlikely that a federal court would find that it could be prudent for a plan administrator to rely on a spouse's consent witnessed only by the interested participant or someone who is subordinate to the interested participant. [ERISA §§ 205(c)(6), 404(a)(1)]

Q 16:81 Who is a *notary*?

ERISA does not define its use of the term *notary public* [ERISA §§ 3, 205], nor does the legislative history of the Retirement Equity Act of 1984 explain what Congress meant by a notary public. [S. Rep. No. 98-575 to accompany H.R. 4280, 98th Cong., 2d Sess. (1984), *reprinted in* 1984 USCCAN 2547, 2560]

Many practitioners assume that Congress intended to describe a person state law recognizes as one whose certificate that he or she witnessed an acknowledgment will be recognized as conclusive evidence that the acknowledgment was made. Usually, a recognized official's certificate that he or she witnessed an acknowledgment is nearly conclusive evidence that the acknowledgment was made. In most states, an acknowledgment may be made before a judge, court clerk, recorder of deeds, or notary. [Unif. Law on Notarial Acts § 3(a)] In New Jersey, a lawyer, if he or she is a licensed attorney, may certify an acknowledgment or affidavit. [N.J.S.A. § 41:2-1]

Q 16:82 How may a person present in a foreign nation make an acknowledgment?

When a person is not present in the United States, his or her acknowledgment may be made before a United States ambassador, consul, consular officer, or consular agent. [22 U.S.C. §§ 4215, 4221]

Further, some states' laws recognize an acknowledgment made before a judge, court clerk, or notary of the nation where the acknowledgment is made. It is unclear, however, whether a plan administrator would adopt such a rule. [ERISA §§ 404(a)(1)(D), 514(a)]

Q 16:83 How may a person in military service make an acknowledgment?

A person who is (1) a member of the armed forces; (2) a former member of the armed forces entitled to retired or retainer pay and legal assistance, or the dependent of an active or former member if the dependent is entitled to legal assistance; (3) a person "serving with, employed by, or accompanying the armed forces outside the United States"; or (4) a person subject to the Uniform Code of Military Justice outside the United States may make his or her acknowledgment, affidavit, deposition, or other statement that calls for a notarial act before a military officer described below. [10 U.S.C. §§ 1044, 1044a(a)(1)-(4)]

The following persons may officiate and certify a notarial act:

1. A judge advocate or reserve judge advocate;
2. A civilian attorney who serves as a legal assistance attorney;
3. An adjutant, assistant adjutant, or personnel adjutant, whether on active or reserve duty; or
4. A person designated by another statute or by a regulation of any of the armed forces.

[10 U.S.C. § 1044a(b)(1)-(4)]

Further, some states' laws recognize an acknowledgment that a person serving in any of the armed forces or his or her dependent, even if not entitled to military legal assistance, makes before a commissioned officer. It is unclear, however, whether a plan administrator would adopt such a rule. [ERISA §§ 404(a)(1)(D), 514(a)]

Q 16:84 Must a notary be independent of the participant?

Yes. Although nothing in ERISA Section 205 requires that a witness to a spouse's consent be independent of the electing participant, at least two courts have interpreted the statute to include such a requirement.

In *Howard v. Branham & Baker Coal Co.*, the district court focused on the fact that the notary public before whom Mr. Jensen had purportedly signed the document was Mrs. Jensen herself—a circumstance that the court concluded would render the document ineffective as a spouse's consent. The court explained its thinking as follows:

> Generally, it is considered contrary to public policy for a notary to take an acknowledgement of an instrument to which he or she is a party, [citation omitted] [C]ongress, through the [Retirement Equity Act], wanted a spouse to carefully consider a decision to waive retirement benefits without pressure from the other spouse and so imposed the requirement that the waiver be witnessed by a plan representative or a notary. To permit a spouse to act as notary to an instrument concerning their own benefits would appear to undermine this congressional intent.

[Howard v. Branham & Baker Coal Co., 968 F.2d 1214 (Table), 1992 WL 154571 *slip op.* at 3 (6th Cir. July 6, 1992) (unpublished disposition), *quoting and affirming* No. 90-00115 (E.D. Ky.) (unpublished order); *accord* Lasche v. George W. Lasche Basic Ret. Plan, 870 F. Supp. 336, 339, Pens. Plan Guide (CCH) ¶ 23905L (S.D. Fla. 1994)]

The federal courts' view is consistent with state laws concerning when a notary properly may officiate and the legal effect of a notary's certificate that he or she witnessed an acknowledgment. [1 Am. Jur. 2nd Acknowledgments § 16]

Q 16:85 Must a plan representative be independent of the participant?

Yes. Although nothing in ERISA Section 205 requires that a witness to a spouse's consent be independent of the electing participant, at least two federal courts have interpreted the statute to include such a requirement. A plan administrator who was the same person as the electing participant could not, even though he was a plan representative (or even if he was the only plan representative), witness his spouse's consent. [Lasche v. George W Lasche Basic Ret. Plan, 870 F. Supp. 336, 339, Pens. Plan Guide (CCH) ¶ 23905L (S.D. Fla. 1994)]

> **Practice Pointer.** If a lawyer who advises a participant about making a beneficiary designation that would provide for anyone other than the participant's spouse knows that the participant also is a plan administrator, trustee, or other fiduciary, the lawyer should advise the participant to ask his or her spouse to sign the consent in the presence of an independent notary.

Because ERISA permits a plan administrator to rely on a spouse's consent witnessed by a notary, it seems unlikely that a federal court would find that it could be prudent for a plan administrator to rely on a spouse's consent witnessed only by the interested participant or someone who is subordinate to the interested participant. [ERISA §§ 205(c)(6), 404(a)(1)]

Q 16:86 May a plan administrator rely on a notary's certificate?

Yes, usually. If a plan administrator acted according to ERISA's fiduciary duties when it decided whether to accept a spouse's consent, the consent, even if not properly witnessed, nonetheless discharges the plan from liability to the extent of the payments made before the plan administrator knew that the consent did not meet the plan's requirements. [ERISA § 205(c)(6)] If a plan administrator acted according to ERISA's fiduciary duties, it is not liable to the nonconsenting spouse. [ERISA § 404(a)(1)] Of course, a plan administrator must promptly correct or restrain payments once it knows that a spouse's consent was not properly witnessed.

Q 16:87 What may a plan administrator do if it relied on a notary's false or incorrect certificate?

If a plan administrator acted according to ERISA's fiduciary duties when it decided to accept a spouse's consent, the consent (or purported consent), even if not properly witnessed, nonetheless discharges the plan from liability to the extent of the payments made before the plan administrator knew that the consent did not meet the requirements of ERISA Section 205 and of the plan. [ERISA § 205(c)(6)] If the plan administrator acted according to ERISA's fiduciary duties, it is not liable to the spouse. [ERISA § 404(a)(1)] Of course, the plan administrator must promptly correct or stop payments once it knows that a spouse's consent was not properly witnessed.

Practice Pointer. A plan administrator may rely on a notary's certificate only if it acted according to ERISA's fiduciary duties, which include relying on a document only if a prudent expert familiar with administering retirement plans would, after exercising sufficient diligence, do so. A plan administrator must not ignore an internal inconsistency or other warning signs of fraud.

Example 1. Harold's election form states that he has no spouse. But the form's part for a spouse's consent is signed and notarized. A prudent administrator would not ignore this inconsistency, and instead must inquire into the facts. [Rice v. Rochester Laborers' Annuity Fund, 888 F. Supp. 494 (W.D.N.Y. 1995)]

Example 2. Wilma submits an election that states that she has no spouse. The form has no inconsistencies or irregularities. The retirement plan's administrator also administers a health plan under which the same group of employees and their spouses are eligible. Would a prudent, expert fiduciary check the health plan's record to confirm that Wilma had not told the other plan that she has a spouse?

If a plan incurs or might incur an expense because the plan administrator relied on a notary's certificate, the plan's fiduciary might have a duty to evaluate whether it is in the plan's best interest to pursue a claim or lawsuit against the notary. [ERISA § 404(a)(1)] A notary is responsible for damages caused by his or her negligent performance of his or her duties. [John D. Perovich, Annotation, Liability of Notary Public or His Bond for Negligence in Performance of Duties, 44 A.L.R. 3d 555 (1972); Kenneth W. Biedzynski, 58 Am. Jur. 2d Notaries Public

(Liability for Notarial Acts—Negligent Acknowledgment) § 60 (2002)] In addition, a spouse who did not receive what he or she would have been entitled to had the notary performed correctly may sue the notary.

Q 16:88 Is a plan administrator protected from liability if it relied on a participant's statement about why his or her spouse's consent was not needed?

Maybe. ERISA includes the following protection from liability: "If a plan fiduciary acts in accordance with part 4 of this subtitle [ERISA's fiduciary-responsibility provisions] in . . . making a determination under paragraph (2) [concerning whether the participant's spouse consented to the participant's election, or whether such a consent was excused], then such . . . determination shall be treated as valid for purposes of discharging *the plan* from liability *to the extent of* payments made pursuant to such Act [*sic*]." [ERISA § 205(c)(6) (emphasis added)]

Some statements in the Retirement Equity Act's legislative history suggest total relief: "If the plan administrator acts in accordance with the fiduciary standards of ERISA . . . in accepting the representations of the participant that the spouse's consent cannot be obtained, then the plan will not be liable for payments to the surviving spouse." [Senate Rep. No. 575, 98th Cong., 2d Sess. 14 (1984), *reprinted in* 1984 U.S.C.C.A.N. 2547, 2560] But one court construed the "to the extent" phrase to mean that a plan must pay the surviving spouse an amount or amounts based on what remains of the benefit that would have been provided in the absence of the participant's false election after subtracting the amounts the plan paid. [Hearn v. Western Conference of Teamsters Pension Trust Fund, 68 F.3d 301 (9th Cir. 1995)]

Caution. Under the Ninth Circuit's precedent, a *plan* might be liable to pay some benefit to a participant's surviving spouse despite the fact that, because the plan administrator did not breach any fiduciary duty, the plan has no claim by which the plan can obtain extra money to pay the surviving spouse. Thus, the expense of paying a benefit to the surviving spouse is an expense that the plan administrator must allocate to other plan accounts and, unless the plan provides otherwise, may allocate to other participants' and beneficiaries' accounts.

Elective-Share Rights

Q 16:89 What is an elective-share right?

In almost all states that do not provide community property (see Qs 16:92–16:97) a decedent's surviving spouse may elect to take a share of the decedent's property, even if the decedent's will and other transfers had not provided for his or her spouse. [Restatement (Third) of Property: Wills and Other Donative Transfers § 9.1(a) (2003)]

Q 16:90 How much is a surviving spouse's elective share?

In many states, a surviving spouse's elective share is one-third of the decedent's estate. In a few, it is one-half. [Restatement (Third) of Property: Wills and Other Donative Transfers § 9.1(a) (2003)]

In some states, the elective-share percentage increases under a schedule based on the duration of the marriage. For those states, a typical schedule has an elective-share percentage that ranges from 3 percent for a marriage that lasted one year to 50 percent for a marriage of 15 years or more. [Unif. Probate Code § 2-202(a), 8 pt. I U.L.A. 102–103 & Supp. 74-77 (2011); *see also* Restatement (Third) of Property: Wills and Other Donative Transfers § 9.2(a) (2003)]

Q 16:91 Is an elective share computed on all property?

Some states compute an elective share only on probate property. However, many states now provide that an elective share is computed on an "augmented estate" that includes several items of non-probate property. [Restatement (Third) of Property: Wills and Other Donative Transfers §§ 9.1(b)-(c), 9.2(b)-(c) (2003)] Some states have detailed rules for counting this augmented estate. [Unif. Probate Code §§ 2-203 to 2-210, 8 pt. I U.L.A. 103–125 (1998) & Supp. 77-90 (2011)]

Community Property

Q 16:92 What is *community property*?

In a separate-property regime, which applies in 41 states and all U.S. territories and possessions other than Puerto Rico, an item of property normally belongs to the person who has title to it, paid for it, earned it, or otherwise acquired it. Although any property owned by a married person may become subject to equitable distribution on a divorce or other marital dissolution, the property belongs to the person who owns it until a court makes an order.

Community property is a term that lawyers use to refer to a regime that treats each item of property or an aggregate of property acquired by either spouse of a married couple during the marriage and while the couple are domiciled in a community-property state (see Q 16:94) as owned equally by each spouse. Each spouse's ownership exists presently, notwithstanding that the other spouse currently may hold title to or have control over the property.

> **Caution.** Income derived from separate property might be separate property or community property based on the kind of property that produced income and which state's laws apply. [*See, e.g.*, Alsenz v. Alsenz, 101 S.W.3d 648 (Tex. Ct. App. 2003) (income received during a marriage from a patent was community property notwithstanding that all work was performed and the patent was issued before the marriage); *see generally* Internal Revenue Manual Part 25.18.1.2.13 (available at http://www.irs.gov/irm/part25/irm_25-018-001.html) (last visited on April 29, 2012)]

Ordinarily, community property is property acquired during marriage, except property acquired by gift (or an inheritance). [*See generally* Black's Law Dictionary 317 (9th ed. 2009)

Note. A typical community-property statute refers to a community of *spouses*, and often provides no useful definition concerning what the word "spouse" means. Even if a state does not recognize same-sex marriages made in the state, it is less clear whether a state would recognize a same-sex couple's marriage or quasi-marriage made in another state. Further, a court might apply community-property law to protect the expectations of a non-spouse in a relationship that, in a judge's view, resembled marriage. (See Q 16:95.)

Q 16:93 How does community-property law apply to a retirement plan benefit?

If community-property law applies, a retirement plan benefit is community property to the extent that it accrued during the marriage and while the participant was domiciled in a community-property state. Beyond the usual tracing and accounting challenges of a community-property regime, a retirement plan might involve extra difficulty because a retirement plan might receive a rollover contribution from an IRA, and indirectly from other eligible retirement plans, and it might be difficult to trace when the contributions to those plans were made.

Practice Pointer. Even a practitioner who works primarily or exclusively in a small geographic area that has no community-property state should maintain some general awareness about community-property law. People in the United States relocate, and property that was community property when a couple was domiciled in a community-property state ordinarily remains community property when the couple relocates to a separate-property state.

In Wisconsin, the nonparticipant's community-property right in a retirement plan or deferred compensation plan ends on the nonparticipant's death if the nonparticipant's death occurs before the participant's death. [Wis. Stat. Ann. §§ 766.31(3), 766.62(5)]

Q 16:94 Which states are community-property states?

Arizona, California, Idaho, Louisiana, Nevada, New Mexico, Puerto Rico, Texas, Washington, and Wisconsin are community-property states.

Alaska gives a married couple a choice of whether to use a separate-property regime or a community-property regime. [Alaska Stat. § 34.77.090] The separate-property regime applies unless the married couple agree to use a community-property regime. If the couple choose community property, they may use a written community-property agreement or a community-property trust to vary some of the state law provisions that otherwise would govern their community property. [Alaska Stat. § 34.77.020]

California law permits a married couple to accept a conveyance as "community property with right of survivorship." [Cal. Civ. Code § 682.1]

In Texas, community-property law is a right protected by the state constitution. [Texas Const. [1845], art. VII, § 19]

Although American community-property regimes are based primarily on the Spanish system, community-property law varies considerably from state to state. For example, if all contributions to a retirement plan were made before the participant was married, but investment earnings accrued during the marriage, some states would classify the entire retirement plan (including investment earnings) as separate property, whereas others might classify the investment earnings that accrued during the marriage as community property.

Wisconsin is the only state to have adopted as its community-property law any form of the Uniform Marital Property Act recommended by the National Conference of Commissioners on Uniform State Laws. [Wis. Stat. Ann. §§ 766.001–766.97; *see generally* Unif. Marital Property Act (1983), 9A pt. I U.L.A. 103–158 (1998) & Supp. 96–101 (2011)] Wisconsin does not apply its marital-property regime to either spouse unless both are domiciled in Wisconsin. [Wis. Stat. § 766.01(5)]

Q 16:95 Can community-property law be applied to nonspouses?

Maybe. In a state that applies community-property law to determine the property rights of married persons but does not recognize common-law marriage, a court might apply community-property law to protect the expectations of a nonspouse in a relationship that, in a judge's view, resembled marriage. Arizona, California, and Louisiana provide community-property rights to a putative spouse, but not to a meretricious nonspouse. [Stevens v. Anderson, 75 Ariz. 331, 256 P.2d 712 (1953); Cal. Civ. Code § 4452; La. Civ. Code Ann. arts. 117–118] Even for a couple in which neither person believed that he or she was married or had a spouse, Washington applies community-property law to a couple who have or had a "committed intimate relationship" (whether opposite-sex or same-sex), and may do so even after a relationship's end that results from either person's death. [Olver v. Fowler, 168 P.3d 348 (2007); Vasquez v. Hawthorne, 145 Wash. 2d 103, 33 P.3d 735 (2001); Connell v. Francisco, 127 Wash. 2d 339, 898 P.2d 831 (1995); Warden v. Warden, 36 Wash. App. 693, 676 P.2d 1037 (1984); *In re* Marriage of Lindsey, 101 Wash. 2d 299, 678 P.2d 328 (1984); *In re* Brenchley's Estate, 96 Wash. 223, 164 P.913(1917)]

Other legal theories for adjusting the property rights of putative spouses or meretricious spouses include express or implied contract, partnership, and unjust enrichment.

Q 16:96 How does community-property law affect payment of benefits under an ERISA plan?

ERISA preempts state laws that relate to an ERISA plan. [ERISA § 514(a)] Nonetheless, a domestic relations court may order a participant to transfer an amount or property to his or her spouse or former spouse.

Q 16:97 How does community-property law affect death benefits under a non-ERISA plan?

If a non-ERISA plan's participant names a beneficiary other than his or her spouse for more than half of (or, more precisely, for more than the participant's separate property plus community-property rights in) his or her benefit under a retirement plan, the participant's spouse might have a right under state law to get a court order invalidating the beneficiary designation, or at least as much of it as would leave the spouse with less than half of (or more precisely, with less than the spouse's community-property rights in) the retirement plan benefit. Nevertheless, a payer may pay based on the beneficiary designation it has on record until a payer receives a court order restraining payment or a written notice that the spouse asserts his or her rights.

Premarital Agreements

Q 16:98 What is a *premarital agreement*?

A *premarital agreement* is an agreement, made between two persons who are about to marry, concerning property rights that arise from marriage. Typically, a premarital agreement provides that each of the soon-to-be spouses waives one or more of the property rights that a spouse otherwise would have. A premarital agreement may waive a spouse's right to a share of the other's estate. Within limits required by public policy and basic fairness, a premarital agreement may specify what property division will apply if the marriage ends by divorce or when it ends by death.

In a state with a law based on the Uniform Premarital Agreement Act, the parties to a premarital agreement may contract concerning property rights, the support of a spouse or former spouse, making a will or trust, and "the ownership rights in and disposition of the death benefit from a life insurance policy." [Unif. Premarital Agreement Act § 3(a)(6), 9C U.L.A. 43–46 (2001) & Supp. 15–16 (2011)] A court will not enforce an agreement to the extent that it would cause a spouse or former spouse to become eligible for public assistance. [*See generally* Unif. Premarital Agreement Act § 6(b), 9C U.L.A. 48-55 (2001) & Supp 17-22 (2011)] A party to a premarital agreement may not waive child support, and a premarital agreement cannot adversely affect child support. [Unif. Premarital Agreement Act § 3(a)(7), 3(b), 9C U.L.A. 43–46 (2001) & Supp. 15-16 (2011)]

Practice Pointer. A guidebook—Gary N. Skoloff, Richard H. Singer Jr., and Ronald L. Brown, *Drafting Prenuptial Agreements* (updated Dec. 20, 2011) (available through http://www.aspenpublishers.com) organizes its authors' explanations of relevant law and drafting suggestions based on whether the couple are both young, both old, or of different ages, and whether the spouses or soon-to-be spouses are similar or different in wealth.

In states that do not regulate premarital agreements by statute, courts apply ordinary contract law, but with extra scrutiny, recognizing the confidential relationship of those engaged to marry. [*See generally* Restatement of Property (Wills and Other Donative Transfers) § 9.4 (2003); *but see* Mallen v. Mallen, 280 Ga. 43, 622 S.E.2d 812, 815 (Ga. 2005) ("Georgia law has not recognized the existence of a confidential relationship between persons who have agreed to marry.")]

Q 16:99 Can a premarital agreement waive a spouse's right to a non-ERISA plan benefit?

Yes. Even if a surviving spouse is entitled to an elective share, community property, or other protective rights under state law, an expertly prepared premarital agreement—or marital agreement (see Qs 16:96–16:98)—should be sufficient to eliminate or waive those rights. [Restatement (Third) of Property: Wills and Other Donative Transfers § 9.4(a) (2003); Unif. Probate Code § 2-207, 8 pt. I U.L.A. 118–121 (1998) & Supp. 83-85 (2011); Unif. Premarital Agreement § 3, 9C U.L.A. 43–46 (2001) & Supp. 15-16 (2011)]

In some circumstances, it might be difficult to enforce the terms of a premarital agreement. At least one court has held that an offset against agreement rights in recognition of a surviving spouse's receipt of retirement plan benefits (that were not provided by the premarital agreement) could be an ERISA violation, notwithstanding that the person applying the offset had no connection to any ERISA plan. This was so because the offset had the effect of "discriminating" against the spouse because she exercised her right to a benefit under an ERISA plan. [*See, e.g.*, Mattei v. Mattei, 126 F.3d 794, 21 Employee Benefits Cas. (BNA) 1745, Pens. Plan Guide (CCH) ¶ 23937W (6th Cir. 1997) (construing ERISA § 510)] Although this case interpreted ERISA's non-interference provision, state law might impose a similar principle concerning a person's rights under a non-ERISA plan.

Q 16:100 Can a premarital agreement waive a spouse's right to a retirement plan benefit under an ERISA plan?

Whether a premarital agreement can waive a spouse's rights under an ERISA plan turns on what rights (if any) the plan provides concerning a spouse.

If a plan includes a spouse's-consent provision similar to the provision that ERISA Section 205 requires for an ERISA plan that is not exempt from Part 2, a premarital agreement likely cannot constitute a spouse's consent to waive those rights. [*See* ERISA § 205; Treas. Reg. § 1.401(a)-20, Q&A 28] Usually, a spouse's consent must be signed by the spouse, and a person making a premarital agreement is not yet a spouse. [*See, e.g.*, Hurwitz v. Sher, 982 F.2d 778 (2d Cir.

1992), *cert. denied*, 113 S. Ct. 2345 (1993); Hagwood v. Newton, 282 F.3d 285 (4th Cir. 2002); Greenebaum Doll & McDonald PLLC v. Sandler, 2007 Fed. App'x 0822N (6th Cir. 2007); Howard v. Branham & Baker Coal Co., 968 F.2d 1214 (6th Cir. 1992); Pedro Enters. Inc. v. Perdue, 998 F.2d 491 (7th Cir. 1993); National Auto Dealers & Assoc. Ret. Trust v. Arbeitman, 89 F.3d 496 (8th Cir. 1996); Ford Motor Co. v. Ross, 129 F. Supp. 2d 1070, 1073–1074 (E.D. Mich. 2001); Callahan v. Hutsell, Callahan & Buchino, 813 F. Supp. 541 (W.D. Ky. 1992), *vacated and remanded,* 14 F.3d 600 (6th Cir. 1993); Nellis v. Boeing, 15 Empl. Benefits Cas. (BNA) 1651, 18 Fam. Law Rep. 1374 (D. Kan. 1992) (not officially reported); Zinn v. Donaldson Co., 799 F. Supp. 69 (D. Minn. 1992)]

At least one court decision has held that a premarital agreement (or, presumably, a marital agreement) cannot waive a QJSA if the spouse could not know what he or she would waive because the plan had not yet been created. [Pedro Enters. v. Perdue, 998 F.2d 491 (7th Cir. 1993)]

Marital Agreements

Q 16:101 What is a *marital agreement*?

A *marital agreement* is an agreement made between two persons who already are spouses concerning property rights that arise from their marriage. Typically, a marital agreement provides that each spouse waives one or more of the property rights that a spouse otherwise would have. A marital agreement can waive a spouse's right to a share of the other's estate. [*See generally* Restatement (Third) of Property: Wills and Other Donative Transfers § 9.4(a) (2003)] Within limits required by public policy and basic fairness, a marital agreement may specify what property division will apply if the marriage ends by divorce or when it ends by a party's death.

Beyond the usual rules of the common law of contracts, many state statutes or court decisions add disclosure and other procedural requirements to decrease the likelihood that a spouse makes a marital agreement without understanding the agreement's provisions. Even if no statute applies specified conditions, courts use heightened scrutiny, recognizing the confidential relationship of spouses. [Restatement (Third) of Property: Wills and Other Donative Transfers § 9.4(b)-(c) (2003)] Typically, each party should fully disclose his or her financial circumstances to the other. The better practice is for each party to get the advice of a lawyer of his or her choosing. Even when the proponent's lawyer warns the other party to seek independent legal advice, an agreement might be invalid if the proponent's lawyer fails to explain to the unrepresented party that person's disadvantages under the agreement and why he or she needs legal advice. [*See, e.g.*, Bonds v. Bonds, 99 Cal. Rptr. 2d 252, 5 P.3d 815 (2000); *In re Estate of Lutz,* 563 N.W.2d 563 N.W.2d 90, 97, 98 (N.D. 1997); *In re Marriage of Foran,* 834 P.2d 834 P.2d 1081 (Wash. Ct. App. 1992)] But Pennsylvania will enforce a premarital or marital agreement even if a party received no disclosure concerning his or her statutory right. [Stoner v. Stoner, 572 Pa. 665, 819 A.2d 529 (2003)]

Caution. An agreement between a couple who are already married might fail to provide what lawyers call consideration—that is, a promise to do something one is not already under a legal duty or obligation to do, or to refrain from doing something that one has a legal right to do. An agreement merely to stay married might be insufficient to support a legally binding marital agreement. [Bratton v. Bratton, No. E2002-00432-SC-R11-CV (Tenn. Apr. 30, 2004)]

A marital agreement is void if it was signed under a threat of a divorce. [*See, e.g.*, *In re* Sharp's Estate, 11 Pa. D&C 3d 371 (Pa. Common Pleas 1979)]

Q 16:102 Can a marital agreement waive a spouse's right to a non-ERISA plan benefit?

Yes. Even if a surviving spouse is entitled to an elective share, community property, or other protective rights under state law, an expertly prepared marital agreement should be sufficient to eliminate or waive those rights. [*See generally* Unif. Probate Code § 2-207, 8 pt. I U.L.A. 118–121 (1998) & Supp. 83–85 (2011)]

Q 16:103 Can a marital agreement waive a spouse's right to an ERISA plan benefit?

Yes, a marital agreement may waive a spouse's right to an ERISA plan benefit if the marital agreement states all of the form requirements necessary to constitute a valid qualified election and spouse's consent under the plan.

Practice Pointer. To accomplish this, a family lawyer should consult an expert employee-benefits lawyer and each plan administrator.

Tenancy by the Entirety

Q 16:104 What is a *tenancy by the entirety*?

Tenancy by the entirety is a form of concurrent property ownership that recognizes the special unity of a married couple.

A tenancy by the entirety can be created only if required unities of title, interest, possession, time, and person (a valid marriage) all exist. [Restatement (First) of Property § 67 (1936)] Along with other requirements, two persons can become co-tenants in a tenancy by the entirety only if they are legally married. Under a tenancy by the entirety, unlike other kinds of joint tenancy, each of the two spouses owns all of the property, but neither spouse acting alone can dispose of the property. A tenancy by the entirety ends on the death of either spouse, or on the divorce or other dissolution of the marriage. [*See, e.g.*, 23 Pa. Cons. Stat. Ann. § 3507; *In re* Sharp's Estate, 11 Pa. D&C 3d 371 (Pa. Common Pleas Orphans Ct. Div. 1979)]

Q 16:105 What kind of property may be owned as a tenancy by the entirety?

Of the states that recognize tenancy by the entirety as an available form of property ownership, some allow it only for real property (for example, a couple's home), and some allow it for both real property and personal property. [Restatement (Third) of Property: Wills and Other Donative Transfers § 6.2, reporter's note 13 to comment f (2003)]

Q 16:106 Why might someone want to own property in a tenancy by the entirety?

Because neither spouse alone can dispose the property (see Q 16:104), a tenancy by the entirety may provide useful protection against the claims of creditors. For example, if only one of the two spouses is bankrupt, a bankruptcy trustee generally cannot reach property held in a tenancy by the entirety. [*See* 11 U.S.C. § 110]

> **Practice Pointer.** A participant might not need the protection that a tenancy-by-the-entirety ownership, when available, could provide. Usually, a retirement plan benefit is excluded from a participant's bankruptcy estate. [11 U.S.C. § 522; *see also* 11 U.S.C. § 541(c)(2); Rousey v. Jacoway, 544 U.S. 320 (2005); Patterson v. Shumate, 504 U.S. 753 (1992)]

> **Note.** For either an ERISA or non-ERISA plan, a federal tax lien supersedes any ERISA, plan, or contract restraints. [I.R.C. §§ 6321, 6331; *cf.* Treas. Reg. § 1.401(a)-13(b)(2)] A federal tax lien may attach to a taxpayer's property rights in a tenancy by the entirety, even if the taxpayer's spouse is not a debtor. [United States v. Craft, 535 U.S. 274 (2002)]

Finally, a married person might prefer tenancy-by-the-entirety ownership simply because it reflects his or her beliefs about the nature of marriage.

Q 16:107 Can a participant transfer a retirement plan benefit into a tenancy by the entirety?

No, a participant will be unable to transfer his or her rights under a retirement plan into a tenancy by the entirety for one or more of the following reasons:

1. State law does not recognize tenancy by the entirety.
2. The retirement plan rights are personal property that cannot be the subject of a tenancy by the entirety.
3. State law precludes a conveyance of property into a tenancy by the entirety.

4. The retirement plan, in a provision required by the Internal Revenue Code, precludes any transfer.

At common law, a married couple cannot hold personal property (property other than land and the buildings fixed onto the land) in a tenancy by the entirety. This is still the rule in some states.

At common law, one spouse who solely owns property cannot convey that property into a tenancy by the entirety. Some states now allow such a transfer; however, those provisions are of no use to a participant because a participant lacks the power to transfer his or her rights under the retirement plan.

A retirement plan usually provides that benefits cannot be assigned, alienated, or transferred. Thus, even in states that recognize a tenancy by the entirety as an available form of property ownership, a tenancy by the entirety cannot apply concerning a retirement plan because a participant cannot transfer ownership of his or her benefit under a retirement plan.

Disclaimers

Q 16:108 What is a *disclaimer*?

A *disclaimer* (also called a *renunciation* in some states) is a writing in which a beneficiary states that he or she does not want to receive a benefit. To be valid and, if desired, to achieve tax purposes, the disclaimer must carefully state specified conditions (see Q 16:113).

Q 16:109 Is a disclaimer permitted under a retirement plan?

A retirement plan (including an IRA) will not permit a participant to disclaim his or her benefit because a retirement plan provides that a participant cannot forfeit or transfer any right he or she has under the contract. But a retirement plan might permit a beneficiary to disclaim a benefit. [*See* G.C.M. 39858 (Sept. 9, 1991); Ltr. Ruls. 9226058, 9037048, 8922036] A trustee, custodian, insurer, or plan administrator may (but need not) accept a beneficiary's disclaimer.

Q 16:110 What is the effect of a disclaimer?

If a beneficiary makes a valid disclaimer that the retirement plan payer accepts, the retirement plan benefit will be distributed (or distributable) as if the beneficiary/disclaimant had died before the participant's death or before the creation of the benefit disclaimed. [Unif. Disclaimer of Property Interests Act (1999, amended 2006), 8A U.L.A. 159–189 (2003) & Supp. 182–201 (2011), Unif. Disclaimer of Property Interests Act (1978) 8A U.L.A. 191–208 (2003) & Supp. 202–203 (2011)]

Q 16:111 What are the tax consequences of a disclaimer?

If a beneficiary makes a valid disclaimer that also meets all requirements of Code Section 2518, the disclaimed benefit will neither be in the disclaimant's estate for federal estate tax purposes nor be included in the disclaimant's income for federal income tax purposes. [I.R.C. § 2518; Treas. Reg. § 25.2518-1] Many states have a similar rule for state estate or inheritance tax purposes. [*See, e.g.*, 72 Pa. Cons. Stat. § 9116(c)]

Q 16:112 Why would someone want to make a disclaimer?

Although most people do not lightly turn away money, sometimes there might be a good reason to make a disclaimer. A typical reason is to complete tax-oriented estate planning. For example, a beneficiary may prefer to make a disclaimer to help accomplish one or more of the following estate-planning objectives:

- Changing a restricted transfer in favor of the beneficiary into an unrestricted transfer to the same beneficiary;
- Changing an unrestricted transfer to the beneficiary into a restricted transfer in favor of the same beneficiary;
- Limiting a transfer to a child or other nonspouse to permit the participant's spouse to delay the required beginning date;
- Limiting a transfer to a child or other nonspouse to permit the participant's spouse to make a rollover;
- Limiting a transfer to a child or other nonspouse to increase the marital deduction;
- Limiting a transfer to a spouse as needed to "equalize" the effective transfer tax rate of each spouse;
- Limiting a transfer to a spouse as needed to fully use the generation-skipping tax exemption of the first spouse to die;
- Limiting a transfer to a spouse as needed to avoid an estate transfer surtax; or
- Providing a designated beneficiary so as to lengthen tax deferral for the plan benefit and thereby increase a gift to charity.

Another frequent use is to correct a "wrong" beneficiary designation.

Example. Matthew saved for retirement using a SEP IRA. When he first "enrolled," he was single and named his parents as beneficiaries. Recently, Matthew married Laura. Shortly after returning from their honeymoon, Matthew was killed in an accident. Matthew's parents believe that if Matthew had thought about it, he would have wanted his wife to be his beneficiary. Therefore, each of them files a disclaimer with the retirement plan custodian. Although the parents cannot directly control who gets the benefit, their lawyer advises them that the IRA's default provision (see Q 16:18), together with their state's intestacy law, will result in Laura getting the benefit. All family members feel that this is what Matthew would have wanted. Disclaimers allow the family to achieve this good result.

Another reason to make a disclaimer is to not receive a benefit that would be taken by the disclaimant's creditors. Some courts find that such a disclaimer is a fraudulent transfer and, thus, is void. And some states by statute bar a disclaimer by an insolvent beneficiary. [Unif. Disclaimer of Property Interests Act (1999, amended 2006) § 13(e) and comment, 8A U.L.A. 183–186 (2003) & Supp. 199–200 (2011)] Federal law or state law is most likely to bar a disclaimer that could interfere with a government's opportunity to collect on a debt to the government. [*See, e.g.*, 42 U.S.C. § 1320a-7b(a)(6); State v. Murtha, 427 A.2d 807 (Conn. 1980); *accord* Department of Income Maint. v. Watts, 558 A.2d 998 (Conn. 1989); *but see In re* Estate of Kirk, 591 N.W.2d 630 (Iowa 1999)] If no rule of this kind applies, a disclaimer is not a fraudulent transfer. [*See, e.g.*, Cal. Probate Code § 283; Essen v. Gilmore, 607 N.W.2d 829 (Neb. 2000)] Even a valid disclaimer does not avoid a federal tax lien. [Drye v. United States, 528 U.S. 49 (1999)]

Q 16:113 What are the requirements for a legally valid disclaimer?

To be effective for federal tax and retirement plan purposes, a disclaimer usually must meet all of the following requirements:

1. The disclaimer must be made before the beneficiary accepts or uses the disclaimed benefit.
2. The disclaimant must not have received any consideration for the disclaimer.
3. The writing must state an irrevocable and unqualified refusal to accept the benefit.
4. The benefit must pass without any direction by the disclaimant.
5. The disclaimer must be in writing and must be signed by the disclaimant.
6. The writing must be delivered to the trustee, custodian, insurer, or plan administrator.
7. The writing must be so delivered no later than nine months after
   a. The date of the participant's death, or
   b. The date the beneficiary attains age 21, whichever is later.
8. The disclaimer must meet all requirements of applicable state law or a relevant state's law.

[I.R.C. § 2518; Treas. Reg. § 25.2518-2; G.C.M. 39858, 1991 WL 776304 (Sept. 9, 1991); *see generally* Unif. Disclaimer of Property Interests Act (1999, amended 2006), 8A U.L.A. 159–189 (2003) & Supp. 182–201 (2011)] A disclaimer may renounce a specified portion of what the beneficiary/disclaimant otherwise would be entitled to.

Note. The Fifth Circuit has interpreted the tax regulations' no-consideration condition as limited to bargained-for consideration. In the view of that court, leading a disclaimant to understand that he or she would otherwise be provided for or that his or her needs would be considered does not necessarily vitiate the tax-qualified treatment of a disclaimer if the disclaimer is valid under non-tax law. [Estate of Monroe v. Commissioner, 124 F.3d 699 (5th Cir. 1997); *see also* Estate of Lute v. United States, 19 F. Supp. 2d 1047 (D. Neb. 1998)]

State law may provide additional requirements. For example, in some states a disclaimer must state the disclaimant's belief that he or she has no creditor that could be disadvantaged by the disclaimer. In some situations, especially when the beneficiary is a minor or an incapacitated person, a disclaimer may require court approval. [*See, e.g.*, N.Y. Est. Powers & Trusts § 2-1.11(c); 20 Pa. Cons. Stat. Ann. § 6202] Even when court approval is not required, under some states' laws a disclaimer is not valid unless it is filed in the appropriate probate court, or delivered to a relevant fiduciary. [Unif. Disclaimer of Property Interests Act (1999, amended 2006) § 12, 8A U.L.A. 181–182 (2003); Unif. Probate Code §§ 2-801, 2-1112, 8 pt I U.L.A. 206–210 (1998) & Supp. 169–172, 199 (2011)]

In addition to state law and tax-law requirements, a retirement plan may impose further requirements.

Caution. Even a valid disclaimer does not defeat a federal tax lien against a disclaimant's property, including property that he or she would receive in the absence of his or her disclaimer and a tax lien. [I.R.C. § 6321; Drye v. United States, 528 U.S. 49 (1999); *see also* United States v. Irvine, 511 U.S. 224 (1994); United States v. Mitchell, 403 U.S. 190 (1971)]

Practice Pointer. If a surviving spouse wishes to make a tax-qualified disclaimer of a portion of what otherwise would be his or her rights under a qualified terminal interest property (QTIP) trust (see Q 16:124), the estate's executor and the QTIP trust's trustee might first divide the QTIP trust into separate trusts. An assignment of any portion of a spouse's interest in a QTIP trust is a taxable gift of that trust's principal. [Treas. Reg. § 25.2519-1(a)] However, a disclaimer is not an assignment. [*Cf.* Ltr. Ruls. 200122036, 200044034; *see generally* Unif. Disclaimer of Property Interests Act (1999, amended 2006) § 5(f), 8A U.L.A. 116–170 (2003) & Supp. 185–186 (2011)]

Q 16:114 Is a disclaimer that harms the disclaimant's creditors invalid?

Often, yes. Some courts find that a disclaimer that hinders a disclaimant's creditors is a fraudulent transfer, and thus is void. And some states, by statute, bar a disclaimer by an insolvent beneficiary. [Unif. Disclaimer of Property Interests Act (1999, amended 2006) § 13(e) and comment, 8A U.L.A. 183–186 (2003) & Supp. 182–183 (2010)] Federal law or state law is most likely to bar a disclaimer that could interfere with a government's opportunity to collect on a debt to the government. [*See, e.g.*, 42 U.S.C. § 1320a-7b(A)(6); State v. Murtha, 427 A.2d 807 (Conn. 1980); *accord* Department of Income Maint. v. Watts, 558 A.2d 998 (Conn. 1989); *but see In re Estate* of Kirk, 591 N.W.2d 630 (Iowa 1999)] If no rule of this kind applies, a disclaimer is not a fraudulent transfer. [*See, e.g.*, Cal. Probate Code § 283; Essen v. Gilmore, 607 N.W.2d 829 (Neb. 2000)] Even a valid disclaimer does not avoid a federal tax lien. [Drye v. United States, 528 U.S. 49 (1999)]

Q 16:115 What is a fraudulent transfer?

Under the Uniform Fraudulent Transfer Act, a transfer is fraudulent concerning a creditor who had a claim before the transfer if the transferor was insolvent when he or she made the transfer (or became insolvent as a result of the transfer) and did not receive "a reasonably equivalent value" in exchange for the transfer. [*See, e.g.*, 12 Pa. Cons. Stat. § 1505] Because a disclaimer is always made without any value in exchange, a disclaimer is fraudulent (if this law applies) when the disclaimant was insolvent when he or she made the disclaimer.

> **Note.** A beneficiary's act in soliciting credit by identifying an inheritance or other benefit might be an acceptance of property that could preclude a disclaimer. [*See, e.g.*, 20 Pa. Cons. Stat. § 6206(a)(4); *In re* Kolb, 326 F.3d 1030 (9th Cir. 2003); *see generally* Ronald A. Brand & William P. LaPiana, Disclaimers in Estate Planning 77–91 (1990)]

Q 16:116 Can a beneficiary's executor or agent disclaim?

If an IRA or other retirement plan permits a beneficiary to disclaim a plan benefit, whether that power can be exercised only by the beneficiary personally or by the beneficiary's executor, personal representative, guardian, or attorney-in-fact as a fiduciary depends on the plan's or contract's language. Unless a plan states that a power to disclaim can be exercised by an executor, personal representative, guardian, or attorney-in-fact, only the beneficiary personally may exercise the power to disclaim. [R. Scott Nickel, as Plan Benefit Adm'r of the Thrift Plan of Phillips Petroleum Co. v. Estate of Lurline Estes, 122 F.3d 294, 21 Employee Benefits Cas. (BNA) 1762, Pens. Plan Guide (CCH) ¶ 23937U (5th Cir. 1997)]

For a non-ERISA plan, it is unclear whether a similar result would apply under state law. In some states, a personal representative may disclaim an interest and the disclaimer relates back to the disclaimant's death or even to the death of the person making the disclaimant a beneficiary. [*See, e.g.*, Tex. Probate Code § 37A; Rolin v. IRS, 588 F.2d 368 (2d Cir. 1978) (applying New York law)]

Even if a fiduciary has power under applicable law to make a disclaimer [*see generally* Unif. Disclaimer of Property Interests Act § 11, 8A U.L.A. 180 (2003)], such a disclaimer might not be a qualified disclaimer for federal tax purposes. [*Cf.* Ltr. Ruls. 200013041, 9615043, 9609052 (disclaimer recognized) *with* Ltr. Rul. 9437042 (disclaimer not recognized); *see also* Rev. Rul. 90-110, 1990-2 C.B. 209 (disclaimer by trustee not a qualified disclaimer)]

Tax-Oriented Estate Planning

Q 16:117 What is the *federal estate tax*?

The *federal estate tax* is a tax on the right to transfer property on death. [I.R.C. § 2001] The tax is imposed on a decedent's taxable estate, which includes non-probate property and rights.

An unlimited marital deduction allows a person to transfer any amount to his or her surviving spouse (if the spouse is a U.S. citizen) without federal estate tax at that time, but tax may apply when the survivor dies. [I.R.C. § 2056]

For an estate of a decedent who dies after 2012, a tax credit allows a person to transfer about $1 million without federal estate tax. [I.R.C. § 2010] For an estate of a decedent who died in 2011 or dies in 2012, a tax credit allows a person to transfer about $5 million without federal estate tax. Further, a surviving spouse's estate may use the unused portion of his or her most recent deceased spouse's applicable exclusion amount. In some circumstances, this could result in an applicable exclusion amount up to $10 million. [I.R.C. § 2010, as amended by the Tax Relief, Unemployment Insurance Reauthorization, and Job Creation Act of 2010, Pub. L. No. 111-312 §§ 301–304 (Dec. 17, 2010), 124 Stat. 3296, 3300–3304 (2010)]

For an estate of a decedent who dies after 2012, the federal estate tax's highest rate is 55 percent; however, a 5 percent surtax is imposed on cumulative taxable transfers between $10 million and $17,184,000, which practically results in a marginal tax rate up to 60 percent. [I.R.C. § 2001] For an estate of a decedent who died in 2011 or dies in 2012, the federal estate tax's highest rate is 35 percent. [I.R.C. § 2001, as amended by the Tax Relief, Unemployment Insurance Reauthorization, and Job Creation Act of 2010, Pub. L. No. 111-312 §§ 301–304 (Dec. 17, 2010), 124 Stat. 3296, 3300-3304 (2010)]

Q 16:118 Should a person who is not "wealthy" be concerned with estate tax planning?

Many people have more wealth (at least for tax purposes) than they think. For estate tax purposes, a taxable estate includes non-probate property, such as the following:

- A home
- Personally owned life insurance benefits
- Employment-based life insurance benefits
- Retirement plan benefits

Q 16:119 What is a *state death transfer tax*?

A *state death transfer tax* is a state tax imposed on the transfer or receipt of wealth at death. Almost every state imposes some form of death transfer tax. An estate tax is a tax on the privilege of transferring property from a decedent. An inheritance tax is a tax on the privilege of receiving property from a decedent, including even property that a person did not own at the time of his or her death. Some states also have a state or local gift tax. Unlike the federal estate tax, which has a marital deduction, an inheritance tax or a state estate tax might apply even when the beneficiary is the decedent's spouse.

Practice Pointer. Although a participant might believe that he or she and his or her beneficiaries likely will not be subject to a *federal* estate tax, many states have a *state* estate or inheritance tax (or both), and most of these have a low exemption amount or none at all.

Q 16:120 Is a retirement plan benefit subject to federal estate tax?

Yes. The value of a participant's account or accrued benefit as of the date of his or her death, or if annuity payments have begun, the value of the remaining payments (if any), is included in the participant's estate for federal estate tax purposes. [*See generally* I.R.C. §§ 2033–2046]

Q 16:121 Is a retirement plan benefit subject to state death tax?

An explanation of the states' death taxes is beyond the scope of this book. Some states tax retirement plan benefits for death tax purposes according to rules similar to the rules of the federal estate tax, but often without an exemption amount. Other states have their own rules. In some states, the tax may vary based on the relationship of the beneficiary to the participant. [*See, e.g.*, 72 Pa. Cons. Stat. § 9116(a)]

Marital Deduction

Q 16:122 Does a beneficiary designation of the spouse qualify for the marital deduction?

Yes, as long as the spouse is the only person who can benefit, at least until his or her death. [I.R.C. § 2056; Ltr. Rul. 199936052]

Q 16:123 Does a beneficiary designation of a QTIP trust qualify for the marital deduction?

Yes. If the trust agreement includes necessary provisions (see Q 16:124) and the executor and the trustee properly make the election, a qualified terminable interest property ("QTIP") trust qualifies for the marital deduction.

Q 16:124 What provisions must a QTIP trust include?

In addition to the usual requirements for a QTIP trust, a participant and his or her estate-planning lawyer should make sure that the trust (or at least the subtrust that will hold the retirement plan benefit) provides all of the following:

1. During the spouse's life, no one (including the spouse) can have any power to appoint any part of the retirement plan benefit or QTIP property resulting from it to anyone other than the surviving spouse.
2. The trustee has power to make the retirement plan and any trust property resulting from it productive or income earning.
3. The spouse has a right to require the trustee to make the retirement plan and any trust property resulting from it productive or income earning.
4. The trust document does not change the definition of principal and income in a way that might result in less income distributable to the spouse.
5. The trustee must have the power under the trust and the right under the retirement plan to get a distribution of the retirement plan benefit, at least for the amount described in item 10.
6. The surviving spouse must have the right to require the trustee to get a retirement plan distribution, at least for the amount described in item 10. (It is enough that the surviving spouse has the right to get the retirement plan's and the QTIP trust's income, and it does not invalidate QTIP treatment that the surviving spouse chooses not to exercise that right.)
7. The QTIP trust's fiduciary accounting income must include the retirement plan's income.
8. To ensure the spouse's right to all of the income, the trust must provide that all administration expenses normally charged to corpus (including any income tax payable with respect to the distribution of principal) be charged to corpus and not to income.
9. The trustee must compute the retirement plan's fiduciary accounting income and the QTIP trust's fiduciary accounting income.
10. If (for a year) the surviving spouse exercises his or her right to get all of the trust's fiduciary accounting income, the QTIP trustee must claim a distribution from the retirement plan in an amount no less than the greater of the Section 401(a)(9) minimum distribution (including any incidental benefit required distribution) or the QTIP trust's fiduciary accounting income attributable to the retirement plan.
11. The participant-decedent's executor and the trustee of the QTIP trust must make the QTIP election for the QTIP trust and for the retirement plan.

[I.R.C. § 2056(b)(7); Treas. Reg. §§ 20.2056(b)-5(f)(8), 20.2056(b)-7; Rev. Rul. 2006-26, 2006-1 C.B. 939]

Caution. A trust creator (and his or her estate-planning lawyer) also should consider what provisions qualify a trust for an exemption or deduction under a state's inheritance, estate, or other transfer tax. Qualifying for a state's marital treatment might require more restrictive, or less restrictive, conditions. For example, a Pennsylvania inheritance tax exemption for "a transfer of property for the sole use of the transferor's surviving spouse" does not require that income be paid if the surviving spouse does not request it.

[72 Pa. Stat. § 9113; *cf.* Estate of Goldman, 781 A.2d 259; 2001 Pa. Commw. LEXIS 533 (2001)]

Practice Pointer. In drafting QTIP trust provisions, an estate-planning lawyer should recognize that a retirement plan does not state provisions for determining fiduciary accounting income. Therefore, the trust must provide for the trustee to make its own determination of fiduciary accounting income based on the information available to it.

Caution. A surviving spouse who does not exercise his or her right to obtain the retirement plan benefit and thereby the QTIP trust's income should consider whether his or her waiver or non-exercise of that right constitutes a taxable gift of a future interest.

Practice Pointer. A careful drafter of a QTIP trust might consider provisions that would preclude (or at least not authorize) an excessive trustee fee. When a trustee is a family member who is a natural object of the QTIP trust beneficiary's bounty, an excessive trustee fee is a taxable gift from the surviving spouse to the trustee. [T.A.M. 200014004; *see generally* Merill v. Fahs, 324 U.S. 308 (1945); Commissioner v. Wemyss, 324 U.S. 303, 306 (1945); Harwood v. Commissioner, 82 T.C. 239, 259 (1984); Estate of Reynolds v. Commissioner, 55 T.C. 172 (1970); Estate of Anderson v. Commissioner, 8 T.C. 706, 720 (1947); Estate of Hendrickson v. Commissioner, T.C. Memo 1999-357] In addition to gift tax on the portion of the trustee's fee that is in excess of reasonable compensation, a surviving spouse's acquiescence in an excessive fee calls into question whether the surviving spouse truly had a right to all of the trust's income, and thereby whether the trust is or was a QTIP trust. [I.R.C. § 2056(b)(7)]

Q 16:125 What is *income* in trust or fiduciary accounting?

In trust or fiduciary accounting, *income* refers to money or property the trust receives as a year's (or shorter period's) return from a principal asset.

Example. Imagine a fruit-bearing tree. A year's harvest of fruit is income. If the tree grows taller and wider (and becomes more valuable if it can bear more fruit than the year before), those are changes in the principal. If the tree's owner chops it down and sells it for more than she paid for the tree, she has a capital gain.

The amount of a retirement plan distribution treated as income is likely to be determined under:

1. A traditional income rule (see Q 16:126)
2. An adjustment rule (see Q 16:127)
3. A unitrust rule (see Q 16:128)

In the absence of an adjustment or a unitrust measure of income, a trust counts as fiduciary accounting income the trust's interest, dividends, rents, and similar income, not, however, on capital gains (or other changes to the principal value of a trust asset).

Q 16:126 What is a traditional income rule for measuring income?

In many states, a trustee ordinarily allocates to principal all of a payment that a retirement plan was not required to make, and 10 percent of a payment that the retirement plan was required to pay. For this rule, a payment is not "required to be made" merely because the trustee exercises its right to a distribution or withdrawal. The rule applies whether the payments begin soon after the beneficiary's right first becomes subject to the trust or are deferred until a future date. As long as the distributee had a right to take a payment, the rule applies whether a distribution is paid in money or delivered in property. The rule is based on the payment right instead of on the assets held under a plan or as a contract under which the payments are made. This rule includes a "fail safe" to preserve QTIP or other marital deduction tax treatment: "If, to obtain an estate tax marital deduction for a trust, a trustee must allocate more of a payment to income than provided for by this [rule], the trustee shall allocate to income the additional amount necessary to obtain the marital deduction." [Unif. Principal and Income Act § 409 (before 2008 amendment), 7B U.L.A. 70–172 (2000)]

In the IRS's view, a trust or subtrust does not qualify as QTIP property unless the surviving spouse has unqualified rights to all of the trust's fiduciary accounting income, including all income attributable to a retirement plan. [Rev. Rul. 2006-26, 2006-1 C.B. 939] A 2008 revision to the recommended uniform law would, to the extent that a state adopts it, provide rules designed to conform to those IRS views. Among other provisions, the uniform law could permit applying a unitrust rule (see Q 16:128) to determine a retirement plan's income that otherwise would be unknown. [Unif. Principal and Income Act § 409, 7B U.L.A. 70–172 (2000)]

Q 16:127 What is the adjustment rule for apportioning income?

If a trustee invests a trust's assets according to a prudent-investor or total-return investment policy, even a trust with very good investment results might have little income. Using a traditional principal-and-income accounting method for a trust that achieves investment returns through capital gains could result in only a small distribution (or none) to a trust's income beneficiary. Under the Uniform Principal and Income Act, a trustee may use fiduciary discretion to make an adjustment between principal and income. [Unif. Principal and Income Act §§ 104, 506, 7B U.L.A. 141–149, 188–190 (2000) & Supp. 37–46, 77–78 (2005)] For example, a trustee might decide to treat a portion of the trust principal's change in value as though it were income. For a QTIP or other marital deduction trust that requires regular income distributions to a surviving spouse, a trustee may use this adjustment power to increase the income to which a surviving spouse is entitled, but not to decrease income. [Unif. Principal and Income Act §§ 104(c)(1), 7B U.L.A. 141–149 (2000) & Supp. 37–46 (2005)] Further, a trustee must use an adjustment power according to applicable law, the terms of the trust, and the trustee's fiduciary duties, including especially the duty to be impartial. [Unif. Trust Code § 803, 7C U.L.A. § 803 (2006) & Supp. 198 (2011)] A court may prevent or remedy an abuse of the trustee's discretion. [Unif. Principal and Income Act § 105, 7B Supp. U.L.A. 46–54 (2005); Restatement (Third) of Trusts § 87 (2007) & Supp. 14–15 (2011)]

Q 16:128 What is the unitrust rule for measuring income?

If a trust is governed by, or its trustee voluntarily adopted, a total-return investment policy, many states provide varying opportunities to treat a percentage of a trust's assets (counted as an average of recent years' closing balances) as income. [*See generally* Unif. Principal Income and Act, general notes 7B U.L.A. 131–135 (2000) & Supp. 4–32 (2006)] For Code provisions that call for income to be distributable, regulations allow a trust to treat this measure of income as meeting those requirements if, along with the necessary total-return investment policy and other conditions, the income percentage is no less than 3 percent and no more than 5 percent. [Treas. Reg. § 1.643(b)-1] In addition to these tax-law constraints on an income percentage, some states specify a presumed percentage (for example, 4 percent). [*See, e.g.*, 20 Pa. Cons. Stat. Ann. § 8105(d)(3)]

Note. During a time when a trustee of a QTIP subtrust must take a minimum distribution, if the subtrust holds only one retirement benefit and counts income as 4 percent of recent years' subtrust assets, that subtrust's income usually will be less than the minimum distribution. Income might be more than the minimum distribution if the minimum distribution is measured based on an age of 72 or younger. [*See* Treas. Reg. § 1.401(a)(9)-9 Q&A 2] Or, income might be more than the minimum distribution if there were investment losses that reduced the balances on which income is determined.

Q 16:129 When would a participant want to name a QTIP trust as beneficiary?

A QTIP trust might be desirable whenever a participant wants the federal estate tax marital deduction, but does not want his or her spouse to receive the retirement plan benefit directly.

Example 1. Bob and Cathy, a married couple, have no children together, but Bob has children from a previous marriage. A QTIP trust can allow Bob to provide for Cathy during Cathy's life, while preserving some of his retirement plan benefit for his children.

Example 2. Annabelle cares very much for her husband, Jim, and wants her retirement plan benefit to provide for Jim if she dies first; but Annabelle believes that Jim is irresponsible in handling money and prefers that a professional trustee manage his financial needs. A QTIP trust can allow Annabelle to provide for Jim without putting all the money in his hands.

Qualified Domestic Trust for an Alien

Q 16:130 How is the marital deduction different when a decedent's spouse is an alien?

Normally, an unlimited deduction is available for property passing to a decedent's surviving spouse. [I.R.C. § 2056] This deduction can apply to all or a portion of a retirement plan benefit to the extent that it becomes payable to the participant's surviving spouse or becomes held under a QTIP trust for the spouse's benefit (see Qs 16:123,-16:124). But if a participant's spouse is an alien, the availability of the marital deduction is severely restricted. These restrictions apply even if the alien spouse resides in the United States. [I.R.C. §§ 2056, 2056A]

Q 16:131 How can a participant preserve the marital deduction when his or her spouse is an alien?

The federal estate tax marital deduction is not available for an alien spouse unless the property passing to the spouse is provided through a qualified domestic trust (QDOT). [I.R.C. § 2056(d)(2)]

Q 16:132 What is a qualified domestic trust?

A *qualified domestic trust (QDOT)* is a trust that holds assets for the benefit of (but not under the control of) a person's spouse during the spouse's life. The trust must restrict distributions during the spouse's life to trust income and hardship distributions, or else pay a special tax on any other distribution. [I.R.C. § 2056A(b)] A QDOT must have at least one trustee who is a U.S. citizen, or a U.S. corporation must be responsible for paying any federal estate tax due from the trust. [I.R.C. § 2056A] Further technical conditions are specified by Treasury regulations. [Treas. Reg. § 20.2056A-1]

Q 16:133 How can a participant obtain QDOT treatment?

It is unlikely that a retirement plan will by its own terms satisfy the conditions for a surviving spouse's benefit to be treated as a QDOT. Therefore, a participant who wants QDOT treatment for his or her spouse's benefit should, with his or her estate-planning lawyer's advice, select an appropriate trustee and create a QDOT. To cause any retirement plan benefit remaining on the participant's death to pass into the QDOT, the participant should change his or her retirement plan beneficiary designation to make the QDOT's trustee the plan beneficiary.

> **Example.** Although a participant should change a beneficiary designation only on his or her expert estate-planning lawyer's advice, the following is a sample beneficiary designation:
>
> *Beneficiary Designation:*
>
> Thomas Tertius, or the duly appointed and then currently serving U.S. trustee of my Qualified Domestic Trust dated February 2, 1991.

The participant and the trustee should be careful to follow any additional requirements particular to QDOT treatment for a retirement plan. [*See, e.g.*, Ltr. Rul. 9713018 (involving a 403(b) arrangement)]

Q 16:134 How can a surviving spouse obtain QDOT treatment?

To preserve the marital deduction for a benefit passing to an alien spouse, the spouse must "transfer" his or her retirement plan distribution to a QDOT before the decedent's estate's federal estate tax return is filed. [I.R.C. § 2056(d)(2)(B)(i)] Of course, a beneficiary cannot assign or transfer a retirement plan distribution. However, if the alien spouse receives a single-sum distribution and pays the proceeds into a QDOT before the estate tax return is filed the distribution might qualify for the marital deduction.

The regulations also provide a special rule for annuity payments, but it is unlikely to be helpful concerning a retirement plan benefit. [Treas. Reg. § 20.2056A-4]

Giving Advice

Q 16:135 May a financial-services representative give advice about beneficiary designations?

A financial-services representative may give practical advice about how to fill in the beneficiary information requested by a plan administrator's form or an application for an IRA that he or she solicits or solicited. However, he or she must not give advice about the legal effect of a beneficiary designation. Further, a nonlawyer must warn a person about the risks of acting without advice. [*See, e.g.*, *In re* Opinion No. 26 of the Committee on Unauthorized Practice, 654 A.2d 1344 (N.J. 1995); *see generally* Restatement (Second) of Torts § 552 (1977)]

Except when done by a properly admitted lawyer, giving legal advice, even for free, is a crime or offense in most states. Even if the nonlawyer explicitly states that he or she is not a lawyer, it is still a crime to give legal advice.

> **Note.** The contributing author asks readers to understand that this description of the law does not reflect his view about what the law ought to be. Rather, he believes that any person should be free to give legal advice (and to bear responsibility for his, her, or its advice).

Unfortunately, many people believe (often incorrectly) that they cannot afford legal advice. Although a financial-services representative should urge a participant to get expert legal advice, it might be impractical to avoid a participant's questions asked in the course of filling out an IRA application. Perhaps it is not unauthorized practice of law to furnish widely known general information that does not involve applying the law to a specific factual situation.

Q 16:136 Is a nonlawyer who gives legal advice liable for damages that result from reliance on his or her incorrect or incomplete advice?

Yes, a nonlawyer is liable if his or her "client" suffered harm because he or she relied on the nonlawyer's inappropriate advice. Courts have not hesitated to impose liability on a nonlawyer for giving incorrect, or even incomplete, advice. Moreover, a nonlawyer is held to at least the same standard of care and expertise as a competent lawyer. [*See, e.g.*, Williams v. Jackson Co., 359 So. 2d 798 (Ala. Civ. App. 1978), *writ denied*, 359 So. 2d 801 (1978); Wright v. Langdon, 274 Ark. 258, 623 S.W.2d 823, 826 (Ark. 1981); Biakanja v. Irving, 49 Cal. 2d 647, 320 P.2d 16 (1958); Banks v. District of Columbia Dep't of Consumer & Regulatory Affairs, 634 A.2d 433 (D.C. 1993); Buscemi v. Intachai, 730 So. 2d 329, 330 (Fla. Dist. Ct. App. 1999), *review denied*, 744 So. 2d 452 (Fla. 1999); Miller v. Whelan, 42 N.E. 59, 63 (Ill. 1895); Torres v. Fiol, 110 Ill. App. 3d 9 (1982); Ford v. Guarantee Abstract & Title Co., 553 P.2d 254, 264 (Kan. 1976); Webb v. Pomeroy, 655 P.2d 465 (Kan. Ct. App. 1982); Busch v. Flangas, 837 P.2d 438, 440 (Nev. 1992); Mezzaluna v. Jersey Mortgage & Title Guar. Co., 162 A. 743, 745 (N.J. 1932); Sandler v. New Jersey Realty Title Ins. Co., 169 A.2d 735, 740–741 (N.J. Super Ct. Law Div. 1961), *rev'd on other grounds*, 178 A.2d 1 (N.J. 1961); Leather v. United States Trust Co. of N.Y., 279 A.D.2d 311; 720 N.Y.S.2d 448; 2001 N.Y. App. Div. LEXIS 154 (2001); Latson v. Eaton, 341 P.2d 247 (Okla. 1959); Jones v. Allstate Ins. Co., 45 P.3d 1068, 1081 (Wash. 2002); Cultum v. Heritage House Realtors, Inc., 694 P.2d 630, 633 (Wash. 1985); Bowers v. Transamerica Title Ins. Co., 675 P.2d 193, 200–201 (Wash. 1983); Tegman v. Accident & Med. Investigations, Inc., 30 P.3d 8, 13 (Wash. Ct. App. 2001); Bishop v. Jefferson Title Co., 28 P.3d 802, 808 (Wash Ct. App. 2001); Hangman Ridge Training Stables, Inc. v. Safeco Title Ins. Co., 652 P.2d 962, 965 (Wash. Ct. App. 1982); Hecomovich v. Nielsen, 518 P.2d 1081, 1085 (Wash. Ct. App. 1974); Burien Motors, Inc. v. Balch, 513 P.2d 582, 586 (Wash. Ct. App. 1974); Andersen v. Northwest Bonded Escrows, Inc., 484 P.2d 488, 491 (Wash. Ct. App. 1971); *see also* McKeown v. First Interstate Bank of Cal., 194 Cal. App. 3d 1225, 240 Cal. Rptr. 127, 1987 Cal. App. LEXIS 2125 (1987); Correll v. Goodfellow, 125 N.W.2d 745 (Iowa 1964); Brown v. Shyne, 242 N.Y. 176 (1926); Mattieligh v. Poe, 57 Wash. 2d 203, 356 P.2d 328, 329 (1960)] Further, a court might treat a nonlawyer's unlicensed practice of law as negligence per se to result in strict liability. [*See generally* Restatement (Second) of Torts § 288A (1965), *accord* Restatement (Third) of Torts: Liability for Physical and Emotional Harm§ 14 (2010)]

> **Practice Pointer.** This duty, even for a nonlawyer, includes the duty to have and use specialist expertise, or to refer one's "client" to an appropriate specialist.

In some circumstances, a nonlawyer is liable if an intended beneficiary or another person suffered harm because the nonlawyer's "client" relied on the nonlawyer's inappropriate advice. [*See, e.g.*, Biakanja v. Irving, 49 Cal. 2d 647, 320 P.2d 16 (1958)]

A nonlawyer plan administrator also will be liable for incorrect or incomplete advice. Although a lawsuit against an ERISA plan's administrator or other fiduciary for negligent misrepresentation or negligent communication is preempted [Griggs v. E.I. DuPont de Nemours & Co., 237 F.3d 371 (4th Cir. 2001); Farr v. U.S. West, 151 F.3d 908 (9th Cir. 1998)], a plan administrator's incorrect statement might be a breach of its fiduciary duty to furnish accurate and non-misleading information. [*See, e.g.*, Griggs v. E.I. DuPont de Nemours & Co., 237 F.3d 371 (4th Cir. 2001)]

Practice Pointer. If a participant expresses a desire to make a beneficiary designation that would provide anything less than all of his or her death benefit to his or her spouse, a practitioner should urge the participant to get the advice of an expert lawyer.

Q 16:137 Can written materials give guidance about beneficiary designations?

Maybe. In Texas, any restriction against the unauthorized practice of law does not preclude "written materials, books, forms, computer software, or similar products if the products clearly and conspicuously state that the products are not a substitute for the advice of an attorney." [Tex. Gov't Code § 81.101(c)]

In other states, it is unclear whether such publications would be so protected. Notwithstanding America's constitutional protections for free speech, at least one court found that mere written publications, without oral communication, was the unauthorized practice of law. [*See, e.g.*, Unauthorized Practice of Law Committee v. Parsons Technology, d/b/a Quicken Family Lawyer, No. 3:97CV-2859H, 1999 WL 47235 (N.D. Tex. Jan. 22, 1999) (before enactment of Tex. Gov't Code § 81.101(c)), *vacated and remanded*, 179 F.3d 956 (5th Cir. 1999)] In the contributing author's view, the court's decision, had it not been vacated, would have been reversed on rehearing, appeal, or review.

Caution. Although some ERISA plan administrators might guess that ERISA preempts state laws, ERISA does not preempt criminal laws, which might include some laws that restrain the unauthorized practice of law. [ERISA § 514(b)(7)]

Q 16:138 Can liability result from a reader's reliance on incorrect information?

Yes, a person who presents information may be liable for damages that result from a reader's reliance on incorrect information. [*See, e.g.*, *In re* Thompson, 574 S.W.2d Thompson, 574 S.W.2d 365, 369 (Mo. 1978) (holding sellers of divorce kits liable to consumers harmed by use of the kits)] In addition to other sources of liability, a person who is or should be aware that a recipient of his or her written or oral communication may rely on it is liable for harm that results because the communication lacks the accuracy, completeness, or other care that would be used by a person who is in the business of presenting that kind of information. [Restatement (Second) of Torts § 552 (1977)]

Q 16:139 Does the lawyer who writes a person's will need to know about his or her beneficiary designation?

Yes. In the early 1980s, Professor John Langbein, an authority on the law of wills, trusts, and estates, observed that many Americans die with several "wills"—maybe one that was written in a lawyer's office, and a dozen others that were filled out on standard forms. For most people, those forms—beneficiary designations—dispose of far more money and property than the will does. [John Langbein, The Nonprobate Revolution and the Future of the Law of Succession," 97 Harv. L. Rev. 1108 (Mar. 1984)] Since then, even more forms of money, property, and rights can be disposed of using nonprobate transfers.

Making a beneficiary designation under a retirement plan is an important part of estate planning. Although a retirement plan benefit will not pass by a will (see Q 16:2), a beneficiary designation affects a person's overall estate plan. A participant should make sure his or her lawyer knows the beneficiary designation he or she made under every retirement plan, including a retirement plan, and should ask for the lawyer's advice about whether to consider changing any beneficiary designation.

Q 16:140 May a lawyer give advice about a beneficiary designation?

Yes. A lawyer may render advice about law as long as he or she writes or speaks his or her advice while present in a state in which he or she is admitted to practice law (even if the advised person is domiciled in a state in which the lawyer is not admitted to practice law). [*See, e.g.*, Estate of Condon, 64 Cal. Rptr. 2d 789 (1997)] In addition, a lawyer may render advice while in a state in which he or she is not admitted if the advice is reasonably related to the lawyer's proper practice in a state in which he or she is admitted. [*See generally* Restatement (Third) Law Governing Lawyers § 3(3) (2001); Model Rules of Professional Conduct, Rule 5.5(c)(4) (ABA 2011)] Also, a lawyer may render advice while in a state in which he or she is not admitted if the lawyer's practice is permitted under federal law. [*See, e.g.*, The Florida Bar re Advisory Opinion—Nonlawyer Preparation of Pension Plans, 571 So. 2d 430 (1990); *see generally* Model Rules of Professional Conduct, Rule 5.5(d)(2) (ABA 2011)]

Common Mistakes

Q 16:141 What are some of the common mistakes people make with beneficiary designations?

Because people enroll in a retirement plan quickly, they sometimes make beneficiary designations that are less than carefully considered. Consider the following explanation of some common mistakes.

1. *Failing to coordinate a beneficiary designation's provisions with those made in other non-probate designations, trusts, and a will.* Although a beneficiary designation's provisions need not be the same as those of a participant's will or other dispositions, if they are different the maker

should understand why he or she has made different provisions and whether they are likely to add up to a combined result that he or she wants.

2. *Failing to consider whether a beneficiary designation is consistent with tax-oriented planning.* A participant might have had a lawyer's advice about how to leave his or her estate, including both probate and non-probate property, to achieve a desired tax outcome. Making a beneficiary designation without counting its effect on the maker's tax-oriented plan could result in an unanticipated tax.
3. *Making a beneficiary designation that a payer will refuse to implement.* For example, a person might try to make a beneficiary designation that refers to terms that one may use in a will or trust but are precluded by his or her retirement plan. A payer's interpretation of the beneficiary designation without the offending terms might result in a disposition quite different from what the participant would have wanted.
4. *Trying to name beneficiaries by writing all my children, equally or describing a class.* Whenever a beneficiary designation refers to information not in a custodian's or insurer's records, a payer may decide that the participant did not make a beneficiary designation, or might allow a claimant an opportunity to name every person in the class and prove that there are no others. Because it is difficult to prove the nonexistence of an unidentified person, even the opportunity to correct such a beneficiary designation would result in significant frustration and delay.
5. *Neglecting to use a beneficiary's Social Security number or individual Taxpayer Identification Number, especially for a daughter.*

   Example. Gary Smith named his three children—Reed Smith, Catherine Smith, and Alice Smith—as his beneficiaries, and used only their names. By the time of Gary's death many years later, Reed and Alice had married. Reed had no special difficulty claiming his benefit. But Alice Carpenter was required to submit proof that she is the same person as Alice Smith. Because an identifying number assigned by the Social Security Administration or IRS is unique, this burden could have been avoided had Gary put Alice's number on the beneficiary designation form.

   Caution. Some participants will want to balance this use of a clear identifier against concerns about a potential for identity theft.
6. *Naming a minor as a beneficiary without considering who the minor's guardian would be.* For example, a divorced person might not want to name his or her young child as a beneficiary if doing so might have the effect of putting money in the hands of the child's other parent—the participant's former spouse (see Q 16:22). Instead, a participant might name a suitable trustee or custodian.
7. *Naming a son or daughter as a beneficiary without considering his or her prudence.*

   Example. Ralph names his daughter, Britney, as beneficiary of Ralph's custodial account. When Ralph dies, Britney is 19 years old, and no longer is a minor under applicable law. Although Britney should pay her sophomore year's $25,000 tuition at the Newark College of Fashion Arts, Britney buys a new car, then neglects to pay the second insurance premium. When the uninsured car is stolen, Britney has nothing left from her father's gift. A participant who wants to benefit his or her son or daughter might consider that person's maturity, and consider whether it could help to choose a suitable trustee to manage the benefit.

A participant who wants to benefit his or her son or daughter might consider that person's maturity, and consider whether it could help to choose a suitable trustee to manage the benefit.

8. *Forgetting to give a copy of the beneficiary designation to the beneficiary.* A retirement plan administrator or IRA custodian or insurer has no duty to contact a participant's beneficiaries to invite them to submit a claim. Indeed, many financial-services providers particularly avoid doing so because such a communication might invite fraudulent claims. A beneficiary might not claim a benefit if he or she is unaware that he or she is a beneficiary. Likewise, a beneficiary might face difficulty in claiming a benefit if he or she does not know the name of the retirement plan administrator or IRA custodian or insurer.
9. *Naming one's estate as his or her beneficiary.* Some people think that naming theirs estate as beneficiary is a way to avoid inconsistency in their estate plan. Although such a beneficiary designation might fulfill a goal of avoiding inconsistency, it bears some disadvantages. For example, amounts paid or payable to an executor or personal representative for the estate are available to a decedent's creditors. And a benefit's "run" through an estate might, because of accounting and timing differences, result in income taxes greater than the income tax that would result if the recipient received the benefit directly. [I.R.C. §§ 1, 72, 641–691]
10. *Failing to make a beneficiary designation.* Although this observation might appear some what inconsistent with some just described, another common mistake is failing to make a beneficiary designation. A person who has difficulty making up his or her mind about a beneficiary designation is unlikely to have read a retirement plan carefully enough to understand the effect of its "default" provision. Although a young person might assume that death is far away, the point of a beneficiary designation is to provide for the possibility of death.

    Practice Pointer. A planner might suggest that the risks of failing to make a beneficiary designation outweigh the risks of a less than perfectly considered beneficiary designation. In those circumstances, a planner might remind a participant that a typical retirement plan allows a participant to change his or her beneficiary designation at anytime.
11. *Forgetting to review one's beneficiary designation.* A participant should review his or her beneficiary designations periodically, and whenever there is a significant change in his or her family or wealth.

Example. Nancy named her husband, Larry, as her beneficiary under a retirement plan. Although Nancy wanted to make sure that her children would be provided for, she trusted her husband to take care of the whole family. Nancy and Larry divorced, and Nancy neglected to change her beneficiary designation. After Nancy's death, Larry submits his claim to the retirement plan custodian. The custodian follows the retirement plan's terms, which do not revoke a beneficiary designation because of a participant's divorce. The custodian pays Larry, and he spends the money without considering any needs of Nancy's children.

The examples and common mistakes explained previously are only a few of the many ways a participant might make an unwise beneficiary designation. A participant should use his or her valuable right to name a beneficiary, and use that right with care.

Chapter 17

Correction Programs

Christine P. Roberts
Mullen & Henzell L.L.P.

This chapter examines the Internal Revenue Service's (IRS's) Employee Plans Compliance Resolution System (EPCRS) and the Department of Labor's (DOL's) Voluntary Fiduciary Correction Program (VFCP). The EPCRS is a comprehensive system of integrated correction programs that plan sponsors may use to correct eligible failures and to continue providing their employees with retirement benefits on a tax-favored basis. The VFCP allows certain persons to avoid potential civil actions and penalties under the Employee Retirement Income Security Act of 1974 (ERISA).

The 2008 streamlined submission procedures for the IRS correction of SEP, SARSEP, and SIMPLE plans, which follow a mostly "check the box" approach, are discussed in this chapter. The Schedules 3 and 4 from Appendix F of Revenue Procedure 2008-50 [2008-35 I.R.B. 464] are used in connection with submissions under the streamlined application procedure. These schedules can be found at: *http://www.irs.gov/pub/irs-tege/vc_appendix_f_schedule_3.pdf* and *http://www.irs.gov/pub/irs-tege/vc_appendix_f_schedule_4.pdf* (visited on Aug. 21, 2012). EPCRS provisions that expand income and excise taxes that the IRS will exercise discretion not to pursue are also discussed.

IRS Correction Program

Q 17:1 Has the IRS provided correction methods for SEPs?

Yes. On June 5, 2003, the IRS issued Revenue Procedure 2003-44 [2003-25 I.R.B. 151], the 2003 version of the correction procedures, which replaced Revenue Procedure 2002-47. [2002-29 I.R.B. 133] Revenue Procedure 2003-44 significantly streamlined the EPCRS program and opened it for the first time to SEPs and SIMPLEs. The EPCRS was first introduced by the IRS in 1998 and has been updated from time to time to reflect more failures and corrections that may be used in plans with such failures. It permits plan sponsors to correct technical and administrative problems with their plans and thereby retain the tax-favored status of their plans.

The EPCRS has three components:

- *Self-Correction Program (SCP):* Employers and/or plan administrators identify and correct problems without the involvement of the IRS.
- *Voluntary Correction Program (VCP):* Employers and/or plan administrators submit their proposed or completed corrections to the IRS for IRS approval. Once approved, employers have written assurance that the method of correction is approved by the IRS.
- *Audit Closing Agreement Program (CAP):* Employers and/or plan administrators correct qualification errors identified on audit and pay a sanction based on the nature, extent, and severity of the failure.

On May 30, 2006, Revenue Procedure 2006-27 [2006-22 I.R.B. 945] modified and superseded Revenue Procedure 2003-44 (see Q 17:3) and was generally effective September 1, 2006. This version of EPCRS did not modify SEP or SIMPLE correction procedures first set forth in Revenue Procedure 2003-44, however.

Revenue Procedure 2006-27 was modified and superseded on September 2, 2008 by Revenue Procedure 2008-50 [2008-35 I.R.B. 464]. Revenue Procedure 2008-50 does not significantly modify or add to correction procedures for SEP, SIMPLE and SEP-IRA plans but does include streamlined VCP application procedures for these types of plans. Revenue Procedure 2008-50 took effect on January 1, 2009 but plan sponsors were permitted to apply its provisions on or after September 2, 2008.

The IRS has also posted on its website documents titled the "SEP Plan Fix-It Guide," the "SIMPLE IRA Fix-It Guide," and the "SARSEP Fix-It Guide," which include grids of potential mistakes, and recommend ways to identify, correct (consistent with Revenue Procedure 2006-27) and avoid such mistakes in the future, along with detailed commentary on same. Links to the Fix-It Guides are available at *http://www.irs.gov/retirement/sponsor/article/0,,id=181908,00.html* (visited on Aug. 21, 2012). Also helpful are "Check-Up" checklists for SIMPLE IRS, SEP and SARSEP arrangements that cover basic operational requirements for these types of plans. Each question on the Check-Up checklist corresponds to correction guidance in the Fix-It Guides, so employers can perform a quick self-audit by filling out the appropriate Check-Up checklist and following instructions in the Fix-It Guides on any checklist item with which it is not in compliance. The Check-Up checklists are available at: *http://www.irs.gov/retirement/article/0,,id=117534,00.html* (visited on Aug. 21, 2012).

Q 17:2 What tax relief is available to successful participants in EPCRS?

Generally speaking, successful completion of the appropriate procedures under EPCRS relieves the participant plan, and its sponsoring employer, from the adverse tax consequences that would occur if one or more "compliance qualification failures" were instead discovered in the course of an audit. A *compliance qualification failure* is any failure that adversely affects the tax-sanctioned status of a qualified plan (i.e., one that satisfies the requirements of Code Section 401(a)), a Section 403(b) plan, a SEP, or a SIMPLE IRA of an employer. EPCRS collectively refers to all of these types of plan—qualified plans, 403(b) plans, and SEP and SIMPLE IRAs—as "retirement plans," and specifically states that successful completion of EPCRS correction procedures will result in a plan being treated as satisfying qualification requirements of the Code as well as qualification requirements for purposes of FICA and FUTA taxes. [*See* Rev. Proc. 2008-50, §§ 3.01, 5.01(2), 2008-35 I.R.B. 464] The four types of compliance qualification failures under EPCRS are described in Q 17:8. Additionally, the Internal Revenue Manual provides in relevant part that a SEP (or SARSEP) that is eligible for EPCRS and that corrects a failure to satisfy the requirements of Code Section 408(k) in accordance with the program will be treated as not failing to meet Code Section 408(k). [IRM § 4.72.17.11 (rev. Sept. 12, 2006)]

Q 17:3 What other changes were made to the EPCRS procedures?

Changes made to the EPCRS in 2003 included the following:

1. Consolidated all of the prior voluntary correction programs into a single program, the EPCRS (see Q 17:6), which eliminates confusion over deciding which program was most appropriate for the employer. The prior terminology stood for the following correction programs (now consolidated into the VCP):

   VCO – Voluntary Correction of Operational Failures

   VCP – Voluntary Correction With Service Approval

   VCT – Voluntary Correction of Tax-Sheltered Annuity Failures

   VCSEP – Voluntary Correction for SEPs
2. Simplified (and reduced) and provided one fixed fee schedule for all voluntary submissions to promote consistency.
3. Simplified and reduced the amount of information that an employer or administrator must send along with the voluntary submission, thereby reducing the paperwork burden on the employer.

4. Streamlined the submission process for third-party administrators and other service providers that submit on behalf of their client's retirement plans and permitted numerous plans to be submitted in a single submission.
5. Expanded EPCRS to cover SIMPLE IRA failures. The Revenue Procedure also covers to a certain extent the reporting requirements for failures under both SEP plans and SIMPLE IRA plans (see Q 17:4).

A new Appendix D was added to provide sample formats for VCP submissions for qualified plans to make it easier for employers to prepare voluntary submissions.

Changes made to the EPCRS in 2006 include the following:

1. Ability under VCP to obtain relief from the excise taxes under Code Section 4972, regarding nondeductible contributions, and Code Section 4979, relating to the 10 percent tax on excess elective contributions (see Q 12:31).
2. Lowered the VCP fee for SEPs and SIMPLE IRA plans from $500 to $250. However, in appropriate circumstances, the IRS reserves the right to impose the normal fee schedule for qualified plans, including the special fees for egregious or intentional failures.
3. Various procedural enhancements making remedial actions easier to implement and less expensive.
4. A submission assembly procedure is provided.
5. Many changes were made in the qualified plan area regarding loans (excess loans, failures to repay, and loan defaults), the exclusion of eligible employees, failure to obtain spousal consent to a distribution, where required, and plan amendments.
6. Revision of corrective contribution requirements for 401(k) plans; when participants are improperly excluded from salary deferral plans, sponsors need only contribute an amount equal to the "missed deferral opportunity," (which is equal to 50 percent of the missed deferral, which may be determined by reference to average deferral percentage for the applicable class of employees) rather than the full average deferral percentage, on behalf of such employees.
7. Availability of EPRCS was extended on a limited basis to terminated plans and orphan plans, which are plans whose sponsor no longer exists, cannot be located, or has abandoned the plan. [Rev. Proc. 2006-27, §§ 4.08, 4.09; 5.06(1), 2006-22 I.R.B. 945] Note, however, that the term *orphan plan* does not include any plan terminated pursuant to DOL regulations governing the termination of abandoned individual account plans.
8. Prohibition on using SCP to correct any operational failure that is directly or indirectly related to an abusive tax avoidance transaction (ATAT), defined as any transaction listed under Treasury Regulations § 1.6011-4(b)(2) and any other transaction identified as an abusive transaction on the IRS Web site titled "EP Abusive Tax Transactions" available at

http://www.irs.gov/retirement/article/0,,id=118821,00.html (visited on Aug. 21, 2012). (VCP or Audit CAP remains available in such instances, depending on the extent to which the qualification failure relates to the ATAT.)

[Rev. Proc. 2006-27, § 2.01, 2006-22 I.R.B. 945]

In addition, the Pension Protection Act of 2006 (PPA) clarified that the Secretary of the Treasury has the full authority to establish and implement EPCRS (or any successor program) and any other employee plans' correction policies, including the authority to waive income, excise, or other taxes to ensure that any tax, penalty, or sanction is not excessive and bears a reasonable relationship to the nature, extent, and severity of the failure. This provision became effective on August 17, 2006. [PPA § 1101]

In addition to the streamlined VCP application procedures for SEPs, SIMPLEs, and SEP-IRAS, changes made to the EPCRS in 2008 include the following:

1. *Revised correction for failure to implement deferral election.* In cases where an employee deferral election has been made but not timely implemented, Revenue Procedure 2008-50 specifies that the "missed deferral opportunity" cost should be equal to 50 percent of the deferral percentage the affected participant actually elected rather than based on the ADP of the participant's compensation grouping.
2. *Expansion of period to complete substantial self-correction.* The new Revenue Procedure expands from 90 to 120 days the "tail" period in which a plan sponsor may complete self-correction of an Operational Failure such that it will be deemed "substantially completed" during the two-year self-correction period and therefore no longer subject to discovery on audit.
3. *Deferral election errors/exclusions.* Revenue Procedure 2008-50 expands corrections for failure to include eligible employees to situations involving catch-up, after-tax and designated Roth contributions. In addition Appendix B of Revenue Procedure 2008-50 provides new illustrations for correcting inadvertent exclusions of eligible employees and failures to implement participants' deferral elections.
4. *Correction of failures relating to catch-up contributions.* Revenue Procedure 2008-50 describes a method to correct failures relating to catch-up contributions for eligible employees age 50 and older. The correction method is for the employer to make a qualified nonelective contribution (QNC) equal to 50 percent of the "missed deferral," with the missed deferral defined as one-half of the catch-up contribution limit for the affected plan year.
5. *Penalty tax relief on excess IRA contributions.* Revenue Procedure 2008-50 provides relief from the 6 percent penalty tax applicable under Code Section 4975 on excess contributions to an IRA resulting from amounts improperly distributed from a plan and rolled to an IRA, provided that the affected participant removes the improperly rolled over amounts.

6. *Correction of plan loan errors.* Revenue Procedure 2008-50 reduces the compliance fee for correction of certain loan violations to half the normal fee and makes other changes expanding VCP procedures for correction of plan loan failures.
7. *Use of VFCP Online Calculator.* Since Revenue Procedure 2006-27, plan sponsors have been allowed to use a "reasonable interest rate" on corrective contributions when it is not possible to make precise calculations or reasonable estimates of actual returns. Revenue Procedure 2008-50 adds for the first time that use of the DOL's Voluntary Fiduciary Correction Program Online Calculator (VFCP Online Calculator) is deemed to be a reasonable interest rate for these purposes. The VFCP Online Calculator is available at *http://askebsa.dol.gov/VFCPCalculator/WebCalculator.aspx* (visited on Aug. 21, 2012). Revenue Procedure 2008-50 does not allow use of the VFCP Online Calculator as a first resort when actual returns can otherwise be calculated or estimated.
8. *Updated Section 415 corrections.* The new program updates the definition of "Excess Amounts" and updates correction methods to accord with final regulations under Code § 415.
9. *Increased* de minimis *distribution amount.* Revenue Procedure 2008-50 increases, from $50 to $75, the definition of a *de minimis* corrective distribution that need not be made provided that the processing costs meet or exceed the *de minimis* amount.
10. *Right to deny program availability.* In Revenue Procedure 2008-50 the Service states that in particular cases it may decline to make one or more correction programs available under EPCRS "in the interest of sound tax administration."
11. *Right to address newly discovered significant failures in Audit CAP.* Revenue Procedure 2008-50 provides that if the IRS, while processing a VCP submission, discovers a failure that is not addressed in the VCP submission and determines that the failure is significant, the IRS retains the right to examine all aspects of the plan and move the plan into Audit CAP and potentially impose the higher sanctions available there. This makes it all the more important to carefully review all aspects of plan operation and documentation before submitting a VCP application.

As this chapter went to press the IRS was in the process of updating Revenue Procedure 2008-50 to include correction of failures arising under final Section 403(b) regulations which went into effect January 1, 2009. Until such time, however, the IRS has stated that VCP corrections are not available for certain Section 403(b) failures and applications based on such failures would be rejected. The IRS specifically referenced instances in which (a) the plan's written program did not satisfy final Section 403(b) regulations, or Code Section 403(b), (b) the plan failed to adopt a written document by December 31, 2009, or (c) the plan was not operated in accordance with its written terms.

Other pending developments at the time of publication include a proposed prototype approval program for Section 403(b) plans. [*See* Rev. Proc. 2007-71 , 2007-51 I.R.B. 1184 and Ann. 2009-34, 2009-18 I.R.B. 916]

Q 17:4 When did the IRS include SIMPLE IRA plan corrections under the EPCRS?

EPCRS was expanded to apply to SIMPLE IRA plans beginning with Revenue Procedure 2003-44, which was generally effective on October 1, 2003, though sponsors were permitted to apply its provisions after June 4, 2003. The IRS anticipated adding correction procedures for "deemed IRAs" and governmental 457(b) plans in the next version of the Revenue Procedure; however, they do not appear in Revenue Procedure 2008-50, other than in Appendix F, Schedule 1, which permits correction of a failure to timely amend a plan to include deemed IRA contributions. Until added to the program, the IRS will accept submissions outside of the EPCRS on failures in governmental 457(b) plans or "deemed IRAs" on a provisional basis. No correction program is currently available for nongovernmental 457(b) plans.

Q 17:5 What are the general principles on which the EPCRS for SEPs and SIMPLE IRAs is based?

The EPCRS for SEPs and SIMPLE IRAs is based on the following general principles:

1. Employers maintaining a 403(b) plans, SEP or SIMPLE IRA should be encouraged to establish administrative practices and procedures that ensure that plans are operated in accordance with the tax qualification requirements.
2. Employers maintaining a SEP or SIMPLE IRA must have an IRS "favorable letter" on the plan.
3. Employers should make voluntary and timely correction of any plan qualification failures, whether involving discrimination in favor of highly compensated employees (HCEs), plan operations, or the terms of the plan document. Timely and efficient correction protects participating employees by providing them with their expected retirement benefits, including favorable tax treatment.
4. Voluntary compliance is promoted by providing for limited fees for voluntary corrections approved by the IRS, thereby reducing employers' uncertainty regarding their potential liability.
5. Taxpayers should be able to rely on the availability of the EPCRS in taking corrective actions to maintain the qualified status of their SEPs under Code Section 408(k), and SIMPLE IRAs under Code Section 408(p).

[Rev. Proc. 2008-50, § 1.02, 2008-35 I.R.B. 464]

Q 17:6 What types of compliance programs exist under the EPCRS?

Depending on the nature and severity of the specific violation, one of three programs may be available to bring a plan into compliance with the Code. The three types of correction programs under the EPCRS are

1. *Self-correction (SCP).* A plan sponsor (generally an employer) that has established compliance practices and procedures may, at any time without paying any fee or sanction, correct insignificant operational failures under a SEP or a SIMPLE IRA plan, provided the SEP or SIMPLE IRA plan is established and maintained on a document approved by the IRS. SCP is only available to correct insignificant operational failures in a SEP or SIMPLE IRA plan (see Q 17:18). In addition, eligibility failures may not be corrected under SCP. [Rev. Proc. 2008-50, §§ 4.01, 6.03, App. F, Schedules 3(A) and 4(A), 2008-35 I.R.B. 464] For example, if an employer maintaining a SARSEP had more than 25 eligible employees in the prior year and did not therefore qualify to offer a salary reduction feature for the current year. SCP is not available to correct this failure. Under VCP, the assets of such plan are to remain in the SEP IRAs of participating employees, and a special fee of 10 percent may apply. [Rev. Proc. 2008-50, § 6.03(1), App. F, Schedule 3(A), 2008-35 I.R.B. 464]
2. *Voluntary correction with IRS approval (VCP)*. A plan sponsor, at any time before audit, may pay a limited fee and receive the IRS's approval for correction of a SEP or SIMPLE IRA plan. Under VCP, there are special procedures for anonymous submissions and group submissions. VCP is available to correct egregious failures. [Rev. Proc. 2008-50, § 4.11, 2008-35 I.R.B. 464]
3. *Correction on audit (Audit CAP)*. If a failure (other than a failure corrected through SCP or VCP) is identified on audit, the plan sponsor may correct the failure and pay a sanction. The sanction imposed will bear a reasonable relationship to the nature, extent, and severity of the failure, taking into account the extent to which correction occurred before audit. [Rev. Proc. 2008-50, § 1.03, 2008-35 I.R.B. 464]

If the plan or plan sponsor is under examination, VCP is not available, and SCP is only available as follows: while the plan or plan sponsor is under examination, insignificant operational failures can be corrected under SCP; if correction of significant operational failures has been completed or substantially completed before the plan or plan sponsor is under examination, correction may be completed under SCP. [Rev. Proc. 2008-50, §§ 5.07, 9.02, 2008-35 I.R.B. 464] An error has been "substantially completed" as long as correction is completed within the (usually two-year) correction period or within 120 days after the end of the applicable correction period. [Rev. Proc. 2008-50, Sec. 9.04, 2008-35 I.R.B. 464]

SCP, VCP, and Audit CAP are not available for qualification failures relating to the diversion or misuse of plan assets (see Q 17:29 *et seq.*). SCP is not available to correct egregious failures. For example, an employer that has consistently or intentionally covered only HCEs under a plan, or has made contributions for the HCEs over the Section 415 limit, has committed an egregious failure. Egregious failures can be corrected under VCP. [Rev. Proc. 2008-50, §§ 4.11, 2008-35 I.R.B. 464] As mentioned previously, SCP is not available to correct an operational failure related to an abusive tax avoidance transaction, but the other EPCRS programs *may* be available.

SEPs and SIMPLE IRAs are eligible to submit corrections under SCP, VCP, and Audit CAP. SCP is not available to correct egregious failures, as defined in § 4.11 of Revenue Procedure 2008-50. [2008-35 I.R.B. 464]

Q 17:7 What correction method must an employer use to correct a SEP or SIMPLE IRA failure using the EPCRS?

Generally, the correction used for a SEP or SIMPLE IRA plan may be (1) "similar" to the correction method required for a qualified plan or 403(b) plan with a similar qualification failure, or (2) a specific correction method listed for SEP or SIMPLE plans.

Under VCP, if a correction method that applies to a qualified plan is not feasible for a SEP plan, or the IRS determines such method is not feasible, the IRS may provide a different correction method.

[Rev. Proc. 2008-50, § 6.10(1)-(2), 2008-35 I.R.B. 464]

The Revenue Procedure lists the following failures as being included in failures that may need a different correction (and for which a special correction fee may apply):

1. Failures relating to the annual limit on salary deferrals (Code Section 402(g)), the limit on "annual additions" (Code Section 415), or the annual limit on compensation (Code Section 401(a)(17));
2. Failures relating to deferral percentages;
3. Discontinuance of contributions to a SARSEP or SIMPLE IRA plan; and
4. Retention of "excess amounts" for situations where there was no violation of a statutory limitation with respect to a SEP or SIMPLE IRA Plan. [Rev. Proc. 2008-50, § 6.10(2), 2008-35 I.R.B. 464]

Correction through plan amendment is permitted under the EPCRS under circumstances primarily relevant to qualified plans.

Q 17:8 What are the types of failures that may occur?

Generally, four types of qualification failures exist:

1. Plan document failures,
2. Operational failures,
3. Demographic failures, and
4. Employer eligibility failures (SCP not available).

With specific respect to SEPs and SARSEPs, the following qualification failures are outlined in the Revenue Procedure:

1. Employer eligibility failure (SARSEPs only), further divided into:
    a. Failure to satisfy the 50 percent eligible employee election requirement for SARSEPs,
    b. Failure to satisfy the 25-employee limitation for SARSEPs; or
    c. Adoption of a SARSEP after December 31, 1996
2. Failure to satisfy the deferral percentage test (SARSEPs only)
3. Failure to make required employer contributions (SEPs or SARSEPs)
4. Failure to provide eligible employees with the opportunity to make elective deferrals (SARSEPs only)
5. Excess amounts contributed, including, for SARSEPs only, contributions in excess of 25 percent of compensation or the applicable limit under Code § 402(g).

[Rev. Proc. 2008-50, §§ 6.10(3), 6.10(4), App. F, Schedule 3(A), 2008-35 I.R.B. 464]

The IRS also notes the following common SARSEP errors in its "Check-Up" Checklist:

1. Failure to make minimum top-heavy contributions for eligible non-key employees
2. Failure to timely deposit employee elective deferrals (this is discussed in more detail under the section of the chapter on the DOL's "Voluntary Fiduciary Compliance Program.")

With specific respect to SIMPLE IRA plans, the following qualification failures are outlined in the Revenue Procedure:

1. Employer eligibility failure, further divided into:
    a. Employer had more than 100 employees;
    b. Employer maintained a qualified plan concurrently with SIMPLE IRA
2. Failure to make required employer contributions (whether matching contributions or the 2 percent employer nonelective contribution, where elected)
3. Failure to provide eligible employees with the opportunity to make elective deferrals
4. Contribution of excess amounts.

[Rev. Proc. 2008-50, §§ 6.10(3), 6.10(4), App. F, Schedule 4(A), 2008-35 I.R.B. 464]

The IRS also notes the following common SIMPLE IRA errors in its "Check-Up" Checklist:

1. Late deposit of salary deferral payments to IRA accounts (see Q 17:37).

2. Failure to meet plan eligibility requirements by not including employees who are eligible (i.e., have earned $5,000 or more during the year), or by including employees who are not yet eligible; and
3. Failure to follow the plan's definition of compensation for purposes of deferrals and allocations;
4. Failure to make contributions on behalf of employees who terminated during the plan year.

Operational SEP and SIMPLE IRA failures corrected under SCP are only available for insignificant failures.

Employer eligibility failures may also be corrected under VCP. Employers may not use a self-correction program for eligibility failures. The IRS has provided guidance on correcting compensation errors (including inclusion, or exclusion, of items in the plan's definition of compensation) at http://www.irs.gov/retirement/article/0,,id = 244236,00.html.

Q 17:9 What requirements must an employer meet to be eligible for the EPCRS?

The requirements differ depending on the type of program under EPCRS:

1. Generally, the plan or employer cannot be under IRS examination. If the employer is under IRS examination, VCP is not available. Under limited circumstances, the error may be corrected under SCP. Audit CAP is, by definition, a consequence of an audit.
2. The plan or employer must not have been party to an ATAT. ATATs disqualify a plan or employer from the SCP component of EPCRS, although VCP or Audit CAP may be available depending on the extent to which the operational failure is directly or indirectly related to the ATAT. [Rev. Proc. 2008-50, § 4.13, 2008-35 I.R.B. 464]
3. Additional requirements apply under SCP:
   (a) The plan must have a favorable letter. SCP (with respect to significant operational failures) is available only if the plan has a favorable opinion, notification, or determination letter from the IRS. A favorable letter is not required in order to participate in VCP but if available should be provided with the application. (See Q 17:11 for what comprises a "favorable letter" for SEP or SIMPLE IRAs.).
   (b) Practices and procedures must be in place. The IRS has been consistent over the past few years in suggesting and requiring for SCP purposes that employers have some sort of practices and procedures in place for qualified plans and 403(b) plans. The practices and procedures must be generally designed to promote and facilitate overall compliance with the applicable IRS requirements. The IRS has stated that checklists, as well as a formal procedural manual, are acceptable. A plan document alone does not satisfy this requirement. Most importantly, these procedures must have been in place and routinely followed. Any operational failure that occurs must occur

through an oversight or mistake in applying the procedures, not because there were no procedures or because the employer ignored the procedures. It is also acceptable if the procedures that were in place, while reasonable, were not sufficient to prevent the failure from happening. [Rev. Proc. 2008-50, § 4.04, 2008-35 I.R.B. 464]

Q 17:10 What is an excess amount for purposes of the EPCRS?

For purposes of the EPCRS, *excess amount* means a qualification failure due to a contribution, allocation, or similar credit that is made on behalf of a participant or beneficiary to a plan in excess of the maximum amount permitted to be contributed, allocated, or credited on behalf of the participant or beneficiary under the terms of the plan, or that exceeds a limitation on contributions or allocations provided in the Code or regulations. Excess amounts include:

1. An overpayment,
2. An excess allocation, including:
   a. An elective deferral returned to satisfy Code Section 415,
   b. An elective deferral that is distributed to satisfy Code Section 401(a)(17) (the compensation limit),
3. An elective deferral in excess of the Code Section 402(g) limit,
4. An amount contributed on behalf of an employee that is in excess of the employee's SEP benefit,
5. An excess contribution that is distributed to satisfy the SARSEP deferral percentage test under Code Section 408(k)(6)(A)(iii), or
6. Any similar amount required to be distributed in order to maintain plan qualification.

[Rev. Proc. 2008-50, §§ 5.01(3), 6.10(5), 12.05(2), 2008-35 I.R.B. 464]

Of these types of Excess Amounts, Revenue Procedure 2008-50 specifies that "Excess Amount" does not include a contribution, allocation or other credit that is made pursuant to a correction method made under EPCRS for a different qualification failure than the one leading to the Excess Amount. [Rev. Proc. 2008-50, § 5.01(3)(a), 2008-35 I.R.B. 464]

Q 17:11 What is a favorable letter in the case of a SEP or SIMPLE IRA?

In the case of a SEP, the term *favorable letter* means

1. A valid model Form 5305-SEP or 5305A-SEP adopted by an employer in accordance with the form's instructions, or
2. A current favorable opinion letter for a plan sponsor that has adopted a prototype SEP that has been amended pursuant to Revenue Procedure 2002-10.

In the case of a SIMPLE IRA, the term *favorable letter* means

1. A valid model Form 5305-SIMPLE or 5304-SIMPLE adopted by an employer in accordance with the form's instructions, or
2. A current favorable opinion letter for a plan sponsor that has adopted a prototype SIMPLE plan that has been amended pursuant to Revenue Procedure 2002-10.

[Rev. Proc. 2008-50, §§ 4.03, 5.01(4), 2008-35 I.R.B. 464]

Revenue Procedure 2008-50 makes clear that model IRS forms or prototype documents constitute a "favorable letter" only if they have been updated to comply with applicable provisions of the Economic Growth & Tax Relief Reconciliation Act of 2001 (EGTRRA). [Rev. Proc. 2008-50, §§ 4.03, 5.01(4), 2008-35 I.R.B. 464] The most current versions of Form 5304-SIMPLE and Form 5305-SIMPLE are dated March 2012.

Q 17:12 What is an *overpayment* under a SEP or SIMPLE IRA?

Revenue Procedure 2008-50 generally defines an overpayment as a qualification failure due to a payment being made to a participant or beneficiary that exceeds the amount payable under the terms of the plan or that exceeds a limitation provided in the Code or regulations. In the specific context of SEP or SIMPLE IRAs, an overpayment is a contribution to an employee or beneficiary that exceeds the employee's or beneficiary's benefit under the terms of the SEP or SIMPLE IRA because of a failure to comply with the compensation limit under Code Section 401(a)(17) or the annual additions limit of the lesser of 25 percent of the participant's taxable compensation or $50,000 ($55,500 with catch-up contribution) under Code Section 415 for 2012 or a payment to a SIMPLE IRA in excess of the employer's contribution maximum. An overpayment generally does not include a distribution of an excess amount (see Q 5:56). [Rev. Proc. 2008-50, §§ 5.01(3)(c), 6.10(5), 12.05(2), 2008-35 I.R.B. 464]

Q 17:13 For how many years must an employer correct a qualification failure after one is discovered?

A qualification failure must be corrected for all taxable years for which adequate data exist, whether or not the year is closed. The correction must generally be a full correction for all years with respect to participants and beneficiaries and should restore current and former participants and beneficiaries and/or the plan to the position of the participants, the beneficiaries, and/or the plan that would have been in if the violation had not occurred. [Rev. Proc. 2008-50, § 6.02(5), 2008-35 I.R.B. 464]

Q 17:14 What is a *reasonable correction method*?

A *reasonable correction method* is a correction method that meets the following requirements:

1. It is listed under the VCP corrections in the Revenue Procedure. (These correction methods are deemed to be reasonable; otherwise reasonableness is determined based on factors 2 through 5, below.)
2. It resembles a method already provided for in the Code and regulations or other guidance for a similar situation. For example, the correction methods for defined contribution plans under Code Section 415 could be used for correcting Section 415 defects, and the correction methods under the Section 402(g) regulations could be used to correct excess elective deferrals.

   Note. Revenue Procedure 2008-50 requires only the replacement of the "missed deferral opportunity" cost when employees improperly are excluded from making salary deferral contributions under a Section 401(k) or 403(b) plan, or have not been permitted to make the catch-up contribution available on and after reaching age 50.
3. It provides benefits to non-highly compensated employees (NHCEs) if it is correcting a nondiscrimination failure. For example, if a plan fails the deferral percentage test, distributions should not be made to HCEs; instead, additional employer contributions should be made to NHCEs.
4. If possible, it keeps the assets in the plan, except when a statute or other guidance provides for distribution to participants and/or the employer.
5. It does not violate another specific qualification requirement such as Code §§ 415, 401(a)(4), 411(d)(6), 408(k), or 408(p).
6. The correction method has been authorized by another government agency, such as the Department of Labor, within the scope of its authority. In such cases the Service may take the correction method into account for purposes of EPCRS. [Rev. Proc. 2008-50, § 6.02(2)(a)–(e), 2008-35 I.R.B. 464]

See Appendix D to this volume for extracts from the Employee Plans Compliance Resolution System procedures.

Q 17:15 Must an employer adjust for earnings when it corrects additional contributions or distributions of excesses?

Yes. If a corrective allocation is made, it should be adjusted for earnings that would have been allocated to the participant's account if the violation had not occurred. There need not be an adjustment for losses, but such an adjustment is permitted. If the plan allowed for participant directed investments at the time of the failure, and therefore a number of different investments were permitted, the plan is permitted to use the highest rate earned in the plan for the year of the failure. This method is applicable if most of the affected participants are NHCEs. For SEP or SIMPLE IRA plans, because the investment vehicles are individual IRAs, the employer may use a "reasonable" interest rate to determine earnings attributable for corrective purposes; use of the VFCP Online Calculator is accepted as use of a reasonable rate. [Rev. Proc. 2008-50, §§ 6.02(4)(e), 6.02(5)(a), 2008-35 I.R.B. 464]

Corrective allocations for a prior plan year are considered an annual addition for the year to which the correction applies, not for the year in which the corrective allocations are made. The normal rules of Code Section 404, however, apply for deduction purposes. This means that the employer will generally not receive a deduction. Corrective allocations can come only from employer contributions. [Rev. Proc. 2008-50, § 6.02(4)(b), 2008-35 I.R.B. 464]

Q 17:16 Are there any exceptions to the requirement that an employer make a full correction?

Yes. Limited exceptions exist, which do not include the fact that full correction will be burdensome or inconvenient. In some cases, however, the full correction may be unreasonable or not feasible. The following exceptions apply:

1. If it is possible to make a precise calculation, but the probable difference between the approximate restoration of benefits and the precise restoration of benefits is insignificant, and the administrative cost of determining the precise restoration would significantly exceed the probable difference, reasonable estimates may be used. [Rev. Proc. 2008-50, § 6.02(5)(a), 2008-35 I.R.B. 464]
2. If it is not possible to make a precise calculation (e.g., where it is impossible to provide plan data), reasonable estimates may be used in calculating appropriate corrections. If it is not feasible to make a reasonable estimate of what the actual investment results would have been, a reasonable interest rate may be used. [Rev. Proc. 2008-50, § 6.02(5)(a), 2008-35 I.R.B. 464] For this purpose, the use of the VFCP Online Calculator is deemed to be a reasonable interest rate. Prime rate plus two percentage points is also an acceptable standard to use.
3. If the total corrective distribution is $75 or less, and the reasonable cost of delivering the distribution (for instance, a fee charged to process a plan distribution) would exceed the amount of the distribution, the employer is not required to make a corrective distribution. [Rev. Proc. 2008-50, § 6.02(5)(b), 2008-35 I.R.B. 464]
4. As long as reasonable actions are taken to locate missing participants and beneficiaries (e.g., use of the IRS Letter Forwarding Program or the Social Security Administration Employer Reporting Service), failure to make corrections with respect to such participants and beneficiaries does not preclude a correction from being a full correction. The IRS reserves the right to decline to perform the letter forwarding request, in which case the plan sponsor must take other reasonable actions to locate participants to whom benefits are due. [Rev. Proc. 2008-50, § 6.02(5)(d), 2008-35 I.R.B. 464]
5. Overpayments of $100 or less need not be recovered from a participant or beneficiary, and the plan sponsor need not provide notice that the amount is not eligible for favorable tax treatment. [Rev. Proc. 2008-50, § 6.02(5)(c), 2008-35 I.R.B. 464]

6. Excess amounts of $100 or less need not be distributed or forfeited; however, if the amount exceeds a statutory limit, the plan sponsor must notify the affected participant that he or she is not eligible for favorable tax treatment including rollover. [Rev. Proc. 2008-50, § 6.02(5)(e), 2008-35 I.R.B. 464]
7. Full correction may not be possible under terminated orphan plans (does not apply to SEPs or SIMPLE IRA plans). [Rev. Proc. 2008-50, § 6.02(5)(f), 2008-35 I.R.B. 464]

Q 17:17 Are penalties and excise taxes waived if an employer corrects a failure under the SCP or the VCP?

Likely upon request under VCP, but not through self-correction. Excise taxes are not waived merely because a correction is made. Instead, Revenue Procedure 2008-50 describes conditions under which the IRS may, upon written request, waive excise taxes under Code Sections 4972 (10 percent tax on nondeductible contributions), 4973 (6 percent tax on excess IRA contributions), 4974 (50 percent tax on required minimum distribution failures), and 4979 (10 percent tax on excess contributions and excess aggregate contributions). Relief from the 50 percent excise tax for failure to make a required minimum distribution may also be available under Audit CAP. Relief from excise taxes under Code Section 4973 for excess contributions to an IRA may be waived when the overpayment or excess amount is removed from the IRA and reported as a taxable distribution; in certain instances relief from the penalty income tax on early distributions under Code Section 72(t) may also be waived in whole or in part where the participant returns to a plan improper distributions that have been rolled over to an IRA. [Rev. Proc. 2008-50, § 6.09, 2008-35 I.R.B. 464] The streamlined VCP applications set forth in Appendices D and F in Revenue Procedure 2008-50 contain requests for relief of excise taxes, however the applicant must explain the specific factual and legal grounds for its relief request. The IRS generally will not waive interest on penalty amounts, however.

Note. The PPA clarifies that the Secretary of the Treasury has the full authority to establish and implement EPCRS (or any successor program) and any other employee plans' correction policies, including the authority to waive income, excise, or other taxes to ensure that any tax, penalty, or sanction is not excessive and bears a reasonable relationship to the nature, extent, and severity of the failure. [PPA § 1101(a), (b)]

Q 17:18 How does an employer determine whether an operational failure is insignificant?

An employer should consider the following factors, among others, to determine whether an operational failure is insignificant:

1. Whether other failures occurred during the period being examined (for this purpose, a failure is not considered to have occurred more than once merely because more than one participant is affected by the failure);

2. The percentage of plan assets and contributions involved in the failure relative to total plan assets;
3. The number of years in which the failure occurred;
4. The number of participants affected relative to the total number of participants in the plan;
5. The number of participants affected as a result of the failure relative to the number of participants who could have been affected by the failure;
6. Whether correction was made within a reasonable time after discovery of the failure; and
7. The reason for the failure (e.g., data errors such as errors in transcription, the transposition of numbers, or minor arithmetic errors).

No single factor is determinative. The IRS indicates that factors 2, 4, and 5 should not be interpreted to exclude small businesses. [Rev. Proc. 2008-50, § 8.02, 2008-35 I.R.B. 464]

Q 17:19 Can an employer correct multiple operational failures using the SCP?

It depends. In the case of a plan with more than one operational failure in a single year, or operational failures that occur in more than one year, the operational failures are eligible for correction under the SCP only if all of the operational failures (other than those that are not treated as resulting in disqualification of the plan under the VCP or the SCP) are insignificant in the aggregate. The IRS does not provide SEP or SIMPLE IRA examples. [Revenue Procedure 2008-50, § 8.04, 2008-35 I.R.B. 464]

Q 17:20 How does an employer correct significant SEP failures?

Significant SEP failures cannot be corrected under the SCP. Therefore, an employer must use the VCP or Audit CAP to correct a significant SEP or SIMPLE IRA failure.

Q 17:21 What must an employer do to correct an operational failure under the VCP?

An employer must do all of the following to correct an operational failure under the VCP:

1. Satisfy submission requirements.
2. Correct the failure identified in accordance with the compliance statement.
3. Pay the required compliance fee.

Q 17:22 Can an employer correct a failure under the VCP when it does not have sufficient information to make a correction?

No. When it is not possible to obtain sufficient information to determine the nature or extent of a failure, or there is insufficient information to effect proper correction, or the application of the VCP would be inappropriate or impractical, the failure cannot be corrected under the VCP.

Q 17:23 Can an employer adopt an amendment to correct a defect in a SEP or SIMPLE IRA?

Yes. If the failure includes the adoption of a permitted amendment (IRS model or prototype), the submission of the amendment with the appropriate fee and submission form should be sent simultaneously with the VCP application.

Q 17:24 What are the submission procedures for the VCP?

Generally, the request under the program from the employer consists of a streamlined VCP application and/or a letter indicating the description of the failures, methods of correction, and any other procedural items. In the case of a VCP submission, the following is required:

1. Identifying information for the applicant;
2. Identifying information for the plan including the type of plan submitted;
3. Plan data including information related to the number of plan participants and the total amount of plan assets;
4. The type of submission (e.g., group submission, anonymous submission, etc.);
5. Identification of the failures, including the years in which they occurred and the number of employees affected;
6. An explanation of how and why the failures arose, including a description of the administrative procedures applicable to the failures in effect at the time the failures occurred (although pre-existing "practices and procedures" are not required in order to participate in VCP);
7. A detailed explanation of the proposed method of correcting the failure, with each step of the correction described in narrative form;
8. A description of the methodology that will be used to calculate earnings or actuarial adjustments;
9. Specific calculations for each affected employee or a representative sample of affected employees;
10. The method that will be used to locate and notify former employees or beneficiaries;
11. A description of the measures that have been implemented to ensure that the same failures will not reoccur;
12. Request for excise tax relief under Code Sections 4972, 4973, 4974, or 4979, or income tax relief under Code Section 72(t);

13. Request for relief from loan failures and income tax reporting relief, where applicable;
14. A statement that neither the employer nor the plan is under examination;
15. A statement that neither the plan nor the employer is party to an ATAT; and
16. A statement, where applicable, that the plan is currently being considered in a determination letter request that is not related to the VCP application.

Additional information must be provided by plan sponsors of Section 403(b) plans, and in regard to orphan plan submissions and group submission. [Rev. Proc. 2008-50, § 11(18), (19), 2008-35 I.R.B. 464]

Documentation required to be submitted with applications includes:

1. A copy of the SEP or SIMPLE plan document;
2. A copy of the most recent opinion letter for a prototype SEP or prototype SIMPLE, or a copy of the IRS current model SEP on Form 5305-SEP or 5305A-SEP, or a copy of the IRS current model SIMPLE plan on Form 5305-SIMPLE or 5304-SIMPLE;
3. The initial VCP fee ($250 for SEP or SIMPLE) must be included with the submission; and
4. The submission must be signed by the employer or their representative, and the "penalty of perjury statement" must be included (one is included in the Sample Format VCP application comprising Appendix D).

It is also advised to submit a completed VCP Checklist (Appendix C of Revenue Procedure 2008-50 and a draft Acknowledgment Form Appendix E) for the Service to return to you upon receipt of the application.

Streamlined VCP applications specific to SEPs, SARSEPs and SIMPLE IRAs that are set forth in Schedules 3 and 4 of Appendix F of Revenue Procedure 2008-50 cover the most typical qualification failures for those types of plans. They are in a "check the box" format that greatly simplifies the application process. Specific correction methods set forth in the streamlined applications are described in Q 17:28.

[Rev. Proc. 2008-50, § 11.03; Appendices C and E, 2008-35 I.R.B. 464]

Q 17:25 Where are VCP applications sent?

VCP applications are sent to:

Internal Revenue Service
Attention: SE:T:EP:RA:VC
P.O. Box 27063
Washington, D.C. 20038-7063

Q 17:26 What are the compliance fees under the VCP?

The fee that applies under the VCP program for SEPs and SIMPLEs is generally $250.

In cases where the employer is using its own correction method (and not one outlined by the IRS under Revenue Procedure 2008-50), the IRS will charge an (undisclosed) additional fee. In addition, if the failure involves an excess amount that is retained in the SEP or SIMPLE IRA, a fee equal to at least 10 percent of the excess amount excluding earnings will be imposed. (Arguably, however, the plan sponsor (generally the employer) is not "retaining" any excess amount in the SEP or SIMPLE IRA due to the employer's lack of control or dominion over participant IRA accounts or annuities.) EPCRS fees are summarized in Tables 17-1 through 17-3. VCP application fees may be reduced by 50 percent where the only failure is participant loans that do not comply with Code Section 72(p)(2) and the failure does not affect more than 25 percent of participants.

[Rev. Proc. 2008-50, §§ 12.02(3), 12.05, 2008-35 I.R.B. 464]

Table 17-1. General VCP Compliance Fee Chart

No. of Participants	*Fee*
20 or fewer	$ 750
21 to 50	$ 1,000
51 to 100	$ 2,500
101 to 500	$ 5,000
501 to 1,000	$ 8,000
1001 to 5,000	$15,000
5001 to 10,000	$20,000
Over 10,000	$25,000

Table 17-2. Group Submissions

(fee based on the number of plans affected by the same failure)

First 20 plans	$10,000
Each additional plan	$ 250
Maximum fee for all plans[1]	$50,000

[1] If additional plans are added after the Group Submission is submitted, the additional fee is paid subject to the maximum $50,000 fee.

Table 17-3. Other Program Fees

Program	*Fee*
Audit CAP	The sanction depends on the severity of the failure(s) and is a negotiated percentage of the maximum payment amount.
Egregious or intentional failures	The maximum compliance fee is increased to 40 percent of the maximum payment amount

Q 17:27 What are the most common failures corrected through VCP?

According to the IRS, the top ten most common failures corrected under VCP are as follows:

1. Failure to amend the plan for tax law changes by the end of the period required by the law, particularly GUST (the General Agreement on Tariffs and Trade, the Uniformed Services Employment and Reemployment Rights Act, the Small Business Job Protection Act, and the Taxpayer Relief Act), EGTRRA, and final and temporary regulations under Code Section 401(a)(9);
2. Failure to follow the plan's definition of compensation for determining contributions;
3. Failure to include eligible employees in the plan or the failure to exclude ineligible employees from the plan;
4. Failure to satisfy plan loan provisions;
5. Impermissible in-service withdrawals;
6. Failure to satisfy Code Section 401(a)(9) minimum distribution rules;
7. Employer eligibility failures;
8. Failure to pass the ADP/ACP nondiscrimination tests under Code Sections 401(k) and 401(m);
9. Failure to properly provide the minimum top-heavy benefit or contribution under Code Section 416 to non-key employees; and
10. Failure to satisfy the limits of Code Section 415.

[*http://www.irs.gov/retirement/article/0,,id=156774,00.html* (visited on Aug. 21, 2012)]

Q 17:28 What are the permitted corrections under SCP and VCP?

The following is a brief description of operational failures and corrections under the SCP and VCP for SEPs and SIMPLE IRAs. In each case, the method described corrects the operational failure identified. Corrective allocations and distributions should reflect earnings. The general rule that the IRS has maintained with regard to SEP and SIMPLE IRAs is that the correction method should be similar to the correction for a qualified plan with a similar qualification failure. [Rev. Proc. 2008-50, § 6.10(1), 2008-35 I.R.B. 464] However, due to the nature of IRA-based plans, plan sponsors generally are not able to make corrections that require restoration of funds improperly contributed to an IRA. The IRS directly addresses such situations for the first time in the "Streamlined VCP Applications" set forth in Appendix F, Schedules 3 and 4 of Revenue Procedure 2008-50, which in some cases allow retention of excess contributions. Payment of an additional VCP fee is required for this type of correction. [Rev. Proc. 2008-50, § 12.05(2), 2008-35 I.R.B. 464]

Table 17-4 summarizes the failures that can be corrected under the EPCRS and the correction procedures applicable to those failures, including the newly described correction of retaining excess amounts.

Corrective allocations and distributions should reflect earnings as described next and in Table 17-4.

Failure to Properly Provide the Minimum Top-Heavy Benefit under Code Section 416 to Non-Key Employees. In a SEP (or SARSEP) plan, the permitted correction method is to properly contribute and allocate the required top-heavy minimums to the SEP IRA in the manner provided for in the plan on behalf of the non-key employees (and any other employees required to receive top-heavy allocations under the plan). [Rev. Proc. 2008-50, App. A § .02, 2008-35 I.R.B.464]

Failure to Satisfy the SARSEP Deferral Percentage Test. The permitted correction method is for the employer to make qualified nonelective contributions (QNCs) (as defined in Treasury Regulations Section 1.401(k)-6) on behalf of the NHCEs to the extent necessary to raise the average deferral percentage of the NHCEs to the percentage needed to pass the test. The contributions must be made on behalf of all eligible NHCEs (to the extent permitted under Code Section 415) and may be calculated as the same percentage of compensation. [Rev. Proc. 2008-50, § 6.10(3), App. F, Schedule 3(B), 2008-35 I.R.B. 464]

The alternative is to use the "one-to-one" correction method discussed later; this is not a correction set forth in the streamlined VCP application, however.

Failure to Timely Distribute Elective Deferrals in Excess of the Code Section 402(g) Limit (in contravention of Section 401(a)(30)). The permitted correction method for a SEP or SIMPLE plan is to distribute the excess deferral to the employee and to report the amount as taxable in the year of deferral *and* the year distributed. Corrective amounts must be adjusted for earnings through the date of correction based on the actual rates of return of the participant's SARSEP or SIMPLE IRA account. A distribution to an HCE is included in the deferral percentage test; a distribution to an NHCE is not included in the deferral percentage test. A distribution is reported as taxable on Form 1099-R for the year of the distribution. The employee is also required to amend his or her tax return for the year of the excess deferral and claim the excess on line 7 of Form 1040. [Rev. Proc. 2008-50, § 6.10(5), App. F, Schedules 3(E), 4(D), 2008-35 I.R.B. 464]

Table 17-4. Summary of Applicable Correction Procedures

		Applicable Correction Procedures					
Failure[1]	*See Revenue Procedure 2008-50*	*SCP (insignificant errors only)*[2]	*Streamlined VCP (App. F)*	*VCP (not under investigation)*	*Audit CAP*	*Remedy*	*Earnings*
Employer Eligibility Failure (SARSEP only) • Established after 1996. • 50% participation rate requirement not met. • 25 employee limit exceeded.	§§ 3.06, 6.03 App. F. Sch. 3, Part 1A	No	Yes	Yes	Yes	Cessation of contributions no later than VCP filing date.	N/A
Failure to satisfy 125% deferral percentage test in a SARSEP	App. F. Sch. 3, Part 1B App. A, § .03	Yes	Yes	Yes	Yes	Contribute fully vested amounts sufficient to pass test.[3]	Calculator[4] and/or actual
Failure to make required employer contributions (including top-heavy)	App. F, Sch. 3, Part 1C App. A, § .02 App A, § .05	Yes	Yes	Yes	Yes	Contribute additional amounts.	Calculator and/or actual
Failure to provide eligible employees opportunity to defer/make catch-up contributions (age 50+) in a SARSEP	App. F, Part 1D App. A, § .05	Yes	Yes	Yes	Yes	Contribute 50% of HCE or NHCE rate.	Calculator and/or actual
Contribution of excess amounts[5,6]	§ 6.06 App. F, Part 1E App. A, § .04 App. A, § .08	Yes	Yes	Yes	Yes	Return excess employer contributions to plan sponsor[11] or distribute excess elective deferrals[12] or retain in IRAs.[13]	Actual earnings under Streamlined VCP; otherwise Calculator is an option.

Table 17-4. Summary of Applicable Correction Procedures (*cont'd*)

		Applicable Correction Procedures					
Failure[1]	*See Revenue Procedure 2008-50*	*SCP (insignificant errors only)*[2]	*Streamlined VCP (App. F)*	*VCP (not under investigation)*	*Audit CAP*	*Remedy*	*Earnings*
> 25% IRC § 402(h) $16,500 IRC § 402(g) $46,000 IRC § 415(c)			Excess may be retained.[7]	Excess may be retained.[8]	Excess may be retained.[9]	Excess may be retained.[10]	
Excess plan compensation[14] IRC § 401(a)(17)	§ 6.10(2)	Yes	Yes Use App. F, Sch. 9	Yes	Yes	Make additional contributions based on ratio by which improper contribution exceeded permitted amount; or reduce account balances by excess amounts.	Up to plan sponsor.
Correction of terminated plan	§ 4.04	No	No	Yes	Yes	Depends.	Not addressed.
Correction of orphan plan	§ 4.07 App. A, § .09	No	No	Yes[15]	Yes[16]	Terminate plan and distribute assets to participants.	N/A
Correction of a tax avoidance transaction	§ 4.13	No	No	Yes[17]	Yes	Depends upon transaction.	Not addressed.
Failure to amend document	§ 5.01(2)(a) App. F, Sch. 1 or 2	Yes	Yes Use App. F, Sch. 1 or 2	Yes	Yes	Amend document and file for determination letter where applicable.	

[1] **Note 1.** Generally, the correction for a SEP or a SIMPLE IRA plan is expected to be similar to the correction required for a qualified plan with a similar qualification failure (i.e., plan document failure, operational failure, demographic failure, and employer eligibility failure). In any case in which correction under Revenue Procedure § 6.10(1) is not feasible for a SEP or SIMPLE IRA plan or in any other case determined by the IRS, in its discretion, the IRS may provide for a different correction for the following:

- Failures relating to Code Section 402(g)
- Failures relating to Code Section 415
- Failures relating to Code Section 401(a)(17)
- Failures relating to deferral percentages
- Discontinuance of contributions to a SARSEP or SIMPLE IRA plan
- Retention of excess amounts for cases in which there has been no violation of a statutory limitation with respect to a SEP or SIMPLE IRA plan.

Note 2. As part of VCP, in appropriate cases, the IRS will not pursue the 6 percent excise tax under Code Section 4973 relating to excess contributions made to IRA, provided the recipient removes the excess amount (plus earnings) from the recipient's IRA and reports that amount (reduced by any applicable after-tax employee contribution) as a taxable distribution for the year in which the excess amount (plus earnings) is removed from the recipient's IRA. The amount removed will generally be taxed in a manner that is similar to the manner in which the corrective disbursement of elective deferrals is taxed, as described in Section 3 of Revenue Procedure 92-93. [Rev. Proc. 2008-50, § 6.09]

In appropriate cases, as a condition for not pursuing all or a portion of the additional 10 percent tax on early distributions, the IRS may require the plan sponsor to pay an additional fee under VCP not in excess of the 10 percent additional income tax under Code Section 72(t). The Plan Sponsor, as part of the submission, must request the relief and provide an explanation supporting the request.

Note 3. Correction under the EPCRS can avoid the 10 percent penalty on nondeductible and excess employer contributions. [I.R.C. §§ 4972, 4979]

Revenue Procedure 2008-50 is available at: *http://www.irs.gov/pub/irs-irbs/irb08-35.pdf* (visited may. 21, 2012).

[2] Rev. Proc. 2008-50, §§ 6.03, 8.02, 8.04 gives examples.

[3] Alternative method under EPCRS § 6.10(3) is to distribute excess contributions, plus earnings, to HCEs and contribute same amount to SEP and allocate to NHCEs.

[4] The "VFCP On-line Calculator" is used. The calculator is available at *http://askebsa.dol.gov/VFCPCalculator/WebCalculator.aspx* (visited on Aug. 21, 2012)

[5] Use new code "E" in Form 1099-R, Box 7 to report distribution of excess amounts.

[6] Excess employer contributions or elective deferrals under $100 (before adjustment for earnings) do not have to be distributed. [Rev. Proc. 2008-50, § 6.05(c)]

[7] If a Code Section 415 excess is retained in SEP plan, must reduce current or subsequent years' Section 415 limit by excess amount. [Rev. Proc. 2008-50, § 6.05(b)]

[8] If a Code Section 415 excess is retained in SEP plan, must reduce current or subsequent years' Section 415 limit by excess amount. [Rev. Proc. 2008-50, § 6.05(b)]

[9] If a Code Section 415 excess is retained in SEP plan, must reduce current or subsequent years' Section 415 limit by excess amount. [Rev. Proc. 2008-50, § 6.05(b)]

[10] If a Code Section 415 excess is retained in SEP plan, must reduce current or subsequent years' Section 415 limit by excess amount. [Rev. Proc. 2008-50, § 6.05(b)]

[11] Excess employer contributions returned to sponsor are not taxed to participants under EPCRS but are reported on Form 1099-R with taxable amount shown as zero (0); plan sponsor not entitled to deduction. [Rev. Proc. 2008-50, § 6.10(5)] Employer must notify participants that amounts are eligible for rollover.

[12] Distribution of excess elective deferrals plus actual earnings—notify participants that amounts are not eligible for rollover.

[13] Retention of excess amounts triggers additional VCP fee equal to 10% of excess amount.

[14] More than statutory limit ($250,000 for 2009–2012) used for plan computations.

[15] Party acting on behalf of plan must be an "Eligible Party." [Rev. Proc. 2008-50, § 5.03(2)]

[16] Party acting on behalf of plan must be an "Eligible Party." [Rev. Proc. 2008-50, § 5.03(2)]

[17] Matter will be referred to IRS Tax Shelter Coordinator; ability to resolve in VCP depends upon extent to which failures are related to a tax avoidance transaction

Exclusion of an Eligible Employee from All Contributions or Accruals under the Plan for One or More Plan Years. The permitted correction method is to make a fully vested contribution to the plan on behalf of the employees excluded from a SEP or SIMPLE IRA plan. If the employee should have been eligible to make an elective contribution under a SARSEP arrangement or SIMPLE IRA, the employer may contribute 50 percent of what the employee would have contributed had he or she been allowed to participate in the plan (the "missed deferral opportunity" cost). Because the employee's deferral decision is not known, the deferral amount should be based on the actual deferral percentage for the employee's group (either HCE or NHCE). Contributing 50 percent of the actual deferral percentage for such employees eliminates the need to redo the deferral percentage test to account for the previously excluded employees. Corrective amounts must be adjusted for earnings through the date of corrective contribution based on actual investment results of the affected IRA, or based on a "reasonable" rate including use of the VFCP Online Calculator. [Rev. Proc. 2008-50, App. F, Schedules 3(D), 4(C) § .05, 2008-35 I.R.B. 464] The SEP Plan Fix-It Guide mentions this error as potentially arising from a plan sponsor's failure properly to identify other companies related by ownership and extend plan coverage to eligible employees of related companies. This correction is also available where a participant has been excluded from participating in elective deferral contributions for a partial plan year, however corrective contributions are not required where an employee has been permitted to defer under the plan for a period of at least nine consecutive months during the plan year. [Rev. Proc. 2008-50, App. A § .05, App. B § 2.02, 2008-35 I.R.B. 464]

Failure to Implement Salary Deferral Election. For an employee who timely elects to make salary deferral elections under a SARSEP or SIMPLE IRA but whose deferral elections are not implemented, the proper correction is to replace the "missed deferral opportunity" cost; i.e., contribute 50 percent of what the employee would have contributed, based on the employee's actual deferral election rather than the ADP of the employee's group. Corrective amounts must be adjusted for earnings as shown above. [Rev. Proc. 2008-50, App. A § 05(5), 2008-35 I.R.B. 464]

Failure to Permit Catch-up Deferrals. Where a participant age 50 or older defers the maximum amount permitted under Code Section 402(g), but is not given the opportunity to make catch-up deferrals of up to $5,500 per year, the correction method is for the employer to replace the "missed deferral opportunity" with a qualified nonelective contribution (QNEC) equal to 50 percent of the "missed deferral attributable to catch-up contributions." The "missed deferral attributable to catch-up contributions" is defined as one-half of the catch-up contribution limit for the affected plan year. For 2009 through 2012, the QNEC is calculated as follows: ($5,500 × 50% = $2,750 "missed deferral") × 50% = $1,375. [Rev. Proc. 2008-50, App. A § 04(4)(a), 2008-35 I.R.B. 464]

Failure to Base Contributions on Plan Definition of Compensation. In a SEP plan, the definition of compensation generally includes items that sometimes are excluded from plan compensation under qualified plans, including bonuses, commissions, tips, shift differential pay, and fringe benefits. If SEP contributions are based on a definition of compensation that excludes these additional amounts, the correction method is to make a corrective contribution, including earnings, on behalf of the affected employees, based on the excluded amounts. [*See* IRS SEP Plan Fix-It Guide, Potential Mistake No. 4]

Failure to Timely Pay the Minimum Distribution Required under Code Section 401(a)(9). In a SEP IRA or SIMPLE plan, the permitted correction method is to distribute the required minimum distributions (RMDs), plus earnings from the date of the failure to the date of distribution. The amount to be distributed for each year in which the failure occurred should be determined by dividing the adjusted account balance on the applicable valuation date by the applicable divisor. For this purpose, *adjusted account balance* means the actual account balance, determined in accordance with the proposed regulations, reduced by the amount of the total missed minimum distributions for prior years. [Rev. Proc. 2008-50, App. A § .06, 2008-35 I.R.B. 464] (Note that under the Worker, Retiree and Employer Recovery Act of 2009 (WRERA), the IRS waived the requirement to take RMDs that otherwise would have been due in 2009, regardless of whether the underlying plan account has experienced gain or loss. This included distributions that retirees would otherwise have taken by December 31, 2009, but did not include first-time distributions for 2008 that were postponed to April 1, 2009.)

Failure to Satisfy the Code Section 415(c) Limits. Contributions to a SEP, SARSEP, or SIMPLE plan almost never exceed the Code Section 415 dollar limit on "annual additions" (the lesser of 100 percent of compensation or $50,000 for 2012, exclusive of catch-up contributions if age 50 or older) because the participant's maximum excludable contribution limit under a SEP/SARSEP (25 percent of taxable compensation) or SIMPLE ($23,000 for 2012, exclusive of catch-up contributions if age 50 or older) is always lower. In the event that the Code Section 415(c) limit is exceeded, the final regulations under Section 415 now specify correction under EPCRS. The correction methods for a qualified plan (including a SIMPLE 401(k)) include removal of excess annual additions from participants' accounts to be held in an unallocated account and used to reduce future employer contributions. Excess amounts are reported on a Form 1099-R as a distribution issued to the affected employees, indicating the taxable amount as zero in box 2a. Where the excess allocations consist of employee salary deferrals, amounts in excess of the Code Section 415 limit are distributed, adjusted for earnings, through the date of correction. However, where the correction procedure applicable to a qualified plan is not feasible when applied to a SEP or SIMPLE IRA plan, the IRS, in its discretion, may provide a different correction. If an excess amount is retained in a SEP or SIMPLE IRA that is attributable to a Code Section 415 excess failure, the excess amount, adjusted for earnings through the date of correction, must reduce the affected participant's Section 415 limit for the year following the year of correction (or for the year of correction if the plan sponsor so chooses) and subsequent years, until the excess is eliminated. A special fee, in addition to the VCP fee, may apply if the excess amounts are retained in a SEP or SIMPLE IRA. [Rev. Proc. 2008-50, § 12.05(2), 2008-35 I.R.B. 464] The plan sponsor is not entitled to a deduction for an excess amount retained in a SEP or SIMPLE IRA attributable to Code Section 415.

Earnings are generally based on the actual rate of return through the date of correction. Insofar as SEP or SIMPLE IRA assets are held in IRAs, however, there is no earnings rate under the SEP or SIMPLE IRA as a whole. If it is not feasible to make a reasonable estimate of what the actual results would have been, a reasonable interest rate may be used. [Rev. Proc. 2008-50, § 6.10(1)-(5); *but see* App. F, Schedule 3(E), 2008-35 I.R.B. 464, which appears to require that actual investment results be determined; *see also* IRS SEP Plan Fix-It Guide, Potential Mistake No. 5] In instances when a reasonable estimate of earnings is appropriate, the plan sponsor may use the VFCP Online Calculator.

Note that the IRS has re-titled Form 1099-R distribution code E from "Excess Annual Additions under Section 415/Certain Excess Amounts under Section 403(b) Plans" to "Distributions under Employee Plans Compliance Resolution System (EPCRS)," and the new code should only be used when excess annual additions are distributed under EPCRS correction procedures. [Rev. Proc. 2008-50, 6.06(2); App. A § .08, 2008-35 I.R.B. 464; IRS SEP Plan Fix-It Guide, Potential Mistake No. 5]

Deferral Percentage Test Failures. The one-to-one correction method has been commonly used under the correction program for the past few years. Under this method, there is a corrective distribution of excess contributions and an equivalent corrective contribution made to the plan that is allocated to NHCEs only.

Correction of Exclusion of Eligible Employees in Employer Contribution to SEPs/SIMPLEs

1. *Corrective Contribution*. Additional nonelective contribution must be made on behalf of the excluded employee, adjusted for earnings. If because of the additional contribution there should be a reduction in another employee's contribution, no reduction is made.
2. *Reallocation method*. The original contribution made is reallocated to include the excluded employee(s). This will require some employees to receive decreases in their account balances. If the aggregate amount of decreases exceeds the aggregate amount of increases, then the employer must make a nonelective contribution to the plan to take care of the difference.

Per the IRS SEP Plan Fix-It Guide, only the contribution method, and not reallocation, is proper for SEPs in most cases since the assets of the plan are held in IRAs. [SEP Plan Fix-It Guide, Potential Mistake No. 2.]

[Rev. Proc. 2008-50, § 6.02(7), App. F, Schedules 3(C), 4(B), 2008-35 I.R.B. 464]

Correction of 415 Overpayment Failures

1. *Forfeiture correction method* (Code Section 415(c) excess). Forfeiture of the applicable amount is a method that may be used for an NHCE who has an excess annual addition and has separated from service with no vested

interest in the matching or nonelective contribution and has not been reemployed at the time of correction.

2. *Return of overpayment correction method* (Code Section 415(c) excess). The employer may take appropriate steps to have the employee return the overpayment (*de minimis* rule of $100 applies) plus earnings, to the plan. The employee must be notified that the returned amount is not eligible for favorable tax treatment (e.g., rollover). To the extent the amount returned is less than the amount of the overpayment, the employer must make up the difference. The overpayment is to be placed in an unallocated account to be used to reduce employer contributions. The employer must also indicate to the employee who received the overpayment that such payment is not eligible for rollover treatment or favorable tax treatment.

[Rev. Proc. 2008-50, App. A § .08, App. B § 2.04, 2008-35 I.R.B. 464]

Other Overpayment Failures. SEP/SIMPLE overpayments are corrected under Code Section 415(c) using the return of overpayment method described above. If the SEP IRA or SIMPLE plan retains the overpayment, the employer is subject to the 10 percent tax in addition to the VCP SEP submission fee. [Rev. Proc. 2008-50, § 6.10(5), 2008-35 I.R.B. 464]

Correction of Code Section 401(a)(17) Failures. Under the reduction of account balance method, the account balance of an employee who received an allocation on the basis of compensation in excess of the Code Section 401(a)(17) limit ($250,000 for 2012) is reduced by this improperly allocated amount (adjusted for earnings). If the improperly allocated amount would have been allocated to other employees in the year of the failure if the failure had not occurred, then that amount (adjusted for earnings) is reallocated to those employees in accordance with the plan's allocation formula. A qualified plan can go further if the improperly allocated amount would not have been allocated to other employees absent the failure; that amount (adjusted for earnings) is placed in an unallocated account, similar to the suspense account described in Treasury Regulations Section 1.415-6(b)(6)(iii), to be used to reduce employer contributions in succeeding year(s). For example, if a plan provides for a fixed level of employer contributions for each eligible employee, and the plan provides that forfeitures are used to reduce future employer contributions, the improperly allocated amount (adjusted for earnings) would be used to reduce future employer contributions. This second step is not available for SEPs or SIMPLEs. [Rev. Proc. 2008-50, App. B §§ 2.06, 2.07(1), 2008-35 I.R.B. 464]

Correction of Inclusion of Ineligible Employee Failure. The plan may be amended retroactively to change the eligibility requirements to allow the ineligible employee to become eligible. All other employees who become eligible due to the amendment must be covered as well. [Rev. Proc. 2008-50, App. B, § 2.07(3), 2008-35 I.R.B. 464]

DOL Correction Program

Q 17:29 Are there any other correction programs?

Yes. The Voluntary Fiduciary Correction Program (VFCP) allows plan sponsors and other plan fiduciaries to voluntarily disclose certain transactions to the DOL and, by correcting the transactions in accordance with the VFCP, to avoid potential civil actions, penalties, and the assessment of civil penalties under Section 502(i) of ERISA. In general, the relief available under the VFCP affects plans, participants, and beneficiaries of such plans in connection with investigation or civil action by the DOL. [VFCP, 71 Fed. Reg. 20262–20285]

Q 17:30 What is the history of the VFCP?

Introduced on an interim basis in 2000, the VFCP was first published in March 2002 and was updated on a "proposed" basis in April 2005. Those proposed changes were finalized and supplemented in April 2006. A final class exemption to permit certain transactions identified in the proposed VFCP, first issued on November 25, 2002, was also updated together with the VFCP in April 2006. [P.T.E. 2002-51 (App. No. D-10933), 67 Fed. Reg. 70623-70628; *amended at* 71 Fed. Reg. 20135-20139] The IRS grants relief from excise taxes under Code Section 4975 consistent with VFCP, but only for certain transactions, including late transmittal of salary deferral contributions, and only upon notification of affected participants. [I.R.S. Ann. 2002-31, 2002-15 I.R.B. 747]

Q 17:31 What is the purpose of the VFCP?

The purpose of the VFCP is to protect the financial security of workers by encouraging identification and correction of transactions that violate Part 4 of Title I of ERISA. Part 4 of Title I of ERISA sets out the responsibilities of employee benefit plan fiduciaries.

Section 409 of ERISA provides that a fiduciary who breaches any of these responsibilities shall be personally liable to make good to the plan any losses to the plan resulting from each breach and to restore to the plan any profits the fiduciary made through the use of the plan's assets.

Section 405 of ERISA provides that a fiduciary may be liable, under certain circumstances, for a co-fiduciary's breach of his or her fiduciary responsibilities. In addition, under certain circumstances, there may be liability for knowing participation in a fiduciary breach. To assist all affected persons in understanding the requirements of ERISA and meeting their legal responsibilities, the Pension and Welfare Benefits Administration (PWBA, now called the Employee Benefits Security Administration (EBSA)) provided guidance on what constitutes adequate correction under Title I of ERISA for the breaches described in the VFCP.

Q 17:32 Who can participate in the VFCP?

Employee benefit plans, fiduciaries, plan sponsors, and other parties in interest may use the VFCP and must fully and accurately correct violations. Incomplete or unacceptable applications may be rejected by the DOL. If an application is rejected, the applicant may be subject to enforcement action, including assessment of civil monetary penalties under ERISA Section 502(l).

Q 17:33 What requirements must an employer meet to be eligible for the VFCP?

An applicant must meet three criteria in order to participate in the VFCP: (1) neither the plan nor the applicant is "under investigation"; (2) there is no evidence of potential criminal violations, as determined by EBSA; and (3) EBSA has not conducted an investigation that resulted in written notice to a plan fiduciary that the transaction has been referred to the IRS.

Q 17:34 How does VFCP define *under investigation*?

VFCP Section 3(b)(3) defines *under investigation* to include the following: (1) EBSA is investigating the plan; (2) EBSA is investigating the potential applicant or plan sponsor in connection with an act or transaction directly related to the plan; (3) any governmental agency is conducting a criminal investigation of the plan, or of the potential applicant or plan sponsor in connection with an act or transaction directly related to the plan; (4) the Tax Exempt/Government Entities (TE/GE) Division of the IRS is conducting an employee plans examination of the plan; and (5) the plan, applicant, or sponsor is under investigation by the Pension Benefit Guaranty Corporation (PBGC), any state attorney general, or any state insurance investigator.

Q 17:35 What relief is available to participants in VFCP?

In general, EBSA will issue to the applicant a no-action letter with respect to a breach identified in the application of an eligible person or entity and provided that the breach is corrected in accordance with the application. Pursuant to the no-action letter it issues, the EBSA will not initiate a civil investigation under Title I of ERISA regarding the applicant's responsibility for any transaction described in the no-action letter, or assess a civil penalty under ERISA Section 502(l) on the correction amount paid to the plan or its participants. Relief from civil penalties applicable to welfare plans and nonqualified pension plans under ERISA Section 502(i) also became available in the revisions finalized in 2006. The IRS grants relief from excise taxes under Code Section 4975 consistent with VFCP, but only for certain transactions, including late transmittal of salary deferral contributions, and subject to certain conditions which may include participant notification.

Q 17:36 What transactions are covered under the program?

Nineteen categories of eligible transactions may be corrected under the VFCP, as follows:

1. Delinquent participant contributions to pension plans
2. Delinquent participant contributions to insured welfare plans
3. Delinquent participant contributions to self-funded welfare plan trusts
4. Fair market interest rate loans with parties in interest
5. Below market interest rate loans with parties in interest
6. Below market interest rate loans with non-parties in interest
7. Below market interest rate loans due to delay in perfecting security interest
8. Participant loans (e.g., in a 401(k) plan) that fail to comply with limits on the loan amount, loan duration, or loan amortization schedule
9. Defaulted loans
10. Purchase of assets by plans from parties in interest
11. Sale of assets by plans to parties in interest
12. Sale and leaseback of property to sponsoring employers
13. Purchase of assets from non-parties in interest at below market value
14. Sale of assets to non-parties in interest at below market value
15. Holding of an illiquid asset previously purchased by the plan
16. Benefit payments based on improper valuation of plan assets
17. Payment of duplicate, excessive, or unnecessary compensation
18. Payment of expenses by the plan that should have been paid by the plan sponsor
19. Payment of dual compensation to plan fiduciaries

Q 17:37 When are participant contributions to a plan considered "delinquent"?

Under the current, long standing rule, employee salary deferrals become "plan assets" under ERISA and must be deposited in the plan (or IRA) as soon as they can reasonably be segregated from the employer's general assets, but no later than the 15th business day of the month following the month in which employee contributions are withheld from the employee's pay. [DOL Reg. § 2510.3-102(a)] Failure to do so is a prohibited transaction because the employer is effectively "borrowing" plan assets. And, because employers with qualified plans must disclose any late deposits of 401(k) deferrals on the Form 5500 annual plan return/report, the error will not escape the attention of the DOL, which has dedicated substantial resources to policing this aspect of plan compliance.

This timing rule consistently has proved confusing to employers. Some incorrectly view the 15-business-day period as a "safe harbor"—which it is not—while others simply have inefficient payroll processing habits that frequently result in 401(k) deposits occurring several days after the employer "reasonably" could have done so. By contrast, the DOL has opined that 401(k) salary deferrals can "reasonably be segregated" as soon as employment taxes are withheld from pay. Thus, a big gap exists between the realities of the situation and the regulatory expectations. Not surprisingly, the DOL has reported that 90 percent of applications to VFCP since its inception in 2000 have involved delinquent deposit of participant contributions and loan repayments. [Final Plan Asset Regulations published at 75 Fed. Reg. 2068, 2069 (Jan. 14, 2010)]

To address confusion and noncompliance in this area, in February 2008 the DOL proposed an amendment to the plan asset regulation that gave employers sponsoring "small" pension or welfare benefit plans (fewer than 100 participants) a seven-business-day "safe harbor" in which to deposit participant contributions, including salary deferrals, into the applicable plan trust account. Final regulations were issued on January 14, 2010. [75 Fed. Reg. 2068] Under the safe harbor, participant contributions, including salary deferrals, that are deposited in a plan account within the seven-business-day period will be deemed to have satisfied the "earliest date of segregation" requirement under the plan asset regulations. Plans with 100 or more participants remain subject to the "as soon as reasonably segregated" standard without benefit of the safe harbor.

Q 17:38 Does the VFCP apply to SEPs, SARSEPs, and SIMPLEs?

Yes, if the plans are subject to ERISA. SEPs, SARSEPs, and SIMPLEs are subject to ERISA if there is at least one common-law employee participating in the plan. The DOL does not currently permit the self-correction of late deposits.

Q 17:39 Does the small plan safe harbor apply to SEPs, SARSEPs, and SIMPLEs?

The final regulations make clear that the safe harbor applies to SARSEP and SIMPLE IRA plans, notwithstanding the 30-calendar-day maximum deadline that applies to SIMPLE IRA contributions under Code Section 408(p) and DOL Regulations Section 2510.3-102(b)(2). The following example illustrates application of the safe harbor both to participant contributions and salary deferrals.

> **Example.** Yvonne's employer maintains a SIMPLE IRA plan and a payroll deduction Roth IRA program. Employees are paid each Wednesday for the previous week. Yvonne makes after-tax contributions of $10 per week to the Roth IRA under her employer's payroll deduction Roth IRA program and elective contributions of $50 per week to the SIMPLE IRA plan which are deposited into her SIMPLE IRA. The safe-harbor seven-day period for the payroll deduction Roth IRA program commences on Monday (the next business day following the date the payroll deduction was made). The safe harbor seven-day period for the SIMPLE IRA, however, starts on Thursday (the next business day following the day the amount would have been

payable in cash). Under the safe harbor seven-day rule, the payroll deduction contributions must be deposited with the trustee or custodian on or before the following Tuesday (the seventh business day that commenced on Monday), and the elective contributions under the SIMPLE IRA program must be deposited with the trustee or custodian on the following Friday (the seventh business day that commenced on Thursday)

Q 17:40 What are the acceptable correction methods under the VFCP?

The VFCP provides acceptable correction methods for the 19 failures listed in Q 17:36. As part of the correction process, applicants must:

1. Conduct valuations of plan assets using generally recognized markets for the assets or obtain written appraisal reports from qualified professionals that are based on generally accepted appraisal standards.
2. Restore to the plan the principal amount involved, plus the greater of
   a. The lost earnings starting on the date of the loss and extending to the recovery date, or
   b. The profits resulting from the use of the principal amount for the same period.
3. Pay the expenses associated with the correction process, such as appraisal costs or the cost of recalculating participant account balances.
4. Make supplemental distributions to former employees, beneficiaries, or alternate payees when appropriate and provide proof of the payments.

The VFCP Online Calculator allows applicants to calculate lost earnings and interest, and compare that amount to restoration of profits. Generally, the greater amount must be paid to the plan. The calculator is also able to calculate corrections involving multiple transactions with different time periods. (See Q 17:49.)

Q 17:41 What is the effective date of the VFCP?

The effective date of the revised VFCP is May 19, 2006.

Q 17:42 What documentation must be filed under the VFCP?

A VFCP applicant must submit the following documentation to the appropriate regional office of the EBSA:

- Copy of relevant portions of the plan and related documents
- Documents supporting transactions such as leases and loan documents and applicable corrections
- Documentation of lost earnings amounts
- Documentation of restored profits, if applicable
- Proof of payment of required amounts

- Certain documents required for relevant transaction
- Signed VFCP checklist
- Penalty of perjury statement

Abbreviated documentation rules apply to delinquent participant contributions and loan repayments to pension plans, and to delinquent participant contributions to insured or self-funded welfare plans. The abbreviated rules apply to applicants correcting breaches involving amounts (1) under $50,000 or (2) greater than $50,000 but that were remitted to the plan within 180 days after receipt by the employer. Full documentation rules apply to applicants who fail to meet the $50,000 and 180-day standards.

EBSA reserves the right to make written request for supplemental documentation needed to complete the review process.

EBSA now provides a model VFCP application form, which is available at *http://www.dol.gov/ebsa/calculator/2006vfcpapplication.html* (visited on Aug. 21, 2012). Use of the model form is voluntary but recommended. It is important to remember to include a completed, signed VFCP checklist—a form which is also provided—as the DOL will not process the application without this document. The VFCP checklist is found at *http://www.dol.gov/ebsa/calculator/2006vfcpchecklist.html* (visited on Aug. 21, 2012).

Practice Pointer. If the VFCP application includes copies of completed Form 5330 (Return of Excise Taxes Related to Employee Benefit Plans), and a copy of proof of payment of those taxes either to the Internal Revenue Service (in the form of a cancelled check) or to the trust of the plan at issue (in the form of a wire transfer, generally), then EBSA will issue a no action letter that omits any mention of referring the matter to the IRS in regards to potential excise tax liability. If no proof of payment of excise taxes is included in the FVCP application, the no action letter will contain that sentence and the possibility of further contact by the IRS exists.

Q 17:43 What general rules apply to the VFCP?

Like an EPCRS applicant, a VFCP applicant must restore the plan, the participants, and their beneficiaries to the condition they would have been in had the breach not occurred. Plans must also file, where necessary, amended returns to reflect corrected transactions or valuations.

Under the VFCP, applicants must also provide proof of payment to participants and beneficiaries or properly segregate affected assets when the plan is unable to locate missing individuals.

Payment of the correction amount may be made directly to the plan when distributions to separated participants would be less than $20 and the cost of correction would exceed the distributions owed. Applicants can use the "blended" or overall earnings rate among all plan investments (in lieu of the highest rate) in calculating the rate of return on affected transactions involving

ERISA Section 404(c) plans only for affected participants who have not made investment allocations.

Q 17:44 Is there an exemption from the prohibited transaction excise tax?

Yes. As mentioned, a prohibited transaction class exemption (P.T.E. 2002-51) issued in conjunction with the VFCP provides limited relief from the excise taxes under Code Section 4975 on certain transactions covered by the VFCP. As amended effective May 19, 2006, the exemption applies to the following transactions:

1. Failure to timely remit participant contributions to plans;
2. Loans made at fair market interest rates by plans to parties in interest;
3. Purchases or sales of assets between plans and parties in interest at fair market value;
4. Sales of real property to plans by employers and leaseback of the property, at fair market value and fair market rental value, respectively;
5. Plan acquisition of an illiquid asset, and subsequent sale to a party in interest; and
6. The use of plan assets to pay for settlor expenses, as opposed to plan expenses.

Q 17:45 What is required in order to qualify for the exemption?

Under the exemption, a VFCP applicant must repay delinquent contributions to the plan no more than 180 days from the date the money was received by the employer or would be payable to plan participants in cash.

The exemption also requires the following:

1. No more than 10 percent of the fair market value of total plan assets may be involved (except for delinquent employee contributions).
2. Notice of the transaction and the correction must be provided to interested persons.
3. Transactions covered under the exemption cannot be part of an arrangement or understanding that benefits a related party.

The exemption does not apply to any transaction similar to a transaction for which an application has been submitted under the VFCP within the past three years.

Additionally, the preamble to the updated P.T.E. 2002-51 makes it clear that neither the prohibited transaction exemption nor VFCP applies to IRAs that are not subject to ERISA. Relief for transactions involving non-ERISA IRAs is only available through the DOL's individual administrative exemption process.

Q 17:46 Is there an exception to the notice requirement under the exemption?

Yes. An exception to the notice requirement applies where the transaction at issue is the failure to timely transmit participant contributions or loan repayments, and the applicable excise tax (as determined using the VFCP Online Calculator) does not exceed $100, provided that the excise tax amount is contributed to the plan and allocated to participants consistent with the plan's allocation formula. This relief is only available if the plan sponsor requests a no-action letter under the VFCP and provides documentation of this correction along with the VFCP application. Late deferral amounts must still be reported on Form 5500.

Q 17:47 How can an employer obtain additional information on the VFCP?

Additional information on the VFCP can be obtained by contacting the EBSA at (866) 275-7922 and requesting the VFCP coordinator. Questions about the prohibited transaction exemption should be directed to the Office of Exemption Determinations at (202) 693-8540. For additional information, see EBSA's "Frequently Asked Questions about the Voluntary Fiduciary Correction Program" at *http://www.dol.gov/ebsa/faqs/faq_vfcp.html* (visited on Aug. 21, 2012).

Q 17:48 Have any amendments been made to the VFCP?

Yes. On May 19, 2006, the DOL revised the VFCP to add certain model forms, reduce documentation required, and add new covered transactions to its program. For example, VFCP now allows a plan that has purchased an asset from a party in interest to retain the asset and to correct the transaction by receiving a settlement amount in cash from the party in interest. Formerly, VFCP required the plan to divest the asset.

Q 17:49 How does the VFCP Online Calculator work?

First of all, the VFCP Online Calculator may be used to calculate lost earnings in the case of deferrals being deposited into the employee's IRA after the deadline.

The VFCP Online Calculator (a manual calculation worksheet is provided as well on the DOL Web site) requires that the employer or administrator know the following: amount of late contribution, loss date (the date that the breach began), recovery date (the date corrected), and final payment date (date earnings restored to plan). Once this information is input, the calculator does all the work.

The Online Calculator allows applicants to view printable inputs and results.

Note. Calculations and data cannot be saved on-line. The employer or administrator may save the results by printing a copy and scanning it, or copying and pasting a copy into a text or spreadsheet file before terminating the on-line session.

Appendix A

Sample Forms

SEP, SARSEP Deferral Form

1. Salary Reduction Deferral

Subject to the requirements of the elective SEP of [*insert name of employer*] I authorize the following amount or percentage of my regular compensation to be withheld from each of my paychecks and contributed to my SEP IRA:

a. _______ percent of my salary (not in excess of 25 percent or [*insert percentage*]);

b. _______ dollar amount (not in excess of $17,000, plus catch-up amount (up to $5,500) if age 50 by the end of the taxable year, for 2012); OR

c. Dollar amount (which equals _______ percent of my current rate of pay).

This salary reduction authorization shall remain in effect until I terminate this authorization or until I give written modification of its terms to my employer.

2. Cash Bonus Deferral

Subject to the requirements of the elective SEP of [*insert name of employer*] I authorize the following amount to be contributed to my SEP IRA rather than being paid to me in cash:

a. _______ dollar amount (not in excess of $17,000, plus catch-up amount (up to $5,500) if age 50 by the end of the taxable year, for 2012).

3. Self-Employed Individuals:

a. I elect to contribute $ _______ for the plan year.

b. If (b) is checked, the following breakdown applies: Regular Elective Deferrals of $ _______ and catch-up deferrals of $ _______.

4. Amount of Deferral

I understand that the total amount I defer in any calendar year to this SEP may not exceed the lesser of:

a. 25 percent of my compensation (determined without including any SEP IRA contributions); or

b. $17,000 (plus catch-up contribution (up to $5,500) if age 50 by the end of the taxable year) for 2012.

Note: $250,000 (the 2012 limit) is the maximum amount of compensation that may be considered for plan purposes. [*See Appendix G—Employee Benefit Limits.*]

5. Commencement of Deferral

The deferral election specified in either item 1 or 2 shall not become effective before:

a. ______ [*Specify a date no earlier than the first day of the first pay period beginning after this authorization.*]

6. Distributions from SEP IRAs

I understand that I should not withdraw or transfer any amounts from my SEP IRA that are attributable to elective deferrals and income on elective deferrals for a particular plan year (except for excess elective deferrals) until two and one-half months after the end of the plan year or, if sooner, when my employer notifies me that the deferral percentage limitation test for that plan year has been completed. Any such amounts that I withdraw or transfer before this time will be includible in income for purposes of Code Sections 72(t) and 408(d)(1).

Signature of employee ______ Date _____

Note. For 2012, the dollar amount may not exceed $17,000, plus catch-up amounts up to $5,500.

Model Notification to Eligible Employees (SIMPLE IRA Plan)

SIMPLE IRA Plan Information

Name of Employer: ______________________

Address of Employer:____________________

Phone: __________________ Plan Year: ___________

Opportunity to Participate in the SIMPLE IRA Plan

You are eligible to make salary reduction contributions to the above referenced Employer's SIMPLE IRA plan. This notice and the attached summary description provide you with information that you should consider before you decide whether to start, continue, or change your salary reduction agreement.

Employer Contribution Election

For the calendar year, the employer elects to contribute to your SIMPLE IRA (*employer must select (1), (2), or (3)*):

☐(1) A matching contribution equal to your salary reduction contributions up to a limit of 3 percent of your compensation for the year;

☐(2) A matching contribution equal to your salary reduction contributions up to a limit of ______ percent (*employer must insert a number from 1 to 3 and is subject to certain restrictions*) of your compensation for the year; or

☐(3) A nonelective contribution equal to 2 percent of your compensation for the year (limited to $250,000*) if you are an employee who makes at least $ ______ (*employer must insert an amount that is $5,000 or less*) in compensation for the year.

Administrative Procedures

To start or change your salary reduction contributions, you must complete the salary reduction agreement and return it to ______ (*employer should designate a place or individual*) by ______ (*employer should insert a date that is not less than 60 days after notice is given*).

Employee Selection of Financial Institution

You must select the financial institution that will serve as the trustee, custodian, or issuer of your SIMPLE IRA and notify your employer of your selection. You may indicate the financial institution on your Salary Reduction Agreement.

* This is the amount for 2012. For later years, the limit may be increased for cost-of-living adjustments. The IRS announces the increase, if any, in a news release, in the Internal Revenue Bulletin, and on the IRS Web site at *http:www.irs.gov* (visited on Aug. 22, 2012).

Model Salary Reduction Agreement (SIMPLE IRA Plan)

SIMPLE IRA Plan Information

Name of Employer: ______

Plan Year: ______

Salary Reduction Election

Name of Employee: ______

Subject to the requirements of the SIMPLE IRA plan of the above named Employer.

- ☐ I authorize ______ percent or $______ (which equals ______ percent of my current rate of pay) to be withheld from my pay for each pay period and contributed to my SIMPLE IRA as a salary reduction contribution.
- ☐ I elect to terminate my salary reduction contributions.
- ☐ I elect not to participate in my Employer's SIMPLE Plan with respect to salary reduction contributions.

Maximum Salary Reduction

I understand that the total amount of my salary reduction contributions in any calendar year cannot exceed the applicable amount for that year. (See SIMPLE IRA Plan Disclosure.)

Date Salary Reduction Begins

I understand that my salary reduction contributions will start as soon as permitted under the SIMPLE IRA plan and as soon as administratively feasible or, if later, ______. (*Fill in the date you want the salary reduction contributions to begin. The date must be after you sign this agreement.*)

Employee Selection of Financial Institution

I select the following financial institution to serve as the trustee, custodian, or issuer of my SIMPLE IRA.

Name of financial institution: ______________________________

Address of financial institution: ______________________________

SIMPLE IRA account name and number: ______________________

Phone: ____________________

I understand that I must establish a SIMPLE IRA to receive any contributions made on my behalf under this SIMPLE IRA plan. If the information regarding my SIMPLE IRA is incomplete when I first submit my salary reduction agreement, I realize that it must be completed by the date contributions must be made under the SIMPLE IRA plan. If I fail to update my agreement to provide this information by that date, I understand that my employer may select a financial institution for my SIMPLE IRA.

Duration of Election

This salary reduction agreement replaces any earlier agreement and will remain in effect as long as I remain an eligible employee under the SIMPLE IRA plan or until I provide my employer with a request to end my salary reduction contributions or provide a new salary reduction agreement as permitted under this SIMPLE IRA plan.

Signature of Employee: ____________________ Date: ____________________

Sample Summary Description (SIMPLE IRA Plan)

Plan Information

1. Name of Employer: ____________________

   Address of Employer: ____________________
2. Name of Trustee/Custodian: ____________________

   Address of Trustee/Custodian: ____________________

Eligibility Requirements

3. All Employees of the Employer shall be eligible to participate under the Plan except:

   ☐a. Employees included in a unit of employees covered under a collective bargaining agreement described in Section __________ of the Plan.

   ☐b. Non-resident alien employees who did not receive US source income described in Section __________ of the Plan.

   ☐c. Employees who are not reasonably expected to earn $__________ (not to exceed $5,000) during the Plan Year for which the contribution is being made.

   ☐d. There are no eligibility requirements. All Employees are eligible to participate upon the later of the plan's effective date or the employee's date of hire.
4. Each Eligible Employee will be eligible to become a Participant after having worked for the Employer during any __________ prior years (not to exceed two) and received at least $ __________ in compensation (not to exceed $5,000), during each of such prior years.

Written Allocation Formula

5. The Employer has agreed to provide contributions for the __________ Plan Year as follows (complete only one choice):

   ☐a. Matching Contribution—The amount of the Participant's Elective Deferral not in excess of 3 percent of such Participant's Compensation.

   ☐b. Matching Contribution—The amount of the Participant's Elective Deferral not in excess of __________ percent (not less than 1 percent nor more than 3 percent) of each Participant's Compensation.

   ☐c. Nonelective Employer Contribution—2 percent of each Eligible Employee's Compensation, who receives at least $5,000, or __________, if less, in Compensation from the Employer for the Plan Year.

Additional Information

The Employer has designated ______________________________ (*insert name & title*) to provide additional information to participants about the Employer's SIMPLE Plan.

General Disclosure Information

The following information explains what a Savings Incentive Match Plan for Employees ("SIMPLE") is, how contributions are made, and how to treat these contributions for tax purposes. For more specific information, refer to the SIMPLE Retirement Plan document itself, the completed Adoption Agreement and the accompanying "Employer Disclosure."

For a calendar year, you may make or modify a salary reduction election during the 60-day period immediately preceding January 1 of that year. However, for the year in which you first become eligible to make salary reduction contributions, the period during which you may make or modify the election is a 60-day period that includes either the date you become eligible or the day before. If indicated on the Adoption Agreement, you may have additional opportunities during a calendar year to make or modify your salary reduction election.

I. SIMPLE Retirement Plan and SIMPLE IRA Defined

A SIMPLE Retirement Plan is a retirement income arrangement established by your employer. Under this SIMPLE Plan, you may choose to defer compensation to your own Simple Individual Retirement Account or Annuity ("IRA"). You may base these "elective deferrals" on a salary reduction basis that, at your election, may be contributed to a SIMPLE IRA or received in cash. This type of plan is available only to an employer with 100 or fewer employees who earned at least $5,000 during the prior calendar year.

A SIMPLE IRA is a separate IRA plan that you establish with an eligible financial institution for the purpose of receiving contributions under this SIMPLE Retirement Plan. Your employer must provide you with a copy of the SIMPLE agreement containing eligibility requirements and a description of the basis upon which contributions may be made. All amounts contributed to your SIMPLE IRA belong to you, even after you quit working for your employer.

II. Elective Deferrals—Not Required

You are not required to make elective deferrals under this SIMPLE Retirement Plan. However, if the Employer is matching your elective deferrals, no Employer contribution will be made on your behalf unless you elect to defer under the plan.

III. Elective Deferrals—Annual Limitation

The maximum amount that you may defer under this SIMPLE Plan for any calendar year is limited to the lesser of the percentage of your compensation indicated in the Deferral Form or "the applicable annual dollar limitation" described below:

Applicable Annual Dollar Limitations

Tax Year	*Contribution Limit*
2012	$11,500

Note. The maximum amount will be adjusted for cost-of-living increases in multiples of $500.

If you attain age 50 or over by the end of a calendar year, you can elect to have your compensation reduced by an additional "catch-up" amount listed below. The maximum additional amount will be adjusted for cost-of-living increases in multiples of $500, as follows:

Tax Year	*Catch-Up Limit*
2012	$2,500

If you work for other employers (unrelated to this Employer) who also maintain a salary deferral plan, there is an overall limit on the maximum amount that you may defer in each calendar year to all elective SEPs, cash or deferred arrangements under Code Section 401(k), other SIMPLE plans and Code Section 403(b) plans regardless of how many employers you may have worked for during the year. This limitation is referred to as the Code Section 402(g) limit. The Code Section 402(g) limit on elective deferrals is listed below and is indexed according to the cost of living.

$17,000 for 2012

IV. Elective Deferrals—Tax Treatment

The amount that you may elect to contribute to your SIMPLE IRA is excludible from gross income, subject to the limitations discussed above, and is not includible as taxable wages on Form W-2. However, these amounts are subject to FICA taxes.

V. Elective Deferrals—Excess Amounts Contributed

When "excess elective deferrals" (i.e., amounts in excess of the SIMPLE elective deferral limit ("the applicable annual dollar limitation" described in Section III above) or the Code Section 402(g) limit) are made, you are responsible for calculating whether you have exceeded these limits in the calendar year. The Code Section 402(g) limit for contributions made to all elective deferral plans is listed in Section III above.

VI. Excess Elective Deferrals—How to Avoid Adverse Tax Consequences

Excess elective deferrals are includible in your gross income in the calendar year of deferral. Income on the excess elective deferrals is includible in your income in the year of withdrawal from the SIMPLE IRA. You should withdraw excess elective deferrals and any allocable income, from your SIMPLE IRA by April 15 following the year to which the deferrals relate. These amounts may not be transferred or rolled over tax-free to another SIMPLE IRA.

VII. Income Allocable To Excess Amounts

The rules for determining and allocating income attributable to excess elective deferrals and other excess SIMPLE contributions are the same as those governing regular IRA excess contributions. The trustee or custodian of your SIMPLE IRA will inform you of the income allocable to such excess amounts.

VIII. Availability of Regular IRA Contribution Deduction

In addition to any SIMPLE contribution, you may contribute to a separate IRA the lesser of 100 percent of compensation or the regular IRA contribution dollar limit to an IRA as a regular IRA contribution. However, the amount that you may deduct is subject to various limitations since you will be considered an "active participant" in an employer-sponsored plan. See Publication 590, *Individual Retirement Arrangements,* for more specific information.

IX. SIMPLE IRA Amounts—Rollover or Transfer to another IRA

You may not roll over or transfer from your SIMPLE IRA any SIMPLE contributions (or income on these contributions) made during the plan year to another IRA (other than a SIMPLE IRA) or to an employer plan until the two years following the date you first participated in the SIMPLE plan. Also, any distribution made before this time will be includible in your gross income and may also be subject to a 25 percent additional income tax for early withdrawal. You may, however, remove excess elective deferrals and income allocable to such excess amounts from your SIMPLE IRA before this time, but you may not roll over or transfer these amounts to another IRA.

If the Adoption Agreement indicates that all initial SIMPLE contributions will be made to a single designated Trustee or Custodian, you may transfer your SIMPLE IRA without cost or penalty to another SIMPLE IRA (if within the two-year period) or thereafter to any other IRA.

After the restriction described above no longer applies, you may withdraw, or receive, funds from your SIMPLE IRA, and no more than 60 days later, place such funds in another IRA, SIMPLE IRA, qualified plan, 403(b) plan, or 457 plan. This is called a "rollover" and may not be done without penalty more frequently than at one-year intervals, if you are rolling to another SIMPLE IRA or IRA. However, there are no restrictions on the number of times that you may make "transfers" if you arrange to have such funds transferred between the trustees/custodians so that you never have possession of the funds. You may not, however, roll over or transfer excess elective deferrals and income allocable to such excess amounts from your SIMPLE IRA to another IRA. These excess amounts may be reduced only by a distribution to you.

Rollover conversion and direct conversion to a Roth IRA are also permitted. See Publication 590—*Individual Retirement Arrangements,* for more specific information.

X. Filing Requirements

You do not need to file any additional forms with the IRS because of your participation in your employer's SIMPLE Plan.

XI. Employer to Provide Information on SIMPLE IRAs and the SIMPLE Agreement

Your employer must provide you with a copy of the executed SIMPLE agreement, this Summary Description, the form you should use to elect to defer amounts to the SIMPLE, and a statement for each taxable year showing any contribution to your SIMPLE IRA.

XII. Financial Institution Where IRA Is Established to Provide Information

The financial institution must provide you with a disclosure statement that contains the following items of information in plain nontechnical language.

1. The statutory requirements that relate to the SIMPLE IRA;
2. The tax consequences that follow the exercise of various options and what those options are;
3. Participation eligibility rules and rules on the deductibility and nondeductibility of retirement savings;

4. The circumstances and procedures under which you may revoke the SIMPLE IRA, including the name, address, and telephone number of the person designated to receive notice of revocation (this explanation must be prominently displayed at the beginning of the disclosure statement);
5. Explanations of when penalties may be assessed against you because of specified prohibited or penalized activities concerning the SIMPLE IRA; and
6. Financial disclosure information which:
   a. Either projects value, growth, rates of the SIMPLE IRA under various contribution and retirement schedules, or describes the method of computing and allocating annual earnings and charges which may be assessed;
   b. Describes whether, and for what period, the growth projections for the plan are guaranteed or a statement of earnings rate and terms on which these projections are based, and;
   c. States the sales commission to be charged in each year expressed as a percentage of $1,000.

See Publication 590, *Individual Retirement Arrangements*, which is available at *http://www.irs.gov/pub/irs-pdf/p590.pdf* (visited on Aug. 22, 2012) or at most IRS offices, for a more complete explanation of the disclosure requirements.

In addition to the disclosure statement, the financial institution is required to provide you with a financial statement each year. It may be necessary to retain and refer to statements for more than one year in order to evaluate the investment performance of your SIMPLE IRA and in order that you will know how to report SIMPLE IRA distributions for tax purposes.

Sample Summary Description for Non-Designated Financial Institution (SIMPLE IRA Plan)

(For use by Institutions where Employer is not known—this form is provided to the employee for his or her employer.)

Employer must complete the following:

ELIGIBILITY REQUIREMENTS

All Employees of the Employer shall be eligible to participate under the Plan except:

☐a. Employees included in a unit of employees covered under a collective bargaining agreement.

☐b. Nonresident alien employees who did not receive U.S. source income.

☐c. Employees who are not reasonably expected to earn $ _______ (not to exceed $5,000) during the Plan Year for which the contribution is being made.

☐d. There are no eligibility requirements. All Employees are eligible to participate upon the later of the plan's effective date or the employee's date of hire.

Each Eligible Employee will be eligible to become a Participant after having worked for the Employer during any _____ prior years (not to exceed two) and received at least $_______ in compensation (not to exceed $5,000), during each of such prior years.

WRITTEN ALLOCATION FORMULA

The Employer has agreed to provide contributions for the _______ Plan Year as follows (complete only one choice):

☐a. Matching Contribution—The amount of the Participant's Elective Deferral not in excess of 3 percent of such Participant's Compensation.

☐b. Matching Contribution—The amount of the Participant's Elective Deferral not in excess of _______ percent (not less than 1 percent nor more than 3 percent) of each Participant's Compensation.

☐c. Nonelective Employer Contribution—2 percent of each Participant's Compensation.

The Employer has designated _______ (*insert name & title*) to provide additional information to participants about the Employer's SIMPLE Plan.

GENERAL DISCLOSURE INFORMATION

The following information explains what a Savings Incentive Match Plan for Employees ("SIMPLE") is, how contributions are made, and how to treat these contributions for tax purposes. For more specific information, refer to the employer's SIMPLE Retirement Plan document itself. For a calendar year, you may make or modify a salary reduction election during the 60-day period immediately preceding January 1 of that year. However, for the year in which you first become eligible to make salary reduction contributions, the period during which you may make or modify the election is a 60 day period that includes either the date you become eligible or the day before. If indicated in your employer's SIMPLE plan, you may have additional opportunities during a calendar year to make or modify your salary reduction election.

I. SIMPLE Retirement Plan and SIMPLE IRA Defined

A SIMPLE Retirement Plan is a retirement income arrangement established by your employer. Under this SIMPLE Plan, you may choose to defer compensation to your own SIMPLE Individual Retirement Account or Annuity ("IRA"). You may base these "elective deferrals" on a salary reduction basis that, at your election, may be contributed to a SIMPLE IRA or received in cash. This type of plan is available only to an employer with 100 or fewer employees who earned at least $5,000 during the prior calendar year. A SIMPLE IRA is a separate IRA plan that you establish with an eligible financial institution for the purpose of receiving contributions under this SIMPLE Retirement Plan. Your employer must provide you with a copy of the SIMPLE agreement containing eligibility requirements and a description of the basis upon which contributions may be made. All amounts contributed to your IRA belong to you, even after you quit working for your employer.

II. Elective Deferrals—Not Required

You are not required to make elective deferrals under this SIMPLE Retirement Plan. However, if the Employer is matching your elective deferrals, no Employer contribution will be made on your behalf unless you elect to defer under the plan.

III. Elective Deferrals—Annual Limitation

The maximum amount that you may defer under this SIMPLE Plan for any calendar year is limited to the lesser of the percentage of your compensation that you select or the following dollar limit, subject to cost-of-living increases.

Applicable Annual Dollar Limitations

Tax Year	*Contribution Limit*
2012	$11,500

If you work for other employers (unrelated to this Employer) who also maintain a salary deferral plan, there is an overall limit on the maximum amount that you may defer in each calendar year to all elective SEPs, cash or deferred arrangements under Code Section 401(k), other SIMPLE plans and 403(b) plans regardless of how many employers you may have worked for during the year. This limitation is referred to as the Code Section 402(g) limit. The Code Section 402(g) limit on elective deferrals is currently $17,000 for 2012 and is indexed according to the cost of living. If you attain age 50 or over by the end of a calendar year, you can elect to have your compensation reduced by an additional "catch-up" amount of $2,500 for 2012, subject to cost-of-living adjustments.

IV. Elective Deferrals—Tax Treatment

The amount that you may elect to contribute to your SIMPLE IRA is excludible from gross income, subject to the limitations discussed above, and is not includible as taxable wages on Form W-2. However, these amounts are subject to FICA taxes.

V. Elective Deferrals—Excess Amounts Contributed

When "excess elective deferrals" (i.e., amounts in excess of the SIMPLE elective deferral limit or the Code Section 402(g) limit) are made, you are responsible for calculating whether you have exceeded these limits in the calendar year. For 2012, the Code Section 402(g) limit for contributions made to all elective deferral plans is $17,000. Excess elective deferrals are calculated on the basis of the calendar year.

VI. Excess Elective Deferrals—How to Avoid Adverse Tax Consequences

Excess elective deferrals are includible in your gross income in the calendar year of deferral. Income on the excess elective deferrals is includible in your income in the year of withdrawal from the IRA. You should withdraw excess elective deferrals and any allocable income, from your SIMPLE IRA by April 15 following the year to which the deferrals relate. These amounts may not be transferred or rolled over tax-free to another SIMPLE IRA. Income on excess elective deferrals is includible in your gross income in the year you withdraw it from your IRA and must be withdrawn by April 15 following the calendar year to which the deferrals relate. Income withdrawn from the IRA after that date may be subject to a 10 percent tax (or 25 percent if withdrawn within the first two years of participation) on early distributions.

VII. Income Allocable to Excess Amounts

The rules for determining and allocating income attributable to excess elective deferrals and other excess SIMPLE contributions are the same as those governing regular IRA excess contributions. The trustee or custodian of your SIMPLE IRA will inform you of the income allocable to such excess amounts.

VIII. Availability of Regular IRA Contribution Deduction

In addition to any SIMPLE contribution, you may contribute to a separate IRA the lesser of 100 percent of compensation or the regular IRA contribution dollar limit to an IRA as a regular IRA contribution. However, the amount that you may deduct is subject to various limitations since you will be considered an "active participant" in an employer-sponsored plan. See Publication 590, *Individual Retirement Arrangements,* for more specific information.

IX. SIMPLE IRA Amounts—Rollover or Transfer to Another IRA

You may not roll over or transfer from your SIMPLE IRA any SIMPLE contributions (or income on these contributions) made during the plan year to another IRA (other than a SIMPLE IRA) or to an employer plan until the two years following the date you first participated in the SIMPLE plan. Also, any distribution made before this time will be includible in your gross income and may also be subject to a 25 percent additional income tax for early withdrawal. You may, however, remove excess elective deferrals and income allocable to such excess amounts from your SIMPLE IRA before this time, but you may not roll over or transfer these amounts to another IRA.

After the two-year restriction no longer applies, you may withdraw, or receive, funds from your SIMPLE IRA, and no more than 60 days later, place such funds in another IRA or SIMPLE IRA. This is called a "rollover" and may not be done without penalty more frequently than at one-year intervals. However, there are no restrictions on the number of times that you may make "transfers" if you arrange to have such funds transferred between the Custodians so that you never have possession of the funds. You may not, however, roll over or transfer excess elective deferrals, and income allocable to such excess amounts from your SIMPLE IRA to another IRA. These excess amounts may be reduced only by a distribution to you.

Rollover conversion and direct conversion to a Roth IRA are also permitted (but before 2010 may be subject to a $100,000 modified adjusted gross income limit restriction and, if married, a joint filing requirement). *See* Publication 590, *Individual Retirement Arrangements,* for more specific information.

X. Filing Requirements

You do not need to file any additional forms with the IRS because of your participation in your employer's SIMPLE Plan.

XI. Employer to Provide Information

Your employer must provide you with a copy of the executed SIMPLE agreement, a Summary Description, the form you should use to elect to defer amounts to your SIMPLE IRA, and a statement for each taxable year showing any contribution to your SIMPLE IRA.

XII. Financial Institution Where IRA Is Established to Provide Information

The financial institution must provide you with a disclosure statement that contains information described in Treasury Regulations Section 1.408-6. The Disclosure Statement that is a part of this SIMPLE IRA account documentation must be read in conjunction with this Summary Description for Non-Designated Financial Institutions. The Disclosure Statement contains important information about the SIMPLE plan rules and the contents of such Disclosure Statement are incorporated herein by reference.

See Publication 590, *Individual Retirement Arrangements,* which is available at *http://www.irs.gov/pub/irs-pdf/p590.pdf* (visited on Aug. 22, 2012) or at most IRS offices, for a more complete explanation of the disclosure requirements. In addition to the disclosure statement, the financial institution is required to provide you with a financial statement each year. It may be necessary to retain and refer to statements for more than one year in order to evaluate the investment performance of your IRA and in order that you will know how to report IRA distributions for tax purposes.

Appendix B

Sample Notices

Notification of Excess SEP Contributions (HCE deferral percentage limitation exceeded)

To: [*name of employee*]

Date: [*generally on or before March 15, 2013*]

Our calculations indicate that the elective deferrals you made to your SEP IRA for the plan year ending __________, 201__________ exceed the maximum permissible limits under Code Section 408(k)(6). You made excess SEP contributions of $_______ for that year.

These excess SEP contributions are includible in your gross income when distributed from your SEP-IRA [*see Notes below*].

These excess SEP contributions must be distributed from your SEP IRA by April 15, 201 _______ [*insert year after the calendar year in which this notice is given*] to avoid possible penalties. Income allocable to the excess amounts must be withdrawn at the same time and is also includible in income in the year withdrawn. Excess SEP contributions remaining in your SEP IRA account (or annuity, if applicable) after that time may be subject to a 6 percent excise tax, and the income on these excess SEP contributions may be subject to a 10 percent penalty when finally withdrawn.

Signature of employer ________________________ Date ___________

Note 1. Excess SEP contributions of an eligible employee who would attain age 50 or over by the end of the calendar year are not includible in income and do not have to be withdrawn to the extent such employee has not reached the catch-up elective deferral contribution limit for the plan year to which the excess SEP contributions relate.

Note 2. If notification is not made by end of the plan year following the plan year in which the excess SEP contribution arose, the SEP is no longer treated as a SEP, and all contributions are treated as traditional IRA contributions. An employer may also be subject to a 10 percent penalty tax if the notice is not provided within 2 months following the close of the plan year (see Q 12:31).

Notification of Disallowed Deferrals (50 percent participation rate requirement not met)

To: [*name of employee*]

Date: [*generally on or before March 15, 2013*]

Our calculations indicate that the elective deferrals you made to your SEP IRA for the plan year ending on ______, 201____ [*enter date plan year ends*], exceed the maximum permissible limits under Code Section 408(k)(6). You made disallowed deferrals (i.e., IRA contributions that are not SEP-IRA contributions) of $______ for 201______. [*See Note.*] The disallowed deferral amount and income allocable to the disallowed deferrals are includible in gross income in the year of withdrawal from the IRA.

These disallowed deferrals must be distributed from your SEP-IRA by April 15, 201______ [*insert year after the calendar year in which this notice is given (2013 or 2014)*] to avoid possible penalties. Income allocable to the disallowed deferral must be withdrawn at the same time and is includible in income in the year withdrawn. Disallowed deferrals remaining in your SEP-IRA account (or annuity, if applicable) after that time may be subject to a 6 percent excise tax, and the income on these excess SEP contributions may be subject to a 10 percent penalty when finally withdrawn.

Signature of employer ______________________ Date ___________

Note. Disallowed deferrals (determined on a plan year basis) are includible in gross income for the calendar year or years in which the amounts deferred would have been received in cash had there been no election to defer. The relevant April 15 follows the calendar year of notification (2012 or 2013).

Notification of Excess Deferrals ($17,000/$22,500 elective deferral limits exceeded)

To: [*name of employee*]

Date: [*on or before January 31, 2013*]

Our calculations indicate that the elective deferrals you made to your SEP IRA for the calendar exceed the maximum permissible limits for the calendar year under Code Section 402(g). The full amount of the elective deferral, including any excess deferrals, was reported in box 12 of Form W-2 for the calendar year to which the deferral relates.

For 2012, the excess deferral amount is $ ______.

The instructions contained on Form W-2, Notice to Employee (Form W-2, box 12) instructs you to include in income elective SEP deferral amounts that exceed the overall elective limit (generally $17,000 plus catch-up contributions ($5,500), if applicable, for 2012). Unless you include the excess deferral in your income on Form 1040, U.S. Individual Income Tax Return (line 7), in the year to which the deferral relates, you may have to file an amended income tax return.

You should generally withdraw the excess deferral and any allocable income by April 15, following this notification, because after that date, the excess deferral is deemed an IRA contribution subject to the IRA contribution limits of Code Sections 219 and 408 and may be considered an excess contribution to your IRA. [I.R.C. §§ 402(g)(2)(A)(ii), 408(d)(4), 408(d)(5)] That is, on April 16, it is no longer treated as an excess deferral, but as an IRA contribution.

If, on the other hand, you withdraw the excess deferral in a proper correcting distribution before April 16 (no extensions) of the year following the calendar year to which the deferral relates, the gain is not subject to the 10 percent premature distribution penalty tax. [I.R.C. §§ 401(k)(8)(D), 408(k)(6)(C)(i)]

Signature of employer ______________________ Date ___________

Note. An employer is not required to provide an employee with any type of formal notification that an elective contribution in excess of the Code Section 402(g) dollar limit (an excess deferral) has been made. However, the full amount of the elective deferral, including any excess, is reported by the employer in box 12 of Form W-2 for the calendar year to which the deferral relates.

Sample Return of Excess Form Request to Return Employer/Employee Contributions (For SIMPLE IRA Plans Under IRS EPCRS Procedure)

I. GENERAL INFORMATION

Name of Participant: Account No:
Participant's Address:
Participant's SSN: Participant's Home Phone #: Participant's Bus. Phone #:
Name of Employer: Employer's Phone #:
Address of Employer:
Trustee/Custodian of SIMPLE IRA:

In accordance with the terms of the IRS' EPCRS program as described under Revenue Procedure 2008-50, the undersigned Participant and the Employer hereby request a distribution from the SIMPLE IRA Account of the above-named Participant as a reportable corrective distribution. Such corrective distribution is described in Section II below.

II. REASON/TYPE OF EXCESS

1. Excess Deferral - The Participant and Employer hereby certify that this distribution is a correction of an excess deferral. This distribution shall be adjusted for earnings through the date of corrective distribution. Such distribution is not eligible for rollover purposes.

Amount of excess deferral: $ ______________ for tax year 201___

Amount of earnings: + $ ______________

Total distribution: = $ ______________

Reporting: The amount distributed to the affected Participant is includible in gross income. Depending upon the timing of the corrective distribution, the Trustee/Custodian may be required to issue multiple forms 1099-R in the name of the Participant.

2. Excess Employer Contributions - The Participant and Employer hereby certify that this distribution is a correction of the Employer Contribution type indicated below. This distribution shall be paid to the Employer and shall be adjusted for earnings through the date of corrective distribution. Such distribution is not eligible for rollover purposes.

☐ **Excess Nonelective Contribution for tax year 201___**

Amount of excess: $ ______________ for tax year 201___

Amount of earnings: + $ ______________

Total distribution: = $ ______________

☐ **Excess Matching Contributions for tax year 201___**

Amount of excess: $ ______________ for tax year 201___

Amount of earnings: + $ ______________

Total distribution: = $ ______________

Reporting: The amount distributed to the Employer is not includible in the gross income of the affected Participant. The Employer is not entitled to a deduction for such employer excess amount. The distribution is reported on Form 1099-A issued to the Participant indicating the taxable amount as zero.

III. DISTRIBUTION AUTHORIZATION BY PARTICIPANT AND EMPLOYER

The above request for a corrective distribution is hereby approved, and the Trustee/Custodian of the SIMPLE IRA is authorized to distribute the amount of the excess, as indicated above, to the Participant (if an excess deferral is indicated) or to the Employer (if an excess employer contribution is indicated). We also certify that no tax advice has been given by the Trustee/Custodian and that all decisions regarding this correction are solely the responsibility of the Participant and the Employer.

Participant's Signature: ______________________ Date: ______________

Employer's Signature: ______________________ Date: ______________

Appendix C

Sample Simplified Employee Pension Allocation Formula Notices

Alternative 1 (nonintegrated or model SEP)

To: All Eligible Employees

Re: Allocation Formula under the Simplified Employee Pension Agreement

Contributions pursuant to the Simplified Employee Pension agreement will be made for (check one) [ ] the calendar year 201 ____ [ ] the employer's taxable year ending __________ [*month*] 201 ____ to employees who will attain at least ____ (not to exceed 21) years of age during such year and who have performed service for the employer during no less than ____ (not to exceed three) years of the immediately preceding five years, at the rate of ____ percent of compensation. The amount contributed excludes compensation in excess of $250,000* for 2012, and the amount of the contributions hereunder may not exceed 25 percent of taxable compensation or $50,000 {Add following if SARSEP} ($55,500 if age 50 or older by December 31) for 2012.

Signature of employer ______________________ Date __________

Note. For 2012, the maximum dollar limit is $50,000 ($55,500 if age 50 by the end of the taxable year).

---

* For 2012, $250,000 is the maximum amount of compensation that may be considered for plan purposes. (See Appendix G—Employee Benefit Limits.)

Alternative 2 (integrated SEP, contribution expressed as a formula)

To: All Eligible Employees

Re: Allocation Formula under the Simplified Employee Pension Agreement

Contributions pursuant to the Simplified Employee Pension agreement will be made for (check one) [ ] the calendar year 201 ____ [ ] the employer's taxable year ending [month] 201 ____ to employees who will attain at least ____ (not to exceed 21) years of age during such year and who have performed service for the employer during no less than ____ (not to exceed three) years of the immediately preceding five years, at the rate of ____ percent, [ ] plus ____ percent of compensation in excess of $ ____ [*an amount not to exceed the TWB for the year*]. The amount contributed excludes compensation in excess of $250,000* for 2012, and the amount of the contributions contributed hereunder may not exceed 25 percent of taxable compensation or $50,000** {*Add following if SARSEP*} ($55,500 if age 50 or older by December 31) for 2012.

Signature of employer ______________________ Date ___________

* The $50,000 amount is a deduction limit. For participant exclusion purposes, the $50,000 amount is reduced if the plan is integrated in the case of an HCE (see Q 9:5).

** For 2012, the maximum dollar limit is $50,000 ($55,500 if age 50 by the end of the taxable year).

Appendix D

Revenue Procedure 2008-50

Revenue Procedure 2008-50 [2008-35 I.R.B. 464 (Sept. 2, 2008)] updates the Employee Plan Compliance Resolution System (EPCRS) for sponsors of retirement plans that are intended to satisfy the requirements of Sections 401(a), 403(a), 403(b), 408(k), or 408(p) of the Internal Revenue Code, but that have not met these requirements for a period of time. EPCRS permits plan sponsors to correct these failures and thereby continue to provide their employees with retirement benefits on a tax-deferred basis. This appendix provides Schedules 3 and 4 of Appendix F of this revenue procedure.

APPENDIX F, SCHEDULE 3
SEPs and SARSEPs

Plan Name: ______________________________ EIN: ______________ Plan #:____

Instructions: This Schedule 3 is available for Simplified Employee Pension plans (SEPs), including SEPs that include salary reduction arrangements (i.e. Salary Reduction Simplified Employee Pension plans (SARSEPs).)

PART I. IDENTIFICATION OF FAILURE(S) AND PROPOSED METHOD(S) OF CORRECTION

The following failure(s) occurred with respect to the plan identified above. Check the failure(s) that apply. Within each failure, check applicable boxes, and provide the information requested:

☐ **A.** **Employer Eligibility Failure** (SARSEPs only)

☐ The Plan Sponsor was not eligible to sponsor a SARSEP because the plan was established on ________ . (Plan Sponsors were not permitted to establish SARSEPs after December 31, 1996.)

☐ The plan was adopted by a Plan Sponsor who was (or subsequently became) ineligible to sponsor a SARSEP under the requirements of § 408(k)(6) because the Plan Sponsor (and, if applicable its related controlled group or affiliated service group employers) had more than 25 employees (including leased employees, if applicable) during the following plan year(s):

____

☐ The plan was adopted by a Plan Sponsor that became ineligible to sponsor a SARSEP under the requirements of § 408(k)(6) because, in one or more plan year(s), fewer than 50% of the employees eligible to participate in the plan elected to make salary reduction contributions. The failure occurred during the following plan year(s): ______________________________

____

Description of Proposed Method of Correction

All contributions ceased as of ____________ (insert date beginning no later than the date this application is filed under VCP). The Plan Sponsor will not permit any new salary reduction contributions to the plan.

☐ **B.** **Failure to satisfy the deferral percentage test** (SARSEPs only)

At least one highly compensated employee ("HCE") deferred an amount which, as a percentage of compensation, was more than 125% of the average deferral percentage ("ADP") for all nonhighly compensated employees ("NHCEs") eligible to participate in the plan (§ 408(k)(6)(A)(iii)). The failure occurred for the following plan year(s):

APPENDIX F, SCHEDULE 3
SEPs and SARSEPs

Plan Name: ________________________________ EIN: ______________ Plan #:____

____

____

The total excess deferrals for each affected plan year were as follows:

Year	Excess Deferrals

Description of the Proposed Method of Correction

The Plan Sponsor has made (or will make) nonforfeitable contributions on behalf of all eligible NHCEs. Each eligible NHCE will receive a contribution equal to a uniform percentage of compensation. The uniform percentage is equal to the difference between the (1) ADP that would have been required for a HCE's deferral percentage to have passed the nondiscrimination test and (2) the actual ADP for NHCEs. (Example: In a particular plan year, an HCE defers 10% of compensation. The ADP for NHCEs for the same plan year is 5% of compensation. However, in order for the plan to pass the nondiscrimination test, the ADP should have been 8% of compensation. The corrective contribution on behalf of each eligible NHCE will be equal to 3% of compensation.) The corrective contribution made on behalf of each NHCE will also be adjusted for earnings. Earnings will be calculated from the last day of the plan year for which the failure occurred through the date of the corrective contribution. The corrective contribution (adjusted for earnings) will be made to each affected NHCE's SARSEP IRA account. If an affected employee does not have a SARSEP IRA account, a SARSEP IRA account will be established for that employee. Earnings will be calculated for an affected NHCE's account on the basis of one of the following methods (check one):

☐ Actual investment results of the affected NHCE's SARSEP IRA account.

☐ The interest rate incorporated in the Department of Labor's Voluntary Fiduciary Correction Program Online Calculator ("VFCP Online Calculator") (http://www.dol.gov/ebsa/calculator/main.html), since the actual earnings of the affected NHCE's SARSEP IRA account cannot be ascertained

APPENDIX F, SCHEDULE 3
SEPs and SARSEPs

Plan Name: ______________________________ EIN: _______________ Plan #:____

☐ Actual investment results for years in which data is available, or the rate incorporated in the VFCP Online Calculator for years in which the actual earnings of the affected NHCE's SARSEP IRA account cannot be ascertained. The VFCP Online Calculator was or will be used for the following years

____

The total corrective contribution (before adjusting for earnings) on behalf of the affected NHCEs for each plan year is as follows:

Year	Corrective contribution

Former employees affected by the failure (check one):

☐ There are no former employees affected by the failure.

☐ Affected former employees will be contacted, and corrective contributions will be made to their SARSEP IRA accounts. To the extent that an affected former employee cannot be located following a mailing to the employee's last known address, the Plan Sponsor will take reasonable actions to locate that employee. Such actions include the use of the Internal Revenue Service Letter Forwarding Program (see Rev. Proc. 94-22, 1994-1 C.B. 608) or the Social Security Administration Employer Reporting Service. After such actions are taken, if an affected employee is not found but is subsequently located on a later date, the Plan Sponsor will make corrective contributions to the affected employee's SARSEP IRA account at that time.

☐ C. **Failure to Make Required Employer Contributions** (SEPs or SARSEPs)

The Plan Sponsor failed to make employer contributions on behalf of eligible employees as required under the terms of the plan.

☐ The failure occurred on account of the erroneous exclusion of eligible employees.

☐ Other (describe): ____

APPENDIX F, SCHEDULE 3
SEPs and SARSEPs

Plan Name: ______________________________ EIN: _____________ Plan #:____

____

The failure occurred for the following plan years: ____________________.

Description of the Proposed Method of Correction

The Plan Sponsor has contributed (or will contribute) additional amounts to the plan on behalf of each affected employee. For each affected employee, the corrective contribution will be determined by calculating the contribution the employee would have been entitled to under the terms of the plan and subtracting any contributions already made on behalf of the participant for the plan year. The required contribution made on behalf of an affected participant will be adjusted for earnings. Earnings will be calculated from the last day of the plan year for which the failure occurred through the date of the corrective contribution. The corrective contribution (adjusted for earnings) will be made to each affected employee's SEP (or SARSEP, if applicable) IRA account. If an affected employee does not have a SEP (or SARSEP, if applicable) IRA account, a SEP (or SARSEP, if applicable) account will be established for that employee.

The total corrective contribution (before adjusting for earnings) for each year is:

Year	Corrective Contribution

Earnings will be calculated for an affected employee on the basis of the following method(s) (check one):

☐ Actual investment results of the affected employee's SEP or SARSEP IRA account.

☐ The interest rate incorporated in the VFCP Online Calculator, since the actual earnings of the affected employee's IRA account cannot be ascertained.

☐ Actual investment results for years in which data is available, or the rate incorporated in the VFCP Online Calculator for years in which the actual earnings of the affected employee's IRA cannot be ascertained. The VFCP Online Calculator was or will be used for the following years

APPENDIX F, SCHEDULE 3
SEPs and SARSEPs

Plan Name: ______________________________ EIN: ______________ Plan #:____

____

Former employees affected by the failure (check one):

☐ There are no former employees affected by the failure.

☐ Affected former employees will be contacted, and corrective contributions will be made to their SEP or SARSEP IRA accounts. To the extent that an affected former employee cannot be located following a mailing to the employee's last known address, the Plan Sponsor will take reasonable actions to locate that employee. Such actions include the use of the Internal Revenue Service Letter Forwarding Program (see Rev. Proc. 94-22, 1994-1 C.B. 608) or the Social Security Administration Employer Reporting Service. After such actions are taken, if an affected employee is not found but is subsequently located on a later date, the Plan Sponsor will make corrective contributions to the affected employee's SEP or SARSEP IRA account at that time.

☐ **D.** **Failure to provide eligible employees with the opportunity to make elective deferrals** (SARSEPs only)

The plan did not provide employee(s) who satisfied the applicable eligibility requirements with the opportunity to make elective deferrals to the SARSEP. The failure occurred for the following plan years: ____________________

____

Description of the Proposed Method of Correction

The Plan Sponsor has contributed (or will contribute) additional amounts to the plan on behalf of each affected employee. The corrective contribution will be made to compensate the affected employee(s) for the missed deferral opportunity. The corrective contribution on behalf of each affected employee is equal to 50% of what the employee's deferral might have been had he or she been provided with the opportunity to make elective deferrals to the plan. Since the employee's deferral decision is not known, the deferral amount is estimated by determining the average of the deferral percentages for the employee's group (highly compensated or nonhighly compensated). (Example: N, an NHCE, was erroneously excluded from the plan. During the year of exclusion, N made $10,000 in compensation. The average of the deferral percentages for other NHCEs who were provided with the opportunity to make elective deferrals was 5%. N's missed deferral is estimated to be: 5% times $10,000 or $500. The required corrective contribution on behalf of N, before adjusting for earnings, is 50% of $500 or $250.)

APPENDIX F, SCHEDULE 3
SEPs and SARSEPs

Plan Name: ________________________________ EIN: ______________ Plan #:____

The total corrective contribution (before adjusting for earnings) on behalf of the affected NHCEs for each plan year is as follows:

Year	Corrective contribution

The corrective contribution made on behalf of each affected employee will also be adjusted for earnings. Earnings will be calculated from the date(s) that the contribution(s) should have been made through the date of the corrective contribution. The corrective contribution (adjusted for earnings) will be made to each affected employee's SARSEP IRA account. If an affected employee does not have a SARSEP IRA account, a SARSEP IRA account will be established for that employee. Earnings will be calculated on the basis of one of the following methods (check one):

☐ Actual investment results of the affected employee's SARSEP IRA account.
☐ The interest rate incorporated in the VFCP Online Calculator, since the actual earnings of the affected employee's IRA account cannot be ascertained.
☐ Actual investment results for years in which data is available, or the rate incorporated in the VFCP Online Calculator for years in which the actual earnings of the affected employee's IRA account cannot be ascertained. The VFCP Online Calculator was or will be used for the following years

____

Former employees affected by the failure (check one):
☐ There are no former employees affected by the failure.
☐ Affected former employees will be contacted, and corrective contributions will be made to their SARSEP IRA accounts. To the extent that an affected former employee cannot be located following a mailing to the employee's last known address, the Plan Sponsor will take reasonable actions to locate that employee. Such actions include the use of the Internal Revenue Service Letter Forwarding Program (see

APPENDIX F, SCHEDULE 3
SEPs and SARSEPs

Plan Name: ______________________ EIN: ____________ Plan #:____

Rev. Proc. 94-22, 1994-1 C.B. 608) or the Social Security Administration Employer Reporting Service. After such actions are taken, if an affected employee is not found but is subsequently located on a later date, the Plan Sponsor will make corrective contributions to the affected employee's SEP or SARSEP IRA account at that time.

☐ **E. Excess Amounts Contributed**

☐ The Plan Sponsor contributed Excess Amounts to the Plan on behalf of participants as follows:
(check boxes that apply)

☐ Amounts were contributed in excess of the benefit the participants were entitled to under the plan.

☐ SARSEP only: Elective deferrals were contributed to the SARSEP in excess of the limitation under the terms of the SARSEP (e.g., the lesser of 25% of compensation or the applicable limit under § 402(g)).

The total of the Excess Amounts for each affected plan year was as follows:

Year	Excess Amounts	Number of Participants Affected

Description of the Proposed Method of Correction
(check all correction methods that apply)

☐ Distribution of Excess Elective Deferrals (SARSEPs only)

The Plan Sponsor has effected (or will effect) a corrective distribution of the Excess Amounts, adjusted for earnings through the date of correction, to the affected participant(s). The earnings adjustment will be based on the actual rates of return of the participant's SARSEP IRA account from the date(s) that the excess deferrals were made through the date of correction.

Affected participants were (or will be) informed that the corrective distribution of an Excess Amount is not eligible for favorable tax

APPENDIX F, SCHEDULE 3
SEPs and SARSEPs

Plan Name: ________________________________ EIN: ______________ Plan #:____

treatment accorded to distributions from a SARSEP and, specifically, is not eligible for tax-free rollover.

The total corrective distribution (before adjusting for earnings) for each affected year is as follows:

Year	Corrective Distribution	Number of Participants Affected

☐ Distribution of Excess Employer Contributions

The Plan Sponsor has effected (or will effect) the return of excess employer contributions, adjusted for earnings through the date of correction, to the Plan Sponsor. The earnings adjustment will be based on the actual rates of return of the SEP or SARSEP from the date(s) that the excess employer contributions were made through the date of correction. The amount returned to the Plan Sponsor is not includible in the gross income of the affected participant(s). The Plan Sponsor is not entitled to a deduction for such excess employer contributions. The amount returned is reported on Form 1099-R as a distribution issued to the affected participant(s), indicating the taxable amount as zero.

The amount to be returned to the Plan Sponsor (before adjusting for earnings) for each affected year is as follows:

Year	Return of Excess Employer Contributions	Number of Participants Affected

☐ Retention of Excess Amounts

APPENDIX F, SCHEDULE 3
SEPs and SARSEPs

Plan Name: ______________________________ EIN: ______________ Plan #:____

Note: If this correction method is selected, an additional VCP fee is required. (See section 12.05(2) of Rev. Proc. 2008-50.)

☐ The Excess Amounts (including earnings) were retained in the SARSEP or SEP IRA accounts of the affected participants as follows:

Year	Excess Amounts Retained	Number of Participants Affected

The earnings adjustment will be based on the actual rates of return of the SEP or SARSEP from the date(s) that the excess employer contributions were made through the date of correction.

☐ Excess Amounts of $100 or less (See section 6.02(5)(e) of Rev. Proc. 2008-50.)

For one or more participants, the total Excess Amount (employer contributions and/or elective deferrals before adjusting for earnings) is $100 or less. The Excess Amount will not be distributed.

PART II. CHANGE IN ADMINISTRATIVE PROCEDURES

The Plan Sponsor has taken the following step(s) to ensure that the failure(s) will not recur:

APPENDIX F, SCHEDULE 3
SEPs and SARSEPs

Plan Name: ______________________________ EIN: ______________ Plan #:____

PART III. REQUEST(S) FOR EXCISE TAX RELIEF
(check applicable boxes)

☐ Excise tax pursuant to § 4979. The Applicant requests that the Service not pursue the excise tax under § 4979. (This applies only to failures to satisfy the nondiscrimination test for elective deferrals. See section 6.09(4) of Rev. Proc. 2008-50 for an example of a situation where a request for relief under § 4979 would be considered. Please enclose a written explanation in support of your request for relief from this excise tax.)

☐ Excise tax pursuant to § 4972. The Applicant requests that the Service not pursue the excise tax under § 4972 (This applies to situations where corrective contributions made in accordance with this submission would be nondeductible contributions for the year of correction and thus would be subject to the excise tax under § 4972. See section 6.09(3) of Rev. Proc. 2008-50. Please enclose a written explanation in support of your request for relief from this excise tax.)

PART IV. ENCLOSURES

In addition to the applicable enclosures listed on Appendix F, the Plan Sponsor encloses the following with this submission:

- The applicable plan document. (This could be an IRS form document, such as a Form 5305-SEP or 5305A-SEP, or a prototype plan document developed by a financial institution. If a prototype plan document is used, please send a copy of the most recent favorable opinion letter issued for such plan document).
- A written explanation of how and why the failure(s) described in this submission occurred, including a description of the administrative procedures applicable to the failure(s) in effect at the time the failure(s) occurred.
- For failures that involve corrective contributions or corrective distributions, a description of assumptions and supporting calculations used to determine the amounts needed for correction:
  1) For failures to satisfy the nondiscrimination test for elective deferrals, Computations in support of the proposed correction, including:
     a) The determination of HCEs and NHCEs,
     b) The deferral percentages of individual employees and the applicable ADP calculations,
     c) The determination of corrective contributions on behalf of NHCEs to correct the ADP test, and,
     d) Calculations showing how the earnings adjustment and the ultimate corrective contribution on behalf of affected employees will be determined. (Please use estimates, including an estimated correction date, if corrective distributions have not been made yet.)

APPENDIX F, SCHEDULE 3
SEPs and SARSEPs

Plan Name: ______________________ EIN: ______________ Plan #:____

2) For failures to make required employer contributions and for failures to provide eligible employees with the opportunity to make elective deferrals:
   a) Computations in support of the corrective contribution amounts attributable to each participant. In the case of a failure to provide eligible employees with the opportunity to make elective deferrals, please include computations showing how the average deferral percentage, missed deferral, and corrective contribution amount was determined.,
   b) Calculations showing how the earnings adjustment and the ultimate corrective contribution on behalf of affected employees will be determined.
3) For failures involving the contribution of Excess Amounts:
   a) Computations in support of the excess contribution amounts attributable to each participant;
   b) Calculations showing how the earnings adjustment and the ultimate corrective distribution amounts are determined. (Please use estimates, including an estimated correction date, if corrective distributions have not been made yet.)

- Explanations in support of requests for excise tax relief.
- Any other information that would be useful for the purpose of understanding the proposals made under the submission.

APPENDIX F, SCHEDULE 4
SIMPLE IRAs

Plan Name: ______________________________ EIN: ______________ Plan #:____

PART I. IDENTIFICATION OF FAILURE(S) AND CORRECTION METHODS

The following failure(s) occurred with respect to the SIMPLE IRA Plan identified above: (Check failure(s) that apply. Within each failure, check applicable boxes, and provide the information requested.)

☐ **A. Employer Eligibility Failure**

☐ The plan was adopted by a Plan Sponsor who was (or subsequently became) ineligible to sponsor a SIMPLE IRA Plan under the requirements of § 408(p) because the Plan Sponsor (and, if applicable, its related controlled group or affiliated service group employers) had more than 100 employees (including leased employees, if applicable) who earned $5,000 or more in compensation during the following plan year(s):

____

☐ The plan was adopted by a Plan Sponsor who was not eligible to sponsor a SIMPLE IRA Plan under the requirements of § 408(p) because the Plan Sponsor established or maintained a Qualified Plan with respect to which contributions were made (or under which benefits were accrued) during any plan year of the SIMPLE IRA Plan. The failure occurred during the following plan year(s):

____

Description of the Proposed Method of Correction

All contributions to the plan ceased as of ____________ (insert a date no later than the date this application is filed under VCP). The Plan Sponsor will not permit any new employer or salary reduction contributions to be made to the plan.

☐ **B. Failure to Make Required Employer Contributions**

The Plan Sponsor failed to make employer contributions on behalf of eligible employees as required under the terms of the plan.

☐ The failure occurred on account of the erroneous exclusion of eligible employees
☐ Other (describe): ______________________________________

____

The failure occurred for the following plan years: ____________________

APPENDIX F, SCHEDULE 4
SIMPLE IRAs

Plan Name: ______________________________ EIN: ______________ Plan #:____

For the applicable plan years, the provisions of the plan document required the Plan Sponsor to make employer contributions based on the following formula:

☐ 2% nonelective contribution on behalf of each eligible employee who earned at least $5,000 in compensation for the year.

☐ Matching contribution on behalf of each eligible employee equal to deferrals up to 3% of compensation.

☐ Grace period applied. The plan provided for a matching contribution on behalf of each eligible employee equal to deferrals up to ____% of compensation.

(Note: If the failure occurred for multiple plan years and different employer contribution criteria applied during those years, check the applicable box, and indicate the plan years for which the formula applied).

Description of the Proposed Method of Correction

The Plan Sponsor has contributed (or will contribute) additional amounts to the plan on behalf of each affected employee. For each affected employee, the corrective contribution will be determined by calculating the contribution the employee would have been entitled to receive under the terms of the plan and subtracting any contributions already made on behalf of the employee for the plan year. The corrective contribution made on behalf of an affected employee will be adjusted for earnings. Earnings will be calculated from the last day of the plan year for which the failure occurred through the date of the corrective contribution. The corrective contribution (adjusted for earnings) will be made to each affected employee's SIMPLE IRA account. If an affected employee does not have a SIMPLE IRA account, an account will be established for that employee.

If the plan did not provide eligible employees with the opportunity to make elective deferrals and the plan provides for matching contributions, the corrective matching contribution will be based on the assumption that the eligible employee would have made an elective deferral equal to 3% of compensation.

The total corrective contribution (before adjusting for earnings) for each plan year is:

Year	Corrective Contribution

- 153 -

APPENDIX F, SCHEDULE 4
SIMPLE IRAs

Plan Name: ______________________________ EIN: _______________ Plan #:____

The earnings calculation for an affected employee will be based on one of the following method(s) (check one):

☐ Actual investment results of the affected employee's SIMPLE IRA account.

☐ The interest rate incorporated in the Department of Labor's Voluntary Fiduciary Correction Program Online Calculator ("VFCP Online Calculator") (http://www.dol.gov/ebsa/calculator/main.html), since the actual earnings of the affected employee's IRA account cannot be ascertained.

☐ Actual investment results for years in which data is available, or the rate incorporated in the VFCP Online Calculator for years in which the actual earnings of the affected employee's IRA account cannot be ascertained. The VFCP Online Calculator was or will be used for the following years

____

Former employees affected by the failure (check one):

☐ There are no former employees affected by the failure.

☐ Affected former employees will be contacted, and corrective contributions will be made to their SIMPLE IRA accounts. To the extent that an affected former employee cannot be located following a mailing to the employee's last known address, the Plan Sponsor will take reasonable actions to locate that employee. Such actions include the use of the Internal Revenue Service Letter Forwarding Program (see Rev. Proc. 94-22, 1994-1 C.B. 608) or the Social Security Administration Employer Reporting Service. After such actions are taken, if an affected employee is not found but is subsequently located on a later date, the Plan Sponsor will make corrective contributions to the affected employee's SIMPLE IRA account at that time.

☐ C. **Failure to provide eligible employees with the opportunity to make elective deferrals**

The plan did not provide employee(s) who satisfied the applicable eligibility requirements with the opportunity to make elective deferrals to the SIMPLE IRA plan. The failure occurred for the following plan years:

- 154 -

APPENDIX F, SCHEDULE 4
SIMPLE IRAs

Plan Name: ______________________________ EIN: ______________ Plan #:____

____.

Description of the Proposed Method of Correction

The Plan Sponsor has contributed (or will contribute) additional amounts to the plan on behalf of each affected employee. The corrective contribution will be made to compensate the affected employee(s) for the missed deferral opportunity. The corrective contribution on behalf of each affected employee is equal to 50% of what the employee's deferral might have been had he or she been provided with the opportunity to make elective deferrals to the plan. Since the employee's deferral decision is not known, the deferral amount is estimated by assuming that the excluded employee would have made an elective deferral equal to 3% of his or her compensation. (Example: N, a nonhighly compensated employee was erroneously excluded from the plan. During the year of exclusion, N made $10,000 in compensation. N's missed deferral is estimated to be: 3% times $10,000 or $300. The required corrective contribution on behalf of N, before adjusting for earnings, is 50% of $300 or $150). Thus, the required corrective contribution for an employee who was erroneously excluded from making elective deferrals from a SIMPLE IRA Plan is equal to 1.5% of compensation (adjusted for earnings).

The total corrective contribution (before adjusting for earnings) on behalf of the affected employees for each plan year is as follows:

Year	Corrective contribution

The corrective contribution made on behalf of each affected employee will also be adjusted for earnings. Earnings will be calculated from the date(s) that the contribution(s) should have been made through the date of the corrective contribution. The corrective contribution (adjusted for earnings) will be made to each affected employee's SIMPLE IRA account. If an affected employee does not have a SIMPLE IRA account, a SIMPLE IRA account will be established for that employee. Earnings will be calculated on the basis of one of the following methods (check one):

APPENDIX F, SCHEDULE 4
SIMPLE IRAs

Plan Name: ______________________________ EIN: ______________ Plan #:____

- ☐ Actual investment results of the affected employee's SIMPLE IRA account.
- ☐ The interest rate incorporated in the VFCP Online Calculator, since the actual earnings of the affected employee's IRA account cannot be ascertained.
- ☐ Actual investment results for years in which data is available, or the rate incorporated in the VFCP Online Calculator for years in which the actual earnings of the affected employee's IRA account cannot be ascertained. The VFCP Online Calculator was or will be used for the following years

  ____

Former employees affected by the failure (check one):

- ☐ There are no former employees affected by the failure.
- ☐ Affected former employees will be contacted, and corrective contributions will be made to their SIMPLE IRA accounts. To the extent that an affected former employee cannot be located following a mailing to the employee's last known address, the Plan Sponsor will take reasonable actions to locate that employee. Such actions include the use of the Internal Revenue Service Letter Forwarding Program (see Rev. Proc. 94-22, 1994-1 C.B. 608) or the Social Security Administration Employer Reporting Service. After such actions are taken, if an affected employee is not found but is subsequently located on a later date, the Plan Sponsor will make a corrective contribution to the affected employee's SIMPLE IRA account at that time.

☐ **D. <u>Excess Amounts Contributed</u>**

The Plan Sponsor contributed Excess Amounts to the plan on behalf of participants as follows:
(check boxes that apply)

- ☐ Amounts were contributed in excess of the benefit the participants were entitled to under the plan.
- ☐ Elective deferrals were made to the SIMPLE IRA in excess of the limitation under the terms of the SIMPLE IRA (e.g., the applicable limit under § 408(p)(2)(E)).

The total of the Excess Amounts for each affected plan year was as follows:

Year	Excess Amounts	Number of Participants Affected

- 156 -

APPENDIX F, SCHEDULE 4
SIMPLE IRAs

Plan Name: ______________________________ EIN: ______________ Plan #:____

Description of the Proposed Method of Correction
(check all correction methods that apply)

☐ Distribution of Excess Elective Deferrals

The Plan Sponsor has effected (or will effect) a distribution of the Excess Amounts, adjusted for earnings through the date of correction, to the affected participant(s). The earnings adjustment will be based on the actual rates of return of the participant's SARSEP IRA account from the date(s) that the excess deferrals were made through the date of correction.

Affected participants were (or will be) informed that the distribution of an Excess Amount is not eligible for favorable tax treatment accorded to distributions from a SIMPLE IRA and, specifically, is not eligible for tax-free rollover.

The total corrective distribution (before adjusting for earnings) for each affected plan year is as follows:

Year	Corrective Distribution	Number of Participants Affected

☐ Distribution of Excess Employer Contributions

The Plan Sponsor has effected (or will effect) the return of excess employer contributions, adjusted for earnings through the date of correction, to the Plan Sponsor. The earnings adjustment will be based on the actual rates of return on the affected participants' SIMPLE IRA accounts from the date(s) that the excess employer contributions were

APPENDIX F, SCHEDULE 4
SIMPLE IRAs

Plan Name: ______________________________ EIN: ______________ Plan #:____

made through the date of correction. The amount returned to the Plan Sponsor is not includible in the gross income of the affected participant(s). The Plan Sponsor is not entitled to a deduction for such excess employer contributions. The amount returned is reported on Form 1099-R as a distribution issued to the affected participant(s), indicating the taxable amount as zero.

The return of the excess employer contributions (before adjusting for earnings) for each affected plan year is as follows:

Year	Return of Excess Employer Contributions	Number of Participants Affected

☐ Retention of Excess Amounts

Note: If this correction method is selected, an additional VCP fee is required. (See section 12.05(2) of Rev. Proc. 2008-50.)

☐ The Excess Amounts (including earnings) were retained in the SIMPLE IRA accounts of the affected participants as follows.

Year	Excess Amounts Retained	Number of Participants Affected

The earnings adjustment will be based on the actual rates of return of the SEP or SARSEP from the date(s) that the excess employer contributions were made through the date of correction.

APPENDIX F, SCHEDULE 4
SIMPLE IRAs

Plan Name: ______________________________ EIN: ______________ Plan #:____

☐ Excess Amounts of $100 or less (See section 6.02(5)(e) of Rev. Proc. 2008-50.)

For one or more participants, the total Excess Amount (employer contributions and/or elective deferrals before adjusting for earnings) is $100 or less. The Excess Amount will not be distributed.

Former employees affected by the Excess Amounts failure (check one):

☐ There are no former employees affected by the failure.

☐ Affected former employees will be contacted, and corrective contributions will be made to their SIMPLE IRA accounts. To the extent that an affected former employee cannot be located following a mailing to the employee's last known address, the Plan Sponsor will take reasonable actions to locate that employee. Such actions include the use of the Internal Revenue Service Letter Forwarding Program (see Rev. Proc. 94-22, 1994-1 C.B. 608) or the Social Security Administration Employer Reporting Service. After such actions are taken, if an affected employee is not found but is subsequently located on a later date, the Plan Sponsor will make corrective contributions to the affected employee's SIMPLE IRA account at that time.

PART II. CHANGE IN ADMINISTRATIVE PROCEDURES

The Plan Sponsor has taken the following step(s) to ensure that the failure(s) will not recur:

PART III. REQUEST(S) FOR EXCISE TAX RELIEF
(check applicable boxes)

☐ Excise tax pursuant to § 4972. The Plan Sponsor requests that the Service not pursue the excise tax under § 4972. (This applies to situations where corrective contributions made in accordance with this submission would be nondeductible contributions for the year of correction and subject to the excise tax under § 4972. See section 6.09(3) of Rev. Proc. 2008-50. Please enclose a written explanation in support of your request for relief from this excise tax.)

- 159 -

APPENDIX F, SCHEDULE 4
SIMPLE IRAs

Plan Name: ______________________________ EIN: ______________ Plan #:____

PART IV. ENCLOSURES

In addition to the applicable enclosures listed on Appendix F, the Plan Sponsor encloses the following with this submission:

- The applicable plan document. (This could be an IRS form document, such as a 5305-SIMPLE or 5304-SIMPLE, or a prototype document developed by a financial institution. If a prototype plan document is used, please send a copy of the most recent opinion letter issued with respect to such plan document.)
- A written explanation of how and why the failure(s) described in this submission occurred, including a description of the administrative procedures applicable to the failure(s) in effect at the time the failure(s) occurred.
- For failures that involve corrective contributions or corrective distributions, a description of assumptions and supporting calculations used to determine the amount needed for correction:
  1) For failures to make required Employer Contributions and for failures to provide eligible employees with the opportunity to make elective deferrals:
     a) Computations in support of the corrective contribution amounts attributable to each participant. In the case of a failure to provide eligible employees with the opportunity to make elective deferrals, please include computations showing how the average deferral percentage, missed deferral, and corrective contribution amount was determined.
     b) Calculations showing how the earnings adjustment and the ultimate corrective contribution on behalf of affected employees will be determined. (Please use estimates, including an estimated correction date, if corrective contributions have not been made yet.)
  2) For failures involving the contribution of Excess Amounts:
     a) Computations in support of the excess contribution amounts attributable to each participant.
     b) Calculations showing how the earnings adjustment and the ultimate corrective distribution amounts are determined. (Please use estimates, including an estimated correction date, if corrective distributions have not been made yet.)
- Explanations in support of requests for excise tax relief.
- Any other information that would be useful for the purpose of understanding the proposals made under the submission.

Appendix E

Comparison of 401(k) Plans and Grandfathered SEP/SARSEP Plans for 2012

	401(k) Plan	*SEP/SARSEP*
Employer Deduction—Percentage Limitation:	25% of eligible employee's plan compensation not in excess of $250,000 for 2012, plus elective contributions	25% of total compensation actually paid to the employees during the employer's taxable year (not taking into account compensation in excess of $250,000 for 2012), provided the SEP is maintained on the basis of the employer's taxable year. In all other cases, the 25% limit is based on compensation paid to the employees for the calendar year ending with or within the employer's business taxable year. Elective contributions are separately deductible.
Employer Deduction—Dollar Limitation:	$50,000/$55,500	$50,000/$55,500
Exclusion by employee of contributions:		The lesser of:
Percentage limitation	a. 100% plus catch-up contributions	a. 25% of includible taxable compensation paid during the plan year.

	401(k) Plan	SEP/SARSEP
Dollar limitation	b. $50,000/$55,500	b. $50,000/$55,500 c. If an HCE, the $50,000 amount is reduced when the plan is integrated. The reduction amount equals the integration level (or compensation if less) multiplied by the spread percentage. [I.R.C. § 402(h)(2)(B)]
Catch-up contribution limit	$5,500 (2012)	$5,500 (2012)
Normal elective contribution limit	$17,000 (2012)	$17,000 (2012)
Maximum salary reduction amount	$22,500 (2012)	$22,500 (2012)
Maximum salary reduction percentage	100% of pre-plan compensation	25% of taxable compensation (20% of pre-plan compensation)
Maximum salary reduction percentage if an HCE	Either NHCE% multiplied by 1.25, or the lesser of: NHCE% plus 2% or NHCE% multiplied by 2. (See chapter 15.)	125% multiplied by the average of the deferral rates (separately calculated) for each eligible NHCE.

NHCE Average	*HCE Average*	*NHCE Average*	*HCE Average*
1.00%	2.00%	1.00%	1.25%
2.00	4.00	2.00	2.50
3.00	5.00	3.00	3.75
4.00	6.00	4.00	5.00
5.00	7.00	5.00	6.25
6.00	8.00	6.00	7.50
7.00	9.00	7.00	8.75
8.00	10.00	8.00	10.00
9.00	11.25	9.00	11.25

Special safe harbor rules also available*

Eligibility based on years of service	2 years of service; 1 year if 401(k) plan	Service during any 3 out of the 5 prior plan years.
Part-time eligibility	1,000 hours	Included, if earning over $550, for 2012.

	401(k) Plan	*SEP/SARSEP*
Employer matching contributions	Permitted if 401(k) plan	Not permitted
5500 preparation	Generally required	Generally not required
Loan provisions	Generally permitted	Not allowed
Total employees	No limit	No limit unless SARSEP. If SARSEP, fewer than 26 eligible employees at all times during the prior plan year.
Participation	Several percentage tests to determine requisite coverage	All eligible employees must receive an employer contribution, if any are made. 50% of eligible employees must actually elect to participate if a SARSEP. Plan must have been in existence on December 31, 1996 if the plan is a SARSEP.
Vesting	Various vesting schedules permitted	100% at all times
Exclusive plan requirement	Participants in SIMPLE 401(k) must not accrue benefits or receive contributions during the year under any other qualified plan, SEP or SIMPLE IRA	Must be only plan of employer (exception for qualified plan covering unionized employees not included in SIMPLE IRA plan)
Designated Roth contribution feature	Allowed Not allowed	
J & S annuity requirements	Generally, yes	N/A
Subject to QDRO rules	Yes	No
Summary plan description	Generally required	Not required
Summary annual report	Generally required	Not required
	401(k) Plan	SEP/SARSEP
Access to funds	Subject to plan's restrictions on withdrawals	Assets may generally be withdrawn at any time

---

* A Code Section 401(k) cash or deferred arrangement may generally satisfy the nondiscrimination requirements by providing matching contributions on behalf of each employee who is not a highly compensated employee in an amount equal to:

(a) 100 percent of the elective contributions of the employee to the extent such elective contributions do not exceed 3 percent of the employee's compensation, and

(b) 50 percent of the elective contributions of the employee to the extent that such elective contributions exceed 3 percent but do not exceed 5 percent of the employee's compensation.

Appendix F

Ten-Year Income Averaging Taxation

Distributions from IRAs are taxable as ordinary income. The purpose of the following chart is to show the tax attributable to distributions from qualified plans that qualify as a lump-sum distribution. The tax rates indicated on this chart do not apply to SEPs, SARSEPs, IRAs, or SIMPLEs, which are generally taxable at the recipient's individual income tax rate of between 10 percent and 35 percent for 2012.

Lump-Sum Distribution	*If Born before 1936; the 1986 10-Year Tax*	*Effective Percentage Rate*
$10,000	$550	5.5
15,000	830	5.5
20,000	1,100	5.5
25,000	1,801	7.2
30,000	2,521	8.4
35,000	3,347	9.6
40,000	4,187	10.5
45,000	5,027	11.2
50,000	5,874	11.8
60,000	7,674	12.8
70,000	9,505	13.6
75,000	10,305	13.7
80,000	11,105	13.9
90,000	12,705	14.1
100,000	14,471	14.5
125,000	19,183	15.3
150,000	24,570	16.4
175,000	30,422	17.4
200,000	36,922	18.5

Lump-Sum Distribution	*If Born before 1936; the 1986 10-Year Tax*	*Effective Percentage Rate*
250,000	50,770	20.3
300,000	66,330	22.1
350,000	83,602	23.9
400,000	102,602	25.7
450,000	122,682	27.3
500,000	143,682	28.7
550,000	164,682	29.9
600,000	187,368	31.2
650,000	211,368	32.5
700,000	235,368	33.6
750,000	259,368	34.6
800,000	283,368	35.4
850,000	307,368	36.2
900,000	332,210	36.9
950,000	357,210	37.6
1,000,000	382,210	38.2
2,000,000	882,210	44.1

* The portion of a qualifying lump-sum distribution attributable to pre-1974 plan participation is eligible for a special capital gains rate of 20 percent in addition to the election to utilize the 10-year special averaging method of taxation for lump-sum distributions. The 1986 tax rates are used and take into account the zero bracket amount under prior law. [TRA '86, § 1122(h)(5); TAMRA '88, § 1111A(b)(15)(B); see Instructions to Form 4972-Tax on Lump-Sum Distributions]

Note. Five-year averaging repealed for years beginning after 1999.

Appendix G

Employee Benefit Limits

Marjorie Martin

Many of the dollar thresholds used in limiting the level of benefits available through tax-advantaged programs are adjusted to reflect changes in the consumer price index (CPI) relative to the base period used for each limit. The limit for a particular year is adjusted based on the cumulative increase through the third quarter of the preceding calendar year. The adjusted limits are then rounded down to the nearest multiplier specified for the particular limit. The limits for 2012, for example, are calculated using the CPI factors through the third quarter of 2011. For 2010 and 2011, the IRS also applied a rule that prevented any of these limits from dropping back to a lower level than the limits for an earlier year (2009).

Indexing of Employee Benefit Limits

	Calendar Year				
Purpose	*2008*	*2009*	*2010*	*2011*	*2012*
Base 402(g) deferral limit	$15,500	$16,500	$16,500	$16,500	$17,000
457 limit	$15,500	$16,500	$16,500	$16,500	$17,000
401(k)/403(b)/457/ SARSEP,[1] catch-up deferrals	$5,000	$5,500	$5,500	$5,500	$5,500
SIMPLE limit	$10,500	$11,500	$11,500	$11,500	$11,500
SIMPLE catch-up deferrals	$2,500	$2,500	$2,500	$2,500	$2,500
IRA/Roth IRA limit	$5,000	$5,000	$5,000	$5,000	$5,000
IRA/Roth IRA catch-up contributions	$1,000	$1,000	$1,000	$1,000	$1,000
DB[2] maximum benefit	$185,000	$195,000	$195,000	$195,000	$200,000
DC[3] maximum addition	$46,000	$49,000	$49,000	$49,000	$50,000
HCE compensation[4]	$105,000	$110,000	$110,000	$110,000	$115,000
Key Employee:					
Officer[5]	$150,000	$160,000	$160,000	$160,000	$165,000

Indexing of Employee Benefit Limits (*Cont'd*)

Purpose	*Calendar Year* 2008	2009	2010	2011	2012
1% Owners	$150,000	$150,000	$150,000	$150,000	$150,000
Compensation[6]	$230,000	$245,000	$245,000	$245,000	$250,000
SEP threshold	$500	$550	$550	$550	$550
ESOP (5-year distribution factor)	$185,000	$195,000	$195,000	$195,000	$200,000
ESOP (account balance)	$935,000	$985,000	$985,000	$985,000	$1,015,000
Taxable wage base[7]	$102,000	$106,800	$106,800	$106,800	$110,100
SECA tax for self-employed individuals, combined rate	15.3%	15.3%	15.3%	13.3%*	13.3%*
Old-age, survivors, and disability insurance tax rate	12.4%	12.4%	12.4%	6.2% (employer) 10.4%* (employee)	6.2% (employer) 10.4%* (employee)
Hospital insurance (Medicare)	2.9%	2.9%	2.9%	2.9%	2.9%
Social Security tax for employees and employers, combined rate	7.65%	7.65%	7.65%	7.65% (employer) 5.65%* (employee)	7.65% (employer) 5.65%* (employee)
Old-age, survivors, and disability insurance tax rate	6.20%	6.20%	6.20%	6.20% (employer) 4.20%* (employee)	6.20% (employer) 4.20%* (employee)
Hospital insurance (Medicare)	1.45%	1.45%	1.45%	1.45%	1.45%

Source: Marjorie Martin. Prepared May 22, 2012.

---

* Reflects 2 percent reduction under the Tax Relief, Unemployment Insurance Reauthorization, and Job Creation Act of 2010 in the employee-paid portion of FICA/SECA tax applicable for 2011, as extended by the Temporary Payroll Tax Cut Continuation Act of 2011 for 2012.

[1] This number represents the catch-up limit available under Code Section 414(v). Code Sections 457(b)(3) and 402(g)(8) provide separate catch-up rules that must also be considered in an appropriate situation.

[2] Defined Benefit limit applies to limitation years ending in indicated year.

[3] Defined Contribution limit applies to limitation years ending in indicated year.

[4] Compensation during the plan year beginning in the indicated year identifies Highly Compensated Employees for the following plan year.

[5] Generally, compensation during the determination year ending in the indicated year identifies Key Employees for the following plan year.

[6] Compensation limit applies to years (generally the plan year) beginning in indicated year. Annual compensation limit for certain eligible participants in governmental plans that followed Code Section 401(a)(17) limits (with indexing) on July 1, 1993 are: $375,000 for 2012; $360,000 for 2011, 2010 and 2009; $345,000 for 2009; and $335,000 for 2008.

[7] Calculation differs from CPI description provided above.

Appendix H

Illustrations of Selected Examples

Many of the examples used in the book are based on the illustrations in this appendix. They were created using QP-SEP Illustrator and SIMPLE Illustrator software programs. Additional information is available at *http://www.GaryLesser.com*.

* UNINCORPORATED SEP PLAN *   * Minimum Earned Income at 25 Percent Rate (see Q 6:30) *   1
07:57 PM
20-Mar-2012

Plan Year Begins:	2012	$50,000.00	- Employer Contribution
Plan Year Ends:	2012	ALL	- DEDUCTIBLE PORTION
Base Percentage:	25.0000000	$50,000.00	- Total Allocated
Integration Level:	$0	24.999999635%	- Allocation % of 402(h) Comp.
Excess Percentage:	25.0000000	None	- Integration
1=P/S 2=MP 3=SEP 4=SARSEP:	3		
E/er Contr. to Owners:	100.00%		
E/er Alloc. Compensation:	100.00%	$50,000.00	- Maximum HCE Allocation Y <-n/a

P	-> No N-Key E/ees; T/H okay Prototype or Model SEP	TOTAL ALLOCATION		IRC 402(h) EMPLOYER CONTRIBUTION		EMPLOYER CONTRIBUTION	Columns reserved for Salary Reduction SEPs	20.000000%	KEY	Col n/a	EMPLOYEE's PRE-PLAN EARNED INCOME	HCE	Col. n/a	Col. n/a
1	Minimum earned income	$50,000.00	h	25.000000%	m	$50,000.00	$0.99		Y	1950	$260,310.19	Y		
2	needed to allocate	$0.00		0.000000%		$0.00	$0.99		Y	1950	$0.00	Y		
3	$50,000 at a 25%	$0.00		0.000000%		$0.00	$0.99		Y	1950	$0.00	Y		
4	contribution rate.	$0.00		0.000000%		$0.00	$0.99		Y	1950	$0.00	Y		
5		$0.00		0.000000%		$0.00	$0.99		Y	1950	$0.00	Y		
6		$0.00		0.000000%		$0.00	$0.99		Y	1950	$0.00	Y		
7		$0.00		0.000000%		$0.00	$0.99		Y	1950	$0.00	Y		
8		$0.00		0.000000%		$0.00	$0.99		Y	1950	$0.00	Y		
	OWNER SUB-TOTALS	$50,000.00				$50,000.00		$0.00			$260,310.19			
9	Participating	$0.00		0.000000%		$0.00	$0.99		N	1950	$0.00	N		
10	Non-Owners	$0.00		0.000000%		$0.00	$0.99		N	1950	$0.00	N		
11		$0.00		0.000000%		$0.00	$0.99		N	1950	$0.00	N		
12		$0.00		0.000000%		$0.00	$0.99		N	1950	$0.00	N		
13		$0.00		0.000000%		$0.00	$0.99		N	1950	$0.00	N		
14		$0.00		0.000000%		$0.00	$0.99		N	1950	$0.00	N		
15		$0.00		0.000000%		$0.00	$0.99		N	1950	$0.00	N		
16		$0.00		0.000000%		$0.00	$0.99		N	1950	$0.00	N		
17		$0.00		0.000000%		$0.00	$0.99		N	1950	$0.00	N		
18		$0.00		0.000000%		$0.00	$0.99		N	1950	$0.00	N		
	NON-OWNER SUB TOTALS	$0.00				$0.00					$0.00			
	GRAND TOTALS	$50,000.00				$50,000.00					$260,310.19			

h or m <-- At a limit/maximum (other solutions possible).

Penny rounding applied.

* Minimum Earned Income at 25 Percent Rate (see Q 6:30) *

* UNINCORPORATED SEP PLAN *

* NON-INTEGRATED CONTRIBUTIONS

2
20-Mar-2012
07:57 PM

* * S P E C I A L   S I T U A T I O N   I N P U T   P A G E * *

ALLOCATION COMPENSATION -Includes- -Elective-	CALCULATE OWNER'S PERCENTAGE	Auto 2	OWNERS SHARE PERCENTAGE	SUBTRACTIONS FOR 402(h) NET COMPENSATION Sum of: 1-E/er Contrib. 2-Basic Elective 4-E/ee Share Cost 5-50% of SE Tax	ADDITIONAL GAIN (LOSS) FOR S-E TAX	$0.00 (4) NON-OWNER CONTRIBUTIONS ALLOCATED	COMPENSATION FOR S-E TAX PURPOSES	TOTAL W-2 WAGES FOR S-E TAX	(5) PRO-RATA S-E TAX DEDUCTION	TOP HEAVY ADDITIONAL AMOUNT FOR 100.00% PERCENTAGE
$200,000.00	0.0000%	A	100.00000%	$60,310.19	$0.00	$0.00	$260,310.19	$0.00	$10,310.19	$0.00
$0.00	0.0000%	A	0.00000%	$0.00	$0.00	$0.00	$0.00	$0.00	$0.00	$0.00
$0.00	0.0000%	A	0.00000%	$0.00	$0.00	$0.00	$0.00	$0.00	$0.00	$0.00
$0.00	0.0000%	A	0.00000%	$0.00	$0.00	$0.00	$0.00	$0.00	$0.00	$0.00
$0.00	0.0000%	A	0.00000%	$0.00	$0.00	$0.00	$0.00	$0.00	$0.00	$0.00
$0.00	0.0000%	A	0.00000%	$0.00	$0.00	$0.00	$0.00	$0.00	$0.00	$0.00
$0.00	0.0000%	A	0.00000%	$0.00	$0.00	$0.00	$0.00	$0.00	$0.00	$0.00
$0.00	0.0000%	A	0.00000%	$0.00	$0.00	$0.00	$0.00	$0.00	$0.00	$0.00
$200,000.00	0.0000%		SUB-TOTALS	$60,310.19	$0.00	$0.00	$260,310.19	$0.00	$10,310.19	$0.00

$0.00	Ownership percentages are--			$0.00
$0.00	A = calculated automatically.			$0.00
$0.00				$0.00
$0.00	Additional amounts (contributions/accounts/gains), if any,entered			$0.00
$0.00	in last column (this page) are considered for Top-Heavy Analysis.			$0.00
$0.00				$0.00
$0.00	KEY-EMPLOYEE TOP-HEAVY ANALYSIS--	DOLLARS	PERCENTAGE	$0.00
$0.00	- Key Employee Accounts/Contributions:	$50,000.00	100.00000%	$0.00
$0.00	- Non-Key Employee Accounts/Contributions:	$0.00	0.00000%	$0.00
$0.00	- - Total Accounts/Contributions:	$50,000.00	100.00000%	$0.00
$0.00	NON-OWNER SUB TOTALS			$0.00
$200,000.00	GRAND TOTALS			$0.00

* UNINCORPORATED SEP PLAN *   * Minimum Earned Income at 20 Percent Rate (see Q 6:30) *   1

07:58 PM
20-Mar-2012

Plan Year Begins:	2012	$50,000.00	- Employer Contribution
Plan Year Ends:	2012	ALL	- DEDUCTIBLE PORTION
Base Percentage:	20.0000000	$50,000.00	- Total Allocated
Integration Level:	$0	20.000000000%	- Allocation % of 402(h) Comp.
Excess Percentage:	20.0000000	None	- Integration
1=P/S 2=MP 3=SEP 4=SARSEP:	3		
E/er Contr. to Owners:	100.00%		
E/er Alloc. Compensation:	100.00%	$50,000.00	- Maximum HCE Allocation Y <-n/a

P	-> No N-Key E/ees; T/H okay Prototype or Model SEP	TOTAL ALLOCATION	IRC 402(h) EMPLOYER CONTRIBUTION	EMPLOYER CONTRIBUTION	Columns reserved for Salary Reduction SEPs	20.000000%	KEY	Col n/a	EMPLOYEE's PRE-PLAN EARNED INCOME	HCE	Col. n/a	Col. n/a
1	Minimum earned income	$50,000.00 h	20.000000%	$50,000.00	$0.99		Y	1950	$310,988.81	Y		
2	needed to allocate	$0.00	0.000000%	$0.00	$0.99		Y	1950	$0.00	Y		
3	$50,000 at a 20%	$0.00	0.000000%	$0.00	$0.99		Y	1950	$0.00	Y		
4	contribution rate.	$0.00	0.000000%	$0.00	$0.99		Y	1950	$0.00	Y		
5		$0.00	0.000000%	$0.00	$0.99		Y	1950	$0.00	Y		
6		$0.00	0.000000%	$0.00	$0.99		Y	1950	$0.00	Y		
7		$0.00	0.000000%	$0.00	$0.99		Y	1950	$0.00	Y		
8		$0.00	0.000000%	$0.00	$0.99		Y	1950	$0.00	Y		
	OWNER SUB-TOTALS	$50,000.00		$50,000.00		$0.00			$310,988.81			
9	Enter Participating	$0.00	0.000000%	$0.00	$0.99		N	1950	$0.00	N		
10	Non-Owners in This Area	$0.00	0.000000%	$0.00	$0.99		N	1950	$0.00	N		
11		$0.00	0.000000%	$0.00	$0.99		N	1950	$0.00	N		
12		$0.00	0.000000%	$0.00	$0.99		N	1950	$0.00	N		
13		$0.00	0.000000%	$0.00	$0.99		N	1950	$0.00	N		
14		$0.00	0.000000%	$0.00	$0.99		N	1950	$0.00	N		
15		$0.00	0.000000%	$0.00	$0.99		N	1950	$0.00	N		
16		$0.00	0.000000%	$0.00	$0.99		N	1950	$0.00	N		
17		$0.00	0.000000%	$0.00	$0.99		N	1950	$0.00	N		
18		$0.00	0.000000%	$0.00	$0.99		N	1950	$0.00	N		
	NON-OWNER SUB TOTALS	$0.00		$0.00					$0.00			
	GRAND TOTALS	$50,000.00		$50,000.00					$310,988.81			

h or m <-- At a limit/maximum (other solutions possible).

Penny rounding applied.

* Minimum Earned Income at 20 Percent Rate (see Q 6:30) *

* UNINCORPORATED SEP PLAN *

* NON-INTEGRATED CONTRIBUTIONS

2
20-Mar-2012
07:58 PM

* * S P E C I A L   S I T U A T I O N   I N P U T   P A G E * *

ALLOCATION COMPENSATION -Includes- -Elective-	CALCULATE OWNER'S PERCENTAGE	A u t o 2	OWNERS SHARE PERCENTAGE	SUBTRACTIONS FOR 402(h) NET COMPENSATION Sum of: 1-E/er Contrib. 2-Basic Elective 4-E/ee Share Cost 5-50% of SE Tax	ADDITIONAL GAIN (LOSS) FOR S-E TAX	$0.00 (4) NON-OWNER CONTRIBUTIONS ALLOCATED	COMPENSATION FOR S-E TAX PURPOSES	TOTAL W-2 WAGES FOR S-E TAX	(5) PRO-RATA S-E TAX DEDUCTION	TOP HEAVY ADDITIONAL AMOUNT FOR 100.00% PERCENTAGE
$250,000.00	0.0000%	A	100.00000%	$60,988.81	$0.00	$0.00	$310,988.81	$0.00	$10,988.81	$0.00
$0.00	0.0000%	A	0.00000%	$0.00	$0.00	$0.00	$0.00	$0.00	$0.00	$0.00
$0.00	0.0000%	A	0.00000%	$0.00	$0.00	$0.00	$0.00	$0.00	$0.00	$0.00
$0.00	0.0000%	A	0.00000%	$0.00	$0.00	$0.00	$0.00	$0.00	$0.00	$0.00
$0.00	0.0000%	A	0.00000%	$0.00	$0.00	$0.00	$0.00	$0.00	$0.00	$0.00
$0.00	0.0000%	A	0.00000%	$0.00	$0.00	$0.00	$0.00	$0.00	$0.00	$0.00
$0.00	0.0000%	A	0.00000%	$0.00	$0.00	$0.00	$0.00	$0.00	$0.00	$0.00
$0.00	0.0000%	A	0.00000%	$0.00	$0.00	$0.00	$0.00	$0.00	$0.00	$0.00
$250,000.00	0.0000%		SUB-TOTALS	$60,988.81	$0.00	$0.00	$310,988.81	$0.00	$10,988.81	$0.00
$0.00	Ownership percentages are--									$0.00
$0.00	A = calculated automatically.									$0.00
$0.00										$0.00
$0.00	Additional amounts (contributions/accounts/gains), if any,entered									$0.00
$0.00	in last column (this page) are considered for Top-Heavy Analysis.									$0.00
$0.00										$0.00
$0.00	KEY-EMPLOYEE TOP-HEAVY ANALYSIS--				DOLLARS	PERCENTAGE				$0.00
$0.00	- Key Employee Accounts/Contributions:				$50,000.00	100.00000%				$0.00
$0.00	- Non-Key Employee Accounts/Contributions:				$0.00	0.00000%				$0.00
$0.00	- - Total Accounts/Contributions:				$50,000.00	100.00000%				$0.00
$0.00			NON-OWNER SUB TOTALS							$0.00
$250,000.00			GRAND TOTALS							$0.00

* UNINCORPORATED SEP PLAN * — * NANCY'S SOLE PROPRIETORSHIP - Percentage Method at 25% (see Q 7:6) — 1
08:01 PM
20-Mar-2012

Plan Year Begins:	2012	$1,858.73	- Employer Contribution
Plan Year Ends:	2012	ALL	- DEDUCTIBLE PORTION
Base Percentage:	25.0000000	$1,858.73	- Total Allocated
Integration Level:	$0	25.000000000%	- Allocation % of 402(h) Comp.
Excess Percentage:	25.0000000	None	- Integration
1=P/S 2=MP 3=SEP 4=SARSEP:	3		
E/er Contr. to Owners:	100.00%		
E/er Alloc. Compensation:	100.00%	$50,000.00	- Maximum HCE Allocation <-n/a

P	-> No N-Key E/ees; T/H okay Prototype or Model SEP	TOTAL ALLOCATION	IRC 402(h) EMPLOYER CONTRIBUTION	EMPLOYER CONTRIBUTION	Columns reserved for Salary Reduction SEPs	KEY	Col n/a	EMPLOYEE's PRE-PLAN EARNED INCOME	HCE	Col. n/a	Col. n/a
1	Nancy	$1,858.73 h	25.000000% m	$1,858.73		Y		$10,000.00	Y		
2		$0.00	0.000000%	$0.00							
3		$0.00	0.000000%	$0.00							
4		$0.00	0.000000%	$0.00							
5		$0.00	0.000000%	$0.00							
6		$0.00	0.000000%	$0.00							
7		$0.00	0.000000%	$0.00							
8		$0.00	0.000000%	$0.00							
	OWNER SUB-TOTALS	$1,858.73		$1,858.73	$0.00			$10,000.00			
9	No employees	$0.00	0.000000%	$0.00							
10		$0.00	0.000000%	$0.00							
11		$0.00	0.000000%	$0.00							
12		$0.00	0.000000%	$0.00							
13		$0.00	0.000000%	$0.00							
14		$0.00	0.000000%	$0.00							
15		$0.00	0.000000%	$0.00							
16		$0.00	0.000000%	$0.00							
17		$0.00	0.000000%	$0.00							
18		$0.00	0.000000%	$0.00							
	NON-OWNER SUB TOTALS	$0.00		$0.00				$0.00			
	GRAND TOTALS	$1,858.73		$1,858.73				$10,000.00			

h or m <-- At a limit/maximum (other solutions possible).

Penny rounding applied.

* NANCY'S SOLE PROPRIETORSHIP - Percentage Method at 25% (see Q 7:6)

* UNINCORPORATED SEP PLAN *

* NON-INTEGRATED CONTRIBUTIONS

2
20-Mar-2012
08:01 PM

* * S P E C I A L   S I T U A T I O N   I N P U T   P A G E * *

ALLOCATION COMPENSATION -Includes- -Elective-	CALCULATE OWNER'S PERCENTAGE	Auto 2	OWNERS SHARE PERCENTAGE	SUBTRACTIONS FOR 402(h) NET COMPENSATION Sum of: 1-E/er Contrib. 2-Basic Elective 4-E/ee Share Cost 5-50% of SE Tax	ADDITIONAL GAIN (LOSS) FOR S-E TAX	$0.00 (4) NON-OWNER CONTRIBUTIONS ALLOCATED	COMPENSATION FOR S-E TAX PURPOSES	TOTAL W-2 WAGES FOR S-E TAX	(5) PRO-RATA S-E TAX DEDUCTION	TOP HEAVY ADDITIONAL AMOUNT FOR 100.00% PERCENTAGE
$7,434.94	0.0000%	A	100.00000%	$2,565.06	$0.00	$0.00	$10,000.00	$0.00	$706.33	$0.00
$0.00	0.0000%	A	0.00000%	$0.00	$0.00	$0.00	$0.00	$0.00	$0.00	$0.00
$0.00	0.0000%	A	0.00000%	$0.00	$0.00	$0.00	$0.00	$0.00	$0.00	$0.00
$0.00	0.0000%	A	0.00000%	$0.00	$0.00	$0.00	$0.00	$0.00	$0.00	$0.00
$0.00	0.0000%	A	0.00000%	$0.00	$0.00	$0.00	$0.00	$0.00	$0.00	$0.00
$0.00	0.0000%	A	0.00000%	$0.00	$0.00	$0.00	$0.00	$0.00	$0.00	$0.00
$0.00	0.0000%	A	0.00000%	$0.00	$0.00	$0.00	$0.00	$0.00	$0.00	$0.00
$0.00	0.0000%	A	0.00000%	$0.00	$0.00	$0.00	$0.00	$0.00	$0.00	$0.00
$7,434.94	0.0000%		SUB-TOTALS	$2,565.06	$0.00	$0.00	$10,000.00	$0.00	$706.33	$0.00
$0.00	Ownership percentages are--									$0.00
$0.00	A = calculated automatically.									$0.00
$0.00										$0.00
$0.00	Additional amounts (contributions/accounts/gains), if any,entered									$0.00
$0.00	in last column (this page) are considered for Top-Heavy Analysis.									$0.00
$0.00										$0.00
$0.00	KEY-EMPLOYEE TOP-HEAVY ANALYSIS--				DOLLARS	PERCENTAGE				$0.00
$0.00	- Key Employee Accounts/Contributions:				$1,858.73	100.00000%				$0.00
$0.00	- Non-Key Employee Accounts/Contributions:				$0.00	0.00000%				$0.00
$0.00	- - Total Accounts/Contributions:				$1,858.73	100.00000%				$0.00
$0.00			NON-OWNER SUB TOTALS							$0.00
$7,434.94			GRAND TOTALS							$0.00

* UNINCORPORATED SEP PLAN * | * UNUSUAL FACTS (see Q 7:19) | 1
08:24 PM
20-Mar-2012

Plan Year Begins:	2012	$45,908.79	- Employer Contribution
Plan Year Ends:	2012	ALL	- DEDUCTIBLE PORTION
Base Percentage:	10.0000000	$45,908.79	- Total Allocated
Integration Level:	$0	10.000000000%	- Allocation % of 402(h) Comp.
Excess Percentage:	10.0000000	None	- Integration
1=P/S 2=MP 3=SEP 4=SARSEP:	3		
E/er Contr. to Owners:	93.47%		
E/er Alloc. Compensation:	93.47%	$50,000.00	- Maximum HCE Allocation <-n/a

P	-> Plan not T/H Prototype or Model SEP	TOTAL ALLOCATION	IRC 402(h) EMPLOYER CONTRIBUTION	EMPLOYER CONTRIBUTION	Columns reserved for Salary Reduction SEPs	KEY	Col n/a	EMPLOYEE's PRE-PLAN EARNED INCOME	HCE	Col. n/a	Col. n/a
1	Joe Normal	$8,398.10	10.000000%	$8,398.10		Y		$100,000.00	Y		
2	Lou - has W-2 income	$8,407.65	10.000000%	$8,407.65		Y		$100,000.00	Y		
3	Tom - has ouside SE loss	$8,462.31	10.000000%	$8,462.31		Y		$100,000.00	Y		
4	Tim - has outside SE gain	$8,397.75	10.000000%	$8,397.75		Y		$100,000.00	Y		
5	Abe - is ineligible	$0.00	0.000000%	$0.00		Y		$0.00	Y		
6	Ros - is a guaranteed	$9,242.98	10.000000%	$9,242.98		Y		$109,400.00	Y		
7	payment partner	$0.00	0.000000%	$0.00							
8		$0.00	0.000000%	$0.00							
	OWNER SUB-TOTALS	$42,908.79		$42,908.79	$0.00			$509,400.00			
9	Nancy Nurse	$1,000.00	10.000000%	$1,000.00		N		$10,000.00	N		
10	Karl Cleaner	$1,000.00	10.000000%	$1,000.00		N		$10,000.00	N		
11	Ruth Ray	$1,000.00	10.000000%	$1,000.00		N		$10,000.00	N		
12		$0.00	0.000000%	$0.00							
13		$0.00	0.000000%	$0.00							
14		$0.00	0.000000%	$0.00							
15		$0.00	0.000000%	$0.00							
16		$0.00	0.000000%	$0.00							
17		$0.00	0.000000%	$0.00							
18		$0.00	0.000000%	$0.00							
	NON-OWNER SUB TOTALS	$3,000.00		$3,000.00				$30,000.00			
	GRAND TOTALS	$45,908.79		$45,908.79				$539,400.00			

Penny rounding applied.

* UNUSUAL FACTS (see Q 7:19)

* UNINCORPORATED SEP PLAN *

* NON-INTEGRATED CONTRIBUTIONS

2
20-Mar-2012
08:24 PM

S P E C I A L   S I T U A T I O N   I N P U T   P A G E

ALLOCATION COMPENSATION -Includes- -Elective-	CALCULATE OWNER'S PERCENTAGE	Man 1	OWNERS SHARE PERCENTAGE	SUBTRACTIONS FOR 402(h) NET COMPENSATION Sum of: 1-E/er Contrib. 2-Basic Elective 4-E/ee Share Cost 5-50% of SE Tax	ADDITIONAL GAIN (LOSS) FOR S-E TAX	$3,000.00 (4) NON-OWNER CONTRIBUTIONS ALLOCATED	COMPENSATION FOR S-E TAX PURPOSES	TOTAL W-2 WAGES FOR S-E TAX	(5) PRO-RATA S-E TAX DEDUCTION	TOP HEAVY ADDITIONAL AMOUNT FOR 93.47% PERCENTAGE
$83,980.98	20.0000%		20.00000%	$16,019.02	$0.00	$600.00	$99,400.00	$0.00	$7,020.92	$0.00
$84,076.55	20.0000%		20.00000%	$15,923.45	$0.00	$600.00	$99,400.00	$20,000.00	$6,915.80	$0.00
$84,623.10	20.0000%		20.00000%	$15,376.90	($10,000.00)	$600.00	$89,400.00	$0.00	$6,314.59	$0.00
$83,977.48	20.0000%		20.00000%	$16,022.52	$10,000.00	$600.00	$109,400.00	$0.00	$7,024.77	$0.00
$0.00	20.0000%	?	20.00000%	$600.00	$0.00	$600.00	$0.00	$0.00	$0.00	$0.00
$92,429.78	0.0000%	?	0.00000%	$16,970.22	$0.00	$0.00	$109,400.00	$0.00	$7,727.25	$0.00
$0.00	0.0000%		0.00000%	$0.00	$0.00	$0.00	$0.00	$0.00	$0.00	$0.00
$0.00	0.0000%		0.00000%	$0.00	$0.00	$0.00	$0.00	$0.00	$0.00	$0.00
$429,087.89	100.0000%		SUB-TOTALS	$80,912.11	$0.00	$3,000.00	$507,000.00	$20,000.00	$35,003.32	$0.00
$10,000.00	Ownership percentages are--									$0.00
$10,000.00	being set manually and total 100%.									$0.00
$10,000.00										$0.00
$0.00	Additional amounts (contributions/accounts/gains), if any, entered									$0.00
$0.00	in last column (this page) are considered for Top-Heavy Analysis.									$0.00
$0.00										$0.00
$0.00	KEY-EMPLOYEE TOP-HEAVY ANALYSIS--				DOLLARS	PERCENTAGE				$0.00
$0.00	- Key Employee Accounts/Contributions:				$42,908.79	93.46530%				$0.00
$0.00	- Non-Key Employee Accounts/Contributions:				$3,000.00	6.53470%				$0.00
$0.00	- - Total Accounts/Contributions:				$45,908.79	100.00000%				$0.00
$30,000.00			NON-OWNER SUB TOTALS							$0.00
$459,087.89			GRAND TOTALS							$0.00

* UNINCORPORATED SEP PLAN * — * MATTY'S SOLE PROPRIETORSHIP - 15% SEP (see Q 7:22, example 1) — 1

07:26 PM
21-Feb-2012

Plan Year Begins:	2012	$15,417.60	- Employer Contribution
Plan Year Ends:	2012	ALL	- DEDUCTIBLE PORTION
Base Percentage:	15.0000000	$15,417.60	- Total Allocated
Integration Level:	$0	15.000000000%	- Allocation % of 402(h) Comp.
Excess Percentage:	15.0000000	None	- Integration
1=P/S 2=MP 3=SEP 4=SARSEP:	3		
E/er Contr. to Owners:	75.68%		
E/er Alloc. Compensation:	75.68%	$50,000.00	- Maximum HCE Allocation <-n/a

-> Plan not T/H

P	Prototype or Model SEP	TOTAL ALLOCATION	IRC 402(h) EMPLOYER CONTRIBUTION	EMPLOYER CONTRIBUTION	Columns reserved for Salary Reduction SEPs	KEY	Col n/a	EMPLOYEE's PRE-PLAN EARNED INCOME	HCE	Col. n/a	Col. n/a
1	Matty	$11,667.60	15.000000%	$11,667.60		Y		$100,000.00	Y		
2		$0.00	0.000000%	$0.00					Y		
3		$0.00	0.000000%	$0.00					Y		
4		$0.00	0.000000%	$0.00					Y		
5		$0.00	0.000000%	$0.00					Y		
6		$0.00	0.000000%	$0.00					Y		
7		$0.00	0.000000%	$0.00					Y		
8		$0.00	0.000000%	$0.00					Y		
	OWNER SUB-TOTALS	$11,667.60		$11,667.60	$0.00			$100,000.00			
9	Employee	$3,750.00	15.000000%	$3,750.00		N		$25,000.00	N		
10		$0.00	0.000000%	$0.00							
11		$0.00	0.000000%	$0.00							
12		$0.00	0.000000%	$0.00							
13		$0.00	0.000000%	$0.00							
14		$0.00	0.000000%	$0.00							
15		$0.00	0.000000%	$0.00							
16		$0.00	0.000000%	$0.00							
17		$0.00	0.000000%	$0.00							
18		$0.00	0.000000%	$0.00							
	NON-OWNER SUB TOTALS	$3,750.00		$3,750.00				$25,000.00			
	GRAND TOTALS	$15,417.60		$15,417.60				$125,000.00			

Penny rounding applied.

* MATTY'S SOLE PROPRIETORSHIP - 15% SEP (see Q 7:22, example 1)

* UNINCORPORATED SEP PLAN *

* NON-INTEGRATED CONTRIBUTIONS

2
21-Feb-2012
07:26 PM

* * S P E C I A L   S I T U A T I O N   I N P U T   P A G E * *

ALLOCATION COMPENSATION -Includes- -Elective-	CALCULATE OWNER'S PERCENTAGE	A u t o 2	OWNERS SHARE PERCENTAGE	SUBTRACTIONS FOR 402(h) NET COMPENSATION Sum of: 1-E/er Contrib. 2-Basic Elective 4-E/ee Share Cost 5-50% of SE Tax	ADDITIONAL GAIN (LOSS) FOR S-E TAX	$3,750.00 (4) NON-OWNER CONTRIBUTIONS ALLOCATED	COMPENSATION FOR S-E TAX PURPOSES	TOTAL W-2 WAGES FOR S-E TAX	(5) PRO-RATA S-E TAX DEDUCTION	TOP HEAVY ADDITIONAL AMOUNT FOR 75.68% PERCENTAGE
$77,783.98	0.0000%	A	100.00000%	$22,216.02	$0.00	$3,750.00	$96,250.00	$0.00	$6,798.42	$0.00
$0.00	0.0000%	A	0.00000%	$0.00	$0.00	$0.00	$0.00	$0.00	$0.00	$0.00
$0.00	0.0000%	A	0.00000%	$0.00	$0.00	$0.00	$0.00	$0.00	$0.00	$0.00
$0.00	0.0000%	A	0.00000%	$0.00	$0.00	$0.00	$0.00	$0.00	$0.00	$0.00
$0.00	0.0000%	A	0.00000%	$0.00	$0.00	$0.00	$0.00	$0.00	$0.00	$0.00
$0.00	0.0000%	A	0.00000%	$0.00	$0.00	$0.00	$0.00	$0.00	$0.00	$0.00
$0.00	0.0000%	A	0.00000%	$0.00	$0.00	$0.00	$0.00	$0.00	$0.00	$0.00
$0.00	0.0000%	A	0.00000%	$0.00	$0.00	$0.00	$0.00	$0.00	$0.00	$0.00
$77,783.98	0.0000%		SUB-TOTALS	$22,216.02	$0.00	$3,750.00	$96,250.00	$0.00	$6,798.42	$0.00
$25,000.00	Ownership percentages are--									$0.00
$0.00	A = calculated automatically.									$0.00
$0.00										$0.00
$0.00	Additional amounts (contributions/accounts/gains), if any,entered									$0.00
$0.00	in last column (this page) are considered for Top-Heavy Analysis.									$0.00
$0.00										$0.00
$0.00	KEY-EMPLOYEE TOP-HEAVY ANALYSIS--				DOLLARS	PERCENTAGE				$0.00
$0.00	- Key Employee Accounts/Contributions:				$11,667.60	75.67714%				$0.00
$0.00	- Non-Key Employee Accounts/Contributions:				$3,750.00	24.32286%				$0.00
$0.00	- - Total Accounts/Contributions:				$15,417.60	100.00000%				$0.00
$25,000.00			NON-OWNER SUB TOTALS							$0.00
$102,783.98			GRAND TOTALS							$0.00

* MATTY'S SOLE PROPRIETORSHIP - 15% SEP (see Q 7:22, example 1)

* UNINCORPORATED SEP PLAN *

* NON-INTEGRATED CONTRIBUTIONS

2012

* * C O N T R I B U T I O N   S U M M A R Y * *

$15,417.60 - Employer Contribution
ALL - DEDUCTIBLE PORTION
$15,417.60 - Total Allocated
15.00% - Allocation % of 402(h) Comp.
None - Integration

None - Integration Level   n\a :TWB Percentage

3
21-Feb-2012
07:26 PM

EMPLOYEE	PRE-PLAN COMPENSATION	TOTAL ALLOCATION	EMPLOYER's CONTRIBUTION	Col. n/a	Col. n/a	ULTRA NET TAXABLE COMPENSATION	Col. n/a	EMPLOYER CONTRIBUTION % OF DEDUCT. COMPENSATION	PERCENTAGE OF EMPLOYER $15,417.60 CONTRIBUTIONS	PERCENTAGE OF TOTAL $15,417.60 ALLOCATIONS
Matty	$100,000.00	$11,667.60	$11,667.60			$81,533.98		15.00%	75.68%	75.68%
		$0.00	$0.00			$0.00		0.00%	0.00%	0.00%
		$0.00	$0.00			$0.00		0.00%	0.00%	0.00%
		$0.00	$0.00			$0.00		0.00%	0.00%	0.00%
		$0.00	$0.00			$0.00		0.00%	0.00%	0.00%
		$0.00	$0.00			$0.00		0.00%	0.00%	0.00%
		$0.00	$0.00			$0.00		0.00%	0.00%	0.00%
		$0.00	$0.00			$0.00		0.00%	0.00%	0.00%
OWNER SUB-TOTALS	$100,000.00	$11,667.60	$11,667.60			$81,533.98			75.68%	75.68%
Employee	$25,000.00	$3,750.00	$3,750.00			$25,000.00		15.00%	24.32%	24.32%
		$0.00	$0.00			$0.00		0.00%	0.00%	0.00%
		$0.00	$0.00			$0.00		0.00%	0.00%	0.00%
		$0.00	$0.00			$0.00		0.00%	0.00%	0.00%
		$0.00	$0.00			$0.00		0.00%	0.00%	0.00%
		$0.00	$0.00			$0.00		0.00%	0.00%	0.00%
		$0.00	$0.00			$0.00		0.00%	0.00%	0.00%
		$0.00	$0.00			$0.00		0.00%	0.00%	0.00%
		$0.00	$0.00			$0.00		0.00%	0.00%	0.00%
		$0.00	$0.00			$0.00		0.00%	0.00%	0.00%
NON-OWNER SUB TOTALS	$25,000.00	$3,750.00	$3,750.00			$25,000.00			24.32%	24.32%
GRAND TOTALS	$25,000.00	$15,417.60	$15,417.60			$106,533.98			100.0%	100.0%

* MATTY'S SOLE PROPRIETORSHIP - 15% SEP (see Q 7:22, example 1)

4
21-Feb-2012
07:26 PM

* UNINCORPORATED SEP PLAN *

* NON-INTEGRATED CONTRIBUTIONS

* * A L L O C A T I O N   O F   D E S I R E D   C O N T R I B U T I O N * *

* * INTEGRATION METHOD: NOT INTEGRATED * *

EMPLOYEES	2012 ALLOCATION COMPENSATION	PLAN ALLOCATION COMPENSATION MULTIPLIED BY 15.000000% BASE PERCENTAGE	PLAN COMPENSATION IN EXCESS OF $0.00	EXCESS COMPENSATION MULTIPLIED BY 0.000000% DISPARITY RATE	UNLIMITED TOTAL PLAN DEPOSIT
Matty	$77,783.98	$11,667.60	$77,783.98	$0.00	$11,667.60
	$0.00	$0.00	$0.00	$0.00	$0.00
	$0.00	$0.00	$0.00	$0.00	$0.00
	$0.00	$0.00	$0.00	$0.00	$0.00
	$0.00	$0.00	$0.00	$0.00	$0.00
	$0.00	$0.00	$0.00	$0.00	$0.00
	$0.00	$0.00	$0.00	$0.00	$0.00
	$0.00	$0.00	$0.00	$0.00	$0.00
	$77,783.98	$11,667.60	$77,783.98	$0.00	$11,667.60
Employee	$25,000.00	$3,750.00	$25,000.00	$0.00	$3,750.00
	$0.00	$0.00	$0.00	$0.00	$0.00
	$0.00	$0.00	$0.00	$0.00	$0.00
	$0.00	$0.00	$0.00	$0.00	$0.00
	$0.00	$0.00	$0.00	$0.00	$0.00
	$0.00	$0.00	$0.00	$0.00	$0.00
	$0.00	$0.00	$0.00	$0.00	$0.00
	$0.00	$0.00	$0.00	$0.00	$0.00
	$0.00	$0.00	$0.00	$0.00	$0.00
	$0.00	$0.00	$0.00	$0.00	$0.00
	$25,000.00	$3,750.00	$25,000.00	$0.00	$3,750.00
	$102,783.98	$15,417.60	$102,783.98	$0.00	$15,417.60

* Do Not contribute amounts shown on this page. Allocation shown is untested or may have been reduced by other factors.

* MATTY'S SOLE PROPRIETORSHIP - 15% SEP (see Q 7:22, example 1)

* UNINCORPORATED SEP PLAN *

* NON-INTEGRATED CONTRIBUTIONS

* CONTRIBUTION LIMITATIONS

5
21-Feb-2012
07:26 PM

2012 M A X I M U M L I M I T A T I O N S

	A	B	D	E	Lesser of: A or B or D or E	
EMPLOYEES	UNLIMITED CONTRIBUTION AMOUNTS	SECTION 415 GENERAL $50,000.00 LIMIT	IRS Model or Prototype SEP - 402(h) LIMIT $50,000.00	SEP IRC 402(h)(2)(b) "HCE" REDUCED DOLLAR LIMIT	2012 MAXIMUM ALLOWABLE PLAN CONTRIBUTION	MULTI-CLASS FORMULA ALLOCATION LIMIT PERCENTAGE (Col. N/A)
Matty	$11,667.60	$50,000.00	$19,445.99	$50,000.00	$11,667.60	0.00000
	$0.00	n/a	$0.00	$0.00	$0.00	0.00000
	$0.00	n/a	$0.00	$0.00	$0.00	0.00000
	$0.00	n/a	$0.00	$0.00	$0.00	0.00000
	$0.00	n/a	$0.00	$0.00	$0.00	0.00000
	$0.00	n/a	$0.00	$0.00	$0.00	0.00000
	$0.00	n/a	$0.00	$0.00	$0.00	0.00000
	$0.00	n/a	$0.00	$0.00	$0.00	0.00000
OWNER SUB-TOTALS						
Employee	$3,750.00	$50,000.00	$6,250.00	$50,000.00	$3,750.00	0.00000
	$0.00	n/a	$0.00	$0.00	$0.00	0.00000
	$0.00	n/a	$0.00	$0.00	$0.00	0.00000
	$0.00	n/a	$0.00	$0.00	$0.00	0.00000
	$0.00	n/a	$0.00	$0.00	$0.00	0.00000
	$0.00	n/a	$0.00	$0.00	$0.00	0.00000
	$0.00	n/a	$0.00	$0.00	$0.00	0.00000
	$0.00	n/a	$0.00	$0.00	$0.00	0.00000
	$0.00	n/a	$0.00	$0.00	$0.00	0.00000
	$0.00	n/a	$0.00	$0.00	$0.00	0.00000

Do not contribute amounts shown on this page.

* MONEY PURCHASE KEOGH PLAN * — * MATTY'S SOLE PROPRIETORSHIP - 15% SEP & 10% Money Purchase Pension (see Q 7:22, example 2) — 1

07:28 PM
21-Feb-2012

Plan Year Begins:	2012	$23,675.63	- Employer Contribution
Plan Year Ends:	2012	ALL	- DEDUCTIBLE PORTION
Base Percentage:	25.0000000	$23,675.63	- Total Contributions
Integration Level:	$0	25.000000000%	- Allocation % of Ded. Comp.
Excess Percentage:	25.0000000	None	- Integration
1=P/S 2=MP 3=SEP 4=SARSEP:	2		
E/er Contr. to Owners:	73.60%		
E/er Alloc. Compensation:	73.60%	$50,000.00	- Maximum Allocation <-n/a

-> Plan not T/H

P	Prototype Plan	TOTAL ALLOCATION	ALLOCATION % OF DEDUCTION COMPENSATION	EMPLOYER CONTRIBUTION	Columns reserved for Salary Reduction SEPs	KEY	Col n/a	EMPLOYEE's PRE-PLAN EARNED INCOME		Col. n/a	Col. n/a
1	Matty	$17,425.63	25.000000%	$17,425.63		Y		$100,000.00	Y		
2		$0.00	0.000000%	$0.00							
3		$0.00	0.000000%	$0.00							
4		$0.00	0.000000%	$0.00							
5		$0.00	0.000000%	$0.00							
6		$0.00	0.000000%	$0.00							
7		$0.00	0.000000%	$0.00							
8		$0.00	0.000000%	$0.00							
	OWNER SUB-TOTALS	$17,425.63		$17,425.63	$0.00			$100,000.00			
9	Employee	$6,250.00	25.000000%	$6,250.00		N		$25,000.00	N		
10		$0.00	0.000000%	$0.00							
11		$0.00	0.000000%	$0.00							
12		$0.00	0.000000%	$0.00							
13		$0.00	0.000000%	$0.00							
14		$0.00	0.000000%	$0.00							
15		$0.00	0.000000%	$0.00							
16		$0.00	0.000000%	$0.00							
17		$0.00	0.000000%	$0.00							
18		$0.00	0.000000%	$0.00							
	NON-OWNER SUB TOTALS	$6,250.00		$6,250.00				$25,000.00			
	GRAND TOTALS	$23,675.63		$23,675.63				$125,000.00			

* MATTY'S SOLE PROPRIETORSHIP - 15% SEP & 10% Money Purchase Pension Plan

* MONEY PURCHASE KEOGH PLAN *

* NON-INTEGRATED CONTRIBUTIONS

2
21-Feb-2012
07:28 PM

* * S P E C I A L   S I T U A T I O N   I N P U T   P A G E * *

ALLOCATION COMPENSATION -Includes- -Elective-	CALCULATE OWNER'S PERCENTAGE	Auto 2	OWNERS SHARE PERCENTAGE	SUBTRACTIONS FOR OWNER'S NET COMPENSATION Sum of: 1-E/er Contrib. 2-Basic Elective 4-E/ee Share Cost 5-50% of SE Tax	ADDITIONAL GAIN (LOSS) FOR S-E TAX	$6,250.00 (4) NON-OWNER CONTRIBUTIONS ALLOCATED	COMPENSATION FOR S-E TAX PURPOSES	TOTAL W-2 WAGES FOR S-E TAX	(5) PRO-RATA S-E TAX DEDUCTION	TOP HEAVY ADDITIONAL AMOUNT FOR 73.60% PERCENTAGE
$69,702.53	0.0000%	A	100.00000%	$30,297.47	$0.00	$6,250.00	$93,750.00	$0.00	$6,621.84	$0.00
$0.00	0.0000%	A	0.00000%	$0.00	$0.00	$0.00	$0.00	$0.00	$0.00	$0.00
$0.00	0.0000%	A	0.00000%	$0.00	$0.00	$0.00	$0.00	$0.00	$0.00	$0.00
$0.00	0.0000%	A	0.00000%	$0.00	$0.00	$0.00	$0.00	$0.00	$0.00	$0.00
$0.00	0.0000%	A	0.00000%	$0.00	$0.00	$0.00	$0.00	$0.00	$0.00	$0.00
$0.00	0.0000%	A	0.00000%	$0.00	$0.00	$0.00	$0.00	$0.00	$0.00	$0.00
$0.00	0.0000%	A	0.00000%	$0.00	$0.00	$0.00	$0.00	$0.00	$0.00	$0.00
$0.00	0.0000%	A	0.00000%	$0.00	$0.00	$0.00	$0.00	$0.00	$0.00	$0.00
$69,702.53	0.0000%		SUB-TOTALS	$30,297.47	$0.00	$6,250.00	$93,750.00	$0.00	$6,621.84	$0.00
$25,000.00	Ownership percentages are--									$0.00
$0.00	A = calculated automatically.									$0.00
$0.00										$0.00
$0.00	Additional amounts (contributions/accounts/gains), if any,entered									$0.00
$0.00	in last column (this page) are considered for Top-Heavy Analysis.									$0.00
$0.00										$0.00
$0.00	KEY-EMPLOYEE TOP-HEAVY ANALYSIS--				DOLLARS	PERCENTAGE				$0.00
$0.00	- Key Employee Accounts/Contributions:				$17,425.63	73.60155%				$0.00
$0.00	- Non-Key Employee Accounts/Contributions:				$6,250.00	26.39845%				$0.00
$0.00	- - Total Accounts/Contributions:				$23,675.63	100.00000%				$0.00
$25,000.00			NON-OWNER SUB TOTALS							$0.00
$94,702.53			GRAND TOTALS							$0.00

* MONEY PURCHASE KEOGH PLAN *		* MATTY'S SOLE PROPRIETORSHIP - 10% Money Purchase Pension Plan		(see Q 7:22, example 3)	1 07:38 PM 21-Feb-2012
Plan Year Begins:	2012	$10,737.57	- Employer Contribution		
Plan Year Ends:	2012	ALL	- DEDUCTIBLE PORTION		
Base Percentage:	10.0000000	$10,737.57	- Total Contributions		
Integration Level:	$0	10.000000000%	- Allocation % of Ded. Comp.		
Excess Percentage:	10.0000000	None	- Integration		
1=P/S 2=MP 3=SEP 4=SARSEP:	2				
E/er Contr. to Owners:	76.72%				
E/er Alloc. Compensation:	76.72%	$50,000.00	- Maximum Allocation	<-n/a	

-> Plan not T/H P	Prototype Plan	TOTAL ALLOCATION	ALLOCATION % OF DEDUCTION COMPENSATION	EMPLOYER CONTRIBUTION	Columns reserved for Salary Reduction SEPs	K E Y	Col n/a	EMPLOYEE's PRE-PLAN EARNED INCOME		Col. n/a	Col. n/a
1	Matty	$8,237.57	10.000000%	$8,237.57		Y		$100,000.00	Y		
2		$0.00	0.000000%	$0.00							
3		$0.00	0.000000%	$0.00							
4		$0.00	0.000000%	$0.00							
5		$0.00	0.000000%	$0.00							
6		$0.00	0.000000%	$0.00							
7		$0.00	0.000000%	$0.00							
8		$0.00	0.000000%	$0.00							
	OWNER SUB-TOTALS	$8,237.57		$8,237.57	$0.00			$100,000.00			
9	Employee	$2,500.00	10.000000%	$2,500.00		N		$25,000.00	N		
10		$0.00	0.000000%	$0.00							
11		$0.00	0.000000%	$0.00							
12		$0.00	0.000000%	$0.00							
13		$0.00	0.000000%	$0.00							
14		$0.00	0.000000%	$0.00							
15		$0.00	0.000000%	$0.00							
16		$0.00	0.000000%	$0.00							
17		$0.00	0.000000%	$0.00							
18		$0.00	0.000000%	$0.00							
	NON-OWNER SUB TOTALS	$2,500.00		$2,500.00				$25,000.00			
	GRAND TOTALS	$10,737.57		$10,737.57				$125,000.00			

* MATTY'S SOLE PROPRIETORSHIP - 10% Money Purchase Pension Plan

* MONEY PURCHASE KEOGH PLAN *

* NON-INTEGRATED CONTRIBUTIONS

2
21-Feb-2012
07:38 PM

* * S P E C I A L   S I T U A T I O N   I N P U T   P A G E * *

ALLOCATION COMPENSATION -Includes- -Elective-	CALCULATE OWNER'S PERCENTAGE	Auto 2	OWNERS SHARE PERCENTAGE	SUBTRACTIONS FOR OWNER'S NET COMPENSATION Sum of: 1-E/er Contrib. 2-Basic Elective 4-E/ee Share Cost 5-50% of SE Tax	ADDITIONAL GAIN (LOSS) FOR S-E TAX	$2,500.00 (4) NON-OWNER CONTRIBUTIONS ALLOCATED	COMPENSATION FOR S-E TAX PURPOSES	TOTAL W-2 WAGES FOR S-E TAX	(5) PRO-RATA S-E TAX DEDUCTION	TOP HEAVY ADDITIONAL AMOUNT FOR 76.72% PERCENTAGE
$82,375.71	0.0000%	A	100.00000%	$17,624.29	$0.00	$2,500.00	$97,500.00	$0.00	$6,886.71	$0.00
$0.00	0.0000%	A	0.00000%	$0.00	$0.00	$0.00	$0.00	$0.00	$0.00	$0.00
$0.00	0.0000%	A	0.00000%	$0.00	$0.00	$0.00	$0.00	$0.00	$0.00	$0.00
$0.00	0.0000%	A	0.00000%	$0.00	$0.00	$0.00	$0.00	$0.00	$0.00	$0.00
$0.00	0.0000%	A	0.00000%	$0.00	$0.00	$0.00	$0.00	$0.00	$0.00	$0.00
$0.00	0.0000%	A	0.00000%	$0.00	$0.00	$0.00	$0.00	$0.00	$0.00	$0.00
$0.00	0.0000%	A	0.00000%	$0.00	$0.00	$0.00	$0.00	$0.00	$0.00	$0.00
$0.00	0.0000%	A	0.00000%	$0.00	$0.00	$0.00	$0.00	$0.00	$0.00	$0.00
$82,375.71	0.0000%		SUB-TOTALS	$17,624.29	$0.00	$2,500.00	$97,500.00	$0.00	$6,886.71	$0.00
$25,000.00	Ownership percentages are--									$0.00
$0.00	A = calculated automatically.									$0.00
$0.00										$0.00
$0.00	Additional amounts (contributions/accounts/gains), if any,entered									$0.00
$0.00	in last column (this page) are considered for Top-Heavy Analysis.									$0.00
$0.00										$0.00
$0.00	KEY-EMPLOYEE TOP-HEAVY ANALYSIS--				DOLLARS	PERCENTAGE				$0.00
$0.00	- Key Employee Accounts/Contributions:				$8,237.57	76.71727%				$0.00
$0.00	- Non-Key Employee Accounts/Contributions:				$2,500.00	23.28273%				$0.00
$0.00	- - Total Accounts/Contributions:				$10,737.57	100.00000%				$0.00
$25,000.00			NON-OWNER SUB TOTALS							$0.00
$107,375.71			GRAND TOTALS							$0.00

* UNINCORPORATED SEP PLAN *   * MYRON's SOLE PROPRIETORSHIP - Combined SEP & 10% MPPP   (see Q 7:22, example 4)   1

08:05 PM
21-Feb-2012

Plan Year Begins:	2012	$50,000.00	- Employer Contribution
Plan Year Ends:	2012	ALL	- DEDUCTIBLE PORTION
Base Percentage:	25.0000000	$50,000.00	- Total Allocated
Integration Level:	$0	24.999999635%	- Allocation % of 402(h) Comp.
Excess Percentage:	25.0000000	None	- Integration
1=P/S 2=MP 3=SEP 4=SARSEP:	3		
E/er Contr. to Owners:	100.00%		
E/er Alloc. Compensation:	100.00%	$50,000.00	- Maximum HCE Allocation <-n/a

-> No N-Key E/ees; T/H okay P Prototype or Model SEP	TOTAL ALLOCATION	IRC 402(h) EMPLOYER CONTRIBUTION	EMPLOYER CONTRIBUTION	Columns reserved for Salary Reduction SEPs		KEY	Col n/a	EMPLOYEE's PRE-PLAN EARNED INCOME	HCE	Col. n/a	Col. n/a
1 Myron	$50,000.00 h	25.000000% m	$50,000.00			Y		$260,310.19	Y		
2	$0.00	0.000000%	$0.00								
3	$0.00	0.000000%	$0.00								
4	$0.00	0.000000%	$0.00								
5	$0.00	0.000000%	$0.00								
6	$0.00	0.000000%	$0.00								
7	$0.00	0.000000%	$0.00								
8	$0.00	0.000000%	$0.00								
OWNER SUB-TOTALS	$50,000.00		$50,000.00		$0.00			$260,310.19			
9 No employees	$0.00	0.000000%	$0.00			N		$0.00	N		
10	$0.00	0.000000%	$0.00								
11	$0.00	0.000000%	$0.00								
12	$0.00	0.000000%	$0.00								
13	$0.00	0.000000%	$0.00								
14	$0.00	0.000000%	$0.00								
15	$0.00	0.000000%	$0.00								
16	$0.00	0.000000%	$0.00								
17	$0.00	0.000000%	$0.00								
18	$0.00	0.000000%	$0.00								
NON-OWNER SUB TOTALS	$0.00		$0.00					$0.00			
GRAND TOTALS	$50,000.00		$50,000.00					$260,310.19			

h or m <-- At a limit/maximum (other solutions possible).

* MYRON's SOLE PROPRIETORSHIP - Combined SEP & 10% MPPP

* UNINCORPORATED SEP PLAN *

* NON-INTEGRATED CONTRIBUTIONS

2
21-Feb-2012
08:05 PM

* * S P E C I A L   S I T U A T I O N   I N P U T   P A G E * *

ALLOCATION COMPENSATION -Includes- -Elective-	CALCULATE OWNER'S PERCENTAGE	Auto 2	OWNERS SHARE PERCENTAGE	SUBTRACTIONS FOR 402(h) NET COMPENSATION Sum of: 1-E/er Contrib. 2-Basic Elective 4-E/ee Share Cost 5-50% of SE Tax	ADDITIONAL GAIN (LOSS) FOR S-E TAX	$0.00 (4) NON-OWNER CONTRIBUTIONS ALLOCATED	COMPENSATION FOR S-E TAX PURPOSES	TOTAL W-2 WAGES FOR S-E TAX	(5) PRO-RATA S-E TAX DEDUCTION	TOP HEAVY ADDITIONAL AMOUNT FOR 100.00% PERCENTAGE
$200,000.00	0.0000%	A	100.00000%	$60,310.19	$0.00	$0.00	$260,310.19	$0.00	$10,310.19	$0.00
$0.00	0.0000%	A	0.00000%	$0.00	$0.00	$0.00	$0.00	$0.00	$0.00	$0.00
$0.00	0.0000%	A	0.00000%	$0.00	$0.00	$0.00	$0.00	$0.00	$0.00	$0.00
$0.00	0.0000%	A	0.00000%	$0.00	$0.00	$0.00	$0.00	$0.00	$0.00	$0.00
$0.00	0.0000%	A	0.00000%	$0.00	$0.00	$0.00	$0.00	$0.00	$0.00	$0.00
$0.00	0.0000%	A	0.00000%	$0.00	$0.00	$0.00	$0.00	$0.00	$0.00	$0.00
$0.00	0.0000%	A	0.00000%	$0.00	$0.00	$0.00	$0.00	$0.00	$0.00	$0.00
$0.00	0.0000%	A	0.00000%	$0.00	$0.00	$0.00	$0.00	$0.00	$0.00	$0.00
$200,000.00	0.0000%		SUB-TOTALS	$60,310.19	$0.00	$0.00	$260,310.19	$0.00	$10,310.19	$0.00
$0.00	Ownership percentages are--									$0.00
$0.00	A = calculated automatically.									$0.00
$0.00										$0.00
$0.00	Additional amounts (contributions/accounts/gains), if any,entered									$0.00
$0.00	in last column (this page) are considered for Top-Heavy Analysis.									$0.00
$0.00										$0.00
$0.00	KEY-EMPLOYEE TOP-HEAVY ANALYSIS--				DOLLARS	PERCENTAGE				$0.00
$0.00	- Key Employee Accounts/Contributions:				$50,000.00	100.00000%				$0.00
$0.00	- Non-Key Employee Accounts/Contributions:				$0.00	0.00000%				$0.00
$0.00	- - Total Accounts/Contributions:				$50,000.00	100.00000%				$0.00
$0.00			NON-OWNER SUB TOTALS							$0.00
$200,000.00			GRAND TOTALS							$0.00

* CORPORATE SEP PLAN *		* DARN KNIT STORE (see Q 9:5, example 1a)		1
				12:59 PM
Plan Year Begins:	2012	$50,860.00	- Employer Contribution	22-Feb-2012
Plan Year Ends:	2012	ALL	- DEDUCTIBLE PORTION	
Base Percentage:	14.3000000	$50,860.00	- Total Allocated	
Integration Level:	$10,000	19.561538462%	- Allocation % of 402(h) Comp	
Excess Percentage:	20.0000000	5.7%	- Maximum Integration Spread	
1=P/S 2=MP 3=SEP 4=SARSEP:	3			
E/er Contr. to Owners:	97.18836020%			
E/er Alloc. Compensation:	96.15384615%	$49,430.00	- Maximum HCE Allocation	<-n/a

-> P	Plan not T/H Integrated Prototype SEP	TOTAL ALLOCATION	IRC 402(h) EMPLOYER CONTRIBUTION	EMPLOYER CONTRIBUTION	Columns reserved for Salary Reduction SEPs	KEY	Col n/a	EMPLOYEE's PRE-PLAN COMPENSATION	HCE	Col. n/a	Col. n/a
1	Donna Darn	$49,430.00 h	19.772000% m	$49,430.00		Y		$250,000.00	Y		
2		$0.00	0.000000%	$0.00							
3		$0.00	0.000000%	$0.00							
4		$0.00	0.000000%	$0.00							
5		$0.00	0.000000%	$0.00							
6		$0.00	0.000000%	$0.00							
7		$0.00	0.000000%	$0.00							
8		$0.00	0.000000%	$0.00							
	OWNER SUB-TOTALS	$49,430.00		$49,430.00	$0.00			$250,000.00			
9	Mona Patch	$1,430.00	14.300000%	$1,430.00		N		$10,000.00	N		
10		$0.00	0.000000%	$0.00							
11		$0.00	0.000000%	$0.00							
12		$0.00	0.000000%	$0.00							
13		$0.00	0.000000%	$0.00							
14		$0.00	0.000000%	$0.00							
15		$0.00	0.000000%	$0.00							
16		$0.00	0.000000%	$0.00							
17		$0.00	0.000000%	$0.00							
18		$0.00	0.000000%	$0.00							
	NON-OWNER SUB TOTALS	$1,430.00		$1,430.00				$10,000.00			
	GRAND TOTALS	$50,860.00		$50,860.00				$260,000.00			

h or m <-- At a limit/maximum (other solutions possible).

* DARN KNIT STORE (see Q 9:5, example 1a)

* CORPORATE SEP PLAN *

* INTEGRATED CONTRIBUTIONS

2012

* * C O N T R I B U T I O N   S U M M A R Y * *

$50,860.00 - Employer Contribution
ALL - DEDUCTIBLE PORTION
$50,860.00 - Total Allocated
19.56% - Allocation % of 402(h) Comp
5.70% - Maximum Integration Spread

$10,000.00 - Integration Level   9.08265213% :TWB Percentage

2
22-Feb-2012
12:59 PM

ALLOCATION COMPENSATION -Includes- -Elective-	TOP HEAVY ADDITIONAL AMOUNT FOR 97.19% PERCENTAGE	PRE-PLAN COMPENSATION	TOTAL ALLOCATION	EMPLOYER's CONTRIBUTION	Col. n/a	Col. n/a	NET TAXABLE COMPENSATION	Col. n/a	EMPLOYER CONTRIBUTION % OF DEDUCT. COMPENSATION	PERCENTAGE OF EMPLOYER $50,860.00 CONTRIBUTIONS	PERCENTAGE OF TOTAL $50,860.00 ALLOCATIONS
$250,000.00	$0.00	$250,000.00	$49,430.00	$49,430.00			$250,000.00		19.77%	97.19%	97.19%
$0.00	$0.00		$0.00	$0.00			$0.00		0.00%	0.00%	0.00%
$0.00	$0.00		$0.00	$0.00			$0.00		0.00%	0.00%	0.00%
$0.00	$0.00		$0.00	$0.00			$0.00		0.00%	0.00%	0.00%
$0.00	$0.00		$0.00	$0.00			$0.00		0.00%	0.00%	0.00%
$0.00	$0.00		$0.00	$0.00			$0.00		0.00%	0.00%	0.00%
$0.00	$0.00		$0.00	$0.00			$0.00		0.00%	0.00%	0.00%
$0.00	$0.00		$0.00	$0.00			$0.00		0.00%	0.00%	0.00%
$250,000.00	$0.00	$250,000.00	$49,430.00	$49,430.00			$250,000.00			97.19%	97.19%
$10,000.00	$0.00	$10,000.00	$1,430.00	$1,430.00			$10,000.00		14.30%	2.81%	2.81%
$0.00	$0.00		$0.00	$0.00			$0.00		0.00%	0.00%	0.00%
$0.00	$0.00		$0.00	$0.00			$0.00		0.00%	0.00%	0.00%
$0.00	$0.00		$0.00	$0.00			$0.00		0.00%	0.00%	0.00%
$0.00	$0.00		$0.00	$0.00			$0.00		0.00%	0.00%	0.00%
$0.00	$0.00		$0.00	$0.00			$0.00		0.00%	0.00%	0.00%
$0.00	$0.00		$0.00	$0.00			$0.00		0.00%	0.00%	0.00%
$0.00	$0.00		$0.00	$0.00			$0.00		0.00%	0.00%	0.00%
$0.00	$0.00		$0.00	$0.00			$0.00		0.00%	0.00%	0.00%
$0.00	$0.00		$0.00	$0.00			$0.00		0.00%	0.00%	0.00%
$10,000.00	$0.00	$10,000.00	$1,430.00	$1,430.00			$10,000.00			2.81%	2.81%
$260,000.00	$0.00	$10,000.00	$50,860.00	$50,860.00			$260,000.00			100.0%	100.0%

* CORPORATE SEP PLAN * — * DARN KNIT STORE (see Q 9:5, example 1b) — 1

05:07 PM
22-Feb-2012

Plan Year Begins:	2012	$52,000.00	- Employer Contribution
Plan Year Ends:	2012	ALL	- DEDUCTIBLE PORTION
Base Percentage:	20.0000000	$52,000.00	- Total Allocated
Integration Level:	$0	19.999999990%	- Allocation % of 402(h) Comp
Excess Percentage:	20.0000000	None	- Integration
1=P/S 2=MP 3=SEP 4=SARSEP:	3		
E/er Contr. to Owners:	96.15384615%		
E/er Alloc. Compensation:	96.15384615%	$50,000.00	- Maximum HCE Allocation

Y <-n/a

-> P	Plan not T/H Prototype or Model SEP	TOTAL ALLOCATION	IRC 402(h) EMPLOYER CONTRIBUTION	EMPLOYER CONTRIBUTION	Columns reserved for Salary Reduction SEPs	KEY	Col n/a	EMPLOYEE's PRE-PLAN COMPENSATION	HCE	Col. n/a	Col. n/a
1	Donna Darn	$50,000.00	20.000000%	$50,000.00		Y		$250,000.00	Y		
2		$0.00	0.000000%	$0.00							
3		$0.00	0.000000%	$0.00							
4		$0.00	0.000000%	$0.00							
5		$0.00	0.000000%	$0.00							
6		$0.00	0.000000%	$0.00							
7		$0.00	0.000000%	$0.00							
8		$0.00	0.000000%	$0.00							
	OWNER SUB-TOTALS	$50,000.00		$50,000.00	$0.00			$250,000.00			
9	Mona Patch	$2,000.00	20.000000%	$2,000.00		N		$10,000.00	N		
10		$0.00	0.000000%	$0.00							
11		$0.00	0.000000%	$0.00							
12		$0.00	0.000000%	$0.00							
13		$0.00	0.000000%	$0.00							
14		$0.00	0.000000%	$0.00							
15		$0.00	0.000000%	$0.00							
16		$0.00	0.000000%	$0.00							
17		$0.00	0.000000%	$0.00							
18		$0.00	0.000000%	$0.00							
	NON-OWNER SUB TOTALS	$2,000.00		$2,000.00				$10,000.00			
	GRAND TOTALS	$52,000.00		$52,000.00				$260,000.00			

* DARN KNIT STORE (see Q 9:5, example 1b)

* CORPORATE SEP PLAN *

* NON-INTEGRATED CONTRIBUTIONS

2012

$52,000.00 - Employer Contribution
ALL - DEDUCTIBLE PORTION
$52,000.00 - Total Allocated
20.00% - Allocation % of 402(h) Comp
None - Integration

2
22-Feb-2012
05:07 PM

* * C O N T R I B U T I O N S U M M A R Y * *

None - Integration Level

ALLOCATION COMPENSATION -Includes- -Elective-	TOP HEAVY ADDITIONAL AMOUNT FOR 96.15% PERCENTAGE	PRE-PLAN COMPENSATION	TOTAL ALLOCATION	EMPLOYER's CONTRIBUTION	Col. n/a	Col. n/a	NET TAXABLE COMPENSATION	Col. n/a	EMPLOYER CONTRIBUTION % OF DEDUCT. COMPENSATION	PERCENTAGE OF EMPLOYER $52,000.00 CONTRIBUTIONS	PERCENTAGE OF TOTAL $52,000.00 ALLOCATIONS
$250,000.00	$0.00	$250,000.00	$50,000.00	$50,000.00			$250,000.00		20.00%	96.15%	96.15%
$0.00	$0.00		$0.00	$0.00			$0.00		0.00%	0.00%	0.00%
$0.00	$0.00		$0.00	$0.00			$0.00		0.00%	0.00%	0.00%
$0.00	$0.00		$0.00	$0.00			$0.00		0.00%	0.00%	0.00%
$0.00	$0.00		$0.00	$0.00			$0.00		0.00%	0.00%	0.00%
$0.00	$0.00		$0.00	$0.00			$0.00		0.00%	0.00%	0.00%
$0.00	$0.00		$0.00	$0.00			$0.00		0.00%	0.00%	0.00%
$0.00	$0.00		$0.00	$0.00			$0.00		0.00%	0.00%	0.00%
$250,000.00	$0.00	$250,000.00	$50,000.00	$50,000.00			$250,000.00			96.15%	96.15%
$10,000.00	$0.00	$10,000.00	$2,000.00	$2,000.00			$10,000.00		20.00%	3.85%	3.85%
$0.00	$0.00		$0.00	$0.00			$0.00		0.00%	0.00%	0.00%
$0.00	$0.00		$0.00	$0.00			$0.00		0.00%	0.00%	0.00%
$0.00	$0.00		$0.00	$0.00			$0.00		0.00%	0.00%	0.00%
$0.00	$0.00		$0.00	$0.00			$0.00		0.00%	0.00%	0.00%
$0.00	$0.00		$0.00	$0.00			$0.00		0.00%	0.00%	0.00%
$0.00	$0.00		$0.00	$0.00			$0.00		0.00%	0.00%	0.00%
$0.00	$0.00		$0.00	$0.00			$0.00		0.00%	0.00%	0.00%
$0.00	$0.00		$0.00	$0.00			$0.00		0.00%	0.00%	0.00%
$0.00	$0.00		$0.00	$0.00			$0.00		0.00%	0.00%	0.00%
$10,000.00	$0.00	$10,000.00	$2,000.00	$2,000.00			$10,000.00			3.85%	3.85%
$260,000.00	$0.00	$10,000.00	$52,000.00	$52,000.00			$260,000.00			100.0%	100.0%

```
* CORPORATE SEP PLAN *                 * BEAVER HAT SHOP (see Q 9:5, example 2a)                                                              1
                                                                                                                                  05:10 PM
Plan Year Begins:                 2012       $45,869.30    - Employer Contribution                                            22-Feb-2012
Plan Year Ends:                   2012              ALL    - DEDUCTIBLE PORTION
Base Percentage:            14.3000000       $45,869.30    - Total Allocated
Integration Level:            $110,100    17.309169811%    - Allocation % of 402(h) Comp
Excess Percentage:          20.0000000             5.7%    - Maximum Integration Spread
1=P/S 2=MP 3=SEP 4=SARSEP:           3
E/er Contr. to Owners:    95.32366964%
E/er Alloc. Compensation: 94.33962264%       $43,724.30    - Maximum HCE Allocation                     Y  <-n/a

->  Plan not T/H                                IRC 402(h)                    Columns reserved for            K                EMPLOYEE's  H
 P  Integrated Prototype SEP        TOTAL         EMPLOYER          EMPLOYER  Salary Reduction SEPs           E    Col          PRE-PLAN   C
                               ALLOCATION     CONTRIBUTION      CONTRIBUTION                                  Y    n/a      COMPENSATION   E    Col. n/a     Col. n/a

 1          Clarence Beaver  $43,724.30 h    17.489720% m        $43,724.30                                   Y             $250,000.00   Y
 2                                $0.00        0.000000%             $0.00
 3                                $0.00        0.000000%             $0.00
 4                                $0.00        0.000000%             $0.00
 5                                $0.00        0.000000%             $0.00
 6                                $0.00        0.000000%             $0.00
 7                                $0.00        0.000000%             $0.00
 8                                $0.00        0.000000%             $0.00

          OWNER SUB-TOTALS   $43,724.30                          $43,724.30                            $0.00                $250,000.00

 9              Joe Skinner   $2,145.00       14.300000%          $2,145.00                                   N              $15,000.00   N
10                                $0.00        0.000000%             $0.00
11                                $0.00        0.000000%             $0.00
12                                $0.00        0.000000%             $0.00
13                                $0.00        0.000000%             $0.00
14                                $0.00        0.000000%             $0.00
15                                $0.00        0.000000%             $0.00
16                                $0.00        0.000000%             $0.00
17                                $0.00        0.000000%             $0.00
18                                $0.00        0.000000%             $0.00

      NON-OWNER SUB TOTALS    $2,145.00                           $2,145.00                                                  $15,000.00
                                        h or m <-- At a limit/maximum (other solutions possible).
              GRAND TOTALS   $45,869.30                          $45,869.30                                                 $265,000.00
```

* BEAVER HAT SHOP (see Q 9:5, example 2a)

* CORPORATE SEP PLAN *

* INTEGRATED CONTRIBUTIONS

2012

$45,869.30 - Employer Contribution
ALL - DEDUCTIBLE PORTION
$45,869.30 - Total Allocated
17.31% - Allocation % of 402(h) Comp
5.70% - Maximum Integration Spread

2
22-Feb-2012
05:10 PM

* * C O N T R I B U T I O N   S U M M A R Y * *

$110,100.00 - Integration Level   100.000000000% :TWB Percentage

ALLOCATION COMPENSATION -Includes- -Elective-	TOP HEAVY ADDITIONAL AMOUNT FOR 95.32% PERCENTAGE	PRE-PLAN COMPENSATION	TOTAL ALLOCATION	EMPLOYER's CONTRIBUTION	Col. n/a	Col. n/a	NET TAXABLE COMPENSATION	Col. n/a	EMPLOYER CONTRIBUTION % OF DEDUCT. COMPENSATION	PERCENTAGE OF EMPLOYER $45,869.30 CONTRIBUTIONS	PERCENTAGE OF TOTAL $45,869.30 ALLOCATIONS
$250,000.00	$0.00	$250,000.00	$43,724.30	$43,724.30			$250,000.00		17.49%	95.32%	95.32%
$0.00	$0.00		$0.00	$0.00			$0.00		0.00%	0.00%	0.00%
$0.00	$0.00		$0.00	$0.00			$0.00		0.00%	0.00%	0.00%
$0.00	$0.00		$0.00	$0.00			$0.00		0.00%	0.00%	0.00%
$0.00	$0.00		$0.00	$0.00			$0.00		0.00%	0.00%	0.00%
$0.00	$0.00		$0.00	$0.00			$0.00		0.00%	0.00%	0.00%
$0.00	$0.00		$0.00	$0.00			$0.00		0.00%	0.00%	0.00%
$0.00	$0.00		$0.00	$0.00			$0.00		0.00%	0.00%	0.00%
$250,000.00	$0.00	$250,000.00	$43,724.30	$43,724.30			$250,000.00			95.32%	95.32%
$15,000.00	$0.00	$15,000.00	$2,145.00	$2,145.00			$15,000.00		14.30%	4.68%	4.68%
$0.00	$0.00		$0.00	$0.00			$0.00		0.00%	0.00%	0.00%
$0.00	$0.00		$0.00	$0.00			$0.00		0.00%	0.00%	0.00%
$0.00	$0.00		$0.00	$0.00			$0.00		0.00%	0.00%	0.00%
$0.00	$0.00		$0.00	$0.00			$0.00		0.00%	0.00%	0.00%
$0.00	$0.00		$0.00	$0.00			$0.00		0.00%	0.00%	0.00%
$0.00	$0.00		$0.00	$0.00			$0.00		0.00%	0.00%	0.00%
$0.00	$0.00		$0.00	$0.00			$0.00		0.00%	0.00%	0.00%
$0.00	$0.00		$0.00	$0.00			$0.00		0.00%	0.00%	0.00%
$0.00	$0.00		$0.00	$0.00			$0.00		0.00%	0.00%	0.00%
$15,000.00	$0.00	$15,000.00	$2,145.00	$2,145.00			$15,000.00			4.68%	4.68%
$265,000.00	$0.00	$15,000.00	$45,869.30	$45,869.30			$265,000.00			100.0%	100.0%

```
* CORPORATE SEP PLAN *                * BEAVER HAT SHOP (see Q 9:5, example 2b)                                        1
                                                                                                                 05:23 PM
Plan Year Begins:                  2012       $53,000.00    - Employer Contribution                            22-Feb-2012
Plan Year Ends:                    2012              ALL    - DEDUCTIBLE PORTION
Base Percentage:             20.0000000       $53,000.00    - Total Allocated
Integration Level:                   $0    20.000000000%    - Allocation % of 402(h) Comp
Excess Percentage:           20.0000000             None    - Integration
1=P/S 2=MP 3=SEP 4=SARSEP:            3
E/er Contr. to Owners:     94.33962264%
E/er Alloc. Compensation:  94.33962264%       $50,000.00    - Maximum HCE Allocation                  Y <-n/a
```

-> Plan not T/H P Prototype or Model SEP		TOTAL ALLOCATION	IRC 402(h) EMPLOYER CONTRIBUTION	EMPLOYER CONTRIBUTION	Columns reserved for Salary Reduction SEPs	KEY	Col n/a	EMPLOYEE's PRE-PLAN COMPENSATION	HCE	Col. n/a	Col. n/a
1	Clarence Beaver	$50,000.00	20.000000%	$50,000.00		Y		$250,000.00	Y		
2		$0.00	0.000000%	$0.00							
3		$0.00	0.000000%	$0.00							
4		$0.00	0.000000%	$0.00							
5		$0.00	0.000000%	$0.00							
6		$0.00	0.000000%	$0.00							
7		$0.00	0.000000%	$0.00							
8		$0.00	0.000000%	$0.00							
	OWNER SUB-TOTALS	$50,000.00		$50,000.00	$0.00			$250,000.00			
9	Joe Skinner	$3,000.00	20.000000%	$3,000.00		N		$15,000.00	N		
10		$0.00	0.000000%	$0.00							
11		$0.00	0.000000%	$0.00							
12		$0.00	0.000000%	$0.00							
13		$0.00	0.000000%	$0.00							
14		$0.00	0.000000%	$0.00							
15		$0.00	0.000000%	$0.00							
16		$0.00	0.000000%	$0.00							
17		$0.00	0.000000%	$0.00							
18		$0.00	0.000000%	$0.00							
	NON-OWNER SUB TOTALS	$3,000.00		$3,000.00				$15,000.00			
	GRAND TOTALS	$53,000.00		$53,000.00				$265,000.00			

* BEAVER HAT SHOP (see Q 9:5, example 2b)

* CORPORATE SEP PLAN *

* NON-INTEGRATED CONTRIBUTIONS

$53,000.00 - Employer Contribution
ALL - DEDUCTIBLE PORTION
$53,000.00 - Total Allocated
20.00% - Allocation % of 402(h) Comp
None - Integration

None - Integration Level

2
22-Feb-2012
05:23 PM

2012

* * C O N T R I B U T I O N   S U M M A R Y * *

ALLOCATION COMPENSATION -Includes- -Elective-	TOP HEAVY ADDITIONAL AMOUNT FOR 94.34% PERCENTAGE	PRE-PLAN COMPENSATION	TOTAL ALLOCATION	EMPLOYER's CONTRIBUTION	Col. n/a	Col. n/a	NET TAXABLE COMPENSATION	Col. n/a	EMPLOYER CONTRIBUTION % OF DEDUCT. COMPENSATION	PERCENTAGE OF EMPLOYER $53,000.00 CONTRIBUTIONS	PERCENTAGE OF TOTAL $53,000.00 ALLOCATIONS
$250,000.00	$0.00	$250,000.00	$50,000.00	$50,000.00			$250,000.00		20.00%	94.34%	94.34%
$0.00	$0.00		$0.00	$0.00			$0.00		0.00%	0.00%	0.00%
$0.00	$0.00		$0.00	$0.00			$0.00		0.00%	0.00%	0.00%
$0.00	$0.00		$0.00	$0.00			$0.00		0.00%	0.00%	0.00%
$0.00	$0.00		$0.00	$0.00			$0.00		0.00%	0.00%	0.00%
$0.00	$0.00		$0.00	$0.00			$0.00		0.00%	0.00%	0.00%
$0.00	$0.00		$0.00	$0.00			$0.00		0.00%	0.00%	0.00%
$0.00	$0.00		$0.00	$0.00			$0.00		0.00%	0.00%	0.00%
$250,000.00	$0.00	$250,000.00	$50,000.00	$50,000.00			$250,000.00			94.34%	94.34%
$15,000.00	$0.00	$15,000.00	$3,000.00	$3,000.00			$15,000.00		20.00%	5.66%	5.66%
$0.00	$0.00		$0.00	$0.00			$0.00		0.00%	0.00%	0.00%
$0.00	$0.00		$0.00	$0.00			$0.00		0.00%	0.00%	0.00%
$0.00	$0.00		$0.00	$0.00			$0.00		0.00%	0.00%	0.00%
$0.00	$0.00		$0.00	$0.00			$0.00		0.00%	0.00%	0.00%
$0.00	$0.00		$0.00	$0.00			$0.00		0.00%	0.00%	0.00%
$0.00	$0.00		$0.00	$0.00			$0.00		0.00%	0.00%	0.00%
$0.00	$0.00		$0.00	$0.00			$0.00		0.00%	0.00%	0.00%
$0.00	$0.00		$0.00	$0.00			$0.00		0.00%	0.00%	0.00%
$0.00	$0.00		$0.00	$0.00			$0.00		0.00%	0.00%	0.00%
$15,000.00	$0.00	$15,000.00	$3,000.00	$3,000.00			$15,000.00			5.66%	5.66%
$265,000.00	$0.00	$15,000.00	$53,000.00	$53,000.00			$265,000.00			100.0%	100.0%

* CORPORATE SEP PLAN *   * BEAVER HAT SHOP (see Q 9:5, example 3a)   1

09:24 AM

17-May-2012

Plan Year Begins:	2012	$65,174.30	- Employer Contribution
Plan Year Ends:	2012	ALL	- DEDUCTIBLE PORTION
Base Percentage:	14.3000000	$65,174.30	- Total Allocated
Integration Level:	$110,100	16.293574999%	- Allocation % of 402(h) Comp
Excess Percentage:	20.0000000	5.7%	- Maximum Integration Spread
1=P/S 2=MP 3=SEP 4=SARSEP:	3		
E/er Contr. to Owners:	67.08825411%		
E/er Alloc. Compensation:	62.50000000%	$43,724.30	- Maximum HCE Allocation <-n/a

-> P	Plan not T/H Integrated Prototype SEP	TOTAL ALLOCATION	IRC 402(h) EMPLOYER CONTRIBUTION	EMPLOYER CONTRIBUTION	Columns reserved for Salary Reduction SEPs	KEY	Col n/a	EMPLOYEE's PRE-PLAN COMPENSATION	HCE	Col. n/a	Col. n/a
1	Clarence Beaver	$43,724.30	17.489720%	$43,724.30		Y		$250,000.00	Y		
2		$0.00	0.000000%	$0.00							
3		$0.00	0.000000%	$0.00							
4		$0.00	0.000000%	$0.00							
5		$0.00	0.000000%	$0.00							
6		$0.00	0.000000%	$0.00							
7		$0.00	0.000000%	$0.00							
8		$0.00	0.000000%	$0.00							
	OWNER SUB-TOTALS	$43,724.30		$43,724.30	$0.00			$250,000.00			
9	Joe Skinner	$4,290.00	14.300000%	$4,290.00		N		$30,000.00	N		
10	Carl Klipper	$4,290.00	14.300000%	$4,290.00		N		$30,000.00	N		
11	Haddie Seller	$4,290.00	14.300000%	$4,290.00		N		$30,000.00	N		
12	Francine Tanner	$4,290.00	14.300000%	$4,290.00		N		$30,000.00	N		
13	Samson DeGuard	$4,290.00	14.300000%	$4,290.00		N		$30,000.00	N		
14		$0.00	0.000000%	$0.00							
15		$0.00	0.000000%	$0.00							
16		$0.00	0.000000%	$0.00							
17		$0.00	0.000000%	$0.00							
18		$0.00	0.000000%	$0.00							
	NON-OWNER SUB TOTALS	$21,450.00		$21,450.00				$150,000.00			
	GRAND TOTALS	$65,174.30		$65,174.30				$400,000.00			

Penny rounding applied.
m <-- at maximum amount or percent
Y <-- highly compensated or key employee. Penny rounding applied.

* BEAVER HAT SHOP (see Q 9:5, example 3a)

* CORPORATE SEP PLAN *

* INTEGRATED CONTRIBUTIONS

2012

* * C O N T R I B U T I O N   S U M M A R Y * *

$65,174.30 - Employer Contribution
ALL - DEDUCTIBLE PORTION
$65,174.30 - Total Allocated
16.29% - Allocation % of 402(h) Comp
5.70% - Maximum Integration Spread

$110,100.00 - Integration Level

100.00000000% :TWB Percentage

2
17-May-2012
09:24 AM

ALLOCATION COMPENSATION -Includes- -Elective-	TOP HEAVY ADDITIONAL AMOUNT FOR 67.09% PERCENTAGE	PRE-PLAN COMPENSATION	TOTAL ALLOCATION	EMPLOYER's CONTRIBUTION	Col. n/a	Col. n/a	NET TAXABLE COMPENSATION	Col. n/a	EMPLOYER CONTRIBUTION % OF DEDUCT. COMPENSATION	PERCENTAGE OF EMPLOYER $65,174.30 CONTRIBUTIONS	PERCENTAGE OF TOTAL $65,174.30 ALLOCATIONS
$250,000.00	$0.00	$250,000.00	$43,724.30	$43,724.30			$250,000.00		17.49%	67.09%	67.09%
$0.00	$0.00		$0.00	$0.00			$0.00		0.00%	0.00%	0.00%
$0.00	$0.00		$0.00	$0.00			$0.00		0.00%	0.00%	0.00%
$0.00	$0.00		$0.00	$0.00			$0.00		0.00%	0.00%	0.00%
$0.00	$0.00		$0.00	$0.00			$0.00		0.00%	0.00%	0.00%
$0.00	$0.00		$0.00	$0.00			$0.00		0.00%	0.00%	0.00%
$0.00	$0.00		$0.00	$0.00			$0.00		0.00%	0.00%	0.00%
$0.00	$0.00		$0.00	$0.00			$0.00		0.00%	0.00%	0.00%
$250,000.00	$0.00	$250,000.00	$43,724.30	$43,724.30			$250,000.00			67.09%	67.09%
$30,000.00	$0.00	$30,000.00	$4,290.00	$4,290.00			$30,000.00		14.30%	6.58%	6.58%
$30,000.00	$0.00	$30,000.00	$4,290.00	$4,290.00			$30,000.00		14.30%	6.58%	6.58%
$30,000.00	$0.00	$30,000.00	$4,290.00	$4,290.00			$30,000.00		14.30%	6.58%	6.58%
$30,000.00	$0.00	$30,000.00	$4,290.00	$4,290.00			$30,000.00		14.30%	6.58%	6.58%
$30,000.00	$0.00	$30,000.00	$4,290.00	$4,290.00			$30,000.00		14.30%	6.58%	6.58%
$0.00	$0.00		$0.00	$0.00			$0.00		0.00%	0.00%	0.00%
$0.00	$0.00		$0.00	$0.00			$0.00		0.00%	0.00%	0.00%
$0.00	$0.00		$0.00	$0.00			$0.00		0.00%	0.00%	0.00%
$0.00	$0.00		$0.00	$0.00			$0.00		0.00%	0.00%	0.00%
$0.00	$0.00		$0.00	$0.00			$0.00		0.00%	0.00%	0.00%
$150,000.00	$0.00	$150,000.00	$21,450.00	$21,450.00			$150,000.00			32.91%	32.91%
$400,000.00	$0.00	$150,000.00	$65,174.30	$65,174.30			$400,000.00			100.0%	100.0%

* CORPORATE SEP PLAN *   * BEAVER HAT SHOP (see Q 9:5, example 3b)   1
05:45 PM
22-Feb-2012

Plan Year Begins:	2012	$80,000.00	- Employer Contribution
Plan Year Ends:	2012	ALL	- DEDUCTIBLE PORTION
Base Percentage:	20.0000000	$80,000.00	- Total Allocated
Integration Level:	$0	19.999999990%	- Allocation % of 402(h) Comp
Excess Percentage:	20.0000000	None	- Integration
1=P/S 2=MP 3=SEP 4=SARSEP:	3		
E/er Contr. to Owners:	62.50000000%		
E/er Alloc. Compensation:	62.50000000%	$50,000.00	- Maximum HCE Allocation <-n/a

P	-> Plan not T/H Prototype or Model SEP	TOTAL ALLOCATION	IRC 402(h) EMPLOYER CONTRIBUTION	EMPLOYER CONTRIBUTION	Columns reserved for Salary Reduction SEPs	KEY	Col n/a	EMPLOYEE's PRE-PLAN COMPENSATION	HCE	Col. n/a	Col. n/a
1	Clarence Beaver	$50,000.00	20.000000%	$50,000.00		Y		$250,000.00	Y		
2		$0.00	0.000000%	$0.00							
3		$0.00	0.000000%	$0.00							
4		$0.00	0.000000%	$0.00							
5		$0.00	0.000000%	$0.00							
6		$0.00	0.000000%	$0.00							
7		$0.00	0.000000%	$0.00							
8		$0.00	0.000000%	$0.00							
	OWNER SUB-TOTALS	$50,000.00		$50,000.00	$0.00			$250,000.00			
9	Joe Skinner	$6,000.00	20.000000%	$6,000.00		N		$30,000.00	N		
10	Carl Klipper	$6,000.00	20.000000%	$6,000.00		N		$30,000.00	N		
11	Haddie Seller	$6,000.00	20.000000%	$6,000.00		N		$30,000.00	N		
12	Francine Tanner	$6,000.00	20.000000%	$6,000.00		N		$30,000.00	N		
13	Samson DeGuard	$6,000.00	20.000000%	$6,000.00		N		$30,000.00	N		
14		$0.00	0.000000%	$0.00							
15		$0.00	0.000000%	$0.00							
16		$0.00	0.000000%	$0.00							
17		$0.00	0.000000%	$0.00							
18		$0.00	0.000000%	$0.00							
	NON-OWNER SUB TOTALS	$30,000.00		$30,000.00				$150,000.00			
	GRAND TOTALS	$80,000.00		$80,000.00				$400,000.00			

* BEAVER HAT SHOP (see Q 9:5, example 3b)

* CORPORATE SEP PLAN *

* NON-INTEGRATED CONTRIBUTIONS

$80,000.00 - Employer Contribution
ALL - DEDUCTIBLE PORTION
$80,000.00 - Total Allocated
20.00% - Allocation % of 402(h) Comp
None - Integration

2
22-Feb-2012
05:45 PM

2012

* * C O N T R I B U T I O N   S U M M A R Y * *

None - Integration Level

ALLOCATION COMPENSATION -Includes- -Elective-	TOP HEAVY ADDITIONAL AMOUNT FOR 62.50% PERCENTAGE	PRE-PLAN COMPENSATION	TOTAL ALLOCATION	EMPLOYER's CONTRIBUTION	Col. n/a	Col. n/a	NET TAXABLE COMPENSATION	Col. n/a	EMPLOYER CONTRIBUTION % OF DEDUCT. COMPENSATION	PERCENTAGE OF EMPLOYER $80,000.00 CONTRIBUTIONS	PERCENTAGE OF TOTAL $80,000.00 ALLOCATIONS
$250,000.00	$0.00	$250,000.00	$50,000.00	$50,000.00			$250,000.00		20.00%	62.50%	62.50%
$0.00	$0.00		$0.00	$0.00			$0.00		0.00%	0.00%	0.00%
$0.00	$0.00		$0.00	$0.00			$0.00		0.00%	0.00%	0.00%
$0.00	$0.00		$0.00	$0.00			$0.00		0.00%	0.00%	0.00%
$0.00	$0.00		$0.00	$0.00			$0.00		0.00%	0.00%	0.00%
$0.00	$0.00		$0.00	$0.00			$0.00		0.00%	0.00%	0.00%
$0.00	$0.00		$0.00	$0.00			$0.00		0.00%	0.00%	0.00%
$0.00	$0.00		$0.00	$0.00			$0.00		0.00%	0.00%	0.00%
$250,000.00	$0.00	$250,000.00	$50,000.00	$50,000.00			$250,000.00			62.50%	62.50%
$30,000.00	$0.00	$30,000.00	$6,000.00	$6,000.00			$30,000.00		20.00%	7.50%	7.50%
$30,000.00	$0.00	$30,000.00	$6,000.00	$6,000.00			$30,000.00		20.00%	7.50%	7.50%
$30,000.00	$0.00	$30,000.00	$6,000.00	$6,000.00			$30,000.00		20.00%	7.50%	7.50%
$30,000.00	$0.00	$30,000.00	$6,000.00	$6,000.00			$30,000.00		20.00%	7.50%	7.50%
$30,000.00	$0.00	$30,000.00	$6,000.00	$6,000.00			$30,000.00		20.00%	7.50%	7.50%
$0.00	$0.00		$0.00	$0.00			$0.00		0.00%	0.00%	0.00%
$0.00	$0.00		$0.00	$0.00			$0.00		0.00%	0.00%	0.00%
$0.00	$0.00		$0.00	$0.00			$0.00		0.00%	0.00%	0.00%
$0.00	$0.00		$0.00	$0.00			$0.00		0.00%	0.00%	0.00%
$0.00	$0.00		$0.00	$0.00			$0.00		0.00%	0.00%	0.00%
$150,000.00	$0.00	$150,000.00	$30,000.00	$30,000.00			$150,000.00			37.50%	37.50%
$400,000.00	$0.00	$150,000.00	$80,000.00	$80,000.00			$400,000.00			100.0%	100.0%

* CORPORATE SEP PLAN *		* BONEFISH, INC. (see Q 9:19, example 1)		1 06:27 PM 22-Feb-2012
Plan Year Begins:	2012	$30,000.00	- Employer Contribution	
Plan Year Ends:	2012	ALL	- DEDUCTIBLE PORTION	
Base Percentage:	10.0000000	$30,000.00	- Total Allocated	
Integration Level:	$0	10.000000000%	- Allocation % of 402(h) Comp	
Excess Percentage:	10.0000000	None	- Integration	
1=P/S 2=MP 3=SEP 4=SARSEP:	3			
E/er Contr. to Owners:	66.66666667%			
E/er Alloc. Compensation:	66.66666667%	$50,000.00	- Maximum HCE Allocation	<-n/a

-> Plan not T/H P	Prototype or Model SEP	TOTAL ALLOCATION	IRC 402(h) EMPLOYER CONTRIBUTION	EMPLOYER CONTRIBUTION	Columns reserved for Salary Reduction SEPs	K E Y	Col n/a	EMPLOYEE's PRE-PLAN COMPENSATION	H C E	Col. n/a	Col. n/a
1	Joe	$10,000.00	10.000000%	$10,000.00		Y		$100,000.00	Y		
2	Sally	$10,000.00	10.000000%	$10,000.00		Y		$100,000.00	Y		
3		$0.00	0.000000%	$0.00							
4		$0.00	0.000000%	$0.00							
5		$0.00	0.000000%	$0.00							
6		$0.00	0.000000%	$0.00							
7		$0.00	0.000000%	$0.00							
8		$0.00	0.000000%	$0.00							
	OWNER SUB-TOTALS	$20,000.00		$20,000.00	$0.00			$200,000.00			
9	Ruth	$3,000.00	10.000000%	$3,000.00				$30,000.00	N		
10	Tom	$2,500.00	10.000000%	$2,500.00				$25,000.00	N		
11	Ned	$2,000.00	10.000000%	$2,000.00				$20,000.00	N		
12	Lee	$1,500.00	10.000000%	$1,500.00				$15,000.00	N		
13	Sarah	$1,000.00	10.000000%	$1,000.00				$10,000.00	N		
14		$0.00	0.000000%	$0.00							
15		$0.00	0.000000%	$0.00							
16		$0.00	0.000000%	$0.00							
17		$0.00	0.000000%	$0.00							
18		$0.00	0.000000%	$0.00							
	NON-OWNER SUB TOTALS	$10,000.00		$10,000.00				$100,000.00			
	GRAND TOTALS	$30,000.00		$30,000.00				$300,000.00			

* BONEFISH, INC. (see Q 9:19, example 1)

* CORPORATE SEP PLAN *

* NON-INTEGRATED CONTRIBUTIONS

2

22-Feb-2012

06:27 PM

$30,000.00 - Employer Contribution
ALL - DEDUCTIBLE PORTION
$30,000.00 - Total Allocated
10.00% - Allocation % of 402(h) Comp
None - Integration

2012

* * C O N T R I B U T I O N   S U M M A R Y * *

None - Integration Level

ALLOCATION COMPENSATION -Includes- -Elective-	TOP HEAVY ADDITIONAL AMOUNT FOR 100.00% PERCENTAGE	PRE-PLAN COMPENSATION	TOTAL ALLOCATION	EMPLOYER's CONTRIBUTION	Col. n/a	Col. n/a	NET TAXABLE COMPENSATION	Col. n/a	EMPLOYER CONTRIBUTION % OF DEDUCT. COMPENSATION	PERCENTAGE OF EMPLOYER $30,000.00 CONTRIBUTIONS	PERCENTAGE OF TOTAL $30,000.00 ALLOCATIONS
$100,000.00	$0.00	$100,000.00	$10,000.00	$10,000.00			$100,000.00		10.00%	33.33%	33.33%
$100,000.00	$0.00	$100,000.00	$10,000.00	$10,000.00			$100,000.00		10.00%	33.33%	33.33%
$0.00	$0.00		$0.00	$0.00			$0.00		0.00%	0.00%	0.00%
$0.00	$0.00		$0.00	$0.00			$0.00		0.00%	0.00%	0.00%
$0.00	$0.00		$0.00	$0.00			$0.00		0.00%	0.00%	0.00%
$0.00	$0.00		$0.00	$0.00			$0.00		0.00%	0.00%	0.00%
$0.00	$0.00		$0.00	$0.00			$0.00		0.00%	0.00%	0.00%
$0.00	$0.00		$0.00	$0.00			$0.00		0.00%	0.00%	0.00%
$200,000.00	$0.00	$200,000.00	$20,000.00	$20,000.00			$200,000.00			66.67%	66.67%
$30,000.00	$0.00	$30,000.00	$3,000.00	$3,000.00			$30,000.00		10.00%	10.00%	10.00%
$25,000.00	$0.00	$25,000.00	$2,500.00	$2,500.00			$25,000.00		10.00%	8.33%	8.33%
$20,000.00	$0.00	$20,000.00	$2,000.00	$2,000.00			$20,000.00		10.00%	6.67%	6.67%
$15,000.00	$0.00	$15,000.00	$1,500.00	$1,500.00			$15,000.00		10.00%	5.00%	5.00%
$10,000.00	$0.00	$10,000.00	$1,000.00	$1,000.00			$10,000.00		10.00%	3.33%	3.33%
$0.00	$0.00		$0.00	$0.00			$0.00		0.00%	0.00%	0.00%
$0.00	$0.00		$0.00	$0.00			$0.00		0.00%	0.00%	0.00%
$0.00	$0.00		$0.00	$0.00			$0.00		0.00%	0.00%	0.00%
$0.00	$0.00		$0.00	$0.00			$0.00		0.00%	0.00%	0.00%
$0.00	$0.00		$0.00	$0.00			$0.00		0.00%	0.00%	0.00%
$100,000.00	$0.00	$100,000.00	$10,000.00	$10,000.00			$100,000.00			33.33%	33.33%
$300,000.00	$0.00	$100,000.00	$30,000.00	$30,000.00			$300,000.00			100.0%	100.0%

* CORPORATE SEP PLAN * * BONEFISH, INC. (see Q 9:19, example 2) 1

06:28 PM
22-Feb-2012

Plan Year Begins:	2012	$30,000.00	- Employer Contribution
Plan Year Ends:	2012	ALL	- DEDUCTIBLE PORTION
Base Percentage:	7.9933330	$30,000.00	- Total Allocated
Integration Level:	$30,000	9.999999667%	- Allocation % of 402(h) Comp
Excess Percentage:	12.2933330	4.3%	- Maximum Integration Spread
1=P/S 2=MP 3=SEP 4=SARSEP:	3		
E/er Contr. to Owners:	73.35555578%		
E/er Alloc. Compensation:	66.66666667%	$48,710.00	- Maximum HCE Allocation <-n/a

-> Plan not T/H

P	Integrated Prototype SEP	TOTAL ALLOCATION	IRC 402(h) EMPLOYER CONTRIBUTION	EMPLOYER CONTRIBUTION	Columns reserved for Salary Reduction SEPs	KEY	Col n/a	EMPLOYEE's PRE-PLAN COMPENSATION	HCE	Col. n/a	Col. n/a
1	Joe	$11,003.33	11.003333%	$11,003.33		Y		$100,000.00	Y		
2	Sally	$11,003.33	11.003333%	$11,003.33		Y		$100,000.00	Y		
3		$0.00	0.000000%	$0.00							
4		$0.00	0.000000%	$0.00							
5		$0.00	0.000000%	$0.00							
6		$0.00	0.000000%	$0.00							
7		$0.00	0.000000%	$0.00							
8		$0.00	0.000000%	$0.00							
	OWNER SUB-TOTALS	$22,006.67		$22,006.67	$0.00			$200,000.00			
9	Ruth	$2,398.00	7.993333%	$2,398.00		N		$30,000.00	N		
10	Tom	$1,998.33	7.993333%	$1,998.33		N		$25,000.00	N		
11	Ned	$1,598.67	7.993333%	$1,598.67		N		$20,000.00	N		
12	Lee	$1,199.00	7.993333%	$1,199.00		N		$15,000.00	N		
13	Sarah	$799.33	7.993333%	$799.33		N		$10,000.00	N		
14		$0.00	0.000000%	$0.00							
15		$0.00	0.000000%	$0.00							
16		$0.00	0.000000%	$0.00							
17		$0.00	0.000000%	$0.00							
18		$0.00	0.000000%	$0.00							
	NON-OWNER SUB TOTALS	$7,993.33		$7,993.33				$100,000.00			
	GRAND TOTALS	$30,000.00		$30,000.00				$300,000.00			

Penny rounding applied.

* BONEFISH, INC. (see Q 9:19, example 2)

* CORPORATE SEP PLAN *

* INTEGRATED CONTRIBUTIONS

2012

$30,000.00 - Employer Contribution
ALL - DEDUCTIBLE PORTION
$30,000.00 - Total Allocated
10.00% - Allocation % of 402(h) Comp
4.30% - Maximum Integration Spread

2
22-Feb-2012
06:28 PM

* * C O N T R I B U T I O N S U M M A R Y * *

$30,000.00 - Integration Level 27.24795640% :TWB Percentage

ALLOCATION COMPENSATION -Includes- -Elective-	TOP HEAVY ADDITIONAL AMOUNT FOR 73.36% PERCENTAGE	PRE-PLAN COMPENSATION	TOTAL ALLOCATION	EMPLOYER's CONTRIBUTION	Col. n/a	Col. n/a	NET TAXABLE COMPENSATION	Col. n/a	EMPLOYER CONTRIBUTION % OF DEDUCT. COMPENSATION	PERCENTAGE OF EMPLOYER $30,000.00 CONTRIBUTIONS	PERCENTAGE OF TOTAL $30,000.00 ALLOCATIONS
$100,000.00	$0.00	$100,000.00	$11,003.33	$11,003.33			$100,000.00		11.00%	36.68%	36.68%
$100,000.00	$0.00	$100,000.00	$11,003.33	$11,003.33			$100,000.00		11.00%	36.68%	36.68%
$0.00	$0.00		$0.00	$0.00			$0.00		0.00%	0.00%	0.00%
$0.00	$0.00		$0.00	$0.00			$0.00		0.00%	0.00%	0.00%
$0.00	$0.00		$0.00	$0.00			$0.00		0.00%	0.00%	0.00%
$0.00	$0.00		$0.00	$0.00			$0.00		0.00%	0.00%	0.00%
$0.00	$0.00		$0.00	$0.00			$0.00		0.00%	0.00%	0.00%
$0.00	$0.00		$0.00	$0.00			$0.00		0.00%	0.00%	0.00%
$200,000.00	$0.00	$200,000.00	$22,006.67	$22,006.67			$200,000.00			73.36%	73.36%
$30,000.00	$0.00	$30,000.00	$2,398.00	$2,398.00			$30,000.00		7.99%	7.99%	7.99%
$25,000.00	$0.00	$25,000.00	$1,998.33	$1,998.33			$25,000.00		7.99%	6.66%	6.66%
$20,000.00	$0.00	$20,000.00	$1,598.67	$1,598.67			$20,000.00		7.99%	5.33%	5.33%
$15,000.00	$0.00	$15,000.00	$1,199.00	$1,199.00			$15,000.00		7.99%	4.00%	4.00%
$10,000.00	$0.00	$10,000.00	$799.33	$799.33			$10,000.00		7.99%	2.66%	2.66%
$0.00	$0.00		$0.00	$0.00			$0.00		0.00%	0.00%	0.00%
$0.00	$0.00		$0.00	$0.00			$0.00		0.00%	0.00%	0.00%
$0.00	$0.00		$0.00	$0.00			$0.00		0.00%	0.00%	0.00%
$0.00	$0.00		$0.00	$0.00			$0.00		0.00%	0.00%	0.00%
$0.00	$0.00		$0.00	$0.00			$0.00		0.00%	0.00%	0.00%
$100,000.00	$0.00	$100,000.00	$7,993.33	$7,993.33			$100,000.00			26.64%	26.64%
$300,000.00	$0.00	$100,000.00	$30,000.00	$30,000.00			$300,000.00			100.0%	100.0%

* BONEFISH, INC. (see Q 9:19, example 2)

* CORPORATE SEP PLAN *

* INTEGRATED CONTRIBUTIONS

3
22-Feb-2012
06:28 PM

** ALLOCATION OF DESIRED CONTRIBUTION **

** INTEGRATION METHOD: IRS PERCENTAGE METHOD **

EMPLOYEES	2012 ALLOCATION COMPENSATION	PLAN ALLOCATION COMPENSATION MULTIPLIED BY 7.993333% BASE PERCENTAGE	PLAN COMPENSATION IN EXCESS OF $30,000.00	EXCESS COMPENSATION MULTIPLIED BY 4.300000% DISPARITY RATE	UNLIMITED TOTAL PLAN DEPOSIT
Joe	$100,000.00	$7,993.33	$70,000.00	$3,010.00	$11,003.33
Sally	$100,000.00	$7,993.33	$70,000.00	$3,010.00	$11,003.33
	$0.00	$0.00	$0.00	$0.00	$0.00
	$0.00	$0.00	$0.00	$0.00	$0.00
	$0.00	$0.00	$0.00	$0.00	$0.00
	$0.00	$0.00	$0.00	$0.00	$0.00
	$0.00	$0.00	$0.00	$0.00	$0.00
	$0.00	$0.00	$0.00	$0.00	$0.00
	$200,000.00	$15,986.67	$140,000.00	$6,020.00	$22,006.67
Ruth	$30,000.00	$2,398.00	$0.00	$0.00	$2,398.00
Tom	$25,000.00	$1,998.33	$0.00	$0.00	$1,998.33
Ned	$20,000.00	$1,598.67	$0.00	$0.00	$1,598.67
Lee	$15,000.00	$1,199.00	$0.00	$0.00	$1,199.00
Sarah	$10,000.00	$799.33	$0.00	$0.00	$799.33
	$0.00	$0.00	$0.00	$0.00	$0.00
	$0.00	$0.00	$0.00	$0.00	$0.00
	$0.00	$0.00	$0.00	$0.00	$0.00
	$0.00	$0.00	$0.00	$0.00	$0.00
	$0.00	$0.00	$0.00	$0.00	$0.00
	$100,000.00	$7,993.33	$0.00	$0.00	$7,993.33
	$300,000.00	$23,980.00	$140,000.00	$6,020.00	$30,000.00

* Do Not contribute amounts shown on this page. Allocation shown is untested or may have been reduced by other factors.

* CORPORATE SEP PLAN *   * BONEFISH, INC. (see Q 9:19, example 3)   1
09:03 PM
21-Mar-2012

Plan Year Begins:	2012	$13,077.60	- Employer Contribution
Plan Year Ends:	2012	ALL	- DEDUCTIBLE PORTION
Base Percentage:	3.0000000	$13,077.60	- Total Allocated
Integration Level:	$32,040	4.359200000%	- Allocation % of 402(h) Comp
Excess Percentage:	6.0000000	3.0%	- Maximum Integration Spread
1=P/S 2=MP 3=SEP 4=SARSEP:	3		
E/er Contr. to Owners:	77.06001101%		
E/er Alloc. Compensation:	66.66666667%	$49,038.80	- Maximum HCE Allocation <-n/a

-> Plan not T/H P Integrated Prototype SEP		TOTAL ALLOCATION	IRC 402(h) EMPLOYER CONTRIBUTION	EMPLOYER CONTRIBUTION	Columns reserved for Salary Reduction SEPs	KEY	Col n/a	EMPLOYEE's PRE-PLAN COMPENSATION	HCE	Col. n/a	Col. n/a
1	Joe	$5,038.80	5.038800%	$5,038.80		Y		$100,000.00	Y		
2	Sally	$5,038.80	5.038800%	$5,038.80		Y		$100,000.00	Y		
3		$0.00	0.000000%	$0.00							
4		$0.00	0.000000%	$0.00							
5		$0.00	0.000000%	$0.00							
6		$0.00	0.000000%	$0.00							
7		$0.00	0.000000%	$0.00							
8		$0.00	0.000000%	$0.00							
	OWNER SUB-TOTALS	$10,077.60		$10,077.60	$0.00			$200,000.00			
9	Ruth	$900.00	3.000000%	$900.00		N		$30,000.00	N		
10	Tom	$750.00	3.000000%	$750.00		N		$25,000.00	N		
11	Ned	$600.00	3.000000%	$600.00		N		$20,000.00	N		
12	Lee	$450.00	3.000000%	$450.00		N		$15,000.00	N		
13	Sarah	$300.00	3.000000%	$300.00		N		$10,000.00	N		
14		$0.00	0.000000%	$0.00							
15		$0.00	0.000000%	$0.00							
16		$0.00	0.000000%	$0.00							
17		$0.00	0.000000%	$0.00							
18		$0.00	0.000000%	$0.00							
	NON-OWNER SUB TOTALS	$3,000.00		$3,000.00				$100,000.00			
	GRAND TOTALS	$13,077.60		$13,077.60				$300,000.00			

* BONEFISH, INC. (see Q 9:19, example 3)

* CORPORATE SEP PLAN *

* INTEGRATED CONTRIBUTIONS

2012

* * C O N T R I B U T I O N   S U M M A R Y * *

$13,077.60 - Employer Contribution
ALL - DEDUCTIBLE PORTION
$13,077.60 - Total Allocated
4.36% - Allocation % of 402(h) Comp
3.00% - Maximum Integration Spread

$32,040.00 - Integration Level

29.10081744% :TWB Percentage

2
21-Mar-2012
09:03 PM

ALLOCATION COMPENSATION -Includes- -Elective-	TOP HEAVY ADDITIONAL AMOUNT FOR 77.06% PERCENTAGE	PRE-PLAN COMPENSATION	TOTAL ALLOCATION	EMPLOYER's CONTRIBUTION	Col. n/a	Col. n/a	NET TAXABLE COMPENSATION	Col. n/a	EMPLOYER CONTRIBUTION % OF DEDUCT. COMPENSATION	PERCENTAGE OF EMPLOYER $13,077.60 CONTRIBUTIONS	PERCENTAGE OF TOTAL $13,077.60 ALLOCATIONS
$100,000.00	$0.00	$100,000.00	$5,038.80	$5,038.80			$100,000.00		5.04%	38.53%	38.53%
$100,000.00	$0.00	$100,000.00	$5,038.80	$5,038.80			$100,000.00		5.04%	38.53%	38.53%
$0.00	$0.00		$0.00	$0.00			$0.00		0.00%	0.00%	0.00%
$0.00	$0.00		$0.00	$0.00			$0.00		0.00%	0.00%	0.00%
$0.00	$0.00		$0.00	$0.00			$0.00		0.00%	0.00%	0.00%
$0.00	$0.00		$0.00	$0.00			$0.00		0.00%	0.00%	0.00%
$0.00	$0.00		$0.00	$0.00			$0.00		0.00%	0.00%	0.00%
$0.00	$0.00		$0.00	$0.00			$0.00		0.00%	0.00%	0.00%
$200,000.00	$0.00	$200,000.00	$10,077.60	$10,077.60			$200,000.00			77.06%	77.06%
$30,000.00	$0.00	$30,000.00	$900.00	$900.00			$30,000.00		3.00%	6.88%	6.88%
$25,000.00	$0.00	$25,000.00	$750.00	$750.00			$25,000.00		3.00%	5.73%	5.73%
$20,000.00	$0.00	$20,000.00	$600.00	$600.00			$20,000.00		3.00%	4.59%	4.59%
$15,000.00	$0.00	$15,000.00	$450.00	$450.00			$15,000.00		3.00%	3.44%	3.44%
$10,000.00	$0.00	$10,000.00	$300.00	$300.00			$10,000.00		3.00%	2.29%	2.29%
$0.00	$0.00		$0.00	$0.00			$0.00		0.00%	0.00%	0.00%
$0.00	$0.00		$0.00	$0.00			$0.00		0.00%	0.00%	0.00%
$0.00	$0.00		$0.00	$0.00			$0.00		0.00%	0.00%	0.00%
$0.00	$0.00		$0.00	$0.00			$0.00		0.00%	0.00%	0.00%
$0.00	$0.00		$0.00	$0.00			$0.00		0.00%	0.00%	0.00%
$100,000.00	$0.00	$100,000.00	$3,000.00	$3,000.00			$100,000.00			22.94%	22.94%
$300,000.00	$0.00	$100,000.00	$13,077.60	$13,077.60			$300,000.00			100.0%	100.0%

* BONEFISH, INC. (see Q 9:19, example 3)

* CORPORATE SEP PLAN *

* INTEGRATED CONTRIBUTIONS

3
21-Mar-2012
09:03 PM

** ALLOCATION OF DESIRED CONTRIBUTION **

** INTEGRATION METHOD: IRS PERCENTAGE METHOD **

EMPLOYEES	2012 ALLOCATION COMPENSATION	PLAN ALLOCATION COMPENSATION MULTIPLIED BY 3.000000% BASE PERCENTAGE	PLAN COMPENSATION IN EXCESS OF $32,040.00	EXCESS COMPENSATION MULTIPLIED BY 3.000000% DISPARITY RATE	UNLIMITED TOTAL PLAN DEPOSIT
Joe	$100,000.00	$3,000.00	$67,960.00	$2,038.80	$5,038.80
Sally	$100,000.00	$3,000.00	$67,960.00	$2,038.80	$5,038.80
	$0.00	$0.00	$0.00	$0.00	$0.00
	$0.00	$0.00	$0.00	$0.00	$0.00
	$0.00	$0.00	$0.00	$0.00	$0.00
	$0.00	$0.00	$0.00	$0.00	$0.00
	$0.00	$0.00	$0.00	$0.00	$0.00
	$0.00	$0.00	$0.00	$0.00	$0.00
	$200,000.00	$6,000.00	$135,920.00	$4,077.60	$10,077.60
Ruth	$30,000.00	$900.00	$0.00	$0.00	$900.00
Tom	$25,000.00	$750.00	$0.00	$0.00	$750.00
Ned	$20,000.00	$600.00	$0.00	$0.00	$600.00
Lee	$15,000.00	$450.00	$0.00	$0.00	$450.00
Sarah	$10,000.00	$300.00	$0.00	$0.00	$300.00
	$0.00	$0.00	$0.00	$0.00	$0.00
	$0.00	$0.00	$0.00	$0.00	$0.00
	$0.00	$0.00	$0.00	$0.00	$0.00
	$0.00	$0.00	$0.00	$0.00	$0.00
	$0.00	$0.00	$0.00	$0.00	$0.00
	$100,000.00	$3,000.00	$0.00	$0.00	$3,000.00
	$300,000.00	$9,000.00	$135,920.00	$4,077.60	$13,077.60

* Do Not contribute amounts shown on this page. Allocation shown is untested or may have been reduced by other factors.

* CORPORATE SEP PLAN * * BONEFISH, INC. (see Q 9:19, example 4)

1
06:53 PM
22-Feb-2012

Plan Year Begins:	2012	$30,000.00	- Employer Contribution
Plan Year Ends:	2012	ALL	- DEDUCTIBLE PORTION
Base Percentage:	6.8285190	$30,000.00	- Total Allocated
Integration Level:	$22,020	9.999999000%	- Allocation % of 402(h) Comp
Excess Percentage:	12.5285190	5.7%	- Maximum Integration Spread
1=P/S 2=MP 3=SEP 4=SARSEP:	3		
E/er Contr. to Owners:	75.15586752%		
E/er Alloc. Compensation:	66.66666667%	$48,744.86	- Maximum HCE Allocation <-n/a

-> P	Plan not T/H Integrated Prototype SEP	TOTAL ALLOCATION	IRC 402(h) EMPLOYER CONTRIBUTION	EMPLOYER CONTRIBUTION	Columns reserved for Salary Reduction SEPs	KEY	Col n/a	EMPLOYEE's PRE-PLAN COMPENSATION	HCE	Col. n/a	Col. n/a
1	Joe	$11,273.38	11.273379%	$11,273.38		Y		$100,000.00	Y		
2	Sally	$11,273.38	11.273379%	$11,273.38		Y		$100,000.00	Y		
3		$0.00	0.000000%	$0.00							
4		$0.00	0.000000%	$0.00							
5		$0.00	0.000000%	$0.00							
6		$0.00	0.000000%	$0.00							
7		$0.00	0.000000%	$0.00							
8		$0.00	0.000000%	$0.00							
	OWNER SUB-TOTALS	$22,546.76		$22,546.76	$0.00			$200,000.00			
9	Ruth	$2,503.42	8.344719%	$2,503.42		N		$30,000.00	N		
10	Tom	$1,876.99	7.507959%	$1,876.99		N		$25,000.00	N		
11	Ned	$1,365.70	6.828519%	$1,365.70		N		$20,000.00	N		
12	Lee	$1,024.28	6.828519%	$1,024.28		N		$15,000.00	N		
13	Sarah	$682.85	6.828519%	$682.85		N		$10,000.00	N		
14		$0.00	0.000000%	$0.00							
15		$0.00	0.000000%	$0.00							
16		$0.00	0.000000%	$0.00							
17		$0.00	0.000000%	$0.00							
18		$0.00	0.000000%	$0.00							
	NON-OWNER SUB TOTALS	$7,453.24		$7,453.24				$100,000.00			
	GRAND TOTALS	$30,000.00		$30,000.00				$300,000.00			

Penny rounding applied.

* BONEFISH, INC. (see Q 9:19, example 4)

* CORPORATE SEP PLAN *

* INTEGRATED CONTRIBUTIONS

2012

* * C O N T R I B U T I O N   S U M M A R Y * *

$30,000.00 - Employer Contribution
ALL - DEDUCTIBLE PORTION
$30,000.00 - Total Allocated
10.00% - Allocation % of 402(h) Comp
5.70% - Maximum Integration Spread

$22,020.00 - Integration Level   20.00000000% :TWB Percentage

2
22-Feb-2012
06:53 PM

ALLOCATION COMPENSATION -Includes- -Elective-	TOP HEAVY ADDITIONAL AMOUNT FOR 75.16% PERCENTAGE	PRE-PLAN COMPENSATION	TOTAL ALLOCATION	EMPLOYER's CONTRIBUTION	Col. n/a	Col. n/a	NET TAXABLE COMPENSATION	Col. n/a	EMPLOYER CONTRIBUTION % OF DEDUCT. COMPENSATION	PERCENTAGE OF EMPLOYER $30,000.00 CONTRIBUTIONS	PERCENTAGE OF TOTAL $30,000.00 ALLOCATIONS
$100,000.00	$0.00	$100,000.00	$11,273.38	$11,273.38			$100,000.00		11.27%	37.58%	37.58%
$100,000.00	$0.00	$100,000.00	$11,273.38	$11,273.38			$100,000.00		11.27%	37.58%	37.58%
$0.00	$0.00		$0.00	$0.00			$0.00		0.00%	0.00%	0.00%
$0.00	$0.00		$0.00	$0.00			$0.00		0.00%	0.00%	0.00%
$0.00	$0.00		$0.00	$0.00			$0.00		0.00%	0.00%	0.00%
$0.00	$0.00		$0.00	$0.00			$0.00		0.00%	0.00%	0.00%
$0.00	$0.00		$0.00	$0.00			$0.00		0.00%	0.00%	0.00%
$0.00	$0.00		$0.00	$0.00			$0.00		0.00%	0.00%	0.00%
$200,000.00	$0.00	$200,000.00	$22,546.76	$22,546.76			$200,000.00			75.16%	75.16%
$30,000.00	$0.00	$30,000.00	$2,503.42	$2,503.42			$30,000.00		8.34%	8.34%	8.34%
$25,000.00	$0.00	$25,000.00	$1,876.99	$1,876.99			$25,000.00		7.51%	6.26%	6.26%
$20,000.00	$0.00	$20,000.00	$1,365.70	$1,365.70			$20,000.00		6.83%	4.55%	4.55%
$15,000.00	$0.00	$15,000.00	$1,024.28	$1,024.28			$15,000.00		6.83%	3.41%	3.41%
$10,000.00	$0.00	$10,000.00	$682.85	$682.85			$10,000.00		6.83%	2.28%	2.28%
$0.00	$0.00		$0.00	$0.00			$0.00		0.00%	0.00%	0.00%
$0.00	$0.00		$0.00	$0.00			$0.00		0.00%	0.00%	0.00%
$0.00	$0.00		$0.00	$0.00			$0.00		0.00%	0.00%	0.00%
$0.00	$0.00		$0.00	$0.00			$0.00		0.00%	0.00%	0.00%
$0.00	$0.00		$0.00	$0.00			$0.00		0.00%	0.00%	0.00%
$100,000.00	$0.00	$100,000.00	$7,453.24	$7,453.24			$100,000.00			24.84%	24.84%
$300,000.00	$0.00	$100,000.00	$30,000.00	$30,000.00			$300,000.00			100.0%	100.0%

* BONEFISH, INC. (see Q 9:19, example 4) — 3

* CORPORATE SEP PLAN * — 22-Feb-2012 06:53 PM

* INTEGRATED CONTRIBUTIONS

* * ALLOCATION OF DESIRED CONTRIBUTION * *

* * INTEGRATION METHOD: IRS PERCENTAGE METHOD * *

EMPLOYEES	2012 ALLOCATION COMPENSATION	PLAN ALLOCATION COMPENSATION MULTIPLIED BY 6.828519% BASE PERCENTAGE	PLAN COMPENSATION IN EXCESS OF $22,020.00	EXCESS COMPENSATION MULTIPLIED BY 5.700000% DISPARITY RATE	UNLIMITED TOTAL PLAN DEPOSIT
Joe	$100,000.00	$6,828.52	$77,980.00	$4,444.86	$11,273.38
Sally	$100,000.00	$6,828.52	$77,980.00	$4,444.86	$11,273.38
	$0.00	$0.00	$0.00	$0.00	$0.00
	$0.00	$0.00	$0.00	$0.00	$0.00
	$0.00	$0.00	$0.00	$0.00	$0.00
	$0.00	$0.00	$0.00	$0.00	$0.00
	$0.00	$0.00	$0.00	$0.00	$0.00
	$0.00	$0.00	$0.00	$0.00	$0.00
	$200,000.00	$13,657.04	$155,960.00	$8,889.72	$22,546.76
Ruth	$30,000.00	$2,048.56	$7,980.00	$454.86	$2,503.42
Tom	$25,000.00	$1,707.13	$2,980.00	$169.86	$1,876.99
Ned	$20,000.00	$1,365.70	$0.00	$0.00	$1,365.70
Lee	$15,000.00	$1,024.28	$0.00	$0.00	$1,024.28
Sarah	$10,000.00	$682.85	$0.00	$0.00	$682.85
	$0.00	$0.00	$0.00	$0.00	$0.00
	$0.00	$0.00	$0.00	$0.00	$0.00
	$0.00	$0.00	$0.00	$0.00	$0.00
	$0.00	$0.00	$0.00	$0.00	$0.00
	$0.00	$0.00	$0.00	$0.00	$0.00
	$100,000.00	$6,828.52	$10,960.00	$624.72	$7,453.24
	$300,000.00	$20,485.56	$166,920.00	$9,514.44	$30,000.00

* Do Not contribute amounts shown on this page. Allocation shown is untested or may have been reduced by other factors.

* CORPORATE SEP PLAN *   * BONEFISH, INC. (see Q 9:19, example 5)   1

12:54 PM

23-Feb-2012

Plan Year Begins:	2012	$71,179.85	- Employer Contribution
Plan Year Ends:	2012	ALL	- DEDUCTIBLE PORTION
Base Percentage:	20.5551365	$71,179.85	- Total Allocated
Integration Level:	$22,020	23.726616500%	- Allocation % of 402(h) Comp
Excess Percentage:	26.2551365	5.7%	- Maximum Integration Spread
1=P/S 2=MP 3=SEP 4=SARSEP:	3		
E/er Contr. to Owners:	70.24458938%		
E/er Alloc. Compensation:	66.66666667%	$48,744.86	- Maximum HCE Allocation <-n/a

P	-> Plan not T/H Integrated Prototype SEP	TOTAL ALLOCATION	IRC 402(h) EMPLOYER CONTRIBUTION	EMPLOYER CONTRIBUTION	Columns reserved for Salary Reduction SEPs	KEY	Col n/a	EMPLOYEE's PRE-PLAN COMPENSATION	HCE	Col. n/a	Col. n/a
1	Joe	$25,000.00 h	24.999997%	$25,000.00		Y		$100,000.00	Y		
2	Sally	$25,000.00 h	24.999997%	$25,000.00		Y		$100,000.00	Y		
3		$0.00	0.000000%	$0.00							
4		$0.00	0.000000%	$0.00							
5		$0.00	0.000000%	$0.00							
6		$0.00	0.000000%	$0.00							
7		$0.00	0.000000%	$0.00							
8		$0.00	0.000000%	$0.00							
	OWNER SUB-TOTALS	$49,999.99		$49,999.99	$0.00			$200,000.00			
9	Ruth	$6,621.40	22.071337%	$6,621.40		N		$30,000.00	N		
10	Tom	$5,308.64	21.234577%	$5,308.64		N		$25,000.00	N		
11	Ned	$4,111.03	20.555137%	$4,111.03		N		$20,000.00	N		
12	Lee	$3,083.27	20.555137%	$3,083.27		N		$15,000.00	N		
13	Sarah	$2,055.51	20.555137%	$2,055.51		N		$10,000.00	N		
14		$0.00	0.000000%	$0.00							
15		$0.00	0.000000%	$0.00							
16		$0.00	0.000000%	$0.00							
17		$0.00	0.000000%	$0.00							
18		$0.00	0.000000%	$0.00							
	NON-OWNER SUB TOTALS	$21,179.86		$21,179.86				$100,000.00			
	GRAND TOTALS	$71,179.85		$71,179.85				$300,000.00			

h or m <-- At a limit/maximum (other solutions possible).

Penny rounding applied.

* BONEFISH, INC. (see Q 9:19, example 5)

* CORPORATE SEP PLAN *

* INTEGRATED CONTRIBUTIONS

2012

* * C O N T R I B U T I O N   S U M M A R Y * *

$71,179.85 - Employer Contribution
ALL - DEDUCTIBLE PORTION
$71,179.85 - Total Allocated
23.73% - Allocation % of 402(h) Comp
5.70% - Maximum Integration Spread

$22,020.00 - Integration Level   20.00000000% :TWB Percentage

2
23-Feb-2012
12:54 PM

ALLOCATION COMPENSATION -Includes- -Elective-	TOP HEAVY ADDITIONAL AMOUNT FOR 70.24% PERCENTAGE	PRE-PLAN COMPENSATION	TOTAL ALLOCATION	EMPLOYER's CONTRIBUTION	Col. n/a	Col. n/a	NET TAXABLE COMPENSATION	Col. n/a	EMPLOYER CONTRIBUTION % OF DEDUCT. COMPENSATION	PERCENTAGE OF EMPLOYER $71,179.85 CONTRIBUTIONS	PERCENTAGE OF TOTAL $71,179.85 ALLOCATIONS
$100,000.00	$0.00	$100,000.00	$25,000.00	$25,000.00			$100,000.00		25.00%	35.12%	35.12%
$100,000.00	$0.00	$100,000.00	$25,000.00	$25,000.00			$100,000.00		25.00%	35.12%	35.12%
$0.00	$0.00		$0.00	$0.00			$0.00		0.00%	0.00%	0.00%
$0.00	$0.00		$0.00	$0.00			$0.00		0.00%	0.00%	0.00%
$0.00	$0.00		$0.00	$0.00			$0.00		0.00%	0.00%	0.00%
$0.00	$0.00		$0.00	$0.00			$0.00		0.00%	0.00%	0.00%
$0.00	$0.00		$0.00	$0.00			$0.00		0.00%	0.00%	0.00%
$0.00	$0.00		$0.00	$0.00			$0.00		0.00%	0.00%	0.00%
$200,000.00	$0.00	$200,000.00	$49,999.99	$49,999.99			$200,000.00			70.24%	70.24%
$30,000.00	$0.00	$30,000.00	$6,621.40	$6,621.40			$30,000.00		22.07%	9.30%	9.30%
$25,000.00	$0.00	$25,000.00	$5,308.64	$5,308.64			$25,000.00		21.23%	7.46%	7.46%
$20,000.00	$0.00	$20,000.00	$4,111.03	$4,111.03			$20,000.00		20.56%	5.78%	5.78%
$15,000.00	$0.00	$15,000.00	$3,083.27	$3,083.27			$15,000.00		20.56%	4.33%	4.33%
$10,000.00	$0.00	$10,000.00	$2,055.51	$2,055.51			$10,000.00		20.56%	2.89%	2.89%
$0.00	$0.00		$0.00	$0.00			$0.00		0.00%	0.00%	0.00%
$0.00	$0.00		$0.00	$0.00			$0.00		0.00%	0.00%	0.00%
$0.00	$0.00		$0.00	$0.00			$0.00		0.00%	0.00%	0.00%
$0.00	$0.00		$0.00	$0.00			$0.00		0.00%	0.00%	0.00%
$0.00	$0.00		$0.00	$0.00			$0.00		0.00%	0.00%	0.00%
$100,000.00	$0.00	$100,000.00	$21,179.86	$21,179.86			$100,000.00			29.76%	29.76%
$300,000.00	$0.00	$100,000.00	$71,179.85	$71,179.85			$300,000.00			100.0%	100.0%

* BONEFISH, INC. (see Q 9:19, example 5)

* CORPORATE SEP PLAN *

* INTEGRATED CONTRIBUTIONS

3
23-Feb-2012
12:54 PM

** ALLOCATION OF DESIRED CONTRIBUTION **

** INTEGRATION METHOD: IRS PERCENTAGE METHOD **

EMPLOYEES	2012 ALLOCATION COMPENSATION	PLAN ALLOCATION COMPENSATION MULTIPLIED BY 20.555137% BASE PERCENTAGE	PLAN COMPENSATION IN EXCESS OF $22,020.00	EXCESS COMPENSATION MULTIPLIED BY 5.700000% DISPARITY RATE	UNLIMITED TOTAL PLAN DEPOSIT
Joe	$100,000.00	$20,555.14	$77,980.00	$4,444.86	$25,000.00
Sally	$100,000.00	$20,555.14	$77,980.00	$4,444.86	$25,000.00
	$0.00	$0.00	$0.00	$0.00	$0.00
	$0.00	$0.00	$0.00	$0.00	$0.00
	$0.00	$0.00	$0.00	$0.00	$0.00
	$0.00	$0.00	$0.00	$0.00	$0.00
	$0.00	$0.00	$0.00	$0.00	$0.00
	$0.00	$0.00	$0.00	$0.00	$0.00
	$200,000.00	$41,110.27	$155,960.00	$8,889.72	$49,999.99
Ruth	$30,000.00	$6,166.54	$7,980.00	$454.86	$6,621.40
Tom	$25,000.00	$5,138.78	$2,980.00	$169.86	$5,308.64
Ned	$20,000.00	$4,111.03	$0.00	$0.00	$4,111.03
Lee	$15,000.00	$3,083.27	$0.00	$0.00	$3,083.27
Sarah	$10,000.00	$2,055.51	$0.00	$0.00	$2,055.51
	$0.00	$0.00	$0.00	$0.00	$0.00
	$0.00	$0.00	$0.00	$0.00	$0.00
	$0.00	$0.00	$0.00	$0.00	$0.00
	$0.00	$0.00	$0.00	$0.00	$0.00
	$0.00	$0.00	$0.00	$0.00	$0.00
	$100,000.00	$20,555.14	$10,960.00	$624.72	$21,179.86
	$300,000.00	$61,665.41	$166,920.00	$9,514.44	$71,179.85

* Do Not contribute amounts shown on this page. Allocation shown is untested or may have been reduced by other factors.

Travel Dreams (see Q 14:64) — SIMPLE IRA PLAN for a Sole-Proprietorship — 03/21/2012

S I M P L E   I R A

2012 <- Plan Year
3.00% <- General Matching
1.00% <- Alternate Matching
I <- SIMPLE IRA
Y <- Catch-Up

S Entity Type (C, P, or S)
C = Corporation
P = Partnership or LLC
S = Sole-Proprietorship

2 <-Auto

Eligible Employees	Year of Birth	If Owner Enter "o"	Pre-Plan W-2 Compensation or Owner Net SE Income	Calculation of Owners Percentage	SE Owner Exp. Share Percentage	Take Home or Desired Salary Reduction Amount $ or % or .999 if K	
Catch-Up Amt $2,500		Totals:	$130,000.00		100.000%		
1 Shannon	1950 .	o	$75,000.00	0.0000%	100.000%	0.999	Max
2 Frank	1950 .	n	$30,000.00	0.0000%	0.000%	4000.000	<- $
3 Delilah	1950 .	n	$25,000.00	0.0000%	0.000%	1000.000	<- $
4	1950 .	n	$0.00	0.0000%	0.000%	0.999	Max
5	1950 .	n	$0.00	0.0000%	0.000%	0.999	Max

#1 _ _ _ _ M A T C H I N G   C O N T R I B U T I O N _ _ _ _ _ _ _ _ _ _

U P   T O   3 %

90.67% <- Owner % of Total E/er
55.19% <- Owner % of Matching
$16,032.16 <- Owner Total
$6,650.00 <- Nonowner Total
$22,682.16 <- Plan Total

S I M P L E   I R A

#	Salary Reduction Amount	W-2 Income/ .9235 NESE after 3% or $1,650.00 Nonowner Allocation	Matching Amounts	Total SIMPLE Contribution	Taxable Income
#	$19,000.00	$122,738.73	$3,682.16	$22,682.16	
1	$14,000.00	$67,738.73	$2,032.16	$16,032.16	$51,706.57
2	$4,000.00	$30,000.00	$900.00	$4,900.00	$26,000.00
3	$1,000.00	$25,000.00	$750.00	$1,750.00	$24,000.00
4	$0.00	$0.00	$0.00	$0.00	$0.00
5	$0.00	$0.00	$0.00	$0.00	$0.00

Travel Dreams (see Q 14:64) — SIMPLE IRA PLAN for a Sole-Proprietorship

#2 _ _ _ _ A L T E R N A T I V E   M A T C H I N G _ _ _ _ _ _ _ _ _ _ _ _ _ _ _

U P   T O: 1.00%

96.39% <- Owner % of Total E/er
55.56% <- Owner % of Matching
$14,687.55 <- Owner Total
$5,550.00 <- Nonowner Total
$20,237.55 <- Plan Total

S I M P L E   I R A

#	Salary Reduction Amount	W-2 Income/ .9235 NESE after $550.00 Nonowner Allocation	Maximum Match 1.00% Matching Amounts	Total SIMPLE Contribution	Taxable Income
#	$19,000.00	$123,754.58	$1,237.55	$20,237.55	
1	$14,000.00	$68,754.58	$687.55	$14,687.55	$54,067.03
2	$4,000.00	$30,000.00	$300.00	$4,300.00	$26,000.00
3	$1,000.00	$25,000.00	$250.00	$1,250.00	$24,000.00
4	$0.00	$0.00	$0.00	$0.00	$0.00
5	$0.00	$0.00	$0.00	$0.00	$0.00

#3 _ _ _ _ N O N E L E C T I V E   C O N T R I B U T I O N _ _ _ _ _ _ _ _

2.00% -- Statutory rate.

93.32% <- Owner % of Total E/er
55.56% <- Owner % of Nonelective
$15,375.09 <- Owner Total
$6,100.00 <- Nonowner Total
$21,475.09 <- Plan Total
$5,000.00 <- Min. Comp.

S I M P L E   I R A

#	Salary Reduction Contribution	W-2 Income/ .9235 NESE after 2% or $1,100.00 Nonowner Allocation	Non-Elective Contribution	Total SIMPLE Contribution	Taxable Income
#	$19,000.00	$233,754.58	$2,475.09	$21,475.09	
1	$14,000.00	$68,754.58	$1,375.09	$15,375.09	$53,379.49
2	$4,000.00	$90,000.00	$600.00	$4,600.00	$86,000.00
3	$1,000.00	$75,000.00	$500.00	$1,500.00	$74,000.00
4	$0.00	$0.00	$0.00	$0.00	$0.00
5	$0.00	$0.00	$0.00	$0.00	$0.00

ALEX Manufacturing Corporation (see Q 14:141) — SIMPLE IRA PLAN for a Corporation — 03/21/2012

S I M P L E   I R A

2012 <- Plan Year
3.00% <- General Matching
1.00% <- Alternate Matching
I <- SIMPLE IRA
Y <- Catch-Up

C Entity Type (C, P, or S)
C = Corporation
P = Partnership or LLC
S = Sole-Proprietorship

#1 _ _ _ _ M A T C H I N G   C O N T R I B U T I O N _ _ _ _ _ _ _ _ _ _ _ _ _ _

U P   T O   3 %

S I M P L E   I R A

62.57% <- Owner % of Total E/er
45.53% <- Owner % of Matching
$28,000.00 <- Owner Total
$70,250.00 <- Nonowner Total
$98,250.00 <- Plan Total

Eligible Employees	Year of Birth	If Owner Enter "o"	Enter Pre-Plan W-2 Compensation		2	<-n/a	Take Home or Desired Salary Reduction Amount $ or % or .999 if K		#	Salary Reduction Amount	W-2 Compensation	Matching Amounts	Total SIMPLE Contribution	Taxable Income
Catch-Up Amt	$2,500	Totals:	$2,205,000.00	Col. n/a					#	$67,500.00	$2,205,000.00	$30,750.00	$98,250.00	
1 Alex	1950 .	o	$1,400,000.00	0.0000%		0.000%	14000.000	<- $	1	$14,000.00	$1,400,000.00	$14,000.00	$28,000.00	$1,386,000.00
2 Beth	1970	n	$250,000.00	0.0000%		0.000%	6000.000	<- $	2	$6,000.00	$250,000.00	$6,000.00	$12,000.00	$244,000.00
3 Chris	1970	n	$150,000.00	0.0000%		0.000%	11500.000	<- $	3	$11,500.00	$150,000.00	$4,500.00	$16,000.00	$138,500.00
4 Dana	1970	n	$125,000.00	0.0000%		0.000%	0.000		4	$0.00	$125,000.00	$0.00	$0.00	$125,000.00
5 Ellen	1970	n	$100,000.00	0.0000%		0.000%	8000.000	<- $	5	$8,000.00	$100,000.00	$3,000.00	$11,000.00	$92,000.00
6 Fred	1970	n	$100,000.00	0.0000%		0.000%	1000.000	<- $	6	$1,000.00	$100,000.00	$1,000.00	$2,000.00	$99,000.00
7 Gary	1950 .	n	$50,000.00	0.0000%		0.000%	14000.000	<- $	7	$14,000.00	$50,000.00	$1,500.00	$15,500.00	$36,000.00
8 Hugh	1970	n	$10,000.00	0.0000%		0.000%	8000.000	<- $	8	$8,000.00	$10,000.00	$300.00	$8,300.00	$2,000.00
9 Isaac	1970	n	$10,000.00	0.0000%		0.000%	1000.000	<- $	9	$1,000.00	$10,000.00	$300.00	$1,300.00	$9,000.00
10 Juan	1970	n	$5,000.00	0.0000%		0.000%	4000.000	<- $	10	$4,000.00	$5,000.00	$150.00	$4,150.00	$1,000.00
11 Kim	1950 .	n	$5,000.00	0.0000%		0.000%	0.000		11	$0.00	$5,000.00	$0.00	$0.00	$5,000.00

ALEX Manufacturing Corporation (see Q 14:141)

#2 _ _ _ _ A L T E R N A T I V E   M A T C H I N G _ _ _ _ _ _ _ _ _ _ _ _ _ _ _ _

U P T O: 1.00%

S I M P L E   I R A

80.58% <- Owner % of Total E/er
67.47% <- Owner % of Matching
$28,000.00 <- Owner Total
$60,250.00 <- Nonowner Total
$88,250.00 <- Plan Total

Maximum Match 1.00%

#	Salary Reduction Amount	W-2 Compensation	Maximum Match 1.00% Matching Amounts	Total SIMPLE Contribution	Taxable Income
#	$67,500.00	$2,205,000.00	$20,750.00	$88,250.00	
1	$14,000.00	$1,400,000.00	$14,000.00	$28,000.00	$1,386,000.00
2	$6,000.00	$250,000.00	$2,500.00	$8,500.00	$244,000.00
3	$11,500.00	$150,000.00	$1,500.00	$13,000.00	$138,500.00
4	$0.00	$125,000.00	$0.00	$0.00	$125,000.00
5	$8,000.00	$100,000.00	$1,000.00	$9,000.00	$92,000.00
6	$1,000.00	$100,000.00	$1,000.00	$2,000.00	$99,000.00
7	$14,000.00	$50,000.00	$500.00	$14,500.00	$36,000.00
8	$8,000.00	$10,000.00	$100.00	$8,100.00	$2,000.00
9	$1,000.00	$10,000.00	$100.00	$1,100.00	$9,000.00
10	$4,000.00	$5,000.00	$50.00	$4,050.00	$1,000.00
11	$0.00	$5,000.00	$0.00	$0.00	$5,000.00

SIMPLE IRA PLAN for a Corporation

#3 _ _ _ _ N O N E L E C T I V E   C O N T R I B U T I O N _ _ _ _ _ _ _ _ _

2.00% -- Statutory rate.

S I M P L E   I R A

54.13% <- Owner % of Total E/er
23.70% <- Owner % of Nonelective
$19,000.00 <- Owner Total
$69,600.00 <- Nonowner Total
$88,600.00 <- Plan Total

$5,000.00 <- Min. Comp.

#	Salary Reduction Contribution	W-2 Compensation	Non-Elective Contribution	Total SIMPLE Contribution	Taxable Income
#	$67,500.00	$2,205,000.00	$21,100.00	$88,600.00	
1	$14,000.00	$1,400,000.00	$5,000.00	$19,000.00	$1,386,000.00
2	$6,000.00	$250,000.00	$5,000.00	$11,000.00	$244,000.00
3	$11,500.00	$150,000.00	$3,000.00	$14,500.00	$138,500.00
4	$0.00	$125,000.00	$2,500.00	$2,500.00	$125,000.00
5	$8,000.00	$100,000.00	$2,000.00	$10,000.00	$92,000.00
6	$1,000.00	$100,000.00	$2,000.00	$3,000.00	$99,000.00
7	$14,000.00	$50,000.00	$1,000.00	$15,000.00	$36,000.00
8	$8,000.00	$10,000.00	$200.00	$8,200.00	$2,000.00
9	$1,000.00	$10,000.00	$200.00	$1,200.00	$9,000.00
10	$4,000.00	$5,000.00	$100.00	$4,100.00	$1,000.00
11	$0.00	$5,000.00	$100.00	$100.00	$5,000.00

Appendix I

IRS Legal Memoranda, General Counsel Memorandum, and Private Letter Rulings

IRS Legal Memorandum

IRS Legal Memorandum 200117003 Dated: January 26, 2001

[Summary: Although the memorandum does not specifically state, it would appear that the payment of earned income to a partner is not properly reportable on Form W-2 and would be treated as earned income under Code Section 401(c) for retirement plan purposes. In a legal memorandum, Michael A. Swim, Chief, Branch 1 (Employment Tax), advised that when a Form SS-8 submission indicates that a party is claiming that a worker is a bona fide member of a partnership, the IRS cannot issue a ruling on that issue.]

SUBJECT: Form SS-8 Submissions Involving Partnership Issues

This memorandum responds to questions raised by a number of Forms SS-8 submissions involving partnership issues. These Forms SS-8 generally involve one of two different types of claims. The first is a claim by a worker that for federal tax purposes, although a valid partnership exists, the worker is an employee of the partnership and not a bona fide member of the partnership. The second is a claim by a worker that a partnership of which he is a purported member is not a bona fide partnership for federal tax purposes, but rather that one of the members (typically one of the general partners) is actually the employer of all the other purported members of the partnership.

Whether or not a person is a partner in a partnership, for federal tax purposes, is a question of federal law. While a person may be recognized as a partner under state law, it is not necessarily determinative of whether they will be treated as a partner for federal tax purposes.

Bona fide members of a partnership cannot be employees for purposes of the employment tax provisions of the Internal Revenue Code (the Code). However, the Form SS-8 is intended to elicit information necessary to determine the worker's proper classification under the common law rules distinguishing employees from independent contractors. The Form SS-8 is not intended to elicit information necessary to determine whether the worker is a bona fide member of a partnership. Therefore, the Service should decline to rule on any Form SS-8 submissions that would require such an analysis in order to determine the worker's classification for purposes of the employment tax provisions.

EMPLOYMENT TAXES AND PARTNERSHIPS

EMPLOYMENT TAXES

Applicable employment taxes are imposed under the Federal Insurance Contributions Act (FICA), Federal Unemployment Tax Act (FUTA) and Collection of Income Tax at Source. See Code sections 3101 and 3111 (FICA tax); Code section 3301 (FUTA tax); and Code section 3402 (Collection of Income Tax at Source). FICA and FUTA taxes are imposed on wages with respect to employment and require an employer-employee relationship (unless a statutory exception applies). In addition, the Collection of Income Tax at Source imposes certain income tax withholding requirements on employers paying wages.

APPLICATION OF EMPLOYMENT TAXES TO MEMBERS OF A PARTNERSHIP

Income received by a bona fide partner from a partnership cannot be wages, but instead may qualify as self-employment income subject to tax under the Self Employment Contributions Act (SECA). See Revenue Ruling 69-184, 1969-1 C.B. 256. As stated in Revenue Ruling 69-184:

> Bona fide members of a partnership are not employees of the partnership within the meaning of the Federal Insurance Contributions Act, the Federal Unemployment Tax Act, and the Collection of Income Tax at Source on Wages . . . Such a partner who devotes his time and energies in the conduct

of the trade or business of the partnership, or in providing services to the partnership as an independent contractor, is, in either event, a self-employed individual rather than an individual who, under the usual common law rules applicable in determining the employer-employee relationship, has the status of an employee.

Thus, to qualify as an employee for purposes of the employment tax provisions, the worker must be classified both as not a bona fide member of a partnership AND as an employee under the common law control test for distinguishing employees from independent contractors (unless a statutory exception applies).

FORM SS-8 (DETERMINATION OF EMPLOYEE WORK STATUS FOR PURPOSES OF FEDERAL EMPLOYMENT TAXES AND INCOME TAX WITHHOLDING)

The Form SS-8 may be submitted by either the worker or the firm for a determination of whether or not the worker is an employee for purposes of the employment tax provisions. The party that does not submit the initial Form SS-8 is offered the opportunity to respond. The forms are processed in either the Austin, Texas or Newport, Vermont IRS Service Centers, except for filings involving federal agencies which are handled by the National Office. An SS-8 ruling applies only for purposes of the employment tax provisions of the Code.

The Form SS-8 consists of a series of questions intended to elicit information necessary to determine whether the parties meet the common law test of control necessary for the finding of an employee-employer relationship. Thus, the form is generally intended to address the issue of whether the worker is an employee or an independent contractor. There are no questions addressing specifically the existence or nonexistence of a partnership arrangement, or any details of such arrangement.

Because the information gathered through the Form SS-8 is not sufficient to determine whether the worker is a bona fide member of a partnership for federal tax purposes, the classification of a worker as an "employee" for purposes of the employment tax provisions cannot be made where there is the potential for the worker to be such a member. Therefore, where the Form SS-8 submission indicates that one or more of the parties is claiming that the worker is a bona fide member of a partnership, the parties should be informed that a ruling cannot be issued.

We hope the information provided is of assistance to you.

General Counsel Memorandum

General Counsel Memorandum 39807 Dated: January 29, 1990

[Summary: A self-employed individual's contribution on his or her own behalf to a Qualified Plan, SEP, SIMPLE, or IRA is not deductible in computing self-employment income.]

ISSUE. At issue in this GCM is whether contributions made by a self-employed person on that individual's own behalf to a qualified section 401(a) plan, that are deductible under section 404(a), are deductible in computing the individual's section 1402 self-employment income for purposes of the Self-Employment Contributions Act of 1954 (SECA). Also at issue is whether contributions made by a self-employed person on that individual's own behalf to a section 408(k) simplified employee pension (SEP), that are deductible under section 404(h), are deductible in computing that person's section 1402 self-employment income for SECA purposes.

Finally, whether contributions made by a self-employed individual to that person's section 408(a) individual retirement account (IRA), that are deductible under section 219(a), are deductible in calculating that person's section 1402 self-employment income.

CONCLUSIONS. Contributions made by a self-employed person, on that individual's own behalf, to a qualified section 401(a) plan, to a SEP, and to an IRA, are not deductible in computing the individual's self-employment income as defined in section 1402.

ANALYSIS. The IRS concluded that it is its "longstanding position" that the deduction for a contribution on behalf of a self-employed individual to a qualified plan is not one "attributable to such trade or business" under section 1402(a). Therefore, the deduction is taken as an adjustment to income on Form 1040, and is not taken as a deduction from the self-employed person's Schedule C income or from the calculation to determine the self-employment tax on the Schedule SE, Form 1040.

Private Letter Rulings

Letter Ruling 200116046 Dated: January 22, 2001

[Summary: The IRS ruled that salary-reduction and employer-matching contributions made to a nonqualified deferred compensation plan may be transferred to a 401(k) subject to Code Sections 402(g) and 401(k)(3) limits. The 401(k) plan assets are protected as a qualified plan, but the nonqualified plan assets are held as the employer's property, subject to the claims of the employer's creditors.

The IRS ruled that elective salary deferrals made to the 401(k) plan from the nonqualified plan would be excluded from participants' income (1) to the extent that the Code Section 402(g) and 401(k) limits were not exceeded; (2) if the transfer election was timely made; and (3) as long as the transfer occurs by March 15. The IRS also ruled that the transfers will be treated as made in the year in which the deferred income was earned rather than in the year of transfer, as will deferrals returned to participants.]

This is in response to your ruling request submitted on your behalf by your authorized representative dated July 23, 1999, and supplemented by additional correspondence dated January 11, 2000, June 23, 2000, September 8, 2000, October 27, 2000, January 8, 2001, and January 16, 2001. The ruling request concerns the tax treatment of elective deferrals to a cash or deferred arrangement in coordination with a nonqualified deferred compensation plan. The following facts and representations were submitted by your authorized representative in support of the rulings requested.

Employer X currently maintains both Plans A and B. Plan A is a qualified plan under section 401(a) of the Internal Revenue Code (the "Code"). Employer X represents that Plan A was established effective January 1, 1998 by adopting a nonstandardized prototype plan and includes a qualified cash or deferred arrangement as described under section 401(k) of the Code. Plan B is an unfunded nonqualified plan established to benefit certain highly compensated management employees of Employer X. Both Plans A and B operate on a calendar year basis.

Plan A provides that participants in Plan A may make pre-tax contributions to the Plan. No after tax contributions may be made to Plan A. Plan A provides that participants may make elective deferral contributions up to 15% of their compensation for the year. Plan A further provides that a participant's elective deferrals are subject to the limitations in effect for year under sections 402(g) and 415 of the Code and by the actual deferral percentage test and the actual contribution percentage test under sections 401(k) and 401(m) of the Code.

Plan A authorizes Employer X to make matching contributions with respect to participant's elective deferrals. Under Plan A, matching contributions are made for a plan year at the discretion of Employer X, and if made, allocated to participants based on the amount of elective deferrals, pursuant to a discretionary formula. Plan A also authorizes Employer X to make a discretionary profit sharing contribution.

Plan B provides that participants in Plan B may elect to defer up to the lesser of $30,000 or 25% of their compensation for the year. Employer X would credit the accounts of participants of Plan B with matching contributions based upon the same formula as set forth in Plan A. Unlike Plan A, however, contributions and matching contributions are not subject to the limitation of Code sections 402(g) or 415 or the limitations imposed by either the actual deferral percentage test or the actual contribution percentage test of sections 401(k) and 401(m) of the Code.

All deferrals, matching contributions and earning credits under Plan B are general assets of Employer X. Those credits may be maintained as a book account or by the allocation of assets to a Rabbi Trust established by Employer X.

Under Plan B the vesting schedule for contributions, other than those contributions made pursuant to an employee deferral election, is the same as the vesting schedule of Plan A.

Plan B requires that a participant make any election to defer on or before December 31 of the calendar year proceeding the year for which the compensation to which the salary deferral relates is earned. For a new participant, an election could be made within thirty days following a participant's initial selection for membership provided the election relates to compensation for services to be performed subsequent to the election to defer.

The terms of Plan B require eligible participants to indicate their respective deferrals by executing a salary reduction agreement. The salary reduction agreement required by the terms of Plan B, in turn, requires the participant to indicate whether he or she authorizes the distribution, in cash of the salary deferrals after the close of the plan year, or to have the salary deferrals transferred to Plan A. Plan B requires the participant's salary reduction agreement to be made on or before December 31 of the calendar year preceding the calendar year during which the compensation to which the salary deferral relates is earned, and, after this date, the salary reduction agreement becomes irrevocable. Plan B further provides that the amount subject to any election to make a contribution to Plan A will be equal to the lesser of:

1. the maximum amount of pre-tax deferrals that could be made to Plan A for the calendar year within the limits imposed under (A) Code section 402(g), (B) the actual deferral percentage test under section 401(k), and (C) the actual contribution percentage test under Code section 401(m); or
2. the amount of the base salary and bonuses such participant actually elects to defer under the terms of Plan B for the calendar year.

Plan B permits the transfer of pre-tax deferrals plus any related matching contribution (but without earnings, gains or losses allocable thereto) from Plan B to Plan A. The transfer must be completed before March 15 of the calendar year following the year in which the salary deferral was made. This transfer provision will enable Employer X to calculate for each participant of Plan B the maximum permitted contribution under Plan A under the limitations of sections 401(k), 401(m) and 402(g) of the Code.

It is represented that Plan A will be amended to provide that any amount transferred to Plan A by Plan B will consist only of amounts attributable to Plan B deferrals that the participant could have deferred directly to Plan A.

The determination of the amount of pre-tax deferrals transferred from Plan B to Plan A will be calculated pursuant to the provisions of Plan A and Plan B as reflected in the election form associated with both Plan A and Plan B. Plan B requires Employer X to contribute this amount to Plan A unless the participant has previously elected to have such amount distributed to himself in the form of cash. These provisions preclude employer discretion with respect to the amount of pre-tax deferrals transferred from Plan B to Plan A on behalf of any participant. The election form for Plan B also serves as the election form for Plan A.

With respect to the foregoing, the following rulings are requested:

1. Assuming that Plan A otherwise satisfies the requirements for a qualified cash or deferred arrangement and that the elective deferral and actual deferral percentage limitations of sections 402(g) and 401(k)(3) of the Code are not exceeded, elective deferrals made by participants under Plan A that are initially held by the Company pursuant to the terms of Plan B will be excluded from gross income under Code section 402(e)(3).
2. For purposes of satisfying section 402(g) of the Code, elective deferrals under Plan A made by participants for a given plan and calendar year that are initially held by the Company pursuant to the terms of Plan B will be treated as having been made in the calendar year in which they would have been otherwise received as wages by the participants.

Section 401(k)(2) of the Code provides, in pertinent part, that a qualified cash or deferred arrangement is any arrangement which is a part of a profit sharing or stock bonus plan, a pre-ERISA money purchase plan, or a rural cooperative plan which meets the requirements of section 401(a), and under which a covered employee may elect to have the employer make payments as contributions to a trust under the plan on behalf of the employee, or to the employee directly in cash.

Section 1.401(k)-1(a)(3)(i) of the Income Tax Regulations ("Regulations") provides that a cash or deferred election is any election (or modification of an earlier election) by an employee to have the employer either (A) provide an amount to the employee in the form of cash or some other taxable benefit that is not currently available, or (B) contribute an amount to a trust, or provide an accrual or other benefit, under a plan deferring the receipt of compensation. A cash or deferred election includes a salary reduction agreement between an employee and employer under which a contribution is made under a plan only if the employee elects to reduce cash compensation or to forgo an increase in cash compensation.

Under section 1.401(k)-1(a)(3)(ii) of the Regulations, a cash or deferred election can only be made with respect to an amount that is not currently available to the employee on the date of the election. Under section 1.401(k)-1(a)(3)(iii) of the Regulations, cash or another taxable amount is currently available to the employee if it has been paid to the employee or if the employee is able currently to receive the cash or other taxable amount at the employee's discretion.

Under section 1.401(k)-1(b)(4)(i) of the Regulations, an elective contribution is taken into account for purposes of the actual deferral percentage test for a plan year only if (A) the elective contribution is allocated to the employee's account under the plan as of a date within that plan year, and (B) the elective contribution relates to compensation that either (1) would have been received by the employee in the plan year but for the employee's election to defer under the arrangement, or (2) is attributable to services performed by the employee in the plan year and, but for the employee's election to defer, would have been received by the employee within two and one-half months after the close of the plan year. An elective contribution is considered allocated as of a date within the plan year only if (i) the allocation is not contingent upon the employee's participation in the plan or performance of services on any date subsequent to that date, and (ii) the elective contribution is actually paid to the trust no later than the end of the 12-month period immediately following the plan year to which the contribution relates.

Section 402(e)(3) of the Code provides, in pertinent part, that contributions made by an employer on behalf of an employee to a trust which is a part of a qualified cash or deferred arrangement (as defined in section 401(k)(2)) shall not be treated as distributed or made available to employee nor as contributions made to a trust by the employee merely because the arrangement includes provisions under which the employee has an election whether the contribution will be made to the trust or received by the employee in cash.

Under section 402(g)(1) of the Code, the elective deferrals of any individual for any taxable year are included in such individual's gross income to the extent the amount of such deferrals for the taxable year exceeds $7,000 (as adjusted under section 402(g)(5) of the Code), notwithstanding section 402(e)(3) of the Code regarding elective deferrals under a qualified cash or deferred arrangement.

With respect to ruling request one, participants may make an irrevocable election to defer compensation under Plan A and Plan B no later than December 31 of the calendar year preceding the year the compensation to which the salary deferral relates is earned. Plan B provides for the transfer of salary deferrals plus any related matching contributions from Plan B to Plan A. The amount to be transferred is determined in accordance with the provisions of Plan A and Plan B. Plan A requires Employer X to contribute such amount to Plan A. These provisions preclude employer discretion with respect to the amount of elective deferrals that will be transferred from Plan B to Plan A. The transfer must be completed on or before March 15 of the calendar year following the year for which the deferral was made under Plan B. If the participant's Plan B salary deferral is more than the salary deferral the participant authorized to be made to Plan A, the difference will be refunded to the participant. Any refund will be taxable income for the year with respect to which the deferral was made.

In addition, for purposes of the actual deferral percentage test under 401(k)(3) of the Code for a calendar year plan year, elective deferrals irrevocably and prospectively elected under Plan B made by the participant for a calendar year plan year that are initially held in the general assets of Employer X and then contributed to Plan A will be treated as having been made under Plan A in the calendar year in which the compensation to which the deferrals relate was earned by the participant, provided that the elective deferrals are allocated to the participant's account by the end of that calendar plan year and the elective deferrals continue to relate to compensation that either would have been received by the participant in the calendar year plan year but for the participant's election, or is attributable to services performed by the participant in the calendar year plan and would have been received by the Participant within $2\frac{1}{2}$ months after the calendar year plan year for participant's election. An election to make a contribution to Plan A is a cash or deferred election within the meaning of section 1.401(k)-1(a)(3)(i) of the Regulations because it is an election to have Employer X provide a benefit under a plan deferring compensation rather than providing an amount in cash to the employee.

Accordingly, we conclude that, assuming Plan A otherwise satisfies the requirements for a qualified cash or deferred arrangement and that the elective deferral and actual deferral percentage limitations of sections 402(g) and 401(k)(3) of the Code are not exceeded, elective deferrals made by the participants under Plan A that are initially held by Employer X pursuant to the terms of Plan B will be excluded from gross income under section 402(e)(3) of the Code when contributed to Plan A, provided such contribution is timely paid and allocated.

With respect to ruling request two, the participant will make an irrevocable election to have his maximum permissible contribution to Plan A transferred from Plan B to Plan A. If the amount permitted to be transferred from Plan B exceeds the permissible contribution that the participant authorized to be contributed to Plan A, then the excess amount will be distributed to the participant. The amount distributed will be taxable income in the year it was earned, rather than the year it was actually distributed. If the maximum permissible deferral under Plan A is contributed to Plan A, it would be subject to the 402(g) limitation applicable to the year when it was earned rather the year in which it was contributed to Plan A.

Accordingly, with respect to ruling request two, we conclude that for purposes of satisfying the limitations of section 402(g) of the Code, contributions made to Plan A by Employer X on behalf of the participants (assuming that such contributions are timely made and timely allocated to participant's account under Plan A), which are initially held by Employer X pursuant to the terms of Plan B, will be treated as deferrals under Plan A having been made in the year in which they would have been taxable to the participant but for the election under Plan B to have such salary contributed to Plan A.

The above rulings are based on the assumption that at all times relevant to these rulings, Plan A is qualified under section 401(a) of the Code, and its cash or deferred arrangement is qualified under section 401(k)(2) of the Code and that the required amendments as proposed by the taxpayer's authorized representative in his above mentioned correspondence are made to the respective Plans. Employer X established Plan A by adopting a nonstandardized prototype plan. Amending Plan A to provide for the transfer of elective deferrals from Plan B may affect the prototype status of Plan A. No opinion is expressed as to the prototype status of Plan A.

Title I of Employee Retirement Income Security Act of 1974 (ERISA) is within the jurisdiction of the Department of Labor. Accordingly, we express no opinion as to whether the subject transactions comply with Title I of ERISA. Finally, no opinion is expressed as to the income tax consequences of establishing Plan B and participating in it except as expressly stated herein.

This ruling is directed only to the taxpayer that requested it and applied only with respect to Plan A as submitted with this request. Section 6110(k)(3) of the Code provides that this private letter ruling may not be used or cited as precedent.

Letter Ruling 9541041 Dated: July 21, 1995

[Summary: The IRS ruled that an employer that joined with other employers to form a new corporation was never under the common control of the new employer, and therefore their plans need not be aggregated. Six different corporations merged to form a new corporation, and the new corporation established a profit-sharing plan. One of the predecessor corporations had a defined benefit plan and a defined contribution plan. The predecessor corporation froze the benefits in the defined benefit plan and began to terminate the plan and distribute the assets a month before the new corporation came into being. In ruling that the plans need not be aggregated, the IRS reasoned that aggregation presupposes the employers are related by virtue of affiliation or common control, neither of which is possible if one of the employers no longer exists. The combined plan limit under Code section 415(e) was repeated for limitation years beginning after 1999.]

This is in response to your request for a ruling dated January 3, 1995, and supplemented by additional correspondence dated March 29, 1995, and May 4, 1995, submitted on your behalf by your authorized representative. Your authorized representative submitted the following facts and representations in support of the ruling request.

Employer B is a professional corporation engaged in the practice of medicine in Delaware. Employer B was formed by six physicians on December 31, 1993, from the merger of each physician's unrelated professional corporation. Before the merger each physician was the sole shareholder of his own corporation. After the merger, each of the six physicians owns one sixth of the stock of Employer B.

Paragraph 2(a) of the Employer B Plan and Agreement of Merger provides that the professional corporations shall be merged in Employer B, which shall be the surviving corporation. Paragraph 2(c) provides, in part, that the separate existence of each of the professional corporations shall cease upon proper execution of the Plan and Agreement of Merger.

Effective December 31, 1993, Employer B adopted Plan X, a profit-sharing plan that does not have a cash or deferred arrangement (CODA) or permit voluntary employee contributions. Plan X received a favorable determination letter dated November 9, 1994.

The Predecessor Employer was one of the six unrelated professional corporations. Individual A was the sole shareholder of the Predecessor Employer. The Predecessor Employer maintained both a defined benefit plan, Plan Y, and a defined contribution plan, Plan Z. Plan Z was terminated and assets were distributed prior to December 31, 1993.

Effective November 30, 1993, the Predecessor Employer froze benefits under Plan Y and began to terminate Plan Y and distribute assets to the participants. Plan Y has not received a TRA '86 determination letter. At the time of this ruling, no application has been filed with the Key District Office for a determination letter upon termination of Plan Y. No contributions have been made by Employer B to Plan Y with respect to compensation earned prior to the merger.

You, Employer B, request the following rulings:

1. that the Predecessor Employer and Employer B are not members of a controlled group of corporations or other entities nor members of an affiliated service group for purposes of section 414(b), (c), and (m) of the Internal Revenue Code; and
2. that, for purposes of section 415(e) of the Code, the Predecessor Employer and Employer B are not the same employer, and that Plan X is not required to be aggregated with Plan Y for purposes of section 415.

Section 415 of the Code provides limitations on contributions and benefits under a qualified plan. Section 415(e) of the Code provides that in any case in which an individual is a participant in both a defined benefit plan and a defined contribution plan maintained by the same employer, the sum of the defined benefit plan fraction and the defined contribution plan fraction for any year may not exceed 1.0.

Section 1.415-8(a) of the Income Tax Regulations provides that for purposes of applying the limitations of section 415(b), (c) and (e) of the Code applicable to a participant for a particular limitation year (1) all qualified defined benefit plans (without regard to whether a plan has been terminated) ever maintained by the employer will be treated as one defined benefit plan, and (2) all qualified defined contribution plans (without regard to whether a plan has been terminated) ever maintained by the employer will be treated as one defined contribution plan.

Section 1.415-8(c) of the Regulations provides that any qualified defined benefit plan or qualified defined contribution plan maintained by any member of a controlled group of corporations (within the meaning of section 414(b) as modified by section 414(h)) or by any trade or business (whether or not incorporated) under common control (within the meaning of section 414(c) as modified by section 415(h)) is deemed maintained by all such members or such trades or businesses.

Section 414(b), (c), and (m) of the Code and the Regulations thereunder apply when determining whether Employer B and the Predecessor Employer are or have been members of a controlled group of corporations, trades or businesses under common control, or members of an affiliated service group for purposes of section 415.

Section 414(b) of the Code provides, in part, that for purposes of sections 401, 408(k), 410, 411, 415, and 416, all employees of all corporations which are members of a controlled group of corporations (within the meaning of section 1563(a), determined without regard to sections 1563(a)(4) and 1563(e)(3)(C)) shall be treated as employed by a single employer.

Section 415(h) of the Code provides that, for purposes of applying section 414(b) and 414(c) to section 415, the phrase "more than 50 percent" shall be substituted for the phrase "at least 80 percent" each place it appears in section 1563(a)(1).

Section 1563(a)(1) of the Code provides that a parent-subsidiary controlled group is one or more chains of corporations connected through stock ownership with a common parent corporation if (A) stock possessing at least 80 percent of the total combined voting power of all classes of stock entitled to vote or at least 80 percent of the total value of shares of all classes of stock of each of the corporations, except the common parent corporation, is owned (within the meaning of subsection (d)(1)) by one or more of the other corporations; and (B) the common parent corporation owns (within the meaning of subsection (d)(1)) stock possessing at least 80 percent of the total combined voting power of all classes of stock entitled to vote or at least 80 percent of the total value of shares of all classes of stock of at least one of the other corporations, excluding, in computing such voting power or value, stock owned directly by such other corporations.

Section 414(c) of the Code provides that, for purposes of sections 401, 408(k), 410, 411, 415, and 416, under regulations prescribed by the Secretary, all employees of trades or businesses (whether or not incorporated) which are under common control shall be treated as employed by a single employer. The regulations prescribed under this subsection shall be based on principles similar to the principles that apply in the case of subsection (b).

Section 1.414(c)-2(a) of the Regulations provides, in general, that for purposes of this section, the term "two or more trades or businesses under common control" means any group of trades or businesses which is either a "parent-subsidiary group of trades or businesses under common control" as defined in paragraph (b) of this section, a "brother-sister group of trades or businesses under common control" as defined in paragraph (c) of this section, or a "combined group of trades or businesses under common control" as defined in paragraph (d) of this section. For purposes of this section and sections 1.414(c)-3 and 1.414(c)-4, the term "organization" means a sole proprietorship, a partnership (as defined in section 7701(a)(2)), a trust, an estate, or a corporation.

Section 1.414(c)-2(b) of the Regulations defines a parent-subsidiary group of trades or businesses under common control as one or more chains of organizations conducting trades or businesses connected through ownership of a controlling interest with a common parent organization if (1) a controlling interest in each of the organizations, except the common parent organization, is owned (directly and with the application of section 1.414(c)-4(b)(1), relating to options) by one or more of the other organizations; and (2) the common parent organization owns (directly and with the application of section 1.414(c)-4(b)(1), relating to options) a controlling interest in at least one of the other organizations, excluding, in computing such controlling interest, any direct ownership interest by such other organizations.

Section 1.414(c)-2(b)(2)(i) of the Regulations defines "controlling interest" as (1) in the case of an organization which is a corporation, ownership of stock possessing at least 80 percent of the total combined voting power of all classes of stock entitled to vote of such corporation or at least 80 percent of the total value of shares of all classes of stock of such corporation; (2) in the case of an organization which is a trust or estate, ownership of an actuarial interest of at least 80 percent of such trust or estate; (3) in the case of an organization which is a partnership, ownership of at least 80 percent of the profits interest or capital interest of such partnership; and (4) in the case of an organization which is a sole proprietorship, ownership of such sole proprietorship.

Section 414(m) of the Code provides that, for purposes of section 415, the term "affiliated service group" means a group consisting of a service organization and one or more other organizations described therein. Section 1.414(m)-1 of the Regulations provides for rules with respect to affiliated service groups.

Based on the facts as represented, Employer B and the Predecessor Employer were never under common control for purposes of sections 414(b), (c), and (m) of the Code. Under the terms of the Employer B Plan and Agreement of Merger, the Predecessor Employer ceased to exist upon its merger with the five unrelated professional corporations which merged to form Employer B. Employer B came into existence upon the merger. The operation of sections 414(b), (c), and (m) and the regulations thereunder necessarily require that controlled group members exist concurrently. Accordingly, with respect to the first ruling, we conclude that the Predecessor Employer and Employer B are not members of a controlled group of corporations or other entities nor members of an affiliated service group for purposes of sections 414(b), (c), and (m).

In order to determine whether plans of separate entities are to be aggregated for purposes of section 415(e) of the Code, it is necessary to determine whether or not the entities were under common control for any period of time during which they were in existence concurrently. We determined in the first ruling that the Predecessor Employer and Employer B are not members of a controlled group of corporations or other entities nor members of an affiliated service group for purposes of sections 414(b), (c), and (m). Accordingly, with respect to the second ruling, we conclude that Plan X and Plan Y do not need to be aggregated for purposes of section 415(e).

This ruling is based on the assumption that Plan X is qualified under section 401(a) of the Code. We express no opinion as to the qualified status of Plan Y.

In accordance with a power of attorney on file in this office, a copy of this ruling is being sent to your authorized representative.

Letter Ruling 9530038 Dated: May 5, 1995

[Summary: The IRS has ruled that elective deferrals, made by a highly compensated employee under a qualified profit-sharing plan and initially held by the employer under the terms of a nonqualified deferred compensation plan, will be excluded from the employee's gross income under Code section 402(e)(3).]

This is in response to your ruling request, dated June 16, 1992, amended by letters dated October 1, November 9, and December 11, 1992, and February 3, March 17, and July 21, 1994, submitted on your behalf as Employee Z, by your authorized representative, concerning certain matters relating to the tax treatment of elective deferrals proposed to be made under Plan A. The following facts and representations were submitted in support of the rulings requested.

Employee Z is a highly compensated employee employed by Employer X. Employer X maintains Plan A and proposes to implement Plan B. Plan A is a qualified profit-sharing plan under section 401(a) of the Internal Revenue Code (the "Code"), which Employer X represents contains a qualified cash-or-deferred arrangement as described in Code section 401(k). Plan B provides that it is intended to be an unfunded nonqualified deferred compensation plan. Deferrals under Plan B are held as part of the general assets of Employer X. The terms of the arrangement provide that assets are subject to the claims of Employer X's general creditors. Employer X intends to implement Plan B upon receipt of this ruling although rulings on Plan B have not been requested or provided.

Employee Z is a participant who is eligible to make pretax elective deferrals under Plan A, subject to the annual dollar limitation of Code section 402(g) and the actual deferral percentage limitation of Code section 401(k)(3). Employer X will also make matching contributions to Plan A with respect to Employee Z's elective deferrals up to the lesser of 100 percent of the participant's elective deferrals or three (3) percent of the participant's annual earnings. Plan A operates with a calendar year plan year.

Employer X represents that Employee Z is a member of the select group of management or highly compensated employees and will be eligible to participate in Plan B. Prior to each January 1 or to the implementation of Plan B, Employee Z may elect to enter into a salary reduction agreement with Employer X, no later than December 31 of the calendar year preceding the year in which the compensation to which the salary deferral election relates is earned. Pursuant to the election, Employee Z will specify the percentage of his compensation otherwise payable to Employee Z for the ensuing calendar year that will be deferred under Plan B. Employer X will also make matching credits to Plan B with respect to Employee Z's salary deferrals up to the lesser of 100 percent of such salary deferrals or three (3) percent of Employee Z's annual earnings. Plan B provides that amounts deferred by Employee Z remain an asset of Employer X and available to Employer X's general creditors.

As soon as practicable each plan year (i.e., calendar year) of Plan A, and not later than January 31 of the next ensuing year, Employer X will perform preliminary actual deferral percentage and actual contribution percentage testing to determine the maximum amount of additional elective contributions that could be made for such current plan year, consistent with section 402(g) and the limitations of section 401(k)(3), on behalf of Employee Z as a participant in Plan A. The lesser of those amounts, or Employee Z's salary deferral under Plan B for that year, will be paid to Employee Z as soon as practicable, but in no event later than March 15 of the plan year following the plan year for which such determination is made, unless Employee Z previously elected to have such amount contributed to Plan A as an elective contribution. Employee Z's election to have such amount contributed to Plan A must be made at the same time as Employee Z's election to enter into a salary reduction agreement with Employer X under Plan B which must be no later than December 31 of the calendar year preceding the year in which the compensation to which the salary deferral relates is earned and, once made, the election is irrevocable. If Employee Z so elects, Employer X shall cause that amount to be contributed directly to Plan A.

Amounts paid to Employee Z, because Employee Z does not elect to have such amounts contributed to Plan A as an elective contribution, will be includible in Employee Z's gross income in the year in which the compensation to which the salary deferral under Plan B relates was earned, and Employer X will include this amount in Employee Z's W-2 compensation for that year.

In addition, to the extent that Employer X is required to make matching contributions under Plan A with respect to such elective contributions, Employer X will make such contributions out of matching amounts previously credited under Plan B. All such Plan A contributions will be debited under Plan B.

No earnings credited under Plan B will be contributed to Plan A. Thus, the elective deferrals under Plan A that result from salary deferred under Plan B will consist solely of amounts that were otherwise payable to Employee Z as current compensation for the plan year involved and for which deferral elections have been made. Any matching contributions associated with such elective contributions shall be in the same amounts as would be made if the elective deferrals were directly made, subject to the actual contribution percentage test of Code section 401(m).

All elective deferrals and matching contributions under Plan A will be treated similarly. Employee Z will be fully vested in his elective deferrals and will not be entitled to a distribution thereof except upon separation from service, attainment of age 59½, death, disability or hardship.

With respect to the foregoing, the following rulings are requested:

1. Assuming that Plan A otherwise satisfies the requirements for a qualified cash or deferred arrangement and that the elective deferral and actual deferral percentage limitations of Code Sections 402(g) and 401(k)(3) are not exceeded, elective deferrals made by Employee Z under Plan A that are initially held by Employer X pursuant to the terms of Plan B will be excluded from gross income under Code section 402(e)(3).
2. For purposes of satisfying the section 402(g) limit, elective deferrals under Plan A made by Employee Z for a given plan and calendar year that are initially held by Employer X pursuant to the terms of Plan B will be treated

as having been made in the calendar year in which they would have been otherwise received as wages by Employee Z.

Code section 402(e)(3) provides, in pertinent part, that contributions made by an employer on behalf of an employee to a trust which is a part of a qualified cash or deferred arrangement (as defined in section 401(k)(2)) shall not be treated as distributed or made available to the employee nor as contributions made to a trust by the employee merely because the arrangement includes provisions under which the employee has an election whether the contribution will be made to the trust or received by the employee in cash.

Code section 401(k)(2) provides, in pertinent part, that a qualified cash or deferred arrangement is any arrangement which is part of a profit-sharing or stock bonus plan, a pre-ERISA money purchase plan, or a rural cooperative plan which meets the requirements of section 401(a), and under which a covered employee may elect to have the employer make payments as contributions to a trust under the plan on behalf of the employee, or to the employee directly in cash.

Section 1.401(k)-1(a)(3)(i) of the Income Tax Regulations provides that a cash or deferred election is any election (or modification of an earlier election) by an employee to have the employer either (A) provide an amount to the employee in the form of cash or some other taxable benefit that is not currently available, or (B) contribute an amount to a trust, or provide an accrual or other benefit, under a plan deferring the receipt of compensation. A cash or deferred election includes a salary reduction agreement between an employee and employer under which a contribution is made under a plan only if the employee elects to reduce cash compensation or to forgo an increase in cash compensation.

Under section 1.401(k)-1(a)(3)(ii) of the regulations, a cash or deferred election can only be made with respect to an amount that is not currently available to the employee on the date of the election. Under section 1.401(k)-1(a)(3)(iii) of the regulations, cash or another taxable amount is currently available to the employee if it has been paid to the employee or if the employee is able currently to receive the cash or other taxable amount at the employee's discretion.

Under section 1.401(k)-1(b)(4)(i) of the regulations, an elective contribution is taken into account for purposes of the actual deferral percentage test for a plan year only if (A) the elective contribution is allocated to the employee's account under the plan as of a date within that plan year, and (B) the elective contribution relates to compensation that either (1) would have been received by the employee in the plan year but for the employee's election to defer under the arrangement, or (2) is attributable to services performed by the employee in the plan year and, but for the employee's election to defer, would have been received by the employee within two and one-half months after the close of the plan year. An elective contribution is considered allocated as of a date within the plan year only if (i) the allocation is not contingent upon the employee's participation in the plan or performance of services on any date subsequent to that date, and (ii) the elective contribution is actually paid to the trust no later than the end of the 12-month period immediately following the plan year to which the contribution relates.

Under Code section 402(g)(1), the elective deferrals of any individual for any taxable year are included in such individual's gross income to the extent the amount of such deferrals for the taxable year exceeds $7,000 (as adjusted under Code section 402(g)(5)), notwithstanding Code section 402(e)(3) regarding elective deferrals under a qualified cash or deferred arrangement.

With respect to issue one, Employee Z may make an irrevocable election to defer compensation under Plan A no later than December 31 of the calendar year preceding the year the compensation to which the salary deferral relates is earned. The amount subject to such election will be equal to the lesser of (i) the maximum amount of elective contributions that could be made for the current plan year on behalf of Employee Z under the actual deferral percentage and actual contribution percentage tests, and subject to the limitation on elective deferrals under Code section 402(g), or (ii) Employee Z's salary deferral amount under Plan B for that current year. Such amount will be distributed in cash to Employee Z as soon as practicable, but in no event later than March 15 of the year following the plan year with respect to which such determination is made, unless Employee Z has previously elected to have such amount contributed to Plan A as an elective contribution. If Employee Z so elects, Employer X shall cause that amount to be contributed directly to Plan A. Any amount distributed to Employee Z shall be includable in Employee Z's gross income in the year in which the compensation to which the salary deferral under Plan B relates was earned.

Accordingly, we conclude that, assuming Plan A otherwise satisfies the requirements for a qualified cash or deferred arrangement and that the elective deferral and actual deferral percentage limitations of Code sections 402(g) and 401(k)(3) are not exceeded, elective deferrals made by Employee Z under Plan A that are initially held by Employer X pursuant to the terms of Plan B will be excluded from gross income under Code section 402(e)(3).

However, no opinion is expressed as to the income tax consequences to Employee Z resulting from the establishment of and participation in Plan B, except as expressly stated herein.

With respect to issue two, we also conclude that, for purposes of satisfying the Code section 402(g) limit, elective deferrals under Plan A made by Employee Z for a given plan and calendar year that are initially held by Employer X pursuant to the terms of Plan B will be treated as having been made in the calendar year in which they would have been otherwise received as wages by Employee Z, provided that elective deferrals are allocated to Employee Z's account by the end of that current plan year and the elective deferrals continue to relate to compensation that either would have been received by Employee Z in the plan year but for his election, or is attributable to services performed by Employee Z in the plan year and would have been received by Employee Z within $2\frac{1}{2}$ months after the plan year but for his election. This conclusion is consistent with the treatment of elective deferrals under section 1.401(k)-1(b)(4)(i) of the regulations for purposes of the actual deferral percentage test under Code section 401(k)(3).

The above rulings are based on the assumption that at all times relevant to these rulings, Plan A is qualified under section 401(a) of the Code, its related trust is tax-exempt under Code section 501(a), and its cash or deferred arrangement is qualified under Code section 401(k)(2).

This ruling is directed only to the taxpayer that requested it and applies only with respect to Plan A, as amended. If the Plan is amended, this ruling may not remain in effect. Section 6110(j)(3) of the Code provides that this private letter ruling may not be used or cited as precedent. Title I of the Employee Retirement Income Security Act of 1974 (ERISA) is within the jurisdiction of the Department of Labor. Accordingly, we express no opinion as to whether the subject transactions comply with Title I of ERISA.

Letter Ruling 9124036 Dated: March 19, 1991

[Summary: The IRS has revoked Ruling Request 1 of LTR 8940013, regarding whether an employer's payments to the trustees of a qualified plan to reimburse the trustees for investment managers' fees incurred in connection with the investment of the assets of the plan are deductible under Code Sections 162 or 212 and, therefore, not contributions to the plan for purposes of Code Sections 404 and 415.]

In a letter dated June 30, 1989, the Internal Revenue Service ruled in Private Letter Ruling 8940013 upon whether an employer's payments to the trustees of a qualified plan to reimburse the trustees for investment managers' fees incurred in connection with the investment of the assets of the plan are deductible under sections 162 or 212 of the Internal Revenue Code and are not deemed to be contributions to the plan for purposes of sections 404 or 415 of the code. In a telephone conversation with a representative of this office on February 6, 1990, your authorized representative indicated that you have not relied upon this ruling, which is Ruling Request 1 of PLR 8940013, since you have not made payments to reimburse the trustees for any investment managers' fees incurred in connection with the investment of the assets of the qualified plan. As a result, your authorized representative indicated that you would waive your right to a conference on the substantive issues involved in this revocation as made available under sections 11.04, 11.05, and 11.06 of Revenue Procedure 91-4, 1991-4 I.R.B. 20. We now believe that the first ruling issued in PLR 8940013 is not in accord with the proper interpretation of the Code and, therefore, we are revoking that ruling, Ruling Request 1 of your private letter ruling, pursuant to section 12.04 of Rev. Proc. 91-4. Thus, you may no longer rely on Ruling Request 1 of PLR 8940013.

Letter Ruling 8941010 Dated: June 30, 1989

[Summary: An employer maintains a plan for its employees. It makes the maximum deductible contribution to the plan each year. Under the terms of the plan's related trust, the employer has the authority to direct the segregation of funds into separate investment accounts and to direct the investment and reinvestment of the assets in those accounts. Accounts have been established with several brokerage firms for investment of plan assets.

In addition to commission costs, the fees charged by the brokerage firms include fees for development of investment policy statements, design of investment packages, provision of data, presentations to participants, provision of transaction analysis, cooperation with an accounting firm, periodic meetings with trustees, custodial fees, and service as broker of record and executor of transactions. These services are recurring and are separate from the cost of assets. If the aggregate value of the plan assets for a period is the same, the broker's fees for the foregoing services are the same, regardless of the number of transactions during the period. The plan provides that the employer may pay all expenses of administering the plan, including trustees' fees, attorney's fees, and expenses incurred by those to whom fiduciary duties have been delegated. All administrative fees are to be charged against the trust funds to the extent that they are not paid directly or reimbursed by the employer.

The trustees hired investment managers, who are paid a fee for managing the plan assets. The employer reimburses the trust for the management fees out of trust assets or pays the fees directly. For administrative convenience, the trustees of the trust entered into a wrap fee arrangement under which one all-inclusive fee is charged for the services rendered by the brokerage firm and the investment managers. Quarterly invoices are rendered to the plan.]

The IRS ruled that the employer's payments to the trustees of the plan to reimburse the trustees for the wrap fees are deductible under Code Sections 162 or 212 and are not deemed contributions to the plan under Code Sections 404 or 415, relying on Revenue Ruling 84-146 (1984-2 C.B. 61) and Revenue Ruling 86-142 (1986-2 C.B. 61), to rule on the two parts of the wrap fee.

The IRS also ruled that the employer's direct payments to the brokerage firms for the fees earned by the investment managers and for the fees for the accounting firm's services are deductible under Code Sections 162 or 212 and are not deemed contributions to the plan under Code Sections 404 and 415.

This is in response to your request for private letter rulings dated * * *, as submitted by your authorized representative, regarding the income tax consequences under the Internal Revenue Code of your payment of a fee for the management and investment of assets of Plan X.

Employer M maintains Plan X for its employees. The plan is qualified under section 401(a) of the Code and the related trust is exempt from tax under section 501(a) of the Code. The plan year of Plan X and the taxable year of Employer M is the fiscal year ending September 30. Employer M makes the maximum deductible contribution to Plan X under section 404 of the Code during the plan year.

Under section 10.01 of Trust Y, Employer M has the authority to direct the segregation of the funds contained in Trust Y into separate investment accounts and to appoint an investment manager to direct the investment and re-investment of the assets in those accounts. Accounts with certain brokerage firms have been established for the purpose of investing the Plan X assets. The brokerage firm will track the share traded volume each quarter for each account, and that number, when compared with institutional trading costs, will provide a factor that represents the approximate percentage of the brokerage firms' fees attributable to pure broker's commissions.

In addition to commission costs, the fees charged by the brokerage firm are generated by services rendered on behalf of Plan X which include:

1. assisting in the development of investment policy statements;
2. assisting in the specific design of investment packages;
3. providing the data necessary to make Investment Manager selection decisions;
4. making presentations to participants outlining and explaining their investment alternatives;
5. providing transaction analysis, portfolio income summaries, asset statements, and performance analysis;
6. working with the accounting firm to ensure that all participants are informed;
7. holding periodic meetings with trustees;
8. serving as custodian; and
9. serving as broker of record and executing all securities and other transactions.

These services are recurring and are separate and apart from the cost of assets purchased or sold. Except for the portion of the broker's fee directly attributable to broker's commissions, the broker's fee for services unrelated to sales rendered to the plan is incurred without regard to the number of securities transactions in a given period. Assuming that the aggregate value of plan assets for a period is the same, the broker's fees for rendering the foregoing services will be the same, regardless of the number of transactions during the period.

Section 3.02 of Trust Y provides that its trustees may employ counsel, accountants and other agents as the Trustees deem advisable. Section 3.02 of Trust Y also provides that all expenses incurred by its trustees in the administration of the Trust Y funds, including, but not limited to, the compensation of counsel, accountants, investment managers, brokers, the trustees, other agents, or fiduciaries are to be charged against the Trust Y funds to the extent that they are not paid directly by or reimbursed by Employer M. Under section 15.01(c)(1)(vi) of Plan X and section 7.01(c)(1)(vi) of Trust Y, Employer M has the authority and responsibility for the appointment of an investment manager.

The trustees of Plan X have hired certain investment managers to manage and invest the assets of Plan X contained in the brokerage accounts. The investment managers provide analysis, research and judgment with respect to selection of investments, and make investment decisions and instruct the brokers on behalf of Plan X and the trustees of Trust Y.

The investment managers are paid a fee for managing the assets of the plan based on a percentage of the assets of Plan X. Employer M reimburses the trust for the management fees paid out of the trust assets, or pays the fees directly. The brokerage firms specify the percentage of the fees which represent broker's commissions.

Employer M requests rulings regarding the income tax consequences of the fees paid to the investment managers, and the fees paid to the brokerage firms, not including broker's commissions, in connection with maintaining Plan X, specifically:

1. Whether Employer M's payments to the trustees of Plan X to reimburse the trustees for the investment managers' fees and the brokerage firms' fees incurred in connection with the investment of the assets of Plan X are deductible under sections 162 or 212 and are not deemed to be contributions to Plan X for purposes of sections 404 and 415 of the Code.
2. Whether Employer M's payments directly to the investment managers and the brokerage firms for fees earned in connection with the investment and management of the assets of Plan X are deductible by Employer M and are not deemed to be contributions to Plan X for purposes of sections 404 and 415 of the Code.

Section 1.404(a)-3(d) of the Income Tax Regulations provides that, in the case of a plan which meets the requirements of section 401(a) of the Code, expenses incurred by the employer in connection with the plan, such as trustees' and actuaries' fees, which are not provided for by contributions under the plan are deductible by the employer under section 162 (relating to trade or business expenses), or 212 (relating to expenses for production of income) to the extent that they are ordinary and necessary.

Rev. Rul. 68-533, 1968-2 C.B. 190, holds that section 1.404(a)-3(d) of the regulations applies to all qualified employees' plans, including those covering self-employed individuals. Trustee's fees paid by a sole proprietor are deductible by the sole proprietor to the extent they are ordinary and necessary.

Section 403(a) of the Employee Retirement Income Security Act of 1974 (ERISA) describes the functions of a trustee as holding all assets of an employee benefit plan in trust, and having exclusive authority and discretion to manage and control assets of the plan. In other words, ERISA recognizes that the trustee has both custodial and investment management functions. A trustee's authority to manage, acquire or dispose of plan assets can be delegated to an investment manager.

Rev. Rul. 84-146, 1984-2 C.B. 61, provides that, consistent with the rules governing deductions in connection with qualified plans, trustee's fees which are separately billed to and paid by an individual who maintains an individual retirement arrangement (IRA) are deductible under section 212 of the Code to the extent the requirements of section 212 of the Code are satisfied.

Concerning the payments to the investment managers in connection with the investment and management of the assets of Plan X contained in the brokerage accounts, these payments reflect a fee charged, on a flat percentage basis, for analysis, research and judgment with respect to selection of investments, and investment decisions and instructions to the brokers made on behalf of Plan X and the trustees of Trust Y. These fees are recurring charges to Plan X, and are unaffected by the number or volume of securities sold. As such, the fees paid for performance of the investment managers' functions are part of the traditional fees charged by trustees.

Accordingly, with respect to the payments to investment managers to manage and invest the assets of Plan X contained in the brokerage accounts, we conclude, with respect to your first ruling request, that Employer M's payments to the trustees of Plan X to reimburse the trustees for such payments incurred are deductible under sections 162 or 212 of the Code and are not deemed to be contributions to Plan X for purposes of sections 404 and 415 of the Code. With respect to your second ruling request, Employer M's payments directly to the investment managers for such fees earned, are deductible under sections 162 or 212 of the Code and are not deemed to be contributions to Plan X for purposes of sections 404 and 415 of the Code.

Rev. Rul. 86-142, 1986-2 C.B. 61, considered the deductibility of broker's commissions charged in connection with the purchase and sale of securities for a qualified employees' trust or an IRA. It notes that broker's fees are not recurring administrative or overhead expenses incurred in connection with the maintenance of the trust or IRA. Rather, brokers' commissions are intrinsic to the value of the trust's or account's assets; buying commissions are part of the cost of securities purchased and selling commissions are an offset against the sales price. Based on this analysis, Rev. Rul. 86-142 held that employer contributions to the trust of a qualified plan, or direct payments by the employer to a broker, to pay brokers' commissions cannot be separately deducted as ordinary and necessary expenses under section 162 or 212 of the Code.

There exist two elements of the payments made to the brokerage firm: the brokerage commissions themselves; and the object of this ruling request, the fees charged by the brokerage firm generated by services rendered on behalf of Plan X. The fee paid for such services rendered is based on a percentage of Plan X's assets and is incurred without regard to the number of securities transactions in a given period. The brokerage firms specify the percentage of the fees which represent broker's commissions.

Because the services rendered by the brokerage firm on behalf of Plan X are analogous to the investment managers' fees we examined above, we find that the fees paid for performance of such functions also are part of the traditional fees charged by trustees. Accordingly, with respect to the portion of the fees paid to the brokerage firm generated by services rendered on behalf of Plan X, not including broker's commissions, we conclude, with respect to your first ruling request, that Employer M's payments to the trustees of Plan X to reimburse the trustees for such portion of the brokerage fees incurred are deductible under sections 162 or 212 of the Code and are not deemed to be contributions to Plan X for purposes of sections 404 or 415 of the Code. Likewise, with respect to your second ruling request, we conclude that Employer M's payments directly to the brokerage firms for services rendered by the firms, are deductible under sections 162 or 212 of the Code and are not deemed to be contributions to Plan X for purposes of sections 404 and 415 of the Code.

The above ruling is based on the assumption that Plan X is qualified under section 401(a) of the Code and its related trusts are exempt from tax under section 501(a) of the Code at all times relevant to this ruling request.

A copy of this ruling is being sent to your authorized representative pursuant to a power of attorney on file in this office.

Letter Ruling 8824019 Dated: March 17, 1988

[Summary: A tax-exempt organization entered into a collective bargaining agreement on July 1, 1984. Under the agreement, the company agreed to contribute amounts into supplemental pension plans for covered employees. Each plan was to be an "individual account-type plan." In 1987, the company adopted a simplified employee pension-individual retirement accounts contribution agreement (SEP-IRA agreement). The agreement was designed to provide the type of plan provided for in the collective bargaining agreement. The SEP-IRA agreement was adopted using the IRS Form 5305-SEP. IRAs were established for the employees with another company, which accepted the employer contributions that were set aside under the agreement. Company contributions to the IRAs are determined at a stated rate per hour, regardless of compensation level. The employees are salaried and are not compensated for overtime. All the employees are credited with 80 hours every 2-week period.]

The IRS has ruled that the contribution formula of the SEP-IRA agreement will be considered uniform and is not in and of itself discriminatory under section 408(k)(3).

This is in response to a ruling request dated December 2, 1987, and a letter amending and updating this request dated January 27, 1988, which were submitted by your authorized representative on your behalf. Your request concerns whether a contribution formula based upon hours worked meets the Simplified Employee Pension (SEP) antidiscrimination requirements of Internal Revenue Code section 408(k)(3).

Your representative submitted the following facts on your behalf:

Company M, a tax exempt organization, entered into a collective bargaining agreement on July 1, 1984. In a revised addendum to this collective bargaining agreement, dated March 13, 1985, Company M agreed to contribute certain amounts for each covered employee into a supplemental pension plan which was to be "an individual account type plan."

On April 1, 1987, Company M adopted a Simplified Employee Pension-Individual Retirement Accounts Contribution Agreement (SEP-IRA Agreement), effective as of December 31, 1986. This SEP-IRA Agreement was designed to provide the individual account type plan provided for in the addendum to the collective bargaining agreement. Further, this SEP-IRA Agreement was adopted using IRS Form 5305-SEP, which you propose to modify in certain respects.

Individual retirement accounts (IRAs) for the employee-participants were established with Company N, which accepted the employer contributions which had been set aside for each employee pursuant to the addendum of the collective bargaining agreement. Pursuant to the SEP-IRA Agreement, SEP contributions by Company M to the IRAs are determined at a stated amount (in cents) for each hour worked by an employee-participant, regardless of the employee's compensation level. The employees of Company M are compensated with a salary and are not compensated for overtime. Further, they are credited with 80 hours of service for each 2-week payroll period, nothing more and nothing less, and it is this number of hours which is used to determine the SEP contributions.

Based on these facts your authorized representative requests a ruling that the contribution formula set-out in the SEP-IRA Agreement satisfies the requirements of Code section 408(k)(3). Section 408(k)(3)(A) of the Code provides that the requirements of this section are met with respect to a SEP for a calendar year if for such year the contributions made by the employer to the SEP for his employees do not discriminate in favor of any highly compensated employee.

Code section 408(k)(3)(C) provides, in relevant part, that employer contributions to SEPs shall be considered discriminatory unless contributions thereto bear a uniform relationship to the total compensation (not in excess of the first $200,000) of each employee maintaining a SEP.

Proposed Income Tax Regulation section 1.408-8(c)(1) provides, in part, that a rate of contribution which decreases as compensation increases shall be considered uniform.

In this case the maximum percentage of compensation contributed on behalf of a member of the highly compensated employee group will not exceed the percentage of compensation contributed on behalf of any participant who is not a highly compensated employee. In fact, since each employee is credited with 80 hours of service for each two week payroll period and the amount of contribution remains constant despite increases in compensation, the rate of contribution is viewed as decreasing.

Accordingly, we conclude that the contribution formula of the SEP-IRA Agreement shall be considered uniform and is not in and of itself discriminatory, within the meaning of section 408(k)(3) of the Code.

This is not a determination as to the actual operation of this contribution formula contained in the plan, but only a determination as to whether Company M's plan in form retains its SEP status when it contains this contribution formula.

Appendix J

Department of Labor Letters

DOL Adv. Opinion 2006-09A—Code Section 4975(c)(1)(A) & (B)

U.S. Department of Labor
Frances Perkins Building
200 Constitution Avenue, NW
Washington, D.C. 20210

December 19, 2006

Edward A. Appelt
24 Winslow Drive
Pittsburg, PA 15229

Dear Mr. Appelt:

This is in response to your request for an advisory opinion under section 4975 of the Internal Revenue Code (Code). Specifically, you ask whether allowing the owner of an individual retirement account (IRA) to direct the IRA to invest in notes being offered by a corporation, in which a relative of the IRA owner is the majority owner and stockholder, would give rise to a prohibited transaction under Code section 4975.[1]

[1] Under Presidential Reorganization Plan No. 4 of 1978, effective December 31, 1978, the authority of the Secretary of the Treasury to issue interpretations regarding section 4975 of the Code has been transferred, with certain exceptions not here relevant, to the Secretary of Labor and the Secretary of the Treasury is bound by the interpretations of the Secretary of Labor pursuant to such authority.

You represent that as the owner of an IRA for which you have retained investment discretion, you would like to direct the investment of these IRA funds into notes (Notes) that are being offered by STARR Life Sciences Corporation (STARR). STARR is currently owned by the founders of the Company who are: Eric (your son-in-law) — 87.5%; Erika (an unrelated party) — 7.5%; and Dr. Strolh (an unrelated party) — 5.0%.

You represent that these Notes are being offered and sold exclusively to persons who qualify as "accredited investors" under rule 501(a) of Regulation D promulgated under the Securities Act of 1933. You represent that you qualify as an accredited investor.

You ask whether the IRA's investment in the Notes would give rise to a prohibited transaction under section 4975 of the Code. Section 4975(c)(1)(A) and (B) of the Code defines a prohibited transaction to include any direct or indirect sale or exchange of property and lending of money or other extension of credit between a plan and a disqualified person.

Section 4975(e)(1) of the Code defines, in relevant part, the term "plan" to include an IRA described in Code section 408(a). Section 4975(e)(3) of the Code defines the term "fiduciary," in relevant part, to include any person who exercises any discretionary authority or discretionary control respecting management of such plan or exercises any authority or control respecting management or disposition of its assets. Because you retain investment discretion over the IRA, you are a fiduciary. Section 4975(e)(2) of the Code defines "disqualified person," in relevant part, to include a fiduciary and certain members of the family of a fiduciary. Consequently, you are also classified as a disqualified person under Code section 4975(e)(2)(A). Sections 4975(e)(2)(F) and 4975(e)(6) of the Code state, in relevant part, that the family of a fiduciary shall include his spouse, ancestor, lineal descendant, and any spouse of a lineal descendant. Consequently, your son-in-law is also classified as a disqualified person because he is a member of the family of a fiduciary.

The IRA's purchase of the Notes would be a transaction between STARR and the IRA. Code section 4975(e)(2)(G)(i) defines "disqualified person," in relevant part, toinclude a corporation of which (or in which) 50 percent or more of the combined voting power of all classes of stock entitled to vote or the total value of shares of all classes of stock of such corporation is owned indirectly by a fiduciary.

In determining indirect stockholdings, Code section 4975(e)(4) requires that for purposes of Code section 4975(e)(2)(G)(i), indirect stockholdings include those which would be taken into account under Code section 267(c), except that members of a family of a fiduciary are members within the meaning of Code section 4975(e)(6). The application of this rule attributes to you the majority stockholdings of your son-in-law. Consequently, STARR is also classified as a disqualified person.

The IRA is a plan and STARR is a disqualified person. Based on the facts and representations in your submissions, it is the opinion of the Department of Labor that the IRA's purchase of the Notes from STARR at your direction would be a transaction described in section 4975(c)(1)(A) and (B) of the Code which prohibit a direct or indirect sale or exchange of property and lending of money or other extension of credit between a plan and a disqualified person.

This letter constitutes an advisory opinion under ERISA Procedure 76-1. Accordingly, this letter is issued subject to the provisions of such procedure, including section 10 relating to the effect of advisory opinions.

Sincerely,

Louis J. Campagna
Chief, Division of Fiduciary Interpretations
Office of Regulations and Interpretations

DOL Adv. Opinion 2006-01A—DOL Reg. Section 2509.75-2

U.S. Department of Labor
Frances Perkins Building
200 Constitution Avenue, NW
Washington, D.C. 20210

January 6, 2006

Debra C. Buchanan, Esq.
Guidant Legal Group, PLLC
225 Commerce Street, Suite 450
Tacoma, WA 98402

Dear Ms. Buchanan,

This is in response to your request for an advisory opinion as to whether the following proposed transaction would be prohibited under section 4975 of the Internal Revenue Code (the "Code"), 26 U.S.C. § 4975.[1]

You represent that Salon Services and Supplies, Inc. is a Washington state "S" Corporation ("S Company") which is 68% owned by Miles and Sydney Berry, a marital community (M). The other 32% is owned by a third-party, George Learned ("G"). Miles Berry (Berry) proposes to create a limited liability corporation ("LLC") that will purchase land, build a warehouse and lease the property to S Company. The investors in the LLC would be Berry's individual retirement account ("IRA") (49%), Robert Payne's ("R") IRA (31%) and G (20%). R is the comptroller of S Company. R and G will manage the LLC. You represent that S Company is a disqualified person with respect to Berry's IRA

[1] Under Reorganization Plan No. 4 of 1978, effective December 31, 1978 [5 U.S.C. App. at 214 (2000 ed.)], the authority of the Secretary of the Treasury to issue interpretations regarding section 4975 of the Code was transferred, with certain exceptions not here relevant, to the Secretary of Labor. As a result, citations to section 406 of the Employee Retirement Income Security Act (ERISA), 29 U.S.C. § 1001 et seq. and applicable regulations also refer to the parallel citations of section 4975 of the Code.

under section 4975(e)(2) of the Code. You represent that R and G are independent of Berry. You also represent that the LLC does not contain plan assets because it is a "real estate operating company" (REOC) as defined by 29 C.F.R. § 2510.3-101(e).

You state that an independent qualified commercial real estate appraiser has appraised the rental value of the lease and has found that the terms of the lease are not less favorable to the LLC and its IRA investors than those obtainable in an arm's length transaction between unrelated parties. Finally, the custodian for Berry's and R's IRAs has reviewed the LLC operating agreement and has approved the investment for those two self-directed IRAs.

Section 4975(c)(1)(A) of the Code prohibits any direct or indirect sale, exchange or leasing of any property between a plan and a "disqualified person." Section 4975(c)(1)(D) of the Code prohibits any direct or indirect transfer to, or use by or for the benefit of, a disqualified person of the income or assets of a plan. A "disqualified person" is defined under section 4975(e)(2)(A) of the Code to include a person who is a fiduciary. Code section 4975(e)(3) defines the term "fiduciary" to include, in pertinent part, any person who exercises any discretionary authority or discretionary control respecting management of such plan or exercises any authority or control respecting management or disposition of its assets. Section 4975(c)(1)(E) prohibits a fiduciary from dealing with the income or assets of a plan in the fiduciary's own interest or for his or her own account. Section 4975(e)(1)(B) of the Code defines the term "plan" to include an individual retirement account described in Code section 408(a).

We first address the proposed lease as it relates to Berry's IRA. Berry is a fiduciary to his own IRA because he exercises authority or control over its assets and management. 26 U.S.C. § 4975(e)(3). As a fiduciary, Berry is a disqualified person under section 4975(e)(2)(A) of the Code. You represent that S Company is a disqualified person under section 4975(e)(2) of the Code. R, the comptroller of S Company, is a disqualified person with respect to Berry's IRA under section 4975(e)(2)(H) as an officer of S Company. R, as an employee of S Company, a company 68% owned by M, cannot be considered independent of Berry.

Based upon your representations, it is the opinion of the Department that a lease of property between the LLC and S Company would be a prohibited transaction under Code section 4975, at least as to Berry's IRA. The lease constitutes a prohibited transaction regardless of whether the LLC qualifies as a REOC under the Department's plan assets regulation. 29 C.F.R. § 2510.3-101.

The Department's regulation at 29 C.F.R. § 2509.75-2(a) (Interpretative Bulletin 75-2), explains that a transaction between a party in interest under ERISA[2] (or disqualified person under the Code, in this case S Company) and a corporation in which a plan has invested (i.e., the LLC) does not generally give rise to a prohibited transaction. However, in some cases it can give rise to a prohibited

[2] Section 3(14) of ERISA defines the term "party in interest" for purposes of Title I of ERISA, including the prohibited transaction provisions of ERISA section 406.

transaction. Regulation section 2509.75-2(c) and Department opinions interpreting it have made clear that a prohibited transaction occurs when a plan invests in a corporation as part of an arrangement or understanding under which it is expected that the corporation will engage in a transaction with a party in interest (or disqualified person).[3]

According to your representations, it appears that Berry's IRA will invest in the LLC under an arrangement or understanding that anticipates that the LLC will engage in a lease with S Company, a disqualified person. Therefore, the lease would amount to a transaction between Berry's IRA and S Company that Code section 4975(c)(1)(A) and (D) prohibits. Additionally, the proposed lease, if consummated, may also constitute a violation by Berry, a fiduciary, of Code section 4975(c)(1)(D) and (E).

Finally, we note the express emphasis in 29 C.F.R. § 2509.75-2(c) that the Department considers "a fiduciary who makes or retains an investment in a corporation or partnership for the purpose of avoiding the application of the fiduciary responsibility provisions of the Act to be in contravention of the provisions of section 404(a) of the Act."

Thus, the proposed lease, which would violate section 4975(c)(1) of the Code, would also have to be referred to the Internal Revenue Service for a determination as to whether it would consider the transaction a violation of the exclusive benefit rule of section 401(a)(2) of the Code, which is the Code's analogue to the fiduciary responsibility provisions of section 404(a) of ERISA.

Because we have concluded that the proposed lease would constitute a prohibited transaction with respect to Berry's IRA, the issue of whether the Code prohibits the lease as it relates to R's IRA is moot, and does not need to be addressed.

This letter constitutes an advisory opinion under ERISA Procedure 76-1, 41 Fed. Reg. 36281 (1976). Accordingly, this letter is issued subject to the provisions of that procedure, including section 10 thereof, relating to the effect of advisory opinions.

Sincerely,

Louis J. Campagna
Chief, Division of Fiduciary Interpretations
Office of Regulations and Interpretations

---

[3] *See* 29 C.F.R. § 2509.75-2(c); Opinion No. 75-103 (Oct. 22, 1975); 1978 WL 170764 (June 13, 1978). Further, prior to the promulgation of the Department's plan assets regulation, 29 C.F.R. § 2510.3-101, the Department had issued Interpretive Bulletin 75-2 which discusses certain prohibited transactions under section 406 of ERISA or section 4975 or the Code. As indicated in the preamble to the plan assets regulation, part of Interpretive Bulletin 75-2 was revised to coordinate it with the final regulation (51 Fed. Reg. 41278). The remainder of the Interpretive Bulletin 75-2, published at 29 C.F.R. § 2509.75-2(c), remains in force and was not affected by the plan assets regulation. Regulation section 2509.75-2(c) sets forth that a transaction between a party in interest and a corporation in which a plan has invested may constitute a prohibited transaction under certain circumstances. Such transactions are prohibited regardless of whether or not they meet the plan assets regulation.

DOL Adv. Opinion 2005-23A—ERISA Section 3(21)

U.S. Department of Labor
Frances Perkins Building
200 Constitution Avenue, NW
Washington, D.C. 20210

December 7, 2005

Michael 'J' Stapley, President
Deseret Mutual Benefit Administrators
Eagle Gate Plaza
60 East South Temple
P.O. Box 45530
Salt Lake City, UT 84145

Dear Mr. Stapley:

This is in response to your request for guidance concerning the fiduciary responsibility provisions of the Employee Retirement Income Security Act of 1974, as amended (ERISA). You have requested guidance concerning the responsibilities of plan fiduciaries regarding the advice and other services provided directly to plan participants by financial planners or advisers. For purposes of this letter, we assume that the planner or adviser is neither chosen nor promoted by plan fiduciaries and is not otherwise a fiduciary with respect to the plan. In that context, you ask a number of questions.

The relevant statutory provisions are as follows. Section 3(21)(A) of ERISA provides that a person is a fiduciary with respect to a plan to the extent (i) he exercises any discretionary authority or discretionary control respecting management of such plan or exercises any authority or control respecting management or disposition of its assets, (ii) he renders investment advice for a fee or other compensation, direct or indirect, with respect to any moneys or other property of such plan, or has any authority or responsibility to do so, or (iii) he has any discretionary authority or discretionary responsibility in the administration of such plan.

Sections 403(c)(1) and 404(a) of ERISA require, among other things, that the assets of a plan be held for the exclusive purpose of providing benefits to participants and beneficiaries of the plan and defraying reasonable administrative expenses of administering the plan, and that a fiduciary with respect to the plan carry out his duties for the exclusive purpose of providing benefits to participants and beneficiaries.

Where an individual account pension plan permits a participant or beneficiary to exercise control over the assets in his or her account and a participant or beneficiary exercises such control, section 404(c) provides that no other person who is otherwise a fiduciary shall be liable for any loss, or by reason of any breach, which results from such participant's or beneficiary's exercise of control.

Section 405(a) of ERISA provides that a fiduciary of a plan may be liable for a breach of fiduciary responsibility committed by another fiduciary of the plan: (1) if he knowingly participates in, or knowingly undertakes to conceal, an act or omission of such other fiduciary, knowing such act or omission is a breach; (2) if, by his failure to comply with section 404(a)(1) of ERISA in the exercise of his fiduciary obligations, he has enabled such other fiduciary to commit a breach; or (3) if he has knowledge of the breach by such other fiduciary, unless he makes reasonable efforts under the circumstances to remedy the breach.

Section 406(a) of ERISA prohibits various types of transactions between a plan and persons who are parties in interest with respect to the plan. In particular, section 406(a)(1)(D) prohibits a fiduciary from engaging in a transaction if the fiduciary knows or should know that the transaction is a direct or indirect transfer to, or use by or for the benefit of any party in interest, of the assets of the plan. Section 406(b) of ERISA prohibits a fiduciary with respect to a plan from dealing with assets of the plan in his own interest or for his own account, acting on behalf of or representing a party dealing with the plan in a transaction involving the assets of the plan, or receiving any consideration for his own personal account from any party dealing with the plan in connection with a transaction involving the assets of the plan.

The following is a summary of the questions presented in your letter and our responses thereto.

Question 1. Is an individual who advises a participant, in exchange for a fee, on how to invest the assets in the participant's account, or who manages the investment of the participant's account, a fiduciary with respect to the plan within the meaning of section 3(21)(A) of ERISA?

Answer. The Department has stated on numerous occasions that directing the investment of a plan constitutes the exercise of authority and control over the management or disposition of plan assets and that the person directing the investments would be a fiduciary, even if the person is chosen by the participant and has no other connection to the plan. In addition, regulation 29 CFR § 2510-3.21(c) further clarifies the meaning of the term "investment advice." Under that regulation, a person will be deemed to be rendering investment advice if such person renders advice to the plan as to the value of securities or other property, or makes a recommendation as to the advisability of investing in, purchasing, or selling securities or other property and such person either directly or indirectly has discretionary authority or control, whether or not pursuant to an agreement, arrangement or understanding, with respect to purchasing or selling securities or other property for the plan; or renders any such advice on a regular basis to the plan pursuant to a mutual agreement, arrangement or understanding, written or otherwise, between such person and the plan or a fiduciary with respect to the plan, that such services will serve as a primary basis for investment decisions with respect to plan assets, and that such person will render individualized investment advice to the plan based on the particular needs of the plan regarding such matters as, among other things, investment policies or strategy, overall portfolio composition, or diversification of plan investments. The Department has taken the position that this definition of fiduciary also applies to investment advice provided to a participant or beneficiary in an individual account plan that allows participants or beneficiaries to direct the investment of their accounts. 29 CFR § 2509.96-1(c).

In the context of a participant-directed individual account plan meeting the requirements of ERISA section 404(c), a person, such as a financial planner or investment manager or adviser, who is selected by a participant to manage the participant's investments would be liable for imprudent investment decisions because those decisions would not have been the direct and necessary result of the participant's exercise of control, even though the participant selected the person to manage the assets in his or her individual account.[1] The other fiduciaries of the plan would not be liable as fiduciaries for either the selection of the investment manager or investment adviser or the results of the investment manager's decisions or investment adviser's recommendations.[2] Nor would the plan fiduciaries have any obligation to advise the participant about the investment manager or investment adviser or their investment decisions or recommendations. See 29 CFR § 2550.404c-1(f)—Example (9).

Question 2. Does a recommendation that a participant roll over his or her account balance to an individual retirement account (IRA) to take advantage of investment options not available under the plan constitute investment advice with respect to plan assets?

Answer. It is the view of the Department that merely advising a plan participant to take an otherwise permissible plan distribution, even when that advice is combined with a recommendation as to how the distribution should be invested, does not constitute "investment advice" within the meaning of the regulation (29 CFR § 2510-3.21(c)).[3] The investment advice regulation defines when a person is a fiduciary by virtue of providing investment advice with respect to the assets of an employee benefit plan. The Department does not view a recommendation to take a distribution as advice or a recommendation concerning a particular investment (i.e., purchasing or selling securities or other property) as contemplated by regulation § 2510.3-21(c)(1)(i). Any investment

---

[1] See Advisory Opinion 84-04A, January 4, 1984 (AO 84-04A). In particular, AO 84-04A stated that if a person is deemed to be giving investment advice within the meaning of regulation § 2510.3-21(c)(1)(ii)(B), the presence of an unrelated second fiduciary acting on the investment advisor's recommendations on behalf of the plan is not sufficient to insulate the investment advisor from fiduciary liability under section 406(b) of ERISA. Regulation § 2510.3-21(c)(1)(B) presupposes the existence of a second fiduciary who by agreement or conduct manifests a mutual understanding to rely on the investment advisor's recommendations as a primary basis for the investment of plan assets. In the presence of such an agreement or understanding, the rendering of investment advice involving self-dealing will subject the investment advisor to liability under section 406(b) of ERISA. We believe that the same principles enunciated in AO 84-04A apply in the context of a financial planner or investment advisor rendering investment advice to a participant in a participant-directed plan.

[2] Other fiduciaries of the plan may have co-fiduciary liability of the plan if, for example, they knowingly participate in a breach committed by the participant's fiduciary. ERISA section 405(a).

[3] We note that a person recommending that a participant take a distribution may be subject to Federal or state securities, banking or insurance regulation.

recommendation regarding the proceeds of a distribution would be advice with respect to funds that are no longer assets of the plan.[4]

Where, however, a plan officer or someone who is already a plan fiduciary responds to participant questions concerning the advisability of taking a distribution or the investment of amounts withdrawn from the plan, that fiduciary is exercising discretionary authority respecting management of the plan and must act prudently and solely in the interest of the participant.[5] Moreover, if, for example, a fiduciary exercises control over plan assets to cause the participant to take a distribution and then to invest the proceeds in an IRA account managed by the fiduciary, the fiduciary may be using plan assets in his or her own interest, in violation of ERISA section 406(b)(1).

Question 3. Would an advisor who is not otherwise a plan fiduciary and who recommends that a participant withdraw funds from the plan and invest the funds in an IRA engage in a prohibited transaction if the advisor will earn management or other investment fees related to the IRA?

Answer. No. For the same reasons explained above, a recommendation by someone who is not connected with the plan, that a participant take an otherwise permissible distribution, even when combined with a recommendation as to how to invest distributed funds, is not investment advice within the meaning of the 29 CFR § 2510-3.21(c), nor is such a recommendation, in and of itself, an exercise of authority or control over plan assets that would make a person a fiduciary within the meaning of section 3(21)(A) of ERISA. Accordingly, a person making such recommendations would not be a fiduciary solely on the basis of making such recommendations, and would not engage in an act of self-dealing if he or she advises the participant to roll over his account balance from the plan to an IRA that will pay management or other investment fees to such person.

However, as indicated above with respect to question 2, this position applies only to advice provided by a person who is not a plan fiduciary on some other basis. Advice of this nature given by someone who is already a fiduciary of the plan would be subject to ERISA's fiduciary duties. Moreover, if the person exercised control over the participant's account in making the distribution and reinvestment outside the plan, the person would be a fiduciary and would be subject to the ERISA's fiduciary obligations.

This letter constitutes an advisory opinion under ERISA Procedure 76-1 (41 Fed. Reg. 36281, August 27, 1976). Accordingly, this letter is issued subject to the provisions of the procedure, including section 10 relating to the effect of advisory opinions.

---

[4] In the view of the Department, the situation described herein is distinguishable from those situations where a plan fiduciary exercises control over the timing of the distribution, the selection of the individual retirement plan provider and the products in which the distributions will be invested. For example, situations such as those involving automatic rollovers of mandatory distributions. See 29 CFR § 2550.404a-2 (69 FR 58018, September 28, 2004). See also, AO 93-24A (September 13, 1993) and the letter from Robert J. Doyle to Judith McCormick, August 11, 1994.

[5] See Varity Corp. v. Howe, 516 U.S. 489, 502–03 (1996).

Sincerely,

Louis Campagna
Chief, Division of Fiduciary Interpretations
Office of Regulations and Interpretations

DOL Opinion 82-3A—ERISA Section 110

U.S. Department of Labor
Labor-Management Services Administration
Washington, DC 20216

January 12, 1982

Reply to the Attention of:

Mr. James M. Thomas
Assistant Vice President
Woburn Five Cents Savings Bank
19 Pleasant Street
Woburn, MA 01801

Dear Mr. Thomas:

You indicate in your letter that, with regard to the non-Model SEP in question, the terms of the SEP require all eligible employees to establish their individual retirement account (IRA) with the Woburn Five Cents Savings Bank (the Bank). In establishing an IRA, the Bank uses IRS Form 5305, which contains no restriction on withdrawal and has added no withdrawal restriction in provisions added under Article IX of Form 5305. Investments under the plan are at the direction of the participant, and not under the control of any other person. Through its IRAs, the Bank offers various investment options, including regular savings, term certificates and "special notice accounts," to participants. You indicate that neither the regular savings or term certificates impose any restriction on withdrawal by the participant; however, "special notice accounts" do not allow withdrawal of funds held on deposit for less than 90 days.

As you note in your letter, the alternative method of compliance under section 2520.104-49 does not apply to a SEP in connection with which the employer who establishes or maintains the SEP selects, recommends, or otherwise influences its employees to choose IRAs into which employer contributions will be made and such IRAs are subject to provisions that prohibit withdrawal of funds by participants for any period of time. Accordingly, you inquire whether an employer who sponsors a non-Model SEP, as described in your letter, would be adversely affected, in terms of using the alternative method of compliance, if a participant directs the Bank to invest his/her funds in the "special notice account" which restricts withdrawal, despite the availability of other investment options which do not have such a restriction.

With regard to your inquiry, it is the view of the Department that if an employer, in connection with sponsoring a non-Model SEP, selects the IRAs into which employer contributions will be made and such IRAs make available to participants an option that imposes a restriction on withdrawals, the administrator for that SEP would not be precluded from using the alternative method of compliance under § 2520.104-49, provided that other meaningful investment options which do not restrict withdrawals are available to participants, the employer does not select, recommend, or otherwise influence any participant's choice of an available investment option under the IRAs and all other conditions of the regulation are satisfied.

This letter constitutes an advisory opinion under ERISA Procedure 76-1. Accordingly, this letter is issued subject to the provisions of that procedure, including section 10 relating to the effect of advisory opinions.

Sincerely,

Jeffrey N. Clayton
Administrator
Pension and Welfare Benefit Programs

Appendix K

Sample Request Form

{{firm name}}

Illustration Request Form for SEP, SARSEP, and SIMPLE Plan

Name of employer: ____

Employer is taxed as a:

a corporation a partnership
a sole-proprietorship a tax-exempt organization

Plan year ends (month): _________. Business's tax year ends (month): _________.

Contribution formula should *primarily* benefit: owners, all employees equally (not integrated with social security benefits), or employees earning above the TWB, or above $ ______________. If "grandfathered" SARSEP, enter total elective deferrals (up to $17,000 for 2012), plus catch-up elective deferrals of up to $5,500 for 2012 if age 50 or older) on census and check here . If SIMPLE, enter elective deferrals up to $11,500 for 2012, plus catch-up elective deferrals of up to $2,500 for 2012 if age 50 or older) on census and check here .

The employer maintains does not maintain an existing SEP, SARSEP, or defined contribution plan? If "yes," this plan will will not replace the existing plan for the current year? Also illustrate a SIMPLE IRA, a 401(k) SIMPLE, or both (to operate on the basis of the calendar year and must also be the only plan of the employer). A tax-exempt organization may establish a SEP or SIMPLE, but may not establish a SARSEP. A SARSEP may be amended, changed, or restated; but may not be *initially* established after 1996.

Employee Code Key for 2012

O **Owners**

F **Officers**. Does not apply to SIMPLE plans.

H **Highly compensated employees**. Does not apply to SIMPLE plans. Use definition of highly compensated employee found in plan document. In general, the term *highly compensated employee* under Code Section 414(q) means (1) an individual is/who was a more than 5 percent owner, at any time during the current or preceding year; OR (2) an individual who had compensation from the employer, exceeding $115,000 for the preceding year (2011) and was in the top-paid group. The employer may elect for a year to limit this to a person who was in the top paid group of employees for the prior year. The rule requiring the highest-paid officer to be treated as a HCE was repealed beginning after 1996.

K **Key employees**. Does not apply to SIMPLE plans. Generally, a *key employee* is any employee or former employee (and the beneficiaries of these employees who was one of the following during the prior year (2011): an officer earning over $165,000, a more than 5 percent owner, or a more than one percent owner earning more than $150,000. Use definition of key employee found in the plan documents. [I.R.C. § 416(i)(1)]

N **Nonresident alien employees** who receive no U.S. source income - (may be excluded and omitted from census if excluded under plan provisions).

U **Unionized employees** covered by a collective bargaining agreement and for whom retirement benefits were the subject of good faith bargaining with the employer - (may be excluded and omitted from census if excluded under plan provisions).

Name of Employer: ______________________________ Page _____ of _____ pages.

Name of Employee	*%*	*Age*	*Circle ALL Codes That Apply:* *O = Owner* *U = Union* *F = Officer* *N = Nonresident* *H = HCE* *K = KEY*	*Date of Hire Month and Year*	*Pre-Plan Earned Income (NESE if SIMPLE*) or W–2 Compensation*	*SIMPLE & SARSEP Estimated Salary Reduction Amount or Percentage*
1			O F H U N K	-	$	$
2			O F H U N K	-	$	$
3			O F H U N K	-	$	$
4			O F H U N K	-	$	$
5			O F H U N K	-	$	$
6			O F H U N K	-	$	$
7			O F H U N K	-	$	$
8			O F H U N K	-	$	$
9			O F H U N K	-	$	$
10			O F H U N K	-	$	$
11			O F H U N K	-	$	$
12			O F H U N K	-	$	$
13			O F H U N K	-	$	$
14			O F H U N K	-	$	$
15			O F H U N K	-	$	$
16			O F H U N K	-	$	$
17			O F H U N K	-	$	$
18			O F H U N K	-	$	$
19			O F H U N K	-	$	$
20			O F H U N K	-	$	$

* Do not apply the 7.65 percent reduction if self-employed.

- If the employer is related to, controlled by or affiliated with another employer, indicate and list each employer separately. Attach additional sheets if necessary. Indicate *all* ownership interests. Enter *full amount* of pre-plan earned income or compensation.
- Indicate all family relationships (e.g., spouses, lineal ancestors and descendants).
- Check if any ☐ nonresident alien employees or if any ☐ unionized employees have been omitted from census.

Prepared by: ______________________ at (___) _____ - ________. Date: __ __ - __ __ - __ __

Appendix L

Chart of Contribution Revocations and CIP Failures

The following chart shows the appropriate code(s) to use when reporting an IRA revocation or when an IRA is closed due to a CIP failure, and the amount to be entered in Box 2a of Form 1099-R for 2012. Report the gross amount of the revoked distribution in Box 1.

Source of Contribution	*Form 1099-R Box 2a*	*Box 7*
Regular contribution to a traditional IRA without earnings	0	Code 8 regardless of age
Regular contribution to a traditional IRA with earnings	Earnings	18 if under age 59½ 8 if at least age 59½
Regular contribution to a Roth IRA without earnings	0	Code J regardless of age
Regular contribution to a Roth IRA with earnings	Earnings	Code J8 regardless of age
Rollover or transfer to a traditional IRA	Same as box 1	Code 7 if at least age 59½; Code 1 if under age 59½
Rollover or transfer to a Roth IRA	Same as box 1	Code J regardless of age
Conversion to a Roth IRA without earnings	0	Code J regardless of age
Conversion to a Roth IRA with earnings	Earnings	Code J regardless of age
SEP IRA or SIMPLE IRA	Same as box 1	Code 1 if under age 59½; Code 7 if at least age 59½; S if SIMPLE IRA less than 2 years

Appendix M

Excess Elective SEP/SARSEP Contributions for 2012

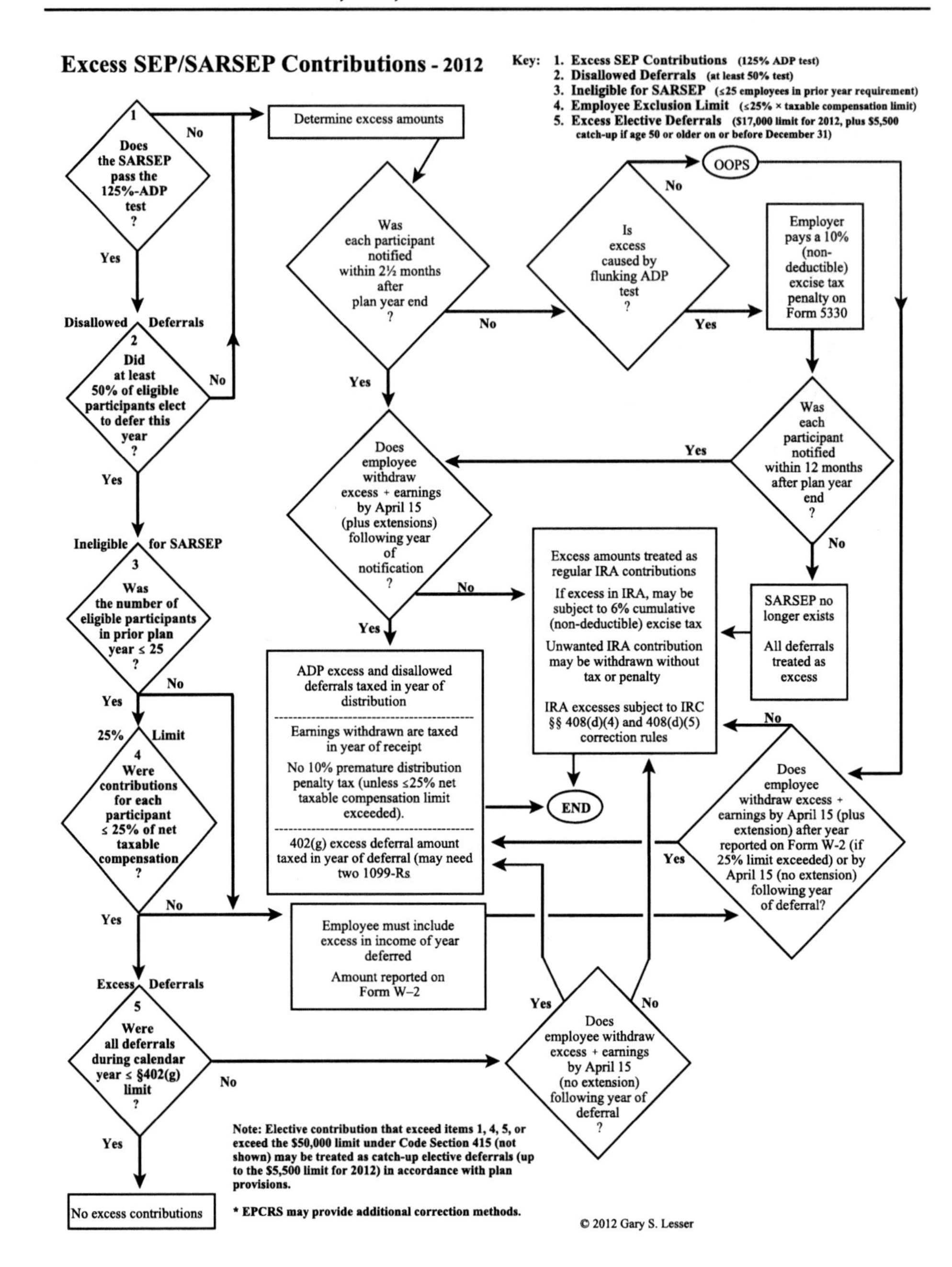

Excess SEP/SARSEP Contributions - 2012
Key: 1. Excess SEP Contributions (125% ADP test)
2. Disallowed Deferrals (at least 50% test)
3. Ineligible for SARSEP (≤25 employees in prior year requirement)
4. Employee Exclusion Limit (≤25% × taxable compensation limit)
5. Excess Elective Deferrals ($17,000 limit for 2012, plus $5,500 catch-up if age 50 or older on or before December 31)
1 Does the SARSEP pass the 125%-ADP test ?
No
Yes
Determine excess amounts
Was each participant notified within 2½ months after plan year end ?
No
Yes
OOPS
Is excess caused by flunking ADP test ?
No
Yes
Employer pays a 10% (non-deductible) excise tax penalty on Form 5330
Disallowed Deferrals
2 Did at least 50% of eligible participants elect to defer this year ?
No
Yes
Was each participant notified within 12 months after plan year end ?
Yes
No
Does employee withdraw excess + earnings by April 15 (plus extensions) following year of notification ?
No
Yes
Ineligible for SARSEP
3 Was the number of eligible participants in prior plan year ≤ 25 ?
No
Yes
Excess amounts treated as regular IRA contributions
If excess in IRA, may be subject to 6% cumulative (non-deductible) excise tax
Unwanted IRA contribution may be withdrawn without tax or penalty
IRA excesses subject to IRC §§ 408(d)(4) and 408(d)(5) correction rules
SARSEP no longer exists
All deferrals treated as excess
ADP excess and disallowed deferrals taxed in year of distribution
Earnings withdrawn are taxed in year of receipt
No 10% premature distribution penalty tax (unless ≤25% net taxable compensation limit exceeded).
402(g) excess deferral amount taxed in year of deferral (may need two 1099-Rs
25% Limit
4 Were contributions for each participant ≤ 25% of net taxable compensation ?
No
Yes
END
Does employee withdraw excess + earnings by April 15 (plus extension) after year reported on Form W-2 (if 25% limit exceeded) or by April 15 (no extension) following year of deferral?
No
Yes
Employee must include excess in income of year deferred
Amount reported on Form W-2
Excess Deferrals
5 Were all deferrals during calendar year ≤ §402(g) limit ?
No
Yes
Does employee withdraw excess + earnings by April 15 (no extension) following year of deferral ?
Yes
No
No excess contributions
Note: Elective contribution that exceed items 1, 4, 5, or exceed the $50,000 limit under Code Section 415 (not shown) may be treated as catch-up elective deferrals (up to the $5,500 limit for 2012) in accordance with plan provisions.
* EPCRS may provide additional correction methods.

Appendix N

2012 Comparison Chart for SIMPLE in IRA Form Versus SIMPLE 401(k)

Provision	*SIMPLE in IRA Form*	*SIMPLE 401(k)*
Eligible Employer	100 or fewer employees in prior year with $5,000 compensation Tax-exempt and government entities, yes	100 or fewer employees in prior year with $5,000 compensation Tax-exempt entities yes; government entities, no
Eligible Employee	$5,000 compensation during any 2 preceding years and expected to earn $5,000 in current year	1 year of service, age 21, 1,000-hour rule. Entry date rules.
Plan Year	Calendar year	Calendar year
Maximum Deferrals	Lesser of 100% of compensation or $11,500 ($14,000 with catch-up contribution)	Lesser of 100% of first $250,000 compensation or $11,500/$14,000 with catch-up contribution Code § 415 limit applies
Matching Contributions	3% of total compensation Maximum of $11,500 ($14,000 with catch-up contribution)	Up to 3% of first $250,000 (part of 100% limit under Code § 415) Maximum of $7,500
Alternative Matching Contributions	1% of total compensation (2 out of 5 years) No maximum compensation rules	Not available
Nonelective Contributions	2% of first $250,000 of compensation, all eligible employees who earn $5,000 in current year—maximum of $5,000	Same or part of 100% limit under Code § 415 Maximum of $5,000

Provision	*SIMPLE in IRA Form*	*SIMPLE 401(k)*
Designated Financial Institution (DFI) Rules	Penalty-free transfers if employee elects	Not applicable
2-Year Holding Period/25% Penalty	Applies, unless another exception	Not applicable, but cannot withdraw money until attainment of age 59 or severance from employment
Withdrawal Restrictions	Available, subject to taxes and penalties	Available only upon severance from employment; hardship, if plan allows; attainment of age 59½; or plan termination
Definition of Compensation	Employee: gross wages, including deferrals Self-employed: net profit × .9235 (see Q 14:63)	Same
Rollovers	Only to another SIMPLE IRA for first 2 years; after 2 years to a qualified plan 403(b) plan, 457(b) plan, IRA, Roth IRA or SIMPLE IRA.	Only to another qualified plan, a 403(b) plan, a 457(b) plan, a Roth IRA, or an IRA (not a SIMPLE IRA)
Transfers	Only to another SIMPLE IRA for first 2 years	Only to another qualified plan
Required Distributions & Beginning Date	April 1 after attaining age 70½, follows IRA rules.	5% owners' April 1 after attaining age 70½ Non-5% owners' April 1 following later of year of retirement or year in which participant attains age 70½ Follows qualified plan rules
Notice & Election Periods	60 days before new calendar year; 60 days before employee is eligible	Same
Trustee Reporting	Forms 5498 and 1099-R, "activity" report; summary description	Form 1099–R
Delivering Elective Deferrals to Trustee	As soon as administratively feasible, but no later than 30 days after end of month. 7-day safe harbor available. **Note.** 15- and 30-day periods are not safe harbors. The 7-day safe harbor applies on a payroll-by-payroll basis.	As soon as administratively feasible, but no later than 15 business days after end of month. 7-day safe harbor available.

Provision	*SIMPLE in IRA Form*	*SIMPLE 401(k)*
Employer Reporting	Notices to employees; summary description	Notices to employees; summary plan description; summary annual report; Form 5500
Employer Deduction	Not limited to 25% of compensation	Limited to 25% of aggregate of all participants gross compensation
Loans	N/A	If plan permits
Code § 415 Limits	N/A	Sum of all contributions: 100% of total compensation
Vesting	100%	100%

Appendix O

Comparison of Elective Deferral Plans for 2012

	SIMPLE IRA	*SIMPLE 401(k)*	*401(k)*	*Design-Based Safe Harbor 401(k)*	*SARSEP*
ADP/ACP	None	None	Yes	No	Yes—Modified
Availability	100 or fewer employees; greater than $5K in compensation during prior year	Nongovernmental organizations; 100 or fewer employees greater than $5K in compensation	Nongovernmental organizations	Satisfy notice requirements; non-governmental organizations	Nongovernmental organizations; fewer than 25 employees
Top-Heavy Rules	None	None	Yes	Yes	Yes
Match	100% of first 3% No $250,000 cap	100% of first 3%, $250,000 cap applies	Flexible, ACP	100% up to 3%, 50% from 3% to 5%	N/A
Flexibility of Match	With prior notification Reduce to 1% for 2 of 5 years	No	Yes	Alternate Rule available	N/A
Nonelective Alternative	With prior notification—2% $250,000 cap; may exclude less than $5,000	With prior notification—2%	QNEC	3% for each NHCE	None
Taxation	Unless Code § 72(t) exception applies, 25% penalty in first 2 years, otherwise 10%	10% early withdrawal penalty	10% early withdrawal penalty	10% early withdrawal penalty	10% early withdrawal penalty
Deferral Maximum	$11,500 Code § 415 does not apply	$11,500	$17,000	$17,000	$17,000

Catch-Up	$2,500	$2,500	$5,500	$5,500	$5,500
Compensation Definition	Form W-2 plus elective deferrals	Form W-2 plus elective deferrals	Form W-2 plus elective deferrals; alternate deferral available	Form W-2 plus elective deferrals; alternate deferral available	Form W-2 plus elective deferrals; alternate deferral available
Effective	Years beginning after 12/31/96	Years beginning after 12/31/96	N/A	Years beginning after 1998	Only for plans established by 12/31/96
Form 5500 Filing	No	Yes	Yes	Yes	No
Special Tax Treatment	No	No	10-year averaging only	10-year averaging only	No
Can maintain another plan?	No (except collectively bargained plan)	Possibly; for employees not covered by SIMPLE	Yes	Yes	Yes (special document needed)
Other employer contributions?	No	No	Yes	Yes	Yes
Vesting on employer contributions?	Full	Full	Immediate, cliff, and graded, except for QNECs and QMACs	100%	100%
Rollovers	To another SIMPLE IRA after 2 years of participation	Triggering event (e.g., plan termination, death, separation from service, disability, or age 59½)	Triggering event (e.g., plan termination, death, separation from service, disability, or age 59½)	Triggering event (e.g., plan termination, death, separation from service, disability, or age 59½)	Same as IRA rules. Must wait until March 15 of following year or notice that ADP test satisfied to remove elective deferrals

	SIMPLE IRA	*SIMPLE 401(k)*	*401(k)*	*Design-Based Safe Harbor 401(k)*	*SARSEP*
Fiduciary Liability Under 404(c)	None after earlier of: a. Affirmative action b. Rollover contribution c. 1 yr. after account established	Yes	Yes	Yes	No
Employee Eligibility	Earned greater than $5K in any 2 prior years; expected to earn $5K this year	Age 21, 12 mos./ 1,000 hrs. of service	Age 21, 12 mos./ 1,000 hrs. of service	Age 21, 12 mos./ 1,000 hrs. of service	Service during 3 of last 5 years
Loans	No	Yes	Yes	No	No

Internal Revenue Code Sections

[References are to question numbers.]

IRC §

IRC §

IRC §

IRC §

IRC §

IRC §

IRC §

IRC §

IRC §

Treasury Regulations Sections

[*References are to question numbers.*]

Treasury Regulations

Treas Reg §

Treas Reg §

Treas Reg §

Treas Reg §

Treas Reg §

Temporary Treasury Regulations

Temp Treas Reg §

Proposed Treasury Regulations

Prop Treas Reg §

ERISA Sections

[References are to question numbers.]

ERISA §

ERISA §

ERISA §

ERISA §

Revenue Procedures and Revenue Rulings

[*References are to question numbers.*]

Revenue Procedures

Rev Proc

Rev Proc

Revenue Rulings

Rev Rul

Rev Rul

Rev Rul

IRS Notices, Announcements, and Letter Rulings

[*References are to question numbers.*]

Notices

Notice

Notice

Announcements

Ann

Ann

Letter Rulings

Ltr Rul

Ltr Rul

Ltr Rul

Ltr Rul

Field Service Advice

Department of Labor Regulations and Advisory Opinions

[*References are to question numbers.*]

Code of Federal Regulations

[*References are to question numbers.*]

United States Code

[References are to question numbers.]

USC

USC

Pension Protection Act of 2006

[References are to question numbers.]

PPA §

PPA §

Cases

[References are to question numbers.]

A

B

C

D

I

J

K

L

M

N

O

P

R

W

Y

Z

Index

[*References are to question numbers and appendices.*]

A

B

C

D

E

F

G

H

I

J

K

L

M

N

O

P

T

U

V

W

Y

Z